Institutions of Government

Congress

http://www.house.gov/

This is the official website of the U.S. House of Representatives.

http://www.senate.gov/

This is the official website of the U.S. Senate.

http://thomas.loc.gov/

This website includes links to current and historical bills and resolutions in Congress, presidential nominations, treaties, and other legislative material.

The Presidency

http://www.whitehouse.gov/

This is the official website of the White House, which contains links to staff offices, Executive Office of the President agencies, and Cabinet Departments. It also contains presidential speeches, historical information on the American Presidency, and other material pertaining to the executive branch.

http://www.archives.gov/

This is the official website of the National Archives and Records Administration, which maintains records of the federal government.

http://www.archives.gov/presidential-libraries/

NARA's extensive resources include presidential libraries located across the country for the administrations of Herbert Hoover to the present, as well as much other material about the executive branch.

The Judiciary

http://www.supremecourtus.gov/

This is the official website of the Supreme Court of the United States.

http://www.landmarkcases.org/

This website provides information on historic Supreme Court decisions in American politics.

Tommy "Pickles" Lipscomb

The following websites were selected for their comprehensiveness in presenting information about the founding, compone American political system. This textbook does not endorse the views of any of the organizations involved in the production

D1443226

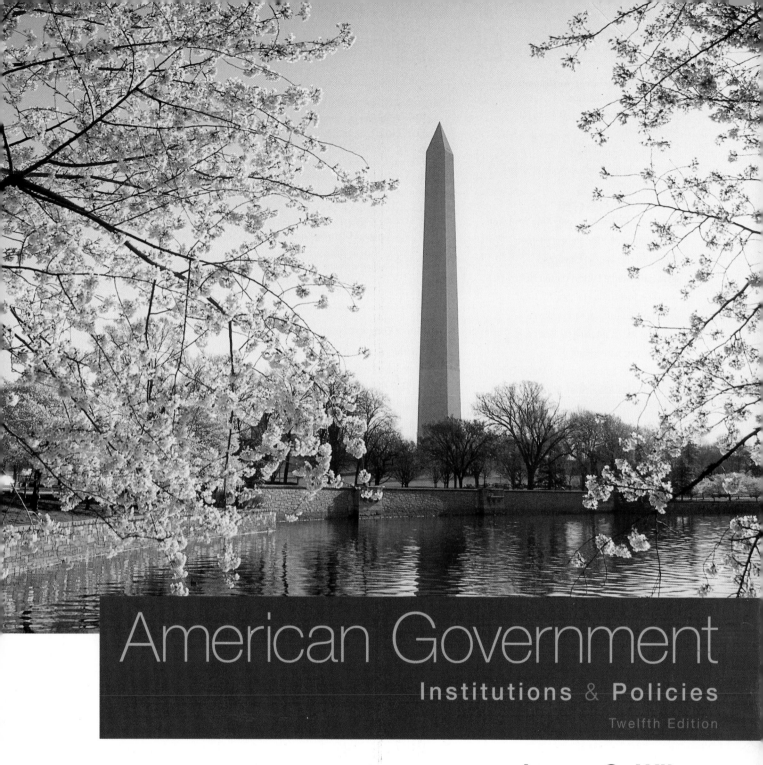

American Government

Institutions & Policies

Twelfth Edition

James Q. Wilson
University of California, Los Angeles, emeritus
Pepperdine University
Boston College

John J. Dilulio, Jr.
University of Pennsylvania

with Meena Bose
Hofstra University

WADSWORTH
CENGAGE Learning

Australia • Brazil • Japan • Korea • Mexico • Singapore • Spain • United Kingdom • United States

WADSWORTH
CENGAGE Learning

American Government: Institutions and Policies, **Twelfth Edition**

James Q. Wilson, John J. DiIulio, Jr., Meena Bose

Publisher: Suzanne Jeans

Executive Acquiring Sponsoring Editor: Carolyn Merrill

Editor in Chief: PJ Boardman

Senior Marketing Manager: Amy Whitaker

Development Editor: Rebecca Green

Media Editor: Laura Hildebrand

Associate Media Editor: Caitlin Holroyd

Art Director: Linda Helcher

Assistant Editor: Katherine Hayes

Editorial Assistant: Angela Hodge

Print Buyer: Karen Hunt

Senior Photo Editor: Jennifer Meyer Dare

Senior Rights Acquisition Manager, Text: Katie Huha

Printer: RR Donnelley

Production Manager: Suzanne St. Clair

Senior Content Project Manager: Joshua Allen

Production Service: Elm Street Publishing Services/Integra Software Services Pvt. Ltd.

© 2011 Cengage Learning

ALL RIGHTS RESERVED. No part of this work covered by the copyright herein may be reproduced, transmitted, stored, or used in any form or by any means graphic, electronic, or mechanical, including but not limited to photocopying, recording, scanning, digitizing, taping, Web distribution, information networks, or information storage and retrieval systems, except as permitted under Section 107 or 108 of the 1976 United States Copyright Act, without the prior written permission of the publisher.

For product information and technology assistance, contact us at **Cengage Learning Customer & Sales Support, 1-800-354-9706**

For permission to use material from this text or product, submit all requests online at **www.cengage.com/permissions.** Further permissions questions can be e-mailed to **permissionrequest@cengage.com.**

Library of Congress Control Number: 2009940835

Instructor's examination copy:

ISBN-13: 978-0-495-89805-4
ISBN-10: 0-495-89805-8

For orders, use student text ISBNs:

ISBN-13: 978-0-495-80281-5
ISBN-10: 0-495-80281-6

Wadsworth
20 Channel Center Street
Boston, MA 02210
USA

Cengage Learning is a leading provider of customized learning solutions with office locations around the globe, including Singapore, the United Kingdom, Australia, Mexico, Brazil, and Japan. Locate your local office at **international.cengage.com/region.**

Cengage Learning products are represented in Canada by Nelson Education, Ltd.

For your course and learning solutions, visit **www.cengage.com.**

Purchase any of our products at your local college store or at our preferred online store **www.ichapters.com.**

For Roberta, Matthew, Rebecca, Annie, and Bob.
J.Q.W.
Dedicated to the memory of
Aaron H. Crasner.
J.J.D.
Dedicated, with respect and appreciation, to
Fred I. Greenstein.
M.B.

Printed in the United States of America
2 3 4 5 6 7 8 9 13 12 11 10

Brief Contents

Contents

PREFACE

We wrote this textbook to explain to students not only how the federal government works but also to make clear how those institutions have developed over time and their effects on public policy. Unlike many authors, we briefly explain the history of Congress, the presidency, the judiciary, and the bureaucracy because the politics we see today are different from those we would have seen a few decades ago. And, of course, change never stops: in another decade, federal politics may be very different from what they are today.

As in the past, we illustrate our discussion with chapter-opening vignettes, landmark court decisions, and clear examples of politics in action. We have added to this edition a new feature: *Research Frontiers*. These are short boxes in most chapters that highlight new findings about how politics works, ask readers to think critically about future implications, and challenge them to conduct their own research for deeper understanding.

We have also refashioned our political trivia boxes into a feature that appears in the margin. They are now much shorter and ask readers to test their knowledge by posing a question on one page (for example, "Who was the first Catholic Supreme Court justice?") and encouraging them to read on to find the answer later in the chapter.

The book is current through mid-2009. It includes an analysis of the 2008 election and the early policy proposals of President Barack Obama.

Professor Meena Bose of Hofstra University contributed vital ideas and assisted in revising each chapter in the eleventh edition and is now a coauthor of this edition.

Boxed items remain focused and clear. For example, the popular *What Would You Do?* boxes are designed to generate classroom discussion and debate. Each highlights an important policy question and briefly states the arguments for and against each option. *How Things Work* boxes give students an understanding of such procedures in American politics as amending the Constitution, becoming a U.S. citizen, and becoming a Congressperson. The *Politically Speaking* feature helps students understand the origins of important terms. The *"Rules" of Politics* boxes give students an insider's insight into how the system really works.

Thanks to the ever-evolving Internet, our students now have virtually limitless access to information on most subjects, including American government. Even when we are not searching for it or paying close attention, news, opinions, and entertainment concerning the latest in American politics stream into our lives. In some ways, this makes teaching and learning about our subject easier than it once was. But it also poses pedagogical challenges for instructors. Information is not knowledge. Instant analysis is no substitute for in-depth study. Strong opinions are hollow unless they are rooted in serious reflection and critical thinking.

Thus, each chapter ends with a Summary, carefully selected World Wide Web Resources, and classic and contemporary Suggested Readings that provide students with reference material and preparation for classroom lectures and examinations. Of course, the most important "examinations" will come later in their lives—lives that, we hope, will include ongoing and serious intellectual and civic interest in American politics and government.

FOR USERS OF THE PREVIOUS EDITION

In addition to the new features, an engaging new design, updated tables, figures, citations, and photographs, and the most current information available throughout, significant chapter-by-chapter changes have been made as follows:

- Chapter 1: A new discussion introduces students to the philosophies of Locke, Hobbes, and others who have influenced the shape of America's government. The *Research Frontiers* feature explores *Do Ballot Initiatives Bolster "Direct Democracy"?*

- Chapter 2: A new *Research Frontiers* feature looks at recent scholarship rediscovering how the competing views about religion and government shaped the debate between the Federalists and the Anti-Federalists.

- Chapter 3: The chapter on Federalism has been reorganized to more closely match the way instructors told us they teach the section, starting with the founding and the debate over the meaning of federalism, and a new section expands upon what the states can do, while the *Research Frontiers* feature explores *The Intergovernmental Trust Gap*.

- Chapter 4: A new section is included on civil society and the individualism of American political culture, along with more comparative data about political culture in other countries.

- Chapter 5: Includes a look at how the right to bear arms may or may not apply to the states, the closing of the Guantanamo prison under Obama, and a *Research Frontiers* feature on *"In Your Face"—Television and Political Tolerance.*

- Chapter 6: The discussion of civil rights includes a new *How Things Work* feature on *How the Court Decides if You Discriminate* and an update on same-sex marriage.

- Chapter 7: The Political Socialization section now includes a brief examination of the role of genetics in our political ideology, a closer look at young adults' views on politics, and more data explaining how faith and gender affect our opinions. The *Research Frontiers* box looks at *How the 2008 Presidential Primary Polling Went Wrong.*

- Chapter 8: Includes a reworked section on the issue of nonvoting, updated in light of the 2008 elections, a look at the youth vote in 2008, new data on the causes and meaning of participation, and a *Research Frontiers* feature that explores *Does Religion Boost Participation?*

- Chapter 9: The Political Parties chapter examines the front-loading of primaries and the role of parties in the 2008 election, while the *Research Frontiers* box asks *Are Republicans the Next Whigs?*

- Chapter 10: Elections and Campaigns contains an overview of the 2008 national elections, including money raised and spent, the prominent campaign issues, and a *Research Frontiers* box about how *Candidate Positions Drive Voter Choices.*

- Chapter 11: A reworked and streamlined chapter on Interest Groups makes the topic more interesting to students and includes a new section explaining earmarks. The *Research Frontiers* box examines whether some powerful lobbies can dominate policymaking on certain issues.

- Chapter 12: The Media chapter delves more deeply into the role of the Internet and other technology in today's politics as well as their future implications.

- Chapter 13: The chapter on Congress contains a new section on legislative productivity.

- Chapter 14: The Presidency chapter has been extensively revised to discuss the Obama presidency.

- Chapter 15: Includes more data on how the public views particular federal agencies and is updated throughout.

- Chapter 16: The Judiciary opens with a closer look at presidential Supreme Court justice nominations and the Senate's increased toughness on confirmations and includes a look at new Justice Sonia Sotomayor.

- Chapter 17: The Policy-Making Process chapter discusses trends by administration and examines public opinion and deregulation.

- Chapter 18: The chapter on America's Economic Policy has been reworked to include an in-depth discussion on *What Caused the 2007–2009 Recession,* as well as ways Washington is trying to stimulate the economy.

- Chapter 19: The Social Welfare chapter takes a closer look at health care policy and the current push for reform, the American Recovery and Reinvestment Act, as well as other policies under the Obama administration.

- Chapter 20: The chapter on Foreign and Military Policy now takes a closer look at Afghanistan and recent foreign policy under the Obama administration.

- Chapter 21: Includes updates to policies on global warming.

- Chapter 22: The closing chapter leaves readers with a portrait of the current political landscape and tasks them with future examination of their government using the tools they've acquired.

LEARNING AND TEACHING ANCILLARIES

The program for *American Government,* Twelfth Edition, includes a number of learning and teaching aids. These ancillaries provide instructors with useful course management and presentation tools and help students get the most from their American Government course.

For the Instructor
PowerLecture DVD with JoinIn™ and ExamView®
ISBN-10: 0495898112 | ISBN-13: 9780495898115

- Interactive **PowerPoint® Lectures**, a one-stop lecture and class preparation tool, makes it easy for you to assemble, edit, publish, and present custom lectures for your course. You will have access to a set of PowerPoints with outlines specific to each chapter of *American Government* as well as photos, figures, and tables found in the book. In addition, we provide media-enhanced PowerPoints for each chapter that can be used on their own or easily integrated with the book-specific outlines. Audio and video clips depicting both historic and current day events; NEW animated learning modules illustrating key concepts; tables, statistical charts, and graphs; and photos from the book as well as outside sources are provided at the appropriate places in the chapter. You can also add your own materials—culminating in a powerful, personalized, media-enhanced presentation.

- A **Test Bank** by P. S. Ruckman of Rock Valley College in Microsoft® Word and ExamView® computerized testing offers a large array of well-crafted multiple-choice and essay questions, along with their answers and page references.

- An **Instructor's Manual** by Allen Trigger of Virginia Western Community College includes learning objectives, chapter outlines, discussion questions, suggestions for stimulating class activities and projects, tips on integrating media into your class (including step-by-step instructions on how to create your own podcasts), suggested readings and Web resources, and a section specially designed to help teaching assistants and adjunct instructors.

- **JoinIn**™ on Turning Point® offers book-specific "clicker" questions that test and track student comprehension of key concepts. Political Polling questions simulate voting, engage students, foster dialogue on group behaviors and values, and add personal relevance; the results can be compared to national data, leading to lively discussions. Visual Literacy questions are tied to images from the book and add useful pedagogical tools and high-interest feedback during your lecture. Save the data from students' responses all semester—track their progress and show them how political science works by incorporating this exciting new tool into your classroom. It is available for college and university adopters only.

- The **Resource Integration Guide** outlines the rich collection of resources available to instructors and students within the chapter-by-chapter framework of the book, suggesting how and when each supplement can be used to optimize learning.

WebTutor

WebTutor™ on WebCT IAC
ISBN-10: 0495898228 | ISBN-13: 9780495898221

WebTutor™ on Blackboard IAC
ISBN-10: 0495898244 | ISBN-13: 9780495898245

WebTutor™ on Angel IAC

Rich with content for your American government course, this Web-based teaching and learning tool includes course management, study/mastery, and communication tools. Use WebTutor™ to provide virtual office hours, post your syllabus, and track student progress with WebTutor's quizzing material. For students, WebTutor™ offers real-time access to interactive online tutorials and simulations, practice quizzes, and Web links—all correlated to *American Government*.

Political Theatre DVD 2.0
ISBN-10: 0495793604 | ISBN-13: 9780495793601

Bring politics home to students with Political Theatre 2.0, up to date through the 2008 election season. This is the second edition of this three-DVD series and includes real video clips that show American political thought throughout the public sector. Clips include both classic and contemporary political advertisements, speeches, interviews, and more. Available to adopters of Cengage textbooks, version 2.0 provides lots of added functionality with this updated edition.

JoinIn™ on Turning Point® for Political Theatre
ISBN-10: 04957982901 | ISBN-13: 9780495798293

For even more interaction, combine Political Theatre with the innovative teaching tool of a classroom response system through JoinIn™. Poll your students with questions created for you or create your own questions. Built within the Microsoft® PowerPoint® software, it's easy to integrate into your current lectures in conjunction with the "clicker" hardware of your choice.

The Wadsworth News Videos for American Government 2010 DVD
ISBN-10: 0495904880 | ISBN-13: 9780495904885

This collection of three- to six-minute video clips on relevant political issues serves as a great lecture or discussion launcher.

Great Speeches Collection
Throughout the ages, great orators have stepped up to the podium and used their communication skills to persuade, inform, and inspire their audiences. Studying these speeches can provide tremendous insight into historical, political, and cultural events that represent a key moment from which to consider what came before, and what followed as a result. The Great Speeches Collection includes the full text of more than 60 memorable orations for you to incorporate into your course. Whether your interest is to examine speech structure, intent, or

effect, you're sure to find an example that fits your needs. Speeches can be collated in a printed reader to supplement your existing course materials or even bound into a core textbook.

ABC Video: Speeches by President Barack Obama

ISBN-10: 1439082472 | ISBN-13: 9781439082478

DVD of nine speeches by President Barack Obama, from 2004 to present day, including his speech at the 2004 Democratic National Convention; his 2008 speech on race, "A More Perfect Union"; and his 2009 inaugural address. Speeches are divided into short video segments for easy, time-efficient viewing. This instructor supplement also features critical thinking questions and answers for each speech, designed to spark classroom discussion.

For the Student

Premium Website with Infotrac® Instant Access Code

ISBN-10: 0495899895 | ISBN-13: 9780495899891

The Premium Website for *American Government* offers a variety of rich online learning resources designed to enhance the student experience. These resources include podcasts, critical thinking activities, simulations, animated learning modules, timelines, flashcards, and videos. Chapter resources are correlated with key chapter learning concepts, and users can browse or search for content in a variety of ways.

Bring the news right into your classroom! Available in both student and instructor versions, CL NewsNow is a combination of Associated Press news stories, videos, and images that bring current events to life. For students, a collection of news stories and accompanying videos is served up each week via the Premium Website that accompanies their American Government text. For instructors, an additional set of multi-media rich PowerPoint® slides are posted each week to the password-protected area of the text's companion. Instructors may use these slides to take a class poll or trigger a lively debate about the events shaping the world right now. And because this all-in-one presentation tool includes the text of the original newsfeed, along with videos, photos, and discussion questions, no Internet connection is required!

MultiMedia eBook

ISBN-10: 0495898198 | ISBN-13: 9780495898191

We provide separate options for the delivery of an interactive, multimedia eBook that contains links to simulations, flashcards, and other interactive activities.

Companion Website

www.cengage.com/politicalscience/wilson/ americangovernment12e

Students will find open access to learning objectives, tutorial quizzes, chapter glossaries, flashcards, and crossword puzzles—all correlated by chapter. Instructors also have access to the Instructor's Manual and PowerPoints.

Election 2008: An American Government Supplement

ISBN-10: 0495567485 | ISBN-13: 9780495567486

The use of real examples in this election booklet, which addresses the 2008 presidential, congressional, and gubernatorial races, makes the concepts covered come alive.

The Handbook of Selected Court Cases

ISBN-10: 0495127744 | ISBN-13: 9780495127741

This handbook includes more than 30 Supreme Court cases.

The Handbook of Selected Legislation and Other Documents

ISBN-10: 0495127825 | ISBN-13: 9780495127826

This handbook features excerpts from laws passed by the U.S. Congress that have had a significant impact on American politics.

ACKNOWLEDGMENTS

A number of scholars reviewed the book and made useful suggestions for the Twelfth Edition. They include:

Lucas Allen, Michigan State University
Roger Ashby, Peace College
Michael Baranowski, Northern Kentucky University
Jack Citrin, University of California, Berkeley
Stan Crippen, Riverside County Office of Education
Kipling Hagopian
Kevin Hassett
Kathleen C Hauger, Abington Senior High School
Halima Asghar Khan, Massasoit Community College
Young-Choul Kim, University of Evansville
Junius H Koonce, Edgecombe Community College
William Lester, Jacksonville State University
Anne F. Presley, McKinney High School
Gayle Randolph, Neosho County Community College
P.S. Ruckman, Rock Valley College
Rebecca Small, Herndon High School

A number of scholars reviewed the Tenth Edition and made useful suggestions for the Eleventh. They include:

Gregory Culver, University of Southern Indiana
Terri Fine, University of Central Florida
Glenn David Garrison, Collin County Community College—Spring Creek Campus
Stephen Kerbow, Southwest Texas Junior College
Brad Lockerbie, University of Georgia
Donald Ranish, Antelope Valley College
Jennifer Walsh, Azusa Pacific University
David Wigg, St. Louis Community College
Teresa Wright, California State University—Long Beach
Jonathan Roberts, Portland, OR, schools
Additional thanks go to Marc Siegal for his research assistance.

About the Authors

JAMES Q. WILSON

James Q. Wilson now teaches at Pepperdine University and Boston College. He is an emeritus professor of management and public policy at the University of California, Los Angeles, and from 1961 to 1987 was a professor of government at Harvard University. Raised in California, he received a B.A. degree from the University of Redlands and a Ph.D. from the University of Chicago. Wilson is the author or coauthor of fourteen books, including *The Marriage Problem* (2002), *Moral Judgment* (1997), *The Moral Sense* (1993), *Bureaucracy* (1989), *Crime and Human Nature* (1985, with Richard J. Herrnstein), *Thinking about Crime* (1983), and *Political Organizations* (1974).

Wilson has served in a number of advisory posts in the federal government. He was chairman of the White House Task Force on Crime in 1967, chairman of the National Advisory Council on Drug Abuse Prevention in 1972–1973, a member of the Attorney General's Task Force on Violent Crime in 1981, and a member of the President's Foreign Intelligence Advisory Board in 1986–1990.

In 1977 the American Political Science Association conferred on him the Charles E. Merriam Award for advancing the art of government through the application of social science knowledge and in 1990 the James Madison Award for distinguished scholarship. In 1991–1992, he was President of the Association.

He is a Fellow of the American Academy of Arts and Sciences and a member of the American Philosophical Society. When not writing, teaching, or advising, he goes scuba diving. In 2003, Wilson received the Presidential Medal of Freedom, this nation's highest civilian award.

JOHN J. DIIULIO, JR.

John J. DiIulio, Jr. is a professor of political science at the University of Pennsylvania. From 1986 to 1999, he was a professor of politics and public affairs at Princeton University's Woodrow Wilson School of Public and International Affairs. He received

B.A. and M.A. degrees from the University of Pennsylvania and M.A. and Ph.D. degrees from Harvard University. He is the author, coauthor, or editor of a dozen books, including *Godly Republic* (2007); *Medicaid and Devolution* (1998, with Frank Thompson); *Deregulating the Public Service* (1994) and *Governing Prisons* (1987).

DiIulio advised both Vice President Al Gore and Governor George W. Bush during the 2000 Presidential campaign. While on leave in academic year 2000–2001, he served as Assistant to the President of the United States. He has advised officials at the National Performance Review, the Office of Management and Budget, the General Accounting Office, the U.S. Department of Justice, and other federal agencies. He has served on the boards of Big Brothers Big Sisters of America and other nonprofit organizations.

In 1995, the Association of Public Policy Analysis and Management conferred on him the David N. Kershaw Award for outstanding research achievements and in 1987 he received the American Political Science Association's Leonard D. White Award in public administration. In 1991–1994, he chaired the latter association's standing committee on professional ethics. Since 2005, he has had a leading role in nonprofit initiatives to assist post-Katrina New Orleans.

MEENA BOSE

Meena Bose is Peter S. Kalikow Chair in Presidential Studies at Hofstra University and Director of Hofstra's Peter S. Kalikow Center for the Study of the American Presidency. She is the author of *Shaping and Signaling Presidential Policy: The National Security Decision Making of Eisenhower and Kennedy* (1998) and editor of the reference volume *The New York Times on the Presidency* (2009) . She also is co-editor (with Rosanna Perotti) of *From Cold War to New World Order: The Foreign Policy of George H. W. Bush* (2002), co-editor (with Mark Landis) of *The Uses and Abuses of Presidential Ratings* (2003), and co-editor (with John J. DiIulio, Jr.) of *Classic Ideas and Current Issues in American Government* (2007).

Bose's current research focuses on the changing role of the United Nations in American foreign policy. She was scholar-in-residence for a nonpartisan course sponsored by The Washington Center in connection with the 2008 Republican National Convention in Minneapolis. She also has designed and taught several courses for Elderhostel, including "The Wisdom of Our Fathers: The Mount Rushmore Presidents"; "Winning the White House in 2008"; and "Another 'Hundred Days' in American Politics?," which compared the early presidential leadership of Franklin D. Roosevelt and Barack Obama. Long Island Business News selected her as one of the "Top 40 Under 40" leaders on Long Island in 2009.

Bose teaches courses on the American Presidency, American Foreign Policy, and American Politics. She taught for six years at the United States Military Academy at West Point, where she also served as Director of American Politics in 2006. She previously taught at Hofstra University from 1996–2000 and represented the American Political Science Association on the Department of State's Historical Advisory Committee from 2001–2004. She earned her undergraduate degree in international politics from Penn State University (1990), and she received her master's (1992) and doctoral (1996) degrees in politics from Princeton University.

Part 1

The American System

In framing a government which is to be administered by men over men, the great difficulty lies in this: You must first enable the government to control the governed; and in the next place oblige it to control itself.

* Federalist No. 51

1

The Study of American Government

WHO GOVERNS?

1. How is political power actually distributed in America?
2. What explains major political change?

TO WHAT ENDS?

1. What value or values matter most in American democracy?
2. Are trade-offs among political purposes inevitable?

After the 9/11 terrorist attacks on the United States, it took the national government many years to implement just a fraction of the bipartisan homeland security policies and programs that nearly everybody favored (such as deploying super-high-tech bomb-detection devices at airports and tightening security for cargo ships, among numerous others). Indeed, a half-decade after the attacks, the failure to act expeditiously on national directives to reinforce vulnerable-to-attack levees and dams figured in the devastation wrought when Hurricanes Katrina and Rita struck the Gulf Coast.

What was behind these historic failures? The answer, you may be surprised to learn, is the same thing that was behind the government's historic achievements in reducing poverty among the elderly, building the interstate highway system, improving public health, and rebuilding war-torn Europe. The answer is that sometimes things get done even when disunity reigns and power is divided between the parties.

The answer, in a word, is politics.

Politics exists in part because people normally differ about two things: who should govern, and the ends toward which they should work.

We want to know the answer to the first question because we believe that those who rule—their personalities and beliefs, their virtues and vices—will affect what they do to and for us. Many people think they already know the answer to the question, and they are prepared to talk and vote on that basis. That is their right, and the opinions they express may be correct. But they may also be wrong. Indeed, many of these opinions *must* be wrong because they are in conflict. When asked, "Who governs?" some people will say "the unions" and some will say "big business"; others will say "the politicians," "the people," or "the special interests." Still others will say "Wall Street," "the military," "crackpot liberals," "the media," "the bureaucrats," or "white males." Not all these answers can be correct—at least not all of the time.

Jean-Pierre Lescourret/Corbis

The answer to the second question is important because it tells us how government affects our lives. We want to know not only who governs, but what difference it makes who governs. In our day-to-day lives, we may not think government makes much difference at all. In one sense that is right, because our most pressing personal concerns—work, play, love, family, health—essentially are private matters on which government touches but slightly. But in a larger and longer perspective government makes a substantial difference. Consider: in 1935, 96 percent of all American families paid no federal income tax, and for the 4 percent or so who did pay, the average rate was only about 4 percent of their incomes. Today almost all families pay federal payroll taxes, and the average rate is 21 percent of their incomes. Or consider: in 1960, in many parts of the country, African Americans could ride only in the backs of buses, had to use washrooms and drinking fountains that were labeled "colored," and could not be served in most public restaurants. Such restrictions have been almost eliminated, in large part because of decisions by the federal government.

It is important to bear in mind that we wish to answer two different questions, and not two versions of the same question. You cannot always predict what goals government will establish knowing only who governs, nor can you always tell who governs by knowing what activities government undertakes. Most people holding national political office are middle-class, middle-aged, white Protestant males, but we cannot then conclude that the government will adopt only policies that are to the narrow advantage of the middle class, the middle-aged, whites, Protestants, or men. If we thought that, we would be at a loss to explain why the rich are taxed more heavily than the poor, why the War on Poverty was declared, why constitutional amendments giving rights to African Americans and women passed Congress by large majorities, or why Catholics and Jews have been appointed to so many important governmental posts.

This book is chiefly devoted to answering the question, Who governs? It is written in the belief that this question cannot be answered without looking at how government makes—or fails to make—decisions about a large variety of concrete issues. Thus in this book we shall inspect government policies to see what individuals, groups, and institutions seem to exert the greatest power in the continuous struggle to define the purposes of government. We shall see that power and purpose are inextricably intertwined.

What Is Political Power?

By **power** we mean the ability of one person to get another person to act in accordance with the first person's intentions. Sometimes an exercise of power is obvious, as when the president tells the air force that it cannot build a new bomber or orders soldiers into combat in a foreign land. Some claim it is exercised in subtle ways that may not be evident even to the participants, as when the president's junior speechwriters, reflecting their own evolving views, adopt a new tone when writing for their boss about controversial social issues like abortion. The speechwriters may not think they are using power—after all, they are the president's subordinates and may rarely see him face-to-face. But if the president lets their words exit his mouth in public, they have used power.

Power is found in all human relationships, but we shall be concerned here only with power as it

power The ability of one person to get another person to act in accordance with the first person's intentions.

Government's Greatest Achievements: A Top 10 List

Based on a survey of 450 history and political science professors and an analysis of over 500 public statutes, here is one list of the government's top 10 post–1950 achievements.

10. Promoted financial security in retirement

9. Reduced the federal budget deficit

8. Increased access to health care for older Americans

7. Strengthened the nation's highway system

6. Ensured safe food and drinking water

5. Reduced workplace discrimination

4. Reduced disease

3. Promoted equal access to public accommodations

2. Expanded the right to vote

1. Rebuilt Europe after World War II

As you read this book and study American government, ponder what might be on the top 10 list for the first quarter of the 21st century.

Source: Adapted from Paul C. Light, "Government's Greatest Achievements of the Past Half Century," Reform Watch Brief #2, Brookings Institution, Washington, D.C., November 2000. Reprinted by permission of the Brookings Institution.

---

is used to affect who will hold government office and how government will behave. This fails to take into account many important things. If a corporation closes a factory in a small town where it was the major employer, it is using power in ways that affect deeply the lives of people. When a university refuses to admit a student or a medical society refuses to license a would-be physician, it is also using power. But to explain how all these things happen would be tantamount to explaining how society as a whole, and in all its particulars, operates. We limit our view here to government, and chiefly to the American federal government. However, we shall repeatedly pay special attention to how things once thought to be "private" matters become "public"—that is, how they manage to become objects of governmental action. Indeed, one of the most striking transformations of American politics has been the extent to which, in recent decades, almost every aspect of human life has found its way onto the governmental agenda. In the 1950s, the federal government would have displayed no interest in a factory closing its doors, a university refusing an applicant, or a profession not accrediting a member. Now government actions can and do affect all these things.

People who exercise political power may or may not have the authority to do so. By **authority** we mean the right to use power. The exercise of rightful power—that is, of authority—is ordinarily easier than the exercise of power not supported by any persuasive claim of right. We accept decisions, often without question, if they are made by people who we believe have the right to make them; we may bow to naked power because we cannot resist it, but by our recalcitrance or our resentment we put the users of naked power to greater trouble than the wielders of authority. In this book, we will on occasion speak of "formal authority." By this we mean that the right to exercise power is vested in a governmental office. A president, a senator, and a federal judge have formal authority to take certain actions.

What makes power rightful varies from time to time and from country to country. In the United States, we usually say a person has political authority if his or her right to act in a certain way is conferred by a law or by a state or national constitution. But what makes a law or constitution a source of right? That is the question of **legitimacy.** In the United States the Constitution today is widely, if not unanimously, accepted as a source of legitimate authority, but that was not always the case.

Much of American political history has been a struggle

authority The right to use power.

legitimacy Political authority conferred by law or by a state or national constitution.

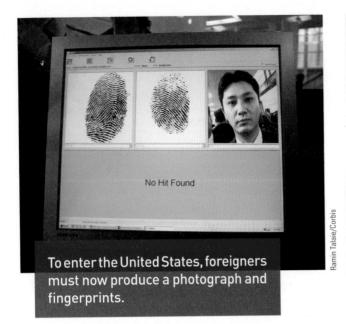

To enter the United States, foreigners must now produce a photograph and fingerprints.

Ramin Talaie/Corbis

An Iraqi woman shows her purple finger indicating that she has voted in 2005, that country's first free election in half a century.

AFP/Getty Images

over what constitutes legitimate authority. The Constitutional Convention in 1787 was an effort to see whether a new, more powerful federal government could be made legitimate; the succeeding administrations of George Washington, John Adams, and Thomas Jefferson were in large measure preoccupied with disputes over the kinds of decisions that were legitimate for the federal government to make. The Civil War was a bloody struggle over the legitimacy of the federal union; the New Deal of Franklin Roosevelt was hotly debated by those who disagreed over whether it was legitimate for the federal government to intervene deeply in the economy. In our own day, even many citizens who take the same view on a hot-button topic like gay marriage disagree over whether it is legitimate to address the issue through an amendment to the Constitution that bans it nationally or whether the matter ought to be left for each state to decide.

On one thing, however, virtually all Americans seem to agree: no exercise of political power by government at any level is legitimate if it is not in some sense democratic. That was hardly always the prevailing view. In 1787, as the Constitution was being debated, Alexander Hamilton worried that the new government he helped create might be too democratic, while George Mason, who refused to sign the Constitution, worried that it was not democratic enough. Today, however, almost everyone believes that democratic government is the only proper kind. Most people believe that American

democracy The rule of the many.

government is democratic; some believe that other institutions of public life—schools, universities, corporations, trade unions, churches—should also be run on democratic principles if they are to be legitimate; and some insist that promoting democracy abroad ought to be a primary purpose of U.S. foreign policy.

Whether democracy is the best way of governing all institutions and whether promoting democracy either has been or ought to be a major objective of U.S. foreign policy are both worthwhile questions. The former question goes beyond the scope of this book, but we will touch upon the latter question later in the text.

What Is Democracy?

Democracy is a word with at least two different meanings. First, the term *democracy* is used to describe those regimes that come as close as possible to Aristotle's definition—the "rule of the many."[1]

Can a Democracy Fight a War Against Terrorists?

On September 11, 2001, a date that will forevermore be referred to as 9/11, war came to the United States when terrorists crashed four hijacked airliners, filled with passengers, into the two towers of the World Trade Center in New York City, into the Pentagon in Washington, D.C., and into some empty land in Pennsylvania. About 3,000 people were killed.

How can a democratic nation respond to a war waged, not by an enemy nation, but by a loose collection of terrorists with cells in many parts of the world? America's new war against terrorism is much more difficult to fight than the one against Nazi Germany and the Japanese warlords in 1941.

- How can we reorganize the military so that it can respond swiftly and effectively against small targets?

- Is it constitutional to try captured terrorists in military tribunals?

- How much new law enforcement authority should be given to police and investigative agencies?

- Should America invade nations that support terrorists?

In the years ahead, these questions will raise profound challenges for American democracy.

Americans felt powerfully connected to their fellow citizens in the immediate aftermath of 9/11.

Matt McDermott/CORBIS SYGMA

A government is democratic if all, or most, of its citizens participate directly in either holding office or making policy. This often is called **direct or participatory democracy.** In Aristotle's time—Greece in the fourth century B.C.—such a government was possible. The Greek city-state, or *polis,* was quite small, and within it citizenship was extended to all free adult male property holders. (Slaves, women, minors, and those without property were excluded from participation in government.) In more recent times, the New England town meeting approximates the Aristotelian ideal. In such a meeting, the adult citizens of a community gather once or twice a year to vote directly on all major issues and expenditures of the town. As towns have become larger and issues more complicated, many town governments have abandoned the pure town meeting in favor of either the representative town meeting (in which a large number of elected representatives, perhaps 200–300, meet to vote on town affairs) or representative government (in which a small number of elected city councilors make decisions).

The second definition of democracy is the principle of governance of most nations that are called democratic. It was most concisely stated by the economist Joseph Schumpeter: "The democratic method is that institutional arrangement for arriving at political decisions in which individuals [that is, leaders] acquire the power to decide by means of

direct or participatory democracy A government in which all or most citizens participate directly.

representative democracy A government in which leaders make decisions by winning a competitive struggle for the popular vote.

a competitive struggle for the people's vote."[2] Sometimes this method is called, approvingly, **representative democracy;** at other times it is referred to, disapprovingly, as the elitist theory of democracy. It is justified by one or both of two arguments: first, it is impractical, owing to limits of time, information, energy, interest, and expertise, for the people to decide on public policy, but it is not impractical to expect them to make reasonable choices among competing leadership groups. Second, some people (including, as we shall see in the next chapter, many of the Framers of the Constitution) believe direct democracy is likely to lead to bad decisions, because people often decide large issues on the basis of fleeting passions and in response to popular demagogues. This concern about direct democracy persists today, as seen from the statements of leaders who do not like what voters have decided. For example, in 2000, voters in Michigan overwhelmingly rejected a referendum that would have increased public funding for private schools. Politicians who opposed the defeated referendum spoke approvingly of the "will of the people," but politicians who favored it spoke disdainfully of "mass misunderstanding."

Is Representative Democracy Best?

Whenever the word *democracy* is used alone in this book, it will have the meaning Schumpeter gave it. As we discuss in the next chapter, the men who wrote the Constitution did not use the word *democracy* in that document. They wrote instead of a "republican form of government," but by that they meant what we call "representative democracy." Whenever we refer to that form of democracy involving the direct participation of all or most citizens, we shall use the term *direct* or *participatory* democracy.

For representative government to work, there must, of course, be an opportunity for genuine leadership competition. This requires in turn that individuals and parties be able to run for office, that communication (through speeches or the press, and in meetings) be free, and that the voters perceive that a meaningful choice exists. Many questions still remain to be answered. For instance: How many offices should be elective and how many appointive? How many candidates or

parties can exist before the choices become hopelessly confused? Where will the money come from to finance electoral campaigns? There is more than one answer to such questions. In some European democracies, for example, very few offices—often just those in the national or local legislature—are elective, and much of the money for campaigning for these offices comes from the government. In the United States, many offices—executive and judicial as well as legislative—are elective, and most of the money the candidates use for campaigning comes from industry, labor unions, and private individuals.

Some people have argued that the virtues of direct or participatory democracy can and should be reclaimed even in a modern, complex society. This can be done either by allowing individual neighborhoods in big cities to govern themselves (community control) or by requiring those affected by some government program to participate in its formulation (citizen participation). In many states, a measure of direct democracy exists when voters can decide on referendum issues—that is, policy choices that appear on the ballot. The proponents of direct democracy defend it as the only way to ensure that the "will of the people" prevails.

The Framers of the Constitution did not think that the "will of the people" was synonymous with the "common interest" or the "public good." They strongly favored representative democracy over direct democracy. They believed that government should mediate, not mirror, popular views and that elected officials should represent, not register, majority sentiments. They supposed that most citizens did not have the time, information, interest, and expertise to make reasonable choices among competing policy positions. They suspected that even highly educated people could be manipulated by demagogic leaders who played on their fears and prejudices. They granted that representative democracy often proceeds slowly and prevents sweeping changes in policy, but they cautioned that a government capable of doing great good quickly also can do great harm quickly. They agreed that majority opinion should figure in the enactment of many or most government policies, but they insisted that the protection of civil rights and civil liberties—the right to a fair trial; the freedom of speech, press, and religion; or the right to vote itself—ought never to hinge on a popular vote. Above all, they embraced representative democracy because they saw it as a way of minimizing the chances that power would be abused either by a tyrannical popular majority or by self-serving officeholders.

The Framers were powerfully influenced by philosophers who had discussed democracy. Aristotle, who lived four centuries before Christ, defined democracy as the rule of the many; that is, rule by ordinary people, most of whom would be poor. But democracy can, he suggested, easily decay into an oligarchy (the rule of the rich) or a tyranny (the rule of a despot). To prevent this, a good political system will be a mixed regime, combining elements of democracy and oligarchy: most people will vote, but talented people will play a large role in managing affairs.

But the decisive influence on the Framers was wielded by John Locke, the 17th-century English writer who argued against powerful kings and in favor of popular consent.[3] People can exist in a state of nature—that is, without any ruler—so long as they can find enough food to eat and a way to protect themselves. But food may not be plentiful and, as a result, life may be poor and difficult.

The human desire for self-preservation will lead people to want a government that will enable them to own property and thereby to increase their supply of food. But unlike his English rival, Thomas Hobbes, Locke did not think it necessary to have an all-powerful government. Hobbes had argued that people live in a "war of all against all" and so an absolute, supreme ruler was essential to prevent civil war.[4] Locke disagreed: people can get along with one another if they can securely own their farms and live off what they produce.

A decent government must exist with the consent of the governed and be managed by majority rule. To prevent a majority from hurting a minority of the people, Locke wrote, the government should separate its powers, with different and competing legislative and executive branches.

As we shall see in the next chapter, what the Framers tried to do in 1787 was to create a government that would protect freedom and private property. And as with Aristotle, they hoped they had created a moderate regime that would simultaneously safeguard people and leave them alone.

How Is Political Power Distributed?

The second question asks how political power has actually been distributed in America's representative democracy. Scholars differ in their interpretations of the American political experience. Where some see a steady march of democracy, others see no such thing; where some emphasize how voting and other rights have been steadily expanded, others stress how they were denied to so many for so long, and so forth. Short of attempting to reconcile these competing historical interpretations, let us step back now for a moment to our definition of representative democracy and four competing views about how political power has been distributed in America.

Representative democracy is defined as any system of government in which leaders are authorized to make decisions—and thereby to wield political power—by winning a competitive struggle for the popular vote. It is obvious then that very different sets of hands can control political power, depending on what kinds of people can become leaders, how the struggle for votes is carried on, how much freedom to act is given to those who win the struggle, and what other sorts of influence (besides the desire for popular approval) affect the leaders' actions.

In some cases, the leaders will be so sharply constrained by what most people want that the actions of officeholders will follow the preferences of citizens very closely. We shall call such cases examples of *majoritarian politics* wherein elected officials are the delegates of the people, acting as the people (or a majority of them) would act were the matter put to a popular vote. The issues handled in a majoritarian fashion can be only those sufficiently important to command the attention of most citizens, sufficiently clear to elicit an informed opinion from citizens, and sufficiently feasible to address so that what citizens want done can in fact be done.

When circumstances do not permit majoritarian decision making, then some group of officials will have to act without knowing (and perhaps without caring) exactly what people want. Indeed, even on issues that do evoke a clear opinion from a majority of citizens, the shaping of the details of a policy will reflect the views of those who are sufficiently motivated to go to the trouble of becoming active participants in policymaking. These active participants usually will be a small, and probably an unrepresentative, minority. Thus the actual distribution of political power, even in a democracy, will depend importantly on the composition of the political elites who are actually involved in the struggles over policy. By **elite** we mean an identifiable group of persons who possess a disproportionate share of some valued resource—in this case, political power.

There are at least four ways of describing political elites: (1) elites reflect a dominant

elite Persons who possess a disproportionate share of some valued resource, like money or power.

RESEARCH FRONTIERS

Do Ballot Initiatives Bolster "Direct Democracy"?

The Framers of the Constitution favored representative democracy over direct democracy, but today in two dozen states voters can make laws directly by putting policy measures on the ballot or indirectly by forcing the governor or state legislature to take up measures the voters like. This process normally starts with a petition signed by a certain number of citizens.

From the 1890's to the present, direct democracy proponents have claimed that ballot initiatives promote citizen engagement and education, check the influence of organized interest groups, and spur major policy reforms. Critics of the system argue that direct democracy weakens the legislature, helps wealthy interest groups to dominate decisions, and leads to the passage of popular but poorly crafted laws. Whichever view is correct, the system has made major decisions on tax policy, gay rights, and criminal justice.

Most states that permit the initiative first adopted it during the Progressive Era, mostly between 1898 and 1918. But why did some Progressive Era state legislatures grant citizens this power while others did not? The conventional answer is that states with populist traditions, led by reform-minded officials, adopted the initiative early and helped citizens to use it often.

That answer, however, has been challenged by political scientist Daniel A. Smith and others. Using sophisticated analytical tools, they find that the level of interparty legislative competition determined whether states embraced or eschewed the initiative: only when and where a majority party's leaders feared that they were losing their grip, or a minority party's leaders barely controlled the body, did either group in effect act to offset the other party's power by empowering the voters.

Progressive Era reforms (women's suffrage, prohibition, eight-hour workdays, and others) probably owed less to ballot initiatives than most historians have hitherto assumed. Recent ballot initiatives have educated citizens about many issues and gotten previously disengaged people into politics. Still, the initiatives have often been crafted and contested by well-financed organized interest groups allied with one or the other major party. Overall, ballot initiatives seem to have little impact on turnout in presidential elections, and draw only slightly more voters to the polls for midterm congressional elections.

Neither Smith nor other experts, however, conclude that ballot initiatives or "direct democracy" itself are bad ideas. Research by Justin H. Phillips suggests that, other things equal, states that permit the initiative process have legislatures that are considerably less prone to political polarization and more likely to produce public laws that, for good or for ill, reflect most citizens' policy preferences.

- Does your home state, the state in which you now reside, or a nearby state have the initiative?

- What, if any, initiatives have been on the ballot in recent years, and which have passed?

- Did the policies stand, or did the state legislature or a state or federal court modify or overturn them?

- What is the evidence concerning whether the policies have proven good or bad, and how does this evidence support or oppose the Framers' case against direct democracy?

Sources: Daniel A. Smith and Dustin Fridkin, "Delegating Direct Democracy: Intraparty Legislative Competition and the Adoption of the Initiative in the American States," *American Political Science Review*, August 2008, pp. 333–350; Daniel A. Smith and Caroline Tolbert, *Educated by the Initiative: The Effects of Direct Democracy on Citizens and Political Organizations in the American States* (University of Michigan Press, 2004); Daniel A. Joseph and Joseph Lubinski, "Direct Democracy During the Progressive Era: A Crack in the Populist Veneer?," *Journal of Policy History*, Vol. 14, No. 2, pp. 349–383; Justin H. Phillips, "Does the Citizen Initiative Weaken Party Government in the United States?" *State Politics and Policy Quarterly*, Summer 2008, pp. 127–149.

social class; (2) a group of business, military, labor union, and elected officials control all decisions; (3) appointed bureaucrats run everything; and (4) representatives of a large number of interest groups are in charge.

The first view began with the theories of Karl Marx who, in the 19th century, argued that governments were dominated by business owners (the "bourgeoisie") until a revolution replaced them with rule by laborers (the "proletariat").[5] But strict Marxism has collapsed in most countries. Today a **class view,** though it may take some inspiration from Marx, is less dogmatic and emphasizes the power of "the rich" or the leaders of multinational corporations.

The second theory ties business leaders together with whatever other elites concern some people: top military officials, labor union leaders, mass media executives, and the heads of a few special interest groups. This **power elite view** argues that American democracy is dominated by a few top leaders, many of them wealthy or privately powerful, who do not hold elective office.[6]

The third concept is that appointed officials run everything despite the efforts of elected officials and the public to control them. The **bureaucratic view** was first set forth by the German scholar, Max Weber (1864–1920). He argued that the modern state, in order to become successful, puts its affairs in the hands of appointed bureaucrats whose competence is essential to the management of complex affairs.[7] These officials, invisible to most people, have mastered the written records and legislative details of the government and do more than just implement democratic policies: they actually make those policies.

The fourth view argues that political resources—such as money, prestige, expertise, and access to the mass media—have become so widely distributed that no single elite, no social class, no bureaucratic arrangement, can control them.[8] Political power is instead based on a **pluralist view.** In the United States, political resources are broadly shared in part because there are so many governmental institutions (cities, states, school boards) and so many rival institutions (legislatures, executives, judges, bureaucrats) that no single group can dominate most, or even much, of the political process.

As you go through this book, it will try to evaluate these rival theories and indicate under what circumstances one or the other is true. A more precise statement of how policies are made can be found in Chapter 17.

Is Democracy Driven by Self-Interest?

Of the four views of how political power has been distributed in the United States, the pluralist view does the most to reassure one that America has been, and continues to be, a democracy in more than name only. But the pluralist view, not less than the other three, may lead some to the cynical conclusion that, whichever view is correct, politics is a self-seeking enterprise in which everybody is out for personal gain. Though there is surely plenty of self-interest among political elites (at least as much as there is among college or high school students!), it does not necessarily follow that the resulting policies will be wholly self-serving. Nor does it follow that democracy itself is driven mainly or solely by people's baser motives or selfish desires.

For one thing, a policy may be good or bad independent of the motives of the person who decided it, just as a product sold on the market may be useful or useless regardless of the profit-seeking or wage-seeking motives of those who produced it. For another thing, the self-interest of individuals often is an incomplete guide to their actions. People must frequently choose between two courses of action, neither of which has an obvious "payoff" to them. We caution against the cynical explanation of politics that Americans seem especially prone to adopt. Alexis de Tocqueville, the French author of a perceptive account of American life and politics in the early 19th century, noticed this trait among us.

> *Americans…are fond of explaining almost all the actions of their lives by the principle of self-interest rightly understood.…In this respect I think they frequently fail to do themselves justice; for in the United States as well as elsewhere people are sometimes seen to give way to those disinterested and spontaneous impulses that are natural to man; but the Americans seldom admit that they yield to emotions of this kind; they are more anxious to do honor to their philosophy than to themselves.*[9]

The belief that people will usually act on the basis of their self-interest, narrowly defined, is a theory to be tested, not an assumption to be made. Sometimes, as happened in New York City on September 11, 2001, elected officials, government workers, and average citizens behave in ways that plainly transcend personal or professional self-interest. There are countless other far less dramatic but still telling examples of people acting publicly in ways that seem anything but self-interested. To understand why people behave as they do, it is not enough to know their incomes or their jobs; one must also know something about their attitudes, their allies, and the temper

class view View that the government is dominated by capitalists.

power elite view View that the government is dominated by a few top leaders, most of whom are outside of government.

bureaucratic view View that the government is dominated by appointed officials.

pluralist view The belief taht competition among all affected interests shapes public policy.

of the times. In short, political preferences cannot invariably be predicted simply by knowing economic or organizational position.

Yet another reason to resist interpreting American democracy as if it were always and everywhere driven by narrowly self-interested individuals and groups is that many of the most important political happenings in U.S. history—the revolutionary movement of the 1770s and 1780s, the battle for civil rights in the 1950s and 1960s, to name just two—were led against long odds by people who risked much knowing that they might not succeed and suspecting that, even if they did succeed, generations might pass before their efforts truly benefited anyone. As we shall see, self-interest figures mightily in politics, but so do ideas about the common good and public-spirited behavior.

What Explains Political Change?

When we see American democracy from the perspective of the past, we will find it hard to accept as generally true any simple interpretation of politics. Economic interests, powerful elites, entrenched bureaucrats, competing pressure groups, and morally impassioned individuals have all played a part in shaping our government and its policies. But the great shifts in the character of our government—its size, scope, institutional arrangements, and the direction of its policies—have reflected complex and sometimes sudden changes in elite or mass *beliefs* about what government is supposed to do.

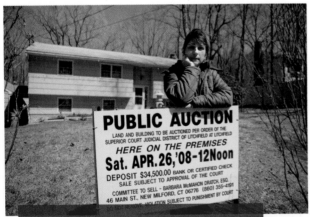

When thousands of people could no longer pay their mortgages, a major recession occurred.

In the 1920s, it was widely assumed that the federal government would play a small role in our lives. From the 1930s through the 1970s, it was generally believed that the federal government would try to solve whatever social or economic problem existed. From 1981 through 1988, the administration of Ronald Reagan sought to reverse that assumption and to cut back on the taxes Washington levied, the money it spent, and the regulations it imposed. It is clear that no simple theory of politics is likely to explain both the growth of federal power after 1932 and the effort to cut back on that power starting in 1981. Every student of politics sooner or later learns that the hardest things to explain usually are the most important ones.

Take the case of foreign affairs. During certain periods in our history we have taken an active interest in the outside world—at the time the nation was founded, when France and England seemed to have it in their power to determine whether or not America would survive as a nation; in the 1840s, when we sought to expand the nation into areas where Mexico and Canada had claims; in the late 1890s, when many leaders believed we had an obligation to acquire an overseas empire in the Caribbean and the Pacific; and in the period from the 1940s to the 1960s, when we openly accepted the role of the world's police officer. At other times America has looked inward, spurning opportunities for expansion and virtually ignoring events that in other periods would have been a cause for war, or at least mobilization. Today, America seems to be looking outward once again, spurred, on the one side, by unprecedented terrorist attacks against the country and, on the other side, by historic opportunities to make new friends with old foreign foes.

Deep-seated beliefs, major economic developments, and widely shared (or competing) opinions about what constitutes the dominant political problem of the time shape the nature of day-to-day political conflict. What this means is that, in any broad historical or comparative perspective, politics is not just about "who gets what," though that is part of the story. It is about how people, or elites claiming to speak for people, define the public interest. Lest one think that such definitions are mere window dressing, bear in mind that on occasion men and women have been prepared to fight and die for one definition or another. Suppose you had been alive in 1861. Do you think you would have viewed slavery as a matter of gains and losses, costs and benefits, winners and losers? Some people did. Or do you think you would have been willing to fight to abolish or preserve it? Many others did just that. The differences in these ways of thinking about such an issue are at least as important as how institutions are organized or elections conducted.

The Nature of Politics

Ideally, political scientists ought to be able to give clear answers, amply supported by evidence, to the questions we have posed about American democracy, starting with "who governs?" In reality they can (at best) give partial, contingent, and controversial answers. The reason is to be found in the nature of our subject. Unlike economists, who assume that people have more or less stable preferences and can compare ways of satisfying those preferences by looking at the relative prices of various goods and services, political scientists are interested in how preferences are formed, especially for those kinds of services, such as national defense or pollution control, that cannot be evaluated chiefly in terms of monetary costs.

Understanding preferences is vital to understanding power. Who did what in government is not hard to find out, but who wielded power—that is, who made a difference in the outcome and for what reason—is much harder to discover. *Power* is a word that conjures up images of deals, bribes, power plays, and arm-twisting. In fact, most power exists because of shared understanding, common friendships, communal or organizational loyalties, and different degrees of prestige. These are hard to identify and almost impossible to quantify.

Nor can the distribution of political power be inferred simply by knowing what laws are on the books or what administrative actions have been taken. The enactment of a consumer protection law does not mean that consumers are powerful, any more than the absence of such a law means that corporations are powerful. The passage of such a law could reflect an aroused public opinion, the lobbying of a small group claiming to speak for consumers, the ambitions of a senator, or the intrigues of one business firm seeking to gain a competitive advantage over another. A close analysis of what the law entails and how it was passed and administered is necessary before much of anything can be said.

This book will avoid sweeping claims that we have an "imperial" presidency (or an impotent one), an "obstructionist" Congress (or an innovative one), or "captured" regulatory agencies. Such labels do an injustice to the different roles that presidents, members of Congress, and administrators play in different kinds of issues and in different historical periods.

The view taken in this book is that judgments about institutions and interests can be made only after one has seen how they behave on a variety of important issues or potential issues, such as economic policy, the regulation of business, social welfare, civil rights and liberties, and foreign and military affairs. The policies adopted or blocked, the groups heeded or ignored, the values embraced or rejected—these constitute the raw material out of which one can fashion an answer to the central questions we have asked: Who governs? and To what ends?

The way in which our institutions of government handle social welfare, for example, differs from the way other democratic nations handle it, and it differs as well from the way our own institutions once treated it. The description of our institutions in Part III will therefore include not only an account of how they work today but also a brief historical background on their workings and a comparison with similar institutions in other countries. There is a tendency to assume that how we do things today is the only way they could possibly be done. In fact, there are other ways to operate a government based on some measure of popular rule. History, tradition, and belief weigh heavily on all that we do.

Although political change is not always accompanied by changes in public laws, the policy process is arguably one of the best barometers of changes in who governs. In Chapter 15, we offer a way of classifying and explaining the politics of different policy issues. The model we present there has been developed, refined, and tested over more than two decades (longer than most of our readers have been alive!). Our own students and others have valued it mainly because, they have found, it helps to answer such questions about who governs: How do political issues get on the public agenda in the first place? How, for example, did sexual harassment, which was hardly ever discussed or debated by Congress, burst onto the public agenda? Once on the agenda, how does the politics of issues like income security for older Americans—for example, the politics of Social Security, a program that has been on the federal books since 1935 (see Chapter 19)—change over time? And if, today, one cares about expanding

WHAT WOULD YOU DO?

MEMORANDUM

To: *Governor Steve Finore*

From: *Edward Heron, chief policy adviser*

Subject: *Initiative Repeal*

You have supported several successful initiatives (life imprisonment for thrice-convicted violent felons, property tax limits), but you have never publicly stated a view on the initiative itself, and the repeal proposal will probably surface during tomorrow's press briefing.

Arguments for a ban:

1. Ours is a representative, not a direct, democracy in which voters elect leaders and elected leaders make policy decisions subject to review by the courts.

2. Voters often are neither rational nor respectful of constitutional rights. For example, many people demand both lower taxes and more government services, and polls find that most voters would prohibit people with certain views from speaking and deprive all persons accused of a violent crime from getting out on bail while awaiting trial.

3. Over the past 100 years, about 800 statewide ballot initiatives have been passed in 24 states. Rather than giving power to the people, special-interest groups have spent billions of dollars manipulating voters to pass initiatives that enrich or benefit them, not the public at large.

Arguments against a ban:

1. When elected officials fail to respond to persistent public majorities favoring tougher crime measures, lower property taxes, and other popular concerns, direct democracy via the initiative is legitimate, and the courts can still review the law.

Friday,

Legal and Policy Experts Call for a Ban on Ballot Initiatives

December 11
SACRAMENTO, CA

A report released yesterday and signed by more than 100 law and public policy professors statewide urges that the state's constitution be amended to ban legislation by initiative. The initiative allows state voters to place legislative measures directly on the ballot by getting enough signatures. The initiative "has led to disastrous policy decisions on taxes, crime, and other issues," the report declared…

2. More Americans than ever have college degrees and easy access to information about public affairs. Studies find that most average citizens are able to figure out which candidates, parties, or advocacy groups come closest to supporting their own economic interests and personal values.

3. All told, the 24 states that passed 35 laws by initiative also passed more than 14,000 laws by the regular legislative process (out of more than 70,000 bills they considered). Studies find that special-interest groups are severely limited in their ability to pass new laws by initiative, while citizens' groups with broad-based public support are behind most initiatives that pass.

Your decision:

Favor ban _____   Oppose ban _____

civil liberties (see Chapter 5) or protecting civil rights (see Chapter 6), what political obstacles and opportunities are you likely to face, and what role are public opinion, organized interest groups, the media, the courts, political parties, and other institutions likely to play in frustrating or fostering your particular policy preferences, whatever they might be?

Peek ahead, if you wish, to the book's policy chapters, but understand that the place to begin a search for how power is distributed in national politics and what purposes that power serves is with the founding of the federal government in 1787: the Constitutional Convention and the events leading up to it. Though the decisions of that time were not made by philosophers or professors, the practical men who made them had a philosophic and professorial cast of mind, and thus they left behind a fairly explicit account of what values they sought to protect and what arrangements they thought ought to be made for the allocation of political power.

SUMMARY

There are two major questions about politics: Who governs? To what ends? This book focuses mainly on answering the first.

Four answers have traditionally been given to the question of who governs.

- The *class*—those who control the economic system will control the political one.
- The *elitist*—a few top leaders, not all of them drawn from business, make the key decisions without reference to popular desires.
- The *bureaucratic*—appointed civil servants run things.
- The *pluralist*—competition among affected interests shapes public policy.

To choose among these theories or to devise new ones requires more than describing governmental institutions and processes. In addition, one must examine the kinds of issues that do (or do not) get taken up by the political system and how that system resolves them.

The distinction between different types of democracies is important. The Framers of the Constitution intended that America be a representative democracy in which the power to make decisions is determined by means of a free and competitive struggle for the citizens' votes.

RECONSIDERING WHO GOVERNS?

1. How is political power actually distributed in America?

Some believe that political power in America is monopolized by wealthy business leaders, by other powerful elites, or by entrenched government bureaucrats. Others believe that political resources such as money, prestige, expertise, organizational position, and access to the mass media are so widely dispersed in American society, and the governmental institutions and offices in which power may be exercised so numerous and varied, that no single group truly has all or most political power. In this view, political power in America is distributed more or less widely. No one, however, argues that political resources are distributed equally in America.

2. What explains major political change?

The great shifts in the character of American government—its size, scope, institutional arrangements, and the direction of its policies—have reflected complex and sometimes sudden changes in elite or mass beliefs about what government is supposed to do. For instance, before Franklin Roosevelt's New Deal, most leaders and citizens did not automatically look to the federal government to improve the economy, and many doubted that Washington had any legitimate role to play in managing economic affairs. Today, however, leaders in both political parties assume that Washington must help reduce unemployment, create jobs, and otherwise actively manage the country's economy. The federal government now has policies on street crime, the environment, homeland security, and many other issues that were not on the federal agenda a half-century (or, in the case of homeland security, a mere half-decade) ago.

RECONSIDERING TO WHAT ENDS?

1. What value or values matter most in American democracy?

The Framers of the Constitution had their vision of American democracy and favored certain values, but neither they nor the Constitution specify what values matter most or how best to make trade-offs among or between competing political ends.

2. Are trade-offs among political purposes inevitable?

Yes. For instance, the government cannot spend more on health care without spending less on something else we may also desire—college loans, police patrols, or toxic waste cleanups. Nor can it maximize one value or purpose (say respecting the rights of persons suspected or accused of terrorist acts) without minimizing others (like liberty and associated legal rights). And, even if everyone agreed that the same one value—say liberty—was supreme, we could not all exercise it at the same time or to the fullest or just as we pleased without all losing it in the bargain: if everybody is at liberty to shout simultaneously, nobody is at liberty to be heard individually. We often cannot have more of some things we desire without having less of other things we desire, too. That is as true in politics and government, and as true for American democracy, as it is in other parts of life.

SUGGESTED READINGS

Banfield, Edward C. *Political Influence.* New York: Free Press, 1961. A method of analyzing politics—in this case, in the city of Chicago—comparable to the approach adopted in this book.

Crick, Bernard, *The American Science of Politics.* London: Routledge & Kegan Paul, 1959. A critical review of the methods of studying government and politics.

Marx, Karl, and Friedrich Engels. "The Manifesto of the Communist Party." In *The Marx-Engels Reader*, 2d ed., edited by Robert C. Tucker. New York: Norton, 1978, 469–500.

Schumpeter, Joseph A. *Capitalism, Socialism, and Democracy*. 3d ed. New York: Harper Torchbooks, 1950, chs. 20–23. A lucid statement of the theory of representative democracy and how it differs from participatory democracy.

Truman, David B. *The Governmental Process*. 2d ed. New York: Knopf, 1971. A pluralist interpretation of American politics.

Weber, Max. *From Max Weber: Essays in Sociology*. Translated and edited by H. H. Gerth and C. Wright Mills. London: Routledge & Kegan Paul, 1948, ch. 8. A theory of bureaucracy and its power.

2

The Constitution

WHO GOVERNS?

1. What is the difference between a democracy and a republic?
2. What branch of government has the greatest power?

TO WHAT ENDS?

1. Does the Constitution tell us what goals the government should serve?
2. Whose freedom does the Constitution protect?

If you had been alive in 1787, you might have wondered what was going on in Philadelphia. A small group of men (all white) were meeting to discuss how the country should be run. They were not chosen by popular election, and they were meeting in secret. There was no press coverage. A few famous men, such as Patrick Henry of Virginia, had refused to be delegates, and one state, Rhode Island, sent no delegates at all.

And just what were these men going to do? They were supposed to fix the defects in the Articles of Confederation, the arrangement under which the former American colonies had waged war against England. But when the convention was over, no defects in the Articles had been fixed; instead, a wholly new constitution had been proposed. And it was a constitution that in the eyes of some people gave too much power to a new national government.

The goal of the American Revolution was liberty. It was not the first revolution with that object; it may not have been the last; but it was perhaps the clearest case of a people altering the political order violently, simply in order to protect their liberties. Subsequent revolutions had more complicated, or utterly different, objectives. The French Revolution in 1789 sought not only liberty, but "equality and fraternity." The Russian Revolution (1917) and the Chinese Revolution (culminating in 1949) chiefly sought equality and were little concerned with liberty as we understand it.

Gregg Newton/Corbis

The Problem of Liberty

What the American colonists sought to protect when they signed the Declaration of Independence in 1776 were the traditional liberties to which they thought they were entitled as British subjects. These liberties included the right to bring their legal cases before truly independent judges rather than ones subordinate to the king; to be free of the burden of having British troops quartered in their homes; to engage in trade without burdensome restrictions; and, of course, to pay no taxes voted by a British Parliament in which they had no direct representation. During the ten years or more of agitation and argument leading up to the War of Independence, most colonists believed their liberties could be protected while they remained a part of the British Empire.

Slowly but surely opinion shifted. By the time war broke out in 1775, a large number of colonists (though perhaps not a majority) had reached the conclusion that the colonies would have to become independent of Great Britain if their liberties were to be assured. The colonists had many reasons for regarding independence as the only solution, but one is especially important: they no longer had confidence in the English constitution. This constitution was not a single document but rather a collection of laws, charters, and traditional understandings that proclaimed the liberties of British subjects. Yet these liberties, in the eyes of the colonists, were regularly violated despite their constitutional protection. Clearly, then, the English constitution was an inadequate check on the abuses of political power. The revolutionary leaders sought an explanation of the insufficiency of the constitution and found it in human nature.

THE COLONIAL MIND

"A lust for domination is more or less natural to all parties," one colonist wrote.[1] Men will seek power, many colonists believed, because they are ambitious, greedy, and easily corrupted. John Adams denounced the "luxury, effeminacy, and venality" of English politics; Patrick Henry spoke scathingly of the "corrupt House of Commons"; and Alexander Hamilton described England as "an old, wrinkled, withered, worn-out hag."[2] This was in part flamboyant rhetoric designed to whip up enthusiasm for the conflict, but it was also deeply revealing of the colonial mind. Their belief that English politicians—and by implication, most politicians—tended to be corrupt was the colonists' explanation of why the English constitution was not an adequate guarantee of the liberty of the citizens. This opinion was to persist and, as we shall see, profoundly affect the way the Americans went about designing their own governments.

The liberties the colonists fought to protect were, they thought, widely understood. They were based not on the generosity of the king or the language of statutes but on a "higher law" embodying "natural rights" that were ordained by God, discoverable in nature and history, and essential to human progress. These rights, John Dickinson wrote, "are born with us; exist with us; and cannot be taken away

Even before the Revolutionary War, many felt some form of union would be necessary if the rebellious colonies were to survive. In 1774, the *Massachusetts Spy* portrayed the colonies as segments of a snake that must "Join or Die."

LC-DIG-ppmsca-02949/Library of Congress

Lafayette College Art Collection

The American colonists' desire to assert their liberties led in time to a deep hostility toward British government, as when these New Yorkers toppled a statue of King George III, melted it down, and used the metal to make bullets.

from us by any human power."[3] There was general agreement that the essential rights included life, liberty, and property long before Thomas Jefferson wrote them into the Declaration of Independence. (Jefferson changed "property" to "the pursuit of happiness," but almost everybody else went on talking about property.)

This emphasis on property did not mean the American Revolution was thought up by the rich and wellborn to protect their interests or that there was a struggle between property owners and the propertyless. In late-18th-century America, most people (except the black slaves) had property of some kind. The overwhelming majority of citizens were self-employed—as farmers or artisans—and rather few people benefited financially by gaining independence from England. Taxes were higher during and after the war than before, trade was disrupted by the conflict, and debts mounted perilously as various expedients were invented to pay for the struggle. There were, of course, war profiteers and those who tried to manipulate the currency to their own advantage, but most Americans at the time of the war saw the conflict clearly in terms of political rather than economic issues. It was a war of ideology.

Everyone recognizes the glowing language with which Jefferson set out the case for independence in the second paragraph of the Declaration:

> *We hold these truths to be self-evident, that all men are created equal, that they are endowed by their Creator with certain unalienable Rights, that among these are Life, Liberty, and the pursuit of Happiness.—That to secure these rights, Governments are instituted among Men, deriving their just powers from the consent of the governed—that whenever any Form of Government becomes destructive of these ends, it is the Right of the People to alter or to abolish it, and to institute new Government, having its foundation on such principles, and organizing its powers in such form, as to them shall seem most likely to effect their Safety and Happiness.*

What almost no one recalls, but what are an essential part of the Declaration, are the next 27 paragraphs, in which Jefferson listed, item by item, the specific complaints the colonists had against George III and his ministers. None of these items spoke of social or economic conditions in the colonies; all spoke instead of specific violations of political liberties. The Declaration was in essence a lawyer's brief prefaced by a stirring philosophical claim that

unalienable A human right based on nature or God.

the rights being violated were **unalienable**—that is, based on nature and Providence, and not on the whims or preferences of people. Jefferson, in his original draft, added another complaint—that the king had allowed the slave trade to continue *and* was inciting slaves to revolt against their masters. Congress, faced with so contradictory a charge, decided to include a muted reference to slave insurrections and omit all reference to the slave trade.

THE REAL REVOLUTION

The Revolution was more than the War of Independence. It began before the war, continued after it, and involved more than driving out the British army by force of arms. The *real* Revolution, as John Adams afterward explained in a letter to

a friend, was the "radical change in the principles, opinions, sentiments, and affections of the people."[4] This radical change had to do with a new vision of what could make political authority legitimate and personal liberties secure. Government by royal prerogative was rejected; instead, legitimate government would require the consent of the governed. Political power could not be exercised on the basis of tradition but only as a result of a direct grant of power contained in a written constitution. Human liberty existed before government was organized, and government must respect that liberty. The legislative branch of government, in which the people were directly represented, should be superior to the executive branch.

These were indeed revolutionary ideas. No government at the time had been organized on the basis of these principles. And to the colonists such notions were not empty words but rules to be put into

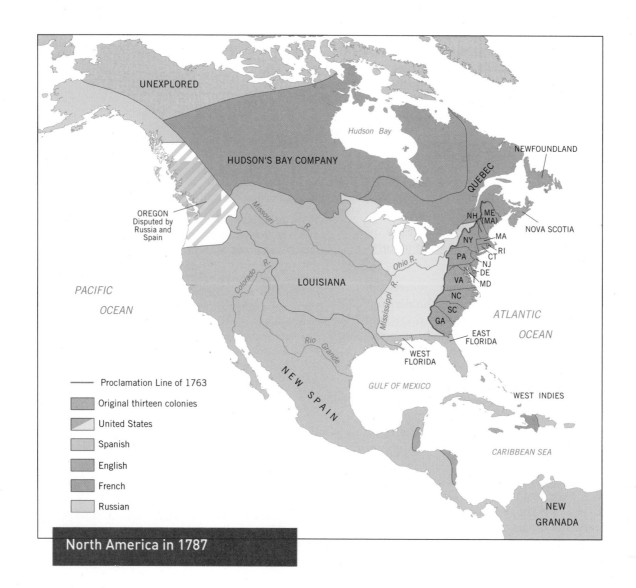

Proclamation Line of 1763
Original thirteen colonies
United States
Spanish
English
French
Russian

North America in 1787

immediate practice. In 1776, eight states adopted written constitutions. Within a few years, every former colony had adopted one except Connecticut and Rhode Island, two states that continued to rely on their colonial charters. Most state constitutions had detailed bills of rights defining personal liberties, and most placed the highest political power in the hands of elected representatives.

Written constitutions, representatives, and bills of rights are so familiar to us now that we forget how bold and unprecedented those innovations were in 1776. Indeed, many Americans did not think they would succeed: such arrangements would be either so strong that they would threaten liberty or so weak that they would permit chaos.

The 11 years that elapsed between the Declaration of Independence and the signing of the Constitution in 1787 were years of turmoil, uncertainty, and fear. George Washington had to wage a bitter, protracted war without anything resembling a strong national government to support him. The supply and financing of his army were based on a series of hasty improvisations, most badly administered and few adequately supported by the fiercely independent states. When peace came, many parts of the nation were a shambles. At least a quarter of New York City was in ruins, and many other communities were nearly devastated. Though the British lost the war, they still were powerful on the North American continent, with an army available in Canada (where many Americans loyal to Britain had fled) and a large navy at sea. Spain claimed the Mississippi River valley and occupied what are now Florida and California. Men who had left their farms to fight came back to discover themselves in debt with no money and heavy taxes. The paper money printed to finance the war was now virtually worthless.

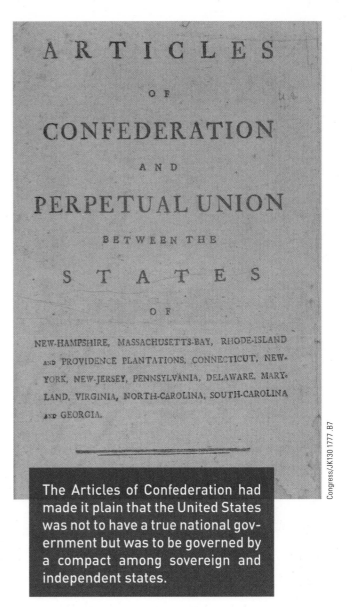

Congress/JK130 1777 .B7

The Articles of Confederation had made it plain that the United States was not to have a true national government but was to be governed by a compact among sovereign and independent states.

WEAKNESSES OF THE CONFEDERATION

The 13 states had formed only a faint semblance of a national government with which to bring order to the nation. The **Articles of Confederation,** which went into effect in 1781, created little more than a "league of friendship" that could not levy taxes or regulate commerce. Each state retained its sovereignty and independence, each state (regardless of size) had one vote in Congress, nine (of 13) votes were required to pass any measure, and the delegates who cast these votes were picked and paid for by the state legislatures. Congress did have the power to make peace, and thus it was able to ratify the treaty with England in 1783. It could coin money, but there was precious little to coin; it could appoint the key army officers, but the army was small and dependent for support on independent state militias; it was allowed to run the post office, then, as now, a thankless task that nobody else wanted. John Hancock, who in 1785 was elected to the meaningless office of "president" under the Articles, never showed up to take the job. Several states claimed the unsettled lands in the West, and they occasionally pressed those claims with guns. Pennsylvania and Virginia went to war near Pittsburgh, and Vermont threatened to become part of Canada. There was no national judicial system to settle these or other claims among the states. To amend the Articles of Confederation, all 13 states had to agree.

Articles of Confederation A weak constitution that governed America during the Revolutionary War.

Library of Congress

John Hancock was proud to have signed the Declaration of Independence but thought so little of the presidency under the Articles of Confederation that he never bothered to accept the job.

they met, they were keenly aware of the problems of the confederacy but far from agreeing as to what should be done about those problems. The protection of life, liberty, and property was their objective in 1787 as it had been in 1776, but they had no accepted political theory that would tell them what kind of national government, if any, would serve that goal.

THE LESSONS OF EXPERIENCE

They had read ancient and modern political history, only to learn that nothing seemed to work. James Madison spent a good part of 1786 studying books sent to by Thomas Jefferson, then in Paris, in hopes of finding some model for a workable American republic. He took careful notes on various confederacies in ancient Greece and on the more modern confederacy of the United Netherlands. He reviewed the history of Switzerland and Poland and the ups and downs of the Roman republic. He concluded that there was no model; as he later put it in one of the *Federalist* papers, history consists only of beacon lights "which give warning of the course to be shunned, without pointing out that which ought to be pursued."[5] The problem seemed to be that confederacies were too weak to govern and tended to collapse from internal dissension, while all stronger forms of government were so powerful as to trample the liberties of the citizens.

State Constitutions

Madison and the others did not need to consult history, or even the defects of the Articles of Confederation, for illustrations of the problem. These could be found in the government of the American states at the time. Pennsylvania and Massachusetts exemplified two aspects of the problem. The Pennsylvania constitution, adopted in 1776, created the most radically democratic of the new state regimes. All power was given to a one-house (unicameral) legislature, the Assembly, the members of which were elected annually for one-year terms. No legislator could serve more than four years. There was no governor or president, only an Executive Council that had few powers. Thomas Paine, whose pamphlets had helped precipitate the break with England, thought the Pennsylvania constitution was the best in America, and in France philosophers hailed it as the very embodiment of the principle of rule by the people. Though popular in France, it was a good deal less popular in Philadelphia. The Assembly disfranchised the Quakers, persecuted conscientious objectors to the war, ignored the requirement of trial by juries, and manipulated the judiciary.[6] To Madison and his friends, the Pennsylvania constitution

Many of the leaders of the Revolution, such as George Washington and Alexander Hamilton, believed a stronger national government was essential. They lamented the disruption of commerce and travel caused by the quarrelsome states and deeply feared the possibility of foreign military intervention, with England or France playing one state off against another. A small group of men, conferring at Washington's home at Mount Vernon in 1785, decided to call a meeting to discuss trade regulation. That meeting, held at Annapolis, Maryland, in September 1786, was not well attended (no delegates arrived from New England), and so another meeting, this one in Philadelphia, was called for the following spring—in May 1787—to consider ways of remedying the defects of the Confederation.

Constitutional Convention A meeting in Philadelphia in 1787 that produced a new constitution.

The Constitutional Convention

The delegates assembled at Philadelphia at the **Constitutional Convention,** for what was advertised (and authorized by Congress) as a meeting to revise the Articles; they adjourned four months later having written a wholly new constitution. When demonstrated how a government, though democratic, could be tyrannical as a result of concentrating all powers into one set of hands.

The Massachusetts constitution, adopted in 1780, was a good deal less democratic. There was a clear separation of powers among the various branches of government, the directly elected governor could veto acts of the legislature, and judges served for life. Both voters and elected officials had to be property owners; the governor, in fact, had to own at least £1,000 worth of property. The principal officeholders had to swear they were Christians.

Shays's Rebellion

But if the government of Pennsylvania was thought too strong, that of Massachusetts seemed too weak, despite its "conservative" features. In January 1787, a group of ex-Revolutionary War soldiers and officers, plagued by debts and high taxes and fearful of losing their property to creditors and tax collectors, forcibly prevented the courts in western Massachusetts from sitting. This became known as **Shays's Rebellion,** after one of the officers, Daniel Shays. The governor of Massachusetts asked the Continental Congress to send troops to suppress the rebellion, but it could not raise the money or the manpower. Then he turned to his own state militia, but discovered he did not have one. In desperation, private funds were collected to hire a volunteer army, which marched on Springfield and, with the firing of a few shots, dispersed the rebels, who fled into neighboring states.

Shays's Rebellion, occurring between the aborted Annapolis and the coming Philadelphia conventions, had a powerful effect on opinion. Delegates who might have been reluctant to attend the Philadelphia meeting, especially those from New England, were galvanized by the fear that state governments were about to collapse from internal dissension. George Washington wrote a friend despairingly: "For God's sake, if they [the rebels] have real grievances, redress them; if they have not, employ the force of government against them at once."[7] Thomas Jefferson, living in Paris, took a more detached view: "A little rebellion now and then is a good thing," he wrote. "The tree of liberty must be refreshed from time to time with the blood of patriots and tyrants."[8] Though Jefferson's detachment might be explained by the fact that he was in Paris and not in Springfield, there were others, like Governor George Clinton of New York, who shared the view that no strong central government was required. (Whether Clinton would have agreed about the virtues of spilled blood, especially his, is another matter.)

The presiding officer at the Constitutional Convention was George Washington (1732–1799). He participated just once in the debates, but the effect of his presence was great. He was a national military hero, and it was generally expected that he would be the nation's first president.

The Free Library of Philadelphia

THE FRAMERS

The Philadelphia convention attracted 55 delegates, only about 30 of whom participated regularly in the proceedings. One state, Rhode Island, refused to send anyone. The convention met during a miserably hot Philadelphia summer, with the delegates pledged to keep their deliberations secret. The talkative and party-loving Benjamin Franklin was often accompanied by other delegates to make sure that neither wine nor his delight in telling stories would lead him to divulge delicate secrets.

Those who attended were for the most part young (Hamilton was 30; Madison 36) but experienced. Eight delegates had signed the Declaration of Independence, seven had been governors, 34 were lawyers and reasonably well-to-do, a few were wealthy. They were not "intellectuals," but men of practical affairs. Thirty-nine had served in the ineffectual Congress of the Confederation; a third were veterans of the Continental Army.

Some names made famous by the Revolution were conspicuously absent. Thomas Jefferson

Shays's Rebellion A 1787 rebellion in which ex-Revolutionary War soldiers attempted to prevent foreclosures of farms as a result of high interest rates and taxes.

and John Adams were serving as ministers abroad; Samuel Adams was ill; Patrick Henry was chosen to attend but refused, commenting that he "smelled a rat in Philadelphia, tending toward monarchy."

The key men at the convention were an odd lot. George Washington was a very tall, athletic man who was the best horseman in Virginia and who impressed everyone with his dignity despite decaying teeth and big eyes. James Madison was the very opposite: quite short with a frail body and not much of an orator, but possessed of one of the best minds in the country. Benjamin Franklin, though old and ill, was the most famous American in the world as a scientist and writer and always displayed shrewd judgment, at least when sober. Alexander Hamilton was the illegitimate son of a French woman and a Scottish merchant; Hamilton had so strong a mind and so powerful a desire that he succeeded in everything he did, from being Washington's aide during the Revolution to a splendid secretary of the treasury during Washington's presidency.

The convention produced not a revision of the Articles of Confederation, as it had been authorized to do, but instead a wholly new written constitution creating a true national government

Shays's Rebellion in western Massachusetts in 1786–1787 stirred deep fears of anarchy in America. The ruckus was put down by a hastily assembled militia, and the rebels were eventually pardoned.

Bettmann/Corbis

unlike any that had existed before. That document is today the world's oldest written national constitution. Those who wrote it were neither saints nor schemers, and the deliberations were not always lofty or philosophical—much hard bargaining, not a little confusion, and the accidents of personality and time helped shape the final product. The delegates were split on many issues—what powers should be given to a central government, how the states should be represented, what was to be done about slavery, the role of the people—each of which was resolved by a compromise. The speeches of the delegates (known to us from the detailed notes kept by Madison) did not explicitly draw on political philosophy or quote from the writings of philosophers. Everybody present was quite familiar with the traditional arguments and, on the whole, well read in history. But though the leading political philosophers were only rarely mentioned, the debate was profoundly influenced by philosophical beliefs, some formed by the revolutionary experience and others by the 11-year attempt at self-government.

From the debates leading up to the Revolution, the delegates had drawn a commitment to liberty, which, despite the abuses sometimes committed in its name, they continued to share. Their defense of liberty as a natural right was derived from the writings of the English philosopher John Locke and based on his view that such rights are discoverable by reason. In a "state of nature," Locke argued, all men cherish and seek to protect their life, liberty, and property. But in a state of nature—that is, a society without a government—the strong can use their liberty to deprive the weak of theirs. The instinct for self-preservation leads people to want a government that will prevent this exploitation. But if the government is not itself to deprive its subjects of their liberty, it must be limited. The chief limitation on it, he said, should derive from the fact that it is created, and governs, by the consent of the governed. People will not agree to be ruled by a government that threatens their liberty; therefore, the government to which they freely choose to submit themselves will be a limited government designed to protect liberty.

The Pennsylvania experience as well as the history of British government led the Framers to doubt whether popular consent alone would be a sufficient guarantor of liberty. A popular government may prove too weak (as in Massachusetts) to prevent one faction from abusing another, or a popular majority can be tyrannical (as in Pennsylvania). In fact, the tyranny of the majority can be an even graver threat than rule by the few. In the former case, there may be no defenses for the individual—one lone person cannot count on the succor of public opinion or the possibility of popular revolt.

The problem, then, was a delicate one: how to devise a government strong enough to preserve order but not so strong that it would threaten liberty. The answer, the delegates believed, was not "democracy" as it was then understood. To many conservatives in the late 18th century, democracy meant mob rule—it meant, in short, Shays's Rebellion (or, if they had been candid about it, the Boston Tea Party). On the other hand, *aristocracy*—the rule of the few—was no solution, since the few were likely to be self-seeking. Madison, writing later in the *Federalist* papers, put the problem this way:

> *If men were angels, no government would be necessary. If angels were to govern men, neither external nor internal controls on government would be necessary. In framing a government which is to be administered by men over men, the great difficulty lies in this: you must first enable the government to control the governed; and in the next place oblige it to control itself.[9]*

Striking this balance could not be done, Madison believed, simply by writing a constitution that set limits on what government could do. The example of British rule over the colonies proved that laws and customs were inadequate checks on political power. As he expressed it, "A mere demarcation on parchment of the constitutional limits [of government] is not a sufficient guard against those encroachments which lead to a tyrannical concentration of all the powers of government in the same hands."[10]

The Challenge

The resolution of political issues, great and small, often depends crucially on how the central question is phrased. The delegates came to Philadelphia in general agreement that there were defects in the Articles of Confederation that ought to be remedied. Had they, after convening, decided to make their business that of listing these defects and debating alternative remedies for them, the document that emerged would in all likelihood have been very different from what in fact was adopted. But immediately after the convention had organized itself and chosen Washington to be its presiding officer, the Virginia delegation, led by Governor Edmund Randolph but relying heavily on the draftsmanship of James Madison, presented to the convention a comprehensive plan for a wholly new national government. The plan quickly became the major item of business of the meeting; it, and little else, was debated for the next two weeks.

THE VIRGINIA PLAN

When the convention decided to make the **Virginia Plan** its agenda, it had fundamentally altered the nature of its task. The business at hand was not to be the Articles and their defects, but rather how one should go about designing a true national government. The Virginia Plan called for a strong national union organized into three governmental branches—the legislative, executive, and judicial. The legislature was to be composed of two houses, the first elected directly by the people and the second chosen by the first house from among the people nominated by state legislatures. The executive was to be chosen by the national legislature, as were members of a national judiciary. The executive and some members of the judiciary were to constitute a "council of revision" that could veto acts of the legislature; that veto, in turn, could be overridden by the legislature. There were other interesting details, but the key features of the Virginia Plan were two: (1) a national legislature would have supreme powers on all matters on which the separate states were not competent to act, as well as the power to veto any and all state laws; and (2) at least one house of the legislature would be elected directly by the people.

THE NEW JERSEY PLAN

As the debate went on, the representatives of New Jersey and other small states became increasingly worried that the convention was going to write a constitution in which the states would be represented in both houses of Congress on the basis of population. If this happened, the smaller states feared they would always be outvoted by the larger ones, and so, with William Paterson of New Jersey as their spokesman, they introduced a new plan. The **New Jersey Plan** proposed to amend, not replace, the old Articles of Confederation. It enhanced the power of the national government (though not as much as the Virginia Plan), but it did so in a way that left the states' representation in Congress unchanged from the Articles—each state would have one vote. Thus not only would the interests of the small states be protected, but Congress itself would remain to a substantial degree the creature of state governments.

If the New Jersey resolutions had been presented first and taken up as the major item of business, it is quite possible they would have become the framework for the document that finally emerged. But they were not. Offered after the

Virginia Plan Proposal to create a strong national government.

New Jersey Plan Proposal to create a weak national government.

convention had been discussing the Virginia Plan for two weeks, the resolutions encountered a reception very different from what they would have received if introduced earlier. The debate had the delegates already thinking in terms of a national government that was more independent of the states, and thus it had accustomed them to proposals that, under other circumstances, might have seemed quite radical. On June 19, the first decisive vote of the convention was taken: seven states preferred the Virginia Plan, three states the New Jersey Plan, and one state was split.

With the tide running in favor of a strong national government, the supporters of the small states had to shift their strategy. They now began to focus their efforts on ensuring that the small states could not be outvoted by the larger ones in Congress. One way was to have the members of the lower house elected by the state legislatures rather than the people, with each state getting the same number of seats rather than seats proportional to its population.

The debate was long and feelings ran high, so much so that

Great Compromise Plan to have a popularly elected House based on state population and a state-selected Senate, with two members for each state.

Benjamin Franklin, at 81 the oldest delegate present, suggested that each day's meeting begin with a prayer. It turned out that the convention could not even agree on this: Hamilton is supposed to have objected that the convention did not need "foreign aid," and others pointed out that the group had no funds with which to hire a minister. And so the argument continued.

THE COMPROMISE

Finally, a committee was appointed to meet during the Fourth of July holidays to work out a compromise, and the convention adjourned to await its report. Little is known of what went on in that committee's session, though some were later to say that Franklin played a key role in hammering out the plan that finally emerged. That compromise, the most important reached at the convention, and later called the **Great Compromise** (or sometimes the Connecticut Compromise), was submitted to the full convention on July 5 and debated for another week and a half. The debate might have gone on even longer, but suddenly the hot weather moderated, and Monday, July 16, dawned cool and fresh after a month of misery. On that day, the plan was adopted: five states were in favor, four were opposed, and two did not vote.* Thus, by the narrowest of margins, the structure of the national legislature was set as follows:

- A House of Representatives consisting initially of sixty-five members apportioned among the states roughly on the basis of population and elected by the people

- A Senate consisting of two senators from each state to be chosen by the state legislatures

The Great Compromise reconciled the interests of small and large states by allowing the former to predominate in the Senate and the latter in the House. This reconciliation was necessary to ensure there would be support for a strong national government from small as well as large states. It represented major concessions on the part of several groups. Madison, for one, was deeply opposed to the idea of having the states equally represented in the Senate. He saw in that a way for the states to hamstring the national government and much preferred some measure of proportional representation in both houses. Delegates from other states worried

Mural by Barry Faulkner of delegates attending the Constitutional Convention.

Courtesy of the National Archives and Records Administration, Washington, D.C.

* The states in favor were Connecticut, Delaware, Maryland, New Jersey, and North Carolina. Those opposed were Georgia, Pennsylvania, South Carolina, and Virginia. Massachusetts was split down the middle; the New York delegates had left the convention. New Hampshire and Rhode Island were absent.

that representation on the basis of population in the House of Representatives would enable the large states to dominate legislative affairs. Although the margin by which the compromise was accepted was razor-thin, it held firm. In time, most of the delegates from the dissenting states accepted it.

After the Great Compromise, many more issues had to be resolved, but by now a spirit of accommodation had developed. When one delegate proposed having Congress choose the president, another, James Wilson, proposed that he be elected directly by the people. When neither side of that argument prevailed, a committee invented a plan for an "electoral college" that would choose the president. When some delegates wanted the president chosen for a life term, others proposed a seven-year term, and still others wanted the term limited to three years without eligibility for reelection. The convention settled on a four-year term with no bar to reelection. Some states wanted the Supreme Court picked by the Senate; others wanted it chosen by the president. They finally agreed to let the justices be nominated by the president and then confirmed by the Senate.

Finally, on July 26, the proposals that were already accepted, together with a bundle of unresolved issues, were handed over to the Committee of Detail, consisting of five delegates. This committee included Madison and Gouverneur Morris, who was to be the chief draftsman of the document that finally emerged. The committee hardly contented itself with mere "details," however. It inserted some new proposals and made changes in old ones, drawing for inspiration on existing state constitutions and the members' beliefs as to what the other delegates might accept. On August 6, the report—the first complete draft of the Constitution—was submitted to the convention. There it was debated, item by item, revised, amended, and finally, on September 17, approved by all 12 states in attendance. (Not all *delegates* approved, however; three, including Edmund Randolph, who first submitted the Virginia Plan, refused to sign.)

The Constitution and Democracy

A debate continues to rage over whether the Constitution created, or was even intended to create, a democratic government. The answer is complex. The Framers did not intend to create a "pure democracy"—one in which the people rule directly. For one thing, the size of the country and the distances between settlements would have made that physically impossible. But more importantly, the Framers worried that a government in which all citizens directly participate, as in the New England town meeting, would be a government excessively subject to temporary popular passions and one in which minority rights would be insecure. They intended instead to create a **republic,** by which they meant a government in which a system of representation operates. In designing that system, the Framers chose, not without argument, to have the members of the House of Representatives elected directly by the people. Some delegates did not want to go even that far. Elbridge Gerry of Massachusetts, who refused to sign the Constitution, argued that though "the people do not want [that is, lack] virtue," they often are the "dupes of pretended patriots." Roger Sherman of Connecticut agreed. But George Mason of Virginia and James Wilson of Pennsylvania carried the day when they argued that "no government could long subsist without the confidence of the people," and this required "drawing the most numerous branch of the legislature directly from the people." Popular elections for the House were approved: six states were in favor, two opposed.

But though popular rule was to be one element of the new government, it was not to be the only one. State legislatures, not the people, would choose the senators; electors, not the people directly, would choose the president. As we have seen, without these arrangements, there would have been no Constitution at all, for the small states adamantly opposed any proposal that would have given undue power to the large ones. And direct popular election of the president would clearly have made the populous states the dominant ones. In short, the Framers wished to observe the principle of majority rule, but they felt that, on the most important questions, two kinds of majorities were essential—a majority of the voters and a majority of the states.

The power of the Supreme Court to declare an act of Congress unconstitutional—**judicial review**—is also a way of limiting the power of popular majorities. It is not clear whether the Framers intended that there be judicial review, but there is little doubt that in the Framers' minds the fundamental law, the Constitution, had to be safeguarded against popular passions. They made the process for amending the Constitution easier than it had been under the Articles but still relatively difficult.

republic A government in which elected representatives make the decisions.

judicial review The power of the courts to declare laws unconstitutional.

An amendment can be proposed either by a two-thirds vote of both houses of Congress *or* by a national convention called by Congress at the request of two-thirds of the states.* Once proposed, an amendment must be ratified by three-fourths of the states, either through their legislatures or through special ratifying conventions in each state. Twenty-seven amendments have survived this process, all of them proposed by Congress and all but one (the Twenty-first Amendment) ratified by state legislatures rather than state conventions.

In short, the answer to the question of whether the Constitution brought into being a democratic government is yes, if by *democracy* one means a system of representative government based on popular consent. The degree of that consent has changed since 1787, and the institutions embodying that consent can take different forms. One form, rejected in 1787, gives all political authority to one set of representatives, directly elected by the people. (That is the case, for example, in most parliamentary regimes, such as Great Britain, and in some city governments in the United States.) The other form of democracy is one in which different sets of officials, chosen directly or indirectly by different groups of people, share political power. (That is the case with the United States and a few other nations where the separation of powers is intended to operate.)

federalism Government authority shared by national and local governments.

enumerated powers Powers given to the national government alone.

reserved powers Powers given to the state government alone.

concurrent powers Powers shared by the national and state governments.

KEY PRINCIPLES

The American version of representative democracy was based on two major principles, the separation of powers and federalism. In America, political power was to be shared by three separate branches of government; in parliamentary democracies, that power was concentrated in a single, supreme legislature. In America, political authority was divided between a national government and several state governments—**federalism**—whereas in most European systems authority was centralized in the national government. Neither of these principles was especially controversial at Philadelphia. The delegates began their work in broad agreement that separated powers and some measure of federalism were necessary, and both the Virginia and New Jersey plans contained a version of each. How much federalism should be written into the Constitution was quite controversial, however.

Under these two principles, governmental powers in this country can be divided into three categories. The powers given to the national government exclusively are the delegated or **enumerated powers.** They include the authority to print money, declare war, make treaties, conduct foreign affairs, and regulate commerce among the states and with foreign nations. Those given exclusively to the states are the **reserved powers** and include the power to issue licenses and to regulate commerce wholly within a state. Those shared by both the national and the state governments are called **concurrent powers** and include collecting taxes, building roads, borrowing money, and having courts.

GOVERNMENT AND HUMAN NATURE

The desirability of separating powers and leaving the states equipped with a broad array of rights and responsibilities was not controversial at the Philadelphia convention because the Framers' experiences with British rule and state government under the Articles had shaped their view of human nature.

These experiences had taught most of the Framers that people would seek their own advantage in and out of politics; this pursuit of self-interest, unchecked, would lead some people to exploit others. Human nature was good enough to make it possible to have a decent government based on popular consent, but it was not good enough to make it inevitable. One solution to this problem would be to improve human nature. Ancient political philosophers such as Aristotle believed that the first task of any government was to cultivate virtue among the governed.

Many Americans were of the same mind. To them, Americans would first have to become good people before they could have a good government. Samuel Adams, a leader of the Boston Tea Party, said that the new nation must become a "Christian Sparta." Others spoke of the need to cultivate frugality, industry, temperance, and simplicity.

But to James Madison and the other architects of the Constitution, the deliberate cultivation of virtue would require a government too strong and thus too

---

* There have been many attempts to get a new constitutional convention. In the 1960s, 33 states, one short of the required number, requested a convention to consider the reapportionment of state legislatures. In the 1980s, efforts were made to call a convention to consider amendments to ban abortions and to require a balanced federal budget.

How Things Work

Checks and Balances

The Constitution creates a system of *separate* institutions that *share* powers. Because the three branches of government share powers, each can (partially) check the powers of the others. This is the system of **checks and balances.** The major checks possessed by each branch are listed below.

Congress

1. Can check the president in these ways:

   a. By refusing to pass a bill the president wants

   b. By passing a law over the president's veto

   c. By using the impeachment powers to remove the president from office

   d. By refusing to approve a presidential appointment (Senate only)

   e. By refusing to ratify a treaty the president has signed (Senate only)

2. Can check the federal courts in these ways:

   a. By changing the number and jurisdiction of the lower courts

   b. By using the impeachment powers to remove a judge from office

   c. By refusing to approve a person nominated to be a judge (Senate only)

The President

1. Can check Congress by vetoing a bill it has passed

2. Can check the federal courts by nominating judges

The Courts

1. Can check Congress by declaring a law unconstitutional

2. Can check the president by declaring actions by him or his subordinates unconstitutional or not authorized by law

In addition to these checks specifically provided for in the Constitution, each branch has informal ways of checking the others. For example, the president can try to withhold information from Congress (on the grounds of "executive privilege"), and Congress can try to get information by mounting an investigation.

The exact meaning of the various checks is explained in Chapter 13 on Congress, Chapter 14 on the presidency, and Chapter 16 on the courts.

---

dangerous to liberty, at least at the national level. Self-interest, freely pursued within reasonable limits, was a more practical and durable solution to the problem of government than any effort to improve the virtue of the citizenry. He wanted, he said, to make republican government possible "even in the absence of political virtue."

Madison argued that the very self-interest that leads people toward factionalism and tyranny might, if properly harnessed by appropriate constitutional arrangements, provide a source of unity and a guarantee of liberty. This harnessing was to be accomplished by dividing the offices of the new government among many people and giving to the holder of each office the "necessary means and personal motives to resist encroachments of the others." In this way, "ambition must be made to counteract ambition" so that "the private interest of every individual may be a sentinel over the public rights."[11]

If men were angels, all this would be unnecessary. But Madison and the other delegates pragmatically insisted on taking human nature pretty much as it was, and therefore they adopted "this policy of supplying, by opposite and rival interests, the defect of better motives."[12] The **separation of powers** would work, not in spite of the imperfections of human nature, but because of them.

So also with federalism. By dividing power between the states and the national government, one level of government can serve as a check on the other. This should provide a "double security" to the rights of the people: "The different governments will control each other, at the same time that each will be controlled by itself."[13] This

checks and balances
Authority shared by three branches of government.

separation of powers
Constitutional authority is shared by three different branches of government.

was especially likely to happen in America, Madison thought, because it was a large country filled with diverse interests—rich and poor, Protestant and Catholic, northerner and southerner, farmer and merchant, creditor and debtor. Each of these interests would constitute a **faction** that would seek its own advantage. One faction might come to dominate government, or a part of government, in one place, and a different and rival faction might dominate it in another. The pulling and hauling among these factions would prevent any single government—say, that of New York—from dominating all of government. The division of powers among several governments would give to virtually every faction an opportunity to gain some—but not full—power.

The Constitution and Liberty

A more difficult question is whether the Constitution created a system of government that would respect personal liberties. And that in fact is the question that was debated in the states when the document was presented for ratification. The proponents of the Constitution called themselves the **Federalists** (though they might more accurately have been called "nationalists"). The opponents came to be known as the **Antifederalists** (though they might more accurately have been called "states' righters").* To be put into effect, the Constitution had to be approved at ratifying conventions in at least nine states. This was perhaps the most democratic feature of the Constitution: it had to be accepted, not by the existing Congress (still limping along under the Articles of Confederation), nor by the state legislatures, but by special conventions elected by the people.

Though democratic, the process established by the Framers for ratifying the Constitution was technically illegal. The Articles of Confederation, which still governed, could be amended only with the approval of all 13 state legislatures. The Framers

faction A group with a distinct political interest.

Federalists Those who favor a stronger national government.

Antifederalists Those who favor a weaker national government.

wanted to bypass these legislatures because they feared that, for reasons of ideology or out of a desire to retain their powers, the legislators would oppose the Constitution. The Framers wanted ratification with less than the consent of all 13 states because they knew that such unanimity could not be attained. And indeed the conventions in North Carolina and Rhode Island did initially reject the Constitution.

THE ANTIFEDERALIST VIEW

The great issue before the state conventions was liberty, not democracy. The opponents of the new Constitution, the Antifederalists, had a variety of objections but were in general united by the belief that liberty could be secure only in a small republic in which the rulers were physically close to—and closely checked by—the ruled. Their central objection was stated by a group of Antifederalists at the ratifying convention in an essay published just after they had lost: "a very extensive territory cannot be governed on the principles of freedom, otherwise than by a confederation of republics."[14]

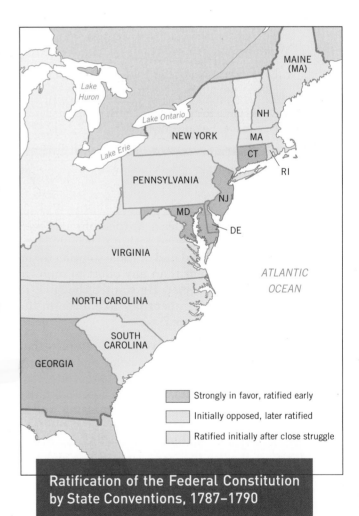

Ratification of the Federal Constitution by State Conventions, 1787–1790

- Strongly in favor, ratified early
- Initially opposed, later ratified
- Ratified initially after close struggle

---

* To the delegates a truly "federal" system was one, like the New Jersey Plan, that allowed for very strong states and a weak national government. When the New Jersey Plan lost, the delegates who defeated it began using the word *federal* to describe their plan even though it called for a stronger national government. Thus men who began as "Federalists" at the convention ultimately became known as "Antifederalists" during the struggle over ratification.

These dissenters argued that a strong national government would be distant from the people and would use its powers to annihilate or absorb the functions that properly belonged to the states. Congress would tax heavily, the Supreme Court would overrule state courts, and the president would come to head a large standing army. (Since all these things have occurred, we cannot dismiss the Antifederalists as cranky obstructionists who opposed without justification the plans of the Framers.) These critics argued that the nation needed, at best, a loose confederation of states, with most of the powers of government kept firmly in the hands of state legislatures and state courts.

But if a stronger national government was to be created, the Antifederalists argued, it should be hedged about with many more restrictions than those in the constitution then under consideration. They proposed several such limitations, including narrowing the jurisdiction of the Supreme Court, checking the president's power by creating a council that would review his actions, leaving military affairs in the hands of the state militias, increasing the size of the House of Representatives so that it would reflect a greater variety of popular interests, and reducing or eliminating the power of Congress to levy taxes. And some of them insisted that a *bill of rights* be added to the Constitution.

James Madison gave his answer to these criticisms in *Federalist* No. 10 and No. 51 (reprinted in the Appendix). It was a bold answer, for it flew squarely in the face of widespread popular sentiment and much philosophical writing. Following the great French political philosopher Montesquieu, many Americans believed liberty was safe only in small societies governed either by direct democracy or by large legislatures with small districts and frequent turnover among members.

Madison argued quite the opposite—that liberty is safest in *large* (or as he put it, "extended") republics. In a small community, he said, there will be relatively few differences in opinion or interest; people will tend to see the world in much the same way. If anyone dissents or pursues an individual interest, he or she will be confronted by a massive majority and will have few, if any, allies. But in a large republic there will be many opinions and interests; as a result, it will be hard for a tyrannical majority to form or organize, and anyone with an unpopular view will find it easier to acquire allies. If Madison's argument seems strange or abstract, ask yourself the following question: if I have an unpopular opinion, an exotic lifestyle, or an unconventional interest, will I find greater security living in a small town or a big city?

By favoring a large republic, Madison was not trying to stifle democracy. Rather, he was attempting to show how democratic government really works, and what can make it work better. To rule, different interests must come together and form a **coalition**—that is, an alliance. In *Federalist* No. 51, he argued that the coalitions that formed in a large republic would be more moderate than those that formed in a small one because the bigger the republic, the greater the variety of interests, and thus the more a coalition of the majority would have to accommodate a diversity of interests and opinions if it hoped to succeed. He concluded that in a nation the size of the United States, with its enormous variety of interests, "a coalition of a majority of the whole society could seldom take place on any other principles than those of justice and the general good." Whether he was right in that prediction is a matter to which we shall return repeatedly.

> **coalition** An alliance of factions.

The implication of Madison's arguments was daring, for he was suggesting that the national government should be at some distance from the people and insulated from their momentary passions, because the people did not always want to do the right thing. Liberty was threatened as much (or even more) by public passions and popularly based factions as by strong governments. Now the Antifederalists themselves had no very lofty view of human nature, as is evidenced by the deep suspicion with which they viewed "power-seeking" officeholders. What Madison did was take this view to its logical conclusion, arguing that if people could be corrupted by office, they could also be corrupted by factional self-interest. Thus the government had to be designed to prevent both the politicians and the people from using it for ill-considered or unjust purposes.

To argue in 1787 against the virtues of small democracies was like arguing against motherhood. Moreover, the Federalists' counterargument involved many steps: representative democracy over direct democracy; a large republic over a small republic; diversity of economic, religious, and other interests over homogeneity of such interests; and barriers, not boosts, to majority group formation and influence. Still, the Federalists prevailed, probably because many citizens were convinced that a reasonably strong national government was essential if the nation were to stand united against foreign enemies, facilitate commerce among the states, guard against domestic insurrections, and keep one faction from oppressing another. The political realities of the moment and the recent bitter experiences with the Articles probably counted for more in ratifying the

The *Federalist* Papers

In 1787, to help win ratification of the new Constitution in the New York state convention, Alexander Hamilton decided to publish a series of articles defending and explaining the document in the New York City newspapers. He recruited John Jay and James Madison to help him, and the three of them, under the pen name "Publius," wrote 85 articles that appeared from late 1787 through 1788. The identity of the authors was kept secret at the time, but we now know that Hamilton wrote 51 of them, Madison 26, and Jay five, and that Hamilton and Madison jointly authored three.

The *Federalist* papers probably played only a small role in securing ratification. Like most legislative battles, this one was not decisively influenced by philosophical writings. But these essays have had a lasting value as an authoritative and profound explanation of the Constitution. Though written for political purposes, the *Federalist* has become the single most important piece of American political philosophy ever produced. Ironically, Hamilton and Madison were later to become political enemies; even at the Philadelphia convention they had different views of the kind of government that should be created. But in 1787–1788, they were united in the belief that the new constitution was the best that could have been obtained under the circumstances.

Although Hamilton wrote most of the *Federalist* papers, Madison wrote the two most famous articles—Nos. 10 and 51, reprinted in the Appendix. After you have finished this chapter, turn to the Appendix and try to read them. On your first reading of the papers, you may find Madison's language difficult to understand and his ideas overly complex. The following pointers will help you decipher his meaning.

In *Federalist* No. 10, Madison begins by stating that "a well constructed Union" can "break and control the violence of faction." He goes on to define a "faction" as any group of citizens who attempt to advance their ideas or economic interests at the expense of other citizens, or in ways that conflict with "the permanent and aggregate interests of the community" or "public good." Thus what Madison terms "factions" are what we today call "special interests."

James Madison

John Jay

Alexander Hamilton

U.S. Government Printing Office

(c) North Wind Picture Archives

Library of Congress/LC-D416-444

One way to defeat factions, according to Madison, is to remove whatever causes them to arise in the first place. This can be attempted in two ways. First, government can deprive people of the liberty they need to organize: "Liberty is to faction what air is to fire." But that is surely a cure "worse than the disease." Second, measures can be taken to make all citizens share the same ideas, feelings, and economic interests. However, as Madison observes, some people are smarter or more hard working than others, and this "diversity in the faculties" of citizens is bound to

For the Independent Journal.

The FŒDERALIST, No. X.

To the People of the State of New-York.

AMONG the numerous advantages promised by a well constructed Union, none deserves to be more accurately developed than its tendency to break and control the violence of faction. The friend of popular governments, never finds himself so much alarmed for their character and fate, as when he contemplates their propensity to this dangerous vice. He will not fail therefore to set a due value on any plan which, without violating the principles to which he is attached, provides a proper cure for it. The instability, injustice and confusion introduced into the public councils, have in truth been the mortal diseases under which popular governments have every where perished; as they continue to be the favorite and fruitful topics from which the adversaries to liberty derive their most specious declamations. The valuable improvements made by the American Constitutions on the popular models, both ancient and modern, cannot certainly be too much admired; but it would be an unwarrantable partiality, to contend that they have as effectually obviated the danger on this side as was wished and expected. Complaints are every where heard from our most considerate and virtuous citizens, equally the friends of public and private faith, and of public and personal liberty; that our governments are too unstable; that the public good is disregarded in the conflicts of rival parties; and that measures are too often decided, not according to the rules of justice, and the rights of the minor party; but by the superior force of an interested and over-bearing majority. However anxiously we may

American Antiquarian Society

result in different economic interests as some people acquire more property than others. Consequently, protecting property rights, not equalizing property ownership, "is the first object of government." Even if everyone shared the same basic economic interests, they would still find reasons "to vex and oppress each other" rather than cooperate "for their common good." Religious differences, loyalties to different leaders, even "frivolous and fanciful distinctions" (not liking how other people dress or their taste in music) can be

fertile soil for factions. In Madison's view, people are factious by nature; the "causes of faction" are "sown" into their very being.

Madison thus proposes a second and, he thinks, more practical and desirable way of defeating faction. The way to cure "the mischiefs of faction" is not by removing its causes but by "controlling its effects." Factions will always exist, so the trick is to establish a form of government that is likely to serve the public good through the even-handed "regulation of these various and interfering interests." Wise and public-spirited leaders can "adjust these clashing interests and render them all subservient to the public good," but, he cautions, "enlightened statesmen will not always be at the helm." (Madison implies that "enlightened statesmen"—such as himself, Washington, and Jefferson—were at the "helm" of government in 1787.)

Madison's proposed cure for the evils of factions is in fact nothing other than a republican form of government. Use the following questions to guide your own analysis of Madison's ideas. Why does Madison think the problem of a "minority" faction is easy to handle? Conversely, why is he so troubled by the potential of a majority faction? How does he distinguish direct democracy from republican government? What is he getting at when he terms elected representatives "proper guardians of the public weal," and why does he think that "extensive republics" are more likely to produce such representatives than small ones?

When you are finished with *Federalist* No. 10, try your hand at *Federalist* No. 51. You will find that the ideas in the former paper anticipate many of those in the latter. And you will find many points on which you may or may not agree with Madison. For example, do you agree with his assumption that people—even your best friends or college roommates—are factious by nature? Likewise, do you agree with his view that government is "the greatest of all reflections on human nature"?

By attempting to meet the mind of James Madison, you can sharpen your own mind and deepen your understanding of American government.

Bill of Rights First ten amendments to the Constitution.

habeas corpus An order to produce an arrested person before a judge.

bill of attainder A law that declares a person, without a trial, to be guilty of a crime.

ex post facto law A law that makes an act criminal although the act was legal when it was committed.

Constitution than Madison's arguments. His cause was helped by the fact that, for all their legitimate concerns and their uncanny instinct for what the future might bring, the Antifederalists could offer no agreed-upon alternative to the new Constitution. In politics, then as now, you cannot beat something with nothing.

But this does not explain why the Framers failed to add a bill of rights to the Constitution. If they were so preoccupied with liberty, why didn't they take this most obvious step toward protecting liberty, especially since the Antifederalists were demanding it? Some historians have suggested that this omission was evidence that liberty was not as important to the Framers as they claimed. In fact, when one delegate suggested that a bill of rights be drawn up, the state delegations at the convention unanimously voted the idea down. There were several reasons for this.

First, the Constitution, as written, *did* contain a number of specific guarantees of individual liberty, including the right of trial by jury in criminal cases and the privilege of the writ of habeas corpus. The liberties guaranteed in the Constitution (before the **Bill of Rights** was added) are listed below.

- Writ of **habeas corpus** may not be suspended (except during invasion or rebellion).

- No **bill of attainder** may be passed by Congress or the states.

- No **ex post facto** law may be passed by Congress or the states.

- Right of trial by jury in criminal cases is guaranteed.

- The citizens of each state are entitled to the privileges and immunities of the citizens of every other state.

- No religious test or qualification for holding federal office is imposed.

- No law impairing the obligation of contracts may be passed by the states.

Second, most states in 1787 had bills of rights. When Elbridge Gerry proposed to the convention that a federal bill of rights be drafted, Roger Sherman rose to observe that it was unnecessary because the state bills of rights were sufficient.[15]

But third, and perhaps most important, the Framers thought they were creating a government with specific, limited powers. It could do, they thought, only what the Constitution gave it the power to do, and nowhere in that document was there permission to infringe on freedom of speech or of the press or to impose cruel and unusual punishments. Some delegates probably feared that if any serious effort were made to list the rights that were guaranteed, later officials might assume that they had the power to do anything not explicitly forbidden.

NEED FOR A BILL OF RIGHTS

Whatever their reasons, the Framers made at least a tactical and perhaps a fundamental mistake. It quickly became clear that without at least the promise of a bill of rights, the Constitution would not be ratified. Though the small states, pleased by their equal representation in the Senate, quickly ratified (in Delaware, New Jersey, and Georgia, the vote in the conventions was unanimous), the battle in the large states was intense and the outcome uncertain. In Pennsylvania, Federalist supporters dragged boycotting Antifederalists to the legislature in order to ensure a quorum was present so a convention could be called. There were rumors of other rough tactics.

In Massachusetts, the Constitution was approved by a narrow majority, but only after key leaders promised to obtain a bill of rights. In Virginia, James Madison fought against the fiery Patrick Henry, whose climactic speech against ratification was dramatically punctuated by a noisy thunderstorm outside. The Federalists won by 10 votes. In New York, Alexander Hamilton argued the case for six weeks against the determined opposition of most of the state's key political leaders; he carried the day, but only by three votes, and then only after New York City threatened to secede from the state if it did not ratify. By June 21, 1788, the ninth state—New Hampshire—had ratified, and the Constitution was law.

Despite the bitterness of the ratification struggle, the new government that took office in 1789–1790, headed by President Washington, was greeted enthusiastically. By the spring of 1790, all 13 states had ratified. There remained, however, the task of fulfilling the promise of a bill of rights. To that end, James Madison introduced into the first session of the First Congress a set of proposals, many based on the existing Virginia bill of rights. Twelve were approved by Congress; 10 of these were ratified by the states and went into effect in 1791. These

How Things Work

The Bill of Rights

The First Ten Amendments to the Constitution Grouped by Topic and Purpose

Protections Afforded Citizens to Participate in the Political Process

Amendment 1: Freedom of religion, speech, press, and assembly; the right to petition the government.

Protections Against Arbitrary Police and Court Action

Amendment 4: No unreasonable searches or seizures.

Amendment 5: Grand jury indictment required to prosecute a person for a serious crime.

No "double jeopardy" (being tried twice for the same offense).

Forcing a person to testify against himself or herself prohibited.

No loss of life, liberty, or property without due process.

Amendment 6: Right to speedy, public, impartial trial with defense counsel and right to cross-examine witnesses.

Amendment 7: Jury trials in civil suits where value exceeds $20.

Amendment 8: No excessive bail or fines, no cruel and unusual punishments.

Protections of States' Rights and Unnamed Rights of People

Amendment 9: Unlisted rights are not necessarily denied.

Amendment 10: Powers not delegated to the United States or denied to states are reserved to the states.

Other Amendments

Amendment 2: Right to bear arms.

Amendment 3: Troops may not be quartered in homes in peacetime.

---

amendments did not limit the power of state governments over citizens, only the power of the federal government. Later, the Fourteenth Amendment, as interpreted by the Supreme Court, extended many of the guarantees of the Bill of Rights to cover state governmental action.

THE CONSTITUTION AND SLAVERY

Though black slaves amounted to one-third of the population of the five southern states, nowhere in the Constitution can one find the word *slave* or *slavery*.

To some, the failure of the Constitution to address the question of slavery was a great betrayal of the promise of the Declaration of Independence that "all men are created equal."[16] For the Constitution to be silent on the subject of slavery, and thereby to allow that odious practice to continue, was to convert, by implication, the wording of the Declaration to "all white men are created equal."

It is easy to accuse the signers of the Declaration and the Constitution of hypocrisy. They knew of slavery, many of them owned slaves, and yet they were silent. Indeed, British opponents of the independence movement took special delight in taunting the colonists about their complaints of being "enslaved" to the British Empire while ignoring the slavery in their very midst. Increasingly, revolutionary leaders during this period spoke to this issue. Thomas Jefferson had tried to get a clause opposing the slave trade put into the Declaration of Independence. James Otis of Boston had attacked slavery and argued that black as well as white men should be free. As revolutionary fervor mounted, so did northern criticism of slavery. The Massachusetts legislature and then the Continental Congress voted to end the slave trade; Delaware prohibited the importation of slaves; Pennsylvania voted to tax it out of existence; and Connecticut and Rhode Island decided that all slaves brought into those states would automatically become free.

Slavery continued unabated in the South, defended by some whites because they thought it right, by others because they found it useful. But even in the South there were opponents, though rarely conspicuous ones. George Mason, a large Virginia slaveholder and a delegate to the convention, warned prophetically that "by an inevitable chain of causes and effects, providence punishes national sins [slavery] by national calamities."[17]

The blunt fact, however, was that any effort to use the Constitution to end slavery would have meant the end of the Constitution. The southern states would never have signed a document that seriously interfered with slavery. Without the southern states, there would have been a continuation of the Articles of Confederation, which would have left each state entirely sovereign and thus entirely free of any prospective challenge to slavery.

Thus the Framers compromised with slavery; political scientist Theodore Lowi calls this their Greatest Compromise.[18] Slavery is dealt with in three places in the Constitution, though never by name. In determining the representation each state was to have in the House, "three-fifths of all other persons" (that is, of slaves) are to be added to "the whole number of free persons."[19] The South originally wanted slaves to count fully even though, of course, none would be elected to the House; they settled for counting 60 percent of them. The Great (or Connecticut) Compromise favored smaller states, which were mostly northern, by giving each state two senators; but the three-fifths compromise even more strongly favored the South's slaveholding states. For example, apportioned according to its free population, the southern states would have had a combined total of 33 House seats rather than the 47 they claimed. The three-fifths compromise is behind the fact that southern-born presidents, House leaders, and Supreme Court justices generally dominated antebellum American national government.[20]

The convention also agreed not to allow the new government by law or even constitutional amendment to prohibit the importation of slaves until 1808.[21] The South thus had 20 years in which it could acquire more slaves from abroad; after that, Congress was free (but not required) to end the importation. Finally, the Constitution guaranteed that if a slave were to escape his or her master and flee to a nonslave state, the slave would be returned by that state to "the party to whom ... service or labour may be due."[22]

The Constitution was silent about slavery, and so buying and selling slaves continued for many years.

Chicago Historical Society

The unresolved issue of slavery was to prove the most explosive question of all. Allowing slavery to continue was a fateful decision, one that led to the worst social and political catastrophe in the nation's history—the Civil War. The Framers chose to sidestep the issue in order to create a union that, they hoped, would eventually be strong enough to deal with the problem when it could no longer be postponed. The legacy of that choice continues to this day.

The Motives of the Framers

The Framers were not saints or demigods. They were men with political opinions who also had economic interests and human failings. It would be a mistake to conclude that everything they did in 1787 was motivated by a disinterested commitment to the public good. But it would be an equally great mistake to think that what they did was nothing but an effort to line their pockets by producing a government that would serve their own narrow interests. As in almost all human endeavors, the Framers acted out of a mixture of motives. What is truly astonishing is that economic interests played only a modest role in their deliberations.

ECONOMIC INTERESTS

Some of the Framers were wealthy; some were not. Some owned slaves; some had none. Some were creditors (having loaned money to the Continental Congress or to private parties); some were deeply in debt. For nearly a century, scholars have argued over just how important these personal interests were in shaping the provisions of the Constitution.

In 1913 Charles Beard, a historian, published a book—*An Economic Interpretation of the Constitution*—arguing that the better-off urban and commercial classes, especially those members who held the IOUs issued by the government to pay for the Revolutionary War, favored the new Constitution because they stood to benefit from it.[23] But in the 1950s, that view was challenged by historians who, after looking carefully at what the Framers owned or owed, concluded that one could not explain the Constitution exclusively or even largely in terms of the economic interests of those who wrote it.[24] Some of the richest delegates, such as Elbridge Gerry of Massachusetts and George Mason of Virginia, refused to sign the document, while many of its key backers—James Madison and James Wilson, for example—were men of modest means or heavy debts.

This late-eighteenth-century cartoon shows the enthusiasm many people had for the new Constitution.

The Granger Collection

In the 1980s, a new group of scholars, primarily economists applying more advanced statistical techniques, found evidence that some economic considerations influenced how the Framers voted on some issues during the Philadelphia convention. Interestingly, however, the economic position of the *states* from which they came had a greater effect on their votes than did their *own* monetary condition.[25]

We have already seen how delegates from small states fought to reduce the power of large states and how those from slaveowning states made certain that the Constitution would contain no provision that would threaten slavery.

But contrary to what Beard asserted, the economic interests of the Framers themselves did not dominate the convention. Some delegates owned a lot of public debt they had purchased for low prices. A strong national government of the sort envisaged by the Constitution was more likely than the weak Continental Congress to pay off this debt at face value, thus making the delegates who owned it much richer. Despite this, the ownership of public debt had no significant effect on how the Framers voted in Philadelphia. Nor did the big land speculators vote their interests. Some, such as George Washington and Robert Morris, favored the Constitution, while others, such as George Mason and William Blount, opposed it.[26]

In sum, the Framers tended to represent their states' interests on important matters. Since they were picked by the states to do so, this is exactly what one would expect. If they had not met in secret, perhaps they would have voted even more often as their constituents wanted.

With the grave and enormous exception of slavery, the Framers usually did not vote their own respective economic interests.

At the popularly elected state ratifying conventions, economic factors played a larger role. Delegates who were merchants, who lived in cities, who owned large amounts of western land, who held government IOUs, and who did not own slaves were more likely to vote to ratify the new Constitution than delegates who were farmers, who did not own public debt, and who did own slaves.[27] There were plenty of exceptions, however. Small farmers dominated the conventions in some states where the vote to ratify was unanimous.

Though interests made a difference, they were not simply elite interests. In most states, the great majority of adult white males could vote for delegates to the ratifying conventions. This means that women and blacks were excluded from the debates, but by the standards of the time—standards that did not change for over a century—the ratification process was remarkably democratic.

THE CONSTITUTION AND EQUALITY

Ideas counted for as much as interests. At stake were two views of the public good. One, espoused by the Federalists, was that a reasonable balance of liberty, order, and progress required a strong national government. The other, defended by the Antifederalists, was that liberty would not be secure in the hands of a powerful, distant government; freedom required decentralization.

Today that debate has a new focus. The defect of the Constitution, to some contemporary critics, is not that the government it created is too strong but that it is too weak. In particular, the national government is too weak to resist the pressures of special interests that reflect and perpetuate social inequality.

This criticism reveals how our understanding of the relationship between liberty and equality has

Elbridge Gerry (left, 1744–1814) was a wealthy Massachusetts merchant and politician who participated in the convention but refused to sign the Constitution. James Wilson (right, 1742–1798) of Pennsylvania, a brilliant lawyer and terrible businessman, was the principal champion of the popular election of the House. Near the end of his life, he was jailed repeatedly for debts incurred as a result of his business speculations.

RESEARCH FRONTIERS

The Founding Debate over Church and State

Over the last decade, diverse scholars have begun to rediscover how competing views about religion and government shaped the debate between the Federalists and the Antifederalists.

In present-day political vernacular, the Antifederalists were the day's religious conservatives. Many Antifederalist leaders condemned the Constitution's no-religious-test provision (Article VI) and denounced the First Amendment because it forbade the Congress from establishing Christianity or any other religion as the national religion.

In stark contrast, most Federalists, even the ortho-dox Reverend John Witherspoon, agreed with James Madison that the Constitution should permit, and the national government should promote, religious plu-ralism. In *Federalist* No. 51, Madison argued that "the security for civil rights" consisted in "the multiplicity of interests" just as "that for religious rights" con-sisted in "the multiplicity of sects."

Scholars have argued about the religious views of the Founders for many years. Some have said they were religious while others have said they were atheists, agnostics, or Deists who believe there is a God but one who does not intervene in human affairs.

We now know that George Washington was not a Deist but rather a fairly typical late 18th-century Anglican. On the other hand, Thomas Jefferson was a Deist. During his two terms as our first president, Washington set many important precedents regarding the relation-ship between government and religion.

Unlike the Antifederalists, Washington, Witherspoon, Madison, and most other Federalists believed that any religious groups including their own might degener-ate into what Madison, in *Federalist* No. 10, famously defined as "factions" that threaten "the rights of other

citizens" and thwart the national interest or common good.

In defeating Antifederalist demands that the Consti-tution privilege Anglo-Protestants, neither Washington nor most other Federalists advocated a total separation between church and state, but neither did they deny the need for government diligence in checking what Madison, in *Federalist* No. 10, termed "a zeal for differ-ent opinions concerning religion."

- Do you think the fact that America today is home to over 300 million citizens representing scores of different Christian and other religious traditions, including tens of millions of citizens who are religiously unaffiliated, vindicates the Federalist vision?

- What might a "neo-Antifederalist" argue regard-ing church and state in America today?

- Finally, do a little research to find out what each of the three most recent presidents—Bill Clinton, George W. Bush, and Barack Obama—have argued about the relationship between religion and government.

Source: Peter R. Henriques, *Realistic Visionary: A Portrait of George Washington* (University of Virginia Press, 2008); Tara Ross and Joseph C. Smith, Jr., *Under God: George Washington and the Question of Church and State* (Spence, 2008); John J. Dilulio, Jr., *Godly Republic: A Centrist Blueprint for America's Faith-Based Future* (University of California Press, 2007); Peter A. Lillback, *George Washington's Sacred Fire* (Providence Forum Press, 2006); Michael Novak and Jana Novak, *Washington's God: Religion, Liberty, and the Father of Our Country* (Basic Books, 2006).

changed since the Founding. To Jefferson and Madison, citizens naturally differed in their talents and qualities. What had to be guarded against was the use of governmental power to create unnatural and undesirable inequalities. This might happen, for example, if political power was concentrated in the hands of a few people (who could use that power to give themselves special privileges) or if it was used in ways that allowed some private parties to acquire exclusive charters and monopolies. To pre-vent the inequality that might result from having

too strong a government, its powers must be kept strictly limited.

Today, some people think of inequality quite differ-ently. To them it is the natural social order—the market-place and the acquisitive talents of people operating in that marketplace—that leads to undesirable inequal-ities, especially in economic power. The government should be powerful enough to restrain these natural tendencies and produce, by law, a greater degree of equality than society allows when left alone.

To the Framers, liberty and (political) equality were not in conflict; to some people today, these two principles are deeply in conflict. To the Framers, the task was to keep government so limited as to prevent it from creating the worst inequality—political privilege. To some modern observers, the task is to make government strong enough to reduce what they believe is the worst inequality—differences in wealth.

Constitutional Reform: Modern Views

Almost from the day it was ratified, the Constitution has been the object of debate over ways in which it might be improved. These debates have rarely involved the average citizen, who tends to revere the document even if he or she cannot recall all its details. Because of this deep and broad popular support, scholars and politicians have been wary of attacking the Constitution or suggesting many wholesale changes. But such attacks have occurred. During the 1980s—the decade in which we celebrated the bicentennial of its adoption—we heard a variety of suggestions for improving the Constitution, ranging from particular amendments to wholesale revisions. In general there are today, as in the 18th century, two kinds of critics: those who think the federal government is too weak and those who think it is too strong.

REDUCING THE SEPARATION OF POWERS

To the first kind of critic, the chief difficulty with the Constitution is the separation of powers. By making every decision the uncertain outcome of the pulling and hauling between the president and Congress, the Constitution precludes the emergence—except perhaps in times of crisis—of the kind of effective national leadership the country needs. In this view, our nation today faces a number of challenges that require prompt, decisive, and comprehensive action. Our problem is gridlock. Our position of international leadership, the dangerous and unprecedented proliferation of nuclear weapons among the nations of the globe, and the need to find ways of stimulating economic growth while reducing our deficit and conserving our environment—all these situations require the president be able to formulate and carry out policies free of some of the pressures and delays from interest groups and members of Congress tied to local interests.

Not only would this increase in presidential authority make for better policies, these critics argue, it would also help the voters hold the president and his party accountable for their actions. As matters now stand, nobody in government can be held responsible for policies: everybody takes the credit for successes and nobody takes the blame for failures. Typically the president, who tends to be the major source of new programs, cannot get his policies adopted by Congress without long delays and much bargaining, the result of which often is some watered-down compromise that neither the president nor Congress really likes but that each must settle for if anything is to be done at all.

Finally, critics of the separation of powers complain that the government agencies responsible for implementing a program are exposed to undue interference from legislators and special interests. In this view, the president is supposed to be in charge of the bureaucracy but in fact must share this authority with countless members of Congress and congressional committees.

Not all critics of the separation of powers agree with all these points, nor do they all agree on what should be done about the problems. But they all have in common a fear that the separation of powers makes the president too weak and insufficiently accountable. Their proposals for reducing the separation of powers include the following:

- Allow the president to appoint members of Congress to serve in the cabinet (the Constitution forbids members of Congress from holding any federal appointive office while in Congress).

- Allow the president to dissolve Congress and call for a special election (elections now can be held only on the schedule determined by the calendar).

- Allow Congress to require a president who has lost its confidence to face the country in a special election before his term would normally end.

- Require the presidential and congressional candidates to run as a team in each congressional district; thus a presidential candidate who carries a given district could be sure the congressional candidate of his party would also win in that district.

- Have the president serve a single six-year term instead of being eligible for up to two four-year terms; this would presumably free the president to lead without having to worry about reelection.

- Lengthen the terms of members of the House of Representatives from two to four years so that the entire House would stand for reelection at the same time as the president.[28]

Some of these proposals are offered by critics out of a desire to make the American system of government

Were Women Left Out of the Constitution?

In one sense, yes: Women were mentioned nowhere in the Constitution when it was written in 1787. Moreover, Article I, which set forth the provisions for electing members of the House of Representatives, granted the vote to those people who were allowed to vote for members of the lower house of the legislature in the states in which they resided. In no state at the time could women participate in those elections. In no state could they vote in any elections or hold any offices. Furthermore, wherever the Constitution uses a pronoun, it uses the masculine form—*he* or *him*.

In another sense, no: Wherever the Constitution or the Bill of Rights defines a right that people are to have, it either grants that right to "persons" or "citizens," not to "men," or it makes no mention at all of people or gender. For example:

- "The *citizens* of each State shall be entitled to all privileges and immunities of citizens of the several States."

  [Art. I, sec. 9]

- "No *person* shall be convicted of treason unless on the testimony of two witnesses to the same overt act, or on confession in open court."

  [Art. III, sec. 3]

- "No bill of attainder or ex post facto law shall be passed." [Art. I, sec. 9]

- "The right of the *people* to be secure in their persons, houses, papers, and effects, against unreasonable searches and seizures, shall not be violated."

  [Amend. IV]

- "No *person* shall be held to answer for a capital, or otherwise infamous crime, unless on presentment or indictment of a grand jury...nor shall any *person* be subject for the same offense to be twice put in jeopardy of life or limb;...nor be deprived of life, liberty, or property, without due process of law."

  [Amend. V]

- "In all criminal prosecutions the *accused* shall enjoy the right to a speedy and public trial, by an impartial jury."

  [Amend. VI]

Moreover, when the qualifications for elective office are stated, the word *person,* not *man,* is used.

- "No *person* shall be a Representative who shall not have attained to the age of twenty-five years."

  [Art. I, sec. 2]

- "No *person* shall be a Senator who shall not have attained to the age of thirty years."

  [Art. I, sec. 3]

- "No *person* except a natural born citizen...shall be eligible to the office of President; neither shall any *person* be eligible to that office who shall not have attained to the age of thirty-five years."

  [Art. II, sec. 1]

In places, the Constitution and the Bill of Rights used the pronoun *he,* but always in the context of referring back to a *person* or *citizen.* At the time, and until quite recently, the male pronoun was often used in legal documents to refer generically to both men and women.

Thus, though the Constitution did not give women the right to vote until the Nineteenth Amendment was ratified in 1920, it did use language that extended fundamental rights, and access to office, to women and men equally.

Of course, what the Constitution permitted did not necessarily occur. State and local laws denied to women rights that in principle they ought to have enjoyed. Except for a brief period in New Jersey, no women voted in statewide elections until, in 1869, they were given the right to cast ballots in territorial elections in Wyoming.

When women were first elected to Congress, there was no need to change the Constitution; nothing in it restricted officeholding to men.

When women were given the right to vote by constitutional amendment, it was not necessary to amend any existing language in the Constitution, because nothing in the Constitution itself denied women the right to vote; the amendment simply added a new right:

- "The right of citizens of the United States to vote shall not be denied or abridged by the United States or any state on account of sex."

  [Amend. XIX]

Source: Adapted from Robert Goldwin, "Why Blacks, Women and Jews Are Not Mentioned in the Constitution," *Commentary* (May 1987): 28–33.

How Things Work

Ways of Amending the Constitution

Under Article V, there are two ways to *propose* **amendments** to the Constitution and two ways to *ratify* them.

To Propose an Amendment

1. Two-thirds of both houses of Congress vote to propose an amendment, *or*

2. Two-thirds of the state legislatures ask Congress to call a national convention to propose amendments.

To Ratify an Amendment

1. Three-fourths of the state legislatures approve it,

or

2. Ratifying conventions in three-fourths of the states approve it.

Some Key Facts

- Only the first method of proposing an amendment has been used.

- The second method of ratification has been used only once, to ratify the Twenty-first Amendment (repealing Prohibition).

- Congress may limit the time within which a proposed amendment must be ratified. The usual limitation has been seven years.

- Thousands of proposals have been made, but only 33 have obtained the necessary two-thirds vote in Congress.

- Twenty-seven amendments have been ratified.

- The first 10 amendments, ratified on December 15, 1791, are known as the Bill of Rights.

---

work more like the British parliamentary system, in which, as we shall see in Chapters 13 and 14, the prime minister is the undisputed leader of the majority in the British Parliament. The parliamentary system is the major alternative in the world today to the American separation-of-powers system.

Both the diagnosis and the remedies proposed by these critics of the separation of powers have been challenged. Many defenders of our present constitutional system believe that nations, such as Great Britain, with a different, more unified political system have done no better than the United States in dealing with the problems of economic growth, national security, and environmental protection. Moreover, they argue, close congressional scrutiny of presidential proposals has improved these policies more often than it has weakened them. Finally, congressional "interference" in the work of government agencies is a good way of ensuring that the average citizen can fight back against the bureaucracy; without that so-called interference, citizens and interest groups might be helpless before big and powerful agencies.

Each of the specific proposals, defenders of the present

amendment A new provision in the Constitution that has been ratified by the states.

constitutional system argue, would either make matters worse or have, at best, uncertain effects. Adding a few members of Congress to the president's cabinet would not provide much help in getting his program through Congress; there are 535 senators and representatives, and probably only about half a dozen would be in the cabinet. Giving either the president or Congress the power to call a special election in between the regular elections (every two or four years) would cause needless confusion and great expense; the country would live under the threat of being in a perpetual political campaign with even weaker political parties. Linking the fate of the president and congressional candidates by having them run as a team in each district would reduce the stabilizing and moderating effect of having them elected separately. A Republican presidential candidate who wins in the new system would have a Republican majority in the House; a Democratic candidate winner would have a Democratic majority. We might as a result expect dramatic changes in policy as the political pendulum swung back and forth. Giving presidents a single six-year term would indeed free them from the need to worry about reelection, but it is precisely that worry that keeps presidents reasonably concerned about what the American people want.

MAKING THE SYSTEM LESS DEMOCRATIC

The second kind of critic of the Constitution thinks the government does too much, not too little. Though the separation of powers at one time may have slowed the growth of government and moderated the policies it adopted, in the last few decades government has grown helter-skelter. The problem, these critics argue, is not that democracy is a bad idea but that democracy can produce bad, or at least unintended, results if the government caters to the special-interest claims of the citizens rather than to their long-term values.

To see how these unintended results might occur, imagine a situation in which every citizen thinks the government grows too big, taxes too heavily, and spends too much. Each citizen wants the government made smaller by reducing the benefits other people get—but not by reducing the benefits he or she gets. In fact, such citizens may even be willing to see their own benefits cut, provided everybody else's are cut as well, and by a like amount.

But the political system attends to individual wants, not general preferences. It gives aid to farmers, contracts to industry, grants to professors, pensions to the elderly, and loans to students. As someone once said, the government is like an adding machine: during elections candidates campaign by promising to do more for whatever group is dissatisfied with what the incumbents are doing for it. As a result, most elections bring to office men and women committed to doing more for somebody. The grand total of all these additions is more for everybody. Few politicians have an incentive to do less for anybody.

To remedy this state of affairs, these critics suggest various mechanisms, but principally a constitutional amendment that would either set a limit on the amount of money the government could collect in taxes each year or require that each year the government have a balanced budget (that is, not spend more than it takes in in taxes), or both. In some versions of these plans, an extraordinary majority (say, 60 percent) of Congress could override these limits, and the limits would not apply in wartime.

The effect of such amendments, the proponents claim, would be to force Congress and the president to look at the big picture—the grand total of what they are spending—rather than just to operate the adding machine by pushing the "add" button over and over again. If they could spend only so much during a given year, they would have to allocate what they spend among all rival claimants. For example, if more money were to be spent on the poor, less could then be spent on the military, or vice versa.

Some critics of an overly powerful federal government think these amendments will not be passed or may prove unworkable; instead, they favor enhancing the president's power to block spending by giving him a **line-item veto.** Most state governors can veto a particular part of a bill and approve the rest using a line-item veto. The theory is that such a veto would better equip the president to stop unwarranted spending without vetoing the other provisions of a bill. In 1996, President Clinton signed the Line Item Veto Act, passed by the 104th Congress. But despite its name, the new law did not give the president full line-item veto power (only a change in the Constitution could confer that power). Instead the law gave the president authority to selectively eliminate individual items in large appropriations bills, expansions in certain income-transfer programs, and tax breaks (giving the president what budget experts call *enhanced rescission authority*). But it also left Congress free to craft bills in ways that would give the president few opportunities to veto (or *rescind*) favored items. For example, Congress could still force the president to accept or reject an entire appropriations bill simply by tagging on this sentence: "Appropriations provided under this act (or title or section) shall not be subject to the provisions of the Line Item Veto Act." In *Clinton et al. v. New York et al.* (1998), the Supreme Court struck down the 1996 law, holding 6 to 3 that the Constitution does not allow the president to cancel specific items in tax and spending legislation. Clinton's successor, President George W. Bush, championed the line-item veto, but to no avail; and, when asked about the line-item veto in February 2009, President Barack Obama's press secretary, Robert Gibbs, quipped that the new president would "love to take that for a test drive."

line-item veto An executive's ability to block a particular provision in a bill passed by the legislature.

Finally, some critics of a powerful government feel that the real problem arises not from an excess of "adding-machine" democracy but from the growth in the power of the federal courts, as described in Chapter 16. These critics would like to devise a set of laws or constitutional amendments that would narrow the authority of federal courts.

The opponents of these suggestions argue that constitutional amendments to restrict the level of taxes or to require a balanced budget are unworkable, even assuming—which they do not—that a smaller government is desirable. There is no precise, agreed-upon way to measure how much the government spends or to predict in advance how much it will receive in taxes during the year; thus defining and enforcing a "balanced budget" is no easy matter. Since the government can always borrow money, it might easily evade any spending limits. It has also

WHAT WOULD YOU DO?

MEMORANDUM

To: *Elizabeth Anthony, Arkansas state senate majority leader*

From: *George Morris, chief of staff*

Subject: *Proposal for a New Constitutional Convention*

In the 1990s, Arkansas and several other states approved term limits for their members of Congress, but the Supreme Court ruled in 1995 that states do not have this authority. Now term-limit advocates are pursuing a broader strategy, calling for states to approve legislation that would require Congress to consider several amendment proposals, including term limits and abolishing the electoral College to permit the direct popular election of the president. The Arkansas General Assembly passed such a bill last week, and several senators in your party have declared their support.

Arguments for:

1. Since the Twenty-second Amendment restricts presidents to two terms, that members of Congress should face similar limits.

2. Term limits will ensure that national leaders do not become career politicians.

3. The public favors the direct popular election of the president; this constitutional convention would make possible abolishing the electoral College.

Arguments against:

1. Limiting members of Congress to two terms would increase the power of lobbyists, congressional staffers, and administrative officials.

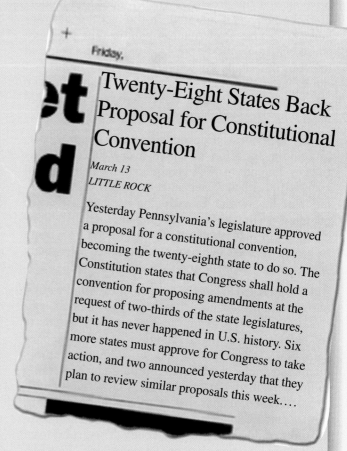

Twenty-Eight States Back Proposal for Constitutional Convention

March 13
LITTLE ROCK

Yesterday Pennsylvania's legislature approved a proposal for a constitutional convention, becoming the twenty-eighth state to do so. The Constitution states that Congress shall hold a convention for proposing amendments at the request of two-thirds of the state legislatures, but it has never happened in U.S. history. Six more states must approve for Congress to take action, and two announced yesterday that they plan to review similar proposals this week....

2. The Electoral College encourages a two-party system; a direct popular vote for the president would require runoff elections if no candidate won a majority.

3. The Constitutional Convention of 1787 was held in secret and involved only a few dozen people; today it would be heavily covered by the press and involve hundreds, perhaps thousands of people. No one knows what changes it might make.

Your decision:

Favor legislation: _____   Oppose legislation: _____

shown great ingenuity in spending money in ways that never appear as part of the regular budget.

The line-item veto may or may not be a good idea. Unless the Constitution is amended to permit it, future presidents will have to do without it. The states, where some governors have long had the veto, are quite different from the federal government in power and responsibilities. Whether a line-item veto would work as well in Washington, D.C., as it does in many state capitals is something that we may simply never know.

Finally, proposals to curtail judicial power are thinly veiled attacks, the opponents argue, on the ability of the courts to protect essential citizen rights. If Congress and the people do not like the way the Supreme Court has interpreted the Constitution, they can always amend the Constitution to change a specific ruling; there is no need to adopt some across-the-board limitation on court powers.

WHO IS RIGHT?

Some of the arguments of these two sets of critics of the Constitution may strike you as plausible or even entirely convincing. Whatever you may ultimately decide, decide nothing for now. One cannot make or remake a constitution based entirely on abstract reasoning or unproven factual arguments. Even when the Constitution was first written in 1787, it was not an exercise in abstract philosophy but rather an effort to solve pressing, practical problems in the light of a theory of human nature, the lessons of past experience, and a close consideration of how governments in other countries and at other times had worked.

In an excellent TV series, John Adams and George Washington discuss politics in the 18th century.

Kent Eanes/HBO/Everett Collection

Just because the Constitution is over 200 years old does not mean it is out-of-date. The crucial questions are these: How well has it worked over the long sweep of American history? How well has it worked compared to the constitutions of other democratic nations?

The only way to answer those questions is to study American government closely—with special attention to its historical evolution and to the practices of other nations. That is what this book is about. Of course, even after close study, people will still disagree about whether our system should be changed. People want different things and evaluate human experience according to different beliefs. But if we first understand how, in fact, the government works and why it has produced the policies it has, we can then argue more intelligently about how best to achieve our wants and give expression to our beliefs.

SUMMARY

The Framers of the Constitution sought to create a government capable of protecting both liberty and order. The solution they chose—one without precedent at that time—was a government that was based on a written constitution that combined the principles of popular consent, the separation of powers, and federalism.

Popular consent was embodied in the procedure for choosing the House of Representatives but limited by the indirect election of senators and the electoral college system for selecting the president. Political authority was to be shared by three branches of government in a manner deliberately intended to produce conflict among these branches. This conflict, motivated by the self-interest of the people occupying each branch, would, it was hoped, prevent tyranny, even by a popular majority.

Federalism came to mean a system in which both the national and state governments had independent authority. Allocating powers between the two levels of government and devising means to ensure that neither large nor small states would dominate the national government required the most delicate compromises at the Philadelphia convention. The decision to do nothing about slavery was another such compromise.

In the drafting of the Constitution and the struggle over its ratification in the states, the positions people took were chiefly determined not by their economic interests but by a variety of factors. Among these were profound differences of opinion over whether the state governments or the national government would be the best protector of personal liberty.

RECONSIDERING WHO GOVERNS?

1. What is the difference between a democracy and a republic?

A democracy means rule by the people; direct democracy means letting every important issue be decided by popular vote. A republic is a government in which authority has been given to elected representatives. The United States is a republic in which members of the House of Representatives are selected in democratic elections, members of the Senate (at least initially) were selected by state legislatures, and the courts are staffed by appointed judges.

2. What branch of government has the greatest power?

Initially, Congress had the most authority. As we shall see in later chapters, the president and the federal courts grew in power, but even so Congress remains the most important institution.

RECONSIDERING TO WHAT ENDS?

1. Does the Constitution tell us what goals the government should serve?

Not really. The preface tells us what the Founders hoped the federal government would do, but that preface has no legal authority. By and large, the government has to set its own goals.

2. Whose freedom does the Constitution protect?

It was intended to protect everybody's freedom, except that of slaves. To create a national government, it was necessary that the Constitution do nothing about slavery, but without the Constitution, there would have been no national government to challenge slavery during the Civil War. Though women are not mentioned, in fact there is nothing in the Constitution to prevent them from holding national office or from voting in federal elections. Voting was to be decided by each state until the passage of a constitutional amendment (the Nineteenth, ratified in 1920) that prohibited the states from denying the vote to women.

WORLD WIDE WEB RESOURCES

To find historical and legal documents:

TeachingAmericanHistory.org

National Constitution Center: **www.constitutioncenter.org**

Congress: **thomas.loc.gov/** (choose Historical Documents)

To look at court cases about the Constitution:

Cornell University: **www.law.cornell.edu/supct**

SUGGESTED READINGS

Bailyn, Bernard. *The Ideological Origins of the American Revolution.* Cambridge: Harvard University Press, 1967. A brilliant account of how the American colonists formed and justified the idea of independence.

Becker, Carl L. *The Declaration of Independence.* New York: Vintage, 1942. The classic account of the meaning of the Declaration.

Farrand, Max. *The Framing of the Constitution of the United States.* New Haven, Conn.: Yale University Press, 1913. A good, brief account of the Philadelphia convention by the editor of Madison's notes on the convention.

Federalist papers. By Alexander Hamilton, James Madison, and John Jay. The definitive edition, edited by Jacob E. Cooke, was published in Middletown,

Conn., in 1961, by the Wesleyan University Press.

Goldwin, Robert A., and William A. Schambra, eds. *How Capitalistic Is the Constitution?* Washington, D.C.: American Enterprise Institute, 1982. Essays from different viewpoints discussing the relationship between the Constitution and the economic order.

————. *How Democratic Is the Constitution?* Washington, D.C.: American Enterprise Institute, 1980. Collection of essays offering different interpretations of the political meaning of the Constitution.

McDonald, Forrest. *Novus Ordo Seclorum.* Lawrence: University of Kansas Press, 1985. A careful study of the intellectual origins of the Constitution. The Latin title means "New World Order," which is what the Framers hoped they were creating.

Sheldon, Garrett W. *The Political Philosophy of James Madison.* Baltimore: Johns Hopkins University Press, 2001. Masterful account of Madison's political thought and its roots in classical republicanism and Christianity.

Storing, Herbert J. *What the Anti-Federalists Were For.* Chicago: University of Chicago Press, 1981. Close analysis of the political views of those opposed to the ratification of the Constitution.

Sundquist, James L. *Constitutional Reform and Effective Government,* rev. ed. Washington, D.C.: Brookings, 1992. An argument in favor of making our national government more like a parliamentary democracy.

Wood, Gordon S. *The Creation of the American Republic.* Chapel Hill: University of North Carolina Press, 1969. A detailed study of American political thought before the Philadelphia convention.

————. *The Radicalism of the American Revolution.* New York: Knopf, 1992. Magisterial study of the nature and effects of the American Revolution and the relationship between the socially radical Revolution and the Constitution.

3

Federalism

Visions of America/Joe Sohm/Digital Vision/Getty Images

WHO GOVERNS?

1. Where is sovereignty located in the American political system?
2. How is power divided between the national government and the states under the Constitution?

TO WHAT ENDS?

1. What competing values are at stake in federalism?
2. Who should decide which matters ought to be governed mainly or solely by national laws?

Like most average citizens, Susette Kelo, a nurse from New London, Connecticut, was not deeply interested in politics and government. But that changed when city officials condemned her little wood-frame home with a view of the Long Island Sound estuary. City officials took it and her neighbors' houses because they wanted to redevelop the area with pricey townhouses, upscale shopping malls, and a huge hotel. Kelo sued the city all the way to the U.S. Supreme Court.

But in *Kelo v. City of New London* (2005), the justices decided, by a 5 to 4 majority, that the Constitution allows the government to seize property, not only for "public use" such as building highways, but also to "promote economic development" in a "distressed" community.

Kelo and her neighbors were outraged, not least of all by the claim that their predominantly middle-class, waterside community was "distressed." But they had lost in the nation's highest court. What more could they or their by-then growing throng of sympathizers all across the country do?

Why Federalism Matters

Plenty, as it turned out. Before the ink had dried on the *Kelo* opinion, public protests, Internet letter-writing campaigns, and grassroots lobbying efforts were begun. Eighteen months later, 34 states had tightened laws to make it much harder for local governments to seize property for economic development purposes.

Similarly, you might suppose that federal law decides the minimum wage that employers must pay to workers. But before Congress moved to raise it (from 1996 into 2007 the standard was $5.15 an hour), over a half-dozen states had a minimum wage above the federal standard (for instance, $7.15 an hour in Pennsylvania).

Okay, you might think, but what about state and local government powers in relation to big federal bureaucracies or huge federal programs? Surely the national government leads in making, administering, and funding important public policies that cost lots of money, right? The short answer is, "It all depends." The main reason is "federalism."

Federalism can be defined as a political system in which the national government shares power with local governments (state governments in the case of the United States, but other sub-national governments in the case of federal systems including Australia, India, and Switzerland).

Constitutionally, in America's federal system, state governments have a specially protected existence and the authority to make final decisions over many governmental activities. Even today, after over a century during which the government headquartered in Washington, D.C., has grown, state and local governments are not mere junior partners in deciding important public policy matters. The national government can pass, and the federal courts can uphold, laws to protect the environment, store nuclear waste, expand low-income housing, guarantee the right to an abortion, provide special services for the handicapped, or toughen public school graduation standards. But whether and how such federal laws are followed or funded often involves decisions by diverse state and local government officials, both elected and appointed.

Federalism or federal-state relations may seem like an arcane or boring subject until you realize that it is behind many things that matter to many people: how much you pay in certain taxes, whether

federalism Government authority shared by national and local governments.

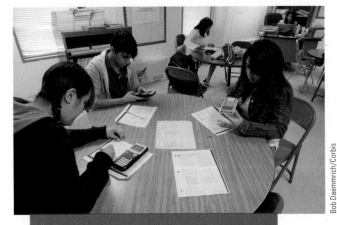

Federal law requires school children to take achievement tests.

Bob Daemmrich/Corbis

you can drive above 55 miles per hour on certain roadways, whether or where you can buy liquor, how much money gets spent on schools, whether all or most children have health insurance coverage, and much more. Federalism affects almost every aspect of crime and punishment in America (penalties for illegal drug sales vary widely from state to state, and persons convicted of murder are subject to the death penalty in some states but not in others). And, as we will see, federalism even figures in how certain civil liberties (Chapter 5) and civil rights (Chapter 6) are defined and protected (for instance, some state constitutions mention God, and some state laws specifically prohibit funding for religious schools).

Federalism matters, but how it matters has changed over time. In 1908, Woodrow Wilson observed that the relationship between the national government and the states "is the cardinal question of our constitutional system," a question that cannot be settled by "one generation, because it is a question of growth, and every successive stage of our political and economic development gives it a new aspect, makes it a new question."[1]

Since the adoption of the Constitution in 1787, the single most persistent source of political conflict has been the relations between the national and state governments. The political conflict over slavery, for example, was intensified because some state governments condoned or supported slavery, while others took action to discourage it. The proponents and opponents of slavery were thus given territorial power centers from which to carry on the dispute. Other issues, such as the regulation of business and the provision of social welfare programs, were in large part fought out, for well over a century, in terms of "national interests" versus "states' rights." While other nations, such as Great Britain, were debating the question of whether the national government *ought* to provide old-age pensions or regulate the railroads, the United States debated a different question—whether the national government *had the right* to do these things.

The Founding

The goal of the Founders seems clear: federalism was one device whereby personal liberty was to be protected. (The separation of powers was another.) They feared that placing final political authority in any one set of hands, even in the hands of persons popularly elected, would so concentrate power as to risk tyranny. But they had seen what happened when independent states tried to form a compact, as under the Articles of Confederation; what the states put together, they could also take apart. The alliance among the states that existed from 1776 to 1787 was a confederation, that is, a system of government in which the people create state governments which in turn create and operate a national government (see Figure 3.1). Since the national government in a confederation derives its powers from the states, it is dependent on their continued cooperation for its survival. By 1786, that cooperation was barely forthcoming.

A BOLD, NEW PLAN

A federation—or a "federal republic," as the Founders called it—derives its powers directly from the people, as do the state governments. As the Founders envisioned it, both levels of government, the national and the state, would have certain powers, but neither would have supreme authority over the other. Madison, writing in *Federalist* No. 46, said that both the state and federal governments "are in fact but different agents and trustees of the people, constituted with different powers." In *Federalist* No. 28, Hamilton explained how he thought the system would work: the people could shift their support between state and federal levels of government as needed to keep the two in balance. "If their rights are invaded by either, they can make use of the other as the instrument of redress."

It was an entirely new plan, for which no historical precedent existed. Nobody came to the Philadelphia convention with a clear idea of what a federal (as opposed to a unitary or a confederal) system would look like, and there was not much discussion at Philadelphia of how the system would work in

Figure 3.1

Lines of Power in Three Systems of Government

UNITARY SYSTEM

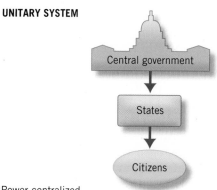

Power centralized.
State or regional governments derive authority from central government. Examples: United Kingdom, France.

FEDERAL SYSTEM

Power divided between central and state or local governments.
Both the government and constituent governments act directly upon the citizens.
Both must agree to constitutional change.
Examples: Canada, United States since adoption of Constitution.

CONFEDERAL SYSTEM (or CONFEDERATION)

Power held by independent states.
Central government is a creature of the constituent governments.
Example: United States under the Articles of Confederation.

practice. Few delegates then used the word *federalism* in the sense in which we now employ it (it was originally used as a synonym for *confederation* and only later came to stand for something different).[2] The Constitution does not spell out the powers that the states are to have, and until the Tenth Amendment was added at the insistence of various states, there was not even a clause in it saying (as did the amendment) that "the powers not delegated to the United States by the Constitution, nor prohibited by it to the states, are reserved to the states respectively, or to the people." The Founders assumed from the outset that the federal government would have only those powers given to it by the Constitution; the Tenth Amendment was an afterthought, added to make that assumption explicit and allay fears that something else was intended.[3]

The Tenth Amendment has rarely had much practical significance, however. From time to time, the Supreme Court has tried to interpret that amendment as putting certain state activities beyond the reach of the federal government, but usually the Court has later changed its mind and allowed Washington to regulate such matters as the hours that employees of a city-owned mass-transit system may work. The Court did not find that running such a transportation system was one of the powers "reserved to the states."[4] But, as we explain later in this chapter, the Court has begun to give new life to the Tenth Amendment and the doctrine of state sovereignty.

ELASTIC LANGUAGE

The need to reconcile the competing interests of large and small states and of northern and southern states, especially as they affected the organization of Congress, was sufficiently difficult without trying to spell out exactly what relationship ought to exist between the national and state systems. For example, Congress was given the power to regulate commerce "among the several states." The Philadelphia convention would have gone on for four years rather than four months if the Founders had decided that it was necessary to describe, in clear language, how one was to tell where commerce *among* the states ended and commerce wholly *within* a single state began. The Supreme Court, as we shall see, devoted over a century to that task before giving up.

Though some clauses bearing on federal-state relations were reasonably clear (see the box on page 56), other clauses were quite vague. The Founders knew, correctly, that they could not make an exact and exhaustive list of everything the federal government was empowered to do—circumstances would change, new exigencies would arise. Thus they added the following elastic language to Article I: Congress shall have the power to "make all laws which shall be necessary and proper for carrying into execution the foregoing powers."

The Founders themselves carried away from Philadelphia different views of what federalism meant. One view was championed by Hamilton.

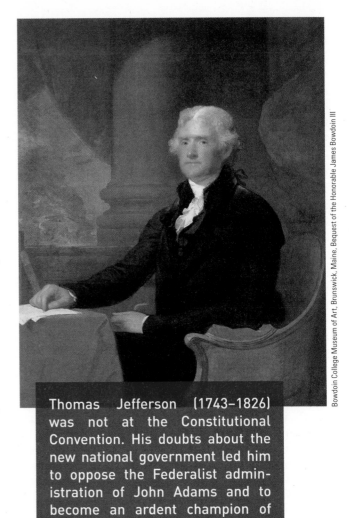

Thomas Jefferson (1743–1826) was not at the Constitutional Convention. His doubts about the new national government led him to oppose the Federalist administration of John Adams and to become an ardent champion of states' rights.

Bowdoin College Museum of Art, Brunswick, Maine, Bequest of the Honorable James Bowdoin III

Since the people had created the national government, since the laws and treaties made pursuant to the Constitution were "the supreme law of the land" (Article VI), and since the most pressing needs were the development of a national economy and the conduct of foreign affairs, Hamilton thought that the national government was the superior and leading force in political affairs and that its powers ought to be broadly defined and liberally construed.

The other view, championed by Jefferson, was that the federal government, though important, was the product of an agreement among the states; and though "the people" were the ultimate sovereigns, the principal threat to their liberties was likely to come from the national government. (Madison, a strong supporter of national supremacy at the convention, later became a champion of states' rights.) Thus the powers of the federal government should be narrowly construed and strictly limited.

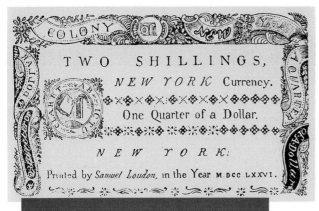

The Granger Collection

At one time the states could issue their own paper money, such as this New York currency worth 25 cents in 1776. Under the Constitution, this power was reserved to Congress.

As Madison put it in *Federalist* No. 45, in language that probably made Hamilton wince, "The powers delegated by the proposed Constitution to the federal government are few and defined. Those which are to remain in the State governments are numerous and indefinite."

Hamilton argued for national supremacy, Jefferson for states' rights. Though their differences were greater in theory than in practice (as we shall see in Chapter 14, Jefferson while president sometimes acted in a positively Hamiltonian manner), the differing interpretations they offered of the Constitution were to shape political debate in this country until well into the 1960s.

The Debate on the Meaning of Federalism

The Civil War was fought, in part, over the issue of national supremacy versus states' rights, but it settled only one part of that argument—namely, that the national government was supreme, its sovereignty derived directly from the people, and thus the states could not lawfully secede from the Union. Virtually every other aspect of the national-supremacy issue continued to animate political and legal debate for another century.

THE SUPREME COURT SPEAKS

As arbiter of what the Constitution means, the Supreme Court became the focal point of that debate. In Chapter 16, we shall see in some detail

how the Court made its decisions. For now it is enough to know that during the formative years of the new Republic, the Supreme Court was led by a staunch and brilliant advocate of Hamilton's position, Chief Justice John Marshall. In a series of decisions, he and the Court powerfully defended the national-supremacy view of the newly formed federal government.

The box on page 59 lists some landmark cases in the history of federal-state relations. Perhaps the most important decision was in a case, seemingly trivial in its origins, that arose when James McCulloch, the cashier of the Baltimore branch of the Bank of the United States, which had been created by Congress, refused to pay a tax levied on that bank by the state of Maryland. He was hauled into state court and convicted of failing to pay a tax. In 1819, McCulloch appealed all the way to the Supreme Court in a case known as *McCulloch v. Maryland*. The Court, in a unanimous opinion, answered two questions in ways that expanded the powers of Congress and confirmed the supremacy of the federal government in the exercise of those powers.

The first question was whether Congress had the right to set up a bank, or any other corporation, since such a right is nowhere explicitly mentioned in the Constitution. Marshall said that, though the federal government possessed only those powers enumerated in the Constitution, the "extent"—that is, the meaning—of those powers required interpretation. Though the word *bank* is not in that document, one finds there the power to manage money: to lay and collect taxes, issue a currency, and borrow funds. To carry out these powers, Congress may reasonably decide that chartering a national bank is "necessary and proper." Marshall's words were carefully chosen to endow the **"necessary and proper" clause** with the widest possible sweep:

> *Let the end be legitimate, let it be within the scope of the Constitution, and all means which are appropriate, which are plainly adapted to that end, which are not prohibited, but consistent with the letter and spirit of the Constitution, are constitutional.*[5]

The second question was whether a federal bank could lawfully be taxed by a state. To answer it, Marshall went back to first principles. The government of the United States was not established by the states,

"necessary and proper" clause Section of the Constitution allowing Congress to pass all laws "necessary and proper" to its duties, and which has permitted Congress to exercise powers not specifically given to it (enumerated) by the Constitution.

How Things Work

The States and the Constitution

The Framers made some attempt to define the relations between the states and the federal government and how the states were to relate to one another. The following points were made in the original Constitution—before the Bill of Rights was added.

Restrictions on Powers of the States

States may not make treaties with foreign nations, coin money, issue paper currency, grant titles of nobility, pass a bill of attainder or an ex post facto law, or, without the consent of Congress, levy any taxes on imports or exports, keep troops and ships in time of peace, or enter into an agreement with another state or with a foreign power.

[Art. I, sec. 10]

Guarantees by the Federal Government to the States

The national government guarantees to every state a "republican form of government" and protection against foreign invasion and (provided the states request it) protection against domestic insurrection.

[Art. IV, sec. 4]

An existing state will not be broken up into two or more states or merged with all or part of another state without that state's consent.

[Art. IV, sec. 3]

Congress may admit new states into the Union.

[Art. IV, sec. 3]

Taxes levied by Congress must be uniform throughout the United States: they may not be levied on some states but not others.

[Art. I, sec. 8]

The Constitution may not be amended to give states unequal representation in the Senate.

[Art. V]

Rules Governing How States Deal with Each Other

"Full faith and credit" shall be given by each state to the laws, records, and court decisions of other states. (For example, a civil case settled in the courts of one state cannot be retried in the courts of another.)

[Art. IV, sec. 1]

The citizens of each state shall have the "privileges and immunities" of the citizens of every other state. (No one is quite sure what this is supposed to mean.)

[Art. IV, sec. 2]

If a person charged with a crime by one state flees to another, he or she is subjected to extradition—that is, the governor of the state that finds the fugitive is supposed to return the person to the governor of the state that wants him or her.

[Art. IV, sec. 2]

---

but by the people, and thus the federal government was supreme in the exercise of those powers conferred upon it. Having already concluded that chartering a bank was within the powers of Congress, Marshall then argued that the only way for such powers to be supreme was for their use to be immune from state challenge and for the products of their use to be protected against state destruction. Since "the power to tax involves the power to destroy," and since the power to destroy a federal agency would confer upon the states supremacy over the federal government, the states may not tax any federal instrument. Hence the Maryland law was unconstitutional.

McCulloch won, and so did the federal government. Half a century later, the Court decided that what was sauce for the goose was sauce for the gander. It held that just as state governments could not tax federal bonds, the federal government could not tax the interest people earn on state and municipal bonds. In 1988, the Supreme Court changed its mind and decided that Congress was now free, if it wished, to tax the interest on such state and local bonds.[6] Municipal bonds, which for nearly a century were a tax-exempt investment protected, so their holders thought, by the Constitution, were now protected only by politics. So far Congress hasn't wanted to tax them.

NULLIFICATION

The Supreme Court can decide a case without settling the issue. The struggle over states' rights versus national supremacy continued to rage in Congress, during presidential elections, and ultimately on the battlefield. The issue came to center on the doctrine of **nullification.** When Congress passed laws (in 1798) to punish newspaper editors who published stories critical of the federal government, James Madison and Thomas Jefferson opposed the laws, suggesting (in statements known as the Virginia and Kentucky Resolutions) that the states had the right to "nullify" (that is, declare null and void) a federal law that, in the states' opinion, violated the Constitution. The laws expired before the claim of nullification could be settled in the courts.

Later the doctrine of nullification was revived by John C. Calhoun of South Carolina, first in opposition to a tariff enacted by the federal government and later in opposition to federal efforts to restrict slavery. Calhoun argued that if Washington attempted to ban slavery, the states had the right to declare such acts unconstitutional and thus null and void. This time the issue was settled—by war. The northern victory in the Civil War determined once and for all that the federal union is indissoluble and that states cannot declare acts of Congress unconstitutional, a view later confirmed by the Supreme Court.[7]

DUAL FEDERALISM

After the Civil War, the debate about the meaning of federalism focused on the interpretation of the commerce clause of the Constitution. Out of this debate emerged the doctrine of **dual federalism,** which held that though the national government was supreme in its sphere, the states were equally supreme in theirs, and that these two spheres of action should and could be kept separate. Applied to commerce, the concept of dual federalism implied that there were such things as *inter*state commerce, which Congress could regulate, and *intra*state commerce, which only the states could regulate, and that the Court could tell which was which.

For a long period the Court tried to decide what was interstate commerce based on the kind of business that was conducted. Transporting things between states was obviously interstate commerce, and so subject to federal regulation. Thus federal laws affecting the interstate shipment of lottery tickets,[8] prostitutes,[9] liquor,[10] and harmful foods and drugs[11] were upheld. On the other hand, manufacturing,[12] insurance,[13] and farming[14] were in the past considered *intra*state commerce, and so only the state governments were allowed to regulate them.

Such product-based distinctions turned out to be hard to sustain. For example, if you ship a case of whiskey from Kentucky to Kansas, how long is it in interstate commerce (and thus subject to federal law), and when does it enter intrastate commerce and become subject only to state law? For a while, the Court's answer was that the whiskey was in interstate commerce so long as it was in its "original package,"[15] but that only precipitated long quarrels as to what was the original package and how one is to treat things, like gas and grain, that may not be shipped in packages at all. And how could one distinguish between manufacturing and transportation when one company did both or when a single manufacturing corporation owned factories in different states? And if an insurance company sold policies to customers both inside and outside a given state, were there to be different laws regulating identical policies that happened to be purchased from the same company by persons in different states?

In time, the effort to find some clear principles that distinguished interstate from intrastate commerce was pretty much abandoned. Commerce was like a stream flowing through the country, drawing to itself contributions from thousands of scattered enterprises and depositing its products in millions of individual homes. The Court began to permit the federal government to regulate almost anything that affected this stream, so that by the 1940s not only had farming and manufacturing been redefined as part of interstate commerce,[16] but even the janitors and window washers in buildings that housed companies engaged in interstate commerce were now said to be part of that stream.[17]

Today lawyers are engaged in interstate commerce but professional baseball players are not. If your state has approved marijuana use for medical purposes, you can still be penalized under federal law even when the marijuana you consume was grown in a small pot in your backyard.[18]

STATE SOVEREIGNTY

It would be a mistake to think that the doctrine of dual federalism is entirely dead. Until recently Congress, provided that it had a good reason, could

nullification. The doctrine that a state can declare null and void a federal law that, in the state's opinion, violates the Constitution.

dual federalism
Doctrine holding that the national government is supreme in its sphere, the states are supreme in theirs, and the two spheres should be kept separate.

Politically Speaking

The Terms of Local Governance

Legally a **city** is a **municipal corporation or municipality** that has been chartered by a state to exercise certain defined powers and provide certain specific services. There are two kinds of charters: special-act charters and general-act charters.

A **special-act charter** applies to a certain city (for example, New York City) and lists what that city can and cannot do. A **general-act charter** applies to a number of cities that fall within a certain classification, usually based on city population. Thus in some states, all cities over 100,000 population will be governed on the basis of one charter, while all cities between 50,000 and 99,999 population will be governed on the basis of a different one.

Under **Dillon's rule,** the terms of these charters are to be interpreted very narrowly. This rule (named after a lawyer who wrote a book on the subject in 1911) authorizes a municipality to exercise only those powers expressly given, implied by, or essential to the accomplishment of its enumerated powers. This means, for example, that a city cannot so much as operate a peanut stand at the city zoo unless the state has specifically given the city that power by law or charter.

A **home-rule charter,** now in effect in many cities, reverses Dillon's rule and allows a city government to do anything not prohibited by the charter or state law. Even under a home-rule charter, however, city laws (called **ordinances**) cannot be in conflict with state laws, and the states can pass laws that preempt or interfere with what home-rule cities want to do.

There are in this country more than 87,500 local governments, only about a fifth (19,500) of which are cities or municipalities. **Counties** (3,000) are the largest territorial units between a state and a city or town. Every state but Connecticut and Rhode Island has county governments. (In Louisiana, counties are called parishes, in Alaska boroughs.)

pass a law regulating almost any kind of economic activity anywhere in the country, and the Supreme Court would call it constitutional. But in *United States v. Lopez* (1995), the Court held that Congress had exceeded its commerce clause power by prohibiting guns in a school zone.

The Court reaffirmed the view that the commerce clause does not justify any federal action when, in May 2000, it overturned the Violence Against Women Act of 1994. This law allowed women who were the victims of a crime of violence motivated by gender to sue the guilty party in federal court. In *United States v. Morrison* the Court, in a five-to-four decision, said that attacks against women are not, and do not substantially affect, interstate commerce, and hence Congress cannot constitutionally pass such a law. Chief Justice William Rehnquist said that "the Constitution requires a distinction between what is truly national and what is truly local." The states, of course, can pass such laws, and many have.

The Court has moved to strengthen states' rights on other grounds as well. In *Printz v. United States* (1997), the Court invalidated a federal law that required local police to conduct background checks on all gun purchasers. The Court ruled that the law violated the Tenth Amendment by commanding state governments to carry out a federal regulatory program. Writing for the five-to-four majority, Justice Antonin Scalia declared, "The Federal government may neither issue directives requiring the states to address particular problems, nor command the states' officers, or those of their political subdivisions, to administer or enforce a Federal regulatory program.... Such commands are fundamentally incompatible with our constitutional system of dual sovereignty."

The Court has also given new life to the Eleventh Amendment, which protects states from lawsuits by citizens of other states or foreign nations. In 1999, the Court shielded states from suits by copyright owners who claimed infringement from state agencies and immunized states from lawsuits by people who argued that state regulations create unfair economic competition. In *Alden v. Maine* (1999), the Court held that state employees could not sue to force state compliance with federal fair-labor laws. In the Court's five-to-four majority opinion, Justice Anthony M. Kennedy stated, "Although the Constitution grants broad powers to Congress, our federalism requires that Congress treat the states in a manner consistent with their status as residuary sovereigns and joint participants in the governance of the nation." A few years later, in *Federal Maritime Commission v. South Carolina Ports*

Landmark Cases

Federal-State Relations

- **McCulloch v. Maryland (1819):** The Constitution's "necessary and proper" clause permits Congress to take actions (in this case, to create a national bank) when it is essential to a power that Congress has (in this case, managing the currency).

- **Gibbons v. Ogden (1824):** The Constitution's commerce clause gives the national government exclusive power to regulate interstate commerce.

- **Wabash, St. Louis and Pacific Railroad v. Illinois (1886):** The states may not regulate interstate commerce.

- **United States v. Lopez (1995):** The national government's power under the commerce clause does not permit it to regulate matters not directly related to interstate commerce (in this case, banning firearms in a school zone).

Authority (2002), the Court further expanded states' sovereign immunity from private lawsuits. Writing for the five-to-four majority, Justice Clarence Thomas declared that dual sovereignty "is a defining feature of our nation's constitutional blueprint," adding that the states "did not consent to become mere appendages of the federal government" when they ratified the Constitution.

Not all Court decisions, however, support greater state sovereignty. In 1999, for example, the Court ruled seven to two that state welfare programs may not restrict new residents to the welfare benefits they would have received in the states from which they moved. In addition, each of the Court's major prostate sovereignty decisions has been decided by a tenuous five-to-four margin. More generally, to empower states is not to disempower Congress, which, as it has done since the late 1930s, can still make federal laws on almost anything as long as it does not go too far in "commandeering" state resources or gutting states' rights.

New debates over state sovereignty call forth old truths about the constitutional basis of state and local government. In general, a state can do anything that is not prohibited by the Constitution or preempted by federal policy and that is consistent

with its own constitution. One generally recognized state power is the **police power,** which refers to those laws and regulations, not otherwise unconstitutional, that promote health, safety, and morals. Thus the states can enact and enforce criminal codes, require children to attend school and citizens to be vaccinated, and restrict (subject to many limitations) the availability of pornographic materials or the activities of prostitutes and drug dealers.

police power State power to enact laws promoting health, safety, and morals.

Governmental Structure

Federalism refers to a political system in which there are local (territorial, regional, provincial, state, or municipal) units of government, as well as a national government, that can make final decisions with respect to at least some governmental activities and whose existence is specially protected. Almost every nation in the world has local units of government of some kind, if for no other reason than to decentralize the administrative burdens of governing. But these governments are not federal unless the local units exist independent of the preferences of the national government and can make decisions on at least some matters without regard to those preferences.

The United States, Canada, Australia, India, Germany, and Switzerland are federal systems, as are a few other nations. France, Great Britain, Italy, and Sweden are not: they are unitary systems, because such local governments as they possess can be altered or even abolished by the national government and cannot plausibly claim to have final authority over any significant governmental activities.

The special protection that subnational governments enjoy in a federal system derives in part from the constitution of the country but also from the habits, preferences, and dispositions of the citizens and the actual distribution of political power in society. The constitution of the former Soviet Union in theory created a federal system, as claimed by that country's full name—the Union of Soviet Socialist Republics—but for most of their history, none of these "socialist republics" were in the slightest degree independent of the central government. Were the American Constitution the only guarantee of the independence of the American states, they would long since have become mere administrative subunits of the government in Washington. Their independence results in large measure from the commitment of Americans to the idea of local

Politically Speaking

Sovereignty, Federalism, and the Constitution

Sovereignty means supreme or ultimate political authority: A sovereign government is one that is legally and politically independent of any other government.

A **unitary system** is one in which sovereignty is wholly in the hands of the national government, so that the states and localities are dependent on its will.

A **confederation or confederal system** is one in which the states are sovereign and the national government is allowed to do only that which the states permit.

A **federal system** is one in which sovereignty is shared, so that in some matters the national government is supreme and in other matters the states are supreme.

The Founding Fathers often took *confederal* and *federal* to mean much the same thing. Rather than establishing a government in which there was a clear division of sovereign authority between the national and state governments, they saw themselves as creating a government that combined some characteristics of a unitary regime with some of a confederal one. Or, as James Madison expressed the idea in *Federalist* No. 39, the Constitution "is, in strictness, neither a national nor a federal Constitution, but a composition of both." Where sovereignty is located in this system is a matter that the Founders did not clearly answer.

In this text, a **federal regime** is defined in the simplest possible terms—as one in which local units of government have a specially protected existence and can make some final decisions over some governmental activities.

sustaining centers of power, prestige, and profit."[19] Political power is locally acquired by people whose careers depend for the most part on satisfying local interests. As a result, though the national government has come to have vast powers, it exercises many of those powers through state governments. What many of us forget when we think about "the government in Washington" is that it spends much of its money and enforces most of its rules not on citizens directly but on other, local units of government. A large part of the welfare system, all of the interstate highway system, virtually every aspect of programs to improve cities, the largest part of the effort to supply jobs to the unemployed, the entire program to clean up our water, and even much of our military manpower (in the form of the National Guard) are enterprises in which the national government does not govern so much as it seeks, by regulation, grant, plan, argument, and cajolery, to get the states to govern in accordance with nationally defined (though often vaguely defined) goals.

In France, welfare, highways, education, the police, and the use of land are all matters that are directed nationally. In the United States, highways and some welfare programs are largely state functions (though they make use of federal money), while education, policing, and land-use controls are primarily local (city, county, or special-district) functions.

FEDERALISM: GOOD OR BAD?

Sometimes, however, confusion or controversy about which government is responsible for which functions surfaces at the worst possible moment and lingers long after attempts have been made to sort it all out. Sadly, in our day, that is largely what "federalism" has meant in practice to citizens from New Orleans and the Gulf Coast region.

Before, during, and after Hurricanes Katrina and Rita struck in 2005, federal, state, and local officials could be found fighting among themselves over everything from who was supposed to maintain and repair the levees to who should lead disaster relief initiatives. In the weeks after the hurricanes hit, it had been widely reported that the main first-responders and disaster relief workers came, not from government, but from myriad religious and other charitable organizations. Not only that, but government agencies, such as the Federal Emergency Management Agency, often acted in ways that made it harder, not easier, for these volunteers and groups to deliver help when and where it was most badly needed.

Federalism needs to be viewed dispassionately through an historical lens wide enough to encompass both its worst legacies (for instance, state and

self-government and from the fact that Congress consists of people who are selected by and responsive to local constituencies.

"The basic political fact of federalism," writes David B. Truman, "is that it creates separate, self

RESEARCH FRONTIERS

Which Governments Do We Trust?

As America readied for the presidential election of 2008, pollsters found a continued decline in public trust and confidence in government:

- Only 26 percent of Americans said they were satisfied with the way that nation was being governed, tying a 1973 result as the lowest ever.

- Only 42 percent said they had "a great deal" or "a fair amount" of trust and confidence in the national government's executive branch; and only 47 percent expressed such support for the U.S. Congress.

Such polling results are nothing new. But scholars who study public opinion on federalism have painted a more complicated picture. Since 1972, the long-term decline in public trust and confidence in Washington has not been matched by similar declines in public support for state and local governments.

For example, Richard L. Cole and John Kincaid have analyzed public opinion data on a wide range of issues:

- After 1972, the fraction of citizens who thought they got the most for their tax money from the federal government fell by 25 percent, while the fraction of citizens who thought they got the most for their tax money from state and local governments rose by 11 percent and 19 percent, respectively.

- After 1987, the fraction of citizens who expressed a "great deal" or a "fair amount" of trust and confidence in the federal government fell by 20 percent, while the fraction who expressed such support for state and local governments fell by 11 percent and 5 percent, respectively.

- Today, citizens are 50 percent more likely to express "not very much" trust and confidence in the federal government or "none at all" than they are to express the same negative view about local government.

The intergovernmental trust and confidence gap is especially wide between the federal government and local governments. Citizens of almost every demographic description are significantly more likely to express a "great deal" or a "fair amount" of trust and confidence in local government than to express such support for the federal government.

James Madison would not be surprised. In *Federalist* No. 46, he doubted that the American people would, in the "future, become more partial to the federal government" than to their respective state and local governments. The people might, he predicted, at times express "transient enthusiasm" for the federal government during wars or national crises, but their "attention and attachment" would ever be more inclined toward "their own particular governments."

- Madison would not be surprised, but are you?

- Do you have greater trust and confidence in the federal government or in state and local governments?

- Do you suppose most people you know feel much the way you do?

Sources: "Trust in Government Remains Low," Gallup Organization, September 2008, reporting results based on telephone interviews with 1,007 adults conducted September 8–11, 2008; Richard L. Cole and John Kincaid, "Public Opinion on U.S. Federal and Intergovernmental Issues," *Publius* 36, Summer 2006, pp. 443–459.

---

local laws that once legalized racial discrimination against blacks) and its best (for instance, blacks winning mayors' offices and seats in state legislatures when no blacks were in the U.S. Senate and not many blacks had been elected to the U.S. House).

Federalism, it is fair to say, has the virtues of its vices and the vices of its virtues. To some, federalism means allowing states to block action, prevent progress, upset national plans, protect powerful local interests, and cater to the self-interest of hack politicians. Harold Laski, a British observer, described American states as "parasitic and poisonous,"[20] and William H. Riker, an American political scientist, argued that "the main effect of federalism since the Civil War has been to perpetuate racism."[21] By contrast, another political scientist, Daniel J. Elazar, argued that the "virtue of the federal system lies in its ability to develop and maintain mechanisms vital to the perpetuation of the unique combination of governmental strength, political flexibility, and individual liberty, which has been the central concern of American politics."[22]

So diametrically opposed are the Riker and Elazar views that one wonders whether they are talking about the same subject. They are, of course, but they are stressing different aspects of the same phenomenon. Whenever the opportunity to exercise political power is widely available (as among the 50 states, 3,000 counties, and many thousands of municipalities in the United States), it is obvious that in different places different people will make use of that power for different purposes. There is no question that allowing states and cities to make autonomous, binding political decisions will allow some people in some places to make those decisions in ways that maintain racial segregation, protect vested interests, and facilitate corruption. It is equally true, however, that this arrangement also enables other people in other places to pass laws that attack segregation, regulate harmful economic practices, and purify politics, often long before these ideas gain national support or become national policy.

The existence of independent state and local governments means that different political groups pursuing different political purposes will come to power in different places. The smaller the political unit, the more likely it is to be dominated by a single political faction. James Madison understood this fact perfectly and used it to argue (in *Federalist* No. 10) that it would be in a large (or "extended") republic, such as the United States as a whole, that one would find the greatest opportunity for all relevant interests to be heard. When William Riker condemns federalism, he is thinking of the fact that in some places the ruling factions in cities and states have opposed granting equal rights to African Americans. When Daniel Elazar praises federalism, he is recalling that, in other states and cities, the ruling factions have taken the lead (long in advance of the federal government) in developing measures to protect the environment, extend civil rights, and improve social conditions. If you live in California, whether you like federalism depends in part on whether you like the fact that California has, independent of the federal government, cut property taxes, strictly controlled coastal land use, heavily regulated electric utilities, and increased (at one time) and decreased (at another time) its welfare rolls.

INCREASED POLITICAL ACTIVITY

Federalism has many effects, but its most obvious effect has been to facilitate the mobilization of political activity. Unlike Don Quixote, the average citizen does not tilt at windmills. He or she is more likely to become involved in organized political activity if he or she feels a reasonable chance exists of having a

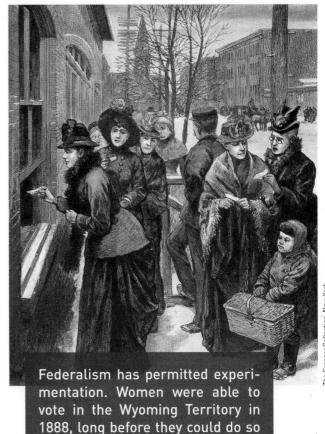

Federalism has permitted experimentation. Women were able to vote in the Wyoming Territory in 1888, long before they could do so in most states.

The Granger Collection, New York

practical effect. The chances of having such an effect are greater where there are many elected officials and independent governmental bodies, each with a relatively small constituency, than where there are few elected officials, most of whom have the nation as a whole for a constituency. In short, a federal system, by virtue of the decentralization of authority, lowers the cost of organized political activity; a unitary system, because of the centralization of authority, raises the cost. We may disagree about the purposes of organized political activity, but the fact of widespread organized activity can scarcely be doubted—or if it can be doubted, it is only because you have not yet read Chapters 8 and 11.

It is impossible to say whether the Founders, when they wrote the Constitution, planned to produce such widespread opportunities for political participation. Unfortunately they were not very clear (at least in writing) about how the federal system was supposed to work, and thus most of the interesting questions about the jurisdiction and powers of our national and state governments had to be settled by a century and a half of protracted, often bitter, conflict.

WHAT THE STATES CAN DO

The states play a key role in social welfare, public education, law enforcement, criminal justice, health and hospitals, roads and highways, and managing water supplies. On these and many other matters, state constitutions are far more detailed and sometimes confer more rights than the federal one. For example, the California constitution includes an explicit right to privacy, says that non-citizens have the same property rights as citizens, and requires the state to use "all suitable means" to support public education.

Many state constitutions are now believed by some to be on the whole more progressive in their holdings on abortion rights (authorizing fewer restrictions on minors), welfare payments (permitting fewer limits on eligibility), employment discrimination (prohibiting discrimination based on sexual preference), and many other matters than federal courts generally are.

As we saw in Chapter 2, the federal Constitution is based on a republican, not a democratic, principle: laws are to be made by the representatives of citizens, not by the citizens directly. But many state constitutions open one or more of three doors to direct democracy. About half of the states provide for some form of legislation by initiative. The **initiative** allows voters to place legislative measures (and sometimes constitutional amendments) directly on the ballot by getting enough signatures (usually between 5 and 15 percent of those who voted in the last election) on a petition. About half of the states permit the **referendum**, a procedure that enables voters to reject a measure adopted by the legislature. Sometimes the state constitution specifies that certain kinds of legislation (for example, tax increases) must be subject to a referendum whether the legislature wishes it or not. The **recall** is a procedure, in effect in over 20 states, whereby voters can remove an elected official from office. If enough signatures are gathered on a petition, the official must go before voters, who can vote to leave the person in office, remove the person from office, or remove the person and replace him or her with someone else.

The existence of the states is guaranteed by the federal Constitution: no state can be divided without its consent, each state must have two representatives in the Senate (the only provision of the Constitutionthat may not be amended), every state is assured of a republican form of government, and the powers not granted to Congress are reserved for the states. By contrast, cities, towns, and counties enjoy no such protection; they exist at the pleasure of the states. Indeed, states have frequently abolished certain kinds of local governments, such as independent school districts.

This explains why there is no debate about city sovereignty comparable to the debate about state sovereignty. The constitutional division of power between them is settled: the state is supreme. But federal-state relations can be complicated, because the Constitution invites elected leaders to struggle over sovereignty. Which level of government has the ultimate power to decide where nuclear waste gets stored, how much welfare beneficiaries are paid, what rights prisoners enjoy, or whether supersonic jets can land at local airports? American federalism answers such questions, but on a case-by-case basis through intergovernmental politics and court decisions.

Federal-State Relations

Though constitutionally the federal government may be supreme, politically it must take into account the fact that the laws it passes have to be approved by members of Congress selected from, and responsive to, state and local constituencies. Thus what Washington lawfully may do is not the same thing as what it politically may wish to do.

GRANTS-IN-AID

The best illustration of how political realities modify legal authority can be found in federal **grants-in-aid.** The first of these programs began even before the Constitution was adopted, in the form of land grants made by the national government to the states in order to finance education. (State universities all over the country were built with the proceeds from the sale of these land grants; hence the name *land-grant colleges.*) Land grants were also made to support the building of wagon roads, canals, railroads, and flood-control projects. These measures were hotly debated in Congress (President Madison thought some were unconstitutional), even though the use to which the grants were put was left almost entirely to the states.

Cash grants-in-aid began almost as early. In 1808, Congress gave $200,000 to the states to pay for their militias,

initiative Process that permits voters to put legislative measures directly on the ballot.

referendum Procedure enabling voters to reject a measure passed by the legislature.

recall Procedure whereby voters can remove an elected official from office.

grants-in-aid Money given by the national government to the states.

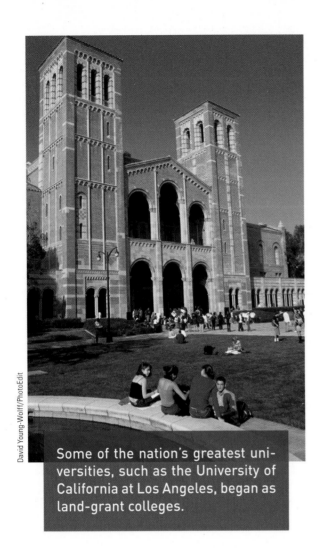

David Young-Wolff/PhotoEdit

Some of the nation's greatest universities, such as the University of California at Los Angeles, began as land-grant colleges.

Table 3.1 Federal Grants to State and Local Governments (2008)

The federal government spent $476 billion on grants to states in 2008.	
Among the biggest items:	
Medicaid	$215.6 billion
Education and training	57.2 billion
Highways	38.8 billion
Community development	17.1 billion
Temporary Assistance to Needy Families	17 billion

Source: Budget of the U.S. Government, Fiscal Year 2009.

Washington in the 1880s had huge budget surpluses. Second, in the 1920s, as those surpluses dwindled, Washington inaugurated the federal income tax. It automatically brought in more money as economic activity (and thus personal income) grew. Third, the federal government, unlike the states, managed the currency and could print more at will. (Technically, it borrowed this money, but it was under no obligation to pay it all back, because, as a practical matter, it had borrowed from itself.) States could not do this: if they borrowed money (and many could not), they had to pay it back, in full.

These three economic reasons for the attractiveness of federal grants were probably not as important as a fourth reason: politics. Federal money seemed to a state official to be "free" money. Governors did not have to propose, collect, or take responsibility for federal taxes. Instead, a governor could denounce the federal government for being profligate in its use of the people's money. Meanwhile, he or she could claim credit for a new public works or other project funded by Washington and, until recent decades, expect little or no federal supervision in the bargain.[23]

That every state had an incentive to ask for federal money to pay for local programs meant, of course, that it would be very difficult for one state to get money for a given program without every state's getting it. The senator from Alabama who votes for the project to improve navigation on the Tombigbee will have to vote in favor of projects improving navigation on every other river in the country if the senator expects his or her Senate colleagues to support such a request. Federalism as practiced in the United States means that when Washington wants to send money to one state or congressional district, it must send money to many states and districts.

with the states in charge of the size, deployment, and command of these troops. However, grant-in-aid programs remained few in number and small in price until the 20th century, when scores of new ones came into being. Today, federal grants go to hundreds of programs, including such giant federal-state programs as Medicaid (see Table 3.1).

The grants-in-aid system, once under way, grew rapidly because it helped state and local officials resolve a dilemma. On the one hand, they wanted access to the superior taxing power of the federal government. On the other hand, prevailing constitutional interpretation, at least until the late 1930s, held that the federal government could not spend money for purposes not authorized by the Constitution. The solution was obviously to have federal money put into state hands: Washington would pay the bills; the states would run the programs.

Federal money seemed, to state officials, so attractive for four reasons. First, the money was there. Thanks to the high-tariff policies of the Republicans,

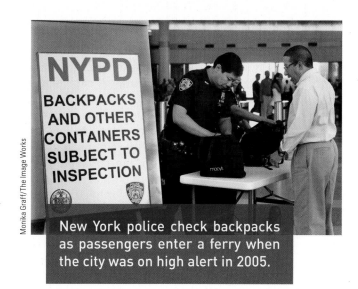

Monika Graft/The Image Works

New York police check backpacks as passengers enter a ferry when the city was on high alert in 2005.

Figure 3.2

The Changing Purpose of Federal Grants to State and Local Governments

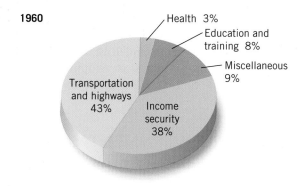

1960

Health 3%
Education and training 8%
Miscellaneous 9%
Transportation and highways 43%
Income security 38%

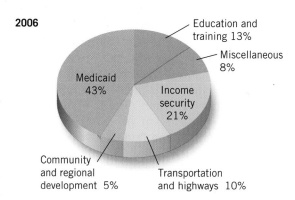

2006

Education and training 13%
Miscellaneous 8%
Medicaid 43%
Income security 21%
Community and regional development 5%
Transportation and highways 10%

Note: Totals may not add up to 100 percent because of rounding.

Source: *Budget of the U.S. Government, Fiscal Year 2007*, table 12.1.

Shortly after September 11, 2001, for example, President George W. Bush and congressional leaders in both parties pledged new federal funds to increase public safety payrolls, purchase the latest equipment to detect bioterror attacks, and so on. Since then, New York City and other big cities have received tens of millions of federal dollars for such purposes, but so have scores of smaller cities and towns. The grants allocated by the Department of Homeland Security were based on so-called fair-share formulas mandated by Congress, which are basically the same formulas the federal government uses to allocate certain highway and other funds among the states. These funding formulas not only spread money around but generally skew funding toward states and cities with low populations. Thus, Wyoming received seven times as much federal homeland security funding per capita as New York State did, and Grand Forks County, North Dakota (population 70,000), received $1.5 million to purchase biochemical suits, a semiarmored van, decontamination tents, and other equipment to deal with weapons of mass destruction.[24]

MEETING NATIONAL NEEDS

Until the 1960s, most federal grants-in-aid were conceived by or in cooperation with the states and were designed to serve essentially state purposes. Large blocs of voters and a variety of organized interests would press for grants to help farmers, build highways, or support vocational education. During the 1960s, however, an important change occurred: the federal government began devising grant programs based less on what states were demanding and more on what federal officials perceived to be important *national* needs (see Figure 3.2.) Federal officials, not state and local ones, were the principal proponents

of grant programs to aid the urban poor, combat crime, reduce pollution, and deal with drug abuse.

The rise in federal activism in setting goals and the occasional efforts, during some periods, to bypass state officials by providing money directly to cities or even local citizen groups, had at least two separate but related effects: one effect was to increase federal grants to state and local governments, and the other was to change the purposes to which those monies were put. Whereas federal aid amounted to less than 2 percent of state general revenue in 1927, by 2006 federal aid accounted for about 30 percent of state general revenue. About 17 percent of the entire federal budget was for grants to state and local governments (about 90 percent went directly to the states). The federal government spent $1,471 per capita on grants to state and local governments.

In 1960, about 3 percent of federal grants to state and local governments were for health care. Today, however, one federal-state health care program alone, Medicaid, accounts for over 43 percent of all federal grants. And whereas in 1960 over 40 percent of all federal grants to state and local governments went to transportation (including highways), today only about 10 percent is used for that purpose (see Figure 3.2). Even in the short term, the purposes to which federal grants are put can shift; for example, after Hurricanes Katrina and Rita, federal grants for "community and regional development" spiked but were slated to return to pre-2005 levels by about 2011.

THE INTERGOVERNMENTAL LOBBY

State and local officials, both elected and appointed, began to form an important new lobby—the "intergovernmental lobby," made up of mayors, governors, superintendents of schools, state directors of public health, county highway commissioners, local police chiefs, and others who had come to count on federal funds.[25] Today, federal agencies responsible for health care, criminal justice, environmental protection, and other programs have people on staff who specialize in providing information, technical assistance, and financial support to state and local organizations, including the "Big 7": the U.S. Conference of Mayors; the National Governors Association; the National Association of Counties; the National League of Cities; the Council of State Governments; the International City/County Management Association; and the National Conference of State Legislatures. Reports by these groups and publications like *Governing* magazine are read routinely by many federal officials to keep a handle on issues and trends in state and local government.

National organizations of governors or mayors press for more federal money, but not for increased funding for any particular city or state. Thus most states, dozens of counties, and over a hundred cities have their own offices in Washington, D.C. Some are small, some share staff with other jurisdictions, but a few are quite large and boast several dozen full-time employees. Back home, state and local governments have created new positions, or redefined old ones, in response to new or changed federal funding opportunities.

The purpose of the intergovernmental lobby has been the same as that of any private lobby—to obtain more federal money with fewer strings attached. For a while, the cities and states did in fact get more money, but since the early 1980s their success in getting federal grants has been more checkered.

categorical grants
Federal grants for specific purposes, such as building an airport.

CATEGORICAL GRANTS

The effort to loosen the strings took the form of shifting, as much as possible, the federal aid from **categorical grants** to block grants. A categorical grant is one for a specific purpose defined by federal law: to build an airport or a college dormitory, for example, or to make welfare payments to low-income mothers. Such grants usually require that the state or locality put up money to "match" some part of the federal grant, though the amount of matching funds can be quite small (sometimes only 10 percent or less). Governors and mayors complained about these categorical grants because their purposes were often so narrow that it was impossible for a state to adapt federal grants to local needs. A mayor seeking federal money to build parks might have discovered that the city could get money only if it launched an urban-renewal program that entailed bulldozing several blocks of housing or small businesses.

One response to this problem was to consolidate several categorical or project grant programs into a single block grant devoted to some general purpose and with fewer restrictions on its use. Block grants began in the mid-1960s, when such a grant was created in the health field. Though many block grants were proposed between 1966 and 1980, only five were enacted. Of the three largest, one consolidated various categorical grant programs aimed at cities (Community Development Block Grants), another created a program to aid local law enforcement (Law Enforcement Assistance Act), and a third authorized new kinds of locally managed programs for the unemployed (CETA, or the Comprehensive Employment and Training Act).

In theory, block grants and revenue sharing were supposed to give the states and cities considerable freedom in deciding how to spend the money while helping to relieve their tax burdens. To some extent they did. However, for four reasons, neither the goal of "no strings" nor the one of fiscal relief was really attained. First, the amount of money available from block grants and revenue sharing did not grow as fast as the states had hoped nor as quickly as did the money available through categorical grants. Second, the federal government steadily increased the number of strings attached to the spending of this supposedly "unrestricted" money.

Third, block grants grew more slowly than categorical grants because of the different kinds of political coalitions supporting each. Congress and the federal bureaucracy liked categorical grants for the same reason the states disliked them—the specificity of these programs enhanced federal control over how the money was to be used. Federal officials, joined by liberal interest groups and organized labor, tended to distrust state governments. Whenever Congress wanted to address some national problem, its natural inclination was to create a categorical grant program so that it, and not the states, would decide how the money would be spent.

Fourth, even though governors and mayors like block grants, these programs cover such a broad range of activities that no single interest group has a vital stake in pressing for their enlargement. Categorical grants, on the other hand, often are a matter of life and death for many agencies—state departments of welfare, of highways, and of health, for example, are utterly dependent on federal aid. Accordingly, the administrators in charge of these programs will press strenuously for their expansion. Moreover, categorical programs are supervised by special committees of Congress, and as we shall see in Chapter 13, many of these committees have an interest in seeing their programs grow.

RIVALRY AMONG THE STATES

The more important federal money becomes to the states, the more likely they are to compete among themselves for the largest share of it. For a century or better, the growth of the United States—in population, business, and income—was concentrated in the industrial Northeast. In recent decades, however, that growth—at least in population and employment, if not in income—has shifted to the South, Southwest, and Far West. This change has precipitated an intense debate over whether the federal government, by the way it distributes its funds and awards its contracts, is unfairly helping some regions and states at the expense of others. Journalists and politicians have dubbed the struggle as one between Snowbelt (or Frostbelt) and Sunbelt states.

Whether in fact there is anything worth arguing about is far from clear: the federal government has had great difficulty in figuring out where it ultimately spends what funds for what purposes. For example, a $1 billion defense contract may go to a company with headquarters in California, but much of the money may actually be spent in Connecticut or New York, as the prime contractor in California buys from subcontractors in the other states. It is even less clear whether federal funds actually affect the growth rate of the regions. The uncertainty about the facts has not prevented a debate about the issue, however. That debate focuses on the formulas written into federal laws by which block grants are allocated. These formulas take into account such

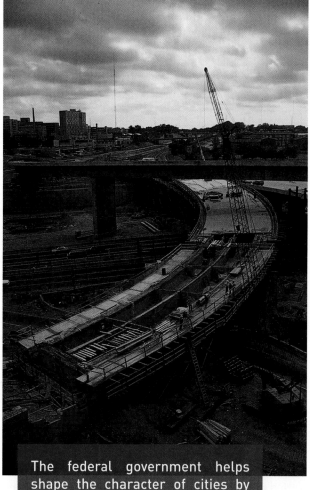

The federal government helps shape the character of cities by giving money to build parts of the federal highway system.

Paul Conklin/PhotoEdit

factors as a county's or city's population, personal income in the area, and housing quality. A slight change in a formula can shift millions of dollars in grants in ways that favor either the older, declining cities of the Northeast or the newer, still-growing cities of the Southwest.

With the advent of grants based on distributional formulas (as opposed to grants for a particular project), the results of the census, taken every 10 years, assume monumental importance. A city or state shown to be losing population may, as a result, forfeit millions of dollars in federal aid. Senators and representatives now have access to computers that can tell them instantly the effect on their states and districts of even minor changes in a formula by which federal aid is distributed. These formulas rely on objective measures, but the exact measure is selected with an eye to its political consequences. There is nothing wrong with this in principle, since any political system must provide some benefits for everybody if it is to stay together. Given the competition among states in a federal system, however, the struggle over allocation formulas becomes especially acute.

Federal Aid and Federal Control

So important has federal aid become for state and local governments that mayors and governors, along with others, began to fear that Washington was well on its way to controlling other levels of government. "He who pays the piper calls the tune," they muttered. In this view, the constitutional protection of state government to be found in the Tenth Amendment was in jeopardy as a result of the strings attached to the grants-in-aid on which the states were increasingly dependent.

Block grants was effort to reverse this trend by allowing the states and localities freedom to spend money as they wished. But as we have seen, the new device did not in fact reverse the trend. Categorical grants—those with strings attached—continued to grow even faster.

There are two kinds of federal controls on state governmental activities. The traditional control tells the state government what it must do if it wants to get some grant money. These strings often are called **conditions of aid.** The newer form of control tells the state government what it must do, period. These rules are called **mandates.** Most mandates have little or nothing to do with federal aid—they apply to all state governments whether or not they accept grants.

conditions of aid Terms set by the national government that states must meet if they are to receive certain federal funds.

mandates Terms set by the national government that states must meet whether or not they accept federal grants.

waiver A decision by an administrative agency granting some other part permission to violate a law or rule that would otherwise apply to it.

MANDATES

Most mandates concern civil rights and environmental protection. States may not discriminate in the operation of their programs, no matter who pays for them. Initially the antidiscrimination rules applied chiefly to distinctions based on race, sex, age, and ethnicity, but of late they have broadened to include physical and mental disabilities as well. Various pollution control laws require the states to comply with federal standards for clean air, pure drinking water, and sewage treatment.[26]

Stated in general terms, these mandates seem reasonable enough. It is hard to imagine anyone arguing that state governments should be free to discriminate against people because of their race or national origin. In practice, however, some mandates create administrative and financial problems, especially when the mandates are written in vague language, thereby giving federal administrative agencies the power to decide for themselves what state and local governments are supposed to do.

But not all areas of public law and policy are equally affected by mandates. Federal-state disputes about who governs on such controversial matters as minors' access to abortion, same-sex marriage, and medical uses for banned narcotics make headlines. It is mandates that fuel everyday friction in federal-state relations, particularly those that Washington foists upon the states but funds inadequately or not at all. One 2006 study concluded that "the number of unfunded federal mandates is high in environmental policy, low in education policy, and moderate in health policy."[27] But why?

Some think that how much Washington spends in a given policy area is linked to how common federal mandates, funded or not, are in that same area. There is some evidence for that view. For instance, in recent years, annual federal grants to state and local governments for a policy area where unfunded mandates are pervasive—environmental protection—were about $4 billion, while federal grants for health care—an area where unfunded mandates have been less pervasive—amounted to about $200 billion. The implication is that when Washington itself spends less on something it wants done, it squeezes the states to spend more for that purpose.

Washington is more likely to grant state and local governments waivers in some areas than in others. A **waiver** is a decision by an administrative agency granting some other party permission to violate a law or administrative rule that would otherwise apply to it. Generally, for instance, education waivers have been easy for state and local governments to get, but environmental protection waivers have proven almost impossible to acquire.[28]

However, caution is in order. Often, the more one knows about federal-state relations in any given area, the harder it becomes to generalize about present-day federalism's fiscal, administrative, and regulatory character, the conditions under which "permissive federalism" prevails, or whether new laws or court decisions will considerably tighten or further loosen Washington's control over the states.

Mandates are not the only way in which the federal government imposes costs on state and local governments. Certain federal tax and regulatory policies make it difficult or expensive for state and local governments to raise revenues, borrow funds, or privatize public functions. Other federal laws expose state and local governments to financial liability, and numerous federal court decisions and administrative regulations require state and local governments to do or not do various things, either by statute or through an implied constitutional obligation.[29]

It is clear that the federal courts have helped fuel the growth of mandates. As interpreted in this century by the U.S. Supreme Court, the Tenth Amendment provides state and local officials no protection against the march of mandates. Indeed, many of the more controversial mandates result not from congressional action but from court decisions. For example, many state prison systems have been, at one time or another, under the control of federal judges who required major changes in prison construction and management in order to meet standards the judges derived from their reading of the Constitution.

School-desegregation plans are of course the best-known example of federal mandates. Those involving busing—an unpopular policy—have typically been the result of court orders rather than of federal law or regulation.

Judges—usually, but not always, in federal courts—ordered Massachusetts to change the way it hires fire fighters, required Philadelphia to institute new procedures to handle complaints of police brutality, and altered the location in which Chicago was planning to build housing projects. Note that in most of these cases nobody in Washington was placing a mandate on a local government; rather a local citizen was using the federal courts to change a local practice.

The Supreme Court has made it much easier of late for citizens to control the behavior of local officials. A federal law, passed in the 1870s to protect newly freed slaves, makes it possible for a citizen to sue any state or local official who deprives that citizen of any "rights, privileges, or immunities secured by the Constitution and laws" of the United States. A century later, the Court decided that this law permitted a citizen to sue a local official if the official deprived the citizen of *anything* to which the citizen was entitled under federal law (and not just those

federal laws protecting civil rights). For example, a citizen can now use the federal courts to obtain from a state welfare office a payment to which he or she may be entitled under federal law.

CONDITIONS OF AID

By far the most important federal restrictions on state action are the conditions attached to the grants the states receive. In theory, accepting these conditions is voluntary—if you don't want the strings, don't take the money. But when the typical state depends for a quarter or more of its budget on federal grants, many of which it has received for years and on which many of its citizens depend for their livelihoods, it is not clear exactly how "voluntary" such acceptance is. During the 1960s, some strings were added, the most important of which had to do with civil rights. But beginning in the 1970s, the number of conditions began to proliferate and have expanded in each subsequent decade to the present.

Some conditions are specific to particular programs, but most are not. For instance, if a state builds something with federal money, it must first conduct an environmental impact study, it must pay construction workers the "prevailing wage" in the area, it often must provide an opportunity for citizen participation in some aspects of the design or location of the project, and it must ensure that the contractors who build the project have nondiscriminatory hiring policies.

The states and the federal government, not surprisingly, disagree about the costs and benefits of such rules. Members of Congress and federal officials feel they have an obligation to develop uniform national policies with respect to important matters and to prevent states and cities from misspending federal tax dollars. State officials, on the other hand, feel

The National Guard is often used to cope with floods and tornados.

Mario Tama/Getty Images

these national rules fail to take into account diverse local conditions, require the states to do things that the states must then pay for, and create serious inefficiencies.

What state and local officials discovered, in short, was that "free" federal money was not quite free after all. In the 1960s, federal aid seemed entirely beneficial; what mayor or governor would not want such money? But just as local officials found it attractive to do things that another level of government then paid for, in time federal officials learned the same thing. Passing laws to meet the concerns of national constituencies—leaving the cities and states to pay the bills and manage the problems—began to seem attractive to Congress.

Because they face different demands, federal and local officials find themselves in a bargaining situation in which each side is trying to get some benefit (solving a problem, satisfying a pressure group) while passing on to the other side most of the costs (taxes, administrative problems).

The bargains struck in this process used to favor the local officials, because members of Congress were essentially servants of local interests: they were elected by local political parties, they were part of local political organizations, and they supported local autonomy. Beginning in the 1960s, however, changes in American politics that will be described in later chapters—especially the weakening of political parties, the growth of public-interest lobbies in Washington, and the increased activism of the courts—shifted the orientation of many in Congress toward favoring Washington's needs over local needs.

A Devolution Revolution?

In 1981, President Ronald Reagan tried to reverse this trend. He asked Congress to consolidate scores of categorical grants into just six large block grants. Congress obliged. Soon state and local governments started getting less federal money but with fewer strings attached to such grants. During the 1980s and into the early 1990s, however, many states also started spending more of their own money and replacing federal rules on programs with state ones.

With the election of Republican majorities in the House and Senate in 1994, a renewed effort was led by Congress to cut total government spending, roll back federal regulations, and shift important functions back to the states. The first key issue was welfare—that is, Aid to Families with Dependent Children (AFDC). Since 1935, there had been a federal guarantee of cash assistance to states that offered support to low-income, unmarried mothers and their children. In 1996, President Bill Clinton signed a new federal welfare law that ended any federal guarantee of support and, subject to certain rules, turned the management of the program entirely over to the states, aided by federal block grants.

These and other Republican initiatives were part of a new effort called devolution, which aimed to pass on to the states many federal functions. It is an old idea but one that actually acquired new vitality because Congress, rather than the president, was leading the effort. Members of Congress traditionally liked voting for federal programs and categorical grants; that way they could take credit for what they were doing for particular constituencies. Under its new conservative leadership, Congress, especially the House, was looking for ways to scale back the size of the national government. President Clinton seemed to agree when, in his 1996 State of the Union address, he proclaimed that the era of big national government was over.

But was it over? No. By 2006, the federal government was spending about $22,000 per year per household, which, adjusted for inflation, was its highest annual per-household spending level since World War II. Federal revenues represented about 18 percent of gross domestic product, close to the post–1966 annual average, and inflation-adjusted federal debt totals hit new highs. Adjusted for inflation, total spending by state and local governments

A woman who heads a faith-based organization works with a jailed teenager to help him overcome his problems.

Robin Nelson/Corbis

also increased every year after 1996, as did state andlocal government debt.

Devolution did not become a revolution. AFDC was ended and replaced by a block grant program called Temporary Assistance for Needy Families (TANF). But far larger federal-state programs, most notably Medicaid, were not turned into block grant programs. Moreover, both federal and state spending on most programs, including the block-granted programs, increased after 1996. Although by no means the only new or significant block grant, TANF now looked like the big exception that proved the rule. The devolution revolution was curtailed by public opinion. Today, as in 1996 and 2006, most Americans favor "shifting responsibility to the states," but not if that also means cuts in government programs that benefit most citizens (not just low-income families), uncertainty about who is eligible to receive benefits, or new hassles associated with receiving them.

Devolution seems to have resulted in more, not fewer, government rules and regulations. Research reveals that, in response to the federal effort to devolve responsibility to state and local governments, states have not only enacted new rules and regulations of their own, but also prompted Washington to issue new rules and regulations on environmental protection (especially greenhouse gas emissions) and other matters.[30]

Still, where devolution did occur, it has had some significant consequences. The devolution of welfare policy has been associated with dramatic decreases in welfare rolls. Scholars disagree about how much the drops were due to the changes in law and how much to economic conditions and other factors. Nor is it clear whether welfare-to-work programs have gotten most participants into decent jobs with adequate health benefits. But few now doubt that welfare devolution has made a measurable difference in how many people receive benefits and for how long.

Subject to state discretion, scores of local governments are now designing and administering welfare programs (job placement, child care, and others) through for-profit firms and a wide variety of nonprofit organizations, including local religious congregations. In some big cities, over a quarter of welfare-to-work programs have been administered through public-private partnerships that included various local community-based organizations as grantees.[31] By 2007, there was preliminary evidence that, at least in some states, such public-private partnerships were closer to the norm than they were only a half-decade or so earlier.[32]

Congress and Federalism

Just as it remains to be seen whether the Supreme Court will continue to revive the doctrine of state sovereignty, so it is not yet clear whether the devolution movement will regain momentum, stall, or be reversed. But whatever the movement's fate, the United States will not become a wholly centralized nation. There remains more political and policy diversity in America than one is likely to find in any other large industrialized nation. The reason is not only that state and local governments have retained certain constitutional protections but also that members of Congress continue to think of themselves as the representatives of localities *to* Washington and not as the representatives *of* Washington to the localities. As we shall see in Chapter 13, American politics, even at the national level, remains local in its orientation.

But if this is true, why do these same members of Congress pass laws that create so many problems for, and stimulate so many complaints from, mayors and governors? One reason is that members of Congress represent different constituencies from the same localities. For example, one member of Congress from Los Angeles may think of the city as a collection of business people, homeowners, and taxpayers, while another may think of it as a group of African Americans, Hispanics, and nature lovers. If Washington wants to simply send money to Los Angeles, these two representatives could be expected to vote together. But if Washington wants to impose mandates or restrictions on the city, they might very well vote on opposite sides, each voting as his or her constituents would most likely prefer.

Another reason is that the organizations that once linked members of Congress to local groups have eroded. As we shall see in Chapter 9, the political parties, which once allowed many localities to speak with a single voice in Washington, have decayed to the point where most members of Congress now operate as free agents, judging local needs and national moods independently. In the 1960s, these needs and moods seemed to require creating new grant programs; in the 1970s, they seemed to require voting for new mandates; in the 1980s and 1990s, they seemed to require letting the cities and states alone to experiment with new ways of meeting their needs; and today, some say they require rethinking devolution before it goes "too far."

There are exceptions. In some states, the parties continue to be strong, to dominate decision making

WHAT WOULD YOU DO?

MEMORANDUM

To: *Representative Sue Kettl*

From: *Grace Viola, chief of staff*

Subject: *Faith-based preemption bill*

As requested, I have researched state-funding poli-cies. The main finding isthat the state laws do hobble getting federal dollars to the relgious groups that have been doing most of the actual recovery work. The immediate question before you is whether to sign on as a co-sponsor to the bill.

Arguments for:

1. Congress has already passed at least four laws that permit federal agencies to fund faith-based groups that deliver social services, subject to prohibitions against using any public funds for proselytizing or such.

2. The faith-based organizations functioned as first responders when the hurricanes hit, and have since supplied billions of dollars worth of manpower and materials.

3. Some legal experts say that the existing laws already preempt the contrary state ones; besides, it polls great (75 percent in favor nationally, even higher in your district).

Arguments against:

1. You have traditionally argued in favor of states' rights and the separation of church and state.

2. Praiseworthy though their civic good works have been, some of the religious groups involved in the cleanup and recovery have beliefs and tenets that seem discriminatory (a few even refuse to hire peo-ple of other faiths).

Congress Debates Requiring States to Follow Feds' Lead on "Faith-Based" Hurricane Recovery Act

January 29
WASHINGTON, D.C.

Today the House begins debate on legislation requiring state governments to comply with federal laws on public funding for religious nonprofit organizations that deliver social services. In cities devastated by hurricanes, so-called faith-based organizations continue to play a major role in disaster recovery and rebuilding efforts. Federal laws already permit these groups to receive federal aid, but a recent audit found that contrary state laws were impeding their implementation....

3. Expressly preempting more state laws could come back to bite us when it comes to state laws that we favor over contrary federal ones.

Your decision:

Support bill _____   Oppose bill _____

in the state legislatures, and to significantly affect the way their congressional delegations behave. Democratic members of Congress from Chicago, for example, typically have a common background in party politics and share at least some allegiance to important party leaders.

But these exceptions are becoming fewer and fewer. As a result, when somebody tries to speak "for" a city or state in Washington, that person has little claim to any real authority. The mayor of Philadelphia may favor one program, the governor of Pennsylvania may favor another, and individual local and state officials—school superintendents, the insurance commissioner, public health administrators—may favor still others. In bidding for federal aid, those parts of the state or city that are best organized often do the best, and increasingly these groups are not the political parties but rather specialized occupational groups such as doctors or schoolteachers. If one is to ask, therefore, why a member of Congress does not listen to his or her state anymore, the answer is, "What do you mean by *the state*? Which official, which occupational group, which party leader speaks for the state?"

Finally, Americans differ in the extent to which we like federal as opposed to local decisions. When people are asked which level of government gives them the most for their money, relatively poor citizens are likely to mention the federal government first, whereas relatively well-to-do citizens are more likely to mention local government. If we add to income other measures of social diversity—race, religion, and region—there emerge even sharper differences of opinion about which level of government works best. It is this social diversity—and the fact that it is represented not only by state and local leaders but also by members of Congress—that keeps federalism alive and makes it so important. Americans simply do not agree on enough things, or even on which level of government ought to decide on those things, to make possible a unitary system.

SUMMARY

States participate actively both in determining national policy and in administering national programs. Moreover, they reserve to themselves or the localities within them important powers over public services, such as schooling and law enforcement, and public decisions, such as land-use control, that in unitary systems are dominated by the national government.

Debates about federalism are as old as the republic itself. After the Civil War, the doctrine of dual federalism emerged, which held that though the national government was supreme in its sphere, the states were equally supreme in theirs. For most of the 20th century, however, changes in public law and court decisions favored national over state power.

After the 1960s, states became increasingly dependent on Washington to fund many activities and programs. Today, however, there is once again a lively debate about the limits of national power, how closely the federal government ought to regulate its grants to states, and the wisdom of devolving ever more federal responsibilities onto state and local governments.

Evaluating federalism is difficult. On the one hand, there is the sordid history of states' rights and legalized racism. On the other hand, there is the open opportunity for political participation afforded by today's 50 states and thousands of local governments. Naturally, federalism permits laws and policies on important public matters to vary from state to state and town to town. But how much, if at all, they should vary on given matters, and who should decide, are questions that every generation of Americans must answer anew.

RECONSIDERING WHO GOVERNS?

1. Where is sovereignty located in the American political system?

Strictly speaking, the answer is "nowhere." Sovereignty means supreme or ultimate political authority. A sovereign government is one that is legally and politically independent of any other government. No government in America, including the national government headquartered in Washington, D.C., meets that definition. In the American political system, federal and state governments share sovereignty in complicated and ever-changing ways. Both constitutional tradition (the doctrine of dual sovereignty) and everyday politicking (fights over federal grants, mandates, and conditions of aid) render the national government supreme in some matters (national defense, for example) and the states supreme in others (education, for instance).

2. How is power divided between the national government and the states under the Constitution?

Early in American history, local governments and the states had most of it. In the 20th century, the national government gained power. In the last two decades, the states have won back some of their power because of Supreme Court decisions and legislative efforts to devolve certain federal programs to the states. But the distribution of power between the national government and the states is never as simple or as settled as it may appear.

RECONSIDERING TO WHAT ENDS?

1. What competing values are at stake in federalism?

Basically two: equality versus participation. Federalism means that citizens living in different parts of the country will be treated differently, not only in spending programs, such as welfare, but in legal systems that assign in different places different penalties to similar offenses or that differentially enforce civil rights laws. But federalism also means more opportunities exist for participation in making decisions—in influencing what is taught in the schools and in deciding where highways and government projects are to be built. Indeed, differences in public policy—that is, unequal treatment—are in large part the result of participation in decision making. It is difficult, perhaps impossible, to have more of one of these values without having less of the other.

2. Who should decide what matters ought to be governed mainly or solely by national laws?

In practice, the federal courts often have been the main or final arbiters of federalism. As we shall see in Chapter 6, it was the U.S. Supreme Court that decided to outlaw state and local laws that kept children in racially segregated public schools. Constitutional amendments initiated by members of Congress have also been used to apply legally enforceable national standards to matters once left to state or local governments. Examples would include the Twenty-sixth Amendment, which gave 18-year-old citizens the right to vote. Not surprisingly, when state and local officials have been permitted to decide, they usually have favored national laws or standards when it served their political interests or desire for "free" money, but decried them as "intrusive" or worse when they have not.

WORLD WIDE WEB RESOURCES

State news: **www.stateline.org**

Council of State Governments: **www.csg.org**

National Governors' Association: **www.nga.org**

Supreme Court decisions: **www.findlaw.com/casecode/supreme.html**

SUGGESTED READINGS

Beer, Samuel H. *To Make a Nation: The Rediscovery of American Federalism.* Cambridge: Harvard University Press, 1993. The definitive study of the philosophical bases of American federalism.

Conlan, Timothy. *From New Federalism to Devolution.* Washington, D.C.: Brookings Institution, 1998. A masterful overview of the politics of federalism from Richard Nixon to Bill Clinton.

Daniel, Ronald, Donald F. Kettl, and Howard Kureuther, eds. *On Risk and Disaster: Lessons from Hurricane Katrina.* Philadelphia: University of Pennsylvania Press, 2006. Several experts evaluate the government response.

Derthick, Martha N. *Keeping the Compound Republic.* Washington, D.C.: Brookings Institution, 2001. A masterful analysis of trends in American federalism from the Founding to the present.

Diamond, Martin. "The Federalist's View of Federalism." In *Essays in Federalism,* edited by George C.S. Benson. Claremont, Calif.: Institute for Studies in Federalism of Claremont Men's College, 1961, 21–64. A profound analysis of what the Founders meant by federalism.

Grodzins, Morton. *The American System.* Chicago: Rand McNally, 1966. Argues that American federalism has always involved extensive sharing of functions between national and state governments.

Melnick, R. Shep. *Between the Lines: Interpreting Welfare Rights.* Washington, D.C.: Brookings Institution, 1994. An examination of how trends in statutory interpretation have affected broader policy developments, including the expansion of the agenda of national government, the persistence of divided government, and the resurgence and decentralization of Congress.

Riker, William H. *Federalism: Origin, Operation, Significance.* Boston: Little, Brown, 1964. A classic explanation and critical analysis of federalism here and abroad.

Teske, Paul. *Regulation in the States.* Washington, D.C.: Brookings Institution, 2004. States have responded to devolution by adding new regulations of their own.

4

American
Political
Culture

Richard Levine/Alamy

WHO GOVERNS?

1. Do Americans trust their government?
2. Why do we accept great differences in wealth and income?

TO WHAT ENDS?

1. Why does our government behave differently than governments in countries with similar constitutions?

The United States, Great Britain, and France are all western nations with well-established representative democracies. Millions of people in each country (maybe including you) have been tourists in one or both of the other two countries. Ask any American who has spent time in either country "what's it like?" and you probably will hear generalizations about the "culture"—"friendly" or "cold," "very different" or "surprisingly like home," and so on.

But "culture" also counts when it comes to politics and government. Politically speaking, there are at least three major differences among and between countries: constitutional, demographic, and cultural. Each difference is important, and the differences tend to feed each other. Arguably, however, the cultural differences are not only the most consequential, but also often the trickiest to analyze. As we will see, that holds not only for cross-national differences between America and other countries, but also when it comes to deciphering political divides within America itself.

Political Culture

Constitutional differences tend to be fairly obvious and easy to summarize. America and France each have a written constitution, while Great Britain does not. The United States separates powers between three equal branches of its national government. By contrast, the United Kingdom has a parliamentary system in which the legislature chooses a prime minister from within its own ranks. And France has a semi-presidential or quasi-parliamentary system divided into three branches: the president selects a prime minister from the majority party in the lower house of the parliament, and the prime minister exercises most executive powers.

Demographic differences are also straightforward. America is a large land with over 300 million citizens. The dominant language is English, but millions of people also speak Spanish. About one-sixth of its population is Hispanic. Over 80 percent of its adults identify themselves as Christians, but they are divided between Catholics (about a quarter) and over a dozen different Protestant denominations. By comparison, France and the United Kingdom are each home to about 60 million people and have small but growing immigrant and foreign-born sub-populations. Most French (over 80 percent) are Catholic; most British belong to the Church of England (Anglican, the official state religion) or the Church of Scotland. But in neither country do many people go to church.

The differences among these three democracies go much deeper. Each country has a different **political culture**—a patterned and sustained way of thinking about how political and economic life ought to be carried out. Most Americans, British, and French think that democracy is good, favor majority rule, and believe in respecting minority rights. And few in each nation would say that a leader who loses office in an election has any right to retake office by force. Even so, their political cultures differ. Cross-national surveys consistently find that Americans are far more likely than the French or British to believe that everybody should be equal politically, but far less likely to think it important that everybody should be equal economically. For example, in one large survey, the French and British were more than twice as likely as Americans to agree that "it is government's responsibility to take care of the very poor," and under a third as likely as Americans to agree that "government should *not* guarantee every citizen food and basic shelter."[1]

political culture A patterned and sustained way of thinking about how political and economic life ought to be carried out.

Alexis de Tocqueville (1805–1859) was a young French aristocrat who came to the United States to study the American prison system. He wrote the brilliant *Democracy in America* (2 vols., 1835–1840), a profound analysis of our political culture.

The Granger Collection

When it comes to ensuring political equality or equality before the law, Americans are more committed from an early age. For instance, a classic study compared how children aged 10–14 in the United States, Great Britain, and France responded to a series of questions about democracy and the law. They were asked to imagine the following:

One day the President (substitute the Queen in England, President of the Republic in France) was driving his car to a meeting. Because he was late, he was driving very fast. The police stopped the car. Finish the story.[2]

The children from each country ended the story quite differently. French children declared that the president would not be reprimanded. British children said the queen would not be punished. But American children were most likely to say that the president would be fined or ticketed, just like any other person should be.

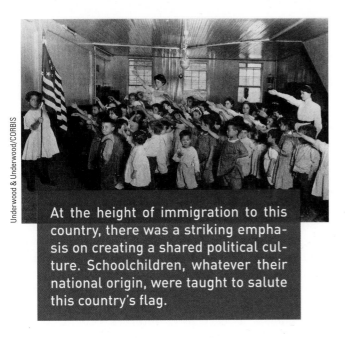

Underwood & Underwood/CORBIS

At the height of immigration to this country, there was a striking emphasis on creating a shared political culture. Schoolchildren, whatever their national origin, were taught to salute this country's flag.

Cross-national differences wrought by political culture seem even sharper between America and such countries as Argentina, Brazil, Mexico, and the Philippines. Why do these countries, whose constitutions are very much like the American one, have so much trouble with corruption, military takeovers, and the rise of demagogues? Each of these nations has had periods of democratic rule, but only for a short period of time, despite having an elected president, a separately elected congress, and an independent judiciary.

Some have argued that democracy took root in the United States but not other countries that copied its constitution because America offered more abundant land and greater opportunities for people. No feudal aristocracy occupied the land, taxes remained low, and when one place after another filled up, people kept pushing west to find new opportunities. America became a nation of small, independent farmers with relatively few landless peasants or indentured servants.

However, as Alexis de Tocqueville, the perceptive French observer of American politics, noted in the 1830s, much of South America contains fertile land and rich resources, but democracy has not flourished there. The constitution and the physical advantages of the land cannot by themselves explain the persistence of any nation's democratic institutions. Nor can they account for the fact that American democracy survived a Civil War and thrived as wave after wave of immigrants became citizens and made the democracy more demographically diverse. What can begin to account for such

differences are the customs of the people—what Tocqueville called their "moral and intellectual characteristics,"[3] and what social scientists today call political culture.

Japan, like the United States, is a democracy. But while America is an immigrant nation that often has favored open immigration policies, Japan remains a Japanese nation in which immigration policies are highly restrictive and foreign-born citizens are few. America, like Saudi Arabia, is a country in which most people profess religious beliefs, and many people identify themselves as orthodox believers. But America's Christian majority favors religious pluralism and church-state separation, while Saudi Arabia's Muslim majority supports laws that maintain Islam as the state religion. In Germany, courts have held that non-Christian religious symbols and dress, but not Christian ones, may be banned from schools and other public places. In France, the government forbids wearing any religious garb in schools. In the United States, such rulings or restrictions would be unthinkable.

THE POLITICAL SYSTEM

There are at least five important elements in the American view of the political system:

- *Liberty:* Americans are preoccupied with their rights. They believe they should be free to do pretty much as they please, with some exceptions, so long as they don't hurt other people.

- *Equality:* Americans believe everybody should have an equal vote and an equal chance to participate and succeed.

- *Democracy:* Americans think government officials should be accountable to the people.

- *Civic duty:* Americans generally feel people ought to take community affairs seriously and help out when they can.[4]

- *Individual responsibility:* A characteristically American view is that, barring some disability, individuals are responsible for their own actions and well-being.

By vast majorities, Americans believe that every citizen should have an equal chance to influence government policy and to hold public office, and they oppose the idea of letting people have titles such as "Lord" or "Duke," as in England. By somewhat smaller majorities, they believe people should be allowed to vote even if they can't read or write or vote intelligently.[5] Though Americans recognize that people differ in their abilities, they overwhelmingly agree with the statement that "teaching children that all people are really equal recognizes that all people are equally worthy and deserve equal treatment."[6]

At least three questions can be raised about this political culture. First, how do we know that the American people share these beliefs? For most of our history there were no public opinion polls, and even after they became commonplace, they were rather crude tools for measuring the existence and meaning of complex, abstract ideas. There is in fact no way to prove that values such as those listed above are important to Americans. But neither is there good reason for dismissing the list out of hand. One can infer, as have many scholars, the existence of certain values by a close study of the kinds of books Americans read, the speeches they hear, the slogans to which they respond, and the political choices they make, as well as by noting the observations of insightful foreign visitors. Personality tests as well as opinion polls, particularly those asking similar questions in different countries, also supply useful evidence, some of which will be reviewed in the following paragraphs.

Second, if these values are important to Americans, how can we explain the existence in our society of behavior that is obviously inconsistent with them? For example, if white Americans believe in equality of opportunity, why did so many of them for so long deny that equality to African Americans? That people act contrary to their professed beliefs is an everyday fact of life: people believe in honesty, yet they steal from their employers and sometimes underreport their taxable income. Besides values, self-interest and social circumstances also shape behavior. Gunnar Myrdal, a Swedish observer of American society, described race relations in this country as "an American dilemma" resulting from the conflict between the "American creed" (a belief in equality of opportunity) and American behavior (denying African Americans full citizenship).[7] But the creed remains important because it is a source of change: as more and more people become aware of the inconsistency between their values and their behavior, that behavior slowly changes.[8] Race relations in this country would take a very different course if instead of an abstract but widespread belief in equality there were an equally widespread belief that one race is inherently inferior to another.

The late political scientist, Samuel P. Huntington, put it this way: "Critics say that America is a lie because its reality falls so far short of its ideals.

America is not a lie, it is a disappointment. And it can be a disappointment only because it is also a hope."[9]

Third, if there is agreement among Americans on certain political values, why has there been so much political conflict in our history? How could a people who agree on such fundamentals fight a bloody civil war, engage in violent labor-management disputes, take to the streets in riots and demonstrations, and sue each other in countless court battles? Conflict, even violent struggles, can occur over specific policies even among those who share, at some level of abstraction, common beliefs. Many political values may be irrelevant to specific controversies: there is no abstract value, for example, that would settle the question of whether steelworkers ought to organize unions. More important, much of our conflict has occurred precisely because we have strong beliefs that happen, as each of us interprets them, to be in conflict. Equality of opportunity seems an attractive idea, but sometimes it can be pursued only by curtailing personal liberty, another attractive idea. The states went to war in 1861 over one aspect of that conflict—the rights of slaves versus the rights of slaveowners.

Indeed, the Civil War illustrates the way certain fundamental beliefs about how a democratic regime ought to be organized have persisted despite bitter conflict over the policies adopted by particular governments. When the southern states seceded from the Union, they formed not a wholly different government but one modeled, despite some important differences, on the U.S. Constitution. Even some of the language of the Constitution was duplicated, suggesting that the southern states believed not that a new form of government or a different political culture ought to be created but that the South was the true repository of the existing constitutional and cultural order.[10]

Perhaps the most frequently encountered evidence that Americans believe themselves bound by common values and common hopes has been the persistence of the word *Americanism* in our political vocabulary. Throughout the 19th and 20th centuries, *Americanism* and *the American dream* were familiar terms not only in Fourth of July speeches but also in everyday discourse. For many years, the House of Representatives had a committee called the House Un-American Activities Committee. There is hardly any example to be found abroad of such a way of thinking: There is no "Britishism" or "Frenchism," and when Britons and French people become worried about subversion, they call it a problem of internal security, not a manifestation of "un-British" or "un-French" activities.

THE PERSISTENCE OF CONFLICT

We have ended slavery, endorsed civil rights, and expanded the scope of free discussion, but these gains have not ended political conflict. We argue about abortion, morality, religion, immigration, and affirmative action. Some people believe that core moral principles are absolute while others feel they are relative to the situation. Some people believe all immigrants should become like every other American while others argue that we should, in the name of diversity and multiculturalism, celebrate group differences.

Much depends on how we define a good citizen. Some people define them as persons who vote, pay their taxes, obey the law, and support the military; others describe them as skeptical of government and ready to join protest movements and boycott products they do not like. A recent study has suggested that these competing opinions reflect differences in age and education. Older people, especially those that experienced the Great Depression and the World War II, are more likely to take the first view, while those born between 1964 and 1984 and who have been to college are more likely to take the second.[11]

These two generations don't quite trust one another. The older generation thinks the younger one is alienated, distrustful, self-centered, and lacking in clear moral guidance. The younger group, often described as Generation X because they were born after the Baby Boomers, responds by saying that older people are rigid, conformist, overly supportive of the status quo, and too impressed by the military.

But these conflicts, though they affect every American, should not obscure the underlying level of agreement. Consider how different ethnic groups

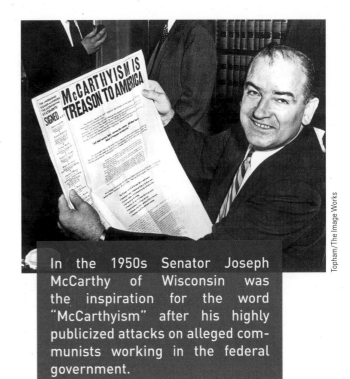

In the 1950s Senator Joseph McCarthy of Wisconsin was the inspiration for the word "McCarthyism" after his highly publicized attacks on alleged communists working in the federal government.

think about this country. When asked whether they "love" this country, the overwhelming majority of whites, blacks, and Hispanics say they do (see Table 4.1).

THE ECONOMIC SYSTEM

Americans judge the economic system using many of the same standards by which they judge the political system, albeit with some very important differences. As it is in American politics, liberty is important in the U.S. economy. Thus Americans support the idea of a free-enterprise economic system, calling the nation's economy "generally fair and efficient" and denying that it "survives by keeping the poor down."[12] However, there are limits to how much freedom they think should exist in the marketplace. People support government regulation of business in order to keep some firms from becoming too powerful and to correct specific abuses.[13]

Americans are more willing to tolerate economic inequality than political inequality. They believe in maintaining "equality of opportunity" in the economy but not "equality of results." If everyone has an equal opportunity to get ahead, then it is all right for people with more ability to earn higher salaries and for wages to be set based on how hard people work rather than on their economic needs. Hardly anyone is upset by the fact that Bill Gates, Warren Buffett, and Donald Trump are rich men. Although

Table 4.1 Patriotism by Race and Ethnicity

Group	How strongly do you love America?
White	91%
Black	80
Hispanic	91

Source: Jack Citrin, et al., "Testing Huntington," *Perspectives on Politics*, 5 (2007), 43. Data are from 2004 National Election Survey.

RESEARCH FRONTIERS

Do Hispanics Embrace American Political Culture?

Hispanics are the largest and fastest-growing minority group in America. The nation's Hispanic population surpassed 45 million in 2007, representing about 15 percent of the total U.S. population. They comprise over a third of the population in several states including California, New Mexico, and Texas.

In recent years, some analysts have asserted that Hispanic immigrants to the U.S., the vast majority of who come from Mexico, will remain strangers to American political culture. Among the most provocative of these analysts is Harvard political scientist Samuel P. Huntington, who has argued that the sheer number, concentration, and ostensible linguistic homogeneity of Hispanics in America will promote ethnic allegiances at odds with bedrock American beliefs about politics and government.

University of California at Berkeley political scientist Jack Citrin and other researchers tested Huntington's controversial contentions about Hispanic immigrants.

Contrary to Huntington's dire predictions, all the evidence suggests that, if anything, Hispanic immigrants over time are far more likely to embrace and emulate, rather than to reject or refashion, American political culture.

- Linguistic adaptation: Regardless of age, educational level, or residential concentration, Hispanic immigrants from one generation to the next speak English as their first language (by the third generation, 71 percent are English dominant).

- Hyphenated-American identity: Most Hispanics think of themselves as both American and Hispanic; and once Hispanic immigrants become citizens, they become far more likely to identify either as "just an American" or as "Hispanic-American."

- Religiosity: Measured by professed importance of religion and rates of church attendance, Hispanics are no more or less religious than non-Hispanic whites.

- Patriotism: 91 percent of Hispanic-Americans say they "love America," and 86 percent express "pride in the American flag."

- Work ethic: The higher the proportion of Hispanics living and working in a given state, the more likely it is that non-Hispanics will agree that Hispanics are especially hard working.

Also contrary to Huntington's Mexican-specific thesis, the data analyses by Citrin and his colleagues, like most other recent empirical studies of the subject, suggest that generation-by-generation, Mexican-born Hispanic immigrants' social, economic, and personal ties to Mexico diminish.

In sum, the latest and best research offers this prediction: most Hispanic immigrant families, like most Italian and other European immigrant families into the early and mid-20th century, will continue to adapt, will adopt American political culture, and will make a hyphenated American identity all their own.

- Do a little research to discover the size and ethnic composition of the Hispanic population in your state. How, if at all, have debates about immigration figured in recent presidential elections or in local politics where you live?

Sources: Jack Citrin et al., "Testing Huntington: Is Hispanic Immigration a Threat to American Identity?," *Perspectives on Politics* 5, March 2007, pp. 31–48; Samuel P. Huntington, *Who are We? The Challenges to America's National Identity* (Simon and Shuster, 2004).

Americans are quite willing to support education and training programs to help disadvantaged people get ahead, they are strongly opposed to anything that looks like preferential treatment (for example, hiring quotas) in the workplace.[14]

The leaders of very liberal political groups, such as civil rights and feminist organizations, are more willing than the average American to support preferential treatment in the hiring and promoting of minorities and women. They do so because, unlike most citizens, they believe that whatever disadvantages minorities and women face are the result of failures of the economic system rather than the fault of individuals. Even so, these leaders strongly support the idea that earnings should be based on ability and oppose the idea of having any top limit on what people can earn.[15]

This popular commitment to economic individualism and personal responsibility may help explain how Americans think about particular public policies, such as welfare and civil rights. Polls show that Americans are willing to help people "truly in need" (this includes the elderly and the disabled) but not those deemed "able to take care of themselves" (this includes, in the public's mind, people "on welfare"). Also, Americans dislike preferential hiring programs and the use of quotas to deal with racial inequality.

At the core of these policy attitudes is a widely (but not universally) shared commitment to economic individualism and personal responsibility. Some scholars, among them Donald Kinder and David Sears, interpret these individualistic values as "symbolic racism"—a kind of plausible camouflage for antiblack attitudes.[16] But other scholars, such as Paul M. Sniderman and Michael Gray Hagen, argue that these views are not a smoke screen for bigotry or insensitivity but a genuine commitment to the ethic of self-reliance.[17] Since there are many Americans on both sides of this issue, debates about welfare and civil rights tend to be especially intense. What is striking about the American political culture is that in this country the individualist view of social policy is by far the most popular.[18]

Views about specific economic policies change. Americans now are much more inclined than they once were to believe that the government should help the needy and regulate business. But the commitment to certain underlying principles has been remarkably enduring. In 1924, almost half of the high school students in Muncie, Indiana, said that "it is entirely the fault of the man himself if he cannot succeed" and disagreed with the view that differences in wealth showed that the system was unjust. Over half a century later, the students in this same high school were asked the same questions again, with the same results.[19]

Comparing America with Other Nations

Americans like their own country more than people in European democracies like theirs. In Table 4.2, we see that 71 percent of Americans are proud to be an American compared to only 21 percent of Germans who are proud to be Germans. There are other differences as well: a majority of the French, Germans, and Italians think success in life is determined by forces outside an individual's own control; Americans deeply disagree. Most Americans think children should be taught the value of hard work and that a belief in God is necessary for morality; most western European countries have the opposite view.

America is not very popular abroad, but these data suggest that the reasons go well beyond the war in Iraq or the criticism of former president George W. Bush. Americans have very different views about important things than Europeans. Following are some examples drawn from politics, the economy, and religion.

Table 4.2 Attitudes in the USA and Other Democracies

	Pride	Outside Control	Teach Value of Work	God and Morality
USA	71%	32%	60%	58%
Canada	66	35	51	30
Britain	45	48	38	25
France	38	54	50	13
Germany	21	68	22	33
Italy	38	66	na	27

Key to columns:

Pride: "I am very proud to be a member of [country]"

Outside Control: "Success in life is determined by forces outside our control"

Teach Value of Work: "Children should be taught the value of hard work"

God and Morality: "It is necessary to believe in God to be moral"

Source: Andrew Kohut, *America Against the World* (New York: Times Books, 2006), 45, 55, 106, 135. The surveys were done in 2000–2005 in these countries.

THE POLITICAL SYSTEM

Sweden has a well-developed democratic government, with a constitution, free speech, an elected legislature, competing political parties, and a reasonably honest and nonpartisan bureaucracy. But the Swedish political culture is significantly different from ours; it is more deferential than participatory. Though almost all adult Swedes vote in national elections, few participate in politics in any other way. They defer to the decisions of experts and specialists who work for the government, rarely challenge governmental decisions in court, believe leaders and legislators ought to decide issues on the basis of "what is best" more than on "what the people want," and value equality as much as (or more than) liberty.[20] Whereas Americans are contentious, Swedes value harmony; while Americans tend to assert their rights, Swedes tend to observe their obligations.

The contrast in political cultures is even greater when one looks at a nation, such as Japan, with a wholly different history and set of traditions. One study compared the values expressed by a small number of upper-status Japanese with those of some similarly situated Americans. Whereas the Americans emphasized the virtues of individualism, competition, and equality in their political, economic, and social relations, the Japanese attached greater value to maintaining good relations with colleagues, having decisions made by groups, preserving social harmony, and displaying respect for hierarchy. The Americans were more concerned than the Japanese with rules and with treating others fairly but impersonally, with due regard for their rights. The Japanese, on the other hand, stressed the importance of being sensitive to the personal needs of others, avoiding conflict, and reaching decisions through discussion rather than the application of rules.[21]

A classic study of political culture in five nations found that Americans, and to a lesser degree citizens of Great Britain, had a stronger sense of **civic duty** (a belief that one has an obligation to participate in civic and political affairs) and a stronger sense of **civic competence** (a belief that one can affect government policies) than the citizens of Germany, Italy, or Mexico. Over half of all Americans and a third of all Britons believed the average citizen ought to "be active in one's community," compared to only a tenth in Italy and a fifth in Germany. Moreover, many more Americans and Britons than Germans, Italians, or Mexicans believed they could

civic duty A belief that one has an obligation to participate in civic and political affairs.

civic competence A belief that one can affect government policies.

"do something" about an unjust national law or local regulation.[22] A more recent study of citizen participation in politics found that while America lagged behind Austria, the Netherlands, Germany, and the United Kingdom in voter participation, when it came to campaigning, attending political meetings, becoming active in the local community, and contacting government officials, Americans were as active—or substantially more active—than citizens elsewhere.[23]

Today the American people have less trust in government than they once did. But even so, popular confidence in political institutions remains higher here than in many places abroad. In cross-national surveys conducted in the United States and 16 other democracies, Americans expressed more confidence in public institutions (the police, the armed forces, the legal system, and the civil service) than the citizens of all but four other countries (Denmark, Ireland, Northern Ireland, and Norway), and greater confidence in private institutions (the church, major companies, the press, trade unions) than the citizens of any other nation.[24] In other cross-national surveys, Americans were more likely than the French or Germans to say they were "very patriotic" (see Figure 4.1). Of course, Americans know that their country has a lot of faults. But even the most disaffected voters believe the United States needs to change only certain policies, not its system of government.[25]

THE ECONOMIC SYSTEM

The political culture of Sweden is not only more deferential than ours but also more inclined to favor equality of results over equality of opportunity. Sidney Verba and Gary Orren compared the views of Swedish and American trade union and political party leaders on a variety of economic issues. In both countries, the leaders were chosen from either blue-collar unions or the major liberal political party (the Democrats in the United States, the Social Democrats in Sweden).

The results are quite striking. By margins of four or five to one, the Swedish leaders were more likely to believe in giving workers equal pay than their American counterparts. Moreover, by margins of at least three to one, the Swedes were more likely than the Americans to favor putting a top limit on incomes.[26]

Just what these differences in beliefs mean in dollars-and-cents terms was revealed by the answers to another question. Each group was asked what should be the ratio between the income of an executive and that of a menial worker (a dishwasher in Sweden, an elevator operator in the United States). The Swedish leaders said the ratio should be a little

Figure 4.1
Political Culture in America and Other Democracies

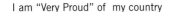
I am "Very Proud" of my country

Number of organizational memberships

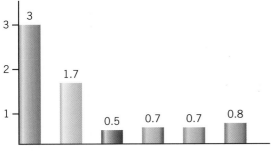

Support for freedom of speech

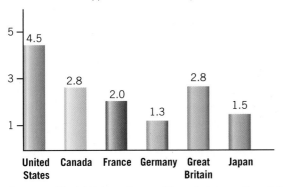

| United States | Canada | France | Germany | Great Britain | Japan |

Sources: World Values Survey Wave 4; International Social Survey Program National Identity Module II (2003–2004)

over two to one. That is, if the dishwasher earned $200 a week, the executive should earn no more than $440 to $480 a week. But the American leaders were ready to let the executive earn between $2,260 and $3,040 per week when the elevator operator was earning $200.

Americans, compared to people in many other countries, are more likely to think that freedom is more important than equality and less likely to think that hard work goes unrewarded or that the government should guarantee citizens a basic standard of living. These cultural differences make a difference in politics. In fact, there is less income inequality in Sweden than in the United States—the government sees to that.

THE CIVIC ROLE OF RELIGION

In the 1830s, Tocqueville was amazed at how religious Americans were in comparison to his fellow Europeans. From the first days of the new Republic to the present, America has been among the most religious countries in the world. The average American is more likely than the average European to believe in God, to pray on a daily basis, and to acknowledge clear standards of right and wrong. [27]

Religious people donate over three times as much money to charity as secular people, even when the incomes of the two groups are the same, and they volunteer their time twice as often. And this is true whether or not religious people go to church or synagogue regularly. Moreover, religious people are more likely to give money and donate time to non-religious organizations, such as the Red Cross, than secular people.[28] It is clear that religion in America has a large effect on our culture.

It also affects our politics. The religious revivalist movement of the late 1730s and early 1740s (known as the First Great Awakening) transformed the political life of the American colonies. Religious ideas fueled the break with England, which, in the words of the Declaration of Independence, had violated "the laws of nature and nature's God." Religious leaders were central to the struggle over slavery in the 19th century and the temperance movement of the early 20th century.

Both liberals and conservatives have used the pulpit to promote political change. The civil rights movement of the 1950s and 1960s was led mainly by black religious leaders, most prominently Martin Luther King, Jr. In the 1980s, a conservative religious group known as the Moral Majority advocated constitutional amendments that would allow prayer in public schools and ban abortion. In

The chaplain of the U.S. House of Representatives leads a prayer.

AP Photo/Ken Lambert

the 1990s, another conservative religious group, the Christian Coalition, attracted an enormous amount of media attention and became a prominent force in many national, state, and local elections.

Candidates for national office in most contemporary democracies mention religion rarely if they mention it at all. Not so in America. During the 2000 presidential campaign, for example, both Democratic candidate Al Gore and Republican candidate George W. Bush gave major speeches extolling the virtues of religion and advocating the right of religious organizations that deliver social services to receive government funding on the same basis as all other nonprofit organizations.

The general feeling about religion became apparent when a federal appeals court in 2002 tried to ban the Pledge of Allegiance because it contained the phrase "under God." There was an overwhelming and bipartisan condemnation of the ruling. To a degree that would be almost unthinkable in many other democracies, religious beliefs will probably continue to shape political culture in America for many generations to come. The Supreme Court, by deciding that the man who brought the case was not entitled to do so, left the Pledge intact without deciding whether it was constitutional.

The Sources of Political Culture

That Americans bring a distinctive way of thinking to their political life is easier to demonstrate than to explain. But even a brief, and necessarily superficial, effort to understand the sources of our political culture can help make its significance clearer.

The American Revolution, as we discussed in Chapter 2, was essentially a war fought over liberty: an assertion by the colonists of what they took to be their rights. Though the Constitution, produced 11 years after the Revolution, had to deal with other issues as well, its animating spirit reflected the effort to reconcile personal liberty with the needs of social control. These founding experiences, and the political disputes that followed, have given to American political thought and culture a preoccupation with the assertion and maintenance of rights. This tradition has imbued the daily conduct of U.S. politics with a kind of adversarial spirit quite foreign to the political life of countries that did not undergo a libertarian revolution or that were formed out of an interest in other goals, such as social equality, national independence, or ethnic supremacy.

The adversarial spirit of the American political culture reflects not only our preoccupation with rights but also our long-standing distrust of authority and of people wielding power. The colonies' experiences with British rule was one source of that distrust. But another, older source was the religious belief of many Americans, which saw human nature as fundamentally depraved. To the colonists, all of mankind suffered from original sin, symbolized by Adam and Eve eating the forbidden fruit in the Garden of Eden. Since no one was born innocent, no one could be trusted with power. Thus, the Constitution had to be designed in such a way as to curb the darker side of human nature. Otherwise, everyone's rights would be in jeopardy.

The contentiousness of a people animated by a suspicion of government and devoted to individualism could easily have made democratic politics so tumultuous as to be impossible. After all one must be willing to trust others with power if there is to be any kind of democratic government, and sometimes those others will be people not of one's own choosing. The first great test case took place around 1800 in a battle between the Federalists, led by John Adams and Alexander Hamilton, and the Democratic-Republicans, led by Thomas Jefferson and James Madison. The two factions deeply distrusted each other: the Federalists had passed laws designed to suppress Jeffersonian journalists; Jefferson suspected the Federalists were out to subvert the Constitution; and the Federalists believed Jefferson intended to sell out the country to France. But as we shall see in Chapter 9, the threat of civil war never materialized, and the Jeffersonians came to power peacefully. Within a few years, the role of an opposition party became legitimate, and people abandoned the idea of making serious efforts to suppress their opponents. By happy circumstance, people came to accept that liberty and orderly political change could coexist.

The Constitution, by creating a federal system and dividing political authority among competing institutions, provided ample opportunity for widespread—though hardly universal—participation in politics. The election of Jefferson in 1800 produced no political catastrophe, and those who had predicted one were, to a degree, discredited. But other, more fundamental features of American life contributed to the same end. One of the most important of these was religious diversity.

The absence of an established or official religion for the nation as a whole, reinforced by a constitutional prohibition of such an establishment and by the migration to this country of people with different religious backgrounds, meant that religious diversity was inevitable. Since there could be no orthodox or official religion, it became difficult for a correspond-ing political orthodoxy to emerge. Moreover, the conflict between the Puritan tradition, with its emphasis on faith and hard work, and the Catholic Church, with its devotion to the sacraments and priestly authority, provided a recurrent source of cleavage in American public life. The differences in values between these two groups showed up not only in their religious practices but also in areas involving the regulation of manners and morals, and even in people's choice of political party. For more than a century, candidates for state and national office were deeply divided over whether the sale of liquor should be prohibited, a question that arose ultimately out of competing religious doctrines.

Even though there was no established church, there was certainly a dominant religious tradition—Protestantism, and especially Puritanism. The Protestant churches provided people with both a set of beliefs and an organizational experience that had profound effects on American political culture. Those beliefs encouraged, or even required, a life of personal achievement as well as religious conviction: a believer had an obligation to work, save money, obey the secular law, and do good works. Max Weber explained the rise of capitalism in part by what he called the Protestant ethic—what we now sometimes call the work ethic.[29] Such values had political consequences, as people holding them were motivated to engage in civic and communal action.

Churches offered ready opportunities for developing and practicing civic and political skills. Since most Protestant churches were organized along congregational lines—that is, the church was controlled by its members, who put up the building, hired the preacher, and supervised the finances—they were, in effect, miniature political systems with leaders and committees, conflict and consensus. Developing a participatory political culture was undoubtedly made easier by the existence of a participatory religious culture. Even some Catholic churches in early America were under a degree of lay control. Parishioners owned the church property, negotiated with priests, and conducted church business.

All aspects of culture, including the political, are preserved and transmitted to new generations primarily by the family. Though some believe that the weakening of the family unit has eroded the extent to which it transmits anything, particularly culture, and has enlarged the power of other sources of values—the mass media and the world of friends and fashion,

leisure, and entertainment—there is still little doubt that the ways in which we think about the world are largely acquired within the family. In Chapter 7, we shall see that the family is the primary source of one kind of political attitude—identification with one or another political party. Even more important, the family shapes in subtle ways how we think and act on political matters. Erik Erikson, the psychologist, noted certain traits that are more characteristic of American than of European families—the greater freedom enjoyed by children, for example, and the larger measure of equality among family members. These familial characteristics promote a belief, carried through life, that every person has rights deserving protection and that a variety of interests have a legitimate claim to consideration when decisions are made.[30]

The combined effect of religious and ethnic diversity, an individualistic philosophy, fragmented political authority, and the relatively egalitarian American family can be seen in the absence of a high degree of **class consciousness** among Americans. Class consciousness means thinking of oneself as a worker whose interests are in opposition to those of management, or vice versa. In this country, most people, whatever their jobs, think of themselves as "middle class."

> *class consciousness*
> A belief that you are a member of an economic group whose interests are opposed to people in other such groups.

Though the writings of Horatio Alger are no longer popular, Americans still seem to believe in the message of those stories—that the opportunity for success is available to people who work hard. This may help explain why the United States is the only large industrial democracy without a significant socialist party and why the nation has been slow to adopt certain welfare programs.

THE CULTURE WAR

Almost all Americans share some elements of a common political culture. Why, then, is there so much cultural conflict in American politics? For many years, the most explosive political issues have included abortion, gay rights, drug use, school prayer, and pornography. Viewed from a Marxist perspective, politics in the United States is utterly baffling: instead of two economic classes engaged in a bitter struggle over wealth, we have two cultural classes locked in a war over values.

As first formulated by sociologist James Davison Hunter, the idea is that there are, broadly defined,

Beth A. Keiser/AP Photo

John Sommers II/Reuters/Corbis

Protests and demonstrations are a common feature of American politics, as with this attack in Seattle on American membership in the World Trade Organization in November 2001. Yet, despite disagreements Americans are a patriotic people, as seen in this photo of baseball fans waving flags and singing "God Bless America," taken a few days after 9/11.

orthodox A belief that morality and religion ought to be of decisive importance.

progressive A belief that personal freedom and solving social problems are more important than religion.

two cultural classes in the United States: the **orthodox** and the **progressive.** On the orthodox side are people who believe that morality is as important as, or more important than, self-expression and that moral rules derive from the commands of God or the laws of nature—commands and laws that are relatively clear, unchanging, and independent of individual preferences. On the progressive side are people who think that personal freedom is as important as, or more important than, certain traditional moral rules and that those rules must be evaluated in light of the circumstances of modern life—circumstances that are quite complex, changeable, and dependent on individual preferences.[31]

Most conspicuous among the orthodox are fundamentalist Protestants and evangelical Christians, and so critics who dislike orthodox views often dismiss them as the fanatical expressions of "the Religious Right." But many people who hold orthodox views are not fanatical or deeply religious or rightwing on most issues: they simply have strong views about drugs, pornography, and sexual morality. Similarly, the progressive side often includes members of liberal Protestant denominations (for example, Episcopalians and Unitarians) and people with no strong religious beliefs, and so their critics often denounce them as immoral, anti-Christian

radicals who have embraced the ideology of secular humanism, the belief that moral standards do not require religious justification. But in all likelihood, few progressives are immoral or anti-Christian, and most do not regard secular humanism as their defining ideology.

Groups supporting and opposing the right to abortion have had many angry confrontations in recent years. The latter have been arrested while attempting to block access to abortion clinics; some clinics have been fire-bombed; and at least seven physicians have been killed. A controversy over what schoolchildren should be taught about homosexuals was responsible, in part, for the firing of the head of the New York City school system; in other states, there have been fierce arguments in state legislatures and before the courts over whether gay and lesbian couples should be allowed to marry or adopt children. Although most Americans want to keep heroin, cocaine, and other drugs illegal, a significant number of people want to legalize (or at least decriminalize) their use. The Supreme Court has ruled that there cannot be state-sponsored prayer in public schools, but this has not stopped many parents and school authorities from trying to reinstate school prayer, or at least prayerlike moments of silence. The discovery that a federal agency, the National Endowment for the Arts, had given money to support exhibitions and performances that many people thought were obscene led to a furious congressional struggle over the future of the agency.

The culture war differs from other political disputes (over such matters as taxes, business regulations, and foreign policy) in several ways: money is not at stake, compromises are almost impossible to arrange, and the conflict is more profound. It is animated by deep differences in people's beliefs about private and public morality—that is, about the standards that ought to govern individual behavior and social arrangements. It is about what kind of country we ought to live in, not just about what kinds of policies our government ought to adopt.

Two opposing views exist about the importance of the culture war. One view, developed by Morris Fiorina and others, holds that politically the culture war is a myth. While political leaders are polarized, most Americans occupy a middle position. Journalists write about the split between "blue states" (those that vote Democratic) and "red states" (those that vote Republican), but in fact popular views across both kinds of states on many policy issues are similar.[32]

The rival view, developed by Alan Abramowitz and others, holds that more and more people are choosing their party affiliations on the basis of the party's position on important issues. Moreover, a growing percentage of the public is politically engaged; that is, they do more about politics than simply vote.[33]

Choosing between these two theories will take time, as we watch what happens in future elections. But even now, popular attitudes about one issue—the war in Iraq—are already deeply polarized.

Mistrust of Government

One aspect of public opinion worries many people. Since the late 1950s, there has been a more or less steady decline in the proportion of Americans who say they trust the government in Washington to do the right thing. In the past, polls showed that about three-quarters of Americans said they trusted Washington most of the time or just about always. The percentage of people who say they trust the government has on occasion gone up (for example, when Ronald Reagan was president and again just after the 9/11 terrorist attacks), but by and large trust has been absent since at least the mid-1960s (see Figure 4.2).

Before we get too upset about this, we should remember that people are talking about government officials, not the system of government. Americans are much more supportive of the country and its institutions than Europeans are of theirs. Even so, the decline in confidence in officials is striking. There are all sorts of explanations for why it has happened. In the 1960s, there was our unhappy war

Some extremists have bombed abortion clinics while opposed activists denounce their behavior.

Chip Somodevilla/Getty Images

in Vietnam; in the 1970s, President Nixon had to resign because of his involvement in the Watergate scandal; and in the 1990s, President Clinton went through scandals that led to his impeachment by the House of Representatives (but not convicted of that charge by the Senate); and in 2004–2007, President Bush presided over a divisive war in Iraq.

But there is another way of looking at the matter. Maybe in the 1950s we had an abnormally *high* level of confidence in government, one that could never be expected to last no matter what any president did. After all, when President Eisenhower took office in 1952, we had won a war against fascism, overcome the Depression of the 1930s, possessed a near monopoly of the atom bomb, had a currency that was the envy of the world, and dominated international trade. Moreover, in those days not much was expected out of Washington. Hardly anybody

Figure 4.2

Trust in the Federal Government, 1958–2004

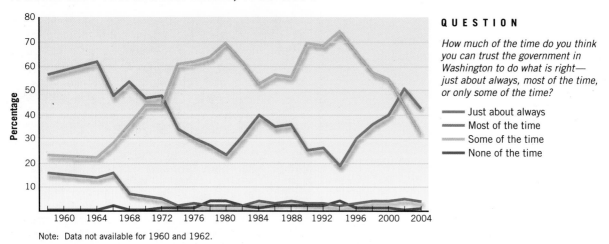

QUESTION

How much of the time do you think you can trust the government in Washington to do what is right— just about always, most of the time, or only some of the time?

—— Just about always
—— Most of the time
—— Some of the time
—— None of the time

Note: Data not available for 1960 and 1962.

Source: University of Michigan, *The American National Election Studies.*

thought there should be important federal laws about civil rights, crime, illegal drugs, the environment, the role of women, highway safety, or almost anything else now on the national agenda. Since nobody expected much out of Washington, nobody was upset that they didn't get much out of it.

The 1960s and 1970s changed all of that. Domestic turmoil, urban riots, a civil rights revolution, the war in Vietnam, economic inflation, and a new concern for the environment dramatically increased what we expected Washington to do. And since these problems are very difficult ones to solve, a lot of people became convinced that our politicians couldn't do much.[34]

Those events also pushed the feelings Americans had about their country—that is, their patriotism—into the background. We liked the country, but there weren't many occasions when expressing that approval seemed to make much sense. But on September 11, 2001, when hijacked airliners were crashed by terrorists into the World Trade Center in New York City and the Pentagon in Washington, all of that changed. There was an extraordinary outburst of patriotic fervor, with flags displayed everywhere, fire and police heroes widely celebrated, and strong national support for our going to war in Afghanistan to find the key terrorist, Osama bin Laden, and destroy the tyrannical Taliban regime that he supported. By November of that year, about half of all Americans of both political parties said they trusted Washington officials to do what is right most of the time, the highest level in many years.

Those who had hoped or predicted that this new level of support would last, not ebb and flow, have been disappointed. In October 2001, 57 percent of Americans (up from just 29 percent in July 2001)

said they trusted the federal government to do what is right just about always or most of the time. But by May 2002, only 40 percent expressed such trust in the federal government, and 57 percent said they trusted Washington only some of the time or never.

Only 12 percent of all Americans have a lot of confidence in Congress, but it—and the rest of the government—should not feel lonely. With few exceptions, Americans have lost confidence in many institutions. As Table 4.3 shows, newspapers, public schools, television news, and labor unions have all suffered a big drop over the last three decades. Only the military has gained support (71 percent of us say we have "a great deal" or "a lot" of confidence in it).

Because Americans are less likely than they once were to hold their leaders in high esteem, to have confidence in government policies, and to believe the system will be responsive to popular wishes, some observers like to say that Americans today are more "alienated" from politics. Perhaps, but careful studies of the subject have not yet been able, for example, to demonstrate any relationship between overall levels of public trust in government or confidence in leaders, on the one hand, and the rates at which people come out to vote, on the other. There is, however, some evidence that the less voters trust political institutions and leaders, the more likely they are to support candidates from the nonincumbent major party (in two-candidate races) and third-party candidates.[35]

CIVIL SOCIETY

Distrust of governmental and other institutions makes more important the role of **civil society,** that collection of private, voluntary groups

Table 4.3 Confidence in American Institutions

Institution	1973	2008
Churches	66%	48%
Public schools	58	33
Newspapers	39	24
Labor unions	30	20
Big business	26	20
Congress	42	12
The military	58	71

Source: Gallup Poll.

that—independent of the government and the commercial market—make human cooperation easier and provide ways of holding the government accountable for its actions.

The individualism of the American political culture makes civil society especially important. As we shall see in Chapter 11, Americans are more likely to join voluntary groups than those in other democracies. These organizations teach people how to cooperate, develop community-serving skills, and increase social capital. This last phrase refers to the connections people have with each other through friendship, personal contact, and group efforts.

Several scholars, such as Robert Putnam, argue that the more a community has social capital, the greater the level of trust among its members. And, the more trust, the easier it is to achieve common

goals such as improving a neighborhood, combating intolerance, and producing useful projects outside of government.

Putnam worries that our social capital may be decreasing because people are less and less likely to join voluntary associations. Once a nation of joiners, we are now "bowling alone." We once bowled in leagues, now we bowl alone. We once joined the PTA, the NAACP, and the Veterans of Foreign Wars, now we stay home and watch television.[36]

There are three qualifications to this argument. First, Americans still join more groups than people in most other democracies. Second, a general measure of our civic health (that combines group membership with informal human contact) has increased of late (see Figure 4.3). Third, in ethnically and racially diverse communities we "hunker down"— that is, we don't trust our neighbors, contribute to charities, cooperate with others, or join voluntary groups.[37] Just where we most need social capital, we do not have as much as we would like.

Political Tolerance

Democratic politics depends crucially on citizens' reasonable tolerance of the opinions and actions of others. If unpopular speakers were always shouted down, if government efforts to censor newspapers were usually met with popular support or even public indifference, if peaceful

civil society Voluntary action that makes cooperation easier.

Figure 4.3
The American Civic Health Index, 1975–2002

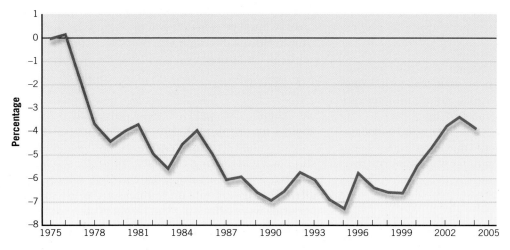

Source: *America's Civic Health Index: Broken Engagement* (Washington, D.C.: National Citizenship Conference and Saguaro Seminar, September 2006), p. 6. Reprinted by permission of the National Conference of Citizenship.

demonstrations were regularly broken up by hostile mobs, if the losing candidates in an election refused to allow their victorious opponents to take office, then the essential elements of a democratic political culture would be missing, and democracy would fail. Democracy does not require perfect tolerance; if it did, the passions of human nature would make democracy forever impossible. But at a minimum, citizens must have a political culture that allows the discussion of ideas and the selection of rulers in an atmosphere reasonably free of oppression.

Public opinion surveys show that the overwhelming majority of Americans agree with concepts such as freedom of speech, majority rule, and the right to circulate petitions—at least in the abstract.[38] But when we get down to concrete cases, a good many Americans are not very tolerant of groups they dislike. Suppose you must decide which groups will be permitted to espouse their causes at meetings held in your community's civic auditorium. Which of these groups would *you* allow to run such a meeting?

1. Protestants holding a revival meeting
2. Right-to-life groups opposing abortion
3. People protesting a nuclear power plant
4. Feminists organizing a march for the Equal Rights Amendment
5. Gays organizing for homosexual rights
6. Atheists preaching against God
7. Students organizing a sit-in to shut down city hall

In general, Americans have become a bit more tolerant and more willing to tolerate communists, people who teach against churches and religions, advocates of government ownership of industries, and people who think that blacks are genetically inferior. People are today more likely than in the past to say they are willing to vote for an otherwise qualified person who ran for president even if the candidate was a Catholic, a Jew, a woman, a black, or a homosexual.[39]

One person's civic intolerance can be another person's heartfelt display of civic concern. Most Americans believe that serious civic problems are rooted in a breakdown of moral values.[40] Correctly or not, most citizens worry that the nation is becoming too tolerant of behaviors that harm society, and they favor defending common moral standards over protecting individual rights.

Nonetheless, this majority tolerance for many causes should not blind us to the fact that for most of us there is some group or cause from which we are willing to withhold political liberties—even though we endorse those liberties in the abstract.

If most people dislike one or another group strongly enough to deny it certain political rights that we usually take for granted, how is it that such groups (and such rights) survive? The answer, in part, is that most of us don't act on our beliefs. We rarely take the trouble—or have the chance—to block another person from making a speech or teaching school. Some scholars have argued that among people who are in a position to deny other people rights—officeholders and political activists, for example—the level of political tolerance is somewhat greater than among the public at large, but that claim has been strongly disputed.[41]

But another reason may be just as important. Most of us are ready to deny *some* group its rights, but we usually can't agree on which group that should be. Sometimes we can agree, and then the disliked group may be in for real trouble. There have been times (1919–1920, and again in the early 1950s) when socialists or communists were disliked by most people in the United States. The government on each occasion took strong actions against them. Today, fewer people agree that these left-wing groups are a major domestic threat, and so their rights are now more secure.

Finally, the courts are sufficiently insulated from public opinion that they can act against majority sentiments and enforce constitutional protections (see Chapter 16). Most of us are not willing to give all rights to all groups, but most of us are not judges.

These facts should be a sober reminder that political liberty cannot be taken for granted. Men and women are not, it would seem, born with an inclination to live and let live, at least politically, and many— possibly most—never acquire that inclination. Liberty must be learned and protected. Happily, the United States during much of its recent history has not been consumed by a revulsion for any one group that has been strong enough to place the group's rights in jeopardy.

Nor should any part of society pretend that it is always more tolerant than another. In the 1950s, for example, ultraconservatives outside the universities were attacking the rights of professors to say and teach certain things. In the 1960s and 1970s, ultra-liberal students and professors inside the universities were attacking the rights of other students and professors to say certain things.

WHAT WOULD YOU DO?

MEMORANDUM

To: *Representative Olivia Kuo*

From: *J. P. Loria, chief of staff*

Subject: *Charitable Choice Expansion Act*

Section 104 of the 1996 federal welfare reform law encourages states to utilize "faith-based organizations" as providers of federal welfare services. Known as Charitable Choice, the law prohibits participating organizations from discriminating against beneficiaries on the basis of religion but permits them to control "the definition, development, practice, and expression" of their religious convictions. The proposed act would expand Charitable Choice to crime prevention and other areas.

Friday,

Religious Leaders Rally to Expand Federal Funding for "Charitable Choice"

August 28
WASHINGTON, D.C.

Yesterday an interfaith coalition of religious leaders conducted an all-day prayer vigil on Capitol Hill and called for increased federal funding for antipoverty programs run by local religious congregations…

Arguments for:

1. Over 90 percent of Americans believe in God, and 80 percent favor government funding for faith-based social programs.

2. Local religious groups are the main nongovernmental providers of social services in poor urban neighborhoods. The primary beneficiaries of faith-based programs are needy neighborhood children who are not affiliated with any congregation.

3. So long as the religious organizations serve civic purposes and do not proselytize, the law is constitutional.

Arguments against:

1. Americans are a richly religious people precisely because we have never mixed church and state in this way.

2. Community-serving religious groups succeed because over 97 percent of their funding is private and they can flexibly respond to people's needs without government or other interference.

3. Constitutional or not, the law threatens to undermine both church and state: Children will have religion slid (if not jammed) down their throats, and religious leaders will be tempted to compromise their convictions.

Your decision:

Favor expansion _____   Oppose expansion _____

SUMMARY

The American system of government is supported by a political culture that fosters a sense of civic duty, takes pride in the nation's constitutional arrangements, and provides support for the exercise of essential civil liberties (albeit out of indifference or diversity more than principle at times). In recent decades, mistrust of government officials (though not of the system itself) has increased, and confidence in their responsiveness to popular feelings has declined.

Although Americans value liberty in both the political system and the economy, they believe equality is important in the political realm. In economic affairs, they wish to see equality of opportunity but accept inequality of results.

Not only is our culture generally supportive of democratic rule, it also has certain distinctive features that make our way of governing different from what one finds in other democracies. Americans are preoccupied with their rights, and this fact, combined with a political system that (as we shall see) encourages the vigorous exercise of rights and claims, gives to our political life an *adversarial* style. Unlike Swedes or Japanese, we do not generally reach political decisions by consensus, and we often do not defer to the authority of administrative agencies. American politics, more than that of many other nations, is shot through at every stage with protracted conflict.

But as we shall learn in the next chapter, that conflict is not easily described as always pitting liberals against conservatives. Not only do we have a lot of conflict, it is often messy conflict, a kind of political Tower of Babel. Foreign observers sometimes ask how we stand the confusion. The answer, of course, is that we have been doing it for over 200 years. Maybe our Constitution is two centuries old—not in spite of this confusion but because of it. We shall see.

RECONSIDERING WHO GOVERNS?

1. Do Americans trust their government?

More than it sometimes appears. Compared to the 1950s, we are much less likely to think the government does the right thing or cares what we think. But when we look at our system of government—the Constitution and our political culture—we are very pleased with it. Americans are much more patriotic than people in many other democracies. And we display a great deal of support for churches in large measure because we are more religious than most Europeans.

2. Why do we accept great differences in wealth and income?

We believe in equality of opportunity and not equality of result. Wealthy people may have more political influence than ordinary folks, but if we think they earned their money through their own efforts and if they follow legal rules, we have no complaint about their wealth.

RECONSIDERING TO WHAT ENDS?

1. Why does our government behave differently than governments in countries with similar constitutions?

Our political culture has imbued it with more tolerance and a greater respect for orderly procedures and personal rights than can be found in nations with constitutions like ours. We are willing to let whoever wins an election govern without putting up a fuss, and our military does not intervene.

WORLD WIDE WEB RESOURCES

Polling organizations that frequently measure aspects of political culture:

www.roper.com

www.gallup.com

U.S. Census Bureau: **www.census.gov**

SUGGESTED READINGS

Almond, Gabriel, and Sidney Verba. *The Civic Culture*. Princeton, N.J.: Princeton University Press, 1963. A survey of the political cultures of five nations—the United States, Germany, Great Britain, Italy, and Mexico—as they were in 1959.

Brooks, Arthur C. *Who Really Cares?* New York: Basic Books, 2006. Fascinating study of who gives to charities in America and Europe.

Hartz, Louis. *The Liberal Tradition in America*. New York: Harcourt Brace Jovanovich, 1955. A stimulating interpretation of American political thought since the Founding, emphasizing the notion of a liberal consensus.

Lipset, Seymour Martin. *The First New Nation*. Rev. ed. New York: Norton, 1979. How the origins of American society gave rise to the partially competing values of equality and achievement and the ways in which these values shape political institutions.

McClosky, Herbert, and John Zaller. *The American Ethos: Public Attitudes Toward Capitalism and Democracy*. Cambridge: Harvard University Press, 1984. Study of the ways in which Americans evaluate political and economic arrangements.

Nivola, Pietro S., and David W. Brady, eds. *Red and Blue Nation?* Washington, D.C.: Brookings Institution, 2006. Compares the arguments of those who do and do not believe that a culture war exists.

Nye, Joseph S., Philip D. Zelikow, and David C. King. *Why People Don't Trust Government*. Cambridge: Harvard University Press, 1997. An effort to explain distrust.

Putnam, Robert D. *Bowling Alone: The Collapse and Revival of American Community*. New York: Simon & Schuster, 2000. An important argument that American political culture has been harmed by the decline in membership in organizations that bring people together for communal activities.

Tocqueville, Alexis de. *Democracy in America*. Edited by Phillips Bradley. 2 vols. New York: Knopf, 1951. First published in 1835–1840, this was and remains the greatest single interpretation of American political culture.

Verba, Sidney, and Gary R. Orren. *Equality in America: The View from the Top*. Cambridge: Harvard University Press, 1985. Elite views on political and economic equality.

5
Civil Liberties

WHO GOVERNS?

1. Why do the courts play so large a role in deciding what our civil liberties should be?

TO WHAT ENDS?

1. Why not display religious symbols on government property?
2. If a person confesses to committing a crime, why is that confession sometimes not used in court?
3. Does the Patriot Act reduce our liberties?

Dogs trained to sniff out drugs go down your high school corridors and detect marijuana in some lockers. The school authorities open and search your locker without permission or a court order. You are expelled from school without any hearing. Have your liberties been violated?

Angry at what you consider unfair treatment, you decide to wear a cloth American flag sewn to the seat of your pants, and your fellow students decide to wear black armbands to class to protest how you were treated. The police arrest you for wearing a flag on your seat, and the school punishes your classmates for wearing armbands contrary to school regulations. Have your liberties, or theirs, been violated?

You go into federal court to find out. We cannot be certain how the court would decide the issues in this particular case, but in similar cases in the past the courts have held that school authorities can use dogs to detect drugs in schools and that these officials can conduct a "reasonable" search of you and your effects if they have a "reasonable suspicion" that you are violating a school rule. But they cannot punish your classmates for wearing black armbands, they cannot expel you without a hearing, and the state cannot make it illegal to treat the flag "contemptuously" (by sewing it to the seat of your pants, for example). In 2007, however, the Court allowed a school principal to punish a student for displaying a flag saying "Bong Hits 4 Jesus" that the official felt endorsed drug use during a school-supervised event. So a student's free speech rights (and a school's authority to enforce discipline) now lie somewhere between disgracing a flag (OK) and encouraging drug use (not OK).[1]

AP Photo/Evan Vucci

Your claim that these actions violated your constitutional rights would have astonished the Framers of the Constitution. They thought they had written a document that stated what the federal government *could* do, not one that specified what state governments (such as school systems) *could not* do. And they thought they had created a national government of such limited powers that it was not even necessary to add a list—a bill of rights—stating what that government was forbidden from doing. It would be enough, for example, that the Constitution did not authorize the federal government to censor newspapers; an amendment prohibiting censorship would be superfluous.

The people who gathered in the state ratifying conventions weren't so optimistic. They suspected—rightly, as it turned out—that the federal government might well try to do things it was not authorized to do, and so they insisted that the Bill of Rights be added to the Constitution. But even they never imagined that the Bill of Rights would affect what *state* governments could do. Each state would decide that for itself, in its own constitution. And if by chance the Bill of Rights did apply to the states, surely its guarantees of free speech and freedom from unreasonable searches and seizures would apply to big issues—the freedom to attack the government in a newspaper editorial, for example, or to keep the police from breaking down the door of your home without a warrant. The courts would not be deciding who could wear what kinds of armbands or under what circumstances a school could expel a student.

Civil liberties are the protections the Constitution provides against the abuse of government power by, for example, censoring your speech. Civil rights, to be discussed in the next chapter, usually refers to protecting certain groups, such as women, gays, and African Americans, against discrimination. In practice, however, there is no clear line between civil liberties and civil rights. For example, is the right to an abortion a civil liberty or a civil right? In this chapter, we take a look at free speech, free press, religious freedom, and the rights of the accused. In the next one, we look at discrimination and abortion.

Culture and Civil Liberties

RIGHTS IN CONFLICT

We often think of "civil liberties" as a set of principles that protect the freedoms of all of us all of the time. That is true—up to a point. But in fact, the Constitution and the Bill of Rights contain a list of *competing* rights and duties. That competition becomes obvious when one person asserts one constitutional right or duty and another person asserts a different one. For example:

- Dr. Samuel H. Sheppard of Cleveland, Ohio, asserted his right to have a fair trial on the charge of having murdered his wife. Bob Considine and Walter Winchell, two radio commentators, as well as other reporters, asserted their right to broadcast whatever facts and rumors they heard about Dr. Sheppard and his love life. Two rights in conflict.

- The U.S. government has an obligation to "provide for the common defense" and, in pursuit of that duty, has claimed the right to keep secret certain military and diplomatic information. The *New York Times* claimed the right to publish such secrets as the "Pentagon Papers" without censorship, citing the Constitution's guarantee of freedom of the press. A duty and a right in conflict.

- Carl Jacob Kunz delivered inflammatory anti-Jewish speeches on the street corners of a Jewish neighborhood in New York City, suggesting, among other things, that Jews be "burnt in incinerators." The Jewish people living in that area were outraged. The New York police commissioner revoked Kunz's license to hold public meetings on the streets. When he continued to air his views on the public streets, Kunz was arrested for speaking without a permit. Freedom of speech versus the preservation of public order.

Even a disruptive high school student's right not to be a victim of arbitrary or unjustifiable expulsion is in partial conflict with the school's obligation to maintain an orderly environment in which learning can take place.

Political struggles over civil liberties follow much the same pattern as interest group politics involving economic issues, even though the claims in question are made by individuals. Indeed, there are formal, organized interest groups concerned with civil liberties. The Fraternal Order of the Police complains about restrictions on police powers, whereas the American Civil Liberties Union defends and seeks to enlarge those restrictions. Catholics have pressed for public support of parochial schools; Protestants and Jews have argued against it. Sometimes the opposed groups are entirely private; sometimes one or both are government agencies. Often their clashes end up in the courts. (When the Supreme Court decided the cases given earlier, Sheppard, the *New York Times,* and Kunz all won.[2])

War has usually been the crisis that has restricted the liberty of some minority. For example:

- The Sedition Act was passed in 1798, making it a crime to write, utter, or publish "any false, scandalous, and malicious writing" with the intention of defaming the president, Congress, or the government or of exciting against the government "the hatred of the people." The occasion was a kind of half-war between the United States and France, stimulated by fear in this country of the violence following the French Revolution of 1789. The policy entrepreneurs were Federalist politicians who believed that Thomas Jefferson and his followers were supporters of the French Revolution and would, if they came to power, encourage here the kind of anarchy that seemed to be occurring in France.

- The Espionage and Sedition Acts were passed in 1917–1918, making it a crime to utter false statements that would interfere with the American military, to send through the mails material "advocating or urging treason, insurrection, or forcible resistance to any law of the United States," or to

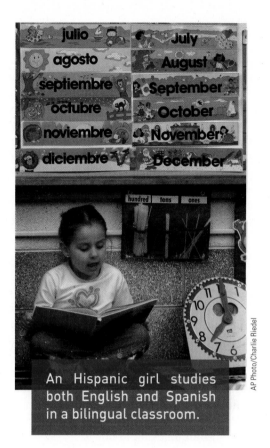

An Hispanic girl studies both English and Spanish in a bilingual classroom.

AP Photo/Charlie Riedel

utter or write any disloyal, profane, scurrilous, or abusive language intended to incite resistance to the United States or to curtail war production. The occasion was World War I; the impetus was the fear that Germans in this country were spies and that radicals were seeking to overthrow the government. Under these laws, more than 2,000 persons were prosecuted (about half were convicted), and thousands of aliens were rounded up and deported. The policy entrepreneur leading this massive crackdown (the so-called Red Scare) was Attorney General A. Mitchell Palmer.

- The Smith Act was passed in 1940, the Internal Security Act in 1950, and the Communist Control Act in 1954. These laws made it illegal to advocate the overthrow of the U.S. government by force or violence (Smith Act), required members of the Communist Party to register with the government (Internal Security Act), and declared the Communist Party to be part of a conspiracy to overthrow the government (Communist Control Act). The occasion was World War II and the Korean War, which, like earlier wars, inspired fears that foreign agents (Nazi and Soviet) were trying to subvert the government. For the latter two laws, the policy entrepreneur was Senator Joseph McCarthy, who attracted a great deal of attention with his repeated (and sometimes inaccurate) claims that Soviet agents were working inside the U.S. government.

These laws had in common an effort to protect the nation from threats, real and imagined, posed by people who claimed to be exercising their freedom to speak, publish, organize, and assemble. In each case, a real threat (a war) led the government to narrow the limits of permissible speech and activity. Almost every time such restrictions were imposed, the Supreme Court was called upon to decide whether Congress (or sometimes state legislatures) had drawn those limits properly. In most instances, the Court tended to uphold the legislatures. But as time passed and the war or crisis ended, popular passions abated and many of the laws proved unimportant.

Though it is uncommon, some use is still made of the sedition laws. In the 1980s, various white supremacists and Puerto Rican nationalists were charged with sedition. In each case, the government alleged that the accused had not only spoken in favor of overthrowing the government but had actually engaged in violent actions such as bombings. Later in this chapter, we shall see how the Court has increasingly restricted the power of Congress and state legislatures to outlaw political speech; to be found guilty of sedition now, it usually is necessary to do something more serious than just talk about it.

CULTURAL CONFLICTS

In the main, the United States was originally the creation of white European Protestants. Blacks were, in most cases, slaves, and American Indians were not citizens. Catholics and Jews in the colonies composed a small minority, and often a persecuted one. The early schools tended to be religious—that is, Protestant—ones, many of them receiving state aid. It is not surprising that under these circumstances a view of America arose that equated "Americanism" with the values and habits of white Anglo-Saxon Protestants.

But immigration to this country brought a flood of new settlers, many of them coming from very different backgrounds (see Figure 5.1). In the mid-19th century, the potato famine led millions of Irish Catholics to migrate here. At the turn of the century, religious persecution and economic disadvantage brought more millions of people, many Catholic or Jewish, from southern and eastern Europe.

In recent decades, political conflict and economic want have led Hispanics (mostly from Mexico but increasingly from all parts of Latin America), Caribbeans, Africans, Middle Easterners, Southeast Asians, and Asians to cross our borders—some

Figure 5.1
Annual Legal Immigration, 1850–2008

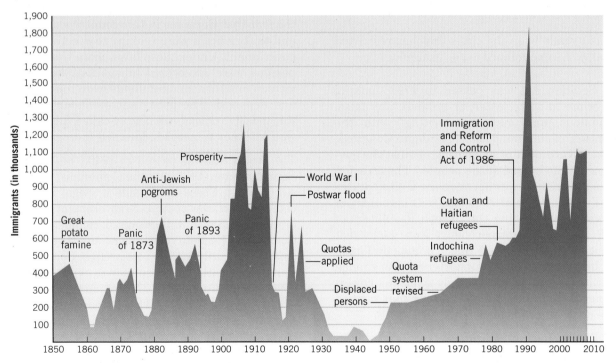

Note: Figures for 1989 and 1990 include persons granted permanent residence under the legalization program of the Immigration and Reform and Control Act of 1986.

Source: Office of Immigration Statistics, *2008 Yearbook of Immigration Statistics.* (Washington, D.C.: Department of Homeland Security, 2009), p. 5.

legally, some illegally. Among them have been Buddhists, Catholics, Muslims, and members of many other religious and cultural groups.

Ethnic, religious, and cultural differences have given rise to different views as to the meaning and scope of certain constitutionally protected freedoms. For example:

- Many Jewish groups find it offensive for a crèche (that is, a scene depicting the birth of Christ in a manger) to be displayed in front of a government building such as city hall at Christmastime, while many Catholics and Protestants regard such displays as an important part of our cultural heritage. Does a religious display on public property violate the First Amendment requirement that the government pass no law "respecting an establishment of religion"?

- Many English-speaking people believe that the public schools ought to teach all students to speak and write English, because the language is part of our nation's cultural heritage. Some Hispanic groups argue that the schools should teach pupils in both English and Spanish, since Spanish is part of the Hispanic cultural heritage. Is bilingual education constitutionally required?

- The Boy Scouts of America refuses to allow homosexual men to become scout leaders even though federal law says that homosexuals may not be the victims of discrimination. Many civil libertarians and homosexuals challenged this policy because it discriminated against gays, while the Boy Scouts defended it because their organization was a private association free to make its own rules. (The Supreme Court in 2000 upheld the Boy Scouts on the grounds of their right to associate freely.)

Even within a given cultural tradition there are important differences of opinion as to the balance between community sensitivities and personal self-expression. To some people the sight of a store carrying pornographic books or a theater showing a pornographic movie is deeply offensive; to others, pornography is offensive but such establishments ought to be tolerated to ensure that laws restricting them do not also restrict politically or artistically important forms of speech; to still others, pornography itself is not especially offensive. What forms of expression are entitled to constitutional protection?

APPLYING THE BILL OF RIGHTS TO THE STATES

For many years after the Constitution was signed and the Bill of Rights was added to it as amendments, the liberties these documents stated applied only to the federal government. The Supreme Court made this clear in a case decided in 1833.[3] Except for Article I which, among other things, banned ex post facto laws and guaranteed the right of habeas corpus, the Constitution was silent on what the states could not do to their residents.

This began to change after the Civil War when new amendments were ratified in order to ban slavery and protect newly freed slaves. The Fourteenth Amendment, ratified in 1868, was the most important addition. It said that no state shall "deprive any person of life, liberty, or property without **due process of law**" (a phrase now known as the "due process clause") and that no state shall "deny to any person within its jurisdiction the **equal protection of the laws**" (a phrase now known as the "equal protection clause").

Beginning in 1897, the Supreme Court started to use these two phrases as a way of applying certain rights to state governments. It first said that no state could take private property without paying just compensation, and then in 1925 held, in the *Gitlow* case, that the federal guarantees of free speech and free press also applied to the states. In 1937, it went much further and said in *Palko v. Connecticut* that certain rights should be applied to the states because, in the Court's words, they "represented the very essence of a scheme of ordered liberty" and were "principles of justice so rooted in the traditions and conscience of our people as to be ranked fundamental."[4]

In these cases, the Supreme Court began the process of **selective incorporation** by which some, but not all, federal rights also applied to the states. But which rights are so "fundamental" that they ought to govern the states? There is no entirely clear answer to this question, but in general the entire Bill of Rights is now applied to the states except for the following:

- The right not to have soldiers forcibly quartered in private homes (Third Amendment)

- The right to be indicted by a grand jury before being tried for a serious crime (Fifth Amendment)

- The right to a jury trial in civil cases (Seventh Amendment)

- The ban on excessive bail and fines (Eighth Amendment)

due process of law Denies the government the right, without due process, to deprive people of life, liberty, and property.

equal protection of the law A standard of equal treatment that must be observed by the government.

selective incorporation Court cases that apply Bill of Rights to states.

RESEARCH FRONTIERS

Does "In Your Face" Television Affect Political Tolerance?

In a representative democracy, constitutional and related legal protections for free speech and other civil liberties ultimately depend on the degree to which average citizens are ready to respect each other's rights and willing to tolerate ideas that the majority dislikes or even despises.

Three separate but related lines of research examine how popular norms relating to political tolerance respecting free speech and other civil liberties arise, persist, and change.

The first and oldest line of research concerns a decades-old disjuncture in public attitudes toward civil liberties: wide majorities favor civil liberties including free speech and assembly, yet only about a third to half favor extending these liberties to groups they strongly dislike.

The second line of research tracks and analyzes changes in public attitudes. For example, in recent decades, there have been successive shifts in public attitudes regarding advocacy for homosexual rights and policies favoring gay rights: tolerance for the expression of homosexual rights has increased steadily; and, in 2009, 59 percent of Americans favored allowing gays to serve openly in the military.

The third line of research attempts to understand more precisely how schooling, the media, and other influences determine mass levels of political toleration and openness to dissent.

One well-established finding here is that, other things equal, more formal schooling is associated with greater political tolerance even toward minority groups that one views as deplorable or even dangerous.

But a newer line of research probes how Americans perceive others whose political views they are strongly inclined to dispute or denounce. For example, through a series of experimental studies, University of Pennsylvania political scientist Diana C. Mutz has examined present-day "television discourse" in relation to whether average citizens' respect and treat their "political foes" as a "legitimate opposition."

As Mutz observes, today much of the political debate carried on television tends to be "highly uncivil in tone," complete with accompanying camera work featuring facial close-ups that "intensify emotional reactions" in the viewing audience.

This televised "in-your-face" politics succeeds in airing oppositional views, but, as Mutz concludes, it also "convinces people that the opposition is even less legitimate than they would have thought without any viewing."

- When, for whatever reasons, average citizens become less willing to perceive even moderate political opponents as legitimate, do they also thereby become less willing to respect or protect civil liberties exercised by citizens they view as "unworthy" or "extreme"? Researchers in various fields are just now asking that question. What is your best guess about what they will find?

- Do you think that newspapers and magazines are less prone to promote "in-your-face" politics than television?

- Do you suppose that "television discourse" used to be less polarizing than it is today?

Source: Diana C. Mutz, "Effects of 'In-Your-Face' Television Discourse on Perceptions of a Legitimate Opposition," *American Political Science Review* 101, November 2007, pp. 623–635; "Opinion About Gays in the Military," Pew Research, March 25, 2009.

The Second Amendment that protects "the right of the people to keep and bear arms" may or may not apply to the states. In 2008, the Supreme Court held for the first time that this amendment did not allow the federal government to ban the private possession of firearms.[5] But the case arose in the District of Columbia, which is governed by federal law. The decision raised two questions: First, will this ban be incorporated, via the Fourteenth Amendment, so that it also applies to state governments? Cases have arisen to test this issue, but as of mid-2009, no decision had been reached. Second, will it still be possible to regulate gun purchases and gun use even if the government cannot ban guns? Based on other court cases, the answer appears to be yes.

Interpreting and Applying the First Amendment

The First Amendment contains the language that has been at issue in most of the cases to which we have thus far referred. It has roughly two parts: one protecting **freedom of expression** ("Congress shall make no law…abridging the freedom of speech, or of the press, or the right of people peaceably to assemble, and to petition the government for a redress of grievances") and the other protecting **freedom of religion** ("Congress shall make no law respecting an establishment of religion; or abridging the free exercise thereof").

SPEECH AND NATIONAL SECURITY

The traditional view of free speech and a free press was expressed by William Blackstone, the great English jurist, in his *Commentaries,* published in 1765. A free press is essential to a free state, he wrote, but the freedom that the press should enjoy is the freedom from **prior restraint**—that is, freedom from censorship, or rules telling a newspaper in advance what it can publish. Once a newspaper has published an article or a person has delivered a speech, that paper or speaker has to take the consequences if what was written or said proves to be "improper, mischievous, or illegal."[6]

The U.S. Sedition Act of 1798 was in keeping with traditional English law. Like it, the act imposed no prior restraint on publishers; it did, however, make them liable to punishment after the fact. The act was an improvement over the English law, however, because unlike the British model, it entrusted the decision to a jury, not a judge, and allowed the defendant to be acquitted if he or she could prove the truth of what had been published. Although several newspaper publishers were convicted under the act, none of these cases reached the Supreme Court. When Jefferson became president in 1801, he pardoned the remaining people who had been convicted under the Sedition Act. Though Jeffersonians objected vehemently to the law, their principal objection was not to the idea of holding newspapers accountable for what they published but to letting the *federal* government do this. Jefferson was perfectly prepared to have the *states* punish what he called the "overwhelming torrent of slander" by means of "a few prosecutions of the most prominent offenders."[7]

It would be another century before the federal government would attempt to define the limits of free speech and writing. Perhaps recalling the widespread opposition to the sweep of the 1798 act, Congress in 1917–1918 placed restrictions not on publications that were critical of the government but only on those that advocated "treason, insurrection, or forcible resistance" to federal laws or attempted to foment disloyalty or mutiny in the armed services.

In 1919, this new law was examined by the Supreme Court when it heard the case of Charles T. Schenck, who had been convicted of violating the Espionage Act because he had mailed circulars to men eligible for the draft, urging them to resist. At issue was the constitutionality of the Espionage Act and, more broadly, the scope of Congress's power to control speech. One view held that the First Amendment prevented Congress from passing *any* law restricting speech; the other held that Congress could punish dangerous speech. For a unanimous Supreme Court, Justice Oliver Wendell Holmes announced a rule by which to settle the matter. It soon became known as the **clear-and-present-danger test:**

> The question in every case is whether the words used are used in such circumstances and are of such a nature as to create a clear and present danger that they will bring about the substantive evils that Congress has a right to prevent.[8]

The Court held that Schenck's leaflets did create such a danger, and so his conviction was upheld. In explaining why, Holmes said that not even the Constitution protects a person who has been "falsely shouting fire in a theatre and causing a panic." In this case things that

---

Landmark Cases

Incorporation

- **Gitlow v. New York (1925):** Supreme Court says the First Amendment applies to states.
- **Palko v. Connecticut (1937):** Supreme Court says that states must observe all "fundamental" liberties.

---

freedom of expression Right of people to speak, publish and assemble.

freedom of religion People shall be free to exercise their religion, and government may not establish a religion.

prior restraint Censorship of a publication.

clear-and-present-danger test Law should not punish speech unless there was a clear and present danger of producing harmful actions.

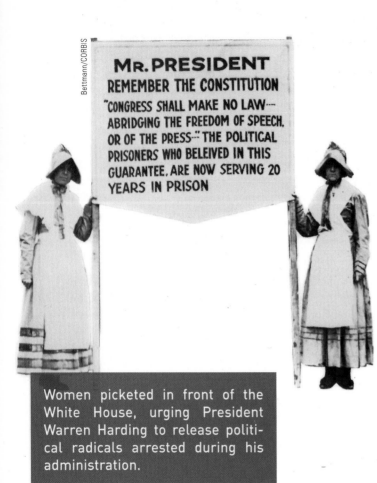

MR. PRESIDENT
REMEMBER THE CONSTITUTION
"CONGRESS SHALL MAKE NO LAW---
ABRIDGING THE FREEDOM OF SPEECH,
OR OF THE PRESS.-" THE POLITICAL
PRISONERS WHO BELEIVED IN THIS
GUARANTEE, ARE NOW SERVING 20
YEARS IN PRISON

Women picketed in front of the White House, urging President Warren Harding to release political radicals arrested during his administration.

The clear-and-present-danger test was a way of balancing the competing demands of free expression and national security. As the memory of World War I and the ensuing Red Scare evaporated, the Court began to develop other tests, ones that shifted the balance more toward free expression. Some of these tests are listed in the box on page 107.

But when a crisis reappears, as it did in World War II and the Korean War, the Court has tended to defer, up to a point, to legislative judgments about the need to protect national security. For example, it upheld the conviction of 11 leaders of the Communist Party for having advocated the violent overthrow of the U.S. government, a violation of the Smith Act of 1940.

This conviction once again raised the hard question of the circumstances under which words can be punished. Hardly anybody would deny that actually *trying* to overthrow the government is a crime; the question is whether *advocating* its overthrow is a crime. In the case of the 11 communist leaders, the Court said that the government did not have to wait to protect itself until "the *putsch* [rebellion] is about to be executed, the plans have been laid and the signal is awaited." Even if the communists were not likely to be successful in their effort, the Court held that specifically advocating violent overthrow could be punished. "In each case," the opinion read, the courts "must ask whether the gravity of the 'evil,' discounted by its improbability, justifies such invasion of free speech as is necessary to avoid the danger."[11]

But as the popular worries about communists began to subside and the membership of the Supreme Court changed, the Court began to tip the balance even farther toward free expression. By 1957, the Court made it clear that for advocacy to be punished, the government would have to show not just that a person believed in the overthrow of the government but also that he or she was using words "calculated to incite" that overthrow.[12]

By 1969, the pendulum had swung to the point where the speech would have to be judged likely to incite "imminent" unlawful action. When Clarence Brandenburg, a Ku Klux Klan leader in Ohio, made a speech before Klan members in which he called for "revengeance" [sic] against blacks and Jews (using racial slurs) and called for a march on Washington, he was arrested and convicted for "advocating" violence. The U.S. Supreme Court reversed the conviction, holding that the First Amendment protects speech that abstractly advocates violence unless that speech will incite or produce "imminent lawless action."[13]

might safely be said in peacetime may be punished in wartime.

The clear-and-present-danger test may have clarified the law, but it kept no one out of jail. Schenck went, and so did the defendants in five other cases in the period 1919–1927, even though during this time Holmes, the author of the test, shifted his position and began writing dissenting opinions in which he urged that the test had not been met and so the defendant should go free.

In 1925, Benjamin Gitlow was convicted of violating New York's sedition law—a law similar to the federal Sedition Act of 1918—by passing out some leaflets. The Supreme Court upheld his conviction but added, as we have seen, a statement that changed constitutional history: freedom of speech and of the press were now among the "fundamental personal rights" protected by the due-process clause of the Fourteenth Amendment from infringements by *state* action.[9] Thereafter, state laws involving speech, the press, and peaceful assembly were struck down by the Supreme Court for being in violation of the freedom-of-expression guarantees of the First Amendment, made applicable to the states by the Fourteenth Amendment.[10]

This means that no matter how offensive or provocative some forms of expression may be, this expression has powerful constitutional protections. In 1977, a group of American Nazis wanted to parade through the streets of Skokie, Illinois, a community with a large Jewish population. The residents, outraged, sought to ban the march. Many feared violence if it occurred. But the lower courts, under prodding from the Supreme Court, held that, noxious and provocative as the anti-Semitic slogans of the Nazis may be, the Nazi party had a constitutional right to speak and parade peacefully.[14]

Similar reasoning led the Supreme Court in 1992 to overturn a Minnesota statute that made it a crime to display symbols or objects, such as a Nazi swastika or a burning cross, that are likely to cause alarm or resentment among an ethnic or racial group, such as Jews or African Americans.[15] On the other hand, if you are convicted of actually hurting someone, you may be given a tougher sentence if it can be shown that you were motivated to assault them by racial or ethnic hatred.[16] To be punished for such a hate crime, your bigotry must result in some direct and physical harm and not just the display of an odious symbol.

What Is Speech?

If most political speaking or writing is permissible, save that which actually incites someone to take illegal actions, what *kinds* of speaking and writing qualify for this broad protection? Though the Constitution says that the legislature may make "no law" abridging freedom of speech or the press, and although some justices have argued that this means literally *no* law, the Court has held that there are at least four forms of speaking and writing that are not automatically granted full constitutional protection: libel, obscenity, symbolic speech, and false advertising.

LIBEL

A **libel** is a written statement that defames the character of another person. (If the statement is oral, it is called a slander.) In some countries, such as England, it is easy to sue another person for libel and to collect. In this country, it is much harder. For one thing, you must show that the libelous statement was false. If it was true, you cannot collect no matter how badly it harmed you.

A beauty contest winner was awarded $14 million (later reduced on appeal) when she proved that *Penthouse* magazine had libeled her. Actress Carol Burnett collected a large sum from a libel

A Ku Klux Klan member uses his constitutional right to free speech to utter "white power" chants in Skokie, Illinois.

Tim Boyle/Newsmakers/Getty Images

suit brought against a gossip newspaper. But when Theodore Roosevelt sued a newspaper for falsely claiming that he was a drunk, the jury awarded him damages of only six cents.[17]

If you are a public figure, it is much harder to win a libel suit. A public figure such as an elected official, an army general, or a well-known celebrity must prove not only that the publication was false and damaging but also that the words were published with "actual malice"—that is, with reckless disregard for their truth or falsity or with knowledge that they were false.[18] Israeli General Ariel Sharon was able to prove that the statements made about him by *Time* magazine were false and damaging but not that they were the result of "actual malice."

OBSCENITY

Obscenity is not protected by the First Amendment. The Court has always held that obscene materials, because they have no redeeming social value and are calculated chiefly to appeal to one's sexual rather than political or literary interests, can be regulated by the state. The problem, of course, arises with the meaning of *obscene*. In the period from 1957 to 1968, the Court decided 13 major cases involving the definition of obscenity, which resulted in 55 separate opinions.[19] Some justices, such as Hugo Black, believed that the First Amendment protected all publications, even wholly obscene ones. Others believed that obscenity deserved no

libel Writing that falsely injures another person.

protection and struggled heroically to define the term. Still others shared the view of former Justice Potter Stewart, who objected to "hard-core pornography" but admitted that the best definition he could offer was "I know it when I see it."[20]

It is unnecessary to review in detail the many attempts by the Court at defining obscenity. The justices have made it clear that nudity and sex are not, by definition, obscene and that they will provide First Amendment protection to anything that has political, literary, or artistic merit, allowing the government to punish only the distribution of "hard-core pornography." Their most recent definition of this is as follows: to be obscene, the work, taken as a whole, must be judged by "the average person applying contemporary community standards" to appeal to the "prurient interest" or to depict "in a patently offensive way, sexual conduct specifically defined by applicable state law" and to lack "serious literary, artistic, political, or scientific value."[21]

After Albany, Georgia, decided that the movie *Carnal Knowledge* was obscene by contemporary local standards, the Supreme Court overturned the distributor's conviction on the grounds that the authorities in Albany failed to show that the film depicted "patently offensive hard-core sexual conduct."[22]

It is easy to make sport of the problems the Court has faced in trying to decide obscenity cases (one conjures up images of black-robed justices leafing through the pages of *Hustler* magazine, taking notes), but these problems reveal, as do other civil liberties cases, the continuing problem of balancing competing claims. One part of the community wants to read or see whatever it wishes; another part wants to protect private acts from public degradation. The first part cherishes liberty above all; the second values decency above liberty. The former fears that *any* restriction on literature will lead to *pervasive* restrictions; the latter believes that reasonable people can distinguish (or reasonable laws can require them to distinguish) between patently offensive and artistically serious work.

Anyone strolling today through an "adult" bookstore must suppose that no restrictions at all exist on the distribution of pornographic works. This condition does not arise simply from the doctrines of the Court. Other factors operate as well, including the priorities of local law enforcement officials, the political climate of the community, the procedures that must be followed to bring a viable court case, the clarity and workability of state and local laws on the subject, and the difficulty of changing the behavior of many people by prosecuting one person.

The current view of the Court is that localities can decide for themselves whether to tolerate hard-core pornography; but if they choose not to, they must meet some fairly strict constitutional tests.

The protections given by the Court to expressions of sexual or erotic interest have not been limited to books, magazines, or films. Almost any form of visual or auditory communication can be considered "speech" and thus protected by the First Amendment. In one case, even nude dancing was given protection as a form of "speech,"[23] although in 1991 the Court held that nude dancing was only "marginally" within the purview of First Amendment protections, and so it upheld an Indiana statute that banned *totally* nude dancing.[24]

Of late some feminist organizations have attacked pornography on the grounds that it exploits and degrades women. They persuaded Indianapolis to pass an ordinance that defined pornography as portrayals of the "graphic, sexually explicit subordination of women" and allowed people to sue the producers of such material. Sexually explicit portrayals of women in positions of equality were not defined as pornography. The Court disagreed. In 1986, it affirmed a lower-court ruling that such an ordinance was a violation of the First Amendment because it represented a legislative preference for one form of expression (women in positions of equality) over another (women in positions of subordination).[25]

One constitutionally permissible way to limit the spread of pornographic materials has been to establish rules governing where in a city they can be sold. When one city adopted a zoning ordinance prohibiting an "adult" movie theater from locating within 1,000 feet of any church, school, park, or residential area, the Court upheld the ordinance, noting that the purpose of the law was not to regulate speech but to regulate the use of land. And in any case, the adult theaters still had much of the city's land area in which to find a location.[26]

With the advent of the Internet, it has become more difficult for the government to regulate obscenity. The Internet spans the globe. It offers an amazing variety of materials—some educational, some entertaining, some sexually explicit. But it is difficult to apply the Supreme Court's standard for judging whether sexual material is obscene—the "average person" applying "contemporary community standards"—to the Internet, because there is no easy way to tell what "the community" is. Is it the place where the recipient lives or the place where the material originates? And since no one is in charge of the Internet, who can

How Things Work

Testing Restrictions on Expression

The Supreme Court has employed various standards and tests to decide whether a restriction on freedom of expression is constitutionally permissible.

1. **Preferred position** The right of free expression, though not absolute, occupies a higher, or more preferred, position than many other constitutional rights, such as property rights. This is still a controversial rule; nonetheless, the Court always approaches a restriction on expression skeptically.

2. **Prior restraint** With scarcely any exceptions, the Court will not tolerate a prior restraint on expression, such as censorship, even when it will allow subsequent punishment of improper expressions (such as libel).

3. **Imminent danger** Punishment for uttering inflammatory sentiments will be allowed only if there is an imminent danger that the utterances will incite an unlawful act.

4. **Neutrality** Any restriction on speech, such as a requirement that parades or demonstrations not disrupt other people in the exercise of their rights, must be neutral—that is, it must not favor one group more than another.

5. **Clarity** If you must obtain a permit to hold a parade, the law must set forth clear (as well as neutral) standards to guide administrators in issuing that permit. Similarly, a law punishing obscenity must contain a clear definition of obscenity.

6. **Least-restrictive means** If it is necessary to restrict the exercise of one right to protect the exercise of another, the restriction should employ the least-restrictive means to achieve its end. For example, if press coverage threatens a person's right to a fair trial, the judge may only do what is minimally necessary to that end, such as transferring the case to another town rather than issuing a "gag order."

Cases cited, by item: (1) *United States v. Carolene Products,* 304 U.S. 144 (1938). (2) *Near v. Minnesota,* 283 U.S. 697 (1931). (3) *Brandenburg v. Ohio,* 395 U.S. 444 (1969). (4) *Kunz v. New York,* 340 U.S. 290 (1951). (5) *Hynes v. Mayor and Council of Oradell,* 425 U.S. 610 (1976). (6) *Nebraska Press Association v. Stuart,* 427 U.S. 539 (1976).

be held responsible for controlling offensive material? Since anybody can send anything to anybody else without knowing the age or location of the recipient, how can the Internet protect children? When Congress tried to ban obscene, indecent, or "patently offensive" materials from the Internet, the Supreme Court struck down the law as unconstitutional. The Court went even further with child pornography. Though it has long held that child pornography is illegal even if it is not obscene because of the government's interest in protecting children, it would not let Congress ban pornography involving computer-designed children. Under the 1996 law, it would be illegal to display computer simulations of children engaged in sex even if no real children were involved. The Court said "no." It held that Congress could not ban "virtual" child pornography without violating the First Amendment because, in its view, the law might bar even harmless depictions of children and sex (for example, in a book on child psychology).[27]

SYMBOLIC SPEECH

You cannot ordinarily claim that an illegal act should be protected because that action is meant to convey a political message. For example, if you burn your draft card in protest against the foreign policy of the United States, you can be punished for the illegal act (burning the card), even if your intent was to communicate your beliefs. The Court reasoned that giving such **symbolic speech** the same protection as real speech would open the door to permitting all manner of illegal actions—murder, arson, rape—if the perpetrator meant thereby to send a message.[28]

On the other hand, a statute that makes it illegal to burn the American flag is an unconstitutional infringement of free speech.[29] Why is there a difference between a draft card and the flag? The Court argues that the government has a right to run a military draft and so can

symbolic speech An act that conveys a political message.

Bettmann/CORBIS

"Symbolic speech": when young men burned their draft cards during the 1960s to protest the Vietnam War, the Supreme Court ruled that it was an illegal act for which they could be punished.

protect draft cards, even if this incidentally restricts speech. But the only motive that the government has in banning flag-burning is to restrict this form of speech, and that would make such a restriction improper.

The American people were outraged by the flag-burning decision, and in response the House and Senate passed by huge majorities (380 to 38 and 91 to 9) a law making it a federal crime to burn the flag. But the Court struck this law down as unconstitutional.[30] Now that it was clear that only a constitutional amendment could make flag-burning illegal, Congress was asked to propose one. But it would not. Earlier members of the House and Senate had supported a law banning flag-burning with over 90 percent of their votes, but when asked to make that law a constitutional amendment they could not muster the necessary two-thirds majorities. The reason is that Congress is much more reluctant to amend the Constitution than to pass new laws. Several members decided that flag-burning was wrong, but not so wrong or so common as to justify an amendment.

Commercial and Youthful Speech

If people have a right to speak and publish, do corporations, interest groups, and children have the same right? By and large the answer is yes, though there are some exceptions.

When the attorney general of Massachusetts tried to prevent the First National Bank of Boston from spending money to influence votes in a local election, the Court stepped in and blocked him. The Court held that a corporation, like a person, has certain First Amendment rights. Similarly, when the federal government tried to limit the spending of a group called Massachusetts Citizens for Life (an antiabortion organization), the Court held that such organizations have First Amendment rights.[31] The Court has also told states that they cannot forbid liquor stores to advertise their prices and informed federal authorities that they cannot prohibit casinos from plugging gambling.[32]

When the California Public Utility Commission tried to compel one of the utilities it regulates, the Pacific Gas and Electric Company, to enclose in its monthly bills to customers statements written by groups attacking the utility, the Supreme Court blocked the agency, saying that forcing it to disseminate political statements violated the firm's free speech rights. "The identity of the speaker is not decisive in determining whether speech is protected," the Court said. "Corporations and other associations, like individuals, contribute to the 'discussion, debate, and the dissemination of information and ideas' that the First Amendment seeks to foster." In this case, the right to speak includes the choice of what *not* to say.[33]

Even though corporations have some First Amendment rights, the government can place more limits on commercial than on noncommercial speech. The legislature can place restrictions on advertisements for cigarettes, liquor, and gambling; it can even regulate advertising for some less harmful products provided that the regulations are narrowly tailored and serve a substantial public interest.[34] If the regulations are too broad or do not serve a clear interest, then ads are entitled to some constitutional protection. For example, the states cannot bar lawyers from advertising or accountants from personally soliciting clients.[35]

A big exception to the free-speech rights of corporations and labor unions groups was imposed by the McCain-Feingold campaign finance reform law passed in 2002. Many groups, ranging from the American Civil Liberties Union and the AFL-CIO to the National Rifle Association and the Chamber of Commerce, felt that the law banned legitimate speech. Under its terms, organizations could not pay for "electioneering communications" on radio or television that "refer" to candidates for federal office within 60 days before the election. But the Supreme Court struck down these arguments,

Landmark Cases

Free Speech and Free Press

- **Schenck v. United States (1919):** Speech may be punished if it creates a clear-and-present-danger test of illegal acts.

- **Chaplinksy v. New Hampshire (1942):** "Fighting words" are not protected by the First Amendment.

- **New York Times v. Sullivan (1964):** To libel a public figure, there must be "actual malice."

- **Tinker v. Des Moines (1969):** Public school students may wear armbands to class protesting against America's war in Vietnam when such display does not disrupt classes.

- **Miller v. California (1973):** Obscenity defined as appealing to prurient interests of an average person with materials that lack literary, artistic, political, or scientific value.

- **Texas v. Johnson (1989):** There may not be a law to ban flag-burning.

- **Reno v. ACLU (1997):** A law that bans sending "indecent" material to minors over the Internet is unconstitutional because "indecent" is too vague and broad a term.

- **McConnell v. Federal Election Commission (2003):** Upholds 2002 campaign finance reform law.

- **FEC v. Wisconsin Right to Life (2007):** Prohibits campaign finance reform law from banning political advocacy.

upholding the law in *McConnell v. Federal Election Commission.* The Court said ads that only mentioned but did not "expressly advocate" a candidate were ways of influencing the election. Some dissenting opinion complained that a Court that had once given free speech protection to nude dancing ought to give it to political speech.[36] In 2007, the Court held that the McCain-Feingold law could not be used to prevent an organization from running an ad urging people to write to Senator Feingold right before a primary election in which he was a candidate, urging him to vote for certain judicial nominees. Since it said nothing about supporting or opposing him, this ad was "issue advocacy" and was protected by the First Amendment.

Under certain circumstances, young people may have less freedom of expression than adults. In 1988, the Supreme Court held that the principal of Hazelwood High School could censor articles appearing in the student-edited newspaper. The newspaper was published using school funds and was part of a journalism class. The principal ordered the deletion of stories dealing with student pregnancies and the impact of parental divorce on students. The student editors sued, claiming their First Amendment rights had been violated. The Court agreed that students do not "shed their constitutional rights to freedom of speech or expression at the schoolhouse gate" and that they cannot be punished for expressing on campus their personal views. But students do not have exactly the same rights as adults if the exercise of those rights impedes the educational mission of the school. Students may lawfully say things on campus, as individuals, that they cannot say if they are part of school-sponsored activities, such as plays or school-run newspapers, that are part of the curriculum. School-sponsored activities can be controlled so long as the controls are "reasonably related to legitimate pedagogical concerns."[37]

Church and State

Everybody knows, correctly, the language of the First Amendment that protects freedom of speech and the press, though most people are not aware of how complex the legal interpretations of these provisions have become. But many people also believe, wrongly, that the language of the First Amendment clearly requires the "separation of church and state." It does not.

What that amendment actually says is quite different and maddeningly unclear. It has two parts. The first, often referred to as the **free-exercise clause,** states that Congress shall make no law prohibiting the "free exercise" of religion. The second, which is called the **establishment clause,** states that Congress shall make no law "respecting an establishment of religion."

THE FREE-EXERCISE CLAUSE

The free-exercise clause is the clearer of the two, though by no means is it lacking in ambiguity. It obviously means that Congress cannot pass a law prohibiting Catholics from

free-exercise clause First Amendment requirement that law cannot prevent free exercise of religion.

establishment clause First Amendment ban on laws "respecting an establishment of religion."

celebrating Mass, requiring Baptists to become Episcopalians, or preventing Jews from holding a bar mitzvah. Since the First Amendment has been applied to the states via the due-process clause of the Fourteenth Amendment, it means that state governments cannot pass such laws either. In general, the courts have treated religion like speech: you can pretty much do or say what you want so long as it does not cause some serious harm to others.

Even some laws that do not appear on their face to apply to churches may be unconstitutional if their enforcement imposes particular burdens on churches or greater burdens on some churches than others. For example, a state cannot apply a license fee on door-to-door solicitors when the solicitor is a Jehovah's Witness selling religious tracts.[38] By the same token, the courts ruled that the city of Hialeah, Florida, cannot ban animal sacrifices by members of an Afro-Caribbean religion called Santeria. Since killing animals generally is not illegal (if it were, there could be no hamburgers or chicken sandwiches served in Hialeah's restaurants, and rat traps would be unlawful), the ban in this case was clearly directed against a specific religion and hence was unconstitutional.[39]

Having the right to exercise your religion freely does not mean, however, that you are exempt from laws binding other citizens, even when the law goes against your religious beliefs. A man cannot have more than one wife, even if (as once was the case with Mormons) polygamy is thought desirable on religious grounds.[40] For religious reasons, you may oppose being vaccinated or having blood transfusions, but if the state passes a compulsory vaccination law or orders that a blood transfusion be given to a sick child, the courts will not block them on grounds of religious liberty.[41] Similarly, if you belong to an Indian tribe that uses a drug, peyote, in religious ceremonies, you cannot claim that your freedom was abridged if the state decides to ban the use of peyote, provided the law applies equally to all.[42] Since airports have a legitimate need for tight security measures, begging can be outlawed in them even if some of the people doing the begging are part of a religious group (in this case, the Hare Krishnas).[43]

Unfortunately, some conflicts between religious belief and public policy are even more difficult to settle. What if you believe on religious grounds that war is immoral? The draft laws have always exempted a conscientious objector from military duty, and the Court has upheld such exemptions. But the Court has gone further: it has said that people cannot be drafted even if they do not believe in a Supreme

Public schools cannot organize prayers, but private ones can.

Judy Griesedieck/Time & Life Pictures/Getty Images

Being or belong to any religious tradition, so long as their "consciences, spurred by deeply held moral, ethical, or religious beliefs, would give them no rest or peace if they allowed themselves to become part of an instrument of war."[44] Do exemptions on such grounds create an opportunity for some people to evade the draft because of their political preferences? In trying to answer such questions, the courts often have had to try to define a religion—no easy task.

And even when there is no question about your membership in a bona fide religion, the circumstances under which you may claim exemption from laws that apply to everybody else are not really clear. What if you, a member of the Seventh-Day Adventists, are fired by your employer for refusing on religious grounds to work on Saturday, and then it turns out that you cannot collect unemployment insurance because you refuse to take an available job—one that also requires you to work on Saturday? Or what if you are a member of the Amish sect, which refuses, contrary to state law, to send its children to public schools past the eighth grade? The Court has ruled that the state must pay you unemployment compensation and cannot require you to send your children to public schools beyond the eighth grade.[45]

These last two decisions, and others like them, show that even the "simple" principle of freedom of religion gets complicated in practice and can lead to the courts' giving, in effect, preference to members of one church over members of another.

THE ESTABLISHMENT CLAUSE

What in the world did the members of the First Congress mean when they wrote into the First

Amendment language prohibiting Congress from making a law "respecting" an "establishment" of religion? The Supreme Court has more or less consistently interpreted this vague phrase to mean that the Constitution erects a "wall of separation" between church and state.

That phrase, so often quoted, is not in the Bill of Rights nor in the debates in the First Congress that drafted the Bill of Rights; it comes from the pen of Thomas Jefferson, who was opposed to having the Church of England as the established church of his native Virginia. (At the time of the Revolutionary War, there were established churches—that is, official, state-supported churches—in at least eight of the 13 former colonies.) But it is not clear that Jefferson's view was the majority view.

During much of the debate in Congress, the wording of this part of the First Amendment was quite different and much plainer than what finally emerged. Up to the last minute, the clause was intended to read "no religion shall be established by law" or "no national religion shall be established." The meaning of those words seems quite clear: whatever the states may do, the federal government cannot create an official, national religion or give support to one religion in preference to another.[46]

But Congress instead adopted an ambiguous phrase, and so the Supreme Court had to decide what it meant. It has declared that these words do not simply mean "no national religion" but mean as well no government involvement with religion at all, even on a nonpreferential basis. They mean, in short, erecting a "wall of separation" between church and state.[47] Though the interpretation of the establishment clause remains a topic of great controversy among judges and scholars, the Supreme Court has more or less consistently adopted this **wall-of-separation** principle.

Its first statement of this interpretation was in 1947. The case involved a New Jersey town that reimbursed parents for the costs of transporting their children to school, including parochial (in this case Catholic) schools. The Court decided that this reimbursement was constitutional, but it made it clear that the establishment clause of the First Amendment applied (via the Fourteenth Amendment) to the states and that it meant, among other things, that the government cannot require a person to profess a belief or disbelief in any religion; it cannot aid one religion, some religions, or all religions; and it cannot spend any tax money, however small the amount might be, in support of any religious activities or institutions.[48]

The reader may wonder, in view of the Court's reasoning, why it allowed the town to pay for busing children to Catholic schools. The answer it gave is that busing is a religiously neutral activity, akin to providing fire and police protection to Catholic schools. Busing, available to public- and private-school children alike, does not breach the wall of separation.

Since 1947, the Court has applied the wall-of-separation theory to strike down as unconstitutional most efforts to have any form of prayer in public schools, even if it is nonsectarian,[49] voluntary,[50] or limited to reading a passage of the Bible.[51] Since 1992, it has even been unconstitutional for a public school to ask a rabbi or minister to offer a prayer—an invocation or a benediction—at the school's graduation ceremony. Since 2000, it has been unconstitutional for a student to lead a prayer at a public high school football game because it was done "over the school's public address system, by a speaker representing the student body, under the supervision of the school faculty, and pursuant to school policy."[52] The Court made it clear, however, that public school students could pray voluntarily during school provided that the school or the government did not sponsor that prayer. Moreover, the Court has held that laws prohibiting teaching the theory of evolution or requiring giving equal time to "creationism" (the biblical doctrine that God created mankind) are religiously inspired and thus unconstitutional.[53] A public school may not allow its pupils to take time out from their regular classes for religious instruction if this occurs within the schools, though "released-time" instruction is all right if it is done outside the public school building.[54] The school prayer decisions in particular have provoked a storm of controversy, but efforts to get Congress to propose to the states a constitutional amendment authorizing such prayers have failed.

Almost as controversial have been Court-imposed restrictions on public aid to parochial schools, though here the wall-of-separation principle has not been used to forbid any and all forms of aid. For example, it is permissible for the federal government to provide aid for constructing buildings on denominational (as well as nondenominational) college campuses[55] and for state governments to loan free textbooks to parochial-school pupils,[56] grant tax-exempt status to parochial schools,[57] allow parents of parochial-school children to deduct

wall of separation
Court ruling that government cannot be involved with religion.

their tuition payments on a state's income tax returns,[58] and pay for computers and a deaf child's sign language interpreter at private and religious schools.[59] But the government cannot pay a salary supplement to teachers who teach secular subjects in parochial schools,[60] reimburse parents for the cost of parochial-school tuition,[61] supply parochial schools with services such as counseling,[62] give money with which to purchase instructional materials, require that "creationism" be taught in public schools, or create a special school district for Hasidic Jews.[63]

The Court sometimes changes its mind on these matters. In 1985, it said the states could not send teachers into parochial schools to teach remedial courses for needy children, but 12 years later it decided they could. "We no longer presume," the Court wrote, "that public employees will inculcate religion simply because they happen to be in a sectarian environment."[64]

Perhaps the most important establishment-clause decision in recent times was the Court ruling that vouchers can be used to pay for children being educated at religious and other private schools. The case began in Cleveland, Ohio, where the state offered money to any family (especially poor ones) whose children attended a school that had done so badly that it was under a federal court order requiring it to be managed directly by the state superintendent of schools. The money, a voucher, could be used to send a child to any other public or private school, including one run by a religious group. The Court held that this plan did not violate the establishment clause because the aid went, not to the school, but to the families who were to choose a school.[65]

If you find it confusing to follow the twists and turns of Court policy in this area, you are not alone. The wall-of-separation principle has not been easy to apply, and the Court has begun to alter its position on church-state matters. The Court has tried to sort out the confusion by developing a three-part test to decide under what circumstances government involvement in religious activities is improper.[66] That involvement is constitutional if it meets these tests:

1. It has a secular purpose.

2. Its primary effect neither advances nor inhibits religion.

3. It does not foster an excessive government entanglement with religion.

No sooner had the test been developed than the Court decided that it was all right for the government of Pawtucket, Rhode Island, to erect a Nativity scene as part of a Christmas display in a local park. But five years later, it said Pittsburgh could not put a Nativity scene in front of the courthouse but could display a menorah (a Jewish symbol of Chanukah) next to a Christmas tree and a sign extolling liberty. The Court claimed that the crèche had to go (because, being too close to the courthouse, a government endorsement was implied) but the menorah could stay (because, being next to a Christmas tree, it would not lead people to think that Pittsburgh was endorsing Judaism).

When the Ten Commandments are displayed in or near a public building, a deeply divided Court has made some complicated distinctions. It held that it was unconstitutional for two Kentucky counties to put up the Ten Commandments in their courthouses because, the Court decided, the purpose was religious. It did no good for one Kentucky courthouse to surround the Ten Commandments with displays of the Declaration of Independence and the Star Spangled Banner so as to make the Commandments part of America's political heritage. The Court said it was still a religious effort, even though it noted that there was a frieze containing Moses in the Supreme Court's own building. (This, the opinion held, was not religious.) But when the Ten Commandments was put up outside the Texas state capitol, this was upheld. The justice, Stephen Breyer, who changed from opposing the Kentucky display to favoring the Texas one, said that in Texas the Commandments now revealed a secular message and, besides, nobody had sued to end this display for 40 years after the Commandments were erected.[67]

Confused? It gets worse. Though the Court has struck down prayer in public schools, it has upheld prayer in Congress (since 1789, the House and Senate open each session with a prayer).[68] A public school cannot have a chaplain, but the armed services can. The Court has said that the government cannot "advance" religion, but it has not objected to the printing of the phrase "In God We Trust" on the back of every dollar bill.

It is obvious that despite its efforts to set forth clear rules governing church-state relations, the Court's actual decisions are hard to summarize. It is deeply divided—some would say deeply confused—on these matters, and so the efforts to define the "wall of separation" will continue to prove to be as difficult as the Court's earlier efforts to decide what is interstate and what is local commerce (see Chapter 3).

How Would You Decide?

Suppose you are on the Supreme Court. In each of the actual cases summarized below, you are asked to decide whether the First Amendment to the Constitution permits or prohibits a particular action. What would be your decision? (How the Supreme Court actually decided is given on page 116.)

Case 1: Jacksonville, Florida, passed a city ordinance prohibiting drive-in movies from showing films containing nudity if the screen was visible to passersby on the street. A movie theater manager protested, claiming he had a First Amendment right to show such films, even if they could be seen from the street. Who is correct?

Case 2: Dr. Benjamin Spock wanted to enter Fort Dix Military Reservation in New Jersey to pass out campaign literature and discuss issues with service personnel. The military denied him access on grounds that regulations prohibit partisan campaigning on military bases. Who is correct?

Case 3: A town passed an ordinance forbidding the placing of "For Sale" or "Sold" signs in front of homes in racially changing neighborhoods. The purpose was to reduce "white flight" and panic selling. A realty firm protested, claiming its freedom of speech was being abridged. Who is correct?

Case 4: A girl in Georgia was raped and died. A local television station broadcast the name of the girl, having obtained it from court records. Her father sued, claiming his family's right to privacy had been violated, and pointed to a Georgia law that made it a crime to broadcast the name of a rape victim. The television station claimed that it had a right under the First Amendment to broadcast the name. Who is correct?

Case 5: Florida passed a law giving a political candidate the right to equal space in a newspaper that had published attacks on him. A newspaper claimed that this violated the freedom of the press to publish what it wants. Who is correct?

Case 6: Zacchini is a "human cannonball" whose entire fifteen-second act was filmed and broadcast by an Ohio television station. Zacchini sued the station, claiming his earning power had been reduced by the film because the station showed for free what he charges people to see at county fairs. The station replied that it had a First Amendment right to broadcast such events. Who is correct?

Crime and Due Process

Whereas the central problem in interpreting the religion clauses of the First Amendment has been to decide what they mean, the central problems in interpreting those parts of the Bill of Rights that affect people accused of a crime have been to decide not only what they mean but also how to put them into effect. It is not obvious what constitutes an "unreasonable search," but even if we settle that question, we still must decide how best to protect people against such searches in ways that do not unduly hinder criminal investigations.

There are at least two ways to provide that protection. One is to let the police introduce in court evidence relevant to the guilt or innocence of a person, no matter how it was obtained and then, after the case is settled, punish the police officer (or his or her superiors) if the evidence was gathered improperly (for example, by an unreasonable search). The other way is to exclude improperly gathered evidence from the trial in the first place, even if it is relevant to determining the guilt or innocence of the accused.

Most democratic nations, including England, use the first method; the United States uses the second. Because of this, many of the landmark cases decided by the Supreme Court have been bitterly controversial. Opponents of these decisions have argued that a guilty person should not go free just because the police officer blundered, especially if the mistake was minor. Supporters rejoin that there is no way to punish errant police officers effectively other than by excluding tainted evidence; moreover, nobody should be convicted of a crime except by evidence that is above reproach.[69]

Landmark Cases

Religious Freedom

- **Pierce v. Society of Sisters (1925):** Though states may require public education, they may not require that students attend only public schools.

- **Everson v. Board of Education (1947):** The wall-of-separation principle is announced.

- **Zorauch v. Clauson (1952):** States may allow students to be released from public schools to attend religious instruction.

- **Engel v. Vitale (1962):** There may not be a prayer, even a nondenominational one, in public schools.

- **Lemon v. Kurtzman (1971):** Three tests are described for deciding whether the government is improperly involved with religion.

- **Lee v. Weisman (1992):** Public schools may not have clergy lead prayers at graduation ceremonies.

- **Santa Fe Independent School District v. Doe (2000):** Students may not lead prayers before the start of a football game at a public school.

- **Zelman v. Simmons-Harris, (2002):** Voucher plan to pay school bills is upheld.

The Threat Operations Center at the National Security Agency in Fort Meade, Virginia.

JASON REED/Reuters/Landov

THE EXCLUSIONARY RULE

The American method relies on what is called the **exclusionary rule.** That rule holds that evidence gathered in violation of the Constitution cannot be used in a trial. The rule has been used to implement two provisions of the Bill of Rights—the right to be free from unreasonable searches and seizures (Fourth Amendment) and the right not to be compelled to give evidence against oneself (Fifth Amendment).*

exclusionary rule
Improperly gathered evidence may not be introduced in a criminal trial.

*We shall consider here only two constitutional limits—those bearing on searches and confessions. Thus we will omit many other important constitutional provisions affecting criminal cases, such as rules governing wiretapping, prisoner rights, the right to bail and to a jury trial, the bar on ex post facto laws, the right to be represented by a lawyer in court, the ban on "cruel and unusual" punishment, and the rule against double jeopardy.

Not until 1949 did the Supreme Court consider whether to apply the exclusionary rule to the states. In a case decided that year, the Court made it clear that the Fourth Amendment prohibited the police from carrying out unreasonable searches and obtaining improper confessions but held that it was not necessary to use the exclusionary rule to enforce those prohibitions. It noted that other nations did not require that evidence improperly gathered had to be excluded from a criminal trial. The Court said that the local police should not improperly gather and use evidence, but if they did, the remedy was to sue the police department or punish the officer.[70]

But in 1961, the Supreme Court changed its mind about the use of the exclusionary rule. It all began when the Cleveland police broke into the home of Dollree Mapp in search of illegal drugs, and not finding them, arrested her for possessing some obscene pictures found there. The Court held that this was an unreasonable search and seizure because the police had not obtained a search warrant, though they had had ample time to do so. Furthermore, such illegally gathered evidence could not be used in the trial of Mapp.[71] Beginning with this case—*Mapp v. Ohio*—the Supreme Court required the use of the exclusionary rule as a way of enforcing a variety of constitutional guarantees.

SEARCH AND SEIZURE

After the Court decided to exclude improperly gathered evidence, the next problem was to decide evidence was improper. What happened to Dollree Mapp was an easy case: hardly anybody argued that it was reasonable for the police to break into someone's home without a warrant, ransack their belongings, and take whatever they could find that

WHAT WOULD YOU DO?

MEMORANDUM

To: *Rebecca Saikia, Supreme Court justice*

From: *David Wilson, law clerk*

Subject: *Patriot Act and libraries*

The Patriot Act allows the FBI to seek the records of possible terrorists from banks, businesses, and libraries. Many libraries claim this will harm the constitutional rights of Americans. You support these rights, but are also aware of the need to protect national security.

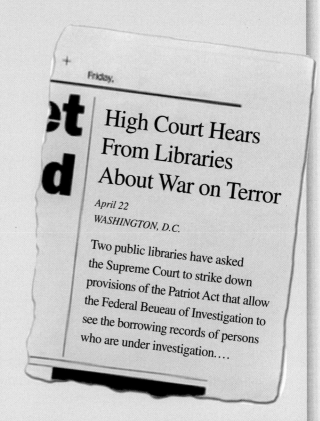

Friday,

High Court Hears From Libraries About War on Terror

April 22
WASHINGTON, D.C.

Two public libraries have asked the Supreme Court to strike down provisions of the Patriot Act that allow the Federal Beueau of Investigation to see the borrowing records of persons who are under investigation....

Arguments supporting the Patriot Act:

1. The Patriot Act does not target individuals who have not violated a criminal law and who do not threaten human life.

2. For the FBI to collect information about borrowers, it must first obtain permission from a federal judge.

3. Terrorists may use libraries to study and plan activities that threaten national security.

Arguments against the Patriot Act:

1. Freedom of speech and expression are fundamental constitutional guarantees that should not be infringed.

2. The law might harm groups engaged in peaceful protests.

3. The law allows the government to delay notifying people that their borrowing habits are being investigated.

Your decision:

Uphold this provision _____   Overturn this provision _____

How the Court Decided

The United States Supreme Court answered the questions on page 113 in the following ways:

Case 1: The drive-in movie won. The Supreme Court, 6–3, decided that the First Amendment protects the right to show nudity; it is up to the unwilling viewer on the public streets to avert his or her eyes.

Erznoznik v. Jacksonville,
422 U.S. 205 (1975)

Case 2: The military won. The Supreme Court, 6–2, decided that military reservations are not like public streets or parks, and thus civilians can be excluded from them, especially if such exclusion prevents the military from appearing to be the handmaiden of various political causes.

Greer v. Spock,
424 U.S. 828 (1976)

Case 3: The realty firm won. The Supreme Court, 8–0, decided that the First Amendment prohibits the banning of signs, even of a commercial nature, without a strong, legitimate state interest. Banning the signs would not obviously reduce "white flight," and the government has no right to withhold information from citizens for fear that they will act unwisely.

Linmark Associates, Inc. v. Willingboro,
431 U.S. 85 (1977)

Case 4: The television station won. The Court, 8–1, decided that the First Amendment protects the right to broadcast the names of rape victims obtained from public (that is, court) records.

Cox Broadcasting Corp. v. Cohn,
420 U.S. 469 (1975)

Case 5: The newspaper won. The Supreme Court decided unanimously that the First Amendment prohibits the state from intruding into the function of editors.

Miami Herald Publishing Co. v. Tornillo,
418 U.S. 241 (1974)

Case 6: Zacchini, the human cannonball, won. The Supreme Court, 5–4, decided that broadcasting the entire act without the performer's consent jeopardized his means of livelihood, even though the First Amendment would guarantee the right of the station to broadcast newsworthy facts about the act.

Zacchini v. Scripps-Howard Broadcasting Co.,
433 U.S. 562 (1977)

---

might be incriminating. But that left a lot of hard choices still to be made.

When can the police search you without it being unreasonable? Under two circumstances—when they have a search warrant and when they have lawfully arrested you. A **search warrant** is an order from a judge authorizing the search of a place; the order must describe what is to be searched and seized, and the judge can issue it only if he or she is persuaded by the police that good reason (**probable cause**) exists to believe that a crime has been committed and that the evidence bearing on that crime will be found at a certain location. (The police can also search a building if the occupant gives them permission.)

In addition, you can be searched if the search occurs when you are lawfully arrested. When can you be arrested? You can be arrested if a judge has issued an arrest warrant for you, if you commit a crime in the presence of a police officer, or if the officer has probable cause to believe you have committed a serious crime (usually a felony). If you are arrested and no search warrant has been issued, the police, and not a judge, decide what they can search. What rules should they follow?

In trying to answer that question, the courts have elaborated a set of rules that are complex, subject to frequent change, and quite controversial. In general the police, after arresting you, can search:

search warrant A judge's order authorizing a search.

probable cause Reasonable cause for issuing a search warrant or making an arrest; more than mere suspicion.

- You

- Things in plain view

- Things or places under your immediate control

As a practical matter, things "in plain view" or "under your immediate control" mean the room in which you are arrested but not other rooms of the house.[72] If the police want to search the rest of your house or a car parked in your driveway, they will first have to go to a judge to obtain a search warrant. But if the police arrest a college student on campus for drinking under age and then accompany that student back to his or her dormitory room so that the student can get proof that he or she was old enough to drink, the police can seize drugs in plain view in that room.[73] And if marijuana is growing in plain view in an open field, the police can enter and search that field even though it is fenced off with a locked gate and a "No Trespassing" sign.[74]

But what if you are arrested while driving your car—how much of it can the police search? The answer to that question has changed almost yearly. In 1979, the Court ruled that the police could not search a suitcase taken from a car of an arrested person, and in 1981 it extended this protection to any "closed, opaque container" found in the car.[75] But the following year, the Court decided that all parts of a car, closed or open, could be searched if the officers had probable cause to believe they contained contraband (that is, goods illegally possessed). And recently, the rules governing car searches have been relaxed even further. Officers who have probable cause to search a car can also search the things passengers are carrying in the car. And if the car is stopped to give the driver a traffic ticket, the car can be searched if the officer develops a "reasonable, articulable suspicion" that the car is involved in other illegal activity.[76]

In this confusing area of the law, the Court is attempting to protect those places in which a person has a "reasonable expectation of privacy." Your body is one such place, and so the Court has held that the police cannot compel you to undergo surgery to remove a bullet that might be evidence of your guilt or innocence in a crime.[77] But the police can require you to take a Breathalyzer test to see whether you have been drinking while driving.[78] Your home is another place where you have an expectation of privacy, but a barn next to your home is not, nor is your backyard viewed from an airplane, nor is your home if it is a motor home that can be driven away, and so the police need not have a warrant to look into these places.[79]

If you work for the government, you have an expectation that your desk and files will be private; nonetheless, your supervisor may search the desk and files without a warrant, provided that he or she is looking for something related to your work.[80] But bear in mind that the Constitution protects you only against *the government;* a private employer has a great deal of freedom to search your desk and files.

CONFESSIONS AND SELF-INCRIMINATION

The constitutional ban on being forced to give evidence against oneself was originally intended to prevent the use of torture or "third-degree" police tactics to extract confessions. But it has since been extended to cover many kinds of statements uttered not out of fear of torture but from lack of awareness of one's rights, especially the right to remain silent, whether in the courtroom or in the police station.

For many decades, the Supreme Court had held that involuntary confessions could not be used in federal criminal trials but had not ruled that they were barred from state trials. But in the early 1960s, it changed its mind in two landmark cases—*Escobedo* and *Miranda.*[81] The story of the latter and of the controversy that it provoked is worth telling.

Ernesto A. Miranda was convicted in Arizona of the rape and kidnapping of a young woman. The conviction was based on a written confession that Miranda signed after two hours of police questioning. (The victim also identified him.) Two years earlier, the Court had decided that the rule against self-incrimination applied to state courts.[82] Now the question arose of what constitutes an "involuntary" confession. The Court decided that a confession should be presumed involuntary unless the person in custody had been fully and clearly informed of his or her right to be silent, to have an attorney present during any questioning, and to have an attorney provided free of charge if he or she could not afford one. The accused may waive these rights and offer to talk, but the waiver must be truly voluntary. Since Miranda did not have a lawyer present when he was questioned and had not knowingly waived his right to a lawyer, the confession was excluded from evidence in the trial and his conviction was overturned.[83]

Miranda was tried and convicted again, this time on the basis of evidence supplied by his girlfriend, who testified that he had admitted to her that he was guilty. Nine years later, he was released from prison; four years after, that he was killed in a barroom fight. When the Phoenix police arrested the prime suspect in Ernesto Miranda's murder, they read him his rights from a "Miranda card."

Everyone who watches cops-and-robbers shows on television probably knows the "Miranda warning" by heart (see the box on page 119). The police now read it routinely to people whom they arrest. It is not clear whether it has much impact on who does or does not confess or what effect, if any, it may have on the crime rate.

In time, the Miranda rule was extended to mean that you have a right to a lawyer when you appear in a police lineup[84] and when you are questioned by a psychiatrist to determine whether you are competent to stand trial.[85] The Court threw out the conviction of a man who had killed a child, because the accused, without being given the right to have a lawyer present, had led the police to the victim's body.[86] You do not have a right to a Miranda warning, however, if while in jail you confess a crime to another inmate who turns out to be an undercover police officer.[87]

Some police departments have tried to get around the need for a Miranda warning by training their officers to question suspects before giving them a Miranda warning and then, if the suspect confessed, giving the warning and asking the same questions over again. But the Supreme Court would not allow this and struck the practice down.[88]

RELAXING THE EXCLUSIONARY RULE

Cases such as *Miranda* were highly controversial and led to efforts in Congress to modify or overrule the decisions by statute—without much coming of the attempts. But as the rules governing police conduct became increasingly more complex, pressure mounted to find an alternative. Some thought that any evidence should be admissible, with the question of police conduct left to lawsuits or other ways of punishing official misbehavior. Others felt that the exclusionary rule served a useful purpose but had simply become too technical to be an effective deterrent to police misconduct (the police cannot obey rules that they cannot understand). And still others felt that the exclusionary rule was a vital safeguard to essential liberties and should be kept intact. The Court has refused to let Congress abolish Miranda because it is a constitutional rule.[89]

The courts themselves began to adopt the second position, deciding a number of cases in ways that retained the exclusionary rule but modified it by limiting its coverage (police were given greater freedom to question juveniles)[90] and by incorporating what was called a **good-faith exception.** For example, if the police obtain a search warrant they believe is valid, the evidence they gather will not be excluded if it later turns out that the warrant was defective for some reason (such as the judge's having used the wrong form).[91] And the Court decided that "overriding considerations of public safety" may justify questioning a person without first reading the person his or her rights.[92] Moreover, the Court changed its mind about the killer who led the police to the place where he had disposed of his victim's body. After the man was convicted a second time and again appealed, the Court in 1984 held that the body would have been discovered anyway; thus evidence will not be excluded if it can be shown that it would "inevitably" have been found.[93]

TERRORISM AND CIVIL LIBERTIES

The attacks of September 11, 2001 raised important questions about how far the government can go in investigating and prosecuting individuals.

A little over one month after the attacks, Congress passed a new law, the USA Patriot Act, designed to increase federal powers to investigate terrorists.*

Its main provisions are these:

- Telephone taps. The government may tap, if it has a court order, any telephone a suspect uses instead of having to get a separate order for each telephone.

- Internet taps. The government may tap, if it has a court order, Internet communications.

- Voice mail. The government, with a court order, may seize voice mail.

- Grand jury information. Investigators can now share with other government officials things learned in secret grand jury hearings.

good-faith exception
An error in gathering evidence sufficiently minor that it may be used in a trial.

---

*The name of the law is an acronym derived from the official title of the bill, drawn from the first letters of the following capitalized words: Uniting and Strengthening America by Providing Appropriate Tools Required to Intercept and Obstruct Terrorism (USA Patriot).

How Things Work

The Miranda Rule

The Supreme Court has interpreted the due-process clause to require that local police departments issue warnings of the sort shown below to people whom they are arresting.

```
PHILADELPHIA POLICE DEPARTMENT

STANDARD POLICE INTERROGATION CARD

WARNINGS TO BE GIVEN ACCUSED

We are questioning you concerning the
crime of (state specific crime).

    We have a duty to explain to
    you and to warn you that you
    have the following legal rights:

A.  You have a right to remain
    silent and do not have to say
    anything at all.

B.  Anything you say can and will
    be used against you in Court.
```

```
C.  You have a right to talk to a
    lawyer of your own choice
    before we ask you any questions,
    and also to have a lawyer here
    with you while we ask questions.

D.  If you cannot afford to hire a
    lawyer, and you want one, we
    will see that you have one
    provided to you free of charge
    before we ask you any questions.

E.  If you are willing to give us a
    statement, you have a right to
    stop any time you wish.

75-Misc.-3                    (Over)

(6-24-70)
```

Philadelphia Police Department

Ernesto A. Miranda was convicted in Arizona of rape and kidnapping. When the Supreme Court overturned the conviction, it issued a set of rules—the "Miranda rules"—governing how police must conduct an arrest and interrogation.

- Immigration. The attorney general may hold any noncitizen who is thought to be a national security risk for up to seven days. If the alien cannot be charged with a crime or deported within that time, he or she may still be detained if he or she is certified to be a security risk.

- Money laundering. The government gets new powers to track the movement of money across U.S. borders and among banks.

- Crime. This provision eliminates the statute of limitation on terrorist crimes and increases the penalties.

About a month later, President Bush, by executive order, proclaimed a national emergency under which any noncitizen who is believed to be a terrorist or has harbored a terrorist will be tried by a military, rather than a civilian, court.

A military trial is carried on before a commission of military officers and not a civilian jury. The tribunal can operate in secret if classified information is used in evidence. Two-thirds of the commission must agree before the suspect can be convicted and sentenced. If convicted, the suspect can appeal to

Inside a cell at the terrorist prison in Guantanamo, where Muslim inmates receive a copy of the Koran, a chess set, and an arrow pointing toward Mecca.

JOE SKIPPER/Reuters/Corbis

the secretary of defense and the president, but not to a civilian court.

These commissions may eventually be used to try some of the men captured by the U.S. military during its campaign in Afghanistan against the Taliban regime and the al Queda terrorist network that was created by Osama bin Laden. These detainees were held in a prison at our Guantanamo naval base in Cuba and are not regarded by the Defense Department as ordinary prisoners of war.

The biggest legal issue created by this country's war on terrorism is whether the people we capture can be held by our government without giving them access to the courts. The traditional view, first announced during World War II, was that spies sent to this country by the Nazis could be tried by a military tribunal instead of by a civilian court. They were neither citizens nor soldiers, but "unlawful combatants."[94] The Bush administration relied on this view when it detained in our military base in Guantanamo Bay, Cuba, men seized by American forces in Afghanistan. These men were mostly members of the al Queda terrorist movement or of the Taliban movement that governed Afghanistan before American armed forces, together with Afghan rebels, defeated them. These men, none of them American citizens, argued that they were neither terrorists nor combatants. They demanded access to American courts. By a vote of six to three, the Supreme Court held that American courts can consider challenges to the legality of the detention of these men. The Court's opinion did not spell out what the courts should do when it hears these petitions.[95]

In another decision given the same day, the Supreme Court ruled on the case of an American citizen who apparently was working with the Taliban regime but was captured by our forces and was imprisoned in South Carolina. The Court said that American citizens were entitled to a hearing before a neutral decision maker in order to challenge the basis for detention.[96]

That "neutral decision maker" was created in 2006 by a law authorizing military commissions to try alien enemy combatants. These are foreign fighters not in uniform, such as members of al Queda, who are captured by American forces. Each commission will be composed of at least five military officers and will allow the defendant certain fundamental rights (such as to see evidence and testify). Appeals from its decisions can be taken to the Court of Military Review, whose members are selected by the secretary of defense. The federal appeals court for the District of Columbia and, if it wishes, the Supreme Court may hear appeals from the Court of Military Review.[97]

Military commissions have conducted hearings about the inmates in the Guantanamo prison. Some were released, some were held, and for some no decision has been made. Right after he became president, Barack Obama issued an order to close the Guantanamo prison. But there is a problem: What do you do with the inmates? While George W. Bush was president, 420 of the more than 700 inmates were released, but another 50 or so, though declared eligible for release, could not find a country willing to accept them. Where will they go?

When it was first passed in 2001, the Patriot Act made certain provisions temporary, perhaps to allay the fears of civil libertarians. When the act was renewed in March 2006, only a few changes were made and almost all of its provisions were made permanent.

In addition to the Patriot Act, Congress passed and the president signed in 2005 a law that requires all states by 2008 to comply with federal standards when they issue driver licenses. States, not Washington, pass out these licenses, but by mid-2008 the Real ID Act says that no federal agency, including those that manage security at airports, may accept a license or state identification card that does not have the person's photograph, address, signature, and full legal name based on documents that prove he or she is legally in this country. Some people think this amounts to a required national ID card.[98]

SEARCHES WITHOUT WARRANTS

For many decades, presidents of both parties authorized telephone taps without warrants when they believed the person being tapped was a foreign spy. Some did this to capture information about their political enemies. In 1978, Congress decided to bring this practice under legislative control. It passed the Foreign Intelligence Surveillance Act (FISA) that required the president to go before a special court, composed of seven judges selected by the Chief Justice, that would approve electronic eavesdropping on persons who were thought to be foreign spies. The FISA court would impose a standard lower than that which governs the issuance of warrants against criminals. For criminals, a warrant must be based on showing "probable cause" that the person is engaged in a crime; for FISA warrants, the government need only show that the person is likely to be working for a foreign government.

Landmark Cases

Criminal Charges

- **Mapp v. Ohio (1961):** Evidence illegally gathered by the police may not be used in a criminal trial.

- **Gideon v. Wainwright (1964):** Persons charged with a crime have a right to an attorney even if they cannot afford one.

- **Miranda v. Arizona (1966):** Court describes ruling that police must give to arrested persons.

- **United States v. Leon (1984):** Illegally obtained evidence may be used in a trial if it was gathered in good faith without violating the principles of the *Mapp* decision.

- **Dickerson v. United States (2000):** The *Mapp* decision is based on the Constitution and it cannot be altered by Congress passing a law.

- **Rasul v. Bush and Hamdi v. Rumsfeld (2004):** Terrorist detainees must have access to a neutral court to decide if they are legally held.

In late 2005, the *New York Times* and other newspapers revealed that the National Security Agency (NSA), this country's code-breaking and electronic surveillance organization, had a secret program to intercept telephone calls and e-mail messages between certain people abroad and Americans.

The Bush administration defended the program, arguing that the intercepts were designed, not to identify criminals or foreign spies, but to alert the country to potential terrorist threats. It could not rely on FISA because its procedures took too long and its standards of proof were too high. Critics of the program said that it imperiled the civil liberties of Americans.

The Supreme Court has never spoken on this matter, but every lower federal court, including the court that hears appeals from the FISA court, has agreed that the president, as commander in chief, has the "inherent authority" to conduct warrantless searches to obtain foreign intelligence information.[99] The administration also argued that after 9/11, when Congress passed a law authorizing the president to exercise "all necessary and appropriate" uses of military force, it included warrantless intercepts of terrorist communications.

In 2008, Congress passed a bill that allowed the government to intercept foreign communications with people in the United States provided the FISA court had approved the surveillance methods. But the administration could begin the surveillance before the FISA ruling was made if it declared the need to be urgent. However, if Americans living overseas are made the target of this surveillance, then there must first be a FISA warrant. In addition, private telephone and Internet companies that aided in the surveillance were exempt from lawsuits so long as they had received "substantial evidence" that the program was authorized by the president.

SUMMARY

Civil liberties questions are in some ways like and in some ways unlike ordinary policy debates. Like most issues, civil liberties problems often involve competing interests—in this case, conflicting rights or conflicting rights and duties—and so we have groups mobilized on both sides of issues involving free speech and crime control. Like some other issues, civil liberties problems can also arise from the successful appeals of a policy entrepreneur, and so we have periodic reductions in liberty resulting from popular fears, usually aroused during or just after a war.

But civil liberties are unlike many other issues in at least one regard: more than struggles over welfare spending or defense or economic policy, debates about civil liberties reach down into our fundamental political beliefs and political culture, challenging us to define what we mean by religion, Americanism, and decency.

The most important of these challenges focuses on the meaning of the First Amendment: What is "speech"? How much of it should be free? How far can the state go in aiding religion? How do we strike a balance between national security and personal expression? The zigzag course followed by the courts in judging these matters has, on balance, tended to enlarge freedom of expression.

Almost as important has been the struggle to strike a balance between the right of society to protect itself from criminals and the right of people (including criminals) to be free from unreasonable searches and coerced confessions. As with free speech cases, the courts generally have broadened the rights at some expense to the power of the police. But in recent years, the Supreme Court has pulled back from some of its more sweeping applications of the exclusionary rule.

The resolution of these issues by the courts is political in the sense that differing opinions about what is right or desirable compete, with one side or another prevailing (often by a small majority). In this competition of ideas federal judges, though not elected, often are sensitive to strong currents of popular opinion. When entrepreneurial politics has produced new action against apparently threatening minorities, judges are inclined, at least for a while, to give serious consideration to popular fears and legislative majorities. And when no strong national mood is discernible, the opinions of elites influence judicial thinking (as described in Chapter 16).

At the same time, courts resolve political conflicts in a manner that differs in important respects from the resolution of conflicts by legislatures or executives. First, the very existence of the courts, and the relative ease with which one may enter them to advance a claim, facilitates challenges to accepted values. An unpopular political or religious group may have little or no access to a legislature, but it will have substantial access to the courts. Second, judges often settle controversies about rights not simply by deciding the case at hand but by formulating a general rule to cover like cases elsewhere. This has an advantage (the law tends to become more consistent and better known) but a disadvantage as well: a rule suitable for one case may be unworkable in another. Judges reason by analogy and sometimes assume two cases are similar when in fact important differences exist. A definition of "obscenity" or of "fighting words" may suit one situation but be inadequate in another. Third, judges interpret the Constitution, whereas legislatures often consult popular preferences or personal convictions. However much their own beliefs influence what judges read into the Constitution, almost all of them are constrained by its language.

Taken together, the desire to find and announce rules, the language of the Constitution, and the personal beliefs of judges have led to a general expansion of civil liberties. As a result, even allowing for temporary reversals and frequent redefinitions, any value thought to hinder freedom of expression and the rights of the accused has generally lost ground to the claims of the First, Fourth, Fifth, and Sixth Amendments.

RECONSIDERING WHO GOVERNS?

1. Why do the courts play so large a role in deciding what our civil liberties should be?

The courts are independent of the executive and legislative branches, both of which will respond to public pressures. In wartime or in other crisis periods, people want "something done." The president and members of Congress know this. The courts usually are a brake on their demands. But of course the courts can make mistakes or get things confused, as many people believe they have with the establishment clause and the rights of criminal defendants.

RECONSIDERING TO WHAT ENDS?

1. Why not display religious symbols on government property?

The courts believe that putting on government property a single religious symbol, such as a Nativity scene, will make Americans believe the government endorses that religion. But if symbols from several different religions are displayed, no one thinks the government has endorsed any one of them. Of course, putting "In God We Trust" on a government dollar bill is all right. Do not look for consistency here.

2. If a person confesses to committing a crime, why is that confession sometimes not used in court?

Because the confession was improperly gathered by the police. Suspects may not be tortured, and they must be given the Miranda warning. There are other ways of protecting the right of people to be free of improper police procedures, such as admitting the confession in court and then punishing the officers who gathered it improperly. The American courts do not think that system would work in this country.

3. Does the Patriot Act reduce our liberties?

There have not yet been any court tests of the law. Passed after 9/11, it improves the ability of the police to obtain search warrants and eliminates the old tension between intelligence and law enforcement.

WORLD WIDE WEB RESOURCES

Court cases: **www.law.cornell.edu**
Civil Rights Division of the Department of Justice: **www.usdoj.gov**
American Civil Liberties Union: **www.aclu.org**

SUGGESTED READINGS

Abraham, Henry J., and Barbara A. Perry, *Freedom and the Court*. 7th ed. New York: Oxford University Press, 1998. Analysis of leading Supreme Court cases on civil liberties and civil rights.

Amar, Akhil Reed. *The Constitution and Criminal Procedure: First Principles*. New Haven, Conn.: Yale University Press, 1997. A brilliant critique of how the Supreme Court has interpreted those parts of the Constitution bearing on search warrants, the exclusionary rule, and self-incrimination.

Berns, Walter. *The First Amendment and the Future of American Democracy*. New York: Basic Books, 1976. A look at what the Founders intended by the First Amendment that takes issue with contemporary Supreme Court interpretations of it.

Clor, Harry M. *Obscenity and Public Morality*. Chicago: University of Chicago Press, 1969. Argues for the legitimacy of legal restrictions on obscenity.

Levy, Leonard W. *Legacy of Suppression: Freedom of Speech and Press in Early American History*. Rev. ed. New York: Oxford University Press, 1985. Careful study of what the Founders and the early leaders meant by freedom of speech and press.

Civil Rights

WHO GOVERNS?

1. Since Congress enacts our laws, why has it not made certain that all groups have the same rights?
2. After the Supreme Court ended racial segregation in the schools, what did the president and Congress do?

TO WHAT ENDS?

1. If the law supports equality of opportunity, why has affirmative action become so important?
2. Under what circumstances can men and women be treated differently?

In 1830, Congress passed a law requiring all Indians east of the Mississippi River to move to the Indian Territory west of the river, and the army set about implementing it. In the 1850s, a major political fight broke out in Boston over whether the police department should be obliged to hire an Irish officer. Until 1920, women could not vote in most elections. In the 1930s, the Cornell University Medical School had a strict quota limiting the number of Jewish students who could enroll. In the 1940s, the army, at the direction of President Franklin D. Roosevelt, removed all Japanese Americans from their homes in California and placed them in relocation centers far from the coast.

In all such cases, some group, usually defined along racial or ethnic lines, was denied access to facilities, opportunities, or services that were available to other groups. Such cases raise the issue of **civil rights.** The pertinent question regarding civil rights is not whether the government has the authority to treat different people differently; it is whether such differences in treatment are reasonable. All laws and policies make distinctions among people—for example, the tax laws require higher-income people to pay taxes at a higher rate than lower-income ones—but not all such distinctions are defensible. The courts have long held that classifying people on the basis of their income and taxing them at different rates is quite permissible because such classifications are not arbitrary or unreasonable and are related to a legitimate public need (that is, raising revenue). Increasingly, however, the courts have said that classifying people on the basis of their race or ethnicity is unreasonable.[1] The tests the courts use are summarised in the box on page 141.

Robert W. Kelley/Time Life Pictures/Getty Images

To explain the victimization of certain groups and the methods by which they have begun to overcome it, we shall consider chiefly the case of African Americans. Black-white relations have in large measure defined the problem of civil rights in this country; most of the landmark laws and court decisions have involved black claims. The strategies employed by or on behalf of African Americans have typically set the pattern for the strategies employed by other groups. At the end of this chapter, we shall look at the related but somewhat different issues of women's rights and gay rights.

The Black Predicament

Though constituting more than 12 percent of the population, African Americans until fairly recently could not in many parts of the country vote, attend integrated schools, ride in the front seats of buses, or buy homes in white neighborhoods.

Although today white citizens generally do not feel threatened when a black family moves into Cicero, Illinois, a black child goes to school at Little Rock Central High School, or a black group organizes voters in Neshoba County, Mississippi, at one time most whites in Cicero, Little Rock, and Neshoba County felt deeply threatened by these things (and some whites still do). This was especially the case in those parts of the country, notably the Deep South, where blacks often were in the majority. There the politically dominant white minority felt keenly the potential competition for jobs, land, public services, and living space posed by large numbers of people of another race. But even in

civil rights The rights of people to be treated without unreasonable or unconstitutional differences.

the North, black gains often appeared to be at the expense of lower-income whites who lived or worked near them, not at the expense of upper-status whites who lived in suburbs.

African Americans were not allowed to vote at all in many areas; they could vote only with great difficulty in others; and even in those places where voting was easy, they often lacked the material and institutional support for effective political organization. If your opponent feels deeply threatened by your demands and can deny you access to the political system that will decide the fate of those demands, you are, to put it mildly, at a disadvantage. Yet from the end of Reconstruction to the 1960s—for nearly a century—many blacks in the South found themselves in just such a position.

To the dismay of those who prefer to explain political action in terms of economic motives, people often attach greater importance to the intangible costs and benefits of policies than to the tangible ones. Thus, even though the average black represented no threat to the average white, antiblack attitudes—racism—produced some appalling actions. Between 1882 and 1946, 4,715 people, about three-fourths of them African Americans, were lynched in the United States.[2] Some lynchings were carried out by small groups of vigilantes acting with much ceremony, but others were the actions of frenzied mobs. In the summer of 1911, a black man charged with murdering a white man in Livermore, Kentucky, was dragged by a mob to the local theater, where he was hanged. The audience, which had been charged admission, was invited to shoot the swaying body (those in the orchestra seats could empty their revolvers; those in the balcony were limited to a single shot).[3]

Though the public in other parts of the country was shocked by such events, little was done: lynching was a local, not a federal, crime. It obviously would not require many lynchings to convince African Americans in these localities that it would be

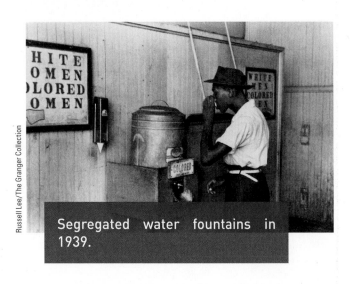

Segregated water fountains in 1939.

Russell Lee/The Granger Collection

foolhardy to try to vote or enroll in a white school. And even in those states where blacks did vote, popular attitudes were not conducive to blacks' buying homes or taking jobs on an equal basis with whites. Even among those professing to support equal rights, a substantial portion opposed African Americans' efforts to obtain them and federal action to secure them. In 1942, a national poll showed that only 30 percent of whites thought black and white children should attend the same schools; in 1956, the proportion had risen, but only to 49 percent, still less than a majority. (In the South, white support for school integration was even lower—14 percent favored it in 1956, about 31 percent in 1963.) As late as 1956, a majority of southern whites were opposed to integrated public transportation facilities. Even among whites who generally favored integration, there was in 1963 (*before* the ghetto riots) considerable opposition to the black civil rights movement: nearly half of the whites classified in a survey as moderate integrationists thought demonstrations hurt the black cause; nearly two-thirds disapproved of actions taken by the civil rights movement; and over a third felt civil rights should be left to the states.[4]

In short, the political position in which African Americans found themselves until the 1960s made it difficult for them to advance their interests through a feasible legislative strategy; their opponents were aroused, organized, and powerful. Thus if black interests were to be championed in Congress or state legislatures, blacks would have to have white allies. Though some such allies could be found, they were too few to make a difference in a political system that gives a substantial advantage to strongly motivated opponents of any new policy. For that to change, one or both of two things would have to happen: additional allies would have to be recruited (a delicate problem, given that many white integrationists disapproved of aspects of the civil rights movement), or the struggle would have to be shifted to a policy-making arena in which the opposition enjoyed less of an advantage.

Partly by plan, partly by accident, black leaders followed both of these strategies simultaneously. By publicizing their grievances and organizing a civil rights movement that (at least in its early stages) concentrated on dramatizing the denial to blacks of essential and widely accepted liberties, African Americans were able to broaden their base of support both among political elites and among the general public and thereby to raise civil rights matters from a low to a high position on the political agenda. By waging a patient, prolonged, but carefully planned legal struggle, black leaders shifted decision-making power on key civil rights issues from Congress, where they had been stymied for generations, to the federal courts.

After this strategy had achieved some substantial successes—after blacks had become enfranchised and legal barriers to equal participation in political and economic affairs had been lowered—the politics of civil rights became more conventional. African Americans were able to assert their demands directly in the legislative and executive branches of government with reasonable (though scarcely certain) prospects of success. Civil rights became less a matter of gaining entry into the political system and more one of waging interest group politics within that system. At the same time, the goals of civil rights politics were broadened. The struggle to gain entry into the system had focused on the denial of fundamental rights (to vote, to organize, to obtain equal access to schools and public facilities); later the dominant issues were manpower development, economic progress, and the improvement of housing and neighborhoods.

The Campaign in the Courts

The Fourteenth Amendment was both an opportunity and a problem for black activists. Adopted in 1868, it seemed to guarantee equal rights for all: "No state shall make or enforce any law which shall abridge the privileges or immunities of citizens of the United States; nor shall any state deprive any person of life, liberty, or property, without due process of law; nor deny to any person within its jurisdiction the equal protection of the laws."

The key phrase was "equal protection of the laws." Read broadly, it might mean that the Constitution should be regarded as color-blind: no state law could have the effect of treating whites and blacks differently. Thus, a law segregating blacks and whites into separate schools or neighborhoods would be unconstitutional. Read narrowly, "equal protection" might mean only that blacks and whites had certain fundamental legal rights in common, among them the right to sign contracts, to serve on juries, or to buy and sell property, but otherwise they could be treated differently.

Historians have long debated which view Congress held when it proposed the Fourteenth Amendment. What forms of racial segregation, if any, were still permissible? Segregated trains? Hotels? Schools? Neighborhoods?

By permission of the Widener Library/Harvard College Library

The cover of the first issue of *The Crisis*, the magazine started by the NAACP in 1910 to raise African American consciousness and publicize racist acts.

The Supreme Court took the narrow view. Though in 1880 it declared unconstitutional a West Virginia law requiring juries to be composed only of white males,[5] it decided in 1883 that it was unconstitutional for Congress to prohibit racial discrimination in public accommodations such as hotels.[6] The difference between the two cases seemed, in the eyes of the Court, to be this: serving on a jury was an essential right of citizenship that the state could not deny to any person on racial grounds without violating the Fourteenth Amendment, but registering at a hotel was a convenience controlled by a private person (the hotel owner), who could treat blacks and whites differently if he or she wished.

separate-but-equal doctrine The doctrine established in *Plessy v. Ferguson* (1896) that African Americans could constitutionally be kept in separate but equal facilities.

The major decision that determined the legal status of the Fourteenth Amendment for over half a century was *Plessy v. Ferguson.* Louisiana had passed a law requiring blacks and whites to occupy separate cars on railroad trains operating in that state. When Adolph Plessy, who was seven-eighths white and one-eighth black, refused to obey the law, he was arrested. He appealed his conviction to the Supreme Court, claiming that the law violated the Fourteenth Amendment. In 1896, the Court rejected his claim, holding that the law treated both races equally even though it required them to be separate. The equal-protection clause guaranteed political and legal but not social equality. "Separate-but-equal" facilities were constitutional because if "one race be inferior to the other socially, the Constitution of the United States cannot put them on the same plane."[7]

"SEPARATE BUT EQUAL"

Thus began the **separate-but-equal doctrine.** Three years later, the Court applied it to schools as well, declaring in *Cumming v. Richmond County Board of Education* that a decision in a Georgia community to close the black high school while keeping open the white high school was not a violation of the Fourteenth Amendment because blacks could always go to private schools. Here the Court seemed to be saying that not only could schools be separate, they could even be unequal.[8]

What the Court has made, the Court can unmake. But to get it to change its mind requires a long, costly, and uncertain legal battle. The National Association for the Advancement of Colored People (NAACP) was the main organization that waged that battle. Formed in 1909 by a group of whites and blacks in the aftermath of a race riot, the NAACP did many things—lobbying in Washington and publicizing black grievances, especially in the pages of *The Crisis,* a magazine edited by W.E.B. Du Bois—but its most influential role was played in the courtroom.

It was a rational strategy. Fighting legal battles does not require forming broad political alliances or changing public opinion, tasks that would have been very difficult for a small and unpopular organization. A court-based approach also enabled the organization to remain nonpartisan.

But it was a slow and difficult strategy. The Court had adopted a narrow interpretation of the Fourteenth Amendment. To get the Court to change its mind would require the NAACP to bring before it cases involving the strongest possible claims that a black had been unfairly treated—and under circumstances sufficiently different from those of earlier cases that the Court could find some grounds for changing its mind.

The steps in that strategy were these: First, persuade the Court to declare unconstitutional laws creating schools that were separate but obviously unequal. Second, persuade it to declare unconstitutional laws supporting schools that were separate but unequal in not-so-obvious ways. Third, persuade it to rule that racially separate schools were inherently unequal and hence unconstitutional.

CAN SEPARATE SCHOOLS BE EQUAL?

The first step was accomplished in a series of court cases stretching from 1938 to 1948. In 1938, the Court held that Lloyd Gaines had to be admitted to an all-white law school in Missouri because no black law school of equal quality existed in that state.[9] In 1948, the Court ordered the all-white University of Oklahoma Law School to admit Ada Lois Sipuel, a black, even though the state planned to build a black law school later. For education to be equal, it had to be equally available.[10] It still could be separate, however: the university admitted Ms. Sipuel but required her to attend classes in a section of the state capitol, roped off from other students, where she could meet with her law professors.

The second step was taken in two cases decided in 1950. Heman Sweatt, an African American, was treated by the University of Texas Law School much as Ada Sipuel had been treated in Oklahoma: "admitted" to the all-white school but relegated to a separate building. Another African American, George McLaurin, was allowed to study for his Ph.D. in a "colored section" of the all-white University of Oklahoma. The Supreme Court unanimously decided that these arrangements were unconstitutional because, by imposing racially based barriers on the black students' access to professors, libraries, and other students, they created unequal educational opportunities.[11]

The third step, the climax of the entire drama, began in Topeka, Kansas, where Linda Brown wanted to enroll in her neighborhood school but could not because she was black and the school was by law reserved exclusively for whites. When the NAACP took her case to the federal district court in Kansas, the judge decided the black school Linda could attend was substantially equal in quality to

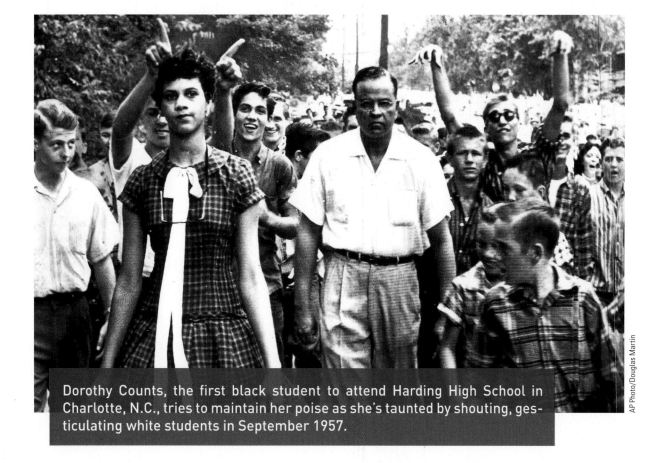

Dorothy Counts, the first black student to attend Harding High School in Charlotte, N.C., tries to maintain her poise as she's taunted by shouting, gesticulating white students in September 1957.

AP Photo/Douglas Martin

WHAT WOULD YOU DO?

MEMORANDUM

To: *Justice Robert Gilbert*

From: *Ella Fitzgerald, law clerk*

Until school segregation ended, southern blacks could attend only all-black colleges. Now they are free to apply to previously all-white colleges, and these schools are integrated. But the traditional black colleges still exist, and very few whites apply to them. In 1992, the Supreme Court held that the state could not solve the problem by requiring a race-neutral admissions policy.* Now the Court must decide whether a predominantly black college can receive state support.

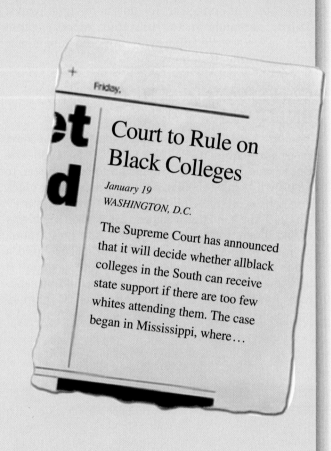

Court to Rule on Black Colleges

January 19
WASHINGTON, D.C.

The Supreme Court has announced that it will decide whether allblack colleges in the South can receive state support if there are too few whites attending them. The case began in Mississippi, where...

Arguments for all-black colleges:

1. These schools have a long tradition that ought to be preserved.

2. Many black students will learn better in an all-black environment.

3. African American organizations, in particular the United Negro College Fund, raise money for these schools.

Arguments against all-black colleges:

1. If the state once required single-race schools, it now has an obligation to dismantle them.

2. Race is a suspect classification, and no state program that chiefly serves one race can be allowed.

Your decision:

Allow all-black colleges _____

Ban all-black colleges _____

*United States v. Fordice, 505 U.S. 717 (1992).

the white school she could not attend. Therefore denying her access to the white school was constitutional. To change that, the lawyers would have to persuade the Supreme Court to overrule the district judge on the grounds that racially separate schools were unconstitutional even if they were equal. In other words, the separate-but-equal doctrine would have to be overturned by the Court.

It was a risky and controversial step to take. Many states, Kansas among them, were trying to make their all-black schools equal to those of whites by launching expensive building programs. If the NAACP succeeded in getting separate schools declared unconstitutional, the Court might well put a stop to the building of these new schools. Blacks could win a moral and legal victory but suffer a practical defeat—the loss of these new facilities. Despite these risks, the NAACP decided to go ahead with the appeal.

BROWN V. BOARD OF EDUCATION

On May 17, 1954, a unanimous Supreme Court, speaking through an opinion written and delivered by Chief Justice Earl Warren, found that "in the field of public education the doctrine of 'separate but equal' has no place" because "separate educational facilities are inherently unequal."[12] *Plessy v. Ferguson* was overruled, and "separate but equal" was dead.

The ruling was a landmark decision, but the reasons for it and the means chosen to implement it were as important and as controversial as the decision itself. There were at least three issues. First, how would the decision be implemented? Second, on what grounds were racially separate schools unconstitutional? Third, what test would a school system have to meet in order to be in conformity with the Constitution?

Implementation

The *Brown* case involved a class-action suit; that is, it applied not only to Linda Brown but to all others similarly situated. This meant that black children everywhere now had the right to attend formerly all-white schools. This change would be one of the most far-reaching and conflict-provoking events in modern American history. It could not be effected overnight or by the stroke of a pen. In 1955, the Supreme Court decided it would let local federal district courts oversee the end of segregation by giving them the power to approve or disapprove local desegregation plans. This was to be done "with all deliberate speed."[13]

In the South, "all deliberate speed" turned out to be a snail's pace. Massive resistance to desegregation broke out in many states. Some communities simply defied the Court; some sought to evade its edict by closing their public schools. In 1956, over 100 southern members of Congress signed a "Southern Manifesto" that condemned the *Brown* decision as an "abuse of judicial power" and pledged to "use all lawful means to bring about a reversal of the decision."

In the late 1950s and early 1960s, the National Guard and regular army paratroopers were used to escort black students into formerly all-white schools and universities. It was not until the 1970s that resistance collapsed and most southern schools were integrated. The use of armed force convinced people that resistance was futile; the disruption of the politics and economy of the South convinced leaders that it was imprudent; and the voting power of blacks convinced politicians that it was suicidal. In addition, federal laws began providing financial aid to integrated schools and withholding it from segregated ones. By 1970, only 14 percent of southern black schoolchildren still attended all-black schools.[14]

The Rationale

As the struggle to implement the *Brown* decision continued, the importance of the rationale for that decision became apparent. The case was decided in a way that surprised many legal scholars. The Court could have said that the equal-protection

In 1963, Governor George Wallace of Alabama stood in the doorway of the University of Alabama to block the entry of black students. Facing him is U.S. Deputy Attorney General Nicholas Katzenbach.

Steve Shapiro/Black Star

clause of the Fourteenth Amendment makes the Constitution, and thus state laws, color-blind. Or it could have said that the authors of the Fourteenth Amendment meant to ban segregated schools. It did neither. Instead, it said segregated education is bad because it "has a detrimental effect upon the colored children" by generating "a feeling of inferiority as to their status in the community" that may "affect their hearts and minds in a way unlikely ever to be undone."[15] This conclusion was supported by a footnote reference to social science studies of the apparent impact of segregation on black children.

Why did the Court rely on social science as much as or more than the Constitution in supporting its decision? Apparently for two reasons. One was the justices' realization that the authors of the Fourteenth Amendment may *not* have intended to outlaw segregated schools. The schools in Washington, D.C., were segregated when the amendment was proposed, and when this fact was mentioned during the debate, it seems to have been made clear that the amendment was not designed to abolish this segregation. When Congress debated a civil rights act a few years later, it voted down provisions that would have ended segregation in schools.[16] The Court could not easily base its decision on a constitutional provision that had, at best, an uncertain application to schools. The other reason grew out of the first. On so important a matter the chief justice wanted to speak for a unanimous court. Some justices did not agree that the Fourteenth Amendment made the Constitution color-blind. In the interests of harmony, the Court found an ambiguous rationale for its decision.

Desegregation versus Integration

That ambiguity led to the third issue. If separate schools were inherently unequal, what would "unseparate" schools look like? Since the Court had not said race was irrelevant, an "unseparate" school could be either one that blacks and whites were free to attend if they chose or one that blacks and whites in fact attended whether they wanted to or not. The first might be called a desegregated school, the latter an integrated school. Think of the Topeka case. Was it enough that there was now no barrier to Linda Brown's attending the white school in her neighborhood? Or was it necessary that there be black children (if not Linda, then some others) actually going to that school together with white children?

de jure segregation
Racial segregation that is required by law.

de facto segregation
Racial segregation that occurs in schools, not as a result of the law, but as a result of patterns of residential settlement.

As long as the main impact of the *Brown* decision lay in the South, where laws had prevented blacks from attending white schools, this question did not seem important. Segregation by law (**de jure segregation**) was now clearly unconstitutional. But in the North, laws had not kept blacks and whites apart; instead, all-black and all-white schools were the result of residential segregation, preferred living patterns, informal social forces, and administrative practices (such as drawing school district lines so as to produce single-race schools). This often was called segregation in fact (**de facto segregation**).

In 1968, the Supreme Court settled the matter. In New Kent County, Virginia, the school board had created a "freedom-of-choice" plan under which every pupil would be allowed without legal restriction to attend the school of his or her choice. As it turned out, all the white children chose to remain in the all-white school, and 85 percent of the black children remained in the all-black school. The Court rejected this plan as unconstitutional because it did not produce the "ultimate end," which was a "unitary, nonracial system of education."[17] In the opinion written by Justice William Brennan, the Court seemed to be saying that the Constitution required actual racial mixing in the schools, not just the repeal of laws requiring racial separation.

This impression was confirmed three years later when the Court considered a plan in North Carolina under which pupils in Mecklenburg County (which includes Charlotte) were assigned to the nearest neighborhood school without regard to race. As a result, about half the black children now attended formerly all-white schools, with the other half attending all-black schools. The federal district court held that this was inadequate and ordered some children to be bused into more distant schools in order to achieve a greater degree of integration. The Supreme Court, now led by Chief Justice Warren Burger, upheld the district judge on the grounds that the court plan was necessary to achieve a "unitary school system."[18]

This case— *Swann v. Charlotte-Mecklenburg Board of Education*—pretty much set the guidelines for all subsequent cases involving school segregation. The essential features of those guidelines are as follows:

- To violate the Constitution, a school system, by law, practice, or regulation, must have engaged in discrimination. Put another way, a plaintiff

Ted Crowell/Black Star

Antibusing protesters buried a school bus (unoccupied) to dramatize their cause.

must show an intent to discriminate on the part of the public schools.

- The existence of all-white or all-black schools in a district with a history of segregation creates a presumption of intent to discriminate.

- The remedy for past discrimination will not be limited to freedom of choice, or what the Court called "the walk-in school." Remedies may include racial quotas in the assignment of teachers and pupils, redrawn district lines, and court-ordered busing.

- Not every school must reflect the social composition of the school system as a whole.

Relying on *Swann,* district courts have supervised redistricting and busing plans in localities all over the nation, often in the face of bitter opposition from the community. In Boston, the control of the city schools by a federal judge, W. Arthur Garrity, lasted for more than a decade and involved him in every aspect of school administration.

One major issue not settled by *Swann* was whether busing and other remedies should cut across city and county lines. In some places, the central-city schools had become virtually all black. Racial integration could be achieved only by bringing black pupils to white suburban schools or moving white pupils into central-city schools. In a series of split-vote decisions, the Court ruled that court-ordered intercity busing could be authorized only if it could be demonstrated that the suburban areas as well as the central city had in fact practiced school segregation. Where that could not be shown, such intercity busing would not be required. The Court was not persuaded that intent had been proved in Atlanta, Detroit, Denver, Indianapolis, and Richmond, but it was persuaded that it had been proved in Louisville and Wilmington.[19]

The importance the Court attaches to intent means that if a school system that was once integrated becomes all black as a result of whites' moving to the suburbs, the Court will not require that district lines constantly be redrawn or new busing plans adopted to adjust to the changing distribution of the population.[20] This in turn means that as long as blacks and whites live in different neighborhoods for whatever reason, there is a good chance that some schools in both areas will be heavily of one race. If mandatory busing or other integration measures cause whites to move out of a city at a faster rate than they otherwise would (a process often called "white flight"), then efforts to integrate the schools may in time create more single-race schools. Ultimately, integrated schools will exist only in integrated neighborhoods or where the quality of education is so high that both blacks and whites want to enroll in the school even at some cost in terms of travel and inconvenience.

Mandatory busing to achieve racial integration has been a deeply controversial program and has generated considerable public opposition. Surveys show that a majority of people oppose it.[21] As recently as 1992, a poll showed that 48 percent of whites in the Northeast and 53 percent of southern whites felt it was "not the business" of the federal government to ensure "that black and white children go to the same schools."[22] Presidents Nixon, Ford, and Reagan opposed busing; all three supported legislation to prevent or reduce it, and Reagan petitioned the courts to reconsider busing plans. The courts refused to reconsider, and Congress has passed only minor restrictions on busing.

The reason why Congress has not followed public opinion on this matter is complex. It has been torn between the desire to support civil rights and uphold the courts and the desire to represent the views of its constituents. Because it faces a dilemma, Congress has taken both sides of the issue simultaneously. By the late 1980s, busing was a dying issue in Congress, in part because no meaningful legislation seemed possible and in part because popular passion over busing had somewhat abated.

Then, in 1992, the Supreme Court made it easier for local school systems to reclaim control over their schools from the courts. In DeKalb County, Georgia (a suburb of Atlanta), the schools had been operating under court-ordered desegregation plans for many years. Despite this effort, full integration had not been achieved, largely because the county's neighborhoods had increasingly become either all black or all white. The Court held that local schools could not be held responsible for segregation caused solely by segregated living patterns and so the courts would have to relinquish their control over the schools. In 2007, the Court said race could not be the decisive factor in assigning students to schools that had either never been segregated (as in Seattle) or where legal segregation had long since ended (as in Jefferson County, Kentucky).[23]

The Campaign in Congress

The campaign in the courts for desegregated schools, though slow and costly, was a carefully managed effort to alter the interpretation of a constitutional provision. But to get new civil rights laws out of Congress required a far more difficult and decentralized strategy, one that was aimed at mobilizing public opinion and overcoming the many congressional barriers to action.

Landmark Cases

Civil Rights

- **Dred Scott Case (Scott v. Sanford, 1857):** Congress had no authority to ban slavery in a territory. A slave was considered a piece of property.

- **Plessy v. Ferguson (1896):** Upheld separate-but-equal facilities for white and black people on railroad cars.

- **Brown v. Board of Education (1954):** Said separate public schools are inherently unequal, thus starting racial desegregation.

- **Green v. County School Board of New Kent County (1968):** Banned a freedom-of-choice plan for integrating schools, suggesting blacks and whites must actually attend racially mixed schools.

- **Swann v. Charlotte-Mecklenburg Board of Education (1971):** Approved busing and redrawing district lines as ways of integrating public schools.

In 1960, black students from North Carolina Agricultural and Technical College staged the first "sit-in" when they were refused service at a lunch counter in Greensboro (left). Twenty years later, graduates of the college returned to the same lunch counter (right). Though prices had risen, the service had improved.

Bettman/Corbis

Bob Jordan/AP Photo

The first problem was to get civil rights on the political agenda by convincing people that something had to be done. This could be achieved by dramatizing the problem in ways that tugged at the conscience of whites who were not racist but were ordinarily indifferent to black problems. Brutal lynchings of blacks had shocked these whites, but lynchings were becoming less frequent in the 1950s.

Those leaders could, however, arrange for dramatic confrontations between blacks claiming some obvious right and the whites who denied it to them. Beginning in the late 1950s, these confrontations began to occur in the form of sit-ins at segregated lunch counters and "freedom rides" on segregated bus lines. At about the same time, efforts were made to get blacks registered to vote in counties where whites had used intimidation and harassment to prevent it.

The best-known campaign occurred in 1955–1956 in Montgomery, Alabama, where blacks, led by a young minister named Martin Luther King, Jr., boycotted the local bus system after it had a black woman, Rosa Parks, arrested because she refused to surrender her seat on a bus to a white man.

These early demonstrations were based on the philosophy of **civil disobedience**—that is, peacefully violating a law, such as one requiring blacks to ride in a segregated section of a bus, and allowing oneself to be arrested as a result.

But the momentum of protest, once unleashed, could not be centrally directed or confined to nonviolent action. A rising tide of anger, especially among younger blacks, resulted in the formation of more militant organizations and the spontaneous eruption of violent demonstrations and riots in dozens of cities across the country. From 1964 to 1968, there were in the North as well as the South four "long, hot summers" of racial violence.

The demonstrations and rioting succeeded in getting civil rights on the national political agenda, but at a cost: many whites, opposed to the demonstrations or appalled by the riots, dug in their heels and fought against making any concessions to "lawbreakers," "troublemakers," and "rioters." In 1964 and again in 1968, over two-thirds of the whites interviewed in opinion polls said the civil rights movement was pushing too fast, had hurt the black cause, and was too violent.[24]

In short, a conflict existed between the agenda-setting and coalition-building aspects of the civil rights movement. This was especially a problem since conservative southern legislators still controlled many key congressional committees that had for years been the graveyard of civil rights legislation. The Senate Judiciary Committee was dominated by a coalition of southern Democrats and conservative Republicans, and the House Rules Committee was under the control of a chairman hostile to civil rights bills, Howard Smith of Virginia. Any bill that passed the House faced an almost certain filibuster in the Senate. Finally, President John F. Kennedy was reluctant to submit strong civil rights bills to Congress.

Four developments made it possible to break the deadlock. First, public opinion was changing. As Figure 6.1 shows, the proportion of whites who were willing to have their children attend a school that was half black increased sharply (though the proportion of whites willing to have their children attend a school that was predominantly black increased by much less). About the same change could be found in attitudes toward allowing blacks equal access to hotels and buses.[25] Of course, support in principle for these civil rights measures was not necessarily the same as support in practice; nonetheless, clearly a major shift was occurring in popular approval of at least the principles of civil rights. At the leading edge of this change were young, college-educated people.[26]

Second, certain violent reactions by white segregationists to black demonstrators were vividly portrayed by the media, especially television, in ways that gave to the civil rights cause a powerful moral force. In May 1963, the head of the Birmingham police, Eugene "Bull" Connor, ordered his men to use attack dogs and high-pressure fire hoses to repulse a peaceful march by African Americans demanding desegregated public facilities and increased job opportunities. The pictures of that confrontation (such as the one on page 137) created a national sensation and contributed greatly to the massive participation, by whites and blacks alike, in the "March on Washington" that summer. About a quarter of a million people gathered in front of the Lincoln Memorial to hear Martin Luther King, Jr., deliver a stirring and widely hailed address, often called the "I Have a Dream" speech. The following summer in Neshoba County, Mississippi, three young civil rights workers (two white and one black) were brutally murdered by Klansmen aided by the local sheriff. When the FBI identified the murderers, the effect on national public opinion was galvanic; no white southern leader could any longer offer persuasive opposition to federal laws protecting voting rights when

civil disobedience
Opposing a law one considers unjust by peacefully disobeying it and accepting the resultant punishment.

Figure 6.1

Changing White Attitudes Toward Differing Levels of School Integration

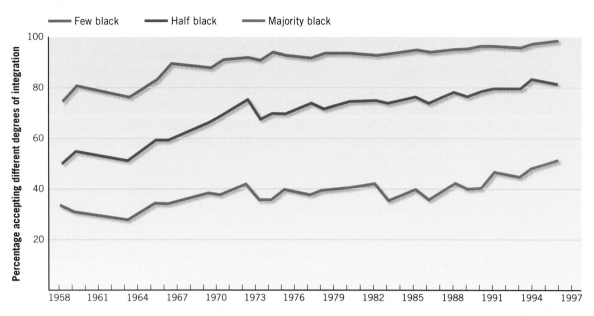

Source: Reprinted by permission of the publisher from *Racial Attitudes in America* by Howard Schuman, Charlotte Steeh, and Lawrence Bobo, p. 69, Cambridge, Mass.: Harvard University Press. Copyright © 1985, 1997, by the Presidents and Fellows of Harvard College.

white law enforcement officers had killed students working to protect those rights. And the next year, a white woman, Viola Liuzzo, was shot and killed while driving a car used to transport civil rights workers. Her death was the subject of a presidential address.

Third, President John F. Kennedy was assassinated in Dallas, Texas, in November 1963. Many people originally (and wrongly) thought he had been killed by a right-wing conspiracy. Even after the assassin had been caught and shown to have left-wing associations, the shock of the president's murder—in a southern city—helped build support for efforts by the new president, Lyndon B. Johnson (a Texan), to obtain passage of a strong civil rights bill as a memorial to the slain president.

Fourth, the 1964 elections not only returned Johnson to office with a landslide victory but also sent a huge Democratic majority to the House and retained the large Democratic margin in the Senate. This made it possible for northern Democrats to outvote or outmaneuver southerners in the House.

The cumulative effect of these forces led to the enactment of five civil rights laws between 1957 and 1968. Three (1957, 1960, and 1965) were chiefly

directed at protecting the right to vote; one (1968) was aimed at preventing discrimination in housing; and one (1964), the most far-reaching of all, dealt with voting, employment, schooling, and public accommodations.

The passage of the 1964 act was the high point of the legislative struggle. Liberals in the House had drafted a bipartisan bill, but it was now in the House Rules Committee, where such matters had often disappeared without a trace. In the wake of Kennedy's murder, a discharge petition was filed, with President Johnson's support, to take the bill out of committee and bring it to the floor of the House. But the Rules Committee, without waiting for a vote on the petition (which it probably realized it would lose), sent the bill to the floor, where it passed overwhelmingly. In the Senate, an agreement between Republican minority leader Everett Dirksen and President Johnson smoothed the way for passage in several important respects. The House bill was sent directly to the Senate floor, thereby bypassing the southern-dominated Judiciary Committee. Nineteen southern senators began an eight-week filibuster against the bill. On June 10, 1964, by a vote of seventy-one to twenty-nine, cloture was invoked and the filibuster ended—the first time in history that a filibuster aimed at blocking civil rights legislation had been broken.

This picture of a police dog lunging at a black man during a racial demonstration in Birmingham, Alabama, in May 1963 was one of the most influential photographs ever published. It was widely reprinted throughout the world and was frequently referred to in congressional debates on the civil rights bill of 1964.

President Lyndon Johnson congratulates Rev. Martin Luther King, Jr., after signing the Civil Rights Act of 1964.

This change partly reflected the growing political strength of southern blacks. In 1960, less than one-third of voting-age blacks in the South were registered to vote; by 1971 more than half were, and by 1984 two-thirds were. In 2001, over 9,000 blacks held elective office (see Table 6.1). But this was only half of the story. Attitudes among white political elites and members of Congress had also changed. This was evident as early as 1968, when Congress passed a law barring discrimination in housing even though polls showed that only 35 percent of the public supported the measure.

Since the 1960s, congressional support for civil rights legislation has grown—so much so, indeed, that labeling a bill a civil rights measure, once the kiss of death, now almost guarantees its passage. For example, in 1984 the Supreme Court decided the federal ban on discrimination in education applied only to the "program or activity" receiving federal aid and not to the entire school or university.[27] In 1988, Congress passed a bill to overturn this decision by making it clear that antidiscrimination rules applied to the entire educational institution and not just to that part (say, the physics lab) receiving federal money. When President Reagan vetoed the bill (because, in his view, it would diminish the freedom of church-affiliated schools), Congress overrode the veto. In the override vote, every southern Democrat in the Senate and almost 90 percent of those in the House voted for the bill. This was a dramatic change from 1964, when over 80 percent of the southern Democrats in Congress voted against the Civil Rights Act (see Figure 6.2).

Figure 6.2

Growing Support Among Southern Democrats in Congress for Civil Rights Bills

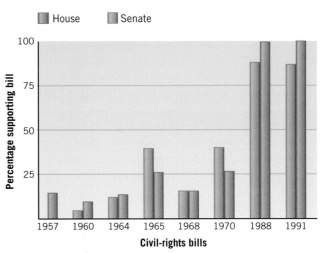

Sources: Congressional Quarterly, *Congress and the Nation,* vols. 1, 2, 3, 7, 8.

Key Provisions of Major Civil Rights Laws

1957 **Voting** Made it a federal crime to try to prevent a person from voting in a federal election. Created the Civil Rights Commission.

1960 **Voting** Authorized the attorney general to appoint federal referees to gather evidence and make findings about allegations that African Americans were deprived of their right to vote. Made it a federal crime to use interstate commerce to threaten or carry out a bombing.

1964 **Voting** Made it more difficult to use devices such as literacy tests to bar African Americans from voting.

Public accommodations Barred discrimination on grounds of race, color, religion, or national origin in restaurants, hotels, lunch counters, gasoline stations, movie theaters, stadiums, arenas, and lodging houses with more than five rooms.

Schools Authorized the attorney general to bring suit to force the desegregation of public schools on behalf of citizens.

Employment Outlawed discrimination in hiring, firing, or paying employees on grounds of race, color, religion, national origin, or sex.

Federal funds Barred discrimination in any activity receiving federal assistance.

1965 **Voter registration** Authorized appointment by the Civil Service Commission of voting examiners who would require registration of all eligible voters in federal, state, and local elections, general or primary, in areas where discrimination was found to be practiced or where less than 50 percent of voting-age residents were registered to vote in the 1964 election.

Literacy tests Suspended use of literacy tests or other devices to prevent African Americans from voting.

1968 **Housing** Banned, by stages, discrimination in sale or rental of most housing (excluding private owners who sell or rent their homes without the services of a real-estate broker).

Riots Made it a federal crime to use interstate commerce to organize or incite a riot.

1972 **Education** Prohibited sex discrimination in education programs receiving federal aid.

1988 **Discrimination** If any part of an organization receives federal aid, no part of that organization may discriminate on the basis of race, sex, age, or physical handicap.

1991 **Discrimination** Made it easier to sue over job discrimination and collect damages; overturned certain Supreme Court decisions. Made it illegal for the government to adjust, or "norm," test scores by race.

Table 6.1 Increase in Number of Black Elected Officials

Office	1970	1991	2001
Congress and state legislatures	182	476	633
City and county offices	715	4,493	5,456
Judges and sheriffs	213	847	1,044
Boards of education	362	1,629	1,928
Total	1,472	7,445	9,061

Sources: *Statistical Abstract of the United States, 2003*, table 417.

Civil rights is not an issue easily confined to schools, housing, and jobs. Sometimes it is extended to crime. When crack cocaine became a popular drug, it was cheap and easily sold on street corners. When the public demanded that the police get tough on crack dealers, arrests followed. Since the great majority of arrested dealers were black, there was a sharp increase in black drug dealers going to prison. Some blacks claimed they were being singled out by the police because of their race. The Supreme Court disagreed, holding that no evidence had been presented to show that drug dealers of other races had not been prosecuted.[28]

RESEARCH FRONTIERS

Civil Rights: Are Guns a Public Nuisance?

Some ideas about public policy grab media attention, garner political support, and go on to become public laws; other ideas never even make it on to the "public agenda." Political scientists have many different theories, taxonomies, and models about the policy process; and, later in this book (Chapter 17) we offer our way of classifying and explaining the politics of issues ranging from economic policy to environmental policy.

When it comes to present-day civil rights policy dynamics, however, new research frontiers are being charted, not mainly by academic theorists, but by practitioner-scholars who have not merely studied change but helped to make it happen.

Take David Kairys, a Temple University law professor who was a full-time civil rights lawyer across four decades. In his 2008 memoir, Kairys illustrates how intricately intertwined with other issues civil rights policies tend to be; how post-1980 civil rights laws on racial discrimination and other matters have often shifted without any legislative changes; and how novel applications of old legal theories can spark new debates about how to define or enforce civil rights.

For example, in the Anglo-American legal tradition, a noisy blacksmith shop teeming with hot objects and other dangers could be declared a "public nuisance" and forced by local government authorities to shut down or pay damages even if it was there before anybody lived nearby, and even if it had always operated legally. But, today, should otherwise law-abiding handgun manufacturers be sued by city officials for creating a "public nuisance," and do citizens have a civil right to live free from violence perpetrated with handguns?

In the late 1990's, the mayors of New Orleans, Chicago, Philadelphia and several dozen other cities, joined in some cases by civil rights groups, brought "public nuisance" lawsuits against handgun manufacturers. In response, many state legislatures passed new laws exempting the handgun industry from these lawsuits; and, in 2005, the U.S. Congress enacted and President George W. Bush signed a new federal law granting the handgun industry broad legal immunity and rejecting related civil rights claims.

- Do you think that freedom from gun violence ought to be counted among "civil rights"?

- Do you think that permitting "public nuisance" or other lawsuits against otherwise law-abiding gun manufacturers might violate their "civil rights"?

- Do you think that a certain minimum standard of living, a certain minimum level of air quality, or a certain minimum degree of privacy ought to be considered a "civil right"?

- Regardless, what, if any, contemporary issues do you think fall outside the domain of "civil rights," and why?

Source: David Kairys, *Philadelphia Freedom: Memoir of a Civil Rights Lawyer* (University of Michigan Press, 2008); John W. Kingdon, *Agendas, Alternatives, and Public Policies*, second edition (Pearson, 1997); James Q. Wilson, ed., *The Politics of Regulation* (Basic Books, 1980); Theodore J. Lowi, "American Business, Public Policy, Case Studies, and Political Theory," *World Politics* 16 (July 1964), pp. 677–715.

RACIAL PROFILING

If law enforcement authorities are more likely to stop and question people because of their race or ethnicity, racial profiling occurs. At first glance, this would seem to be a bad idea. For example, African Americans often complain that they are stopped by the police for "driving while black." This complaint became a national issue in 1998 when the governor of New Jersey fired the head of the state police for saying blacks were stopped more frequently than whites because they broke the law more frequently. Soon President Clinton and later President Bush made statements condemning racial profiling.

But there is another side to this issue. Perhaps people of a certain race are more likely to break the speed limit or smuggle drugs in their cars; if that is the case, then stopping them more frequently, even if it means stopping more innocent people, may make sense. A study of police stops in Oakland, California, by the RAND Corporation showed that, at least in that city, officers stopped cars without knowing the race of the occupants because the share of blacks stopped at night, when the drivers could not been seen, was the same as the share stopped during the day when they could be seen.[29]

The terrorist attacks of 9/11 added a new dimension to the issue. If young Middle Eastern men are more likely to smuggle weapons onto airplanes, searching them more carefully than one searches an elderly white Caucasian woman may make sense. But federal officials are leery of doing anything that might get them labeled as "racial profilers."

Women and Equal Rights

The political and legal efforts to secure civil rights for African Americans were accompanied by efforts to expand the rights of women. There was an important difference between the two movements, however: whereas African Americans were arguing against a legal tradition that explicitly aimed to keep them in a subservient status, women had to argue against a tradition that claimed to be protecting them. For example, in 1908 the Supreme Court upheld an Oregon law that limited female laundry workers to a 10-hour workday against the claim that it violated the Fourteenth Amendment. The Court justified its decision with this language:

> *The two sexes differ in structure of body, in the functions to be performed by each, in the amount of physical strength, in the capacity for long-continued labor, particularly when done standing. . . . the self-reliance which enables one to assert full rights, and in the capacity to maintain the struggle for subsistence. This difference justifies a difference in legislation and upholds that which is designed to compensate for some of the burdens which rest upon her.*[30]

The origin of the movement to give more rights to women was probably the Seneca Falls Convention held in 1848. Its leaders began to demand the right to vote for women. Though this was slowly granted by several states, especially in the West, it was not until 1920 that the Nineteenth Amendment made it clear that no state may deny the right to vote on the basis of sex. The great change in the status of women, however, took place during World War II when the demand for workers in our defense plants led to the employment of millions of women, such as "Rosie the Riveter," in jobs they had rarely held before. After the war, the feminist movement took flight with the publication in 1963 of *The Feminine Mystique* by Betty Friedan.

Congress responded by passing laws that required equal pay for equal work, prohibited discrimination on the basis of sex in employment and among students in any school or university receiving federal

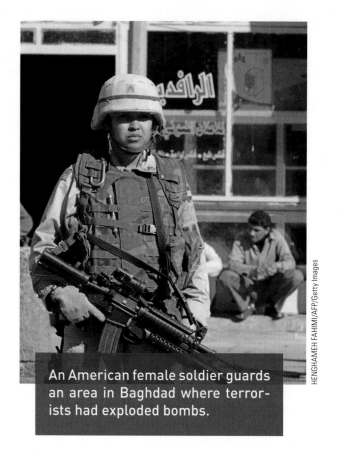

An American female soldier guards an area in Baghdad where terrorists had exploded bombs.

HENGHAMEH FAHIMI/AFP/Getty Images

funds, and banned discrimination against pregnant women on the job.[31]

At the same time, the Supreme Court was altering the way it interpreted the Constitution. The key passage was the Fourteenth Amendment, which prohibits any state from denying to "any person" the "equal protection of the laws." For a long time the traditional standard, as we saw in the 1908 case, was a kind of protective paternalism. By the early 1970s, however, the Court had changed its mind. In deciding whether the Constitution bars all, some, or no sexual discrimination, the Court had a choice among three standards. The first is the *reasonableness* standard. This says that when the government treats some classes of people differently from others—for example, applying statutory rape laws to men but not to women—the different treatment must be reasonable and not arbitrary.

The second standard is *intermediate scrutiny*. When women complained that some laws treated them unfairly, the Court adopted a standard somewhere between the reasonableness and strict scrutiny tests. Thus, a law that treats men and women differently must be more than merely reasonable, but the allowable differences need not meet the strict scrutiny test.

How Things Work

How the Court Decides if You Discriminate

The Supreme Court has produced three different tests to decide if a government policy produces unconstitutional discrimination. Don't be surprised if you find it a bit hard to tell them apart.

1. **Rational Basis**   If the policy uses reasonable means to achieve a legitimate government goal, it is constitutional.

   Examples: If the government says you can't buy a drink until you are 21, this meets the rational basis test: the government wants to prevent children from drinking, and age 21 is a reasonable means to define when a person is an adult. And a state can ban advertising on trucks unless the ad is about the truck owner's own business.

2. **Intermediate Scrutiny**   If the policy "serves an important government interest" and is "substantially related" to serving that interest, it is constitutional.

   Examples: Men can be punished for statutory rape even if women are not punished because men and women are not "similarly situated." And men can be barred from entering hospital delivery rooms even though (obviously) women are admitted.

3. **Strict scrutiny**   To be constitutional, the discrimination must serve a "compelling government interest," it must be "narrowly tailored" to attain that interest, and it must use "the least restrictive means" to attain it.

   Examples: Distinctions based on race, ethnicity, religion, or voting must pass the strict scrutiny test. You cannot bar black children from a public school or black adults from voting and you cannot prevent one religion from knocking on your door to promote its views.

And so in 1971, the Court held that an Idaho statute was unconstitutional because it required that males be preferred over females when choosing people to administer the estates of deceased children. To satisfy the Constitution, a law treating men and women differently "must be reasonable, not arbitrary, and must rest on some ground of difference having a fair and substantial relation to the object of legislation so that all persons similarly circumstanced shall be treated alike."[32] In later decisions, some members of the Court wanted to make classifications based on sex inherently suspect and subject to the strict scrutiny test, but no majority has yet embraced this position.[33]

The third standard is *strict scrutiny*. This says that some instances of drawing distinctions between different groups of people—for example, by treating whites and blacks differently—are inherently suspect; thus, the Court will subject them to strict scrutiny to ensure they are clearly necessary to attain a legitimate state goal.

But sexual classifications can also be judged by a different standard. The Civil Rights Act of 1964 prohibits sex discrimination in the hiring, firing, and compensation of employees. The 1972 Civil Rights Act bans sex discrimination in local education programs receiving federal aid. These laws apply to *private* and not just government action.

Over the years, the Court has decided many cases involving sexual classification. The following lists provide several examples of illegal sexual discrimination (violating either the Constitution or a civil rights act) and legal sexual distinctions (violating neither).

Illegal Discrimination

- A state cannot set different ages at which men and women legally become adults.[34]

- A state cannot set different ages at which men and women are allowed to buy beer.[35]

- Women cannot be barred from jobs by arbitrary height and weight requirements.[36]

- Employers cannot require women to take mandatory pregnancy leaves.[37]

- Girls cannot be barred from Little League baseball teams.[38]

- Business and service clubs, such as the Junior Chamber of Commerce and Rotary Club, cannot exclude women from membership.[39]

Landmark Cases

Women's Rights

- **Reed v. Reed (1971):** Gender discrimination violates the equal protection clause of the Constitution.

- **Craig v. Boren (1976):** Gender discrimination can only be justified if it serves "important governmental objectives" and be "substantially related to those objectives."

- **Rostker v. Goldberg (1981):** Congress can draft men without drafting women.

- **United States v. Virginia (1996):** State may not finance an all-male military school.

- Though women as a group live longer than men, an employer must pay them monthly retirement benefits equal to those received by men.[40]

- High schools must pay the coaches of girls' sports the same as they pay the coaches of boys' sports.[41]

Decisions Allowing Differences Based on Sex

- A law that punishes males but not females for statutory rape is permissible; men and women are not "similarly situated" with respect to sexual relations.[42]

- All-boy and all-girl public schools are permitted if enrollment is voluntary and quality is equal.[43]

- States can give widows a property-tax exemption not given t8 widowers.[44]

- The navy may allow women to remain officers longer than men without being promoted.[45]

The lower federal courts have been especially busy in the area of sexual distinctions. They have said that public taverns may not cater to men only and that girls may not be prevented from competing against boys in noncontact high school sports; on the other hand, hospitals may bar fathers from the delivery room. Women may continue to use their maiden names after marriage.[46]

In 1996, the Supreme Court ruled that women must be admitted to the Virginia Military Institute, until then an all-male state-supported college that had for many decades supplied what it called an "adversative method" of training to instill physical and mental discipline in cadets. In practical terms, this meant the school was very tough on students. The Court said that for a state to justify spending tax money on a single-sex school, it must supply an "exceedingly persuasive justification" for excluding the other gender. Virginia countered by offering to support an all-female training course at another college, but this was not enough.[47] This decision came close to imposing the strict scrutiny test, and so it has raised important questions about what could happen to all-female or traditionally black colleges that accept state money.

Perhaps the most far-reaching cases defining the rights of women have involved the draft and abortion. In 1981, the Court held in *Rostker v. Goldberg* that Congress may require men but not women to register for the draft without violating the due-process clause of the Fifth Amendment.[48] In the area of national defense, the Court will give great deference to congressional policy (Congress had already decided to bar women from combat roles). For many years, women could be pilots and sailors but not on combat aircraft or combat ships. In 1993, the secretary of defense opened air and sea combat positions to all persons regardless of gender; only ground-troop combat positions are still reserved for men. The issue played a role in preventing the ratification of the Equal Rights Amendment to the Constitution, because of fears that it would reverse *Rostker v. Goldberg*.

SEXUAL HARASSMENT

When Paula Corbin Jones accused President Clinton of sexual harassment, the judge threw the case out of court because she had not submitted enough evidence such that, if the jury believed her story, she would have made a legally adequate argument that she had been sexually harassed.

What, then, is sexual harassment? Drawing on rulings by the Equal Employment Opportunities Commission, the Supreme Court has held that harassment can take one of two forms. First, it is illegal for someone to request sexual favors as a condition of employment or promotion. This is the "quid pro quo" rule. If a person does this, the employer is "strictly liable." Strict liability means the employer can be found at fault even if he or she did not know a subordinate was requesting sex in exchange for hiring or promotion.

Second, it is illegal for an employee to experience a work environment that has been made hostile or intimidating by a steady pattern of offensive sexual teasing, jokes, or obscenity. But employers are not strictly liable in this case; they can be found at fault only if they were "negligent"—that is, they knew about the hostile environment but did nothing about it.

In 1998, the Supreme Court decided three cases that made these rules either better or worse, depending on your point of view. In one, it determined that a school system was not liable for the conduct of a teacher who seduced a female student because the student never reported the actions. In a second, it held that a city was liable for a sexually hostile work environment confronting a female lifeguard even though she did not report this to her superiors. In the third, it decided that a female employee who was not promoted after having rejected the sexual advances of her boss could recover financial damages from the firm. But, it added, the firm could have avoided paying this bill if it had put in place an "affirmative defense" against sexual exploitation, although the Court never said what such a policy might be.[49]

Sexual harassment is a serious matter, but because there are almost no federal laws governing it, we are left with somewhat vague and often inconsistent court and bureaucratic rules to guide us.

PRIVACY AND SEX

Regulating sexual matters has traditionally been left up to the states, which do so by exercising their **police powers.** These powers include more than the authority to create police departments; they include all laws designed to promote public order and secure the safety and morals of the citizens. Some have argued that the Tenth Amendment to the Constitution, by reserving to the states all powers not delegated to the federal government, meant that states could do anything not explicitly prohibited by the Constitution. But that changed when the Supreme Court began expanding the power of Congress over business and when it started to view sexual matters under the newly discovered right to privacy.

Until that point, it had been left up to the states to decide whether and under what circumstances a woman could obtain an abortion. For example, New York allowed abortions during the first 24 weeks of pregnancy, while Texas banned it except when the mother's life was threatened.

That began to change in 1965 when the Supreme Court held that the states could not prevent the sale of contraceptives because by so doing it would invade a "zone of privacy." Privacy is nowhere mentioned in

Landmark Cases

Privacy and Abortion

- **Griswold v. Connecticut (1965):** Found a "right to privacy" in the Constitution that would ban any state law against selling contraceptives.

- **Roe v. Wade (1973):** State laws against abortion were unconstitutional.

- **Webster v. Reproductive Health Services (1989):** Allowed states to ban abortions from public hospitals and permitted doctors to test to see if fetuses were viable.

- **Planned Parenthood v. Casey (1992):** Reaffirmed *Roe v. Wade* but upheld certain limits on its use.

- **Gonzales v. Carhart (2007):** Federal law may ban certain forms of partial birth abortion.

the Constitution, but the Court argued that it could be inferred from "penumbras" (literally, shadows) cast off by various provisions of the Bill of Rights.[50]

Eight years later the Court, in its famous *Roe v. Wade* decision, held that a "right to privacy" is "broad enough to encompass a woman's decision whether or not to terminate a pregnancy."[51] The case, which began in Texas, produced this view: during the first three months (or trimester) of pregnancy, a woman has an unfettered right to an abortion. During the second trimester, states may regulate abortions but only to protect the mother's health. In the third trimester, states might ban abortions.

In reaching this decision, the Court denied that it was trying to decide when human life began—at the moment of conception, at the moment of birth, or somewhere in between. But that is not how critics of the decision saw things. To them, life begins at conception, and so the human fetus is a "person" entitled to the equal protection of the laws guaranteed by the Fourteenth Amendment. People feeling this way began to use the slogans "right to life" and "pro-life." Supporters of the Court's action saw matters differently. In their view, no one can say for certain when human life begins; what one *can* say, however, is that a woman is entitled to choose whether or not to

police powers State power to effect laws promoting health, safety, and morals.

have a baby. These people took the slogans "right to choose" and "pro-choice."

Almost immediately, the congressional allies of pro-life groups introduced constitutional amendments to overturn *Roe v. Wade,* but none passed Congress. Nevertheless, abortion foes did persuade Congress, beginning in 1976, to bar the use of federal funds to pay for abortions except when the life of the mother is at stake. This provision is known as the Hyde Amendment, after its sponsor, Representative Henry Hyde. The chief effect of the amendment has been to deny the use of Medicaid funds to pay for abortions for low-income women.

Despite pro-life opposition, the Supreme Court for 16 years steadfastly reaffirmed and even broadened its decision in *Roe v. Wade*. It struck down laws requiring, before an abortion could be performed, a woman to have the consent of her husband, an "emancipated" but underage girl to have the consent of her parents, or a woman to be advised by her doctor as to the facts about abortion.[52]

But in 1989, under the influence of justices appointed by President Reagan, it began in the *Webster* case to uphold some state restrictions on abortions. When that happened, many people predicted that in time *Roe v. Wade* would be overturned, especially if President George H.W. Bush was able to appoint more justices. He appointed two (Souter and Thomas), but *Roe* survived. The key votes were cast by Justices O'Connor, Souter, and Kennedy. In 1992, in its *Casey* decision, the Court by a vote of five to four explicitly refused to overturn *Roe,* declaring that there was a right to abortion. At the same time, however, it upheld a variety of restrictions imposed by the state of Pennsylvania on women seeking abortions. These included a mandatory 24-hour waiting period between the request for an abortion and the performance of it, the requirement that teenagers obtain the consent of one parent (or, in special circumstances, of a judge), and a requirement that women contemplating an abortion be given pamphlets about alternatives to it. Similar restrictions had been enacted in many other states, all of which looked to the Pennsylvania case for guidance as to whether they could be enforced. In allowing these restrictions, the Court overruled some of its own earlier decisions.[53] On the other hand, the Court did strike down a state law that would have required married women to obtain the consent of their husbands before having an abortion.

After a long political and legal struggle, the Court in 2007 upheld a federal law that bans certain kinds of partial-birth abortions. The law does not allow an abortion in which the fetus, still alive, is withdrawn until its head is outside the mother and then it is killed. The law does not ban a late-term abortion if it is necessary to protect the physical health of the mother or if it is performed on an already dead fetus, even if the doctor has already killed it.[54]

There is one irony in all of this: "Roe," the pseudonym for the woman who started the suit that became *Roe v. Wade,* never had an abortion and many years later, using her real name, Norma McCorvey, became an evangelical Christian who published a book and started a ministry to denounce abortions.

Affirmative Action

A common thread running through the politics of civil rights is the argument between **equality of results** and equality of opportunity.

EQUALITY OF RESULTS

One view, expressed by most civil rights and feminist organizations, is that the burdens of racism and sexism can be overcome only by taking race or sex into account in designing remedies. It is not enough to give rights to people; they must be given benefits. If life is a race, everybody must be brought up to the same starting line (or possibly even to the same finish line). This means that the Constitution is not and should not be color-blind or sex-neutral. In education, this implies that the races must actually be mixed in the schools, by busing if necessary. In hiring, it means that **affirmative action**—preferential hiring practices—must be used to find and hire women, African Americans, and other minorities. Women should not simply be free to enter the labor force; they should be given the material necessities (for example, free daycare) that will help them enter it. On payday, workers' checks should reflect not just the results of people's competing in the marketplace but the results of plans designed to ensure that people earn comparable amounts for comparable jobs. Of late, affirmative action has been defended in the name of diversity or multiculturalism—the view that every institution (firm, school, or agency) and every

equality of result Making certain that people achieve the same result.

affirmative action Programs designed to increase minority participation in some institution (businesses, schools, labor unions, or government agencies) by taking positive steps to appoint more minority-group members.

How Things Work

Becoming a Citizen

For persons born in the United States, the rights of U.S. citizenship have been ensured, in constitutional theory if not in everyday practice, since the passage of the Fourteenth Amendment in 1868 and the civil rights laws of the 1960s. The Fourteenth Amendment conferred citizenship upon "all persons born in the United States . . . and subject to the jurisdiction thereof." Subsequent laws also gave citizenship to children born outside the United States to parents who are American citizens.

But immigrants, by definition, are not born with the rights of U.S. citizenship. Instead, those seeking to become U.S. citizens must, in effect, assume certain responsibilities in order to become citizens. The statutory requirements for naturalization, as they have been broadly construed by the courts, are as follows:

• Five years' residency, or three years if married to a citizen.

• Continuous residency since filing of the naturalization petition.

• Good moral character, which is loosely interpreted to mean no evidence of criminal activity.

• Attachment to constitutional principles. This means that potential citizens have to answer basic factual questions about American government (e.g., "Who was the first president of the United States?") and publicly denounce any and all allegiance to their native country and its leaders (e.g., Italy and the king of Italy), but devotion to constitutional principles is now regarded as implicit in the act of applying for naturalization.

• Being favorably disposed to "the good order and happiness of the United States."*

Today, about 97 percent of aliens who seek citizen-ship are successful in meeting these requirements and becoming naturalized citizens of the United States.

*8 U.S.C. 1423, 1427 (1970); *Girouard v. United States*, 328 U.S. 61 (1946).

Source: *New York Times* (July 25, 1993), 33. Copyright © 1993 by the *New York Times*. Reprinted by permission.

---

college curriculum should reflect the cultural (that is, ethnic) diversity of the nation.

EQUALITY OF OPPORTUNITY

The second view holds that if it is wrong to discriminate *against* African Americans and women, it is equally wrong to give them preferential treatment over other groups. To do so constitutes **reverse discrimination.** The Constitution and laws should be color-blind and sex-neutral.[55] In this view, allowing children to attend the school of their choice is sufficient; busing them to attain a certain racial mixture is wrong. Eliminating barriers to job opportunities is right; using numerical "targets" and "goals" to place minorities and women in specific jobs is wrong. If people wish to compete in the market, they should be satisfied with the market verdict concerning the worth of their work.

These two views are intertwined with other deep philosophical differences. Supporters of **equality of opportunity** tend to have orthodox beliefs; they favor letting private groups behave the way that they want (and so may defend the right of a men's club to exclude women). Supporters of the opposite view are likely to be progressive in their beliefs and insist that private clubs meet the same standards as schools or business firms. Adherents to the equality-of-opportunity view often attach great importance to traditional models of the family and so are skeptical of daycare and federally funded abortions. Adherents to the equality-of-results view prefer greater freedom of choice in lifestyle questions and so take the opposite position on daycare and abortion.

Of course, the debate is more complex than this simple contrast suggests. Take, for example, the question of affirmative action. Both the advocates of equality of opportunity and those of equality of results might agree that there is something odd about a factory or university that hires no African Americans or women, and both might press it to prove that its hiring policy is fair. Affirmative

reverse discrimination
Using race to sex to give preferential treatment to some people.

equality of opportunity
Giving people an equal chance to succeed.

How Things Work

The Rights of Aliens

America is a nation of immigrants. Some have arrived legally, others illegally. An illegal, or undocumented, alien is subject to deportation. With the passage in 1986 of the Immigration Reform and Control Act, illegal aliens who have resided in this country continuously before January 1, 1982, are entitled to amnesty—that is, they can become legal residents. However, the same legislation stipulated that employers (who once could hire undocumented aliens without fear of penalty) must now verify the legal status of all newly hired employees; if they knowingly hire an illegal alien, they face civil and criminal penalties.

Aliens—people residing in this country who are not citizens—cannot vote or run for office. Nevertheless, they must pay taxes just as if they were citizens. And they are entitled to many constitutional rights, even if they are in this country illegally. This is because most of the rights mentioned in the Constitution refer to "people" or "persons," not to "citizens." For example, the Fourteenth Amendment bars a state from depriving " *any person* of life, liberty, or property, without due process of law" or from denying "to *any person* within its jurisdiction the equal protection of the laws" [italics added]. As a result, the courts have held that:

- The children of illegal aliens cannot be excluded from the public school system.[1]

- Legally admitted aliens are entitled to welfare benefits.[2]

- Illegal aliens cannot be the object of reprisals if they attempt to form a labor union where they work.[3]

- The First Amendment rights of free speech, religion, press, and assembly and the Fourth Amendment protections against arbitrary arrest

and prosecution extend to aliens as well as to citizens.[4]

- Aliens are entitled to own property.

The government can make rules that apply to aliens only, but they must justify the reasonableness of the rules. For example:

- The Immigration and Naturalization Service has broader powers to arrest and search illegal aliens than police departments have to arrest and search citizens.[5]

- States can limit certain jobs, such as police officer and schoolteacher, to citizens.[6]

- The president or Congress can bar the employment of aliens by the federal government.[7]

- States can bar aliens from serving on a jury.[8]

- Illegal aliens are not entitled to obtain a Social Security card.

[1]*Plyler v. Doe*, 457 U.S. 202 (1982).

[2]*Graham v. Richardson*, 403 U.S. 365 (1971).

[3]*Sure-Tan v. National Labor Relations Board*, 467 U.S. 883 (1984).

[4]*Chew v. Colding*, 344 U.S. 590 (1953).

[5]*U.S. v. Brignoni-Ponce*, 422 U.S. 873 (1975); *INS v. Delgado*, 466 U.S. 210 (1984); *INS v. Lopez-Mendoza*, 486 U.S. 1032 (1984).

[6]*Cabell v. Chavez-Salido*, 454 U.S. 432 (1982); *Foley v. Connelie*, 435 U.S. 291 (1978); *Amblach v. Norwick*, 441 U.S. 68 (1979).

[7]*Hampton v. Mow Sun Wong*, 436 U.S. 67 (1976).

[8]*Schneider v. New Jersey*, 308 U.S. 147 (1939).

action in this case can mean *either* looking hard for qualified women and minorities and giving them a fair shot at jobs *or* setting a numerical goal for the number of women and minorities that should be hired and insisting that that goa l be met. Persons who defend the second course of action call these goals "targets"; persons who criticize that course call them "quotas."

The issue has largely been fought in the courts. Between 1978 and 1990, about a dozen major cases involving affirmative action were decided by the

Supreme Court; in about half it was upheld, and in the other half it was overturned. The different outcomes reflect two things—the differences in the facts of the cases and the arrival on the Court of three justices (Kennedy, O'Connor, and Scalia) appointed by a president, Ronald Reagan, who was opposed to at least the broader interpretation of affirmative action. As a result of these decisions, the law governing affirmative action is now complex and confusing.

Consider one issue: should the government be allowed to use a quota system to select workers,

How Things Work

The Rights of the Disabled

In 1990, the federal government passed the Americans with Disabilities Act (ADA), a sweeping law that extended many of the protections enjoyed by women and racial minorities to disabled persons.

Who Is a Disabled Person?

Anyone who *has* a physical or mental impairment that substantially limits one or more major life activities (for example, holding a job), anyone who has a *record* of such impairment, or anyone who is *regarded* as having such an impairment is considered disabled.

What Rights Do Disabled Persons Have?

Employment   Disabled persons may not be denied employment or promotion if, with "reasonable accommodation," they can perform the duties of that job. (Excluded from this protection are people who currently use illegal drugs, gamble compulsively, or are homosexual or bisexual.) Reasonable accommodation need not be made if this would cause "undue hardship" on the employer.

Government Programs and Transportation
Disabled persons may not be denied access to government programs or benefits. New buses, taxis, and trains must be accessible to disabled persons, including those in wheelchairs.

Public Accommodations   Disabled persons must enjoy "full and equal" access to hotels, restaurants, stores, schools, parks, museums, auditoriums, and the like. To achieve equal access, owners of existing facilities must alter them "to the maximum extent feasible"; builders of new facilities must ensure they are readily accessible to disabled persons, unless this is structurally impossible.

Telephones   The ADA directs the Federal Communications Commission to issue regulations to ensure telecommunications devices for hearing- and speech-impaired people are available "to the extent possible and in the most efficient manner."

Congress   The rights under this law apply to employees of Congress.

Rights Compared   The ADA does not enforce the rights of disabled persons in the same way as the Civil Rights Act enforces the rights of African Americans and women. Racial or gender discrimination must end *regardless of cost*; denial of access to disabled persons must end unless "undue hardship" or excessive costs would result.

---

enroll students, award contracts, or grant licenses? In the *Bakke* decision in 1978, the Court said the medical school of the University of California at Davis could not use an explicit numerical quota in admitting minority students but could "take race into account."[56] So no numerical quotas, right? Wrong. Two years later, the Court upheld a federal rule that set aside 10 percent of all federal construction contracts for minority-owned firms.[57] All right, maybe quotas can't be used in medical schools, but they can be used in the construction industry. Not exactly. In 1989, the Court overturned a Richmond, Virginia, law that set aside 30 percent of its construction contracts for minority-owned firms.[58] Well, maybe the Court just changed its mind between 1980 and 1989. No. One year later it upheld a federal rule that gave preference to minority-owned firms in the awarding of broadcast licenses.[59] Then in 1993, it upheld the right of white contractors to challenge minority set-aside laws in Jacksonville, Florida.[60]

It is too early to try to make sense of these twists and turns, especially since a deeply divided Court is still wrestling with these issues and Congress (as

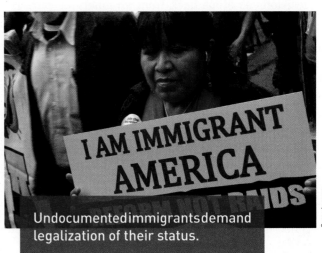

Undocumented immigrants demand legalization of their status.

Getty Images

with the Civil Rights Act of 1991) is modifying or superseding some earlier Court decisions. But a few general standards seem to be emerging. In simplified form, they are as follows:

- The courts will subject any quota system created by state or local governments to "strict scrutiny" and will look for a "compelling" justification for it.

- Quotas or preference systems cannot be used by state or local governments without first showing that such rules are needed to correct an actual past or present pattern of discrimination.[61]

- In proving there has been discrimination, it is not enough to show that African Americans (or other minorities) are statistically underrepresented among employees, contractors, or union members; you must identify the actual practices that have had this discriminatory impact.[62]

- Quotas or preference systems created by *federal* law will be given greater deference, in part because Section 5 of the Fourteenth Amendment gives to Congress powers not given to the states to correct the effects of racial discrimination.[63]

- It may be easier to justify in court a voluntary preference system (for example, one agreed to in a labor-management contract) than one that is required by law.[64]

- Even when you can justify special preferences in *hiring* workers, the Supreme Court is not likely to allow racial preferences to govern who gets *laid off*. A worker laid off to make room for a minority worker loses more than a worker not hired in preference to a minority applicant.[65]

Complex as they are, these rulings still generate a great deal of passion. Supporters of the decisions barring certain affirmative action plans hail these decisions as steps back from an emerging pattern of reverse discrimination. In contrast, civil rights organizations have denounced those decisions that have overturned affirmative action programs. In 1990, their congressional allies introduced legislation that would reverse several decisions. In particular, this legislation would put the burden of proof on the employer, not the employee, to show that the underrepresentation of minorities in the firm's work force was the result of legitimate and necessary business decisions and not the result of discrimination. If the employer could not prove this, the aggrieved employee would be able to collect large damage awards. (In the past, he or she could collect only back pay.) In 1991, the bill was passed and was signed by President Bush.

In thinking about these matters, most Americans distinguish between compensatory action and preferential treatment. They define *compensatory action* as "helping disadvantaged people catch up, usually by giving them extra education, training, or services." A majority of the public supports this. They define preferential treatment as "giving minorities preference in hiring, promotions, college admissions, and contracts." Large majorities oppose this.[66] These views reflect an enduring element in American political culture—a strong commitment to individualism ("nobody should get something without deserving it") coupled with support for help for the disadvantaged ("somebody who is suffering through no fault of his or her own deserves a helping hand").

Where does affirmative action fit into this culture? Polls suggest that if affirmative action is defined as "helping," people will support it, but if it is defined as "using quotas," they will oppose it. On this matter, blacks and whites see things differently. Blacks think they should receive preferences in employment to create a more diverse work force and to make up for past discrimination; whites oppose using goals to create diversity or to remedy past ills. In sum, the controversy over affirmative action depends on what you mean by it and on your racial identity.[67]

A small construction company named Adarand tried to get a contract to build guardrails along a highway in Colorado. Though it was the low bidder, it lost the contract because of a government policy that favors small businesses owned by "socially and economically disadvantaged individuals"—that is, by racial and ethnic minorities. In a five-to-four decision, the Court agreed with Adarand and sent the case back to Colorado for a new trial.

The essence of its decision was that *any* discrimination based on race must be subject to strict scrutiny, even if its purpose is to help, not hurt, a racial minority. Strict scrutiny means two things:

- Any racial preference must serve a "compelling government interest."

- The preference must be "narrowly tailored" to serve that interest.[68]

To serve a compelling governmental interest, it is likely that any racial preference will have to remedy a clear pattern of past discrimination. No such pattern had been shown in Colorado.

This decision prompted a good deal of political debate about affirmative action. In California, an initiative was put on the 1996 ballot to prevent state authorities from using "race, sex, color, ethnicity, or national origin as a criterion for either

Landmark Cases

Affirmative Action

- **Regents of the University of California v. Bakke (1978):** In a confused set of rival opinions, the decisive vote was cast by Justice Powell, who said that a quota-like ban on Bakke's admission was unconstitutional but that "diversity" was a legitimate goal that could be pursued by taking race into account.

- **United Steelworkers v. Weber (1979):** Despite the ban on racial classifications in the 1964 Civil Rights Act, this case upheld the use of race in an employment agreement between the steelworkers union and steel plant.

- **Richmond v. Croson (1989):** Affirmative action plans must be judged by the strict scrutiny standard that requires any race-conscious plan to be narrowly tailored to serve a compelling interest.

- **Grutter v. Bollinger and Gratz v. Bollinger (2003):** Numerical benefits cannot be used to admit minorities into college, but race can be a "plus factor" in making those decisions.

- **Parents v. Seattle School District (2007):** Race cannot be used to decide which students may attend especially popular high schools because this was not "narrowly tailored" to achieve a "compelling" goal.

Landmark Cases

Gay Rights

- **Lawrence v. Texas (2003):** State law may not ban sexual relations between same-sex partners.

- **Boy Scouts of America v. Dale (2000):** A private organization may ban gays from its membership.

discriminating against, or granting preferential treatment to, any individual or group" in public employment, public education, or public contracting. When the votes were counted, it passed. Michigan, Nebraska, and Washington have adopted similar measures, and other states may.

But the *Adarand* case and the passage of the California initiative did not mean affirmative action was dead. Though the federal Court of Appeals for the Fifth Circuit had rejected the affirmative action program of the University of Texas Law School,[69] the Supreme Court did not take up that case. It waited for several more years to rule on a similar matter arising from the University of Michigan. In 2003, the Supreme Court overturned the admissions policy of the University of Michigan that had given to every African American, Hispanic, and Native American applicant a bonus of 20 points out of the 100 needed to guarantee admission to the

University's undergraduate program.[70] This policy was not "narrowly tailored." In rejecting the bonus system, the Court reaffirmed its decision in the *Bakke* case made in 1978 in which it had rejected a university using a "fixed quota" or an exact numerical advantage to the exclusion of "individual" considerations.

But that same day, the Court upheld the policy of the University of Michigan Law School that used race as a "plus factor" but not as a numerical quota.[71] It did so even though using race as a plus factor increased by threefold the proportion of minority applicants who were admitted. In short, admitting more minorities serves a "compelling state interest" and doing so by using race as a plus factor is "narrowly tailored" to achieve that goal.

Gays and the Constitution

At first, the Supreme Court was willing to let states decide how many rights homosexuals should have. Georgia, for example, passed a law banning sodomy (that is, any sexual contact involving the sex organs of one person and the mouth or anus of another). Though the law applied to all persons, homosexuals sued to overturn it. In *Bowers v. Hardwick,* the Supreme Court decided, by a five-to-four majority, that there was no reason in the Constitution to prevent a state from having such a law. There was a right to privacy, but it was designed simply to protect "family, marriage, or procreation."[72]

But ten years later, the Court seemed to take a different position. The voters in Colorado had adopted a state constitutional amendment that made it illegal to pass any law to protect persons based on their "homosexual, lesbian, or bisexual orientation." The law did not penalize gays and lesbians; instead it said they could not become the object of specific legal protection of the sort that had traditionally been given to racial or ethnic minorities. (Ordinances to give specific protection to homosexuals had been adopted in some Colorado cities.) The Supreme Court struck down the Colorado constitutional amendment because it violated the equal protection clause of the federal Constitution.[73]

Now we faced a puzzle: a state can pass a law banning homosexual sex, as Georgia had, but a state cannot adopt a rule preventing cities from protecting homosexuals, as Colorado had. The matter was finally put to rest in 2003. In *Lawrence v. Texas,* the Court, again by a five-to-four vote, overturned a Texas law that banned sexual contact between persons of the same sex. The Court repeated the language it had used earlier in cases involving contraception and abortion. If "the right to privacy means anything, it is the right of the individual, married or single, to be free from unwanted governmental intrusion" into sexual matters. The right of privacy means the "right to define one's own concept of existence, of meaning, of the universe, and of the mystery of human life." It specifically overruled *Bowers v. Hardwick.*[74]

The *Lawrence* decision had a benefit and a cost. The benefit was to strike down a law that was rarely enforced and if introduced today probably could not be passed. The cost was to create the possibility that the Court, and not Congress or state legislatures, might decide whether same-sex marriages were legal.

That same year, the Massachusetts Supreme Judicial Court decided, by a four-to-three vote, that gays and lesbians must be allowed to be married in the state.[75] The Massachusetts legislature responded by passing a bill that, if it becomes a state constitutional amendment, will reverse the state court's decision. For that to happen, the legislature would have to vote again on this matter, but that did not happen.

By mid-2009, six states had authorized same-sex marriages. In three of them it was by a decision of the state's supreme court (Connecticut, Iowa, and Massachusetts) while in the other three (Maine, New Hampshire, and Vermont) it was by a vote of the legislature. A few other places had authorized "civil unions" for gays and lesbians.

In 2008 the California Supreme Court ruled, five to four, that the state's ban on same-sex marriage violated the state's constitution. In November of that year the voters were asked to decide whether the constitution should be amended to ban such marriages. The initiative (Proposition 8) passed.

When the state supreme court was asked to decide whether this popular vote was binding, it upheld it but at the same time allowed existing same-sex marriages to remain in effect.

Many states have passed laws banning same-sex marriages, and in 1996 Congress enacted a bill, signed by President Clinton, called the Defense of Marriage Act. Under it, no state would have to give legal status to a same-sex marriage performed in another state, and it would define marriage as a lawful union of husband and wife. But state and federal laws on this matter could be overturned if the Supreme Court should decide in favor of same-sex marriage, using language that appears in the *Lawrence* case. That could be prevented by an amendment to the Constitution, but Congress is not willing to propose one and, if proposed, it is not clear the states would ratify it.

Private groups, however, can exclude homosexuals from their membership. In another five-to-four decision, the Supreme Court decided that the Boy Scouts of America could exclude gay men and boys because that group had a right to determine its own membership.[76]

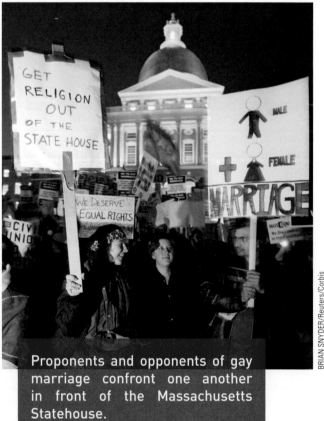

Proponents and opponents of gay marriage confront one another in front of the Massachusetts Statehouse.

BRIAN SNYDER/Reuters/Corbis

SUMMARY

The civil rights movement in the courts and in Congress profoundly changed the nature of African American participation in politics by bringing southern blacks into the political system so they could become an effective interest group. The decisive move was to enlist northern opinion in this cause, a job made easier by the northern perception that civil rights involved simply an unfair contest between two minorities—southern whites and southern blacks. That perception changed when it became evident the court rulings and legislative decisions would apply to the North as well as the South, leading to the emergence of northern opposition to court-ordered busing and affirmative action programs.

By the time this reaction developed, the legal and political system had been changed sufficiently to make it difficult if not impossible to limit the application of civil rights laws to the special circumstances of the South or to alter by legislative means the decisions of federal courts. Though the courts can accomplish little when they have no political allies (as revealed by the massive resistance to early school-desegregation decisions), they can accomplish a great deal, even in the face of adverse public opinion, when they have some organized allies (as revealed by their ability to withstand antibusing moves).

The feminist movement has paralleled in organization and tactics many aspects of the black civil rights movement, but with important differences. Women sought to repeal or reverse laws and court rulings that in many cases were ostensibly designed to protect rather than subjugate them. The conflict between protection and liberation was sufficiently intense to defeat the effort to ratify the Equal Rights Amendment.

The most divisive civil rights issues in American politics are abortion and affirmative action. From 1973 to 1989, the Supreme Court seemed committed to giving constitutional protection to all abortions within the first trimester; since 1989, it has approved various state restrictions on the circumstances under which abortions can be obtained.

There has been a similar shift in the Court's view of affirmative action. Though it will still approve some quota plans, it now insists they pass strict scrutiny to ensure they are used only to correct a proven history of discrimination, they place the burden of proof on the party alleging discrimination, and they be limited to hiring and not extended to layoffs. Congress has modified some of these rulings with new civil rights legislation.

RECONSIDERING WHO GOVERNS?

1. Since Congress enacts our laws, why has it not made certain that all groups have the same rights?

Congress responds to public demands. During much of our history, people have expected women, African Americans, Native Americans, and many other groups to be treated differently than others. The Bill of Rights is a check on congressional and state authority; to be effective, it must be enforced by independent courts.

2. After the Supreme Court ended racial segregation in the schools, what did the president and Congress do?

For a while, not much. But in time, these institutions began spending federal money and using federal troops and law enforcement officials in ways that greatly increased the rate of integration.

RECONSIDERING TO WHAT ENDS?

1. If the law supports equality of opportunity, why has affirmative action become so important?

There are several reasons. If there has been active discrimination in the past, affirmative action can be a way to help disadvantaged groups catch up. But the Supreme Court has also held, though by narrow majorities, that even when there has not been a legacy of discrimination, pursuing "diversity" is a "compelling" interest. The real issue is what diversity means and how best to achieve it.

2. Under what circumstances can men and women be treated differently?

A difference in treatment can be justified constitutionally if the difference is fair, reasonable, and not arbitrary. Sex differences need not meet the "strict scrutiny" test. It is permissible to punish men for statutory rape and to bar them from hospital delivery rooms; men are different from women in these respects. Congress may draft men without drafting women.

WORLD WIDE WEB RESOURCES

Court cases: **www.law.cornell.edu**

Department of Justice: **www.usdoj.gov**

Civil rights organizations: National Association for the Advancement of Colored People: **www.naacp.org**

National Organization for Women: **www.now.org**

National Gay and Lesbian Task Force: **www.thetaskforce.org**

National Council of La Raza: **www.nclr.org**

American Arab Anti-Discrimination Committee: **www.adc.org**

Anti-Defamation League: **www.adl.org**

SUGGESTED READINGS

Branch, Taylor. *Parting the Waters: America in the King Years*. New York: Simon and Schuster, 1988. A vivid account of the civil rights struggle.

Flexner, Eleanor. *Century of Struggle: The Women's Rights Movement in the United States*. Rev. ed. Cambridge: Harvard University Press, 1975. A historical account of the feminist movement and its political strategies.

Friedan, Betty. *The Feminine Mystique*. New York: Norton, 1963. Tenth anniversary edition, 1974. A well-known call for women to become socially and culturally independent.

Foreman, Christopher A. *The African-American Predicament*. Washington, D.C.: Brookings Institution, 1999. Thoughtful essays on problems faced by African Americans today.

Franklin, John Hope. *From Slavery to Freedom*. 5th ed. New York: Knopf, 1980. A survey of black history in the United States.

Kluger, Richard. *Simple Justice*. New York: Random House/Vintage Books, 1977. Detailed and absorbing account of the school-desegregation issue, from the Fourteenth Amendment to the *Brown* case.

Kull, Andrew. *The Color-Blind Constitution*. Cambridge: Harvard University Press, 1992. A history of efforts, none yet successful, to make the Constitution color-blind.

Mansbridge, Jane J. *Why We Lost the ERA*. Chicago: University of Chicago Press, 1986. Explains why the Equal Rights Amendment did not become part of the Constitution.

Thernstrom, Stephan, and Abigail Thernstrom. *America in Black and White*. New York: Simon and Schuster, 1997. Detailed history and portrait of African Americans.

Wilhoit, Francis M. *The Politics of Massive Resistance*. New York: George Braziller, 1973. The methods—and ultimate collapse—of all-out southern resistance to school desegregation.

Woodward, C. Vann. *The Strange Career of Jim Crow*. New York: Oxford University Press, 1957. Brief, lucid account of the evolution of Jim Crow practices in the South.

Part 2

Opinions, Interests, and Organizations

The latent causes of faction are thus sown in the nature of man; and we see them everywhere brought into different degrees of activity, according to the different circumstances of civil society.

* Federalist No. 10

7

Public Opinion

Spencer Grant/PhotoEdit

WHO GOVERNS?

1. How does public opinion in America today vary by race, gender, and other differences?
2. What is political ideology, and how does it affect political behavior and influence public policy?

TO WHAT ENDS?

1. What role did the Framers of the Constitution think public opinion should play in American democracy?
2. When, if ever, should public policies mirror majority opinion?

The lead story on the Internet home page had this headline: "Americans See Gloom, Doom in 2007."[1] Two hours later, however, the lead story had this headline: "Americans Optimistic for 2007."[2] The same news organization released both stories. Each story was based on the same telephone poll of the same 1,000 adults conducted a little over two weeks earlier. Each story cited numerous statistics from the poll. For instance, the former story reported that 60 percent believed America would suffer another terrorist attack in the year ahead, and that 90 percent believed higher gas prices were likely. The latter story reported that 89 percent believed the new year would be good for themselves and their families, and that just 25 percent felt pessimistic about what it would bring for the country.

So far as one can tell, the poll on which all the statistics cited in each story were based was well-designed and well-conducted. The statistics in each case were correct. Each story, however, had a different writer.

You have now learned a not-to-be-forgotten lesson about our topic: even a good survey and valid statistics do not speak for themselves when it comes to interpreting "what the public really thinks."

Defined simply, **public opinion** refers to how people think or feel about particular things. In this chapter, we take a close look at what "public opinion" is, how it is formed, and how opinions differ. In later chapters, we examine the workings of political parties, interest groups, and government institutions and consider what impact they have on whether public opinion affects government policy. We begin, however, by exploring the role public opinion is meant to play in the country's representative democracy.

Public Opinion and Democracy

public opinion How people think or feel about particular things.

In the Gettysburg Address, Abraham Lincoln said the United States has a government "of the people, by the people, and for the people." That suggests the government should do what the people want. If that is the case, it is puzzling that:

- The federal government often has had a large budget deficit, but the people want a balanced budget.

- The Equal Rights Amendment to the Constitution was not ratified, but polls showed that most people supported it.

- Most people believe there should be a limit on the number of terms to which U.S. senators and members of the U.S. House of Representatives can be elected, but Congress has not approved term limits.

Some people, reflecting on the many gaps between what the government does and what the people want, may become cynical and think our system is democratic in name only. That would be a mistake. There are several very good reasons why government policy often will appear to be at odds with public opinion.

First, the Framers of the Constitution did not try to create a government that would do from day to day "what the people want." They created a government for the purpose of achieving certain substantive goals. The preamble to the Constitution lists six of these: "to form a more perfect Union, establish Justice, ensure domestic Tranquility, provide for the common defense, promote the general Welfare, and secure the Blessings of Liberty."

One means of achieving these goals was popular rule, as provided for by the right of the people to vote for members of the House of Representatives (and later for senators and presidential electors). But other means were provided as well: representative government, federalism, the separation of powers, a Bill of Rights, and an independent judiciary. These were all intended to be checks on public opinion. In addition, the Framers knew that in a nation as large and diverse as the United States there would rarely be any such thing as "public opinion"; rather there would be many "publics" (that is, factions) holding many opinions. The Framers hoped the struggle among these many publics would protect liberty (no one "public" would dominate) while at the same time permitting the adoption of reasonable policies that commanded the support of many factions.

Second, it is not as easy as one may suppose to know what the public thinks. We are so inundated these days with public opinion polls that we may imagine that they tell us what the public believes. That may be true on a few rather simple, clear-cut, and widely discussed issues, but it is not true with respect to most matters on which the government must act. The best pollsters know the limits of their methods, and the citizen should know them as well.

What Is Public Opinion?

Some years ago, researchers at the University of Cincinnati asked 1,200 local residents whether they favored passage of the Monetary Control Bill. About 21 percent said they favored the bill, 25 percent said they opposed it, and the rest said they hadn't thought much about the matter or didn't know. But there was no such thing as the Monetary Control Bill. The researchers made it up. About 26 percent of the people questioned in a national survey also expressed opinions on the same nonexistent piece of legislation.[3] In many surveys, wide majorities favor expanding most government programs *and* paying less in taxes. On some issues, the majority in favor one month gives way to the majority opposed the next, often with no obvious basis for the shift.

How much confidence should we place in surveys that presumably tell us "what the American people

American politics is intensely local, as when Rep. Loretta Sanchez shakes hands with a voter in her California district.

Jonathan Nourok/PhotoEdit

think" about legislation and other issues, and how should we assess "public opinion"?

For businesses, understanding how people think or feel about particular things—for example, knowing whether consumers are likely to want a new product or be willing to pay more for an old one—can spell the difference between profit and loss. In the early 20th century, corporations and marketing firms pioneered attempts to systematically measure public views. But political scientists were not far behind them.

The first major academic studies of public opinion and voting, published in the 1940s, painted a distressing picture of American democracy. The studies found that, while a small group of citizens knew lots about government and had definite ideas on many issues, the vast majority knew next to nothing about government and had only vague notions even on much-publicized public policy matters that affected them directly.[4] In the ensuing decades, however, other studies painted a somewhat more reassuring picture. These studies suggested that, while most citizens are poorly informed about government and care little about most public policy issues, they are nonetheless pretty good at using limited information (or cues) to figure out what policies, parties, or candidates most nearly reflect their values or favor their interests, and then acting (or voting) accordingly.[5]

The closer scholars have studied public opinion on particular issues, the less uniformed, indifferent, or fickle it has appeared to be. For example, a study by political scientist Terry M. Moe analyzed public opinion concerning whether the government should provide parents with publicly funded grants, or vouchers, that they can apply toward tuition at private schools. He found that although most people are unfamiliar with the voucher issue, "they do a much better job of formulating their opinions than skeptics would lead us to expect." When supplied with basic information, average citizens adopt "their positions for good substantive reasons, just as the informed do."[6]

HOW POLLING WORKS

If properly conducted, a survey of public opinion—popularly called a **poll**—can capture the opinions of 300 million citizens by interviewing as few as 1,500 of them. There are many keys to good polling: posing comprehensible questions (asking people about things they have some basis for forming an opinion about); wording questions fairly (not using "loaded" or "emotional" words or indicating what the "right" answer is); and others.

But no poll, whatever it asks and however worded, can provide us with a reasonably accurate measure of how people think or feel unless the persons polled are a **random sample** of the entire population, meaning that any given voter or adult has an equal chance of being interviewed. Through a process called stratified or multistage area sampling, the pollster makes a list of all the geographical units in the country—say all the counties—and groups (or "stratifies") them by size of their population. The pollster then selects at random units from each group or stratum in proportion to its total population. Within each selected county, smaller and smaller geographical units (down to particular blocks or streets) are chosen, and then, within the smallest unit, individuals are selected at random (by, for example, choosing the occupant of every fifth house). Repeat the process using equally randomized methods, and the pollster might get slightly different results. The difference between the results of two surveys or samples is called **sampling error.** For example, if one random sample shows that 70 percent of all Americans approve of the way the president is handling his job, and another random sample taken at the same time shows that 65 percent do, the sampling error is 5 percent.

Even if properly conducted, polls are hardly infallible. Since 1952, every major poll has in fact picked the winner of the presidential election. Likewise, **exit polls,** interviews with randomly selected voters conducted at polling places on election day in a representative sample of voting districts, have proven quite accurate. But as a result of sampling error and for other reasons, it is very hard for pollsters to predict the winner in a close election.

For any population over 500,000, pollsters need to make about 15,000 telephone calls to reach a number of respondents (technically, the number computes to 1,065) sufficient to ensure that the opinions of the sample differ only slightly (by a 3 percent plus or minus margin) from what the results would have been had they interviewed the entire population from which the sample was drawn. That can be very expensive to do. Polling firms can economize by using smaller than ideal samples or by undersampling

poll A survey of public opinion.

random sample Method of selecting from a population in which each person has an equal probability of being selected.

sampling error The difference between the results of random samples taken at the same time.

exit polls Polls based on interviews conducted on Election Day with randomly selected voters.

RESEARCH FRONTIERS

How the 2008 Presidential Primary Polling Went Wrong

In 2008, opinion polls made a lot of mistakes during the primary contests. They picked the wrong Democratic and Republican winners in New Hampshire and made other bad judgments in California, South Carolina, and Wisconsin.

To figure out what went wrong, opinion experts studied the matter and reported in early 2009 on how several polling firms operated. Here is what they found:

Many polls thought Democrat Barack Obama would carry New Hampshire. Instead, Hillary Clinton did. They made these mistakes because they did not spend the time and money to get and interview a representative sample of voters.

The pollsters did not reach out to find hard-to-locate voters, they interviewed too few union members and people without much schooling, and often interviewed whoever answered the telephone instead of the particular person named in the sample.

In part, this happened because it is getting harder to conduct reliable polling. A lot of people use cell phones; some do not even own a regular home phone. How do you find them? And a lot of people are getting tired of answering telephone polls and just hang up. How do you reach them?

Imagine you are trying to accurately poll students at your school.

- How big a sample should you have?
- How do you identify a representative sample?
- If you interview students by phone, what do you do if you can't find them or they hang up on you?

Source: American Association for Public Opinion Research, *Report of the Ad Hoc Committee on the 2008 Presidential Primary Polling* (March 2009).

hard-to-contact people, but then they risk getting things wrong. As summarized in the "Research Frontiers" box above, that is the story behind why so many 2008 presidential primary polls performed so poorly.

HOW OPINIONS DIFFER

Nobody fully understands how public opinion influences everything from who wins an election to what gets politicians' attention to whether given bills become law, but a few things are clear: some people care more about certain issues than other people do (*opinion saliency*); on some issues or choices, opinions are pretty steady, while on others they tend to be more volatile (*opinion stability*); and, on some issues government seems largely in sync with popular views or majority sentiments, while on other issues it seems significantly out of sync (*opinion-policy congruence*). For example, most Americans have an opinion on U.S. involvement in Iraq, but some feel more strongly about it than others do, and opinions have changed in response to news of positive or negative developments. From 2004 through 2006, for example, much news on the situation in Iraq was negative, and mass public support for U.S. involvement fell.[7]

Jim Cole/AP Photo

The polls predicted she would lose the 2008 New Hampshire primary, but Hillary Clinton had a surprise win over Barack Obama and John Edwards.

Studies also tell us that people with certain characteristics in common sometimes hold certain political beliefs in common. By no means do people with similar or even virtually identical family histories, religious affiliations, formal educations,

Bob Daemmrich/The Image Works

political socialization
Process by which background traits influence one's political views.

elite People who have a disproportionate amount of some valued resource.

or job experiences think or vote exactly the same way on all or most issues. But **political socialization**—the process by which personal and other background traits influence one's views about politics and government—matters. It is behind the fact, to be discussed in the next section, that children tend to share their parents' party affiliations; and it helps to explain why, as we shall see, opinions seem to vary in interesting ways associated with class, race, religion, gender, and other characteristics.

Research has also made clear that mass and elite opinion differ. By "elite" we do not mean people who are "better" than others. Rather, as we discussed in Chapter 1, **elite** is a term used by social scientists to refer to people who have a disproportionate amount of some valued resource—money, schooling, prestige, political power, or whatever. Not only do political elites *know more* about politics than the rest of us, they *think differently* about it—they have different views and beliefs. As we explain later in this v , they are more likely than average citizens to hold a more or less consistent set of opinions as to the policies government ought to pursue. The government attends more to the elite views than to popular views, at least on many matters.

Children grow up learning, but not always following, their parents' political beliefs.

Political Socialization

GENES AND THE FAMILY

For a long time, scholars believed people acquired their political views from their families. There is still a lot of truth in that argument. The great majority of high school students know the party affiliation of their parents and only a tiny minority of the children support a party opposite that of their parents.[8]

But of late we have learned that our genetic background explains much of our political ideology though rather little of our party affiliation. When we compare how identical twins (who are genetically the same) feel about politics with how fraternal twins (who share only half of their genes) think about politics, we discover that identical twins are much more likely to have similar political views than fraternal twins. Roughly one-third of the differences among people about political beliefs comes from our genetic makeup, but only one-tenth of these differences come from family influences.[9]

This should not surprise us. We know that children in the same family have different personalities even though they have the same parents. Genes play a big role in this. This is also true of basic political beliefs. If you add together the big effect of genes and the much smaller effect of parental influences, then half of our political views come from our family backgrounds. The other half comes from our individual life experiences, such as the friends we acquire, the schools we attend, and what happens to us as adults.

But our political beliefs are not necessarily the same as our party affiliation. We can be a liberal or conservative Democrat, a liberal or conservative Republican. Studies that have shown that genes affect our political beliefs suggest also that they do not have much of an effect on our party affiliation. Whether we are Democrats, Republicans, or something else depends on what we learn from our parents.

The ability of the family to inculcate a strong sense of party identification has declined in recent years. The proportion of citizens who say they consider themselves Democrats or Republicans has become steadily smaller since the early 1950s. Accompanying this decline in partisanship has been a sharp rise in the proportion of citizens describing themselves as independents.[10]

Part of this change results from the fact that young voters have always had a weaker sense of partisanship than older ones. But the youthfulness of the *gender gap* Difference in political views between men and women.

population cannot explain all the changes, for the decline in partisanship has occurred at all age levels. Moreover, those who reached voting age in the 1960s were less apt than those who matured in the 1950s to keep the party identification of their parents.[11]

There are also sizeable age-related differences in opinions on several issues. In some ways, the opinions of younger citizens break old ideological molds. For instance, compared to older Americans, citizens aged 18 to 29 are more likely to favor gay marriage and women's rights (generally labeled the liberal view on these issues), but also more likely to favor giving parents tax money in the form of vouchers for private or religious schools and letting people invest some of their Social Security contribution in the stock market (generally labeled the conservative view on these issues).[12] More generally, most of today's 18- to 24-year-olds think that politics has become too partisan, but most also think that getting involved in politics is an honorable thing to do (see Table 7.1).

But where do such views about politics come from? In most families, the dinner table is not a seminar in political philosophy but a place where people discuss school, jobs, dates, and chores. In some families, however, the dinner table is a political classroom. Studies of the participants in various student radical movements in the 1960s suggested that college radicals often were the sons and daughters of people who had themselves been young radicals; some commentators dubbed them the "red-diaper babies." Presumably, deeply conservative people come disproportionately from families that were also deeply conservative. This transfer of political beliefs from one generation to the next reflects both heredity and, to a lesser extent, family teaching.

RELIGION

One way in which the family forms and transmits political beliefs is by its religious tradition. Religious differences make for political differences, but the differences generally are more complicated than first meets the eye.

While most Americans remain somewhat or deeply religious, most seriously question religion's role in politics and government.[13] Religious influences on public opinion are pronounced with respect to social issues like abortion or gay rights, but they matter less on most other issues; and, when a war is perceived to be going badly or the economy is in trouble, most Americans of all faiths or of no faith agree that these are the issues that matter most.[14]

Opinions about politics and government vary not only across but within given religious traditions. For instance, Table 7.2 shows four Christian religious groups' respective opinions on three issues. White evangelicals and Hispanic Catholics differ significantly on health insurance and abortion, but all four groups have wide majorities that favor giving faith-based organizations government grants to deliver social services.

THE GENDER GAP

Journalists often point out that women have "deserted" Republican candidates to favor Democratic ones. In some cases, this is true. But it would be more correct to say that men have "deserted" Democratic candidates for Republican ones. The **gender gap** is the difference in political views between men and women. That gap has existed for a long time, and it is a problem for both political parties.

Women obtained the right to vote in 1920 when the Nineteenth Amendment to the Constitution was

Table 7.1 Young Adults on Politics and Politicians (2008)

Percent of 18- to 24-year-olds who agree that:	
politics has become too partisan	74%
elected officials don't have the same priorities I have	69%
getting involved in politics is an honorable thing to do	68%
people like me don't have any say about what government does	47%
it is difficult to find ways to be involved in politics	40%
politics is not relevant to my life right now	28%

Source: Institute of Politics, The 15th Biannual Youth Survey on Politics and Public Service, John F. Kennedy School of Government, Harvard University, October 2008.

Table 7.2 Opinions by Four Christian Groups on Three Issues (2008)

	Government-guaranteed health insurance	Abortion legal in all cases	Grants to faith based groups
	Percent in favor		
All Americans	63%	17%	67%
White Evangelicals	53	9	78
Black Protestants	66	17	83
White Catholics	62	13	71
Hispanic Catholics	78	21	75

Source: Pew Forum on Religion and Public Life, Survey: More Americans Question Religion's Role in Politics, August 21, 2008, sections 3 and 4.

ratified. Until 1980, women voted at significantly lower rates than men. Since 1980, however, women have voted at somewhat higher rates than men, a difference amplified by the fact that women are also a larger proportion of the voting-age population. In every presidential election from 1980 through 2008, women were more likely than men to favor the Democratic candidate.

As Table 7.3 shows, the Democratic advantage among women, especially women ages 18 to 29, has widened in recent years. Behind this gender gap in partisan self-identification are differences between men and women regarding what issues matter most (see Figure 7.1), and the view held by most voting-age women that the Democratic party sees these issues more as they do than the Republican party does.

Cleavages in Public Opinion

The way in which political opinions are formed helps explain the cleavages that exist among these opinions and why these cleavages do not follow any single political principle but instead overlap and crosscut in bewildering complexity. If, for example, the United States lacked regional differences and was composed almost entirely of white Protestants who had never attended college, there would still be plenty of political conflict—the rich would have different views from the poor; workers would have different views from farmers—but that conflict would be much simpler to describe and explain. It might even lead to political parties that

Table 7.3 Gender Gaps in Partisan Identification, 1992–2008

	Men			Women		
	Rep %	Dem %	D-R diff	Rep %	Dem %	D-R diff
All Voters						
2008	43	46	+3	33	56	+22
2004	48	43	−5	40	51	+11
2000	47	42	−5	38	51	+13
1996	49	43	−6	39	53	+14
1992	45	46	+1	40	52	+12
Voters Ages 18–29						
2008	38	52	+14	28	63	+35
2004	44	47	+3	36	54	+18
2000	46	44	−2	37	53	+16
1996	50	44	−6	38	55	+17
1992	52	42	−10	42	50	+8

Source: Pew Research Center for the People & the Press, Gen Dems: The Party's Advantage Among Young Voters Widens, April 28, 2008.

Figure 7.1

Gender Gaps on Issue Importance (2006)

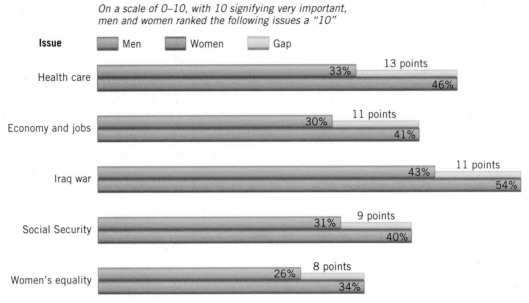

On a scale of 0–10, with 10 signifying very important, men and women ranked the following issues a "10"

Source: Ms. magazine/WDN Poll, Lake Research Partners, surveying 1,000 randomly selected likely voters November 6–7, 2006.

were more clearly aligned with competing political philosophies than those we now have. In fact, some democratic nations in the world today have a population very much like the one we have asked you to imagine, and the United States itself, during the first half of the 19th century, was overwhelmingly white, Protestant, and without much formal schooling.

Today, however, there are crosscutting cleavages based on race, ethnicity, religion, region, and education, in addition to those created by income and occupation. To the extent that politics is sensitive to public opinion, it is sensitive to a variety of different and even competing publics. Not all these publics have influence proportionate to their numbers or even to their numbers adjusted for the intensity of their feelings. As will be described later, a filtering process occurs that makes the opinions of some publics more influential than those of others.

Whatever this state of affairs may mean for democracy, it creates a messy situation for political scientists. It would be so much easier if everyone's opinion on political affairs reflected some single feature of his or her life, such as income, occupation, age, race, or sex. Of course, some writers have argued that political opinion is a reflection of one such feature, social class, usually defined in terms of income or occupation, but that view, though containing some

truth, is beset with inconsistencies: poor blacks and poor whites disagree sharply on many issues involving race; well-to-do Jews and well-to-do Protestants often have opposing opinions on social welfare policy; and low-income elderly people are much more worried about crime than low-income graduate students. Plumbers and professors may have similar incomes, but they rarely have similar views, and business people in New York City often take a very different view of government than business people in Houston or Birmingham.

In some other democracies, a single factor such as class may explain more of the differences in political attitudes than it does in the more socially heterogeneous United States. Most blue-collar workers in America think of themselves as "middle-class," whereas most such workers in Britain and France describe themselves as "working-class."

SOCIAL CLASS

Americans speak of "social class" with embarrassment. The norm of equality tugs at our consciences, urging us to judge people as individuals, not as parts of some social group (such as "the lower class"). Social scientists speak of "class" with confusion. They know it exists but quarrel constantly about how to define it: by income? occupation? wealth? schooling? prestige? personality?

cartoonbank.com

*"Good God! He's giving the
white-collar voters' speech to the blue collars."*

Let's face up to the embarrassment and skip over the confusion. Truck drivers and investment bankers look different, talk differently, and vote differently. There is nothing wrong with saying that the first group consists of "working-class" (or "blue-collar") people and the latter of "upper-class" (or "management") people. Moreover, though different definitions of class produce slightly different groupings of people, most definitions overlap to such an extent that it does not matter too much which we use.

However defined, public opinion and voting have been less determined by class in the United States than in Europe, and the extent of class cleavage has declined in the last few decades in both the United States and Europe. In the 1950s, V. O. Key, Jr., found that differences in political opinion were closely associated with occupation. He noted that people holding managerial or professional jobs had distinctly more conservative views on social welfare policy and more internationalist views on foreign policy than manual workers.[15]

During the next decade, this pattern changed greatly. Opinion surveys done in the late 1960s showed that business and professional people had views quite similar to those of manual workers on matters such as the poverty program, health insurance, American policy in Vietnam, and government efforts to create jobs.[16]

The voting patterns of different social classes have also become somewhat more similar. Class voting has declined sharply since the late 1940s in the United States, France, Great Britain, and Germany and declined moderately in Sweden.

Class differences remain, of course. Unskilled workers are more likely than affluent white-collar workers to be Democrats and to have liberal views on economic policy. And when economic issues pinch—for example, when farmers are hurting or steelworkers are being laid off—the importance of economic interests in differentiating the opinions of various groups rises sharply.

Still, many of the issues that now lead us to choose which party to support and that determine whether we think of ourselves as liberals or conservatives are noneconomic issues. In recent years, our political posture has been shaped by the positions we take on race relations, abortion, school prayer, environmentalism, and terrorism, issues that do not clearly affect the rich differently than the poor (or at least do not affect them as differently as do the union movement, the minimum wage, and unemployment). Moral, symbolic, and foreign policy matters do not divide rich and poor in the same way as economic ones. Thus, we have many well-off people who think of themselves as liberals because they take liberal positions on these noneconomic matters, and many not-so-well-off people who think of themselves as conservatives because that is the position they take on these issues.

RACE AND ETHNICITY

African Americans are overwhelmingly Democratic, though younger ones are a bit more likely than older ones to identify with the Republican party.[17] Younger blacks are also much more likely to support the idea of using school vouchers to pay for education than older ones. There are sharp differences between white and black attitudes on many public policy questions. For example, blacks are much more likely than whites to support affirmative action, to think that the criminal justice system is biased against them, to oppose the use of military force, to doubt that we all should be willing to fight for our country, and to think that believing in God is essential for a person to be moral.[18]

But there are also many areas of agreement. Both blacks and whites want our courts to be tougher in handling criminals, oppose the idea of making abortion legal in all cases, agree that people have become too dependent on government aid, and think that everyone has it in their own power to succeed.[19]

Latinos are now the largest minority group in America, numbering over 40 million people. Unfortunately, studies of Latino public opinion have been called "small, disproportionately oriented toward immigration, and relatively silent on the influence of gender"

Los Angeles Mayor Antonio Villaraigosa speaks to supporters.

Lester Cohen/WireImage.com/Getty Images

and other possible intragroup opinion cleavages.[20] Likewise, despite the country's growing Asian population, there is as yet also virtually no literature on Asian public opinion. However, an early survey of ethnic groups in California, a state where fully one-third of all recent immigrants to this country live, gives us some hint of how Latinos and Asian Americans feel about political parties and issues. Latinos identify themselves as Democrats, but much less so than blacks, and Asian Americans are even more identified with the Republican party than Anglo whites. On issues such as spending on the military and welfare programs, prayer in public schools, and the imposition of the death penalty for murder, Asian American views are much more like those of Anglo whites than those of either blacks or Hispanics. Latinos are somewhat more liberal than Anglos or Asian Americans, but much less liberal than blacks, except with respect to bilingual education programs.[21]

These figures conceal important differences within these ethnic groups. For example, Japanese Americans are among the more conservative Asian Americans, whereas Korean Americans (perhaps because they are among the most recent immigrants) are more liberal. Similarly, Latinos, the fastest-growing ethnic group in the United States, are a diverse mix of Cuban Americans, Mexican Americans, Central Americans, and Puerto Ricans, each with distinct political views. Most studies of Latino voting show that people from Mexico vote heavily Democratic, those from Cuba mostly Republican, and those from Puerto Rico somewhere in between.[22] But local conditions will affect these views. Hispanics in Texas often vote for more conservative candidates than do those in California.

Hispanic majorities seem to favor bigger government, oppose making abortions generally available, and think that the Democratic party cares more about them and is better able to handle economic and other issues. But these views are complicated not only because Latinos come from many nations but also because some were born here and some abroad. For example, in 2005 most Latinos believed U.S. troops should be withdrawn from Iraq, but there were important differences in the views of native-born and foreign-born Latinos.[23]

Latinos have less money and are younger than non-Hispanic white Americans. About four-fifths of all Latinos, but only half of all non-Hispanic whites, are younger than 45. It is possible that these differences affect their views.[24]

Despite these differences, there are broad areas of agreement between Latinos and non-Hispanic whites here. Almost exactly the same percentage of both groups favor allowing people to invest some of their Social Security taxes into stock-market funds.[25] We would like to know more about these opinions, but pollsters have not yet fully explored Hispanic attitudes.

REGION

It is widely believed that geographic region affects political attitudes and in particular that southerners and northerners disagree significantly on many policy questions. At one time, white southerners were conspicuously less liberal than easterners, midwesterners, or westerners on questions such as aid to minorities, legalizing marijuana, school busing, and enlarging the rights of those accused of crimes. Although more conservative on these issues, they held views on economic issues similar to those of whites in other regions of the country. This helps to explain why the South was for so long a part of the Democratic party coalition: on national economic and social welfare policies, southerners expressed views not very different from those of northerners. That coalition was always threatened, however, by the divisiveness produced by issues of race and liberty.

The southern lifestyle is in fact different from that of other regions of the country. The South has, on the whole, been more accommodating to business enterprise and less so to organized labor than, for example, the Northeast; it gave greater support to the third-party candidacy of George Wallace in 1968, which was a protest against big government and the growth of national political power as well as against civil rights; and it was in the South that the greatest opposition arose to income-redistribution plans such as the Family Assistance Plan of 1969. Moreover, there is some evidence that white southerners became by the 1970s more conservative than they had been in the 1950s, at least when compared to white northerners.[26] Finally, white southerners have become less attached to the Democratic party: no Democratic candidate for president has won a majority of white southern votes since Lyndon Johnson did so in 1964; in 2008, Barack Obama won the presidency with about half the white vote nationally but only about 30 percent of the white vote in the South.

Political Ideology

Up to now the words *liberal* and *conservative* have been used here as if everyone agreed on what they meant and as if they accurately described general sets of political beliefs held by large segments of the population. Neither of these assumptions is correct. Like many useful words—*love, justice, happiness*—they are as vague as they are indispensable.

When we refer to people as liberals, conservatives, socialists, or radicals, we are implying that they have a patterned set of beliefs about how government and other important institutions in fact operate and how they ought to operate, and in particular about what kinds of policies government ought to pursue. They are said to display to some degree a **political ideology**—that is, a more or less consistent set of beliefs about what policies government ought to pursue. Political scientists measure the extent to which people have a political ideology in two ways: first, by seeing how frequently people use broad political categories (such as "liberal," "conservative," "radical") to describe their own views or to justify their preferences for various

political ideology A more or less consistent set of beliefs about what policies government ought to pursue.

Politically Speaking

Liberals and Conservatives

Both words—*liberal* and *conservative*—first came into use in the early 19th century. At that time, a liberal was a person who favored personal and economic liberty—that is, freedom from the controls and powers of government or the state. An economic liberal, for example, supported the free market and opposed government regulation of trade. By contrast, a conservative was a person who opposed the bloody excesses of the French Revolution and its emphasis on personal freedom and favored instead a restoration of the power of the church and the aristocracy.

The terms' meanings changed in the 1930s. President Franklin Delano Roosevelt used *liberal* to refer to his New Deal program calling for an active national government that would intervene in the economy, create social welfare programs, and help certain groups (such as labor unions) acquire greater bargaining power. Roosevelt's opponents began using the term *conservative* to describe themselves. In 1964, Barry Goldwater was the first presidential candidate to declare himself a "conservative," by which he meant someone favoring a free market rather than a regulated one, states' rights over national supremacy, and greater reliance on individual choice in economic affairs.

Roosevelt was a Democrat. Goldwater was a Republican. Roosevelt, however, would not instantly recognize as liberals today's staunchly pro-choice, secular Democrats. Several times before he died in 1998, Goldwater scolded Republicans who invoked religious reasons for wanting to outlaw abortion and gay rights; they were not, he insisted, conservatives. And today we have self-described "neo-liberals," "neo-conservatives," "compassionate conservatives," and many other twists on these terms.

Still, the two words remain in general use, convey some significant meaning, and point to real and persistent differences on many issues between, for example, the liberal and conservative wings of the Democratic and Republican parties.

candidates and policies, and second, by seeing to what extent the policy preferences of a citizen are consistent over time or are based at any one time on consistent principles.

This second method involves a simple mathematical procedure: measuring how accurately one can predict a person's view on a subject at one time based on his or her view on that subject at an earlier time, or measuring how accurately one can predict a person's view on one issue based on his or her view on a different issue. The higher the accuracy of such predictions (or correlations), the more we say a person's political opinions display "constraint" or ideology.

Despite annual fluctuations, ideological self-identification surveys from the last three decades typically find that moderates are the largest group among American voters (roughly 40 percent), conservatives the second largest (about 30 percent), and liberals the smallest (about 20 percent).[27] For three reasons, however, these self-identification survey averages do not really tell us much at all about how or whether most people think about politics in an ideological manner. First, except when asked by pollsters, most Americans do not actually employ the words *liberal, conservative,* or *moderate* in explaining or justifying their preferences for parties, candidates or policies, and not many more than half can give plausible definitions of these terms. The vast majority of Americans simply do not think about politics in an ideological or very coherent manner.

Second, over the last decade, survey research scholars have rediscovered old truths about the limitations of polling as a window into "the public mind."[28] Public opinion polls must of necessity ask rather simple questions. The apparent "inconsistency" in the answers people give at different times may mean only that the nature of the problem and the wording of the question have changed. Or it could simply mean that many people consistently want from politics or government things that, as a practical matter, they cannot have, or at least cannot have all at once or at a price they are willing to pay—for instance, a bigger military, more expansive public health insurance coverage for all, and greater funding for public schools, but no military draft, no new or increased taxes, and no government budget deficits, either. Ideological liberals might consistently covet everything on that list except the bigger military, and be willing to pay higher taxes to get it. Ideological conservatives might want only the bigger military, but only if getting it requires no tax increases. But most citizens are more inclined to pick and choose their positions without regard to conventional liberal or conservative views, and without feeling any need to be "consistent."

Third, when surveyed in person (including by telephone), some people will hide what they think to be socially or morally unacceptable self-identifications or positions behind a "don't know" or "middle-ground" response.[29] This can happen not only when the questions concern specific labels like "liberal" or "conservative," or particular issues like racial integration or immigration restrictions, but also when the question seems to ask about fundamental values, patriotism, or "Americanism." As we saw in Chapter 4, most Americans share a distinctive political culture—a belief in freedom, in equality of political condition and economic opportunity, and in civic duty. Trying to determine precisely where political culture ends and ideology begins often is difficult or impossible.

MASS IDEOLOGIES: A TYPOLOGY

Partly in recognition of these and related limitations, pollsters have increasingly taken a fresh approach to documenting and analyzing average Americans' ideological cast and character. Essentially, rather than ask people to identify themselves as "liberal," "conservative," or "moderate," they ask people multiple questions about politics and government, and then use the answers to sort them into a half-dozen or more different groups.

The oldest ideological typology survey of this sort started in 1987 and has been updated three times since. (To see where you fit, you can take the survey for yourself at **http://typology.people-press .org/typology**). Americans, it finds, are divided into nine different groups, each defined by certain key values (see Table 7.4). Measured by both their presence among registered voters and in the general population, "liberals" are the largest single ideological bloc. Together with "disadvantaged Democrats," they number nearly one in three registered voters and over a quarter of the general public.

But various types of conservatives ("social," "pro-government," and conservative Democrats), together with heavily Republican "enterprisers," comprise nearly one in two registered voters and over 40 percent of the general population. And nearly one in five Americans ("disaffected" plus "bystanders") hold views that lead them to be cynical about politics or pay it no mind. Dig deeper into the data on these nine groups (also available via the same web site cited above), such as the related survey findings regarding each group's socioeconomic status and views on religion and other matters that affect politics, and you will see that the old three-way (liberal-conservative-moderate) self-identification surveys probably obscured more than they revealed about what most average Americans think about politics.

Table 7.4 Ideology Typology: Nine Groups and Their Key Values

Key Values of Nine Groups	Registered Voters	Adult Population	Democrat/ Republican/ Independent
Liberals			
(Seculars; 60s Democrats)	19%	17%	59%/1%/40%
Pro-choice; diplomacy over military force; protect the environment			
Conservative Democrats			
(Socially Conservative Democrats; New Dealers)	15	14	89/0/11
Religion vital to morality; oppose same-sex marriage; support antipoverty programs			
Social Conservatives			
(Moralists)	13	11	0/82/18
Pro-life; assertive foreign policy; oppose welfare			
Upbeats			
(New Prosperity Independents)	13	11	39/5/56
Economic growth; pro-government and pro-business; pro-immigration			
Pro-Government Conservatives			
(Populist Republicans)	10	9	2/58/40
Government must promote morality; for anti-poverty programs and business regulation			
Enterprisers			
(Staunch Conservatives)	10	9	1/81/18
Patriotic; anti-regulation, including the environment			
Disaffecteds			
(Disaffected Voters)	10	9	30/2/68
Cynical about government; unhappy with own economic situation; anti-immigration			
Disadvantaged Democrats			
(Partisan Poor)	10	10	84/0/16
Extremely anti-business; strong support for anti-poverty programs; deep mistrust of elected leaders			
Bystanders			
(N/A)	0	10	22/22/56
Vote in single digits even in presidential elections; ignore most political news			

Source: Adapted from "Profiles of the Typology Groups: Beyond Red and Blue," Pew Research Center for the People and the Press, 2005.

LIBERAL AND CONSERVATIVE ELITES

Still, while the terms *liberal* and *conservative* do not describe the political views held by most average Americans, they do capture the views held by many, perhaps most, people who are in the country's political elite. As we discussed in Chapter 1, every society has an elite, because in every society government officials will have more power than ordinary folk, some persons will make more money than others, and some people will be more popular than others. In the former Soviet Union, they even had an official name for the political elite—the *nomenklatura*.

political elites Persons with a disproportionate share of political power.

But, in America, we often refer to **political elites** more casually as "activists"—people who hold office, run for office, work in campaigns or on newspapers, lead interest groups and social movements, and speak out on public issues. Being an activist is not an all-or-nothing proposition: people display differing degrees of activism, from full-time politicians to persons who occasionally get involved in a campaign (see Chapter 8). But the more a person is an activist, the more likely it is that he or she will display ideological consistency on the conventional liberal-conservative spectrum.

The reasons for this greater consistency seem to be information and peers. First, information: in general, the better informed people are about politics and the more interest they take in politics, the more likely they are to have consistently liberal or conservative views.[30] This higher level of information and interest may lead them to find relationships among issues that others don't see and to learn from the media and elsewhere what are the "right" things to believe. This does not mean there are no differences within liberal elites (or within conservative ones), only that the differences occur within a liberal (or conservative) consensus that is more well defined, more consistent, and more important to those who share it than would be the case among ordinary citizens.

Second, peers: politics does not make strange bedfellows. On the contrary, politics is a process of likes attracting likes. The more active you are in politics, the more you will associate with people who agree with you on some issues; and the more time you spend with those people, the more your other views will shift to match theirs.

The greater ideological consistency of political elites can be seen in Congress. As we shall note in Chapter 13, Democratic members of Congress tend to be consistently liberal, and Republican members of Congress tend to be consistently conservative—*far more* consistently than Democratic voters and Republican voters. By the same token, we shall see in Chapter 9 that the delegates to presidential nominating conventions are far more ideological (liberal in the Democratic convention, conservative in the Republican one) than is true of voters who identify with the Democratic or Republican party.

Still, on a large number of issues, the policy preferences of average Republican and Democratic voters do differ significantly from one another. Some

political scientists argue that Republican and Democratic leaders in Congress are more polarized because voters are more polarized.

Other political scientists, however, analyze the available polling and election data differently. They find that ideological changes among voters have been small while public opinion among Democrats voting in districts represented by Democrats and among Republicans voting in districts represented by Republicans has been remarkably stable. Which side is right? We have no data that will allow us to compare in each district what voters think and how their representatives behave. To amass such data would require polls of perhaps 500 voters in each congressional district taken several years apart. Nobody thinks it is worth spending millions of dollars to interview over 10,000 voters at different times just to answer this one academic puzzle.

Political Elites, Public Opinion, and Public Policy

Though the elites and the public see politics in very different ways, and though there often are intense antagonisms between the two groups, the elites influence public opinion in at least two important ways.

First, elites, especially those in or having access to the media (see Chapter 12), raise and frame political issues. At one time, environmentalism was not on the political agenda; at a later time, not only was it on the agenda, it was up near the top of government concerns. At some times the government had little interest in what it should do in South Africa or Central America; at other times the government was preoccupied with these matters. Though world events help shape the political agenda, so also do political elites. A path-breaking study by John Zaller shows in fact that elite views shape mass views by influencing both what issues capture the public's attention and how those issues are debated and decided.[31] Contrary to the myth of the pandering politician, recent evidence suggests that what scholars of the subject call opinion-policy congruence (essentially the rate at which governments adopt crime, health, trade, and other policies supported by majorities in polls) has been declining, not rising, since 1980, a trend that may reflect greater elite influence over how policy options are presented to the public.[32]

WHAT WOULD YOU DO?

MEMORANDUM

To: *Cecilia Kennedy, U.S. Representative*

From: *Ronald Edwards, legislative assistant*

Subject: *Vote on comprehensive immigration reform*

The 1986 Immigration Reform and Control Act (IRCA) sought to stem illegal immigration by imposing penalties on employers who hire them, while permitting the estimated 3 million illegal immigrants at the time to attain legal status. Since then, however, the number of illegal immigrants in the United States has quadrupled, while law enforcement efforts to punish employers or deport those immigrants have been minimal. Your district is not directly affected by immigration, but voters have concerns both about maintaining law and order, and providing economic opportunities for people who have resided in this country for many years.

Arguments for:

1. Your district contains a large proportion of first-generation Americans, who favor a "path to citizenship" for immigrants who have lived in this country for years, regardless of their legal status.

2. Illegal immigrants often take menial jobs that nobody else wants, and contribute to the U.S. economy by paying taxes and buying goods and services.

3. A "path to citizenship," with fines and other penalties for being in the country illegally, is the most realistic option for individuals who have family and other long-term ties in the United States.

Friday,

U.S. House Considers Comprehensive Immigration Reform

March 4
WASHINGTON, D.C.

The U.S. House of Representatives is weighing a bill that would result in the most comprehensive immigration reform in more than a decade. Proponents say it will both improve border security and provide opportunities for legal residency for the more than 11 million illegal immigrants in the United States. The bill received a mixed reception, however, as critics denounced the provisions for illegal immigrants, saying they amount to "amnesty" for law-breakers...

Arguments against:

1. Your party leaders oppose comprehensive immigration reform, saying that enhanced border security must be a higher priority.

2. Illegal immigrants take jobs away from native-born Americans and cost more in public services, such as education and emergency health care, than they contribute to the economy.

3. People who entered the country illegally must not be rewarded for breaking the law, and enforcement can be effective with sufficient resources.

Your decision:

Vote for bill _____   Vote against bill _____

Second, elites state the norms by which issues should be settled. (A **norm** is a standard of right or proper conduct.) By doing this, they help determine the range of acceptable and unacceptable policy options. For example, elites have for a long time emphasized that racism is wrong. Of late they have emphasized that sexism is wrong. Over a long period, the steady repetition of views condemning racism and sexism will at least intimidate, and perhaps convince, those who are racist and sexist.

A recent example of this process has been the public discussion of AIDS and its relationship to homosexuality. The initial public reaction to AIDS was one of fear and loathing. But efforts to quarantine people infected with AIDS were met with firm resistance from the medical community and from other policy elites. The elites even managed to persuade some legislatures to bar insurance companies from testing insurance applicants for the disease.

norm A standard of right or proper conduct.

There are limits to how much influence elites can have on the public. For instance, elites do not define economic problems—people can see for themselves the existence of unemployment, raging inflation, or high interest rates. Elite opinion may shape the policies, but it does not define the problem. Similarly, elite opinion has little influence on whether we think there is a crime or drug problem; it is, after all, *our* purses being snatched, cars being stolen, and children being drugged. On the other hand, elite opinion does define the problem as well as the policy options with respect to most aspects of foreign affairs; the public has little firsthand experience with which to judge what is going on in Iraq.

Because elites affect how we see some issues and determine how other issues get resolved, it is important to study the differences between elite and public opinion. But it is wrong to suppose there is one elite, unified in its interests and opinions. Just as there are many publics, and hence many public opinions, there are many elites, and hence many different elite opinions. Whether there is enough variety of opinion and influence among elites to justify calling our politics "pluralist" is one of the central issues confronting any student of government.

SUMMARY

"Public opinion" is a slippery notion, partly because there are many publics, with many different opinions, and partly because opinion on all but relatively simple matters tends to be uninformed, unstable, and sensitive to different ways of asking poll questions. Polling is a difficult and expensive art, not an exact science.

Political attitudes are shaped by family, schooling, and other experiences. Opinions vary in America according to class, gender, and other characteristics. Americans are also divided by their political ideologies but not along a single liberal-conservative dimension. There are several kinds of issues on which people may take "liberal" or "conservative" positions, and they often do not take the same position on all issues. The most comprehensive and up-to-date surveys sort average Americans into a half-dozen or more ideological groupings.

Political elites are much more likely to display a consistently liberal or consistently conservative ideology. Elites are important because they have a disproportionate influence on public policy and even an influence on mass opinion (through the dissemination of information and the evocation of political norms).

RECONSIDERING WHO GOVERNS?

1. How does public opinion in America today vary by race, gender, and other differences?

There are cleavages in American public opinion, but they change over time, and it is hard to generalize meaningfully about how they affect politics and government. For example, on some issues, the opinions of whites and blacks are similar or narrowing, but on other issues, wide opinion gaps remain between whites and blacks. Surprisingly, little major research exists on the opinions and partisan preferences of the country's over 40 million Latinos. People who attend worship services regularly are more conservative and far more likely to vote Republican in presidential elections than people who attend worship services rarely if ever. Women are far more sympathetic to liberal causes and Democratic candidates than men, but these so-called gender gaps in opinion and voting behavior are more pronounced in some elections than in others.

2. What is political ideology, and how does it affect political behavior and influence public policy?

Political ideology is a more or less consistent set of beliefs about the policies government ought to pursue. Political scientists measure the extent to which people have a political ideology by seeing how frequently people use broad political categories (such as "liberal" and "conservative") to describe their own views or to justify their preferences for candidates and policies. They also measure it by seeing to what extent the policy preferences of a citizen are consistent over time or are based at any one time on consistent principles. Many scholars believe that Americans are becoming more ideological. On many issues, for example, the policy preferences of average Republican and Democratic voters now differ significantly from one another. There is clear evidence that political elites are more ideological today than they were just a generation or two ago. The government attends more to the elite views than to popular views, at least on many matters.

RECONSIDERING TO WHAT ENDS?

1. What role did the Framers of the Constitution think public opinion should play in American democracy?

Basically, a rather limited role. Turn to the Appendix and read *Federalist* No. 10 by James Madison. In it, Madison makes plain his view that the public interest is not always, or even often, the same as what most people demand from the government. Instead members of Congress are to be "proper guardians of the public weal," representatives who serve "the permanent and aggregate interests" of the country. He holds that "the regulation of these various and interfering interests" is the "principal task" of representatives.

2. When, if ever, should public policies mirror majority opinion?

For most of us, the answer depends on the issue in question. (Which, if any, of the gaps between majority opinion and public policy mentioned on the first page of this chapter would you wish to see closed?) When it comes to civil rights and civil liberties (see Chapters 5 and 6), few of us would be willing, strictly speaking, to trust our freedoms to a popular vote. On the other hand, few of us would consider our system truly democratic if government only rarely did pretty much what most people wanted. The Framers of the Constitution offer one principled answer. They believed temporary or transient popular majorities should carry little weight with representatives, but persistent popular majorities—for example, ones that persist over the staggered terms of House and Senate and over more than a single presidential term—should be heard and in many, though not in all, cases heeded.

WORLD WIDE WEB RESOURCES

Roper Center for Public Opinion Research: **www.ropercenter.uconn.edu**

CBS News poll: **cbsnews.cbs.com**

Gallup opinion poll: **www.gallup.com**

Los Angeles Times poll: **www.latimes.com/news/custom/timespoll**

The Pew Research Center for the People & the Press: **www.people-press.org**

Zogby International: **www.zogby.com**

SUGGESTED READINGS

Berinsky, Adam J. *Silent Voices: Public Opinion and Political Participation in America.* Princeton, N.J.: Princeton University Press, 2004. Shows how opinion polls can bias the results and induce people with unpopular views to say "don't know."

Caplan, Bryan. *The Myth of the Rational Voter: Why Democracies Choose Bad Policies.* Princeton, N.J.: Princeton University Press, 2007. Democracy often lets people support economic policies that make them worse off.

Erikson, Robert S., and Kent L. Tedin. *American Public Opinion.* 5th ed. Boston: Allyn and Bacon, 1995. An excellent summary of how opinion is measured, what it shows, and how it affects politics.

Jennings, M. Kent, and Richard G. Niemi. *Generations and Politics.* Princeton, N.J.: Princeton University Press, 1981. A study of persistence and change in the political views of young adults and their parents.

——— *The Political Character of Adolescence: The Influence of Families and Schools.* Princeton, N.J.: Princeton University Press, 1974. A study of political attitudes among high school students.

Key, V. O., Jr. *The Responsible Electorate.* Cambridge: Harvard University Press, 1966. An argument, with evidence, that American voters are not fools.

Lewis-Beck, Michael S., et al. *The American Voter Revisited.* Ann Arbor, Mich.: University of Michigan Press, 2008. A careful comparison of how voters in the early 2000s compare to those in the mid-1950s.

Lipset, Seymour Martin. *Political Man: The Social Bases of Politics.* Garden City, N.Y.: Doubleday, 1959. An exploration of the relationship between society, opinion, and democracy in America and abroad.

Moe, Terry M. *Schools, Vouchers, and the American Public.* Washington, D.C.: Brookings Institution Press, 2001. A masterful study of how public opinion matters to education policy, suggesting that most people, with only slight information, form reasonable views.

Nie, Norman H., Sidney Verba, and John R. Petrocik. *The Changing American Voter.* Cambridge: Harvard University Press, 1976. Traces shifts in American voter attitudes since 1960.

Weissberg, Robert. *Polling, Policy, and Public Opinion.* New York: Palgrave Macmillan, 2002. A critique of what we think we know from opinion polling, showing the many ways in which polls can give us misleading answers.

Zaller, John. *The Nature and Origins of Mass Opinion.* Cambridge, England: Cambridge University Press, 1992. A path-breaking study of how the public forms an opinion, illustrating the ways in which elite views help shape mass views.

8

Political
Participation

WHO GOVERNS?

1. Who votes, who doesn't?
2. Why do some people participate in politics at higher rates than others?

TO WHAT ENDS?

1. How did the Framers of the Constitution think average citizens should participate in America's representative democracy?
2. Should today's college-age citizens participate more in politics?

Every American loves democracy, but a lot of them do not do much about it. Think about the simplest action: voting. In much of Europe, about 80 percent of all citizens vote, but in the United States the turnout is only about half as great. In 2008, 62 percent of Americans voted, but that was a 40-year high. Some observers are embarrassed by our low turnout rate, blame it on voter apathy, and urge the government and private groups to do something about it.

There are three things wrong with this advice. First, it is not an accurate description of the problem; second, it is an incorrect explanation of the problem; and third, it proposes a remedy that probably won't work.

David McNew/Getty Images News/Getty Images

A Closer Look at Nonvoting

First, let's look at how best to describe the problem. Since 1996, about 60 percent of U.S. citizens eligible to vote—the **voting-age population**—has been registered to vote during mid-term congressional election years, and about two-thirds has been registered to vote during presidential election years. For instance, in the 2006 mid-term congressional elections, 61.6 percent of the voting-age population was registered to vote, and 43.6 percent of the voting-age population actually voted, meaning that 70.7 percent (43.6 percent divided by 61.6 percent) of all **registered voters** voted.[1] In other words, in 2006 the turnout rate among registered voters (70.7 percent) was far higher than the turnout rate among the voting-age population (43.6 percent).

Thus has it been to varying degrees in every national election from 1944 through 2008. This is one reason why cross-national comparisons in voter turnout rates can be somewhat misleading. Another reason is because most other countries simply do not have so many national and other elections.

For example, ranked in terms of average voter turnout as a percentage of the voting-age population, from 1945 to 2007, the United States ranks last behind well-established democracies from Germany (81 percent) to India (61 percent).[2] But ranked in terms of voter turnout among registered voters, the United States would be in the middle of the pack between France (67 percent) and the United Kingdom (75 percent). The United States would be in the top half of the pack, ahead of Japan (68 percent) and Canada (69 percent), if the cross-national comparisons were restricted to presidential elections, which typically draw over 70 percent of registered U.S. voters to the polls.

Apathy on national election days is clearly not the source of the problem. Of those registered, the overwhelming majority vote in those elections. The real source of the voter turnout problem is because a relatively low percentage of the voting-age population is registered to vote.

So what can be done? Mounting a get-out-the-vote (GOTV) drive can make only a small difference depending on what tactic is used. In a 2008 study, political scientists Donald P. Green and Alan Gerber examined the findings from over a hundred scientific studies of diverse GOTV tactics: door-to-door canvassing, leaflets, direct mail, e-mail, phone calls, radio ads, television ads, and election-day festivals.[3] Door-to-door canvassing and phone calls were the only two tactics that demonstrated statistically significant results; but even most prospective voters touched by these tactics did not turn out. In a separate 2008 study, they found that "social pressure" exerted through mailings increased turnout, yet 62 percent of those pressured still did not vote.[4]

If U.S. turnout rates are to rise significantly and rival average turnout rates in most other democracies, at least two things must happen. First, more registered voters must vote. Even though, as we have seen, the vast majority of registered voters do vote, the roughly 30 percent of all registered voters who did not vote in recent national elections represent over 40 million voting-age citizens.

When registered nonvoters were asked why they did not vote, three answers were most common: about a quarter of registered nonvoters said they were too busy or had scheduling conflicts (work or school mostly); about 12 percent cited family chores or obligations; and another 12 percent believed their vote would make no difference.[5]

In response to the number one reason why registered voters fail to vote (school, work, or other scheduling conflicts), some have proposed making Election Day a national holiday or holding national elections on weekends. Such proposals, though popular, remain only proposals; but all states now give voters the option to vote prior to election day via mail-in ballots; and, by 2004, twenty-six states afforded voters the option of "no-fault" absentee voting, meaning that voters can vote absentee without having to demonstrate they are residing outside their home state or giving any other explanation. By 2008, however, so far as most researchers were able to determine, and with a few dramatic exceptions (for example, Oregon's 1996 all-mail-in election for the U.S. Senate), the greater flexibility and convenience of these voting procedures had done little or nothing to increase voter turnout.[6]

Second, if voter turnout rates are to rise substantially in the United States, then nonregistered voters must become registered to vote in ever greater numbers. In addition to the roughly 40 million registered nonvoters, another 40 million or so voting-age citizens were not registered to vote in the 2006 and 2008 national elections.

In most European nations, registration is done for you—automatically—by the government. By contrast, in America, the entire burden of registering to

---

voting-age population Citizens who are eligible to vote after reaching the minimum age requirement.

registered voters People who are registered to vote.

vote falls on the individual voters: they must learn how and when and where to register; they must take the time and trouble to go somewhere and fill out a registration form; and they must register if they happen to move. Since it is costly to register to vote in this country and costless to register in other democracies, it should not be surprising that fewer people are registered here than abroad.

But would making it less burdensome to register necessarily result in higher percentages of Americans becoming registered voters *and* voting? In 1993, Congress passed a law designed to make it easier to register to vote. Known as the motor-voter law, the law allows people in all fifty states to register to vote when applying for driver's licenses and to provide registration through the mail and at some state offices that serve the disabled or provide public assistance (such as checks for eligible low-income families).

As with mail-in and absentee balloting, the evidence regarding the motor-voter law's impact on voter participation remains less than encouraging. In 2001, eight years after the law was enacted, millions of citizens had registered to vote via state motor vehicles bureaus or other state offices, but a study found "that those who register when the process is costless are less likely to vote."[7] By 2006, motor-voter law-related means of registration were widely used (see Figure 8.1). But between 1993 and 2006,

while voter registration rates had increased somewhat over pre-1993 levels, there still was no solid evidence that the law had substantially increased voter turnout.

Of course, voting is only one way of participating in politics. It is important (we could hardly be considered a democracy if nobody voted), but it is not all-important. Joining civic associations, supporting social movements, writing to legislators, fighting city hall—all these and other activities are ways of participating in politics. It is possible that, by these measures, Americans participate in politics *more* than most Europeans—or anybody else, for that matter. Moreover, it is possible that low rates of registration indicate that people are reasonably well satisfied with how the country is governed. If 100 percent of all adult Americans registered and voted (especially under a system that makes registering relatively difficult), it could mean that people were deeply upset about how things were run. In short, it is not at all clear whether low voter turnout is a symptom of political disease or a sign of political good health.

The important question about participation is not how much participation there is but how different kinds of participation affect the kind of government we get. This question cannot be answered just by looking at voter turnout, the subject of this chapter; it also requires us to look at the composition and activities of political parties, interest groups, and the media (the subjects of later chapters).

Nonetheless, voting is important. To understand why participation in American elections takes the form that it does, we must first understand how laws have determined who shall vote and under what circumstances.

The Rise of the American Electorate

It is ironic that relatively few citizens vote in American elections, since it was in this country that the mass of people first became eligible to vote. At the time the Constitution was ratified, the vote was limited to property owners or taxpayers, but by the administration of Andrew Jackson (1829–1837) it had been broadened to include virtually all white male adults. Only in a few states did property restrictions persist: they were not abolished in New Jersey until 1844 or in North Carolina until 1856. And, of course, African American males could not vote in many states, in the North as well as the South, even if they were not slaves. Women could not vote in most states until the twentieth century;

Figure 8.1

Method of Registration to Vote, 2006
Percent Distribution of Registered Voters

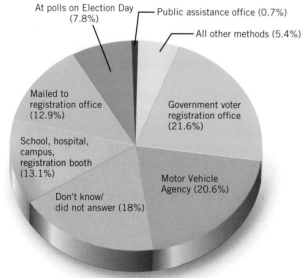

Source: U.S. Bureau of the Census, Current Population Survey, "Voting and Registration," June 2008.

Chinese Americans were widely denied the vote; and being in prison is grounds for losing the franchise even today. Aliens, on the other hand, often were allowed to vote if they had at least begun the process of becoming citizens. By 1880, only an estimated 14 percent of all adult males in the United States could not vote; in England in the same period, about 40 percent of adult males were disfranchised.[8]

FROM STATE TO FEDERAL CONTROL

Initially, it was left entirely to the states to decide who could vote and for what offices. The Constitution gave Congress the right to pick the day on which presidential electors would gather and to alter state regulations regarding congressional elections. The only provision of the Constitution requiring a popular election was the clause in Article I stating that members of the House of Representatives be chosen by the "people of the several states."

Because of this permissiveness, early federal elections varied greatly. Several states picked their members of the House at large (that is, statewide) rather than by district; others used districts but elected more than one representative from each. Still others had their elections in odd-numbered years, and some even required that a congressional candidate win a majority, rather than simply a plurality, of votes to be elected (when that requirement was in effect, runoff elections—in one case as many as twelve—were necessary). Furthermore, presidential electors were at first picked by state legislatures rather than by the voters directly.

Congress, by law and constitutional amendment, has steadily reduced state prerogatives in these matters. In 1842, a federal law required that all members of the House be elected by districts; other laws over the years required that all federal elections be held in even-numbered years on the Tuesday following the first Monday in November.

The most important changes in elections have been those that

literacy test A requirement that citizens show that they can read before registering to vote.

poll tax A requirement that citizens pay a tax in order to register to vote.

grandfather clause A clause in registration laws allowing people who do not meet registration requirements to vote if they or their ancestors had voted before 1867.

white primary The practice of keeping blacks from voting in the southern states' primaries through arbitrary use of registration requirements and intimidation.

Landmark Cases

Right to Vote

- *Smith v. Allwright* (1944): Since political parties select candidates for public office, they may not exclude blacks from voting in their primary elections.

extended the suffrage to women, African Americans, and 18 year-olds and made mandatory the direct popular election of U.S. senators. The Fifteenth Amendment, adopted in 1870, said that the "right of citizens of the United States to vote shall not be denied or abridged by the United States or by any state on account of race, color, or previous condition of servitude." Reading those words today, one would assume they gave African Americans the right to vote. That is not what the Supreme Court during the 1870s thought they meant. By a series of decisions, it held that the Fifteenth Amendment did not necessarily confer the right to vote on anybody; it merely asserted that if someone was denied that right, the denial could not be explicitly on the grounds of race. And the burden of proving that it was race that led to the denial fell on the black who was turned away at the polls.[9]

This interpretation opened the door to all manner of state stratagems to keep blacks from voting. One was a **literacy test** (a large proportion of former slaves were illiterate); another was a requirement that a **poll tax** be paid (most former slaves were poor); a third was the practice of keeping blacks from voting in primary elections (in the one-party South, the only meaningful election was the Democratic primary). To allow whites who were illiterate or poor to vote, a **grandfather clause** was added to the law, saying that a person could vote, even if he did not meet the legal requirements, if he or his ancestors voted before 1867 (blacks, of course, could not vote before 1867). When all else failed, blacks were intimidated, threatened, or harassed if they showed up at the polls.

There began a long, slow legal process of challenging in court each of these restrictions in turn. One by one, the Supreme Court set most of them aside. The grandfather clause was declared unconstitutional in

WHITE SUPREMACY!

Attention, White Men!

Grand Torch-Light Procession

At JACKSON,

On the Night of the

Fourth of January, 1890.

The Final Settlement of Democratic Rule and White Supremacy in Mississippi.

GRAND PYROTECHNIC DISPLAY!
Transparencies and Torches Free for all.

All in Sympathy with the Grand Cause are Cordially and Earnestly Invited to be on hand, to aid in the Final Overthrow of Radical Rule in our State.

Come on foot or on horse-back; come any way, but be sure to get there.
Brass Bands, Cannon, Flambeau Torches, Transparencies, Sky-rockets, Etc.

A GRAND DISPLAY FOR A GRAND CAUSE.

After Reconstruction ended in 1876, black voting shrank under the attacks of white supremacists.

Department of Social History/Smithsonian Institution

After the Civil Rights Act of 1964 was passed, blacks and whites voted together in a small Alabama town.

Flip Schulke/CORBIS

1915,[10] and the **white primary** finally fell in 1944.[11] Some of the more blatantly discriminatory literacy tests were also overturned.[12] The practical result of these rulings was slight: only a small proportion of voting-age blacks were able to register and vote in the South, and they were found mostly in the larger cities. A dramatic change did not begin until 1965, with the passage of the Voting Rights Act. This act suspended the use of literacy tests and authorized the appointment of federal examiners who could order the registration of blacks in states and counties (mostly in the South) where fewer than 50 percent of the voting-age population were registered or had voted in the last presidential election. It also provided criminal penalties for interfering with the right to vote.

Though implementation in some places was slow, the number of African Americans voting rose sharply throughout the South. For example, in Mississippi the proportion of voting-age blacks who registered rose from 5 percent to over 70 percent from 1960 to 1970. These changes had a profound effect on the behavior of many white southern politicians: Governor George Wallace stopped making prosegregation speeches and began courting the black vote.

Women were kept from the polls by law more than by intimidation, and when the laws changed, women almost immediately began to vote in large numbers. By 1915, several states, mostly in the West, had begun to permit women to vote. But it was not until the Nineteenth Amendment to the Constitution was ratified in 1920, after a struggle lasting many decades, that women generally were allowed to vote. At one stroke, the size of the eligible voting population almost doubled. Contrary to the hopes of some and the fears of others, no dramatic changes occurred in the conduct of elections, the identity of the winners, or the substance of public policy. Initially, at least, women voted more or less in the same manner as men, though not quite as frequently.

The political impact of the youth vote was also less than expected. The Voting Rights Act of 1970 gave 18-year-olds the right to vote in federal elections beginning January 1, 1971. It also contained a provision lowering the voting age to 18 in state elections, but the Supreme Court declared this unconstitutional. As a result a constitutional amendment, the Twenty-sixth, was proposed by Congress and ratified by the states in 1971. The 1972 elections became the first in which all people between the ages of 18 and 21 could cast ballots (before then, four states had allowed those under 21 to vote). About 25 million people suddenly became eligible to participate in elections, but their turnout

The campaign to win the vote for women nationwide succeeded with the adoption of the Nineteenth Amendment in 1920.

(42 percent) was lower than for the population as a whole, and they did not flock to any particular party or candidate. Every presidential election year since 1972 has been accompanied by predictions that the "youth vote" was likely to surge. Such predictions were especially prevalent in 2008. But as Table 8.1 suggests, the surge has yet to happen. Over the 26 years and seven national elections from 1994 to 2006, registration and turnout rates among younger voters have fluctuated but remained anemic both in absolute terms and relative to rates among senior citizens.

In 2008, 23 million citizens under age 30, representing 52 percent of the 18- to 29-year-old voting population, voted. That was a higher fraction than in 1996 (37 percent), 2000 (41 percent), and 2004 (48 percent), but lower than 1972 (55 percent) and the same as 1992 (52 percent). Moreover, in every presidential election from 1996 through 2004, the under-30 youth vote accounted for 17 percent of the total Election Day electorate; in 2008 the fraction rose, but only to 18 percent of the total Election Day electorate.

National standards now govern almost every aspect of voter eligibility. All persons 18 years of age and older may vote; there may be no literacy test or poll tax; states may not require residency of more than 30 days in that state before a person may vote; areas with significant numbers of citizens not speaking English must give those people ballots written in their own language; and federal voter registrars and poll watchers may be sent into areas where less than 50 percent of the voting-age population participates in a presidential election. Before 1961, residents of

Table 8.1 Voter Registration and Turnout by Age

Age	Percent Registered/Voted, Midterm Elections			
	1994	**1998**	**2002**	**2006**
18–20	37/17	32/14	33/15	37/17
21–24	46/22	35/19	43/19	45/22
25–34	52/32	52/28	50/27	50/28
65+	76/61	75/60	76/61	75/61
Age	**Percent Registered/Voted, Presidential Elections**			
	1996	**2000**	**2004**	
18–20	46/31	41/28	51/41	
21–24	51/33	49/35	52/43	
25–34	57/43	55/44	56/47	
65+	77/67	76/68	77/69	

Source: Adapted from U.S. Bureau of the Census, Current Population Reports, June 2008, Table 400.

the District of Columbia could not vote in presidential elections; the Twenty-third Amendment to the Constitution gave them this right.

VOTER TURNOUT

Given all these legal safeguards, one might expect that participation in elections would have risen sharply. In fact, the proportion of the voting-age population that has gone to the polls in presidential elections has remained about the same—between 50 and 63 percent of those eligible—at least since 1928 and appears today to be much smaller than it was in the latter part of the 19th century (see Figure 8.2). In every presidential election between 1860 and 1900, at least 70 percent of the eligible population apparently went to the polls, and in some years (1860 and 1876) almost 80 percent seem to have voted. Since 1900, not a single presidential election turnout has reached 70 percent, and on two occasions (1920 and 1924), it did not even reach 50 percent.[13] Even outside the South, where efforts to disenfranchise African Americans make data on voter turnout especially hard to interpret, turnout seems to have declined: over 84 percent of the voting-age population participated in presidential elections in nonsouthern states between 1884 and 1900, but only 68 percent participated between 1936 and 1960, and even fewer have done so since 1960.[14]

Scholars have vigorously debated the meaning of these figures. One view is that this decline in turnout, even allowing for the shaky data on which the estimates are based, has been real and is the result of a decline of popular interest in elections and a weakening of the competitiveness of the two major parties. During the 19th century, according to this theory, the parties fought hard, worked strenuously to get as many voters as possible to the polls, afforded the mass of voters a chance to participate in party politics through caucuses and conventions, kept the legal barriers to participation (such as complex registration procedures) low, and looked forward to close, exciting elections. After 1896, by which time the South had become a one-party Democratic region and the North heavily Republican, both parties became more conservative, national elections usually resulted in lopsided victories for the Republicans, and citizens began to lose interest in politics because it no longer seemed relevant to their needs. The parties ceased functioning as organizations to mobilize the mass of voters and fell under the control of leaders, mostly conservative, who resisted mass participation.[15]

There is another view, however. It argues that the decline in voter turnout has been more apparent than real. Though elections were certainly more of a popular sport in the 19th century than they are today, the parties were no more democratic then than now, and voters then may have been more easily manipulated. Until around the beginning of the 20th century, voting fraud was commonplace, because it was easy to pull off. The political parties, not the government, printed the ballots; they often were cast in public, not private, voting booths; there were few serious efforts to decide who was eligible to vote, and the rules that did operate were easily evaded.

Figure 8.2

Voter Participation in Presidential Elections, 1860–2008

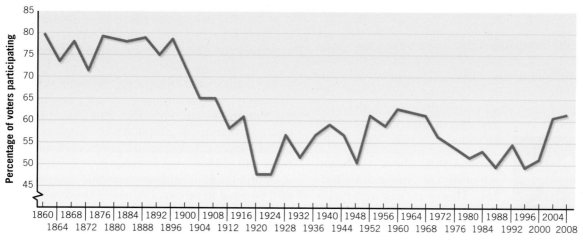

Note: Several southern states did not participate in the 1864 and 1868 elections.

Sources: For 1860–1928: Bureau of the Census, *Historical Statistics of the United States, Colonial Times to 1970*, part 2, 1071; 1932–1944: *Statistical Abstract of the United States*, 1992, 517; 1948–2000: Michael P. McDonald and Samuel L. Popkin, "The Myth of the Vanishing Voter," *American Political Science Review* 95 (December 2001): table 1, 966; 2004 and 2008 elections, American National Election Studies (ANES).

MARC SEROTA/Reuters/Landov

A celebrity urges young people to vote at a Rock the Vote meeting.

Under these circumstances, it was easy for a person to vote more than once, and the party machines made heavy use of these "floaters," or repeaters. "Vote early and often" was not a joke but a fact. The parties often controlled the counting of votes, padding the totals whenever they feared losing. As a result of these machinations, the number of votes counted often was larger than the number cast, and the number cast was in turn often larger than the number of individuals eligible to vote.

Australian ballot A government-printed ballot of uniform dimensions to be cast in secret that many states adopted around 1890 to reduce voting fraud associated with party-printed ballots cast in public.

Around 1890, the states began adopting the **Australian ballot**. This was a government-printed ballot of uniform size and shape that was cast in secret, created to replace the old party-printed ballots cast in public. By 1910, only three states were without the Australian ballot. Its use cut back on (but certainly did not eliminate) vote buying and fraudulent vote counts.

In short, if votes had been legally cast and honestly counted in the 19th century, the statistics on election turnout might well be much lower than the inflated figures we now have.[16] To the extent that this is true, we may not have had a decline in voter participation as great as some have suggested. Nevertheless, most scholars believe that turnout probably did actually decline somewhat after the 1890s. One reason was that voter-registration regulations became more burdensome: there were longer residency requirements; aliens who had begun but not completed the process of becoming citizens could no longer vote in most states; it became harder for African Americans to vote; educational qualifications for voting were adopted by several states; and voters had to register long in advance of the elections. These changes, designed to purify the electoral process, were aspects of the progressive reform impulse (described in Chapter 9) and served to cut back on the number of people who could participate in elections.

Strict voter-registration procedures tended, like most reforms in American politics, to have unintended as well as intended consequences. These changes not only reduced fraudulent voting but also reduced voting generally, because they made it more difficult for certain groups of perfectly honest voters—those with little education, for example, or those who had recently moved—to register and vote. This was not the first time, and it will not be the last, that a reform designed to cure one problem created another.

Following the controversy over Florida's vote count in the 2000 presidential election, many proposals were made to overhaul the nation's voting system. In 2002, Congress passed a measure that for the first time requires each state to have in place a system for counting the disputed ballots of voters whose names were left off official registration lists. In addition, the law provides federal funds for upgrading voting equipment and procedures and for training election officials. But it stops short of creating a uniform national voting system. Paper ballots, lever machines, and punch-card voting systems will still be used in some places, while optical scan and direct recording electronic equipment will still be used in others. Following the 2004 national elections, however, calls to overhaul the nation's voting system were more muted, partly because the popular vote for president was not terribly close (President Bush received 51 percent, John Kerry received 48 percent), and partly because in most states there were few reported problems.

Even after all the legal changes are taken into account, there seems to have been a decline in citizen participation in elections. Between 1960 and 1980, the proportion of voting-age people casting a ballot in presidential elections fell by about 10 percentage points, a drop that cannot be explained by how ballots were printed or how registration rules were rewritten. Nor can these factors explain why 1996 witnessed not only the lowest level of turnout (49 percent) in a presidential election since 1924 but also the single steepest four-year decline (from 55 percent in 1992) since 1920.

There is, however, one alternative theory: voter turnout has not, in fact, been going down. There are different ways of calculating voter turnout. Turnout means the percentage of the voting-age population that votes; an accurate measure of turnout means having an accurate count of both how many people voted and how many people could have voted. In fact, we do not have very good measures of either number. Eligible voters are derived from census reports that tell us what the voting-age population (VAP) is—that is, how many people exist who are 18 and over (or before younger people were allowed to vote, the number 21 and over). But within the VAP are a lot of people who cannot vote, such as prisoners, felons, and aliens.

Political scientists Michael P. McDonald and Samuel L. Popkin have adjusted the VAP to take into account these differences.[17] They call their alternate measure of turnout the voting eligible population (VEP). Table 8.2 shows how turnout percentages differ depending on which measure, VAP or VEP, is used. Calculated by the VEP, national voter turnout in presidential elections has *not* fallen since the early 1970s. Some state-level differences are striking. Calculated by the VAP, California's turnout rate in the 2008 presidential election was 49.4 percent, but calculated by the VEP, it was 61.7 percent (same as the VEP national average). Whichever measure one uses, however, two things are the same: the days when turnout routinely exceeded 60 percent (1952–1968) in presidential elections are gone, and post-1970 turnout in midterm congressional elections has been anemic, averaging only 38 to 40 percent, however it is calculated.[18]

Actual trends in turnout aside, what if they gave an election and everyone came? Would universal

Table 8.2 Two Methods of Calculating Turnout in Presidential Elections, 1948–2008

Year	Voting Age Population (VAP)	Voting Eligible Population (VEP)
1948	51.1%	52.2%
1952	61.6	62.3
1956	59.3	60.2
1960	62.8	63.8
1964	61.9	62.8
1968	60.9	61.5
1972	55.2	56.2
1976	53.5	54.8
1980	52.8	54.7
1984	53.3	57.2
1988	50.3	54.2
1992	55.0	60.6
1996	48.9	52.6
2000	51.2	55.6
2004	55.0	60.0
2008	56.8	61.7

Source: Updated from Michael P. McDonald and Samuel L. Popkin, "The Myth of the Vanishing Voter," *American Political Science Review* 95 (December 2001): table 1, 966. Reprinted with permission of Cambridge University Press; Michael P. McDonald, "2008 General Election Turnout Rates," updated April 26, 2009, at http://elections.gmu.edu, accessed May 8, 2009.

turnout change national election outcomes and the content of public policy? It has long been argued that because the poor, less educated, and minorities are overrepresented among nonvoters, universal turnout would strongly benefit Democratic candidates and liberal causes. But a careful study of this question found that the "party of nonvoters" largely mirrors the demographically diverse and ideologically divided population that goes to the polls.[19]

Who Participates in Politics?

To understand better why voter turnout declined and what, if anything, that decline may mean, we must first look at who participates in politics.

FORMS OF PARTICIPATION

Voting is by far the most common form of political participation, while giving money to a candidate and being a member of a political organization are the least common. Many Americans exaggerate how frequently they vote or how active they are in politics.

In a study by Sidney Verba and Norman Nie, 72 percent of those interviewed said they voted "regularly" in presidential elections.[20] Yet we know that since 1960, on average under 60 percent of the voting-age population has actually cast presidential ballots. Obviously, many people claim to have voted when in fact they have not. If people misreport their voting behavior, it is likely that they also misreport—that is, exaggerate—the extent to which they participate in other ways.

Indeed, most research shows that "politics is not at the heart of the day-to-day life of the American people."[21] Work, family, church, and other voluntary activities come first, both in terms of how Americans spend their time and in terms of the money they donate. For example, a study by Verba and others found that a higher proportion of citizens take part in nonpolitical than political activities: "More citizens reported giving time to church-related or charitable activities than indicated contacting a government official or working informally on a community problem, two of the most frequent forms of political participation beyond the vote."[22]

In an earlier study, Verba and Nie analyzed the ways in which people participate in politics and came up with six forms of participation that are characteristic of six different kinds of U.S. citizens. About one-fifth (22 percent) of the population is completely inactive: they rarely vote, they do not get involved in organizations, and they probably do not even talk about politics very much. These inactives typically have little education and low incomes and are relatively young. Many of them are African American. At the opposite extreme are the complete **activists,** constituting about

> **activists** People who tend to participate in all forms of politics.

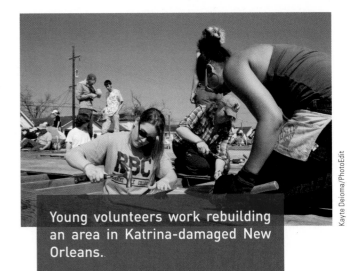

Young volunteers work rebuilding an area in Katrina-damaged New Orleans.

Kayte Deioma/PhotoEdit

one-ninth of the population (11 percent). These people are highly educated, have high incomes, and tend to be middle-aged rather than young or old. They tend to participate in all forms of politics.

Between these extremes are four categories of limited forms of participation. The *voting specialists* are people who vote but do little else; they tend not to have much schooling or income and to be substantially older than the average person. *Campaigners* not only vote but also like to get involved in campaign activities. They are better educated than the average voter, but what seems to distinguish them most is their interest in the conflicts, passions, and struggle of politics; their clear identification with a political party; and their willingness to take strong positions. *Communalists* are much like campaigners in social background but have a very different temperament: they do not like the conflict and tension of partisan campaigns. They tend to reserve their energy for community activities of a more nonpartisan nature—forming and joining organizations to deal with local problems and contacting local officials about these problems. Finally, there are some *parochial participants*, who do not vote and stay out of election campaigns and civic associations but are willing to contact local officials about specific, often personal, problems.[23]

PARTICIPATION: CAUSES AND MEANING

Whether participation takes the form of voting or being a complete activist, it is higher among people who have gone to college than it is among those who have not, higher among people who are employed than among the unemployed, and higher among whites and blacks than among Hispanics.

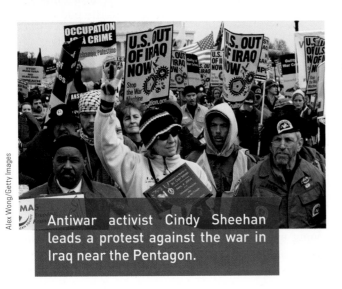

Antiwar activist Cindy Sheehan leads a protest against the war in Iraq near the Pentagon.

Alex Wong/Getty Images

Figure 8.3

Voter Turnout in Presidential Elections, by Schooling, Employment, and Race, 1996–2004

Source: Adapted from U.S. Bureau of the Census, Current Population Reports, June 2008, Table 400.

The differences in voting rates for these groups are shown in Figure 8.3.

It is, however, far easier to describe differences in voting rates by schooling, employment status, race, and other characteristics than it is to explain them. Not long ago, political scientists thought they had a pretty firm handle on how education, occupation, race, gender, religion, political ideology, and other factors mattered to who votes.

For instance, a rich, older, professional woman with a graduate degree who strongly identifies as liberal or conservative and has strong partisan attachments is far more likely to vote than a poor, young, unemployed male who dropped out of high school and has no interest in politics. And, other things equal, the more schooling one has—independent of age, occupation, race, or income—the more likely one is to vote.

All true, but the more sophisticated research into voting behavior has become—and the more that this research has attempted to explain not just intergroup differences but intragroup differences in voting behavior (some rich, old, politically engaged professional women don't vote; some poor, young, politically disaffected men do vote)—the less confidence we can retain in broad generalizations about the causes of participation.

One interesting explanation is religion. As the research frontiers box on page 186 explains, by at least some measures, religion does seem to boost participation in politics and in civic life more generally.

But, even with all the latest and best data at our disposal, it is wise to generalize with care: "religion increases participation" would be too sweeping, but "certain types of religious expression increase participation under some conditions" is about right.

The same caution applies when it comes to interpreting the meaning of participation. Although Americans are going to the polls less than earlier generations did, they are campaigning, contacting government officials, and (here the evidence is clearest, especially for younger Americans) volunteering and working on community issues no less and perhaps even more. And while the proportion of the population that votes is lower in the United States than in many other democracies, the percentage of Americans who engage in one or more political activities beyond voting is higher (see Table 8.3).

Although we vote at lower rates here than people do abroad, the meaning of our voting is different. For one thing, we elect far more public officials than the citizens of any other nation. There are over a half

RESEARCH FRONTIERS

Does "Religion" Boost "Participation"?

For decades now, political scientists have studied participation in relation to income, race, gender, age, religion, marital status, and other variables. In recent years, however, scholars from many different disciplines have joined the fray, many with a special interest in understanding participation in relation to religion. What, if anything, have they discovered so far?

The cutting-edge studies of the subject are synthesized in a 2008 book co-authored by political scientist Corwin E. Smidt. The book's findings are fascinating but complicated. Start with religion in relation to civic participation:

> Americans vary not only by religious tradition, but also even within a given religious tradition according to their level of public religious practice (high or low) and their level of private religious practice (high or low).

> Other things (income, race, gender, age, marital status) being equal, Mainline Protestants are more likely than citizens in most other religious traditions, and more likely than religiously unaffiliated citizens, to be members of voluntary associations.

> But, regardless of religious tradition, persons whose form of religious expression involves high levels of both public and private religious practice are most likely to become voluntary association members.

> While religious citizens at all income levels give to charities at higher rates than otherwise comparable citizens who are religiously unaffiliated, the impact of religion on philanthropy is smaller than the impact of religion on volunteering.

What about religion in relation to political engagement?

> Religion is a significant factor in determining who votes and who doesn't, but no more significant than such variables as education and income.

> When it comes to attention to public matters, religion—other things equal—generally is less important than education and age.

> Overall, "one's form of religious expression appears to be a stronger factor in shaping civic than in shaping political participation."

- Are you surprised by the finding that religion seems to matter more in relation to whether citizens volunteer or give to charity than it does to whether they vote or follow the political news?

- Smidt and his colleagues also report the same form of religious expression—namely, high levels of public and private religious practice—associated with higher rates of volunteering and donating is also associated with higher rates of political intolerance. Does that finding surprise you? Regardless, what other questions about religion and participation do you think would be worth exploring?

Source: Corwin Smidt et al., *Pews, Prayers, & Participation: Religion & Civic Responsibility in America* (Georgetown University Press, 2008).

Table 8.3 Political Participation Here and Abroad

Percent of People Who . . .	USA	Rank Among Twenty Democracies	Outranked By
Tried to persuade others to vote for a candidate	44%	2nd	Canada
Supported party by attending meeting, putting up poster	30%	2nd	Canada
Donated money to political group	21%	1st	None
Were contacted by party or candidate	47%	3rd	Canada, Ireland

Source: Professor Martin Wattenberg, University of California-Irvine, using data from the *Comparative Study of Electoral Systems*.

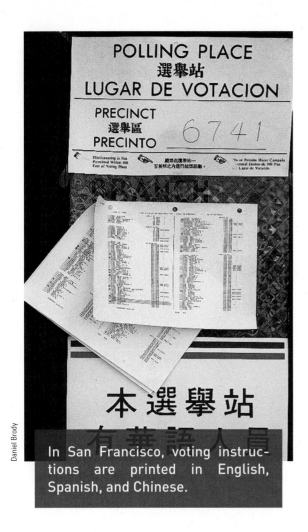

Daniel Brody

In San Francisco, voting instructions are printed in English, Spanish, and Chinese.

million elective offices in the United States and just about every other week of the year there is an election going on somewhere in this country.

A citizen of Massachusetts, for example, votes not only for the U.S. president but also for two senators, the state governor, the member of the House of Representatives for his or her district, a state representative, a state senator, the state attorney general, the state auditor, the state treasurer, the secretary of state, a county commissioner, a sheriff, and clerks of various courts, as well as (in the cities) for the mayor, the city councillor, and school committee members and (in towns) for selectmen, town-meeting members, a town moderator, library trustees, health board members, assessors, water commissioners, the town clerk, housing authority

members, the tree warden, and the commissioner of the public burial ground. (There are probably others whom we have forgotten.)

In many European nations, by contrast, the voters get to make just one choice once every four or five years: they can vote for or against a member of parliament. When there is only one election for one office every several years, that election is bound to assume more importance to voters than many elections for scores of offices. But one election for one office probably has less effect on how the nation is governed than many elections for thousands of offices. Americans may not vote at high rates, but voting affects a far greater part of the political system here than abroad.

The kinds of people who vote here are also different from those who vote abroad. Since almost everybody votes in many other democracies, the votes cast there mirror almost exactly the social composition of those nations. Since only slightly over half of the voting-age population turns out even for presidential elections here, the votes cast in the United States may not truly reflect the country.

Latinos are the largest and fastest-growing minority group in America. Although they remain the most underrepresented group among all voters, the Latino share of the Election Day electorate nearly doubled between 1996 (5 percent) and 2008 (9 percent). Until recently, little was known about the relationship between political participation and variables such as command of the language and involvement in nonpolitical institutions such as workplaces, voluntary associations, and churches that provide information or impart skills relevant to politics.

But together with other recent research, a detailed 2008 study examined how ever more of the nation's Latino citizens are participating in politics in conjunction with their participation in diverse urban church communities.[24] Latino politics, it now seems clear, increasingly is taking shape as a form of hyphenated-American identity politics in which many Latino voters, including the young and the poor, not only gain information and hone politically relevant skills via church membership but attach quasi-religious meaning to many forms of civic engagement.

WHAT WOULD YOU DO?

MEMORANDUM

To: *Senator Henry Gilbert*

From: *Peter Clark, legislative analyst*

Subject: *Voting reform legislation*

In the 1990s, barely half of the electorate voted for president, and only a third or so cast ballots for congressional elections. In a few recent presidential primaries and statewide special elections, turnout has run 10 percent or below. Studies show that often citizens miss the opportunity to vote because of complications with work or child care. To address this problem, legislators from both parties support celebrating Veterans Day on Election Day, which would create a national holiday for voting. Eligible voters who do not go to the polls would be fined.

Arguments for:

1. This proposal honors veterans by recognizing their service with the fundamental requirement of representative democracy, rule by the people through voting.

2. A voting holiday ensures that people who cannot take off time from work or other responsibilities to vote have the opportunity to exercise their democratic right.

3. Imposing a fine for nonvoting sends a moral message that voting is a civic duty in a democracy. More citizens will feel morally obliged to vote if all citizens are legally obliged to do so.

Arguments against:

1. Just as veterans volunteer their service, so, too, should citizens volunteer to exercise their democratic responsibilities.

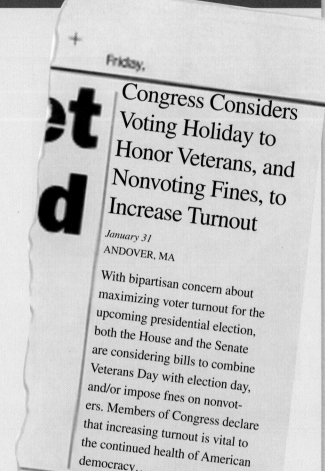

Congress Considers Voting Holiday to Honor Veterans, and Nonvoting Fines, to Increase Turnout

January 31
ANDOVER, MA

With bipartisan concern about maximizing voter turnout for the upcoming presidential election, both the House and the Senate are considering bills to combine Veterans Day with election day, and/or impose fnes on nonvoters. Members of Congress declare that increasing turnout is vital to the continued health of American democracy…

2. Voting is a right, but citizens have a civic duty to exercise that right, and the government should not, in effect, exercise that duty on their behalf. Moreover, people can vote by absentee ballot at their convenience.

3. Compulsory voting does not guarantee informed voting. It is both unwise and undemocratic to legally oblige people to vote.

Your decision:

Vote for bill _____   Vote against bill _____

SUMMARY

The popular view that Americans don't vote as a result of apathy is not quite right. It is nearer to the truth to say that we don't all register to vote and don't always vote even when registered. There are many factors having nothing to do with apathy that shape our participation rates—age, race, party organization, the barriers to registration, and popular views about the significance of elections.

Compared to other nations, Americans vote at lower rates but more frequently and for many more offices, so elections make a bigger difference in the conduct of public affairs here than abroad. We also engage somewhat more frequently than people abroad in various nonelectoral forms of participation.

RECONSIDERING WHO GOVERNS?

1. Who votes, who doesn't?

The most powerful determinants of voting are age (older people vote more than younger people) and education (college graduates vote more than high school graduates). Race makes a difference, but black participation rates approximate white rates once you control for socioeconomic status.

2. Why do some people participate in politics at higher rates than others?

Older people and college graduates have learned to have a greater interest in politics, in part because they see ways in which government policies will affect them, in part because they may have acquired a political ideology that makes politics intrinsically interesting. As we have seen, Americans vote less than people in most other democratic nations. That gap is in part the result of the failure of many Americans to register to vote; efforts to increase registration, such as the motor-voter law, have got more names onto the voting rolls, but these new additions often do not vote as often as other registered voters.

RECONSIDERING TO WHAT ENDS?

1. How did the Framers of the Constitution think average citizens should participate in America's representative democracy?

The Framers believed citizens should play an important but not the decisive role in the American Republic. They elect the House, but until the Constitution was amended in 1913, they did not elect the Senate; the president and senators, not ordinary people, select federal judges; and the president is chosen by electors. Over time, the system has become much more responsive to public opinion. Voters now help pick party candidates through party primaries, and their views are regularly solicited by opinion polls.

2. Should today's college-age citizens participate more in politics?

We would say yes, but the fact is that many young adults seem less disposed to traditional forms of political activity, including voting, than they are toward other types of civic engagement, such as community service or volunteer work. One forecast to ponder: unless youth voting rates increase relative to those of senior citizens, then, on Election Day 2020, persons 65 and older (about 22 percent of the general population) will cast a quarter of all ballots, while persons 18 to 29 (about 21 percent of the general population) will account for less than an eighth of the voting electorate.

WORLD WIDE WEB RESOURCES

Information for voters

DemocracyNet: **www.congress.org/congressorg/e4/**

League of Women Voters: **www.lwv.org/**

Voter Information Services: **www.vis.org/**

Women's Voting Guide: **www.womenvote.org/resources**

National Mail Voter Registration Form: **www.fec.gov/votregis/vr.shtml**

The Vanishing Voter: **www.vanishingvoter.org/**

Voter turnout statistics: **www.fec.gov/pages/electpg.htm**

SUGGESTED READINGS

Burnham, Walter Dean. *Critical Elections and the Mainsprings of American Politics*. New York: Norton, 1970. An argument about the decline of voter participation, linking it to changes in the economic system.

Green, Donald P., and Alan S. Gerbec. *Get Out the Vote!: How to Increase Voter Turnout*. Washington, D.C.: Brookings Institution Press, 2nd edition, 2008. Excellent review of the evidence on what works—and what doesn't—to get more people to the polls.

Eisner, Jane. *Taking Back the Vote: Getting American Youth Involved in Our Democracy*. Boston: Beacon Press, 2004. Highly readable account of why today's college-age Americans volunteer lots but vote little, with recommendations for getting young people more interested in politics.

Verba, Sidney, Norman H. Nie, and Jae-on Kim. *Participation and Political Equality*. Cambridge: Cambridge University Press, 1978. Classic comparative study of political participation in seven nations.

Wilson, Catherine E. *The Politics of Latino Faith: Religion, Identity, and Urban Community*. New York: New York University Press, 2008. Richly detailed study of how Latino religious life intersects with politics in three cities.

Political Parties

WHO GOVERNS?

1. How has America's two-party system changed, and how does it differ from the party systems of other representative democracies?
2. How much do parties affect how Americans vote?

TO WHAT ENDS?

1. Did the Founding Fathers think political parties were a good idea?
2. How, if at all, should America's two-party system be reformed?

Beginning in 2006 and culminating in 2008, Democratic party leaders had reason to smile. In 2006 they won control of the House and the Senate and in 2008 elected Barack Obama as president. But party control of Congress and the presidency changes and no doubt will change again unless there has been a big shift in the partisan affiliation of American voters.

There is no reason to think that this shift has occurred. The party loyalty of voters remains about what it has been for many decades: In June 2009, about one-third are Democrats and another third are Republicans, with the rest describing themselves as independents. These numbers change a bit over time: beginning in 2006, the Republican share went down and then when President Obama ran into trouble with his health care plan the Republican affiliation increased a bit.

The central fact is that party attachment explains much but far from all of any election's results. Political parties must cope with economic conditions, personal popularity, crises in foreign policy, and various social issues. The attachment of voters to parties is weaker today than it was a century ago.

Max Whittaker/Getty Images

Parties—Here and Abroad

political party A group that seeks to elect candidates to public office.

A **political party** is a group that seeks to elect candidates to public office by supplying them with a label—a "party identification"—by which they are known to the electorate.[2] This definition is purposefully broad so that it will include both familiar parties (Democratic, Republican) and unfamiliar ones (Whig, Libertarian, Socialist Workers) and will cover periods in which a party is very strong (having an elaborate and well-disciplined organization that provides money and workers to its candidates) as well as periods in which it is quite weak (supplying nothing but the label to candidates). The label by which a candidate is known may or may not actually be printed on the ballot opposite the candidate's name: in the United States, it does appear on the ballot in all national elections but in only a minority of municipal ones; in Australia and Israel (and in Great Britain before 1969), it never appears on the ballot at all.

American political parties are the oldest in the world. They may be in decline, but they are not dead or dying. New parties (like the Green party launched in 2000 by consumer advocate Ralph Nader) still come and go. Two old parties (Democratic and Republican) still dominate the country's campaigns and elections. Nor have party leaders been wholly replaced by media consultants, pollsters, or others whose profession is raising money or devising strategies for whichever candidates bid highest for their services.

Still, America's political parties do not matter as much, or in the same ways, as they once did. For instance, one reason voter turnout is higher abroad than in this country is that political parties in other democratic nations are more effective at mobilizing voters. The sense of belonging to a party and the inclination to vote the party ticket are greater in France, Italy, and Sweden than in the United States.

It was not always thus. At one time, being a Democrat or a Republican was a serious commitment that people did not make lightly or abandon easily. In those days, it would have been hard to find anything in Europe that could match the vote-getting power of such party organizations as those in Chicago, New York, and Philadelphia.

Parties in the United States are relatively weak today mainly because the laws and rules under which they operate have taken away much of their power at the same time that many voters have lost their sense of commitment to party identification. This weakening has proceeded unevenly, however, because our constitutional system has produced a decentralized party system just as it has produced a decentralized governmental system, with the result that parties are strong in some places and almost nonexistent in other places.

There are three political arenas in which parties may be found and in which changes in their strength may be assessed. A party exists as a *label* in the minds of the voters, as an *organization* that recruits and campaigns for candidates, and as a *set of leaders* who try to organize and control the legislative and executive branches of government. A powerful party is one whose label has a strong appeal for voters, whose organization can decide who will be candidates and how their campaigns will be managed, and whose leaders can dominate one or all branches of government.

American parties have become weaker in all three arenas. As a *label* with which voters identify, the parties probably are much weaker than they were in the 19th century but only somewhat weaker than they were 40 years ago (see Figure 9.1). In 1952, a total of 36 percent of the electorate identified strongly as Democrats (22 percent) or Republicans (14 percent), while a total of 23 percent of the electorate identified as independents. By 2004, total strong party identifiers had dropped to 33 percent of the electorate, while all independents had risen to 39 percent of the electorate. But the best evidence of weakening party identification is what voters *do*. As we shall see in the next chapter, in some elections many people vote split tickets—supporting a president from one party and members of Congress from the other.

As a *set of leaders* who organize government, especially Congress, political parties remain somewhat strong in ways that will be described in Chapter 13. As *organizations* that nominate and elect candidates, parties have become dramatically weaker since the 1960s. In most states, parties have very little control over who gets nominated to office. The causes and consequences of that change are the subject of this chapter.

In Europe, things are very different. Almost the only way a person can become a candidate for elective office is to be nominated by party leaders. Campaigns are run by the party, using party funds and workers, not by the candidate. Once in office, the elected officials are expected to vote and act together with other members of their party.

Figure 9.1

Decline in Party Identification, 1952–2004

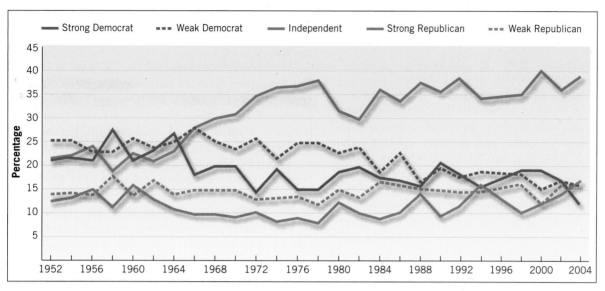

Legend: —— Strong Democrat   ••• Weak Democrat   —— Independent   —— Strong Republican   ••• Weak Republican

Source: *American National Election Studies*, November 2005, table 2A.1.

The principal criterion by which voters choose among candidates is their party identification or label. This has been changing somewhat of late: European parties, like American ones, have not been able to count as heavily as in the past on party loyalty among the voters.

Several factors explain the striking differences between American and European political parties. First, the federal system of government in the United States decentralizes political authority and thus decentralizes political party organizations. For nearly two centuries, most of the important governmental decisions were made at the state and local levels—decisions regarding education, land use, business regulation, and public welfare—and thus it was at the state and local levels that the important struggles over power and policy occurred. Moreover, most people with political jobs—either elective or appointive—worked for state and local government, and thus a party's interest in obtaining these jobs for its followers meant it had to focus attention on who controlled city hall, the county courthouse, and the state capitol. Federalism, in short, meant political parties would acquire jobs and money from local sources and fight local contests. This, in turn, meant the national political parties would be coalitions of local parties, and though these coalitions would have a keen interest in capturing the presidency (with it, after all, went control of large numbers of federal jobs), the national party leaders rarely had as much power as the local ones. The Republican leader of Cuyahoga County, Ohio, for example, could often ignore the decisions of the

Republican national chairman and even the Ohio state chairman.

Political authority in the United States has recently become far more centralized: the federal government now makes decisions affecting almost all aspects of our lives, including those—such as schooling and welfare—once left entirely in local hands. Yet the political parties have not become more centralized as a result. If anything, they have become even weaker and more decentralized. One reason for this apparent paradox is that in the United States, unlike in most other democratic nations, political parties are closely regulated by state and federal laws, and these regulations have weakened the power of parties substantially.

Election posters put up in 2005 during Iraq's first free election in half a century.

Wisam Ahmad/Reuters/Corbis

Perhaps the most important of these regulations are those that prescribe how a party's candidates are selected.

In the great majority of American states, the party leaders do not select people to run for office; by law, those people are chosen by the voters in primary elections. Though sometimes the party can influence who will win a primary contest, in general people running for state or national office in this country owe little to party leaders. In Europe, by contrast, there is no such thing as a primary election—the only way to become a candidate for office is to persuade party leaders to put your name on the ballot. In a later section of this chapter, the impact of the direct primary will be discussed in more detail; for now, it is enough to note that its use removes from the hands of the party leadership its most important source of power over officeholders.

Furthermore, if an American political party wins control of Congress, it does not—as in most European nations with a parliamentary system of government—also win the right to select the chief executive of the government. The American president, as we have seen, is independently elected, and this means that he will choose his principal subordinates not from among members of Congress but from among persons out of Congress. Should he pick a representative or senator for his cabinet, the Constitution requires that person to resign from Congress in order to accept the job. Thus, an opportunity to be a cabinet secretary is not an important reward for members of Congress, and so the president cannot use the prospect of that reward as a way of controlling congressional action. All this weakens the significance and power of parties in terms of organizing the government and conducting its business.

The Rise and Decline of the Political Party

Our nation began without parties, and today's parties, though far from extinct, are about as weak as at any time in our history. In between the Founding and the present, however, parties arose and became powerful. We can see this process in four broad periods of party history: when political parties were created (roughly from the Founding to the 1820s); when the more or less stable two-party system emerged (roughly from the time of President Jackson to the Civil War); when parties developed a comprehensive organizational form and appeal (roughly from the Civil War to the 1930s); and finally when party "reform" began to alter the party system (beginning in the early 1900s but taking effect chiefly since the New Deal).

THE FOUNDING

The Founders disliked parties, thinking of them as "factions" motivated by ambition and self-interest. George Washington, dismayed by the quarreling between Hamilton and Jefferson in his cabinet, devoted much of his Farewell Address to condemning parties. This hostility toward parties was understandable: the legitimacy and success of the newly created federal government were still very much in doubt. When Jefferson organized his followers to oppose Hamilton's policies, it seemed to Hamilton and *his* followers that Jefferson was opposing not just a policy or a leader but also the very concept of a national government. Jefferson, for his part, thought Hamilton was not simply pursuing bad policies but was subverting the Constitution itself. Before political parties could become legitimate, it was necessary for people to separate in their minds quarrels over policies and elections from disputes over the legitimacy of the new government itself. The ability to make that distinction was slow in coming; thus, parties were objects of profound suspicion, at first defended only as temporary expedients.

The first organized political party in American history was made up of the followers of Jefferson, who, beginning in the 1790s, called themselves *Republicans* (hoping to suggest thereby that their opponents were secret monarchists).* The followers of Hamilton kept the label *Federalist*, which once referred to all supporters of the new Constitution (hoping to imply that their opponents were "Antifederalists," or enemies of the Constitution).

These parties were loose caucuses of political notables in various localities, with New England strongly Federalist and much of the South passionately Republican. Jefferson and ally James Madison thought their Republican party was a temporary arrangement designed to defeat John Adams, a Federalist, in his bid to succeed Washington in 1796. (Adams narrowly defeated Jefferson, who, under the system then in effect, became vice president because he had the second most electoral votes.) In 1800, Adams's bid to succeed himself intensified party activity even more, but this time Jefferson

---

* The Jeffersonian Republicans were not the party that today we call Republican. In fact, present-day Democrats consider Jefferson to be the founder of their party.

Question

1. *Who was the first African American to receive votes at a National party convention?*

"The man who has filled the measure of his Country's Glory."
JEFFERSON.

Jackson,

DEMOCRACY,

And our Country.

"The Union must be Preserved."

I. Samuel M'Kean.

When Andrew Jackson ran for president in 1828, over a million votes were cast for the first time in American history. This poster, from the 1832 election, was part of the emergence of truly mass political participation.

Tennessee Historical Society

essentially small groups of local notables. Political participation was limited, and nominations for most local offices were arranged rather casually.

THE JACKSONIANS

What often is called the second party system emerged around 1824 with Andrew Jackson's first run for the presidency and lasted until the Civil War became inevitable. Its distinctive feature was that political participation became a mass phenomenon. For one thing, the number of voters to be reached had become quite large. Only about 365,000 popular votes were cast in 1824. But as a result of laws that enlarged the number of people eligible to vote and an increase in the population, by 1828 well over a million votes were tallied. By 1840, the figure was well over 2 million. (In England at this time, there were only 650,000 eligible voters.) In addition, by 1832 presidential electors were selected by popular vote in virtually every state. (As late as 1816, electors were chosen by the state legislatures, rather than by the people, in about half the states.) Presidential politics had become a truly national, genuinely popular activity; in many communities, election campaigns had become the principal public spectacle.

The party system of the Jacksonian era was built from the bottom up rather than—as during the period of the Founding—from the top down. No change better illustrates this transformation than the abandonment of the system of having caucuses composed of members of Congress nominate presidential candidates. The caucus system was an effort to unite the legislative and executive branches by giving the former some degree of control over who would have a chance to capture the latter. The caucus system became unpopular when the caucus candidate for president in 1824 ran third in a field of four in the general election. It was completely discredited that same year when Congress denied the presidency to Jackson, the candidate with the greatest share of the popular vote.

To replace the caucus, the party convention was invented. The first convention in American history was held by the Anti-Masonic party in 1831; the first convention of a major political party was held by the anti-Jackson Republicans later that year (it nominated Henry Clay for president). The Democrats held a convention in 1832 that ratified Jackson's nomination for reelection and picked Martin Van Buren as his running mate. The first convention to select a man who would be elected president and who was not already the incumbent president was held by the Democrats in 1836; they chose Van Buren.

won and the Republicans assumed office. The Federalists feared that Jefferson would dismantle the Constitution, but Jefferson adopted a conciliatory posture, saying in his inaugural address that "we are all Republicans, we are all Federalists."[3] It was not true, of course: the Federalists detested Jefferson, and some were planning to have New England secede from the Union. But it was good politics, expressive of the need that every president has to persuade the public that, despite partisan politics, the presidency exists to serve all the people.

So successful were the Republicans that the Federalists virtually ceased to exist as a party. Jefferson was reelected in 1804 with almost no opposition; Madison easily won two terms; James Monroe carried 16 out of 19 states in 1816 and was reelected without opposition in 1820. Political parties had seemingly disappeared, just as Jefferson had hoped. The parties that existed in these early years were

Answer

1. *Frederick Douglas, by the Republicans in 1888.*

THE CIVIL WAR AND SECTIONALISM

Though the party system created in the Jacksonian period was the first truly national system, with Democrats (followers of Jackson) and Whigs (opponents of Jackson) fairly evenly balanced in most regions, it could not withstand the deep split in opinion created by the agitation over slavery. Both parties tried, naturally, to straddle the issue, since neither wanted to divide its followers and thus lose the election to its rival. But slavery and sectionalism were issues that could not be straddled. The old parties divided and new ones emerged. The modern Republican party (not the old Democratic-Republican party of Thomas Jefferson) began as a third party. As a result of the Civil War, it became a major party (the only third party ever to gain major-party status) and dominated national politics, with only occasional interruptions, for three-quarters of a century.

mugwumps or *progressives* Republican party faction of the 1890s to the 1910s, composed of reformers who opposed patronage.

Republican control of the White House, and to a lesser extent Congress, was in large measure the result of two events that gave to Republicans a marked advantage in the competition for the loyalties of voters. The first of these was the Civil War. This bitter, searing crisis deeply polarized popular attitudes. Those who supported the Union side became Republicans for generations; those who supported the Confederacy, or who had opposed the war, became Democrats.

As it turned out, this partisan division was nearly even for a while: though the Republicans usually won the presidency and the Senate, they often lost control of the House. There were many northern Democrats. In 1896, however, another event—the presidential candidacy of William Jennings Bryan—further strengthened the Republican party. Bryan, a Democrat, alienated many voters in the populous northeastern states while attracting voters in the South and Midwest. The result was to confirm and deepen the split in the country, especially North versus South, begun by the Civil War. From 1896 to the 1930s, with rare exceptions northern states were solidly Republican, southern ones solidly Democratic.

This split had a profound effect on the organization of political parties, for it meant that most states were now one-party states. As a result, competition for office at the state level had to go on *within* a single dominant party (the Republican party in Massachusetts, New York, Pennsylvania, Wisconsin, and elsewhere; the Democratic party in Georgia, Mississippi, South Carolina, and elsewhere). Consequently, there emerged two major factions within each party, but especially within the Republican party. One was composed of the party regulars—the professional politicians, the "stalwarts," the Old Guard. They were preoccupied with building up the party machinery, developing party loyalty, and acquiring and dispensing patronage—jobs and other favors—for themselves and their faithful followers. Their great skills were in organization, negotiation, bargaining, and compromise; their great interest was in winning.

The other faction, variously called **mugwumps** or **progressives** (or "reformers"), was opposed to the heavy emphasis on patronage; disliked the party machinery because it permitted only bland candidates to rise to the top; was fearful of the heavy influx of immigrants into American cities and of the ability of the party regulars to organize them into "machines;" and wanted to see the party take unpopular positions on certain issues (such as free trade). Their great skills lay in the areas of advocacy and articulation; their great interest was in principle.

At first the mugwumps tried to play a balance-of-power role, sometimes siding with the Republican party of which they were members, at other times defecting to the Democrats (as when they bolted the Republican party to support Grover Cleveland, the Democratic nominee, in 1884). But later, as the Republican strength in the nation grew, progressives within that party became increasingly less able to play a balance-of-power role, especially at

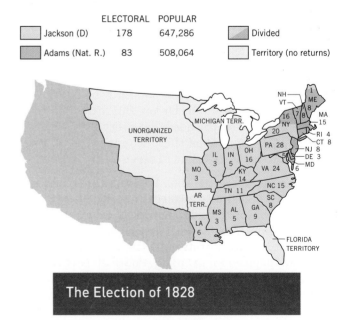

	ELECTORAL	POPULAR		
Jackson (D)	178	647,286		Divided
Adams (Nat. R.)	83	508,064		Territory (no returns)

The Election of 1828

	ELECTORAL	POPULAR
Lincoln (R)	180	1,866,452
Douglas (No. D)	12	1,375,157
Breckenridge (So. D)	76	847,953
Bell (Const. Union)	39	590,631
Divided		
Territory (no returns)		

The Election of 1860

	ELECTORAL	POPULAR
F.D. Roosevelt (D)	472	22,821,857
Hoover (R)	59	15,761,841

The Election of 1932

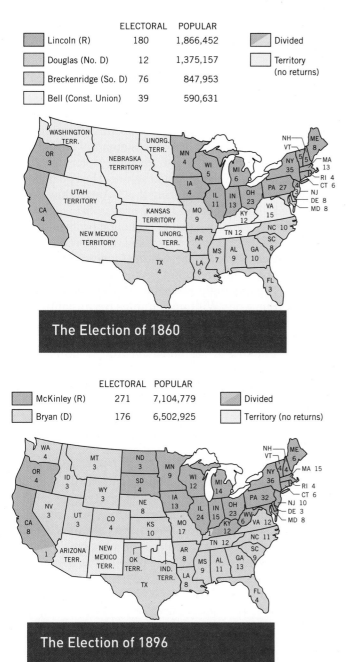

	ELECTORAL	POPULAR
McKinley (R)	271	7,104,779
Bryan (D)	176	6,502,925
Divided		
Territory (no returns)		

The Election of 1896

the state level. If the progressives were to have any power, it would require, they came to believe, an attack on the very concept of partisanship itself.

THE ERA OF REFORM

Progressives began to espouse measures to curtail or even abolish political parties. They favored primary elections to replace nominating conventions because the latter were viewed as manipulated by party bosses; they favored nonpartisan elections at the city level and in some cases at the state level as well; they argued against corrupt alliances between parties and businesses. They wanted strict voter-registration

requirements that would reduce voting fraud (but would also, as it turned out, keep ordinary citizens who found the requirements cumbersome from voting); they pressed for civil service reform to eliminate patronage; and they made heavy use of the mass media as a way of attacking the abuses of partisanship and of promoting their own ideas and candidacies.

The progressives were more successful in some places than in others. In California, for example, progressives led by Governor Hiram Johnson in 1910–1911 were able to institute the direct primary and to adopt procedures—called the *initiative* and the *referendum*—so citizens could vote directly on proposed legislation, thereby bypassing the state legislature. Governor Robert La Follette brought about similar changes in Wisconsin.

The effect of these changes was to reduce substantially the worst forms of political corruption and ultimately to make boss rule in politics difficult if not impossible. But they also had the effect of making political parties, whether led by bosses or by statesmen, weaker, less able to hold officeholders accountable, and less able to assemble the power necessary for governing the fragmented political institutions created by the Constitution. In Congress, party lines began to grow fainter, as did the power of congressional leadership. Above all, the progressives did not have an answer to the problem first faced by Jefferson: if there is not a strong political party, by what other means will candidates for office be found, recruited, and supported?

PARTY REALIGNMENTS

There have clearly been important turning points in the strength of the major parties, especially in the 20th century, when for long periods we have not so much had close competition between two parties as we have had an alternation of dominance by one party and then the other. To help explain these major shifts in the tides of politics, scholars have developed the theory of **critical** or **realigning periods.** During such periods a sharp, lasting shift occurs in the popular coalition supporting one or both parties. The issues that separate the two parties change, and so the kinds of voters supporting each party change. This shift may occur at the time of the election or just after, as the new administration draws in new supporters.[4] There seem to have been five realignments so far, during or just after these elections: 1800, when the Jeffersonian Republicans defeated the Federalists; 1828, when the Jacksonian Democrats came to power; 1860, when the Whig party collapsed and the Republicans under Lincoln came to power; 1896, when the Republicans defeated William Jennings Bryan; and 1932, when the Democrats under Roosevelt came into office.

> *critical* or *realignment period* Periods when a major, lasting shift occurs in the popular coalition supporting one or both parties.

There are at least two kinds of realignments—one in which a major party is so badly defeated that it disappears and a new party emerges to take its place (this happened to the Federalists in 1800 and to the Whigs in 1856–1860), and another in which the two existing parties continue but voters shift their support from one to the other (this happened in 1896 and 1932).

The three clearest cases seem to be 1860, 1896, and 1932. By 1860, the existing parties could no longer straddle the fence on the slavery issue. The Republican party was formed in 1856 on the basis of clear-cut opposition to slavery; the Democratic party split in half in 1860, with one part (led by Stephen A. Douglas and based in the North) trying to waffle on the issue and the other (led by John C. Breckinridge and drawing its support from the South) categorically denying that any government had any right to outlaw slavery. The remnants of the Whig party, renamed the Constitutional Union party, tried to unite the nation by writing no platform at all, thus remaining silent on slavery. Lincoln and the antislavery Republicans won in 1860; Breckinridge and the proslavery Southern Democrats came in second. From that moment on, the two major political parties acquired different sources of support and stood (at least for a decade) for different principles. The parties that had tried to straddle the fence were eliminated. The Civil War fixed these new party loyalties deep in the popular mind, and the structure of party competition was set for nearly 40 years.

In 1896, a different kind of realignment occurred. Economics rather than slavery was at issue. A series of depressions during the 1880s and 1890s fell especially hard on farmers in the Midwest and parts of the South. The prices paid to farmers for their commodities had been falling more or less steadily since the Civil War, making it increasingly difficult for them to pay their bills. A bitter reaction against the two major parties, which were straddling this issue as they had straddled slavery, spread like a prairie fire, leading to the formation of parties of economic protest—the Greenbackers and the Populists. Reinforcing the economic cleavages were cultural ones: Populists tended to be fundamentalist Protestants; urban voters were increasingly Catholic. Matters came to a head in 1896 when William Jennings Bryan captured the Democratic nomination for president and saw to it that the party adopted a Populist platform. The existing Populist party endorsed the Bryan candidacy. In the election, anti-Bryan Democrats deserted the party in droves to support the Republican candidate, William McKinley. Once again, a real issue divided the two parties: the Republicans stood for industry, business, hard money, protective tariffs, and urban interests; the Democrats for farmers, small towns, low tariffs, and rural interests. The Republicans won, carrying the cities, workers, and business people the Democrats lost, carrying most of the southern and midwestern farm states. The old split between North and South that resulted from the Civil War was now replaced in part by an East versus West, city versus farm split.[5] It was not, however, only an economic cleavage—the Republicans

William Jennings Bryan giving a campaign speech during one of his three unsuccessful presidential campaigns.

CORBIS

had been able to appeal to Catholics and Lutherans who disliked fundamentalism and its hostility toward liquor and immigrants.

This alignment persisted until 1932. Again change was triggered by an economic depression; again more than economic issues were involved. The New Deal coalition that emerged was based on bringing together into the Democratic party urban workers, northern blacks, southern whites, and Jewish voters. Unlike in 1860 and 1896, it was not preceded by any third-party movement; it occurred suddenly (though some groups had begun to shift their allegiance in 1928) and gathered momentum throughout the 1930s. The Democrats, isolated since 1896 as a southern and midwestern sectional party, had now become the majority party by finding a candidate and a cause that could lure urban workers, blacks, and Jews away from the Republican party, where they had been for decades. It was obviously a delicate coalition—blacks and southern whites disagreed on practically everything except their liking for Roosevelt; Jews and the Irish bosses of the big-city machines also had little in common. But the federal government under Roosevelt was able to supply enough benefits to each of these disparate groups to keep them loyal members of the coalition and to provide a new basis for party identification.

In short, an electoral realignment occurs when a new issue of utmost importance to the voters (slavery, the economy) cuts across existing party divisions and replaces old issues that formerly were the basis of party identification.

Some people wondered whether the election of 1980, since it brought into power the most conservative administration in half a century, signaled a new realignment. Many of President Reagan's supporters began talking of a "mandate" to adopt major new policies in keeping with the views of the "new majority." But Reagan won in 1980 less because of what he stood for than because he was not Jimmy Carter, and he was reelected in 1984 primarily because people were satisfied with how the country was doing, especially economically.[6]

Just because we have had periods of one-party dominance in the past does not mean we will have them in the future. Reagan's election could not have been a traditional realignment, because it left Congress in the hands of the Democratic party. Moreover, some scholars are beginning to question the theory of critical elections, or at least the theory that they occur with some regularity.

Nevertheless, one major change has occurred of late—the shift in the presidential voting patterns

of the South. From 1972 through 2008, the South was more Republican than the nation as a whole. The proportion of white southerners describing themselves to pollsters as "strongly Democratic" fell from more than one-third in 1952 to about one-seventh in 1984. There has been a corresponding increase in "independents." As it turns out, southern white independents have voted overwhelmingly Republican in recent presidential elections.[7] If you lump independents together with the parties for which they actually vote, the party alignment among white southerners has gone from 6 to 1 Democratic in 1952 to about 50/50 Democrats and Republicans. If this continues, it will constitute a major realignment in a region of the country that is growing rapidly in population and political clout.

In general, however, the kind of dramatic realignment that occurred in the 1860s or after 1932 may not occur again, because party labels have lost their meaning for a growing number of voters. For these people politics may *de*align rather than *re*align.

PARTY DECLINE

The evidence that the parties are decaying, not realigning, is of several sorts. We have already noted that the proportion of people identifying with one or the other party declined between 1960 and 1980. Simultaneously, the proportion of those voting a **split ticket** (as opposed to a **straight ticket**) increased.

Split-ticket voting rose between 1952 and 1972 and hovered around 25 percent until it declined somewhat after 1992 (see Figure 9.2). For example, in 1988 more than *half* of all House Democrats were elected in districts that voted for Republican George Bush as president. This ticket splitting was greatest in the South, but it was common everywhere. If every district that voted for Bush had also elected a Republican to Congress, the Republican party would have held a 2-to-1 majority in the House of Representatives. Ticket splitting creates divided government—the White House and Congress are controlled by different parties (see Chapter 14). Ticket splitting helped the Democrats keep control of the House of Representatives from 1954 to 1994.

Ticket splitting was almost unheard of in the 19th century, and for a very good reason. In those days, the voter was either given a ballot by the party of his choice and he dropped it, intact, into the ballot box

split ticket Voting for candidates of different parties for various offices in the same election.

straight ticket Voting for candidates of the same party.

Figure 9.2

Split-Ticket Voting for President/House, 1952–2004

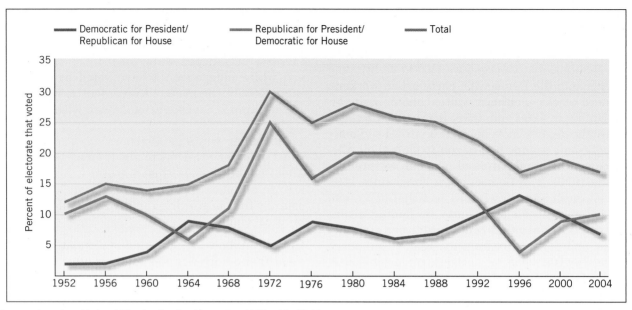

Source: *American National Election Studies*, November 2005, table 9B.2.

(thereby voting for everybody listed on the ballot), or he was given a government-printed ballot that listed in columns all the candidates of each party. All the voter had to do was mark the top of one column in order to vote for every candidate in that column. (When voting machines came along, they provided a single lever that, when pulled, cast votes for all the candidates of a particular party.) Around the turn of the century progressives began to persuade states to adopt the **office-bloc** (or "Massachusetts") **ballot** in place of the **party-column** (or "Indiana") **ballot.** The office-bloc ballot lists all candidates by office; there is no way to vote a straight party ticket by making one mark. Not surprisingly, states using the office-bloc ballot show much more ticket splitting than those without it.[8]

office-bloc ballot A ballot listing all candidates of a given office under the name of that office; also called a "Massachusetts" ballot.

party-column ballot A ballot listing all candidates of a given party together under the name of that party; also called an "Indiana" ballot.

The National Party Structure Today

It would be a mistake, however, to conclude that parties have declined simply because many voters now split tickets in national elections. Despite many changes and challenges (see Figure 9.3), America's two-party system remains strong. In most elections—national, state, and local—voters registered as Democrats still vote for Democratic candidates, and voters registered as Republicans still vote for Republican candidates. In Congress, state legislatures, and city councils, members still normally vote along party lines. Local political machines have died, but as we shall now explain, national party structures remain alive and well.

Since political parties exist at the national, state, and local levels, you might suppose they are arranged like a big corporation, with a national board of directors giving orders to state managers who in turn direct the activities of rank-and-file workers at the county and city level.

Nothing could be further from the truth. At each level, a separate and almost entirely independent organization exists that does pretty much what it wants, and in many counties and cities there is virtually no organization at all.

State party organizations, all determined to pick their delegates to the presidential nominating convention first, moved their primary elections to earlier and earlier dates. For example, the Iowa caucus and the New Hampshire primary in the 1980s were held in March; in 2008, they were held in January. California moved its primary from June to February. This front-loaded set of primaries made

Figure 9.3
Cleavages and Continuity in the Two-Party System

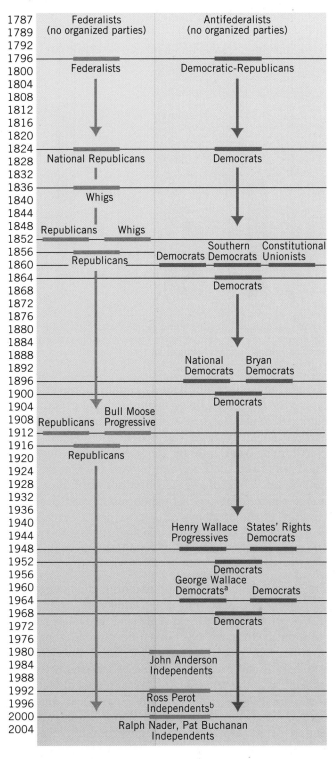

1787
1789
1792
1796   Federalists (no organized parties)   Antifederalists (no organized parties)
1800   Federalists   Democratic-Republicans
1804
1808
1812
1816
1820
1824
1828   National Republicans   Democrats
1832
1836
1840   Whigs
1844
1848   Republicans   Whigs
1852
1856   Republicans   Southern / Constitutional
1860   Democrats Democrats Unionists
1864   Democrats
1868
1872
1876
1880
1884
1888   National / Bryan
1892   Democrats / Democrats
1896
1900   Democrats
1904
1908   Bull Moose
        Republicans   Progressive
1912
1916   Republicans
1920
1924
1928
1932
1936
1940   Henry Wallace / States' Rights
1944   Progressives / Democrats
1948
1952   Democrats
1956   George Wallace
1960   Democrats[a]   Democrats
1964
1968   Democrats
1972
1976
1980   John Anderson
1984   Independents
1988
1992   Ross Perot
1996   Independents[b]
2000   Ralph Nader, Pat Buchanan
2004   Independents

[a]American Independent party.

[b]United We Stand American or Reform Party.

the campaign much longer and more expensive, but the national party organizations were almost powerless to prevent it.

On paper, the national Democratic and Republican parties look quite similar. In both parties, ultimate authority is in the hands of the **national convention** that meets every four years to nominate a presidential candidate. Between these conventions, party affairs are managed by a **national committee** made up of delegates from each state and territory. In Congress, each party has a **congressional campaign committee** that helps members of Congress running for reelection or would-be members running for an open seat or challenging a candidate from the opposition party. The day-to-day work of the party is managed by a full-time, paid **national chairman** elected by the committee.

> ***national convention*** A meeting of party delegates held every four years.
>
> ***national committee*** Delegates who run party affairs between national conventions.
>
> ***congressional campaign committee*** A party committee in Congress that provides funds to members and would-be members.
>
> ***national chairman*** Day-to-day party manager elected by the national committee.

For a long time, the two national parties were alike in behavior as well as description. The national chairman, if his party held the White House, would help decide who among the party faithful would get federal jobs. Otherwise, the parties did very little.

But beginning in the late 1960s and early 1970s, the Republicans began to convert their national party into a well-financed, highly staffed organization devoted to finding and electing Republican candidates, especially to Congress. At about the same time, the Democrats began changing the rules governing how presidential candidates are nominated in ways that profoundly altered the distribution of power within the party. As a consequence, the Republicans became a bureaucratized party and the Democrats became a factionalized one. After the Republicans won four out of five presidential elections from 1968 to 1984 and briefly took control of the Senate, the Democrats began to suspect that maybe an efficient bureaucracy was better than a collection of warring factions, and so they made an effort to emulate the Republicans.

The Republicans had taken advantage of a new bit of technology—computerized mailings. They built up a huge file of names of people who had given or might give money to the party, usually in small amounts, and used that list to raise a big budget for the national party. The Republican National Committee (RNC) used this money to run, in effect, a national political consulting firm. Money went to recruit and train Republican candidates, give them legal and financial advice, study issues and analyze voting trends, and conduct national advertising campaigns on behalf of the party as a whole.

When the Democratic National Committee (DNC) decided to play catch-up, it followed the RNC strategy. Using the same computerized direct-mail techniques, the Democratic party committees—the National Committee, Senatorial Committee, and Congressional Committee—raised more money than ever before, though not as much as the Republicans. In 2004, the Democrats and their allies outspent the Republicans. The Democrats, like the Republicans, ship a lot of their national party money to state organizations to finance television ads supporting their parties.

Despite the recent enactment of campaign finance laws intended to check the influence of money on national elections, in 2004 both Democrats and Republicans redoubled efforts to raise *soft money*—that is, funds to aid parties (and their ads and polls). In the Democratic presidential primary, Howard Dean alone raised $30 million over the Internet with average contributions under $100. In 2006, new records were also set for spending on congressional races. In 39 House races, challengers raised over $1 million. About three-quarters of these "million-dollar challengers" were Democrats (see Figure 9.4).

NATIONAL CONVENTIONS

The national committee selects the time and place of the next national convention and issues a "call" for the convention that sets forth the number of delegates each state and territory is to have and the rules under which delegates must be chosen. The number of delegates and their manner of selection can significantly influence the chances of various presidential candidates, and considerable attention is thus devoted to these matters. In the Democratic party, for example, a long struggle took place between those who wished to see southern states receive a large share of delegates to the convention, in recognition of their firm support of Democratic candidates in presidential elections, and those who preferred to see a larger share of delegates allotted to northern and western states, which, though less solidly Democratic, were larger or more liberal. A similar conflict within the Republican party has pitted conservative Republican leaders in the Midwest against liberal ones in the East.

Figure 9.4

House Challengers Who Raised $1 Million or More (2000–2006)

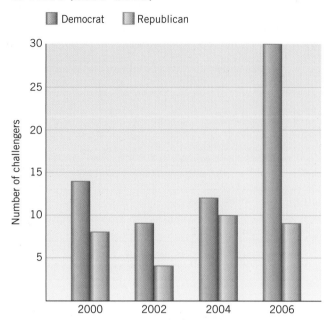

Source: Campaign Finance Institute, George Washington University, Washington, D.C., October 19, 2006, figure 1, summarizing data from the Federal Election Commission.

A compromise formula usually is chosen; nevertheless, over the years these formulas have gradually changed, shifting voting strength in the Democratic convention away from the South and toward the North and West and in the Republican convention away from the East and toward the South and Southwest. These delegate allocation formulas are but one sign (others will be mentioned later in this chapter) of the tendency of the two parties' conventions to move in opposite ideological directions—Democrats more to the left, Republicans more to the right.

The exact formula for apportioning delegates is extremely complex. For the Democrats, it takes into account the vote each state cast for Democratic candidates in past elections and the number of electoral votes of each state; for the Republicans, it takes into account the number of representatives in Congress and whether the state in past elections cast its electoral votes for the Republican presidential candidate and elected Republicans to the Senate, the House, and the governorship. Thus, the Democrats give extra delegates to large states, while the Republicans give extra ones to loyal states.

The way in which delegates are chosen can be even more important than their allocation. The Democrats, beginning in 1972, developed an

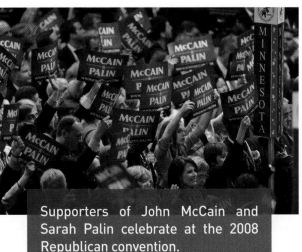

Democratic National Committee

The Internet is the latest means through which people are becoming politically informed and active. It has also become an important way to raise money for candidates and parties.

reforms were aimed at creating *intra*party democracy as well as *inter*party democracy. Rules for the 1980 Democratic convention required:

- Equal division of delegates between men and women

- Establishment of "goals" for the representation of African Americans, Hispanics, and other groups in proportion to their presence in a state's Democratic electorate

- Open delegate selection procedures, with advance publicity and written rules

- Selection of 75 percent of the delegates at the level of the congressional district or lower

- No "unit rule" that would require all delegates to vote with the majority of their state delegation

- Restrictions on the number of party leaders and elected officials who could vote at the convention

- A requirement that all delegates pledged to a candidate vote for that candidate

elaborate set of rules designed to weaken the control over delegates by local party leaders and to increase the proportion of women, young people, African Americans, and Native Americans attending the convention. These rules were first drafted by a party commission chaired by Senator George McGovern (who later made skillful use of these new procedures in his successful bid for the Democratic presidential nomination). They were revised in 1974 by another commission, chaired by Barbara Mikulski, whose decisions were ratified by the 1974 midterm convention. After the 1976 election, a third commission, chaired by Morley Winograd, produced still another revision of the rules, which took effect in 1980. Then a fourth commission, chaired by North Carolina governor James B. Hunt, recommended in 1981 another set of rules, which became effective with the 1984 convention.

The general thrust of the work of the first three rules commissions was to broaden the antiparty changes started by the progressives at the beginning of this century. Whereas the earlier reformers had tried to minimize the role of parties in the election process, those of the 1970s sought to weaken the influence of leaders within the party. In short, the newer

In 1981, the Hunt Commission changed some of these rules—in particular, the last two—in order to increase the influence of elected officials and to make the convention a somewhat more deliberative body. The commission reserved about 14 percent of the delegate seats for party leaders and elected officials (the "**superdelegates**"), who

superdelegates Party leaders and elected officials who become delegates to the national convention without having to run in primaries or caucuses.

Supporters of John McCain and Sarah Palin celebrate at the 2008 Republican convention.

Stan Honda/AFP/Getty Images

Table 9.1 Who Are the Party Delegates?

Characteristics of delegates to Democratic and Republican national conventions in 2004		
	Democrats	**Republicans**
Sex and Race		
Women	50%	43%
Blacks	18	6
Religion		
Protestant	43	65
Catholic	32	—
Jewish	8	—
Education		
College degree and beyond	77	73
Post graduate	53	44
Family Income		
Under $50,000	15	8
$100,000 and over	42	44
Belong to union	25	8
Born-again Christian	13	33
Gun owner in household	22	45

Sources: New York Times (August 29, 2004); CBSNEWS.COM, July 24, 2004; Boston Globe, August 31, 2004.

would not have to commit themselves in advance to a presidential candidate, and it repealed the rule requiring that delegates pledged to a candidate vote for that candidate.

But the "reform" of the parties, especially the Democratic party, has had far more profound consequences than merely helping one candidate or another. Before 1968, the Republican party represented, essentially, white-collar voters and the Democratic party represented blue-collar ones. After a decade of "reform," the Republican and the Democratic parties each represented two ideologically different sets of upper-middle-class voters (see Table 9.1). In the terminology of Chapter 7, the Republicans came to represent the more conservative wing of the traditional middle class and the Democrats the more leftist wing of the liberal middle class.

This was more troubling to the Democrats than the Republicans, because the traditional middle class is somewhat closer to the opinions of most citizens than the liberal middle class (and thus the Republican national convention more closely reflected public opinion than the Democratic national convention).

And for whatever reason, the Republicans won five out of six presidential races between 1968 and 1988.

The DNC changed the rules for the 1992 campaign. Former DNC chairman Ronald H. Brown (later President Clinton's secretary of commerce) won approval for three important requirements:

- The winner-reward systems of delegate distribution, which gave the winner of a primary or caucus extra delegates, were banned. (In 1988, fifteen states used winner-reward systems, including such vote-rich states as Florida, Illinois, New Jersey, and Pennsylvania.)

- The proportional representation system was put into use. This system divides a state's publicly elected delegates among candidates who receive at least 15 percent of the vote.

- States that violate the rules are now penalized with the loss of 25 percent of their national convention delegates.

Even though the Democrats have retreated a bit from the reforms of the 1960s and 1970s, the conventions of both parties have changed fundamentally, and probably permanently. Delegates once selected by party leaders are now chosen by primary elections and grassroots caucuses. As a result, the national party conventions are no longer places where party leaders meet to bargain over the selection of their presidential candidates; they are instead places where delegates come together to ratify choices already made by party activists and primary voters.

Most Americans dislike bosses, deals, and manipulation and prefer democracy, reform, and openness. These are commendable instincts. But such instincts, unless carefully tested against practice, may mislead us into supposing that anything carried out in the name of reform is a good idea. Rules must be judged by their practical results as well as by their conformity to some principle of fairness. Rules affect the distribution of power: they help some people win and others lose. Later in this chapter, we shall try to assess delegate selection rules by looking more closely at how they affect who attends conventions and which presidential candidates are selected there.

State and Local Parties

While the national party structures have changed, the grassroots organizations have withered. In between, state party systems have struggled to redefine their roles.

In every state, a Democratic and a Republican state party is organized under state law. Each typically

2. *Who was the first Catholic nominated for president by a major party?*

consists of a state central committee, below which are county committees and sometimes city, town, or even precinct committees. The members of these committees are chosen in a variety of ways—sometimes in primary elections, sometimes by conventions, sometimes by a building-block process whereby people elected to serve on precinct or town committees choose the members of county committees, who in turn choose state committee members.

Knowing these formal arrangements is much less helpful than knowing the actual distribution of power in each state party. In a few places strong party bosses handpick the members of these committees; in other places, powerful elected officials—key state legislators, county sheriffs, or judges—control the committees. And in many places no one is in charge, so that either the party structure is largely meaningless or it is made up of the representatives of various local factions.

To understand how power is distributed in a party, we must first know what *incentives* motivate people in a particular state or locality to become active in a party organization. Different incentives lead to different ways of organizing parties.

THE MACHINE

A **political machine** is a party organization that recruits its members by the use of tangible incentives—money, political jobs, an opportunity to get favors from government—and is characterized by a high degree of leadership control over member activity. At one time, many local party organizations

Ex-Senator George Washington Plunkitt of Tammany Hall explains machine politics from atop the bootblack stand in front of the New York County Courthouse around 1905.

were machines, and the struggle over political jobs—patronage—was the chief concern of their members. Though Tammany Hall in New York City began as a caucus of well-to-do notables in the local Democratic party, by the late 19th century, it had become a machine organized on the basis of political clubs in each assembly district. These clubs were composed of party workers whose job it was to get out the straight party vote in their election districts and who hoped for a tangible reward if they were successful.

And there were abundant rewards to hope for. During the 1870s, it was estimated that one out of every eight voters in New York City had a federal, state, or city job.[9] The federal bureaucracy was one important source of those jobs. The New York Customhouse alone employed thousands of people, virtually all of whom were replaced if their party lost the presidential election. The postal system was another source, and it was frankly recognized as such. When James N. Tyner became postmaster general in 1876, he was "appointed not to see that the mails were carried, but to see that Indiana was carried."[10] Elections and conventions were so frequent and the intensity of party competition so great that being a party worker was for many a full-time paid occupation.

Well before the arrival of vast numbers of poor immigrants from Ireland, Italy, and elsewhere, old-stock Americans had perfected the machine, run up the cost of government, and systematized voting fraud. Kickbacks on contracts, payments extracted from officeholders, and funds raised from business people made some politicians rich but also paid the huge bills of the elaborate party organization. When the immigrants began flooding the eastern cities, the party machines were there to provide them with all manner of services in exchange for their support at the polls: the machines were a vast welfare organization operating before the creation of the welfare state.

political machine A party organization that recruits members by dispensing patronage.

The abuses of the machine were well known and gradually curtailed. Stricter voter registration laws reduced fraud, civil service reforms cut down the number of patronage jobs, and competitive bidding laws made it harder to award overpriced contracts to favored businesses. The Hatch Act (passed by Congress in 1939) made it illegal for federal civil service employees to take an active part in political management or political campaigns by serving as party officers, soliciting campaign funds, running for partisan office, working in a partisan campaign,

Answer

2. Al Smith, by the Democrats in 1928.

ideological party A party that values principled stands on issues above all else.

endorsing partisan candidates, taking voters to the polls, counting ballots, circulating nominating petitions, or being delegates to a party convention. (They may still vote and make campaign contributions.)

These restrictions gradually took federal employees out of machine politics, but they did not end the machines. In many cities—Chicago, Philadelphia, and Albany—ways were found to maintain the machines even though city employees were technically under the civil service. Far more important than the various progressive reforms that weakened the machines were changes among voters. As voters grew in education, income, and sophistication, they depended less and less on the advice and leadership of local party officials. And as the federal government created a bureaucratic welfare system, the parties' welfare systems declined in value.

It is easy either to scorn the political party machine as a venal and self-serving organization or to romanticize it as an informal welfare system. In truth, it was a little of both. Above all, it was a frank recognition of the fact that politics requires organization; the machine was the supreme expression of the value of organization. Even allowing for voting fraud, in elections where party machines were active, voter turnout was huge: more people participated in politics when mobilized by a party machine than when appealed to via television or good-government associations.[11] Moreover, because the party machines were interested in winning, they would subordinate any other consideration to that end. This has meant that the machines usually were willing to support the presidential candidate with the best chance of winning, regardless of his policy views (provided, of course, that he was not determined to wreck the machines once in office). Republican machines helped elect Abraham Lincoln as well as Warren G. Harding; Democratic machines were of crucial importance in electing Franklin D. Roosevelt and John F. Kennedy.

The old-style machine is almost extinct, though important examples still can be found in the Democratic organization in Cook County (Chicago) and the Republican organization in Nassau County (New York). But a new-style machine has emerged in a few places. It is a machine in the sense that it uses money to knit together many politicians, but it is new in that the money comes not from patronage and contracts but from campaign contributions supplied by wealthy individuals and the proceeds of direct-mail campaigns.

IDEOLOGICAL PARTIES

At the opposite extreme from the machine is the **ideological party.** Where the machine values winning above all else, the ideological party values principle above all else. Where the former depends on money incentives, the latter spurns them. Where the former is hierarchical and disciplined, the latter usually is contentious and factionalized.

The most firmly ideological parties have been independent "third parties," such as the Socialist, Socialist Workers, Libertarian, and Right-to-Life parties. But there have been ideological factions within the Democratic and Republican parties as well, and in some places these ideological groups have taken over the regular parties.

In the 1950s and 1960s, these ideological groups were "reform clubs" within local Democratic and Republican parties. In Los Angeles, New York, and many parts of Wisconsin and Minnesota, issue-oriented activists fought to take over the party from election-oriented regulars. Democratic reform clubs managed to defeat the head of Tammany Hall in Manhattan; similar activist groups became the dominant force in California state politics.[12] Democratic club leaders were more liberal than rank-and-file Democrats, and Republican club leaders were often more conservative than rank-and-file Republicans.

The 1960s and 1970s saw these "reform" movements replaced by more focused social movements. The reform movement was based on a generalized sense of liberalism (among Democrats) or conservatism (among Republicans). With the advent of social movements concerned with civil rights, peace, feminism, environmentalism, libertarianism, and abortion, the generalized ideology of the clubs was replaced by the specific ideological demands of single-issue activists.

The result is that in many places, the party has become a collection of people drawn from various social movements. For a candidate to win the party's support, he or she often has to satisfy the "litmus test" demands of the ideological activists in the party. Democratic senator Barbara Mikulski put it this way: "The social movements are now our farm clubs."

With social movements as their farm clubs, the big-league teams—the Democrats and Republicans at the state level—behave very differently than they did when political machines were the farm clubs. Internal factionalism is more intense, and the freedom of action of the party leader (say, the chairperson of the state committee) has been greatly reduced. A leader who demands too little or gives up too much, or who says the wrong thing on a key issue, is quickly accused of having "sold out." Under these circumstances, many are "leaders" in name only.

SOLIDARY GROUPS

Many people who participate in state and local politics do so not in order to earn money or vindicate some cause, but simply because they find it fun. They enjoy the game, they meet interesting people, and they like the sense of being "in the know" and rubbing shoulders with the powerful. When people get together out of gregarious or game-loving instincts, they are responding to **solidary incentives;** if they form an organization, it is a solidary association.

Some of these associations were once machines. When a machine loses its patronage, some of its members—especially the older ones—may continue to serve in the organization out of a desire for camaraderie. In other cases precinct, ward, and district committees are built up on the basis of friendship networks. One study of political activists in Detroit found that most of them mentioned friendships and a liking for politics—rather than an interest in issues—as their reasons for joining the party organization.[13] Members of ward and town organizations in St. Louis County gave the same answers when asked why they joined.[14] Since patronage has declined in value and since the appeals of ideology are limited to a minority of citizens, the motivations for participating in politics have become very much like those for joining a bowling league or a bridge club.

The personal following of former President George Bush was passed on to his sons, George W. (left) and Jeb (right), both of whom became governors of large states, and the former of whom became president.

The advantage of such groups is that they are neither corrupt nor inflexible; the disadvantage is that they often do not work very hard. Knocking on doors on a rainy November evening to try to talk people into voting for your candidate is a chore under the best of circumstances; it is especially unappealing if you joined the party primarily because you like to attend meetings or drink coffee with your friends.[15]

SPONSORED PARTIES

Sometimes a relatively strong party organization can be created among volunteers without heavy reliance on money or ideology and without depending entirely on people's finding the work fun. This type of **sponsored party** occurs when another organization exists in the community that can create, or at least sponsor, a local party structure. The clearest example of this is the Democratic party in and around Detroit, which has been developed, led, and to a degree financed by the political-action arm of the United Auto Workers union. The UAW has had a long tradition of rank-and-file activism, stemming from its formative struggles in the 1930s, and since the city virtually is a one-industry town, it was not hard to transfer some of this activism from union organizing to voter organizing.

> *solidary incentives* The social rewards (sense of pleasure, status, or companionship) that lead people to join political organizations.
>
> *sponsored party* A local or state political party largely supported by another organization in the community.

By the mid-1950s, union members and leaders made up over three-fourths of all the Democratic party district leaders within the city.[16] On election day, union funds were available for paying workers to canvass voters; between elections, political work on an unpaid basis was expected of union leaders. Though the UAW-Democratic party alliance in Detroit has not always been successful in city elections (the city is nonpartisan), it has been quite successful in carrying the city for the Democratic party in state and national elections.

Not many areas have organizations as effective or as dominant as the UAW that can bolster, sponsor, or even take over the weak formal party structure. Thus sponsored local parties are not common in the United States.

PERSONAL FOLLOWING

Because most candidates can no longer count on the backing of a machine, because sponsored parties are limited to a few unionized areas, and because

two-party system An electorial system with two dominant parties that compete in national elections.

plurality system An electoral system in which the winner is the person who gets the most votes, even if he or she does not receive a majority; used in almost all American elections.

personal following The political support provided to a candidate on the basis of personal popularity and networks.

solidary groups are not always productive, a person wanting to get elected often will try to form a **personal following** that will work for him or her during a campaign and then disband until the next election rolls around. Sometimes a candidate tries to meld a personal following with an ideological group, especially during the primary election campaign, when candidates need the kind of financial backing and hard work that only highly motivated activists are likely to supply.

To form a personal following, the candidate must have an appealing personality, a lot of friends, or a big bank account. The Kennedy family has all three, and the electoral success of the personal followings of John F. Kennedy, Edward M. Kennedy, Robert Kennedy, and Joseph P. Kennedy II are legendary. President George H.W. Bush also established such a following. After he left office, one son (Jeb) became governor of Florida and another one (George W.) became governor of Texas and the 43rd president of the United States.

Southern politicians who operate in one-party states with few, if any, machines have become grand masters at building personal followings, such as those of the Talmadge family in Georgia, the Long family in Louisiana, and the Byrd family in Virginia. But the strategy is increasingly followed wherever party organization is weak. The key asset is to have a known political name. This has helped the electoral victories of the son of Hubert Humphrey in Minnesota, the son and daughter of Pat Brown in California, the son of Birch Bayh in Indiana, the son of George Wallace in Alabama, and the son and grandson of Robert La Follette in Wisconsin.

By the mid-1980s, the traditional party organization—one that is hierarchical, lasting, based on material incentives, and capable of influencing who gets nominated for office—existed, according to political scientist David Mayhew, in only about eight states, mostly the older states of the Northeast. Another five states, he found, had faction-ridden versions of the traditional party organization.[17] The states in the rest of the country displayed the weak party system of solidary clubs, personal followings, ideological groups, and sponsored parties. What that meant could also be seen in the composition of Democratic national conventions. In 1984, over half of the delegates were drawn from the ranks of the AFL-CIO, the National Education Association, and the National Organization for Women.[18] By 2004, both national party organizations and their respective conventions had been dominated for at least two decades by ideological groups and the like.

The Two-Party System

With so many different varieties of local party organizations (or nonorganizations), and with such a great range of opinion found within each party, it is remarkable that we have had only two major political parties for most of our history. In the world at large a **two-party system** is a rarity; by one estimate only 15 nations have one.[19] Most European democracies are multiparty systems. We have only two parties with any chance of winning nationally, and these parties have been, over time, rather evenly balanced—between 1888 and 2004, the Republicans won 17 presidential elections and the Democrats 13. Furthermore, whenever one party has achieved a temporary ascendancy and its rival has been pronounced dead (as were the Democrats in the first third of this century and the Republicans during the 1930s and the 1960s), the "dead" party has displayed remarkable powers of recuperation, coming back to win important victories.

At the state and congressional district levels, however, the parties are not evenly balanced. For a long time, the South was so heavily Democratic at all levels of government as to be a one-party area, while upper New England and the Dakotas were strongly Republican. All regions are more competitive today than once was the case. Parties are not as competitive in state elections as they are in presidential ones. States have rarely had, at least for any extended period, political parties other than the Democratic and Republican.

Scholars do not entirely agree on why the two-party system should be so permanent a feature of American political life, but two explanations are of major importance. The first has to do with the system of elections, the second with the distribution of public opinion.

Elections at every level of government are based on the plurality, winner-take-all method. The **plurality system** means that in all elections for representative, senator, governor, or president, and in almost all elections for state legislator, mayor, or city councilor, the winner gets the *most* votes, even if he or she does not get a *majority* of all votes cast. We are so familiar with this system that we sometimes forget there are other ways of running an election. For example, one could require that the winner get a majority of the votes, thus producing runoff elections if nobody got a majority on the first try. France does this in choosing its national legislature. In the first election, candidates for parliament who win an absolute majority of the votes cast are declared elected. A week later, remaining candidates who received at least one-eighth, but less than one-half of the vote, go into a runoff election; those who then win an absolute majority are also declared elected.

The French method encourages many political parties to form, each hoping to win at least one-eighth of the vote in the first election and then to enter into an alliance with its ideologically nearest rival in order to win the runoff. In the United States, the plurality system means that a party must make all the alliances it can before the first election—there is no second chance. Hence, every party must be as broadly based as possible; a narrow, minor party has no hope of winning.

The winner-take-all feature of American elections has the same effect. Only one member of Congress is elected from each district. In many European countries, the elections are based on proportional representation. Each party submits a list of candidates for parliament, ranked in order of preference by the party leaders. The nation votes. A party winning 37 percent of the vote gets 37 percent of the seats in parliament; a party winning 2 percent of the vote gets 2 percent of the seats. Since even the smallest parties have a chance of winning something, minor parties have an incentive to organize.

The most dramatic example of the winner-take-all principle is the electoral college (see Chapter 14). In every state but Maine and Nebraska, the candidate who wins the most popular votes in a state wins *all* of that state's electoral votes. In 1992, for example, Bill Clinton won only 45 percent of the popular vote in Missouri, but he got all of Missouri's 11 electoral votes because his two rivals (George H. W. Bush and Ross Perot) each got fewer popular votes. Minor parties cannot compete under this system. Voters often are reluctant to "waste" their votes on a minor-party candidate who cannot win.

The United States has experimented with other electoral systems. Proportional representation was used for municipal elections in New York City at one time and still is in use in Cambridge, Massachusetts. Many states have elected more than one state legislator from each district. In Illinois, for example, three legislators have been elected from each district, with each voter allowed to cast two votes, thus virtually guaranteeing that the minority party will be able to win one of the three seats. But none of these experiments has altered the national two-party system, probably because of the existence of a directly elected president chosen by a winner-take-all electoral college.

The presidency is the great prize of American politics; to win it, you must form a party with as broad appeal as possible. As a practical matter, this means there will be, in most cases, only two serious parties—one made up of those who support the party already in power, and the other made up of everybody else. Only one third party ever won the presidency—the Republicans in 1860—and it had by then pretty much supplanted the Whig party. No third party is likely to win, or even come close to winning, the presidency anytime soon. Despite the decline in mass party attachment, among Americans who actually vote in presidential elections, party voting is almost as strong today as it was in the early 1950s. As Table 9.2 shows, in the presidential elections of 1992 through 2008, the vast majority of Democrats voted for the Democrat, and the vast majority of Republicans voted for the Republican. Meanwhile, most independents voted for the winning Republican in 1988 and 2000, and pluralities of independents voted for the winning Democrat in 1992 and 1996 and again in 2008.

The second explanation for the persistence of the two-party system is found in the opinions of the voters. Recent national surveys have found that most Americans see "a difference in what Democratic and Republican parties stand for."[20] For the most part, the majority has deemed Democrats better at handling such issues as poverty, the environment, and health

Table 9.2 Party Voting in Presidential Elections

Party Affiliation of Voter	1992			1996			2000			2004			2008		
	Dem.	Rep.	Ind.	Dem.	Rep.	Ind.	Dem.	Rep.	Ind.	Dem.	Rep.	Ind.	Dem.	Rep.	Ind.
Democrat	82%	8%	10%	84%	10%	5%	85%	10%	3%	89%	11%	0%	89	10	0
Republican	7	77	16	13	80	6	7	91	1	6	93	0	9	89	0
Independent	39	30	31	43	35	17	37	42	9	49	48	1	52	44	0

Source: Data from CNN exit polls for each year.

care and the Republicans better at handling such issues as national defense, foreign trade, and crime; but voters generally have split on which party is best at handling the economy and taxes.[21] And when it comes to which party is best able to handle whatever individuals see as the "most important problem" facing the nation, normally about 15 percent to a quarter each choose either Democrats or Republicans, while about 45 to 55 percent answer "not much difference."[22]

As we learned in Chapter 7, however, public opinion often is dynamic, not static. Mass perceptions concerning the parties are no exception. For instance, by 2004, a few years after President George W. Bush passed his No Child Left Behind education plan, Republicans cut into the Democrats' traditional slight edge in public school support concerning which party does better on public schools. After 2004, as the war in Iraq became unpopular, Republicans lost ground to Democrats on national defense. And on certain complicated or controversial issues, such as immigration policy, opinions can shift overnight in response to real or perceived changes in policy by those the public views as each party's respective leaders or spokespersons.

Though there have been periods of bitter dissent, most of the time most citizens have agreed enough to permit them to come together into two broad coalitions. There has not been a massive and persistent body of opinion that has rejected the prevailing economic system (and thus we have not had a Marxist party with mass appeal); there has not been in our history an aristocracy or monarchy (and thus there has been no party that has sought to restore aristocrats or monarchs to power). Churches and religion have almost always been regarded as matters of private choice that lie outside politics (and thus there has not been a party seeking to create or abolish special government privileges for one church or another). In some European nations, the organization of the economy, the prerogatives of the monarchy, and the role of the church have been major issues with long and bloody histories. So divisive have these issues been that they have helped prevent the formation of broad coalition parties.

But Americans have had other deep divisions—between white and black, for example, and between North and South—and yet the two-party system has endured. This suggests that our electoral procedures are of great importance—the winner-take-all, plurality election rules have made it useless for anyone to attempt to create an all-white or an all-black national party except as an act of momentary defiance or in the hope of taking enough votes away from the two major parties to force the presidential election into the House of Representatives. (That may have been George Wallace's strategy in 1968.)

For many years, there was an additional reason for the two-party system: the laws of many states made it difficult, if not impossible, for third parties to get on the ballot. In 1968, for example, the American Independent party of George Wallace found that it would have to collect 433,000 signatures (15 percent of the votes cast in the last statewide election) in order to get on the presidential ballot in Ohio. Wallace took the issue to the Supreme Court, which ruled, 6 to 3, that such a restriction was an unconstitutional violation of the equal-protection clause of the Fourteenth Amendment.[23] Wallace got on the ballot. In 1980, John Anderson, running as an independent, was able to get on the ballot in all 50 states; in 1992, Ross Perot did the same. But for the reasons already indicated, the two-party system will probably persist even without the aid of legal restrictions.

Minor Parties

The electoral system may prevent minor parties from winning, but it does not prevent them from forming. Minor parties—usually called, erroneously, "third parties"—have been a permanent feature of American political life. Four major kinds of minor parties, with examples of each, are described in the box on page 213.

The minor parties that have endured are the ideological ones. Their members feel outside the mainstream of American political life and sometimes, as in the case of various Marxist parties, look forward to a time when a revolution or some other dramatic change in the political system will vindicate them. They usually are not interested in immediate electoral success and thus persist despite their poor showing at the polls. One such party, however, the Socialist party of Eugene Debs, won nearly 6 percent of the popular vote in the 1912 presidential election. During its heyday, 1,200 candidates were elected to local offices, including 79 mayors. Part of the Socialist appeal arose from its opposition to municipal corruption, its opposition to American entry into World War I, and its critique of American society. No ideological party has ever carried a state in a presidential election.

Apart from the Republicans, who quickly became a major party, the only minor parties to carry states and thus win electoral votes were one party of economic protest (the Populists, who carried five states in 1892) and several factional parties (most recently, the States' Rights Democrats in 1948 and

3. *Who was the first presidential candidate to make an acceptance speech at a national convention?*

How Things Work

Types of Minor Parties

1. **Ideological parties:** Parties professing a comprehensive view of American society and government radically different from the established parties. Most have been Marxist in outlook, but some are quite the opposite, such as the Libertarian party.

   Examples:

   Socialist party (1901 to 1960s)

   Socialist Labor party (1888 to present)

   Socialist Workers party (1938 to present)

   Communist party (1920s to present)

   Libertarian party (1972 to present)

   Green party (1984 to present)

2. **One-issue parties:** Parties seeking a single policy, usually revealed by their names, and avoiding other issues.

   Examples:

   Free-Soil party—to prevent the spread of slavery (1848–1852)

   American or "Know-Nothing" party—to oppose immigration and Catholics (1856)

   Prohibition party—to ban the sale of liquor (1869 to present)

   Woman's party—to obtain the right to vote for women (1913–1920)

3. **Economic-protest parties:** Parties, usually based in a particular region, especially involving farmers, that protest against depressed economic conditions. These tend to disappear as conditions improve.

   Examples:

   Greenback party (1876–1884)

   Populist party (1892–1908)

4. **Factional parties:** Parties created by a split in a major party, usually over the identity and philosophy of the major party's presidential candidate.

   Examples:

   Split off from the Republican party:

   "Bull Moose" Progressive party (1912)

   La Follette Progressive party (1924)

   Split off from the Democratic party:

   States' Rights ("Dixiecrat") party (1948)

   Henry Wallace Progressive party (1948)

   American Independent (George Wallace) party (1968)

   Split off from both Democrats and Republicans:

   Reform party (Ross Perot)

the American Independent party of George Wallace in 1968). Though factional parties may hope to cause the defeat of the party from which they split, they have not always been able to achieve this. Harry Truman was elected in 1948 despite the defections of both the leftist progressives, led by Henry Wallace, and the right-wing Dixiecrats, led by J. Strom Thurmond. In 1968, it seems likely that Hubert Humphrey would have lost even if George Wallace had not been in the race (Wallace voters would probably have switched to Nixon rather than to Humphrey, though of course one cannot be certain). It is quite possible, on the other hand, that a Republican might have beaten Woodrow Wilson in 1912 if the Republican party had not split in two (the regulars supporting William Howard Taft, the progressives supporting Theodore Roosevelt).

What is striking is not that we have had so many minor parties but that we have not had more. There have been several major political movements that did not produce a significant third party: the civil rights movement of the 1960s, the antiwar movement of the same decade, and, most important, the labor movement of the 20th century. African Americans were part of the Republican party after the Civil War and part of the Democratic party after the New Deal (even though the southern wing of that party for a long time kept them from voting). The

Answer

3. Franklin D. Roosevelt at the 1932 Democratic convention.

antiwar movement found candidates with whom it could identify within the Democratic party (Eugene McCarthy, Robert F. Kennedy, George McGovern), even though it was a Democratic president, Lyndon B. Johnson, who was chiefly responsible for the U.S. commitment in Vietnam. After Johnson only narrowly won the 1968 New Hampshire primary, he withdrew from the race. Unions have not tried to create a labor party—indeed, they were for a long time opposed to almost any kind of national political activity. Since labor became a major political force in the 1930s, the largest industrial unions have been content to operate as a part (a very large part) of the Democratic party.

One reason some potential sources of minor parties never formed such parties, in addition to the dim chance of success, is that the direct primary and the national convention made it possible for dissident elements of a major party—unless they become completely disaffected—to remain in the party and influence the choice of candidates and policies. The antiwar movement had a profound effect on the Democratic conventions of 1968 and 1972; African Americans have played a growing role in the Democratic party, especially with the candidacy of Jesse

Jackson in 1984 and 1988; only in 1972 did the unions feel that the Democrats nominated a presidential candidate (McGovern) unacceptable to them.

The impact of minor parties on American politics is hard to judge. One bit of conventional wisdom holds that minor parties develop ideas that the major parties later come to adopt. The Socialist party, for example, supposedly called for major social and economic policies that the Democrats under Roosevelt later embraced and termed the New Deal. It is possible the Democrats did steal the thunder of the Socialists, but it hardly seems likely that they did it because the Socialists had proposed these things or proved them popular. (In 1932, the Socialists received only 2 percent of the vote and in 1936 less than one-half of 1 percent.) Roosevelt probably adopted the policies in part because he thought them correct and in part because dissident elements within his *own* party—leaders such as Huey Long of Louisiana—were threatening to bolt the Democratic party if it did not move to the left. Even Prohibition was adopted more as a result of the efforts of interest groups such as the Anti-Saloon League than as the consequence of its endorsement by the Prohibition party.

The Socialist party and the Progressive party were both minor parties, but their origins were different. The Socialist party was an ideological party; the "Bull Moose" Progressive party split off from the Republicans to support Theodore Roosevelt.

Library of Congress/LC-DIG pga-01130

Bettmann/CORBIS

The minor parties that have probably had the greatest influence on public policy have been the factional parties. Mugwumps and liberal Republicans, by bolting the regular party, may have made that party more sensitive to the issue of civil service reform; the Bull Moose and La Follette Progressive parties probably helped encourage the major parties to pay more attention to issues of business regulation and party reform; the Dixiecrat and Wallace movements probably strengthened the hands of those who wished to go slow on desegregation. The threat of a factional split is a risk that both major parties must face, and it is in the efforts that each makes to avoid such splits that one finds the greatest impact, at least in this century, of minor parties.

In 1992 and again in 1996, Ross Perot led the most successful recent third-party movement. It began as United We Stand America and was later renamed the Reform party. Perot's appeal seemed to reflect a growing American dissatisfaction with the existing political parties and a heightened demand for bringing in a leader who would "run the government without politics." In 2000 and again in 2004, Ralph Nader led the Green party and rallied supporters by promising to remain above partisan politics and avoid making compromises if elected. Of course, it is no more possible to take politics out of governing than it is to take churches out of religion. Though unrealistic, some people seem to want policies without bargaining.

Nominating a President

The major parties face, as we have seen, two contrary forces: one, generated by the desire to win the presidency, pushes them in the direction of nominating a candidate who can appeal to the majority of voters and who will thus have essentially middle-of-the-road views. The other, produced by the need

Ross Perot founded the independent Reform party in 1996.

to keep dissident elements in the party from bolting and forming a third party, leads them to compromise with dissidents or extremists in ways that may damage the party's standing with the voters.

The Democrats and Republicans have always faced these conflicting pressures, but of late they have become especially acute. When the presidential nomination was made by a party convention heavily influenced, if not controlled, by party leaders and elected officials, it was relatively easy to ignore dissident factions and pick candidates on the basis of who could win. The *electoral* objectives of the party were predominant. The result was that often a faction left the party and ran a separate ticket—as in 1912, 1924, 1948, 1968, and 1980. Today the power of party leaders and elected officials within the parties is greatly diminished, with most delegates now selected by primary elections. A larger proportion of the delegates is likely more interested in issues and less amenable to compromise over those issues than formerly. In these circumstances, the *policy* interests of the party activists are likely important.

ARE THE DELEGATES REPRESENTATIVE OF THE VOTERS?

There would be no conflict between the electoral and policy interests of a political party if the delegates to its nominating convention had the same policy views as most voters, or at least as most party supporters. In fact, this is not the case: in parties, as in many organizations, the activists and leaders tend to have views different from those of the rank and file.[24] In American political parties in recent years, this difference has become very great.

In 1964, the Republican party nominated the highly conservative Barry Goldwater for president. We have no opinion data for delegates to that convention as detailed and comprehensive as those available for subsequent conventions, but it seems clear that the Republican delegates selected as their nominee a person who was not the most popular candidate among voters at large and thus not the candidate most likely to win.

At every Democratic national convention since 1972, the delegates have had views on a variety of important issues vastly different from those of rank-and-file Democrats. On welfare, military policy, school desegregation, crime, and abortion, Democratic delegates expressed opinions almost diametrically opposed to those of most Democrats. The delegates to the 1980, 1984, and (to a lesser extent) 1988, 1992, 1996, 2000, and 2004 conventions were ideologically very different from the

Reed Saxon/APPhoto

voters at large. The Democratic delegates were more liberal than the Democratic voters, and the Republican delegates were more conservative than the Republican voters.[25]

What accounts for the sharp disparity between delegate opinion (and often delegate candidate preference) and voter attitudes? Some blame the discrepancy on the rules, described earlier in this chapter, under which Democratic delegates are chosen, especially those that require increased representation for women, minorities, and the young. Close examination suggests this is not a complete explanation. For one thing, it does not explain why the Republicans nominated Goldwater in 1964 (and almost nominated Ronald Reagan instead of Gerald Ford in 1976). In addition, women, minorities, and youth have among them all shades of opinions: there are many middle-of-the-road women and young people, as well as very liberal or very conservative ones. (There are not many very conservative African Americans, at least on race issues, but there are certainly plenty who are moderate on race and conservative on other issues.) The question is why only *certain* elements of these groups are heavily represented at the conventions.

caucus A meeting of party members to select delegates backing one or another primary candidate.

WHO VOTES IN PRIMARIES?

Maybe delegates are unrepresentative of the party rank and file because they are chosen in caucuses and primary elections whose participants are unrepresentative. Before 1972, most delegates were picked by party leaders; primaries were relatively unimportant, and voter caucuses were almost unheard of. Adlai Stevenson in 1952 and Hubert Humphrey in 1968 won the Democratic presidential nominations without even entering a primary. Harry Truman once described primaries as "eyewash."[26]

After 1972, the vast majority of delegates were selected in primaries and caucuses. In 1992, forty states and territories held primaries, and 20 held caucuses (some places had primaries and caucuses).

Only about half as many people vote in primaries as in general elections. If these primary voters have more extreme political views than rank-and-file party followers, then they might support presidential delegates who also have extreme views. However, little evidence suggests that such is the case. Studies comparing the ideological orientations of primary voters with those of rank-and-file party voters show few strong differences.[27]

When it comes to presidential primaries, a good fight draws a crowd. For example, in 12 of the first 18 Republican presidential primaries in 2000, voter turnout hit record highs as Governor George W. Bush battled state by state to stay ahead of Senator John McCain. But the "crowd" represented only 13.6 percent of the voting-age population, up 4.3 percent from the 1996 turnout, and the highest since Senator Barry Goldwater's campaign for the nomination divided Republicans in 1964.[28] In the states that voted after Bush had the nomination all but won, turnout was considerably lower. Likewise, the contest between Vice President Al Gore and Senator Bill Bradley resulted in the second-lowest Democratic presidential primary turnout since 1960.

Primaries differ from caucuses. A **caucus** is a meeting of party followers, often lasting for hours and held in the dead of winter in a schoolhouse miles from home, in which party delegates are picked. Only the most dedicated partisans attend. For the Democrats, these have been liberals; for the Republicans, conservatives. In 1988, the most liberal Democratic candidate, Jesse Jackson, got more delegates in the Alaska, Delaware, Michigan, and Vermont caucuses than Michael Dukakis, the eventual nominee. Republican evangelist Pat Robertson did not win any primary, but he won the caucuses in Alaska, Hawaii, and Washington.

WHO ARE THE NEW DELEGATES?

However delegates are chosen, they are a different breed today than they once were. Whether picked by caucuses or primaries, and whatever their sex and race, a far larger proportion of convention delegates, both Republican and Democratic, are issue-oriented activists—people with an "amateur" or "purist" view of politics. Far fewer delegates are in it for the money (there is no longer much patronage to pass around) or to help their own reelection prospects. For example, in 1980 only 14 percent of the Democratic senators and 15 percent of the Democratic members of the House were delegates to the national convention. In 1956, by contrast, 90 percent of the senators and 33 percent of the representatives were delegates.[29] Party activists, especially those who work without pay and who are in politics out of an interest in issues, are not likely to resemble the average citizen for whom politics is merely an object of observation, discussion, and occasional voting.

The changing incentives for participation in party work, in addition to the effects of the primary system, have contributed to the development of a national presidential nominating system different from that which once existed. The advantage of the new system is that it increases the opportunity for those with strong policy preferences to play a role in the party and thus reduces the chance that they

RESEARCH FRONTIERS

Are Republicans the Next Whigs?

Since the Founding era, there have been five lasting shifts in the popular coalition supporting one or both major parties. The third of these so-called realigning periods occurred in 1850's when the Whig Party collapsed.

In the 1830's, the Whigs were born in opposition to President Andrew Jackson and the day's Democratic Party. Two Whigs (William Henry Harrison and Zachary Taylor) won the presidency. Lincoln himself had been a Whig leader in Illinois. But in 1852, many Whigs like Lincoln who opposed the expansion of slavery defected to the new Republican Party.

In 2009, Republican Party leaders were publicly debating whether "the party of Lincoln" might go the way of the Whigs. In 2006, Republicans lost control of the U.S. House of Representatives. In 2008, they lost the White House. But the debates about the Republican Party's condition were also fueled by fresh survey evidence indicating a deep and wide decline in post-2001 Republican affiliation among American voters:

- Between 2001 and 2009, only frequent churchgoers maintained their level of support for the GOP, with conservative voters and senior citizens dropping off only slightly, and with long anemic levels of support among African-Americans unchanged.

- Among every other demographic group in every region of the country (men, women, old, young, rich, middle class, poor, married, unmarried, college graduates, and others) affiliation with the Republican Party fell significantly.

- Whereas in 2001 partisan self-identification was split between the two parties, by mid-2009 the electorate was running 53 percent Democratic versus 39 percent Republican.

In a two-party democracy like America, demography is electoral destiny. Still, it is unlikely that the Republicans will follow their Whig forbearers into political party oblivion, at least not anytime soon:

- Republicans remain relatively strong in parts of the country that are experiencing robust population growth.

- Over the next several election cycles, Republicans are likely to recruit and run more candidates who appeal to broad popular coalitions.

- In the past, realignments have occurred only when a new issue of utmost importance to the voters (like slavery in the 1850's) has cut across existing party divisions.

- Do you think that there is any such issue on the political horizon today?

- Regardless, what is the relative strength of two parties where you reside?

- If you were a political consultant with no partisan loyalties toward either party, what would you advise the Republican Party's leaders to do in order to improve their electoral fortunes, and what would you advise the Democratic Party's leaders to do to maintain their present electoral edge or expand it?

Source: Gallup Organization, "GOP Losses Span Nearly All Demographic Groups," May 2009, reporting data from January-April 2009 telephone interviews with 7,139 nationalk adults aged 18 and older; James L. Sundquist, *Dynamics of the Party System*, second edition (Brookings Institution Press, 1983); William Nisbet Chambers et al, eds., *The American Party Systems: Stages of Political Development*, second edition (Oxford University Press, 1975).

---

will bolt the party and form a factional minor party. The disadvantage of the system is that it increases the chances that one or both parties may nominate presidential candidates who are not appealing to the average voter or even to a party's rank and file.

In sum, presidential nominating conventions are now heavily influenced by ideologically motivated activists. Democratic conventions have heavy representation from organized feminists, unionized schoolteachers, and abortion rights activists; Republican conventions have large numbers of antiabortion activists, Christian conservatives, and small government libertarians. As a result the presidential nominating system is now fundamentally different from what it was as late as the mid-1960s.

WHAT WOULD YOU DO?

MEMORANDUM

To: *Elizabeth Bunting, All for Life president*

From: *Ralph Marx, political consultant*

Subject: *Upcoming presidential election*

Without regard to your organization's cause or issue, I have been hired to brief you on the pros and cons of backing or beginning a third-party candidate in the presidential election.

Arguments for:

1. Independent and third-party candidates can garner votes for president or tip an election result. In 1992, Ross Perot won nearly a fifth of the votes. In 2000, Green party candidate Ralph Nader got only 3 percent, but that included 100,000 votes in Florida where Republican Bush was credited with only 600 votes more than Democrat Gore.

2. Third-party candidates (Eugene Debs, Robert La Follette, George Wallace) can make a mark on American politics. Third parties have advocated policies later championed by the two main parties: abolishing slavery (Free-Soil party), women's right to vote (Woman's party), direct election of U.S. senators (Progressive party), and many others.

Arguments against:

1. It is virtually impossible to win, thanks to the winner-take-all system of elections. Since the 1850s, over a hundred third parties have come and gone. There will be a brief media frenzy when you bolt; but, after that, you might be ignored. Better to grumble but be heard inside a major party than to shout but not be heard with a minor party.

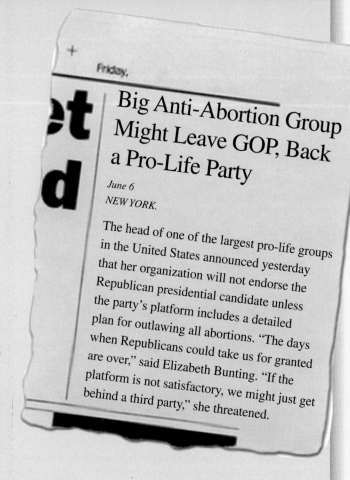

Friday,

Big Anti-Abortion Group Might Leave GOP, Back a Pro-Life Party

June 6
NEW YORK.

The head of one of the largest pro-life groups in the United States announced yesterday that her organization will not endorse the Republican presidential candidate unless the party's platform includes a detailed plan for outlawing all abortions. "The days when Republicans could take us for granted are over," said Elizabeth Bunting. "If the platform is not satisfactory, we might just get behind a third party," she threatened.

2. Splitting off from a major party could weaken support for your issue and lead one or the other major party to "resolve" it in a watered-down way. In the 1930s, the Democrats plucked Social Security from the Socialist party's far-reaching plan. In the 1980s, the Republicans' position on taxes only faintly echoed the Libertarian party's.

Your decision:

Back or begin a third party _____   Stay with the major party _____

Parties versus Voters

Since 1968, the Democratic party has had no trouble winning congressional elections but great difficulty winning presidential contests. Except for 1994–2006, the Democrats have controlled both houses of Congress; except for 1976, 1992, 1996, and 2008, they have lost every presidential election. The Republican party has had the opposite problem: though it won five out of seven presidential elections between 1968 and 1992, it did not control Congress for the 40 years preceding its big win in 1994.

There are many reasons for this odd state of affairs, most of which will be discussed later. But one requires attention here. The difficulty the Democrats have had in competing for the presidency is in part because their candidates for the presidency have had, on certain issues—chiefly social and taxation issues—views very different from those of the average voter. That disparity to a large degree mirrors (and may be caused by) the gulf that separates the opinions of delegates to Democratic nominating conventions from the opinions of most citizens.

The Republicans have not been immune to this problem. In 1964, they nominated Barry Goldwater, whose beliefs placed him well to the right of most voters. Not surprisingly, he lost. And the delegates to recent Republican conventions have held opinions on some matters that continue to be very different from most people's. Still, the problem has been somewhat more acute for the Democrats.

The problem can be seen in Table 9.3. A lot of information is shown there; to understand it, study the table step by step. First, look at the middle column, which summarizes the views of voters in 2004. (Because there are about the same number of Democratic and Republican voters, the opinion of the average voter is about halfway between those of the followers of the two parties.) Now look at the columns on the far left and the far right. These show the views of delegates to the 2004 Democratic and Republican conventions. On almost every issue, the delegates are in sharp disagreement. There were hardly any conservatives at the Democratic convention or liberals at the Republican convention. On each and every issue, the delegates were at opposite ends of the spectrum.

Still, either party can win if its delegates nominate a candidate whose views put him or her closer to the average citizen than to the average delegate or if the campaign is fought out over issues on which the delegates and the voters agree. For example, if the election turned on what to do about an economic recession, the delegates, the voters, and the candidate would probably all agree: do whatever is necessary to end the recession. Exactly that happened in 1992, and the Democrats won.

Of course, even without a scandal, recession, or some other unifying issue, the need to win an election will lead all candidates to move toward the middle of the road. That is where the votes are. But this creates a dilemma for a candidate of either party. The stance one takes to win support from party activists in the caucuses and primaries often will be quite different

Table 9.3 Political Opinions of Delegates and Voters, 2004

	Democratic Delegates	Voters	Republican Delegates
Who They Are			
Male	50%	49%	57%
Female	50	51	43
African American	18	14	6
Income over $75,000	61	28	58
What They Think			
Government should do more to solve national problems.	79	42	9
Abortion should be generally available.	75	34	13
Religion is extremely important in daily life.	21	28	39
Government's antiterrorism laws restrict civil liberties.	77	43	15
The penalty for murder should be death, not life in prison.	19	50	57
Protect the environment even if jobs are lost because of it.	62	52	25
There should be no legal recognition of a gay couple's relationship.	5	39	49

Source: *New York Times*/CBS News polls as reported in Katharine Q. Seeley and Marjorie Connelly, "The Conventioneers; Delegates Leaning to the Right of G.O.P. and the Nation," *New York Times*, August 29, 2004.

from the stance one should take to win votes from the general public. In the next chapter, we shall look more closely at how politicians try to cope with that dilemma.

SUMMARY

A political party exists in three arenas: among the voters who psychologically identify with it, as a grassroots organization staffed and led by activists, and as a group of elected officials who follow its lead in lawmaking. In this chapter, we looked at the party primarily as an organization and saw the various forms it takes at the local level—the machine, the ideological party, the solidary group, the sponsored party, and the personal following.

The spread of the direct primary has made it harder for parties to control who is nominated for elective office, thus making it harder for the parties to influence the behavior of these people once elected. Delegate selection rules, especially in the Democratic party, have helped shift the center of power in the national nominating convention. Because of the changes in rules, power has moved away from officeholders and party regulars and toward the more ideological wings of the parties.

Minor parties have arisen from time to time, but the only ones that have affected the outcome of presidential elections have been those that represented a splinter group within one of the major parties (such as the Bull Moose progressives). The two-party system is maintained, and minor parties are discouraged by an election system (winner-take-all, plurality elections) that makes voters reluctant to waste a vote on a minor party and by the ability of potential minor parties to wield influence within a major party by means of the primary system.

In the next chapter, we shall look at the role of parties in shaping voter attitudes, and, in Chapter 13, we shall look at the role of parties in Congress. In each of these areas, we will find more evidence of party decay.

RECONSIDERING WHO GOVERNS?

1. How has America's two-party system changed, and how does it differ from the party systems of other representative democracies?

American parties during the 19th century and the first half of the 20th century were strong organizations that picked their candidates for office. Parties in European democracies still do that, but America has changed. Now, candidates usually are picked by direct primary elections as the American voters' loyalty to parties has weakened.

2. How much do parties affect how Americans vote?

Registered Democrats are more likely to vote for Democratic candidates, and registered Republicans are more likely to vote for Republican candidates, but more voters now register as independents, the proportion of people identifying with one or the other party has declined, and split-ticket voting has been common in the American electorate. The declining attachment of voters to parties and their weaknesses as organizations have led many candidates for president and other offices to run more as individuals than as party members.

RECONSIDERING TO WHAT ENDS?

1. Did the Founding Fathers think political parties were a good idea?

No. For example, George Washington denounced parties as "factions." But as soon as it was time to select his replacement, the republic's first leaders realized they had to organize their followers to win the election, and parties were born. It was not, however, until well into the 19th century that the idea of a permanent two-party system was considered legitimate by virtually all of the country's political leaders.

2. How, if at all, should America's two-party system be reformed?

Any answer should depend, at least in part, on how one evaluates the many reforms already made. For instance, some argue that the parties should become more open to popular influences. To a large extent, however, that has already happened. Whereas once presidential candidates were selected by party leaders, today they are selected by primaries. Others maintain that there is little real difference between the two parties. That opinion, however, is at variance with the wide differences on many important issues one finds in party platforms, as well a[s] fact that delegates to the Republic[an] Convention and delegates to the D[emocratic] National Convention differ widely [on] issues. Still others contend that th[e] system in which the winner is the candidate with the most votes, even if he or she does not receive a majority, is unfair to minor or third-party candidates. Perhaps, but Bill Clinton was twice (1992 and 1996) a popular plurality president. Besides, America has had little experience with other voting or party systems, and democracies that have proportional voting or multiparty systems have other shortcomings (such as unduly empowering small parties with extreme views).

WORLD WIDE WEB RESOURCES

Democratic National Committee: **www.democrats.org**

Republican National Committee: **www.rnc.org**

Green party: **www.greens.org**

Libertarian party: **www.lp.org**

Reform party: **www.reformparty.org**

SUGGESTED READINGS

Aldrich, John H. *Why Parties?*: (Chicago: University of Chicago Press, 1995). Explain why we have parties.

Goldwin, Robert A., ed. *Political Parties in the Eighties*. Washington, D.C.: American Enterprise Institute, 1980. Essays evaluating parties and efforts at reform.

Key, V. O., Jr. *Southern Politics*. New York: Knopf, 1949. A classic account of the one-party South.

Mayhew, David R. *Placing Parties in American Politics*. Princeton, N.J.: Princeton University Press, 1986. A state-by-state description of state party organizations.

Nader, Ralph. *Crashing the Party: Taking on the Corporate Government in an Age of Surrender*. New York: St. Martin's Press, 2002. An impassioned attack on the two-party system by a well-known activist who ran for president as a minor-party candidate in 2000 and 2004.

Polsby, Nelson W. *Consequences of Party Reform*. New York: Oxford University Press, 1983. Fine analysis of how changed party rules have affected the parties and the government.

Ranney, Austin. *Curing the Mischiefs of Faction: Party Reform in America*. Berkeley: University of California Press, 1975. History and analysis of party "reforms," with special attention to the 1972 changes in the Democratic party rules.

Riordan, William L. *Plunkitt of Tammany Hall*. New York: Knopf, 1948. (First published in 1905.) Insightful account of how an old-style party boss operated.

Schattschneider, E. E. *Party Government*. New York: Holt, Rinehart and Winston, 1942. An argument for a more disciplined and centralized two-party system.

Shafer, Byron E. *Quiet Revolution: The Struggle for the Democratic Party and the Shaping of Post-Reform Politics*. New York: Russell Sage Foundation, 1983. Detailed, insightful history of how the Democratic party came to be reformed.

Sundquist, James L. *Dynamics of the Party System*. Rev. ed. Washington, D.C.: Brookings Institution, 1983. History of the party system, emphasizing the impact of issues on voting.

Wilson, James Q. *The Amateur Democrat*. Chicago: University of Chicago Press, 1962. Analysis of the issue-oriented political clubs that rose in the 1950s and 1960s.

10

Elections and Campaigns

WHO GOVERNS?

1. How do American elections determine the kind of people who govern us?
2. What matters most in deciding who wins presidential and congressional elections?

TO WHAT ENDS?

1. Do elections make a real difference in what laws get passed?

The 2008 presidential sweepstakes started in 2006. By early 2007, over a dozen candidates had come forward, and at least one had declared then dropped out. For the first time in four-score years, neither a sitting president nor a sitting vice president was in the race. With hundreds of days left to go before election day in November 2008, several frontrunners were each on their way to raising around $100 million.

It is difficult to imagine how different things were not all that long ago. In 1968, Vice President Hubert Humphrey won the Democratic presidential nomination without competing in a single state primary. His party's bosses pretty much delivered the nomination to him. He competed in a three-way race for president without having to raise nearly as much money as many also-ran candidates routinely do today. (He lost in a close race to Republican Richard M. Nixon.)

In 1988, Vice President George H.W. Bush won the Republican presidential nomination. He had to win primaries and raise tens of millions of dollars, too. His party's leaders played a big role in his campaign, but so did consultants, pollsters, and others with no traditional ties to the party organization. (He won in a landslide over Democrat Michael Dukakis.) Still, even his 1988 campaign would not be close to presidential politics in 2008.

J. Scott Applewhite/AP Photo

Campaigns, Then and Now

Many things have changed, but the key changes are related to one another: parties are less important; media (or "media buys") are more important; polling is ubiquitous; and money—or the nonstop fund-raising that keeps it coming—matters more than ever.

As we saw in Chapter 9, political parties once determined, or powerfully influenced, who got nominated. In the 19th century, the members of Congress from a given caucus would meet to pick their presidential candidate. After the caucuses were replaced by the national nominating conventions, the real power was wielded by local party leaders, who came together (sometimes in the legendary "smoke-filled rooms") to choose the candidate, whom the rest of the delegates would then endorse. Congressional candidates were also often hand-picked by local party bosses. Most people voted a straight party ticket.

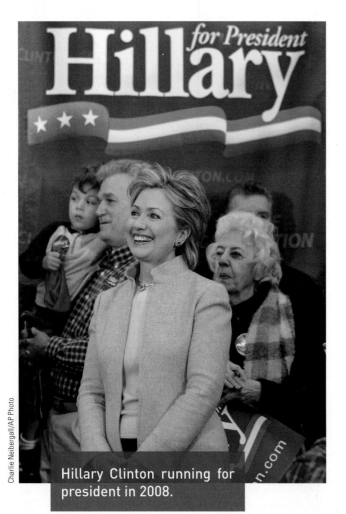

Charlie Neibergall/AP Photo

Hillary Clinton running for president in 2008.

That was then, but by 2008 that system's last remaining remnants had faded to the point where only older party workers or political history buffs paid any real attention to them. With the parties' ability to control nominations weakened, candidates are now pretty much on their own. Most, however, do not go it alone. Rather, they hire people to perform several separate but related campaign tasks:[1]

- *Media consultants* who create advertisements and buy airtime from stations and networks.
- *Direct mail firms* that design and produce mailings to promote the candidate or solicit money.
- *Polling firms* to survey voters on their attitudes toward issues and candidates and run focus groups.
- *Political technology firms* to supply services such as web site design, online advertising, online fund-raising, and voter-targeting.

To pay for all this help, today's candidates must raise and spend enormous sums of money. As Table 10.1 shows, in 2008, all candidates for national office raised and spent around $3.2 billion: about $1 billion in House races, over $400 million in Senate races, and over $1.75 billion by candidates in the race for the White House. These campaign finance sums are unprecedented.

In the 2004 elections, all candidates for national office raised and spent "only" about $1.85 billion; the leap to about $3.1 billion in 2008 represented a 67 percent increase in just four years.

In particular, presidential campaign fund-raising and expenditures more than doubled between 2004 and 2008; presidential campaign spending in 2008 (about $1.81 billion) rivaled total 2004 House, Senate, and presidential campaign spending (about $1.85 billion). As Table 10.2 shows, even adjusted for inflation, the amounts of money raised and spent by presidential candidates have exploded since 1976.

Today's presidential candidates spend more on media consultants, television and radio ads, and diverse other forms of "media messages" than on any other category of campaign expenses. For example, 2008 presidential candidates spent about $569 million on media, representing about 31 percent of all their campaign expenditures (see Figure 10.1).

With so much money spent by candidates for media outlets and media consultants, you might think there is clear and convincing evidence that media exposure makes a critical difference in who wins elections, or that some types of televised appeals work better than others, or both.

Table 10.1 The 2008 National Elections: Money Raised and Spent

	Total Raised	Total Spent
House candidates	$978,308,660	$937,263,589
Senate candidates	$410,411,573	$428,569,374
Presidential candidates	$1,812,975,610	$1,759,232,744
Total, all candidates	$3,201,605,843	$3,125,065,707

Source: Federal Election Commission, 2008 election summary reports, May 2009.

Table 10.2 Presidential Fundraising and Expenditures, 1976–2008

Year	$ Raised	$ Spent	Percent change from previous election Raised	Percent change from previous election Spent
1976	$171 million	$70 million	—%	—%
1980	$162 million	$92 million	−5.2	+31.4
1984	$202 million	$104 million	+24.6	+13.0
1988	$324 million	$211 million	+60.3	+102.6
1992	$331 million	$192 million	−00.9	−9.00
1996	$426 million	$240 million	+28.7	+25.0
2000	$529 million	$343 million	+24.1	+42.9
2004	$881 million	$718 million	+66.6	+109
2008	$1.81 billion	$1.76 billion	+105	+145
1976–2008 Increase	+$1.63 billion	+$1.69 billion	+953	+2,414
Inflation-Adjusted	+$436 million	+$452 million	+255	+645

Source: Adapted from Federal Election Commission, summary reports, January 2009 and May 2009. Dollar figures rounded. Inflation adjustment keyed to consumer price index 1976–2008, 3.74 (i.e., assumes that what cost $1.00 in 1976 cost $3.74 in 2008).

Figure 10.1

Presidential Campaigns' Spending on Media, 2009

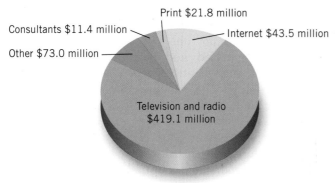

Print $21.8 million

Consultants $11.4 million

Internet $43.5 million

Other $73.0 million

Television and radio $419.1 million

Total: $568.8 million

Source: Federal Election Commission, summary reports, May 2009. Figures rounded.

But you would be wrong. About the only safe generalizations one can presently make on the subject concern not that "media buys" matter, but how common it is for today's candidates to purchase political ads embodying emotional appeals.

A comprehensive 2006 study carefully analyzed thousands of political ads broadcast from 1999 through 2004.[2] A plurality, it found, were purposely designed (everything from the images used to the music playing in the background) to appeal mainly to voters' fears (impending war, losing a job, and so on). A smaller but significant fraction were more focused on stirring positive emotions (patriotism and community pride). You might suppose that candidates favor such ads because they are particularly effective in reaching voters who know little and care less about politics.

Once again, you would be wrong. The political ads, televised and other, that appealed to emotion (fear or enthusiasm, mainly) wielded the greatest influence over voters with the greatest interest in politics and the most information about government.[3] Still, experts don't know how or whether televised political ads influence election outcomes.

BETTER OR WORSE?

There is less mystery in political polling. Today, even many candidates running in relatively low-budget local races do extensive pre- and post-election voter polling, and often use the results to shape television ads, other campaign communications, positions on the issues, and even what words candidates repeat (or eschew) and how they dress when in public.

It is, however, still only in the national political big leagues that many candidates do extensive polling designed not merely to test voters' existing attitudes, but to discover how to change them. And it is still only in presidential races and especially well-funded contests for Congress (mostly for the Senate) that sophisticated surveys, much like those traditionally done by big corporations to identify markets where their goods or services are especially likely to sell, are used to mobilize voters.

In the elections of 2004, 2006, and again in 2008, these survey techniques "micro-targeted" people by using data about their consumer and recreational habits (small car or SUV, drink high-cost coffees or cheap brews, like watching professional sports or loathe it, and more). In 2008, micro-targeting software, databases, and techniques became highly refined and were used intensively by both the Obama and the McCain presidential campaigns.[4]

Of course, it is one thing to know where "your voters" are, but quite another thing to reach them through door-to-door drives like the ones that once were the political parties' chief stock in trade. In 2008, both parties' national leaders stressed building or expanding grassroots get-out-the-vote organizations not dissimilar from those that, precinct by precinct, once dominated election days in most American cities. Such "high-tech canvassing," if it continues, may yet re-create something somewhat like the party organizations of old.

Patrick Caddell pioneered present-day political polling techniques when he served as Jimmy Carter's consultant in the mid-1970s. By the time Ronald Reagan followed Carter as president in 1980, pollsters like Caddell were the new political bosses, at least in presidential campaigns. As veteran political reporter Joe Klein has reflected, when they "endorsed" a candidate, "fund-raising, media buzz, and support from the party's special interests suddenly became easier."[5]

In 2006, republican presidential hopeful, Senator John McCain, hired into his campaign political consultants who had previously worked against him and developed harshly negative ads that he had in years past objected to as dishonest (and worse). But nobody who knows how the game is played today was really surprised. Today, candidates in both parties, whether ideologically liberal, conservative, or in between, routinely practice what the political professionals preach and purchase what they produce.

This is the main reason for the unceasing spiral in campaign spending, and hence for the fact that "campaigning" has become largely synonymous with "fund-raising." Candidates for major offices have two top needs: money for television ads, followed by time for fund-raising to generate the cash needed to pay for the ads.[6] Once elected, the permanent fund-raising campaign continues for House members, and almost as much for senators and even for the president (who, especially when popular, also makes many trips to raise money for his party's candidates).

The American Association for Political Consultants (AAPC) is a trade association. In 1980, it had about 50 members. By 1990, it had around 700 members. Today, it has over 1,100 members representing a campaign industry with over 2,500 firms.[7] The industry's expansion coincided with decreased political participation, and—the only development that can definitely be laid at its door—a dramatic rise in negative, slick, and super-costly political ads. If that leads you to wonder whether, all told, campaigns were better for democracy when party bosses in smoke-filled rooms were more common than political consultants in high-tech firms, you are not alone.

HERE AND ABROAD

Even the best American political consultants probably would have trouble exporting their wares. A campaign plan that will work here would be useless in almost any other democratic nation; one that would work abroad would be useless here.

Unlike in many other democratic nations, in America, elections have not one but two crucial phases—getting nominated and getting elected. Getting nominated means getting your name on the ballot. In the great majority of states, winning your party's nomination for either the presidency or Congress requires an *individual* effort—*you* decide to run, *you* raise money, *you* and your friends collect signatures to get your name on the ballot, and *you* appeal to voters in primary elections on the basis of your personality and your definition of the issues. In most European nations winning your party's nomination for parliament involves an *organizational* decision—*the party* looks you over, *the party* decides whether to allow you to run, and *the party* puts your name on its list of candidates.

American political parties do play a role in determining the outcome of the final election, but even that

Question

1. *Who was the first woman to run for national office?*

Campaign workers celebrating
during the 2008 vote count.

Sara D. Davis/AP Photo

role involves parties more as labels in the voters' minds than as organizations that get out the vote. By contrast, many other democratic nations conduct campaigns almost entirely a contest between parties as organizations. In Israel and the Netherlands, the names of the candidates for the legislature do not even appear on the ballot; only the party names are listed there. And even where candidate names are listed, as in Great Britain, the voters tend to vote "Conservative" or "Labour" more than they vote for Smith or Jones. European nations (except France) do not have a directly elected president; instead, the head of the government—the prime minister—is selected by the party that has won the most seats in parliament.

Presidential versus Congressional Campaigns

Presidential and congressional races differ in important ways. The most obvious, of course, is size: more voters participate in the former than the latter contests, and so presidential candidates must work harder and spend more. But there are some less obvious differences that are equally important.

First, presidential races are more competitive than those for the House of Representatives. In the 39 elections from 1932 to 2008 the Republicans won control of the House only eight times (20 percent of the time); in the 20 presidential elections during the same period the Republicans won the White House on nine occasions (45 percent of the time). In the typical presidential race, the winner gets less than 55 percent of the two-party vote; in the typical House race, the **incumbent** wins with over 60 percent of the vote.

incumbent The person already holding an elective office.

Second, a much smaller proportion of people vote in congressional races during off years (that is, when there is no presidential contest) than vote for president. This lower turnout (around 36 percent of the voting-age population) means that candidates in congressional races must be appealing to the more motivated and partisan voter.

Third, members of Congress can do things for their constituents that a president cannot. They take credit—sometimes deserved, sometimes not—for every grant, contract, bridge, canal, and highway that the federal government provides the district or state. They send letters (at the government's expense) to large factions of their constituents and visit their districts every weekend. Presidents get

Answer

1. *Geraldine Ferraro, candidate for vice president in 1984.*

little credit for district improvements and must rely on the mass media to communicate with voters.

Fourth, a candidate for Congress can deny that he or she is responsible for "the mess in Washington," even when the candidate is an incumbent. Incumbents tend to run as individuals, even to the point of denouncing the very Congress of which they are a part. An incumbent president can't get away with this; rightly or wrongly, he often is held responsible for whatever has gone wrong, not only in the government but in the nation as a whole.

These last three factors—low voter turnout, services to constituents, and the ability to duck responsibility—probably help explain why so high a percentage of congressional incumbents get reelected.

But they do not enjoy a completely free ride. Members of Congress who belong to the same party as the president often feel voters' anger about national affairs, particularly economic conditions. When the economy turns sour and a Republican is in the White House, Republican congressional candidates lose votes; if a Democrat is in the White House, Democratic congressional candidates lose votes.

coattails The alleged tendency of candidates to win more votes in an election because of the presence at the top of the ticket of a better-known candidate, such as the president.

At one time the **coattails** of a popular presidential candidate could help congressional candidates in his own party. But there has been a sharp decline in the value of presidential coattails; indeed, some scholars doubt they still exist.

The net effect of all these factors is that, to a substantial degree, congressional elections have become independent of presidential ones. Though economic factors may still link the fate of a president and some members of his party, by and large the incumbent members of Congress enjoy enough of a cushion to protect them against whatever political storms engulf an unpopular president. This fact further reduces the meaning of party—members of Congress can get reelected even though their party's "leader" in the White House has lost popular support, and nonincumbent candidates for Congress may lose despite the fact that a very popular president from their party is in the White House.

RUNNING FOR PRESIDENT

The first task facing anyone who wishes to be president is to get "mentioned" as someone who is of "presidential caliber." No one is quite sure why some people are mentioned and others are not. Journalist

David Broder has suggested that somewhere there is "The Great Mentioner" who announces from time to time who is of presidential caliber (and only The Great Mentioner knows how big that caliber is).

But if The Great Mentioner turns out to be as unreal as the Easter Bunny, you have to figure out for yourself how to get mentioned. One way is to let it be known to reporters, "off the record," that you are thinking about running for president. Another is to travel around the country making speeches (Ronald Reagan, while working for General Electric, made a dozen or more speeches *a day* to audiences all over the country). Another way is to already have a famous name (John Glenn, the former astronaut, was in the public eye long before he declared for the presidency in 1984). Another way to get mentioned is to be identified with a major piece of legislation. Former Senator Bill Bradley of New Jersey was known as an architect of the Tax Reform Act of 1986; Representative Richard Gephardt of Missouri was known as an author of a bill designed to reduce foreign imports. Still another way is to be the governor of a big state. Former New York governors, such as Mario Cuomo, often are viewed as presidential prospects, partly because New York City is the headquarters of the television and publishing industries.

Once you are mentioned, it is wise to set aside a lot of time to run, especially if you are only "mentioned" as opposed to being really well known. Ronald Reagan devoted the better part of six years to running; Walter Mondale spent four years campaigning; Howard Baker resigned from the Senate in 1984 to prepare to run in 1988 (he finally dropped out of the race). However, many post-1988 candidates—senators Bob Dole, John Kerry, John McCain and Barack Obama; governors Michael Dukakis, Bill Clinton, and George W. Bush; vice presidents George Bush and Al Gore; and House members Ron Paul and Dennis Kucinich—made the run while holding elective office.

Though presidential candidates come from various backgrounds, in general the voters tend to prefer those with experience as governors or military leaders rather than those who come immediately from Congress. Some candidates, such as John F. Kennedy, have been elected president directly after being a senator, but most are either war heroes (Dwight Eisenhower), former governors (George W. Bush, Bill Clinton, Ronald Reagan, Jimmy Carter, and Franklin D. Roosevelt) or former members of Congress who have already had experience as vice presidents (Gerald Ford, Richard Nixon, Lyndon Johnson, and Harry Truman).

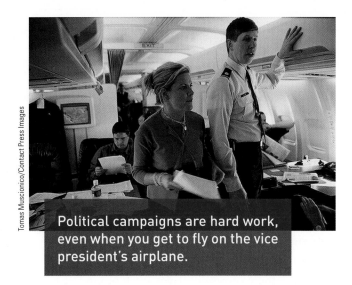

Political campaigns are hard work, even when you get to fly on the vice president's airplane.

Tomas Muscionico/Contact Press Images

Money

One reason why running takes so much time is that it takes so long to raise the necessary money and build up an organization of personal followers. As we shall see later in this chapter, federal law restricts the amount that any single individual can give a candidate to $2,000 in each election. (A **political action committee,** or PAC, which is a committee set up by and representing a corporation, labor union, or other special-interest group, can give up to $5,000.) Moreover, to be eligible for federal matching grants to pay for your primary campaign, you must first raise at least $5,000, in individual contributions of $250 or less, in each of 20 states.

Organization

Raising and accounting for this money requires a staff of fund-raisers, lawyers, and accountants. You also need a press secretary, a travel scheduler, an advertising specialist, a direct-mail company, and a pollster, all of whom must be paid, plus a large number of volunteers in at least those states that hold early primary elections or party caucuses. These volunteers will brief you on the facts of each state, try to line up endorsements from local politicians and celebrities, and put together a group of people who will knock on doors, make telephone calls, organize receptions and meetings, and try to keep you from mispronouncing the name of the town in which you are speaking. Finally, you have to assemble advisers on the issues. These advisers will write "position papers" for you on all sorts of things you are supposed to know about (but probably don't). Because a campaign usually is waged around a few broad themes, these position papers rarely get used or even read. The papers exist so you can show important interest groups that

you have taken "sound" positions, so you can be prepared to answer tough questions, and so journalists can look up your views on matters that may become topical.

> *political action committee (PAC)* A committee set up by a corporation, labor union, or interest group that raises and spends campaign money from voluntary donations.

Strategy and Themes

Every candidate picks a strategy for the campaign. In choosing one, much depends on whether you are the incumbent. Incumbents must defend their records, like it or not. (An incumbent ran for president in 1964, 1972, 1976, 1980, 1984, 1992, 1996, and 2004.) The challenger attacks the incumbent. When there is no incumbent (as in 1960, 1968, 1988, 2000, and 2008), both candidates can announce their own programs; however, the candidate from the party that holds the White House must take, whether he thinks he deserves it or not, some of the blame for whatever has gone wrong in the preceding four years. Within these limits, a strategy consists of the answers to questions about tone, theme, timing, and targets:

- What *tone* should the campaign have? Should it be a positive (build-me-up) or negative (attack-the-opponent) campaign? In 1988, George H.W. Bush began with a negative campaign; Michael Dukakis followed suit.

- What *theme* can I develop? A theme is a simple, appealing idea that can be repeated over and over again. For Jimmy Carter in 1976, it was "trust"; for Ronald Reagan in 1980, it was "competence" and in 1984, it was "it's morning again in America"; for Bush in 1988, it was "stay the course"; for Clinton in 1992, it was "we need to change"; for George W. Bush in 2000, it was "compassionate conservatism"; for Barack Obama in 2008, it was "yes we can" and also "change you can belive in."

- What should be the *timing* of the campaign? If you are relatively unknown, you will have to put everything into the early primaries and caucuses, try to emerge a frontrunner, and then hope for the best. If you are already the frontrunner, you may either go for broke early (and try to drive out all your opponents) or hold back some reserves for a long fight.

- Whom should you *target*? Only a small percentage of voters change their vote from one election to the next. Who is likely to change this time—unemployed steelworkers? Unhappy farmers? People upset by inflation?

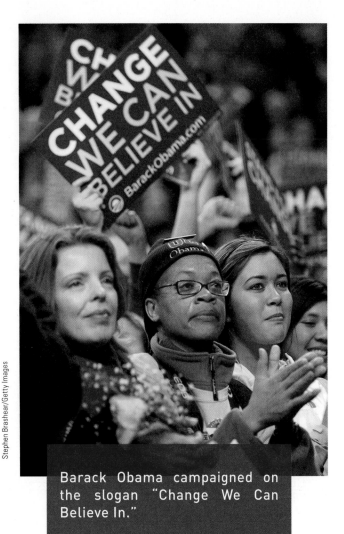

Barack Obama campaigned on the slogan "Change We Can Believe In."

Stephen Brashear/Getty Images

GETTING ELECTED TO CONGRESS

A president cannot serve more than two terms, so at least once every eight years you have a chance of running against a nonincumbent; members of Congress can serve for an unlimited number of terms, and so chances are you will run against an incumbent. If you decide to run for the House, the odds are very much against you. Since 1962, over 90 percent of the House incumbents who sought reelection won it.

But the incredible incumbency advantage enjoyed by modern-day House members is hardly the whole story of getting elected to Congress. Who serves in Congress, and what interests are represented there, is affected by how its members are elected. Each state is entitled to two senators who serve six-year terms and at least one representative who serves a two-year term. How many more representatives a state has depends on its population; what local groups these representatives speak for depends in part on how the district lines are drawn.

The Constitution says very little about how representatives will be selected except to require that they be inhabitants of the states from which they are chosen. It says nothing about districts and originally left it up to the states to decide who would be eligible to vote for representatives. The size of the first House was set by the Constitution at 65 members, and the apportionment of the seats among the states was spelled out in Article I, section 2. From that point on, it has been up to Congress to decide how many representatives each state would have (provided that each had at least one).

Initially, some states did not create congressional districts; all their representatives were elected at large. In other states, representatives were elected from multimember as well as single-member districts. In time, all states with more than one representative elected each from a single-member district. How those district boundaries were drawn, however, could profoundly affect the outcomes of elections. There were two problems. One was **malapportionment,** which results from having districts of very unequal size. If one district is twice as populous as another, twice as many votes are needed in the larger district to elect a representative. Thus, a citizen's vote in the smaller district is worth twice as much as a vote in the larger.

The other problem was **gerrymandering,** which means drawing a district boundary in some bizarre or unusual shape to make it easy for the candidate of one party to win election in that district. In a state entitled to ten representatives, where half the voters are Democrats and half are Republicans, district lines could be drawn so that eight districts would have a slight majority of citizens from one party and two districts would have lopsided majorities from the other. Thus, it can be made easy for one party to win eight of the 10 seats.

Malapportionment and gerrymandering have been conspicuous features of American congressional politics. In 1962, for example, one district in Texas had nearly a million residents, while another had less than a quarter million. In California, Democrats in control of the state legislature drew district lines in the early 1960s so that two pockets of Republican

malapportionment
Drawing the boundaries of legislative districts so that they are unequal in population.

gerrymandering
Drawing the boundaries of legislative districts in bizarre or unusual shapes to favor one party.

strength in Los Angeles separated by many miles were connected by a thin strip of coastline. In this way, most Republican voters were thrown into one district, while Democratic voters were spread more evenly over several.

Hence, there are four problems to solve in deciding who gets represented in the House:

1. Establishing the total size of the House
2. Allocating seats in the House among the states
3. Determining the size of congressional districts within states
4. Determining the shape of those districts

By and large, Congress has decided the first two questions, and the states have decided the last two—but under some rather strict Supreme Court rules.

In 1911, Congress decided the House had become large enough and voted to fix its size at 435 members. There it has remained ever since (except for a brief period when it had 437 members owing to the admission of Alaska and Hawaii to the Union in 1959). Once the size was decided, it was necessary to find a formula for performing the painful task of apportioning seats among the states as they gained and lost population. The Constitution requires such reapportionment every 10 years. A more or less automatic method was selected in 1929 based on a complex statistical system that has withstood decades of political and scientific testing. Since 1990, under this system 18 states have lost representation in the House and 11 have gained it. Florida and California posted the biggest gains, while New York and Pennsylvania suffered the largest losses (see Table 10.3).

The states did little about malapportionment and gerrymandering until ordered to do so by the Supreme Court. In 1964, the Court ruled that the Constitution requires districts be drawn so that, as nearly as possible, one person's vote would be worth as much as another's.[8] The Court rule, "one person, one vote," seems clear but in fact leaves a host of questions unanswered. How much deviation from equal size is allowable? Should other factors be considered besides population? (For example, a state legislature might want to draw district lines to make it easier for African Americans, Italian Americans, farmers, or some other group with a distinct interest to elect a representative; the requirement of exactly equal districts might make this impossible.) And the gerrymandering problem remains: districts of the same size can be drawn to favor one party or another. The courts have struggled to find answers to these questions, but they remain far from settled.

Winning the Primary

However the district lines are drawn, getting elected to Congress first requires getting one's name on the ballot. At one time, the political parties nominated candidates and even printed ballots with the party slates listed on them. All the voter had to do was take the ballot of the preferred party and put it in the ballot box. Today, with rare exceptions, a candidate wins a party's nomination by gathering enough voter signatures to get on the ballot in a primary election, the outcome of which often is beyond the ability of political parties to influence. Candidates tend to form organizations of personal followings and win "their party's" nomination simply by getting more primary votes than the next candidate. It is quite unusual for an incumbent to lose a primary: from 1990 through 2008, only about 10 percent of incumbent senators and 5 percent of incumbent representatives seeking reelection failed to win renomination in primaries. These statistics suggest how little opportunity parties have to control or punish their congressional members.

Most newly elected members become strong in their districts very quickly; this is called the **sophomore surge.** It is the difference between the votes candidates get the first time they are elected (and thus become freshman members) and the votes they get when they run for reelection (in hopes of becoming sophomore members). Before the 1960s, House candidates did not do much better the second time they ran. Beginning then, however, the sophomore surge kicked in, so that today freshman candidates running for reelection will get 8 to 10 percent more votes than when they were first elected. Senate candidates also benefit now from a sophomore surge, though to a lesser degree.

The reason for this surge is that members of Congress have figured out how to use their offices to run *personal* rather than party campaigns. They make use of free ("franked") mail, frequent trips home, radio and television broadcasts, and the distribution of services to their districts to develop among their constituents a good opinion of themselves, not their party. They also cater to their constituents' distrust of the federal government by promising to "clean things up" if reelected. They run *for* Congress by running *against* it.[9]

To the extent that they succeed, they enjoy great freedom in voting on particular issues and have less need to explain away votes that their

sophomore surge An increase in the votes congressional candidates usually get when they first run for reelection.

Table 10.3 Changes in State Representation in the House of Representatives

States	Number of Seats			
	Before 1990 Census	After 1990 Census	After 2000 Census	Change
Gained Seats				
After Both 1990 and 2000 Census				
Arizona	6	8	10	+4
California	45	52	53	+8
Florida	15	23	25	+10
Georgia	10	11	13	+3
North Carolina	11	12	13	+2
Texas	27	30	32	+5
Lost Seats				
After Both 1990 and 2000 Census				
Illinois	22	20	19	–3
Michigan	18	16	15	–3
New York	34	31	29	–5
Ohio	21	19	18	–3
Pennsylvania	23	21	19	–4

Source: U.S. Bureau of the Census.

constituents might not like. If, however, any single-issue groups are actively working in their districts for or against abortion, gun control, nuclear energy, or tax cuts, muting the candidates' voting record may not be possible.

Staying in Office

The way people get elected to Congress has two important effects. First, it produces legislators closely tied to local concerns (their districts, their states), and second, it ensures that party leaders will have relatively weak influence over them (because those leaders cannot determine who gets nominated for office).

The local orientation of legislators has some important effects on how policy is made. For example:

- Every member of Congress organizes his or her office to do as much as possible for people back home.

- If your representative serves on the House Transportation and Infrastructure Committee, your state has a much better chance of getting a new bridge or canal than if you do not have a representative on this committee.[10]

- If your representative serves on the House Appropriations Committee, your district is more likely to get approval for a federal grant to improve your water and sewage-treatment programs than if your representative does not serve on that committee.[11]

Former House Speaker Thomas P. "Tip" O'Neill had this in mind when he said, "All politics is local." Some people think this localism is wrong; in their view members of Congress should do what is best for "the nation as a whole." This argument is about the role of legislators: are they supposed to be *delegates* who do what their district wants or *trustees* who use their best judgment on issues without regard to the preferences of their district?

Naturally, most members are some combination of delegate and trustee, with the exact mix depending on the nature of the issue. But some, as we shall see, definitely lean one way or the other. All members want to be reelected, but "delegates" tend to value this over every other consideration and so seek out committee assignments and projects that will produce benefits for their districts. On the other hand, "trustees" will seek out committee assignments that give them a chance to address large questions, such as foreign affairs, that may have no implications at all for their districts.

Question

2. *Who was the presidential candidate who won the largest percentage of the popular vote?*

Primary versus General Campaigns

When you run for federal office, you must run in two elections, not just one. The first consists of primary elections designed to choose each party's nominee, the second is the general election that picks the winner who will hold office. If you are running for president, some states, such as Iowa, hold caucuses instead of primary elections. A caucus is a meeting of people, often in an auditorium or church basement, where they vote on who they would like for their party's nominee.

Each election or caucus attracts a different mix of voters. What may help you win a primary or a caucus may be very different from what will help you win the general election. To win a primary or a caucus, you must mobilize political activists who will give money, do volunteer work, and attend local caucuses. As we saw in Chapters 7 and 8, activists are more ideologically stringent than the voters at large. To motivate these activists, you must be more liberal (if you are a Democrat) in your tone and theme than rank-and-file Democrats, or more conservative (if you are a Republican) than rank-and-file Republicans.

Consider the caucuses held in Iowa in the winter preceding a presidential election year. This is the first real test of the candidates vying for the nomination. Anyone who does poorly here is at a disadvantage, in terms of media attention and contributor interest, for the rest of the campaign.

The several thousand Iowans who participate in their parties' caucuses are not representative of the followers of their party in the state, much less nationally. In 1988, Senator Robert Dole came in first and evangelist Pat Robertson came in second in the Iowa Republican caucus, with Vice President George Bush finishing third. As it turned out, there was little support for Dole or Robertson in the rest of the country.

Democrats who participate in the Iowa caucus tend to be more liberal than Democrats generally. Moreover, the way the caucuses are run is a far cry from how most elections are held. To vote in the Republican caucus, you need not prove you are a Republican or even a voter. The Democratic caucus is not an election at all; instead, a person supporting a certain candidate stands in one corner of the room with people who also support him, while those supporting other candidates stand in other corners with other groups. There is a lot of

calling back and forth, intended to persuade people to leave one group and join another. No group with fewer than 15 percent of the people in attendance gets to choose any delegates, so people in these small groups then go to other, larger ones. It is a cross between musical chairs and fraternity pledge week.

Suppose you are a Democrat running for president and you do well in the Iowa caucus. Suppose you go on to win your party's nomination. Now you have to go back to Iowa to campaign for votes in the general election. Between 1940 and 2008, Iowa has voted Republican in every presidential election but seven (1948, 1964, 1988, 1992, 1996, 2000, and 2008). Your Republican opponent is not going to let you forget all of the liberal slogans you uttered nine months before. The Republican candidate faces the mirror image of this problem—sounding very conservative to get support from Republican activists in states such as Massachusetts and New York and then having to defend those speeches when running against his Democratic opponent in those states.

The problem is not limited to Iowa but exists in every state where activists are more ideologically polarized than the average voter. To get activist support for the nomination, candidates move to the ideological extremes; to win the general election, they try to move back to the ideological center. The typical voter looks at the results and often decides that neither candidate appeals to him or her very much, and so casts a "clothespin vote" (see the box on this page).

Early in the 2004 presidential caucuses and primaries, John Kerry claimed he was an opponent of the American invasion of Iraq in order to defeat Howard Dean, the Vermont governor who seemed to be capturing the antiwar vote among Democrats. But after he won his party's nomination, Kerry backed away from an antiwar stance in order to be more attractive to centrist voters. He had learned a lesson that George McGovern did not understand in 1972. McGovern maintained his liberal views on the war in Vietnam, decriminalizing marijuana, and providing amnesty for draft dodgers.[12] His opponent, Richard Nixon, defeated him easily by taking more centrist positions.

One last thing: if you decide to run for president as a Democrat, do not trust too much in the early polls indicating the frontrunner for the nomination. Edmund Muskie (1972), George Wallace (1976), Ted Kennedy (1980), Gary Hart (1988), Mario Cuomo (1992), and Joseph Lieberman (2004) were all early frontrunners among Democrats, but none got the party's nomination. Only frontrunners Walter Mondale (1984) and Al Gore (2000) prevailed (though neither

2. Lyndon Johnson won 61.7 percent in 1964.

How Things Work

Qualifications for Entering Congress and Privileges of Serving in Congress

Representative

- Must be 25 years of age (when seated, not when elected)

- Must have been a citizen of the United States for seven years

- Must be an inhabitant of the state from which elected (*Note:* Custom, but *not* the Constitution, requires that a representative live in the district that he or she represents.)

Senator

- Must be 30 years of age (when seated, not when elected)

- Must have been a citizen of the United States for nine years

- Must be an inhabitant of the state from which elected

Judging Qualifications

Each house is the judge of the "elections, returns, and qualifications" of its members. Thus, Congress alone can decide disputed congressional elections. On occasion, it has excluded a person from taking a seat on the grounds that the election was improper.

Either house can punish a member—by reprimand, for example—or, by a two-thirds vote, expel a member.

Privileges

Members of Congress have certain privileges, the most important of which, conferred by the Constitution, is that "for any speech or debate in either house they shall not be questioned in any other place." This doctrine of "privileged speech" has been interpreted by the Supreme Court to mean that members of Congress cannot be sued or prosecuted for anything that they say or write in connection with their legislative duties.

When Senator Mike Gravel read the Pentagon Papers—some then-secret government documents about the Vietnam War—into the *Congressional Record* in defiance of a court order restraining their publication, the Court held that this was "privileged speech" and beyond challenge [*Gravel v. United States*, 408 U.S. 606 (1972)]. But when Senator William Proxmire issued a press release critical of a scientist doing research on monkeys, the Court decided the scientist could sue him for libel because a press release was not part of the legislative process [*Hutchinson v. Proxmire*, 443, U.S. 111 (1979)].

---

went on to win the office). By contrast, since 1972, every early Republican frontrunner except one has won the nomination. In 2007, the Republican frontrunner was former New York City Mayor Rudolph Guiliani, and the Democratic frontrunner was then New York State Senator Hillary Rodham Clinton. By early 2008, Guiliani faded, and Arizona Senator John McCain went on to win the Republican nomination. McCain lost the general election to Illinous Senator Barack Obama following Obama's protracted nomination battle with Clinton.

TWO KINDS OF CAMPAIGN ISSUES

In election campaigns, there are two different kinds of issues.[13] A **position issue** is one in which the rival candidates have opposing views on a question that also divides the voters. For example, in

the 2008 election, John McCain wanted to let people put some of their Social Security money into private savings accounts; Barack Obama opposed this.

Since 1860, many of the great party realignments have been based on differing position issues. After the Civil War, the question was whether African Americans should be slaves or free. In the 1890s, it was whether tariffs should be high or low and whether the dollar should be made cheaper. In the 1960s, it was whether broad new civil rights legislation was needed.

But sometimes voters are not divided on important issues. Instead, the question is whether a candidate fully supports the public's view on a matter about which nearly everyone agrees. These are called **valence issues.** For example, everybody wants a strong economy and low crime rates, and so no candidate favors high unemployment or more crime.

Politically Speaking

Clothespin Vote

The vote cast by a person who does not like either candidate and so votes for the less objectionable of the two, putting a clothespin over his or her nose to keep out the unpleasant stench.

What voters look for on valence issues is which candidate seems most closely linked to a universally shared view.

Valence issues are quite common. In 1968, Richard Nixon seemed more supportive of anticrime measures than his rival; in 1976, Jimmy Carter seemed more likely to favor honesty in government than his opponent; in 1984, Ronald Reagan seemed more closely identified with a strong economy than his opponent; in 1988, George H.W. Bush seemed more closely linked to patriotism than his opponent. Notice that we have said "seemed." This is how voters perceived the winners; it does not mean the opponents favored crime, corruption, unemployment, or anti-Americanism.

position issue an issue about which the public is divided and rival candidates or political parties adopt different policy positions.

valence issue an issue about which the public is united and rival candidates or political parties adopt similar positions in hopes that each will be thought to best represent those widely shared beliefs.

In 1992, Bill Clinton was beset with charges that he was guilty of dodging the draft, marital infidelity, and smoking pot. But his strategists decided to focus the campaign on the valence issue of the economy, and they went about rescuing Clinton from the other criticisms. One observer later reported, "Retooling the image of a couple who had already been in the public eye for five battering months required a campaign of behavior modification and media manipulation so elaborate that its outline ran to 14 single-spaced pages."[14] Bill and Hillary Clinton made joint appearances on television during which they demonstrated their affection for each other. The plan even called for staging an event where Bill Clinton and his daughter would surprise Hillary Clinton on Mother's Day.[15]

The 2008 campaign relied on both valence issues (Obama and McCain supported "reforming" the health-care system to make it more "affordable," while differing on many details related to government-paid health insurance) and position issues (McCain supported tax cuts while Obama favored increasing taxes for people earning over $200,000 a year).

Campaigns usually combined both position and valence questions, but the latter increased in importance in recent years. This has happened in part because presidential campaigns are now conducted largely on television, where it is important to project popular symbols and manipulate widely admired images. Candidates try to show they are likable, and they rely on televised portraits of their similarity to ordinary people.

TELEVISION, DEBATES, AND DIRECT MAIL

Once campaigns mostly involved parades, big rallies, "whistle-stop" train tours, and shaking hands outside factory gates and near shopping centers. All of this still goes on, but increasingly presidential and senatorial candidates (and those House candidates with television stations in their districts) use broadcasting.

There are two ways to use television—by running paid advertisements and by getting on the nightly news broadcasts. Short television ads are called *spots,* and a campaign activity that appears on a news broadcast is called a *visual.* Much has been written about the preparation of spots, usually under titles such as "the selling of the president" or "packaging the candidate" (and mostly by advertising executives, who are not especially known for underestimating their own influence).

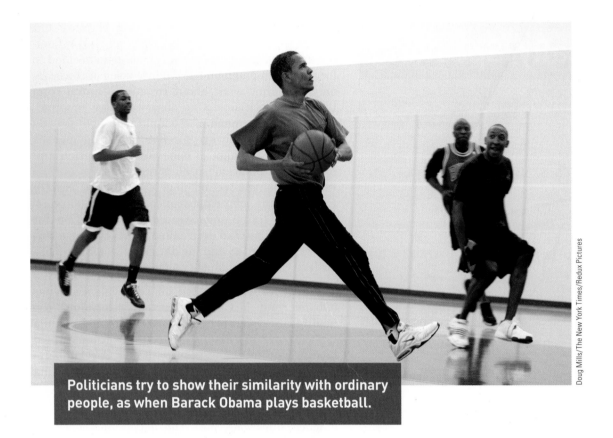

Politicians try to show their similarity with ordinary people, as when Barack Obama plays basketball.

Doug Mills/The New York Times/Redux Pictures

No doubt spots can have an important effect in some cases. A little-known candidate can increase his or her visibility by frequent use of spots (this is what Jimmy Carter did in the 1976 presidential primaries).

The effect of television advertising on general elections is probably a good deal less than its effect on primaries; indeed, as we shall see in Chapter 12, most scientific studies of television's influence on voting decisions have shown that either it has no effect or the effect is subtle and hard to detect. Nor is it surprising that this should be the case. In a general election, especially one for a high-visibility office (such as president or governor), the average voter has many sources of information—his or her own party or ideological preference, various kinds of advertising, the opinions of friends and family, and newspaper and magazine stories. Furthermore, both sides will use TV spots; if well done,

they are likely to cancel each other out. In short, it is not yet clear that a gullible public is being sold a bill of goods by slick Madison Avenue advertisers, whether the goods are automobiles or politicians.

Visuals are a vital part of any major campaign effort because, unlike spots, they cost the campaign little and, as "news," they may have greater credibility with the viewer. A visual is a brief, filmed episode showing the candidate doing something that a reporter thinks is newsworthy. Simply making a speech, unless the speech contains important new facts or charges, often is thought by TV editors to be uninteresting: television viewers are not attracted by pictures of "talking heads," and in the highly competitive world of TV, audience reactions are all-important determinants of what gets on the air. Knowing this, campaign managers will strive to have their candidates do something visually interesting every day, no later than 3:00 P.M. (if the visual is to be on the 6:00 P.M. news)—talk to elderly folks in a nursing home, shake hands with people waiting in an unemployment line, or sniff the waters of a polluted lake. Obviously, all these efforts are for naught if a TV camera crew is not around; great pains therefore are taken to schedule these visuals at times and in places that make it easy for photographers to be present.

general election An election held to choose which candidate will hold office.

primary election An election held to choose candidates for office.

closed primary A primary election in which voting is limited to already registered party members.

open primary A primary election in which voters may choose in which party to vote as they enter the polling place.

How Things Work

Kinds of Elections

There are two kinds of elections in the United States: general and primary. A **general election** is used to fill an elective office. A **primary election** is used to select a party's candidates for an elective office, though in fact those who vote in a primary election may not consider themselves party members. Some primaries are closed. In a **closed primary**, you must declare in advance (sometimes several weeks in advance) that you are a registered member of the political party in whose primary you wish to vote. About 40 states have closed primaries.

Other primaries are open. In an **open primary**, you can decide when you enter the voting booth which party's primary you wish to participate in. You are given every party's ballot; you may vote on one. Idaho, Michigan, Minnesota, Montana, North Dakota, Utah, Vermont, and Wisconsin have open primaries. A variant on the open primary is the **blanket** (or "free love") **primary**—in the voting booth, you mark a ballot that lists the candidates of all the parties, and thus you can help select the Democratic candidate for one office and the Republican candidate for another. Alaska and Washington have blanket primaries.

The differences among these kinds of primaries should not be exaggerated, for even the closed primary does not create any great barrier for a voter who wishes to vote in the Democratic primary in one election and the Republican in another. Some states also have a **runoff primary:** if no candidate gets a majority of the votes, there is a runoff between the two with the most votes. Runoff primaries are common in the South.

A special kind of primary, a presidential primary, is used to pick delegates to the presidential nominating conventions of the major parties. Presidential primaries come in a bewildering variety. A simplified list looks like this:

- **Delegate selection only** Only the names of prospective delegates to the convention appear on the ballot. They may or may not indicate their presidential preferences.

- **Delegate selection with advisory presidential preference** Voters pick delegates and indicate their preferences among presidential candidates. The delegates are not legally bound to observe these preferences.

- **Binding presidential preference** Voters indicate their preferred presidential candidates. Delegates must observe these preferences, at least for a certain number of convention ballots. The delegates may be chosen in the primary or by a party convention.

In 1981, the Supreme Court ruled that political parties, not state legislatures, have the right to decide how delegates to national conventions are selected. Thus, Wisconsin could not retain an open primary if the national Democratic party objected (*Democratic Party v. La Follette,* 101 Sup. Ct. 1010, 1981). Now the parties can insist that only voters who declare themselves Democrats or Republicans can vote in presidential primaries. The Supreme Court's ruling may have relatively little practical effect, however, since the "declaration" might occur only an hour or a day before the election.

Ironically, visuals—and television newscasts generally—may give the viewer less information than commercial spots. This, of course, is the exact opposite of what many people believe. It is commonplace to deplore political advertising, especially the short spot, on the grounds that it is either devoid of information or manipulative, and to praise television news programs, especially longer debates and interviews, because they are informative and balanced. In fact, the best research we have so far suggests that the reverse is true: news programs covering elections tend to convey very little information (they often show scenes of crowds cheering or candidates shouting slogans) and make little or no impression on viewers, if indeed they are watched at all. Paid commercials, on the other hand, especially the shorter spots, often contain a good deal of information seen, remembered, and evaluated by a public quite capable of distinguishing between fact and humbug.[16]

blanket primary A primary election in which each voter may vote for candidates from both parties.

runoff primary A second primary election held when no candidate wins a majority of the votes in the first primary.

A special kind of television campaigning is the campaign debate. Incumbents or well-known candidates have little incentive to debate their opponents; by so doing, they only give more publicity to lesser-known rivals. Despite the general rule among politicians never to help an opponent, Vice President Nixon debated the less-well-known John Kennedy in 1960, and President Gerald Ford debated the less-well-known Jimmy Carter in 1976. Nixon and Ford lost. Lyndon Johnson would not debate Barry Goldwater in 1964, nor would Nixon debate Humphrey in 1968 or McGovern in 1972. Johnson and Nixon won. Carter debated the equally well-known Reagan in 1980 (but refused to join in a three-way debate with Reagan and John Anderson). Carter lost. It is hard to know what effect TV debates have on election outcomes, but poll data suggest that in 1980 voters who watched the debates were reassured by Reagan's performance; after the second debate with Carter, he took a lead in the polls that he never relinquished.[17] In 1984, most people thought that Mondale did better than Reagan in the first debate, but there is little evidence that the debate affected the outcome of the election. In 1992 and 1996, Clinton was probably the better debater, but he most likely would have won even if he had stumbled.

In 2008, Barack Obama and John McCain held three televised debates. Opinions differ as to who did better, but there is little evidence that these encounters affected the election results.

Though TV visuals and debates are free, they are also risky. The risk is the slip of the tongue. You may have spent 30 years of your life in unblemished public service, you may have thought through your position on the issues with great care, you may have rehearsed your speeches until your dog starts to howl, but just make one verbal blunder and suddenly the whole campaign focuses on your misstep. In 1976, President Ford erroneously implied that Poland was not part of the Soviet bloc. For days, the press dwelt on this slip. His opponent, Jimmy Carter, admitted in a *Playboy* interview that he sometimes had lust in his heart. It is hard to imagine anyone who has not, but apparently presidents are supposed to be above that sort of thing. In 1980, Ronald Reagan said trees cause pollution—oops, here we go again.

Because of the fear of a slip, because the voters do not want to hear long speeches about complex issues, and because general-election campaigns are fights to attract the centrist voter, the candidates will rely on a stock speech that sets out the campaign theme as well as on their ability to string together several proven applause-getting lines. For

Library of Congress

In the 1888 presidential campaign, supporters of Benjamin Harrison rolled a huge ball covered with campaign slogans across the country. The gimmick, first used in 1840, gave rise to the phrase "keep the ball rolling."

reporters covering the candidate every day, it can be a mind-numbing experience. Nelson Rockefeller spoke so often of the "brotherhood of man and the fatherhood of God" that the reporters started referring to it as his BOMFOG speech. Occasionally this pattern is interrupted by a "major" address—that is, a carefully composed talk on some critical issue, usually delivered before a live audience and designed to provide issue-related stories for the reporters to write.

If you dislike campaign oratory, put yourself in the candidate's shoes for a moment. Every word you say will be scrutinized, especially for slips of the tongue. Interest group leaders and party activists will react sharply to any phrase that departs from their preferred policies. Your opponent stands ready to pounce on any error of fact or judgment. You must give countless speeches every day. The rational reaction to this state of affairs is to avoid controversy, stick to prepared texts and tested phrases, and shun anything that sounds original (and hence untested). You therefore wind up trying to sell yourself as much as or more than your ideas. Voters may *say* they admire a blunt, outspoken person, but in a tough political campaign they would probably find such bluntness a little unnerving.

Television is the most visible example of modern technology's effect on campaigns. Since 1960, presidential elections have been contested largely through television. Without television, the campaign waged in 1992 by independent candidate Ross Perot might not have happened at all. Perot launched his candidacy with successive appearances on Cable News Network's call-in program "Larry King Live," and he bought several half-hour chunks of television time to air his views on the federal budget deficit. In early October, before the first of three televised debates featuring Perot, Republican incumbent George H.W. Bush, and Democratic challenger Bill Clinton, most national polls showed Perot with only 10 percent of the vote. But after the debates, Perot's support in the polls doubled, and he ended up with about 19 percent of the votes cast on election day.

In 1996, the big television networks agreed to make some free television time available to the major presidential candidates. The Federal Communications Commission approved the plan to limit the free TV to "major" candidates, thus denying it to minor third-party nominees.

Less visible than television but perhaps just as important is the Internet. The computer makes possible sophisticated direct-mail campaigning, and this in turn makes it possible for a candidate to address specific appeals to particular voters easily and rapidly solicit campaign, contributions. In the 2004 presidential campaign, Vermont Governor Howard Dean, at first largely unknown, raised a huge amount of money from Internet appeals in which he emphasized his opposition to our war in Iraq. Other candidates will no doubt do the same. However, the Internet lends itself to ideological appeals that motivate small contributions, and not every candidate will want to make such arguments.

Whereas television is heard by everybody—and thus leads the candidate using it to speak in generalities to avoid offending anyone—direct mail is aimed at particular groups (college students, Native Americans, bankers, autoworkers) to whom specific views can be expressed with much less risk of offending someone. So important are the lists of names of potential contributors to whom a computer may send appeals that a prized resource of any candidate, guarded as if it were a military secret, is "The List." Novices in politics must slowly develop their own lists or beg sympathetic incumbents for a peek at theirs.

The chief consequence of the new style of campaigning is not, as some think, that it is more manipulative than old-style campaigning (picnics with free

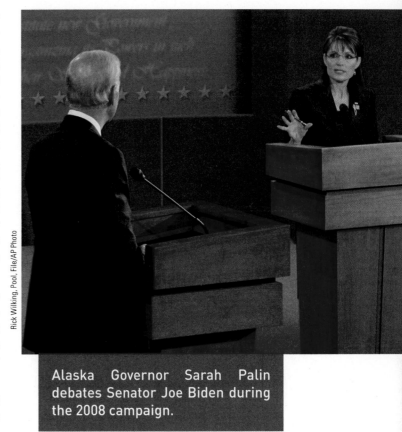

Rick Wilking, Pool, File/AP Photo

Alaska Governor Sarah Palin debates Senator Joe Biden during the 2008 campaign.

beer and $5 bills handed to voters can be just as manipulative as TV ads); rather, it is that running campaigns has become divorced from the process of governing. Previously, the party leaders who ran the campaigns would take part in the government once it was elected, and since they were *party* leaders, they had to worry about getting their candidate *re*elected. Modern political consultants take no responsibility for governing, and by the time the next election rolls around, they may be working for someone else.

Money

As we outlined earlier in this chapter, all these consultants, TV ads, and computerized mailings cost money—lots of it. A powerful California politician once observed that "money is the mother's milk of politics," and many people think that our democracy is drowning in it. In Chapter 11, we will consider what, if anything, interest groups get for the money they give to politicians; in Chapter 12, we shall summarize what we know about the effects of television advertising on elections. Here let us try to answer four questions: Where does campaign money

Candidates first made phonographic recordings of their speeches in 1908. Warren G. Harding is shown here recording a speech during the 1920 campaign.

John F. Kennedy and Richard Nixon debate during the 1960 presidential campaign.

come from? What rules govern how it is raised and spent? What has been the effect of campaign finance reform? What does campaign spending buy?

THE SOURCES OF CAMPAIGN MONEY

Presidential candidates get part of their money from private donors and part from the federal government; congressional candidates get all of their money from private sources. In the presidential primaries, candidates raise money from private citizens and interest groups. The federal government will provide matching funds, dollar for dollar, for all monies raised from individual donors who contribute no more than $250. (To prove they are serious candidates, they must first raise $5,000 in each of 20 states from such small contributors.) The government also gives a lump-sum grant to each political party to help pay the costs of its nominating convention. In the general election, the government pays all the costs (upto a legal limit) of major-party candidates and part of the cost of minor-party candidates (those winning between 5 and 25 percent of the vote).

Congressional candidates get no government funds; all their money must come out of their own pockets or be raised from individuals, interest groups (PACs), or the political parties. Contrary to what many people think, most of that money comes from—and has always come from—individual donors. Because the rules sharply limit how much any individual can give, these donors tend not to be fat cats but people

of modest means who contribute $100 or $200 per person.

CAMPAIGN FINANCE RULES

During the 1972 presidential election, men hired by President Nixon's campaign staff broke into the headquarters of the Democratic National Committee in the Watergate office building. They were caught by an alert security guard. The subsequent investigation disclosed that the Nixon people had engaged in dubious or illegal money-raising schemes, including taking large sums from wealthy contributors in exchange for appointing them to ambassadorships. Many individuals and corporations were indicted for making illegal donations (since 1925, it had been against the law for corporations or labor unions to contribute money to candidates, but the law had been unenforceable). Some of the accused had given money to Democratic candidates as well as to Nixon.

When the break-in was discovered, the Watergate scandal unfolded. It had two political results: President Nixon was forced to resign, and a new campaign finance law was passed.

Under the new law, individuals could not contribute more than $1,000 to a candidate during any single election. Corporations and labor unions had for many decades been prohibited from spending money on campaigns, but the new law created a substitute: political action committees. A PAC must have at least 50 members (all of whom enroll voluntarily),

How Things Work

Major Federal Campaign Finance Rules

General

- All federal election contributions and expenditures are reported to a Federal Election Commission.

- All contributions over $100 must be disclosed, with name, address, and occupation of contributor.

- No *cash* contributions over $100 or foreign contributions.

- No ceiling on how much candidates may spend out of their own money (unless they accept federal funding for a presidential race).

Individual Contributions

- An individual may not give more than $2,000 to any candidate in any election.

- An individual may not make federal political gifts exceeding $95,000 every two years, of which only $37,500 may go to candidates.

Political Action Committees (PACs)

- Each corporation, union, or association may establish one.

- A PAC must register six months in advance, have at least 50 contributors, and give to at least five candidates.

- PAC contributions may not exceed $5,000 per candidate per election or $15,000 to a national political party.

Ban on Soft Money

- No corporation or union may give money from its own treasury to any national political party.

Independent Expenditures

- Corporations, unions, and associations may not use their own money to fund "electioneering communications" that refer to clearly identified candidates 60 days before a general election or 30 days before a primary contest.

- PACs may fund electioneering communications up to their expenditure limits.

Presidential Primaries

- Federal matching funds can be given to match individual contributions of $250 or less.

- To be eligible, a candidate must raise $5,000 in each of 20 states in contributions of $250 or less.

Presidential Election

- The federal government will pay all campaign costs (up to a legal limit) of major-party candidates and part of the cost of minor-party candidates (those winning between 5 and 25 percent of the vote).

---

give to at least five federal candidates, and must not give more than $5,000 to any candidate in any election or more than $15,000 per year to any political party.

In addition, the law made federal tax money available to help pay for presidential primary campaigns and for paying all of the campaign costs of a major-party candidate and a fraction of the costs of a minor-party candidate in a presidential general election.

The new law helped increase the amount of money spent on elections and, in time, changed the way money was spent. There are now more than 4,000

PACs (see Figure 10.2). In each election since 2002, PACs have given over $250 million to congressional candidates. But PACs are not a dominant influence on candidates because they give rather little (often no more than $500). A small contribution is enough to ensure that a phone call to a member of Congress from a PAC sponsor will be returned but not enough, in most cases, to guarantee that the member will act as the PAC wishes.

Moreover, most money for congressional candidates still comes from individuals. But since the limit until 2002 was $1,000 per election (a limit set in the early 1970s), candidates had to devise clever ways of reaching a lot of individuals to raise the amount of

Figure 10.2

Growth of PACs 1979–2009

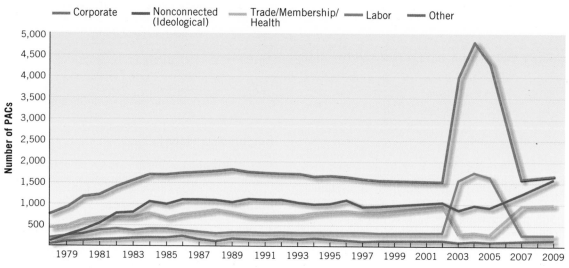

Source: Federal Election Commission, March 9, 2009.

money they needed. This usually meant direct mail and telephone solicitations. If you are bothered by constant appeals for campaign funds, remember— that's what the law requires.

By contrast, when George McGovern ran against Richard Nixon in 1972, he was chiefly supported by the large contributions of one wealthy donor, and when Eugene McCarthy ran against Lyndon Johnson in 1968, he benefited from a few big donations and did not have to rely on massive fund-raising appeals.

A candidate gets federal money to match, dollar for dollar, what he or she has raised in contributions of $250 or less. But a presidential candidate can decide to forgo federal primary funding and raise his or her own money. In 2000, George W. Bush relied entirely on his own fund-raising, while his chief rival, John McCain, used federal matching funds. In 2004, Bush, Kerry, and Dean all declined federal matching funds in the primary elections. In 2008, John McCain declined public financing for the primaries but accepted it for the general election; Barack Obama relied entirely on his own fund-raising for both the primaries and the general election.

If you are a minor-party candidate, you can get some support from the federal government provided you have won at least 5 percent of the vote in the last election. In 2000, both Pat Buchanan (Reform party) and Ralph Nader (Green party) got partial support from Washington because their parties had won more than 5 percent of the vote in 1996. But

no minor party won more than 5 percent in either 2004 or 2008, so none received partial support.

The 1973 campaign finance law produced two problems. The first was **independent expenditures.** A PAC, a corporation, or a labor union could spend whatever it wanted supporting or opposing a candidate, so long as this spending was "independent," that is, not coordinated with or made at the direction of the candidate's wishes. Simply put, independent expenditures are ordinary advertising directed at or against candidates.

The second was **soft money.** Under the law, individuals, corporations, labor unions, and other groups could give unlimited amounts of money to political parties provided the money was not used to back candidates by name. But the money could be used in ways that helped candidates by financing voter-registration and get-out-the-vote drives. Over half a billion dollars in soft money was spent during each of the last three presidential campaigns (2000, 2004, 2008).

independent expenditures Spending by political action committees, corporations, or labor unions to help a party or candidate but done independently of them.

soft money Funds obtained by political parties that are spent on party activities, such as get-out-the-vote drives, but not on behalf of a specific candidate.

A SECOND CAMPAIGN FINANCE LAW

Reform is a tricky word. We like to think it means fixing something gone wrong. But some reforms can make matters worse. For example, the campaign finance reforms enacted in the early 1970s helped matters in some ways by ensuring that all campaign contributors would be identified by name. But they made things worse in other ways by, for example, requiring candidates to raise small sums from many donors. This made it harder for challengers to run (incumbents are much better known and raise more money) and easier for wealthy candidates to

run because, under the law as interpreted by the Supreme Court, candidates can spend as much of their own money as they want.

After the 2000 campaign, a strong movement developed in Congress to reform the reforms of the 1970s. The result was the Bipartisan Campaign Finance Reform Act of 2002, which passed easily in the House and Senate and was signed by President Bush. After the 1970s laws were passed, the Supreme Court, in *Buckley v. Valeo* (1976), upheld federal limits on campaign contributions even as it ruled that spending money to influence elections is a form of constitutionally protected free speech (hence candidates were free to give unlimited amounts of money to their own

The 2008 Election

It was a most unusual election. It was the first race in which either an African American (Barack Obama) or a woman (Sarah Palin) could win national office. It was the first race since 1960 that a senator would win. It was the first election since 1980 (with one exception) in which the last Gallup poll taken before the primaries began did not predict who would be the candidates. Up until December 2007, the polls predicted Rudolph Giuliani would be the Republican candidate, but he did not win a single primary. In December 2007, Hillary Clinton led Barack Obama by 18 points in the polls, but she eventually lost to him.

But perhaps the strangest fact was this: it was a year in which the party out of power (the Democrats) confronted a very unpopular president (George W. Bush), a war in Iraq that had divided the country, and a sagging economy brought about by the collapse of the financial markets that had invested much too heavily in mortgage payments to people who could not afford them. In those circumstances, the candidate out of power should have been ahead by 15 points in the polls. But Obama was not; it was a relatively close race right to the end.

When Obama won, he received only 52 percent of the vote. That was the first time since 1964 that a Democratic candidate received more than 51 percent and only the second time over 50 percent. The Democrats increased their majorities in both the House and Senate, and they did acquire the 60 Senate seats that would guarantee they could defeat any filibuster.

Why was the election so close in a year that should have given the Democrats an overwhelming advantage?

Scholars do not (yet) know. Perhaps it was because Obama, though a personally appealing and eloquent candidate, had little political experience and no clear record of action on many important issues. Or perhaps it is simply because America is a deeply divided nation.

Obama won 95 percent of the vote among African American voters but lost among white voters (see Figure 10.3). He also carried by a decisive margin the votes of Hispanics and Asians. He won a big majority among young voters but lost among voters over the age of 45. He barely won a majority of college graduates but got a large majority among persons with postgraduate degrees.

Naturally, Democrats gave a huge majority to Obama, and Republicans gave an equally large one to McCain, but Obama won the vote of self-described independents, 52 to 44 percent.

The weakness of the economy was the major issue among voters, dwarfing every other consideration.

There remains one puzzle to which no one has an answer. Would Obama have won by a much larger margin if he had not been black? One study has shown that in the early 1990s, the votes won by black candidates for governor and senator were smaller than what the pre-election polls had predicted, but by the mid-1990s, that gap had disappeared. Black candidates won just what the pre-election polls indicated. But, of course, none of these black candidates was running for president. It is unlikely that scholars will ever be able to answer this question.

Figure 10.3

Presidential Exit Poll Results, 2008

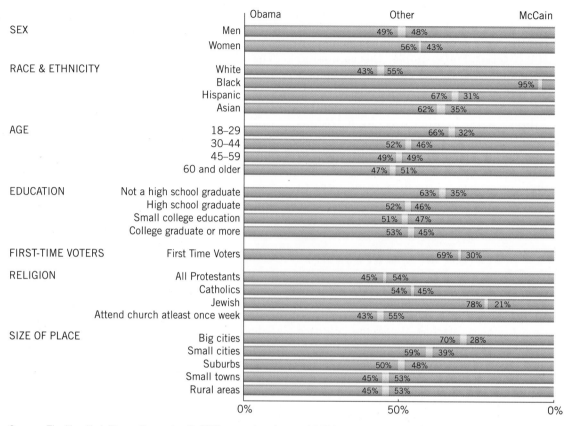

Source: *The New York Times*, November 5, 2008, reporting data on 17,836 votes from 300 polling places around the country on Election Day and telephone interviews with 2,378 absentee and early voters.

campaigns). That precedent had pretty much held, but the new law made three important changes.

First, it banned "soft money" contributions to national political parties from corporations and unions. After the federal elections in 2002, no national party or party committee can accept soft money. Any money the national parties get must come from "hard money"—that is, individual donations or PAC contributions as limited by federal law.

Second, the limit on individual contributions was raised from $1,000 per candidate per election to $2,000.

Third, "independent expenditures" by corporations, labor unions, trade associations, and (under certain circumstances) nonprofit organizations are sharply restricted. Now none of these organizations can use their own money to refer to a clearly identified federal candidate in any advertisement during the 60 days preceding a general election or the 30 days preceding a primary contest. (PACs can still refer

to candidates in their ads, but of course PACs are restricted to "hard money"—that is, the amount they can spend under federal law.)

Immediately after the law was signed, critics filed suit in federal court claiming it was unconstitutional. The suit brought together a number of organizations that rarely work together, such as the American Civil Liberties Union and the National Right to Life Committee.

The suit claimed that the ban on independent spending that "refers to" clearly identified candidates 60 days before an election is unconstitutional because it is an abridgement of the right of free speech. Under the law, an organization need not even endorse or oppose a candidate; it is enough that it mention a politician. This means that 60 days before an election, an organization cannot say it "supports (or opposes) a bill proposed by Congresswoman Pelosi."

Newspapers, magazines, and radio and television stations are not affected by the law, so they can say

Map 10.1
Election by County, 2008

Election08

Obama wins

Electoral votes

270 needed to win

Obama	365
McCain	173

Nationwide popular vote

Obama	52.5%
McCain	46.1%
Others	1.2%

State breakdown of electoral votes

OBAMA • BIDEN

| DC 86.3 | VT 35.5 | MA 25.8 | NY 25.4 | DE 24.9 | IL 24.6 | MD 24.1 | CA 23.9 | CT 22.3 | WA 16.7 | MI 16.4 | OR 16.2 | NJ 14.7 | NM 14.5 | NV 12.4 | PA 10.3 | MN 10.2 | IA 9.2 | CO 8.6 | VA 5.5 | OH 3.9 | FL 2.5 | IN 0.9 | NC 0.3 | MO 0.1 | MT 2.4 | GA 5.2 | SD 8.4 | ND 8.6 | TX 11.7 | WV 13.1 | TN 15 | KS 15.3 | KY 16.3 | AR 19.9 | AL 21.6 | UT 28.7 | WY 32.5 |
| HI 45.1 | RI 28.2 | | | | | | | ME 17.1 | | | | | | WI 13.9 | | | NH 9.5 | | | | | NE* 0.5 | | | | AZ 8.5 | SC 8.9 | | MS 13.7 | NE* 16.1 | LA 18.7 | AL 25.4 | ID 31.2 | OK | | |

MARGIN OF VICTORY
AS PERCENTAGE

270 electoral votes needed to win the presidency

* McCain won Nebraska, although one electoral vote went to Obama who won a congressional district; McCain's margin of victory based on state total

MCCAIN • PALIN

State winner

Not called/
no data

OBAMA   MCCAIN

CHANGED PARTY
from 2004 election

Geography of the popular vote

99.6% of precincts reporting nationwide in presidential race

LEADER'S PERCENTAGE

OBAMA
MCCAIN
OTHER

– 50% 55% 60% +
Percentage of total vote

Not called/no data

Tie/runoff

STATE POPULAR VOTE

RI
DE
MD
DC

COUNTY POPULAR VOTE

ELECTORAL COLLEGE VOTE ALLOCATION:

All states and D.C. are winner-takes-all, except for Maine and Nebraska where two electoral votes go to the state winner and one goes to the winner of each congressional district

Unofficial results as of Nov. 19, 2008

NOTE: Alaska results are statewide only

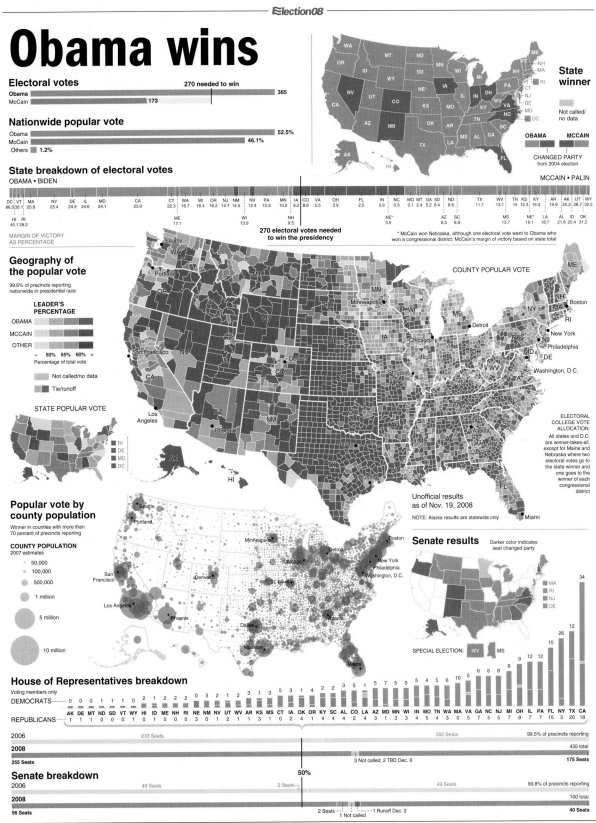

Popular vote by county population

Winner in counties with more than 70 percent of precincts reporting

COUNTY POPULATION
2007 estimates

- 50,000
- 100,000
- 500,000
- 1 million
- 5 million
- 10 million

Senate results

Darker color indicates seat changed party

MA
RI
NJ
DE

SPECIAL ELECTION: WY   MS

										34
									12	
								26		
							10			
				9	12	12				
6	8	8	8							

House of Representatives breakdown

Voting members only

DEMOCRATS	AK	DE	MT	ND	SD	VT	WY	HI	ID	ME	NH	RI	NE	NM	NV	UT	WV	AR	KS	MS	CT	IA	OK	OR	KY	SC	AL	CO	LA	AZ	MD	MN	WI	IN	MO	TN	MA	VA	GA	NC	NJ	MI	OH	IL	PA	FL	NY	TX	CA
	0	0	0	1	1	1	0	2	1	2	2	2	0	3	2	1	2	3	1	3	5	3	1	4	2	2	3	5	1	5	7	5	5	4	5	6	10	5	6	8	8	8	9	12	12	10	12	26	34
REPUBLICANS	1	1	1	0	0	0	1	0	1	0	0	0	3	0	1	2	1	1	3	1	0	2	4	1	4	4	4	2	4	3	1	3	3	4	5	4	0	5	7	5	5	7	8	7	7	15	3	20	18

2006	233 Seats		202 Seats	99.5% of precincts reporting
2008				435 total
255 Seats		3 Not called; 2 TBD Dec. 6		175 Seats

Senate breakdown

50%

2006	49 Seats	2 Seats	49 Seats	99.8% of precincts reporting
2008				100 total
56 Seats		2 Seats / 1 Not called / 1 Runoff Dec. 2		40 Seats

SOURCES: AP Election Research; USGS; Census Bureau

J. Balestrieri, C. Osgood, N. Rapp • AP

whatever they want for or against a candidate. One way of evaluating the law is to observe that it shifts influence away from businesses and unions and toward the media.

In *McConnell v. Federal Election Commission* (2002), the Supreme Court decided to uphold almost all of the law. As we saw in Chapter 5, it rejected the argument of those who claimed that speech requires money and decided it was no violation of the free speech provisions of the First Amendment to eliminate the ability of corporations and labor unions (and the organizations that use their money) to even *mention* a candidate for federal office for 60 days before the national election. In 2007, however, the Court backed away from this view. An ad by a right-to-life group urged people to write to Senator Russell Feingold to convince him to vote for certain judicial nominees, but it did not tell people how to vote. The Court decided this was "issue advocacy" protected by the First Amendment and so could not be banned by the McCain-Feingold law.

If the past is any guide, however, neither recent changes nor the existing legal maze will do much to keep individuals, PACs, party leaders, and others from funding the candidates they favor. Nor should we be surprised if groups continue to steer contributions much as one might expect.

For instance, PACS dedicated to a party, a policy position, or a cause (for example, pro-choice PACS that favor Democrats and pro-life PACS that favor Republicans) generally do not change how they give to candidates depending on who is in power. By contrast, trade and corporate PAC money tends to follow power: after the Democrats regained the House in 2006, scores of trade and corporate PACS started giving Democrats far more money and Republicans far less. The Wine and Spirits Wholesalers PAC gave 23 percent of its money to Democrats in 2005 and 65 percent of its money to Democrats in 2007; the Home Depot Inc. PAC gave 13 percent of its money to Democrats in 2005 and 46 percent of its money to Democrats in 2007—and so it went for numerous other trade or corporate PACS (See Table 10.4 for a list of the top 20 PAC contributors in 2007–2008).

NEW SOURCES OF MONEY

If money is, indeed, the mother's milk of politics, efforts to make the money go away are not likely to work. The Bipartisan Campaign Reform Act, once enforced, immediately stimulated people to find other ways to spend political money.

Senators John McCain and Russell Feingold wrote the campaign finance reform act that passed in 2002.

Alex Wong/Newsmakers/Getty Images

The most common were **527 organizations.** These groups, named after a provision of the Internal Revenue Code, are designed to permit the kind of soft money expenditures once made by political parties. In 2004, the Democrats created the Media Fund, America Coming Together, America Votes, and many other groups. George Soros, the wealthy businessman, gave more than $23 million to organizations pledged to defeat George Bush. The Republicans responded by creating Progress for America, The Leadership Forum, America for Job Security, and other groups. Under the law, as it is now interpreted, 527 organizations can spend their money on politics so long as they do not coordinate with a candidate or

527 organizations
Organizations under section 527 of the Internal Revenue Code that raise and spend money to advance political causes.

Table 10.4 Top 20 PAC Contributors to Federal Candidates, Democratic and Republican (2007–2008)

PAC Name	Total Amount	Dem Pct	Repub Pct
National Assn of Relators	$4,013,900	58%	42%
Intl Brotherhood of Electrical Workers	3,344,650	98	2
AT&T Inc	3,108,200	47	52
National Auto Dealers Assn	2,864,000	34	66
National Beer Wholesalers Assn	2,860,000	53	47
American Bankers Assn	2,834,643	42	58
International Assn of Fire Fighters	2,703,900	77	23
American Assn for Justice	2,700,500	95	4
Operating Engineers Union	2,692,667	87	13
Laborers Union	2,540,350	92	8
Honeywell International	2,512,116	52	48
National Assn of Home Builders	2,482,000	46	54
Airline Pilots Assn	2,387,000	85	15
Machinists/Aerospace Workers Union	2,326,800	97	3
Credit Union National Assn	2,313,549	53	47
Plumbers/Pipefitters Union	2,304,639	95	5
Service Employees International Union	2,287,250	94	6
American Federation of Teachers	2,279,750	99	1
Teamsters Union	2,257,000	97	3
National Air Traffic Controllers Assn	2,226,475	80	20

Source: Federal Election Commission, March 2, 2009.

lobby directly for that person. In 2004, 527 organizations raised and spent over one-third of a billion dollars. So far, the lesson seems to be this: campaign finance laws are not likely to take money out of politics.

MONEY AND WINNING

In the general election for president, money does not make much difference, because both major-party candidates have the same amount, contributed by the federal government. During peacetime, presidential elections usually are decided by three things: political party affiliation, the state of the economy, and the character of the candidates.

For all the talk about voting for "the person, not the party," history teaches that at least 80 percent of the presidential vote will go to the candidates of the two main parties. This means that a presidential election will normally be decided by the 20 percent of voters who cannot be counted on to vote either Democratic or Republican.

In good economic times, the party holding the White House normally does well; in poor times, it does badly. This is sometimes called the "pocketbook vote." But it is not clear whose pocketbook determines how a person will vote. Many who are doing well financially will vote against the party in power if the country as a whole is not doing well. A person doing well may have friends or family members who are doing poorly. Or the well-off voter may think that if the country is doing poorly, he or she will soon feel the pinch by losing a job or losing customers.

Voters also care about character, and so some money from presidential campaign coffers goes to fund "character ads." *Character* here means several things: Is the candidate honest and reliable? Does the candidate think as the voter thinks about social issues such as crime, abortion, and school prayer? Does the candidate act presidential? Acting presidential seems to mean being an effective speaker, displaying dignity and compassion, sounding like someone who can take charge and get things done,

Landmark Cases

Financing Elections

- *Buckley v. Valeo* (1976): Held that a law limiting contributions to political campaigns was constitutional but that one restricting a candidate's expenditures of his or her own money was not.

- *McConnell v. Federal Election Commission* (2002): Upheld a law prohibiting corporations and labor unions from running ads that mention candidates and their positions for 60 days before a federal general election.

and coming across consistently as a reasonable, likable person. Rash, disagreeable extremists need not apply.

Since both major candidates usually get the same amount of federal money for the general election campaign, money does not make much of a difference in determining the winner. Other factors that also do not make a difference include the following:

- *Vice-presidential nominee:* There has rarely been an election in which his or her identity has made a difference.

- *Political reporting:* It may make a difference in some elections, but not in presidential ones.

- *Religion:* Being a Catholic was once a barrier, but since John F. Kennedy was elected president in 1960, this is no longer true.

- *Abortion:* This probably affects who gets a party's nomination, but in the general election ardent supporters and ardent opponents are about evenly balanced.

In congressional races, however, in general it seems that money does make a decisive difference. Scholars are not entirely agreed on the facts, but strong evidence suggests that how much the challenger spends is most important, because the challenger usually must become known to the public. Buying name recognition is expensive. Gary Jacobson has shown that, other things equal, in every congressional election from 1972 to the mid-1980s, challengers who spent more money did better than those who spent less.[19] Jacobson also suggested that how much the incumbents spent was not very important, presumably because they already had all the name recognition they needed (as well as the other benefits of holding office, such as free mail and travel). Other scholars, applying different statistical methods to the same facts, have come to different conclusions. It now seems that, other things equal, high-spending incumbents do better than low-spending ones.[20] As noted earlier in this chapter, "million-dollar challenges" are becoming more common in House races; but it remains to be seen if that will continue, and if so, whether it narrows the gap with incumbents.

Incumbents find it easier to raise money than challengers; incumbents provide services to their districts that challengers cannot; incumbents regularly send free ("franked") mail to their constituents, while challengers must pay for their mailings; incumbents can get free publicity by sponsoring legislation or conducting an investigation. Thus, it is hardly surprising that incumbents who run for reelection win in the overwhelming majority of races.

What Decides the Election?

To the voter, it all seems quite simple—he or she votes for "the best person" or maybe "the least-bad person." To scholars, it is all a bit mysterious. How do voters decide who the best person is? What does "best" mean, anyway?

PARTY

One answer to these questions is party identification. People may say they are voting for the "best person," but for many people the best person is always a Democrat or a Republican. Moreover, we have seen in Chapter 7 that many people know rather little about the details of political issues. They may not even know what position their favored candidate has taken on issues the voters care about. Given these facts, many scholars have argued that party identification is the principal determinant of how people vote.[21]

If it were only a matter of party identification, though, the Democrats would always win the presidency, since usually more people identify with the Democratic than the Republican party. But we know that the Democrats lost seven of the 10 presidential elections between 1968 and 2004. There are three reasons for this.

First, those people who consider themselves Democrats were less firmly wedded to their party

Table 10.5 Percentage of Popular Vote by Groups in Presidential Elections, 1960–2008

		National	Republicans	Democrats	Independents
1960	Kennedy	50%	5%	84%	43%
	Nixon	50	95	16	57
1964	Johnson	61	20	87	56
	Goldwater	39	80	13	44
1968	Humphrey	43	9	74	31
	Nixon	43	86	12	44
	Wallace	14	5	14	25
1972	McGovern	38	5	67	31
	Nixon	62	95	33	69
1976	Carter	51	11	80	48
	Ford	49	89	20	52
1980[a]	Carter	41	11	66	30
	Reagan	51	84	26	54
	Anderson	7	4	6	12
1984	Mondale	41	7	73	35
	Reagan	59	92	26	63
1988	Dukakis	46	8	82	43
	Bush	54	91	17	55
1992	Clinton	43	10	77	38
	Bush	38	73	10	32
	Perot	19	17	13	30
1996	Clinton	49	13	84	43
	Dole	41	80	10	35
	Perot	8	6	5	17
2000	Gore	49	8	86	45
	Bush	48	91	11	47
2004	Kerry	49	6	89	49
	Bush	51	93	11	48
2008	Obama	52	9	89	52
	McCain	46	89	10	44

[a]The figures for 1980, 1984, 1988, and 1996 fail to add up to 100 percent because of missing data.

than Republicans. Table 10.5 shows how people identifying themselves as Democrats, Republicans, or independents voted in presidential elections from 1960 to 2004. In every election except 1992, at least 80 percent of Republican voters supported the Republican candidate in each election. By contrast, there have been more defections among Democratic voters—in 1972 a third of Democrats supported Nixon, and in 1984, 26 percent supported Reagan.

The second reason, also clear from Table 10.5, is that the Republicans did much better than the Democrats

among the self-described "independent" voters. In the dozen presidential elections since 1960, the Democratic candidate won a large share of the independent vote five times (1964, 1992, 1996, 2004, and 2008) while the Republican candidate won it seven times (1968, 1972, 1976, 1980, 1984, 1988, and 2000).

Finally, a higher percentage of Republicans than Democrats vote in elections. In every presidential contest in the past 34 years, those describing themselves as "strongly Republican" have been more likely to vote than those describing themselves as "strongly Democratic."

ISSUES, ESPECIALLY THE ECONOMY

Even though voters may not know a lot about the issues, that does not mean issues play no role in elections or that voters respond irrationally to them. For example, V. O. Key, Jr., looked at those voters who switched from one party to another between elections and found that most of them switched in a direction consistent with their own interests. As Key put it, the voters are not fools.[22]

Moreover, voters may know a lot more than we suppose about issues that really matter to them. They may have hazy, even erroneous, views about monetary policy, business regulation, and the trade deficit, but they likely have a very good idea about whether unemployment is up or down, prices at the supermarket are stable or rising, or crime is a problem in their neighborhoods. And on some issues—such as abortion, school prayer, and race relations—they likely have some strong principles they want to see politicians obey.

Contrary to what we learn in our civics classes, representative government does not require voters to be well informed on the issues. If it were our duty as citizens to have accurate facts and sensible ideas about how best to negotiate with foreign adversaries, stabilize the value of the dollar, revitalize failing industries, and keep farmers prosperous, we might as well forget about citizenship and head for the beach. It would be a full-time job, and then some, to be a citizen. Politics would take on far more importance in our lives than most of us would want, given our need to earn a living and our belief in the virtues of limited government.

To see why our system can function without well-informed citizens, we must understand the differences between two ways in which issues can affect elections.

Prospective Voting

Prospective means "forward-looking"—we vote prospectively when we examine the views the rival candidates have on the issues of the day and then cast our ballots for the person we think has the best ideas for handling these matters. **Prospective voting** requires a lot of information about issues and candidates. Some of us vote prospectively. Those who do tend to be political junkies. They are either willing to spend a lot of time learning about issues or are so concerned about some big issue (abortion, school busing, nuclear energy) that all they care about is how a candidate stands on that question.

prospective voting
Voting for a candidate because you favor his or her ideas for handling issues.

retrospective voting
Voting for a candidate because you like his or her past actions in office.

Prospective voting is more common among people who are political activists, have a political ideology that governs their voting decision, or are involved in interest groups with a big stake in the election. They are a minority of all voters, but (as we saw in Chapters 7 and 8) they are more influential than their numbers would suggest. Some prospective voters (by no means all) are organized into single-issue groups, to be discussed in the next section.

Retrospective Voting

Retrospective means "backward-looking"—**retrospective voting** involves looking at how things have gone in the recent past and then voting for the party that controls the White House if we like what has happened and voting against that party if we don't like what has happened. Retrospective voting does not require us to have a lot of information—all we need to know is whether things have, in our view, gotten better or worse.

Elections are decided by retrospective voters.[23] In 1980, they decided to vote against Jimmy Carter because inflation was rampant, interest rates were high, and we seemed to be getting the worst of things overseas. The evidence suggests rather clearly that they did not vote *for* Ronald Reagan; they voted for *an alternative to* Jimmy Carter. (Some people did vote for Reagan and his philosophy; they were voting prospectively, but they were in the minority.) In 1984, people voted for Ronald Reagan because unemployment, inflation, and interest rates were down and because we no longer seemed to be getting pushed around overseas. In 1980, retrospective voters wanted change; in 1984, they wanted continuity. In 1988, there was no incumbent running, but George H.W. Bush portrayed himself as the candidate who would continue the policies that had led to prosperity and depicted Michael Dukakis as a "closet liberal" who would change those policies. In 1992, the economy had once again turned sour, and so voters turned away from Bush and toward his rivals, Bill Clinton and Ross Perot.

Though most incumbent members of Congress get reelected, those who lose do so, it appears, largely because they are the victims of retrospective voting. After Reagan was first elected, the economy went into a recession in 1981–1982. As a result, Republican members of Congress were penalized by the voters, and Democratic challengers were helped. But it is not just the economy that can hurt congressional candidates. In most midterm elections, the party holding the White House has lost seats in Congress. Just why this should be is not entirely clear, but it probably has something to do with the tendency of some voters to change their opinions

Figure 10.4

The Economy and Vote for President, 1948–2004

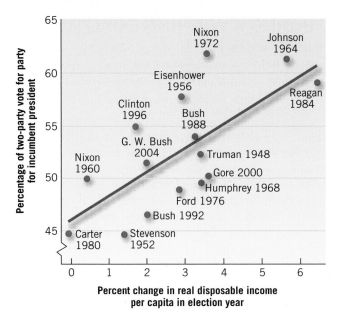

Notes: (1) Each dot represents a presidential election, showing the popular vote received by the incumbent president's party. (2) 1992 data do not include votes for independent candidate H. Ross Perot. (3) 2004 value on RDI is projection from data available in December 2004.

Source: From *American Public Opinion*, 5th ed., by Robert S. Erikson and Kent L. Tedin. Copyright © 1995 by Addison-Wesley Educational Publishers, Inc. Reprinted by permission of Pearson Education, Inc.

of the presidential party once that party has had a chance to govern—which is to say, a chance to make some mistakes, disappoint some supporters, and irritate some interests.

Some scholars believe that retrospective voting is based largely on economic conditions. Figure 10.4 certainly provides support for this view. Each dot represents a presidential election (15 of them, from 1948 to 2004). The horizontal axis is the percentage increase or decrease in per capita disposable income (adjusted for inflation) during the election year. The vertical axis is the percentage of the two-party vote won by the party already occupying the White House. You can see that, as per capita income goes up (as you move to the right on the horizontal axis), the incumbent political party tends to win a bigger share of the vote.

Other scholars feel that matters are more complicated than this. As a result, a small industry has grown up consisting of people who use different techniques to forecast the outcome of elections. If you know how the president stands in the opinion polls several months before the election and how

well the economy is performing, you can make a pretty good guess as to who is going to win the presidency. For congressional races, predicting the result is a lot tougher because so many local factors affect these contests. Election forecasting remains an inexact science. As one study of the performance of presidential election forecasting models concluded: "Models may be no improvement over pundits."[24]

THE CAMPAIGN

If party loyalty and national economic conditions play so large a role in elections, is the campaign just sound and fury, signifying nothing?

No. Campaigns can make a difference in three ways. First, they reawaken the partisan loyalties of voters. Right after a party's nominating convention selects a presidential candidate, that person's standing with voters of both parties goes way up in the polls. The reason is that the just-nominated candidate has received a lot of media attention during the summer months, when not much else is happening. When the campaign gets under way, however, both candidates get publicity, and voters return to their normal Democratic or Republican affiliations.

Second, campaigns give voters a chance to watch how the candidates handle pressure, and they give candidates a chance to apply that pressure. The two rivals, after promising to conduct a campaign "on the issues" without mudslinging, immediately start searching each other's personal histories and records to find acts, statements, or congressional votes that can be shown in the worst possible light in newspaper or television ads. Many voters don't like these "negative ads"—but they work. Careful statistical studies based on actual campaigns (as opposed to voter surveys or laboratory-like focus group studies) suggest that negative ads work by stimulating voter turnout.[25] As a result, every politician constantly worries about how an opponent might portray his or her record, a fact that helps explain why so many politicians never do or say anything that can't be explained in a 30-second television spot.

Third, campaigns allow voters an opportunity to judge the character and core values of the candidates. Most voters don't study in detail a candidate's positions on issues; even if they had the time, they know you can't predict how politicians will behave just from knowing what a campaign manager has written in a position paper. The voters want some guidance as to how a candidate will behave once elected. They get that guidance by listening not to the details of what a candidate says but to the themes and tone of those statements. Is the

3. Andrew Johnson ran with Abraham Lincoln in 1864.

Union members were once heavily Democratic, but since Ronald Reagan began winning white union votes in 1980, these votes have been up for grabs.

candidate tough on crime and drugs? Are his or her statements about the environment sincere or perfunctory? Does the candidate favor having a strong military? Does the candidate care more about not raising taxes or more about helping the homeless?

The desire of voters to discern character, combined with the mechanics of modern campaigning—short radio and television ads and computer-targeted direct mail—lend themselves to an emphasis on themes at the expense of details. This tendency is reinforced by the expectations of ideological party activists and single-issue groups.

Thematic campaigning, negative ads, and the demands of single-issue groups are not new; they are as old as the republic. In the 19th century, the theme was slavery and the single-issue groups were abolitionists and their opponents; their negative ads make the ones we have today sound like Sunday school sermons. At the turn of the century, the themes were temperance and the vote for women; both issues led to no-holds-barred, rough-and-tumble campaigning. In the 1970s and 1980s, new themes were advanced by fundamentalist Christians and by pro- and antiabortion groups.

What has changed is not the tone of campaigning but the advent of primary elections. Once, political parties picked candidates out of a desire to win elections. Today, activists and single-issue groups influence the selection of candidates, sometimes out of a belief that it is better to lose with the "right" candidate than to win with the wrong one. In a five-candidate primary, a minority of the voters can pick the winner. Single-issue groups can make a

big difference under these conditions, even though they may not have much influence in the general election.

FINDING A WINNING COALITION

Putting together a winning electoral coalition means holding on to your base among committed partisans and attracting the swing voters who cast their ballots in response to issues (retrospectively or prospectively) and personalities.

There are two ways to examine the nature of the parties' voting coalitions. One is to ask what percentage of various identifiable groups in the population supported the Democratic or Republican candidate for president. The other is to ask what proportion of a party's total vote came from each of these groups. The answer to the first question tells us how *loyal* African Americans, farmers, union members, and others are to the Democratic or Republican party or candidate; the answer to the second question tells us how *important* each group is to a candidate or party.

At a public meeting, Samuel Joseph Wurzelbacher challenged Barack Obama on his tax plan and quickly became known as "Joe the Plumber."

Table 10.6 Who Likes the Democrats?

	1968[a]	1972	1976	1980[c]	1984	1988	1992[d]	1996	2000	2004	2008
Percentage of various groups saying they voted for the Democratic presidential candidate, 1964–2008.											
Sex											
Men	41%	37%	53%	37%	37%	41%	41%	43%	42%	45%	49%
Women	45	38	48	45	42	49	46	54	54	52	56
Race											
White	38	32	46	36	34	40	39	43	42	42	43
Nonwhite	85	87	85	82	90	86	82	84	90	89	95
Education											
College	37	37	42	35	40	43	44	47	45	47	50
Graduate school	52	49	58	43	49	56	55	52	52	55	58
Age											
Under 30	47	48	53	43	41	47	44	53	48	54	66
50 and over	41	36	52	41[e]	39	49	50	48[g]	48	49	48
Religion											
Protestant	35	30	46	NA	NA	33[f]	33	36	42	41	45
Catholic	59	48	57	40	44	47	44	53	50	48	54
Jewish[b]	85	66	68	45	66	64	78	78	79	76	78
Southerners	31	29	54	47	36	41	42	46	NA	41	45

[a]1968 election had three major candidates (Humphrey, Nixon, and Wallace). [b]Jewish vote estimated from various sources; since the number of Jewish persons interviewed often is less than 100, the error in this figure, as well as that for nonwhites, may be large. [c]1980 election had three major candidates (Carter, Reagan, and Anderson). [d]1992 election had three major candidates (Clinton, Bush, and Perot). [e]For 1980–1992, refers to age 60 and over. [f]For 1988, white Protestants only. [g]For 1996, refers to age 45 and over.

Sources: For 1964–1976: Gallup poll data, as tabulated in Jeane J. Kirkpatrick, "Changing Patterns of Electoral Competition," in *The New American Political System*, ed. Anthony King (Washington, D.C.: American Enterprise Institute, 1978), 254–256. For 1980–1992: Data from *New York Times*/CBS News exit polls. For 1996: *Congressional Quarterly Weekly Report*, 1997, p. 188, For 2000: Exit polls supplied by ABC News. For 2004 and 2008, CNN exit polls.

For the Democratic coalition, African Americans are the most loyal voters. In every election but one since 1952, two-thirds or more of all African Americans voted Democratic; since 1964, four-fifths have gone Democratic. Usually, Jewish voters are almost as solidly Democratic. Most Hispanics have been Democrats, though the label "Hispanic" conceals differences among Cuban Americans (who often vote Republican) and Mexican Americans and Puerto Ricans (who are strongly Democratic). The turnout among most Hispanic groups has been quite low (many are not yet citizens), so their political power is not equivalent to their numbers.

The Democrats have lost their once strong hold on Catholics, southerners, and union members. In 1960, Catholics supported John F. Kennedy (a Democrat and fellow Catholic), but they also voted for Eisenhower, Nixon, and Reagan—all Republicans. Union members deserted the Democrats in 1968 and 1972, came back in 1980 and 1988, and divided about evenly between the two parties in 1952, 1956,

and 1980. White southerners have voted Republican in national elections but Democratic in many local ones (see Table 10.6).

The Republican party often is described as the party of business and professional people. The loyalty of these groups to Republicans is strong: only in 1964 did they desert the Republican candidate to support Lyndon Johnson. Farmers usually have been Republican, but they are a volatile group, highly sensitive to the level of farm prices—and thus quick to change parties.

In sum, the loyalty of most identifiable groups of voters to either party is not overwhelming. Only African Americans, businesspeople, and Jews usually give two-thirds or more of their votes to one party or the other; other groups display tendencies, but none that cannot be overcome.

The contribution that each of these groups makes to the party coalitions is a different matter. Though African Americans are overwhelmingly and persistently Democratic, they make up so small a portion

RESEARCH FRONTIERS

Candidate Positions Drive Voter Choices

When asked why they voted for one candidate over another, most people will say they chose the best person for the job. But how do voters decide who the "best person" is?

In a 2008 article, political scientists Michael Tomz and Robert P. Van Houweling address this question with surveys and other data regarding candidate positions and voter choice. Their focus is mainly on health care policy, but their research spans dozens of studies of how voters make decisions and tests three leading theories—proximity, discounting, and direction:

> Proximity: Voters believe candidates will deliver on campaign pledges and prefer candidates whose positions on the issues are closest to their own.

> Discounting: Doubting candidates will deliver on campaign pledges, voters discount pledges and prefer candidates who—whatever their positions—voters think might get something good done in government.

> Direction: Voters see issues as essentially two-sided; prefer candidates who take their side or "direction"; and, given a choice between two candidates who are both on their side, will prefer the candidate whose position is most intense.

As Tomz and Van Houweling emphasize, each theory yields a different prediction about the relationship between candidate positioning and voter choice. For example, if a voter has a position on an issue (abortion, for example), but does not feel strongly about it (say the voter is moderately pro-choice), proximity theory predicts that the voter will choose the candidate closest to his or her position even if that candidate is on the opposite side (say a candidate who is moderately pro-life). Direction theory predicts that the voter will

instead choose the competing candidate who advocates his or her side of the issue most intensely (say, a candidate who is very strongly pro-choice).

And the winner is?

Proximity: Tomz and Van Houweling find proximity voting about twice as common as discounting and four times as common as direction voting. Thus, a voter who favors a 5 percent increase in government spending on health care will most likely prefer a candidate who advocates much the same position.

- Does that finding surprise you, and just how inclined are you to behave like a proximity voter?

- Do you strongly prefer candidates whose positions on the issues are closest to your own? Or might you vote for a candidate who—though espouses positions at odds with your own—seems more likely than an opponent whose positions more nearly mirror your own to "get things done" in government?

- Do you think candidates who advocate extreme positions are more likely to stay committed if elected than candidates who advocate more moderate positions on the same issues?

- In sum, what most influences your way of deciding who is the "best person" for the job?

Source: Michael Tomz and Robert P. Van Houweling, "Candidate Positioning and Voter Choice," *American Political Science Review* 102, August 2008, pp. 303–318.

of the total electorate that they have never accounted for more than a quarter of the total Democratic vote. The groups that make up the largest part of the Democratic vote—Catholics, union members, southerners—are also the least dependable parts of that coalition.[26]

When representatives of various segments of society make demands on party leaders and presidential candidates, they usually stress their numbers

or their loyalty, but rarely both. African American leaders, for example, sometimes describe the black vote as of decisive importance to Democrats and thus deserving of special consideration from a Democratic president. But African Americans are so loyal that a Democratic candidate, can almost take their votes for granted, and in any event they are not as numerous as other groups. Union leaders emphasize how many union voters there are, but a president will know that union leaders cannot "deliver" the union vote and that this vote may go to the president's opponent, whatever the leaders say. For any presidential candidate, a winning coalition must be put together anew for each election. Only a few voters can be taken for granted or written off as a lost cause.

The Effects of Elections on Policy

To the candidates, and perhaps to the voters, the only interesting outcome of an election is who won. To a political scientist, the interesting outcomes are the broad trends in winning and losing and what they imply about the attitudes of voters, the operation of the electoral system, the fate of political parties, and the direction of public policy.

Figure 10.5 shows the trend in the popular vote for president since before the Civil War. From 1876 to 1896, the Democrats and Republicans were hotly competitive. The Republicans won three times, the Democrats twice in close contests. Beginning in 1896, the Republicans became the dominant party, and except for 1912 and 1916, when Woodrow Wilson, a Democrat, was able to win owing to a split in the Republican party, the Republicans carried every presidential election until 1932. Then

Franklin Roosevelt put together what has since become known as the "New Deal coalition," and the Democrats became the dominant party. They won every election until 1952, when Eisenhower, a Republican and a popular military hero, was elected for the first of his two terms. In the presidential elections since 1952, power has switched hands between the parties frequently.

Still, cynics complain that elections are meaningless: no matter who wins, crooks, incompetents, or self-serving politicians still hold office. The more charitable argue that elected officials usually are decent enough, but that public policy remains more or less the same no matter which official or party is in office.

There is no brief and simple response to this latter view. Much depends on which office or policy you examine. One reason it is so hard to generalize about the policy effects of elections is that the offices to be filled by the voters are so numerous and the ability of the political parties to unite these office-holders behind a common policy is so weak that any policy proposal must run a gauntlet of potential opponents. Though we have but two major parties, and though only one party can win the presidency, each party is a weak coalition of diverse elements that reflect the many divisions in public opinion. The proponents of a new law must put together a majority coalition almost from scratch, and a winning coalition on one issue tends to be somewhat

Figure 10.5

Partisan Division of the Presidential Vote in the Nation, 1856–2008

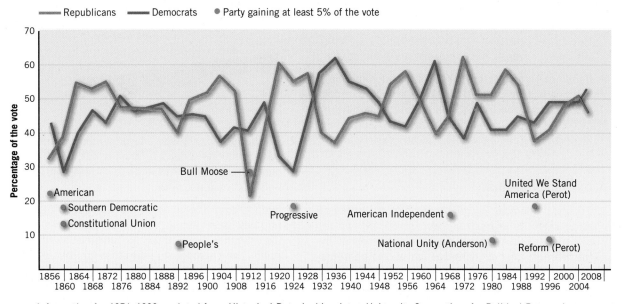

Sources: Information for 1856–1988, updated from Historical Data Archive, Inter-University Consortium for Political Research, as reported in William H. Flanigan and Nancy H. Zingale, *Political Behavior of the American Electorate*, 3rd ed., 32. For 1992: *World Almanac and Book of Facts 1994*, 73.

WHAT WOULD YOU DO?

MEMORANDUM

To: *Arjun Bruno, National Party Chairman*

From: *Arlene Marcus, State Party Chairwoman*

Subject: *Supporting a National Primary*

In the past few election cycles, our state's role in the party nomination for president virtually has disappeared with a May primary date. Several states have leapfrogged ahead of us, and party leaders have indicated that they do not want any more states to move up their primary date. The national party needs to find a way to ensure that all states, large and small, have a real voice in nominating a presidential candidate.

Arguments for:

1. A single national primary permits equal participation by all states and presents a fair compromise with the increased number of delegates that larger states send to the national conventions, much like the compromises during the original constitutional debates.

2. The nominating process needs to be less costly, particularly when presidential candidates realistically need to raise $100 million a year before the general election to be competitive for the nomination. Holding all primaries and caucuses on a single day will reduce overall election expenses significantly.

3. If the American electorate knows presidential nominations will be decided by each party on one day, then they will be more likely to vote, a significant factor for elections in which historically, fewer than 20 percent of eligible voters typically participate.

Arguments against:

1. Each state decides in conjunction with the national party when its primary or caucus will take place, and the federal system of government designed by the Framers did not guarantee that all states would be treated equally at all times.

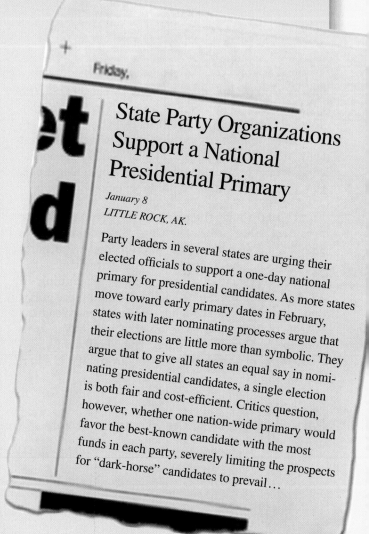

State Party Organizations Support a National Presidential Primary

January 8
LITTLE ROCK, AK.

Party leaders in several states are urging their elected officials to support a one-day national primary for presidential candidates. As more states move toward early primary dates in February, states with later nominating processes argue that their elections are little more than symbolic. They argue that to give all states an equal say in nominating presidential candidates, a single election is both fair and cost-efficient. Critics question, however, whether one nation-wide primary would favor the best-known candidate with the most funds in each party, severely limiting the prospects for "dark-horse" candidates to prevail…

2. A national primary would favor candidates with high name recognition and funding to further that recognition and would severely disadvantage lesser-known candidates within the party.

3. Even though the general election takes place on one day, voter turnout in the United States still is lower than in other advanced industrialized democracies, which suggests that other factors influence who participates.

Your decision:

Support National Primary _____   Oppose National Primary _____ different—quite often dramatically different—from a winning coalition on another issue.

In a parliamentary system with strong parties, such as that in Great Britain, an election often can have a major effect on public policy. When the Labour party won office in 1945, it put several major industries under public ownership and launched a comprehensive set of social services, including a nationalized health care plan. Its ambitious and controversial campaign platform was converted, almost item by item, into law. When the Conservative party returned to power in 1951, it accepted some of these changes but rejected others (for example, it denationalized the steel industry).

American elections, unless accompanied by a national crisis such as a war or a depression, rarely produce changes of the magnitude of those that occurred in Britain in 1945. The constitutional system within which our elections take place was designed to moderate the pace of change—to make it neither easy nor impossible to adopt radical proposals. But the fact that the system is intended to moderate the rate of change does not mean it will always work that way.

The election of 1860 brought to national power a party committed to opposing the extension of slavery and southern secession; it took a bloody war to vindicate that policy. The election of 1896 led to the dominance of a party committed to high tariffs, a strong currency, urban growth, and business prosperity—a commitment that was not significantly altered until 1932. The election of that year led to the New Deal, which produced the greatest single enlargement of federal authority since 1860. The election of 1964 gave the Democrats such a large majority in Congress (as well as control of the presidency) that there began to issue forth an extraordinary number of new policies of sweeping significance—Medicare and Medicaid, federal aid to education and to local law enforcement, two dozen environmental and consumer protection laws, the Voting Rights Act of 1965, a revision of the immigration laws, and a new cabinet-level Department of Housing and Urban Development.

The election of 1980 brought into office an administration determined to reverse the direction of policy over the preceding half century. Reagan's administration succeeded in obtaining large tax cuts, significant reductions in spending (or in the rate of increase of spending) on some domestic programs, and changes in the policies of some regulatory agencies. The election of 1982, in which the Democrats made gains in the House of Representatives, stiffened congressional resistance to further spending cuts and stimulated renewed interest in tax increases as a way of reducing the deficit. Following the election of 1984, a major tax reform plan was passed. After the 1996 election, Clinton and Republican congressional leaders agreed on a plan to balance the budget.

In view of all these developments, it is hard to argue that the pace of change in our government is always slow or that elections never make a difference. Studies by scholars confirm that elections often are significant, despite the difficulty of getting laws passed. One analysis of about 1,400 promises made between 1944 and 1964 in the platforms of the two major parties revealed that 72 percent were put into effect.[27]

Another study examined the party platforms of the Democrats and Republicans from 1844 to 1968 and all the laws passed by Congress between 1789 and 1968. By a complex statistical method, the author of the study was able to show that during certain periods the differences between the platforms of the two parties were especially large (1856, 1880, 1896, 1932) and that there was at about the same time a high rate of change in the kinds of laws being passed.[28] This study supports the general impression conveyed by history that elections often can be central to important policy changes.

Why then do we so often think elections make little difference? It is because public opinion and the political parties enter a phase of consolidation and continuity between periods of rapid change. During this phase, the changes are digested, and party leaders adjust to the new popular consensus, which may (or may not) evolve around the merits of these changes. During the 1870s and 1880s, Democratic politicians had to come to terms with the failure of the southern secessionist movement and the abolition of slavery; during the 1900s, the Democrats had to adjust again, this time to the fact that national economic policy was going to support industrialization and urbanization, not farming; during the 1940s and 1950s, the Republicans had to learn to accept the popularity of the New Deal.

Elections in ordinary times are not "critical"—they do not produce any major party realignment, they are not fought out over a dominant issue, and they provide the winners with no clear mandate. In most cases, an election is little more than a retrospective judgment on the record of the incumbent president and the existing congressional majority. If times are good, incumbents win easily; if times are bad, incumbents may lose—even though their opponents may have no clear plans for change. But even a "normal" election can produce dramatic results if the winner is a person such as Ronald Reagan, who helped give his party a distinctive political philosophy, or Barack Obama, the nation's first African American president.

SUMMARY

Political campaigns have changed dramatically since the mid-20th century, with many important changes occurring in just the last two decades. Today's candidates must create a temporary organization that can raise money from large numbers of small donors, pay for political consultants and pollsters, mobilize enthusiastic supporters, and win a nomination in a way that will not harm their ability to appeal to a broader, more diverse constituency in the general election. There are important differences between presidential and congressional campaigns, but both involve position-taking on different types of issues. Federal election laws have changed several times since the early 1970s, and restrictions on fund-raising by individuals and organizations are now many and complicated, but each new election cycle breaks previous total spending records. Money alone, however, does not decide elections. Campaigning itself has an uncertain effect on election outcomes, but election outcomes can have important effects on public policy, especially at those times—during critical or "realigning" elections—when new voters are coming into the electorate in large numbers, old party loyalties are weakening, or a major issue is splitting the majority party. Most people vote retrospectively rather than prospectively.

RECONSIDERING WHO GOVERNS?

1. How do American elections determine the kind of people who govern us?

American democracy rewards candidates who have personal appeal rather than party endorsements. Politics here produces individualists who usually have a strong ideological orientation toward liberal or conservative causes, but only a weak sense of loyalty to the political parties who endorse those ideologies.

2. What matters most in deciding who wins presidential and congressional elections?

The party identification of the voters matters the most. Only 10 to 20 percent of the voters are available to have their votes changed. For them, the state of the economy, and in wartime the success or failures we have while fighting abroad, make the most difference. Closely allied with those issues, at least for presidential candidates, is the voters' assessment of their character.

RECONSIDERING TO WHAT ENDS?

1. Do elections make a real difference in what laws get passed?

Yes. During campaigns parties may try to sound alike, in order to attract centrist voters, but when in office they differ greatly in the policies they put into law.

WORLD WIDE WEB RESOURCES

Federal Election Commission: **www.fec.gov**
Project Vote Smart: **www.vote-smart.org**
Election history: **clerkweb.house.gov**
Electoral college: **www.fec.gov/pages/ecmenu2**
Campaign finance: **www.opensecrets.org**

SUGGESTED READINGS

Black, Earl, and Merle Black. *Divided America: The Ferocious Power Struggle in American Politics.* New York: Simon and Schuster, 2007. Detailed account of how evenly balanced the two parties are in all parts of the country.

Burnham, Walter Dean. *Critical Elections and the Mainsprings of American Politics.* New York: Norton, 1970. An argument about the decline in voting participation and the significance of the realigning election of 1896.

Bader, Ted. *Campaigning for Hearts and Minds: How Emotional Appeals in Political Ads Work.* Chicago: University of Chicago Press, 2006. Masterful analysis of how ads move voters and influence people who are most well-informed about politics.

Klein, Joe. *Politics Lost? How American Democracy Was Trivialized By People Who Think You're Stupid.* New York: Doubleday, 2006. A veteran political reporter claims that political consultants are to blame for negative political developments.

Sundquist, James L. *Dynamics of the Party System: Alignment and Realignment of Political Parties in the United States.* Rev. ed. Washington, D.C.: Brookings Institution, 1983. Historical analysis of realigning elections from 1860 to the nonrealignment of 1980.

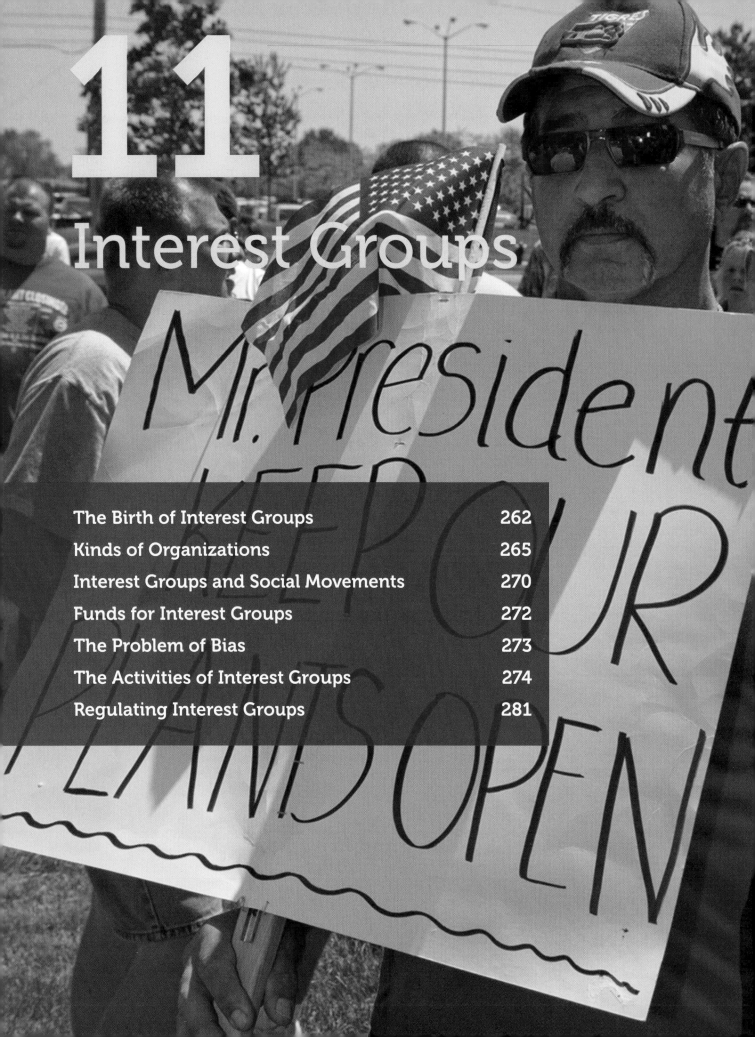

11

Interest Groups

Jim West/Alamy

WHO GOVERNS?

1. Do interest groups dominate government, and is any particular lobby politically unbeatable?
2. Why do people join interest groups?

TO WHAT ENDS?

1. Is the proliferation of political action committees (PACs) and other groups good or bad for America's representative democracy?
2. Should interest groups' political activities be restricted by law?

Like most people, you probably think lobbyists are one reason why our government does not work as well as it should. Lobbyists, after all, represent special interest groups and are the enemies of doing what the public interest requires.

But before you embrace that view, ask yourself what interest groups you or your parents or your friends have joined. Does your father build houses? Does your mother teach school or go to PTA meetings? Is your sister a lawyer? Are you or your friends part of an effort to improve the environment?

If these things are true, then your father probably belongs to a labor union, your mother to the National Education Association, your sister to the American Bar Association, and you and your friends may help support the Sierra Club or the Audubon Society. In short, you and your family belong to interest groups.

In America, this is not only commonplace, but inevitable. The size and diversity of our country, the decentralizing effects of our Constitution, the vast number of nonprofit organizations, and the weakness of our political parties make it certain that interest groups will be an important way for people to have their voices heard.

Suppose we were a small country that had no state governments and operated under a parliamentary system that made the prime minister the only important official. Suppose further that strong parties dominated how policies were made and that our tax laws made it hard to support nonprofit organizations. If these things were true, then interest groups would be much less important. Most of the political decisions would be made by the ruling party. If you wanted to affect how those decisions were made, you would have to be a leader of that party or part of one or two very powerful interest groups.

But here these things are not true. This country has a great variety of ethnic groups, more than 70 religious organizations, and a Constitution that requires power to be shared by three branches of government and that ensures independent authority for 50 state governments. In our diverse nation, political authority is so decentralized that it invites the creation of interest groups that try to affect some part of every decision.

And the Constitution makes it clear that lobbyists are protected: they are exercising freedom of speech and petitioning the government for a redress of grievances, just as the First Amendment guarantees.

Compare the United States with Great Britain. Both nations are democratic, but in Great Britain only a few big interest groups exist; here, there are thousands. In Britain, only one lobbying organization represents farmers; here, there are at least three. Or compare the United States and Germany. Both are democratic, but German environmentalists formed an influential political party (the Green Party), which by 2005 had won more than 50 seats in the national legislature. In this country, the Green Party has won no seats in Congress; most environmentalists have instead worked through a score of interest groups.

The Birth of Interest Groups

The number of interest groups has grown rapidly since 1960. A study of Washington-based political associations revealed that roughly 70 percent of them established their Washington offices after 1960, and nearly half opened their doors after 1970.[1]

The 1960s and 1970s were boom years for interest groups, but there have been other periods in our history when political associations were created in especially large numbers. During the 1770s, many groups arose to agitate for American independence; during the 1830s and 1840s, the number of religious associations increased sharply, and the antislavery movement began. In the 1860s, trade unions based on crafts emerged in significant numbers, farmers formed the Grange, and various fraternal organizations were born. In the 1880s and 1890s, business associations proliferated. The great era of organization building, however, was in the first two decades of the 20th century. Within this 20-year period, many of the best-known and largest associations with an interest in national politics were formed: the Chamber of Commerce, the National Association of Manufacturers, the American Medical Association, the National Association for the Advancement of Colored People (NAACP), the Urban League, the American Farm Bureau Federation, the Farmers' Union, the National Catholic Welfare Conference, the American Jewish Committee, and the Anti-Defamation League. The wave of interest group formation that occurred in the 1960s led to the emergence of environmental, consumer, and political reform organizations such as those sponsored by consumer activist Ralph Nader.

The fact that associations in general, and political interest groups in particular, are created more rapidly in some periods than in others suggests that these groups do not arise inevitably out of natural social processes. There have always been farmers in this country, but there were no national farm organizations until the latter part of the 19th century. Blacks had been victimized by various white-supremacy policies from the end of the Civil War on, but the NAACP did not emerge until 1910. Men and women worked in factories for decades before industrial unions were formed.

At least four factors help explain the rise of interest groups. The first consists of broad economic developments that create new interests and redefine old ones. Farmers had little reason to become organized for political activity so long as most of them consumed what they produced. The importance of regular political activity became evident only after most farmers began to produce cash crops for sale in markets that were unstable or affected by forces (the weather, the railroads, foreign competition)

In 2009 many people launched "Tea Party" protests against the Obama administration.

George Guajardo/NBC NewsWire/AP Photos

that farmers could not control. Similarly, for many decades most workers were craftspeople working alone or in small groups. Such unions as existed were little more than craft guilds interested in protecting members' jobs and in training apprentices. The reason for large, mass-membership unions did not exist until there arose mass-production industry operated by large corporations.

Second, government policy itself helped create interest groups. Wars create veterans, who in turn demand pensions and other benefits. The first large veterans organization, the Grand Army of the Republic, was made up of Union veterans of the Civil War. By the 1920s, these men were receiving about a quarter of a billion dollars a year from the government, and naturally they created organizations to watch over the distribution of this money. The federal government encouraged the formation of the American Farm Bureau Federation (AFBF) by paying for county agents who would serve the needs of farmers under the supervision of local farm organizations; these county bureaus eventually came together as the AFBF. The Chamber of Commerce was launched at a conference attended by President William Howard Taft.

Professional societies, such as those made up of lawyers and doctors, became important in part because state governments gave to such groups the authority to decide who was qualified to become a lawyer or a doctor. Workers had a difficult time organizing

so long as the government, by the use of injunctions enforced by the police and the army, prevented strikes. Unions, especially those in mass-production industries, began to flourish after Congress passed laws in the 1930s that prohibited the use of injunctions in private labor disputes, that required employers to bargain with unions, and that allowed a union representing a majority of the workers in a plant to require all workers to join it.[2]

Third, political organizations do not emerge automatically, even when government policy permits them and social circumstances seem to require them. Somebody must exercise leadership, often at substantial personal cost. These organizational entrepreneurs are found in greater numbers at certain times than others. They often are young, caught up in a social movement, drawn to the need for change, and inspired by some political or religious doctrine. Antislavery organizations were created in the 1830s and 1840s by enthusiastic young people influenced by a religious revival sweeping the country. The period from 1890 to 1920, when so many national organizations were created, was a time when the college-educated middle class was growing rapidly. (The number of men and women who received college degrees each year tripled between 1890 and 1920.)[3] During this era, natural science and fundamentalist Christianity were locked in a bitter contest, with the Gospels and Darwinism offering competing ideas about personal salvation and social progress. The 1960s, when many

RESEARCH FRONTIERS

No Lobby Can't Be Beat

Nobody doubts that interest groups have proliferated, but is any one lobby so powerful as to dominate policymaking on certain issues? Three interest groups strike many observers as uniquely powerful:

- NRA: The National Rifle Association lobbies for promoting gun ownership as a civil liberty protected by the Second Amendment to the Constitution; it opposes most gun-control legislation. It has about four million members and takes in over $200 million a year.

- AIPAC: The American Israel Public Affairs Committee lobbies for U.S. foreign aid and diplomatic policies favorable to Israel. It has about 100,000 members. Together with other pro-Israel groups, it steers millions of dollars in campaign contributions to candidates it favors.

- The AARP lobbies for policies that provide financial benefits and services to people over age 50. The 40-million-member AARP is widely considered to be the dominant lobby on issues relating to such mammoth federal programs as Social Security and Medicare.

The NRA has won legislative battles for "shall-carry" laws giving people the right to bear concealed weapons; the AIPAC boasts national leaders in both parties who support spending billions of dollars a year in U.S. financial and military aid to Israel; and the AARP has driven successive health care policy debates, like one in 2003 that resulted in increased federal subsidies for prescription drugs.

But recent and often highly critical writings on each lobby by political scientists and others remind us that no one group controls policymaking on any big issue:

- The NRA's legislative battles over "shall-carry" laws were protracted in many states. In 2004 it successfully stymied the renewal of the 1994 federal ban on various assault weapons; but it had lost its fight against that ban a decade earlier.

- The AIPAC has made U.S. support for Israel a bipartisan norm, but it has hardly always had its aid proposals adopted; and it has been subjected to espionage allegations and criticized by diverse past and present top U.S. government officials.

- The AARP has loomed large in debates over Social Security and Medicare, but it has often been more successful at blocking proposals that it opposes than in getting proposals that it favors into law; and it has faced congressional investigations.

Do a little research of your own on these three important, but not all-powerful or never-defeated, lobbies.

- What, if any, influence do each of these three lobbies wield in your state?

- What would you say are the main sources of each lobby's significant but not solitary influence over federal policy?

Sources: Richard Feldman, *Ricochet: Confessions of a Gun Lobbyist* (Wiley, 2007); John J. Mearsheimer and Stephen M. Walt, *The Israel Lobby and U.S. Foreign Policy* (Farrar, Straus, and Giroux, 2008); and Dale Van Natta, *Trust Betrayed: Inside the AARP* (Regnery, 1998), and "This Isn't the Old AARP," *Los Angeles Times*, November 24, 2003.

---

new organizations were born, was a decade in which young people were powerfully influenced by the civil rights and antiwar movements and when college enrollments more than doubled.

Finally, the more activities government undertakes, the more organized groups that will be interested in those activities. Most Washington offices representing corporations, labor unions, and trade and professional associations were established before 1960—in some cases many decades before—because it was during the 1930s or even earlier that the government began making policies important to business and labor. The great majority of "public-interest" lobbies (those concerned with the environment or consumer protection), social welfare associations, and organizations concerned with civil rights, the elderly, and the handicapped established offices in Washington after 1960. Policies of interest to these groups, such as the major civil rights and environmental laws, were adopted after that date. In fact, over half the public-interest lobbies opened their doors after 1970.

Kinds of Organizations

An **interest group** is any organization that seeks to influence public policy. When we think of an organization, we usually think of something like the Boy Scouts or the League of Women Voters—a group consisting of individual members. In Washington, however, many organizations do not have individual members at all but are offices—corporations, law firms, public relations firms, or "letterhead" organizations that get most of their money from foundations or from the government—out of which a staff operates. It is important to understand the differences between the two kinds of interest groups—institutional and membership interests.[4]

INSTITUTIONAL INTERESTS

Institutional interests are individuals or organizations representing other organizations. General Motors, for example, has a Washington representative. Over 500 firms have such representatives in the capital, most of whom have opened their offices since 1970.[5] Firms that do not want to place their own full-time representative in Washington can hire a Washington lawyer or public relations expert on a part-time basis. Washington now has more lawyers than Los Angeles, a city three times its size.[6] Another kind of institutional interest is the trade or governmental association, such as the National Independent Retail Jewelers or the National Association of Counties.

Individuals or organizations that represent other organizations tend to be interested in bread-and-butter issues of vital concern to their clients. Some of the people who specialize in this work can earn very large fees. Top public relations experts and Washington lawyers can charge $500 an hour or more for their time. Since they earn a lot, they are expected to deliver a lot.

Just what they are expected to deliver, however, varies with the diversity of the groups making up

Landmark Cases

Lobbying Congress

- *U.S. v. Harriss* (1954): The Constitution protects the lobbying of Congress, but the government may require information from groups that try to influence legislation.

the organization. The American Cotton Manufacturers Institute represents southern textile mills. Those mills are few enough in number and similar enough in outlook to allow the institute to carry out clear policies squarely based on the business interests of its clients.

> *interest group* An organization of people sharing a common interest or goal that seeks to influence public policy.

For example, the institute works hard to get the federal government to adopt laws and rules that will keep foreign-made textiles from competing too easily with American-made goods. Sometimes the institute is successful, sometimes not, but it is never hard to explain what it is doing.

By contrast, the U.S. Chamber of Commerce represents thousands of different businesses in hundreds of different communities. The Chamber has led all interest groups in annual lobbying expenditures. All told, from 1998 to 2004, it spent $205 million on lobbying (see Figure 11.1). Its membership is so large and diverse that the Chamber in Washington can speak out clearly and forcefully on only those relatively few matters in which all, or most, businesses take the same position. Since all businesses would like lower taxes, the Chamber favors that. On the other hand, since some businesses (those that import goods) want low tariffs and other businesses (those that face competition

Figure 11.1

What the Top Lobby Spent, 1998–2004

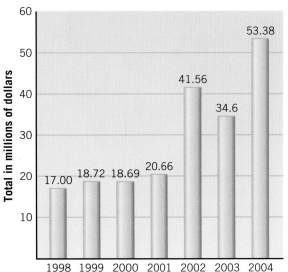

Annual lobbying expenditures by the Chamber of Commerce for the United States

Source: Center for Public Integrity, Georgetown University, Washington, D.C., 2006.

from imported goods) want higher tariffs, the Chamber says little or nothing about tariffs.

Institutional interests do not just represent business firms; they also represent governments, foundations, and universities. For example, the American Council on Education claims to speak for most institutions of higher education, the American Public Transit Association represents local mass-transit systems, and the National Association of Counties argues on behalf of county governments.

MEMBERSHIP INTERESTS

It often is said that Americans are a nation of joiners, and so we take for granted the many organizations around us supported by the activities and contributions of individual citizens. But we should not take this multiplicity of organizations for granted; in fact, their existence is something of a puzzle.

Americans join only certain kinds of organizations more frequently than citizens of other democratic countries. We are no more likely than the British, for example, to join social, business, professional, veterans, or charitable organizations, and we are *less* likely to join labor unions. Our reputation as a nation of joiners arises chiefly out of our unusually high tendency to join religious and civic or political associations. About three times as many Americans as Britons say they are members of a civic or political organization.[7]

This proclivity of Americans to get together with other citizens to engage in civic or political action reflects,

apparently, a greater sense of political efficacy and a stronger sense of civic duty. When Gabriel Almond and Sidney Verba asked citizens of five nations what they would do to protest an unjust local regulation, 56 percent of the Americans—but only 34 percent of the British and 13 percent of the Germans—said they would try to organize their neighbors to write letters, sign petitions, or otherwise act in concert.[8] Americans are also more likely than Europeans to think organized activity is an effective way to influence the national government, remote as that institution may seem. And this willingness to form civic or political groups is not a product of higher levels of education in this country; Americans of every level of schooling are political joiners.[9]

But explaining the American willingness to join politically active groups by saying that Americans feel a "sense of political efficacy" is not much of an explanation; we might as well say people vote because they think their vote makes a difference. But one vote clearly makes no difference at all in almost any election; similarly, one member, more or less, in the Sierra Club, the National Rifle Association, or the NAACP clearly will make no difference in the success of those organizations.

And most people who are sympathetic to the aims of a mass-membership interest group do not join it. The NAACP, for example, enrolls as members only a tiny fraction of all African Americans. This is not because people are selfish or apathetic but because they are rational and numerous. A single African American, for example, knows that he or she can make no difference in the success of the NAACP, just as a single nature enthusiast knows that he or she cannot enhance the power of the Sierra Club. Moreover, if the NAACP or the Sierra Club succeeds, African Americans and nature lovers will benefit even if they are not members. Therefore, rational people who value their time and money would no more join such organizations than they would attempt to empty a lake with a cup—unless they got something out of joining.

INCENTIVES TO JOIN

Every interest group faces a free rider problem. That is, many people who do not give it money or join as members are likely to benefit if the organization achieves its goal. They ride free on the organization's efforts. To overcome this, interest groups must offer people some **incentive** to join the group. There are three kinds.

Solidary incentives are the sense of pleasure, status, or companionship that arises out of meeting together in small groups. Such rewards are extremely

W.E.B. Du Bois, scholar and activist, was one of the founders of the NAACP.

C M Battey/Hulton Archive/Getty Images

Teachers organized by the National Education Association campaign for more money for public schools.

important, but because they tend to be available only from face-to-face contact, national interest groups offering them often have to organize themselves as coalitions of small local units. For example, the League of Women Voters, the Parent Teacher Association (PTA), the NAACP, the Rotary Club, and the American Legion all consist of small local chapters that support a national staff. It is the task of the local chapters to lure members and obtain funds from them; the state or national staff can then pursue political objectives by using these funds. Forming organizations made up of small local chapters is probably easier in the United States than in Europe because of the great importance of local government in our federal system. There is plenty for a PTA, an NAACP, or a League of Women Voters to do in its own community, and so its members can be kept busy with local affairs while the national staff pursues larger goals.

A second kind of incentive consists of **material incentives**—that is, money, or things and services readily valued in monetary terms. Farm

"If you still want to belong to an organization dedicated to killing Americans, there's always the tobacco lobby."

organizations have recruited many members by offering a wide range of services. The Illinois Farm Bureau, for example, offers to its members—and *only* to its members—a chance to buy farm supplies at discount prices, market their products through cooperatives, and purchase low-cost insurance. These material incentives help explain why the Illinois Farm Bureau has been able to enroll nearly every farmer in the state as well as many nonfarmers who also value these rewards.[10]

Similarly, the American Association of Retired Persons (AARP) has recruited over 30 million members by supplying them with everything from low-cost life insurance and mail-order discount drugs to tax advice and group travel plans. About 45 percent of the nation's population aged 50 and older—one out of every four registered voters—belongs to the AARP. With an annual operating budget of over $200 million and a cash flow estimated at a whopping $10 billion, the AARP seeks to influence public policy in many areas, from health and housing to taxes and transportation. To gain additional benefits for members, interest groups like the AARP also seek to influence how public laws are administered and who gets government grants. For example, the Environmental Protection Agency funds the AARP to hire senior citizens as temporary workers for various environmental projects.[11]

The third—and most difficult—kind of incentive is the *purpose* of the organization. Many associations rely chiefly on this **purposive incentive**—the appeal of their stated goals—to recruit members. If the attainment of those goals will also benefit people who do not join, individuals who do join will have to be those who feel passionately about the goal, who have a strong sense of duty (or who cannot say no to a friend who asks them to join), or for whom the cost of joining is so small that they are indifferent to joining or not. Organizations that attract members by appealing to their interest in a coherent set of (usually) controversial principles are sometimes called **ideological interest groups.**

incentive Something of value one cannot get without joining an organization.

solidary incentives The social rewards (sense of pleasure, status, or companionship) that lead people to join political organizations.

material incentives Money or things valued in monetary terms.

purposive incentive A benefit that comes from serving a cause or principle.

ideological interest groups Political organizations that attract members by appealing to their political convictions or principles.

Public-Interest Law Firms

A special kind of public-interest lobby is an organization that advances its cause by bringing lawsuits to challenge existing practices or proposed regulations. A public-interest law firm will act in one of two ways: First, it will find someone who has been harmed by some public or private policy and bring suit on his or her behalf. Second, it will file a brief with a court supporting somebody else's lawsuit (this is called an amicus curiae brief; it is explained in Chapter 16).

Here are some examples of liberal and conservative public-interest law firms:

Liberal	*Conservative*
American Civil Liberties Union	Atlantic Legal Foundation
Asian American Legal Defense Fund	The Center for Individual Rights
Lawyers' Committee for Civil Rights	Criminal Justice Legal Foundation
Mexican American Legal Defense Fund	Landmark Legal Foundation
NAACP Legal Defense and Education Fund	Mountain States Legal Foundation
Natural Resources Defense Council	Pacific Legal Foundation
Women's Legal Defense Fund	Washington Legal Foundation

public-interest lobby
A political organization whose goals will principally benefit nonmembers.

When the purpose of the organization, if attained, will principally benefit nonmembers, it is customary to call the group a **public-interest lobby.** (Whether the public at large will really benefit, of course, is a matter of opinion, but at least the group members think they are working selflessly for the common good.)

Though some public-interest lobbies may pursue relatively noncontroversial goals (for example, persuading people to vote or raising money to house orphans), the most visible of these organizations are highly controversial. It is precisely the controversy that attracts the members, or at least those members who support one side of the issue. Many of these groups can be described as markedly liberal or decidedly conservative in outlook.

Perhaps the best known of the liberal public-interest groups are those founded by or associated with Ralph Nader. Nader became a popular figure in the mid-1960s after General Motors made a clumsy attempt to investigate and discredit his background at a time when he was testifying in favor of an auto-safety bill. Nader won a large out-of-court settlement against General Motors, his books began to earn royalties, and he was able to command substantial lecture fees. Most of this money was turned over to various organizations he created that dealt with matters of interest to consumers. In addition, he founded a group called Public Citizen that raised money by direct-mail solicitation from thousands of small contributors and sought foundation grants. Finally, he helped create Public Interest Research Groups (PIRGs) in a number of states, supported by donations from college students (voluntary at some colleges, a compulsory assessment levied on all students at others) and concerned with organizing student activists to work on local projects.

Recently, cracks have begun to appear in the Nader movement. When Hawaii and California considered plans to develop no-fault automobile insurance, some former allies of Nader led the effort to reduce auto insurance prices by adopting a no-fault system. Nader denounced this effort and urged Hawaii's governor to veto the no-fault bill. Each side criticized the other.

Conservatives, though slow to get started, have also adopted the public-interest organizational strategy. As with such associations run by liberals, they are of two kinds: those that engage in research and lobbying and those that bring lawsuits designed to advance their cause. The boxes on this page and page 269 list

Think Tanks in Washington

Think tanks are public-interest organizations that do research on policy questions and disseminate their findings in books, articles, conferences, op-ed essays for newspapers, and (occasionally) testimony before Congress. Some are nonpartisan and ideologically more or less neutral, but others—and many of the most important ones—are aligned with liberal or conservative causes. Here are some examples of each:

Liberal

Center on Budget and Policy Priorities

Center for Defense Information

Children's Defense Fund

Economic Policy Institute

Institute for Policy Studies

Joint Center for Political and
   Economic Studies

Progressive Policy Institute

Conservative

American Enterprise Institute

Cato Institute

Center for Strategic and
   International Studies

Competitive Enterprise Institute

Ethics and Public Policy Center

Free Congress Foundation

Heritage Foundation

Note that the labels "liberal" and "conservative," while generally accurate, conceal important differences among the think tanks in each list.

---

some examples of public-interest organizations that support liberal or conservative causes.

Membership organizations that rely on purposive incentives, especially appeals to deeply controversial purposes, tend to be shaped by the mood of the times. When an issue is hot—in the media or with the public—such organizations can grow rapidly. When the spotlight fades, the organization may lose support. Thus, such organizations have a powerful motive to stay in the public eye. To remain visible, public-interest lobbies devote a lot of attention to generating publicity by developing good contacts with the media and issuing dramatic press releases about crises and scandals.

Because of their need to take advantage of a crisis atmosphere, public-interest lobbies often do best when the government is in the hands of an administration that is *hostile,* not sympathetic, to their views. Environmentalist organizations could mobilize more resources when James Watt, an opponent of much of the environmental movement, was secretary of the interior than they could when Cecil D. Andrus, his proenvironment predecessor, was in office. By the same token, many conservative interest groups were able to raise more money with the liberal Jimmy Carter or Bill Clinton in the White House than with the conservative Ronald Reagan or George W. Bush.

THE INFLUENCE OF THE STAFF

We often make the mistake of assuming that what an interest group does politically is simply to exert influence on behalf of its members. That is indeed the case when all the members have a clear and similar stake in an issue. But many issues affect different members differently. In fact, if the members joined to obtain solidary or material benefits, they may not care at all about many of the issues with which the organization gets involved. In such cases, what the interest group does may reflect more what the staff wants than what the members believe.

For example, a survey of the white members of a large labor union showed that one-third of them believed the desegregation of schools, housing, and job opportunities had gone too fast; only one-fifth thought it had gone too slowly. But among the staff members of the union, *none* thought desegregation had gone too fast, and over two-thirds thought it had gone too slowly.[12] As a result, the union staff aggressively lobbied Congress for the passage of tougher civil rights laws, even though most of the union's members did not feel they were needed. The members stayed in the union for reasons unrelated to civil rights, giving the staff the freedom to pursue its own goals.

Interest Groups and Social Movements

social movement A widely shared demand for change in some aspect of the social or political order.

Because it is difficult to attract people with purposive incentives, interest groups employing them tend to arise out of social movements. A **social movement** is a widely shared demand for change in some aspect of the social or political order. The civil rights movement of the 1960s was such an event, as was the environmentalist movement of the 1970s. A social movement need not have liberal goals. In the 19th century, for example, there were various nativist movements that sought to reduce immigration to this country or to keep Catholics or Masons out of public office. Broad-based religious revivals are social movements.

No one is quite certain why social movements arise. At one moment, people are largely indifferent to some issue; at another moment, many of these same people care passionately about religion, civil rights, immigration, or conservation. A social movement may be triggered by a scandal (an oil spill on the Santa Barbara beaches helped launch the environmental movement), the dramatic and widely publicized activities of a few leaders (lunch counter sit-ins helped stimulate the civil rights movement), or the coming of age of a new generation that takes up a cause advocated by eloquent writers, teachers, or evangelists.

THE ENVIRONMENTAL MOVEMENT

Whatever its origin, the effect of a social movement is to increase the value some people attach to purposive incentives. As a consequence, new interest groups are formed that rely on these incentives. In the 1890s, as a result of the emergence of conservation as a major issue, the Sierra Club was organized. In the 1930s, conservation once again became popular, and the Wilderness Society and the National Wildlife Federation took form. In the 1960s and 1970s, environmental issues again came to the fore, and we saw the emergence of the Environmental Defense Fund and Environmental Action.

The smallest of these organizations (Environmental Action and the Environmental Defense Fund) tend to

have the most liberal members. This often is the case with social movements. A movement will spawn many organizations. The most passionately aroused people will be the fewest in number, and they will gravitate toward the organizations that take the most extreme positions; as a result, these organizations are small but vociferous. The more numerous and less passionate people will gravitate toward more moderate, less vociferous organizations, which will tend to be larger.

THE FEMINIST MOVEMENT

There have been several feminist social movements in this country's history—in the 1830s, in the 1890s, in the 1920s, and in the 1960s. Each period brought new organizations, some of which have endured to the present. For example, the League of Women Voters was founded in 1920 to educate and organize women for the purpose of using effectively their newly won right to vote.

Though a strong sense of purpose may lead to the creation of organizations, each will strive to find some incentive that will sustain it over the long haul. These permanent incentives will affect how the organization participates in politics.

There are at least three kinds of feminist organizations. First, there are those that rely chiefly on solidary incentives, enroll middle-class women with relatively high levels of schooling, and tend to support those causes that command the widest support among women generally. The League of Women Voters and the Federation of Business and Professional Women are examples. Both supported the campaign to ratify the Equal Rights Amendment (ERA), but as Jane Mansbridge has observed in her history of the ERA, they were uneasy with the kind of intense, partisan fighting displayed by some

The Million Moms March in 2004 demanded a federal ban on assault weapons.

STACI MCKEE/AFP/Getty Images

other women's organizations and with the tendency of more militant groups to link the ERA to other issues, such as abortion. The reason for their uneasiness is clear: to the extent they relied on solidary incentives, they had a stake in avoiding issues and tactics that would divide their membership or reduce the extent to which membership provided camaraderie and professional contacts.[13]

Second, there are women's organizations that attract members with purposive incentives. The National Organization for Women (NOW) and the National Abortion Rights Action League (NARAL) are two of the largest such groups, though there are many smaller ones. Because they rely on purposes, these organizations must take strong positions, tackle divisive issues, and employ militant tactics. Anything less would turn off the committed feminists who make up the rank and file and contribute the funds. But because these groups take controversial stands, they are constantly embroiled in internal quarrels between those who think they have gone too far and those who think they have not gone far enough, between women who want NOW or NARAL to join with lesbian and socialist organizations and those who want them to steer clear. Moreover, as Mansbridge showed, purposive organizations often cannot make their decisions stick on the local level (local chapters will do pretty much as they please).[14]

The third kind of women's organization is the caucus that takes on specific issues that have some material benefit to women. The Women's Equity Action League (WEAL) is one such group. Rather than relying on membership dues for financial support, it obtains grants from foundations and government agencies. Freed of the necessity of satisfying a large rank-and-file membership, WEAL has concentrated its efforts on bringing lawsuits aimed at enforcing or enlarging the legal rights of women in higher education and other institutions. In electoral politics, the National Women's Political Caucus (officially nonpartisan, but generally liberal and Democratic) and the National Federation of Republican Women (openly supportive of the Republican party) work to get more women active in politics and more women elected or appointed to office.

The feminist movement has, of course, spawned an antifeminist movement, and thus feminist organizations have their antifeminist counterparts. The campaign by NOW for the ERA was attacked by a women's group called STOP ERA; the pro-choice position of NARAL has been challenged by the various organizations associated with the right-to-life movement. These opposition groups have their own tactical problems, which arise in large part from their reliance on

different kinds of incentives. In the chapter on civil rights, we shall see how the conflict between these opposing groups shaped the debate over the ERA.

THE UNION MOVEMENT

When social movements run out of steam, they leave behind organizations that continue the fight. But with the movement dead or dormant, the organizations often must struggle to stay alive. This has happened to labor unions.

The major union movement in this country occurred in the 1930s when the Great Depression, popular support, and a sympathetic administration in Washington led to a rapid growth in union membership. In 1945, union membership peaked; at that time, nearly 36 percent of all nonfarm workers were union members.

Since then, union membership has fallen more or less steadily. Today, only about 10 percent of all workers are covered by unions. Between 1983 and 2005, the number of union members fell by 2.2 million, and the number of people who, though not union members themselves, worked for organizations in which wages and labor conditions were set at least in part by agreements with unions fell by 3.3 million. This decline was caused by several factors. There has been a shift in the nation's economic life away from industrial production (where unions have traditionally been concentrated) and toward service delivery (where unions have usually been weak). But accompanying this decline, and perhaps contributing to it, has been a decline in popular approval of unions. Approval has moved down side by side with a decline in membership and declines in union victories in elections held to see whether workers in a plant want to join a union. The social movement that supported unionism has faded.

But unions will persist because most can rely on incentives other than purposive ones to keep them going. In many industries, they can require workers to join if they wish to keep their jobs, and in other industries workers believe they get sufficient benefits from the union to make even voluntary membership worthwhile. And in a few industries, such as teaching and government, there has been a growth in membership as some white-collar workers have turned to unions to advance their interests.

Unions composed of government workers are becoming the most important part of the union movement. They are almost the only part growing in size. Between 1983 and 2005, the number of private sector union members fell from 11.9 million to 8.2 million, but the number of public sector union members grew from 5.7 million to 7.4 million. Also, the most significant unions with respect to lobbying and campaigns are the public teachers' unions like the American Federation of Teachers and the National Education Association. Together, during the 2005–2006 election cycle, the PACs for these two groups contributed nearly $4 million to federal candidates, 95 percent of it to Democrats.

Funds for Interest Groups

All interest groups have some trouble raising money, but membership organizations have more trouble than most, especially membership organizations relying on appeals to purpose—to accomplishing stated goals. As a result, the Washington office of a public-interest lobbying group is likely to be small, stark, and crowded, whereas that of an institutional lobby, such as the AFL-CIO or the American Council on Education, will be rather lavish.

To raise more money than members supply in dues, lobbying organizations have turned to three sources that have become important in recent years: foundation grants, government grants, and direct-mail solicitation.

FOUNDATION GRANTS

One study of 83 (primarily liberal) public-interest lobbying groups found that one-third of them received half or more of all their funds from foundation grants; one-tenth received over 90 percent from such sources.[15] In one 10-year period, the Ford Foundation alone contributed about $21 million to liberal public-interest groups. Many of these organizations were law firms that, other than the staff lawyers, really had no members at all. The Environmental Defense Fund is supported almost entirely by grants from foundations such as the Rockefeller Family Fund. The more conservative Scaife foundations gave $1.8 million to a conservative public-interest group, the National Legal Center for the Public Interest.[16]

FEDERAL GRANTS AND CONTRACTS

The expansion of federal grants during the 1960s and 1970s benefited interest groups as well as cities and states; the cutbacks in those grants during the early 1980s hurt interest groups even more than they hurt local governments. Of course, the federal government usually does not give the money to support lobbying itself; it is given instead to support some project the organization has undertaken.

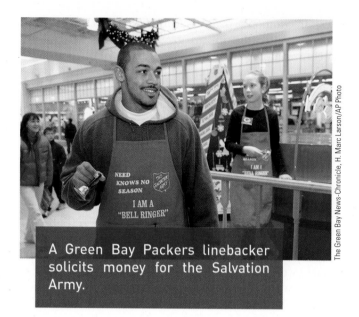

A Green Bay Packers linebacker solicits money for the Salvation Army.

The Green Bay News-Chronicle, H. Marc Larson/AP Photo

For example, many large national for-profit firms with trade representatives or other lobbyists in Washington (sometimes unflatteringly referred to as "beltway bandits") do most or all of their business by winning federal grants and contracts. Even large national religious nonprofit organizations such as Lutheran Social Services, Catholic Charities, the Salvation Army, and the Jewish Federations have received millions of dollars in government grants to provide diverse social services and run various community projects. But money for a service or project helps support the organization as a whole and thus enables the organization to press Congress for policies it favors (including, of course, policies that will supply it with more grants and contracts).

In the 1980s, the Reagan administration attempted to cut back on federal funds going to nonprofit groups that conservatives claimed also lobbied for liberal causes. Some writers called this an effort to "de-fund the left." In 2001, the Bush administration attempted to increase federal funds going to faith-based organizations. Some writers construed this as an effort to "fund the religious right." Neither effort, however, made a significant difference either in which organizations won or lost federal grants and contracts, or in how much federal money was available overall.

DIRECT MAIL

If there is any one technique unique to the modern interest group, it is the sophistication with which mailings are used both to raise money and to mobilize supporters. By using computers, membership interest groups can mail directly to specialized audiences identified from lists developed by the staff or purchased from other organizations. Letters can be tailor-made, for example, to appeal to upper-income residents of Oregon who belong to the Sierra Club, live near the Columbia River, own four-wheel-drive vehicles, and thus might be interested in maintaining a local wilderness area.

A classic example of an interest group created and maintained by direct-mail solicitation is Common Cause, a liberal organization founded in 1970. Its creator, John Gardner, sent letters to tens of thousands of people selected from mailing lists it had acquired, urging them to join the organization and to send in money. Over 200,000 members were obtained in this way, each of whom mailed in dues (initially $15 a year) in return for nothing more than the satisfaction of belonging.

But raising money by mail costs money—lots of money. To bring in more money than it spends, the interest group must write a letter that will galvanize enough readers to send in a check. "Enough" usually amounts to at least 2 percent of the names on the list. Techniques include the following:

- Have the endorsement of a famous name. For liberals, it was often Senator Kennedy; for conservatives, it may be former House Speaker Newt Gingrich.

- Personalize the letter by instructing the computer to insert the recipient's name into the text of the letter to create the impression it was written personally to him or her.

The Problem of Bias

Many observers believe interest groups active in Washington reflect an upper-class bias. There are two reasons for this belief: first, well-off people are more likely than poor people to join and be active in interest groups, and second, interest groups representing business and the professions are much more numerous and better financed than organizations representing minorities, consumers, or the disadvantaged.

Many scholars have shown that people with higher incomes, those whose schooling went through college or beyond, and those in professional or technical jobs were much more likely to belong to a voluntary association than people with the opposite characteristics. Just as we would expect, higher-income people can afford more organizational memberships than lower-income ones; people in business and the professions find it easier to attend meetings (they have more control over their own work schedules) and more necessary to do so than people in blue-collar jobs; and people with college degrees often have a

wider range of interests than those without. One study found that over half of the many thousand groups represented in Washington were corporations, and another third were professional and trade associations. Only 4 percent were public-interest groups; fewer than 2 percent were civil rights or minority groups.[17] About 170 organizations represented in Washington were concerned just with the oil industry.

But the question of an upper-class bias cannot be settled by these two facts taken alone. In the first place, they describe only certain *inputs* into the political system; they say nothing about the *outputs*—that is, who wins and who loses on particular issues. Even if 170 interest groups are trying to protect the oil industry, this is important only if the oil industry in fact gets protected. Sometimes it does; sometimes it does not. At one time, when oil prices were low, oil companies were able to get Congress to pass a law that sharply restricted the importation of foreign oil. A few years later, after oil prices had risen and people were worried about energy issues, these restrictions were ended.

In the second place, business-oriented interest groups often are divided among themselves. Take one kind of business: farming. Once, farm organizations seemed so powerful in Washington that scholars spoke of an irresistible "farm bloc" in Congress that could get its way on almost anything. Today, dozens of agricultural organizations operate in the capital, with some (such as the Farm Bureau) attempting to speak for all farmers and others (such as the Tobacco

Farmers once had great influence in Congress and could get their way with a few telephone calls. Today, they often must use mass protest methods.

Institute and Mid-America Dairymen) representing particular commodities and regions.

Whenever American politics is described as having an upper-class bias, it is important to ask exactly what this bias is. Most of the major conflicts in American politics—over foreign policy, economic affairs, environmental protection, or equal rights for women—are conflicts *within* the upper middle class; they are conflicts, that is, among politically active elites. As we saw in Chapter 7, there are profound cleavages of opinion among these elites. Interest group activity reflects these cleavages.

Nonetheless, it would be a mistake to ignore the over-representation of business in Washington. A student of politics should always take differences in the availability of political resources as an important clue to possible differences in the outcomes of political conflicts. But they are only clues, not conclusions.

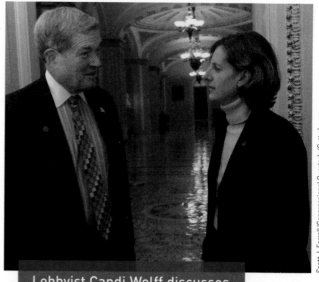

Lobbyist Candi Wolff discusses public policy with Senator Christopher S. Bond (R-MO).

The Activities of Interest Groups

Size and wealth are no longer entirely accurate measures of an interest group's influence—if indeed they ever were. Depending on the issue, the key to political influence may be the ability to generate a dramatic newspaper headline, mobilize a big letter-writing campaign, stage a protest demonstration, file a suit in federal court to block (or compel) some government action, or quietly supply information to key legislators. All of these things require organization, but only some of them require big or expensive organizations.

INFORMATION

Of all these tactics, the single most important one—in the eyes of virtually every lobbyist and every academic student of lobbying—is supplying credible information. The reason why information is so valuable is that, to busy legislators and bureaucrats, information is in short supply. Legislators in particular must take positions on a staggering number of issues about which they cannot possibly become experts.

Though there are nonpolitical sources of information, such as encyclopedias, they often do not provide the kind of detailed, specific, up-to-date information that politicians need. This kind of information will ordinarily be gathered only by a group that has a strong interest in some issue. Lobbyists, for the most part, are not flamboyant, party-giving arm-twisters; they are specialists who gather information (favorable to their clients, naturally) and

present it in as organized, persuasive, and factual a manner as possible. All lobbyists no doubt exaggerate, but few can afford to misrepresent the facts or mislead a legislator, and for a very simple reason: almost every lobbyist must develop and maintain the confidence of a legislator over the long term, with an eye on tomorrow's issues as well as today's. Misrepresentation or bad advice can embarrass a legislator who accepts it or repel one who detects it, leading to distrust of the lobbyist. Maintaining contacts and channels of communication is vital; to that end, maintaining trust is essential.

The value of the information provided by a lobbyist often is greatest when the issue is fairly narrow, involving only a few interest groups or a complex economic or technical problem. The value of information, and thus the power of the lobbyist, is likely to be least when the issue is one of broad and highly visible national policy.

Sometimes the nature of an issue or the governmental process by which an issue is resolved gives a great advantage to the suppliers of certain information and imposes a great burden on would-be suppliers of contrary information. This is an example of "client politics." For example, the Civil Aeronautics Board (CAB) once set airline fares and decided what airlines would fly to what cities. Historically, the only organizations with any incentive to appear before the CAB and supply the necessary information were, naturally, the airlines. Until the CAB began to deregulate civil aviation, CAB decisions often tended to favor the established airlines.

Scott J. Ferrell/Congressional Quarterly/Getty Images

Public officials not only want technical information, they also want political cues. A **political cue** is a signal telling the official what values are at stake in an issue—who is for, who against a proposal—and how that issue fits into his or her own set of political beliefs. Some legislators feel comfortable when they are on the liberal side of an issue, and others feel comfortable when they are on the conservative side, especially when they are not familiar with the details of the issue. A liberal legislator will look to see whether the AFL-CIO, the NAACP, the Americans for Democratic Action, the Farmers' Union, and various consumer organizations favor a proposal; if so, that is often all he or she has to know. If these liberal groups are split, then the legislator will worry about the matter and try to look into it more closely. Similarly, a conservative legislator will feel comfortable taking a stand on an issue if the Chamber of Commerce, the National Rifle Association, the American Medical Association, various business associations, and Americans for Constitutional Action are in agreement about it; he or she will feel less comfortable if such conservative groups are divided. As a result of this process, lobbyists often work together in informal coalitions based on general political ideology.

One important way in which these cues are made known is by **ratings** that interest groups make of legislators. These are regularly compiled by the AFL-CIO (on who is prolabor), by the Americans for Democratic Action (on who is liberal), by the Americans for Constitutional Action (on who is conservative), by the Consumer Federation of America (on who is proconsumer), and by the League of Conservation Voters (on who is pro-environment). These ratings are designed to generate public support for (or opposition to) various legislators. They can be helpful sources of information, but they are sometimes biased by the arbitrary determination of what constitutes a liberal, proconsumer, or conservative vote.

Both political information and political cues now arrive in the offices of politicians at a faster rate than ever before, thanks to fax machines and the Internet. Many interest groups and political activists have banks of computer-operated fax machines that can get a short, snappy document into the hands of every legislator within minutes. William Kristol, a Republican activist, used this technique to good effect in 1993 when he bombarded Republican members of Congress with arguments concerning why they should oppose President Clinton's health care plan. Many believe he played a major role in the defeat of that plan.

EARMARKS

Information can be linked to influence. Lobbyists not only tell members of Congress facts, they learn from these members what Washington is doing and then look for ways to sell that information to their clients. What often results is an **earmark**, that is, a provision in a law that provides a direct benefit to a client without the benefit having been reviewed on the merits by all of Congress.

political cue A signal telling a legislator what values are at stake in a vote, and how that issue fits into his or her own political views on party agenda.

ratings Assessments of a representative's voting record on issues important to an interest group.

Earmarks have always existed but they became much more common in the 1970s and later. There were two reasons for this. First, the federal government was doing much more and thus affecting more parts of the society. Second, lobbying organizations figured out they could sell to their clients information about how to convert some bit of federal activity to their benefit.

One recent study showed how a new kind of lobbying firm was born. Cassidy and Associates prospered by helping clients get earmarks. The firm charged a flat fee ($10,000 or more per month) and devoted its energy to studying congressional laws to find opportunities for its clients. [18]

Its first big client was a university that wanted federal money to pay for a nutrition center it hoped to build. The Cassidy firm discovered that Congress had authorized a "national" nutrition center and then set about persuading key congressional leaders that such a center should be located at the university that was paying Cassidy a fee. Soon many more universities pushed for earmarks for their pet ideas (a foreign service school, defense software institutes, and computer centers). Not long after that, business firms joined the hunt.

In 2008, the Office of Management and Budget estimated that more than 11,000 earmarks had been approved by Congress at a cost of more than $16 billion. Soon a movement started among some legislators to stop earmarks. But they faced a problem. Many members of Congress think earmarks are good: why should only the president or congressional committees decide on what things Congress should spend its money? Why not let individual legislators do good things for their constituents?

To balance these competing views, one could try to tell the difference between a good and a bad earmark. Is a university nutrition center a good thing but a study on wood utilization a bad one? Is a computer center desirable but a bridge to a (largely) uninhabited island in Alaska a bad one? There is no easy way to make these judgments, and so earmarks continue to thrive in Washington. Interest groups suggest ways legislators can help people who vote for them.

PUBLIC SUPPORT: THE RISE OF THE NEW POLITICS

Once upon a time, when the government was small, Congress was less individualistic, and television was nonexistent, lobbyists mainly used an *insider strategy:* they worked closely with a few key members of Congress, meeting them privately to exchange information and (sometimes) favors. Matters of mutual interest could be discussed at a leisurely pace, over dinner or while playing golf. Public opinion was important on some highly visible issues, but there were not many of these.

Following an insider strategy is still valuable, but increasingly interest groups have turned to an *outsider strategy*. The newly individualistic nature of Congress has made this tactic useful, and modern technology has made it possible. Radio, fax machines, and the Internet can now get news out almost immediately. Satellite television can be used to link interested citizens in various locations across the country. Toll-free phone numbers can be publicized, enabling voters to call the offices of their members of Congress without charge. Public opinion polls can be done by telephone, virtually overnight, to measure (and help generate) support for or opposition to proposed legislation. Mail can be directed by computers to people already known to have an interest in a particular matter.

This kind of *grassroots lobbying* is central to the outsider strategy. It is designed to generate public pressure directly on government officials. The "public" that exerts this pressure is not every voter or even most voters; it is that part of the public (sometimes called an *issue public*) directly affected by or deeply concerned with a government policy. What modern technology has made possible is the overnight mobilization of specific issue publics.

Not every issue lends itself to an outsider strategy: it is hard to get many people excited about, for example, complex tax legislation affecting only a few firms. But as the government does more and more, its policies affect more and more people, and so more and more will join in grassroots lobbying efforts over matters such as abortion, Medicare, Social Security, environmental protection, and affirmative action.

Undoubtedly, the new politics creates new conflicts. Since conflict is the essence of politics, it may seem strange that politicians dislike controversy. But they do, and for perfectly human reasons: no one enjoys dealing with people who are upset or who find one's viewpoint objectionable or unworthy. Consequently, most legislators tend to hear what they want to hear and deal with interest groups that agree with them.[19] Two senators from the same state may choose to listen to very different constituencies in that state and to take very different policy positions. Neither senator may feel "pressured" or "lobbied," because each has heard mostly from groups or persons who share his or her views. (Politicians define "pressure" as arguments and inducements supplied by somebody with whom they disagree.)

Members of an interest group will also tend to work primarily with legislators with whom they agree; lobbyists do not like to argue with people who are suspicious of them or who are unlikely to change their minds no matter what is said. For the lobbyist, the key target is the undecided or wavering legislator or bureaucrat. Sometimes lobbyists will make a major effort to persuade an undecided legislator that public opinion is strongly inclined in one direction. A lobbyist will do this by commissioning public opinion polls, stimulating local citizens to write letters or send telegrams, arranging for constituents to pay personal visits to the legislator, or getting newspapers to run editorials supporting the lobbyist's position.

Though most lobbying organizations cultivate the goodwill of government officials, there are important exceptions. Some groups, especially those that use an ideological appeal to attract supporters or that depend for their maintenance and influence on media publicity, will deliberately attack actual or potential allies in government in order to embarrass them. Ralph Nader is as likely to denounce as to praise those officials who tend to agree with him, if their agreement is not sufficiently close or public. He did this with Senator Edmund Muskie, the author of the Clean Air Act, and with William Haddon, Jr., an early administrator of the National Highway Traffic Safety Administration. The head of the Fund for Animals is not reluctant to attack those officials in the Forest Service and the Interior Department on whose cooperation the fund must rely if it is to achieve its goals.[20] Sometimes, as we shall see later in this chapter, the use of threats instead of rewards extends to physical confrontations.

Of late, interest groups have placed great emphasis on developing grassroots support. Sometimes it is impossible to develop such support, as when a complicated tax regulation of interest to only a few firms is changed. But sometimes a proposed bill touches a public nerve such that even businesses can help generate an outpouring of mail: when the Food and Drug Administration announced it was going to ban saccharin on the grounds that it caused cancer in laboratory animals, the Calorie Control Council (closely tied to the Coca-Cola Company, a big user of saccharin in soft drinks such as Tab) ran newspaper ads denouncing the policy. The public, worried about losing access to an artificial sweetener important to dieters, responded with an avalanche of mail to Congress, which promptly passed a law reversing the ban.

The press sometimes depicts certain large, well-funded interest groups as all-powerful, but few are. Take, for example, the National Rifle Association (NRA). Founded in 1871 as a group dedicated to shooting instruction, the NRA in the 1960s and 1970s became a lobby opposing policies that would restrict citizens' rights to own and use firearms for sporting and other legal purposes. By the 1980s, the NRA's dues-paying membership had increased from 1 million to nearly 3 million. Its members receive magazines, decals, and other direct benefits. From 1983 to 1992, the NRA spent $8 million on congressional races both in direct contributions to their favored candidates and in independent expenditures supporting or opposing various candidates. Still, in the mid-1990s, the NRA lost a major battle to repeal New Jersey's ban on certain types of semiautomatic weapons and lost similar battles in Connecticut, Virginia, and other states. In 1993, over fierce opposition from the NRA, Congress passed the Brady bill, a major piece of gun control legislation named after Jim Brady, the press secretary who was shot and permanently disabled during an attempt to assassinate President Reagan. By the late 1990s, the NRA had a negative image even among most gun owners, and the organization found itself constantly in the political crosshairs of small but media-savvy pro-gun control lobbies such as Handgun Control, Inc. As the NRA's recent history teaches, in American politics no interest group, no matter how big its budget or mammoth its membership, is a lobby that cannot be beat.

MONEY AND PACS

Contrary to popular suspicions, money is probably one of the less effective ways by which interest groups advance their causes. That was not always the case. Only a few decades ago, powerful interests used their bulging wallets to buy influence in Congress. The passage of the campaign finance reform law in 1973 changed that. The law had two effects. First, it sharply restricted the amount any interest could give to a candidate for federal office (see Chapter 10).

Second, it made it legal for organizations to create political action committees (PACs) that could make political contributions. A PAC is an organization created by a business firm, labor union, trade association, or ideological group that recruits members from whom it obtains campaign contributions. There are strict limits on how much a member can contribute and how much the PAC can give to candidates and parties. How they work is shown in Figure 11.2.

Once PACs became legal, they grew rapidly in numbers. By 1993, there were six times as many as there had been in 1975. In 2008, there were more than 4,000; in the 2003–2004 election cycle, they gave more than $300 million to candidates running for the House and Senate.

Some people worry that the existence of all this political money has resulted in our having, as Senator Edward Kennedy put it, "the finest Congress that money can buy." More likely, the increase in the number of PACs has had just the opposite effect. The reason is simple: with PACs so numerous and so easy to form, it is now probable that money will be available on every side of almost every conceivable issue. As a result, members of Congress can take money and still decide for themselves how to vote. As we shall see, there is not much scholarly evidence that money buys votes in Congress.

Indeed, some members of Congress tell PACs what to do rather than take orders from them. Members will frequently inform PACs that they "expect" money from them; grumbling PAC officials feel they have no choice but to contribute for fear of alienating the members. Moreover, some members have created their *own* PACs—organizations set up to raise money from individual donors that is then given to favored political allies in and out of Congress or used to advance the members' own political ambitions. When Charles Rangel, congressman from New York, was hoping to be elected whip of the Democratic party in the House, he set up a PAC that made campaign contributions to fellow representatives in hopes that they might vote for him as whip. There are many other examples from both sides of the aisle. An ironic consequence of this is that a conservative Republican may give money to a PAC set up by a moderate Democrat, who then gives the money to a liberal Democrat (or vice versa), with the result that the original donor winds up having his or her money go to somebody that he or she profoundly dislikes.

Almost any kind of organization—corporation, labor union, trade association, public-interest lobby, citizens group—can form a PAC. Over half of all PACs are sponsored by corporations, about a tenth

Figure 11.2
Political Action Committees (PACs)

Can be formed by:

- Business firms
- Labor unions
- Trade associations
- Ideological organizations

Must have at least 50 individual members

- Each member can give up to $5,000 per election
- The sponsoring firm, union, association, or ideological group cannot contribute money

Each PAC may contribute:

- $5,000 to any federal candidate in any election (must give to at least five candidates)
- $15,000 to any national political party
- $5,000 to any state or local party

Where the money goes:

- Business PACs give slightly more to Republicans than to Democrats
- Labor unions give more than 90 percent to Democrats
- Ideological PACs give to Democrats and Republicans in about equal amounts

by labor unions, and the rest by various groups, including ideological ones.

The rise of ideological PACs has been the most remarkable development in interest group activity in recent years. They have increased in number at a faster rate than business or labor PACs, and in several elections they raised more money than either business or labor. One study calculated more than one thousand ideological PACs; about one-third were liberal, about two-thirds conservative.[21]

Though the ideological PACs raised more money than business or labor ones, they spent less on campaigns and gave less to candidates. The reason for this anomaly is that an ideological PAC usually has to raise its money by means of massive direct-mail solicitations, expensive efforts that can consume all the money raised, and more. By contrast, a typical business or labor PAC solicits money from within a single corporation or union. Even a well-run ideological PAC must spend 50 cents to raise a dollar; some spend much more than that.[22]

Of the 10 PACs that gave the most money to candidates in the 2004 election, most were labor unions, business organizations, and groups that represented doctors, lawyers, realtors, and government employees. Incumbents received more PAC money than challengers. Labor PACs gave almost exclusively to Democrats. Business PACs favored Republicans.

Both parties have become dependent on PAC money. Still, the popular image of rich PACs stuffing huge sums into political campaigns and thereby buying the attention and possibly the favors of the grateful candidates is a bit overdrawn. For one thing, the typical PAC contribution is rather small. The average PAC donation to a House candidate is only a few hundred dollars. Most PACs spread small sums of money over many candidates, and despite their great growth in numbers and expenditures, PACs still provide only about one-third of all the money spent by candidates for the House.[23]

Moreover, scholars have yet to find systematic evidence that PAC contributions generally affect how members of Congress vote. On most issues, how legislators vote can be explained primarily by their general ideological outlooks and the characteristics of their constituents; how much PAC money they have received turns out to be a small factor. On the other hand, when an issue arises in which most of their constituents have no interest and ideology provides little guidance, there is a slight statistical correlation between PAC contributions and votes. But even here the correlation may be misleading. The same groups that give money also wage intensive lobbying campaigns, flooding representatives with information, press releases, and letters from interested constituents. These studies may be measuring the effect of persuasive arguments, not dollars; no one can be certain.[24]

It is possible that money affects legislative behavior in ways that will never appear in studies of roll-call votes in Congress. Members of Congress may be more willing to set aside time in their busy schedules for a group that has given money than for a group that has not. What the money has bought is access: it has helped open the door. Or contributions might influence how legislators behave on the committees on which they serve, subtly shaping the way in which they respond to arguments and the facts on which they rely. No one knows, because the research has not been done.

In any event, if interest group money makes a difference at all, it probably makes it on certain kinds of issues more than others. In the chapter on policymaking we define the kind of issues—we call them "client politics"—on which a given interest group is likely to be especially influential, whether by means of arguments, money, or both. After reading that chapter and considering the examples given there, it will be easier to put the present discussion of PAC money into context.

THE "REVOLVING DOOR"

Every year, hundreds of people leave important jobs in the federal government to take more lucrative positions in private industry. Some go to work as lobbyists, others as consultants to business, still others as key executives in corporations, foundations, and universities. Many people worry that this "revolving door" may give private interests a way of improperly influencing government decisions. If a federal official uses his or her government position to do something for a corporation in exchange for a cushy job after leaving government, or if a person who has left government uses his or her personal contacts in Washington to get favors for private parties, then the public interest may suffer.

From time to time, certain incidents seem to confirm these fears. Michael K. Deaver, former deputy chief of staff in the Reagan White House, was convicted of perjury in connection with a grand jury investigation of his having used his former government contacts to help the clients of his public relations firm. Lyn Nofziger, a former Reagan White House aide, was convicted of violating the Ethics in Government Act by lobbying the White House, soon after he left it, on behalf of various businesses and labor unions. In Chapter 15, we will have more to say about more innocent, if no less costly, bureaucratic dysfunctions related to contracting.

How Things Work

Conflict of Interest

In 1978, a new federal law, the Ethics in Government Act, codified and broadened the rules governing possible conflicts of interest among senior members of the executive branch. The key provisions were as follows.

The president, vice president, and top-ranking (GS-16 and above) executive branch employees must each year file a public financial disclosure report that lists:

- The source and amount of all earned income as well as income from stocks, bonds, and property; the worth of any investments or large debts; and the source of a spouse's income, if any

- Any position held in business, labor, or certain nonprofit organizations

Employment after government service is restricted. Former executive branch employees may *not:*

- Represent anyone before their former agencies in connection with any matter that the former employees had been involved in before leaving the government

- Appear before an agency, for two years after leaving government service, on matters that came within the former employees' official sphere of responsibility, even if they were not personally involved in the matter

- Represent anyone on any matter before their former agencies, for one year after leaving them, even if the former employees had no connection with the matter while in the government

In addition, another law prohibits bribery. It is illegal to ask for, solicit, or receive anything of value in return for being influenced in the performance of one's duties.

Finally, an executive order forbids outside employment. An official may not hold a job or take a fee, even for lecturing or writing, if such employment or income might create a conflict of interest or an apparent conflict of interest.

Sources: *National Journal* (November 19, 1977): 1796–1803; *Congressional Quarterly Weekly Report* (October 28, 1978): 3121–3127.

How systematic is this pattern of abuse? We don't know. Studies of the revolving door in federal regulatory agencies have found no clear pattern of officials' tilting their decisions in hopes of landing a lucrative business job.[25] Over the years, more than a few scandals took place concerning corrupt dealings between federal department officials and industry executives. Many have involved contractors or their consultants bribing procurement officials. Far more common, however, have been major breakdowns in the procurement process itself. For example, in 2006, the Department of Homeland Security revealed the results from an internal audit.[26] In the previous year, the department had spent $17.5 billion on contracts for airport security, radiation-monitor detectors, and other goods and services. But records for nearly three dozen contracts were completely missing, and records for many other contracts lacked evidence that the department had followed federal rules in negotiating best prices. (The internal audit itself was performed by private consultants, presumably in compliance with all relevant rules.)

Agencies differ in their vulnerability to outside influences. If the Food and Drug Administration is not vigilant, people in that agency who help decide whether a new drug should be placed on the market may have their judgment affected somewhat by the possibility that, if they approve the drug, the pharmaceutical company that makes it will later offer them a lucrative position.

On the other hand, lawyers in the Federal Trade Commission who prosecute businesses that violate the antitrust laws may decide that their chances for getting a good job with a private law firm later on will increase if they are particularly vigorous and effective prosecutors. The firm, after all, wants to hire competent people, and winning a case is a good test of competence.[27]

CIVIL DISOBEDIENCE

Public displays and disruptive tactics—protest marches, sit-ins, picketing, and violence—have always been a part of American politics. Indeed, they were among the favorite tactics of the American colonists seeking independence in 1776.

Both ends of the political spectrum have used display, disruption, and violence. On the left feminists, antislavery agitators, coal miners, autoworkers, welfare mothers, African Americans, antinuclear power groups, public housing tenants, the American Indian Movement, the Students for a

Lawsuits, such as this one against Proposition 8 which banned same sex marriage in California, are often more effective than protest demonstrations in changing policies.

Fred Prouser/Reuters/Landov

Democratic Society, and the Weather Underground have created "trouble" ranging from peaceful sit-ins at segregated lunch counters to bombings and shootings. On the right, the Ku Klux Klan has used terror, intimidation, and murder; parents opposed to forced busing of schoolchildren have demonstrated; business firms have used strong-arm squads against workers; right-to-life groups have blockaded abortion clinics; and an endless array of "anti-" groups (anti-Catholics, anti-Masons, anti-Jews, anti-immigrants, antisaloons, antiblacks, antiprotesters, and probably even anti-antis) have taken their disruptive turns on stage. These various activities are not morally the same—a sit-in demonstration is quite different from a lynching—but politically they constitute a similar problem for a government official.

An explanation of why and under what circumstances disruption occurs is beyond the scope of this book. To understand interest group politics, however, it is important to remember that making trouble has, since the 1960s, become a quite conventional political resource and is no longer simply the last resort of extremist groups. Making trouble is now an accepted political tactic of ordinary middle-class citizens as well as the disadvantaged or disreputable.

There is of course a long history of the use of disruptive methods by "proper" people. In a movement that began in England at the turn of the century and then spread here, feminists would chain themselves to lampposts or engage in what we now call "sit-ins" as part of a campaign to win the vote for women. The object then was much the same as the object of similar tactics today: to disrupt the working of some institution so that it is forced to negotiate with you, or, failing that, to enlist the sympathies of third parties (the media, other interest groups) who will come to your aid and press your target to negotiate with you, or, failing that, to goad the police into making attacks and arrests so that martyrs are created.

The civil rights and antiwar movements of the 1960s gave experience in these methods to thousands of young people and persuaded others of the effectiveness of such methods under certain conditions. Though these movements have abated or disappeared, their veterans and emulators have put such tactics to new uses—trying to block the construction of a nuclear power plant, for example, or occupying the office of a cabinet secretary to obtain concessions for a particular group.

Government officials dread this kind of trouble. They usually find themselves in a no-win situation. If they ignore the disruption, they are accused of being "insensitive," "unresponsive," or "arrogant." If they give in to the demonstrators, they encourage more demonstrations by proving that this is a useful tactic. If they call the police, they run the risk of violence and injuries, followed not only by bad publicity but by lawsuits.

Regulating Interest Groups

Interest group activity is a form of political speech protected by the First Amendment to the Constitution: it cannot lawfully be abolished or even much curtailed. In 1946, Congress passed the Federal Regulation of Lobbying Act, which requires groups and individuals seeking to influence legislation to register with the secretary of the Senate and the clerk of the House and to file quarterly financial reports. The Supreme Court upheld the law but restricted its application to lobbying efforts involving direct contacts with members of Congress.[28] More general "grassroots" interest group activity may not be restricted by the government. The 1946 law had little practical effect. Not all lobbyists took the trouble to register, and there was no guarantee that the financial statements were accurate. There was no staff in charge of enforcing the law.

After years of growing popular dissatisfaction with Congress, prompted in large measure by the (exaggerated) view that legislators were the pawns of powerful special interests, Congress in late 1995 unanimously passed a bill that tightened up the registration and disclosure requirements. Signed by the president, the law restated the obligation of lobbyists to register with the House and Senate, but it broadened the definition of a lobbyist to include the following:

- People who spend at least 20 percent of their time lobbying
- People who are paid at least $5,000 in any six-month period to lobby
- Corporations and other groups that spend more than $20,000 in any six-month period on their own lobbying staffs

The law covered people and groups who lobbied the executive branch and congressional staffers as well as elected members of Congress, and it included law firms that represent clients before the government. Twice a year, all registered lobbyists were required to report the following:

- The names of their clients
- Their income and expenditures
- The issues on which they worked

The registration and reporting requirements did not, however, extend to so-called grassroots organizations—that is, campaigns (sometimes led by volunteers, sometimes by hired professionals) to mobilize citizens to write or call the government about some issue. Nor was any new enforcement organization created, although congressional officials may refer violations to the Justice Department for investigation. Fines for breaking the law could amount to $50,000. In addition, the law barred tax-exempt, nonprofit advocacy groups that lobby from getting federal grants.

Just as the Republicans moved expeditiously to pass new regulations on interest groups and lobbying when they regained majorities in Congress in the November 1994 elections, the Democrats' first order of business after retaking Congress in the November 2006 elections was to adopt sweeping reforms. Beginning March 1, 2007, many new regulations took effect, including the following:

- No gifts of any value from registered lobbyists or firms that employ lobbyists
- No reimbursement for travel costs from registered lobbyists or firms that employ lobbyists

WHAT WOULD YOU DO?

MEMORANDUM

To: *Kathleen Moore, Senate majority leader*

From: *Christopher Franklin, chief of staff*

Subject: *Full federal financing of presidential campaigns*

Every presidential election since 1976 has been financed in part by federal funds. Now presidential candidates say they will forego public funding for the general election, given the vastly greater resources available through private fund-raising. Congress needs to decide whether elections are a publicinvestment or a political free market for citizens and candidates.

Arguments for:

1. Legal precedents are promising. Federal matching funds already go to presidential primary candidates who have raised at least $5,000, in contributions of $250 or less, in each of twenty states. For the general election, each major party nominee already is eligible for federal funding if he or she agrees to spend no more than that amount.

2. The funding required would be small. Allocating $1 billion out of the public treasury for a presidential election every four years is hardly a fiscal drain on a nearly $2 trillion annual budget.

3. The effects would be pervasive. Candidates and party leaders would stop covertly courting big donors with phone calls, lunches, and personal visits, and would focus instead on the needs of average citizens.

Arguments against:

1. Constitutional precedent for requiring political candidates to accept public fundsis weak. In *Buckley v. Valeo* (1976), the Supreme Court upheld limits on campaign contributions for candidates who accept public money, but it also defined spending money for political purposes as expression protected by the First Amendment, thereby giving individuals

---

Friday,

Bipartisan Group in Senate Proposes Full Public Financing of Presidential Campaigns

February 15
WASHINGTON, D.C.

With the upcoming presidential election expected to cost more than $1 billion, a bipartisan group of senators has proposed that Congress control those expenses by fully funding and setting an upperlimit on financing for presidential campaigns. Presidential contendes so far have refrained from taking a position on the legislation…

---

the right to raise and spend as much of their own money as they choose, if they forego federal funds.

2. Campaign spending would soon spiral once again. The federal government may not restrict spending by individuals or organizations working independently from the political parties, and federal funds would merely supplement, not supplant, private fund-raising.

3. Less than 10 percent of taxpayers currently supports public financing through voluntary federal income tax checkoffs, and voters likely would view bankrolling elections as serving politicians, not the people.

Your decision:

Support legislation _____   Oppose legislation _____

- No reimbursement for travel costs, no matter the source, if the trip is in any part organized or requested by a registered lobbyist or firm that employs lobbyists

Strictly speaking, these and related new rules mean that a House member cannot go on a "fact-finding" trip to a local site or a foreign country and have anyone associated with lobbying arrange to pay for it. Even people who are not themselves registered lobbyists, but who work for a lobbying firm, are not permitted to take members of Congress to lunch or give them any other "thing of value," no matter how small.

But, if past experience is any guide, "strictly speaking" is not how the rules will be followed or enforced. For instance, buried in the new rules' fine print are provisions that permit members of Congress to accept reimbursement for travel from lobbyists if the travel is for "one-day trips," so long as the lobbyists themselves do not initiate the trip, make the reservations, or pick up incidental expenses unrelated to the visit. Moreover, these rules have not yet been adopted in precisely the same form by the Senate; and neither chamber had yet clarified language or closed loopholes related to lobbying registration and reporting.

Do not suppose, however, that such remaining gaps in lobbying laws render the system wide open to abuses or evasions. For one thing, loopholes and all, the lobbying laws are now tighter than ever. For another, as we intimated earlier in this chapter, the most significant legal constraints on interest groups come not from the current federal lobbying law (though that may change) but from the tax code and the campaign finance laws. A nonprofit organization—which includes not only charitable groups but almost all voluntary associations that have an interest in politics—need not pay income taxes, and financial contributions to it can be deducted on the donor's income tax return, provided that the organization does not devote a "substantial part" of its activities to "attempting to influence legislation."[29] Many tax-exempt organizations do take public positions on political questions and testify before congressional committees. If the organization does any serious lobbying, however, it will lose its tax-exempt status (and thus find it harder to solicit donations and more expensive to operate). Exactly this happened to the Sierra Club in 1968 when the Internal Revenue Service revoked its tax-exempt status because of its extensive lobbying activities. Some voluntary associations try to deal with this problem by setting up separate organizations to collect tax-exempt money—for example, the NAACP, which lobbies, must pay taxes, but the NAACP Legal Defense and Education Fund, which does not lobby, is tax-exempt.

Finally, the campaign finance laws, described in detail in Chapter 10, limit to $5,000 the amount any political action committee can spend on a given candidate in a given election. These laws have sharply curtailed the extent to which any *single* group can give money, though they have increased the *total* amount that different groups are providing.

Beyond making bribery or other manifestly corrupt forms of behavior illegal and restricting the sums that campaign contributors can donate, there is probably no system for controlling interest groups that would both make a useful difference and leave important constitutional and political rights unimpaired. Ultimately, the only remedy for imbalances or inadequacies in interest group representation is to devise and sustain a political system that gives all affected parties a reasonable chance to be heard on matters of public policy. That, of course, is exactly what the Founders thought they were doing. Whether they succeeded or not is a question to which we shall return at the end of this book.

SUMMARY

Interest groups in the United States are more numerous and more fragmented than those in nations such as Great Britain, where the political system is more centralized. The goals and tactics of interest groups reflect not only the interests of their members but also the size of the groups, the incentives with which they attract supporters, and the role of their professional staffs. The chief source of interest group influence is information; public support, money, and the ability to create "trouble" are also important. The right to lobby is protected by the Constitution, but the tax and campaign finance laws impose significant restrictions on how money may be used.

RECONSIDERING WHO GOVERNS?

1. Do interest groups dominate government, and is any particular lobby politically unbeatable?

The answers are "not really" and "no," respectively. There are so many governmental institutions in which power may be exercised that no single group can dominate most public policy decisions. What the government does is often the outcome of a complex pattern of political haggling, innumerable compromises, and shifting alliances among and between different groups and their leaders. Even supposedly all-powerful lobbies (like the National Rifle Association [NRA] on gun control, or the American Association of Retired Persons [AARP] on senior citizens' health care benefits) sometimes find themselves on the losing side of legislative decisions and court opinions.

2. Why do people join interest groups?

Pretty much for the same basic reasons that people join any organization. There are three kinds of incentives: solidary, material, and purposive. Organizations, including interest groups, can attract members through one, two, or all three incentives. Some interest groups rely mainly on one incentive. For example, ideological political action committees (PACs) rely largely on purposive incentives, attracting members by appealing to their beliefs in a coherent set of principles or their passions on a particular set of issues. Even these groups, however, normally provide their members with certain tangible, members-only benefits (for example, magazines or special discounts on various products). Organizations that principally benefit nonmembers are sometimes called public-interest lobbies.

RECONSIDERING TO WHAT ENDS?

1. Is the proliferation of political action committees (PACs) and other groups good or bad for America's representative democracy?

What would James Madison say? Go back to the Appendix and *Federalist* No. 10. Madison recognized that freedom begat factions, but he hoped that the government proposed under the Constitution would succeed in "regulating these various and interfering interests" in ways that secured the "public good." The mere proliferation of interest groups in our time does not justify a negative answer to that question. Rather, one would also have to believe the political process is dominated by groups that seek to serve their members with little or no regard for the well-being and rights of other citizens. To some pro-choice voters, certain pro-life groups may appear as factions, and to some pro-life citizens, certain pro-choice groups may appear as factions. Both these and other ideological groups have proliferated in recent decades. Whether this is good or bad for American's representative democracy is a question on which reasonable minds can and do differ. But this much is clear: in contemporary American politics, one citizen's special-interest group often is another citizen's public-interest lobby.

2. Should interest groups' political activities be restricted by law?

The first thing to notice is that there literally scores of such laws are already on the books. For example, Washington lobbyists must register with the House or Senate. All registered lobbyists must publicly divulge their client list and expenditures. There are legal limits on PAC contributions. Every new wave of campaign finance laws (see Chapter 10) has resulted in more rules regulating interest groups. The Internal Revenue Service (IRS) has tightly restricted political activity by religious groups, private schools, and other organizations as a condition for their exemption from federal income tax. The courts have consistently upheld such restrictions and ruled that they do not, under most circumstances, violate freedom of speech or other constitutional protections. On the other hand, the courts have effectively afforded even tax-exempt groups ways of legally, but indirectly, engaging in political activity. Finally, states and cities have their own laws regulating interest groups, and some places are more restrictive than others.

WORLD WIDE WEB RESOURCES

Conservative interest groups

American Conservative Union: **www.conservative.org**

Christian Coalition: **www.cc.org**

Liberal interest groups

American Civil Liberties Union: **www.aclu.org**

Americans for Democratic Action: **www.adaction.org**

Environmental groups

Environmental Defense: **www.environmentaldefense.org**

National Resources Defense Council: **www.nrdc.org**

Civil rights groups

NAACP: **www.naacp.org**

Center for Equal Opportunity: **www.ceousa.org**

Feminist group

National Organization for Women: **www.now.org**

SUGGESTED READINGS

Bauer, Raymond A., Ithiel de Sola Pool, and Lewis A. Dexter. *American Business and Public Policy*. New York: Atherton, 1963. A classic study of how business groups tried to shape foreign-trade legislation, set in a broad analysis of pressure groups and Congress.

Berry, Jeffrey M. *Lobbying for the People*. Princeton, N.J.: Princeton University Press, 1977. Analyzes more than eighty "public-interest" lobbies, with a detailed discussion of two.

Cigler, Allan J., and Burdett A. Loomis, eds. *Interest Group Politics*. 7th ed. Washington, D.C.: Congressional Quarterly Press, 2007. Essays on several interest groups active in Washington.

Lowi, Theodore J. *The End of Liberalism*. New York: Norton, 1969. A critique of the role of interest groups in American government.

Mansbridge, Jane J. *Why We Lost the ERA*. Chicago: University of Chicago Press, 1986. Insightful analysis of the relationship between organizational incentives and tactics in the ERA campaign.

Olson, Mancur. *The Logic of Collective Action*. Cambridge: Harvard University Press, 1965. An economic analysis of interest groups, especially the "free-rider" problem.

Sabato, Larry. *PAC Power*. New York: Norton, 1985. A full discussion of the nature and activities of political action committees.

Schlozman, Kay Lehman, and John T. Tierney. *Organized Interests and American Democracy*. New York: Harper and Row, 1985. Comprehensive treatise on interest groups based on original research.

Truman, David B. *The Governmental Process*. 2d ed. New York: Knopf, 1971. First published in 1951, this was the classic analysis—and defense—of interest group pluralism.

Wilson, James Q. *Political Organizations*. Rev. ed. Princeton, N.J.: Princeton University Press, 1995. A theory of interest groups emphasizing the incentives they use to attract members.

12

WHAT IF?

The Media

TO WIN: 2025

PENNSYLVANIA
100 TOTAL DELEGATES

PROPOR

AMERICA VOTES | 2008

WHO GOVERNS?

1. How much power do the media have?
2. Can we trust the media to be fair?

TO WHAT ENDS?

1. What public policies will the media support?

Suppose you want to influence how other people think about health, politics, sports, or celebrities. What would you do? At one time, you might write a book or publish an essay in a newspaper or magazine. But unless you were very lucky, the book or article would only reach a few people. Today, you will have a much bigger impact if you can get on television or invent a controversial web log (or blog). Vastly more people watch "American Idol" than read newspaper editorials; many more get opinions from blogs—such as the Daily Kos on the left or Power Line on the right—than read essays in magazines.

Television and the Internet are key parts of the New Media; newspapers and magazines are part of the Old Media. And when it comes to politics, the New Media are getting stronger and the Old Media weaker. In 2004, "60 Minutes," a CBS television news program, ran a story claiming that President Bush had performed poorly during his time in the Air National Guard. Within a few hours, bloggers produced evidence that the documents underlying this charge were forgeries, something CBS later conceded was true. Not long afterward, the producer and newscaster responsible for the charges left CBS.

By 2008, more than four-fifths of all young Americans (ages 18 to 29) used the Internet and about half of them used it to get news about the presidential election, share their views with others, and mobilize others. This use of the Internet is three times greater than it was in 2000. Young people use the Internet much more than they read newspapers: four-fifths rely on the Internet; only one-third read newspapers (see Figure 12.1).

Not only was the Internet used more, it was used differently. In 2008, a third of all Americans watched online videos related to the political campaign, and about one-tenth of the public donated money to candidates by going online.[1] And the Internet makes more demands on politicians. If a candidate says something controversial, it might take a few days before a newspaper gets the facts right. But with millions of people on the Internet, challenges to a controversial position will occur within minutes.[2]

But not all of the users are convinced that the Internet is entirely trustworthy. One-third think it lets the loudest and most extreme voices prevail and feel that it is full of

Ozier Muhammad/The New York Times/Redux Pictures

misinformation. And though newspapers are rapidly losing their audience, they remain vitally important: much of what is on the Internet comes from newspaper reporters, and politicians devote at least as much time to getting good newspaper coverage as they devote to expanding their Internet coverage.

The Media and Politics

The Internet is an important new way for politics to be carried on, but it is only the latest episode in the love-hate relationship between politicians and the nations' changing ways of communicating with one another. From the beginning of the Republic, public officials have tried to get the media on their side while knowing that, since the media love controversy, they are as likely to attack as to praise. The Internet may strike some politicians as the solution to this problem: they think that if they put their own web pages out there, they can reach the voters directly. They can, but so can rival politicians with their own web pages and with their allies attacking their competitors.

All of this takes place in a country so committed to a free press that there is little the government can do to control the process. As we shall see, there have been efforts to control radio and television as a result of the government's right to license broadcasters, but most of these attempts have evaporated.

Even strongly democratic nations restrict the press more than the United States. For example, the laws governing libel are much stricter in Great Britain than in the United States. As a result, it is easier in Great Britain for politicians to sue newspapers for publishing articles that defame or ridicule them. In this country, the libel laws make it almost impossible to prevent press criticisms of public figures. Moreover, England has an Official Secrets Act that can be used to punish any past or present public officials who leak information to the press.[3] In this country, leaking information occurs all the time, and our Freedom of Information Act makes it relatively easy for the press to extract documents from the government.

European governments can be much tougher on what people say than in the American one. In 2006, an Austrian court sentenced a man to three years in prison for having denied that the Nazi death camp at Auschwitz killed its inmates. A French court convicted a distinguished American historian for telling a French newspaper that the slaughter of Armenians may not have been the result of planned effort. An Italian journalist stood trial for having written things "offensive to Islam." In this country, such statements would be protected by the Constitution even if, as with the man who denied the existence of the Holocaust, they were profoundly wrong.[4]

America has a long tradition of privately owned media. By contrast, private ownership of television has come only recently to France. And the Internet is not owned by anybody: here and in many nations, people can say or read whatever they want on their computers.

Newspapers in this country require no government permission to operate, but radio and television stations need licenses granted by the Federal Communications Commission (FCC). These licenses must be renewed periodically. On occasion, the White House has made efforts to use license renewals as a way of influencing station owners who were out of political favor, but of late the level of FCC control over what is broadcast has lessened.

There are two potential limits to the freedom of privately owned newspapers and broadcast stations. First, they must make a profit. Some critics believe the need for profit will lead media outlets to distort the news in order to satisfy advertisers or to build an audience. Though there is some truth to this argument, it is too simple. Every media outlet must satisfy a variety of people—advertisers, subscribers, listeners, reporters, and editors—and balancing those demands is complicated and will be done differently by different owners.

The second problem is media bias. If most of the reporters and editors have similar views about politics and if they act on those views, then the media will give us only one side of many stories. Later in this chapter, we shall take a close look at this possibility.

Journalism in American Political History

Important changes in the nature of American politics have gone hand in hand with major changes in the organization and technology of the press. It is

blog A series, or log, of discussion items on a page of the World Wide Web.

the nature of politics, essentially a form of communication, to respond to changes in how communications are carried on. This can be seen by considering four important periods in journalistic history.

THE PARTY PRESS

In the early years of the Republic, politicians of various factions and parties created, sponsored, and controlled newspapers to further their interests. This was possible because circulation was of necessity small (newspapers could not easily be distributed to large audiences, owing to poor transportation) and newspapers were expensive (the type was set by hand and the presses printed copies

slowly). Furthermore, there were few large advertisers to pay the bills. These newspapers circulated chiefly among the political and commercial elites who could afford the high subscription prices. Even with high prices, the newspapers often required subsidies that frequently came from the government or a political party.

During the Washington administration, the Federalists, led by Alexander Hamilton, created the *Gazette of the United States*. The Republicans, led by Thomas Jefferson, retaliated by creating the *National Gazette* and made its editor, Philip Freneau, "clerk for foreign languages" in the State Department at $250 a year to help support

Blogs, both conservative and liberal, have become an important form of political advertising.

powerlineblog.com. Reprinted with permission.

As appeared on www.dailykos.com. Reprinted with permission.

him. After Jefferson became president, he induced another publisher, Samuel Harrison Smith, to start the *National Intelligencer,* subsidizing him by giving him a contract to print government documents. Andrew Jackson, when he became president, aided in the creation of the *Washington Globe.* By some estimates, there were over 50 journalists on the government payroll during this era. Naturally, these newspapers were relentlessly partisan in their views. Citizens could choose among different party papers, but only rarely could they find a paper that presented both sides of an issue.

THE POPULAR PRESS

Changes in society and technology made possible the rise of a self-supporting, mass-readership daily newspaper. The development of the high-speed rotary press enabled publishers to print thousands of copies of a newspaper cheaply and quickly. The invention of the telegraph in the 1840s meant that news from

Washington could be flashed almost immediately to New York, Boston, Philadelphia, and Charleston, thus providing local papers with access to information that once only the Washington papers enjoyed. The creation in 1848 of the Associated Press allowed telegraphic dissemination of information to newspaper editors on a systematic basis. Since the AP provided stories that had to be brief and that went to newspapers of every political hue, it could not afford to be partisan or biased; to attract as many subscribers as possible, it had to present the facts objectively. Meanwhile, the nation was becoming more urbanized, with large numbers of people brought together in densely settled areas. These people could support a daily newspaper by paying only a penny per copy and by patronizing merchants who advertised in its pages. Newspapers no longer needed political patronage to prosper, and soon such subsidies began to dry up. In 1860, the Government Printing Office was established, thereby putting an end to most of the printing contracts that Washington newspapers had once enjoyed.

The *National Gazette,* edited by Phlip Freneau, supported the Thomas Jefferson faction in national ploitics, Jefferson, as secretary of state, helped Freneau by giving him a job in the State Department. The *Gazette of the United States,* published by John Fenno, supported Jefferson's rival, Alexander Hamilton.

By permission of the Houghton Library/Harvard University

The mass-readership newspaper was scarcely non-partisan, but the partisanship it displayed arose from the convictions of its publishers and editors rather than from the influence of its party sponsors. And these convictions blended political beliefs with economic interest. The way to attract a large readership was with sensationalism: violence, romance, and patriotism, coupled with exposés of government, politics, business, and society. As practiced by Joseph Pulitzer and William Randolph Hearst, founders of large newspaper empires, this editorial policy had great appeal for the average citizen and especially for the immigrants flooding into the large cities.

Strong-willed publishers could often become powerful political forces. Hearst used his papers to agitate for war with Spain when the Cubans rebelled against Spanish rule. Conservative Republican political leaders were opposed to the war, but a steady diet of newspaper stories about real and imagined Spanish brutalities whipped up public opinion in favor of intervention. At one point, Hearst sent the noted artist Frederic Remington to Cuba to supply paintings of the conflict. Remington cabled back: "Everything is quiet. ... There will be no war." Hearst supposedly replied: "Please remain. You furnish the pictures and I'll furnish the war."[5] When the battleship USS *Maine* blew up in Havana harbor, President William McKinley felt helpless to resist popular pressure, and war was declared in 1898.

For all their excesses, the mass-readership newspapers began to create a common national culture, to establish the feasibility of a press free of government control or subsidy, and to demonstrate how exciting (and profitable) could be the criticism of public policy and the revelation of public scandal.

MAGAZINES OF OPINION

The growing middle class often was repelled by what it called "yellow journalism" and was developing around the turn of the century a taste for political reform and a belief in the doctrines of the progressive movement. To satisfy this market, a variety of national magazines appeared that—unlike those devoted to manners and literature—discussed issues of public policy. Among the first of these were the *Nation,* the *Atlantic Monthly,* and *Harper's,* founded in the 1850s and 1860s; later came the more broadly based mass-circulation magazines such as *McClure's, Scribner's,* and *Cosmopolitan.* They provided the means for developing a national constituency for certain issues such as regulating business (or in the language of the times, "trust-busting"), purifying municipal politics, and reforming the civil service system. Lincoln Steffens and other so-called muckrakers were frequent contributors to the magazines, setting a pattern for what we now call "investigative reporting."

The national magazines of opinion provided an opportunity for individual writers to gain a nationwide following. The popular press, though initially under the heavy influence of founder-publishers, made the names of certain reporters and columnists household words. In time, the great circulation wars between the big-city daily newspapers started to wane, as the more successful papers bought up or otherwise eliminated their competition. This reduced the need for the more extreme forms of sensationalism, a change reinforced by the growing sophistication and education of America's readers. And the founding publishers gradually were replaced by less flamboyant managers. All of these changes—in circulation needs, audience interests, managerial style, the emergence of nationally known writers—helped increase the power of editors and reporters and make them a force to be reckoned with.

Although politics dominated the pages of most national magazines in the late 19th century, today national magazines that focus mainly on politics and government affairs account for only a small and declining portion of the national magazine market. Among all magazines in circulation today, only a fraction focus on politics—the majority of today's magazines focus on popular entertainment and leisure activities.

ELECTRONIC JOURNALISM

Radio came on the national scene in the 1920s, television in the late 1940s. They represented a major change in the way news was gathered and disseminated, though few politicians at first understood the importance of this change. A broadcast permits public officials to speak directly to audiences without their remarks being filtered through editors and reporters. This was obviously an advantage to politicians, provided they were skilled enough to use it: they could in theory reach the voters directly on a national scale without the services of political parties, interest groups, or friendly editors.

But there was an offsetting disadvantage—people could easily ignore a speech broadcast on a radio or television station, either by not listening at all or by tuning to a different station. By contrast, the views of at least some public figures would receive prominent and often unavoidable display in newspapers, and in a growing number of cities there was only one daily paper. Moreover, space in a newspaper is cheap compared to time on a television broadcast.

Bettmann/Corbis

Before television and the Internet, news came by radio, as here in 1939.

Table 12.1 Decline in Viewership of the Television Networks

"Big Three" Networks: Average Shares of Prime-Time Viewing Audience	
Year	Share
1961	94%
1971	91
1981	83
1991	41
1997	33
2002	29
2005	28

Source: Updated from 2005 Cabletelevision Advertising Bureau analysis of Nielsen data.

Adding one more story, or one more name to an existing story, costs the newspaper little. By contrast, less news can be carried on radio or television, and each news segment must be quite brief to avoid boring the audience. As a result, the number of political personalities that can be covered by radio and television news is much smaller than is the case with newspapers, and the cost (to the station) of making a news item or broadcast longer often is prohibitively large.

sound bite A radio or video clip of someone speaking.

Thus, to obtain the advantages of electronic media coverage, public officials must do something sufficiently bold or colorful to gain free access to radio and television news—or they must find the money to purchase radio and television time. The president of the United States, of course, is routinely covered by radio and television and can ordinarily get free time to speak to the nation on matters of importance. All other officials must struggle for access to the electronic media by making controversial statements, acquiring a national reputation, or purchasing expensive time.

The rise of the talk show as a political forum has increased politicians' access to the electronic media, as has the televised "town meeting." But such developments need to be understood as part of a larger story.

Until the 1990s, the "big three" television networks (ABC, CBS, and NBC) together claimed 80 percent or more of all viewers (see Table 12.1). Their evening newscasts dominated electronic media coverage of politics and government affairs. When it came to presidential campaigns, for example, the three networks were the only television games in town—they reported on the primaries, broadcast the party conventions, and covered the general election campaigns, including any presidential debates. But over the last few decades, the networks' evening newscasts have changed in ways that have made it harder for candidates to use them to get their messages across. For instance, the average **sound bite**—a video clip of a presidential contender speaking—dropped from about 42 seconds in 1968 to 7.3 seconds in 2000.[6]

Today, politicians have sources other than the network news for sustained and personalized television exposure. Cable television, early-morning news and entertainment programs, and prime-time "news-magazine" shows have greatly increased and diversified politicians' access to the electronic media.

Naturally, many politicians favor the call-in format, town-meeting setups, lengthy human interest interviews, and casual appearances on entertainment shows to televised confrontations on policy issues with seasoned network journalists who push, probe, and criticize. And naturally, they favor being a part of visually interesting programs rather than traditional "talking heads" news shows. But what is preferable to candidates is not necessarily helpful to the selection process that voters must go through in choosing a candidate.

One thing is clear: most politicians crave the media spotlight, both on the campaign trail and in office. The efforts made by political candidates to get "visuals"—filmed stories—on television continue after they are elected. Since the president is always news, a politician wishing to make news is well advised to attack the president.

THE INTERNET

Half of all Americans used the Internet to get political news in 2008.[7] The political news found there ranges from summaries of stories from newspapers and magazines to political rumors and hot gossip. Many blogs exist on which viewers can scan political ideas posted there; many blogs specialize in offering liberal, conservative, or libertarian perspectives. The Internet is the ultimate free market in political news: no one can ban, control, or regulate it, and no one can keep facts, opinions, or nonsense off of it.

The Internet is beginning to play a big role in politics. When Howard Dean ran for the Democratic presidential nomination in 2004, he raised most of his money from Internet appeals. When John Kerry, who won the nomination, was campaigning, the Internet and the blogs on it were a major source of discussion of the criticisms made of him by former Vietnam war veterans. Now every candidate for important offices has a web site.

The rise of the Internet has completed a remarkable transformation in American journalism. In the days of the party press, only a few people read newspapers. When mass-circulation newspapers arose, mass politics also arose. When magazines of opinion developed, interest groups also developed. When radio and television became dominant, politicians could build their own bridges to voters without party or interest group influence. And now, with the Internet, voters and political activists can talk to each other.

Most users think the Internet is a wonderful device, but some worry that using e-mail, YouTube, Facebook, text messaging, blogs, and Twitter to communicate will isolate people from one another and make public opinion more extreme. There have been several studies of this possibility but they have not produced a clear answer. A Stanford study argued that the Internet isolates people from ordinary human contact and makes them become anonymous. A study at Carnegie Mellon University came to much the same conclusion.

By contrast, a study done at UCLA found that Internet users are more likely to consult newspapers and magazines and that they spend just as much time on the telephone as people not on the Internet. And a Pew survey suggested that e-mail make people feel more, not less, connected to others.[8]

But one thing is clear: the Internet has profoundly affected politics by making it easier to (1) raise money in small donations, (2) organize people to attend meetings, (3) take instant (though probably unreliable) opinion polls, (4) disseminate instant criticism of your opponent, (5) mobilize local followers, and (6) target campaigners with the names of people they should contact.

The Structure of the Media

The relationship between journalism and politics is a two-way street: though politicians take advantage as best they can of the communications media available to them, these media in turn attempt to use politics and politicians as a way of both entertaining and informing their audiences. The mass media, whatever their disclaimers, are not simply a mirror held up to reality or a messenger that carries the news. There is inevitably a process of selection, of editing, and of emphasis, and this process reflects, to some degree, the way in which the media are organized, the kinds of audiences they seek to serve, and the preferences and opinions of the members of the media.

DEGREE OF COMPETITION

There has been a large decline in the numbers of daily newspapers that serve large communities. There were competing papers in 60 percent of American cities in 1900 but in only 4 percent in 1972. Several large cities—Boston, Chicago, Detroit, Los Angeles, New York, Philadelphia, and Washington, D.C.—have more than one paper, but in some of these the same business owns both papers. And newspaper circulation has fallen in recent years, with more and more people getting their news from radio and television. Young people especially have turned away from political news. In the 1940s and 1950s, age did not make much difference; people under the age of 30 read about the same amount of news as people over the age of 50. But by the 1970s, that had changed dramatically; from then until now, young people read less political news than older people. In Figure 12.1, we can see that today only half as many people between the ages of 18 and 34 read newspapers as was true in 1970.

To a degree that would astonish most foreigners, the American press—radio, television, and newspapers—is made up of locally owned and managed enterprises. In Britain, France, Germany, Japan, Sweden, and elsewhere, the media are owned and operated with a national audience in mind. The *Times* of London may be published in that city, but it is read throughout Great Britain, as are the *Guardian,* the *Daily Telegraph,* and the *Daily Mirror.* Radio and television broadcasts are centrally planned and nationally aired.

Figure 12.1

Percentage of Newspaper Readers Ages 18–34

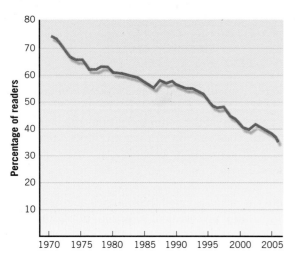

Notes: 18–34 readership represents the average of 18–24 readership and 25–34 readership. 2006 data is through September

Source: *The Wall Street Journal* (February 15, 2007). Copyright © 2007 Dow Jones & Company, Inc. Reprinted with the permission of Dow Jones & Company, Inc., via Copyright Clearance Center.

The American newspaper, however, is primarily oriented to its local market and local audience, and there is typically more local than national news in it. Radio and television stations accept network programming, but the early- and late-evening news programs provide a heavy diet of local political, social, and sports news. Government regulations developed by the Federal Communications Commission (FCC) are in part responsible for this. Until the mid-1990s, no one could own and operate more than one newspaper, one AM radio station, one FM radio station, or one television station in a given market. The networks still today may not compel a local affiliate to accept any particular broadcast. (In fact, almost all network news programs are carried by the affiliates.) The result has been the development of a decentralized broadcast industry.

THE NATIONAL MEDIA

The local orientation of much of the American communications media is partially offset, however, by the emergence of certain publications and broadcast services that constitute a kind of national press. The wire services—the Associated Press and United Press International—supply most of the national news that local papers publish. Certain newsmagazines, such as *Time* and *Newsweek*, have a national readership. The network evening news broadcasts produced by ABC, CBS, and NBC are carried by most television stations with a network affiliation. Both CNN (Cable News Network) and Fox News broadcast news around the clock and have large audiences, as does MSNBC.

Though most newspapers have only local audiences, several have acquired national influence. The *New York Times* and the *Wall Street Journal* are printed in several locations and can be delivered to many homes early in the morning. *USA Today* was created as a national newspaper and is distributed everywhere, aimed especially at people who travel a lot.

These newspapers have national standing for several reasons. First, they distribute a lot of copies: over 1 million each day for the *Times* and the *Journal,* and over 2 million a day for *USA Today.* Second, these papers, as well as the *Washington Post,* are carefully followed by political elites. Unlike most people, the elites even read the editorials. By contrast, local newspapers and radio stations may be invisible to Washington politicians. Third, radio and television stations often decide what to broadcast by looking at the front pages of the *Times* and the *Post.* The front page of the *Times* is a model for each network's evening news broadcast.[9] Finally, the editors and reporters for the national press tend to be better educated and more generously paid than their counterparts in local outlets. And as we shall see, the writers for the national press tend to have distinctly liberal political views. Above all they seek—and frequently obtain—the opportunity to write stories that are not accounts of a particular news event but "background," investigative, or interpretive stories about issues and policies.

The national press plays the role of gatekeeper, scorekeeper, and watchdog for the federal government.

Gatekeeper

As gatekeeper, the national media can influence what subjects become national political issues and for how long. Automobile safety, water pollution, and the quality of prescription drugs were not major political issues before the national press began giving substantial attention to these matters and thus helped place them on the political agenda. When crime rates rose in the early 1960s, the subject was given little political attention in Washington, in part because the media did not cover it extensively. Media attention to crime increased in the late 1960s and early 1970s, slackened in the late 1970s, and rose again in the 1980s and early 1990s. Throughout most of these years, crime went up. In short, *reality* did not change during this time; only the focus of media and political attention shifted. Elite opinion about the war in Vietnam also changed significantly as the attitude toward the war expressed by the national media changed.

Scorekeeper

As scorekeepers, the national media keep track of and help make political reputations, note who is "mentioned" as a presidential candidate, and help decide who is winning and losing in Washington

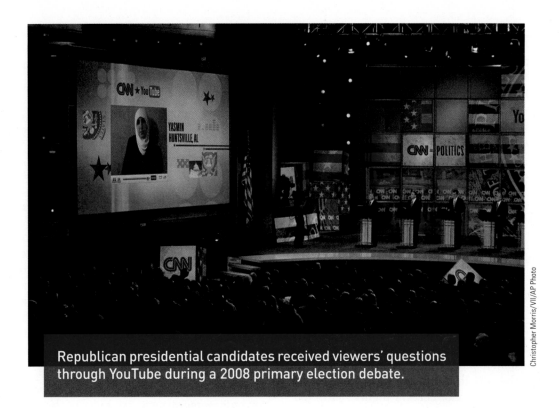

Republican presidential candidates received viewers' questions through YouTube during a 2008 primary election debate.

Christopher Morris/VII/AP Photo

politics. When Jimmy Carter, a virtually unknown former governor of Georgia, was planning his campaign to get the Democratic nomination for president, he understood clearly the importance of being "mentioned." So successful was he in cultivating members of the national press that, before the first primary election was held, he was the subject of more stories in the *New York Times,* the *Washington Post,* and the *Columbus Dispatch* than any other potential Democratic presidential candidate.

The scorekeeper role of the media often leads the press to cover presidential elections as if they were horse races rather than choices among policies. Consider the enormous attention the media give to the Iowa caucus and the New Hampshire primary election, despite the fact that these states produce only a tiny fraction of the delegates to either party's nominating convention and that neither state is representative of the nation as a whole. The results of the Iowa caucus, the first in the nation, are given great importance by the press. Consequently, the coverage received by a candidate who does well in Iowa constitutes a tremendous amount of free publicity that can help him or her in the New Hampshire primary election. Doing well in that primary results in even more media attention, thus boosting the candidate for the next primaries, and so on.

Watchdog

Once the scorekeepers decide you are the person to watch, they adopt their watchdog role. When Gary

Hart was the front-runner for the 1988 Democratic presidential nomination, the press played its watchdog role right from the start. When rumors circulated that he was unfaithful to his wife, the *Miami Herald* staked out his apartment in Washington, D.C., and discovered he had spent several evening hours there with an attractive young woman, Donna Rice. Soon other stories appeared about his having taken Rice on a boat trip to Bimini. Not long thereafter, Hart dropped out of the presidential race, accusing the press of unfair treatment.

This close scrutiny is natural. The media have an instinctive—and profitable—desire to investigate personalities and expose scandals. To some degree, all reporters probably share the belief that the role of the press is to "comfort the afflicted and afflict the comfortable." They tend to be tolerant of underdogs, tough on front-runners. Though some reporters develop close relations with powerful personages, many—especially younger ones—find the discovery of wrongdoing both more absorbing and more lucrative. Bob Woodward and Carl Bernstein, who wrote most of the Watergate stories for the *Washington Post,* simultaneously performed an important public service, received the accolades of their colleagues, and earned a lot of money.

Newspapers and television stations play these three roles in somewhat different ways. A newspaper can cover more stories in greater depth than a TV station and faces less competition from other papers than TV stations face from other broadcasters. A TV station faces brutal competition, must select its programs in part for their visual impact, and must keep its stories short and punchy. As a result, newspaper reporters have more freedom to develop their own stories, but they earn less money than television news broadcasters. The latter have little freedom (the fear of losing their audience is keen), but they can make a lot of money (if they are attractive personalities who photograph well).

Rules Governing the Media

Ironically, the least competitive media outlets—the big-city newspapers—are almost entirely free from government regulation, while the most competitive ones—radio and television stations—must have a government license to operate and must adhere to a variety of government regulations.

Newspapers and magazines need no license to publish, their freedom to publish may not be restrained in advance, and they are liable for punishment for what they do publish only under certain highly restricted circumstances. The First Amendment has been interpreted as meaning that no government, federal or state, can place "prior restraints" (that is, censorship) on the press except under very narrowly defined circumstances.[10] When the federal government sought to prevent the *New York Times* from publishing the Pentagon Papers, a set of secret government documents stolen by an antiwar activist, the Court held that the paper was free to publish them.[11]

Once something is published, a newspaper or magazine may be sued or prosecuted if the material is libelous or obscene or if it incites someone to commit an illegal act. But these usually are not very serious restrictions, because the courts have defined *libelous, obscene,* and *incitement* so narrowly as to make it more difficult here than in any other nation to find the press guilty of such conduct. For example, for a paper to be found guilty of libeling a public official or other prominent person, the person must not only show that what was printed was wrong and damaging but must also show, with "clear and convincing evidence," that it was printed maliciously—that is, with "reckless disregard" for its truth or falsity.[12] When in 1984 Israeli General Ariel Sharon sued *Time* magazine for libel, the jury decided the story *Time* printed was false and defamatory but that *Time* had not published it as the result of malice, and so Sharon did not collect any damages.

There are also laws intended to protect the privacy of citizens, but they do not really inhibit newspapers. In general, your name and picture can be printed without your consent if they are part of a news story of some conceivable public interest. And if a paper attacks you in print, the paper has no legal obligation to give you space for a reply.[13]

It is illegal to use printed words to advocate the violent overthrow of the government if by your advocacy you incite others to action, but this rule has only rarely been applied to newspapers.[14]

CONFIDENTIALITY OF SOURCES

Reporters believe they should have the right to keep confidential the sources of their stories. Some states agree and have passed laws to that effect. Most states and the federal government do not agree, so the courts must decide in each case whether the need of a journalist to protect confidential sources does or does not outweigh the interest of the government in gathering evidence in a criminal investigation. In general, the Supreme Court has upheld the right of the government to compel reporters to divulge information as part of a properly conducted criminal investigation, if it bears on the commission of a crime.[15]

This conflict arises not only between reporters and law enforcement agencies but also between reporters and persons accused of committing a crime. Myron Farber, a reporter for the *New York Times,* wrote a series of stories that led to the indictment and trial of a physician on charges he had murdered five patients. The judge ordered Farber to show him his notes to determine whether they should be given to the defense lawyers. Farber refused, arguing that revealing his notes would infringe upon the confidentiality he had promised to his sources. Farber was sent to jail for contempt of court. On appeal, the New Jersey Supreme Court and the

Activists urge Congress to pass a law shielding reporters from being required to testify about their sources.

Bebeto Matthews/AP Photo

U.S. Supreme Court decided against Farber, holding that the accused person's right to a fair trial includes the right to compel the production of evidence, even from reporters.

In 2005, two reporters were sentenced to jail when they refused to give prosecutors information about who in the Bush administration had told them that a woman was in fact a CIA officer. A federal court decided they were not entitled to any protection for their sources in a criminal trial. The *New York Times* reporter, Judith Miller, spent 85 days in jail; she was released after a government official authorized her to talk about their conversation. There is no federal shield law that will protect journalists, though such laws exist in 34 states.

In another case, the Supreme Court upheld the right of the police to search newspaper offices, so long as they have a warrant. But Congress then passed a law forbidding such searches (except in special cases), requiring instead that the police subpoena the desired documents.[16]

REGULATING BROADCASTING

Although newspapers and magazines by and large are not regulated, broadcasting is regulated by the government. No one may operate a radio or television station without a license from the Federal Communications Commission, renewable every seven years for radio and every five for television stations. An application for renewal is rarely refused, but until recently the FCC required the broadcaster to submit detailed information about its programming and how it planned to serve "community needs" in order to get a renewal. Based on this information or on the complaints of some group, the FCC could use its powers of renewal to influence what the station put on the air. For example, it could induce stations to reduce the amount of violence shown, increase the proportion of "public service" programs on the air, or alter the way it portrayed various ethnic groups.

Of late a movement has arisen to deregulate broadcasting, on the grounds that so many stations are now on the air that competition should be allowed to determine how each station defines and serves community needs. In this view, citizens can choose what they want to hear or see without the government's shaping the content of each station's programming. For example, since the early 1980s, a station can simply submit a postcard requesting that its license be renewed, a request automatically granted unless some group formally opposes the renewal. In that case, the FCC holds a hearing. As a result, some of the old rules—for instance, that each hour on TV could contain only 16 minutes of commercials—are no longer rigidly enforced.

Landmark Cases

The Rights of the Media

- *Near v. Minnesota* (1931): Freedom of the press applies to state governments, so that they cannot impose prior restraint on newspapers.

- *New York Times v. Sullivan* (1964): Public officials may not win a libel suit unless they can prove that the statement was made knowing it to be false or with reckless disregard of its truth.

- *Miami Herald v. Tornillo* (1974): A newspaper cannot be required to give someone a right to reply to one of its stories.

Radio broadcasting has been deregulated the most. Before 1992, one company could own one AM and one FM station in each market. In 1992, this number was doubled. And in 1996, the Telecommunications Act allowed one company to own as many as eight stations in large markets (five in smaller ones) and as many as it wished nationally. This trend has had two results. First, a few large companies now own most of the big-market radio stations. Second, the looser editorial restrictions that accompanied deregulation mean that a greater variety of opinions and shows can be found on radio. There are many more radio talk shows than would have been heard when content was more tightly controlled.

Deregulation has also lessened the extent to which the federal government shapes the content of broadcasting. At one time, for example, a Fairness Doctrine required broadcasters that air one side of a story to give time to opposing points of view. But there are now so many radio and television stations that the FCC relies on competition to manage differences of opinion. The abandonment of the Fairness Doctrine permitted the rise of controversial talk radio shows. If the doctrine had stayed in place, there would be no Rush Limbaugh or Al Franken. The FCC decided that competition among news outlets protected people by giving them many different sources of news.

equal time rule An FCC rule that if a broadcaster sells time to one candidate, it must sell equal time to other candidates.

There still exists an **equal time rule** that obliges stations that sell advertising time to one political candidate to sell equal time to that person's opponents.

CAMPAIGNING

When candidates wish to campaign on radio or television, the equal time rule applies. A broadcaster must provide equal access to candidates for office and charge them rates no higher than the cheapest rate applicable to commercial advertisers for comparable time.

At one time, this rule meant that a station or network could not broadcast a debate between the Democratic and Republican candidates for an office without inviting all other candidates as well—Libertarian, Prohibitionist, or whatever. Thus, a presidential debate in 1980 could be limited to the major candidates, Reagan and Carter (or Reagan and Anderson), only by having the League of Women Voters sponsor it and then allowing radio and TV to cover it as a "news event." Now stations and networks can themselves sponsor debates limited to major candidates.

Though laws guarantee that candidates can buy time at favorable rates on television, not all candidates take advantage of this. The reason is that television is not always an efficient way to reach voters. A television message is literally "broad cast"—spread out to a mass audience without regard to the boundaries of the district in which a candidate is running. Presidential candidates, of course, always use television because their constituency is the whole nation. Candidates for senator or representative, however, may or may not use television, depending on whether the boundaries of their state or district conform well to the boundaries of a television market.

A *market* is an area easily reached by a television signal; there are about 200 such markets in the country. If you are a member of Congress from South Bend, Indiana, you come from a television market based there. You can buy ads on the TV stations in South Bend at a reasonable fee. But if you are a member of Congress from northern New Jersey, the only television stations are in nearby New York City. In that market, the costs of a TV ad are very high because they reach a lot of people, most of whom are not in your district and so cannot vote for you. Buying a TV ad is a waste of money. As a result, a much higher percentage of Senate than House candidates use television ads.

Horse-race journalism news coverage that focuses on who is ahead rather than on the issues.

One aspect of campaigning that worries scholars is the media's reliance on **horse-race journalism**, that is, covering a campaign based on guesses about who is ahead rather than on candidates' positions on the issues. For example, in 2008 the journalists talked about how Barack Obama would win the New Hampshire primary because that is what the polls and political insiders told them. But then Hillary Clinton won. Nowhere in the press coverage was any attention given to the positions Clinton and Obama had on the issues. The public says they want more such coverage, though one suspects that they actually like horse-race journalism.

Are the National Media Biased?

Everyone believes the media have a profound effect, for better or for worse, on politics. Many think the political opinions of writers and editors influence that effect. To decide whether these statements are true, we must answer three questions:

1. Do members of the media have a distinctive political attitude?
2. Does that attitude affect what they write or say?
3. Does what they write or say affect what citizens believe?

The answers to these questions, to be discussed below, are yes, yes, and probably.

A LIBERAL MAJORITY

Many studies, dating back to the early 1980s, all conclude that members of the national press are more liberal than the average citizen.[17] In 1992, 91 percent of the media members interviewed said they had voted for the Democratic candidate for president. By contrast, only 43 percent of the public voted that way.[18]

Not only are the media more liberal, they tend to be secular. About 70 percent say they never or only a few times a year attend a religious service. And in recent years, the surveys suggest they have become more liberal. For example, between 1980 and 1995, the proportion of media members who believe the government should guarantee jobs to people rose, and the proportion who think government should reduce the regulation of business fell.[19]

The public certainly believes that members of the media are liberals. A Gallup Poll done in 2003 found that 45 percent of Americans believe the media are "too liberal" (15 percent thought they were "too conservative"). In another study, even Democrats agreed with this view.[20]

Conservative media outlets, have become more visible in recent years. Radio talk shows, such as those hosted by Rush Limbaugh and Sean Hannity, are conservative, as is some of the TV reporting broadcast on Fox News, such as on the "O'Reilly Factor."

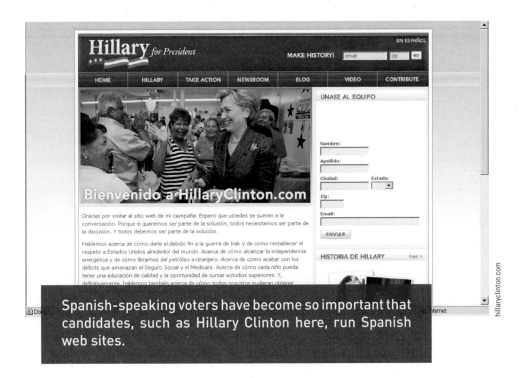

Spanish-speaking voters have become so important that candidates, such as Hillary Clinton here, run Spanish web sites.

hillaryclinton.com

Limbaugh and Hannity have large audiences, and Fox News has grown in popularity.

One-fifth of all Americans listen to radio talk shows every day and another tenth listen several times a week. A puzzling fact is that talk radio, which has grown rapidly in importance, is predominately conservative. Almost half of the 28 largest talk shows were hosted by outspoken conservatives.

None of this dominance is the result of radio station owners plotting to put conservatives on the air. Media owners are interested in ratings—that is, in measures of how big their audiences are. Liberal talk show hosts have had big corporate sponsors, but they dropped away when the show did not get good ratings. If Fidel Castro got high ratings by playing the harmonica, Castro would be on the air.

William G. Mayer, a political scientist, has speculated as to why conservative talk shows are so common. First, there are more self-described conservatives than liberals in this country. Second, conservative listeners do not think their views are reflected in what big-city newspapers, the major television networks, and the leading newsmagazines display. Liberals, by contrast, think their views are encouraged by newspapers and television stations. Third, much of the liberal audience is broken up into distinctive racial and ethnic groups that have their own radio outlets. Many Hispanics listen to stations that broadcast in Spanish; many African Americans prefer stations that have black hosts and focus on black community issues.[21]

NEUTRAL AND OBJECTIVE?

In the United States, the journalistic philosophy in many media documents is that the press, when it reports the news (though not in editorial pages), should be neutral and objective. That view, of course, does not cover radio talk shows, but it is supposed to cover newspapers. A different view can be found in France or Great Britain where newspapers often clearly identify with one party or another.

But it is hard to measure whether the American commitment to objectivity is actually achieved. One would have to take into account not only how much space a politician or policy receives, but the tone in which it is handled and the adjectives used to describe people who are part of those stories.

New stories differ significantly in the opportunity for bias. **Routine stories** cover major political events that will be covered by many reporters and that involve relatively simple matters. For example: the president takes a trip, Congress passes a major bill, or the Supreme Court issues a ruling. **Feature stories** cover events that, though public, a reporter has to seek out because they are not routinely covered by

routine stories Media stories about events regularly covered by reporters.

feature stories Media stories about events that, though public, are not regularly covered by reporters.

insider stories Media stories about events that are not usually made public.

How to Read a Newspaper

Newspapers don't simply report the news; they report somebody's idea of what is news, written in language intended to persuade as well as inform. To read a newspaper intelligently, look for three things: what is covered, who are the sources, and how language is used.

Coverage

Every newspaper will cover a big story, such as a flood, fire, or presidential trip, but newspapers can pick and choose among lesser stories. One paper will select stories about the environment, business fraud, and civil rights; another will prefer stories about crime, drug dealers, and "welfare cheats." What do these choices tell you about the beliefs of the editors and reporters working for these two papers? What do these people want you to believe are the important issues?

Sources

For some stories, the source is obvious: "The Supreme Court decided ... ," "Congress voted ... ," or "The president said. ..." For others, the source is not so obvious. There are two kinds of sources you should beware of. The first is an anonymous source. When you read phrases such as "a high official said today ..." or "White House sources revealed that ..." always ask yourself this question: Why does the source want me to know this? The answer usually will be this: because if I believe what he or she said, it will advance his or her interests. This can happen in one of three ways. First, the source may support a policy or appointment and want to test public reaction to it. This is called floating a **trial balloon.** Second, the source may oppose a policy or appointment and hope that by leaking word of it, the idea will be killed. Third, the source may want to take credit for something good that happened or shift blame onto somebody else for something bad that happened. When you read a story based on anonymous sources,

ask yourself these questions: Judging from the tone of the story, is this leak designed to support or kill an idea? Is it designed to take credit or shift blame? In whose interest is it to accomplish these things? By asking these questions, you often can make a pretty good guess as to the identity of the anonymous source.

Some stories depend on the reader's believing a key fact, previously unknown. For example: "The world's climate is getting hotter because of manmade pollution," "drug abuse is soaring," "the death penalty will prevent murder," "husbands are more likely to beat up on their wives on Super Bowl Sunday." Each of these "facts" is wrong, grossly exaggerated, or stated with excessive confidence. But each comes from an advocate organization that wants you to believe it, because if you do, you will take that organization's solution more seriously. Be skeptical of key facts if they come from an advocacy source. Don't be misled by the tendency of many advocacy organizations to take neutral or scholarly names like "Center for the Public Interest" or "Institute for Policy Research." Some of these really are neutral or scholarly, but many aren't.

Language

Everybody uses words to persuade without actually making a clear argument. This is called using **loaded language.** For example: if you like a politician, call him "Senator Smith"; if you don't like him, refer to him as "right-wing (or left-wing) senators such as Smith." If you like an idea proposed by a professor, call her "respected"; if you don't like the idea, call her "controversial." If you favor abortion, call somebody who agrees with you "pro-choice" ("choice" is valued by most people); if you oppose abortion, call those who agree with you "pro-life" ("life," like "choice," is a good thing). Recognizing loaded language in a newspaper article can give you important clues to the writer's own point of view.

the press. The reporter has to find the story and persuade an editor to publish it. For example: an interest group works hard to get a bill passed, a government agency adopts a new ruling, or a member of Congress conducts an unusual investigation. **Insider stories** cover things that are often secret. Investigative reporters are often credited with uncovering these stories, though it is often the case that some government insider leaked the story to the press. Which leak a reporter

picks up on may be influenced by the reporter's view as to what is important to him or her.

Routine stories often are covered in much the same way by reporters. The space given to the story and the headline attached to it may reflect the political views of the editor, but the story itself often is written about the same way by every reporter. Feature and insider stories, by contrast, may more easily reflect the political views of reporters and editors. On these stories, journalists have to make choices.

Early in American history, newspapers had virtually no routine stories; almost everything they printed was an expression of opinion. By the 20th century, with the advent of telephone and telegraph lines that made it easy for news organizations such as the Associated Press to send the same story to almost every newspaper, routine stories became commonplace. But with the advent of radio and television and the rise of around-the-clock news broadcasting, feature and insider stories became much more important to newspapers. If people got their routine news from radio and television, newspapers had to sell something different; feature and insider stories were different.

A conservative newspaper might print feature or insider stories about crime, drug abuse, or welfare cheats, while a liberal newspaper might run ones on feminism, the environment, or civil rights. There are, however, very few conservative newspapers with a national audience.

A key question is whether there are facts to back up these generalizations. There are no definitive answers; here we can take a look at a few of the better studies.

One looked at 12 years' worth of political stories published in the *New York Times* and the *Washington Post*. It asked how these papers described the 10 most liberal and the 10 most conservative senators. The authors found that conservative senators were about three times more likely to be called conservative than liberal senators were to be called liberal.[22] The difference in the use of adjectives may influence how readers feel about the story. Politically independent readers might (no one knows) take more seriously the views of senators that are given no ideological labels than they will of those to which such labels have been attached.

There have been efforts to see how newspapers and magazines cover specific issues. When *Time* and *Newsweek* ran stories about nuclear power, scholars found they tended to avoid quoting scientists and engineers working in this field because these specialists were in favor of nuclear power at a time when the magazines were opposed to it.[23]

Another study looked at how the top 10 newspapers and the Associated Press cover economic news when there is either a Democratic or Republican president in office. The news was based on government reports about sales, unemployment, and economic growth over a 13-year period. The authors decided whether a newspaper's headline covering that news (on the day

it was released) was either positive, negative, or neutral. In general, these headlines gave a more positive spin when there was a Democrat in the White House and a more negative one when there was a Republican there.[24]

Newspapers are privately owned, so perhaps some of their bias comes from decisions made by the publishers. When scholars looked at 400 daily newspapers, they found that the "ideology of the owners doesn't correlate in any significant way with the political slant of their newspapers' coverage." Instead, a newspaper's bias tends to reflect the political views of its readers. If the same person owns several newspapers, each paper's style is tailored to its own market more than to the owner's beliefs.[25]

But perhaps the easiest evidence to understand comes from reporters themselves. The *New York Times* has a "public editor," that is, a person charged with receiving complaints from the public. When asked, "Is the *New York Times* a liberal newspaper?" he answered, in print, very simply: "Of course it is."

Public distrust of the media has grown. As shown in Figure 12.2, the proportion of people saying that news stories are often inaccurate has grown significantly since 1985.

MEDIA'S INFLUENCE

Some people will be influenced by what they read or hear, but others will not be. There is a well-known psychological process called **selective attention.** It means that people remember or believe only what they want to. If they see or hear statements inconsistent with their existing beliefs, they will tune out these messages.[26]

After the 1964 presidential election, one study suggested that in the northern part of the United States a newspaper endorsement favoring Democratic candidate Lyndon Johnson added about five percentage points to the vote he received.[27]

Another study examined the vote in more than 60 contests for the U.S. Senate held over a five-year period. Newspaper stories about the rival candidates were scored as positive, negative, or neutral. How voters felt about the candidates were learned from public opinion polls. Obviously, many things other than newspaper stories will affect how voters

trial balloon Information leaked to the media to test public reaction to a possible policy.

loaded language Words that imply a value judgment, used to persuade a reader without having made a serious argument.

selective attention Paying attention only to those news stories with which one already agrees.

Figure 12.2

Public Perception of Accuracy in the Media

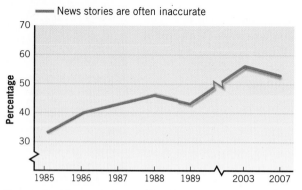

Source: Pew Research Center, "The People and the Press" (August 2007).

feel, and so the authors of this study tried to control for these factors. They held constant the seniority of incumbent candidates, the level of political experience of challengers, the amount of campaign spending, how close each race was, and the political ideology and party identification of voters. After doing all of this, they discovered two things. First, newspapers that endorsed incumbents on their editorial pages gave more positive news coverage to them than newspapers that did not endorse them. Second, the voters had more positive feelings about endorsed incumbents than they did about nonendorsed ones. In short, editorial views affect news coverage, and news coverage affects public attitudes.[28]

A fascinating natural experiment occurred when Fox News, a network that generally favors Republicans, went on the air at different times in different cities. When two scholars compared the effects on voting patterns in cities where Fox News was on the air with similar cities in which it was not, they found that there was a 3 to 8 percent increase in the vote for Republican candidates and about a half a percent increase in the Republican vote for president in the Fox towns.[29] Another study even manufactured an experiment: the authors gave, at no charge, the *Washington Post* (a liberal newspaper) or the *Washington Times* (a conservative newspaper) to people who subscribed to neither in a northern Virginia county. In the next election, those people receiving the *Post* were more likely to vote for the Democratic candidate for governor.[30]

What the press covers affects the policy issues that people think are important. Experiments conducted in New Haven, Connecticut, and a study done in North Carolina show that what citizens believe about some policy questions reflects what newspapers and television stations say about them.[31]

But there are limits to media influence. If people are unemployed, the victims of crime, or worried about high gasoline prices, they do not have to be told these things by the media.[32] But most people have no personal knowledge of highway fatalities, the condition of the environment, or American foreign policy in Europe. On these matters, the media are likely to have much more influence.

But the best evidence of how important the media are comes from the behavior of people trying to get elected. In 1950, Estes Kefauver was a little-known senator from Tennessee. Then he chaired a Senate committee investigating organized crime. When these dramatic hearings were televised, Kefauver became a household name. In 1952, he ran for the Democratic nomination for president and won a lot of primary votes before losing to Adlai Stevenson.

From that time on, developing a strong media presence became a top priority for political candidates. Sometimes it backfires. In 2004, Howard Dean, then a candidate for the Democratic presidential nomination, saw his campaign start to sputter after television carried a speech he gave to his supporters that seemed to end in a kind of anguished scream. And every White House staffer spends a lot of time worrying about how to get the press, especially television, to cover the president. Studies show that television commentary about presidents affects their popularity.[33] President Lyndon Johnson reportedly concluded that the war he was supporting in Vietnam was a hopeless cause after Walter Cronkite, then the star of the popular CBS News program, turned against the war.

Government and the News

Every government agency, every public official, spends a great deal of time trying to shape public opinion. From time to time, somebody publishes an exposé of the efforts of the Pentagon, the White House, or some bureau to "sell" itself to the people, but in a government of separated powers, weak parties, and a decentralized legislature, any government agency that fails to cultivate public opinion will sooner or later find itself weak, without allies, and in trouble.

PROMINENCE OF THE PRESIDENT

Theodore Roosevelt was the first president to raise the systematic cultivation of the press to an art form. From the day he took office, he made it clear that he would give inside stories to friendly reporters and withhold them from hostile ones. He made sure that scarcely a day passed without his doing something newsworthy. In 1902, he built the West Wing of the White House and included in it, for the first time, a special room for reporters near his office, and he invited the press to become fascinated by the antics of his children. In return, the reporters adored him. Teddy's nephew Franklin Roosevelt institutionalized this system by making his press secretary (a job created by Herbert Hoover) a major instrument for cultivating and managing, as well as informing, the press.

Today, the press secretary heads a large staff that meets with reporters, briefs the president on questions he is likely to be asked, attempts to control the flow of news from cabinet departments to the press, and arranges briefings for out-of-town editors (to bypass what many presidents think are the biases of the White House press corps).

All this effort is directed primarily at the White House press corps, a group of men and women who have a lounge in the White House where they wait for a story to break, attend the daily press briefing, or take advantage of a "photo op"—an opportunity to photograph the president with some newsworthy person.

No other nation in the world has brought the press into such close physical proximity to the head of its government. The result is that the actions of our government are personalized to a degree not found in most other democracies. Whether the president rides a horse, comes down with a cold, greets a Boy Scout, or takes a trip, the press is there. The prime minister of Great Britain does not share his home with the press or expect to have his every sneeze recorded for posterity.

COVERAGE OF CONGRESS

Congress has watched all this with irritation and envy. It resents the attention given the president, but it is not certain how it can compete. The 435 members of the House are so numerous and play such specialized roles that they do not get much individualized press attention. In the past, the House was quite restrictive about television or radio coverage of its proceedings. Until 1978, it prohibited television cameras on the floor except on purely ceremonial occasions (such as the annual State of the Union message delivered by the president). From 1952 to 1970, the House would not even allow electronic coverage of its committee hearings (except for a few occasions during those periods when the Republicans were in the

The "Rules" of Politics

The Maxims of Media Relations

The importance of the national media to politicians has given rise to some shared understandings among officeholders about how one deals with the media. Some of these are caught in the following maxims:

- **All secrets become public knowledge.** The more important the secret, the sooner it becomes known.

- **All stories written about me are inaccurate; all stories written about you are entirely accurate.**

- **The rosier the news, the higher ranking the official who announces it.**

- **Always release bad news on Saturday night.** Fewer people notice it.

- **Never argue with a person who buys ink by the barrel.**

majority). Significant live coverage of committee hearings began in 1974 when the House Judiciary Committee was discussing the possible impeachment of President Nixon. Since 1979, cable TV (C-SPAN) has provided gavel-to-gavel coverage of speeches on the House floor.

The Senate has used television much more fully, heightening the already substantial advantage that senators have over representatives in getting the public eye. Although radio and television coverage of the Senate floor was not allowed until 1978 (when the debates on the Panama Canal treaties were broadcast live), Senate committee hearings have frequently been televised for either news films or live broadcasts ever since Estes Kefauver demonstrated the power of this medium in 1950. Since 1986, the Senate has allowed live C-SPAN coverage of its sessions.

Senatorial use of televised committee hearings has helped turn the Senate into the incubator for presidential candidates. At least in most states, if you are a governor, you are located far from network television news cameras; the best you can hope for is that some disaster—a flood or a blizzard—will bring the cameras to you and focus them on your leadership. But senators all work in Washington, a city filled with cameras. No disaster is necessary to get on the air; only an investigation, a scandal, a major political conflict, or an articulate and telegenic personality is needed.

WHY DO WE HAVE SO MANY NEWS LEAKS?

American government is the leakiest in the world. The bureaucracy, members of Congress, and the White House staff regularly leak stories favorable to their interests. Of late, the leaks have become geysers, gushing forth torrents of insider stories. Many people in and out of government find it depressing that our government seems unable to keep anything secret for long. Others think the public has a right to know even more and that there are still too many secrets.

However you view leaks, you should understand why we have so many. The answer is found in the Constitution. Because we have separate institutions that must share power, each branch of government competes with the others to get power. One way to compete is to try to use the press to advance your pet projects and to make the other side look bad. There are far fewer leaks in other democratic nations in part because power is centralized in the hands of a prime minister, who does not need to leak in order to get the upper hand over the legislature, and because the legislature has too little information to be a good source of leaks. In addition, we have no Official Secrets Act of the kind that exists in England; except for a few matters, it is not against the law for the press to receive and print government secrets.

Even if the press and the politicians loved each other, the competition between the various branches of government would guarantee plenty of news leaks. But since the Vietnam War, the Watergate scandal, and the Iran-contra affair, the press and the politicians have come to distrust one another. As a result, journalists today are far less willing to accept at face value the statements of elected officials and are far more likely to try to find somebody who will leak "the real story." We have come, in short, to have an **adversarial press**—that is, one that (at least at the national level) is suspicious of officialdom and eager to break an embarrassing story that will win for its author honor, prestige, and (in some cases) a lot of money.

adversarial press The tendency of the national media to be suspicious of officials and eager to reveal unflattering stories about them.

This cynicism and distrust of government and elected officials have led to an era of attack journalism—seizing upon any bit of information or rumor that might call into question the qualifications or character of a public official. Media coverage of gaffes—misspoken words, misstated ideas, clumsy

When President Theodore Roosevelt cultivated the media, reporters usually were unknown and poorly paid.

Brown Brothers

moves—has become a staple of political journalism. At one time, such "events" as President Ford slipping down some stairs, Governor Dukakis dropping the ball while playing catch with a Boston Red Sox player, or Vice President Quayle misspelling the word *potato* would have been ignored, but now they are hot news items. Attacking public figures has become a professional norm, where once it was a professional taboo.

During the 1992 election, most of the national press clearly supported Bill Clinton. The love affair between Clinton and reporters lasted for several months after his inauguration. But when stories began to appear about Whitewater (an Arkansas real estate deal in which the Clintons were once involved), Clinton's alleged sexual escapades, and Hillary Rodham Clinton's profits in commodities trading, the press went into a feeding frenzy. The Clintons learned the hard way the truth of an old adage: if you want a friend in Washington, buy a dog.

Many people do not like this type of journalism, and the media's rising cynicism about the government is mirrored by the public's increasing cynicism about the media. In a national survey of registered voters conducted shortly before the 2000 presidential election, 89 percent of respondents agreed that the media's "political views influence coverage" often (57 percent) or sometimes (32 percent); 47 percent believed that "most journalists" were "pulling for" Gore to win; and 23 percent believed that most journalists were partial to Bush.[34] Most Americans really dislike biased journalism (or journalism they perceive as biased): 53 percent say they would require a license to practice journalism, and 70 percent favor court-imposed fines for inaccurate or biased reporting.[35]

Given their experiences with Watergate and Irangate, given the highly competitive nature of national newsgathering, and given their political ideology (which tends to put them to the left of the administration in power), American editors and reporters, at least at the national level, are likely to have an adversarial relationship with government for a long time to come. Given our constitutional system, there will always be plenty of people in government eager to help them with leaks hostile to one faction or another.

SENSATIONALISM IN THE MEDIA

Back in the 1930s, newspaper reporters knew President Franklin Roosevelt had a romantic affair with a woman other than his wife. They did not report it. In the early 1960s, many reporters knew President John Kennedy had many sexual affairs outside his marriage. They did not report this. In 1964, the director of the Federal Bureau of Investigation played for reporters secret tape recordings of the Reverend Martin Luther King, Jr., having sex with women other than his wife. They did not report it.

By the 1980s, sex and politics were extensively covered. When presidential candidate Gary Hart was caught in adultery and when President Bill Clinton was accused of adultery by Gennifer Flowers, of asking for sexual favors by Paula Jones, and of having sex with Monica Lewinsky in the Oval Office, these were headline news stories.

What had changed? Not politics: all of the people whom the press protected or reported on were Democrats. The big change was in the economics of journalism and the ideas of reporters.

Until the 1970s, Americans gathered their political news from one of three networks—ABC, CBS, or NBC. For a long time, these networks had only one half-hour news show a day. Today, however, viewers have the same three networks plus three cable news networks, two sports networks, 10 weekly newsmagazine shows, countless radio talk shows, and the Internet. Many of the cable networks, such as CNN, carry news 24 hours a day. The result of this intense competition is that each radio or television network has a small share of the audience. Today, less than half the public watches the evening network news shows. Dozens of news programs are trying to reach a shrinking audience, with the result that the audience share of each program is small. To attract any audience at all, each program has a big incentive to rely on sensational news stories—sex, violence, and intrigue. Reinforcing this desire to go with sensationalism is the fact that covering such stories is cheaper than investigating foreign policy or analyzing the tax code. During its first month, the Lewinsky story consumed more than one-third of the on-air time of the news networks—more than the U.S. showdown with Iran, the Winter Olympics, the pope's visit to Cuba, and the El Niño weather pattern combined.

Since the days of Vietnam and Watergate, journalists have become adversaries of the government.

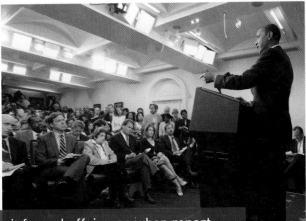

In 1933, White House press conferences were informal affairs, as when reporters gathered around Franklin Roosevelt's desk in the Oval Office. Today, they are huge gatherings held in a special conference room, as on the right. Obama press conference showing large number of reporters and the room around them as much as possible.

Bettmann/Corbis

JASON REED/Reuters/Landov

They instinctively distrust people in government. But to that attitude change can be added an economic one: in their desperate effort to reclaim market share, journalists are much more likely to rely on unnamed sources than once was the case. When the *Washington Post* broke the Watergate story in the 1970s, it required the reporters to have at least two sources for their stories. Now many reporters break stories that have only one unnamed source, and often not a source at all but a rumor posted on the Internet.

Before the terrorist attack on the United States on September 11, 2001, the big stories were the sexual conduct of President Clinton and the connection between California representative Gary Condit and a missing young woman. After September 11, the press focused on a more important matter—defeating terrorism at home and abroad. By early 2002, surveys indicated that the number of people who said they followed national news closely had increased slightly from 48 percent to 53 percent, and the number who said the media usually get the facts straight rose from 35 percent to 46 percent (the best public grade for accuracy in a decade). But within a year after the terrorist attack, public confidence in the media had collapsed, with more people than before saying the press was often inaccurate.[36] The television networks did not seem to gain any viewers back as a result of the crisis: fully 53 percent cited cable as their primary source for news on terrorism, versus 18 percent for local television and 17 percent for national networks.[37]

GOVERNMENT CONSTRAINTS ON JOURNALISTS

background A public official's statement to a reporter given on condition that the official not be named.

An important factor works against the influence of ideology and antiofficial attitudes on reporters—the need every reporter has for access to key officials. A reporter is only as good as his or her sources, and it is difficult to cultivate good sources if you regularly antagonize them. Thus, Washington reporters must constantly strike a balance between expressing their own views (and risk losing a valuable source) and keeping a source (and risk becoming its mouthpiece).

The great increase in the number of congressional staff members has made striking this balance easier than it once was. Since it is almost impossible to keep anything secret from Congress, the existence

"*Those are the headlines, and we'll be back in a moment to blow them out of proportion.*"

© 1991 Dana Fradon/The New Yorker Collection from cartoonbank.com. All Rights Reserved.

of 15,000 to 20,000 congressional staffers means there is a potential source for every conceivable issue and cause. Congress has become a gold mine for reporters. If a story annoys one congressional source, another source can easily be found.

The government is not without means to fight back. The number of press officers on the payroll of the White House, Congress, and the executive agencies has grown sharply in recent decades. Obviously, these people have a stake in putting out news stories that reflect favorably on their elected superiors. They can try to do this with press releases, but adversarial journalists are suspicious of "canned news" (although they use it nonetheless). Or the press officers can try to win journalistic friends by offering leaks and supplying background stories to favored reporters.

There are four ways in which reporters and public officials, or their press officers, can communicate:

- On the record: The reporter can quote the official by name.

- Off the record: What the official says cannot be used.

- On **background:** What the official says can be used but may not be attributed to him or her by name. Reporters often call these anonymous source "a high-ranking official" or "a knowledgeable member of Congress."

- On deep background: What the official says can be used but not attributed to anybody, even an anonymous source.

To get around the national press, public officials and their press officers can try to reach the local media directly by giving interviews or appearing on radio talk shows. The local media are a bit less likely than the national media to have an adversarial attitude toward the national government, and

RESEARCH FRONTIERS

Are "Tweeting" Politicians and "Digital Democracy" to Be Desired?

John McCain and Al Gore have something in common, and it's not just that both men once ran for president (Gore as a Democrat in 2000, McCain as a Republican in 2008) and lost. It's that both McCain and Gore are master micro-bloggers.

Gore was talking about the Internet and the "information superhighway" back in the 1980s before most people had ever seen a personal computer let alone used one daily, so he is a natural for cyber-social networking. McCain, however, is another story entirely. In 2008 he told reporters that he needed help logging onto the Internet.

But, in 2009, McCain and ABC News reporter (and former Clinton administration staff aide) George Stephanopoulos did an entire news interview via Twitter, the free service that enables users to send and read each others' "tweets" of up to 140 characters. As of mid-2009, McCain supposedly had some 300,000 "followers" (Twitter users who read his now-regular posts).

Gore and McCain are not the only politicians tweeting. Other 2008 presidential hopefuls, including Republican Ron Paul and Democrat Chris Dodd, are micro-bloggers. So are President Barrack Obama and House Speaker Nancy Pelosi. Many state and local politicians have gotten fully into the cyber-social networking act. For instance, in mid-2009, Newark Mayor Cory Booker had over 125,000 followers, and San Francisco Mayor Gavin Newsom had nearly 500,000 followers.

Given the growing popularity of tweeting and related high-technology communications, you might suppose that researchers have been carefully studying what, if any, impact they are having on campaigns, elections, and policymaking.

You might, but you would be wrong. Believe it or not, as late as the early 1980s, many reputable scholars still actually argued that television's influence on politics was minimal or ambiguous. It wasn't that they claimed that most voters did not watch television or were totally unaffected by what they watched.

Rather, the claim was essentially that, all things considered, most citizens' opinions, partisan attachments, and voting behavior was pretty much what it would have been had they not been "exposed" to television or been regular consumers of televised political news reports or the like.

Today, nobody doubts that television, other electronic communications, and the Internet in all its manifestations matter to campaign politics, legislative agenda-setting, and more.

Still, the nature, scope, and direction of these "media effects," and how they vary under different conditions, are points on which the experts don't all agree. Many unresolved research questions divide scholars that study the media and politics. For example, some argue that the Internet revolution has improved political coverage, while others argue that the Internet (and instant communications more generally) has created a shallow "digital democracy."

- Who is right? I don't know, but consider the source: I don't "tweet."

Sources: Jennings Bryant and Susan Thompson, *Fundamentals of Media Effects* (New York: McGraw Hill, 2008); Megan Boler, ed., *Digital Media and Democracy: Tactics in Hard Times* (Cambridge, Mass: MIT University Press, 2008); "Mayors in New Jersey and California Popular 'Tweeters,'" Associated Press, June 6, 2009.

one can select talk-show hosts on the basis of their known ideology.

The ultimate weapon in the government's effort to shape the press to its liking is the president's rewarding of reporters and editors who treat him well and his punishing of those who treat him badly. President Kennedy regularly called in offending reporters for brutal tongue-lashings and favored friendly reporters with tips and inside stories. Johnson did the same, with special attention to television reporters. Nixon made the mistake of attacking the press publicly, thereby allowing it to defend itself with appeals to the First Amendment. (Kennedy's and Johnson's manipulative skills were used privately.) Probably every president tries to use the press with whatever means are at his disposal, but in the long run it is the press, not the president,

WHAT WOULD YOU DO?

MEMORANDUM

To: *Matthew Wilson, senator*

From: *Margaret Drinker, legislative assistant*

Subject: *Protecting Journalists*

The Supreme Court has held that forcing a reporter to testify does not violate the First Amendment to the Constitution. But Congress could pass a law, similar to that in many states, banning such testimony if it reveals a confidential source.

Arguments for:

1. Thirty-four states now have shield laws similar to the one proposed by Congress.

2. Effective journalism requires protecting sources from being identified; without protection, a lot of important stories would not be written.

Arguments against:

1. Every person accused in a criminal trial has a right to know all of the evidence against him or her and to confront witnesses. A shield law would deprive people of this right.

2. A shield law would allow any government official to leak secret information with no fear of being detected.

Journalist Immunity Debated

October 5
WASHINGTON, D.C.

Congress today began deliberating over whether it should pass a law that would ban federal prosecutors from asking a reporter to reveal his or her confidential sources in a criminal trial. It has been a hot issue since reporter Judith Miller went to jail because she refused to reveal who had told her that Valerie Plame was a CIA officer. . .

Your decision:

Support bill _____   Oppose bill_____

who wins. Johnson decided not to run again in 1968 in part because of press hostility to him; Nixon was exposed by the press; Carter and Bush came to be disliked by national reporters. The press and the president need but do not trust one another; it is inevitably a stormy relationship.

SUMMARY

Changes in the nature of American politics have been accompanied by—and influenced by—changes in the nature of the mass media. The rise of strong national political party organizations was facilitated by the emergence of mass-circulation daily newspapers. Political reform movements depended in part on the development of national magazines catering to middle-class opinion. The weakening of political parties was accelerated by the ability of candidates to speak directly to constituents by radio and television.

The role of journalists in a democratic society poses an inevitable dilemma: if they are to serve well their functions as information gatherer, gatekeeper, scorekeeper, and watchdog, they must be free of government controls. But to the extent that they are free of such controls, they are also free to act in their own interests, whether political or economic. In the United States, a competitive press largely free of government controls (except in the area of broadcast licenses) has produced both a substantial diversity of opinion and a general (though not unanimous) commitment to the goal of fairness in news reporting. The national media are in general more liberal than the local media, but the extent to which a reporter's beliefs affect reporting varies greatly with the kind of story—routine, feature, or insider.

RECONSIDERING WHO GOVERNS?

1. How much power do the media have?

A lot, but it is limited by selective attention and personal knowledge. Selective attention means that people tend to believe only those arguments consistent with their own beliefs. Personal knowledge means people know a lot based on their own experiences regardless of what the press says. Politicians in and out of office spend a great deal of time cultivating the media, but in many campaigns it is clear that the press is more likely to favor some people over others.

2. Can we trust the media to be fair?

The public does not believe we can trust the press and that hostility has increased in recent years. Members of the national media are disproportionately liberal and secular, and there is evidence that these liberal views affect what they say or write. The extent of that political influence will differ, however, depending on whether a story is a routine feature or an insider account.

RECONSIDERING TO WHAT ENDS?

1. What public policies will the media support?

The media will lead the public to think about issues remote from their personal experiences, such as foreign policy. But the press can take up or drop issues, not because the issue has changed, but because the issue has become, to journalists, stale. Crime and drug abuse may be big topics some years and minor ones in other years. Liberal newspapers, such as the *New York Times,* will be much more interested in gay rights, gun control, and the environment than will conservative newspapers or even the general public.

WORLD WIDE WEB RESOURCES

To search many newspapers: **www.ipl.org**

To get analyses of the press

    Nonpartisan view: **www.cmpa.org**

    Liberal view: **www.fair.org**

    Conservative view: **www.mrc.org**

Public opinion about the press

    Pew Research Center: **people-press.org**

National media:

    New York Times: **www.nytimes.com**

    Wall Street Journal: **www. wsj.com**

    Washington Post: **www.washingtonpost.com**

SUGGESTED READINGS

Crouse, Timothy. *The Boys on the Bus.* New York: Random House, 1973. A lively, irreverent account by a participant of how reporters cover a presidential campaign.

Epstein, Edward J. *Between Fact and Fiction: The Problem of Journalism.* New York: Random House, 1975. Essays by a perceptive student of the press on media coverage of Watergate, the Pentagon Papers, the deaths of Black Panthers, and other major stories.

_____. *News from Nowhere.* New York: Random House, 1973. Analysis of how television network news programs are produced and shaped.

Garment, Suzanne. *Scandal.* New York: Random House, 1991. A careful look at the role of the media (and others) in fostering the "culture of mistrust."

Graber, Doris A. *Mass Media and American Politics.* 6th ed. Washington, D.C.: Congressional Quarterly Press, 2002. A good summary of what we know about the press and politics.

Iyengar, Shanto, and Donald R. Kinder. *News That Matters.* Chicago: University of Chicago Press, 1987. The report of experiments testing the effect of television news on public perceptions of politics.

Kurtz, Howard. *Spin Cycle: Inside the Clinton Propaganda Machine.* New York: Free Press, 1998. A journalistic account of how one president's staff tried to influence the media.

Lichter, S. Robert, Stanley Rothman, and Linda S. Lichter. *The Media Elite.* Bethesda, Md.: Adler and Adler, 1986. A study of the political beliefs of "elite" journalists and how those beliefs influence what we read and hear.

McGowan, William. *Coloring the News.* San Francisco: Encounter Books, 2001. An argument about the harmful effects of affirmative action and "identity politics" on news coverage.

Sabato, Larry J. *Feeding Frenzy.* New York: Free Press, 1991. Explains the press focus on political misconduct.

Part 3

Institutions of Government

But the great security against a gradual concentration of the several powers in the same department consists in giving to those who administer each department the necessary constitutional means and personal motives to resist encroachments of the others.

* Federalist No. 51

13

Congress

WHO GOVERNS?

1. Are members of Congress representative of the American people?
2. Does Congress normally do what most citizens want it to do?

TO WHAT ENDS?

1. Should Congress run under strong leadership?
2. Should Congress act more quickly?

If you are like most Americans, you trust the Supreme Court, respect the presidency (whether or not you like the president), and dislike Congress (even if you like your own member of Congress). Congress is the most unpopular branch of government. Some people think of it as the broken branch, badly in need of fixing. But it is also the most important one. You cannot understand the national government without first understanding Congress.

Glance at the Constitution and you will see why Congress is so important: the first four and a half pages are about Congress, while the presidency gets only a page and a half and the Supreme Court about three-quarters of one page. And when you go beyond the Constitution and discover how Congress actually operates, you may come to think it is not a broken branch at all, but rather one that is remarkably sensitive to American public opinion.

The late senator Daniel Patrick Moynihan once remarked that the United States is the only democratic government with a legislature. Of course, lots of democracies have parliaments that can pass laws. What he meant is that among the world's major democracies, only the U.S. Congress has great powers it can exercise independently of the executive branch. To see why this is so, we must understand the difference between a congress and a parliament.

Marc C. Burnett/Stock Boston

Congress versus Parliament

The United States (along with many Latin American nations) has a congress; Great Britain (along with most Western European nations) has a parliament. A hint as to the difference between the two kinds of legislatures can be found in the original meanings of the words: *Congress* derives from a Latin term that means "a coming together," a meeting, as of representatives from various places. *Parliament* comes from a French word, parler, that means "to talk."

There is of course plenty of talking—some critics say there is nothing *but* talking—in the U.S. Congress, and certainly members of a parliament represent to a degree their local districts. But the differences implied by the names of the lawmaking groups are real ones, with profound significance for how laws are made and how the government is run. These differences affect two important aspects of lawmaking bodies: how one becomes a member and what one does as a member.

Ordinarily, a person becomes a member of a parliament (such as the British House of Commons) by persuading a political party to put his or her name on the ballot. Though usually a local party committee selects a person to be its candidate, that committee often takes suggestions from national party headquarters. The local group selects as its candidate someone willing to support the national party program and leadership. In the election, voters in the district choose not between two or three personalities running for office, but between two or three national parties.

By contrast, a person becomes a candidate for representative or senator in the U.S. Congress by running in a primary election. Except in a very few places, political parties exercise little control over the choice of who is nominated to run for congressional office. (This is the case even though the person who wins the primary will describe himself or herself in the general election as a Democrat or a Republican.) Voters select candidates in the primaries because of their personalities, positions on issues, or overall reputation. Even in the general election, where the party label affects who votes for whom, many citizens vote "for the man" (or for the woman), not for the party. As a result of these different systems, a parliament tends to be made up of people loyal to the national party leadership who meet to debate and vote on party issues. A congress, on the other hand, tends to be made up of people who think of themselves as independent representatives of their districts or states and who, while willing to support their party on many matters, expect to vote as their (or their constituents') beliefs and interests require.

House Speaker Nancy Pelosi of California (center), flanked by House Majority Leader Steny Hoyer of Maryland (left) and House Minority Leader John Boehner of Ohio, speak with President Bush by telephone in the Speaker's office on Capitol Hill as the first day of the 111th Congress began.

AP Photo/Lauren Victoria Burke

How Things Work

The Powers of Congress

The powers of Congress are found in Article I, section 8, of the Constitution.

- To lay and collect taxes, duties, imposts, and excises
- To borrow money
- To regulate commerce with foreign nations and among the states
- To establish rules for naturalization (i.e., is becoming a citizen) and bankruptcy
- To coin money, set its value, and punish counterfeiting
- To fix the standard of weights and measures
- To establish a post office and post roads
- To issue patents and copyrights to inventors and authors
- To create courts inferior to (below) the Supreme Court
- To define and punish piracies, felonies on the high seas, and crimes against the law of nations

- To declare war
- To raise and support an army and navy and make rules for their governance
- To provide for a militia (reserving to the states the right to appoint militia officers and to train the militia under congressional rules)
- To exercise exclusive legislative powers over the seat of government (the District of Columbia) and other places purchased to be federal facilities (forts, arsenals, dockyards, and "other needful buildings")
- To "make all laws which shall be necessary and proper for carrying into execution the foregoing powers, and all other powers vested by this Constitution in the government of the United States" (*Note:* This "necessary and proper," or "elastic," clause has been generously interpreted by the Supreme Court, as explained in Chapter 16.)

Once they are in the legislature, members of a parliament discover they can make only one important decision—whether or not to support the government. The government in a parliamentary system such as Britain's consists of a prime minister and various cabinet officers selected from the party that has the most seats in parliament. As long as the members of that party vote together, that government will remain in power (until the next election). Should members of a party in power in parliament decide to vote against their leaders, the leaders lose office, and a new government must be formed. With so much at stake, the leaders of a party in parliament have a powerful incentive to keep their followers in line. They insist that all members of the party vote together on almost all issues. If someone refuses, the penalty is often drastic: the party does not renominate the offending member in the next election.

Members of the U.S. Congress do not select the head of the executive branch of government—that is done by the voters when they choose a president. Far from making members of Congress less powerful,

this makes them more powerful. Representatives and senators can vote on proposed laws without worrying that their votes will cause the government to collapse and without fearing that a failure to support their party will lead to their removal from the ballot in the next election. Congress has independent powers, defined by the Constitution, that it can exercise without regard to presidential preferences. Political parties do not control nominations for office, and thus they cannot discipline members of Congress who fail to support the party leadership. Because Congress is constitutionally independent of the president, and because its members are not tightly disciplined by a party leadership, individual members of Congress are free to express their views and vote as they wish. They are also free to become involved in the most minute details of lawmaking, budget making, and supervision of the administration of laws. They do this through an elaborate set of committees and subcommittees.

A real parliament, such as that in Britain, is an assembly of party representatives who choose a

Three powerful Speakers of the House: Thomas B. Reed (1889–1891, 1895–1899) (left), Joseph G. Cannon (1903–1911) (center), and Sam Rayburn (1941–1947, 1949–1953, 1955–1961) (right). Reed put an end to a filibuster in the House by refusing to allow dilatory motions and by counting as "present"—for purposes of a quorum—members in the House even though they were not voting. Cannon further enlarged the Speaker's power by refusing to recognize members who wished to speak without Cannon's approval and by increasing the power of the Rules Committee, over which he presided. Cannon was stripped of much of his power in 1910. Rayburn's influence rested more on his ability to persuade than on his formal powers.

government and discuss major national issues. The principal daily work of a parliament is debate. A congress, such as that in the United States, is a meeting place of the representatives of local constituencies—districts and states. Members of the U.S. Congress can initiate, modify, approve, or reject laws, and they share with the president supervision of the administrative agencies of the government. The principal work of a congress is representation and action, most of which takes place in committees.

What this means in practical terms to the typical legislator is easy to see. Since members of the British House of Commons have little independent power, they get rather little in return. They are poorly paid, may have no offices of their own and virtually no staff, are allowed only small sums to buy stationery, and can make a few free local telephone calls. Each is given a desk, a filing cabinet, and a telephone, but not always in the same place.

By contrast, a member of the U.S. House of Representatives, even a junior one, has power and is rewarded accordingly. For example, in 2009, each member earned a substantial salary ($174,000) and was entitled to a large office (or "clerk-hire") allowance, to pay for as many as 22 staffers. Each member also received individual allowances for travel, computer services, and the like. In addition, each member could mail newsletters and certain other documents to constituents for free using the "franking privilege." Senators, and representatives with seniority, received even larger benefits. Each senator is entitled to a generous office budget and legislative assistance allowance and is free to hire as many staff members as he or she wishes with the money. These examples are not given to suggest that members of Congress are overrewarded, but only that their importance as individuals in our political system can be inferred from the resources they command.

Question

1. *Who was the only former Speaker of the House to be elected President?*

Because the United States has a congress made up of people chosen to represent their states and districts, rather than a parliament made up to represent competing political parties, no one should be surprised to learn that members of the U.S. Congress are more concerned with their own constituencies and careers than with the interests of any organized party or program of action. And since Congress does not choose the president, members of Congress know that worrying about the voters they represent is much more important than worrying about whether the president succeeds with his programs. These two factors taken together mean that Congress tends to be a decentralized institution, with each member more interested in his or her own views and those of his or her voters than with the programs proposed by the president.

Indeed, Congress was designed by the Founders in ways that almost inevitably make it unpopular with voters. Americans want government to take action, follow a clear course of action, and respond to strong leaders. Americans dislike political arguments, the activities of special-interest groups, and the endless pulling and hauling that often precede any congressional decision. But the people who feel this way are deeply divided about what government should do: Be liberal? Be conservative? Spend money? Cut taxes? Support abortions? Stop abortions? Since they are divided, and since members of Congress must worry about how voters feel, it is inevitable that on controversial issues Congress will engage in endless arguments, worry about what interest groups (who represent different groups of voters) think, and work out compromise decisions. When it does those things, however, many people feel let down and say they have a low opinion of Congress.

Of course, a member of Congress might explain all these constitutional facts to the people, but not many members are eager to tell their voters that they do not really understand how Congress was created and organized. Instead they run for reelection by promising voters they will go back to Washington and "clean up that mess."

The Evolution of Congress

The Framers chose to place legislative powers in the hands of a congress rather than a parliament for philosophical and practical reasons. They did not want to have all powers concentrated in a single governmental institution, even one that was popularly elected, because they feared such a concentration could lead to rule by an oppressive or impassioned majority. At the same time, they knew the states were jealous of their independence and would never consent to a national constitution if it did not protect their interests and strike a reasonable balance between large and small states. Hence, they created a **bicameral** (two-chamber) **legislature**—with a House of Representatives, elected directly by the people, and a Senate, consisting of two members from each state, chosen by the legislatures of each state. Though "all legislative powers" were vested in Congress, those powers would be shared with the president (who could veto acts of Congress), limited to powers explicitly conferred on the federal government, and, as it turned out, subject to the power of the Supreme Court to declare acts of Congress unconstitutional.

For decades, critics of Congress complained that the body cannot plan or act quickly. They are right, but two competing values are at stake: centralization versus decentralization. If Congress acted quickly and decisively as a body, then there would have to be strong central leadership, restrictions on debate, few opportunities for stalling tactics, and minimal committee interference. If, on the other hand, the interests of individual members—and the constituencies they represent—were protected or enhanced, then there would have to be weak leadership, rules allowing for delay and discussion, and many opportunities for committee activity.

Though there have been periods of strong central leadership in Congress, the general trend, especially since the mid-20th century, has been toward decentralizing decision-making and enhancing the power of the individual member at the expense of the congressional leadership. This decentralization may not have been inevitable. Most American states have constitutional systems quite similar to the federal one, yet in many state legislatures, such as those in New York, Massachusetts, and Indiana, the leadership is quite powerful. In part, the position of these strong state legislative leaders may be the result of the greater strength of political parties in some states than in the nation as a whole. In large measure, however, it is a consequence of permitting state legislative leaders to decide who shall chair what committee and who shall receive what favors.

bicameral legislature A lawmaking body made up of two chambers or parts.

Answer

1. *James K. Polk (1844)*

House History: Six Phases

Phase One: The Powerful House

During the first three administrations—of George Washington, John Adams, and Thomas Jefferson—leadership in Congress often was supplied by the president or his cabinet officers. Rather quickly, however, Congress began to assert its independence. The House of Representatives was the preeminent institution, overshadowing the Senate.

Phase Two: The Divided House

In the late 1820s, the preeminence of the House began to wane. Andrew Jackson asserted the power of the presidency by vetoing legislation he did not like. The party unity necessary for a Speaker, or any leader, to control the House was shattered by the issue of slavery. Of course, representatives from the South did not attend during the Civil War, and their seats remained vacant for several years after it ended. A group called the Radical Republicans, led by men such as Thaddeus Stevens of Pennsylvania, produced strong majorities for measures aimed at punishing the defeated South. But as time passed, the hot passions the war had generated

One of the most powerful Speakers of the House, Henry Clay is shown here addressing the U.S. Senate around 1850.

Library of Congress

The House of Representatives, though always powerful, often has changed the way in which it is organized and led. In some periods, it has given its leader, the Speaker, a lot of power; in other periods, it has given much of that power to the chairmen of the House committees; and in still other periods, it has allowed individual members to acquire great influence. To simplify a complicated story, the box starting on this page outlines six different periods in the history of the House.

The House faces fundamental problems: it wants to be big (it has 435 members) and powerful, and its members want to be powerful as individuals and as a group. But being big makes it hard for the House to be powerful unless some small group is given the authority to run it. If a group runs the place, however, the individual members lack much power. Individuals can gain power, but only at the price of making the House harder to run and thus reducing its collective power in government. There is no lasting solution to these dilemmas, and so the House will always be undergoing changes.

The Senate does not face any of these problems. It is small enough (100 members) that it can be run began to cool, and it became clear that the leadership of the House remained weak.

Phase Three: The Speaker Rules

Toward the end of the 19th century, the Speaker of the House gained power. When Thomas B. Reed of Maine became Speaker in 1889, he obtained by vote of the Republican majority more authority than any of his predecessors, including the right to select the chairmen and members of all committees. He chaired the Rules Committee and decided what business would come up for a vote, any limitations on debate, and who would be allowed to speak and who would not. In 1903, Joseph G. Cannon of Illinois became Speaker. He tried to maintain Reed's tradition, but he had many enemies within his Republican ranks.

Phase Four: The House Revolts

In 1910–1911, the House revolted against "Czar" Cannon, voting to strip the Speaker of his right to appoint committee chairmen and to remove him from the Rules Committee. The powers lost by the Speaker flowed to the party caucus, the Rules Committee, and the chairmen of the standing committees. It was not, however, until the 1960s and 1970s that House members struck out against all forms of leadership.

Phase Five: The Members Rule

Newly elected Democrats could not get the House to vote on a meaningful civil rights bill until 1964 because powerful committee chairmen, most of them from the South, kept such legislation bottled up. In response, Democrats changed their rules so that chairmen lost much of their authority. Beginning in the 1970s, committee chairmen would no longer be selected simply on the basis of seniority: they had to be elected by the members of the majority party. Chairmen could no longer refuse to call committee meetings, and most meetings had to be public. Committees without subcommittees had to create them and allow their members to choose subcommittee chairmen. Individual members' staffs were greatly enlarged, and half of all majority-party members were chairmen of at least one committee or subcommittee.

Phase Six: The Leadership Returns

Since every member had power, it was harder for the House to get anything done. By slow steps, culminating in some sweeping changes made in 1995, there were efforts to restore some of the power the Speaker had once had. The number of committees and subcommittees was reduced. Republican Speaker Newt Gingrich dominated the choice of committee chairmen, often passing over more senior members for more agreeable junior ones. But Gingrich's demise was as quick as his rise. His decision not to pass some appropriations bills forced many government offices to close for a short period, he had to pay a fine for using tax-exempt funds for political purposes, and then the Republicans lost a number of seats in the 1998 election. Gingrich resigned as Speaker and as a member of the House and was replaced by a more moderate Speaker, Republican Dennis Hastert of Illinois, with a penchant for accommodating his colleagues. As the 110th Congress began in 2007, Democrat Nancy Pelosi of California held the Speaker's gavel. She was the first woman to lead the House.

without giving much authority to any small group of leaders. In addition, it has escaped some of the problems the House once faced. During the period leading up to the Civil War, it was carefully balanced so that the number of senators from slaveowning states exactly equaled the number from free states. Hence, fights over slavery rarely arose in the Senate.

From the first, the Senate was small enough that no time limits had to be placed on how long a senator could speak. This meant there never was anything like a Rules Committee that controlled the amount of debate.

Finally, senators were not elected by the voters until this century. Prior to that, they were picked instead by state legislatures. Thus senators often were the leaders of local party organizations, with an interest in funneling jobs and contracts back to their states.

The big changes in the Senate came not from any fight about how to run it (nobody ever really ran it), but from a dispute over how its members should be chosen. For more than a century after, the Founding members of the Senate were chosen by state legislatures. Though often these legislatures

Politically Speaking

Filibuster

A filibuster is a technique by which a small number of senators attempt to defeat a measure by talking it to death—that is, by speaking continuously and at such length as to induce the supporters of the measure to drop it in order to get on with the Senate's business.

The right to filibuster is governed by the Senate's Rule 22, which allows for unlimited debate unless at least 60 senators agree to a motion to cut it off.

Originally *filibusterers* were 16th-century English and French pirates and buccaneers who raided Spanish treasure ships. The term came from a Dutch word, *vrijbuiter*, meaning "free-booter," which was converted into the English word *filibuster*.

The word came into use in America as a term for "continuous talking" in the mid-19th century. One of its first appearances was in 1854, when a group of senators tried to talk to death the Kansas-Nebraska Act.

Source: From *Safire's Political Dictionary* by William Safire. Copyright © 1968, 1972, 1978 by William Safire. Reprinted by permission of Random House, Inc. and the author.

A cartoon from *Puck* in 1890 expressed popular resentment over the "Millionaires Club," as the Senate had become known.

New York Public Library

filibuster An attempt to defeat a bill in the Senate by talking indefinitely, thus preventing the Senate from taking action on the bill.

picked popular local figures to be senators, just as often there was intense political maneuvering among the leaders of various factions, each struggling to win (and sometimes buy) the votes necessary to become senator. By the end of the 19th century the Senate was known as the Millionaires' Club because of the number of wealthy party leaders and businessmen in it. There arose a demand for the direct, popular election of senators.

Naturally the Senate resisted, and without its approval the necessary constitutional amendment could not pass Congress. When some states threatened to demand a new constitutional convention, the Senate feared that such a convention would change more than just the way in which senators were chosen. A protracted struggle ensued, during which many state legislatures devised ways to ensure that the senators they picked would already have won a popular election. The Senate finally agreed to a constitutional amendment that required the popular election of its members, and in 1913 the Seventeenth Amendment was approved by the necessary three-fourths of the states. Ironically, given the intensity of the struggle over this question, no great change in the composition of the Senate resulted; most of those members who had first been chosen by state legislatures managed to win reelection by popular vote.

The other major issue in the development of the Senate was the filibuster. A **filibuster** is a prolonged speech, or series of speeches, made to delay action in a legislative assembly. It had become a common—and unpopular—feature of Senate life by the end of the 19th century. It was used by liberals and conservatives alike and for lofty as well as self-serving purposes. The first serious effort to restrict the filibuster came in 1917, after an important foreign policy measure submitted by President Wilson had been talked to death by, as Wilson put it, "eleven willful men." Rule 22 was adopted by a Senate fearful of tying a president's hands during a wartime crisis. The rule provided that debate could be cut off if two-thirds of the senators present and voting agreed to a "cloture" motion (it has since been revised to allow 60 senators to cut off debate). Two years later, it was first invoked successfully when the Senate voted cloture to end, after 55 days, the debate over the Treaty of Versailles. Despite the existence of Rule 22, the tradition of unlimited debate remains strong in the Senate.

Who Is in Congress?

With power so decentralized in Congress, the kind of person elected to it is especially important. Since each member exercises some influence,

the beliefs and interests of each individual affect policy. Viewed simplistically, most members of Congress seem the same: the typical representative or senator is a middle-aged white Protestant male lawyer. If all such persons usually thought and voted alike, that would be an interesting fact, but they do not, and so it is necessary to explore the great diversity of views among seemingly similar people.

SEX AND RACE

Congress has gradually become less male and less white. Between 1950 and 2009, the number of women in the House increased from nine to 77 and the number of African Americans from two to 42. There are also 25 Hispanic members.

Until recently, the Senate changed much more slowly (see Table 13.1). Before the 1992 election, there were no African Americans and only two women in the Senate. But in 1992, four more women, including one black woman, Carol Mosely Braun of Illinois, were elected. Two more were elected in 1994, when a Native American, Ben Nighthorse Campbell of

Table 13.1 Blacks, Hispanics, and Women in Congress, 1971–2010

Congress	Blacks	Senate Hispanics	Women	Blacks	House Hispanics	Women
111th (2009–2010)	1	3	17	42	25	77
110th	1	3	16	38	23	74
109th	1	0	14	37	23	59
108th	0	0	13	39	23	62
107th	0	0	13	36	19	59
106th	0	0	9	39	19	58
105th	1	1	9	37	18	51
104th	1	0	8	38	18	48
103rd	1	0	6	38	17	47
102nd	0	0	2	26	10	29
101st	0	0	2	24	11	25
100th	0	0	2	23	11	23
99th	0	0	2	20	11	22
98th	0	0	2	21	10	22
97th	0	0	2	17	6	19
96th	0	0	1	16	6	16
95th	1	0	2	16	5	18
94th	1	1	0	15	5	19
93rd	1	1	0	15	5	14
92nd (1971–1972)	1	1	2	12	5	13

Source: *Congressional Quarterly*, various years.

When the Democrats regained control of the House, the very liberal John Conyers (ADA score = 100%) became chairman of the House Judiciary Committee in place of the very conservative James Sensenbrenner (ADA score = 10%).

Marcy Kaptur (D., OH) discusses the war on terrorism in front of the capitol.

Colorado, also became a senator. By 2009, there was one African American and 17 women in the Senate.

The relatively small number of African Americans and Hispanics in the House understates their influence, at least when the Democrats are in the majority. In 1994, four House committees were chaired by blacks and three by Hispanics. In the same year, however, no woman chaired a committee. The reason for this difference in power is that the former tend to come from safe districts and thus have more seniority than the latter. When the Democrats retook control of Congress in 2007, African Americans and Hispanics became chairpersons of several important committees.

INCUMBENCY

The most important change that has occurred in the composition of Congress has been so gradual that most people have not noticed it. In the 19th century, a large fraction—often a majority—of congressmen served only one term. In 1869, for example, more than half the members of the House were serving their first term in Congress. Being a congressman in those days was not regarded as a career. This was in part because the federal government was not very important (most of the interesting political decisions were made by the states); in part because travel to Washington, D.C., was difficult and the city was not a pleasant place in which to live; and in part because being a congressman did not pay well. Furthermore, many congressional districts were highly competitive, with the two political parties fairly evenly balanced in each.

By the 1950s, however, serving in Congress had become a career. Between 1863 and 1969, the proportion of first-termers in the House fell from 58 percent to 8 percent.[1] As the public took note of this shift, people began to complain about "professional politicians" being "out of touch with the people." A movement to impose term limits was started. In 1995, the House approved a constitutional amendment to do just that, but it died in the Senate. Then the Supreme Court struck down an effort by a state to impose term limits on its own members of Congress.

As it turned out, natural political forces were already doing what the term limits amendment was supposed to do. The 1992 and 1994 elections brought scores of new members to the House, with the result that by 1995 the proportion of members who were serving their first or second terms had risen sharply. Three things were responsible for this change. First, when congressional district lines were redrawn after the 1990 census, a lot of incumbents found themselves running in new districts they couldn't carry. Second, voter disgust at a variety of Washington political scandals made them receptive to appeals from candidates who could describe themselves as "outsiders." And third, the Republican victory in 1994—made possible in part by the conversion of the South from a Democratic bastion to a Republican stronghold—brought a lot of new faces to the Capitol.

This influx of freshman members should not obscure the fact that incumbents still enjoy enormous advantages in congressional elections.[2] Even in 1994, when 35 incumbent Democrats lost to Republicans, over 90 percent of all House members who ran for reelection were reelected. In the Senate, 92 percent of incumbents who ran again were reelected. In 2004 and 2006, two of the most hotly contested elections in recent history, only a handful of House incumbents who ran for reelection lost.

The arrival of scores of new faces in Congress should not obscure the fact that most House members still win big in their districts. Political scientists call districts that have close elections (when the winner gets less than 55 percent of the vote) **marginal districts** and districts where incumbents win by wide margins (55 percent or more) **safe districts.** The proportion of House incumbents who have won reelection with at least 60 percent of the vote increased from about three-fifths in the 1950s and early 1960s to three-quarters in the 1970s and almost nine-tenths in the late 1980s (see Figure 13.1). Even as this trend began to change in 1990, most House districts remained safe. Senators remained less secure. Just the same, over half of Senate incumbents won with 60 percent or more of the vote in one half the elections since 1980; in 2008, nearly two-thirds of Senate incumbents won with 60 percent or more of the vote.

Why congressional seats have become less marginal—that is, safer—is a matter on which scholars do not agree. Some feel it is the result of television and other media. But challengers can go on television, too, so why should this benefit incumbents? Another possibility is that voters are becoming less and less likely to automatically support whatever candidate wins the nomination of their own party. They are more likely, in short, to vote for the person rather than the party. And they are more likely to have heard of a person who is an incumbent: incumbents can deluge the voter with free mailings, they can travel frequently (and at public expense) to meet constituents, and they can get their names in the newspaper by sponsoring bills or conducting investigations. Simply having a familiar name is important in getting elected, and incumbents find it easier than challengers to make their names known.

Finally, some scholars argue that incumbents can use their power to get programs passed or funds spent to benefit their districts—and thereby to benefit themselves. They can help keep an army base open, support the building of a new highway (or block the building of an unpopular one), take credit for federal grants to local schools and hospitals, make certain a particular industry or labor union is protected by tariffs against foreign competition, and so on.[3]

marginal districts Political districts in which candidates elected to the House of Representatives win in close elections, typically by less than 55 percent of the vote.

safe districts Districts in which incumbents win by margins of 55 percent or more.

Probably all of these factors make some difference. Whatever the explanation, the tendency of voters to return incumbents to office means that in ordinary times no one should expect any dramatic changes in the composition of Congress.

PARTY

Thirty-nine Congresses convened between 1933 and 2009 (a new Congress convenes every two years). The Democrats controlled both houses in 27 of these

Figure 13.1
Percentage of Incumbents Reelected to Congress

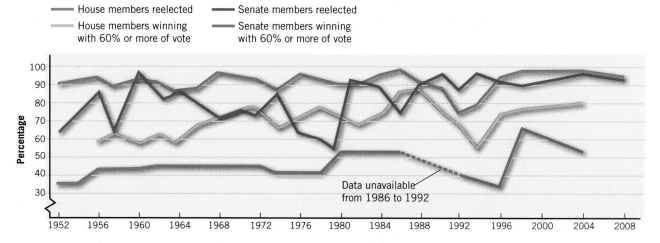

Source: Harold W. Stanley and Richard G. Niemi, *Vital Statistics on American Politics, 1999–2000* (Washington, D.C.: Congressional Quarterly Press, 2000), table 1-18; 2004 update by Marc Siegal.

Congresses and at least one house in 29 of them. Scholars differ in their explanations of why the Democrats have so thoroughly dominated Congress. Most of the research on the subject has focused on the reasons for Democratic control of the House.

In every election from 1968 to 1992, the percentage of the popular vote for Republican candidates to the House was higher than the percentage of House seats that actually went to Republicans. For example, in 1976 the Republicans won 42.1 percent of the vote but received only 32.9 percent of the seats. Some argued that this gap between votes and seats occurred because Democratic-controlled state legislatures redrew congressional district maps in ways that make it hard for Republicans to win House seats. Some striking anecdotal evidence supports this conclusion. For example, following the 1990 census, the Democratic-controlled Texas legislature crafted a new congressional district map clearly designed to benefit Democrats. In 1992, Republicans won 48 percent of the House vote in Texas but received only 30 percent of the seats. But after Republicans won control of more state legislatures, matters began to change. In Texas, a new districting plan was adopted that ensured more House seats would be won by Republicans. And when a court, rather than the Democratic legislature, redrew California's district lines, both parties won the same proportion of seats as their share of the popular vote.[4] In 2006, things had evened out nationally: both parties won about the same share of House seats as their percentage of the vote.

Partisan tinkering with district maps and other structural features of House elections is not a sufficient explanation of why Democrats dominated the House until 1994. As one study concluded, "Virtually all the political science evidence to date indicates that the electoral system has little or no partisan bias, and that the net gains nationally from redistricting for one party over another are very small."[5] To control the redistricting process, one party must control both houses of the legislature, the governor's office, and, where necessary, the state courts. These conditions simply do not exist in most states. And even if district lines were consistently drawn with scrupulous fairness, the Democrats would still win control of the House, because they win more votes. The pre-1994 Republican vote-seat gap is accounted for in part by the fact that the Democrats tend to do exceptionally well in low-turnout districts such as minority-dominated inner cities, while the Republicans tend to do well in high-turnout districts such as affluent white suburbs.

Congressional incumbents have come to enjoy certain built-in electoral advantages over challengers.

Democrats were in the majority as the advantages of incumbency grew, but Republicans enjoyed the same or greater advantages from 1994 to 2006. Studies suggest the incumbency advantage was worth about two percentage points prior to the 1960s but has grown to six to eight points today.

It is important to remember that from time to time major electoral convulsions do alter the membership of Congress. For example, in the election of 1938 the Democrats lost 70 seats in the House; in 1942, they lost 50; in 1950, they lost 29; and in 1966, they lost 48. Despite these big losses, the Democrats retained a majority in the House in each of these years. Not so, however, in 1994, when the Democrats lost 52 House seats (the largest loss by either party since the Republicans lost 75 seats in 1948), and Republicans gained majorities in both the House and the Senate.

Just as it is not easy to explain why Democrats dominated Congress for half a century, so it is not easy to explain why that domination ended when and as it did in 1994, or why Democrats regained control in 2006. Several reasons, however, stand out. By the 1990s, the advantages of incumbency had turned into disadvantages: voters increasingly came to dislike "professional politicians," whom they held responsible for "the mess in Washington." Just what "the mess" was varied according to which voter you asked, but it included chronic budget deficits, the congressional habit of exempting itself from laws that affected everybody else, constant bickering between Congress and the White House, and various congressional scandals. During the 1980s, about 40 members of Congress were charged with misconduct ranging from having sex with minors to accepting illegal gifts. When it was disclosed that the House had its own bank that would cash checks even for members who (temporarily) had no funds in their accounts, public indignation exploded, even though almost no taxpayer money was lost. Public respect for Congress, as measured by the polls, plummeted.

The Democrats had the misfortune of being the majority party in Congress when all of this happened. The anti-incumbent mood, coupled with the effects of redistricting after the 1990 census and the shift of the South to the Republican party, brought the Republicans into power in the House and Senate in the 1994 elections. By 2006, however, with an unpopular Republican president in the White House, and with most voters blaming congressional leaders for moving the country in the "wrong direction," Democrats regained control of both chambers.

In the past, the Democratic party was more deeply divided than the Republicans because of the

Question

2. *Who were the three sitting Senators to be elected President?*

presence in Congress of conservative Democrats from the South. These southern Democrats often would vote with the Republicans in the House or Senate, thereby forming what came to be called the **conservative coalition.** During the 1960s and 1970s, that coalition came together in about one-fifth of all roll-call votes. When it did, it usually won, defeating northern Democrats. But since the 1980s, and especially since the watershed election of 1994, the conservative coalition has become much less important. The reason is simple: many southern Democrats in Congress have been replaced by southern Republicans, and the southern Democrats who remain (many of them African Americans) are as liberal as northern Democrats. The effect of this change is to make Congress, and especially the House, more ideologically partisan—Democrats are liberals, Republicans are conservatives—and this in turn helps explain why there is more party unity in voting—no matter which party is in charge.

Do Members Represent Their Voters?

In a decentralized, individualistic institution such as Congress, it is not obvious how its members will behave. They could be devoted to doing whatever their constituents want or, since most voters are not aware of what their representatives do, act in accordance with their own beliefs, the demands of pressure groups, or the expectations of congressional leaders. You may think it would be easy to figure out whether members are devoted to their constituents by analyzing how they vote, but that is not quite right. Members can influence legislation in many ways other than by voting: they can conduct hearings, help mark up bills in committee meetings, and offer amendments to the bills proposed by others. A member's final vote on a bill may conceal as much as it reveals: some members may vote for a bill that contains many things they dislike because it also contains a few things they value.

There are at least three theories about how members of Congress behave: representational, organizational, and attitudinal.

The *representational* explanation is based on the reasonable assumption that members want to get reelected, and therefore they vote to please their constituents. The *organizational* explanation is based on the equally reasonable assumption that since most constituents do not know how their legislator has voted, it is not essential to please them. But it is important to please fellow members of Congress, whose goodwill is valuable in getting things done and in acquiring status and power in Congress. The *attitudinal* explanation is based on the assumption that there are so many conflicting pressures on members of Congress that they cancel one another out, leaving them virtually free to vote on the basis of their own beliefs.

> **conservative coalition**
> An alliance between Republican and conservative Democrats.

Political scientists have studied, tested, and argued about these (and other) explanations for decades, and nothing like a consensus has emerged. Some facts have been established, however.

REPRESENTATIONAL VIEW

The representational view has some merit under certain circumstances—namely, when constituents have a clear view on some issue and a legislator's vote on that issue is likely to attract their attention. Such is often the case for civil rights laws: representatives with significant numbers of black voters in their districts are not likely to oppose civil rights bills; representatives with few African Americans in their districts are comparatively free to oppose such bills. (Until the late 1960s, many southern representatives were able to oppose civil rights measures because the African Americans in their districts were prevented from voting. On the other hand, many representatives without black constituents have supported civil rights bills, partly out of personal belief and partly perhaps because certain white groups in their districts—organized liberals, for example—have insisted on such support.)

Keith Ellison (D., MN), the first Muslim elected to Congress.

Craig Lassig/EPA/Corbis

Answer

One study of congressional roll-call votes and constituency opinion showed that the correlation between the two was quite strong on civil rights bills. There was also a positive (though not as strong) correlation between roll-call votes and constituency opinion on social welfare measures. Scarcely any correlation, however, was found between congressional votes and hometown opinion on foreign policy measures.[6] Foreign policy generally is remote from the daily interests of most Americans, and public opinion about such matters can change rapidly. It is not surprising, therefore, that congressional votes and constituent opinion should be different on such questions.

From time to time, an issue arouses deep passions among the voters, and legislators cannot escape the need either to vote as their constituents want, whatever their personal views, or to anguish at length about which side of a divided constituency to support. Gun control has been one such question, the use of federal money to pay for abortions has been another, and the effort to impeach President Clinton was a third. Some fortunate members of Congress get unambiguous cues from their constituents on these matters, and no hard decision is necessary. Others get conflicting views, and they know that whichever way they vote, it may cost them dearly in the next election. Occasionally, members of Congress in this fix will try to be out of town when the matter comes up for a vote. One careful study found that constituency influences were an important factor in Senate votes,[7] but no comparable study has been done for the House.

You might think that members of Congress who won a close race in the last election—who come from a "marginal" district—would be especially eager to vote the way their constituents want. Research so far has shown that is not generally the case. There seem to be about as many independent-minded members of Congress from marginal as from safe districts. Perhaps it is because opinion is so divided in a marginal seat that one cannot please everybody; as a result, the representative votes on other grounds.

In general, the problem with the representational explanation is that public opinion is not strong and clear on most measures on which Congress must vote. Many representatives and senators face constituencies that are divided on key issues. Some constituents go to special pains to make their views known (these interest groups were discussed in Chapter 11). But as we indicated, the power of interest groups to affect congressional votes depends, among other things, on whether a legislator sees them as united and powerful or as disorganized and marginal.

This does not mean that constituents rarely have a direct influence on voting. The influence they have probably comes from the fact that legislators risk defeat should they steadfastly vote in ways that can be held against them by a rival in the next election. Though most congressional votes are not known to most citizens, blunders (real or alleged) quickly become known when an electoral opponent exploits them.

Still, any member of Congress can choose the positions he or she takes on most roll-call votes (and on all voice or standing votes, where names are not recorded). And even a series of recorded votes against constituency opinion need not be fatal: a member of Congress can win votes in other ways—for example, by doing services for constituents or by appealing to the party loyalty of the voters.

ORGANIZATIONAL VIEW

When voting on matters where constituency interests or opinions are not vitally at stake, members of Congress respond primarily to cues provided by their colleagues. This is the organizational explanation of their votes. The principal cue is party; as already noted, what party a member of Congress belongs to explains more about his or her voting record than any other single factor. Additional organizational cues come from the opinions of colleagues with whom the member of Congress feels a close ideological affinity: for liberals in the House, it is the Democratic Study Group; for conservatives, it often has been the Republican Study Committee or the Wednesday Club. But party and other organizations do not have clear positions on all matters. For the scores of votes that do not involve the "big questions," a representative or senator is especially likely to be influenced by the members of his or her party on the sponsoring committee.

It is easy to understand why. Suppose you are a Democratic representative from Michigan who is summoned to the floor of the House to vote on a bill to authorize a new weapons system. You haven't the faintest idea what issues might be at stake. There is no obvious liberal or conservative position on this matter. How do you vote? Simple. You take your cue from several Democrats on the House Armed Services Committee that handled the bill. Some are liberal; others are conservative. If both liberals and conservatives support the bill, you vote for it unhesitatingly. If they disagree, you vote with whichever Democrat is generally closest to your own political ideology. If the matter is one that affects your state, you can take your cue from members of your state's delegation to Congress.

ATTITUDINAL VIEW

Finally, there is evidence that the ideology of a member of Congress affects how he or she votes. We have seen that Democratic and Republican legislators differ sharply on a liberal-versus-conservative scale. On both domestic and foreign policy issues, many tend to be consistently liberal or conservative.[8]

This consistency isn't surprising. As we saw in Chapter 7, political elites generally think more ideologically than the public.

On many issues, the average member of the House has opinions close to those of the average voter. Senators, by contrast, often are less in tune with public opinion. In the 1970s, they were much more liberal than voters; in the early 1980s, more conservative. Two senators from the same state often mobilize quite different bases of support. The result is that many states, such as California, Delaware, and New York, have been represented by senators with almost diametrically opposed views.

Of late, the Senate has gone through three phases. In the first, during the 1950s and early 1960s, it was a cautious, conservative institution dominated by southern senators and displaying many of the features of a "club" that welcomed members into its inner circle only after they had displayed loyalty to its gentlemanly (and, in effect, conservative) customs. This was the era when the Senate was the graveyard of civil rights bills.

The second period began in the mid-1960s as liberal senators rose steadily in number, seniority, and influence, helped along by the Johnson reforms, which made it easier for junior senators to gain chairmanships. The decentralization of the Senate gave more power to individual senators, including liberals. In 1972, there were about 24 liberal senators, but among them they held 40 subcommittee chairmanships.[9]

The third period began in the late 1970s and became most visible after the 1980 elections when many liberals lost their seats to conservative Republicans. The conservatism of the present Senate is based more on ideology than on the rules of the southern "club" that characterized it in the 1950s.

The Democratic party is more deeply divided than the Republican. There are only a few liberal Republicans, but there have been many more conservative Democrats from the South and West. Southern Democrats often teamed up with Republicans to form a conservative coalition. In a typical year, a majority of Republicans and southern Democrats would vote together against a majority of northern Democrats about 20 to 25 percent of the time. When the conservative coalition did form, it usually won: between 1970 and 1982, it won about two-thirds of the votes on which it held together. After the Reagan victory and the Republican gain of 30 seats in the House in 1981, the conservative coalition became even more effective, dominating key votes on the Reagan budget and tax plans.

But the conservative coalition was important only when there were a lot of conservative southern Democrats. Many of these have now been replaced with southern Republicans. As a result, almost all of the conservatives are now in the Republican party, so there is not much of a coalition left to form. The map and accompanying tables (on page 329) show the most liberal and most conservative state delegations in the House.

A Polarized Congress

Figure 13.2 shows that a generation ago, the more liberal half of the House had 29 Republicans.[10] About three decades later, however, it had only 10 Republicans. Similarly, a generation ago, the more conservative half of the House had 56 Democrats. By 1998, however, it had zero. (Zero!) The picture for the 111th Congress would not be radically different from that for the 105th Congress. Today, as it had been for over a decade now, Congress is polarized along ideological and partisan lines.

Congress has become an increasingly ideological organization, that is, its members are more sharply divided by political ideology than they once were and certainly more divided than American voters. In short, the attitudinal explanation of how members vote has increased in importance, while the organizational explanation has declined. All of Congress's most liberal members are Democrats, and all of its most conservative ones are Republicans. That is not what you would find among ordinary voters. A lot of us split our tickets, voting for one party's presidential nominee and a different party's congressional candidate.

This higher level of congressional ideology does not mean that its existing members have changed how they think. Rather, it means that new kinds of members have been elected, bringing to Congress a more ideological perspective.[11] In 1974 (the election right after Watergate), a large number of more ideological

Figure 13.2

Distribution of House Members in Terms of Their "Liberal" or "Conservative" Characteristics, by Party

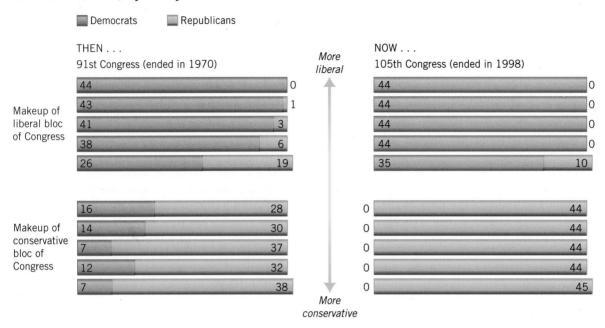

Source: "A Polarized Congress," *National Journal*, January 21, 2006, p. 21, reporting data compiled and depicted by Duke University political scientists David Rohde and John Aldrich. Reprinted with permission from *National Journal*. Copyright © 2007 National Journal. All rights reserved.

Democrats entered Congress. In 1994, there was a large influx of more ideological Republicans.

Congress has become more polarized than voters in terms of political beliefs. Among voters, the average Democrat and the average Republican—though they surely disagree—nonetheless have views that put them close to the center of the political spectrum. But among members of Congress, the average Democrat is very liberal and the average Republican very conservative, a fact that keeps them far from the political center. There are, of course, some conservative Democrats and some liberal Republicans, but their numbers have been getting smaller and smaller.

One result of this polarization is that members of Congress, especially those in the House, do not get along as well as they once did with members who disagree with them, and they are more likely to challenge, investigate, and denounce one another. Two Speakers of the House, Jim Wright and Newt Gingrich, were investigated and resigned. Many presidential nominees have been subjected to withering investigations, some based on ideological differences and some on charges of ethical violations, many of which were dubious. President Clinton was impeached on a nearly party-line vote. Members regularly accuse one another of misconduct. When they run for reelection, they often use negative ads

of the sort discussed in Chapter 10. The mass media feed on and aggravate this tendency because of their interest in scandal.

The result is that the public—already puzzled by the constitutional need members have to discuss policy matters for long periods, listen to interest groups, and reach compromise settlements—are now put off even more by the political disposition members have to attack one another. At one time, the constitutional need to negotiate was facilitated by reasonably good relationships between Democrats and Republicans, most of whom treated one another with politeness and socialized together after hours. This congenial social relationship no longer exists in most cases, and the public has noticed.

The Organization of Congress: Parties and Caucuses

Congress is not a single organization; it is a vast and complex collection of organizations by which the business of the legislative branch is carried on and through which its members form alliances (see Figure 13.3). If we were to look inside the British

Map 13.1

State Delegations in the House

This map shows the most-liberal to most-conservative state delegations in the House, based on each delegation's average composite liberal score in *National Journal's* 2005 vote ratings.

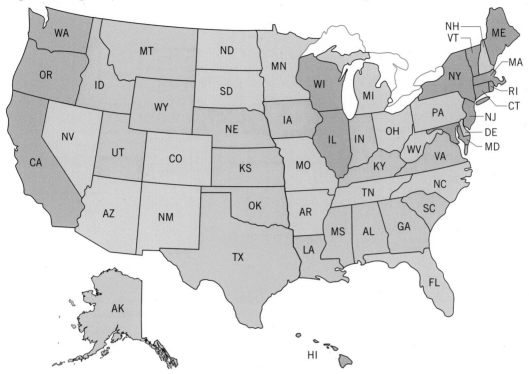

MOST-LIBERAL STATE DELEGATIONS			
Massachusetts	90	Oregon	65
Vermont	90	Connecticut	64
Maine	80	Illinois	63
Rhode Island	74	New Jersey	62
New York	69	California	61
Maryland	68	Washington	61
Hawaii	67	Wisconsin	61

CENTRIST STATE DELEGATIONS			
North Dakota	60	Missouri	46
South Dakota	59	North Carolina	46
West Virginia	58	Pennsylvania	46
Minnesota	56	Colorado	44
New Mexico	54	Nevada	43
Delaware	53	Tennessee	43
Arkansas	52	New Hampshire	42
Michigan	52	Arizona	40
Ohio	48	Florida	40

MOST-CONSERVATIVE STATE DELEGATIONS			
Mississippi	39	Alaska	31
Virginia	39	Alabama	30
Georgia	38	Louisiana	30
Idaho	38	Utah	30
Iowa	36	Kansas	28
Texas	34	Nebraska	27
South Carolina	33	Kentucky	26
Indiana	32	Montana	25
Wyoming	32	Oklahoma	23

Source: Reprinted with permission from National Journal, February 25, 2006. Copyright © 2006 National Journal. All rights reserved.

House of Commons, we would find only one kind of organization of any importance—the political party. Though party organization is important in the U.S. Congress, it is only one of many important elements. In fact, other organizations have grown in number as the influence of the parties has declined.

The Democrats and Republicans in the House and the Senate are organized by party leaders. The key leaders in turn are elected by the full party membership within the House and Senate. The description that follows is confined to the essential positions.

PARTY ORGANIZATION OF THE SENATE

The majority party chooses one of its members—usually the person with the greatest seniority—to be president pro tempore of the Senate. It is largely an honorific position, required by the Constitution so that the Senate will have a presiding officer in the absence of the vice president of the United States (who is also, according to the Constitution, the president of the Senate). In fact, presiding over the Senate is a tedious chore that neither the vice

Figure 13.3
The U.S. Congress

HOUSE OF REPRESENTATIVES
1. House Minority Whip
2. Lobby
3. House chamber
4. Cloakrooms
5. Speaker of the House
6. Ways and Means Committee
7. House Minority Leader

SENATE
8. Senate Minority Leader
9. Office of the Secretary
10. Senate chamber
11. Cloakrooms
12. Senate Majority Leader
13. Vice President

The House and Senate meet at opposite ends of the Capitol building. When there is a joint session of Congress—for example, to hear the president's State of the Union address—the senators sit with the representatives in the House chamber. Though the most important work of Congress goes on in committee meetings, which are held in office buildings behind the Capitol, some important political negotiations occur in the offices surrounding the chambers—especially in the cloakrooms (actually, lounges) and the offices of the majority and minority leaders, the Speaker and the vice president, and the secretary of the Senate.

president nor the president pro tem relishes, and so the actual task of presiding usually is assigned to a junior senator.

The real leadership is in the hands of the **majority leader** (chosen by the senators of the majority party) and the **minority leader** (chosen by the senators of the other party). In addition, the senators of each party elect a whip. The principal task of the majority leader is to schedule the business of the Senate, usually in consultation with the minority leader. The majority leader has the right to be recognized first in any floor debate. A majority leader with a strong personality who is skilled at political bargaining may do much more. Lyndon Johnson, Senate majority leader for the Democrats during much of the 1950s, used his prodigious ability to serve the needs of fellow senators. He helped them with everything from obtaining extra office space to getting choice committee assignments, and in this way he acquired substantial influence over the substance as well as the schedule of Senate business. Johnson's successor, Mike Mansfield, was a less assertive majority leader and had less influence.

The **whip** is a senator who helps the party leader stay informed about what party members are thinking, rounds up members when important votes are to be taken, and attempts to keep a nose count on how the voting on a controversial issue is likely to go. The whip has several senators who assist him or her in this task.

Each party in the Senate also chooses a Policy Committee composed of a dozen or so senators who

majority leader The legislative leader elected by party members holding the majority of seats in the House or the Senate.

minority leader The legislative leader elected by party members holding a minority of seats in the House or the Senate.

whip A senator or representative who helps the party leader stay informed about what party members are thinking.

Politically Speaking

Whip

A whip is a party leader who makes certain that party members are present for a vote and vote the way the party wishes. In the British House of Commons, the whips produce strong party votes; in the U.S. Congress, whips are a lot less successful.

The word comes from *whipper-in,* a term from fox hunting denoting the person whose job it is to keep the hounds from straying off the trail. It became a political term in England in the 18th century, and from there came to the United States.

Source: From *Safire's Political Dictionary* by William Safire. Copyright © 1968, 1972, 1978 by William Safire. Reprinted by permission of Random House, Inc. and the author.

Nancy Pelosi, the first woman to serve as House Speaker.

Zach Seckler/Corbis

help the party leader schedule Senate business, choosing what bills are to be given major attention and in what order.

From the point of view of individual senators, however, the key party organization is the group that assigns senators to the standing committees of the Senate. The Democrats have a Steering Committee that does this; the Republicans have a Committee on Committees. These assignments are especially important for newly elected senators: their political careers, their opportunities for favorable publicity, and their chances for helping their states and their supporters depend in great part on the committees to which they are assigned.

Party control of the Senate has changed frequently. When George W. Bush took office in 2001, the Republicans briefly retained control by having 50 seats plus a tie-breaking vote cast by Vice President Cheney. But then Senator James Jeffords, a Republican, became an independent and voted to let the Democrats control it, 51 to 49. But that ended when the Republicans won enough seats in the 2002 election to regain control. Having a tiny majority in the Senate does not affect most important votes since the other side can filibuster, but having your own party control the chairmanships is very important because it helps determine what issues will get to the floor for a vote.

The key—and delicate—aspect of selecting party leaders, of making up the important party committees, and of assigning freshman senators to Senate committees is achieving ideological and regional balance. Liberals and conservatives in each party

How Things Work

Party Leadership Structure in 2009

Senate

President Pro Tempore   Selected by majority party

Democrats

Majority Leader   Leads the party

Majority Whip   Assists the leader, rounds up votes, heads group of deputy whips

Chairman of the Conference   Presides over meetings of all Senate Democrats

Policy Committee   Schedules legislation

Steering Committee   Assigns Democratic senators to committees

Democratic Senatorial Campaign Committee   Provides funds, assistance to Democratic candidates for the Senate

Republicans

Minority Leader   Leads the party

Minority Whip   Assists the leader, rounds up votes

Chairman of the Conference   Presides over meetings of all Senate Republicans

Policy Committee   Makes recommendations on party policy

Committee on Committees   Assigns Republican senators to committees

Republican Senatorial Committee   Provides funds, advice to Republican candidates for the Senate

House

Speaker of the House   Selected by majority party

Democrats

Majority Leader   Leads the party

Majority Whip   Assists the leader, rounds up votes, heads group of deputy and assistant whips

Chairman of the Caucus   Presides over meetings of all House Democrats

Steering and Policy Committee   Schedules legislation, assigns Democratic representatives to committees

Democratic Congressional Campaign Committee   Provides funds, advice to Democratic candidates for the House

Republicans

Minority Leader   Leads the party

Minority Whip   Assists the leader, rounds up votes, heads large group of deputy and assistant whips

Chairman of the Conference   Presides over meetings of all House Republicans

Committee on Committees   Assigns Republican representatives to committees

Policy Committee   Advises on party policy

National Republican Congressional Committee Provides funds, advice to Republican candidates for the House

Research Committee   On request, provides information about issues

---

will fight over the choice of majority and minority leader, but factors in addition to ideology play a part in the choice. These include personal popularity, the ability of the leader to make an effective television appearance, and who owes whom what favors.

PARTY STRUCTURE IN THE HOUSE

Though the titles of various posts are different, the party structure essentially is the same in the House as in the Senate. Leadership carries more power in the House than in the Senate because of the House rules. Being so large (435 members), the House must restrict debate and schedule its business with

great care; thus, leaders who do the scheduling and who determine how the rules shall be applied usually have substantial influence.

The Speaker is the most important person in the House. Elected by whichever party has a majority, the Speaker presides over all House meetings. Unlike the president pro tem of the Senate, however, the Speaker's position is anything but honorific. He or she is the principal leader of the majority party as well as the presiding officer of the entire House. Though Speakers-as-presiders are expected to be fair, Speakers-as-party-leaders are expected to use their powers to help pass legislation favored by their party.

In helping his or her party, the Speaker has some important formal powers: deciding who shall be recognized to speak on the floor of the House; ruling whether a motion is relevant and germane to the business at hand; and deciding (subject to certain rules) the committees to which new bills shall be assigned. The Speaker influences what bills are brought up for a vote and appoints the members of special and select committees (explained on page 336). Since 1975, the Speaker has been able to nominate the majority-party members of the Rules Committee. He or she also has some informal powers: controlling some patronage jobs in the Capitol building and the assignment of extra office space. Even though the Speaker is far less powerful than in the days of Clay, Reed, and Cannon, he or she still is an important person to have on one's side. Sam Rayburn of Texas exercised great influence as Speaker, and Tip O'Neill, Jim Wright, Tom Foley, and Newt Gingrich tried to do the same.

In the House, as in the Senate, the majority party elects a floor leader, called the majority leader. The other party also chooses a leader—the minority leader. Traditionally, the majority leader becomes Speaker when the person in that position dies or retires—provided, of course, the departing Speaker's party still is in the majority. Each party also has a whip, with several assistant whips in charge of rounding up votes from various state delegations. Committee assignments are made and the scheduling of legislation is discussed, by the Democrats, in a Steering and Policy Committee, chaired by the Speaker. The Republicans have divided committee assignments and policy discussions, with the former task assigned to a Committee on Committees and the latter to a Policy Committee. Each party also has a congressional campaign committee to provide funds and other assistance to party members running for election or reelection to the House.

THE STRENGTH OF PARTY STRUCTURES

One important measure of the strength of the parties in Congress is the ability of party leaders to get their members to vote together on the rules and structure of Congress. When Newt Gingrich became Speaker of the Republican-controlled House in 1995, he proposed sweeping changes in House rules, many not popular with some Republican members. For example, he wanted no one to serve as a committee chairman for more than six years, for three committees to be abolished, and for other committees to lose either functions or members. He also wanted to pass over some senior members in picking committee chairmen. Though these moves adversely affected some Republican representatives, they all voted in favor of the new rules.[12] Of course, Gingrich would not have made these proposals unless he was certain he could get them adopted. But it was a measure of his influence and support among newly elected Republicans that even major changes in congressional procedures would get unanimous party support.[13] Getting support on proposed legislation is a harder task.

The Senate is another matter. As Barbara Sinclair has argued, in the last few decades the Senate has been transformed by changes in norms (informal understandings governing how members ought to behave toward their colleagues), without any far-reaching changes in the written Senate rules.[14] Compared to the Senate of the 1950s and 1960s, today's Senate is less party-centered, less leader-oriented, more hospitable to freshmen (who no longer have to "pay their dues" before assuming major roles as legislators), more heavily staffed, and more subcommittee-oriented.

PARTY UNITY

The strength of Congress's elaborate party machinery can also be measured by the extent to which members of a party vote together in the House and Senate. **Party polarization** is defined as a vote in which a majority of voting Democrats oppose a majority of voting Republicans. In seven of the 13 years from 1953 to 1965, at least half of all House votes pitted a majority of voting Democrats against a majority of voting Republicans. But in 1966, the number dropped to 41 percent, and it was not until 1983 that voting in the House once again took on a distinctively partisan cast. By the 1990s, party unity voting was the norm in both the House and the Senate.

> ***party polarization***
> A vote in which a majority of Democratic legislators oppose a majority of Republican legislators.

As these recent trends make plain, party unity in Congress is hardly a thing of the past. Specific issues can trigger an extraordinary degree of party cohesion. For example, in 1993 every single Republican in both the House and Senate voted against the Clinton budget plan, the first budget offered by a Democratic president since Jimmy Carter left office in 1980. This may be an extreme example, but it reflects the increasingly adversarial relationship between Democrats and Republicans, especially in the House.

Still, it is worth remembering that even today's Congress is less divided along party lines than many of its predecessors were. During 1890–1910, for example, two-thirds of all votes evoked a party split, and in several sessions more than half the roll calls found 90 percent of each party's members opposing the other party.[15] Whereas the party splits of the past often reflected the routine operations of highly disciplined parties interested mainly in winning elections, dispensing patronage, and keeping power, today's party splits often reflect sharp ideological differences between the parties (or at least between their respective leaders).

The sharp increase in party votes among members of Congress since 1970 is remarkable, since it is not obvious that the Americans who vote for these members are as deeply divided by party. When social scientists describe a trait among people—say, their height—they usually note that there are a few very short ones and a few very tall ones, but that most people are in the middle. They call this distribution "unimodal." But when one describes voting in Congress, except on matters of national urgency, the votes are "bimodal"—that is, almost all of the Democrats vote one way and almost all of the Republicans vote a different way.

For example, when President Clinton was impeached, 98 percent of the House Republicans voted for at least one of the four impeachment articles and 98 percent of the House Democrats voted against all four, and this happened despite the fact that most Americans did not want to have the president impeached. In fact, the Republican vote did not even match how people felt who lived in districts represented by Republicans. On abortion, most Americans favor it but with some important limitations, but in Congress Democrats almost always support it with no restrictions and Republicans usually want to put on lots of restrictions. Votes on less emotional matters, like the tax bills, often show the same pattern of Democrats and Republicans at loggerheads.

How could these things happen in a democratic nation? If the American people usually are in the center on political issues, why are congressional Democrats almost always liberal and congressional Republicans almost always conservative?

There is no simple or agreed-upon answer to this question. Some scholars have argued that in the last 30 years or so, voters have in fact become more partisan. "More partisan" means they see important differences between the two parties, they identify themselves as either conservatives or liberals, and they favor parties that share their ideological preferences.[16]

One reason this has happened has been the way congressional districts are drawn for House members.

The vast majority are drawn so as to protect one party or the other. This means that if you are a Republican voter living in a pro-Democratic district (or a Democrat living in a pro-Republican one), your votes don't make much difference in an election. Most House districts are not competitive, meaning that in them the only election that counts is the primary used to pick a candidate. In primaries voter turnout is lower, so that the most motivated (and thus most ideological) voters play a disproportionate role in choosing candidates.

A second possibility is that the voters have become more partisan as a result of Congress having become more partisan. When House Democrats vote liberal and House Republicans vote conservative, a lot of voters follow this cue and take positions based on a similar ideology.[17] People who don't see the world this way have either become less numerous or vote less often.

And a third is the role of seniority. On one hand, the so-called seniority rule is no longer strictly followed. The tradition whereby the most senior majority-member of a committee (usually a three-plus-term Republican or Democratic stalwart from a safe district) received the chair position broke down in the mid-1990s. By the 107th Congress (2001–2002), chair selection was determined more by a majority-party member's support of party goals and party unity.[18] On the other hand, the system never broke down entirely; for instance, in the 110th Congress (2007–2008), the most senior majority-party member was selected for every committee chair position except one (Silvestre Reyes over Jane Harman as Intelligence Committee Chairperson). Since the chairpersons have a lot of influence over how bills are written, their views—shaped by a lifetime of dedication to Democratic or Republication causes—will be very important.

Still, just how much congressmen are influenced by committee chairmen and other party leaders is hard to know. In several sophisticated studies, political scientists Keith T. Poole and Howard Rosenthal have suggested that, while parties and their leaders matter, individual members' ideological views (see Chapter 7) probably matter as much or more than party discipline does in explaining how Congress works and how congressmen behave. "Members of Congress," they find, "come to Washington with a staked-out position on the (liberal-conservative) continuum, and then, largely 'die with their ideological boots on."[19] Everything from which "ideological boots" a given member chooses to wear in the first place to how he or she votes on a particular issue "may result as much from external pressures

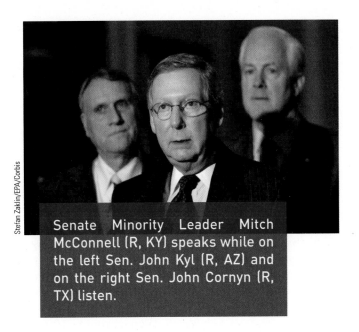

Stefan Zaklin/EPA/Corbis

Senate Minority Leader Mitch McConnell (R, KY) speaks while on the left Sen. John Kyl (R, AZ) and on the right Sen. John Cornyn (R, TX) listen.

of campaign donors and primary voters as from the internal pressures of the congressional party."[20]

In short, party *does* make a difference in Congress—not as much as it once did, and not nearly as much as it does in a parliamentary system, but enough so that party affiliation is still the most important thing to know about a member of Congress. Knowing whether a member is a Democrat or a Republican will not tell you everything about the member, but it will tell you more than any other single fact.

CAUCUSES

Congressional caucuses are a growing rival to the parties as a source of policy leadership. A **caucus** is an association of members of Congress created to advocate a political ideology or a regional or economic interest. In 1959, there were only four caucuses; by the late 1980s, there were over a hundred.

As Congress expert Susan Webb Hammond has observed, "The pace of caucus formation accelerated rapidly during the 1970s as members, operating with increased and more equitably distributed resources within a decentralized institution, sought to respond to increased external demands. . . . Members derive benefits—gaining information, being identified as a 'leader,' symbolically showing that they care about an issue of importance to constituents—from caucus activities."[21] In January 1995, at the beginning of the Republican-led 104th Congress, it was widely reported that the House of Representatives would "abolish" congressional caucuses. By 2009, there were about 300 congressional caucuses (most using that name, but a few styling themselves instead as "task forces" or "committees"). Table 13.2 offers a sample.

It is no longer easy to know whether any given caucus matters much to life in Congress, but there are some well-established exceptions. Perhaps the most notable is the Congressional Black Caucus (CBC). Founded in 1969, it received its name in 1971 on the motion of Representative Charles Rangel, a Democrat from New York. As the 110th Congress convened in 2007, Rangel served as chairman of the powerful House Ways and Means Committee. Officially nonpartisan, all CBC members are Democrats. In the 1990s, former Representative J. C. Watts, a black Republican from Oklahoma, refused to join. In January 2007, Representative Stephen Cohen, a Democrat from Tennessee, attempted to join. Cohen is Jewish, but more than half of his constituents are African Americans. He was rejected. The "death" of caucuses was greatly exaggerated.

caucus An association of Congress members created to advance a political ideology or a regional, ethnic, or economic interest.

Table 13.2 Congressional Caucuses: A Sample, 2009

Caucus
Animal Protection
Bike
Black
Blue Dog (Democratic)
Green Jobs
Hispanic
Human Trafficking
Internet
Israel Allies
Musicians
Nanotechnology
Nuclear Safety
Prayer
Real Estate
Rural
Shellfish
Soccer
Tourism
Ukranian
Wildlife
World Economic Forum

Source: U.S. House of Representatives, 2009.

The Organization of Congress: Committees

The most important organizational feature of Congress is the set of legislative committees of the House and Senate. It is there that the real work of Congress is done, and it is in the chairmanships of these committees and their subcommittees that most of the power in Congress is found. The number and jurisdiction of these committees are of the greatest interest to members of Congress, since decisions on these subjects determine what group of members, with what political views, will pass on legislative proposals, oversee the workings of agencies in the executive branch, and conduct investigations.

There are three kinds of committees: **standing committees** (more or less permanent bodies with specified legislative responsibilities), **select committees** (groups appointed for a limited purpose and usually lasting for only a few congresses), and **joint committees** (those on which both representatives and senators serve). An especially important kind of joint committee is the **conference committee,** made up of representatives and senators appointed to resolve differences in the Senate and House versions of the same piece of legislation before final passage.

Though members of the majority party could, in theory, occupy all of the seats on all of the committees, in practice they take the majority of seats on each committee, name the chairperson, and allow the minority party to have the other seats. Usually the ratio of Democrats to Republicans on a committee roughly corresponds to their ratio in that house of Congress, but on occasion the majority party will try to take extra seats on some key panels, such as the House Appropriations or Ways and Means Committees. Then the minority party complains, as the Republicans did in 1981 and the Democrats did in 1999, usually with little effect. In 2001, with the Senate evenly divided between Democrats and Republicans, each committee had the same number of members from each party with Republicans serving as chairmen.

standing committees Permanently established legislative committees that consider and are responsible for legislation within a certain subject area.

select committees Congressional committees appointed for a limited time and purpose.

joint committees Committees on which both senators and representatives serve.

conference committees A joint committee appointed to resolve differences in the Senate and House versions of the same bill.

Standing committees are the important ones, because, with few exceptions, they are the only ones that can propose legislation by reporting a bill out to the full House or Senate. Each member of the House usually serves on two standing committees, unless he or she is on an "exclusive" committee—Appropriations, Rules, or Ways and Means. In such a case, the representative is limited to one. Each senator may serve on two "major" committees and one "minor" committee.

When party leaders were strong, as under Speakers Reed and Cannon, committee chairmen were picked on the basis of loyalty to the leader. Now that this leadership has been weakened, seniority on the committee governs the selection of chairmen. Of late, however, even seniority has been under attack. In 1971, House Democrats decided in their caucus to elect committee chairmen by secret ballot. From then through 1991, they used that procedure to remove six committee chairmen. When the Republicans took control of the House in 1995, they could have returned to the strict seniority rule, but they did not. When the Democrats regained control of the House in 2007, they returned to it but not without exceptions (a semi-strict seniority rule).

Traditionally, the committees of Congress were dominated by the chairmen. They often did their most important work behind closed doors (though their hearings and reports were almost always published in full). In the early 1970s, Congress further decentralized and democratized its operations by a series of changes that some members regarded as a "bill of rights" for representatives and senators, especially those with relatively little seniority. These changes were by and large made by the Democratic Caucus, but since the Democrats were in the majority, the changes, in effect, became the rules of Congress. The more important ones were as follows.

House

- Committee chairmen to be elected by secret ballot in party caucus

- No member to chair more than one committee

- All committees with more than 20 members to have at least four subcommittees (at the time, Ways and Means had no subcommittees)

- Committee and personal staffs to be increased in size

- Committee meetings to be public unless members vote to close them

Politically Speaking

Caucus

A *caucus* is a closed meeting of the members of a political party either to select a candidate for office or to agree on a legislative position.

The term is from an American Indian word meaning "elder" or "counselor." It quickly entered political usage in the United States, with a Caucus Club in Boston as early as 1763.

The first national political caucuses were in Congress, where legislators would gather to select their party's candidate for president. Persons who did not get a caucus endorsement soon began denouncing the entire procedure, referring contemptuously to the "decrees of King Caucus." Popular resentment led in the 1830s to the creation of the nominating convention as a way of choosing presidential candidates.

Today, congressional caucuses are organizations of legislators from a single party (Democrats or Republicans), with a common background (for example, women, African Americans, Hispanics), sharing a particular ideology (liberals or conservatives), or having an interest in a single issue (such as mushrooms, steel mills, or the environment).

Source: From *Safire's Political Dictionary* by William Safire. Copyright © 1968, 1972, 1978 by William Safire. Reprinted by permission of Random House, Inc. and the author.

Senate

- Committee meetings to be public unless members vote to close them

- Committee chairmen to be selected by secret ballot at the request of one-fifth of the party caucus

- Committees to have larger staffs

- No senator to chair more than one committee

The effect of these changes, especially in the House, was to give greater power to individual members and to lessen the power of party leaders and committee chairmen. The decentralization of the House meant that it was much harder for chairmen to block legislation they did not like or to discourage junior members from playing a large role. House members were quick to take advantage of these enlarged opportunities. In the 1980s, they proposed three times as many amendments to bills as they had in the 1950s.[22]

There was a cost to be paid, however, for this empowerment of the membership. The 435 members of the House could not get much done if they all talked as much as they liked and introduced as many amendments as they wished. And with the big increase in the number of subcommittees, many subcommittee meetings were attended by (and thus controlled by) only one person, the chairman. To deal with this, the Democratic leaders began reclaiming some of their lost power. They made greater use of restrictive rules that sharply limited debate and the introduction of amendments. Committee chairmen began casting proxy votes. (A proxy is a written authorization to cast another person's vote.) In this way, a chairman could control the results of committee deliberations by casting the proxies of absent members.

Republican House members were angered by all of this. They suspected that restrictive rules and proxy voting were designed to keep them from having any voice in House affairs. When they took control of the House in 1995, they announced some changes:

- They banned proxy voting.

- They limited committee and subcommittee chairmen's tenures to three terms (six years) and the Speaker's to four terms (eight years).

- They allowed more frequent floor debate under open rules.

- They reduced the number of committees and subcommittees.

- They authorized committee chairmen to hire subcommittee staffs.

How Things Work

Standing Committees of the Senate

Major Committees

No senator is supposed to serve on more than two (but some do).

Agriculture, Nutrition, and Forestry

Appropriations

Armed Services

Banking, Housing, and Urban Affairs

Budget

Commerce, Science, and Transportation

Energy and Natural Resources

Environment and Public Works

Finance

Foreign Relations

Governmental Affairs

Health, Education, Labor, and Pensions

Judiciary

Minor Committees

No senator is supposed to serve on more than one (but some do).

Rules and Administration

Small Business

Veterans' Affairs

Select Committees

Aging

Ethics

Indian Affairs

Intelligence

The endless arguments about rules illustrate a fundamental problem that the House faces. Closed rules, proxy voting, powerful committee chairmen, and strong Speakers make it easier for business to get done; they put the House in a good bargaining position with the president and the Senate; and they make it easier to reduce the number of special-interest groups with legislative power. But this system also keeps individual members weak. The opposite arrangements—open rules, weak chairmen, many subcommittees, meetings open to the public—help individual members be heard and increase the amount of daylight shining on congressional processes. But if everyone is heard, no one is heard, because the noise is deafening and the speeches endless. And though open meetings and easy amending processes may be intended to open up the system to "the people," the real beneficiaries are the lobbyists.

The House Republican rules of 1995 gave back some power to the chairmen (for example, by letting them pick all staff members) but further reduced it in other ways (for example, by imposing term limits and banning proxy voting). The commitment to public meetings remained.

In the Senate, there have been fewer changes, in part because individual members of the Senate have always had more power than their counterparts in the House. Two important changes were made by the Republicans in 1995:

- A six-year term limit on all committee chairmen (no limit on the majority leader's term)

- A requirement that committee members select their chairmen by secret ballot

Despite these new rules and under Democratic or Republican control, the committees remain the place where the real work of Congress is done. The different types of committees tend to attract different kinds of members. Some, such as the committees that draft tax legislation (the Senate Finance Committee and the House Ways and Means Committee) or that oversee foreign affairs (the Senate Foreign Relations Committee and the House International Relations Committee) are attractive to members who want to shape public policy, become experts on important issues, or have influence with their colleagues. Others, such as the House and Senate committees dealing with public lands, small business,

How Things Work

Standing Committees of the House

Exclusive Committees

Members may not serve on any other committee except Budget.

Appropriations

Rules

Ways and Means

Major Committees

Members may serve on only one major committee.

Agriculture

Armed Services

Education and the Workforce

Energy and Commerce

Financial Services

International Relations

Judiciary

Transportation and Infrastructure

Nonmajor Committees

Members may serve on one major and one nonmajor committee, or on two nonmajor committees.

Budget

Government Reform

House Administration

Resources

Science

Small Business

Standards of Official Conduct

Veterans' Affairs

Note: In 1995 the House Republican majority abolished three committees—District of Columbia, Post Office and Civil Service, and Merchant Marine and Fisheries—and gave their duties to other standing committees.

and veterans' affairs, are attractive to members who want to serve particular constituents.[23]

The Organization of Congress: Staffs and Specialized Offices

In 1900, representatives had no personal staffs, and senators averaged fewer than one staff member each. As recently as 1935, the typical representative had but two aides. By 1998, the average representative had 17 assistants and the average senator over 40. To the more than 10,000 individuals who served on the personal staffs of members of the 103rd Congress must be added 3,000 more who worked for congressional committees and yet another 3,000 employed by various congressional research agencies. Until the 1990s, Congress had the most rapidly growing bureaucracy in Washington—the personal staffs of legislators increased more than fivefold from 1947 to 1991, then leveled off and declined slightly. Though some staffers perform routine chores, many

help draft legislation, handle constituents, and otherwise shape policy and politics.

TASKS OF STAFF MEMBERS

Staff members assigned to a senator or representative spend most of their time servicing requests from constituents—answering mail, handling problems, sending out newsletters, and meeting with voters. In short, a major function of a member of Congress's staff is to help constituents solve problems and thereby help the member get reelected. Indeed, over the last two decades, a larger and larger portion of congressional staffs—now about one-third—work in the local (district or state) office of the member of Congress rather than in Washington. Almost all members of Congress have such offices on a full-time basis; about half maintain two or more offices in their constituencies. Some scholars believe that this growth in constituency-serving staffs helps explain why it is so hard to defeat an incumbent representative or senator.

The legislative function of congressional staff members is also important. With each senator serving on an average of more than two committees and seven subcommittees and each representative serving on an average of six committees and subcommittees, it is virtually impossible for members of Congress to become familiar in detail with all the proposals that come before them or to write all the bills that they feel ought to be introduced. As the workload of Congress has grown (over 6,000 bills are introduced, about 600 public laws are passed, and uncounted hearings and meetings are held during a typical Congress), the role of staff members in devising proposals, negotiating agreements, organizing hearings, writing questions for members of Congress to ask of witnesses, drafting reports, and meeting with lobbyists and administrators has grown correspondingly.

Those who work for individual members of Congress, as opposed to committees, see themselves entirely as advocates for their bosses. As the mass media have supplanted political parties as ways of communicating with voters, the advocacy role of staff members has led them to find and promote legislation for which a representative or senator can take credit. This is the entrepreneurial function of the staff. While it is sometimes performed under the close supervision of the member of Congress, just as often a staff member takes the initiative, finds a policy, and then "sells" it to his or her employer. Lobbyists and reporters understand this completely and therefore spend a lot of time cultivating congressional staffers, both as sources of information and as consumers of ideas.

One reason for the rapid growth in the size and importance of congressional staffs is that a large staff creates conditions that seem to require an even larger staff. As the staff grows in size, it generates more legislative work. Subcommittees proliferate to handle all the issues with which legislators are concerned. But as the workload increases, legislators complain that they cannot keep up and need more help.

The increased reliance on staff has changed Congress, not because staffers do things against the wishes of their elected masters but because the staff has altered the environment within which Congress does its work. In addition to their role as entrepreneurs promoting new policies, staffers act as negotiators. As a result members of Congress are more likely to deal with one another through staff intermediaries than personally. Congress has thereby become less collegial, more individualistic, and less of a deliberative body.[24]

STAFF AGENCIES

In addition to increasing the number of staff members, Congress has also created a set of staff agencies that work for Congress as a whole. These staff agencies have come into being in large part to give Congress specialized knowledge equivalent to what the president has by virtue of his position as chief of the executive branch.

Congressional Research Service (CRS)

Formerly the Legislative Reference Service, the CRS is part of the Library of Congress. Since 1914, it has responded to congressional requests for information and now employs nearly 900 people, many with advanced academic training, to respond to more than a quarter of a million questions each year. As a politically neutral body, it does not recommend policy, but it will look up facts and indicate the arguments for and against a proposed policy. CRS also keeps track of the status of every major bill before Congress and produces a summary of each bill introduced. This information is instantly available to legislators via computer terminals located in almost all Senate and most House offices.

General Accounting Office (GAO)

Created in 1921, this agency once performed primarily routine financial audits of the money spent by executive-branch departments. Today, it also investigates agencies and policies and makes recommendations on almost every aspect of government—defense contracting, drug enforcement policies, the domestic security investigations of the FBI, Medicare and Medicaid programs, water pollution programs, and so forth. Though the head of the GAO—the comptroller general—is appointed by the president (with the consent of the Senate), he or she serves for a 15-year term and is very much the servant of Congress rather than of the president. The GAO employs about 5,000 people, many of whom are permanently assigned to work with various congressional committees.

Office of Technology Assessment (OTA)

Established in 1972 to study and evaluate policies and programs with a significant use of or impact on technology, the OTA had a staff of more than a hundred. Staff members looked into matters such as a plan to build a pipeline to transport coal slurry. The agency had little impact and was abolished in 1995.

Congressional Budget Office (CBO)

Created in 1974, the CBO advises Congress on the likely economic effects of different spending programs and provides information on the costs of proposed policies. This latter task has been more useful to Congress than the more difficult job of estimating future economic trends. The CBO prepares analyses of the president's budget and economic projections that often come to conclusions different from those of the administration, thus giving members of Congress arguments to use in the budget debates.

Question

3. *Who was the first woman elected to serve in Congress?*

How a Bill Becomes Law

Some bills zip through Congress; others make their way slowly and painfully. Congress, an English observer once remarked, is like a crowd, moving either sluggishly or with great speed.

Bills that have sped through on the fast track include ones to reduce drug abuse, reform Defense Department procurement procedures, end the mandatory retirement age, and help the disabled. Those that have plodded through on the slow track include ones dealing with health care, tax laws, energy conservation, and foreign trade, as well as several appropriations bills.

Why the difference? Studying the list above gives some clues. Bills to spend a lot of money move slowly, especially during times (such as the 1980s and early 2000s) when the government is running up big deficits. Bills to tax or regulate businesses move slowly because so many different interests have to be heard and accommodated. On the other hand, bills that seem to embody a clear, appealing idea ("stop drugs," "help old folks," "end scandal") gather momentum quickly, especially if the government doesn't have to spend a lot of its money (as opposed to requiring other people to spend their money) on the idea.

In the following account of how a bill becomes law, keep in mind the central fact that the complexity of these procedures ordinarily gives a powerful advantage to the opposition. There are many points at which action can be blocked. This does not mean that nothing gets done but that, to get something done, a member of Congress must *either* assemble a majority coalition slowly and painstakingly or take advantage of temporary enthusiasm for some new cause that sweeps away the normal obstacles.

INTRODUCING A BILL

Any member of Congress may introduce a bill—in the House simply by handing it to a clerk or dropping it in a box (the "hopper"), in the Senate by being recognized by the presiding officer and announcing the bill's introduction. Bills are numbered and sent to the printer: a House bill bears the prefix H.R., a Senate bill the prefix *S*. A bill can be either a **public bill** (pertaining to public affairs generally) or a **private bill** (pertaining to a particular individual, such as a person pressing a financial claim against the government or seeking special permission to become a naturalized citizen). Private bills were once very numerous; today, many such matters have been delegated to administrative agencies or the courts. If a bill is not passed by both houses and signed by the president within the life of one Congress, it is dead and must be reintroduced during the next

Congress. Pending legislation does not carry over from one Congress to the next. (A new Congress is organized every two years.)

We often hear that legislation is initiated by the president and enacted by Congress—the former proposes, the latter disposes. The reality is more complicated. Congress frequently initiates legislation; in fact, most of the consumer and environmental protection legislation passed since 1966 began in Congress, not in the executive branch. And even laws formally proposed by the president often represent presidential versions of proposals that have incubated in Congress. This was the case, for example, with some civil rights laws and with the proposal that eventually became Medicare. Even when the president is the principal author of a bill, he usually submits it (if he is prudent) only after careful consultation with key congressional leaders. In any case, the president cannot himself introduce legislation; he must get a member of Congress to do it for him.

One study showed that of 90 major laws passed between 1880 and 1945, 77 were introduced without presidential sponsorship. In shaping the final contents, congressional influence dominated in 35 cases, presidential influence dominated in 19, and influence was mixed in the remaining 36. Another study, covering the period 1940 to 1967, found that Congress was the major contributor to the contents of about half of all laws passed.[25]

In addition to bills, Congress can pass resolutions. A **simple resolution** (passed by either the House or the Senate) is used for matters such as establishing the rules under which each body will operate. A **concurrent resolution** settles housekeeping and procedural matters that affect both houses. Simple and concurrent resolutions are not signed by the president and do not have the force of law. A **joint resolution** requires the approval of both houses and the signature of the president; it is essentially the same as a law. A joint resolution is also used to propose a constitutional amendment; in this case, it must be approved by a two-thirds vote of both houses, but it does not require the signature of the president.

public bill A legislative bill that deals with matters of general concern.

private bill A legislative bill that deals only with specific, private, personal, or local matters.

simple resolution An expression of opinion either in the House or Senate to settle procedural matters in either body.

concurrent resolution An expression of opinion without the force of law that requires the approval of both the House and the Senate, but not the president.

joint resolution A formal expression of congressional opinion that must be approved by both houses of Congress and by the president; constitutional amendments need not be signed by the president.

How Things Work

How a Bill Becomes Law

Introduction

Draft and Introduce You do not need to be a member of Congress to draft a bill; lobbyists, congressional staff, and others draft legislation all the time. But you do need to be a member of Congress to introduce legislation. The bill or resolution gets a number preceded by *H.R.* for House bills and *S.* for Senate bills.

Refer to Committee Numbered bills get referred to standing committees depending on their content and in accordance with detailed rules and procedures that differ somewhat between the House and the Senate. Once referred, the bill gets on the committee's calendar for review by a subcommittee or by the full committee.

Committee Action

Get Committee Action Not every bill on the calendar gets action. Many bills get referred to subcommittees for staff analysis and hearings held in public. But getting a hearing is not the same thing as getting action. Even after study, hearings, and other consideration of the bill, if the committee fails to act, the bill is dead.

Go to Mark Up If, however, the committee so chooses, the bill then goes to "mark up," a process that normally works by subcommittee members and staff editing or amending the bill, often extensively. But even after "the mark," the subcommittee may decide not to recommend the bill to the full committee, and the bill dies there.

Order the Bill Once the full committee gets the bill, it may or may not conduct more analysis and hold more hearings on the legislation, consider amendments thereto, and vote its recommendation to the House or Senate (a procedure called "ordering the bill" or "ordering the bill reported"). If the bill is ordered, it still has a chance; if not, it is dead.

Publish a Report The committee chairman orders a public report on the bill. Most such reports are prepared by committee staff and describe the nature and purpose of the bill; what various experts have said or testified concerning it; what, if any, position the president has taken on it; what, if any, public comments the relevant cabinet agencies or other executive branch units have offered on it; and what dissenting members of the committee have to say about it.

Floor Action and Conference Action

Get a Date The bill goes back to the chamber that originated it and is scheduled for floor debate and a vote. The House has many different scheduling procedures or "calendars," while the Senate has but one. Even having come this far, the bill might or might not get a date, or come up in an order that makes it likely to keep going.

Win Two Chambers The debate over the bill and any amendments having concluded, the members vote. If the bill is defeated, it is dead. If the bill is approved, it next goes to the other chamber, which begins the process again, starting with the bill being referred to committee. Anything can happen. The second chamber can accept the bill as is, change it, or never even consider it. The bill can go back to the first chamber with few or no changes, go to a "conference committee" to reconcile any significant differences between the two versions of the bill, or go nowhere. If the two chambers agree, a conference report on the final bill is prepared. Only if the two chambers approve exactly the same final bill with identical language does the bill get sent to the president for consideration.

President

Get President's Signature If the president signs the bill, it becomes law. If the president takes no action for ten days after receiving the bill, and Congress is still in session, the bill becomes law. If the president takes no action after the Congress has adjourned, the bill dies from his "pocket veto." Or, the president can veto the bill outright, in which case it goes back to Congress.

Override President's Veto If the president vetoes a bill, Congress can still turn it into law, but that requires a two-thirds vote of the members, and there must be enough members present to form a quorum.

LEGISLATIVE PRODUCTIVITY

In recent years, political scientists have studied how productive Congress has been and whether the post–9/11 Congress (led first by Republicans and then by Democrats) has performed especially well or especially poorly.

The first issue concerns how best to measure the body's major and minor "legislative productivity." It is clear that Congress passed and funded an enormous number of bills in response to the Great Depression in the 1930s and in the mid-1960s, mainly in conjunction with that era's "war on

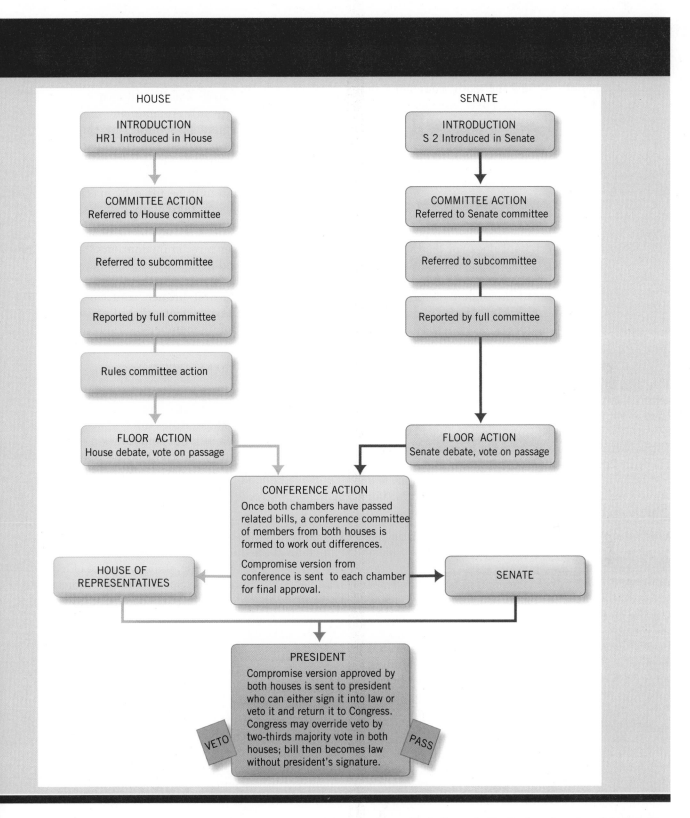

HOUSE

INTRODUCTION
HR1 Introduced in House

COMMITTEE ACTION
Referred to House committee

Referred to subcommittee

Reported by full committee

Rules committee action

FLOOR ACTION
House debate, vote on passage

SENATE

INTRODUCTION
S 2 Introduced in Senate

COMMITTEE ACTION
Referred to Senate committee

Referred to subcommittee

Reported by full committee

FLOOR ACTION
Senate debate, vote on passage

CONFERENCE ACTION
Once both chambers have passed related bills, a conference committee of members from both houses is formed to work out differences.

Compromise version from conference is sent to each chamber for final approval.

HOUSE OF REPRESENTATIVES

SENATE

PRESIDENT
Compromise version approved by both houses is sent to president who can either sign it into law or veto it and return it to Congress. Congress may override veto by two-thirds majority vote in both houses; bill then becomes law without president's signature.

VETO

PASS

poverty." And most scholars agree that, by whatever measures, during the 1980s and 1990s, the body's legislative output slowed or declined.[26]

The second issue is how best to evaluate changes in the legislation Congress produces from one time period to the next. For instance, some scholars argue that the relatively low levels of legislative output of the late 1990s, together with decreases in the body's oversight hearings and related activities, betokened an institutional decline of Congress; others, however, reject the view that Congress, by passing fewer laws and holding fewer hearings, had thereby become a "broken branch."[27]

divided government
One party controls the White House and another party controls one or both houses of Congress.

unified government The same party controls the White House and both houses of Congress.

earmarks "Hidden" congressional provisions that direct the federal government to fund specific projects or that exempt specific persons or groups from paying specific federal taxes or fees

The third issue is whether **divided government** (one party in control of the presidency and the other in charge of one or both chambers of Congress) decreases legislative productivity. Although there are some exceptions, most studies of the subject suggest that divided party government only reduces the passage of the most far-reaching and costly legislation.[28] As we shall discuss in Chapter 14, divided party government does not lead inevitably to "policy gridlock" anymore than having **unified government** (a single party in power in the White House and in both chambers of Congress) makes enacting ever more sweeping laws easy or inevitable.

The fourth issue involves so-called **earmarks**—congressional provisions that direct the federal government to fund specific projects or exempt specific persons or groups from needing to pay specific federal taxes or fees. Earmarks have tripled since 1994; in 2006, nearly 13,000 earmarks cost about $64 billion.[29] Earmarks are legally binding, but few appear in a bill's text; rather, most are "hidden" in conference reports not subject to amendment.

This form of "legislative productivity" is criticized by most scholars and, in principle at least, by most citizens. Earmarks figured in the scandals surrounding lobbyist Jack Abramoff and the convicted Congressman Randy "Duke" Cunningham; Barack Obama and John McCain argued against earmarks during the 2008 presidential campaign. Still, earmarks, in one form or another, have proliferated because individuals and institutions—including not just businesses but private universities, hospitals, and other nonprofit organizations—persist in demanding them from constituency-oriented members of Congress.

The fifth issue is how the post–9/11 Congress has legislated on matters directly relevant to homeland security, especially its own. The Framers crafted Congress as an institution that favors deliberation over dispatch; to act boldly only when backed by a persistent popular majority, or a broad consensus among its leaders, or both; and to be slow to change its time-honored procedures and structures.

But intelligence officials believe that a fourth plane involved in the 9/11 terrorist attacks was headed for the Capitol. In its June 2003 report, the bipartisan Continuity of Government Commission concluded that "the greatest hole in our constitutional system is the possibility of a terrorist attack that would kill or injure many members of Congress."[30]

This "hole" is relatively small with respect to the Senate. The Seventeenth Amendment allows the emergency replacement of senators by the governors of their states provided the state legislature allows it; otherwise, the governors must call for new elections. But the problem is greater for the House, where vacancies can only be filled by special elections, a process that can take many months.

Congress has enacted some, but by no means all, of the 9/11 Commission's recommendations.[31] But, as of 2009, it had failed to enact comprehensive legislation or proposals for constitutional amendments to ensure that "the first branch" can continue to function should a terrorist attack kill or incapacitate many or most of its members.

STUDY BY COMMITTEES

A bill is referred to a committee for consideration by either the Speaker of the House or the presiding officer of the Senate. Rules govern which committee will get which bill, but sometimes a choice is possible. In the House, the right of the Speaker to make such choices is an important component of his powers. (His decisions can be appealed to the full House.) In 1963, a civil rights bill was referred by the presiding officer of the Senate to the Commerce Committee in order to keep it out of the hands of the chairman of the Judiciary Committee, who was hostile to the bill. In the House, the same piece of legislation was referred by the Speaker to the Judiciary Committee in order to keep it out of the grasp of the hostile chairman of the Interstate and Foreign Commerce Committee.

The Constitution requires that "all bills for raising revenue shall originate in the House of Representatives." The Senate can and does amend such bills, but only after the House has acted first. Bills that are not for raising revenue—that is, bills that do not change the tax laws—can originate in either house. In practice, the House also originates appropriations bills—that is, bills directing how money shall be spent. Because of the House's special position in relation to revenue legislation, the committee that handles those bills—the Ways and Means Committee—is particularly powerful.

Most bills die in committee. They often are introduced only to get publicity for the member of Congress or to enable the member to say to constituents or pressure groups that he or she "did something" on a matter concerning them. Bills of general interest—many of

---

H.R.1661

Children's Health Insurance Accountability Act of 1999 (Introduced in the House)

HR 1661 IH

106th CONGRESS

1st Session

H. R. 1661

To amend title XXVII of the Public Health Service Act and part 7 of subtitle B of title I of the Employee Retirement Income Security Act of 1974 to establish standards for the health quality improvement of children in managed care plans and other health plans.

IN THE HOUSE OF REPRESENTATIVES

May 4, 1999

Mrs. MORELLA (for herself, Mr. BALDACCI, Mr. SAWYER, and Mr. HILLIARD) introduced the following bill; which was referred to the Committee on Commerce, and in addition to the Committee on Education and the Workforce, for a period to be subsequently determined by the Speaker, in each case for consideration of such provisions as fall within the jurisdiction of the committee concerned

---

A BILL

To amend title XXVII of the Public Health Service Act and part 7 of subtitle B of title I of the Employee Retirement Income Security Act of 1974 to establish standards for the health quality improvement of children in managed care plans and other health plans.

Be it enacted by the Senate and House of Representatives of the United States of America in Congress assembled,

A bill (H.R. 1661) as it looks when introduced in the House.

which are drafted in the executive branch but introduced by a member of Congress—are assigned to a subcommittee for a hearing, where witnesses appear, evidence is taken, and questions are asked. These hearings are used to inform members of Congress, to permit interest groups to speak out (whether or not they have anything helpful to say), and to build public support for a measure favored by the majority of the committee.

Though committee hearings are necessary and valuable, they also fragment the process of considering bills dealing with complex matters. Both power and information are dispersed in Congress, and thus it is difficult to take a comprehensive view of matters cutting across committee boundaries.

To deal with this problem Congress has established a process whereby a bill may now be referred to several committees that simultaneously consider it in whole or in part. This process, called **multiple referral,** was used in 1977 to send President Carter's energy proposals to six different committees in both the House and Senate. An even bigger multiple referral was used for the 1988 trade bill, which was considered by 14 committees in the House and nine in the Senate. The advantage of this procedure is that all views have a chance to be heard; the disadvantage is that it takes a lot of time and gives opponents a greater chance to kill or modify the bill. And if the different committees disagree about the bill, their members have to come together in a gargantuan joint meeting to iron out their differences. In these cases, the

advantages of the committee system—providing expert knowledge and careful deliberation—are often lost. Before the practice was abolished in 1995, about a quarter of all House bills and resolutions went through multiple referrals. Under the new rules, the Speaker is allowed to send a bill to a second committee after the first is finished acting, or he may refer parts of a bill to separate committees. This process, called **sequential referral,** has not noticeably slowed down the pace of legislative activity in Congress. In the 108th Congress, House rules were changed to give the Speaker, "under exceptional circumstances the right to not designate a primary committee." It is still too soon to know what, if any, difference this change will make.

After the hearings, the committee or subcommittee will "mark up" the bill—that is, make revisions and additions, some of which are extensive. These changes do not become part of the bill unless they are approved by the house of which the committee is a part. If a majority of the committee votes to report a bill out to the House or Senate, it goes forward. It is accompanied by a report that explains why the committee favors the bill and why it wishes to see its amendments, if any, adopted. Committee members who oppose the bill have an opportunity to include their dissenting opinions in the report.

multiple referral A congressional process whereby a bill may be referred to several important committees.

sequential referral A congressional process by which a Speaker may send a bill to a second committee after the first is finished acting.

How Things Work

Congressional Calendars

House

Union Calendar Bills to raise revenue or spend money

Example: an appropriations bill

House Calendar Nonmoney bills of major importance

Example: a civil rights bill

Private Calendar Private bills

Example: a bill to waive the immigration laws so that a Philadelphia woman could be joined by her Italian husband

Consent Calendar Noncontroversial bills

Example: a resolution creating National Stenographers Week

Discharge Calendar Discharge petitions

Senate

Executive Calendar Presidential nominations, proposed treaties

Calendar of Business All legislation

If the committee does not report the bill out favorably, that ordinarily kills it. There is a procedure whereby the full House or Senate can get a bill that is stalled in committee out and onto the floor, but it is rarely used. In the House, a **discharge petition** must be signed by 218 members; if the petition is approved by a vote of the House, the bill comes before it directly. In the Senate, a member can move to discharge a committee of any bill, and if the motion passes, the bill comes before the Senate. During the last century, there have been over 800 efforts in the House to use discharge petitions; only two dozen have succeeded. Discharge is rarely tried in the Senate, in part because Senate rules permit almost any proposal to get to the floor as an amendment to another bill.

For a bill to come before either house, it must first be placed on a calendar. There are five such calendars in the House and two in the Senate (see the box above).

Though the bill goes onto a calendar, it is not necessarily considered in chronological order or even considered at all. In the House, the Rules Committee reviews most bills and adopts a rule that governs the procedures under which they will be considered by the House. A **closed rule** sets a strict time limit on debate and forbids the introduction of any amendments from the floor, or forbids amendments except those offered by the sponsoring committee. Obviously, such a rule can make it very difficult for opponents to do anything but vote yes or no on the measure. An **open rule** permits amendments from the floor. A **restrictive rule** permits some amendments but not others.

In the early 1970s, most bills were debated under open rules. In the 1980s, the Rules Committee—which is controlled by the Speaker—increasingly introduced bills for consideration under closed or restrictive rules in an effort to reduce the number of amendments from the floor (and, the Republicans argued, to reduce Republican influence). By the end of the 1980s, roughly half of all bills and nearly three-fourths of all important ones were debated under restrictive or closed rules. In 1992, only one-third of all bills were considered under an open rule.[32]

The House has at least three ways of bypassing the Rules Committee: (1) a member can move that the rules be suspended, which requires a two-thirds vote; (2) a discharge petition, as explained above, can be filed; or (3) the House can use the "Calendar Wednesday" procedure.* These methods are not used very often, but they are available if the Rules

discharge petition
A device by which any member of the House, after a committee has had the bill for 30 days, may petition to have it brought to the floor.

closed rule An order from the House Rules Committee that sets a time limit on debate; forbids a bill from being amended on the floor.

open rule An order from the House Rules Committee that permits a bill to be amended on the floor.

restrictive rule An order from the House Rules Committee that permits certain kinds of amendments but not others to be made into a bill on the floor.

---

* On Wednesdays the list of committees of the House is called more or less in alphabetical order, and any committee can bring up for action a bill of its own already on a calendar. Action on a bill brought to the floor on Calendar Wednesday must be completed that day, or the bill goes back to committee. Since major bills rarely can be voted on in one day, this procedure is not often used.

Committee departs too far from the sentiments of the House.

In theory, few such barriers to floor consideration exist in the Senate. There bills may be considered in any order at any time whenever a majority of the Senate chooses. The majority leader, in consultation with the minority leader, schedules bills for consideration. In practice, however, getting proposals to the Senate floor is far more complicated. Whereas the House normally plows through its legislative schedule, ignoring individual members' complaints in favor of getting its work done, the Senate majority leader must accommodate the interests of individual senators before proceeding with the Senate's business.

FLOOR DEBATE—THE HOUSE

Once on the floor, the bills are debated. In the House, all revenue and most other bills are discussed by the "Committee of the Whole," which is nothing more than whoever happens to be on the floor at the time. The **quorum,** or minimum number of members who must be present for business to be conducted, is only 100 members for the Committee of the Whole. Obviously, this number is easier to assemble than a quorum for the House itself, which the Constitution specifies as a majority, or 218 members. The Speaker does not preside but chooses another person to wield the gavel. The Committee of the Whole debates, amends, and generally decides the final shape of the bill, but technically cannot pass it. To do that, the Committee of the Whole reports the bill back to the House (that is, to itself), which takes final action. During the debate in the Committee of the Whole, the committee sponsoring the bill guides the discussion, divides the time equally between proponents and opponents, and decides how long each member will be permitted to speak. If amendments are allowed under the rule, they must be germane to the purpose of the bill—extraneous matters (riders) are not allowed—and no one may speak for more than five minutes on an amendment. During this process, people wishing to take time out to huddle about strategy or to delay action can demand a **quorum call**—a calling of the roll to find out whether the necessary minimum number of members are present. If a quorum is not present, the House must either adjourn or dispatch the sergeant at arms to round up missing members. The sponsoring committee almost always wins; its bill, as amended by it, usually is the version that the House passes.

FLOOR DEBATE—THE SENATE

Things are a good deal more casual in the Senate. Short of cloture (discussed below), there is no rule limiting debate, and members can speak for as long

Politically Speaking

Riders and Christmas Trees

A *rider* is a provision added to a piece of legislation not germane to the bill's purpose. The goal is usually to achieve one of two outcomes: either to get the president (or governor) to sign an otherwise objectionable bill by attaching to it, as an amendment, a provision that the chief executive desperately wants to see enacted, or to get the president to veto a bill that he would otherwise sign by attaching to it, as an amendment, a provision that the chief executive strongly dislikes.

A rider is a convenient way for a legislator to get a pet project approved that might not be approved if it had to be voted on by itself. The term can be traced back to 17th-century England.

When a bill has lots of riders, it becomes a *Christmas tree bill*. In 1966, for example, the Foreign Investors Act, a bill designed to solve the balance-of-payments problem, had added to it riders giving assistance to hearse owners, the mineral ore business, importers of scotch whiskey, and presidential candidates.

Source: From *Safire's Political Dictionary* by William Safire. Copyright © 1968, 1972, 1978 by William Safire. Reprinted by permission of Random House, Inc. and the author.

as they can stay on their feet. A senator's remarks need not be relevant to the matter under consideration (some senators have read aloud from the *quorum* The minimum number of members who must be present for business to be conducted in Congress.

quorum call A roll call in either house of Congress to see whether the minimum number of representatives required to conduct business is present.

cloture rule A rule used by the Senate to end or limit debate.

double-tracking A procedure to keep the Senate going during a filibuster in which the disputed bill is shelved temporarily so that the Senate can get on with other business.

Washington telephone directory), and anyone can offer an amendment at any time. There is no Committee of the Whole. Amendments need not be germane to the purpose of the bill, and thus the Senate often attaches riders to bills.

In fact, the opportunity to offer nongermane amendments gives a senator a chance to get a bill onto the floor without regard to the calendar or the schedule of the majority leader: he or she need only offer a pet bill as an "amendment" to a bill already under discussion. (This cannot be done to an appropriations bill.) Indeed, the entire committee hearing process can be bypassed in the Senate if the House has already passed the bill. In that case a senator can get the House-passed measure put directly onto the Senate calendar without committee action. In 1957 and again in 1964, this was done with House-passed civil rights bills to make certain that they would not be bottled up in the conservative Senate Judiciary Committee.

A Senate filibuster is difficult to break. The current **cloture rule** requires that 16 senators sign a petition to move cloture. The motion is voted on two days after the petition is introduced; to pass, three-fifths of the entire Senate membership (60 senators if there are no vacancies) must vote for it. If it passes, each senator is thereafter limited to one hour of debate on the bill under consideration. The total debate, including roll calls and the introduction of amendments, cannot exceed 100 hours.

In recent years, both filibusters and cloture votes have become more common. The filibuster occurs more frequently because it is now easier to stage one. It often consists not of a senator's making a long speech but of endless requests for the clerk to call the roll. More filibusters means more cloture votes, which are now easier to win since the 1975 change lowering the required number of supporters from two-thirds to three-fifths of all senators. During the 100th Congress (1987–1988), there were almost as many cloture votes—43—as there had been in the half century after the procedure was invented. Since 1975, about 40 percent of all cloture votes have succeeded in cutting off debate.

Conservatives have used the filibuster to try to block civil rights laws; liberals have used it to try to block decontrol of gas prices. Since both factions have found the filibuster useful, it seems most unlikely it will ever be abolished, though it has been somewhat curtailed. One way to keep the Senate going during a filibuster is through **double-tracking,** whereby the disputed bill is shelved temporarily so that the Senate can get on with other business. Because double-tracking permits the Senate to discuss and vote on matters other than the bill that is filibustered, it is less costly to individual senators to stage a filibuster. In the past, before double-tracking, a senator and his allies had to keep talking around the clock to keep their filibuster alive. If they stopped talking, the Senate was free to take up other business. Opponents of the filibuster would bring cots and blankets to the Senate so they could sleep and eat there, ready to take the floor the moment the filibuster faltered. But with double-tracking other business can go on while the stalled bill is temporarily set aside. As a result, the number of filibusters has skyrocketed. In the words of two expert Senate watchers, the "Senate has become increasingly unmanageable as filibusters have become virtually commonplace on both major and minor pieces of legislation, raising the standard for passage of even routine bills from fifty to sixty votes and resulting in frequent delays in scheduling, stop-and-go patterns of floor debate," and the use of other procedures "that make the institution hostage to the whims of individual senators."[33]

What the threat of a filibuster means in practice is this: neither political party can control the Senate unless it has at least sixty votes. Neither party had that many Senate seats between 1979 and 2008, but in 2009 the Democrats had sixty.

METHODS OF VOTING

Some observers of Congress make the mistake of deciding who was for and who was against a bill by the final vote. This can be misleading—often a member of Congress will vote for final passage of a bill after having supported amendments that, if they had passed, would have made the bill totally different. To keep track of various members' voting records, therefore, it is often more important to know how they voted on key amendments than to know how they voted on the bill itself.

Finding that out is not always easy, though it has become more so in recent years. There are four procedures for voting in the House. A **voice vote** consists of the members' shouting "yea" or "nay"; a **division** (or standing) **vote** involves the members' standing and being counted. In neither a voice nor

How Things Work

House-Senate Differences: A Summary

House

- 435 members serve two-year terms.

- House members have only one major committee assignment, thus tend to be policy specialists.

- Speaker's referral of bills to committee is hard to challenge.

- Committees almost always consider legislation first.

- Scheduling and rules are controlled by the majority party.

- Rules Committee is powerful; controls time of debate, admissibility of amendments.

- Debate usually is limited to one hour.

- Nongermane amendments may not be introduced from the floor.

Senate

- 100 members serve rotating six-year terms.

- Senators have two or more major committee assignments, thus tend to be policy generalists.

- Referral decisions are easy to challenge.

- Committee consideration is easily bypassed.

- Scheduling and rules generally are agreed to by majority and minority leaders.

- Rules Committee is weak; few limits on debate or amendments.

- Debate is unlimited unless shortened by unanimous consent or by invoking cloture.

- Nongermane amendments may be introduced.

---

a standing vote are the names of members recorded as having voted one way or the other.

To learn how an individual votes, there must be either a recorded teller vote or a roll call. In a **teller vote**, the members pass between two tellers, the yeas first and then the nays. Since 1971, a teller vote can be "recorded," which means that, at the request of 20 members, clerks write down the names of those favoring or opposing a bill as they pass the tellers. Since teller votes but not roll calls may be taken in the Committee of the Whole, the use of a recorded teller vote enables observers to find out how members voted in those important deliberations.

A **roll-call vote,** of course, consists of people answering "yea" or "nay" to their names. It can be done at the request of one-fifth of the representatives present in the House. When roll calls were handled orally, it was a time-consuming process, since the clerk had to drone through 435 names. Since 1973, an electronic voting system has been in operation that permits each member, by inserting a plastic card into a slot, to record his or her own vote and to learn the total automatically. Owing to the use of recorded teller votes and the advent of electronic roll-call votes, the number of recorded votes has gone up sharply in the House. There were only 73 House roll calls in 1955; twenty years later,

there were over eight times that many. Voting in the Senate is much the same, only simpler: there is no such thing as a teller vote, and no electronic counters are used.

If a bill passes the House and Senate in different forms, the differences must be reconciled if the bill is to become law. If they are minor, the last house to act may simply refer the bill back to the other house, which then accepts the alterations. If the differences are major, it often is necessary to appoint a conference committee to iron them out. Only a minority of bills require a conference. Each house must vote to form such a committee. The members are picked by the chairmen of the House and Senate standing committees that have been handling the legislation, with representation given to the minority as well as the majority party. There usually are between three and 15 members from each house. No decision

voice vote A congressional voting procedure in which members shout "yea" in approval or "nay" in disapproval, permitting members to vote quickly or anonymously on bills.

division vote A congressional voting procedure in which members stand and are counted.

teller vote A congressional voting procedure in which members pass between two tellers, the "yeas" first and the "nays" second.

roll-call vote A congressional voting procedure that consists of members answering "yea" or "nay" to their names.

Cartoon by Mark Cullum/The Birmingham News. Reprinted with permission.

can be made unless approved by a majority of both delegations.

Bargaining is long and hard; in the past it was also secret. Now some conference sessions are open to the public. Often—as with President Carter's energy bill—the legislation is substantially rewritten in conference. Complex bills can lead to enormous conference committees. The 1988 trade bill went before a conference committee of 200 members. Theoretically, the conferees are not supposed to change anything already agreed to by both the House and Senate, but in the inevitable give-and-take even matters already approved may be changed.

In most cases, the conference reports tend to favor, slightly, the Senate version of the bill. Whoever wins (and both sides always claim they got everything out of the bargaining that they possibly could have), conferees report their agreement back to their respective houses, which usually consider the report immediately. The report can be accepted or rejected; it cannot be amended. In the great majority of cases, it is accepted: the alternative is to have no bill at all, at least for that Congress. The bill, now in final form, goes to the president for signature or veto. If a veto is cast, the bill returns to the house of origin. There an effort can be made to override the veto. This requires that two-thirds of those present (provided that there is a quorum) must vote to

override; this vote must be a roll call. If both houses override in this manner, the bill becomes law without the president's approval.

Reducing Power and Perks

While most citizens are only vaguely familiar with the rules and procedures under which Congress operates, they do care whether Congress as an institution serves the public interest and fulfills its mission as a democratic body. Over the last several decades, many proposals have been made to reform and improve Congress—term limitations, new ethics and campaign finance laws, and organizational changes intended to reduce the power and perks of members while making it easier for Congress to pass needed legislation in a timely fashion. Some of these proposals—for example, campaign finance reforms (see Chapter 10)—have recently become law.

Many would-be reformers share the view that Congress is overstaffed and self-indulgent. It is, they complain, quick to impose new laws on states, cities, businesses, and average citizens but slow to apply those same laws to itself and its members. It is quick to pass **pork-barrel legislation**—bills that give tangible benefits (highways, dams, post offices) to constituents in the hope of winning their votes in return—but slow to tackle complex and controversial questions of national policy. The reformers' image of Congress is unflattering, but is it wholly unwarranted?

No perk is more treasured by members of Congress than the frank. Members of Congress are allowed by law to send material through the mail free of charge by substituting their facsimile signature (*frank*) for postage. But rather than using this **franking privilege** to keep their constituents informed about the government, most members use franked newsletters and questionnaires as campaign literature. That is why use of the frank soars in the months before an election.

Thus, the frank amounts to a taxpayer subsidy of members' campaigns, a perk that bolsters the electoral fortunes of incumbents. Some reformers do not believe it is possible to fence in congressional use of the frank for public education or other legitimate purposes, and so they propose abolishing it outright. Other reformers argue that the frank can be fenced in by prohibiting mailings just before primaries and general elections.

For years, Congress routinely exempted itself from many of the laws it passed. In defense of this practice, members said that if members of Congress were subject to, for example, the minimum wage laws, the executive branch, charged with enforcing these laws, would acquire excessive power over Congress. This would violate the separation of powers. But as public criticism of Congress grew and confidence in government declined, more and more people demanded that Congress subject itself to the laws that applied to everybody else. In 1995, the 104th Congress did this by passing a bill that obliges Congress to obey 11 important laws governing things such as civil rights, occupational safety, fair labor standards, and family leave.

The bipartisan Congressional Accountability Act of 1995 had to solve a key problem: under the constitutional doctrine of separated powers, it would have been unwise and perhaps unconstitutional for the executive branch to enforce congressional compliance with executive-branch regulations. So Congress created the independent Office of Compliance and an employee grievance procedure to deal with implementation. Now Congress, too, must obey laws such as the Civil Rights Act, the Equal Pay Act, the Age Discrimination Act, and the Family and Medical Care Leave Act.

As already mentioned, bills containing money for local dams, bridges, roads, and monuments are referred to disparagingly as pork-barrel legislation. Reformers complain that when members act to "bring home the bacon," Congress misallocates tax dollars by supporting projects with trivial social benefits in order to bolster their reelection prospects.

No one can doubt the value of trimming unnecessary spending, but pork is not necessarily the villain it is made out to be. For example, the main cause of the budget deficit was the increase in spending on entitlement programs (like health care and interest on the

Politically Speaking

Pork Barrel

Before the Civil War, it was the custom to take salt pork from barrels and distribute it to the slaves. Often, the eagerness of the slaves to get the food would result in a rush on the barrels, with each slave trying to get as much as possible.

By the 1870s, members of Congress were using the term *pork* to refer to benefits for their districts and *pork barrel* to mean the piece of legislation containing those benefits.

Today, the classic example of pork-barrel legislation is the rivers and harbors bill, which provides appropriations for countless dams, bridges, and canals to be built in congressional districts all over the country.

Source: From *Safire's Political Dictionary* by William Safire. Copyright © 1968, 1972, 1978 by William Safire. Reprinted by permission of Random House, Inc. and the author.

pork-barrel legislation
Legislation that gives tangible benefits to constituents in several districts or states in the hope of winning their votes in return.

franking privilege
The ability of members to mail letters to their constituents free of charge by substituting their facsimile signature for postage.

Answer

How Things Work

Rules on Congressional Ethics

Senate

Gifts: No gifts (in money, meals, or things) totaling $100 or more from anyone except a spouse or personal friend.

Lobbyists may not pay for gifts, official travel, legal defense funds, or charitable contributions to groups controlled by senators.

Fees: No fees for lectures or writing ("honoraria"), except that fees of up to $2,000 may go to a senator-designated charity.

Outside earned income may not exceed 15 percent of a senator's salary.

Ex-senators may not try to influence members of Congress for one year after leaving the Senate.

Mass mailings: No senator may receive more than $50,000 from the Senate to send out a mailing to constituents.

House

Gifts: No gifts (in money, meals, or things) totaling $100 or more from anyone except a spouse or personal friend.

Lobbyists may not offer gifts or pay for travel, even if lobbyist is a spouse or personal friend.

Travel: House members may travel at the expense of others if travel is for officially connected meetings.

Fees: No honoraria for House members.

Ex–House members may not lobby Congress for one year after leaving office.

How Things Work

How Congress Raises Its Pay

For over 200 years, Congress has tried to find a politically painless way to raise its own pay. It has managed to vote itself a pay increase 23 times in those two centuries, but usually at the price of a hostile public reaction. Twice during the 19th century, a pay raise led to a massacre of incumbents in the next election.

Knowing this, Congress has invented various ways to get a raise without actually appearing to vote for it. These have included the following:

- Voting for a tax deduction for expenses incurred as a result of living in Washington

- Creating a citizens commission that could recommend a pay increase that would take effect automatically, provided Congress did not vote against it

- Linking increases in pay to decreases in honoraria (that is, speaking fees)

In 1989, a commission recommended a congressional pay raise of over 50 percent (from $89,500 to $135,000) and a ban on honoraria. The House planned to let it take effect automatically. But the public wouldn't have it, demanding that Congress vote on the raise—and vote it down. It did.

Embarrassed by its maneuvering, Congress retreated. At the end of 1989, it voted itself (as well as most top executive and judicial branch members) a small pay increase (7.9 percent for representatives, 9.9 percent for senators) that also provided for automatic cost-of-living adjustments (up to 5 percent a year) in the future. But the automatic adjustments in congressional pay have been rejected every year in recorded roll-call votes. Apparently nobody in Congress wants to be accused of "getting rich" at the taxpayers' expense.

WHAT WOULD YOU DO?

MEMORANDUM

To: *Representative Peter Skerry*

From: *Martha Bayles, legislative aide*

Subject: *The Size of the House of Representatives*

The House can decide how big it wishes to be. When it was created, there was one representative for every 30,000 people. Now there is one for every 600,000. In most other democracies, each member of parliament represents far fewer than 600,000 people. Doubling the size of the House may be a way of avoiding term limits.

Arguments for:

1. Doubling the size of the House would reduce the huge demand for constituent services each member now faces.

2. A bigger House would represent more shades of opinion more fairly.

3. Each member could raise less campaign money because his or her campaign would be smaller.

Arguments against:

1. A bigger House would be twice as hard to manage, and it would take even longer to pass legislation.

2. Campaigns in districts of 300,000 people would cost as much as ones in districts with 600,000 people.

3. Interest groups do a better job of representing public opinion than would a House with more members.

Should We Have a Bigger Congress?

November 15
WASHINGTON, D.C.

A powerful citizens organization has demanded that the House of Representatives be made larger so that voters can feel closer to their members. Each representative now speaks for about 600,000 people—far too many, the group argues, to make it possible for all points of view to be heard. In its petition…

Your decision:

Increase size of House: _____   Do not increase size of House: _____

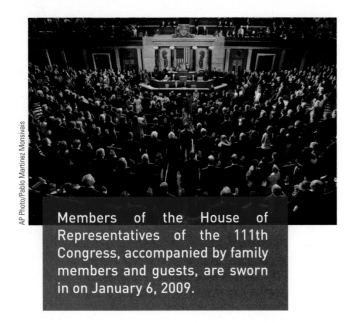

Members of the House of Representatives of the 111th Congress, accompanied by family members and guests, are sworn in on January 6, 2009.

AP Photo/Pablo Martinez Monsivais

another person's necessity. No doubt some congressional districts get an unnecessary bridge or highway, but others get bridges and highways that are long overdue. The notion that every bridge or road a member of Congress gets for his or her district is wasteful pork is tantamount to saying that no member attaches any importance to merit.

Even if all pork were bad, it would still be necessary. Congress is an independent branch of government, and each member is, by constitutional design, the advocate of his or her district or state. No member's vote can be won by coercion, and few can be had by mere appeals to party loyalty or presidential needs. Pork is a way of obtaining consent. The only alternative is bribery, but bribery, besides being wrong, would benefit only the member, whereas pork usually benefits voters in the member's district. If you want to eliminate pork, you must eliminate Congress, by converting it into a parliament under the control of a powerful party leader or prime minister. In a tightly controlled parliament, no votes need be bought; they can be commanded. But members of such a parliament can do little to help their constituents cope with government or to defend them against bureaucratic abuses, nor can they investigate the conduct of the executive branch. The price of a citizen-oriented Congress is a pork-oriented Congress.

national debt) without a corresponding increase in taxes. Spending on pork is a small fraction of total annual federal spending (about 2.5 percent, on average, from 1993 to 2005).[34] But many categories of pork spending have increased in the last 10 or 15 years. Of course, one person's pork is

SUMMARY

As complicated as congress seems (and is), even a single legislator among 535 can make a big difference in what ideas get considered and which bills become law. Constitutionally speaking, Congress was and remains the first branch of American government. Party control may shift—as it did in 1994 to the Republicans and in 2006 to the Democrats—but the features that make Congress a representative institution with lawmaking functions persist. The House and the Senate both differ greatly from any parliamentary bodies. Over the last half-century or so Congress, especially the House, has evolved through three stages.

During the first stage, lasting from the end of World War I until the early 1960s, the House was dominated by powerful committee chairmen who controlled the agenda, decided which members would get what services for their constituents, and tended to follow the leadership of the Speaker. Newer members

were expected to be seen but not heard; power and prominence came only after a long apprenticeship. Congressional staffs were small, and so members dealt with each other face to face.

The second stage emerged in the early 1970s, in part as the result of trends already under way (for example, the steady growth in the number of staffers assigned to each member) and in part as a result of changes in procedures and organization brought about by younger, especially northern, members. Dissatisfied with southern resistance to civil rights bills and emboldened by a sharp increase in the number of liberals who had been elected in the Johnson landslide of 1964, the House Democratic caucus adopted rules that allowed the caucus to select committee chairmen without regard to seniority, dramatically increased the number and staffs of subcommittees (for the first time, the Ways and Means Committee was required to have subcommittees), authorized individual committee members (instead of the chairman) to choose the chairmen of these subcommittees, ended the ability of chairmen to refuse to call meetings, and made it much harder for those meetings to be closed to the public. The installation of electronic voting made it easier to require recorded votes, and so the number of times each member had to go on record rose sharply. The Rules Committee was instructed to issue more rules that would allow floor amendments.

At the same time, the number of southern Democrats in leadership positions began to decline, and the conservatism of the remaining ones began to lessen. (In 1990, southerners held only a quarter of committee chairmanships in the House and none of the major party leadership posts.) Moreover, northern and southern Democrats began to vote together a bit more frequently (though the conservative Boll Weevils remained a significant—and often swing—group).

These changes created a House ideally suited to serve the reelection needs of its members. Each representative could be an individual political entrepreneur, seeking publicity, claiming credit, introducing bills, holding subcommittee hearings, and assigning staffers to work on constituents' problems. There was no need to defer to powerful party leaders or committee chairmen. But because representatives in each party were becoming more alike ideologically, there was a rise in party voting. Congress became a career attractive to men and women skilled in these techniques, and these people entered Congress in large numbers. Their skill was manifest in the growth of the sophomore surge—the increase in their winning percentage during their first reelection campaign.

Even junior members could now make their mark on legislation. In the House, more floor amendments were offered and passed; in the Senate, filibusters became more commonplace. Owing to multiple referrals and overlapping subcommittee jurisdictions, more members could participate in writing bills and overseeing government agencies.

But lurking within the changes that defined the second stage were others, less noticed at the time, that created the beginnings of a new phase. The third stage was an effort in the House to strengthen and centralize party leadership. The Speaker acquired the power to appoint a majority of the members of the Rules Committee. That body, worried by the flood of floor amendments, began issuing more restrictive rules. By the mid-1980s, this had reached the point where Republicans were complaining that they were being gagged. The Speaker also got control of the Democratic Steering and Policy Committee (it assigns new members to committees) and was given the power to refer bills to several committees simultaneously.

The evolution of the House remains an incomplete story; it is not yet clear whether it will remain in stage two or find some way of moving decisively into stage three. For now it has elements of both.

Meanwhile, the Senate remains as individualistic and decentralized as ever—a place where it has always been difficult to exercise strong leadership.

Though its members may complain that Congress is collectively weak, to any visitor from abroad it seems extraordinarily powerful, probably the most powerful legislative body in the world. Congress has always been jealous of its constitutional independence and authority. Three compelling events led to Congress's reasserting its authority: the increasingly unpopular war in Vietnam; the Watergate scandals, which revealed a White House meddling illegally in the electoral process; and the advent of divided governments—with one party in control of the presidency and the other in control of Congress. It remains to be seen, however, whether Congress will function differently with the return of unified party government or in response to the threat of terrorism.

Claims that Congress became weak as the president grew stronger are a bit overdrawn. As we shall see in the next chapter, the view from the White House is quite different. Recent presidents have complained bitterly of their inability to get Congress even to act on, much less approve, many of their key proposals and have resented what they regard as congressional interference in the management of executive-branch agencies and the conduct of foreign affairs. If the past is prologue, the present era of unified party government will involve plenty of legislative-executive intraparty conflicts.

RECONSIDERING WHO GOVERNS?

1. *Are members of Congress representative of the American people?*

Demographically, no: most Americans are not middle-aged white males with law degrees or past political careers. Some groups (for example, women) are much less prevalent in Congress than they are in the nation as a whole, while other groups (for example, Catholics) constitute about the same fraction of Congress as they do of the American people. Ideologically, Republican members of Congress are more conservative than average Americans, and Democratic members of Congress are more liberal than average Americans.

2. *Does Congress normally do what most citizens want it to do?*

On most issues most of the time, Congress is in step with the public. But on some issues, most representatives' opinions generally are out of sync with mass public preferences. For example, most Americans have long favored protectionist trade policies, but most members of Congress have consistently voted for free trade policies. Likewise, most citizens are less solicitous of laws that reinforce civil liberties than the Congress has traditionally been. This, however, is much as the Framers of the Constitution had hoped and expected. They believed that representatives should refine, not reflect, public wishes, and mediate, not mirror, public views.

RECONSIDERING TO WHAT ENDS?

1. *Should Congress run under strong leadership?*

Congress has tried it both ways. Sometimes the House has had a strong Speaker, sometimes a weak one; sometimes committee chairmen were selected by seniority, sometimes by the Speaker, and sometimes by party vote. If we want a Congress that can act quickly and decisively as a body, then we should desire strong leadership, place restrictions on debate, provide few opportunities for stalling tactics, and brook only minimal committee interference. But if we want a Congress in which the interests of individual members and the people they represent are routinely protected or enhanced, then we must reject strong leadership, proliferate rules allowing for delay and discussion, and permit many opportunities for committee activity. Unfortunately, the public often wants both systems to operate, the first for some issues and the second for others.

2. *Should Congress act more quickly?*

The Framers of the Constitution knew that Congress would normally proceed slowly and err in favor of deliberative, not decisive, action. Congress was intended to check and balance strong leaders in the executive branch, not automatically cede its authority to them, not even during a war or other national crisis. Today, the increased ideological and partisan polarization among members has arguably made Congress even less capable than it traditionally has been of planning ahead or swiftly adopting coherent changes in national policies. There is, however, only conflicting evidence concerning whether so-called policy gridlock has become more common than in decades past. Since the September 11, 2001 terrorist attacks on the United States, Congress has passed a host of new laws intended to enhance America's homeland security. Still, Congress took its time with several major proposals to reorganize the government around homeland security priorities. Some cite this as but the latest, and potentially the gravest, example of what's wrong with Congress. But others cite it as a salutary reminder that a Congress that could move swiftly to enact wise homeland security or other policies could also move swiftly to adopt unwise ones.

WORLD WIDE WEB RESOURCES

House of Representatives: **www.house.gov**

Senate: **www.senate.gov**

Library of Congress: **www.loc.gov**

For news about Congress

   Roll Call magazine: **www.rollcall.com**

   C-SPAN: **www.c-span.org**

SUGGESTED READINGS

Arnold, R. Douglas. *The Logic of Congressional Action*. New Haven and London: Yale University Press, 1990. Masterful analysis of how Congress sometimes passes bills that serve the general public, not just special interests.

Black, Amy E. *From Inspiration to Legislation: How An Idea Becomes a Bill*. Upper Saddle River, N.J.: Pearson, 2007. An insider's account of the creation of the Safe Haven Act of 2001.

Fenno, Richard F., Jr. *Congressmen in Committees*. Boston: Little, Brown, 1973. Classic study of the styles of 12 standing committees.

Fiorina, Morris P. *Congress: Keystone of the Washington Establishment*. 2d ed. New Haven, Conn.: Yale University Press, 1989. Argues that congressional behavior is aimed at guaranteeing their chances for reelection.

Jacobson, Gary. *The Politics of Congressional Elections*. 6th ed. New York: Longman, 2004. Authoritative study of how members of Congress are elected.

Maass, Arthur. *Congress and the Common Good*. New York: Basic Books, 1983. Insightful account of congressional operations, especially those involving legislative-executive relations. Disputes Fiorina's argument that reelection needs explain congressional behavior.

Mann, Thomas E. and Norman J. Ornstein, *Broken Branch: How Congress Is Failing America and How to Get It Back on Track*, 2nd edition. New York: Oxford University Press, 2008. Criticially compares the post–1994 Congress its predecessors and suggests several major reforms.

Poole, Keith T., and Howard Rosenthal. *Congress: A Political-Economic History of Roll Call Voting*. New York: Oxford University Press, 1997. Sophisticated study of why members of Congress vote as they do and how relatively stable congressional voting patterns have been throughout American history.

Sundquist, James L. *The Decline and Resurgence of Congress*. Washington, D.C.: Brookings Institution, 1981. A history of the fall and, after 1973, the rise of congressional power vis-à-vis the president.

14

The
Presidency

J. Scott Applewhite/AP Photo

WHO GOVERNS?

1. Did the Founders expect the presidency to be the most important political institution?
2. How important is the president's character in determining how he governs?

TO WHAT ENDS?

1. Should we abolish the electoral college?
2. Is it harder to govern when the presidency and the Congress are controlled by different political parties?

Professor Jones speaks to his political science class: "The president of the United States occupies one of the most powerful offices in the world. Presidents Kennedy and Johnson sent American troops to Vietnam, President Bush sent them to Saudi Arabia, and President Clinton sent them to Kosovo, all without war being declared by Congress. In fact, Clinton ordered our air force to bomb parts of the old Yugoslavia despite the fact that the House of Representatives had rejected a resolution that would have authorized the bombing. President Nixon imposed wage and price controls on the country. Between them, Presidents Carter and Reagan selected most of the federal judges now on the bench; thus the political philosophies of these two men were stamped on the courts. President George W. Bush created military tribunals to try captured terrorists and persuaded Congress to toughen antiterrorist laws. President Barack Obama, within just months of taking office, got Congress to go along with his plans for giving the executive branch new and sweeping powers to regulate financial markets. No wonder people talk about our having an 'imperial presidency.'"

A few doors down the hall, Professor Smith speaks to her class: "The president, compared to the prime ministers of other democratic nations, is one of the weakest chief executives anywhere. President Carter signed an arms-limitation treaty with the Soviets, but the Senate wouldn't ratify it. President Reagan was not allowed even to test antisatellite weapons, and in 1986 Congress rejected his budget before the ink was dry. President Clinton's health care plan was ignored, and the House voted to impeach him. The federal courts struck down several parts of President Bush's antiterrorist policies. Even with his party in control of both houses of Congress, President Obama's first budget proposals were nixed on Capitol Hill, and his first health care reform plans were quickly recast by congressional committee chairpersons. Regularly, subordinates who are supposed to be loyal to the president leak his views to the press and undercut his programs before Congress. No wonder people call the U.S. president a 'pitiful, helpless giant.'"

Can Professors Jones and Smith be talking about the same office? Who is right? In fact, they are both right. The American presidency is a unique office, with elements of great strength and profound weakness built into it by its constitutional origins.

Presidents and Prime Ministers

The popularly elected president is an American invention. Of the roughly five dozen countries in which there is some degree of party competition and thus, presumably, some measure of free choice for the voters, only 16 have a directly elected president, and 13 of these are nations of North and South America. The democratic alternative is for the chief executive to be a prime minister, chosen by and responsible to the parliament. This system prevails in most Western European countries as well as in Israel and Japan. There is no nation with a purely presidential political system in Europe; France combines a directly elected president with a prime minister and parliament.[1]

In a parliamentary system, the prime minister is the chief executive. The prime minister is chosen not by the voters but by the legislature, and he or she in turn selects the other ministers from the members of parliament. If the parliament has only two major parties, the ministers usually will be chosen from the majority party; if there are many parties (as in Israel), several parties may participate in a coalition cabinet. The prime minister remains in power as long as his or her party has a majority of the seats in the legislature or as long as the coalition he or she has assembled holds together. The voters choose who is to be a member of parliament—usually by voting for one or another party—but cannot choose who is to be the chief executive officer.

Whether a nation has a presidential or a parliamentary system makes a big difference in the identity and powers of the chief executive.

Presidents Are Often Outsiders
People become president by winning elections, and sometimes winning is easier if you can show the voters that you are not part of "the mess in Washington." Prime ministers are selected from among people already in parliament, and so they are always insiders.

Jimmy Carter, Ronald Reagan, Bill Clinton, and George W. Bush did not hold national office before becoming president. Franklin Roosevelt had been assistant secretary of the navy, but his real political experience was as governor of New York. Dwight Eisenhower was a general, not a politician. John F. Kennedy, Lyndon Johnson, and Richard Nixon had been in Congress, but only Nixon had had top-level experience in the executive branch (he had been vice president). George H.W. Bush had had a great

Bettmann/Corbis

The first cabinet: left to right, Secretary of War Henry Knox, Secretary of State Thomas Jefferson, Attorney General Edmund Randolph, Secretary of the Treasury Alexander Hamilton, and President George Washington.

deal of executive experience in Washington—as vice president, director of the CIA, and representative to China, whereas Bill Clinton and George W. Bush both served as governors. Barack Obama is the third president to be elected directly from the U.S. Senate to the White House—the other two were Warren G. Harding and John F. Kennedy.

Thirty-one different people were elected president between 1828 and 2000. Of these, the great majority were governors, military leaders, or vice presidents; only 13 percent were legislators just before becoming president.

Presidents Choose Cabinet Members from Outside Congress

Under the Constitution, no sitting member of Congress can hold office in the executive branch. The persons chosen by a prime minister to be in the cabinet are almost always members of parliament.

Of the 15 heads of cabinet-level departments in the first George W. Bush administration, only four had been members of Congress. The rest, as is customary with most presidents, were close personal friends or campaign aides, representatives of important constituencies (for example, farmers, blacks, or women), experts on various policy issues, or some combination of all three.

The prime minister of Great Britain, by contrast, picks all of his or her cabinet ministers from among members of Parliament. This is one way by which the prime minister exercises control over the legislature. If you were an ambitious member of Parliament, eager to become prime minister yourself someday, and if you knew that your main chance of realizing that ambition was to be appointed to a series of ever-more-important cabinet posts, then you would not likely antagonize the person doing the appointing.

Presidents Have No Guaranteed Majority in the Legislature

A prime minister's party (or coalition) always has a majority in parliament; if it did not, somebody else would be prime minister. A president's party often does not have a congressional majority; instead, Congress often is controlled by the opposite party, creating a divided government. Divided government means that cooperation between the two branches, hard to achieve under the best of circumstances, is often further reduced by partisan bickering.

Even when one party controls both the White House and Congress, the two branches often work at cross-purposes. The U.S. Constitution created a system of separate branches sharing powers. The authors of the document expected there would be conflict between the branches, and they have not been disappointed.

When Kennedy was president, his party, the Democrats, held a big majority in the House and the Senate. Yet Kennedy was frustrated by his inability to get Congress to approve proposals to enlarge civil rights, supply federal aid for school construction, create a Department of Urban Affairs and Housing, or establish a program of subsidized medical care for the elderly. During his last year in office, Congress passed only about one-fourth of his proposals. Carter did not fare much better; even though the Democrats controlled Congress, many of his most important proposals were defeated or greatly modified. Only Franklin Roosevelt (1933–1945) and Lyndon Johnson (1963–1969) had even brief success in leading Congress, and for Roosevelt most of that success was confined to his first term or to wartime.

Presidents and Prime Ministers at War

These differences in political position are illustrated by how George W. Bush and Tony Blair managed the war in Iraq.

- Once Bush decided to fight, he had to cajole Congress, even though it was controlled by his own party, to support him. Once Blair decided to fight, there could not be any meaningful political resistance in parliament.

- When public opinion turned against Bush, he continued the fight because he could not be removed from office. When public opinion turned against Blair, he announced he would resign from office and turn over the job of prime minister to another person in his party.

Divided Government

In the 56 years between 1952 and 2008, there were 28 Congressional elections and 14 presidential elections. Eighteen of the 28 produced **divided government**—a government in which one party controls the White House and a different party controls one or both houses of Congress. When Barack Obama became president in 2009, it was only the fourth time since 1969 that the same party controlled the White House and Congress, creating a **unified government.** And it was only the

divided government One party controls the White House and another party controls one or both houses of Congress.

unified government The same party controls the White House and both houses of Congress.a

gridlock The inability of the government to act because rival parties control different parts of the government.

first time since 1953 when the Republicans were in charge. But not long after the Senate convened, one Republican, James Jeffords of Vermont announced that he was an independent and voted with the Democrats. Divided government had returned until an additional Republican was elected to the Senate in 2002. But the Democrats retook control in 2007 and increased their majorities in both chambers two years later, even gaining the 60 votes necessary to halt filibusters in the senate following a contested Minnesota race that ended with Democrat Al Franken being declared the winner and seated.

Americans say they don't like divided government. They, or at least the pundits who claim to speak for them, think divided government produces partisan bickering, political paralysis, and policy gridlock. During the 1990 battle between President Bush and a Democratic Congress, one magazine compared it to a movie featuring the Keystone Kops, characters from the silent movies who wildly chased each other around while accomplishing nothing.[2] In the 1992 campaign, Bush, Clinton, and Ross Perot bemoaned the "stalemate" that had developed in Washington. When Clinton was sworn in as president, many commentators spoke approvingly of the "end of gridlock."

There are two things wrong with these complaints. First, it is not clear that divided government produces a gridlock that is any worse than that which exists with unified government. Second, it is not clear that, even if **gridlock** does exist, it is always, or even usually, a bad thing for the country.

DOES GRIDLOCK MATTER?

Despite the well-publicized stories about presidential budget proposals being ignored by Congress (Democrats used to describe Reagan's and Bush's budgets as being "dead on arrival"), it is not easy to tell whether divided governments produce fewer or worse policies than unified ones. The scholars who have looked closely at the matter have, in general, concluded that divided governments do about as well as unified ones in passing important laws, conducting important investigations, and ratifying significant treaties.[3] Political scientist David Mayhew studied 267 important laws that were enacted between 1946 and 1990. These laws were as likely to be passed when different parties controlled the White House and Congress as when the same party controlled both branches.[4] For example, divided governments produced the 1946 Marshall Plan to rebuild war-torn Europe and the 1986 Tax Reform Act. The

Divided Government at Work: Six Examples

President George W. Bush and the Democratic-controlled Congress expand federal laws that fund health care for low-income and elderly citizens.

President Bill Clinton and the Republican-controlled Congress overhaul the nation's welfare system and balance the federal budget.

President George H. W. Bush and a Democratic-controlled Congress enact far-reaching federal laws to aid disabled persons.

President Ronald Reagan and the Democratic-controlled Congress reform the federal tax system.

President Richard Nixon and the Democratic-controlled Congress create new batteries of federal environmental policies and programs.

President Dwight D. Eisenhower and the Democratic-controlled Congress establish the interstate highway system.

Source: Eisenhower to Clinton, adapted from Associated Press, "Major Laws Passed in Divided Government," November 9, 2006.

Question

1. Who was the only bachelor president?

box nearby lists six examples of divided government in action.

Why do divided governments produce about as much important legislation as unified ones? The main reason is that "unified government" is something of a myth. Just because the Republicans control both the presidency and Congress does not mean that the Republican president and the Republican senators and representatives will see things the same way. For one thing, Republicans are themselves divided between conservatives (mainly from the South) and liberals (mainly from the Northeast and Midwest). They disagree about policy almost as much as Republicans and Democrats disagree. For another thing, the Constitution ensures that the president and Congress will be rivals for power and thus rivals in policymaking. That's what the separation of powers and checks and balances are all about.

As a result, periods of unified government often turn out not to be so unified. Democratic president Lyndon Johnson could not get many Democratic members of Congress to support his war policy in Vietnam. Democratic president Jimmy Carter could not get the Democratic-controlled Senate to ratify his strategic arms limitation treaty. Democratic president Bill Clinton could not get the Democratic Congress to go along with his policy on gays in the military or his health proposals; and when the heavily revised Clinton budget did pass in 1993, it was by just one vote.

The only time there really is a unified government is when not just the same party but the same *ideological wing* of that party is in effective control of both branches of government. This was true in 1933 when Franklin Roosevelt was president and change-oriented Democrats controlled Congress, and it was true again in 1965 when Lyndon Johnson and liberal Democrats dominated Congress. Both were periods when many major policy initiatives became law: Social Security, business regulations, Medicare, and civil rights legislation. But these periods of ideologically unified government are very rare.

IS POLICY GRIDLOCK BAD?

An American president has less ability to decide what laws get passed than does a British prime minister. If you think the job of a president is to "lead the country," that weakness will worry you. The only cure for that weakness is either to change the Constitution so that our government resembles the parliamentary system in effect in Great Britain, or always to vote into office members of Congress who not only are of the same party as the president but also agree with him on policy issues.

We suspect that even Americans who hate gridlock and want more leadership aren't ready to make sweeping constitutional changes or to stop voting for presidents and members of Congress from different parties. This unwillingness suggests they like the idea of somebody being able to block a policy they don't like. Since all of us don't like something, we all have an interest in some degree of gridlock.

And we seem to protect that interest. In a typical presidential election, about one-fourth of all voters will vote for one party's candidate for president and the other party's candidate for Congress. As a result, about one-fourth of all congressional districts will be represented in the House by a person who does not belong to the party of the president who carried that district. Some scholars believe that voters split tickets deliberately in order to create divided government and thus magnify the effects of the checks and balances built into our system, but the evidence supporting this belief is not conclusive.

Gridlock, to the extent that it exists, is a necessary consequence of a system of representative democracy. Such a system causes delays, intensifies deliberations, forces compromises, and requires the creation of broad-based coalitions to support most new policies. This system is the opposite of direct democracy. If you believe in direct democracy, you believe that what the people want on some issue should become law with as little fuss and bother as possible. Political gridlocks are like traffic gridlocks—people get overheated, things boil over, nothing moves, and nobody wins except journalists who write about the mess and lobbyists who charge big fees to steer their clients around the tie-up. In a direct democracy, the president would be a traffic cop with broad powers to decide in what direction the traffic should move and to make sure that it moves that way.

But if unified governments are not really unified—if in fact they are split by ideological differences within each party and by the institutional rivalries between the president and Congress—then this change is less important than it may seem. What *is* important is the relative power of the president and Congress. That has changed greatly.

Answer

1. James Buchanan was the only bachelor president.

The Evolution of the Presidency

In 1787, few issues inspired as much debate or concern among the Framers as the problem of defining the chief executive. The delegates feared anarchy and monarchy in about equal measure. When the Constitutional Convention met, the existing state constitutions gave most, if not all, power to the legislatures. In eight states, the governor actually was chosen by the legislature, and in ten states, the governor could not serve more than one year. Only in New York, Massachusetts, and Connecticut did governors have much power or serve for any length of time.

Some of the Framers proposed a plural national executive (that is, several people would each hold the executive power in different areas, or they would exercise the power as a committee). Others wanted the executive power checked, as it was in Massachusetts, by a council that would have to approve many of the chief executive's actions. Alexander Hamilton strongly urged the exact opposite: in a five-hour speech, he called for something very much like an elective monarchy, patterned in some respects after the British kind. No one paid much attention to this plan or even, at first, to the more modest (and ultimately successful) suggestion of James Wilson for a single, elected president.

In time, those who won out believed that the governing of a large nation, especially one threatened by foreign enemies, required a single president with significant powers. Their cause was aided, no doubt, by the fact that everybody assumed George Washington would be the first president, and confidence in him—and in his sense of self-restraint—was widely shared. Even so, several delegates feared the presidency would become, in the words of Edmund Randolph of Virginia, "the foetus of monarchy."

CONCERNS OF THE FOUNDERS

The delegates in Philadelphia, and later the critics of the new Constitution during the debate over its ratification, worried about aspects of the presidency that were quite different from those that concern us today. In 1787–1789, some Americans suspected that the president, by being able to command the state militia, would use the militia to overpower state governments. Others were worried that if the president were allowed to share treaty-making power with the Senate, he would be "directed by minions and favorites" and become a "tool of the Senate."

But the most frequent concern was over the possibility of presidential reelection: Americans in the late 18th century were sufficiently suspicious of human nature and sufficiently experienced in the arts of mischievous government to believe that a president, once elected, would arrange to stay in office in perpetuity by resorting to bribery, intrigue, and force. This might happen, for example, every time the presidential election was thrown into the House of Representatives because no candidate had received a majority of the votes in the electoral college, a situation that most people expected to happen frequently.

In retrospect, these concerns seem misplaced, even foolish. The power over the militia has had little significance; the election has gone to the House only twice (1800 and 1824); and though the Senate dominated the presidency off and on during the second half of the 19th century, it has not done so recently. The real sources of the expansion of presidential power—the president's role in foreign affairs, his ability to shape public opinion, his position as head of the executive branch, and his claims to have certain "inherent" powers by virtue of his office—were hardly predictable in 1787. And not surprisingly. There was nowhere in the world at that time, nor had there been at any time in history, an example of an American-style presidency. It was a unique and unprecedented institution, and the Framers and their critics can easily be forgiven for not predicting accurately how it would evolve. At a more general level, however, they understood the issue quite clearly. Gouverneur Morris of Pennsylvania put the problem of the presidency this way: "Make him too weak: the Legislature will usurp his powers. Make him too strong: he will usurp on the Legislature."

The Framers knew very well that the relations between the president and Congress and the manner in which the president is elected were of profound importance, and they debated both at great length. The first plan was for Congress to elect the president—in short, for the system to be quasi-parliamentary. But if that were done, some delegates pointed out, Congress could dominate an honest or lazy president, while a corrupt or scheming president might dominate Congress.

After much discussion, it was decided that the president should be chosen directly by voters. But by which voters? The emerging nation was large and diverse. It seemed unlikely that every citizen would be familiar enough with the candidates to cast an informed vote for a president directly. Worse, a direct popular election would give inordinate weight to the large, populous states, and no plan with that outcome had any chance of adoption by the smaller states.

THE ELECTORAL COLLEGE

Thus the **electoral college** was invented, whereby each of the states would select electors in whatever manner it wished. The electors would then meet in each state capital and vote for president and vice president. Many Framers expected that this procedure would lead to each state's electors' voting for a favorite son, and thus no candidate would win a majority of the popular vote. In this event, it was decided, the House of Representatives should make the choice, with each state delegation casting one vote.

The plan seemed to meet every test: large states would have their say, but small states would be protected by having a minimum of three electoral votes no matter how tiny their population. The small states together could wield considerable influence in the House, where, it was widely expected, most presidential elections would ultimately be decided. Of course, it did not work out quite this way: the Framers did not foresee the role that political parties would play in producing nationwide support for a slate of national candidates.

Once the manner of electing the president was settled, the question of his powers was much easier to decide. After all, if you believe the procedures are fair and balanced, then you are more confident in assigning larger powers to the president within this system. Accordingly, the right to make treaties and the right to appoint lesser officials, originally reserved for the Senate, were given to the president "with the advice and consent of the Senate."

THE PRESIDENT'S TERM OF OFFICE

Another issue was put to rest soon thereafter. George Washington, the unanimous choice of the electoral college to be the first president, firmly limited himself to two terms in office (1789–1797), and no president until Franklin D. Roosevelt (1933–1945) dared to run for more (though Ulysses S. Grant tried). In 1951, the Twenty-second Amendment to the Constitution was ratified, formally limiting all subsequent presidents to two terms. The remaining issues concerning the nature of the presidency, and especially the relations between the president and Congress, have been the subject of continuing dispute. The pattern of relationships that we see today is the result of an evolutionary process that has extended over more than two centuries.

The first problem was to establish the legitimacy of the presidency itself: that is, to ensure, if possible, public acceptance of the office, its incumbent, and its powers and to establish an orderly transfer of power from one incumbent to the next.

Today, we take this for granted. When George W. Bush was inaugurated in January 2001 as our 43rd president, Bill Clinton, the 42nd, quietly left the White House. In the world today, such an uneventful succession is unusual. In many nations, a new chief executive comes to power with the aid of military force or as a result of political intrigue; his predecessor often leaves office disgraced, exiled, or dead. At the time the Constitution was written, the Founders could only hope that an orderly transfer of power from one president to the next would occur. France had just undergone a bloody revolution; England in the not-too-distant past had beheaded a king; and in Poland the ruler was elected by a process so manifestly corrupt and so open to intrigue that Thomas Jefferson, in what may be the first example of ethnic humor in American politics, was led to refer to the proposed American presidency as a "bad edition of a Polish king."

Yet by the time Abraham Lincoln found himself at the helm of a nation plunged into a bitter, bloody civil war, 15 presidents had been elected, served their time, and left office without a hint of force being used to facilitate the process and with the people accepting the process—if not admiring all the presidents. This orderly transfer of authority occurred despite passionate opposition and deeply divisive elections (such as that which brought Jefferson to power). And it did not happen by accident.

THE FIRST PRESIDENTS

Those who first served as president were among the most prominent men in the new nation, all active either in the movement for independence or in the Founding or in both. Of the first five presidents, four (all but John Adams) served two full terms. Washington and Monroe were not even opposed. The first administration had at the highest levels the leading spokesmen for all of the major viewpoints: Alexander Hamilton was Washington's secretary of the treasury (and was sympathetic to the urban commercial interests), and Thomas Jefferson was

electoral college The people chosen to cast each state's votes in a presidential election. Each state can cast one electoral vote for each senator and representative it has. The District of Columbia has three electoral votes, even though it cannot elect a representative or senator.

America witnessed peaceful transfers of power not only between leaders of different parties (such as Woodrow Wilson and William Howard Taft in 1913), but also after a popular leader was assassinated (Lyndon Johnson is sworn in after John F. Kennedy's death).

secretary of state (and more inclined toward rural, small-town, and farming views). Washington spoke out strongly against political parties, and though parties soon emerged, there was a stigma attached to them: many people believed that it was wrong to take advantage of divisions in the country, to organize deliberately to acquire political office, or to make legislation depend upon party advantage. As it turned out, this hostility to party (or "faction," as it was more commonly called) was unrealistic: parties are as natural to democracy as churches are to religion.

Establishing the legitimacy of the presidency in the early years was made easier by the fact that the national government had relatively little to do. It had, of course, to establish a sound currency and to settle the debt accrued during the Revolutionary War. The Treasury Department inevitably became the principal federal office, especially under the strong leadership of Hamilton. Relations with England and France were important—and difficult—but otherwise government took little time and few resources.

In appointing people to federal office, a general rule of "fitness" emerged: those appointed should have some standing in their communities and be well thought of by their neighbors. Appointments based on partisanship soon arose, but community stature could not be neglected.

The presidency was kept modest. Washington clearly had not sought the office and did not relish the exercise of its then modest powers. He traveled widely so that as many people as possible could see their new president. His efforts to establish a semiregal court etiquette were quickly rebuffed; the presidency was to be kept simple. Congress decided that not until after a president was dead might his likeness appear on a coin or on currency; no president until Eisenhower was given a pension on his retirement.

The president's relations with Congress were correct but not close. Washington appeared before the Senate to ask its advice on a proposed treaty with some Indian tribes. He got none and instead was politely told that the Senate would like to consider the matter in private. He declared that he would be "damned if he ever went there again," and he never did. Thus ended the responsibility of the Senate to "advise" the president. Vetoes were sometimes cast by the president, but sparingly, and only when the president believed the law was not simply unwise but unconstitutional. Washington cast only two vetoes; Jefferson and Adams cast none.

THE JACKSONIANS

At a time roughly corresponding to the presidency of Andrew Jackson (1829–1837), broad changes began to occur in American politics. These changes, together with the personality of Jackson himself, altered the relations between president and Congress and the nature of presidential leadership.

The Granger Collection

President Andrew Jackson thought of himself as the "Tribune of the People," and he symbolized this by throwing a White House party that anyone could attend. Hundreds of people showed up and ate or carried away most of a 1,400-pound block of cheese.

As so often happens, few people at the time Jackson took office had much sense of what his presidency would be like. Though he had been a member of the House of Representatives and of the Senate, he was elected as a military hero—and an apparently doddering one at that. Sixty-one years old and seemingly frail, he nonetheless used the powers of his office as no one before him had.

Jackson vetoed 12 acts of Congress, more than all his predecessors combined and more than any subsequent president until Andrew Johnson 30 years later. His vetoes were not simply on constitutional grounds but on policy ones: as the only official elected by the entire voting citizenry, he saw himself as the "Tribune of the People." None of his vetoes were overridden. He did not initiate many new policies, but he struck out against the ones he did not like. He did so at a time when the size of the electorate was increasing rapidly, and new states, especially in the West, had entered the Union. (There were then 24 states in the Union, nearly twice the original number.)

Jackson demonstrated what could be done by a popular president. He did not shrink from conflict with Congress, and the tension between the two branches of government that was intended by the Framers became intensified by the personalities of those in government: Jackson in the White House, and Henry Clay, Daniel Webster, and John Calhoun in Congress. These powerful figures walked the political stage at a time when bitter sectional conflicts—over

slavery and commercial policies—were beginning to split the country. Jackson, though he was opposed to a large and powerful federal government and wished to return somehow to the agrarian simplicities of Jefferson's time, was nonetheless a believer in a strong and independent presidency. This view, though obscured by nearly a century of subsequent congressional dominance of national politics, was ultimately to triumph—for better or for worse.

THE REEMERGENCE OF CONGRESS

With the end of Jackson's second term, Congress quickly reestablished its power, and except for the wartime presidency of Lincoln and brief flashes of presidential power under James Polk (1845–1849) and Grover Cleveland (1885–1889, 1893–1897), the presidency for a hundred years was the subordinate branch of the national government. Of the eight presidents who succeeded Jackson, two (William H. Harrison and Zachary Taylor) died in office, and none of the others served more than one term. Schoolchildren, trying to memorize the list of American presidents, always stumble in this era of the "no-name" presidents. This is hardly a coincidence: Congress was the leading institution, struggling, unsuccessfully, with slavery and sectionalism.

It was also an intensely partisan era, a legacy of Jackson that lasted well into the 20th century. Public opinion was closely divided. In nine of the 17 presidential elections between the end of Jackson's term in 1837 and Theodore Roosevelt's election in 1904, the winning candidate received less than half the popular vote. Only two candidates (Lincoln in 1864 and Ulysses S. Grant in 1872) received more than 55 percent of the popular vote.

During this long period of congressional—and usually senatorial—dominance of national government, only Lincoln broke new ground for presidential power. Lincoln's expansive use of that power, like Jackson's, was totally unexpected. He was first elected in 1860 as a minority president, receiving less than 40 percent of the popular vote in a field of four candidates. Though a member of the new Republican party, he had been a member of the Whig party, a group that had stood for limiting presidential power. He had opposed America's entry into the Mexican War and had been critical of Jackson's use of executive authority. But as president during the Civil War, he made unprecedented use of the vague gift of powers in Article II of the Constitution, especially those that he felt were "implied" or "inherent" in the phrase "take care that the laws be faithfully executed" and in the express authorization for him to act as commander in chief.

How Things Work

The Electoral College

Until November 2000, it was almost impossible to get a student interested in the electoral college. But in the 2000 presidential election, Florida's electoral vote hung in the balance for weeks, with Bush finally winning it and (though he had fewer popular votes than Al Gore) the presidency.

Here are the essential facts: each state gets electoral votes equal to the number of its senators and representatives (the District of Columbia also gets 3, even though it has no representatives in Congress). There are 538 electoral votes. To win, a candidate must receive at least half, or 270.

In all but two states, the candidate who wins the most popular votes wins all of the state's electoral votes. Maine and Nebraska have a different system. They allow electoral votes to be split by awarding some votes on the basis of a candidate's statewide total and some on the basis of how the candidate did in each congressional district.

The winning slates of electors assemble in their state capitals about six weeks after the election to cast their ballots. Ordinarily this is a pure formality. Occasionally, however, an elector will vote for a presidential candidate other than the one who carried the state. Such "faithless electors" have appeared in several elections since 1796. The state electoral ballots are opened and

Electrol Votes per State

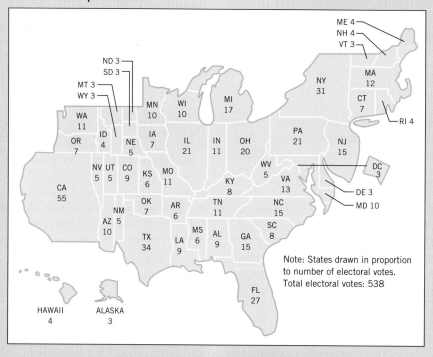

Note: States drawn in proportion to number of electoral votes.
Total electoral votes: 538

Lincoln raised an army, spent money, blockaded southern ports, temporarily suspended the writ of habeas corpus, and issued the Emancipation Proclamation to free the slaves—all without prior congressional approval. He justified this, as most Americans probably would have, by the emergency conditions created by civil war. In this he acted little differently from Thomas Jefferson, who while president waged undeclared war against various North African pirates.

After Lincoln, Congress reasserted its power and became, during Reconstruction and for many decades thereafter, the principal federal institution. But it had become abundantly clear that a national emergency could equip the president with great powers and that a popular and strong-willed president could expand his powers even without an emergency.

Except for the administrations of Theodore Roosevelt (1901–1909) and Woodrow Wilson counted before a joint session of Congress during the first week of January. The candidate with a majority is declared elected.

If no candidate wins a majority, the House of Representatives chooses the president from among the three leading candidates, with each state casting one vote. By House rules, each state's vote is allotted to the candidate preferred by a majority of the state's House delegation. If there is a tie within a delegation, that state's vote is not counted.

The House has had to decide two presidential contests. In 1800, Thomas Jefferson and Aaron Burr tied in the electoral college because of a defect in the language of the Constitution—each state cast two electoral votes, without indicating which was for president and which for vice president. (Burr was supposed to be vice president, and after much maneuvering he was.) This problem was corrected by the Twelfth Amendment, ratified in 1804. The only House decision under the modern system was in 1824, when it chose John Quincy Adams over Andrew Jackson and William H. Crawford, even though Jackson had more electoral votes (and probably more popular votes) than his rivals.

Today the winner-take-all system in effect in 48 states makes it possible for a candidate to win at least 270 electoral votes without winning a majority of the popular votes. This happened in 2000, 1888, and 1876, and almost happened in 1960 and 1884. Today a candidate who carries the 10 largest states wins 256 electoral votes, only 14 short of a presidential victory.

This means that the candidates have a strong incentive to campaign hard in big states they have a chance of winning. In 2000, Gore worked hard in California, New York, and Pennsylvania but pretty much ignored Texas, where Bush was a shoo-in. Bush campaigned hard in Florida, Illinois, and Ohio, but not so much in New York, where Gore was an easy winner.

But the electoral college can also help small states. South Dakota, for example, has 3 electoral votes (about 0.5 percent of the total), even though it casts only about 0.3 percent of the popular vote. South Dakota and other small states are thus overrepresented in the electoral college.

Most Americans would like to abolish the electoral college. But doing away with it entirely would have some unforeseen effects. If we relied just on the popular vote, there would have to be a runoff election among the two leading candidates if neither got a majority because third-party candidates won a lot of votes. This would encourage the formation of third parties (we might have a Jesse Jackson party, a Pat Buchanan party, a Pat Robertson party, and a Ralph Nader party). Each third party would then be in a position to negotiate with one of the two major parties between the first election and the runoff about favors it wanted in return for its support. American presidential politics might come to look like the multiparty systems in France and Italy.

There are other changes that could be made. One is for each state to allocate its electoral votes proportional to the popular vote the candidates receive in that state. Voters in Colorado acted on that measure in November 2004, but that proposal failed. If every state did that, several past elections would have been decided in the House of Representatives because no candidate got a majority of the popular vote.

And the electoral college serves a larger purpose: it makes candidates worry about carrying states as well as popular votes, and so heightens the influence of states in national politics.

(1913–1921), the president was, until the New Deal, at best a negative force—a source of opposition to Congress, not a source of initiative and leadership for it. Grover Cleveland was a strong personality, but for all his efforts he was able to do little more than veto bills that he did not like. He cast 414 vetoes—more than any other president until Franklin Roosevelt. A frequent target of his vetoes were bills to confer special pensions on Civil War veterans.

Today we are accustomed to thinking that the president formulates a legislative program to which Congress then responds, but until the 1930s the opposite was more the case. Congress ignored the initiatives of such presidents as Grover Cleveland, Rutherford Hayes, Chester Arthur, and Calvin Coolidge. Woodrow Wilson in 1913 was the first president since John Adams to deliver personally the State of the Union address, and he was one of the first to develop and argue for a presidential legislative program.

Our popular conception of the president as the central figure of national government, devising a legislative program and commanding a large staff of advisers, is very much a product of the modern era and of the enlarged role of government. In the past, the presidency became powerful only during a national crisis (the Civil War, World War I) or because of an extraordinary personality (Andrew Jackson, Theodore Roosevelt, Woodrow Wilson). Since the 1930s, however, the presidency has been powerful no matter who occupied the office and whether or not there was a crisis. Because government now plays such an active role in our national life, the president is the natural focus of attention and the titular head of a huge federal administrative system (whether he is the real boss is another matter).

But the popular conception of the president as the central figure of national government belies the realities of present-day legislative-executive relations. During national policymaking from the Eisenhower years through the Reagan administration, Congress, not the president, often took the lead in setting the legislative agenda.[5] For example, the 1990 Clean Air Act, like the 1970 Clean Air Act before it, was born and bred mainly by congressional, not presidential, action. Indeed, administration officials played almost no role in the legislative process that culminated in these laws.[6] When President Bush signed the 1990 Clean Air Act or President Clinton signed the 1996 Welfare Reform Act, each took credit for it, but in fact both bills were designed by members of Congress, not by the president.[7] Likewise, although presidents dominated budget policymaking from the 1920s into the early 1970s, they no longer do. Instead, the "imperatives of the budgetary process have pushed congressional leaders to center stage."[8] Thus, as often as not, Congress proposes, the president disposes, and legislative-executive relations involve hard bargaining and struggle between these two branches of government.

The Powers of the President

Though the president, unlike a prime minister, cannot command an automatic majority in the legislature, he does have some formidable, albeit vaguely defined, powers. These are mostly set forth in Article II of the Constitution and are of two sorts: those he can exercise in his own right without formal legislative approval, and those that require the consent of the Senate or of Congress as a whole.

A military officer carrying "the football"—the briefcase containing the secret codes the president can use to launch a nuclear attack.

Mark Wilson/Getty Images News/Getty Images

Powers of the President Alone

- Serve as commander in chief of the armed forces
- Commission officers of the armed forces
- Grant reprieves and pardons for federal offenses (except impeachment)
- Convene Congress in special sessions
- Receive ambassadors
- Take care that the laws be faithfully executed
- Wield the "executive power"
- Appoint officials to lesser offices

Powers the President Shares with the Senate

- Make treaties
- Appoint ambassadors, judges, and high officials

Powers the President Shares with Congress as a Whole

• Approve legislation

Taken alone and interpreted narrowly, this list of powers is not very impressive. Obviously, the president's authority as commander in chief is important, but literally construed, most of the other constitutional grants seem to provide for little more than a president who is chief clerk of the country. A hundred years after the Founding, that is about how matters appeared to even the most astute observers. In 1884, Woodrow Wilson wrote a book about American politics titled *Congressional Government,* in which he described the business of the president as "usually not much above routine," mostly "*mere* administration." The president might as well be an officer of the civil service. To succeed, he need only obey Congress and stay alive.[9]

But even as Wilson wrote, he was overlooking some examples of enormously powerful presidents, such as Lincoln, and was not sufficiently attentive to the potential for presidential power to be found in the more ambiguous clauses of the Constitution as well as in the political realities of American life. The president's authority as commander in chief has grown—especially, but not only, in wartime—to encompass not simply the direction of the military forces, but also the management of the economy and the direction of foreign affairs as well. A quietly dramatic reminder of the awesome implications of

the president's military powers occurs at the precise instant that a new president assumes office. A military officer carrying a locked briefcase moves from the side of the outgoing president to the side of the new one. In the briefcase are the secret codes and orders that permit the president to authorize the launching of American nuclear weapons.

The president's duty to "take care that the laws be faithfully executed" has become one of the most elastic phrases in the Constitution. By interpreting this broadly, Grover Cleveland was able to use federal troops to break a labor strike in the 1890s, and Dwight Eisenhower was able to send troops to help integrate a public school in Little Rock, Arkansas, in 1957.

The greatest source of presidential power, however, is not found in the Constitution at all but in politics and public opinion. Increasingly since the 1930s, Congress has passed laws that confer on the executive branch broad grants of authority to achieve some general goals, leaving it up to the president and his deputies to define the regulations and programs that will actually be put into effect. In Chapter 15, we shall see how this delegation of legislative power to the president has contributed to the growth of the bureaucracy. Moreover, the American people—always in times of crisis, but increasingly as an everyday matter—look to the president for leadership and hold him responsible for a large and growing portion of our national affairs. The public thinks, wrongly, that the presidency is the "first branch" of government.

How Things Work

The President: Qualifications and Benefits

Qualifications

• A natural-born citizen (can be born abroad of parents who are American citizens)

• 35 years of age

• A resident of the United States for at least 14 years (but not necessarily the 14 years just preceding the election)

Benefits

• A nice house

• A salary of $400,000 per year (taxable)

• An expense account of $50,000 per year (tax-free)

• Travel expenses of $100,000 per year (tax-free)

• A pension, on retirement, equal to the pay of a cabinet member (taxable)

• Staff support and Secret Service protection for 10 years on leaving the presidency

• A White House staff of 400 to 500

• A place in the country—Camp David

• A personal airplane—Air Force One

• A fine chef

The Office of the President

It was not until 1857 that the president was allowed to have a private secretary paid for with public funds, and it was not until after the assassination of President McKinley in 1901 that the president was given a Secret Service bodyguard. He was not able to submit a single presidential budget until after 1921, when the Budget and Accounting Act was passed and the Bureau of the Budget (now called the Office of Management and Budget) was created. Grover Cleveland personally answered the White House telephone, and Abraham Lincoln often answered his own mail.

Today, of course, the president has hundreds of people assisting him, and the trappings of power—helicopters, guards, limousines—are plainly visible. The White House staff has grown enormously. (Just how big the staff is, no one knows. Presidents like to pretend that the White House is not the large bureaucracy that it in fact has become.) Add to this the opportunities for presidential appointments to the cabinet, the courts, and various agencies, and the resources at the disposal of the president would appear to be awesome. That conclusion is partly true and partly false, or at least misleading, and for a simple reason. If the president was once helpless for lack of assistance, he now confronts an army of assistants so large that it constitutes a bureaucracy he has difficulty controlling.

The ability of a presidential assistant to affect the president is governed by the rule of propinquity: in general, power is wielded by people in the room when a decision is made. Presidential appointments can thus be classified in terms of their proximity, physical and political, to the president. There are three degrees of propinquity: the White House Office, the Executive Office, and the cabinet.

THE WHITE HOUSE OFFICE

The president's closest assistants have offices in the White House, usually in the West Wing of that building. Their titles often do not reveal the functions that they actually perform: "counsel," "counselor,"

pyramid structure A president's subordinates report to him through a clear chain of command headed by a chief of staff.

circular structure Several of the president's assistants report directly to him.

ad hoc structure Several subordinates, cabinet officers, and committees report directly to the president on different matters.

"assistant to the president," "special assistant," "special consultant," and so forth. The actual titles vary from one administration to another, but in general the men and women who hold them oversee the political and policy interests of the president. As part of the president's personal staff, these aides do not have to be confirmed by the Senate; the president can hire and fire them at will. In 2001, the Bush White House had 400 staff members and a budget of $35.4 million.

There are essentially three ways in which a president can organize his personal staff—through the "pyramid," "circular," and "ad hoc" methods. In a **pyramid structure,** used by Eisenhower, Nixon, Reagan, Bush, and (after a while) Clinton, most assistants report through a hierarchy to a chief of staff, who then deals directly with the president. In a **circular structure,** used by Carter, cabinet secretaries and assistants report directly to the president. In an **ad hoc structure,** used for a while by President Clinton, task forces, committees, and informal groups of friends and advisers deal directly with the president. For example, the Clinton administration's health care policy planning was spearheaded not by Health and Human Services secretary Donna E. Shalala, but by First Lady Hillary Rodham Clinton and a White House adviser, Ira Magaziner. Likewise, its initiative to reform the federal bureaucracy (the National Performance Review) was led not by Office of Management and Budget director Leon E. Panetta, but by an adviser to Vice President Gore, Elaine Kamarck.[10]

It is common for presidents to mix methods; for example, Franklin Roosevelt alternated between the circular and ad hoc methods in the conduct of his domestic policy and sometimes employed a pyramid structure when dealing with foreign affairs and military policy. Taken individually, each method of organization has advantages and disadvantages. A pyramid structure provides for an orderly flow of information and decisions, but does so at the risk of isolating or misinforming the president. The circular method has the virtue of giving the president a great deal of information, but at the price of confusion and conflict among cabinet secretaries and assistants. An ad hoc structure allows great flexibility, minimizes bureaucratic inertia, and generates ideas and information from disparate channels, but it risks cutting the president off from the government officials who are ultimately responsible for translating presidential decisions into policy proposals and administrative action.

How Things Work

The Myth and Reality of the White House Office

The Myth

The White House Office was created in the 1930s following recommendations made by the President's Commission on Administrative Management. The principles underlying those recommendations have been endorsed by almost every presidential chief of staff since then. The key ones are:

1. *Small is beautiful.* The presidential staff should be small. At first, there were only six assistants.

2. *A passion for anonymity.* The president's personal assistants should stay out of the limelight.

3. *Honest brokers.* The presidential staff should not make decisions for the president; it should only coordinate the flow of information to the president.

The Reality

Increasingly, the operations of the White House Office seem to reflect almost the exact opposite of these principles.

1. *Big is better.* The White House staff has grown enormously in size. Hundreds now work there.

2. *Get out front.* Key White House staffers have become household words—Henry Kissinger (under Nixon and Ford), H.R. Haldeman (under Nixon), Hamilton Jordan (under Carter), Howard Baker (under Reagan), George Stephanopoulos (under Clinton), and Karl Rove (under G.W. Bush).

3. *Be in charge.* Cabinet officers regularly complain that White House staffers are shutting them out and making all the important decisions. Congressional investigations have revealed the power of such White House aides as Haldeman, John Poindexter, and Lieutenant Colonel Oliver North.

Why the Gap Between Myth and Reality?

The answer is—the people and the government. The people expect much more from presidents today; no president can afford to say, "We're too busy here to worry about that." The government is much more complex, and so leadership requires more resources. Even conservatives such as Ronald Reagan have been activist presidents.

Source: Adapted from Samuel Kernell and Samuel L. Popkin, eds., *Chief of Staff* (Berkeley: University of California Press, 1986), 193–232.

All presidents claim they are open to many sources of advice, and some presidents try to guarantee that openness by using the circular method of staff organization. President Carter liked to describe his office as a wheel with himself as the hub and his several assistants as spokes. But most presidents discover, as did Carter, that the difficulty of managing the large White House bureaucracy and of conserving their own limited supply of time and energy makes it necessary for them to rely heavily on one or two key subordinates. Carter, in July 1979, dramatically altered the White House staff organization by elevating Hamilton Jordan to the post of chief of staff, with the job of coordinating the work of the other staff assistants.

At first, President Reagan adopted a compromise between the circle and the pyramid, putting the White House under the direction of three key aides. At the beginning of his second term in 1985, however, the president shifted to a pyramid, placing all his assistants under a single chief of staff. Clinton began with an ad hoc system and then changed to one more like a pyramid. Each assistant has, of course, others working for him or her, sometimes a large number. There are, at a slightly lower level of status, "special assistants to the president" for various purposes. (Being "special" means, paradoxically, being less important.)

Typically, senior White House staff members are drawn from the ranks of the president's campaign staff—longtime associates in whom he has confidence. A few members, however, will be experts brought in after the campaign: such was the case, for example, with Henry Kissinger, a former Harvard professor who became President Nixon's assistant for national security affairs. The offices these men and women occupy often are small and crowded (Kissinger's was not much bigger than the one he had while a professor at Harvard), but their occupants willingly put up with any discomfort in exchange for the privilege (and the power) of being *in* the White House. The arrangement of offices—their size, and especially their proximity to the president's Oval Office—is a good measure of the relative influence of the people in them.

To an outsider, the amount of jockeying among the top staff for access to the president may seem comical or even perverse. The staff attaches enormous significance to whose office is closest to the president's, who can see him on a daily as opposed to a weekly basis, who can get an appointment with the president and who cannot, and who has a right to see documents and memoranda just before they go to the Oval Office. To be sure, there is ample grist here for Washington political novels. But there is also something important at stake: it is not simply a question of power plays and ego trips. Who can see the president and who sees and "signs off" on memoranda going to the president affect in important ways who influences policy and thus whose goals and beliefs become embedded in policy.

For example, if a memo from a secretary of the treasury who believes in free trade can go directly to the president, the president may be more likely to support free trade (low tariffs). On the other hand, if that memo must be routed through the office of the assistant to the president for political affairs, who is worried about the adverse effects of foreign competition on jobs in the American steel industry because the votes of steelworkers are important to the president's reelection campaign, then the president may be led to support higher tariffs.

THE EXECUTIVE OFFICE OF THE PRESIDENT

Agencies in the Executive Office report directly to the president and perform staff services for him but are not located in the White House itself. Their members may or may not enjoy intimate contact with him; some agencies are rather large bureaucracies. The top positions in these organizations are filled by presidential appointment, but unlike the White House staff positions, these appointments must be confirmed by the Senate.

cabinet The heads of the 15 executive branch departments of the federal government.

The principal agencies in the Executive Office are:

- Office of Management and Budget (OMB)
- Director of National Intelligence (DNI)
- Council of Economic Advisers (CEA)
- Office of Personnel Management (OPM)
- Office of the U.S. Trade Representative

Of all the agencies in the Executive Office of the President, perhaps the most important in terms of the president's need for assistance in administering the federal government is the Office of Management and Budget. First called the Bureau of the Budget when it was created in 1921, it became OMB in 1970 to reflect its broader responsibilities. Today it does considerably more than assemble and analyze the figures that go each year into the national budget the president submits to Congress. It also studies the organization and operations of the executive branch, devises plans for reorganizing various departments and agencies, develops ways of getting better information about government programs, and reviews proposals that cabinet departments want included in the president's legislative program.

OMB has a staff of over five hundred people, almost all career civil servants, many of high professional skill and substantial experience. Traditionally, OMB has been a nonpartisan agency—experts serving all presidents, without regard to party or ideology. Starting with the Reagan administration, however, OMB has played a major role in advocating policies rather than merely analyzing them. David Stockman, President Reagan's OMB director, was the primary architect of the 1981 and 1985 budget cuts proposed by the president and enacted by Congress. Stockman's proposals often were adopted over the objections of the affected department heads. In 2001, President George W. Bush's OMB director, Mitch Daniels, also participated fully in West Wing political strategy sessions; he later was elected governor of Indiana. In 2009, President Obama appointed Peter Orzag, a former think tank and university researcher who had served as an economic adviser to President Clinton and as a budget analyst in Congress, to head OMB. Whether Orzag's appointment presaged a return to OMB's earlier tradition as a mostly nonpartisan body remains to be seen.

THE CABINET

The **cabinet** is a product of tradition and hope. At one time, the heads of the federal departments met regularly with the president to discuss matters, and some people, especially those critical of strong presidents, would like to see this kind of collegial decision making reestablished. But in fact this role of the cabinet is largely a fiction. Indeed, the Constitution does not even mention the cabinet (though the Twenty-fifth Amendment implicitly defines it as consisting of "the principal offices of the executive departments"). When Washington tried to get his cabinet members to work together, its two strongest members—Alexander Hamilton and Thomas Jefferson—spent most of their time feuding. The cabinet, as a presidential committee, did not work any better for John Adams or Abraham Lincoln, for Franklin Roosevelt or John Kennedy. Dwight Eisenhower is almost the only modern president who came close to making the cabinet a truly deliberative body: he gave it a large staff, held regular meetings, and listened to opinions expressed there. But even under Eisenhower, the cabinet did not have much influence over presidential decisions, nor did it help him gain more power over the government.

By custom, cabinet officers are the heads of the 15 major executive departments. These departments, together with the dates of their creation and the approximate number of their employees, are given in Table 14.1. The order of their creation is unimportant except in terms of protocol: where one sits at cabinet meetings is determined by the age of the department that one heads. Thus, the secretary of

Table 14.1 The Cabinet Departments

Department	Created	Approximate Employment (2007)
State	1789	34,657
Treasury	1789	111,577
Defense[a]	1947	673,722
Justice	1789	106,946
Interior	1849	70,256
Agriculture[b]	1889	99,629
Commerce	1913	40,163
Labor	1913	15,855
Health and Human Services[c]	1953	61,217
Housing and Urban Development	1965	9,718
Transportation	1966	53,536
Energy	1977	14,696
Education	1979	4,146
Veterans Affairs	1989	245,537
Homeland Security	2002	155,397

[a]Formerly the War Department, created in 1789. Figures are for civilians only.

[b]Agriculture Department created in 1862; made part of cabinet in 1889.

[c]Originally Health, Education and Welfare; reorganized in 1979.

Source: *Statistical Abstract of the United States, 2009*, table 481.

state sits next to the president on one side and the secretary of the treasury next to him on the other. Down at the foot of the table are the heads of the newer departments.

The president appoints or directly controls vastly more members of his cabinet departments than does the British prime minister. The reason is simple: the president must struggle with Congress for control of these agencies, while the prime minister has no rival branch of government that seeks this power. Presidents get more appointments than prime ministers to make up for what the separation of powers denies them.

This abundance of political appointments, however, does not give the president ample power over the departments. The secretary of Health and Human Services (HHS) reports to the president and has a few hundred political appointees to assist him or her in responding to the president's wishes. But the secretary of HHS heads an agency with over 60,000 employees, 11 operating divisions, hundreds of grantmaking programs, and a budget of more than $460 billion. Likewise, the secretary of Housing and Urban Development (HUD) spends most of his or her time on departmental business and vastly less on talking to the president. It is hardly surprising that the secretary is largely a representative of HUD to the president than his representative to HUD. And no one should be surprised that the secretary of HUD rarely finds much to talk about with the secretary of defense at cabinet meetings.

Having the power to make these appointments does give the president one great advantage: he has a lot of opportunities to reward friends and political supporters. In the Education Department, for example, President Clinton found jobs for onetime mayors, senators, state legislators, and campaign aides.

INDEPENDENT AGENCIES, COMMISSIONS, AND JUDGESHIPS

The president also appoints people to four dozen or so agencies and commissions that are not considered part of the cabinet and that by law often have a quasi-independent status. The difference between an "executive" and an "independent" agency is not precise. In general, it means the heads of executive agencies serve at the pleasure of the president and can be removed at his discretion. On the other hand, the heads of many independent agencies serve for fixed terms of office and can be removed only "for cause."

The president can also appoint federal judges, subject to the consent of the Senate. Judges serve for life unless they are removed by impeachment and conviction. The reason for the special barriers to the removal of judges is that they represent an independent branch of government as defined by the Constitution, and limits on presidential removal powers are necessary to preserve that independence.

One new feature of appointing top government officials is the increasing use of "acting" appointments. An acting appointee holds office until the Senate acts on his or her nomination. In 1998, acting officials held one-fifth of all of the Clinton administration's cabinet-level (or subcabinet-level)* jobs. Some were in office for many months. Many senators feel that this violates their right to consent to appointments and in particular violates the Vacancies Act passed in 1868. That law limits acting appointees to 120 days in office. If the Senate takes no action during those 120 days, the acting official may stay in office until he or she, or someone else, is confirmed for the post. Administration officials defend the practice as necessary given the slow pace of confirmations; senators attack it as an opportunity for a president to fill up his administration with unconfirmed officials.

Who Gets Appointed

As we have seen, a president can make a lot of appointments, but he rarely knows more than a few of the people whom he does appoint.

Unlike cabinet members in a parliamentary system, the president's cabinet officers and their principal deputies usually have not served with the chief executive in the legislature. Instead they come from private business, universities, think tanks, foundations, law firms, labor unions, and the ranks of former and present members of Congress as well as past state and local government officials. A president is fortunate if most cabinet members turn out to agree with him on major policy questions. President Reagan made a special effort to ensure that his cabinet members were ideologically in tune with him, but even so Secretary of State Alexander Haig soon got into a series of quarrels with senior members of the White House staff and had to resign.

The men and women appointed to the cabinet and to the subcabinet usually will have had some prior federal experience. One study of over a thousand such appointments made by five presidents (Franklin Roosevelt through Lyndon Johnson) found that about 85 percent of the cabinet, subcabinet, and independent-agency appointees had some prior federal experience. In fact, most were in government service (at the federal, state, or local levels) just before they received their cabinet or subcabinet appointment.[11] Clearly, the executive branch is not, in general, run by novices.

Many of these appointees are what Richard Neustadt has called "in-and-outers": people who alternate between jobs in the federal government and ones in the private sector, especially in law firms and in universities. Donald Rumsfeld, before becoming secretary of defense to President George W. Bush, had been secretary of defense and chief of staff under President Ford and before that a member of Congress. Between his Ford and Bush services, he was an executive in a large pharmaceutical company. This pattern is quite different from that of parliamentary systems, where all the cabinet officers come from the legislature and typically are full-time career politicians.

At one time, the cabinet had in it many people with strong political followings of their own—former senators and governors and powerful local party leaders. Under Franklin Roosevelt, Truman, and Kennedy, the postmaster general was the president's campaign manager. George Washington, Abraham Lincoln, and other presidents had to contend with cabinet members who were powerful figures in their own right: Alexander Hamilton and Thomas Jefferson worked with Washington; Simon Cameron (a Pennsylvania political boss) and Salmon P. Chase (formerly governor of Ohio) worked for—and against—Lincoln. Before 1824, the post of secretary of state was regarded as a stepping stone to the presidency; and after that at least 10 persons ran for president who had been either secretary of state or ambassador to a foreign country.[12]

Of late, however, a tendency has developed for presidents to place in their cabinets people known for their expertise or administrative experience rather than for their political following. This is in part because political parties are now so weak that party leaders can no longer demand a place in the cabinet and in part because presidents want (or think they want) "experts." A remarkable illustration of this is the number of people with Ph.D.'s who have entered the cabinet. President Nixon, who supposedly did

---

Subcabinet refers to under secretary, deputy secretary, and assistant secretaries in each cabinet department.

How Things Work

Federal Agencies

The following agencies are classified by whether the president has unlimited or limited right of removal.

"Executive" Agencies

Head can be removed at any time.

- Action
- Arms Control and Disarmament Agency
- Commission on Civil Rights
- Energy Research and Development Agency
- Environmental Protection Agency
- Federal Mediation and Conciliation Service
- General Services Administration
- National Aeronautics and Space Administration
- Postal Service
- Small Business Administration
- All cabinet departments
- Executive Office of the President

"Independent" or "Quasi-Independent" Agencies

Members serve for a fixed term.

- Federal Reserve Board (14 years)
- Consumer Product Safety Commission (6 years)
- Equal Employment Opportunity Commission (5 years)
- Federal Communications Commission (7 years)
- Federal Deposit Insurance Corporation (6 years)
- Federal Energy Regulatory Commission (5 years)
- Federal Maritime Commission (5 years)
- Federal Trade Commission (7 years)
- National Labor Relations Board (5 years)
- National Science Foundation (6 years)
- Securities and Exchange Commission (5 years)
- Tennessee Valley Authority (9 years)

not like Harvard professors, appointed two—Henry Kissinger and Daniel Patrick Moynihan—to important posts; Gerald Ford added a third, John Dunlop.

A president's desire to appoint experts who do not have independent political power is modified—but not supplanted—by his need to recognize various politically important groups, regions, and organizations. Since Robert Weaver became the first African American to serve in the cabinet (as secretary of HUD under President Johnson), it is clear that it would be quite costly for a president *not* to have one or more blacks in his cabinet. The secretary of labor must be acceptable to the AFL-CIO, the secretary of agriculture to at least some organized farmers. Each of the last three presidents (Bill Clinton, George W. Bush, and Barack Obama) appointed several women and minorities to his cabinet.

Because political considerations must be taken into account in making cabinet and agency appointments and because any head of a large organization will tend to adopt the perspective of that organization, there is an inevitable tension—even a rivalry—between the White House staff and the department heads. Staff members see themselves as extensions of the president's personality and policies; department heads see themselves as repositories of expert knowledge (often knowledge of why something will not work as the president hopes). White House staffers, many of them young men and women in their 20s or early 30s with little executive experience, will call department heads, often persons in their 50s with substantial executive experience, and tell them "the president wants" this or that or "the president asked me to tell you" one thing or another. Department heads try to conceal their irritation and then maneuver for some delay so they can develop their own counterproposals. On the

Secretary of Labor Frances Perkins (left), appointed by President Franklin Roosevelt, was the first woman cabinet member. When Condoleezza Rice was selected by President George W. Bush to be National Security Advisor, she became the first woman to hold that position (and later the first African American woman to be Secretary of State).

other hand, when department heads call a White House staff person and ask to see the president, unless they are one of the privileged few in whom the president has special confidence, they often are told that "the president can't be bothered with that" or "the president doesn't have time to see you."

Presidential Character

Every president brings to the White House a distinctive personality; the way the White House is organized and run will reflect that personality. Moreover, the public will judge the president not only in terms of what he accomplished, but also in terms of its perception of his character. Thus, personality plays a more important role in explaining the presidency than it does in explaining Congress.

Dwight Eisenhower brought an orderly, military style to the White House. He was accustomed to delegating authority and to having careful and complete staff work done for him by trained specialists. Though critics often accused him of having a bumbling, incoherent manner of speaking, in fact much

of that was a public disguise—a strategy for avoiding being pinned down in public on matters where he wished to retain freedom of action. His private papers reveal a very different Eisenhower—sharp, precise, deliberate.

John Kennedy brought a very different style to the presidency. He projected the image of a bold, articulate, and amusing leader who liked to surround himself with talented amateurs. Instead of clear, hierarchical lines of authority, there was a pattern of personal rule and an atmosphere of improvisation. Kennedy did not hesitate to call very junior subordinates directly and tell them what to do, bypassing the chain of command.

Lyndon Johnson was a master legislative strategist who had risen to be majority leader of the Senate on the strength of his ability to persuade other politicians in face-to-face encounters. He was a consummate deal maker who, having been in Washington for 30 years before becoming president, knew everybody and everything. As a result he tried to make every decision himself. But the style that served him well in political negotiations did not serve him

Question

2. Who were the three presidents who died on the Fourth of July?

well in speaking to the country at large, especially when trying to retain public support for the war in Vietnam.

Richard Nixon was a highly intelligent man with a deep knowledge of and interest in foreign policy, coupled with a deep suspicion of the media, his political rivals, and the federal bureaucracy. In contrast to Johnson, he disliked personal confrontations and tended to shield himself behind an elaborate staff system. Distrustful of the cabinet agencies, he tried first to centralize power in the White House and then to put into key cabinet posts former White House aides loyal to him. Like Johnson, his personality made it difficult for him to mobilize popular support. Eventually, he was forced to resign under the threat of impeachment arising out of his role in the Watergate scandal.

Gerald Ford, before being appointed vice president, had spent his political life in Congress and was at home with the give-and-take, discussion-oriented procedures of that body. He was also a genial man who liked talking to people. Thus, he preferred the circular to the pyramid system of White House organization. But this meant that many decisions were made in a disorganized fashion in which key people—and sometimes key problems—were not taken into account.

Jimmy Carter was an outsider to Washington and boasted of it. A former Georgia governor, he was determined not to be "captured" by Washington insiders. He also was a voracious reader with a wide range of interests and an appetite for detail. These dispositions led him to try to do many things and to do them personally. Like Ford, he began with a circular structure; unlike Ford, he based his decisions on reading countless memos and asking detailed questions. His advisers finally decided that he was trying to do too much in too great detail, and toward the end of his term he shifted to a pyramid structure.

Ronald Reagan was also an outsider, a former governor of California. But unlike Carter, he wanted to set the broad directions of his administration and leave the details to others. He gave wide latitude to subordinates and to cabinet officers, within the framework of an emphasis on lower taxes, less domestic spending, a military buildup, and a tough line with the Soviet Union. He was a superb leader of public opinion, earning the nickname "The Great Communicator."

George H.W. Bush lacked Reagan's speaking skills and was much more of a hands-on manager. Drawing on his extensive experience in the federal government (he had been vice president, director of the CIA, ambassador to the United Nations, representative to China, and a member of the House), Bush made decisions on the basis of personal contacts with key foreign leaders and Washington officials.

Bill Clinton, like Carter, paid a lot of attention to public policy and preferred informal, ad hoc arrangements for running his office. Unlike Carter, he was an effective speaker who could make almost any idea sound plausible. He was elected as a centrist Democrat but immediately pursued liberal policies such as comprehensive health insurance. When those failed and the Republicans won control of Congress in 1994, Clinton became a centrist again. His sexual affairs became the object of major investigations, and he was impeached by the House but acquitted by the Senate.

George W. Bush, the 43rd president, entered office as an outsider from Texas, but he was an outsider with a difference: his father had served as the 41st president of the United States, his late paternal grandfather had served as a United States senator from Connecticut, and he won the presidency only after the U.S. Supreme Court halted a recount of ballots in Florida, where his brother was governor. During the campaign, he focused almost entirely on domestic issues, especially cutting taxes and reforming education. A deeply religious man, he talked openly about how he had stopped excessive drinking only after he had found God. He ran as a "compassionate conservative" concerned about America's needy children and families. Bush, who had earned an advanced degree in business administration from Harvard, ran a very tight White House ship, insisting that meetings run on time and that press contacts be strictly controlled. He turned back public doubts about his intellect through self-deprecating humor. Following the terrorist attack on America on September 11, 2001, his agenda shifted almost entirely to foreign and military affairs, the war on terror, and the issue of homeland security.

Barack Obama succeeded Bush in 2009. He was the first African American to win a major party's presidential nomination and only the third person elected to the presidency while a sitting U.S. Senator. After Harvard, he taught constitutional law part-time at the University of Chicago. After entering politics and winning an Illinois State Senate seat, he was elected to the U.S. Senate in 2004. His electrifying speech at the 2004 Democratic National Convention catapulted him to national attention. He criticized Democratic presidential candidates who had supported military action against Iraq,

Answer
2. These presidents died on the Fourth of July: Thomas Jefferson (1826), John Adams (1826), James Monroe (1831).

and he campaigned in 2008 as the candidate of change and hope ("Yes we can!" was his most popular mantra). He came to office in January 2009 amid a global economic crisis that included devastating losses in America's real estate sector and financial markets. By mid-2009, he had proposed the largest budget in U.S. history and unveiled his plans for comprehensive health insurance.

The Power to Persuade

The sketchy constitutional powers given the president, combined with the lack of an assured legislative majority, mean that he must rely heavily on persuasion if he is to accomplish much. Here, the Constitution gives him some advantages: he and the vice president are the only officials elected by the whole nation, and he is the ceremonial head of state as well as the chief executive of the government. The president can use his national constituency and ceremonial duties to enlarge his power, but he must do so quickly: the second half of his first term in office will be devoted to running for reelection, especially if he faces opposition for his own party's nomination (as was the case with Carter and Ford).

THE THREE AUDIENCES

The president's persuasive powers are aimed at three audiences. The first, and often the most important, is his Washington, D.C., audience of fellow politicians and leaders. As Richard Neustadt points out in his book *Presidential Power,* a president's reputation among his Washington colleagues is of great importance in affecting how much deference his views receive and thus how much power he can wield.[13] If a president is thought to be "smart," "sure of himself," "cool," "on top of things," or "shrewd," and thus "effective," he *will* be effective. Franklin Roosevelt had that reputation, and so did Lyndon Johnson, at least for his first few years in office. Truman, Ford, and Carter often did not have that reputation, and they lost ground accordingly. Power, like beauty, exists largely in the eye of the beholder.

A second audience is composed of party activists and officeholders outside Washington—the partisan grassroots. These persons want the president to exemplify their principles, trumpet their slogans, appeal to their fears and hopes, and help them get reelected. Since, as we explained in Chapter 9, partisan activists increasingly have

President Bush shakes hands with Speaker Nancy Pelosi after his State of the Union address.

an ideological orientation toward national politics, these people will expect "their" president to make fire-and-brimstone speeches that confirm in them a shared sense of purpose and, incidentally, help them raise money from contributors to state and local campaigns.

The third audience is "the public." But of course that audience is really many publics, each with a different view or set of interests. A president on the campaign trail speaks boldly of what he will accomplish; a president in office speaks quietly of the problems that must be overcome. Citizens often are irritated at the apparent tendency of officeholders, including the president, to sound mealy-mouthed and equivocal. But it is easy to criticize the cooking when you haven't been the cook. A president learns quickly that his every utterance will be scrutinized closely by the media and by organized groups here and abroad, and his errors of fact, judgment, timing, or even inflection will be immediately and forcefully pointed out. Given the risks of saying too much, it is a wonder that presidents say anything at all.

Presidents have made fewer and fewer impromptu remarks in the years since Franklin Roosevelt held office and have instead relied more and more on prepared speeches from which political errors can be removed in advance. Hoover and Roosevelt held six or seven press conferences each month, but every president from Nixon through Clinton has held barely one a month. Instead, modern presidents make formal speeches. A president's use of these speeches often is called the **bully pulpit,** a

bully pulpit The president's use of his prestige and visibility to guide or enthuse the American public.

phrase that means taking advantage of the prestige and visibility of the presidency to try to guide or mobilize the American people.

POPULARITY AND INFLUENCE

The object of all this talk is to convert personal popularity into congressional support for the president's legislative programs (and improved chances for reelection). It is not obvious, of course, why Congress should care about a president's popularity. After all, as we saw in Chapter 13, most members of Congress are secure in their seats, and few need fear any "party bosses" who might deny them renomination. Moreover, the president cannot ordinarily provide credible electoral rewards or penalties to members of Congress. By working for their defeat in the 1938 congressional election, President Roosevelt attempted to "purge" members of Congress who opposed his program, but he failed. Nor does presidential support help a particular member of Congress: most representatives win reelection anyway, and the few who are in trouble are rarely saved by presidential intervention. When President Reagan campaigned hard for Republican senatorial candidates in 1986, he, too, failed to have much impact.

For a while, scholars thought congressional candidates might benefit from the president's coattails: they might ride into office on the strength of the popularity of a president of their own party. It is true, as can be seen from Table 14.2, that a winning president will find that his party's strength in Congress increases.

But there are good reasons to doubt whether the pattern observed in Table 14.2 is the result of presidential coattails. For one thing, there are some exceptions. Eisenhower won 57.4 percent of the vote in 1956, but the Republicans lost seats in the House and Senate. Kennedy won in 1960, but the Democrats lost seats in the House and gained but one in the Senate. When Nixon was reelected in 1972 with one of the largest majorities in history, the Republicans lost seats in the Senate.

Careful studies of voter attitudes and of how presidential and congressional candidates fare in the same districts suggest that, whatever may once have been the influence of coattails, their effect has declined in recent years and is quite small today. The weakening of party loyalty and of party organizations, combined with the enhanced ability of members of Congress to build secure relations with their constituents, has tended to insulate congressional elections from presidential ones. When voters choose as members of Congress people of the same party as an incoming president, they probably do so

Table 14.2 Partisan Gains or Losses in Congress in Presidential Election Years

Year	President	Party	Gains or Losses of President's Party In: House	Senate
1932	Roosevelt	Dem.	+90	+9
1936	Roosevelt	Dem.	+12	+7
1940	Roosevelt	Dem.	+7	-3
1944	Roosevelt	Dem.	+24	-2
1948	Truman	Dem.	+75	+9
1952	Eisenhower	Rep.	+22	+1
1956	Eisenhower	Rep.	-3	-1
1960	Kennedy	Dem.	-20	+1
1964	Johnson	Dem.	+37	+1
1968	Nixon	Rep.	+5	+7
1972	Nixon	Rep.	+12	-2
1976	Carter	Dem.	+1	+1
1980	Reagan	Rep.	+33	+12
1984	Reagan	Rep.	+16	-2
1988	Bush	Rep.	-3	-1
1992	Clinton	Dem.	-9	+1
1996	Clinton	Dem.	+9	-2
2000	Bush	Rep.	-3	-4
2004	Bush	Rep.	+4	+4
2008	Obama	Dem.	+21	+9

Sources: Updated from Congressional Quarterly, *Guide to U.S. Elections*, 928; and *Congress and the Nation*, vol. 4 (1973–1976), 28.

out of desire for a general change and as an adverse judgment about the outgoing party's performance as a whole, not because they want to supply the new president with members of Congress favorable to him.[14] The big increase in Republican senators and representatives that accompanied the election of Ronald Reagan in 1980 was probably as much a result of the unpopularity of the outgoing president and the circumstances of various local races as it was of Reagan's coattails.

Nonetheless, a president's personal popularity may have a significant effect on how much of his program Congress passes, even if it does not affect the reelection chances of those members of Congress. Though they do not fear a president who threatens to campaign against them (or cherish one who promises to support them), members of Congress do have a sense that it is risky to oppose too adamantly the policies of a popular president. Politicians share

Figure 14.1
Presidential Popularity

a sense of a common fate: they tend to rise or fall together. Statistically, a president's popularity, as measured by the Gallup poll (see Figure 14.1), is associated with the proportion of his legislative proposals approved by Congress (see Figure 14.2). Other things equal, the more popular the president, the higher the proportion of his bills Congress will pass.

But use these figures with caution. How successful a president is with Congress depends not just on the numbers reported here, but on a lot of other factors as well. First, he can be "successful" on a big bill or on a trivial one. If he is successful on a lot of small matters and never on a big one, the measure of presidential victories does not tell us much. Second, a president can keep his victory score high by not taking a position on any controversial measure. (President Carter made his views known on only 22 percent of the House votes, while President Eisenhower made his views known on 56 percent of those votes.) Third, a president can appear successful if a few bills he likes are passed, but most of his legislative program is bottled up in Congress and never comes to a vote. Given these problems, "presidential victories" are hard to measure accurately.

A fourth general caution: presidential popularity is hard to predict and can be greatly influenced by factors over which nobody, including the president, has much control. For example, when he took office in 2001, President George W. Bush's approval

rating was 57 percent, nearly identical to what President Bill Clinton received in his initial rating (58 percent) in 1993. But Bush also had the highest initial *dis*approval rating (25 percent) of any president since polling began. This was undoubtedly partly due to his becoming president on the heels of the Florida vote-count controversy (see Chapter 10). Bush's approval ratings through his first six months were fairly typical for post-1960 presidents. But from the terrorist attack on the United States on September 11, 2001 through mid-2002, his approval ratings never dipped below 70 percent, and the approval ratings he received shortly after the attack (hovering around 90 percent) were the highest ever recorded. Through his first six months in office, President Barack Obama's approval rating averaged 63 percent.

THE DECLINE IN POPULARITY

Though presidential popularity is an asset, its value tends inexorably to decline. As can be seen from Figure 14.1, every president except Eisenhower, Reagan, and Clinton lost popular support between his inauguration and the time that he left office, except when his reelection gave him a brief burst of renewed popularity. Truman was hurt by improprieties among his subordinates and by the protracted Korean War; Johnson was crippled by the increasing unpopularity of the Vietnam War; Nixon was severely damaged by the Watergate scandal; Ford was hurt by having pardoned Nixon for his part

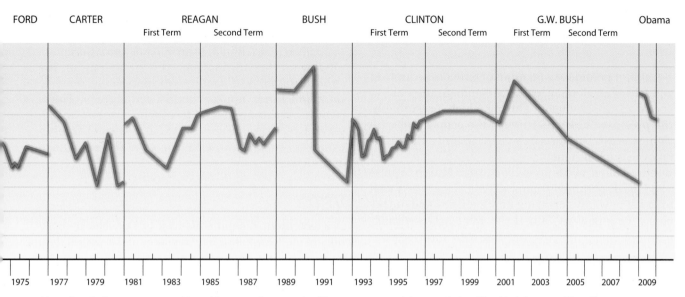

| FORD | CARTER | REAGAN First Term | Second Term | BUSH | CLINTON First Term | Second Term | G.W. BUSH First Term | Second Term | Obama |

1975 1977 1979 1981 1983 1985 1987 1989 1991 1993 1995 1997 1999 2001 2003 2005 2007 2009

Note: Popularity was measured by asking every few months, "Do you approve of the way is handling his job as president?"

Source: Thomas E. Cronin, *The State of the Presidency* (Boston: Little, Brown, 1975), 110–111. Copyright © 1975 by Little, Brown and Company, Inc. Reprinted by permission. Updated with Gallup poll data, 1976–2004. Reprinted by permission of the Gallup Poll News Service.

Figure 14.2

Presidential Victories on Votes in Congress, 1953–2006

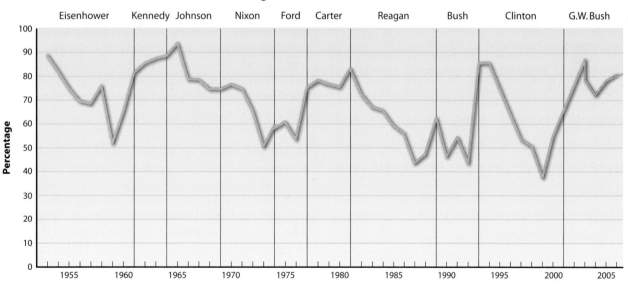

Note: Percentages indicate number of congressional votes supporting the president divided by the total number of votes on which the president has taken a position.

Sources: *Congressional Quarterly Almanac* (Washington, D.C.: Congressional Quarterly, various years); *Congressional Quarterly Weekly Report (CQ Weekly)* (1992), 3894; (1993), 3473; (1994), 3620; (1996), 3428; (1998), 14; (1999), 76, 2972; (2001) 54; (2002), 142, 3237; (2004), 54–55, 2947–2948; (2006), 87; (2007), 50.

Answer

3. William Howard Taft was the first president to own a car.

in Watergate; Carter was weakened by continuing inflation, staff irregularities, and the Iranian kidnapping of American hostages; George H.W. Bush was harmed by an economic recession. George W. Bush suffered from public criticism of the war in Iraq.

Because a president's popularity tends to be highest right after an election, political commentators like to speak of a "honeymoon," during which, presumably, the president's love affair with the people and with Congress can be consummated. Certainly, Roosevelt enjoyed such a honeymoon. In the legendary "first hundred days" of his presidency, from March to June 1933, FDR obtained from a willing Congress a vast array of new laws creating new agencies and authorizing new powers. But those were extraordinary times: the most serious economic depression of this century had put millions out of work, closed banks, impoverished farmers, and ruined the stock market. It would have been political suicide for Congress to have blocked, or even delayed, action on measures that appeared designed to help the nation out of the crisis.

veto message A message from the president to Congress stating that he will not sign a bill it has passed. Must be produced within 10 days of the bill's passage.

pocket veto A bill fails to become law because the president did not sign it within 10 days before Congress adjourns.

Other presidents, serving in more normal times, have not enjoyed such a honeymoon. Truman had little success with what he proposed; Eisenhower proposed little. Kennedy, Nixon, Ford, and Carter had some victories in their first year in office, but nothing that could be called a honeymoon. Only Lyndon Johnson enjoyed a highly productive relationship with Congress; until the Vietnam War sapped his strength, he rarely lost. Reagan began his administration with important victories in his effort to cut expenditures and taxes, but in his second year in office he ran into trouble.

The decay in the reputation of the president and his party in midterm is evident in Table 14.3. Since 1934, in every off-year election but two, the president's party has lost seats in one or both houses of Congress. In 1998, the Democrats won five seats in the House and lost none in the Senate; in 2002, the Republicans gained eight House seats and two in the Senate. The ability of the president to persuade is important but limited. However, he also has a powerful bargaining chip to play: the ability to say no.

The Power to Say No

The Constitution gives the president the power to veto legislation. In addition, most presidents have asserted the right of "executive privilege," or the right to withhold information that Congress may want to obtain from the president or his subordinates, and some presidents have tried to impound funds appropriated by Congress. These efforts by the president to say no are not only a way of blocking action but also a way of forcing Congress to bargain with him over the substance of policies.

VETO

If a president disapproves of a bill passed by both houses of Congress, he may veto it in one of two ways. One is by a **veto message.** This is a statement that the president sends to Congress accompanying the bill, within 10 days (not counting Sundays) after the bill has been passed. In it he sets forth his reasons for not signing the bill. The other is the **pocket veto.** If the president does not sign the bill within 10 days *and* Congress has adjourned within that time, then the bill will not become law. Obviously, a pocket veto can be used only during a certain time of the year—just before Congress adjourns at the end of its second session. At times, however, presidents have pocket-vetoed a bill just before Congress recessed for a summer vacation or to permit its members to campaign during an off-year election. In 1972, Senator Edward M. Kennedy of Massachusetts protested that this was unconstitutional, since a recess is not the same thing as an adjournment. In a case brought to federal court, Kennedy was upheld, and it is now understood that the pocket veto can be used only just before the life of a given Congress expires.

A bill not signed or vetoed within 10 days while Congress is still in session becomes law automatically, without the president's approval. A bill returned to Congress with a veto message can be passed over the president's objections if at least two-thirds of each house votes to override the veto. A bill that has received a pocket veto cannot be brought back to life by Congress (since Congress has adjourned), nor does such a bill carry over to the next session of Congress. If Congress wants to press the matter, it will have to start all over again by passing the bill anew in its next session, and then hope the president will sign it or, if he does not, that they can override his veto.

The president must either accept or reject the entire bill. Presidents did not have the power, possessed

Table 14.3 Partisan Gains or Losses in Congress in Off-Year Elections

Year	President	Party	Gains or Losses of President's Party In:	
			House	Senate
1934	Roosevelt	Dem.	+9	+9
1938	Roosevelt	Dem.	-70	-7
1942	Roosevelt	Dem.	-50	-8
1946	Truman	Dem.	-54	-11
1950	Truman	Dem.	-29	-5
1954	Eisenhower	Rep.	-18	-1
1958	Eisenhower	Rep.	-47	-13
1962	Kennedy	Dem.	-5	+2
1966	Johnson	Dem.	-48	-4
1970	Nixon	Rep.	-12	+1
1974	Ford	Rep.	-48	-5
1978	Carter	Dem.	-12	-3
1982	Reagan	Rep.	-26	0
1986	Reagan	Rep.	-5	-8
1990	Bush	Rep.	-9	-1
1994	Clinton	Dem.	-52	-9
1998	Clinton	Dem.	+5	0
2002	G. W. Bush	Rep.	+8	+2
2006	G. W. Bush	Rep.	-32	-6

Source: Norman J. Ornstein, Thomas E. Mann, and Michael J. Malbin, *Vital Statistics on Congress, 2001–2002* (Washington, D.C.: Congressional Quarterly Press, 2001), 207 (upated).

by most governors, to exercise a **line-item veto,** with which the chief executive can approve some provisions of a bill and disapprove others. Congress could take advantage of this by putting items the president did not like into a bill he otherwise favored, forcing him to approve those provisions along with the rest of the bill or reject the whole thing. In 1996, Congress passed a bill, which the president signed into law, that gives the president the power of "enhanced rescission." This means the president could cancel parts of a spending bill passed by Congress without vetoing the entire bill. The president had five days after signing a bill to send a message to Congress rescinding some parts of what he had signed. These rescissions would take effect unless Congress, by a two-thirds vote, overturned them. Congress could choose which parts of the president's cancellations it wanted to overturn. But the Supreme Court has decided that

this law is unconstitutional. The Constitution gives the president no such power to carve up a bill: he must either sign the whole bill, veto the whole bill, or allow it to become law without his signature.[15]

Nevertheless, the veto power is a substantial one, because Congress rarely has the votes to override it. From George Washington to Bill Clinton, over 2,500 presidential vetoes were cast; about 4 percent were overridden (see Table 14.4). Cleveland, Franklin Roosevelt, Truman, and Eisenhower made the most extensive use of vetoes, accounting for 65 percent of all vetoes ever cast. George W. Bush did not veto a single bill in his first term. Often the vetoed legislation is revised by Congress and passed in a form suitable to the president. There is no tally of how often this happens, but it is frequent enough so that both branches of government recognize that the veto, or even the threat of it, is part of an elaborate process of political negotiation in which the president has substantial powers.

EXECUTIVE PRIVILEGE

The Constitution says nothing about whether the president is obliged to divulge private communications between himself and his principal advisers, but presidents have acted as if they do have that privilege of confidentiality. The presidential claim is based on two grounds. First, the doctrine of the separation of powers means that one branch of government does not have the right to inquire into the internal workings of another branch headed by constitutionally named officers. Second, the principles of statecraft and of prudent administration require that the president have the right to obtain confidential and candid advice from subordinates; such advice could not be obtained if it would quickly be exposed to public scrutiny.

line-item veto An executive's ability to block a particular provision in a bill passed by the legislature.

For almost 200 years, there was no serious challenge to the claim of presidential confidentiality. The Supreme Court did not require the disclosure of confidential communications to or from the president.[16] Congress was never happy with this claim but until 1973 did not seriously dispute it. Indeed, in 1962, a Senate committee explicitly accepted a claim by President Kennedy that his secretary of defense, Robert S. McNamara, was not obliged to divulge the identity of Defense Department officials who had censored certain speeches by generals and admirals.

In 1974, the Supreme Court for the first time met the issue directly. A federal special prosecutor

Table 14.4 Presidential Vetoes, 1789–2009

	Regular Vetoes	Pocket Vetoes	Total Vetoes	Vetoes Overridden
Washington	2	—	2	—
Madison	5	2	7	—
Monroe	1	—	1	—
Jackson	5	7	12	—
Tyler	6	3	9	1
Polk	2	1	3	—
Pierce	9	—	9	5
Buchanan	4	3	7	—
Lincoln	2	4	6	—
A. Johnson	21	8	29	15
Grant	45	49	94	4
Hayes	12	1	13	1
Arthur	4	8	12	1
Cleveland	304	109	413	2
Harrison	19	25	44	1
Cleveland	43	127	170	5
McKinley	6	36	42	—
T. Roosevelt	42	40	82	1
Taft	30	9	39	1
Wilson	33	11	44	6
Harding	5	1	6	—
Coolidge	20	30	50	4
Hoover	21	16	37	3
F. Roosevelt	372	263	635	9
Truman	180	70	250	12
Eisenhower	73	108	181	2
Kennedy	12	9	21	—
L. Johnson	16	14	30	—
Nixon	26	17	43	7
Ford	48	18	66	12
Carter	13	18	31	2
Reagan	39	39	78	9
Bush	29	15	44	1
Clinton	36	1	37	2
G. W. Bush	12	0	12	4

Source: Norman J. Ornstein, Thomas E. Mann, and Michael J. Malbin, *Vital Statistics on Congress, 2002–2003* (Washington, D.C.: Congressional Quarterly Press, 2003), 207 (upated).

sought tape recordings of White House conversations between President Nixon and his advisers as part of his investigation of the Watergate scandal.

In the case of *United States v. Nixon,* the Supreme Court, by a vote of eight to zero, held that while there may be a sound basis for the claim of executive privilege, especially where sensitive military or diplomatic matters are involved, there is no "absolute unqualified Presidential privilege of immunity from judicial process under all circumstances."[17] To admit otherwise would be to block the constitutionally defined function of the federal courts to decide criminal cases.

Thus, Nixon was ordered to hand over the disputed tapes and papers to a federal judge so that the judge could decide which were relevant to the case at hand and allow those to be introduced into evidence. In the future, another president may well persuade the Court that a different set of records or papers is so sensitive as to require protection, especially if there is no allegation of criminal misconduct requiring the production of evidence in court. As a practical matter, it seems likely that presidential advisers will be able, except in unusual cases such as Watergate, to continue to give private advice to the president.

In 1997 and 1998, President Clinton was sued while in office by a private person, Paula Jones, who claimed he had solicited sex from her in ways that hurt her reputation. In defending himself against that and other matters, his lawyers attempted to claim executive privilege for Secret Service officers and government-paid lawyers who worked with him, but federal courts held that not only could a president be sued, but these other officials could not claim executive privilege.[18] One unhappy consequence of this episode is that the courts have greatly weakened the number of officials with whom the president can speak in confidence. It is not easy to run an organization when the courts can later compel your associates to testify about everything you said.

IMPOUNDMENT OF FUNDS

From time to time, presidents have refused to spend money appropriated by Congress. Truman did not spend all that Congress wanted spent on the armed forces, and Johnson did not spend all that Congress made available for highway construction. Kennedy refused to spend money appropriated for new weapons systems that he did not like. Indeed, the precedent for impounding funds goes back at least to the administration of Thomas Jefferson.

But what has precedent is not thereby constitutional. The Constitution is silent on whether the president *must* spend the money that Congress appropriates; all it says is that the president

Landmark Cases

Powers of the President

- *U.S. v. Nixon* (1974) Though the president is entitled to receive confidential advice, he can be required to reveal material related to a criminal prosecution.

- *Nixon v. Fitzgerald* (1982) The president may not be sued while in office.

- *Clinton v. Jones* (1997) The president may be sued for actions taken before he became president.

cannot spend money that Congress has *not* appropriated. The major test of presidential power in this respect occurred during the Nixon administration. Nixon wished to reduce federal spending. He proposed in 1972 that Congress give him the power to reduce federal spending so that it would not exceed $250 billion for the coming year. Congress, under Democratic control, refused. Nixon responded by pocket-vetoing 12 spending bills and then impounding funds appropriated under other laws that he had not vetoed.

Congress in turn responded by passing the Budget Reform Act of 1974, which, among other things, requires the president to spend all appropriated funds unless he first tells Congress what funds he wishes not to spend and Congress, within 45 days, agrees to delete the items. If he wishes simply to delay spending the money, he need only inform Congress, but Congress then can refuse the delay by passing a resolution requiring the immediate release of the money. Federal courts have upheld the rule that the president must spend, without delay for policy reasons, money that Congress has appropriated.

SIGNING STATEMENTS

Since at least the presidency of James Monroe, the White House has issued statements at the time the president signs a bill that has been passed by Congress. These statements have had several purposes: to express presidential attitudes about the law, to tell the executive branch how to implement it, or to declare that the president thinks some part of the law is unconstitutional. President Andrew

Jackson, for example, issued a statement in 1830 saying that a law designed to build a road from Chicago to Detroit should not cross the Michigan boundary (and so not to get to Chicago). Congress complained, but Jackson's view prevailed and the road did not get to Chicago.

In the 20th century, these statements became common. President Reagan issued 71, President George H.W. Bush signed 141, and President Clinton inked 105. By the late 1980s, they were published in legal documents as part of the legislative history of a bill.[19] By mid-2006, President George W. Bush had signed over 750.

Naturally, members of Congress are upset by this practice. To them, a **signing statement** often blocks the enforcement of a law Congress has passed and so it is equivalent to an unconstitutional line-item veto. But presidential advisers have defended these documents, arguing (as did an assistant attorney general in the Clinton administration) that they not only clarify how the law should be implemented but allow the president to declare what part of the law is in his view unconstitutional and thus ought not to be enforced at all.[20]

signing statement A presidential document that reveals what the president thinks of a new law and how it ought to be enforced.

While the Supreme Court has allowed signing statements to clarify the unclear legislative intent of a law, it has never given a clear verdict about the constitutional significance of such documents.[21] By 2007, the Democratic Congress was considering a challenge to the practice. The struggle over signing statements is another illustration of what one scholar has called the "invitation to struggle" that the Constitution has created between the president and Congress.[22]

The President's Program

Imagine you have just spent three or four years running for president, during which time you have given essentially the same speech over and over again. You have had no time to study the issues in any depth. To reach a large television audience, you have couched your ideas largely in rather simple—if not simple-minded—slogans. Your principal advisers are political aides, not legislative specialists.

You win. You are inaugurated. Now you must *be* a president instead of just talking about it. You must fill hundreds of appointive posts, but you know personally only a handful of the candidates. You must deliver a State of the Union message to Congress only two or three weeks after you are sworn in. It is quite possible you have never read, much less written, such a message before. You must submit a new budget; the old one is hundreds of pages long, much of it comprehensible only to experts. Foreign governments, as well as the stock market, hang on your every word, interpreting many of your remarks in ways that totally surprise you. What will you do?

The Constitution is not much help. It directs you to report on the state of the union and to recommend "such measures" as you shall judge "necessary and expedient." Beyond that, you are charged to "take care that the laws be faithfully executed."

At one time, of course, the demands placed on a newly elected president were not very great, because the president was not expected to do very much. The president, on assuming office, might speak of the tariff, or relations with England, or the value of veterans' pensions, or the need for civil service reform, but he was not expected to have something to say (and offer) to everybody. Today he is.

PUTTING TOGETHER A PROGRAM

To develop policies on short notice, a president will draw on several sources, each with particular strengths and weaknesses:

- **Interest groups**

Strength: Will have specific plans and ideas.

Weakness: Will have narrow view of the public interest.

- **Aides and campaign advisers**

Strength: Will test new ideas for their political soundness.

Weakness: Will not have many ideas to test; inexperienced in government.

- **Federal bureaus and agencies**

Strength: Will know what is feasible in terms of governmental realities.

Weakness: Will propose plans that promote own agencies and will not have good information on whether plans will work.

- **Outside, academic, and other specialists and experts**

Strength: Will have many general ideas and criticisms of existing programs.

Weakness: Will not know the details of policy or have good judgment as to what is feasible.

There are essentially two ways for a president to develop a program. One, exemplified by Presidents Carter and Clinton, is to have a policy on almost everything. To do this, they worked endless hours and studied countless documents, trying to learn something about, and then state their positions on, a large number of issues. The other method, illustrated by President Reagan, is to concentrate on three or four major initiatives or themes and leave everything else to subordinates.

But even when a president has a governing philosophy, as did Reagan, he cannot risk plunging ahead on his own. He must judge public and congressional reaction to this program before he commits himself fully to it. Therefore, he often will allow parts of his program to be "leaked" to the press, or "floated" as a trial balloon. Reagan's commitment to a 30 percent tax cut and larger military expenditures was so well known that it required no leaking, but he did have to float his ideas on Social Security and certain budget cuts to test popular reaction. His opponents in the bureaucracy did exactly the same thing, hoping for the opposite effect. They leaked controversial parts of the program in an effort to discredit the whole policy. This process of testing the winds by a president and his critics helps explain why so many news stories coming from Washington mention no person by name but only an anonymous "highly placed source."

In addition to the risks of adverse reaction, the president faces three other constraints on his ability to plan a program. One is the sheer limit of his time and attention span. Every president works harder than he has ever worked before. A 90-hour week is typical. Even so, he has great difficulty keeping up with all the things he is supposed to know and make decisions about. For example, Congress during an average year passes between 400 and 600 bills, each of which the president must sign, veto, or allow to take effect without his signature. Scores of people wish to see him. Hundreds of phone calls must be made to members of Congress and others in order to ask for help, to smooth ruffled feathers, or to get information. He must receive all newly appointed ambassadors and visiting heads of state and in addition have his picture taken with countless people, from a Nobel Prize winner to a child whose likeness will appear on the Easter Seal.

The second constraint is the unexpected crisis. Franklin Roosevelt obviously had to respond to a depression and to the mounting risks of world war. But most presidents get their crises when they least expect them. Consider these crises:

4. Who was the only divorced president?

Kennedy

- Failure of Bay of Pigs invasion of Cuba
- Soviets put missiles in Cuba
- China invades India
- Federal troops sent to the South to protect blacks

Johnson

- Vietnam War
- Black riots in major cities
- War between India and Pakistan
- Civil war in Dominican Republic
- Arab-Israeli war
- Civil rights workers murdered in South

Nixon

- Watergate scandal
- Arab-Israeli war
- Value of dollar falls in foreign trade
- Arabs raise the price of oil

Carter

- OMB director Bert Lance accused of improprieties
- Lengthy coal strike
- Seizure of American hostages in Iran
- Soviet invasion of Afghanistan

Reagan

- Poland suppresses Solidarity movement
- U.S. troops sent to Lebanon
- U.S. hostages held in Lebanon
- Civil war in Nicaragua
- Iran-contra crisis

Bush (the elder)

- Soviet Union dissolves
- Iraq invades Kuwait

Clinton

- Civil war continues in Bosnia and other parts of the former Yugoslavia
- Investigation of possible wrongdoing of President and Mrs. Clinton in Whitewater real estate development
- Clinton impeached

Bush (the younger)

- Terrorist attacks on World Trade Center and Pentagon kill close to 3,000 people
- U.S.-led war against terrorists in Afghanistan and Iraq

Obama

- Economic crisis affecting financial markets, industry, and employment

The third constraint is that the federal government and most federal programs, as well as the federal budget, can only be changed marginally, except in special circumstances. The vast bulk of federal expenditures are beyond control in any given year: the money must be spent whether the president likes it or not. Many federal programs have such strong congressional or public support that they must be left intact or modified only slightly. And this means that most federal employees can count on being secure in their jobs, whatever a president's views on reducing the bureaucracy.

The result of these constraints is that the president, at least in ordinary times, has to be selective about what he wants. He can be thought of as having a stock of influence and prestige the way that he might have a supply of money. If he wants to get the most "return" on his resources, he must "invest" that influence and prestige carefully in enterprises that promise substantial gains—in public benefits and political support—at reasonable costs. Each president tends to speak in terms of changing everything at once, calling his approach a "New Deal," a "New Frontier," a "Great Society," or the "New Federalism." But beneath the rhetoric, he must identify a few specific proposals on which he wishes to bet his resources, mindful of the need to leave a substantial stock of resources in reserve to handle the inevitable crises and emergencies. In recent decades, events have required every president to devote much of his time and resources to two key issues: the state of the economy and foreign affairs. What he manages to do beyond this will depend on his personal views and his sense of what the nation, as well as his reelection, requires.

And it will depend on one other thing: opinion polls. The last president who never used polls was Herbert Hoover. Franklin Roosevelt began making heavy use of them, and every president since has relied on them. Bill Clinton had voters polled about almost everything—where he should go on vacation (the West) and how to deal with Bosnia (no ground troops).

Answer

4. Ronald Reagan was divorced.

A group of Civilian Conservation Corps workers hired by the government during the Great Depression.

Once, when polls did not exist, politicians often believed they should do what they thought the public interest required. Now that polls are commonplace, some politicians act on the basis of what their constituents want. Scholars call the first view the trustee approach: do what the public good requires, even if the voters are skeptical. The second view is the delegate model: do what your constituents want you to do.

But there is another way of looking at polls. They may be a device not for picking a policy, but for deciding what language to use in explaining that policy. Choose a policy that helps you get reelected or that satisfies an interest group, but then explain it with poll-tested words. President Clinton wanted to keep affirmative action (described in the chapter titled "Civil Rights"), but knew that most voters disliked it. So he used a poll-tested phrase—"mend it but don't end it"—and then did nothing to mend it.

Finally, a president's program can be radically altered by a dramatic event or prolonged crisis. George W. Bush ran as a candidate interested in domestic issues and with little background in foreign affairs, but the terrorist attack of September 11, 2001, on the World Trade Center and the Pentagon dramatically changed his presidency into one preoccupied with foreign and military policy. Barack Obama campaigned against the war in Iraq but spent the first months of his presidency focused mainly on the country's sagging economy.

ATTEMPTS TO REORGANIZE

One item on the presidential agenda has been the same for almost every president since Herbert Hoover: reorganizing the executive branch of government. In the wake of the terrorist attack on the United States on September 11, 2001, the president, by executive order, created a new White House Office of Homeland Security, headed by his friend and former Pennsylvania governor, Tom Ridge. In the months that followed, it became clear to all, including the president, that he had given Ridge an impossible job. For one thing, despite its obvious importance, Ridge's office, like most units with the Executive Office of the President, had only a dozen or so full-time staff, little budgetary authority, and virtually no ability to make and enforce decisions regarding how cabinet agencies operated. Nobody could meaningfully coordinate the literally dozens of administrative units that the administration's new homeland security blueprint required Ridge's office to somehow manage.

To address this problem, President Bush called for a reorganization that would create the third-largest cabinet department encompassing 22 federal agencies, nearly 180,000 employees, and an annual budget of close to $40 billion. Among the federal agencies placed under the new Department of Homeland Security are the Coast Guard, the Customs Service, the Federal Emergency Management Agency, and the Immigration and Naturalization Service. A law authorizing the new Department of Homeland Security was enacted in November 2002, but it will take years and much effort for the new agency to become fully operational.

Important as it is, the ongoing attempt to reorganize the federal government around homeland security goals is neither the first, nor even the largest, reorganization effort made by a sitting president. With few exceptions, every president since 1928 has

"15% LIKE YOU AS A CONSERVATIVE, 15% LIKE YOU LIBERAL, 70% DON'T CARE ... SO MY ADVICE IS TO REINVENT YOURSELF AS THE 'I DON'T CARE' CANDIDATE."

tried to change the structure of the staff, departments, and agencies that are theoretically subordinate to him. Every president has been appalled by the number of agencies that report to him and by the apparently helter-skelter manner in which they have grown up. But this is only one—and often not the most important—reason for wanting to reorganize. If a president wants to get something done, put new people in charge of a program, or recapture political support for a policy, it often is easier to do so by creating a new agency or reorganizing an old one than by abolishing a program, firing a subordinate, or passing a new law. Reorganization serves many objectives and thus is a recurring theme.

Legally, the president can reorganize his personal White House staff anytime he wishes. To reorganize in any important way the larger Executive Office of the President or any of the executive departments or agencies, however, Congress must first be consulted. For over 40 years, this consultation usually took the form of submitting to Congress a reorganization plan that would take effect provided that neither the House nor the Senate passed, within 60 days, a concurrent resolution disapproving the plan (such a resolution was called a **legislative veto**). This procedure, first authorized by the Reorganization Act of 1939, could be used to change, but not create or abolish, an executive agency. In 1981, authority under that act expired, and Congress did not renew it. Two years later, the Supreme Court declared all legislative vetoes unconstitutional (see Chapter 15), and so today any presidential reorganization plan would have to take the form of a regular law, passed by Congress and signed by the president.

What has been said so far may well give the reader the impression that the president is virtually helpless. That is not the case. The *actual* power of the president can only be measured in terms of what he can accomplish. What this chapter has described so far is the office as the president finds it—the burdens, restraints, demands, complexities, and resources that he encounters on entering the Oval Office for the first time. Every president since Truman has commented feelingly on how limited the powers of the president seem from the inside compared to what they appear to be from the outside. Franklin Roosevelt compared his struggles with the bureaucracy to punching a feather bed; Truman wrote that the power of the president was chiefly the power to persuade people to do what they ought to do anyway. After in office a year or so, Kennedy spoke to interviewers about how much more complex the world appeared than he had first supposed. Johnson and Nixon were broken by the office and the events that happened there.

Yet Franklin Roosevelt helped create the modern presidency, with its vast organizational reach, and directed a massive war effort. Truman ordered two atomic bombs dropped on Japanese cities. Eisenhower sent American troops to Lebanon; Kennedy supported an effort to invade Cuba. Johnson sent troops to the Dominican Republic and to Vietnam; Nixon ordered an invasion of Cambodia; Reagan launched an invasion of Grenada and sponsored an antigovernment insurgent group in Nicaragua; Bush invaded Panama and sent troops to the Persian Gulf to fight Iraq; Clinton sent troops to Haiti and Bosnia. George W. Bush ordered a U.S. military operation in Afghanistan and Iraq. Obviously Europeans, Russians, Vietnamese, Cambodians, Dominicans, Panamanians, and Iraqis do not think the American president is "helpless."

Presidential Transition

No president but Franklin Roosevelt has ever served more than two terms, and since the ratification of the Twenty-second Amendment in 1951, no president will ever again have the chance. But more than tradition or the Constitution escorts presidents from office. Only about one-third of the presidents since George Washington have been elected to a second term. Of the 27 not reelected, four died in office during their first term. But the remainder either did not seek or (more usually) could not obtain reelection.

Of the eight presidents who died in office, four were assassinated: Lincoln, Garfield, McKinley, and Kennedy. At least six other presidents were the objects of unsuccessful assassination attempts: Jackson, Theodore Roosevelt, Franklin Roosevelt, Truman, Ford, and Reagan. (There may have been attempts on other presidents that never came to public notice; the attempts mentioned here involved public efforts to fire weapons at presidents.)

The presidents who served two or more terms fall into certain periods, such as the Founding (Washington, Jefferson, Madison, Monroe) or wartime (Lincoln, Wilson, Roosevelt), or they happened to be in office during especially tranquil times (Monroe, McKinley, Eisenhower, Clinton), or some combination of the above. When the country was deeply divided, as during the years just before the Civil War and during the period of Reconstruction after it, it was the rare president who was reelected.

legislative veto The authority of Congress to block a presidential action after it has taken place. The Supreme Court has held that Congress does not have this power.

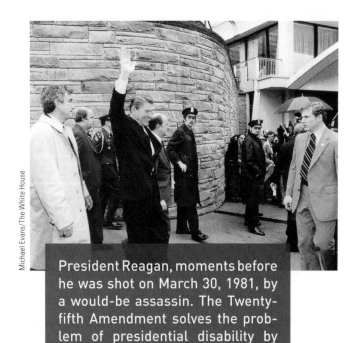

Michael Evans/The White House

President Reagan, moments before he was shot on March 30, 1981, by a would-be assassin. The Twenty-fifth Amendment solves the problem of presidential disability by providing for an orderly transfer of power to the vice president.

THE VICE PRESIDENT

Eight times a vice president has become president because of the death of his predecessor. It first happened to John Tyler, who became president in 1841 when William Henry Harrison died peacefully after only one month in office. The question for Tyler and for the country was substantial: was Tyler simply to be the acting president and a kind of caretaker until a new president was elected, or was he to be *president* in every sense of the word? Despite criticism and despite what might have been the contrary intention of the Framers of the Constitution, Tyler decided on the latter course and was confirmed in that opinion by a decision of Congress. Ever since, the vice president has automatically become president, in title and in powers, when the occupant of the White House has died or resigned.

But if vice presidents frequently acquire office because of death, they rarely acquire it by election. Since the earliest period of the Founding, when John Adams and Thomas Jefferson were each elected president after having first served as vice president under their predecessors, there have only been three occasions when a vice president was later able to win the presidency without his president's having died in office. One was in 1836, when Martin Van Buren was elected president after having served as Andrew Jackson's vice president; the second was in 1968, when Richard Nixon became president after having served as Dwight Eisenhower's

vice president eight years earlier; the third was in 1988, when George Bush succeeded Ronald Reagan. Many vice presidents who entered the Oval Office because their predecessors died were subsequently elected to terms in their own right—Theodore Roosevelt, Calvin Coolidge, Harry Truman, and Lyndon Johnson. But no one who wishes to become president should assume that to become vice president first is the best way to get there.

The vice-presidency is just what so many vice presidents have complained about its being: a rather empty job. John Adams described it as "the most insignificant office that ever the invention of man contrived or his imagination conceived," and most of his successors would have agreed. Thomas Jefferson, almost alone, had a good word to say for it: "The second office of the government is honorable and easy, the first is but a splendid misery."[23] Daniel Webster rejected a vice-presidential nomination in 1848 with the phrase, "I do not choose to be buried until I am really dead."[24] (Had he taken the job, he would have become president after Zachary Taylor died in office, thereby achieving a remarkable secular resurrection.) For all the good and bad jokes about the vice-presidency, however, candidates still struggle mightily for it. John Nance Garner gave up the speakership of the House to become Franklin Roosevelt's vice president (a job he valued as "not worth a pitcher of warm spit"*), and Lyndon Johnson gave up the majority leadership of the Senate to become Kennedy's. Truman, Nixon, Humphrey, Mondale, and Gore all left reasonably secure Senate seats for the vice-presidency.

The only official task of the vice president is to preside over the Senate and to vote in case of a tie. Even this is scarcely time-consuming, as the Senate chooses from among its members a president pro tempore, as required by the Constitution, who (along with others) presides in the absence of the vice president. The vice president's leadership powers in the Senate are weak, especially when the vice president is of a different party from the majority of the senators. But on occasion the vice president can become very important. Right after the terrorists attacked the United States in 2001, President Bush was in his airplane while his advisers worried that he might be attacked next. Vice President Cheney was quickly hidden away in a secret, secure location so he could run the government if anything happened to President Bush. And for many months thereafter, Cheney stayed in this location in case he suddenly became president. But absent a crisis,

*The word he actually used was a good deal stronger than *spit*, but historians are decorous.

the vice president is, at best, only an adviser to the president.

PROBLEMS OF SUCCESSION

If the president should die in office, the right of the vice president to assume that office has been clear since the time of John Tyler. But two questions remain: What if the president falls seriously ill, but does not die? And if the vice president steps up, who then becomes the new vice president?

The first problem has arisen on a number of occasions. After President James A. Garfield was shot in 1881, he lingered through the summer before he died. President Woodrow Wilson collapsed from a stroke and was a virtual recluse for seven months in 1919 and an invalid for the rest of his term. Eisenhower had three serious illnesses while in office; Reagan was shot during his first term and hospitalized during his second.

The second problem has arisen on eight occasions when the vice president became president owing to the death of the incumbent. In these cases, no elected person was available to succeed the new president, should he die in office. For many decades, the problem was handled by law. The Succession Act of 1886, for example, designated the secretary of state as next in line for the presidency should the vice president die, followed by the other cabinet officers in order of seniority. But this meant that a vice president who became president could pick his own successor by choosing his own secretary of state. In 1947, the law was changed to make the Speaker of the House and then the president pro tempore of the Senate next in line for the presidency. But that created still other problems: a Speaker or a president pro tempore is likely to be chosen because of seniority, not executive skill, and in any event might well be of the party opposite to that occupying the White House.

Both problems were addressed in 1967 by the Twenty-fifth Amendment to the Constitution. It deals with the disability problem by allowing the vice president to serve as "acting president" whenever the president declares he is unable to discharge the powers and duties of his office or whenever the vice president and a majority of the cabinet declare that the president is incapacitated. If the president disagrees with the opinion of his vice president and a majority of the cabinet, then Congress decides the issue. A two-thirds majority is necessary to confirm that the president is unable to serve.

The amendment deals with the succession problem by requiring a vice president who assumes the presidency (after a vacancy is created by death or resignation) to nominate a new vice president. This person takes office if the nomination is confirmed by a majority vote of both houses of Congress. When there is no vice president, then the 1947 law governs: next in line are the Speaker, the Senate president, and the 15 cabinet officers, beginning with the secretary of state.

The disability problem has not arisen since the adoption of the amendment, but the succession problem has. In 1973, Vice President Spiro Agnew resigned, having pleaded no contest to criminal charges. President Nixon nominated Gerald Ford as vice president, and after extensive hearings he was confirmed by both houses of Congress and sworn in. Then on August 9, 1974, Nixon resigned the presidency—the first man to do so—and Ford became president. He nominated as his vice president Nelson Rockefeller, who was confirmed by both houses of Congress—again, after extensive hearings—and was sworn in on December 19, 1974. For the first time in history, the nation had as its two principal executive officers men who had not been elected to either the presidency or the vice-presidency. It is a measure of the legitimacy of the Constitution that this arrangement caused no crisis in public opinion.

IMPEACHMENT

There is one other way—besides death, disability, or resignation—by which a president can leave office before his term expires, and that is by impeachment. Not only the president and vice president, but also all "civil officers of the United States" can be removed by being impeached and convicted. As a practical matter civil officers—cabinet secretaries, bureau chiefs, and the like—are not subject to impeachment, because the president can remove them at any time and usually will if their behavior makes them a serious political liability. Federal judges, who serve during "good behavior"* and who are constitutionally independent of the president and Congress, have been the most frequent objects of impeachment.

An **impeachment** is like an indictment in a criminal trial: a set of charges against somebody, voted by (in this case) the House of Representatives. To be removed from office, the impeached officer must be convicted by a two-thirds vote of the Senate, which sits as a court, is presided over by the Chief Justice, hears the evidence, and makes its decision under whatever rules it wishes to adopt. Sixteen persons

> *impeachment* Charges against a president approved by a majority of the House of Representatives.

---

*"Good behavior" means a judge can stay in office until he retires or dies, unless he or she is impeached and convicted.

Politically Speaking

Lame Duck

A **lame duck** is a politician whose power has diminished because he or she is about to leave office as a result of electoral defeat or statutory limitation (for example, the president can serve no more than two terms).

The expression was first used in 18th-century England, where it meant a "bankrupt businessman." Soon it was used to refer to "bankrupt" politicians. Perhaps they were called "lame ducks" because they had been shot on the wing and, though still alive, could no longer fly.

A lame duck is not to be confused with a "sitting duck" (somebody who is an easy target).

Source: From *Safire's Political Dictionary* by William Safire. Copyright © 1968, 1972, 1978 by William Safire. Reprinted by permission of Random House, Inc. and the author.

have been impeached by the House, and seven have been convicted by the Senate. The last conviction was in 1989, when two federal judges were removed from office.

Only two presidents have ever been impeached—Andrew Johnson in 1868 and Bill Clinton in 1998. Richard Nixon would surely have been impeached in 1974, had he not resigned after the House Judiciary Committee voted to recommend impeachment.

The Senate did not convict either Johnson or Clinton by the

lame duck A person still in office after he or she has lost a bid for reelection.

necessary two-thirds vote. The case against Johnson was entirely political—Radical Republicans, who wished to punish the South after the Civil War, were angry at Johnson, a southerner, who had a soft policy toward the South. The argument against him was flimsy.

The case against Clinton was more serious. The House Judiciary Committee, relying on the report of independent counsel Kenneth Starr, charged Clinton with perjury (lying under oath about his sexual affair with Monica Lewinsky), obstruction of justice (trying to block the Starr investigation), and abuse of power (making false written statements to the Judiciary Committee). The vote to impeach was passed by the House along party lines. A majority, but not two-thirds, of the Senate voted to convict.

Why did Clinton survive? There were many factors. The public disliked his private behavior, but did not think it amounted to an impeachable offense. (In fact, right after Lewinsky revealed her sexual affair with him, his standing in opinion polls went up.) The economy was strong, and the nation was at peace. Clinton was a centrist Democrat who did not offend most voters.

The one casualty of the entire episode was the death of the law creating the office of the Independent Counsel. Passed in 1978 by a Congress that was upset by the Watergate crisis, the law directed the attorney general to ask a three-judge panel to appoint an independent counsel whenever a high official is charged with serious misconduct. (In 1993, when the 1978 law expired, President Clinton asked that it be passed again. It was.) Eighteen people were investigated by various independent counsels from 1978 to 1999. In about half the cases, no charges were brought to court.

For a long time, Republicans disliked the law because the counsels were investigating them. After Clinton came to office, the counsels started investigating him and his associates, and so the Democrats began to oppose it. In 1999, when the law expired, it was not renewed.

A problem remains, however. How will any high official, including the president, be investigated when the attorney general, who does most investigations, is part of the president's team? One answer is to let Congress do it, but Congress may be controlled by the president's party. No one has yet solved this puzzle.

Some Founders may have thought that impeachment would be used frequently against presidents, but as a practical matter it is so complex and serious an undertaking that we can probably expect it to be reserved in the future only for the gravest forms of

WHAT WOULD YOU DO?

MEMORANDUM

To: *Delegate James Nagle*

From: *Amy Wilson, legal staff*

Subject: *Six-year presidential term*

The proposal to give the president a single six-year term is perhaps the most popular amendment now before the convention. Polls suggest that it is supported by a sizable percentage of the American people.

Arguments for:

1. Today, a president no sooner learns the ropes after being elected for the first time than he or she has to start preparing for the next election. A six-year term will give the president a chance to govern for several years after learning how to be president. This will lessen the extent to which political pressures dictate what the president does.

2. Limited to a single term, the president need not cater to special-interest groups or the media in deciding on policy. He or she can concentrate on what is good for the country.

3. Many states have limited their governors to a single term.

Friday,

Six-Year Term for President

October 15
EUDORA, KS

Here at the convention called to propose amendments to the United States Constitution, the major isssue facing the delegates is the proposal to limit the president to a single six-year term. Proponents of the measure claim…

Arguments against:

1. It is the need to win reelection that keeps the president (like any politician) attentive to what the people want. A president unable to succeed himself or herself will be tempted to ignore public opinion.

2. Limiting a president to a single term will not free him or her from the need to play to the media or special-interest groups, since the formal powers of the presidency are too weak to permit the incumbent to govern without the aid of Congress and the press.

3. There is no evidence that presidents (such as Dwight Eisenhower) who served a second term knowing that they could not run for reelection did a better or less "political" job in the second term than in the first.

Your decision:

Favor amendment _____   Oppose amendment _____

presidential misconduct. No one quite knows what a high crime or misdemeanor is, but most scholars agree that the charge must involve something illegal or unconstitutional, not just unpopular. Unless a president or vice president is first impeached and convicted, many experts believe he is not liable to prosecution as would an ordinary citizen. (No one is certain, because the question has never arisen.) President Ford's pardon of Richard Nixon meant that he could not be prosecuted under federal law for things he may have done while in office.

Students may find the occasions of misconduct or disability remote and the details of succession or impeachment tedious. But the problem is not remote—succession has occurred nine times and disability at least twice—and what may appear tedious goes, in fact, to the heart of the presidency. The first and fundamental problem is to make the office legitimate. That was the great task George Washington set himself, and that was the substantial accomplishment of his successors. Despite bitter and sometimes violent partisan and sectional strife, beginning almost immediately after Washington stepped down, presidential succession has always occurred peacefully, without a military coup or a political plot. For centuries, in the bygone times of kings as well as in the present times of dictators and juntas, peaceful succession has been a rare event among the nations of the world. Many of the critics of the Constitution believed in 1787 that peaceful succession would not happen in the United States either: somehow the president would connive to hold office for life or to handpick his successor. Their predictions were wrong, though their fears are understandable.

How Powerful Is the President?

Just as members of Congress bemoan their loss of power, so presidents bemoan theirs. Can both be right?

In fact, they can. If Congress is less able to control events than it once was, it does not mean that the president is thereby more able to exercise control. The federal government *as a whole* has become more constrained, so it is less able to act decisively. The chief source of this constraint is the greater complexity of the issues with which Washington must deal.

It was one thing to pass the Social Security Act in 1935; it is quite another thing to keep the Social Security system adequately funded. It was one thing for the nation to defend itself when attacked in 1941; it is quite another to maintain a constant

military preparedness while simultaneously exploring possibilities for arms control. It was not hard to give pensions to veterans; it seems almost impossible today to find the cure for drug abuse or juvenile crime.

In the face of modern problems, all branches of government, including the presidency, seem both big and ineffectual. Add to this the much closer and more critical scrutiny of the media and the proliferation of interest groups, and it is small wonder that both presidents and members of Congress feel that they have lost power.

Presidents have come to acquire certain rules of thumb for dealing with their political problems. Among them are these:

- *Move it or lose it.* A president who wants to get something done should do it early in his term, before his political influence erodes.

- *Avoid details.* President Carter's lieutenants regret having tried to do too much. Better to have three or four top priorities and forget the rest.

- *Cabinets don't get much accomplished; people do.* Find capable White House subordinates and give them well-defined responsibility; then watch them closely.[25]

Barack Obama is sworn in as the 44th president.

SUMMARY

Presidents have greater powers in military and foreign policy than they do in domestic policy. Congress has not used its power to declare war since 1942, but modern presidents at war face many challenges to their powers. President George W. Bush, the war in Iraq, and controversies surrounding his administration's strong stance on presidential powers are only the latest examples. Both with respect to war powers and more generally, there are basic differences between presidents and prime ministers. A U.S. president, chosen by the people and with powers derived from a written constitution, has less power than does a British prime minister, even though the latter depends entirely on the support of his or her party in Parliament. The separation of powers between the executive and legislative branches, the distinguishing feature of the American system, means that the president must deal with a competitor—Congress—in setting policy and even in managing executive agencies.

Presidential power, though still sharply limited, has grown from its constitutional origins as a result of congressional delegation, the increased importance of foreign affairs, and public expectations. But if the president today has more power, more is also demanded of him. As a result how effective he is depends not on any general grant of authority, but on the nature of the issue that he confronts and the extent to which he can mobilize informal sources of power (public opinion, congressional support).

Though the president seemingly controls a vast executive-branch apparatus, in fact he appoints but a small portion of the officials, and the behavior of even these often is beyond his easy control. Moreover, public support, high at the beginning of any new presidency, usually declines as the term proceeds. Consequently each president must conserve his power (and his energy and time), concentrating these scarce resources to deal with a few matters of major importance. Virtually every president since Franklin Roosevelt has tried to enlarge his ability to manage the executive branch—by reorganization, by appointing White House aides, by creating specialized staff agencies—but no president has been satisfied with the results.

The extent to which a president will be weak or powerful will vary with the kind of issue and the circumstances of the moment. It is a mistake to speak of an "imperial presidency" or of an ineffectual one. A president's power is better assessed by considering how he behaves in regard to specific issues.

RECONSIDERING WHO GOVERNS?

1. Did the Founders expect the presidency to be the most important political institution?

Most did not. They worried about whether the presidency would be too strong or too weak, but designed a Constitution hoping that Congress would be the most important institution. And it was, with a few exceptions, until the 20th century. Today, the strength of the presidency depends chiefly on two things: the importance of military and foreign affairs and the president's personal popularity.

2. How important is the president's character in determining how he governs?

Very important. Presidents with great personal skills, such as Franklin Roosevelt, Dwight Eisenhower, Ronald Reagan, and Bill Clinton can influence public opinion and that in turn influences Congress. But character is not the whole story. Having a majority of fellow believers in Congress, though rare, is important (as it was for Roosevelt and Lyndon Johnson), and so are unexpected events, such as wars and other crises.

RECONSIDERING TO WHAT ENDS?

1. Should we abolish the electoral college?

There are big risks in doing that. If no president were to win a majority of the popular vote (which happens quite often), there would either have to be a runoff election or the House would make the final decision. With an electoral college, small parties would play a bigger role and the United States could politically come to look like France or Italy. And without the college, a presidential campaign might be waged in just a few big states with the candidates ignoring most places.

2. Is it harder to govern when the presidency and Congress are controlled by different parties?

Not really. Both the Democratic and Republican parties have legislators who often vote with their party rivals. Unless the president has a big ideological majority in Congress, something that does not happen too often, he can easily lose legislative struggles. Gridlock does not in fact prevent major new pieces of legislation from being passed.

WORLD WIDE WEB RESOURCES

Official White House blog: **www.whitehouse.gov**

Studies of Presidents: **www.millercenter.virginia.edu/academic/americanpresident**

SUGGESTED READINGS

General

Corwin, Edward S. *The President: Office and Powers.* 5th ed. New York: New York University Press, 1985. Historical, constitutional, and legal development of the office.

Greenstein, Fred I. *The Presidential Difference: Leadership Style from FDR to Barack Obama.* Princeton, NJ: Princeton University Press, 2009. Explores how, independent of other influences, modern presidents' respective leadership styles account for consequential changes in domestic and foreign policy decisions.

Kernell, Samuel. *Going Public: New Strategies of Presidential Leadership,* 4th ed. New Haven, Conn.: Yale University Press, 2007. Examines how modern presidents develop policies with an eye fixed on how best to communicate with multiple public audiences.

Neustadt, Richard E. *Presidential Power: The Politics of Leadership.* Rev. ed. New York: Wiley, 1976. How presidents try to acquire and hold political power in the competitive world of official Washington, by a man who has been both a scholar and an insider.

Peterson, Mark A. *Legislating Together: The White House and Congress from Eisenhower to Reagan.* Cambridge: Harvard University Press, 1990. Challenges the conventional view that "the president proposes, Congress disposes." Contains many excellent examples of bargaining and cooperation between Congress and the executive branch.

Polsby, Nelson W., and Aaron Wildausky. *Presidential Elections.* 10th ed. New York: Chatham House, 2000. Excellent analysis of how campaigns and the electoral college shape the presidency.

Tulis, Jeffrey K. *The Rhetorical Presidency.* Princeton, NJ: Princeton University Press, 1987. Facinating study of how once-powerful constitutional customs that proscribed presidents rallying the public for political support on a routine basis changed in the early 20th century.

On Franklin D. Roosevelt

Leuchtenberg, William E. *Franklin D. Roosevelt and the New Deal, 1932–1940*. New York: Harper & Row, 1963.

Maney, Richard J. *The Roosevelt Presence*. New York: Twayne, 1992.

On Harry S Truman

Hamby, A. L. *Beyond the New Deal: Harry S Truman and American Liberalism*. New York: Columbia University Press, 1973.

McCullough, David. *Truman*. New York: Simon and Schuster, 1984.

On Dwight D. Eisenhower

Ambrose, Stephen E. *Eisenhower*. New York: Simon and Schuster, 1984.

Greenstein, Fred I. *The Hidden-Hand Presidency: Eisenhower as Leader*. New York: Basic Books, 1982.

On John F. Kennedy

Paper, Lewis J. *The Promise and the Performance: The Leadership of John F. Kennedy*. New York: Crown, 1975.

Parmet, Herbert C. *Jack*. New York: Dial Press, 1980.

On Lyndon B. Johnson

Caro, Robert A. *The Years of Lyndon Johnson*. 3 vols. New York: Alfred Knopf, 1982–2002.

Dallek, Robert. *Lone Star Rising and Flawed Giant*. New York: Oxford University Press, 1991 and 1996.

Kearns, Doris. *Lyndon Johnson and the American Dream*. New York: Harper and Row, 1976.

On Richard M. Nixon

Ambrose, Stephen E. *Nixon*. 3 vols. New York: Simon and Schuster, 1987, 1989, 1991.

On Jimmy Carter

Bourne, Peter G. *Jimmy Carter*. New York: Scribner, 1997.

On Ronald Reagan

Cannon, Lou. *President Reagan*. New York: Simon and Schuster, 1991.

On George H.W. Bush

Parmet, Herbert C. *George Bush*. New York: Scribner, 1997.

On Bill Clinton

Klein, Joe. *The Natural: The Misunderstood Presidency of Bill Clinton*. New York: Doubleday, 2002.

15

The
Bureaucracy

WHO GOVERNS?

1. What happened to make the bureaucracy a "fourth branch" of American national government?
2. What are the actual size and scope of the federal bureaucracy?

TO WHAT ENDS?

1. What should be done to improve bureaucratic performance?
2. Is "red tape" all bad?

There is probably not a man or woman in the United States who has not, at some time or other, complained about "the bureaucracy." Your letter was slow in getting to Aunt Minnie? The Internal Revenue Service took months to send you your tax refund? The Defense Department paid $400 for a hammer? The Occupational Safety and Health Administration told you that you installed the wrong kind of portable toilet for your farm workers? The "bureaucracy" is to blame.

For most people and politicians, *bureaucracy* is a pejorative word implying waste, confusion, red tape, and rigidity. But for scholars—and for bureaucrats themselves—*bureaucracy* is a word with a neutral, technical meaning. A **bureaucracy** is a large, complex organization composed of appointed officials. By *complex*, we mean that authority is divided among several managers; no one person is able to make all the decisions. A large corporation is a bureaucracy; so also are a big university and a government agency. With its sizable staff, even Congress has become, to some degree, a bureaucracy.

What is it about complex organizations in general, and government agencies in particular, that leads so many people to complain about them? In part, the answer is to be found in their very size and complexity. But in large measure the answer is to be found in the political context within which such agencies must operate. If we examine that context carefully, we will discover that many of the problems that we blame on "the bureaucracy" are in fact the result of what Congress, the courts, and the president do.

David Sailors/Encyclopedia/Corbis

Distinctiveness of the American Bureaucracy

Bureaucratic government has become an obvious feature of all modern societies, democratic and non-democratic. In the United States, however, three aspects of our constitutional system and political traditions give to the bureaucracy a distinctive character. First, political authority over the bureaucracy is not in one set of hands but is shared among several institutions. In a parliamentary regime, such as in Great Britain, the appointed officials of the national government work for the cabinet ministers, who are in turn dominated by the prime minister. In theory, and to a considerable extent in practice, British bureaucrats report to and take orders from the ministers in charge of their departments, do not deal directly with Parliament, and rarely give interviews to the press. In the United States, the Constitution permits both the president and Congress to exercise authority over the bureaucracy. Every senior appointed official has at least two masters: one in the executive branch and the other in the legislative. Often there are many more than two: Congress, after all, is not a single organization but a collection of committees, subcommittees, and individuals. This divided authority encourages bureaucrats to play one branch of government against the other and to make heavy use of the media.

Second, most of the agencies of the federal government share their functions with related agencies in state and local government. Though some federal agencies deal directly with American citizens—the Internal Revenue Service collects taxes from them, the Federal Bureau of Investigation looks into crimes for them, the Postal Service delivers mail to them—many agencies work with other organizations at other levels of government. For example, the Department of Education gives money to local school systems; the Health Care Financing Administration in the Department of Health and Human Services reimburses states for money spent on health care for the poor; the Department of Housing and Urban Development gives grants to cities for community development; and the Employment and Training Administration in the Department of Labor supplies funds to local governments so that they can run job-training programs. In France, by contrast, government programs dealing with education, health, housing, and employment are centrally run, with little or no control exercised by local governments.

Third, the institutions and traditions of American life have contributed to the growth of what some writers have described as an "adversary culture," in which the definition and expansion of personal rights, and the defense of rights and claims through lawsuits as well as political action, are given central importance. A government agency in this country operates under closer public scrutiny and with a greater prospect of court challenges to its authority than in almost any other nation. Virtually every important decision of the Occupational Safety and Health Administration or of the Environmental Protection Agency is likely to be challenged in the courts or attacked by an affected party; in Sweden the decisions of similar agencies go largely uncontested.

The scope as well as the style of bureaucratic government differs. In most Western European nations, the government owns and operates large parts of the economy: the French government operates the railroads and owns companies that make automobiles and cigarettes, and the Italian government owns many similar enterprises and also the nation's oil refineries. In just about every large nation except the United States, the telephone system is owned by the government. Publicly operated enterprises account for about 12 percent of all employment in France but less than 3 percent in the United States.[1] The U.S. government regulates privately owned enterprises to a degree not found in many other countries, however. Why we should have preferred regulation to ownership as the proper government role is an interesting question to which we shall return.

Proxy Government

Much of our federal bureaucracy operates on the principle of **government by proxy**.[2] In every representative government, the voters elect legislators who make the laws, but in this country the bureaucrats often pay other people to do the work. These "other people" include state and local governments, business firms, and nonprofit organizations.

Among the programs run this way are Social Security, Medicare, much environmental protection, and the collection of income taxes by withholding money from your paycheck. Even many military duties are contracted out.[3] In the first Gulf War in

bureaucracy A large, complex organization composed of appointed officials.

government by proxy Washington pays state and local governments and private groups to staff and administer federal programs.

Ric Feld/AP Photo

When the floodwaters of Hurricane Rita hit Lake Charles, LA, they created a crisis for the federal and state bureaucracies.

1991, American soldiers outnumbered private contractors in the region by 60 to one. But by 2006, there were nearly as many private workers as soldiers in Iraq. One company was paid $7.2 billion to get food and supplies to our troops there.[4]

When Hurricanes Katrina and Rita hit our Gulf Coast, the nation's response was managed by a small and weak group, the Federal Emergency Management Agency (FEMA). When the levees broke, it had only 2,600 employees; most of the help it was to provide came through "partners," such as state and local agencies, and some of these were not very competent.

Critics of our government-by-proxy system argue that it does not keep track of how the money we send to public and private agencies is used. Congress, of course, could change matters around, but it has an interest in setting policies and defining goals, not in managing the bureaucracy or levying taxes. Moreover, the president and Congress like to keep the size of the federal bureaucracy small by giving jobs to people not on the federal payroll.[5]

Defenders of government by proxy claim that the system produces more flexibility, takes advantage of private and nonprofit skills, and defends the principle of federalism embodied in our Constitution. The defenders make fair points, but the system does produce certain everyday oddities like the fact that many average citizens receive costly federal government services over long periods of time without ever directly interacting with civil servants. In 2008, Donald F. Kettl, a University of Maryland political scientist, dubbed this the "Mildred Paradox": in her last several years of life, his aged and ill mother-in-law, Mildred, applied successfully for multiple federal health insurance programs and received several

years' worth of different types of expensive institutional care and top-quality medical treatment—all at government expense—but without ever actually encountering a single government worker.[6]

The Growth of the Bureaucracy

The Constitution made scarcely any provision for an administrative system other than to allow the president to appoint, with the advice and consent of the Senate, "ambassadors, other public ministers and consuls, judges of the Supreme Court, and all other officers of the United States whose appointments are not herein otherwise provided for, and which shall be established by law."[7] Departments and bureaus were not mentioned.

In the first Congress, in 1789, James Madison introduced a bill to create a Department of State to assist the new secretary of state, Thomas Jefferson, in carrying out his duties. People appointed to this department were to be nominated by the president and approved by the Senate, but they were "to be removable by the president" alone. These six words, which would confer the right to fire government officials, occasioned six days of debate in the House. At stake was the locus of power over what was to become the bureaucracy. Madison's opponents argued that the Senate should consent to the removal of officials as well as their appointment. Madison responded that, without the unfettered right of removal, the president would not be able to control his subordinates, and without this control he would not be able to discharge his constitutional obligation to "take care that the laws be faithfully executed."[8] Madison won, 29 votes to 22. When the issue went to the Senate, another debate resulted in a tie vote, broken in favor of the president by Vice President John Adams. The Department of State, and all cabinet departments subsequently created, would be run by people removable only by the president.

That decision did not resolve the question of who would really control the bureaucracy, however. Congress retained the right to appropriate money, to investigate the administration, and to shape the laws that would be executed by that administration—more than ample power to challenge any president who claimed to have sole authority over his subordinates. And many members of Congress expected the cabinet departments, even though headed by people removable by the president, to report to Congress.

The government in Washington was at first minuscule. The State Department started with only nine employees; the War Department did not have 80 civilian employees until 1801. Only the Treasury Department, concerned with collecting taxes and finding ways to pay the public debt, had much power, and only the Post Office Department provided any significant service.

THE APPOINTMENT OF OFFICIALS

Small as the bureaucracy was, people struggled, often bitterly, over who would be appointed to it. From George Washington's day to modern times, presidents have found appointment to be one of their most important and difficult tasks. The officials they select affect how the laws are interpreted (thus the political ideology of the job holders is important), what tone the administration will display (thus personal character is important), how effectively the public business is discharged (thus competence is important), and how strong the political party or faction in power will be (thus party affiliation is important). Presidents trying to balance the competing needs of ideology, character, fitness, and partisanship have rarely pleased most people. As John Adams remarked, every appointment creates one ingrate and 10 enemies.

Because Congress, during most of the 19th and 20th centuries, was the dominant branch of government, congressional preferences often controlled the appointment of officials. And since Congress was, in turn, a collection of people who represented local interests, appointments were made with an eye to rewarding the local supporters of members of Congress or building up local party organizations. These appointments made on the basis of political considerations—patronage—were later to become a major issue. They galvanized various reform efforts that sought to purify politics and to raise the level of competence of the public service. Many of the abuses the reformers complained about were real enough, but patronage served some useful purposes as well. It gave the president a way to ensure that his subordinates were reasonably supportive of his policies; it provided a reward the president could use to induce recalcitrant members of Congress to vote for his programs; and it enabled party organizations to be built up to perform the necessary functions of nominating candidates and getting out the vote.

Though at first there were not many jobs to fight over, by the middle of the 19th century, there were a lot. From 1816 to 1861, the number of federal employees increased eightfold. This expansion was not, however, the result of the government's taking on new functions but simply a result of the increased demands on its traditional functions. The Post Office alone accounted for 86 percent of this growth.[9]

The Civil War was a great watershed in bureaucratic development. Fighting the war led, naturally, to hiring many new officials and creating many new offices. Just as important, the Civil War revealed the administrative weakness of the federal government and led to demands by the civil service reform movement for an improvement in the quality and organization of federal employees. And finally, the war was followed by a period of rapid industrialization and the emergence of a national economy. The effects of these developments could no longer be managed by state governments acting alone. With the creation of a nationwide network of railroads, commerce among the states became increasingly important. The constitutional powers of the federal government to regulate interstate commerce, long dormant for want of much commerce to regulate, now became an important source of controversy.

A SERVICE ROLE

From 1861 to 1901, new agencies were created, many to deal with particular sectors of society and the economy. Over 200,000 new federal employees were added, with only about half of this increase in the Post Office. The rapidly growing Pension Office began paying benefits to Civil War veterans; the Department of Agriculture was created in 1862 to help farmers; the Department of Labor was founded in 1882 to serve workers; and the Department of Commerce was organized in 1903 to assist business people. Many more specialized agencies, such as the National Bureau of Standards, also came into being.

In the 19th century, railroads were so important to the nation that the Interstate Commerce Commission was created to regulate their rates.

Bettmann/Corbis

These agencies had one thing in common: their role was primarily to serve, not to regulate. Most did research, gathered statistics, dispensed federal lands, or passed out benefits. Not until the Interstate Commerce Commission (ICC) was created in 1887 did the federal government begin to regulate the economy (other than by managing the currency) in any large way. Even the ICC had, at first, relatively few powers.

There were several reasons why federal officials primarily performed a service role. The values that had shaped the Constitution were still strong: these included a belief in limited government, the importance of states' rights, and the fear of concentrated discretionary power. The proper role of government in the economy was to promote, not to regulate, and a commitment to **laissez-faire**—a freely competitive economy—was strongly held. But just as important, the Constitution said nothing about giving any regulatory powers to bureaucrats. It gave to *Congress* the power to regulate commerce among the states. Now obviously Congress could not make the necessary day-to-day decisions to regulate, for example, the rates that interstate railroads charged to farmers and other shippers. Some agency or commission composed of appointed officials and experts would have to be created to do that. For a long time, however, the prevailing interpretation of the Constitution was that no such agency could exercise such regulatory powers unless Congress first set down clear standards that would govern the agency's decisions. As late as 1935, the Supreme Court held that a regulatory agency could not make rules on its own; it could only apply the standards enacted by Congress.[10] The Court's view was that the legislature may not delegate its powers to the president or to an administrative agency.[11]

These restrictions on what administrators could do were set aside in wartime. During World War I, for example, President Woodrow Wilson was authorized by Congress to fix prices, operate the railroads, manage the communications system, and even control the distribution of food.[12] This kind of extraordinary grant of power usually ended with the war.

Some changes in the bureaucracy did not end with the war. During the Civil War, World War I, World War II, the Korean War, and the war in Vietnam, the number of civilian (as well as military) employees of the government rose sharply. These increases were not simply in the number of civilians needed to help serve the war effort; many of the additional people were hired by agencies, such as the Treasury Department, not obviously connected with the war. Furthermore, the number of federal officials did not return to prewar levels after each war. Though there was some reduction, each war left the number of federal employees larger than before.[13]

It is not hard to understand how this happens. During wartime, almost every government agency argues that its activities have *some* relation to the war effort, and few legislators want to be caught voting against something that may help that effort. Hence in 1944, the Reindeer Service in Alaska, an agency of the Interior Department, asked for more employees because reindeer are "a valued asset in military planning."

A CHANGE IN ROLE

Today's bureaucracy is largely a product of two events: the depression of the 1930s (and the concomitant New Deal program of President Roosevelt) and World War II. Though many agencies have been added since then, the basic features of the bureaucracy were set mainly as a result of changes in public attitudes and in constitutional interpretation that occurred during these periods. The government was now expected to play an active role in dealing with economic and social problems. In the late 1930s, the Supreme Court reversed its earlier decisions (see Chapter 16) on the question of delegating legislative powers to administrative agencies and upheld laws by which Congress merely instructs agencies to make decisions that serve "the public interest" in some area.[14] As a result, it was possible for President Nixon to set up in 1971 a system of price and wage controls based on a statute that simply authorized the president "to issue such orders and regulations as he may deem appropriate to stabilize prices, rents, wages, and salaries."[15] The Cost of Living Council and other agencies that Nixon established to carry out this order were run by appointed officials who had the legal authority to make sweeping decisions based on general statutory language.

> **laissez-faire** An economic theory that government should not regulate or interfere with commerce.

World War II was the first occasion during which the government made heavy use of federal income taxes—on individuals and corporations—to finance its activities. Between 1940 and 1945, total federal tax collections increased from about $5 billion to nearly $44 billion. The end of the war brought no substantial tax reduction: the country believed that a high level of military preparedness continued to be necessary and that various social programs begun before the war should enjoy the heavy funding made possible by wartime taxes. Tax receipts continued, by and large, to grow. Before 1913, when the Sixteenth Amendment to the Constitution was passed, the federal government could not collect income taxes at all (it financed itself largely from customs duties and excise taxes). From 1913 to 1940, income taxes were small (in 1940, the average American paid only $7 in federal income taxes). World War II created the first great financial boom for the government, permitting the sustained expansion of a wide variety of programs and thus entrenching a large number of administrators in Washington.[16]

Although it is still too soon to tell, a third event—the September 11, 2001, terrorist attacks on the United States—could affect bureaucracy as profoundly as the depression of the 1930s and World War II. A law creating a massive new cabinet agency, the Department of Homeland Security (DHS), was passed in late 2002. Within two years of its creation, the DHS had consolidated under its authority 22 smaller federal agencies with nearly 180,000 federal employees (third behind Defense and Veterans Affairs) and over $40 billion in budgets (fourth behind Defense, Health and Human Services, and Education). In addition, dozens of intergovernmental grant-making programs came under the authority of the DHS. In late 2004, Congress passed another law that promised, over time, to centralize under a single director of national intelligence the work of the over seventy federal agencies authorized to spend money on counterterrorist activities. But even after related reforms in 2006, dozens of different agencies were still authorized to spend money on counterterrorism activities; and, in 2008, the General Accounting Office (GAO) once again ranked the DHS, which by then had grown to over 155,000 employees, among those agencies with especially serious management problems.[17]

The Federal Bureaucracy Today

No president wants to admit that he has increased the size of the bureaucracy. He can avoid saying this by pointing out that the number of civilians working for the federal government, excluding postal workers, has not increased significantly in recent years and is about the same today (2 million persons) as it was in 1960, and less than it was during World War II. This explanation is true but misleading, for it neglects the roughly 13 million people who work *indirectly* for Washington as employees of private firms and state or local agencies that are largely, if not entirely, supported by federal funds.

There are nearly three persons earning their living indirectly from the federal government for every one earning it directly. While federal employment has remained quite stable, employment among federal contractors and consultants and in state and local governments has mushroomed. Indeed, most federal bureaucrats, like most other people who work for the federal government, live outside Washington, D.C.

In recent decades, federal spending as a percentage of the gross domestic product has fluctuated, but usually within a narrow range, hovering around 20 percent on average (or about twice what it was, on average, in the decades just before World War II). Also, since the mid-1970s, the number of pages in the *Federal Register*—a rough measure of how expansive federal regulations are—dipped in the 1980s but rose steeply in the 1990s, ending the decade at around 70,000 pages (about the number it had in 1975). But the total number of federal civilian employees fell by about 10 percent from 1970 to 2007.

As Table 15.1 shows, from 1990 to 2007, nearly every federal executive department reduced its workforce. The U.S. Department of State grew by over a third, but that represented fewer than 10,000 new staff. The single major exception was the U.S. Department of Justice (DOJ). This exception is explained almost entirely by the growth in just one DOJ unit—and one of the few federal agencies anywhere in the bureaucracy that was slow to join the trend toward what we described earlier in this chapter as government by proxy—the Federal Bureau of Prisons (BOP). The BOP administers over a hundred facilities, from maximum-security prisons to community corrections centers, all across the country. Between 1990 and 2009, its staff grew by 90 percent, or about 17,000 new employees; but the prisoner populations these federal workers supervised grew by 355 percent, or nearly 150,000.

The power of the federal bureaucracy cannot be measured by the number of employees, however. A bureaucracy of 5 million persons would have little power if each employee did nothing but type letters or file documents, whereas a bureaucracy of only 100 persons would have awesome power if each member were able to make arbitrary life-and-death decisions affecting the rest of us. The power of the bureaucracy depends on the extent to which appointed officials have **discretionary authority**—that is, the ability to choose courses of action and to make policies not spelled out in advance by laws. The volume of regulations issued and the amount of money spent

Table 15.1 Federal Civilian Employment, 1990–2007

	1990	2007	Percent Change
All executive departments (in millions)	2.065	1.696	−17.8
(In thousands)			
State	25.2	34.6	+37.3%
Treasury	158.6	111.5	−29.6
Defense	1,034	673.7	−34.8
Justice	83.9	106.9	+27.4
Interior	77.6	70.2	−9.5
Agriculture	122.5	99.6	−18.6
Commerce	69.9	40.1	−42.6
Labor	17.7	15.8	−10.7
Health and Human Services	123.9	61.2	−50.6
Housing and Urban Development	13.5	9.7	−28.1
Transportation	67.3	53.5	−20.5
Energy	17.7	14.6	−17.5
Education	4.70	4.1	−12.7
Veterans Affairs	248.1	245.5	−1
Homeland Security	N/A	155.3	N/A

Source: *Statistical Abstract of the United States 2009*. Table 481.

Federal Bureau of Prisons	1990	2009	Percent Change
Staff	19.0	36.2	+90.5
Inmates	58.0	206.1	+355

Sources: Federal Bureau of Prisons Weekly Population Report and Quick Facts (available at http://www.bop.gov/locations/weekly_report.jsp; and http://www.bop.gov/news/quick.jsp#5).

have risen much faster than the number of federal employees who write the regulations and spend the money.

By this test, the power of the federal bureaucracy has grown enormously. Congress has delegated substantial authority to administrative agencies in three areas: (1) paying subsidies to particular groups and organizations in society (farmers, veterans, scientists, schools, universities, hospitals); (2) transferring money from the federal government to state and local governments (the grant-in-aid programs described in Chapter 3); and (3) devising and enforcing regulations for various sectors of society and the economy. Some of these administrative functions, such as grants-in-aid to states, are closely monitored by Congress; others, such as the regulatory programs, usually operate with a greater degree of independence. These delegations of power, especially in the areas of paying subsidies and regulating the economy, did not become commonplace until the 1930s, and then only after the Supreme Court decided that such delegations were constitutional. Today, by contrast, appointed officials can decide, within rather broad limits, who shall own a television station, what safety features automobiles shall have, what kinds of scientific research shall be specially encouraged, what drugs shall appear on the market, which dissident groups shall be investigated, what fumes an industrial smokestack may emit, which corporate mergers shall be allowed, what use shall be made of national forests, and what prices crop and dairy farmers shall receive for their products.

discretionary authority The extent to which appointed bureaucrats can choose courses of action and make policies not spelled out in advance by laws.

If appointed officials have this kind of power, then how they use it is of paramount importance in understanding modern government. There are, broadly, four factors that may explain the behavior of these officials:

1. The manner in which they are recruited and rewarded
2. Their personal attributes, such as their socioeconomic backgrounds and their political attitudes
3. The nature of their jobs
4. The constraints that outside forces—political superiors, legislators, interest groups, journalists—impose on their agencies

RECRUITMENT AND RETENTION

The federal civil service system was designed to recruit qualified people on the basis of merit, not political patronage, and to retain and promote employees on the basis of performance, not political favoritism. Many appointed federal officials belong to the **competitive service.** This means they are appointed only after they have passed a written examination administered by the Office of Personnel Management (OPM) or met certain selection criteria (such as training, educational attainments, or prior experience) devised by the hiring agency and approved by the OPM. Where competition for a job exists and candidates can be ranked by their scores or records, the agency must usually appoint one of the three top-ranking candidates.

competitive service
The government offices to which people are appointed on the basis of merit, as ascertained by a written exam or by applying certain selection criteria.

In recent years, the competitive service system has become decentralized, so that each agency now hires its own people without an OPM referral, and examinations have become less common. In 1952, more than 86 percent of all federal employees were civil servants hired by the competitive service; by 1996, that figure had fallen to less than 54 percent. This decentralization and the greater use of ways other than exams to hire employees were caused by three things. First, the old OPM system was cumbersome and often not relevant to the complex needs of departments. Second, these agencies had a need for more professionally trained employees—lawyers, biologists, engineers, and computer specialists—who could not be ranked on the basis of some standard exam. And third, civil rights groups pressed Washington to make the racial composition of the federal bureaucracy look more like the racial composition of the nation.

Moreover, the kinds of workers being recruited into the federal civil service have changed. For example, blue-collar employment has fallen while the federal government's white-collar work force has become more diverse occupationally. As one expert on civil service reform has noted, the "need to recruit and retain physicists, biologists, oceanographers, nurses, statisticians, botanists, and epidemiologists, as well as large numbers of engineers, lawyers, and accountants, now preoccupies federal personnel managers."[18]

Employees hired outside the competitive service are part of the excepted service. They now make up almost half of all workers. Though not hired by the OPM, they still are typically hired in a nonpartisan fashion. Some are hired by agencies—such as the CIA, the FBI, and the Postal Service—that have their own selection procedures.

About 3 percent of the excepted employees are appointed on grounds other than or in addition to merit. These legal exceptions exist to permit the president to select, for policymaking and politically sensitive posts, people who are in agreement with his policy views. Such appointments are generally of three kinds:

1. Presidential appointments authorized by statute (cabinet and subcabinet officers, judges, U.S. marshals and U.S. attorneys, ambassadors, and members of various boards and commissions).
2. "Schedule C" appointments to jobs described as having a "confidential or policy-determining character" below the level of cabinet or subcabinet posts (including executive assistants, special aides, and confidential secretaries).
3. Noncareer executive assignments (NEAs) given to high-ranking members of the regular competitive civil service or to persons brought into the civil service at these high levels. These people are deeply involved in the advocacy of presidential programs or participate in policymaking.

These three groups of excepted appointments constitute the patronage available to a president and his administration. When President Kennedy took office in 1961, he had 451 political jobs to fill. When President Barack Obama took office in 2009, he had more than four times that number, including nearly four times the number of top cabinet posts. Scholars disagree over whether this proliferation of political appointees has improved or worsened Washington's performance, but one thing is clear: widespread presidential patronage is hardly unprecedented. In the 19th century, practically every federal job was a patronage job. For example, when Grover Cleveland, support. Though presidents may have liked in theory the idea of hiring and firing subordinates at will, most felt that the demands for patronage were impossible either to satisfy or to ignore. Furthermore, by increasing the coverage of the merit system a president could "blanket in" patronage appointees already holding office, thus making it difficult or impossible for the next administration to fire them.

The Buddy System

The actual recruitment of civil servants, especially in middle- and upper-level jobs, is somewhat more complicated, and slightly more political, than the laws and rules might suggest. Though many people enter the federal bureaucracy by learning of a job, filling out an application, perhaps taking a test, and being hired, many also enter on a "name-request" basis. A **name-request job** is one that is filled by a person whom an agency has already identified. In this respect, the federal government is not so different from private, business. A person learns of a job from somebody who already has one, or the head of a bureau decides in advance whom he or she wishes to hire. The agency must still send a form describing the job to the OPM, but it also names the person whom the agency wants to appoint. Sometimes the job is even described in such a way that the person named is the only one who can qualify for it. Occasionally, this tailor-made, name-request job is offered to a person at the insistence of a member of Congress who wants a political supporter taken care of; more often it is made available because the bureaucracy itself knows whom it wishes to hire and wants to circumvent an elaborate search. This is the "buddy system."

name-request job A job filled by a person whom an agency has already identified.

The buddy system does not necessarily produce poor employees. Indeed, it is frequently a way of hiring people known to the agency as capable of handling the position. It also opens up the possibility of hiring people whose policy views are congenial to those already in office. Such networking is based on shared policy views, not (as once was the case) on narrow partisan affiliations. For example, bureaucrats in consumer protection agencies recruit new staff from private groups with an interest in consumer protection, such as the various organizations associated with Ralph Nader, or from academics who have a proconsumer inclination.

There has always been an informal "old boys' network" among those who move in and out of high-level government posts; with the increasing appointment of women to these jobs, there has begun to emerge

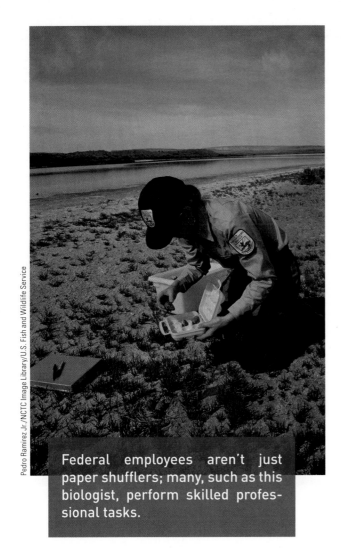

Pedro Ramirez, Jr./NCTC Image Library/U.S. Fish and Wildlife Service

Federal employees aren't just paper shufflers; many, such as this biologist, perform skilled professional tasks.

a Democrat, became president in 1885, he replaced some 40,000 Republican postal employees with Democrats.

Ironically, two years earlier, in 1883, the passage of the Pendleton Act had begun a slow but steady transfer of federal jobs from the patronage to the merit system. It may seem strange that a political party in power (the Republicans) would be willing to relinquish its patronage in favor of a merit-based appointment system. Two factors made it possible for the Republicans to pass the Pendleton Act: (1) public outrage over the abuses of the spoils system, highlighted by the assassination of President James Garfield by a man always described in the history books as a "disappointed office seeker" (*lunatic* would be a more accurate term); and (2) the fear that if the Democrats came to power on a wave of antispoils sentiment, existing Republican officeholders would be fired. (The Democrats won anyway.)

The merit system spread to encompass most of the federal bureaucracy, generally with presidential

How Things Work

A Day in the Life of a Bureaucrat

Here is how the commissioner of the Social Security Administration (SSA), a high-level bureaucrat, spent a typical day:

5:45 A.M.	Arise.
6:50 A.M.	Leave for the office.
7:30 A.M.	Read newspapers.
8:00 A.M.	Meet with deputy commissioner.
8:30 A.M.	Brief cabinet secretary on Social Security data.*
9:45 A.M.	Decide how to respond to press criticisms.
10:05 A.M.	Leave for meeting in another building.
11:30 A.M.	Meet with top staff.
1:00 P.M.	Meet with bureau chiefs on half a dozen issues.
2:45 P.M.	Meet with a deputy to discuss next year's budget.
3:30 P.M.	Meet with business executive about use of computers in SSA.
4:30 P.M.	Meet with deputy in charge of Medicare to discuss plan for national health insurance.
5:10 P.M.	Catch up on phone calls; meet with committee concerned with drug abuse.
6:10 P.M.	Leave for home. Get out of attending a dinner meeting in Washington.

As is obvious, high-level bureaucrats spend most of their time discussing things in meetings. It is in such meetings that government policy is made.

*SSA was part of the Department of Health and Human Services but no longer is.

Source: Adapted from "A Day in the Life of a Government Executive," in *Inside the System*, ed. Charles Peters and Nicholas Leamann, 4th ed. (New York: Holt, Rinehart and Winston, 1979), 205–213.

an old girls' network as well.[19] In a later section, we will consider whether, or in what ways, these recruitment patterns make a difference.

Firing a Bureaucrat

The great majority of bureaucrats who are part of the civil service and who do not hold presidential appointments have jobs that are, for all practical purposes, beyond reach. An executive must go through elaborate steps to fire, demote, or suspend a civil servant. Realistically, this means no one is fired or demoted unless his or her superior is prepared to invest a great deal of time and effort in the attempt. In 1987, about 2,600 employees who had completed their probationary period were fired for misconduct or poor performance. That is about one-tenth of 1 percent of all federal employees. It is hard to believe that a large private company would fire only one-tenth of 1 percent of its workers in a given year. It's also impossible to believe that, as is often the case in Washington, it would take a year to fire anyone. To cope with this problem, federal executives have devised a number of stratagems for bypassing

or forcing out civil servants with whom they cannot work—denying them promotions, transferring them to undesirable locations, or assigning them to meaningless work.

With the passage of the Civil Service Reform Act of 1978, Congress recognized that many high-level positions in the civil service have important policy-making responsibilities and that the president and his cabinet officers ought to have more flexibility in recruiting, assigning, and paying such people. Accordingly, the act created the Senior Executive Service (SES), about 8,000 top federal managers who can (in theory) be hired, fired, and transferred more easily than ordinary civil servants. Moreover, the act stipulated that members of the SES would be eligible for substantial cash bonuses if they performed their duties well. (To protect the rights of SES members, anyone who is removed from the SES is guaranteed a job elsewhere in the government.)

Things did not work out quite as the sponsors of the SES had hoped. Though most eligible civil servants joined it, there was only a modest increase in the

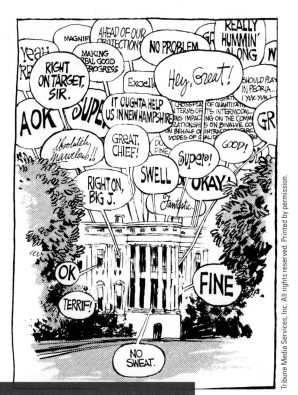

Tribune Media Services, Inc. All rights reserved. Printed by permission.

One barrier to improving presidential control of the federal bureaucracy is that even the White House has become a large bureaucracy.

proportion of higher-ranking positions in agencies that were filled by transfer from another agency; the cash bonuses did not prove to be an important incentive (perhaps because the base salaries of top bureaucrats did not keep up with inflation); and hardly any member of the SES was actually fired. Two years after the SES was created, less than one-half of 1 percent of its members had received an unsatisfactory rating, and none had been fired. Nor does the SES give the president a large opportunity to make political appointments: only 10 percent of the SES can be selected from outside the existing civil service. And no SES member can be transferred involuntarily.

The Agency's Point of View

When one realizes that most agencies are staffed by people recruited by those agencies, sometimes on a name-request basis, and virtually immune from dismissal, it becomes clear that the recruitment and retention policies of the civil service work to ensure that most bureaucrats will have an "agency" point of view. Even with the encouragement for transfers created by the SES, most government agencies are dominated by people who have not served in any other agency and who have been in government service most of their lives. This fact has some

advantages: it means that most top-tier bureaucrats are experts in the procedures and policies of their agencies and that there will be a substantial degree of continuity in agency behavior no matter which political party happens to be in power.

But the agency point of view has its costs as well. A political executive entering an agency with responsibility for shaping its direction will discover that he or she must carefully win the support of career subordinates. A subordinate has an infinite capacity for discreet sabotage and can make life miserable for a political superior by delaying action, withholding information, following the rule book with literal exactness, or making an "end run" around a superior to mobilize members of Congress sympathetic to the bureaucrat's point of view. For instance, when one political executive wanted to downgrade a bureau in his department, he found, naturally, that the bureau chief was opposed. The bureau chief spoke to some friendly lobbyists and a key member of Congress. When the political executive asked the congressman whether he had any problem with the contemplated reorganization, the congressman replied, "No, you have the problem, because if you touch that bureau, I'll cut your job out of the budget."[20]

How Things Work

Firing a Bureaucrat

To fire or demote a member of the competitive civil service, these procedures must be followed:

1. The employee must be given written notice at least thirty days in advance that he or she is to be fired or demoted for incompetence or misconduct.

2. The written notice must contain a statement of reasons, including specific examples of unacceptable performance.

3. The employee has the right to an attorney and to reply, orally or in writing, to the charges.

4. The employee has the right to appeal any adverse action to the Merit Systems Protection Board

(MSPB), a three-person, bipartisan body appointed by the president with the consent of the Senate.

5. The MSPB must grant the employee a hearing, at which the employee has the right to have an attorney present.

6. The employee has the right to appeal the MSPB decision to a U.S. court of appeals, which can hold new hearings.

PERSONAL ATTRIBUTES

A second factor that might shape the way bureaucrats use their power is their personal attributes. These include their social class, education, and personal political beliefs. The federal civil service as a whole looks very much like a cross section of American society in the education, sex, race, and social origins of its members (see Figure 15.1). But as with many other employers, African Americans and other minorities are most likely heavily represented in the lowest grade levels and tend to be underrepresented at the executive level. At the higher-ranking levels, where the most power is found—say, in the supergrade ranks

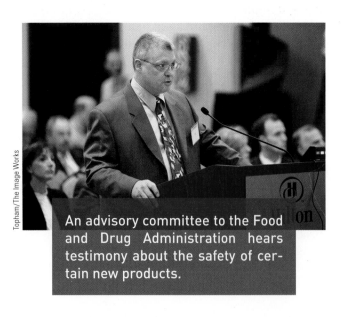

Topham/The Image Works

An advisory committee to the Food and Drug Administration hears testimony about the safety of certain new products.

of GS 16 through GS 18—the typical civil servant is a middle-aged white male with a college degree whose father was somewhat more advantaged than the average citizen. In the great majority of cases, this individual is in fact very different from the typical American in both background and personal beliefs.

Because political appointees and career bureaucrats are unrepresentative of the average American, and because of their supposed occupational self-interest, some critics have speculated that the people holding these jobs think about politics and government in ways very different from the public at large. Some surveys do find that career bureaucrats are more likely than other people to hold liberal views, to trust government, and to vote for Democrats.[21]

It is important, however, not to overgeneralize from such differences. For example, whereas Clinton appointees (virtually all of them strong Democrats) were more liberal than average citizens, Reagan appointees (virtually all of them loyal Republicans) were undoubtedly more conservative than average citizens. Likewise, career civil servants are more pro-government than the public at large, but on most specific policy questions, federal bureaucrats do not have extreme positions. Still, those employed in "activist" agencies such as the Federal Trade Commission, Environmental Protection Agency, and Food and Drug Administration tend to have more liberal views than those who work for the more "traditional" agencies such as the departments of Agriculture, Commerce, and the Treasury. Even when the bureaucrats come from roughly the

Figure 15.1

Characteristics of Federal Civilian Employees, 1960 and 2005

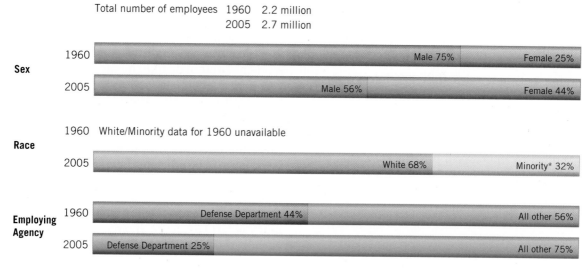

Total number of employees 1960 2.2 million
2005 2.7 million

*Blacks, Native Americans, Hispanics, Asians, and Pacific Islanders

Sources: Statistical Abstract of the United States, 1961, 392–394; Statistical Abstract of the United States, 2009, table 482.

same social backgrounds, their policy views seem to reflect the type of government work that they do. For example, studies dating back decades have found that Democrats and people with liberal views tend to be overrepresented in social service agencies, whereas Republicans and people with conservative views tend to be overrepresented in defense agencies.[22] But it is not clear whether such differences in attitudes are produced by the jobs that people hold or whether certain jobs attract people with certain beliefs. Probably both forces are at work.

DO BUREAUCRATS SABOTAGE THEIR POLITICAL BOSSES?

Because it is so hard to fire career bureaucrats, it is often said that these people will sabotage any actions by their political superiors with which they disagree. And since civil servants tend to have liberal views, it has been conservative presidents and cabinet secretaries who have usually expressed this worry.

There is no doubt that some bureaucrats will drag their heels if they don't like their bosses, and a few will block actions they oppose. However, most bureaucrats try to carry out the policies of their superiors even when they personally disagree with them. When David Stockman was director of the OMB, he set out to make sharp cuts in government spending programs in accordance with the wishes of his boss, President Reagan. He later published a book complaining about all the people in the White House and Congress who worked against him.[23] But nowhere in the book is there any major criticism of the civil servants at the OMB. It appears that whatever these people thought about Stockman and Reagan, they loyally tried to carry out Stockman's policies.

Bureaucrats tend to be loyal to political superiors who deal with them cooperatively and constructively. An agency head who tries to ignore or discredit them can be in for a tough time, however. The powers of obstruction available to aggrieved bureaucrats are formidable. Such people can leak embarrassing stories to Congress or to the media, help interest groups mobilize against the agency head, and discover a thousand procedural reasons why a new course of action won't work.

The exercise of some of those bureaucratic powers is protected by the Whistle Blower Protection Act. Passed in 1989, the law created the Office of Special Counsel, charged with investigating complaints from bureaucrats that they were punished after reporting to Congress about waste, fraud, or abuse in their agencies.

It may seem odd that bureaucrats, who have great job security, would not always act in accordance with their personal beliefs instead of in accordance with the wishes of their bosses. Bureaucratic sabotage, in this view, ought to be very common. But bureaucratic cooperation with superiors is not odd, once you take into account the nature of a bureaucrat's job.

If you are a voter at the polls, your beliefs will clearly affect how you vote (see Chapter 7). But if you are the second baseman for the Boston Red Sox, your political beliefs, social background, and education will have nothing to do with how you field ground balls. Sociologists like to call the different things that people do in their lives "roles" and to distinguish between roles that are loosely structured (such as the role of voter) and those that are highly structured (such as that of second baseman). Personal attitudes greatly affect loosely structured roles and only slightly affect highly structured ones. Applied to the federal bureaucracy, this suggests that civil servants performing tasks that are routinized (such as filling out forms), tasks that are closely defined by laws and rules (such as issuing welfare checks), or tasks that are closely monitored by others (supervisors, special-interest groups, the media) will probably perform them in ways that can only partially be explained, if at all, by their personal attitudes. Civil servants performing complex, loosely defined tasks that are not closely monitored may carry out their work in ways powerfully influenced by their attitudes.

Among the loosely defined tasks are those performed by professionals, and so the values of these people may influence how they behave. An increasing number of lawyers, economists, engineers, and physicians are hired to work in federal agencies. These men and women have received extensive training that produces not only a set of skills, but also a set of attitudes as to what is important and valuable. For example, the Federal Trade Commission (FTC), charged with preventing unfair methods of competition among businesses, employs two kinds of professionals—lawyers, organized into a Bureau of Competition, and economists, organized into a Bureau of Economics. Lawyers are trained to draw up briefs and argue cases in court and are taught the legal standards by which they will know whether they have a chance of winning a case or not. Economists are trained to analyze how a competitive economy works and what costs consumers must bear if the goods and services are produced by a monopoly (one firm controlling the market) or an oligopoly (a small number of firms dominating the market).

Because of their training and attitudes, lawyers in the FTC prefer to bring cases against a business firm that has done something clearly illegal, such as attending secret meetings with competitors to rig the prices that will be charged to a purchaser. These cases appeal to lawyers because there is usually a victim (the purchaser or a rival company) who complains to the government, the illegal behavior can be proved in a court of law, and the case can be completed rather quickly.

Economists, on the other hand, are trained to measure the value of a case not by how quickly it can be proved in court, but by whether the illegal practice imposes large or small costs on the consumer. FTC economists often dislike the cases that appeal to lawyers. The economists feel that the amount of money that such cases save the consumer is often small and that the cases are a distraction from the major issues—such as whether IBM unfairly dominates the computer business or whether General Motors is too large to be efficient. Lawyers, in turn, are leery of big cases, because the facts are hard to prove and they may take forever to decide (one blockbuster case can drag through the courts for ten years). In many federal agencies divergent professional values such as these help explain how power is used.

CULTURE AND CAREERS

Unlike the lawyers and economists working in the FTC, the government bureaucrats in a typical agency don't have a lot of freedom to choose a course of action. Their jobs are spelled out not only by the laws, rules, and routines of their agency, but also by the informal understandings among fellow employees as to how they are supposed to act. These understandings are the *culture* of the agency.[24]

If you belong to the air force, you can do a lot of things, but only one thing really counts: flying airplanes, especially advanced jet fighters and bombers. The culture of the air force is a pilots' culture. If you belong to the navy, you have more choices: fly jet aircraft or operate nuclear submarines. Both jobs provide status and a chance for promotion to the highest ranks. By contrast, sailing minesweepers or transport ships (or worse, having a desk job and not sailing anything at all) is not a very rewarding job. The culture of the CIA emphasizes working overseas as a clandestine agent; staying in Washington as a report writer is not as good for your career. The culture of the State Department rewards skill in political negotiations; being an expert on international economics or embassy security is much less rewarding.

You can usually tell what kind of culture an agency has by asking an employee, "If you want to get ahead here, what sort of jobs should you take?" The jobs that are career enhancing are part of the culture; the jobs that are not career enhancing (NCE in bureaucratic lingo) are not part of it.

Being part of a strong culture is good—up to a point. It motivates employees to work hard in order

The "Rules" of Politics

Learning Bureaucratese

A few simple rules, if remembered, will enable you to speak and write in the style of a government official.

- **Use nouns as if they were verbs.** Don't say, "We must set priorities"; say instead, "We must prioritize."

- **Use adjectives as if they were verbs.** Don't say, "We put the report in final form"; say instead, "We finalized the report."

- **Use several words where one word would do.** Don't say, "now"; say instead, "at this point in time."

- **Never use ordinary words where unusual ones can be found.** Don't say that you "made a choice"; say that you "selected an option."

- **No matter what subject you are discussing, employ the language of sports and war.** Never say, "progress"; say, "breakthrough." Never speak of a "compromise"; instead consider "adopting a fallback position."

- **Avoid active verbs.** Never say, "Study the problem"; say instead, "It is felt that the problem should be subjected to further study."

MISS WATSON, TURN SOME OF THESE NOUNS INTO VERBS FOR ME. I WANT THIS TO SOUND IMPORTANT.

© 1986 by NEA, Inc. THAVES 4-11

Thaves. Reprinted with permission.

to win the respect of their coworkers as well as the approval of their bosses. But a strong culture also makes it hard to change an agency. FBI agents for many years resisted getting involved in civil rights or organized crime cases, and diplomats in the State Department didn't pay much attention to embassy security. These important jobs were not a career-enhancing part of the culture.

CONSTRAINTS

The biggest difference between a government agency and a private organization is the vastly greater number of constraints on the agency. Unlike a business firm, the typical government bureau cannot hire, fire, build, or sell without going through procedures set down in laws. How much money it pays its members is determined by statute, not by the market. Not only the goals of an agency but often its exact procedures are spelled out by Congress.

At one time, the Soil Conservation Service was required by law to employ at least 14,177 full-time workers. The State Department has been forbidden by law from opening a diplomatic post in Antigua or Barbuda but forbidden from closing a post anywhere else. The Agency for International Development (which administers our foreign-aid program) has been given by Congress 33 objectives and 75 priorities and must send to Congress 288 reports each year. When it buys military supplies, the Defense Department must give a "fair proportion" of its contracts to small businesses, especially those operated by "socially and economically disadvantaged individuals," and must buy from American firms even if, in some cases, buying abroad would be cheaper. Some of the more general constraints include the following:

- Administrative Procedure Act (1946). Before adopting a new rule or policy, an agency must give notice, solicit comments, and (often) hold hearings.

- Freedom of Information Act (1966). Citizens have the right to inspect all government records except those containing military, intelligence, or trade secrets or revealing private personnel actions.

- National Environmental Policy Act (1969). Before undertaking any major action affecting the environment, an agency must issue an environmental impact statement.

- Privacy Act (1974). Government files about individuals, such as Social Security and tax records, must be kept confidential.

- Open Meeting Law (1976). Every part of every agency meeting must be open to the public unless certain matters (for example, military or trade secrets) are being discussed.

One of the biggest constraints on bureaucratic action is that Congress rarely gives any job to a single agency. Stopping drug trafficking is the task of the Customs Service, the FBI, the Drug Enforcement Administration, the Border Patrol, and the Defense Department (among others). Disposing of the assets of failed savings-and-loan associations is the job of the Resolution Funding Corporation, Resolution Trust Corporation, Federal Housing Finance Board, Office of Thrift Supervision in the Treasury Department, Federal Deposit Insurance Corporation, Federal Reserve Board, and Justice Department (among others).

The effects of these constraints on agency behavior are not surprising.

- The government will often act slowly. (The more constraints that must be satisfied, the longer it will take to get anything done.)

- The government will sometimes act inconsistently. (What is done to meet one constraint—for example, freedom of information—may endanger another constraint—for example, privacy.)

- It will be easier to block action than to take action. (The constraints ensure that lots of voices will be heard; the more voices heard, the more they may cancel each other out.)

- Lower-ranking employees will be reluctant to make decisions on their own. (Having many constraints means having many ways to get into trouble; to avoid trouble, let your boss make the decision.)

- Citizens will complain of red tape. (The more constraints to serve, the more forms to fill out.)

These constraints do not mean government bureaucracy is powerless, only that, however great its power, it tends to be clumsy. That clumsiness arises not from the fact that the people who work for agencies are dull or incompetent, but from the complicated political environment in which that work must be done.

The "Rules" of Politics

"Laws" of Bureaucratic Procedure

Acheson's Rule A memorandum is written not to inform the reader but to protect the writer.

Boren's Laws

When in doubt, mumble.

When in trouble, delegate.

When in charge, ponder.

Chapman's Rules of Committees

Never arrive on time, or you will be stamped a beginner.

Don't say anything until the meeting is half over; this stamps you as being wise.

Be as vague as possible; this prevents irritating others.

When in doubt, suggest that a subcommittee be appointed.

Meskimen's Law There's never time to do it right but always time to do it over.

Murphy's Law If anything can go wrong, it will.

O'Toole's Corollary to Murphy's Law Murphy was an optimist.

Parkinson's First Law Work expands to fill the time available for its completion.

Parkinson's Second Law Expenditure rises to meet income.

Peter Principle In every hierarchy, each employee tends to rise to his level of incompetence; thus, every post tends to be filled by an incompetent employee.

Robertson's Rule The more directives you issue to solve a problem, the worse it gets.

Smith's Principle Never do anything for the first time.

The moral of the story: the next time you get mad at a bureaucrat, ask yourself, Why would a rational, intelligent person behave that way? Chances are you will discover there are good reasons for that action. You would probably behave the same way if you were working for the same organization.

Topham/The Image Works

The real federal bureaucracy is bigger than just who works for the national government. Because defense contractors depend on government contracts, the bureaucracy includes people who work in these private firms.

Why So Many Constraints?

Government agencies behave as they do in large part because of the many different goals they must pursue and the complex rules they must follow. Where does all this red tape come from?

From us. From us, the people.

Every goal, every constraint, every bit of red tape, was put in place by Congress, the courts, the White House, or the agency itself responding to the demands of some influential faction. Civil rights groups want every agency to hire and buy from women and minorities. Environmental groups want every agency to file environmental impact statements. Industries being regulated want every new agency policy to be formulated only after a lengthy public hearing with lots of lawyers present. Labor unions also want those hearings so that they can argue against industry lawyers. Everybody who sells something to the government wants a "fair chance" to make the sale, and so everybody insists that government contracts be awarded only after complex procedures are followed. A lot of people don't trust the government, and so they insist that everything it does be done in the sunshine—no secrets, no closed meetings, no hidden files.

If we wanted agencies to pursue their main goal with more vigor and less encumbering red tape, we would have to ask Congress, the courts, or the White House to repeal some of these constraints. In other words, we would have to be willing to give up something we want in order to get something else we want even more. But politics does not encourage

people to make these trade-offs; instead it encourages us to expect to get everything—efficiency, fairness, help for minorities—all at once.

AGENCY ALLIES

Despite these constraints, government bureaucracies are not powerless. In fact, some of them actively seek certain constraints. They do so because it is a way of cementing a useful relationship with a congressional committee or an interest group.

At one time scholars described the relationship between an agency, a committee, and an interest group as an **iron triangle.** For example, the Department of Veterans Affairs, the House and Senate committees on veterans' affairs, and veterans' organizations (such as the American Legion) would form a tight, mutually advantageous alliance. The department would do what the committees wanted and in return get political support and budget appropriations; the committee members would do what the veterans' groups wanted and in return get votes and campaign contributions. Iron triangles are examples of what are called *client politics*.

> *iron triangle* A close relationship between an agency, a congressional committee, and an interest group.

Many agencies still have important allies in Congress and the private sector, especially those bureaus that serve the needs of specific sectors of the economy or regions of the country. The Department of Agriculture works closely with farm organizations, the Department of the Interior with groups interested in obtaining low-cost irrigation or grazing rights, and the Department of Housing and Urban Development with mayors and real-estate developers.

Sometimes these allies are so strong that they can defeat a popular president. For years, President Reagan tried to abolish the Small Business Administration (SBA), arguing that its program of loans to small firms was wasteful and ridden with favoritism. But Congress, reacting to pressures from small-business groups, rallied to the SBA's defense. As a result, Reagan had to oversee an agency that he didn't want.

But iron triangles are much less common today than once was the case. Politics of late has become far more complicated. For one thing, the number and variety of interest groups have increased so much in recent years that scarcely any agency is not subject to pressures from several competing interests instead of only from one powerful interest. For another, the growth of subcommittees in Congress has meant most agencies are subject to control by many different legislative groups, often with very different concerns. Finally, the courts have made it much easier for all kinds of individuals and interests to intervene in agency affairs.

As a result, nowadays government agencies face a bewildering variety of competing groups and legislative subcommittees that constitute not a loyal group of allies, but a fiercely contentious collection of critics.

The Environmental Protection Agency is caught between the demands of environmentalists and those of industry organizations, the Occupational Safety and Health Administration between the pressures of labor and those of business, and the Federal Communications Commission between the desires of broadcasters and those of cable television companies. Even the Department of Agriculture faces not a unified group of farmers, but many different farmers split into rival groups, depending on the crops they raise, the regions in which they live, and the attitudes they have toward the relative merits of farm subsidies or free markets.

issue network A network of people in Washington, D.C.–based interest groups, on congressional staffs, in universities and think tanks, and in the mass media, who regularly discuss and advocate public policies.

authorization legislation Legislative permission to begin or continue a government program or agency.

appropriation A legislative grant of money to finance a government program or agency.

Political scientist Hugh Heclo has described the typical government agency today as being embedded not in an iron triangle, but in an **issue network**.[25] These issue networks consist of people in Washington-based interest groups, on congressional staffs, in universities and think tanks, and in the mass media, who regularly debate government policy on a certain subject—say, health care or auto safety. The networks are contentious, split along political, ideological, and economic lines. When a president takes office, he often recruits key agency officials from those members of the issue network who are most sympathetic to his views.

When Jimmy Carter, a Democrat, became president, he appointed to key posts in consumer agencies people who were from that part of the consumer issue network associated with Ralph Nader. Ronald Reagan, a conservative Republican, filled these same jobs with people who were from that part of the issue network holding free market or antiregulation views. When George Bush the elder, a more centrist Republican, took office, he filled these posts with more centrist members of the issue network. Bill Clinton brought back the consumer activists.

Congressional Oversight

The main reason why some interest groups are important to agencies is that they are important to Congress. Not every interest group in the country has substantial access to Congress, but those that do and that are taken seriously by the relevant committees or subcommittees must also be taken seriously by the agency. Furthermore, even apart from interest groups, members of Congress have constitutional powers over agencies and policy interests in how agencies function.

Congressional supervision of the bureaucracy takes several forms. First, no agency may exist (except for a few presidential offices and commissions) without congressional approval. Congress influences—and sometimes determines precisely—agency behavior by the statutes it enacts.

Second, no money may be spent unless it has first been authorized by Congress. **Authorization legislation** originates in a legislative committee (such as Agriculture, Education and Labor, or Public Works) and states the maximum amount of money that an agency may spend on a given program. This authorization may be permanent, it may be for a fixed number of years, or it may be annual (that is, it must be renewed each year, or the program or agency goes out of business).

Third, even funds that have been authorized by Congress cannot be spent unless (in most cases) they are also appropriated. Appropriations usually are made annually, and they originate not with the legislative committees but with the House Appropriations Committee and its various (and influential) subcommittees. An **appropriation** (money formally set aside for a specific use) may be, and often is, for less than the amount authorized. The Appropriations Committee's action thus tends to have a budget-cutting effect. There are some funds that can be spent without an appropriation, but in virtually every part of the bureaucracy, each agency is keenly sensitive to congressional concerns at the time that the annual appropriations process is going on.

THE APPROPRIATIONS COMMITTEE AND LEGISLATIVE COMMITTEES

The fact that an agency budget must be both authorized and appropriated means that each agency serves not one congressional master but several, and that these masters may be in conflict. The real power over an agency's budget is exercised by the Appropriations Committee; the legislative committees are especially important when a substantive law is first passed or an agency is first created, or when an agency is subject to annual authorization.

In the past, the power of the Appropriations Committee was rarely challenged: from 1947 through 1962, fully 90 percent of the House Appropriations Committee's recommendations on expenditures were approved by the full House without change.[26] Furthermore, the Appropriations Committee tends to recommend less money than an agency requests (though some specially favored agencies, such as the FBI, the Soil Conservation Service, and the Forest Service, have tended to get almost everything that they have asked for). Finally, the process of "marking up" (revising, amending, and approving) an agency's budget request gives to the Appropriations Committee, or one of its subcommittees, substantial influence over the policies that the agency follows.

Of late, the appropriations committees have lost some of their great power over government agencies. This has happened in three ways:

First, Congress has created trust funds to pay for the benefits many people receive. The Social Security trust fund is the largest of these. In 2008, it took in $695 billion in Social Security taxes and paid out $516 billion in old-age benefits. There are several other trust funds as well. **Trust funds** operate outside the regular government budget, and the appropriations committees have no control over these expenditures. They are automatic.

Second, Congress has changed the authorization of many programs from permanent or multiyear to annual authorizations. This means that every year the legislative committees, as part of the reauthorization process, get to set limits on what these agencies can spend. This limits the ability of the appropriations committees to determine the spending limits. Before 1959, most authorizations were permanent or multiyear. Now a long list of agencies must be reauthorized every year—the State Department, NASA, military procurement programs of the Defense Department, the Justice Department, the Energy Department, and parts or all of many other agencies.

Third, the existence of huge budget deficits during the 1980s and in the 2000s has meant that much of Congress's time has been taken up with trying (usually not very successfully) to keep spending down. As a result, there has rarely been much time to discuss the merits of various programs or how much ought to be spent on them; instead, attention has been focused on meeting a target spending limit. In 1981, the budget resolution passed by Congress mandated cuts in several programs before the appropriations committees had even completed their work.[27]

In addition to the power of the purse, there are informal ways by which Congress can control the bureaucracy. An individual member of Congress can call an agency head on behalf of a constituent. Most such calls merely seek information, but some result in, or attempt to obtain, special privileges for particular people. Congressional committees may also obtain the right to pass on certain agency decisions. This is called **committee clearance,** and though it usually is not legally binding on the agency, few agency heads will ignore the expressed wish of a committee chair that he or she be consulted before certain actions (such as transferring funds) are taken.

trust funds Funds for government programs collected and spent outside the regular government budget.

committee clearance The ability of a congressional committee to review and approve certain agency decisions in advance and without passing a law.

legislative veto The authority of Congress to block a presidential action after it has taken place. The Supreme Court has held that Congress does not have this power.

THE LEGISLATIVE VETO

For many decades, Congress made frequent use of the legislative veto to control bureaucratic or presidential actions. A **legislative veto** is a requirement that an executive decision must lie before Congress for a specified period (usually 30 or 90 days) before it takes effect. Congress could then veto the decision if a resolution of disapproval was passed by either house (a "one-house veto") or both houses (a "two-house veto"). Unlike laws, such resolutions were not signed by the president. Between 1932 and 1980, about 200 laws were passed providing for a legislative veto, many of them involving presidential proposals to sell arms abroad.

But in June 1983, the Supreme Court declared the legislative veto to be unconstitutional. In the *Chadha* case, the Court held that the Constitution clearly requires in Article I that "every order, resolution, or vote to which the concurrence of the Senate and House of Representatives may be necessary" (with certain minor exceptions) "shall be presented to the President of the United States," who must either approve it or return it with his veto attached. In short, Congress cannot take any action that has the force of law unless the president concurs in that action.[28] At a stroke of the pen parts of 200 laws suddenly became invalid.

At least that happened in theory. In fact, since the *Chadha* decision, Congress has passed a number of laws that contain legislative vetoes, despite the Supreme Court's having ruled against them! (Someone will have to go to court to test the constitutionality of these new provisions.)

Opponents of the legislative veto hope future Congresses will have to pass laws that state much more clearly than before what an agency may or may not do. But it is just as likely that Congress will continue to pass laws stated in general terms and require that agencies implementing those laws report their plans to Congress, so that it will have a chance to enact and send to the president a regular bill disapproving the proposed action. Or Congress may rely on informal (but scarcely weak) means of persuasion, including threats to reduce the appropriations of an agency that does not abide by congressional preferences.

CONGRESSIONAL INVESTIGATIONS

Perhaps the most visible and dramatic form of congressional supervision of an agency is the investigation. Since 1792, when Congress investigated an army defeat by a Native American tribe, congressional investigations of the bureaucracy have been a regular feature—sometimes constructive, sometimes destructive—of legislative-executive relations. The investigative power is not mentioned in the Constitution, but has been inferred from the power to legislate. The Supreme Court has consistently upheld this interpretation, though it has also said that such investigations should not be solely for the purpose of exposing the purely personal affairs of private individuals and must not operate to deprive citizens of their basic rights.[29] Congress may compel a person to attend an investigation by issuing a subpoena; anyone who ignores the subpoena may be punished for contempt. Congress can vote to send the person to jail or can refer the matter to a court for further action. As explained in Chapter 14, the president and his principal subordinates have refused to answer certain congressional inquiries on grounds of "executive privilege."

Although many areas of congressional oversight—budgetary review, personnel controls, investigations—are designed to control the exercise of bureaucratic

red tape Complex bureaucratic rules and procedures that must be followed to get something done.

discretion, other areas are intended to ensure the freedom of certain agencies from effective control, especially by the president. In dozens of cases, Congress has authorized department heads and bureau chiefs to operate independent of presidential preferences. Congress has resisted, for example, presidential efforts to ensure that policies to regulate pollution do not impose excessive costs on the economy, and interest groups have brought suit to prevent presidential coordination of various regulatory agencies. If the bureaucracy sometimes works at cross-purposes, it usually is because Congress—or competing committees in Congress—wants it that way.

Bureaucratic "Pathologies"

Everyone complains about bureaucracy in general (though rarely about bureaucratic agencies that everyone believes are desirable). This chapter should persuade you that it is difficult to say anything about bureaucracy "in general"; there are too many different kinds of agencies, kinds of bureaucrats, and kinds of programs to label the entire enterprise with some single adjective. Nevertheless, many people who recognize the enormous variety among government agencies still believe they all have some general features in common and suffer from certain shared problems or pathologies.

This is true enough, but the reasons for it—and the solutions, if any—are often not understood. There are five major (or at least frequently mentioned) problems with bureaucracies: red tape, conflict, duplication, imperialism, and waste. **Red tape**

At the world's busiest border crossing, cars line up to enter the United States in Tijuana, Mexico.

David McNew/Getty Images

refers to the complex rules and procedures that must be followed to get something done. *Conflict* exists because some agencies seem to be working at cross-purposes with other agencies. (For example, the Agricultural Research Service tells farmers how to grow crops more efficiently, while the Agricultural Stabilization and Conservation Service pays farmers to grow fewer crops or to produce less.) *Duplication* (usually called "wasteful duplication") occurs when two government agencies seem to be doing the same thing, as when the Customs Service and the Drug Enforcement Administration both attempt to intercept illegal drugs being smuggled into the country. *Imperialism* refers to the tendency of agencies to grow without regard to the benefits that their programs confer or the costs that they entail. *Waste* means spending more than is necessary to buy some product or service.

These problems all exist, but they do not necessarily exist because bureaucrats are incompetent or power-hungry. Most exist because of the very nature of government itself. Take red tape: partly we encounter cumbersome rules and procedures because any large organization, governmental or not, must have some way of ensuring that one part of the organization does not operate out of step with another. Business corporations have red tape also; it is to a certain extent a consequence of bigness. But a great amount of governmental red tape is also the result of the need to satisfy legal and political requirements. Government agencies must hire on the basis of "merit," must observe strict accounting rules, must supply Congress with detailed information on their programs, and must allow for citizen access in countless ways. Meeting each need requires rules; enforcing the rules requires forms.

Or take conflict and duplication: they do not occur because bureaucrats enjoy conflict or duplication. (Quite the contrary!) They exist because Congress, in setting up agencies and programs, often wants to achieve a number of different, partially inconsistent goals or finds that it cannot decide which goal it values the most. Congress has 535 members and little strong leadership; it should not be surprising that 535 people will want different things and will sometimes succeed in getting them.

Imperialism results in large measure from government agencies' seeking goals so vague and so difficult to measure that it is hard to tell when they have been attained. When Congress is unclear as to exactly what an agency is supposed to do, the agency will often convert that legislative vagueness into bureaucratic imperialism by taking the largest

possible view of its powers. It may do this on its own; more often it does so because interest groups and judges rush in to fill the vacuum left by Congress. As we saw in Chapter 3, the 1973 Rehabilitation Act was passed with a provision barring discrimination against people with disabilities in any program receiving federal aid. Under pressure from people with disabilities, that lofty but vague goal was converted by the Department of Transportation into a requirement that virtually every big-city bus have a device installed to lift people in wheelchairs on board.

Waste is probably the biggest criticism that people have of the bureaucracy. Everybody has heard stories of the Pentagon's paying $91 for screws that cost 3 cents in the hardware store. President Reagan's "Private Sector Survey on Cost Control," generally known as the Grace Commission (after its chairman, J. Peter Grace), publicized these and other tales in a 1984 report.

No doubt there is waste in government. After all, unlike a business firm worried about maximizing profits, in a government agency there are only weak incentives to keep costs down. If a business employee cuts costs, he or she often receives a bonus or raise, and the firm gets to add the savings to its profits. If a government official cuts costs, he or she receives no reward, and the agency cannot keep the savings—they go back to the Treasury.

But many of the horror stories are either exaggerations or unusual occurrences.[30] Most of the screws, hammers, and light bulbs purchased by the government are obtained at low cost by means of competitive bidding among several suppliers. When the government does pay outlandish amounts, the reason typically is that it is purchasing a new or one-of-a-kind item not available at your neighborhood hardware store—for example, a new bomber or missile.

Even when the government is not overcharged, it still may spend more money than a private firm in buying what it needs. The reason is red tape—the rules and procedures designed to ensure that when the government buys something, it will do so in a way that serves the interests of many groups. For example, it often must buy from American rather than foreign suppliers, even if the latter charge a lower price; it must make use of contractors that employ minorities; it must hire only union laborers and pay them the "prevailing" (that is, the highest) wage; it must allow public inspection of its records; it frequently is required to choose contractors favored by influential members of Congress; and so on. Private firms do not have to comply with all these rules and thus can buy for less.

From this discussion, it should be easy to see why these five basic bureaucratic problems are so hard to correct. To end conflicts and duplication, Congress would have to make some policy choices and set some clear priorities, but with all the competing demands that it faces, Congress finds it difficult to do that. You make more friends by helping people than by hurting them, and so Congress is more inclined to add new programs than to cut old ones, whether or not the new programs are in conflict with existing ones. To check imperialism some way would have to be found to measure the benefits of government, but that is often impossible; government exists in part to achieve precisely those goals—such as national defense—that are least measurable. Furthermore, what might be done to remedy some problems would make other problems worse: if you simplify rules and procedures to cut red tape, you are also likely to reduce the coordination among agencies and thus to increase the extent to which there is duplication or conflict. If you want to reduce waste, you will have to have more rules and inspectors—in short, more red tape. The problem of bureaucracy is inseparable from the problem of government generally.

Just as people are likely to say they dislike Congress but like their own member of Congress, they are inclined to express hostility toward "the bureaucracy" but goodwill for that part of the bureaucracy with which they have dealt personally. While most Americans have unfavorable impressions of government agencies and officials in general, they have quite favorable impressions about government agencies and officials with whom they have had direct contact or about which they claim to know something specific.

For example, Table 15.2 shows that wide majorities have very or somewhat favorable impressions of diverse federal government agencies. Surveys dating back decades suggest that, despite persistent public complaints about "the bureaucracy," most Americans have judged, and continue to judge, each federal agency to be fair and useful.[31] Even the tax-collecting IRS has more public fans than foes, as did the new Transportation Safety Administration (TSA) whose workers people routinely encounter at airport security checkpoints.

This finding helps explain why government agencies are rarely reduced in size or budget: whatever the popular feelings about the bureaucracy, any given agency tends to have many friends. Even the much-criticized FEMA, viewed unfavorably by half the public, was able to fend off budget cuts in the several years following its failed response to Hurricane Katrina.

Table 15.2 How the Public Views Particular Federal Agencies

Percent reporting a "favorable or unfavorable impression"*

AGENCY	% FAVORABLE Very/Somewhat/Total	% UNFAVORABLE Very/Somewhat/Total	Favorable minus Unfavorable
Postal Service	58/31/89	5/5/10	+79
FBI	31/46/77	10/7/17	+60
Defense Department	31/34/65	15/2/17	+48
Social Security Admin.	24/40/64	19/13/32	+32
EPA	23/40/63	15/15/31	+32
CIA	22/36/58	16/14/30	+28
Homeland Security	24/36/60	17/17/34	+26
Transportation Safety	15/41/56	16/9/25	+26
Education Department	22/37/59	19/19/38	+21
IRS	14/42/56	21/18/39	+17
FEMA	16/33/49	24/26/50	−1

Source: Adapted from results of a nationally representative Associated Press/IPSOS Public Agenda poll conducted December 17–19, 2007.

*Other response categories were "never heard of" and "can't rate," and only the newest agency, the Transportation Safety Administration, drew significant numbers in each category (9 percent for each).

Politically Speaking

Red Tape

As early as the seventh century, legal and government documents in England were bound together with a tape of pinkish red color. In the 1850s, historian Thomas Carlyle described a British politician as "little other than a red tape Talking Machine," and later the American writer Washington Irving said of an American figure that "his brain was little better than red tape and parchment."

Since then *red tape* has come to mean "bureaucratic delay or confusion," especially that accompanied by unnecessary paperwork.

Source: From *Safire's Political Dictionary* by William Safire. Copyright © 1968, 1972, 1978 by William Safire. Reprinted by permission of Random House, Inc. and the author.

Reforming the Bureaucracy

The history of American bureaucracy has been punctuated with countless efforts to make it work better and cost less. There were 11 major attempts in the 20th century alone. The latest was the National Performance Review (NPR)—popularly called the plan to "reinvent government"—led by Vice President Al Gore.

The NPR differed from many of the preceding reform efforts in one important way. Most of the earlier ones suggested ways of increasing central (that is, presidential) control of government agencies: the Brownlow Commission (1936–1937) recommended giving the president more assistants, the First Hoover Commission (1947–1949) suggested ways of improving top-level management, and the Ash Council (1969–1971) called for consolidating existing agencies into a few big "super departments." The intent was to make it easier for the president and his cabinet secretaries to run the bureaucracy. The key ideas were efficiency, accountability, and consistent policies.

The NPR, by contrast, emphasized customer satisfaction (the "customers" in this case being the citizens who come into contact with federal agencies). To the authors of the NPR report, the main problem with the bureaucracy was that it had become too centralized, too rule-bound, too little concerned with making programs work, and too much concerned with avoiding scandal. The NPR report contained many horror stories about useless red tape, excessive regulations, and cumbersome procurement systems that make it next to impossible for agencies to do what they were created to do. (For example, before it could buy an ashtray, the General Services Administration issued a nine-page document that described an ashtray and specified how many pieces it must break into, should it be hit with a hammer.)[31] To solve these problems, the NPR called for less centralized management and more employee initiative, fewer detailed rules and more emphasis on customer satisfaction. It sought to create a new kind of organizational culture in government agencies, one more like that found in the more innovative, quality-conscious American corporations. The NPR was reinforced legislatively by the Government Performance and Results Act (GPRA) of 1993, which required agencies "to set goals, measure performance, and report on the results." President George W. Bush built on the Clinton-Gore NPR efforts and the GPRA using the Performance Assessment Rating Tool (PART). The main goal of the PART was to link management reform to the budget process.

But making these changes is easier said than done. Most of the rules and red tape that make it hard for agency heads to do a good job are the result either of the struggle between the White House and Congress for control over the agencies or of the agencies' desire to avoid irritating influential voters. Silly as the rules for ashtrays may sound, they were written so that the government could say it had an "objective" standard for buying ashtrays. If it simply went out and bought ashtrays at a department store the way ordinary people do, it would risk being accused by the Acme Ashtray Company of buying trays from its competitor, the A-1 Ashtray Company, because of political favoritism.

The rivalry between the president and Congress for control of the bureaucracy makes bureaucrats

WHAT WOULD YOU DO?

MEMORANDUM

To: *Dr. Robert Smith, president of Cybersystems Engineering*

From: *James Logan, secretary of defense*

Subject: *Becoming an assistant secretary of defense*

As both secretary and a dear old college buddy of yours, I write again to express my hope that you will accept the president's call to service. We all desperately want you aboard. Yes, conflict-of-interest laws will require you to sell your stock in your present company and drop out of its generous pension plan. No, the government won't even pay moving costs. And once you leave office, you will be barred for life from lobbying the executive branch on matters in which you were directly involved while in office, and you will be barred for two years from lobbying on matters that were under your general official authority. Your other concerns have teeth, too, but let me help you weigh your options.

New Administration Struggling to Fill Top Posts

Cabinet Secretaries Say "The President Needs Help!"

May 20
WASHINGTON, D.C.

Four months into the new administration, hundreds of assistant secretary and deputy assistant secretary positions remain unfilled. In 1960 the total number of presidential political appointees was just 450. Today the total is over 2,400, but sheer growth is not the whole story. Rather, say experts on fed-eral bureau-cracy, plum public service posts go unfilled because the jobs have become so unreward-ing, even punishing...

Arguments for:

1. I hate to preach, but it is one's duty to serve one's country when called. Your sacrifice would honor your family and benefit your fellow Americans for years to come.

2. As an accomplished professional and the head of a company that has done business with the government, you could help the president succeed in reforming the department so that it works better and costs less.

3. Despite the restrictions, you could resume your career once your public service was complete.

Arguments against:

1. Since you will have to be confirmed by the Senate, your life will be put under a microscope, and everything (even some of our old college mischief together) will be fair game for congressional staffers and reporters.

2. You will face hundreds of rules telling you what you can't do and scores of congressmen telling you what you should do. Old friends will get mad at you for not doing them favors. The president will demand loyalty. The press will pounce on your every mistake, real or imagined.

3. Given the federal limits on whom in the government you can deal with after you leave office, your job at Cybersystems may well suffer.

Your decision:

Accept position _____

Reject position _____

nervous about irritating either branch, and so they issue rules designed to avoid getting into trouble, even if these rules make it hard to do their job. Matters become even worse during periods of divided government when different parties control the White House and Congress. As we saw in Chapter 14, divided government may not have much effect on *making* policy, but it can have a big effect on *implementing* it. Presidents of one party have tried to increase political control over the bureaucracy ("executive micromanagement"), and Congresses of another party have responded by increasing the number of investigations and detailed rule-making ("legislative micromanagement"). Divided government intensifies the cross-fire between the executive and legislative branches, making bureaucrats dig into even deeper layers of red tape to avoid getting hurt.

This does not mean that reform is impossible, only that it is very difficult. For example, despite a lack of clear-cut successes in other areas, the NPR's procurement reforms stuck: government agencies can now buy things costing as much as $100,000 without following any complex regulations. Still, the main effect of the NPR, the GPRA, and the PART was to get federal agencies collecting far more information than in the past concerning what they do without, however, using the information to improve the way they do it.[32]

Transportation Safety Administration workers check our luggage at airports.

Mike Derer/AP Photo

It might be easier to make desirable changes if the bureaucracy were accountable to only one master—say, the president—instead of to several. But that situation, which exists in many parliamentary democracies, creates its own problems. When the bureaucracy has but one master, it often ends up having none: it becomes so powerful that it controls the prime minister and no longer listens to citizen complaints. A weak, divided bureaucracy, such as exists in the United States, may strike us as inefficient, but that very inefficiency may help protect our liberties.

SUMMARY

Bureaucracy is characteristic of almost all aspects of modern life, not simply the government. Government bureaucracies, however, pose special problems because they are subject to competing sources of political authority, must function in a constitutional system of divided powers and federalism, have vague goals, and lack incentive systems that will encourage efficiency. The power of a bureaucracy should be measured by its discretionary authority, not by the number of its employees or the size of its budget.

Since the mid-20th century, the federal bureaucracy has increasingly paid state and local governments, business firms, and nonprofit organizations to administer programs. Opinions are divided about the success of government by proxy.

War and depression have been the principal sources of bureaucratic growth, aided by important changes in constitutional interpretation in the 1930s that permitted Congress to delegate broad grants of authority to administrative agencies. With only partial success Congress seeks to check or recover those grants by controlling budgets, personnel, and policy decisions and by the exercise of legislative vetoes. The uses to which bureaucrats put their authority can be explained in part by their recruitment and security (they have an agency orientation), their personal political views, and the nature of the tasks that their agencies are performing.

Many of the popular solutions for the problems of bureaucratic rule—red tape, duplication, conflict, agency imperialism, and waste—fail to take into account that these problems are to a degree inherent in any government that serves competing goals and is supervised by rival elected officials. Nevertheless, some reform efforts have succeeded in making government work better and cost less to operate.

RECONSIDERING WHO GOVERNS?

1. What happened to make bureaucracy a "fourth branch" of American national government?

The Constitution made no provision for an administrative system other than to allow the president to appoint, with the advice and consent of the Senate, ambassadors, Supreme Court judges, and "all other officers . . . which shall be provided by law." By the early twentieth century, however, Washington's role in making, administering, and funding public policies had already grown far beyond what the Framers had contemplated. Two world wars, the New Deal, and the Great Society each left the government with expanded powers and requiring new batteries of administrative agencies to exercise them. Today, the federal bureaucracy is as vast as most people's expectations about Washington's responsibility for every public concern one can name. It is the appointed officials—the bureaucrats—not the elected officials or policymakers, who command the troops, deliver the mail, audit the tax returns, run the federal prisons, decide who qualifies for public assistance, and do countless other tasks. Unavoidably, many bureaucrats exercise discretion in deciding what public laws and regulations mean and how to apply them. Still, the president, cabinet secretaries, and thousands of political appointees are ultimately their bosses. Congress and the courts have ample, if imperfect, means of checking and balancing even the biggest bureaucracy, old or new.

2. What are the actual size and scope of the federal bureaucracy?

A few million civil servants work directly for the federal government, but over five times as many people work indirectly for Washington as employees of business firms or of nonprofit organizations that receive federal grants or contracts, or as state and local government employees working under federal mandates. For example, the U.S. Department of Health and Human Services (HHS) has about 60,000 employees, runs over 300 different programs, and makes over 60,000 grants a year. But millions more people work indirectly for the HHS—as state and local government employees whose entire jobs involve the administration of one or more HHS programs (for example, Medicaid), and as people who work for community-serving nonprofit organizations that receive HHS grants to administer social services.

RECONSIDERING TO WHAT ENDS?

1. What should be done to improve bureaucratic performance?

There have been numerous efforts to make the bureaucracy work better and cost less, including eleven presidential or other major commissions in the twentieth century. Among the latest was the National Performance Review (NPR), popularly called the plan to "reinvent government." Vice President Gore led the NPR during the two terms of the Clinton administration. The NPR was predicated on the view that bureaucracy had become too centralized, too rule-bound, too little concerned with program results, and too much concerned with avoiding scandal. In the end, the NPR produced certain money-saving changes in the federal procurement process (how government purchases goods and services from private contractors), and it also streamlined parts of the federal personnel process (how Washington hires career employees). Most experts, however, gave the NPR mixed grades. The Bush Administration abolished the NPR but began the Performance Asscessment Rating Tool (PART). Most experts judged the PART to be only mildly successful.

2. Is "red tape" all bad?

No, not all. Red tape refers to the complex rules and procedures that must be followed to get something done. All large organizations, including business firms, have some red tape. Some red tape in government agencies is silly and wasteful (or worse), but try imagining government without any red tape at all. Imagine no rules about hiring on the basis of merit, no strict financial accounting procedures, and no regulations concerning citizen access to information or public record keeping. As the

Yale political scientist Herbert Kaufman once quipped, one citizen's "red tape" often is another's "treasured procedural safeguard."

WORLD WIDE WEB RESOURCES

For addresses and reports of various cabinet departments

Web addresses: **www.whitehouse.gov**

Documents and bulletin boards: **www.fedworld.gov**

National Performance Review: **www.npr.gov**

A few specific web sites of federal agencies

Department of Defense: **www.defenselink.mil**

Department of Education: **www.ed.gov**

Department of Health and Human Services: **www.dhhs.gov**

Department of State: **www.state.gov**

Federal Bureau of Investigation: **www.fbi.gov**

Department of Labor: **www.dol.gov**

SUGGESTED READINGS

Burke, John P. *Bureaucratic Responsibility.* Baltimore: Johns Hopkins University Press, 1986. Examines the problem of individual responsibility—for example, when to be a whistle blower—in government agencies.

Downs, Anthony. *Inside Bureaucracy.* Boston: Little, Brown, 1967. An economist's explanation of why bureaucrats and bureaus behave as they do.

Halperin, Morton H. *Bureaucratic Politics and Foreign Policy.* Washington, D.C.: Brookings Institution, 1974. Insightful account of the strategies by which diplomatic and military bureaucracies defend their interests.

Heclo, Hugh. *A Government of Strangers.* Washington, D.C.: Brookings Institution, 1977. Analyzes how political appointees attempt to gain control of the Washington bureaucracy and how bureaucrats resist those efforts.

Kettl, Donald F. *Government by Proxy.* Washington, D.C.: Congressional Quarterly Press, 1988. An account of how the federal government pays others to staff and run its programs.

Kettl, Donald F. *The Next Government of the United States: Why Our Institutions Fail Us and How to Fix Them.* New York: W. W. Norton, 2008. A masterful study of how proxy government functions and often fails today, and what might be done to remedy its worst failures.

Moore, Mark H. *Creating Public Value: Strategic Management in Government.* Cambridge: Harvard University Press, 1995. A thoughtful account of how wise bureaucrats can make government work better.

Parkinson, C. Northcote. *Parkinson's Law.* Boston: Houghton Mifflin, 1957. Half-serious, half-joking explanation of why government agencies tend to grow.

Wilson, James Q. *Bureaucracy: What Government Agencies Do and Why They Do It.* New York: Basic Books, 1989. A comprehensive review of what we know about bureaucratic behavior in the United States.

EQUAL JUSTICE UNDER LAW

Joe Sohm/The Image Works

WHO GOVERNS?

1. Why should federal judges serve for life?

TO WHAT ENDS?

1. Why should federal courts be able to declare laws unconstitutional?
2. Should federal judges only interpret existing laws or should they be able to create new laws?

Until recently, most Supreme Court justice nominees were routinely approved. When President Ronald Reagan nominated Antonin Scalia, he was confirmed by the Senate in 1986 by a vote of 98–0. But one year later, when President Reagan nominated Robert Bork, he was rejected by the Senate. Four years after that, Clarence Thomas barely survived a confirmation vote, and in 2005, Samuel Alito won a narrow confirmation victory.

Not all justices had such close calls. In recent years, Stephen Breyer, Ruth Bader Ginsburg, Anthony Kennedy, and David Souter were easily confirmed. One reason for this difference may have been that Bork, Thomas, and Alito were regarded as conservatives whereas Breyer, Ginsburg, and Souter were regarded as liberals (or, in the case of Souter, ones with unknown views). The Senate tends to be tougher on the former than on the latter.

But an equally important and closely related reason is that the federal judiciary has played an increasingly important role in making public policy. It, and not Congress, decided that abortions should be legal; settled the closely contested 2000 presidential election; and allowed private homes to be seized in order to build a residential hotel and other private structures aimed at affluent clientele. In these and many other cases, the federal courts have become major political actors; as a result, Congress has become concerned about who will be federal judges. As you will see on page 439, by the 1980s, the senatorial habit of confirming every nominee to federal appeals courts had collapsed. As federal judges make more policy decisions, the Senate pays more close attention to who they are.

One aspect of this power is **judicial review**—the right of the federal courts to declare laws of Congress and acts of the executive branch void and unenforceable if they are judged to be in conflict with the Constitution. Since 1789, the Supreme Court has declared over 160 federal laws to be unconstitutional. In Britain, by contrast, Parliament is supreme, and no court may strike down a law that it passes. As the second earl of Pembroke is supposedly said, "A parliament can do anything but make a man a woman and a woman a man." All that prevents Parliament from acting contrary to the (unwritten) constitution of Britain are the consciences of its members and the opinions of the citizens. About 60 nations do have something resembling judicial review, but in only a few cases does this power mean much in practice. Where it means something—in Australia, Canada, Germany, India, and some other nations—one finds a stable, federal system of government with a strong tradition of an independent judiciary.[1] (Some other nations—France, for example—have special councils, rather than courts, that can under certain circumstances decide that a law is not authorized by the constitution.)

judicial review The power of courts to declare laws unconstitutional.

judicial restraint approach The view that judges should decide cases strictly on the basis of the language of the laws and the Constitution.

activist approach The view that judges should discern the general principles underlying laws or the Constitution and apply them to modern circumstances.

Judicial review is the federal courts' chief weapon in the system of checks and balances on which the American government is based. Today, few people would deny to the courts the right to decide that a legislative or executive act is unconstitutional, though once that right was controversial. What remains controversial is the method by which such review is conducted.

There are two competing views, each ardently pressed during the fight to confirm Clarence Thomas. The first holds that judges should only judge—that is, they should confine themselves to applying those rules stated in or clearly implied by the language of the Constitution. This often is called the **judicial restraint approach.** The other argues that judges should discover the general principles underlying the Constitution and its often vague language, amplify those principles on the basis of some moral or economic philosophy, and apply them to cases. This is sometimes called the **activist approach.**

Note that the difference between activist and strict-constructionist judges is not necessarily the same as the difference between liberals and conservatives. Judges can be political liberals and still believe they are bound by the language of the Constitution. A liberal justice, Hugo Black, once voted to uphold a state law banning birth control because nothing in the Constitution prohibited such a law. Or judges can be conservative and still think they have a duty to use their best judgment in deciding what is good public policy. Rufus Peckham, one such conservative, voted to overturn a state law setting maximum hours of work because he believed the Fourteenth Amendment

Table 16.1 Chief Justices of the United States

Chief Justice	Appointed by	Years of Service
John Jay	Washington	1789–1795
Oliver Ellsworth	Washington	1796–1800
John Marshall	Adams	1801–1835
Roger B. Taney	Jackson	1836–1864
Salmon P. Chase	Lincoln	1864–1873
Morrison R. Waite	Grant	1874–1888
Melville W. Fuller	Cleveland	1888–1910
Edward D. White	Taft	1910–1921
William Howard Taft	Harding	1921–1930
Charles Evans Hughes	Hoover	1930–1941
Harlan Fiske Stone	F. Roosevelt	1941–1946
Fred M. Vinson	Truman	1946–1953
Earl Warren	Eisenhower	1953–1969
Warren E. Burger	Nixon	1969–1986
William H. Rehnquist	Reagan	1986–2005
John G. Roberts, Jr.	Bush	2005–present

Note: Omitted is John Rutledge, who served for only a few months in 1795 and who was not confirmed by the Senate.

guaranteed something called "freedom of contract," even though those words are not in the amendment.

Seventy years ago, judicial activists tended to be conservatives and strict-constructionist judges tended to be liberals; today the opposite usually is the case.

The Development of the Federal Courts

Most of the Founders probably expected the Supreme Court to have the power of judicial review (though they did not say that in so many words in the Constitution), but they did not expect federal courts to play so large a role in making public policy. The traditional view of civil courts was that they judged disputes between people who had direct dealings with each other—they had entered into a contract, for example, or one had dropped a load of bricks on the other's toe—and decided which of the two parties was right. The court then supplied relief to the wronged party, usually by requiring the other person to pay him or her money ("damages").

This traditional understanding was based on the belief that judges would find and apply existing law. The purpose of a court case was not to learn what the judge believes but what the law requires. The later rise of judicial activism occurred when judges questioned this traditional view and argued instead that judges do not merely find the law, they make the law.

The view that judges interpret the law and do not make policy made it easy for the Founders to justify the power of judicial review and led them to predict that the courts would play a relatively neutral, even passive, role in public affairs. Alexander Hamilton, writing in *Federalist* No. 78, described the judiciary as the branch "least dangerous" to political rights. The president is commander in chief and thus holds the "sword of the community"; Congress appropriates money and thus "commands the purse" as well as decides what laws shall govern. But the judiciary "has no influence over either the sword or the purse" and "can take no active resolution whatever." It has "neither force nor will but merely judgment," and thus is "beyond comparison the weakest of the three departments of power." As a result, "liberty can have nothing to fear from the judiciary alone." Hamilton went on to state clearly that the Constitution intended to give to the courts the right to decide whether a law is contrary to the Constitution. But this authority, he explained, was designed not to enlarge the power of the courts but to confine that of the legislature.

Obviously, things have changed since Hamilton's time. The evolution of the federal courts, especially the Supreme Court, toward the present level of activism and influence has been shaped by the political, economic, and ideological forces of three historical eras. From 1787 to 1865, nation building, the legitimacy of the federal government, and slavery were the great issues; from 1865 to 1937, the great issue was the relationship between the government and the economy; from 1938 to the present, the major issues confronting the Court have

involved personal liberty and social equality and the potential conflict between the two. In the first period, the Court asserted the supremacy of the federal government; in the second, it placed important restrictions on the powers of that government; and in the third, it enlarged the scope of personal freedom and narrowed that of economic freedom.

NATIONAL SUPREMACY AND SLAVERY

"From 1789 until the Civil War, the dominant interest of the Supreme Court was in that greatest of all the questions left unresolved by the Founders—the nation-state relationship."[2] The answer the Court gave, under the leadership of Chief Justice John Marshall, was that national law was in all instances the dominant law, with state law having to give way, and that the Supreme Court had the power to decide what the Constitution meant. In two cases of enormous importance—*Marbury v. Madison* in 1803 and *McCulloch v. Maryland* in 1819—the Court, in decisions written by Marshall, held that the Supreme Court could declare an act of Congress unconstitutional; that the power granted by the Constitution to the federal government flows from the people and thus should be generously construed (and thus any federal laws that are "necessary and proper" to the attainment of constitutional ends are permissible); and that federal law is supreme over state law, even to the point that a state may not tax an enterprise (such as a bank) created by the federal government.[3]

The supremacy of the federal government was reaffirmed by other decisions as well. In 1816, the Supreme Court rejected the claim of the Virginia courts that the Supreme Court could not review the decisions of state courts. The Virginia courts were ready to acknowledge the supremacy of the U.S. Constitution but believed they had as much right as the U.S. Supreme Court to decide what the Constitution meant. The Supreme Court felt otherwise, and in this case and another like it, the Court asserted its own broad powers to review any state court decision if that decision seemed to violate federal law or the federal Constitution.[4]

The power of the federal government to regulate commerce among the states was also established. When New York gave to Robert Fulton, the inventor of the steamboat, the monopoly right to operate his steamboats on the rivers of that state, the Marshall Court overturned the license because the rivers connected New York and New Jersey and thus trade on those rivers would involve *inter*state commerce, and federal law in that area was supreme. Since there

Marbury v. Madison

The story of *Marbury v. Madison* is often told, but it deserves another telling because it illustrates so many features of the role of the Supreme Court—how apparently small cases can have large results, how the power of the Court depends not simply on its constitutional authority but also on its acting in ways that avoid a clear confrontation with other branches of government, and how the climate of opinion affects how the Court goes about its task.

When President John Adams lost his bid for reelection to Thomas Jefferson in 1800, he—and all members of his party, the Federalists—feared that Jefferson and the Republicans would weaken the federal government and turn its powers to what the Federalists believed were wrong ends (states' rights, an alliance with the French, hostility to business). Feverishly, as his hours in office came to an end, Adams worked to pack the judiciary with 59 loyal Federalists by giving them so-called midnight appointments before Jefferson took office.

John Marshall, as Adams's secretary of state, had the task of certifying and delivering these new judicial commissions. In the press of business, he delivered all but 17; these he left on his desk for the incoming secretary of state, James Madison, to send out. Jefferson and Madison, however, were furious at Adams's behavior and refused to deliver the 17. William Marbury and three other Federalists who had been promised these commissions hired a lawyer and brought suit against Madison to force him to produce the documents. The suit requested the Supreme Court to issue a writ of mandamus (from the Latin, "we command") ordering Madison to do his duty. The right to issue such writs had been given to the Court by the Judiciary Act of 1789.

Marshall, the man who had failed to deliver the commissions to Marbury and his friends in the first place, had become the chief justice and was now in a position to decide the case. These days a justice who had been involved in an issue before it came to the Court would probably disqualify himself or herself, but Marshall had no intention of letting others decide this question. He faced, however, not simply a partisan dispute over jobs but what was nearly a constitutional crisis. If he ordered the commission delivered, Madison might still refuse, and the Court had no way—if Madison was determined to resist—to compel him. The Court had no police force, whereas Madison had the support of

was a conflicting federal law on the books, the state law was void.[5]

All of this may sound rather obvious to us today, when the supremacy of the federal government is largely unquestioned. In the early 19th century, however, these were almost revolutionary decisions. The Jeffersonian Republicans were in power and had become increasingly devoted to states' rights; they were aghast at the Marshall decisions. President Andrew Jackson attacked the Court bitterly for defending the right of the federal government to create a national bank and for siding with the Cherokee Indians in a dispute with Georgia. In speaking of the latter case, Jackson is supposed to have remarked, "John Marshall has made his decision; now let him enforce it!"[6]

Though Marshall seemed to have secured the supremacy of the federal government over the state governments, another even more divisive issue had arisen; that, of course, was slavery. Roger B. Taney

succeeded Marshall as chief justice in 1836. He was deliberately chosen by President Jackson because he was an advocate of states' rights, and he began to chip away at federal supremacy, upholding state claims that Marshall would have set aside. But the decision for which he is famous—or infamous—came in 1857, when in the *Dred Scott* case, he wrote perhaps the most disastrous judicial opinion ever issued. A slave, Dred Scott, had been taken by his owner to a territory (near what is now St. Paul, Minnesota) where slavery was illegal under federal law. Scott claimed that since he had resided in a free territory, he was now a free man. Taney held that Negroes were not citizens of the United States and could not become so, and that the federal law—the Missouri Compromise—prohibiting slavery in northern territories was unconstitutional.[7] The public outcry against this view was enormous, and the Court and Taney were discredited in the North, at least. The Civil War was ultimately fought over what the Court mistakenly had assumed was a purely legal question.

the president of the United States. And if the order were given, whether or not Madison complied, the Jeffersonian Republicans in Congress would probably try to impeach Marshall. On the other hand, if Marshall allowed Madison to do as he wished, the power of the Supreme Court would be seriously reduced.

Marshall's solution was ingenious. Speaking for a unanimous Court, he announced that Madison was wrong to withhold the commissions, that courts could issue writs to compel public officials to do their prescribed duty—*but* that the Supreme Court had no power to issue such writs in this case because the law (the Judiciary Act of 1789) giving it that power was unconstitutional. The law said the Supreme Court could issue such writs as part of its "original jurisdiction"—that is, persons seeking such writs could go *directly* to the Supreme Court with their request (rather than go first to a lower federal court and then, if dissatisfied, appeal to the Supreme Court). Article III of the Constitution, Marshall pointed out, spelled out precisely the Supreme Court's original jurisdiction; it did not mention issuing writs of this sort and plainly indicated that on all matters not mentioned in the Constitution, the Court would have only

John Adams   James Madison

Library of Congress

appellate jurisdiction. Congress may not change what the Constitution says; hence, the part of the Judiciary Act attempting to do this was null and void.

The result was that a showdown with the Jeffersonians was avoided—Madison was not ordered to deliver the commissions—but the power of the Supreme Court was unmistakably clarified and enlarged. As Marshall wrote, "It is emphatically the province and duty of the judicial department to say what the law is." Furthermore, "a law repugnant to the Constitution is void."

GOVERNMENT AND THE ECONOMY

The supremacy of the federal government may have been established by John Marshall and the Civil War, but the scope of the powers of that government or even of the state governments was still to be defined. During the period from the end of the Civil War to the early years of the New Deal, the dominant issue the Supreme Court faced was deciding when the economy would be regulated by the states and when by the nation.

The Court revealed a strong though not inflexible attachment to private property. In fact, that attachment had always been there: the Founders thought political and property rights were inextricably linked, and Marshall certainly supported the sanctity of contracts. But now, with the muting of the federal supremacy issue and the rise of a national economy with important unanticipated effects, the property question became

the dominant one. In general, the Court developed the view that the Fourteenth Amendment, adopted in 1868 primarily to protect African American claims to citizenship from hostile state action, also protected private property and the corporation from unreasonable state action. The crucial phrase was this: no state shall "deprive any person of life, liberty, or property, without due process of law." Once it became clear that a "person" could be a firm or a corporation as well as an individual, business and industry began to flood the courts with cases challenging various government regulations.

The Court quickly found itself in a thicket: it began ruling on the constitutionality of virtually every effort by any government to regulate any aspect of business or labor, and its workload rose sharply. Judicial activism was born in the 1880s and 1890s as the Court set itself up as the arbiter of what kind of regulation was permissible. In the first 75 years of this country's history, only two federal laws were

The Granger Collection, New York

Roger B. Taney, chief justice from 1836 to 1864, wrote the *Dred Scott* decision, which asserted that blacks were not citizens of the United States. Dred Scott claimed that when his master brought him north to a free state, he ceased to be a slave. The public outcry against the decision was intense, at least in the North, as is evident from this poster announcing a mass meeting "to consider the atrocious decision."

held to be unconstitutional; in the next 75 years, 71 were.[8] Of the roughly 1,300 state laws held to be in conflict with the federal Constitution since 1789, about 1,200 were overturned after 1870. In one decade alone—the 1880s—five federal and 48 state laws were declared unconstitutional.

Many of these decisions provided clear evidence of the Court's desire to protect private property: it upheld the use of injunctions to prevent labor strikes,[9] struck down the federal income tax,[10] sharply limited the reach of the antitrust law,[11] restricted the powers of the Interstate Commerce Commission to set railroad rates,[12] prohibited the federal government from eliminating child labor,[13] and prevented the states from setting maximum hours of work.[14] In 184 cases between 1899 and 1937, the Supreme Court struck down state laws for violating the Fourteenth Amendment, usually by economic regulation.[15]

But the Court also rendered decisions that authorized various kinds of regulation. It allowed states to regulate businesses "affected with a public interest,"[16] changed its mind about the Interstate Commerce Commission and allowed it to regulate railroad rates,[17] upheld rules requiring railroads to improve their safety,[18] approved state antiliquor laws,[19] approved state mine safety laws,[20] supported state workers' compensation laws,[21] allowed

Landmark Cases

Power of the Supreme Court

- *Marbury v. Madison* (1803): Upheld judicial review of congressional acts.

- *Martin v. Hunter's Lessee* (1816): The Supreme Court can review the decisions of the highest state courts if they involve a federal law or the federal Constitution.

- *McCulloch v. Maryland* (1819): Said that creating a federal bank, though not mentioned in the Constitution, was a "necessary and proper" exercise of the government's right to borrow money.

- *Ex Parte McCardle* (1869): Allowed Congress to change the appellate jurisdiction of the Supreme Court.

states to regulate fire-insurance rates,[22] and in time upheld a number of state laws regulating wages and hours. Indeed, between 1887 and 1910, in 558 cases involving the Fourteenth Amendment, the Supreme

Bettmann/Corbis

The "nine old men"—the Supreme Court in 1937, not long after President Franklin D. Roosevelt tried, unsuccessfully, to "pack" it by appointing six additional justices who would have supported his New Deal legislation. Justice Owen J. Roberts (standing, second from the left) changed his vote on these matters, and the Court ceased to be a barrier to the delegation of power to the bureaucracy.

Court upheld state regulations over 80 percent of the time.[23]

To characterize the Court as probusiness or antiregulation is both simplistic and inexact. More accurate, perhaps, is to characterize it as supportive of the rights of private property but unsure how to draw the lines that distinguish "reasonable" from "unreasonable" regulation. Nothing in the Constitution clearly differentiates reasonable from unreasonable regulation, and the Court has been able to invent no consistent principle of its own to make this determination. For example, what kinds of businesses are "affected with a public interest"? Grain elevators and railroads are, but are bakeries? Sugar refiners? Saloons? And how much of commerce is "interstate"—anything that moves? Or only something that actually crosses a state line? The Court found itself trying to make detailed judgments that it was not always competent to make and to invent legal rules where no clear legal rules were possible.

In one area, however, the Supreme Court's judgments were clear: the Fourteenth and Fifteenth Amendments were construed so narrowly as to give African Americans only the most limited benefits of their provisions. In a long series of decisions, the Court upheld segregation in schools and on railroad cars and permitted blacks to be excluded from voting in many states.

GOVERNMENT AND POLITICAL LIBERTY

After 1936, the Supreme Court stopped imposing any serious restrictions on state or federal power to regulate the economy, leaving such matters in the hands of the legislatures. From 1937 to 1974, the Supreme Court did not overturn a single federal law designed to regulate business but did overturn 36 congressional enactments that violated personal political liberties. It voided as unconstitutional laws that restricted freedom of speech,[24] denied passports to communists,[25] permitted the government to revoke a person's citizenship,[26] withheld a person's mail,[27] or restricted the availability of government benefits.[28]

This new direction began when one justice changed his mind, and it continued as the composition of the Court changed. At the outset of the New Deal, the Court was by a narrow margin dominated by

Map 16.1

U.S. District and Appellate Courts

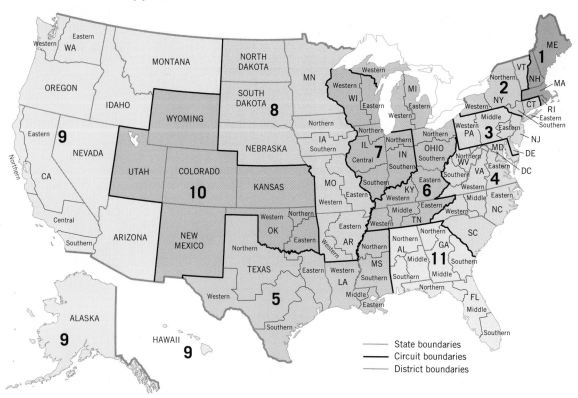

Note: Washington, D.C., is in a separate court. Puerto Rico is in the first circuit; the Virgin Islands are in the third; Guam and the Northern Mariana Islands are in the ninth.

Source: Administrative Office of the United States Courts (January 1983).

justices who opposed the welfare state and federal regulation based on broad grants of discretionary authority to administrative agencies. President Franklin Roosevelt, who was determined to get just such legislation implemented, found himself powerless to alter the composition of the Court during his first term (1933–1937): because no justice died or retired, he had no vacancies to fill. After his overwhelming reelection in 1936, he moved to remedy this problem by "packing" the Court.

Roosevelt proposed a bill that would have allowed him to appoint one new justice for each one over the age of 70 who refused to retire, up to a total membership of 15. Since there were six men in this category then on the Supreme Court, he would have been able to appoint six new justices, enough to ensure a comfortable majority supportive of his economic policies. A bitter controversy ensued, but before the bill could be voted on, the Supreme Court, perhaps reacting to Roosevelt's big win in the 1936 election, changed its mind. Whereas it had been striking down several New Deal measures by votes of 5 to 4, now it started approving them by the same vote. One justice, Owen Roberts, had switched his

position. This was called the "switch in time that saved nine," but in fact Roberts had changed his mind *before* the FDR plan was announced.

The "Court-packing" bill was not passed, but it was no longer necessary. Justice Roberts had yielded before public opinion in a way that Chief Justice Taney a century earlier had not, thus forestalling an assault on the Court by the other branches of government. Shortly thereafter, several justices stepped down, and Roosevelt was able to make his own appointments (he filled seven seats during his four terms in office). From then on, the Court turned its attention to new issues—political liberties and, in time, civil rights.

With the arrival in office of Chief Justice Earl Warren in 1953, the Court began its most active period yet. Activism now arose to redefine the relationship of citizens to the government and especially to protect the rights and liberties of citizens from governmental trespass. Although the Court has always seen itself as protecting citizens from arbitrary government, before 1937 that protection was of a sort that conservatives preferred; after 1937, it was of a kind that liberals preferred.

THE REVIVAL OF STATE SOVEREIGNTY

For many decades, the Supreme Court allowed Congress to pass almost any law authorized by the Constitution, no matter how it affected the states. As we saw in Chapter 3, the Court had long held that Congress could regulate almost any activity if it affected interstate commerce, and in the Court's opinion virtually every activity did affect it. The states were left with few rights to challenge federal power. But since around 1992, the Court has backed away from this view. By narrow majorities, it has begun to restore the view that states have the right to resist some forms of federal action.

When Congress passed a bill that forbade anyone from carrying a gun near a school, the Court held that carrying guns did not affect interstate commerce, and so the law was invalid.[29] One year later, it struck down a law that allowed Indian tribes to sue the states in federal courts, arguing that Congress lacks the power to ignore the "sovereign immunity" of states—that is, the right, protected by the Eleventh Amendment, not to be sued in federal court. (It has since upheld that view in two more cases.) And the next year, it held that the Brady gun control law could not be used to require local law enforcement officers to do background checks on people trying to buy weapons.[30] These cases are all hints that there are some real limits to the supremacy of the federal government created by the existence and powers of the several states.

The Structure of the Federal Courts

The only federal court the Constitution requires is the Supreme Court, as specified in Article III. All other federal courts and their jurisdictions are creations of Congress. Nor does the Constitution indicate how many justices shall be on the Supreme Court (there were originally six, now there are nine) or what its appellate jurisdiction shall be.

Congress has created two kinds of lower federal courts to handle cases that need not be decided by the Supreme Court: constitutional and legislative courts. A **constitutional court** is one exercising the judicial powers found in Article III of the Constitution, and therefore its judges are given constitutional protection: they may not be fired (they serve during "good behavior"), nor may their salaries be reduced while they are in office. The most important of the constitutional courts are the **district courts** (a total of 94, with at least one in each state, the District of Columbia, and the commonwealth of Puerto Rico) and the **courts of appeals** (one in each of 11 regions, plus one in the District of Columbia and one federal circuit). There are also various specialized constitutional courts, such as the Court of International Trade.

A **legislative court** is one set up by Congress for some

Louis Brandeis, creator of the "Brandeis Brief" that developed court cases based on economic and social more than legal arguments, became the first Jewish Supreme Court justice. He served in the Court from 1916 until 1939.

Topham/The Image Works

constitutional court A federal court authorized by Article III of the Constitution that keeps judges in office during good behavior and prevents their salaries from being reduced. They are the Supreme Court (created by the Constitution) and appellate and district courts created by Congress.

district courts The lowest federal courts; federal trials can be held only here.

courts of appeals Federal courts that hear appeals from district courts; no trials.

legislative courts Courts created by Congress for specialized purposes whose judges do not enjoy the protections of Article III of the Constitution.

specialized purpose and staffed with people who have fixed terms of office and can be removed or have their salaries reduced. Legislative courts include the Court of Military Appeals and the territorial courts.

SELECTING JUDGES

Party background makes a difference in how judges behave. An analysis has been done of over 80 studies of the link between party and either liberalism or conservatism among state and federal judges in cases involving civil liberties, criminal justice, and economic regulation. It shows that judges who are Democrats are more likely to make liberal decisions and Republican judges are more likely to make conservative ones.* The party effect is not small.[31] We should not be surprised by this, since we have already seen that among political elites (and judges are certainly elites), party identification influences personal ideology.

But ideology does not entirely determine behavior. So many other things shape court decisions—the facts of the case, prior rulings by other courts, the arguments presented by lawyers—that there is no reliable way of predicting how judges will behave in all matters. Presidents often make the mistake of thinking they know how their appointees will behave, only to be surprised by the facts. Theodore Roosevelt appointed Oliver Wendell Holmes to the Supreme Court, only to remark later, after Holmes had voted in a way that Roosevelt did not like, that "I could carve out of a banana a judge with more backbone than that!" Holmes, who had plenty of backbone, said he did not "give a damn" what Roosevelt thought. Richard Nixon, an ardent foe of court-ordered school busing, appointed Warren Burger chief justice. Burger promptly sat down and wrote the opinion upholding busing. Another Nixon appointee, Harry Blackmun, wrote the opinion declaring the right to an abortion to be constitutionally protected.

Sex, race, and ethnicity have also become important factors in selecting judges as is evident in Figure 16.1.

Senatorial Courtesy

In theory, the president nominates a "qualified" person to be a judge, and the Senate approves or

litmus test An examination of the political ideology of a nominated judge.

---

* A "liberal" decision is one that favors a civil right, a criminal defendant or an economic regulation; a "conservative" one opposes the right or the regulation or supports the criminal prosecutor.

rejects the nomination based on those "qualifications." In fact, the tradition of *senatorial courtesy* gives heavy weight to the preferences of the senators from the state where a federal district judge is to serve. Ordinarily, the Senate will not confirm a district court judge if the senior senator from the state where the district is located objects (if he is of the president's party). The senator can exercise this veto power by means of the "blue slip"—a blue piece of paper on which the senator is asked to record his or her views on the nominee. A negative opinion, or even failure to return the blue slip, usually kills the nomination. This means that as a practical matter the president nominates only persons recommended to him by that key senator. Someone once suggested that, at least with respect to district judges, the Constitution has been turned on its head. To reflect reality, he said, Article II, section 2, ought to read: "The senators shall nominate, and by and with the consent of the President, shall appoint" federal judges.

The "Litmus Test"

Of late, presidents have tried to exercise more influence on the selection of federal district and appellate court judges by getting the Justice Department to find candidates that not only are supported by their party's senators, but also reflect the political and judicial philosophy of the president. Presidents Carter and Clinton sought out liberal, activist judges; President Reagan sought out conservative, strict-constructionist ones. The party membership of federal judges makes a difference in how they vote.[32]

Because different courts of appeals have different combinations of judges, some will be more liberal than others. For example, there are more liberal judges in the court of appeals for the ninth circuit (which includes most of the far western states) and more conservative ones in the fifth circuit (Texas, Louisiana, and Mississippi). The ninth circuit takes liberal positions, the fifth more conservative ones. Since the Supreme Court does not have time to settle every disagreement among appeals courts, different interpretations of the law may exist in different circuits. In the fifth, for instance, it was for a while unconstitutional for state universities to have affirmative action programs, but in the ninth circuit that was permitted.

These differences make some people worry about the use of a political **litmus test**—a test of ideological purity—in selecting judges. When conservatives are out of power, they complain about how liberal presidents use such a test; when liberals are out power, they complain about how conservative

Question
1. Who was the first Catholic Supreme Court justice?

Figure 16.1

Female and Minority Judicial Appointments, 1963–2004

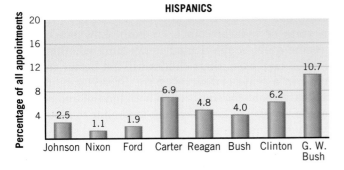

Source: Updated from Harold W. Stanley and Richard G. Niemi, *Vital Statistics on American Politics, 2005–2006* (Washington, D.C.: Congressional Quarterly, 2006), table 7.5.

presidents use it. Many people would like to see judges picked on the basis of professional qualifications, without reference to ideology, but the courts are now so deeply involved in political issues that it is hard to imagine what an ideologically neutral set of professional qualifications might be.

The litmus test has grown in importance. There has been a sharp drop in the percentage of nominees to federal appeals courts who are confirmed (see Figure 16.2). From 1945 until 1970, almost every nominee was confirmed, but by 1995 only about half got through the Senate and by 2000 it was less than 40 percent. (Nominees to the federal district court are, obviously, much less controversial because the president rarely nominates someone who is not supported by the state's senators.)

A judicial nominee's view on abortion is the chief motive for using the litmus test. Since it is easy to mount a filibuster and it takes 60 votes to end one, the nominee usually must be assured of 60 Senate votes to be confirmed. In theory, the Senate could adopt a rule preventing filibusters of nominations—but it never has. In 2005, a group of 14 senators, half from each party, agreed they would vote to block a filibuster on court nominees unless there were "extraordinary circumstances." This group—called the Gang of Fourteen—made it possible for several nominees (including Samuel Alito) to be confirmed even though they had fewer than 60 votes (but still, of course, more than 50).

The litmus test issue is of greatest importance in selecting Supreme Court justices. Here, there is no tradition of senatorial courtesy. The president takes a keen personal interest in the choices and, of late, has sought to find nominees who share his philosophy. In the Reagan administration, there were bruising fights in the Senate over the nomination of William Rehnquist to be chief justice (he won) and Robert Bork to be an associate justice (he lost), with liberals pitted against conservatives. When President George H.W. Bush nominated David Souter, there were lengthy hearings as liberal senators tried to pin down Souter's views on issues such as abortion. Souter refused to discuss matters on which he might later have to judge, however. Clarence Thomas, another Bush nominee, also tried to avoid the litmus test by saying he had not formed an opinion on prominent abortion cases. In his case, however, the litmus test issue was overshadowed by sensational allegations from a former employee, Anita Hill, that Thomas had sexually harassed her.

Of the 145 Supreme Court nominees presented to it, the Senate has rejected 29. Only five of these were in the 20th century. The reasons for rejecting a Supreme Court nominee are complex—each senator may have a different reason—but have involved such matters as the nominee's alleged hostility to civil rights, questionable personal

Answer

1. *Roger B. Taney (on bench: 1836–1864)*

Figure 16.2

Confirmation Rates for Nominees to the U.S. Court of Appeals (1947–2005)

Source: "The Consequences of Polarization: Congress and the Courts" by Sarah A. Binder, in David Brady and Pietro Nivola, Eds., *Red and Blue Nation?* (Vol. 2) *Consequences and Correction of America's Polarized Politics* (figure 3.3, p. 116). Brookings Institution Press. Reprinted by permission of the author.

financial dealings, a poor record as a lower-court judge, and Senate opposition to the nominee's political or legal philosophy. Nominations of district court judges are rarely defeated, because typically no nomination is made unless the key senators approve in advance.

The Jurisdiction of the Federal Courts

We have a dual court system—one state, one federal—and this complicates enormously the task of describing what kinds of cases federal courts may hear and how cases beginning in the state courts may end up before the Supreme Court. The Constitution lists the kinds of cases over which federal courts have jurisdiction (in Article III and the Eleventh Amendment); by implication, all other matters are left to state courts. Federal courts (see Figure 16.3) can hear all cases "arising under the Constitution, the laws of the United States, and treaties" (these are **federal-question cases**), and cases involving citizens of different states (called **diversity cases**).

federal-question cases Cases concerning the Constitution, federal laws, or treaties.

diversity cases Cases involving citizens of different states who can bring suit in federal courts.

Some kinds of cases can be heard in either federal or state courts. For example, if citizens of different states wish to sue one another and the matter involves more than $75,000, they can do so in either a federal or a state court. Similarly, if someone robs a federally insured bank, he or she has broken both state and federal law and thus can be prosecuted in state or federal courts, or both. Lawyers have become quite sophisticated in deciding whether, in a given civil case, their clients will get better treatment in a state or federal court. Prosecutors often send a person who has broken both federal and state law to whichever court system is likelier to give the toughest penalty.

Sonia Sotomayor became the third female and first Hispanic justice on the Supreme Court.

Karen Bleier/AFP/Getty Images

Figure 16.3

The Jurisdiction of the Federal Courts

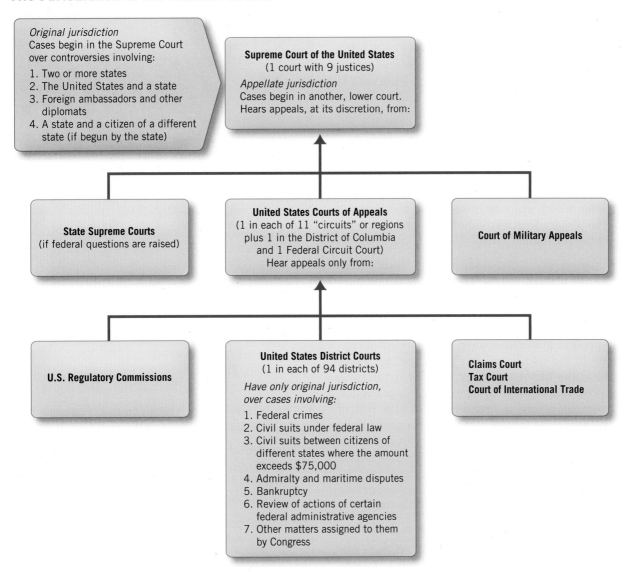

Original jurisdiction
Cases begin in the Supreme Court over controversies involving:

1. Two or more states
2. The United States and a state
3. Foreign ambassadors and other diplomats
4. A state and a citizen of a different state (if begun by the state)

Supreme Court of the United States
(1 court with 9 justices)
Appellate jurisdiction
Cases begin in another, lower court. Hears appeals, at its discretion, from:

State Supreme Courts
(if federal questions are raised)

United States Courts of Appeals
(1 in each of 11 "circuits" or regions plus 1 in the District of Columbia and 1 Federal Circuit Court)
Hear appeals only from:

Court of Military Appeals

U.S. Regulatory Commissions

United States District Courts
(1 in each of 94 districts)
Have only original jurisdiction, over cases involving:

1. Federal crimes
2. Civil suits under federal law
3. Civil suits between citizens of different states where the amount exceeds $75,000
4. Admiralty and maritime disputes
5. Bankruptcy
6. Review of actions of certain federal administrative agencies
7. Other matters assigned to them by Congress

Claims Court
Tax Court
Court of International Trade

Sometimes defendants may be tried in both state and federal courts for the same offense. In 1992, four Los Angeles police officers accused of beating Rodney King were tried in a California state court and acquitted of assault charges. They were then prosecuted in federal court for violating King's civil rights. This time, two of the four were convicted. Under the dual sovereignty doctrine, state and federal authorities can prosecute the same person for the same conduct. The Supreme Court has upheld this doctrine on two grounds: first, each level of government has the right to enact laws serving its own purposes.[33] As a result, federal civil rights charges could have been brought against the officers even if they had already been convicted of assault in state court (though as a practical matter this would have been unlikely). Second, neither level of government wants the other to be able to block prosecution of an accused person who has the sympathy of the authorities at one level. For example, when certain southern state courts were in sympathy with whites who had lynched blacks, the absence of the dual sovereignty doctrine would have meant that a trumped-up acquittal in state court would have barred federal prosecution.

Furthermore, a matter that exclusively within the province of a state court—for example, a criminal case in which the defendant is charged with violating only a state law—can be appealed to the U.S. Supreme Court under certain circumstances (described below). Thus federal judges can overturn state court rulings even when they had no jurisdiction over the original matter. Under what circumstances this should occur has been the subject of long-standing controversy between the state and federal courts.

Some matters, however, are exclusively under the jurisdiction of federal courts. When a federal criminal law is broken—but not a state one—the case is heard in federal district court. If you wish to appeal the decision of a federal regulatory agency, such as the Federal Communications Commission, you can do so only before a federal court of appeals. And if you wish to declare bankruptcy, you do so in federal court. If there is a controversy between two state governments—say, California and Arizona sue each other over which state is to use how much water from the Colorado River—the case can be heard only by the Supreme Court.

The vast majority of all cases heard by federal courts begin in the district courts. The volume of business there is huge. In 2007, the 650 or so district court judges received over 250,000 cases (about 380 per judge). Most of the cases heard in federal courts involve rather straightforward applications of law; few lead to the making of new public policy. Cases that do affect how the law or the Constitution is interpreted can begin with seemingly minor events. For example, a major broadening of the Bill of Rights—requiring for the first time that all accused persons in *state* as well as federal criminal trials be supplied with a lawyer, free if necessary—began when impoverished Clarence Earl Gideon, imprisoned in Florida, wrote an appeal in pencil on prison stationery and sent it to the Supreme Court.[34]

The Supreme Court does not have to hear any appeal it does not want to hear. At one time, it was required to listen to certain appeals, but Congress has changed the law so that now the Court can pick the cases it wants to consider.

It does this by issuing a **writ of certiorari**. *Certiorari* is a Latin word meaning, roughly, "made more certain"; lawyers and judges have abbreviated it to *cert*. It works this way: the Court considers all the petitions it receives to review lower-court decisions. If four justices agree to hear a case, cert is issued and the case is scheduled for a hearing.

In deciding whether to grant certiorari, the Court tries to reserve its time for cases decided by lower federal courts or by the highest state courts in which a significant federal or constitutional question has

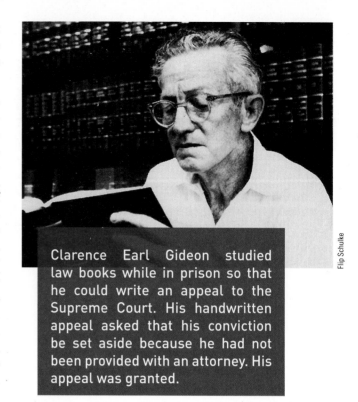

Clarence Earl Gideon studied law books while in prison so that he could write an appeal to the Supreme Court. His handwritten appeal asked that his conviction be set aside because he had not been provided with an attorney. His appeal was granted.

Flip Schulke

been raised. For example, the Court often will grant certiorari when one or both of the following is true:

- Two or more federal circuit courts of appeals have decided the same issue in different ways.

- The highest court in a state has held a federal or state law to be in violation of the Constitution or has upheld a state law against the claim that it is in violation of the Constitution.

In a typical year, the Court may consider over seven thousand petitions asking it to review decisions of lower or state courts. It rarely accepts more than about one hundred of them for full review.

In exercising its discretion in granting certiorari, the Supreme Court is on the horns of a dilemma. If it grants it frequently, it will be inundated with cases. As it is, the Court's workload has quintupled in the last fifty years. If, on the other hand, the Court grants certiorari only rarely, then the federal courts of appeals have the last word on the interpretation of the Constitution and federal laws, and since there are twelve of these, staffed by about 167 judges, they may well be in disagreement. In fact this has already happened: because the Supreme Court reviews only about 1 or 2 percent of appeals court cases, applicable federal law may be different in different parts of the country.[35] One proposal to deal with this dilemma is to devote the Supreme Court's time entirely to major questions of constitutional interpretation and to create a national

writ of certiorari An order by a higher court directing a lower court to send up a case for review.

2. Who was the first Jewish Supreme Court justice?

court of appeals that would ensure that the twelve circuit courts of appeals are producing uniform decisions.[36]

Because the Supreme Court has a heavy workload, the influence wielded by law clerks has grown. These clerks—recent graduates of law schools hired by the justices—play a big role in deciding which cases should be heard under a writ of *certiorari.*Indeed, some of the opinions written by the justices are drafted by the clerks. Since the reasons for a decision may be as important as the decision itself, and since these reasons are sometimes created by the clerks, the power of the clerks can be significant.

Getting to Court

In theory, the courts are the great equalizer in the federal government. To use the courts to settle a question, or even to alter fundamentally the accepted interpretation of the Constitution, one need not be elected to any office, have access to the mass media, be a member of an interest group, or be otherwise powerful or rich. Once the contending parties are before the courts, they are legally equal.

It is too easy to believe this theory uncritically or to dismiss it cynically. In fact, it is hard to get before the Supreme Court: it rejects over 96 percent of the applications for *certiorari* that it receives. And the costs involved in getting to the Court can be high. To apply for *certiorari* costs only $300 (plus 40 copies of the petition), but if *certiorari* is granted and the case is heard, the costs—for lawyers and for copies of the lower-court records in the case—can be very high. And by then one has already paid for the cost of the first hearing in the district court and probably one appeal to the circuit court of appeals. Furthermore, the time it takes to settle a matter in federal court can be quite long.

But there are ways to make these costs lower. If you are indigent—without funds—you can file and be heard as a pauper for nothing; about half the petitions arriving before the Supreme Court are **in forma pauperis** (such as the one from Gideon, described earlier). If your case began as a criminal trial in the district courts and you are poor, the government will supply you with a lawyer at no charge. If the matter is not a criminal case and you cannot afford to hire a lawyer, interest groups representing a wide spectrum of opinion sometimes are willing to take up the cause if the issue in the case seems sufficiently important. The American Civil Liberties Union (ACLU), a liberal group, represents some people who believe their freedom of speech has been abridged or their constitutional rights in criminal proceedings have been violated. The Center for Individual Rights, a conservative group, represents some people who feel that they have been victimized by racial quotas.

But interest groups do much more than just help people pay their bills. Many of the most important cases decided by the Court got there because an interest group organized the case, found the plaintiffs, chose the legal strategy, and mobilized legal allies. The NAACP has brought many key civil rights cases on behalf of individuals. Although in the past most such cases were brought by liberal interest groups, of late conservative interest groups have entered the courtroom on behalf of individuals. One helped sue CBS for televising a program that allegedly libeled General William Westmoreland, once the American commander in Vietnam. (Westmoreland lost the case.) And many important issues are raised by attorneys representing state and local governments. Several price-fixing cases have been won by state attorneys general on behalf of consumers in their states.

FEE SHIFTING

Unlike what happens in most of Europe, each party to a lawsuit in this country must pay its own way. (In England, by contrast, if you sue someone and lose, you pay the winner's costs as well as your own.) But various laws have made it easier to get someone else to pay. **Fee shifting** enables the **plaintiff** (the party that initiates the suit) to collect its costs from the defendant if the defendant loses, at least in certain kinds of cases. For example, if a corporation is found to have violated the antitrust laws, it must pay the legal fees of the winner. If an environmentalist group sues the Environmental Protection Agency, it can get the EPA to pay the group's legal costs. Even more important to individuals, Section 1983 of Chapter 42 of the *United States Code* allows a citizen to sue a state or local government official—say, a police officer or a school superintendent—who has deprived the citizen of some constitutional right or withheld some benefit to which the citizen is entitled. If the citizen wins, he or she can collect money damages and lawyers' fees from the government. Citizens, more aware of their legal rights, have become more litigious, and a flood of such "Section 1983" suits has burdened the

in forma pauperis A method whereby a poor person can have his or her case heard in federal court without charge.

fee shifting A rule that allows a plaintiff to recover costs from the defendant if the plaintiff wins.

plaintiff The party that initiates a lawsuit.

courts. The Supreme Court has restricted fee shifting to cases authorized by statute,[37] but it is clear that the drift of policy has made it cheaper to go to court—at least for some cases.

STANDING

There is, in addition, a nonfinancial restriction on getting into federal court. To sue, one must have **standing,** a legal concept that refers to who is entitled to bring a case. It is especially important in determining who can challenge the laws or actions of the government itself. A complex and changing set of rules governs standings; some of the more important ones are these:

- There must be an actual controversy between real adversaries. (You cannot bring a "friendly" suit against someone, hoping to lose in order to prove your friend right. You cannot ask a federal court for an opinion on a hypothetical or imaginary case or ask it to render an advisory opinion.)

- You must show that you have been harmed by the law or practice about which you are complaining. (It is not enough to dislike what the government or a corporation or a labor union does; you must show that you were actually harmed by that action.)

- Merely being a taxpayer does not ordinarily entitle you to challenge the constitutionality of a federal governmental action. (You may not want your tax money to be spent in certain ways, but your remedy is to vote against the politicians doing the spending; the federal courts will generally require that you show some other personal harm before you can sue.)

Congress and the courts have recently made it easier to acquire standing. It has always been the rule that a citizen could ask the courts to order federal officials to carry out some act that they were under a legal obligation to perform or to refrain from some action that was contrary to law. A citizen can also sue a government official personally to collect damages if the official acted contrary to law. For example, it was for long the case that if an FBI agent broke into your office without a search warrant, you could sue the agent and, if you won, collect money. However, you cannot sue the government itself without its consent. This is the doctrine of **sovereign immunity.** For instance, if the army accidentally kills your cow while testing a new cannon, you cannot sue the government to recover the cost of the cow unless the government agrees to be sued. (Since testing cannons is legal, you cannot sue the army officer who fired the cannon.) By statute, Congress has given its consent for the government to be sued in many cases involving a dispute over a contract or damage done as a result of negligence (for example, the dead cow). Over the years, these statutes have made it easier to take the government into court as a defendant.

Even some of the oldest rules defining standing have been liberalized. The rule that merely being a taxpayer does not entitle you to challenge in court a government decision has been relaxed where the citizen claims that a right guaranteed under the First Amendment is being violated. The Supreme Court allowed a taxpayer to challenge a federal law that would have given financial aid to parochial (or church-related) schools on the grounds that this aid violated the constitutional requirement of separation between church and state. On the other hand, another taxpayer suit to force the CIA to make public its budget failed because the Court decided that the taxpayer did not have standing in matters of this sort.[38]

CLASS-ACTION SUITS

Under certain circumstances, a citizen can benefit directly from a court decision, even though the citizen himself or herself has not gone into court. This can happen by means of a **class-action suit:** a case brought into court by a person on behalf not only of himself or herself, but of all other persons in similar circumstances. Among the most famous of these was the 1954 case in which the Supreme Court found that Linda Brown, a black girl attending the fifth grade in the Topeka, Kansas, public schools, was denied the equal protection of the laws (guaranteed under the Fourteenth Amendment) because the schools in Topeka were segregated. The Court did not limit its decision to Linda Brown's right to attend an unsegregated school but extended it—as Brown's lawyers from the NAACP had asked—to cover all "others similarly situated."[39] It was not easy to design a court order that would eliminate segregation in the schools, but the principle was clearly established in this class action.

Since the *Brown* case, many other groups have been quick to take advantage of the opportunity created by class-action suits. By this means, the courts could be used to give relief not simply to a

standing A legal rule stating who is authorized to start a lawsuit.

sovereign immunity The rule that a citizen cannot sue the government without the governments consent.

class-action suit A case brought by someone to help him or her and all others who are similarly situated.

particular person but to all those represented in the suit. A landmark class-action case challenged the malapportionment of state legislative districts (see Chapter 13).[40] There are thousands of class-action suits in the federal courts involving civil rights, the rights of prisoners, antitrust suits against corporations, and other matters. These suits became more common partly because people were beginning to have new concerns that were not being met by Congress and partly because some class-action suits became quite profitable. The NAACP got no money from Linda Brown or from the Topeka Board of Education in compensation for its long and expensive labors, but beginning in the 1960s court rules were changed to make it financially attractive for lawyers to bring certain kinds of class-action suits.

Suppose, for example, that you think your telephone company overcharged you by $75. You could try to hire a lawyer to get a refund, but not many lawyers would take the case, because there would be no money in it. Even if you were to win, the lawyer would stand to earn no more than perhaps one-third of the settlement, or $25. Now suppose you bring a class action against the company on behalf of everybody who was overcharged. Millions of dollars might be at stake; lawyers would line up eagerly to take the case, because their share of the settlement, if they won, would be huge. The opportunity to win profitable class-action suits, combined with the possibility of having the loser pay the attorneys' fees, led to a proliferation of such cases.

In response to the increase in its workload, the Supreme Court decided in 1974 to tighten drastically the rules governing these suits. It held that it would no longer hear (except in certain cases defined by Congress, such as civil rights matters) class-action suits seeking monetary damages unless each

and every ascertainable member of the class was individually notified of the case. To do this often is prohibitively expensive (imagine trying to find and send a letter to every customer that may have been overcharged by the telephone company!), and so the number of such cases declined and the number of lawyers seeking them out dropped.[41]

Linda Brown was refused admission to a white elementary school in Topeka, Kansas. On her behalf, the NAACP brought a class-action suit that resulted in the 1954 landmark Supreme Court decision *Brown v. Board of Education.*

Carl Iwasaki/Time Life Pictures/Getty Images

Table 16.2 Supreme Court Justices in Order of Seniority, 2009

Name (Birth Date)	Home State	Prior Experience	Appointed by (Year)
John G. Roberts, Jr., Chief Justice (1955)	Maryland	Federal judge	G. W. Bush (2005)
John Paul Stevens (1916)	Illinois	Federal judge	Ford (1975)
Antonin Scalia (1936)	Virginia	Federal judge	Reagan (1986)
Anthony Kennedy (1936)	California	Federal judge	Reagan (1988)
Clarence Thomas (1948)	Georgia	Federal judge	G. H. W. Bush (1991)
Ruth Bader Ginsburg (1933)	New York	Federal judge	Clinton (1993)
Stephen Breyer (1938)	Massachusetts	Federal judge	Clinton (1994)
Samuel Alito (1950)	New Jersey	Federal judge	G. W. Bush (2006)
Sonia Sotomayor	New York	Federal judge	Obama (2009)

But it remains easy to bring a class-action suit in most state courts. State Farm automobile insurance company was told by a state judge in a small Illinois town that it must pay over $1 billion in damages on behalf of a "national" class, even though no one in this class had been notified. Big class-action suits powerfully affect how courts make public policy. Such suits have forced into bankruptcy companies making asbestos and silicone breast implants and have threatened to put out of business tobacco companies and gun manufacturers. (Ironically, in some of these cases, such as the one involving breast implants, there was no scientific evidence showing that the product was harmful.) Some class-action suits, such as the one ending school segregation, are good, but others are frivolous efforts to get companies to pay large fees to the lawyers who file the suits.

In sum, getting into court depends on having standing and having resources. The rules governing standing are complex and changing, but generally they have been broadened to make it easier to enter the federal courts, especially for the purpose of challenging the actions of the government. Obtaining the resources is not easy but has become easier because laws in some cases now provide for fee shifting, private interest groups are willing to finance cases, and it is sometimes possible to bring a class-action suit that lawyers find lucrative.

The Supreme Court in Action

If your case should find its way to the Supreme Court—and of course the odds are that it will not—you will be able to participate in one of the more impressive, sometimes dramatic ceremonies of American public life. The Court is in session in its white marble building for 36 weeks out of each year, from early October until the end of June. The nine justices read briefs in their individual offices, hear oral arguments in the stately courtroom, and discuss their decisions with one another in a conference room where no outsider is ever allowed.

Most cases, as we have seen, come to the Court on a writ of *certiorari*. The lawyers for each side may then submit their briefs. A **brief** is a document that sets forth the facts of the case, summarizes the lower-court decision, gives the arguments for the side represented by the lawyer who

brief A written statement by an attorney that summarizes a case and the laws and rulings that support it.

amicus curiae A brief submitted by a "friend of the court."

wrote the brief, and discusses the other cases that the Court has decided bear on the issue. Then the lawyers are allowed to present their oral arguments in open court. They usually summarize their briefs or emphasize particular points in them, and they are strictly limited in time—usually to no more than a half hour. (The lawyer speaks from a lectern that has two lights on it. When the white light goes on, the attorney has five minutes remaining; when the red flashes, he or she must stop—instantly.) The oral arguments give the justices a chance to question the lawyers, sometimes searchingly.

Since the federal government is a party—as either plaintiff or defendant—to about half the cases that the Supreme Court hears, the government's top trial lawyer, the solicitor general of the United States, appears frequently before the Court. The solicitor general is the third-ranking officer of the Department of Justice, right after the attorney general and deputy attorney general. The solicitor general decides what cases the government will appeal from lower courts and personally approves every case the government presents to the Supreme Court. In recent years, the solicitor general often has been selected from the ranks of distinguished law school professors.

In addition to the arguments made by lawyers for the two sides in a case, written briefs and even oral arguments may also be offered by "a friend of the court," or **amicus curiae.** An amicus brief is from an interested party not directly involved in the suit. For example, when Allan Bakke complained that he had been the victim of "reverse discrimination" when he was denied admission to a University of California medical school, 58 amicus briefs were filed supporting or opposing his position. Before such briefs can be filed, both parties must agree or the Court must grant permission. Though these briefs sometimes offer new arguments, they are really a kind of polite lobbying of the Court that declare which interest groups are on which side. The ACLU, the NAACP, the AFL-CIO, and the U.S. government itself have been among the leading sources of such briefs.

These briefs are not the only source of influence on the justices' views. Legal periodicals such as the *Harvard Law Review* and the *Yale Law Journal* are frequently consulted, and citations to them often appear in the Court's decisions. Thus the outside world of lawyers and law professors can help shape, or at least supply arguments for, the conclusions of the justices.

The justices retire every Friday to their conference room, where in complete secrecy they debate the cases they have heard. The chief justice speaks first, followed by the other justices in order of seniority. After the arguments they vote, traditionally in reverse order of seniority: the newest justice votes first, the chief justice last. By this process an able chief justice can exercise considerable influence—in guiding or limiting debate, in setting forth the issues, and in handling sometimes temperamental personalities. In deciding a case, a majority of the justices must be in agreement: if there is a tie, the lower-court decision is left standing. (There can be a tie among nine justices if one is ill or disqualifies himself or herself because of prior involvement in the case.)

Though the vote is what counts, by tradition the Court usually issues a written opinion explaining its decision. Sometimes the opinion is brief and unsigned (called a **per curiam opinion**); sometimes it is quite long and signed by the justices agreeing with it. If the chief justice is in the majority, he will either write the opinion or assign the task to a justice who agrees with him. If he is in the minority, the senior justice on the winning side will decide who writes the Court's opinion. There are three kinds of opinions—an **opinion of the Court** (reflecting the majority's view), a **concurring opinion** (an opinion by one or more justices who agree with the majority's conclusion but for different reasons that they wish to express), and a **dissenting opinion** (the opinion of the justices on the losing side). Each justice has three or four law clerks to help him or her review the many petitions the Court receives, study cases, and write opinions.

Many Supreme Court decisions, perhaps two-fifths of them, are decided unanimously. In these cases, the law is clear and no difficult questions of interpretation exist. But for the remaining ones, there appear to be two main blocs and one swing vote on today's Court:

- A conservative bloc of Samuel Alito, John Roberts, Antonin Scalia, and Clarence Thomas

- A liberal bloc of Stephen Breyer, Ruth Bader Ginsburg, John Paul Stevens, and (probably) Sonia Sotomayor

- A swing vote of Anthony Kennedy. He often votes with the conservatives on criminal law but on some other cases (abortion, gay rights, and foreign combatants detained at Guantanamo Bay) votes with the liberals.

per curiam opinion A brief, unsigned court opinion.

opinion of the court A signed opinion of a majority of the Supreme Court.

concurring opinion A signed opinion in which one or more members agree with the majority view but for different reasons.

dissenting opinion A signed opinion in which one or more justices disagree with the majority view.

The members of the Supreme Court, front row, from left are: Anthony Kennedy, John Paul Stevens, Chief Justice John Roberts, Antonin Scalia, and Clarence Thomas. Back row, from left are: Samuel Alito, Ruth Bader Ginsburg, Stephen Breyer, and Sonia Sotomayor.

Charles Dharapak/AP Photo

The Power of the Federal Courts

The great majority of the cases heard in the federal courts have little or nothing to do with changes in public policy: people accused of bank robbery are tried, disputes over contracts are settled, personal-injury cases are heard, and the patent law is applied. In most instances, the courts are simply applying a relatively settled body of law to a specific controversy.

THE POWER TO MAKE POLICY

The courts make policy whenever they reinterpret the law or the Constitution in significant ways, extend the reach of existing laws to cover matters not previously thought to be covered by them, or design remedies for problems that involve the judges' acting in administrative or legislative ways. By any of these tests the courts have become exceptionally powerful.

One measure of that power is the fact that more than 160 federal laws have been declared unconstitutional. And as we shall see, on matters where Congress feels strongly, it can often get its way by passing slightly revised versions of a voided law.

stare decisis "Let the decision stand," or allowing prior rulings to control the current case.

political question An issue the Supreme Court will allow the executive and legislative branches decide.

Another measure, and perhaps a more revealing one, is the frequency with which the Supreme Court changes its mind. An informal rule of judicial decision-making has been **stare decisis,** meaning "let the decision stand." It is the principle of precedent: a court case today should be settled in accordance with prior decisions on similar cases. (What constitutes a similar case is not always clear; lawyers are especially gifted at finding ways of showing that two cases are different in some relevant way.) There are two reasons why precedent is important. The practical reason should be obvious: if the meaning of the law continually changes, if the decisions of judges become wholly unpredictable, then human affairs affected by those laws and decisions become chaotic. A contract signed today might be invalid tomorrow. The other reason is at least as important: if the principle of equal justice means anything, it means that similar cases should be decided in a similar manner. On the other hand, times change, and the Court can make mistakes. As Justice Felix Frankfurter once said, "Wisdom too often never comes, and so one ought not to reject it merely because it comes late."[42]

However compelling the arguments for flexibility, the pace of change can become dizzying. By one count, the Court has overruled its own previous decisions in over 260 cases since 1810.[43] In fact, it may have done it more often, because sometimes the Court does not say that it is abandoning a precedent, claiming instead that it is merely distinguishing the present case from a previous one.

A third measure of judicial power is the degree to which courts are willing to handle matters once left to the legislature. For example, the Court refused for a long time to hear a case about the size of congressional districts, no matter how unequal their populations.[44] The determination of congressional district boundaries was regarded as a **political question**—that is, as a matter that the Constitution left entirely to another branch of government (in this case, Congress) to decide for itself. Then in 1962, the Court decided that it was competent after all to handle this matter, and the notion of a "political question" became a much less important (but by no means absent) barrier to judicial power.[45]

Alex Webb/Magnum Photos

The activism of federal courts is exemplified by the sweeping orders they have issued to correct such problems as overcrowded prisons.

By all odds the most powerful indicator of judicial power can be found in the kinds of remedies that the courts will impose. A **remedy** is a judicial order setting forth what must be done to correct a situation that a judge believes to be wrong. In ordinary cases, such as when one person sues another, the remedy is straightforward: the loser must pay the winner for some injury that he or she has caused, the loser must agree to abide by the terms of a contract he or she has broken, or the loser must promise not to do some unpleasant thing (such as dumping garbage on a neighbor's lawn). Today, however, judges design remedies that go far beyond what is required to do justice to the individual parties who actually appear in court. The remedies now imposed often apply to large groups and affect the circumstances under which thousands or even millions of people work, study, or live. For example, when a federal district judge in Alabama heard a case brought by a prison inmate in that state, he issued an order not simply to improve the lot of that prisoner but to revamp the administration of the entire prison system. The result was an improvement in the living conditions of many prisoners, at a cost to the state of an estimated $40 million a year. Similarly, a person who feels entitled to welfare payments that have been denied him or her may sue in court to get the money, and the court order will in all likelihood affect all welfare recipients. In one case certain court orders made an additional 100,000 people eligible for welfare.[46]

The basis for sweeping court orders can sometimes be found in the Constitution; the Alabama prison decision, for example, was based on the judge's interpretation of the Eighth Amendment, which prohibits "cruel and unusual punishments."[47] Others are based on court interpretations of federal laws. The Civil Rights Act of 1964 forbids discrimination on grounds of "race, color, or national origin" in any program receiving federal financial assistance. The Supreme Court interpreted that as meaning the San Francisco school system was obliged to teach English to Chinese students unable to speak it.[48] Since a Supreme Court decision is the law of the land, the impact of that ruling was not limited to San Francisco. Local courts and legislatures elsewhere decided that that decision meant that classes must be taught in Spanish for Hispanic children. What Congress meant by the Civil Rights Act is not clear; it may or may not have believed that teaching Hispanic children in English rather than Spanish was a form of discrimination. What is important is that it was the Court, not Congress, that decided what Congress meant.

VIEWS OF JUDICIAL ACTIVISM

Judicial activism has, of course, been controversial. Those who support it argue that the federal courts must correct injustices when the other branches of the federal government, or the states, refuse to do so. The courts are the institution of last resort for those without the votes or the influence to obtain new laws, and especially for the poor and powerless. After all, Congress and the state legislatures tolerated segregated public schools for decades. If the Supreme Court had not declared segregation unconstitutional in 1954, it might still be law today.

remedy A judicial order enforcing a right or redressing a wrong.

Those who criticize judicial activism rejoin that judges usually have no special expertise in matters of school administration, prison management, environmental protection, and so on; they are lawyers, expert in defining rights and duties but not in designing and managing complex institutions. Furthermore, however desirable court-declared rights and principles may be, implementing those principles means balancing the conflicting needs of various interest groups, raising and spending tax monies, and assessing the costs and benefits of complicated alternatives. Finally, federal judges are not elected; they are appointed and are thus immune to popular control. As a result, if they depart from their traditional role of making careful and cautious interpretations of what a law or the Constitution means and instead begin formulating wholly new policies, they become unelected legislators.

Some people think we have activist courts because we have so many lawyers. The more we take matters to courts for resolution, the more likely it is that the courts will become powerful. It is true that we have more lawyers in proportion to our population than most other nations. There is one lawyer for every 325 Americans, but only one for every 970 Britons, every 1,220 Germans, and every 8,333 Japanese.[49] But that may well be a symptom, not a cause, of court activity. As we suggested in Chapter 4, we have an adversary culture based on an emphasis on individual rights and an implicit antagonism between the people and the government. Generally speaking, lawyers do not create cases; contending interests do, thereby generating a demand for lawyers.[50] Furthermore, we had more lawyers in relation to our population in 1900 than in 1970, yet the courts at the turn of the 20th century were far less active in public affairs. In fact, in 1932 there were more court cases per 100,000 people than there were in 1972.

A more plausible reason for activist courts has been the developments discussed earlier in this chapter that have made it easier for people to get standing in the courts, to pay for the costs of litigation, and to bring class-action suits. The courts and Congress have gone a long way toward allowing private citizens to become "private attorneys general." Making it easier to get into court increases the number of cases being heard. For example, in 1961 civil rights cases, prisoners' rights cases, and cases under the Social Security laws were relatively uncommon in federal court. Between 1961 and 1990, the increase in the number of such matters was phenomenal: civil rights cases rose over sixtyfold and prisoners' petitions over fortyfold. Such matters are the fastest-growing portion of the courts' civil workload.

LEGISLATION AND THE COURTS

An increase in cases will not by itself lead to sweeping remedies. For that to occur, the law must be sufficiently vague to permit judges wide latitude in interpreting it, and the judges must want to exercise that opportunity fully. The Constitution is filled with words of seemingly ambiguous meaning—"due process of law," the "equal protection of the laws," the "privileges or immunities of citizens." Such phrases may have been clear to the Framers, but to the Supreme Court they have become equivocal or elastic. How the Court has chosen to interpret such phrases has changed greatly over the last two centuries in ways that can be explained in part by the personal political beliefs of the justices.

Increasingly, Congress has passed laws that also contain vague language, thereby adding immeasurably to the courts' opportunities for designing remedies. Various civil rights acts outlaw discrimination but do not say how one is to know whether discrimination has occurred or what should be done to correct it if it does occur. That is left to the courts and the bureaucracy. Various regulatory laws empower administrative agencies to do what the "public interest" requires but say little about how the public interest is to be defined. Laws intended to alleviate poverty or rebuild neighborhoods speak of "citizen participation" or "maximum feasible participation" but do not explain who the citizens are that should participate, or how much power they should have.

In addition to laws that require interpretation, other laws induce litigation. Almost every agency that regulates business will make decisions that cause the agency to be challenged in court—by business firms if the regulations go too far, by consumer or labor organizations if they do not go far enough.

One study showed that the federal courts of appeals heard over 3,000 cases in which they had to review the decision of a regulatory agency. In two-thirds of them, the agency's position was supported; in the other third, the agency was overruled.[51] Perhaps one-fifth of these cases arose out of agencies or programs that did not even exist in 1960. The federal government today is much more likely to be on the defensive in court than it was 20 or 30 years ago.

Finally, the attitudes of the judges powerfully affect what they will do, especially when the law gives them wide latitude. Their decisions and opinions have been extensively analyzed—well enough, at least, to know that different judges often decide the same case in different ways. Conservative southern federal judges in the 1950s, for example, often resisted plans to desegregate public schools, while judges with a different background authorized bold plans.[52] Some of the greatest disparities in judicial behavior can be found in the area of sentencing criminals.[53]

Checks on Judicial Power

No institution of government, including the courts, operates without restraint. The fact that judges are not elected does not make them immune to public opinion or to the views of the other branches of government. How important these restraints are varies from case to case, but in the broad course of history they have been significant.

One restraint exists because of the very nature of courts. A judge has no police force or army; decisions that he or she makes can sometimes be resisted or ignored, *if* the person or organization resisting is not highly visible and is willing to run the risk of being caught and charged with contempt of court. For example, long after the Supreme Court had decided that praying and Bible reading could not take place in public schools,[54] schools all over the country were still allowing prayers and Bible reading.[55] Years after the Court declared segregated schools to be unconstitutional, scores of school systems remained segregated. On the other hand, when a failure to comply is easily detected and punished, the courts' power is usually unchallenged. When the Supreme Court declared the income tax to be unconstitutional in 1895, income tax collections promptly ceased. When the Court in 1952 declared illegal President Truman's effort to seize the steel mills in order to stop a strike, the management of the mills was immediately returned to their owners.

Question

3. *Who was the first black Supreme Court justice?*

Judicial Review in Canada and Europe

Courts outside the United States can declare laws to be unconstitutional, but most can do so in ways that are very different from that in the United States.

Canada: The highest court can declare a law unconstitutional, but not if the legislature has passed it with a special provision that says the law will survive judicial scrutiny notwithstanding the country's Charter of Rights. Such laws must be renewed every five years.

Europe: The European Court of Human Rights in Strasbourg can decide human rights cases that begin in any of the nations that make up the European Community.

France: Its Constitutional Council can declare a law unconstitutional, but only if asked to do so by government officials and only before (not after) the law goes into effect.

Germany: The Federal Constitutional Court can declare in an advisory opinion, before a case has emerged, that a law is unconstitutional, and it can judge the constitutionality of laws when asked to do so by a lower court (which itself cannot rule a law unconstitutional). The Federal Constitutional Court may hold an administrative or judicial action to be unjustified when a citizen, having exhausted all other remedies, files a petition.

CONGRESS AND THE COURTS

Congress has a number of ways of checking the judiciary. It can gradually alter the composition of the judiciary by the kinds of appointments the Senate is willing to confirm, or it can impeach judges it does not like. Fifteen federal judges have been the object of impeachment proceedings in our history, and nine others have resigned when such proceedings seemed likely. Of the 15 who were impeached, seven were acquitted, four were convicted, and one resigned. The most recent convictions were those of Alcee Hastings of Florida and Walter Nixon of Mississippi, both in 1989.[56] In practice, however, confirmation and impeachment proceedings do not make much of an impact on the federal courts because simple policy disagreements are not generally regarded as adequate grounds for voting against a judicial nominee or for starting an impeachment effort.

Congress can alter the number of judges, though, and by increasing the number sharply, it can give a president a chance to appoint judges to his liking. As described above, a "Court-packing" plan was proposed (unsuccessfully) by Franklin Roosevelt in 1937 specifically to change the political persuasion of the Supreme Court. In 1978, Congress passed a bill creating 152 new federal district and appellate judges to help ease the workload of the federal judiciary. This bill gave President Carter a chance to appoint over 40 percent of the federal bench. In 1984, an additional 84 judgeships were created; by 1988, President Reagan had appointed about half of all federal judges. In 1990, an additional 72 judges were authorized.

During and after the Civil War, Congress may have been trying to influence Supreme Court decisions when it changed the size of the Court three times in six years (raising it from nine to 10 in 1863, lowering it again from 10 to seven in 1866, and raising it again from seven to nine in 1869).

Congress and the states can also undo a Supreme Court decision interpreting the Constitution by amending that document. This happens, but rarely: the Eleventh Amendment was ratified to prevent a citizen from suing a state in federal court; the Thirteenth, Fourteenth, and Fifteenth were ratified to undo the *Dred Scott* decision regarding slavery; the Sixteenth was added to make it constitutional for Congress to pass an income tax; and the Twenty-sixth was added to give the vote to 18-year-olds in state elections.

On over 30 occasions, Congress has merely repassed a law that the Court has declared unconstitutional. In one case, a bill to aid farmers, voided in 1936, was accepted by the Court in slightly revised form three years later.[57] (In the meantime, of course, the Court had changed its collective mind about the New Deal.)

One of the most powerful potential sources of control over the federal courts, however, is the authority of Congress, given by the Constitution, to decide what the entire jurisdiction of the lower courts and the appellate jurisdiction of the Supreme Court shall be. In theory, Congress could prevent matters on which it did not want federal courts to act from ever coming before the courts. This happened in 1868. A Mississippi newspaper editor named McCardle was

Answer

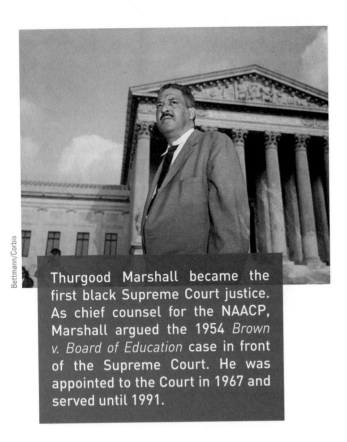

Thurgood Marshall became the first black Supreme Court justice. As chief counsel for the NAACP, Marshall argued the 1954 *Brown v. Board of Education* case in front of the Supreme Court. He was appointed to the Court in 1967 and served until 1991.

Furthermore, laws narrowing jurisdiction or restricting the kinds of remedies that a court can impose often are blunt instruments that might not achieve the purposes of their proponents. Suppose that you, as a member of Congress, would like to prevent the federal courts from ordering schoolchildren to be bused for the purpose of achieving racial balance in the schools. If you denied the Supreme Court appellate jurisdiction in this matter, you would leave the lower federal courts and all state courts free to do as they wished, and many of them would go on ordering busing. If you wanted to attack that problem, you could propose a law that would deny to all federal courts the right to order busing as a remedy for racial imbalance. But the courts would still be free to order busing (and of course a lot of busing goes on even without court orders), provided that they did not say that it was for the purpose of achieving racial balance. (It could be for the purpose of "facilitating desegregation" or making possible "redistricting.") Naturally you could always make it illegal for children to enter a school bus for any reason, but then many children would not be able to get to school at all. Finally, the Supreme Court might well decide that if busing were essential to achieve a constitutional right, then any congressional law prohibiting such busing would itself be unconstitutional. Trying to think through how *that* dilemma would be resolved is like trying to visualize two kangaroos simultaneously jumping into each other's pouches.

PUBLIC OPINION AND THE COURTS

Though they are not elected, judges read the same newspapers as members of Congress, and thus they, too, are aware of public opinion, especially elite opinion. Though it may be going too far to say the Supreme Court follows the election returns, it is nonetheless true that the Court is sensitive to certain bodies of opinion, especially of those elites—liberal or conservative—to which its members happen to be attuned. The justices will keep in mind historical cases in which their predecessors, by blatantly disregarding public opinion, very nearly destroyed the legitimacy of the Court itself. This was the case with the *Dred Scott* decision, which infuriated the North and was widely disobeyed. No such crisis exists today, but it is altogether possible that changing political moods affect the kinds of remedies that judges will think appropriate.

jailed by federal military authorities who occupied the defeated South. McCardle asked the federal district court for a writ of habeas corpus to get him out of custody; when the district court rejected his plea, he appealed to the Supreme Court. Congress at that time was fearful that the Court might find the laws on which its Reconstruction policy was based (and under which McCardle was in jail) unconstitutional. To prevent that from happening, it passed a bill withdrawing from the Supreme Court appellate jurisdiction in cases of this sort. The Court conceded that Congress could do this and thus dismissed the case because it no longer had jurisdiction.[58]

Congress has threatened to withdraw jurisdiction on other occasions, and the mere existence of the threat may have influenced the nature of Court decisions. In the 1950s, for example, congressional opinion was hostile to Court decisions in the field of civil liberties and civil rights, and legislation was proposed that would have curtailed the Court's jurisdiction in these areas. It did not pass, but the Court may have allowed the threat to temper its decisions.[59] On the other hand, as congressional resistance to the Roosevelt Court-packing plan shows, the Supreme Court enjoys a good deal of prestige in the nation, even among people who disagree with some of its decisions, and so passing laws that would frontally attack it would not be easy except perhaps in times of national crisis.

Opinion not only restrains the courts; it may also energize them. The most activist periods in Supreme Court history have coincided with times when the political system was undergoing profound and lasting changes. The assertion by the Supreme Court, under John Marshall's leadership, of the principles

Question

4. Who was the first female Supreme Court justice?

Bettmann/Corbis

of national supremacy and judicial review occurred at the time when the Jeffersonian Republicans were coming to power and their opponents, the Federalists, were collapsing as an organized party. The proslavery decisions of the Taney Court came when the nation was so divided along sectional and ideological lines as to make almost any Court decision on this matter unpopular. Supreme Court review of economic regulation in the 1890s and 1900s came at a time when the political parties were realigning and the Republicans were acquiring dominance that would last for several decades. The Court decisions of the 1930s corresponded to another period of partisan realignment. (The meaning of a realigning election was discussed in Chapter 10.)

Pollsters have been measuring how much confidence the public has in the Supreme Court. The results are shown in Figure 16.4. The percentage of people saying that they had a "great deal of confidence" in the Court rose sharply from 1971 to 1974, fell again until 1976, seesawed up and down until 1989, took a sharp dip and then recovered from 1989 to 1991, and again seesawed before rising in 1996. These movements seem to reflect the public's reaction not only to what the Court does but also to what the government as a whole is doing. The upturn in the early 1970s was probably caused by the Watergate scandal, an episode that simultaneously discredited the presidency and boosted the stock of those institutions (such as the courts) that seemed to be checking the abuses of the White House. The gradual upturn in the 1980s may have reflected a general restoration of public confidence in government during that decade.[60]

Though popular support is now relatively low for the Supreme Court, this decline has so far not resulted in any legal checks placed on it. In the 1970s and 1980s, several bills were introduced in Congress that would have restricted the jurisdiction of federal courts over busing for purposes of racial integration or altered the Supreme Court's decisions regarding school prayer and abortion. None passed.

The changes that have occurred in the Court have been caused by changes in its personnel. Presidents Nixon and Reagan attempted to produce a less activist Court by appointing justices who were more inclined to be strict constructionists and conservatives. To some extent, they succeeded: Justices Kennedy, O'Connor, Rehnquist, and Scalia were certainly less inclined than Justice Thurgood Marshall to find new rights in the Constitution or to overturn the decisions of state legislatures. But as of yet, there has been no wholesale retreat from the positions staked out by the Warren Court. As noted above, a Nixon appointee, Justice Blackmun, wrote the decision making antiabortion laws unconstitutional; and another Nixon appointee, Chief Justice Burger, wrote the opinion upholding court-ordered school busing to achieve racial integration. A Reagan appointee, Justice O'Connor, voted to uphold a right to an abortion. The Supreme Court has become somewhat less willing to impose restraints on police practices, and it has not blocked the use of the death penalty. But in general, the major features of Court activism and liberalism during the Warren years—school integration, sharper limits on police practice,

Figure 16.4

Patterns of Public Confidence in the Court, 1974–2006

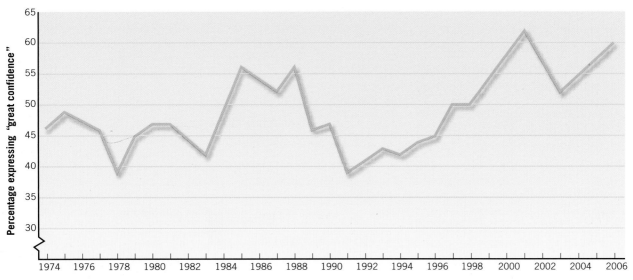

Source: The Gallup Poll.

Answer

4. Sandra Day O'Connor (on bench: 1981–2006)

What Would You Do?

MEMORANDUM

To: *Senator Ann Gilbert*

From: *Amy Wilson, legislative assistant*

The Supreme Court has held that the attorney general cannot use his authority over federally controlled drugs to block the implementation of the Oregon "Death With Dignity" law. Now some of your colleagues want to enact a federal equivalent of that law that would allow physicians to prescribe deadly drugs to patients who request them.

Legalizing Assisted Suicide

February 24
WASHINGTON, D.C.

Congress is discussing a federal law that would allow physicians to administer drugs that will lead to the death of patients who request them. Oregon already has a "Death With Dignity" statute and now some legislators wish …

Arguments for:

1. The law respects the people's rights to choose the time and place of their own death.

2. It is already permissible to post "Do Not Resuscitate" orders on the charts of terminally ill patients.

3. Physicians can be held to high standards in implementing the law.

Arguments against:

1. The law will corrupt the role of doctors as many think has happened in Holland, where a similar law has led some physicians to kill patients prematurely or without justification.

2. Such a law will lead some physicians to neglect or ignore the desires of the patient.

3. This law will undermine the more important goal of helping patients overcome pain and depression.

Your decision:

Support the law _____   Oppose the law _____

greater freedom of expression—have remained intact.

The reasons for the growth in court activism are clear. One is the sheer growth in the size and scope of the government as a whole. The courts have come to play a larger role in our lives because Congress, the bureaucracy, and the president have come to play larger ones. In 1890, hardly anybody would have thought of asking Congress—much less the courts—to make rules governing the participation of women in college sports or the district boundaries of state legislatures. Today such rules are commonplace, and the courts are inevitably drawn into interpreting them. And when the Court decided how the vote in Florida would be counted during the 2000 presidential election, it created an opportunity in the future for scores of new lawsuits challenging election results.

The other reason for increased activism is the acceptance by a large number of judges, conservative as well as liberal, of the activist view of the function of the courts. If courts once existed solely to "settle disputes," today they also exist in the eyes of their members to "solve problems."

SUMMARY

An independent judiciary with the power of judicial review—the right to decide the constitutionality of acts of Congress, the executive branch, and state governments—can be a potent political force in American life. That influence has been realized from the earliest days of the nation, when Marshall and Taney put the Supreme Court at the center of the most important issues of the time. From 1787 to 1865, the Supreme Court was preoccupied with the establishment of national supremacy. From 1865 to 1937, it struggled with defining the scope of political power over the economy. In the present era, it has sought to expand personal liberties.

The scope of the courts' political influence has increasingly widened as various groups and interests have acquired access to the courts, as the judges serving on them have developed a more activist stance, and as Congress has passed more laws containing vague or equivocal language. Whereas in other political arenas (the electorate, Congress, the bureaucracy) the influence of contending groups is largely dependent on their size, intensity, prestige, and political resources, the influence of contending groups before the courts depends chiefly on their arguments and the attitudes of the judges.

Though the Supreme Court is the pinnacle of the federal judiciary, most decisions, including many important ones, are made by the several courts of appeals and the 94 district courts. The Supreme Court can control its own workload by deciding when to grant *certiorari*. It has become easier for citizens and groups to gain access to the federal courts (through class-action suits, by *amicus curiae* briefs, by laws that require government agencies to pay legal fees, and because of the activities of private groups such as the NAACP and the ACLU).

At the same time, the courts have widened the reach of their decisions by issuing orders that cover whole classes of citizens or affect the management of major public and private institutions. However, the courts can overstep the bounds of their authority and bring upon themselves a counterattack from both the public and Congress. Congress has the right to control much of the courts' jurisdiction, but it rarely does so. As a result, the ability of judges to make law is only infrequently challenged directly.

RECONSIDERING WHO GOVERNS?

1. Why should federal judges serve for life?

Strictly speaking, they serve during "good behavior," but that means they would have to be impeached and convicted in order to be removed. The reason for this protection is clear: the judiciary cannot be independent of the other two branches of government if judges could be easily removed by the president or Congress, and this independence ensures that they are a separate branch of government.

RECONSIDERING TO WHAT ENDS?

1. Why should federal courts be able to declare laws unconstitutional?

Though the Constitution does not explicitly give them that power, they have acquired it on the reasonable assumption that the Constitution would become meaningless if the president and Congress could ignore its provisions. The Constitution, after all, states that it shall be the "supreme law of the land."

2. Should federal judges only interpret existing laws or should they be able to create new laws?

The federal courts rarely think their decisions create entirely new laws, but in fact their interpretations sometimes come close to just that. One reason is that many provisions of the Constitution are vague. What does the Constitution mean by "respecting an establishment of religion," the "equal protection of the law," or a "cruel and unusual punishment"? The courts must give concrete meaning to these phrases. But another reason is the personal ideology of judges. Some think a free press is more important than laws governing campaign finance, while others think a free press must give way to such laws. Some believe the courts ought to use federal law to strike down discrimination, but others think affirmative action programs must be put in place.

World Wide Web Resources

Federal Judicial Center: **www.fjc.gov**

Federal courts: **www.uscourts.gov**

Supreme Court decisions: **www.law.cornell.edu**

Finding laws and reports: **www.findlaw.com**

SUGGESTED READINGS

Abraham, Henry J. *The Judicial Process*. 7th ed. New York: Oxford University Press, 1998. An excellent, comprehensive survey of how the federal courts are organized and function.

Abraham, Henry J., and Barbara A. Perry. *Freedom and the Court*. 8th ed. Lawrence, KS: University of Kansas Press, 2003. Careful summary of civil liberties and civil rights cases.

Cardozo, Benjamin N. *The Nature of the Judicial Process*. New Haven, Conn.: Yale University Press, 1921. Important statement of how judges make decisions, by a former Supreme Court justice.

Ely, John Hart. *Democracy and Distrust*. Cambridge: Harvard University Press, 1980. Effort to create a theory of judicial review that is neither strict-constructionist nor activist.

Greenburg, Jan Crawford. *Supreme Conflict*. New York: Penguin, 2007. A fascinating journalistic account of how the Supreme Court operates.

Hall, Kermit L., ed. *The Oxford Companion to the Supreme Court of the United States*. New York: Oxford University Press, 1992. Everything you ever wanted to know about the Supreme Court, its justices, and its major decisions, arranged in more than a thousand alphabetical entries.

Lasser, William. *The Limits of Judicial Power*. Chapel Hill: Univer-sity of North Carolina Press, 1988. Shows how the Court through history has withstood the political storms created by its more controversial decisions.

McCloskey, Robert G. *The American Supreme Court*. 4th ed. Edited by Sanford Levinson. Chicago: University of Chicago Press, 2005.

Superb brief history of the Supreme Court, updated by one of McCloskey's former students who now teaches law at the University of Texas.

Rabkin, Jeremy. *Judicial Compulsions*. New York: Basic Books, 1989. Explains (and argues against) the extensive Court intervention in the work of administrative agencies.

Wolfe, Christopher. *The Rise of Modern Judicial Review*. New York: Basic Books, 1986. An excellent history of judicial review from 1787 to the present.

Part 4

The Politics of Public Policy

In the extended republic of the United States, and among the great variety of interests, parties, and sects, which it embraces, a coalition of a majority of the whole society could seldom take place on any other principles than those of justice and the general good.

* Federalist No. 51

17

The Policy-Making Process

WHO GOVERNS?
1. Does some political elite dominate American politics?
2. Do powerful interest groups decide what policies our government should adopt?

TO WHAT ENDS?
1. Why are Social Security payments popular but welfare payments to unwed mothers unpopular?
2. Why were government regulations on certain industries repealed over the objection of those industries?

If all you wanted to know about American politics is how our leaders are chosen and the ways in which they operate, you could close this book now. But if you are interested in how our public policies get made, you should keep reading because not all policies are made the same way.

Of course, some people claim that big business, or top bureaucrats, or powerful interest groups decide everything. But the Marxist, the Weberian, and the pluralist views are only partially correct.

Consider some outcomes that need to be explained if we are to understand the political influence wielded by just one kind of institution—the business corporation. Certain oil companies were once able to persuade the government to restrict sharply the amount of foreign oil imported into the United States, to give them preferential tax treatment, and to permit them to drill for new oil just about anywhere they liked. Today, the restrictions on foreign oil imports have ended, the tax breaks the oil companies enjoy have been reduced considerably (though they still exist), and their freedom to drill in certain places, particularly offshore locations, has been restricted.

Automobile manufacturers once faced virtually no federal controls on the products they manufactured; now they face many. In the past, some corporations have been regulated in ways that have increased their profitability (the airlines), reduced it (the railroads), or had no appreciable effect one way or the other (electric utilities). These outcomes of government action or inaction are complicated. To understand why they happen, we need some theory of policymaking. This chapter will provide one; subsequent chapters will apply it.

Setting the Agenda

The most important decision that affects policymaking is also the least noticed one: deciding what to make policy *about,* or in the language of political science, deciding what belongs on the **political agenda.** We take for granted that politics is about certain familiar issues such as taxes, energy, welfare, and civil rights. We forget that there is nothing inevitable about having these issues—rather than some other ones—on the nation's agenda. At one time, it was unconstitutional for the federal government to levy income taxes; energy was a nonissue because everybody (or at least everybody who could chop down trees for a fireplace) had enough; welfare was something for cities and towns to handle; and civil rights were supposed to be a matter of private choice rather than government action. Until the 1930s, the national political agenda was quite short, and even in the 1950s many people would have been astonished or upset to be told that the federal government was supposed to worry about the environment, consumerism, or civil rights.

political agenda Issues that people believe require governmental action.

"He who decides what politics is about runs the country."[1] This is a statement of profound significance, though it exaggerates the extent to which somebody—some person—actually "decides" what politics is all about. The statement correctly suggests that, at any given time, certain shared beliefs determine what is legitimate (proper, right) for the government to do. This legitimacy is affected by several forces:

- Shared political values—for example, if many people believe that poverty is the result of individual failure rather than social forces, then there is no reason for a government program to combat poverty.

- The weight of custom and tradition—people will usually accept what the government has customarily done, even if they are leery of what it proposes to do.

- The impact of events—wars, depressions, and the like—alter our sense of the proper role of government.

- Changes in the way political elites think and talk about politics.

THE LEGITIMATE SCOPE OF GOVERNMENT ACTION

Because many people believe that whatever the government now does it ought to continue doing, and because changes in attitudes and the impact of events tend to increase the number of things that government does, the scope of legitimate government action is always getting larger. As a result, the scope of what is illegitimate for the government to do steadily gets smaller. This means that today we hear far fewer debates about the legitimacy of a proposed government policy than we heard in the 1920s or the 1930s. The existence of "big government" is sustained by these expanded beliefs about legitimacy and is not the consequence of some sinister power grab by politicians or bureaucrats. When President Gerald Ford, a Republican, ran for election in 1976, a favorite slogan of his was that a government big enough to give you everything you want is also big enough to take away everything you have. No doubt he thought he was criticizing liberal Democrats. But it was his immediate predecessor, President Nixon, also a Republican, who had imposed peacetime wage and price controls and proposed a guaranteed annual income for every family, working or not working. It was another Republican president, Dwight Eisenhower, who had sent federal troops to Little Rock, Arkansas, to enforce a school-desegregation order. And it was yet another Republican president, Ronald Reagan, who was in office when federal payments to farmers grew to be six times larger than they had been in the 1970s. For better or worse, the expansion of government has been the result, fundamentally, of a nonpartisan process.

Popular views on the legitimate scope of government action, and thus on the kinds of issues that ought to be on the political agenda, are changed by the impact of events. During wartime or after a terrorist attack on this country, the people expect the government to do whatever is necessary to win, whether or not such actions are clearly authorized by the Constitution. (As we saw in Chapter 15, the federal bureaucracy enjoys its most rapid growth in wartime.) A depression, such as the one that began in 1929, also leads people to expect the government to do something. As we shall see in Chapter 19, public opinion favored federal action to deal with the problems of the unemployed, the elderly, and the poor well in advance of the actual decisions of the government to take action. A coal mine disaster leads to an enlarged role for the government in promoting mine safety. A series of airplane hijackings leads to a change in public opinion so great that what once would have been unthinkable—requiring all passengers at airports to be searched before boarding their flights—becomes routine.

But sometimes the government enlarges its agenda of policy issues, often dramatically, without any crisis or widespread public demand. This may happen even at a time when the conditions at which a policy is directed are improving. There was no public demand for government action to make automobiles safer before 1966, when a law was passed imposing safety standards on cars. Though the number of auto fatalities (per 100 million miles driven) had gone up slightly just before the law was passed, the long-term trend in highway deaths had been more or less steadily downward. The Occupational Safety and Health Act was passed in 1970 at a time when the number of industrial deaths (per 100,000 workers) had been steadily dropping for almost 20 years.[2] Programs to combat urban poverty and unemployment were adopted in the mid-1960s at a time when the number of persons, black as well as white, living below the poverty line was declining and when the adult unemployment rate—for blacks as well as whites—was lower than it had been at any time in the preceding 10 years.[3] Affirmative action programs were introduced to increase the flow of minorities into jobs and colleges at a time when minorities were already making rapid progress.

It is not easy to explain why the government adds new issues to its agenda and adopts new programs when there is little public demand and when, in fact, there has been an improvement in the conditions to which the policies are addressed. In general, the explanation may be found in the behavior of groups, the workings of institutions, the opinions of political elites, and the action of state governments.

Groups

Many policies are the result of small groups of people enlarging the scope of government by their demands. Sometimes these are organized interests (for example, corporations or unions); sometimes they are intense but unorganized groups (urban minorities). The organized groups often work quietly, behind the scenes; the intense, unorganized ones may take their causes to the streets.

Organized labor favored a tough federal safety law governing factories and other workplaces not because it was unaware that factory conditions had been improving but because the standards by which union leaders and members judged working conditions had risen even faster. As people became better off, conditions that once were thought normal suddenly became intolerable. When Alexis de Tocqueville sought to explain the French Revolution, he observed that citizens are most restless and easily aroused not when they are living in abject poverty or under grinding repression but when they have started to become better off.[4] Social scientists sometime refer to this as a sense of "relative deprivation."

On occasion, a group expresses in violent ways its dissatisfaction with what it judges to be intolerable conditions. The black riots in American cities during the mid-1960s had a variety of causes, and people participated out of a variety of motives. For many, rioting was a way of expressing pent-up anger at what they regarded as an unresponsive and unfair society. This sense of relative deprivation—of being worse off than one thinks one *ought* to be—helps explain why so large a proportion of the rioters were not uneducated, unemployed recent migrants to the city, but rather young men and women born in the North, educated in its schools, and employed in its factories.[5] Life under these conditions turned out to be not what they had come to expect or what they were prepared to tolerate.

The new demands of such groups need not result in an enlarged political agenda, and they do not when society and its governing institutions are confident of the rightness of the existing state of affairs. Unions could have been voted down on the occupational safety bill; rioting blacks could have been jailed and ignored. At one time, exactly this would have happened. But society itself had changed: many people who were not workers sympathized with the plight of the injured worker and distrusted the good intentions of business in this matter. Many whites felt that a constructive as well as a punitive response to the urban riots was required and thus urged the formation of commissions to study—and the passage of laws to deal with—the problems of inner-city life. Such changes in the values and beliefs of people generally—or at least of people in key government positions—are an essential part of any explanation of why policies not demanded by public opinion nonetheless become part of the political agenda.

On May Day, 2006, immigrants demonstrate in Las Vegas and many other cities to show their importance in the American economy.

Ethan Miller/Getty Images

Institutions

Among the institutions whose influence on agenda-setting has become especially important are the courts, the bureaucracy, and the Senate.

The courts can make decisions that force the hand of the other branches of government. When in 1954 the Supreme Court ordered schools desegregated, Congress and the White House could no longer ignore the issue. Local resistance to implementing the order led President Eisenhower to send troops to Little Rock, Arkansas, despite his dislike for using force against local governments. When the Supreme Court ruled in 1973 that the states could not ban abortions during the first trimester of pregnancy, abortion suddenly became a national political issue. Right-to-life activists campaigned to reverse the Court decision or, failing that, to prevent federal funds from being used to pay for abortions. Pro-choice activists fought to prevent the Court from changing its mind and to get federal funding for abortions. In these and many other cases, the courts act like trip-wires: when activated, they set off a chain reaction of events that alters the political agenda and creates a new constellation of political forces.

Indeed, they are more than tripwires. As the government agenda has expanded, the courts have become the favorite method for doing things for which there is no popular majority. There may be no electoral support for allowing abortion on demand, eliminating school prayer, creating affirmative action, ordering school busing, or attacking tobacco companies, but in the courts elections do not matter. The courts are the preferred vehicles for the advocates of unpopular causes.

The bureaucracy has acquired a new significance in American politics not simply because of its size or power but also because it is now a source of political innovation. At one time, the federal government *reacted* to events in society and to demands from segments of society; ordinarily it did not itself propose changes and new ideas. Today, the bureaucracy is so large and includes within it so great a variety of experts and advocates, that it has become a *source* of policy proposals as well as an implementer of those that become law. Daniel Patrick Moynihan called this the "professionalization of reform," by which he meant, in part, that the government bureaucracy had begun to think up problems for government to solve rather than simply to respond to the problems identified by others.[6] In the 1930s, many of the key elements of the New Deal—Social Security, unemployment compensation, public housing, old-age benefits—were ideas devised by nongovernment experts and intellectuals here and abroad and then, as the crisis of the depression deepened, taken up by the federal government. In the 1960s, by contrast, most of the measures that became known as part of Lyndon Johnson's "Great Society"—federal aid to education, manpower development and training, Medicare and Medicaid, the "War on Poverty," the "safe-streets" act providing federal aid to local law enforcement agencies—were developed, designed, and advocated by government officials, bureaucrats, and their political allies.

Chief among these political allies are U.S. senators and their staffs. Once the Senate was best described as a club that moved slowly, debated endlessly, and resisted, under the leadership of conservative southern Democrats, the plans of liberal presidents. With the collapse of the one-party South and the increase in the number of liberal activist senators, the Senate became in the 1960s an incubator for developing new policies and building national constituencies.[7] As the Senate became more conservative in the 1980s, it retained the initiative, but now on behalf of reversing some of the changes wrought earlier. The Senate has thus become one of the sources of political change rather than, as the Founders intended, a balance wheel designed to moderate change.[8]

Media

The national press can either help place new matters on the agenda or publicize those matters placed there by others. There was a close correlation between the political attention given in the Senate to proposals for new safety standards for industry, coal mines, and automobiles and the amount of space devoted to these questions in the pages of the *New York Times*. Newspaper interest in the matter, low before the issue was placed on the agenda, peaked at about the time the bill was passed.[9] It is hard, of course, to decide which is cause and which effect. The press may have stimulated congressional interest in the matter or merely reported on what Congress had already decided to pursue. Nonetheless, the press must choose which of thousands of proposals it will cover. The beliefs of editors and reporters led it to select the safety issue. In later chapters, we shall discuss the kinds of issues for which the national press is important.

In short, the political agenda can change because of changes in popular attitudes, elite interest, critical events, or government actions. An overly simple but essentially correct generalization might be this: popular attitudes usually change slowly, often in response to critical events; elite attitudes and government actions are more volatile and interdependent and thus change more quickly, often in response to each other.

ACTION BY THE STATES

National policy is increasingly being made by the actions of state governments. You may wonder how. After all, a state can only pass laws that affect its own people. Of course, the national government may later adopt ideas pioneered in the states, as it did when Congress passed a "Do Not Call" law to reduce how many phone calls you will get from salespeople while you are trying to eat dinner. The states had taken the lead in this.

But there is another way in which state governments can make national policy directly without Congress ever voting on the matter. The attorneys general of states may sue a business firm and settle the suit with an agreement that binds the industry throughout the country. The effect of that suit was to raise prices for consumers and create a new set of regulations. This is what happened in 1998 with the tobacco agreement negotiated between cigarette companies and some state attorneys general. The companies agreed to raise their prices, pay more than $240 billion to state governments (to use as they wished) and several billion dollars to private lawyers, and to agree to a massive regulatory program. A decade later, the federal government passed laws that reinforced the states' regulations, culminating in the Family Smoking Prevention Tobacco Control Act of 2009.

Making a Decision

Once an issue is on the political agenda, its nature affects the kind of politicking that ensues. Some issues provoke intense interest group conflict; others allow one group to prevail almost unchallenged. Some issues involve ideological appeals to broad national constitu-encies; others involve quiet bargaining in congressional offices. We all know that private groups try to influence government policies; we often forget that the nature of the issues with which government is dealing influences the kinds of groups that become politically active.

One way to understand how an issue affects the distribution of political power among groups and institutions is to examine what appear to be the costs and benefits of the proposed policy. The **cost** is any burden, monetary or nonmonetary, that some people must bear, or think they must bear, if the policy is adopted. The costs of a government spending program are the taxes it entails; the cost of a foreign policy initiative may be the increased chance of having the nation drawn into war. The **benefit** is any satisfaction, monetary or

cost A burden that people believe they must bear if a policy is enacted.

benefit A satisfaction that people believe they will enjoy if a policy is adopted.

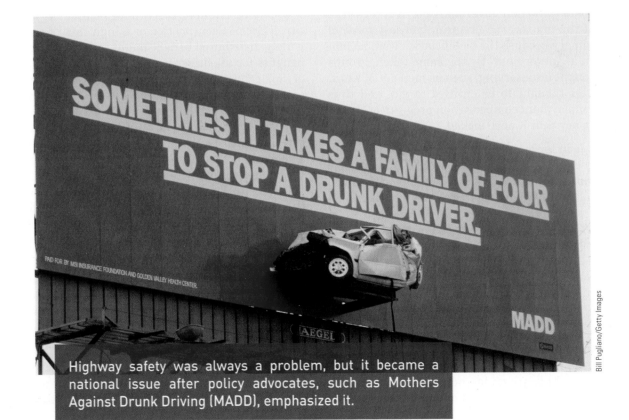

Highway safety was always a problem, but it became a national issue after policy advocates, such as Mothers Against Drunk Driving (MADD), emphasized it.

Bill Pugliano/Getty Images

nonmonetary, that people believe they will enjoy if the policy is adopted. The benefits of a government spending program are the payments, subsidies, or contracts received by some people; the benefits of a foreign policy initiative may include the enhanced security of the nation, the protection of a valued ally, or the vindication of some important principle such as human rights.

Two aspects of these costs and benefits should be borne in mind. First, it is the *perception* of costs and benefits that affects politics. People may think the cost of an auto emissions control system is paid by the manufacturer, when it is actually passed on to the consumer in the form of higher prices and reduced performance. Political conflict over pollution control will take one form when people think that Ford and GM pay the costs and another form when they think that the consumers pay.

Second, people take into account not only who benefits but also whether it is *legitimate* for that group to benefit. When programs providing financial assistance to women with dependent children were first developed in the early part of this century, they were relatively noncontroversial because people saw the money as going to widows and orphans who deserved such aid. Later on, giving aid to mothers with dependent children became controversial because some people now perceived the recipients not as deserving widows but as sexually loose women who had never married. Whatever the truth of the matter, the program had lost some of its legitimacy because the beneficiaries were no longer seen as "deserving." By the same token, groups once thought undeserving, such as men out of work, were later thought to be entitled to aid, and thus the unemployment compensation program acquired a legitimacy that it once lacked.

Politics is in large measure a process of raising and settling disputes over who *will* benefit or pay for a program and who *ought* to benefit or pay. Since beliefs about the results of a program and the rightness of those results are matters of opinion, it is evident that ideas are at least as important as interests in shaping politics. In recent years, ideas have become especially important with the rise of issues whose consequences are largely intangible, such as abortion, school prayer, and racial integration.

Though perceptions about costs and benefits change, most people most of the time prefer government programs that provide substantial benefits to them at low cost. This rather obvious fact can have important implications for how politics is carried out. In a political system based on some measure of popular rule, public officials have a strong incentive to offer programs that confer—or appear to confer—benefits on people with costs either small in amount, remote in time, or borne by "somebody else." Policies that seem to impose high, immediate costs in return for small or remote benefits will be avoided, enacted with a minimum of publicity, or proposed only in response to a real or apparent crisis.

Ordinarily, no president would propose a policy that would immediately raise the cost of fuel, even if he were convinced that future supplies of oil and gasoline were likely to be exhausted unless higher prices reduced current consumption. But when a crisis occurs, such as the Arab oil cartel's price increases beginning in 1973, it becomes possible for the president to offer such proposals—as did Nixon, Ford, and Carter in varying ways. Even then, however, people are reluctant to bear increased costs, and thus many are led to dispute the president's claim that an emergency actually exists.

These entirely human responses to the perceived costs and benefits of proposed policies can be organized into a simple theory of politics.[10] It is based on the observation that the costs and benefits of a policy may be *widely distributed* (spread over many, most, or even all citizens) or *narrowly concentrated* (limited to a relatively small number of citizens or to some identifiable, organized group). For instance, a widely distributed cost would include an income tax, a Social Security tax, or a high rate of crime; a widely distributed benefit might include retirement benefits for all citizens, clean air, national security, or low crime rates. Examples of narrowly concentrated costs include the expenditures by a factory to reduce its pollution, government regulations imposed on doctors and hospitals participating in the Medicare program, or restrictions on freedom of speech imposed on a dissident political group. Examples of narrowly concentrated benefits include subsidies to farmers or merchant ship companies, the enlarged freedom to speak and protest afforded a dissident group, or protection against competition given to an industry because of favorable government regulation.

The perceived distribution of costs and benefits shapes the *kinds of political coalitions that will form*—but it will not necessarily determine *who wins*. A given popular majority, interest group, client, or entrepreneur may win or lose depending on its influence and the temper of the times.

In the remainder of this chapter, we shall describe the politics of four kinds of policies and then illustrate each kind with examples drawn from government efforts to regulate business.

Majoritarian Politics: Distributed Benefits, Distributed Costs

Some policies promise benefits to large numbers of people at a cost that large numbers of people will have to bear (see Figure 17.1). For example, almost everybody will sooner or later receive Social Security benefits, and almost everybody who works has to pay Social Security taxes. Similarly, defending the nation against military attack benefits everyone, and every taxpayer contributes to its cost. If government-sponsored research to find cures for cancer and heart disease is successful, a large proportion of the citizenry will benefit from a program that all taxpayers have been obliged to support.

Such **majoritarian politics** are usually not dominated by pulling and hauling among rival interest groups; instead they involve making appeals to large blocs of voters and their representatives in hopes of finding a majority. The reason why interest groups are not so important in majoritarian politics is that, as we saw in Chapter 11, citizens rarely will have much incentive to join an interest group if the policy that such a group supports will benefit everybody, whether or not they are members of the group. This is the "free-rider" problem. Why join the Committee to Increase (or Decrease) the Defense Budget when what you personally contribute to that committee makes little difference in the outcome and when you will enjoy the benefits of more (or less) national defense even if you have stayed on the sidelines?

Majoritarian politics may be controversial, but the controversy is usually over matters of cost or ideology, not between rival interest groups. When Congress passed three laws to reduce drug use, this was a majoritarian issue (that is, there were no interest groups active on behalf of drug dealers). The arguments were over matters such as the desirability of the death penalty for big traffickers. The military budget went up during the early 1980s, down in the late 1980s, and up again after 2001; the changes reflected different views on how much we should spend and the relationship between military spending and arms-control negotiations.

Interest Group Politics: Concentrated Benefits, Concentrated Costs

In **interest group politics,** a proposed policy will confer benefits on some relatively small, identifiable group and impose costs on another small, equally identifiable group. For example, when Congress passed a bill requiring companies to give 60 days' notice of a plant closing or a large-scale layoff, labor unions (whose members would benefit) backed the bill, and many business firms (which would pay the costs) opposed it.

majoritarian politics
A policy in which almost everybody benefits and almost everybody pays.

interest group politics
A policy in which one small group benefits and another small group pays.

Figure 17.1

A Way of Classifying and Explaining the Politics of Different Policy Issues

PERCEIVED COSTS

PERCEIVED BENEFITS

Distributed — Concentrated

Distributed:
Majoritarian Politics | Entrepreneurial Politics

Concentrated:
Client Politics | Interest Group Politics

During the Great Depression, depositors besiege a bank hoping to get their savings out.

client politics A policy in which one small group benefits and almost everybody pays.

Issues of this kind tend to be fought out by organized interest groups. Each side will be so powerfully affected by the outcome that it has a strong incentive to mobilize: union members who worry about layoffs will have a personal stake in favoring the notice bill; business leaders who fear government control of investment decisions will have an economic stake in opposing it.

Interest group politics often produces decisions about which the public is uninformed. The bitter debates between television broadcasters and cable companies over who may send what kind of signals to which homes hardly draws any public notice—until after a law is passed and people can see their cable charges. Similarly, the long struggle to give banks the right to sell insurance involved not the public, but banks and insurance companies. In time, the public will discover whether they like the results.

Though many issues of this type involve monetary costs and benefits, they can also involve intangible considerations. If the American Nazi party wants to march through a predominantly Jewish neighborhood carrying flags with swastikas on them, the community may organize itself to resist out of revulsion against the disgraceful treatment of Jews by Nazi Germany. Each side may hire lawyers to debate the issue before the city council and in the courts.

Client Politics: Concentrated Benefits, Distributed Costs

With **client politics** some identifiable, often small group will benefit, but everybody—or at least a large part of society—will pay the costs. Because the benefits are concentrated, the group to receive those benefits has an incentive to organize and work to get them. But because the costs are widely distributed, affecting many people only slightly, those who pay the costs may be either unaware of any costs or indifferent to them, because per capita they are so small.

This situation gives rise to client politics (sometimes called clientele politics); the beneficiary of the policy is the "client" of the government. For example, many farmers benefit substantially from agricultural price supports, but the far more numerous food consumers have no idea what these price supports cost them in taxes and higher food prices. In the same way, airlines for a long time benefited from the higher prices they were able to charge on certain routes as a result of government regulations that restricted competition over prices. But the average passenger

Texas high school students protest against smoking during an event sponsored by Teens Against Tobacco Use, a peer-based tobacco use prevention program.

was either unaware that his or her costs were higher or did not think the higher prices were worth making a fuss about.

Not all clients are economic interests. Localities can also benefit as clients when, for example, a city or county obtains a new dam, a better harbor, or an improved irrigation system. Some of these projects may be worthwhile, others may not; by custom, however, they are referred to as *pork-barrel projects.* Usually several pieces of "pork" are put into one barrel—that is, several projects are approved in a single piece of **pork-barrel legislation,** such as the "rivers and harbors" bill that Congress passes almost every year. Trading votes in this way attracts the support of members of Congress from each affected area; with enough projects a majority coalition is formed. This process is called **logrolling.**

Not every group that wants something from government at little cost to the average citizen will get it. Welfare recipients cost the typical taxpayer a small amount each year, yet there was great resistance to increasing these benefits. The homeless have not organized themselves to get benefits; indeed, most do not even vote. Yet benefits are being provided (albeit in modest amounts so far). These examples illustrate the importance of popular views concerning the legitimacy of client claims as a factor in determining the success of client demands. As we shall see in Chapter 19, welfare recipients have never enjoyed much legitimacy in the public's eye, and so programs to increase their benefits were hard to sell to Congress. The plight of the homeless, on the other hand, has aroused a good deal of sympathy and produced bipartisan agreement on a bill providing emergency aid. Moreover, that agreement seems to have persisted.

A Superfund site in Houston, Texas, where bacteria were used to clean up harmful industrial waste.

Paul S. Howell/Liaison/Getty Images

By the same token, groups can lose legitimacy that they once had. People who grow tobacco once were supported simply because they were farmers, and were thus seen as both "deserving" and politically important. But when people began worrying about the health risks associated with using tobacco, farmers who produce tobacco lost some legitimacy compared to those who produce corn or cotton. As a result, it became harder to get votes for maintaining tobacco price supports and easier to slap higher taxes on cigarettes.

Entrepreneurial Politics: Distributed Benefits, Concentrated Costs

In **entrepreneurial politics,** society as a whole or some large part of it benefits from a policy that imposes substantial costs on some small, identifiable segment of society. The antipollution and safety requirements for automobiles were proposed as ways of improving the health and well-being of all people at the expense (at least initially) of automobile manufacturers. Similarly, Congress enacted the Brady bill, which requires a background check on gun buyers before they can purchase a firearm.

No policies exist unchallenged; for example, the entrepreneurial politics that got the Brady bill enacted failed to keep certain of its key provisions from being elemenated a decade later. Still, it is remarkable that policies of this sort are ever adopted, and in fact many are not. After all, the American political system creates many opportunities for checking and blocking the actions of others. The Founders deliberately arranged things so that it would be difficult to pass a new law; a determined minority therefore has an excellent chance of blocking a new policy. And any organized group that fears the loss of some privilege or the imposition of some burden will become a very determined minority indeed. The opponent has every incentive to work hard; the large group of prospective beneficiaries may be unconvinced of the benefit or regard it as too small to be worth fighting for.

pork-barrel legislation Legislation that gives tangible benefits to constituents in several districts or states in the hope of winning their votes in return.

logrolling A legislator supports a proposal favored by another in return for support of his or hers.

entrepreneurial politics A policy in which almost everybody benefits and a small group pays the cost.

Nonetheless, policies with distributed benefits and concentrated costs are in fact adopted, and in recent decades they have been adopted with increasing frequency. A key element in the adoption of such policies has been the work of people who act on behalf of the unorganized or indifferent majority. Such people, called **policy entrepreneurs,** are those both in and out of government who find ways of pulling together a legislative majority on behalf of interests that are not well represented in the government.

policy entrepreneurs Activists in or out of government who pull together a political majority on behalf of unorganized interests.

These policy entrepreneurs may or may not represent the interests and wishes of the public at large, but they do have the ability to dramatize an issue in a convincing manner. Ralph Nader is perhaps the best-known example of a policy entrepreneur, or as he might describe himself, a "consumer advocate." But there are other examples from both ends of the political spectrum, conservative as well as liberal.

Entrepreneurial politics can occur without the leadership of a policy entrepreneur if voters or legislators in large numbers suddenly become disgruntled by the high cost of some benefit that a group is receiving (or become convinced of the urgent need for a new policy to impose such costs). For example, voters may not care about government programs that benefit the oil industry when gasoline costs only one dollar a gallon, but they might care very much when the price rises to three dollars a gallon, even if the government benefits had nothing to do with the price increase. By the same token, legislators may not worry much about the effects of smog in the air until a lot of people develop burning eyes and runny noses during an especially severe smog attack.

Likewise, most legislators did not worry very much about toxic or hazardous wastes until 1977, when the Love Canal dump site near Buffalo, New York, spilled some of its toxic waste into the backyards of an adjacent residential neighborhood and people were forced to leave their homes. Five years later, anyone who had forgotten about Love Canal was reminded of it when the town of Times Beach, Missouri, had to be permanently evacuated because it had become contaminated with the chemical dioxin. Only then did it become widely known that there were more than thirty thousand toxic waste sites nationwide that posed public safety risks. Although researchers have yet to find any conclusive evidence of health damage at either site, the Superfund program was born in 1980 of the political pressure that developed in the wake of these and other highly publicized tales of toxic waste dangers. Superfund was intended to force industries to clean up their own toxic waste sites. It also authorized the Environmental Protection Agency (EPA) to act speedily, with or without cooperation from industries, in identifying and cleaning up any sites that posed a large or imminent danger.

Superfund has suffered a number of political and administrative problems, and only a few of the 1,300 sites initially targeted by the EPA had been cleaned up a dozen years after the program went into effect.[11] However, Superfund is a good illustration of entrepreneurial politics in action. Special taxes on once largely unregulated oil and chemical companies have funded the program. Previously, these companies enjoyed special tax privileges as beneficiaries of client politics; today they face special tax burdens as the targets of entrepreneurial politics.

For many reasons—including the enlarged political role of the media, the decentralization of Congress, and a change in the attitudes of many citizens—entrepreneurial politics has become more common and policy entrepreneurs more visible in recent decades.

The Case of Business Regulation

Efforts by government to regulate business not only illustrate these four kinds of policymaking processes, but also shed light on an issue that many people think is central to the study of politics—namely, the relationship between wealth and power.

To some observers, the very existence of large corporations is a threat to popular rule. Economic power will dominate political power, they believe, for one or more of three reasons: first, because wealth can be used to buy influence; second, because politicians and business leaders have similar class backgrounds and thus similar beliefs about public policy; and third, because elected officials must defer to the preferences of business so as to induce corporations to keep the economy healthy and growing. Karl Marx, of course, proposed the most sweeping version of the view that economics controls politics; for him the state in a capitalist society was nothing more than the executive committee of the propertied classes.[12] But there are other non-Marxist or neo-Marxist versions of the same concern.[13]

To other observers politics, far from being subordinate to economic power, is a threat to the very existence of a market economy and the values—economic growth, private property, personal freedom—that they believe such an economy protects. In this view, politicians will find it in their interest, in their struggle for votes, to take the side of the nonbusiness majority against that of the business minority. The heads of large corporations, few in number but great in wealth, fear that they will be portrayed as a sinister elite on whom politicians can blame war, inflation, unemployment, and pollution. Defenders of business worry that corporations will be taxed excessively to pay for social programs that in turn will produce more votes for politicians. Just as bad, in this view, is the tendency of universities (on which corporations must rely for technical experts) to inculcate antibusiness values in their students.[14]

The theory of the policymaking process presented earlier in this chapter should suggest that neither of these two extreme views of business-government relations is entirely correct. These relations depend on many things, including the *kind* of policy proposed. Instead of clenching our fists and shouting probusiness or antibusiness slogans at each other, we should be able, after applying this theory to the available facts, to make more careful and exact statements of the following sort: "If certain conditions exist, then business-government relations will take certain forms."

MAJORITARIAN POLITICS

Not all efforts to regulate business pit one group against another. From time to time, laws are passed that reflect the views of a majority of voters that is neither imposing its will on a hostile business community nor acceding to the desires of a privileged industry.

Much of the antitrust legislation passed in this country, including the Sherman Act (1890) and parts of the Federal Trade Commission Act (1914) and the Clayton Act (1914), has been the result of majoritarian politics. Toward the end of the 19th century, a broadly based criticism arose of business monopolies (then called trusts) and, to a lesser extent, of large corporations, whether or not they monopolized trade. The Grange, an organization of farmers, was especially outspoken in its criticism, and popular opinion generally— insofar as we can know it in an era without pollsters—seems to have been indignant about trusts and in favor of "trustbusting." Newspaper editorials and magazine articles frequently dwelt on the problem.[15]

But though antitrust feeling was strong, it was also relatively unfocused: no single industry was the special target of this criticism (the oil industry, and especially the Standard Oil Company, came as close as any), and no specific regulation was proposed. In fact, there was no general agreement about how to define the problem: for some it was monopoly; for others sheer bigness; and for still others the legal basis of the modern corporation. The bill proposed by Senator John Sherman did not clarify matters much: while it made it a crime to "restrain" or "monopolize" trade, it did not define these terms, nor did it create any new regulatory agency charged with enforcing the law.[16]

No doubt some large corporations worried about what all this would mean for them, but few felt sufficiently threatened to try very hard to defeat the bill. It passed the Senate by a voice vote and the House by a vote of 242 to 0.

Laws are not self-executing, and vague laws are especially likely to lie dormant unless political leaders work hard at bringing them to life. For the first decade or so after 1890, only one or two antitrust cases a year were filed in the courts. In 1904, President Theodore Roosevelt persuaded Congress to provide enough money to hire five full-time lawyers, and soon the number of prosecutions increased to about seven a year. Then in 1938, President Franklin Roosevelt appointed as head of the Antitrust Division of the Justice Department a vigorous lawyer named Thurman Arnold, who began bringing an average of 50 cases a year.[17] Today, over 400 lawyers in the division sift through complaints alleging monopolistic or other unfair business practices. Though controversy exists over the kinds of cases that should be brought, there is no serious effort among either politicians or business leaders to abandon the commitment to a firm antitrust policy, the strongest such policy found in any industrial nation.

The antitrust laws were strengthened in 1914 by bills that created the Federal Trade Commission and made (via the Clayton Act) certain specific practices, such as price discrimination, illegal. As with the earlier Sherman Act, the advocates of these measures had a variety of motives. Some proponents favored these laws because they would presumably help consumers (by preventing unfair business practices); other proponents supported them because they might help business (by protecting firms against certain tactics that competitors might employ).

President Woodrow Wilson endorsed both of these bills and helped create a broad coalition on behalf of the legislation; the Federal Trade Commission Act and the Clayton Act passed Congress by lopsided majorities.[18]

As with the Sherman Act, there has been continual controversy about how these laws should be administered. But this controversy, like the debate over the initial passage of the laws, has not been dominated by interest groups.[19] The reason for the relative absence of interest group activity is that these laws do not divide society into permanent and identifiable blocs of proponents and opponents. Any given business firm can be either helped or hurt by the enforcement of the antitrust laws. One year, the XYZ Widget Company may be sued by the government to prevent it from unfairly advertising its widgets, and the next year the same XYZ Company may ask the government to prosecute its competitor for trying to drive XYZ out of business by selling widgets at prices below cost.

The amount of money the federal government devotes to antitrust enforcement and the direction those enforcement efforts take are determined more by the political ideology and personal convictions of the administration in power than by interest group pressures. For example, the Reagan administration decided the benefits of trying to break up IBM were not worth the costs, and thus it ended its antitrust prosecution of the giant computer firm. At the same time, however, it decided it was desirable to break up American Telephone and Telegraph (AT&T), making the local phone companies independent of AT&T and forcing AT&T to compete with other long-distance service providers. In the 1990s, the Clinton administration brought an antitrust suit against computer software giant Microsoft.

Between 2001 and 2008, the Bush administration, through a high-level White House task group led by Vice President Dick Cheney, reversed many Clinton-era policies and reinstated Reagan-era ones. Then, in 2009, with the country beset by a major economic crisis, the Obama administration proposed overhauling antitrust policies yet again, folding its plan into a proposal that would centralize all relevant financial regulatory powers in just a few federal agencies. And Christine Varney, a strong antitrust enforcement advocate, was appointed to head the new administration's antitrust investigations within the U.S. Department of Justice.

In sum, as with most majoritarian policies, antitrust regulation tends to reflect broad philosophies of governance more than interest group activity.

INTEREST GROUP POLITICS

Organized interest groups are very powerful, however, when the regulatory policies confer benefits on a particular group and costs on another, equally distinct group.

In 1935, labor unions sought government protection for their right to organize, to bargain collectively with industry, and to compel workers in unionized industries to join the unions. Business firms opposed these plans. The struggle was fought out in Congress, where the unions won. The Wagner Act, passed that year, created the National Labor Relations Board (NLRB) to regulate the conduct of union organizing drives and to hear complaints of unfair labor practices brought by workers against management.

But the struggle was far from over. In 1947, management sought to reverse some of the gains won by unions by pressing for a law (the Taft-Hartley Act) that would make illegal certain union practices (such as the closed shop and secondary boycotts) and would authorize the president to obtain a court order blocking for up to eighty days any strike that imperiled the "national health or safety." Business won.

Business and labor fought round three in 1959 over a bill (the Landrum-Griffin Act) intended to prevent corruption in unions, to change the way in which organizing drives were carried out, and

The Grange sought to warn farmers of the dangers of a railroad monopoly.

The Granger Collection, New York

to prohibit certain kinds of strikes and picketing. Business won.

In each of these cases, the struggle was highly publicized. The winners and losers were determined by the partisan composition of Congress (Republicans and southern Democrats tended to support business, northern Democrats to support labor) and by the existence of economic conditions (a depression in 1935, revelations of labor racketeering in 1959) that affected public opinion on the issue.

But the interest group struggle did not end with the passage of the laws; it continued throughout their administration. The National Labor Relations Board, composed of five members appointed by the president, had to adjudicate countless disputes between labor and management over the interpretation of these laws. The losing party often appealed the NLRB decision to the courts, where the issue was fought out again. Moreover, each president has sought to tilt the NLRB in one direction or another by means of whom he appoints to it. Democratic presidents favor labor and thus tend to appoint prounion board members; Republican presidents favor business and thus tend to appoint promanagement members. Since NLRB members serve five-year terms, a new president cannot immediately appoint all of the board's members; thus there is often a split on the board between two factions.

A similar pattern of interest group influence is revealed by the history of the Occupational Safety and Health Act, passed in 1970. Labor unions wanted a strict bill with tough standards set by a single administrator; business organizations wanted a more flexible bill with standards set by a commission that would include some business representatives. After a long struggle labor won, and the Occupational Safety and Health Administration (OSHA), headed by a single administrator, was set up inside the Department of Labor.

As with the NLRB, conflict did not end with the passage of the law, and OSHA decisions were frequently appealed to the courts. The politics swirling about OSHA were all the more contentious because of the vast mandate of the agency: it is supposed to determine the safe limits for worker exposure to hundreds of chemicals and to inspect tens of thousands of workplaces to see whether they should be cited for violating any standards. During the Carter administration, an appointed OSHA administrator was sympathetic to the labor view and thus set many standards and issued many citations; during the Reagan administration, the selected administrator was admired by business because he set fewer standards and issued fewer citations.

CLIENT POLITICS

Many people suppose that when government sets out to regulate business, the firms that are supposed to be regulated will in fact "capture" the agency that is supposed to do the regulating. But as we have already seen, certain kinds of policies—those that give rise to majoritarian and interest group politics—do not usually lead to capture, because the agency either faces no well-organized, enduring opponent (as with majoritarian politics) or is caught in a crossfire of competing forces (as with interest group politics).

But when a policy confers a benefit on one group at the expense of many other people, client politics arises, and so agency "capture" is likely. More precisely, nothing needs to be captured at all, since the agency will have been created from the outset to serve the interests of the favored group. We sometimes think regulations are always resisted. But a regulation need not be a burden; it can be a great benefit.

How this works can be seen close to home. State and city laws regulate the practice of law and medicine as well as a host of other occupations—barbers, beauticians, plumbers, dry cleaners, taxi drivers, and undertakers. These regulations are sometimes designed and always defended as ways of preventing fraud, malpractice, and safety hazards. But they also have the effect of restricting entry into the regulated occupation, thereby enabling its members to charge higher prices than they otherwise might.[20] Ordinarily, citizens do not object to this, in part because they believe, rightly or wrongly, that the regulations in fact protect them, and in part because the higher prices are spread over so many customers as to be unnoticed.

Much the same thing can be found at the national level. In the early 1930s, the American dairy industry was suffering from rapidly declining prices for milk. As the farmers' incomes fell, many could no longer pay their bills and were forced out of business. Congress responded with the Agricultural Adjustment Act, which authorized an agency of the Department of Agriculture to regulate the milk industry. This agency, the Dairy Division of the Agricultural Marketing Service, would issue "market orders" that had the effect of preventing price competition among dairy farmers and thus kept the price of milk up. If this guaranteed minimum price leads to the production of more milk than people want to drink, then another part of the Agriculture Department—the Commodity Credit Corporation—stands ready to buy up the surplus with tax dollars.[21]

Consumers wind up paying more for milk than they otherwise would, but they have no way of knowing the difference between the regulated and unregulated price of milk (economists estimate that it amounts to between five and 21 cents per gallon).[22] Consumers have little incentive to organize politically to do much about it. The total cost, however, can be very high; in 2006 it was over $4 billion. Although consumers are not helped by high prices, not every dairy farmer is helped either. More milk is produced than people will buy, and so many dairy farmers have gone out of business.

A similar system works with sugar. Sugar produced abroad, in countries such as Brazil and the Philippines, costs much less than sugar produced here, in states such as Louisiana. To keep the incomes of U.S. sugar producers high, Congress decided to restrict the importation of cheap foreign sugar by imposing quotas. This costs the consumer money—maybe as much as $3 billion a year—but the extra cost per pound of sugar is not noticeable.[23]

From time to time, various officials attempt to change the regulations that benefit a client group. But they must confront some sobering political facts. Dairy farmers are found scattered through scores of congressional districts; sugar beet growers are concentrated in southern states important in any presidential election. Efforts have been made in Congress to cut milk subsidies and sugar quotas, but with only limited success.

In 1996, Congress passed and President Clinton signed a bill that began, at least for wheat and corn crops, to phase out the practice of paying farmers the difference between what they can sell their crops for and what the government thinks the crops ought to be worth. It replaced these crop subsidies with direct cash payments to farmers that they can use for anything, including not farming.

Dairy farmers get government subsidies for their milk production.

But the 1996 plan to lure farmers into a free-market economy did not last. Between 1996 and 2001, the subsidies they got increased rather than decreased. In 2002, President Bush signed a new farm bill that did away with the 1996 law and authorized paying farmers $171 billion in new subsidies by 2012. Though defended as a way of protecting "the little farmer," most of the money will go to big farmers who produce wheat, corn, rice, cotton, and soybeans (but not to those who produce cattle, hogs, poultry, fruits, or vegetables).

Farm subsidies are justified by the fact that the prices farmers earn swing wildly, but subsidies don't go to people who make computer chips or raise cattle even though they also experience big swings in the prices they can charge. The existence of farm subsidies is the result of history (a legacy of the time, during the Great Depression, when the government wanted to help nearly one-fourth of all employed Americans who then worked on farms) and politics (farmers are key and changeable voters in many important states).

Client politics has become harder to practice in this country unless a group is widely thought to be a "deserving" client. Dairy farmers, sugar producers, and tobacco growers struggle (sometimes successfully, sometimes unsuccessfully) to keep their benefits, but the struggle relies on "insider politics"—that is, on dealing with key Washington decision makers and not on building widespread public support. By contrast, when a devastating flood, tornado, earthquake, or hurricane strikes a community, the victims are thought to be eminently deserving of help. After all, people say, it was not their fault that their homes were destroyed. (In some cases, it was because they built homes in areas they knew were at high risk for hurricanes or floods.) They receive client benefits.

Although client politics for "special interests" seems to be on the decline, that is true mostly for programs that actually send certain groups money. Pietro Nivola reminds us of a different form of client politics: using regulations instead of cash to help groups. For example, regulations encourage the use of ethanol (a kind of alcohol made from corn) in gasoline, which benefits corn farmers and ethanol manufacturers. Clients that might not be thought legitimate increasingly get their way by means of regulations rather than subsidies.[24]

But regulation that starts out by trying to serve a client can end up hurting it. Radio broadcasters supported the creation of the Federal Communications Commission (FCC), which would, broadcasters and telephone companies thought, bring order and stability to their industries. It did. But then it started doing a bit more than the industries had hoped for. It began reviewing efforts by companies to merge. When one telephone company tried to merge with another, the FCC said it would have to review the consolidation even though the law did not give it the power to do so. After long (and secret) negotiations, it extracted concessions from the companies as a condition of their merger. Because there was no law requiring such concessions, the firms accepted them "voluntarily." But if they had not agreed, they would have been in deep trouble with the FCC in the future.

Regulatory agencies created to help clients can become burdens to those clients when the laws the agencies enforce are sufficiently vague so as to provide freedom of action for the people who run them. For a long time, most of these laws were hopelessly vague. The FCC, for example, was told to award licenses as "the public interest, convenience, and necessity" required. In time, such language can give an agency wide, undefined powers.

ENTREPRENEURIAL POLITICS

During the 1960s and 1970s some two dozen consumer- and environmental-protection laws were passed, including laws that regulated the automobile industry, oil companies, toy manufacturers, poultry producers, the chemical industry, and pharmaceutical companies.*

When measures such as these become law, it is often because a policy entrepreneur has dramatized an issue, galvanized public opinion, and mobilized congressional support. Sometimes that entrepreneur is in the government (a senator or an outspoken bureaucrat); sometimes that entrepreneur is a private person (the best known, of course, is Ralph Nader). The motives of such entrepreneurs can be either self-serving or public-spirited; the policies they embrace may be either good or bad. (Just because someone succeeds in regulating business does not mean that the public will necessarily benefit; by the same token, just because business claims that a new regulation will be excessively costly does not mean that business will in fact have to pay those costs.)

An early example of a policy entrepreneur inside the government was Dr. Harvey Wiley, a chemist in the Department of Agriculture, who actively campaigned for what was to become the Pure Food and Drug Act of 1906. Later, Senator Estes Kefauver held hearings that built support for the 1962 drug laws (and incidentally for his presidential bid), and Senator Edmund Muskie called attention to the need for air and water pollution control legislation (and incidentally to his own 1972 presidential aspirations).

When a policy entrepreneur is outside the government, he or she will need a sympathetic ear within it. Occasionally, the policy needs of the entrepreneur and the political needs of an elected official coincide. When Ralph Nader was walking the corridors of the Capitol looking for someone interested in auto safety, he found Senators Abraham Ribicoff and Warren Magnuson, who themselves were looking for an issue with which they could be identified.

The task of the policy entrepreneur is made easier when a crisis or scandal focuses public attention on a problem. Upton Sinclair's book *The Jungle*[25] dramatized the frightful conditions in meatpacking plants at the turn of the century and helped pave the way for the Meat Inspection Act of 1906. The stock market collapse of 1929 helped develop support for the Securities and Exchange Act. When some people who had taken a patent medicine (elixir of sulfanilamide) died as a result, the passage of the 1938 drug laws became easier. Oil spilled on the beaches of Santa Barbara, California, drew attention to problems addressed by the Water Quality Improvement Act of 1970.

The dramatic event need not be an actual crisis; in some cases, a political scandal will do. Highway fatalities were not a matter of great concern to most citizens when Congress began considering the auto-safety act in 1965–1966, but support for the bill grew when it was revealed that General Motors had hired a private detective who made a clumsy effort to collect (or manufacture) gossip harmful to Ralph Nader, whose book *Unsafe at Any Speed* had criticized the safety of certain GM cars.

In some cases, no dramatic event at all is required for entrepreneurial politics to succeed. Most of the air and water pollution control bills were passed despite the absence of any environmental catastrophe.[26] Support for such measures was developed by holding carefully planned committee hearings that were closely followed by the media. For example, by drawing attention to the profits of the pharmaceutical companies, Senator Kefauver was able to convince many people that these firms were insensitive to public needs. By drawing on information made available to him by environmentalists, Senator

---

* The Motor Vehicle Air Pollution Control Act of 1965, the National Traffic and Motor Vehicle Safety Act of 1966, the Clean Air Act of 1970, the Water Quality Improvement Act of 1970, the Children's Protection and Toy Safety Act of 1969, the Wholesome Poultry Act of 1968, the Toxic Substances Control Act of 1976, and the 1962 amendments to the Pure Food and Drug Act.

Muskie was able to capitalize on and help further a growing perception in the country during the early 1970s that nature was in danger.

Because political resistance must be overcome without the aid of a powerful economic interest group, policy entrepreneurs seeking to regulate an industry often adopt a moralistic tone, with their opponents portrayed as devils, their allies viewed with suspicion, and compromises fiercely resisted. When Senator Muskie was drafting an air pollution bill, Ralph Nader issued a highly publicized report *attacking* Muskie, his nominal ally, for not being tough enough. This strategy forced Muskie—who wanted acclaim, not criticism, for his efforts—to revise the bill so that it imposed even more stringent standards.[27] Other allies of Nader, such as Dr. William Haddon, Jr., and Joan Claybrook, got the same treatment when they later became administrators of the National Highway Traffic Safety Administration. They came under attack not only from the auto industry, for designing rules that the companies thought were too strict, but also from Nader, for devising rules that he thought were not strict enough.

Once a policy entrepreneur manages to defeat an industry that is resisting regulation, he or she creates—at least for a while—a strong impetus for additional legislation of the same kind. A successful innovator produces imitators, in politics as in rock music. After the auto safety law was passed in 1966, it became easier to pass a coal mine safety bill in 1969 and an occupational safety and health bill in 1970.

The great risk faced by policy entrepreneurs is not that their hard-won legislative victories will later be reversed but that the agency created to do the regulating will be captured by the industry it is supposed to regulate. The Food and Drug Administration (FDA), which regulates the pharmaceutical industry, has fallen victim during much of its history to precisely this kind of capture. Once the enthusiasm of its founders had waned and public attention had turned elsewhere, the FDA seemed to develop a cozy and rather uncritical attitude toward the drug companies. (In 1958, the head of the FDA received an award from the Pharmaceutical Manufacturers' Association.)[28] In the mid-1960s, under the spur of renewed congressional and White House attention, the agency was revitalized. During the Reagan administration, environmentalists worried that the leadership of the Environmental Protection Agency had been turned over to persons who were unduly sympathetic to polluters.

There are at least five reasons, however, why the newer consumer and environmental protection agencies may not be as vulnerable to capture as some critics contend. First, these agencies often enforce laws that impose specific standards in accordance with strict timetables, and so they have relatively little discretion. (The Environmental Protection Agency, for example, is required by law to reduce certain pollutants by a fixed percentage within a stated number of years.) Second, the newer agencies, unlike the FDA, usually regulate many different industries and so do not confront a single, unified opponent. The Occupational Safety and Health Administration, for example, deals with virtually every industry. Third, the very existence of these agencies has helped strengthen the hand of the "public interest" lobbies that initially demanded their creation. Fourth, these lobbies can now call upon many sympathetic allies in the media who will attack agencies thought to have a probusiness bias.

Finally, as explained in Chapter 16, it has become easier for groups to use the federal courts to put pressure on the regulatory agencies. These groups do not have to be large or broadly representative of the public; all they need are the services of one or two able lawyers. If the Environmental Protection Agency (EPA) issues a rule disliked by a chemical company, the company will promptly sue the EPA; if it issues a ruling that pleases the company, the Environmental Defense Fund will sue.

Entrepreneurial politics: Upton Sinclair's book *The Jungle,* published in 1906, shocked readers with its description of conditions in the meatpacking industry and helped bring about passage of the Meat Inspection Act of 1906.

Bettmann/Corbis

AP Photos

Perceptions, Beliefs, Interests, and Values

The politics of business regulation provides a good illustration of the theory of policymaking offered in this book, but the reader should not be misled by a discussion of costs and benefits into thinking that all or even most of politics is about getting or losing money or that it is an easy matter to classify the costs and benefits of a policy and thus put it into the correct pigeonhole.

For one thing, what constitutes a cost or a benefit is a matter of opinion, and opinions change. We have already said it is the *perception* of costs and benefits that affects politics. If people think that laws requiring factories to install devices to remove from their smokestacks chemicals that contribute to acid rain can be implemented in ways that make the companies but not the consumers pay the bills, they will favor such measures, and the affected industries will oppose them. But if people believe that the cost of preventing acid rain will be borne by them—in the form of fewer jobs or higher prices—then these citizens may be less enthusiastic about such measures.

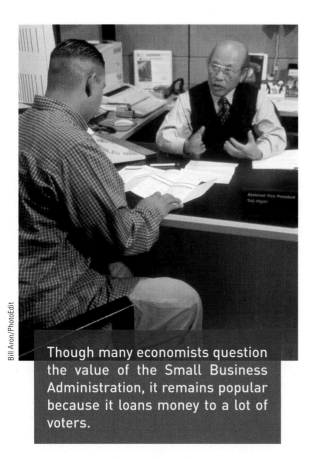

Though many economists question the value of the Small Business Administration, it remains popular because it loans money to a lot of voters.

Bill Aron/PhotoEdit

Some people favor having the government regulate the price of natural gas, and others oppose it. One reason for the conflict, obviously, is that people who use natural gas in their homes want to buy it cheaply, whereas people who work in the natural gas industry want gas prices to go up so they can earn more. Interests are clearly in conflict.

Yet some users may oppose regulating the price of gas because they believe that keeping the price of gas artificially low now will discourage exploration for new gas fields, thereby creating shortages—and much higher prices—in the future. Thus, *beliefs* are also in conflict; in this case, some users believe that it is more important to take the long view and worry about gas shortages 10 years from now, while others believe that what counts is how much you have to pay for natural gas today.

A political conflict is in large measure a struggle to make one definition of the costs and benefits of a proposal prevail over others; that is, it is a struggle to alter perceptions and beliefs. Material interests do play a part in all this: the more you stand to gain or lose in hard cash from a proposal, the harder it will be for someone else to change your mind about your position. But many, perhaps most, government proposals will not have an immediate, unambiguous impact on your pocketbook, and so your perceptions and beliefs about what will happen in the future become the prize for which political activists compete.

In that competition, certain arguments enjoy a natural advantage over others. One might be called the *here-and-now* argument. What happens now or in the near future is more important to most people than what happens in the distant future. (Economists refer to this as the human tendency to "discount the future.") Thus, most users of natural gas probably care more about present prices than future shortages, and so many will tend to favor price regulation today.

Another political tactic that enjoys a natural advantage might be called the *cost* argument. People seem to react more sharply to what they will lose if a policy is adopted than to what they may gain. Thus, there usually will be strong opposition to putting a tax on imported oil, even if the benefit gained will be to reduce our dependence on foreign oil.

Politicians know the value of the here-and-now and the cost arguments and so try to present their proposals in ways that take advantage of these sentiments. Regulations aimed at new drugs, for example, will emphasize the harm that will be prevented now from keeping dangerous drugs off the market, not the harm that may come later if lifesaving drugs with some dangerous side effects are kept off the market. Plans to solve the problems of our Social Security system stress keeping intact the benefits now received by people already retired, postponing into the future the tax increases necessary to pay for these benefits.

Policies are affected not only by our perceptions and beliefs about where our interests lie but also by our *values*—that is, by our conceptions of what is good for the country or for our community. Many whites, for example, want to see opportunities increased for minorities, not because such opportunities will make whites better off but because they think it is the right thing to do. Many citizens worry about political conditions in the Middle East, not because they fear having to fight a war there or because they work for a company that does business there but because they wish a better life for people who live in that region and want them to be free of terrorists and dictatorships. Some citizens oppose restrictions on the sale of obscene magazines and others favor those restrictions; neither group stands to benefit—those who oppose censorship usually don't plan to read the publications, and those who favor it would not thereby have their own lives improved—yet both groups often advocate their opposing views with great passion.

All this may seem obvious, but the reader should recall how often he or she assumes that people are only "looking out for themselves" and so politics only is about "who gets what." We all have a tendency to be a bit cynical about government—that is, to impute self-seeking motives to whoever is involved. Since there is plenty of self-interest in politics, this assumption is often a pretty good one. But following it blindly can lead us to ignore those cases in which ideas—beliefs, perceptions, and values—are the decisive forces in political conflict.

DEREGULATION

In the 1980s, several industries were deregulated over the objections of those industries. Airline fares were once set by the Civil Aeronautics Board. The airlines liked it that way—it kept competition down and prices up. But today airline fares are set by the market, with the result that in some (but not all) areas fares are lower than they once were. Not only did most airlines fight tooth and nail to prevent this deregulation from occurring, but some couldn't adjust to the new era of competition and, like Eastern Airlines, went bankrupt.

Long-distance telephone services were once provided on a monopoly basis by AT&T; its prices were set by the Federal Communications Commission. Today there are several long-distance telephone systems—MCI, Sprint, AT&T—and prices are heavily influenced by competition. AT&T was not eager to have this happen, but it couldn't prevent it.

Once, the number of trucking companies and the prices they charged were set by the Interstate Commerce Commission (ICC). The trucking companies and the Teamsters Union favored this pattern of regulation—as with the airlines, the system kept competition down and prices up. But then Congress changed the law, and in January 1996 the ICC was abolished.

People who think politics is simply the result of deals struck between certain favored industries and friendly or "captured" agencies would have a hard time explaining this period of deregulation. Client politics—the cozy relationship (or "iron triangle") between a private client, a government agency, and a supportive Congress—was ended. How did it happen?

Martha Derthick and Paul Quirk, two political scientists, answered the question in their book *The Politics of Deregulation*.[29] The key to that answer is the power of ideas. Academic economists were in agreement that regulating prices in industries that were competitive, or could easily be made so, was a bad idea; the regulations hurt consumers by keeping prices artificially high. But academic ideas by themselves are powerless. In the three cases described above, key political leaders—Presidents Carter, Ford, and Reagan, and Senators Edward Kennedy and Howard Cannon—accepted and acted on these ideas, albeit for very different reasons. The regulatory commissions—the Civil Aeronautics Board (CAB), the Federal Communications Commission (FCC), the ICC—were led by people who wanted to deregulate. In one case, the breakup of AT&T, a federal judge made many of the key decisions. The public did not support deregulation, but it was concerned about inflation, and deregulation could be defended as a way of bringing prices down. Finally, the industries that fought to save their client relationships with government—the airlines, the trucking companies, the phone company—were not wildly popular businesses; once they were subjected to political criticism, they found that they had relatively few allies.

Since the mid-1970s, every president has put in place machinery to bring government regulation of industry under more central review. President Ford in 1974 ordered all regulatory agencies to assess the inflationary impact of their decisions. President Carter in 1978 directed each agency to consider

WHAT WOULD YOU DO?

MEMORANDUM

To: *J. Peter, assistant to the president*

From: *Daniel Gilbert, special assistant to the president*

Subject: *Department of Energy Nuclear Waste Plan*

The president must decide whether to sign the bill allowing the department to establish a safe repository for the nation's nuclear waste beneath mountains in Nevada. The waste is produced mainly by 131 commercial nuclear reactors and by national defense weapons programs. It is presently stored at 126 sites in over three dozen states.

Friday,

Congress Approves Plan to Store Nuclear Waste in Nevada

July 23
LAS VEGAS, NEVADA

Yesterday the U.S. Congress approved a bill allowing the U.S. Department of Energy to proceed with a plan to site 70,000 tons of highly radioactive nuclear waste in Nevada. Under the plan, beginning in 2010, irradiated fuel from nuclear reactors would be shipped to Nevada from cities all over the country...

Arguments for:

1. For over 50 years, radioactive waste that remains deadly to humans for 10,000 years has been accumulating in cities and towns throughout the country.

2. According to many experts, encasing the waste in well-engineered tunnels beneath mountains in remote locations is both safer and more cost-effective than such alternatives as storing it in ocean tunnels or propelling it into space.

3. The bill achieved a bipartisan majority. Polls find that most people know little about the problem but believe that something should be done to increase safety.

Arguments against:

1. The department admits that transporting nuclear waste to the Nevada site through dozens of states on trucks, trains, and barges would take decades and pose safety risks.

2. Some experts argue that constructing a 100-mile network of tunnels that safely stores nuclear waste in disposal canisters for 10,000 years will prove technologically difficult and financially burdensome.

3. The plan is strongly opposed by many elected officials in Nevada and surrounding states, and a coalition of environmental groups is threatening to challenge it in court.

Your decision:

Advise president to sign _____

Advise president not to sign _____

alternative ways of achieving the goals of regulation. President Reagan in 1981 created the Task Force on Regulatory Relief and instructed those agencies under his control not to issue a regulation if, in the judgment of the Office of Management and Budget, its potential benefits to society did not outweigh its costs.[30] President Bush the elder essentially continued the Reagan system.

Deregulation is opposed, of course, by groups that benefit from regulation. But it is controversial in at least two other ways. First, some members of the public do not like the results, especially if the world becomes more complicated as a result of relying on the market. Many people liked CAB control of the airlines, for example, because the higher prices kept the number of air travelers down, and so airports were less congested. Second, some people who favor deregulating *prices* oppose deregulating *processes.* **Process regulation** (sometimes called social regulation) includes rules aimed at improving consumer or worker safety and reducing environmental damage. There are good and bad ways of achieving these goals, and much of the dispute about regulation concerns the question of means, not ends. The intensity of that dispute shows how important perceptions and beliefs are even when economic interests are at stake.

process regulation Rules governing commercial activities designed to improve consumer, worker, or environmental conditions. Also called social regulation.

It is too soon to know, but we might be entering into a new period in which "deregulation," whether of financial markets, consumer products, telecommunications, or other domains, is treated by many politicians in both parties as a dirty word.

For instance, among the many reasons widely believed to be behind the financial meltdown that many observers date to September 2008 is how the Securities and Exchange Commission (SEC) and other financial regulatory bodies exempted brokerage firms from old regulations that limited the amount of debt they could take on, and thereby freed them to make unconventional and, as it turned out, unsafe and unstable investments (such as so-called mortgage-backed securities and credit derivatives).

Similarly, in 2008 and 2009, opinion polls suggested that most average Americans did not believe that the Food and Drug Administration (FDA) does enough to regulate the safety of drugs; meanwhile, the Consumer Product Safety Commission (CPSC) was challenged regarding public scares about lead paint in imported toys, and the Federal Communications Commission (FCC) was widely criticized regarding rising cell phone, cable television, and Internet service bills.

Whether what critics call the "drive to deregulate" actually has weakened these or other agencies or otherwise produced perverse and unintended consequences that obviate the benefits of deregulation is less important politically than what most people and their elected representatives believe to be true.

THE LIMITS OF IDEAS

Ideas can be powerful, but there are limits to their power. There are many forms of client politics that persist—some because people agree that the client deserves to benefit, others because the conditions do not exist for mounting an effective challenge to the client.

Dairy, sugar, and other agricultural price supports are paid for by tax payers. Regulations that increased above market levels the prices charged by airlines and trucking companies were successfully challenged; regulations that increased above market levels the prices charged by oceangoing freighters were not. The wages paid to airline pilots and truck drivers are no longer protected by federal rules; the wages paid to merchant seamen and construction workers employed on federal projects still are.

It is not entirely clear why it is easier to challenge client politics in some industries and occupations than in others. We can say, however, why it generally is harder to maintain client politics free of challenge today than once was the case.

SUMMARY

Policymaking involves two stages—placing an issue on the governmental agenda and deciding what to do about that issue once it is on the agenda. The agenda steadily expands as the result of historical crises, interest group activity, the competition for votes, and the operation of key institutions, especially the courts, the bureaucracy, and the mass media.

Decision-making requires that a majority coalition be formed. The kinds of coalitions that form will depend in large measure on the nature of the issue, especially the perceived distribution of costs and benefits. We have identified four kinds of coalitions, or distinctive political processes: majoritarian, client, interest group, and entrepreneurial.

Government regulation of business illustrates the relationship between these four kinds of policies and the sorts of coalitions that will form in each instance. These case studies make clear that there is no single, simple answer to the question of how much influence business has over government (or vice versa).

The outcome of these political struggles will depend not only on who gains and who loses but also on the perceptions, beliefs, and values of key political actors. The example of airline deregulation shows that changes in how people think can make a big difference even in the case of policies where money interests are at stake.

RECONSIDERING WHO GOVERNS?

1. Does some political elite dominate American politics?

People active in politics are an elite in the sense that they play a larger role than most citizens. But there are so many American elections and so many places where political action can be blocked that no single elite can dominate. Business corporations, for example, are an important interest group, but they only dominate client politics, and even then their influences can be overcome by entrepreneurial politics.

2. Do powerful interest groups decide what policies our government should adopt?

Over the last half century, there has been a sharp increase in the number and variety of interest groups so that in interest group politics there are always rival organizations competing for influence. In client politics, one interest group can dominate decision-making, but client politics is becoming rarer as new interest groups emerge.

RECONSIDERING TO WHAT ENDS?

1. Why are Social Security payments popular but welfare payments to unwed mothers unpopular?

For two reasons: First, people who get retirement benefits have paid money into the program, while those who get welfare benefits have not. Second, many people think elderly people who have retired are legitimate recipients of payments but that unwed mothers are not.

2. Why were government regulations on certain industries repealed over the objection of those industries?

There were several reasons, but the most important were new ideas. When enough political leaders became convinced that government-regulated airfares, bank interest rates, and trucking charges made people pay more money than would fares, rates, and charges set by the market, government regulation was abandoned.

WORLD WIDE WEB RESOURCES

Nonpartisan reviews of public policy issues

www.policy.com

www.publicagenda.org

For partisan discussion of issues, use the World Wide Web addresses of the Washington, D.C., think tanks listed in Chapter 11.

SUGGESTED READINGS

Derthick, Martha. *Up in Smoke.* Washington, D.C.: Congressional Quarterly Press, 2002. Fascinating account of how lawyers and tobacco companies created a private regulation of smoking.

Derthick, Martha, and Paul J. Quirk. *The Politics of Deregulation.* Washington, D.C.: Brookings Institution, 1985. A brilliant analysis of how three industries—airlines, trucking, and telecommunications—were deregulated, often in the teeth of industry opposition.

Kingdon, John W. *Agendas, Alternatives, and Public Policies.* Boston: Little, Brown, 1984. An insightful account of how issues, especially those involving health and transportation, get on (or drop off) the federal agenda.

Lowi, Theodore J. "American Business, Public Policy, Case Studies, and Political Theory."

World Politics 16 (July 1964). A theory of policy-making somewhat different from that offered in this book.

Nadel, Mark V. *The Politics of Consumer Protection.* 2d ed. Indianapolis: Bobbs-Merrill, 1975. An analysis of the sources and uses of political influence in consumer legislation.

Polsby, Nelson W. *Political Innovation in America.* New Haven, Conn.: Yale University Press, 1984. Explains how eight policy innovations were adopted by the federal government.

Wilson, James Q., ed. *The Politics of Regulation.* New York: Basic Books, 1980. Analyzes regulatory politics in nine agencies and provides a more detailed statement of the theory presented in this text.

18

Economic
Policy

TIMOTHY A. CLARY/AFP/Getty Images

WHO GOVERNS?

1. Who in the federal government can make our economy strong?
2. Who was responsible for the recession?

TO WHAT ENDS?

1. Why does the federal government ever have a budget deficit?
2. How do you end a recession?

Like most Americans, you probably think about the way the government spends its money the same way you think about how you ought to spend yours. If you spend more than you earn, you will have to borrow money and pay it back to the bank. If you want to buy a car or a house, you will have to get a loan and make monthly payments on it. It you run up so many charges on your credit card that it is maxed out, you won't be able to charge anything more on it. If you keep spending more than you earn, you will have to declare bankruptcy. Surely, the government ought to work the same way: spend no more than it earns and pay back its loans.

But it doesn't. With just a few exceptions, the government has spent more money than it takes in every year since at least 1960. The amount it spends in excess of what it takes in each year is called the **deficit.** It is financed by selling government bonds, issued by the Treasury Department, to Americans and foreigners. The total amount of all deficits is the **national debt** (see Figure 18.1). How can the government in Washington get away with this?

There are three reasons: one economic, one substantive, and one political. The economic reason is that a debt is important only insofar as the government cannot make the payments on its bonds in a currency that people regard as stable and valuable. Happily, almost everybody around the world regards the American dollar as stable and valuable. As a result, people line up to buy Treasury bonds whenever they are sold. And so the government in Washington, like the owners of Wal-Mart, can pay for whatever they want. But to keep our currency stable, people must believe that the dollar will always be valuable and that the government is not borrowing more than it can pay back. Some observers have complained that a big government debt will cause prices to rise (inflation) or investment in new businesses to suffer. But inflation will not occur if the government does not print a lot of money. And low levels of investment will not occur if the government does not take a lot of money out of circulation. Later in this chapter, we will explain how these things might occur.

The government must pay the interest on the federal debt just as you have to pay the interest on your car loan. The total federal debt is a very large number (over $9 trillion), but the number, while huge, does not mean much when taken alone. The key is what fraction of our federal spending is used to pay interest on the debt. In 2008, that interest was about 8 percent of all federal expenditures, making interest the third most expensive program (behind social welfare and defense). It is a lot of money, but the percentage is a lot less than what many families pay in interest on their car and home.

The economy can afford paying this interest. Federal interest payments take up about 1.7 percent of the total value of all the goods and services the nation produces. This output is called **gross domestic product,** or GDP. In two years, while Bill Clinton was president we had no deficit, but those brief surpluses did not reduce the total debt by very much.

The American economy can easily pay the annual deficit, but it may have greater trouble managing the total public debt after one realizes two things. First, there can be a serious recession when businesses fail, unemployment rises, and economic growth stops. This happened, starting in 2007 and continuing through 2009 and perhaps beyond. Second, our population is getting older. This creates huge new demands for Social Security retirement benefits and medical payments under Medicare (see Chapter 19). When a recession and an older population occur together, our national debt and interest payments to support it will shoot up.

The substantive argument about our debt is what we buy with this money. Most families borrow to buy long-lasting items, like a home, a new car, or a college education. We don't really know what the federal debt is used for. It would be nice if we knew that we borrowed only to pay for long-lasting things that enhanced security and economic growth, such as schools, aircraft carriers, and basic health care research. But our government borrows whenever it needs the money without much regard for what it gets.

The political argument is easier to understand: since they know the public is opposed to the government going into debt, politicians will also oppose the debt, but they offer two opposed ways to combat it. One, advanced by conservatives, is by cutting spending; the other, offered by liberals, is raising taxes. But since the people do not want less spending on programs they favor and certainly don't want higher taxes, these contradictory political strategies are hard to reconcile.

The Politics of Economic Prosperity

The health of the American economy creates majoritarian politics. Hardly anyone wants inflation or unemployment; everyone wants rapid increases in income and wealth. But this fact is a bit puzzling.

You might think that people would care about their own jobs and worry only about avoiding their own unemployment. If that were the case, they would vote for politicians who promised to award contracts to firms that would hire them or who would create programs that would benefit them, regardless of how well other people were getting along. In fact, though, people see connections between their own well-

Figure 18.1

Federal Budget Deficit (or Surplus), FY 1960–2008 in Billions of CONSTANT FY 2003 Dollars (President's Proposals)

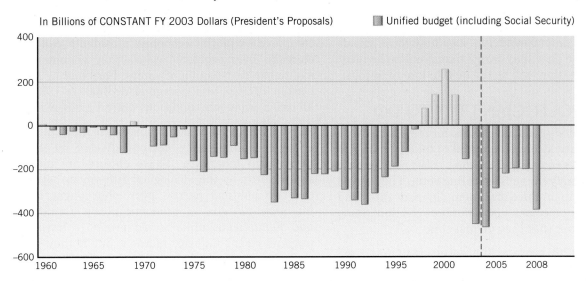

Source: Budget of the U.S. Government, FY 2009 updated by OMB's Mid-Session Review, July 2009 © 2003, AAAS. Reprinted with permission.

being and that of the nation, and they tend to hold politicians responsible for the state of the country.

Everybody knows that just before an election politicians worry about the *pocketbook issue*. We have seen in Chapter 10 that economic conditions are strongly associated with how much success the incumbent party has in holding on to the White House and to the seats held by the White House's party in Congress. But whose pocketbook are voters worried about?

In part, of course, it is their own. We know that low-income people are more likely to worry about unemployment and to vote Democratic, and higher-income people are more likely to worry about inflation and to vote Republican.[1] We also know that people who tell pollsters that their families' finances have gotten worse are more likely than other people to vote against the incumbent president.[2] In 1980, about two-thirds of those who said they had become worse off economically voted for Ronald Reagan, the challenger, while over half of those who felt they had become better off voted for Jimmy Carter, the incumbent.[3] In 1992, people who felt economically pinched were more likely to vote for Clinton than for Bush. Clinton campaign aides often reminded each other, "It's the economy, stupid!"

But people do not simply vote their own pocketbooks. In any recession, the vast majority of people still have jobs; nevertheless, these people say unemployment is the nation's biggest problem, and many of them vote accordingly—against the incumbent during whose watch unemployment went up.[4] Why

should employed people worry about other people's unemployment?

By the same token, younger voters—whose incomes tend to go up each year—often worry less about inflation than retired people living on fixed incomes, the purchasing power of which goes down with inflation.[5] In presidential elections, those who think national economic trends are bad are much more likely to vote against the incumbent, *even when* their own personal finances have not worsened.[6]

In technical language, voting behavior and economic conditions are strongly correlated at the national level but not at the individual level, and this is true both in the United States and in Europe.[7] Such voters are behaving in an "other-regarding" or "sociotropic" way. In ordinary language, voters seem to respond more to the condition of the national economy than to their own personal finances.

It is not hard to understand why this might be true. Part of the explanation is that people understand what government can and cannot be held accountable for. If you lose your job at the aircraft plant because the government has not renewed the plant's contract, you will be more likely to hold the government responsible than if you lose your job because

> *deficit* The result of when the government in one year spends more money than it takes in from taxes.
>
> *national debt* The total deficit from the first presidency down to the present.
>
> *gross domestic product* The total of all goods and services produced in the economy during a given year.

you were always showing up drunk or because the plant moved out of town.

And part of the explanation is that people see general economic conditions as having indirect effects on them even when they are still doing pretty well. They may not be unemployed, but they may have friends who are, and they may worry that if unemployment grows worse, they will be the next to lose their jobs.

WHAT POLITICIANS TRY TO DO

Elected officials, who have to run for reelection every few years, are strongly tempted to take a short-run view of the economy and to adopt those policies that will best satisfy the self-regarding voter. They would dearly love to produce low unemployment rates and rising family incomes just before an election. Some scholars think that they do just this.

Since the 19th century, the government has used money to affect elections. At first this mostly took the form of patronage passed out to the party faithful and money benefits given to important blocs of voters. The massive system of Civil War pensions for Union army veterans was run in a way that did no harm to the political fortunes of the Republican party. After the Social Security system was established, Congress voted to increase the benefits in virtually every year in which there was an election (see Chapter 19).

But it is by no means clear that the federal government can or will do whatever is necessary to reduce unemployment, cut inflation, lower interest rates, and increase incomes just to win an election. For one thing, the government does not know how to produce all of these desirable outcomes. Moreover, doing one of these things often may be possible only at the cost of not doing another. For example, reducing inflation can, in many cases, require the government to raise interest rates, and this in turn can slow down the economy by making it harder to sell

Tea Party protests demonstrate against deficit financing.

houses, automobiles, and other things purchased with borrowed money.

If it were easy to stimulate the economy just before an election, practically every president would serve two full terms. But because of the uncertainties and complexities of the economy, presidents can lose elections over economic issues they do not manage to the satisfaction of voters. Ford lost in 1976, Carter in 1980, and George H.W. Bush in 1992. In all cases, economic conditions played a major role.

All this means that politicians must make choices about economic policy, choices affected by uncertainty and ignorance. Those choices are shaped significantly by the ideological differences between the two political parties over what ought to be the principal goal of economic policy. Democrats and Republicans alike would prefer to have low unemployment and no inflation, but if they must choose (and choose they must), then the Democrats mainly attempt to reduce unemployment and the Republicans chiefly attempt to reduce inflation.[8]

This tendency mirrors to some degree what Democratic and Republican voters want their parties to do. Polls regularly show that those who think of themselves as Democrats are much more worried about unemployment than those who think of themselves as Republicans.[9] (There is not as much of a difference between Democratic and Republican voters in worrying about inflation.) Because of these beliefs, voters concerned about unemployment not only are more likely to vote against the incumbent but also are more likely to vote Democratic.

The Politics of Taxing and Spending

People want prosperity, but they also want no tax increases, no government deficit, and continued (or higher) government spending on the things they like, such as education, medical care, the environment, and retirement benefits. Politicians confront two inconsistent kinds of majoritarian politics: everybody wants general prosperity, and large majorities want more government spending on popular programs. But the more the government spends on popular programs, the more money it requires, and the more it takes in, the less that is left over for private investment that produces prosperity.

Most voters would like to have all three things—lower taxes, less debt, and new programs. But the difficulty with this is that the policies endorsed are inconsistent with one another. We cannot have

What Caused the 2007–2009 Recession?

It was a perfect storm. The Federal Reserve Bank made borrowed money cheap by lowering interest rates (see page 494). Firms invented new ways of selling mortgages to investors. The government made it easy for poor people to get mortgages. They were called "subprime" because they went to people with low credit ratings who put up a small (if any) deposit. Investment firms invented new ways of selling mortgages. Cheap money combined with a big market for mortgages produced a housing boom and made it easy to get loans.

Investment banks packaged good and subprime mortgages together and sold them as "mortgage-backed securities." The theory was that since each of these securities was backed by so many mortgages, a few could fail without hurting the value of the stock. Credit agencies were optimistic and said these were good deals.

For a while, it was a great success. More people bought homes, the price of these homes shot up, and people and firms used borrowed money to buy whatever they wanted. The unemployment rate was low. Everybody was happy.

But these changes led people and businesses to borrow more money than they could afford to pay back. The problem began with banks. Under federal rules, banks must have at least $1 of their own capital for every $12 dollars of deposits they accept. This makes it easier to fund mortgages. But there is a risk: if a lot of people who have mortgages stop making payments, then the bank may go out of business. Suppose a bank has $10 million in capital and issues mortgages worth $100 million. Suppose further that these mortgages decline in value by $10 million. The bank's capital ($10 million) is wiped out. Worried depositors will start withdrawing their money, and worried investors will sell their stock in the bank. The bank will fail.

The recession began when some people could no longer make their mortgage payments. Private and public regulatory agencies told the people who owned these mortgages that they had to write down their value. Suddenly, banks and investment companies with valueless mortgages began to fail. The firms that had insured these loans could not afford to pay for them. The market for credit froze. Many firms started firing people and others went out of business. The recession was underway.

Some people think all of this simply showed a weakness in America's private economy. They are wrong. Government was a big part of the problem. The two biggest purchasers of bank mortgages were the Federal National Mortgage Association (known as Fannie Mae) and the Federal Home Loan Mortgage Corporation (known as Freddie Mac). By 2007, they owned $5 *trillion* worth of mortgages.

These firms were created and sponsored by the federal government, but they were owned by private investors. Despite being privately owned, many people believed the federal government would stand behind Fannie Mae and Freddie Mac. One reason for this belief was that Washington politicians told the two firms how to behave. In particular, they told them to issue "subprime" mortgages. The goal was to extend home ownership to poor people. The problem is that poor people often cannot afford a mortgage.

When some people stopped paying for their mortgages, the federal government took over Fannie Mae and Freddie Mac because they were bankrupt. Private investment houses were also in trouble; a few went out of business or were sold to other firms.

The credit squeeze was on. Banks were reluctant to lend money and people were worried about borrowing it. Without credit, contractors stopped building homes and auto dealers stopped selling cars. As firms lost business, they began laying off workers. The unemployment rate went up. The value of homes sharply declined. The stock market collapsed. The recession was in full swing.

---

lower taxes, no debt, and higher spending on politically popular programs such as health care, education, the environment, and retirement benefits. If we have more spending, we have to pay for it, either with higher taxes or with more borrowing.

People who want new programs have to either cut existing programs, let the government go deeper in debt, or raise taxes. But how do you raise taxes without alienating voters? The answer is that you raise taxes on *other people*.

The "other people" are always a minority of the voters. For example, if you want to put more money into medical research (something that everybody likes), you raise taxes on cigarettes (only a minority smoke

During the recession, people, including middle class workers, line up at the unemployment office.

Yellow Dog Productions/Getty Images

them). If you want to pay for new education programs or bigger environmental programs, you raise taxes on affluent voters. In this way, you can find a majority of voters who will support—or at least not oppose very strongly—tax increases on a small group of voters—cigarette smokers or high-income people.

Legislators who like high rates say that "people who can afford it should pay a lot." Legislators who want low rates say that their opponents are trying to "soak the rich" by denying tax cuts to the people who now pay the biggest share of taxes.

Economic Theories and Political Needs

There are four main theories about how to improve the economy. When presidents select economic advisers, they often choose people who identify with one of these theories. In general, conservative economists tend to support monetarism and supply-side economics, while liberal economists are more likely to embrace Keynesianism and planning. Here, we give a highly simplified account of them and what each implies about ending a recession.

monetarism The belief that inflation occurs when too much money is chasing too few goods.

Keynesianism The belief the government must manage the economy by spending more money when in a recession and cutting spending when there is inflation.

economic planning The belief that government plans, such as wage and price controls or the direction of investment, can improve the economy.

MONETARISM

A monetarist, such as the late economist Milton Friedman, believes that inflation occurs when too much money chases too few goods. The federal government has the power to create money (in ways to be described on page 494); according to monetarists, inflation occurs when it prints too much money. When inflation becomes rampant and government tries to do something, it often cuts back sharply on the amount of money in circulation. Then a recession will occur, with slowed economic growth and an increase in unemployment. Since the government does not understand that economic problems result from its own start-and-stop habit of issuing new money, it will try to cure some of these problems with policies that make matters worse—such as having an unbalanced budget or creating new welfare programs. **Monetarism** suggests that the proper thing for government to do is to have a steady, predictable increase in the money supply at a rate about equal to the growth in the economy's productivity. When the economy goes into a recession, however, many monetarists think the Federal Reserve Bank ("the Fed") should cut interest rates to make it easier for people and businesses to borrow money. That is what the Fed did during 2008.

KEYNESIANISM

John Maynard Keynes, an English economist who died in 1946, believed that the market will not automatically operate at a full-employment, low-inflation level. Its health depends on what fraction of people's incomes they save or spend. If they save too much, there will be too little demand, production will decline, and unemployment will rise. If they spend too much, demand will rise too fast, prices will go up, and shortages will develop. According to **Keynesianism,** the key is to create the right level of demand. This is the task of government. When demand is too little, the government should pump more money into the economy (by spending more than it takes in in taxes and by creating public-works programs). When demand is too great, the government should take money out of the economy (by increasing taxes or cutting federal expenditures). There is no need for the government's budget to be balanced on a year-to-year basis; what counts is the performance of the economy.

PLANNING

Some economists have too little faith in the workings of the free market to be pure Keynesians, much less monetarists. They believe the government should plan, in varying ways, some part of the country's economic activity. One form of **economic planning** is price and wage controls, as advocated by John Kenneth Galbraith and others. In this view, big corporations can raise prices because the forces of competition are too weak to restrain them, and labor

Washington Tries to Stimulate the Economy

First Stimulus Bill (February, 2008)

- $125 billion paid to people in checks of $600 each

  Results: Almost none. People paid down loans or saved the money; only one-fifth spent it.

Troubled Asset Relief Program (October, 2008)

- $700 billion invested

- Buy shares in troubled banks and insurance companies

- Make loans to Chrysler and General Motors

- Make payments to troubled mortgage owners

  Results: No one knows.

American Recovery and Reinvestment Act (February 2009)

- $787 billion (over 11 years)

- Tax cuts and benefit checks for people earning less than $75,000 (total = $237 billion)

- Tax cuts for some businesses (total = $51 billion)

- Paying for unemployment benefits, health insurance, food stamps, etc. (total = $322 billion)

- Grants to states for Medicaid, highways, school construction, etc. (total = $155 billion)

- Money to repair or manage federal facilities (total = $57 billion)

  Results: No one knows.

Federal Reserve Board

- Federal Reserve spending $1.8 trillion (The Fed can create money by writing a check)

- Fed will help banks borrow money at low rates, purchase some corporate debt, and help bail out some investment houses (Bear Stearns) and insurance companies (AIG).

  Results: Too early to tell.

Public-Private Investment Program (March 23, 2009)

- A program to help banks and others get rid of bad loans.

- An auction will be held in which investors can buy up bad loans at low prices, with the federal government paying for much of the cost.

  Results: Not much so far. Banks are reluctant to sell bad loans at the low prices the auction might produce.

Source: Updated from "Sorting Out the Bailouts," *Congressional Quarterly Weekly* (February 23, 2009).

---

unions can force up wages because management finds it easy to pass the increases along to consumers in the form of higher prices. Thus during inflationary times, the government should regulate the maximum prices that can be charged and wages that can be paid, at least in the larger industries.

Planning has never been popular in America, but when the TARP program began investing in banks, some people began to suggest that perhaps the government should own the banks. That way, they said, the government might get back some of the money it had spent on them. The government was already the largest single stockholder in Bank of America and Citigroup (though in each case it owned less than half the stocks).

SUPPLY-SIDE TAX CUTS

Exactly the opposite remedy for declining American productiv-ity is suggested by people who call themselves supply-siders. The view of economists such as Arthur Laffer and Paul Craig Roberts is that the market, far from having failed, has not been given an adequate chance. According to **supply-side theory,** what is needed is not more planning but less government interference. In particular, sharply cutting taxes will increase people's incentive to work, save, and invest. Greater investments will then lead to more jobs, and if the earnings

> *supply-side theory* The belief that lower taxes and fewer regulations will stimulate the economy.

Landmark Cases

Federal Laws About Commerce

- *Lochner v. New York* (1905): Struck down as unconstitutional a New York law limiting the number of hours that may be worked by bakers.

- *Muller v. Oregon* (1980): Upheld as constitutional an Oregon law limiting the number of hours worked by women; in effect, it overruled the Lochner decision.

- *West Coast Hotel Co. v. Parrish* (1937): Upheld as constitutional a Washington State minimum wage law for women.

- *Youngstown Sheet & Tube Co. v. Sawyer* (1952): The president does not have the authority to seize private steel mills even in wartime.

from these investments and jobs are taxed less, it will lessen the tendency of many individuals to shelter their earnings from the tax collector by taking advantage of various tax loopholes or cheating on their income tax returns. The greater productivity of the economy will produce more tax revenue for the government. Even though tax *rates* will be lower, the total national income to which these rates are applied will be higher.

DID THE FEDERAL GOVERNMENT END THE RECESSION?

The box on page 491 summarizes the complicated efforts the federal government made to end the recession that began in 2007. If you take a course in economics, you may be able to learn what effect these efforts have had. But here you can learn about the *politics* of these attempts.

Proponents (in Congress, almost entirely the Democrats) of the second stimulus law enacted in early 2009 believed that several things had to be done:

- Give money to people so they could spend more.

- Spend more money on state, local, and federal projects to create jobs.

- Borrow the money to pay for these programs.

Critics of the second stimulus plan (in Congress, almost every Republican) believed this approach was wrong because:

- Spending more money on government projects would not help because much of it would not produce benefits for several years.

- Borrowing a lot of money would vastly increase the federal debt.

- More could be accomplished by sharply cutting tax rates on people and businesses so that they would spend and invest more.

The Machinery of Economic Policy Making

Predicting what will happen to the economy is very hard. Few economists, for example, foresaw the 2007–2009 recession. But even if the president knew exactly the right thing to do, he would still have to find some way of doing it. In our government, that is no easy task. The machinery for making decisions about economic matters is complex and not under the president's full control. Within the executive branch, three people other than the president are of special importance. Sometimes called the troika,* these are the chairman of the Council of Economic Advisers (CEA), the director of the Office of Management and Budget (OMB), and the secretary of the treasury.

The CEA, composed of three professional economists plus a small staff, has existed since 1946. In theory, it is an impartial group of experts responsible for forecasting economic trends, analyzing economic issues, and helping prepare the economic report that the president submits to Congress each year. Though quite professional in tone, the CEA is not exactly impartial in practice, since each president picks members sympathetic to his point of view. Kennedy picked Keynesians; Reagan picked supply-siders and monetarists. But whatever its philosophical tilt, the CEA is seen by other executive agencies as the advocate of the opinion of professional economists, who despite their differences generally tend to favor reliance on the market.

The OMB originally was the Bureau of the Budget, which was created in 1921 and made part of the executive office of the president in 1939; in 1970, it was renamed the Office of Management and Budget. Its chief function is to prepare estimates of the amount that will be spent by federal agencies,

*From the Russian word for a carriage pulled by three horses.

Karen Vismara/Black Star

Milton Friedman

Bettmann/Corbis

John Maynard Keynes

Bettmann/Corbis

John Kenneth Galbraith

Corbis/Corbis Sygma

Arthur B. Laffer

to negotiate with other departments over the size of their budgets, and to make certain (insofar as it can) that the legislative proposals of these other departments are in accord with the president's program. Of late it has acquired something of a split personality; it is in part an expert, nonpartisan agency that analyzes spending and budget patterns and in part an activist, partisan organization that tries to get the president's wishes carried out by the bureaucracy.

The secretary of the treasury often is close to or drawn from the world of business and finance and is expected to argue the point of view of the financial community. (Since its members do not always agree, this is not always easy.) The secretary provides estimates of the revenue that the government can expect from existing taxes and what will be the result of changing tax laws. He or she represents the United States in its dealings with the top bankers and finance ministers of other nations.

A good deal of pulling and hauling takes place among members of the troika, but if that were the extent of the problem, presidential leadership would be fairly easy. The problem is far more complex. One study found 132 separate government bureaus engaged in formulating economic policy. They regulate business, make loans, and supply subsidies. For example, as foreign trade becomes increasingly important to this country, the secretary of state (among many others) acquires an interest in economic policy. One-third of corporate profits come from overseas investments, and one-fourth of farm output is sold abroad.

THE FED

Among the most important of these other agencies is the board of governors of the Federal Reserve

System (the "Fed"). Its seven members are appointed by the president, with the consent of the Senate, for 14-year, nonrenewable terms and may not be removed except for cause. (No member has been removed since it was created in 1913.) The chairman serves for four years. In theory, and to some degree in practice, the Fed is independent of both the president and Congress. Its most important function is to regulate, insofar as it can, the supply of money (both in circulation and in bank deposits) and the price of money (in the form of interest rates). The Fed sets **monetary policy,** that is, the effort to shape the economy by controlling the amount of money and bank deposits and the interest rates charged for money. The box on page 494 shows how the Fed does this. In 2001, it lowered interest rates eleven times in order to help reduce the recession. From 2004 to 2007, it raised these rates 17 times in order to prevent inflation.

Just how independent the Fed is can be a matter of dispute. During the 1980 election, Fed policies helped keep interest rates at a high level, a circumstance that did not benefit President Carter's reelection bid. On the other hand, whenever a president is determined to change monetary policy, he usually can do so. For example, the term of Fed chairman Arthur F. Burns, appointed by President Nixon, came up for renewal in 1978. President Carter, seeking to influence Burns's decisions, held out the prospect of reappointing him chairman. When Burns balked, he was passed over, and G. William Miller was appointed in his stead. Presidents Truman, Johnson, and Nixon were all able to obtain changes in monetary policy. When Alan Greenspan, a conservative, became Fed chairman in 1987 under President Reagan, he was so successful

monetary policy
Managing the economy by altering the supply of money and interest rates.

How Things Work

The Federal Reserve Board

The Tools by which the Fed Implements Its Monetary Policy

1. **Buying and selling federal government securities** (bonds, Treasury notes, and other pieces of paper that constitute government IOUs). When the Fed buys securities, it in effect puts more money into circulation and takes securities out of circulation. With more money around, interest rates tend to drop, and more money is borrowed and spent. When the Fed sells government securities, it in effect takes money out of circulation, causing interest rates to rise and making borrowing more difficult.

2. **Regulating the amount of money that a member bank must keep in hand as reserves** to back up the customer deposits it is holding. A bank lends out most of the money deposited with it. If the Fed says that it must keep in reserve a larger fraction of its deposits, then the amount that it can lend drops, loans become harder to obtain, and interest rates rise.

3. **Changing the interest charged banks** that want to borrow money from the Federal Reserve System. Banks borrow from the Fed to cover short-term needs. The interest that the Fed charges for this is called the *discount* rate. The Fed can raise or lower that rate; this will have an effect, though usually rather small, on how much money the banks will lend.

Federal Reserve Board (7 members)

- Determines how many government securities will be bought or sold by regional and member banks.

- Determines interest rates to be charged by regional banks and amount of money member banks must keep in reserve in regional banks.

Regional Federal Reserve Banks (12)

- Buy and sell government securities.

- Loan money to member banks.

- Keep percentage of holdings for member banks.

Member Banks (6,000)

- Buy and sell government securities.

- May borrow money from regional banks.

- Must keep percentage of holdings in regional banks.

- Interest rates paid to regional banks determine interest rates charged for business and personal loans and influence all bank interest rates.

---

in curbing inflation that he was reappointed by President Clinton, a Democrat.

CONGRESS

The most important part of the economic policy making machinery, of course, is Congress. It must approve all taxes and almost all expenditures; there can be no wage or price controls without its consent; and it has the ability to alter the policy of the nominally independent Federal Reserve Board by threatening to pass laws that would reduce its powers. And Congress itself is fragmented, with great influence wielded by the members of key committees, especially the House and Senate Budget Committees, the House and Senate Appropriations

fiscal policy Managing the economy by the use of tax and spending laws.

Committees, the House Ways and Means Committee, and the Senate Finance Committee. The decisions Congress makes about how high taxes should be and how much money the government should spend create the nation's **fiscal policy.**

In sum, no matter what economic theory the president may have, if he is to put that theory into effect he needs the assistance of many agencies within the executive branch, such independent agencies as the Federal Reserve Board, and the various committees of Congress. Though members of the executive and legislative branches are united by their common desire to get reelected (and thus have a common interest in producing sound economic growth), each part of this system may also be influenced by different economic theories and will be motivated by the claims of interest groups.

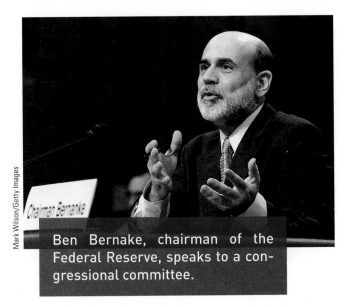

Ben Bernake, chairman of the Federal Reserve, speaks to a congressional committee.

Mark Wilson/Getty Images

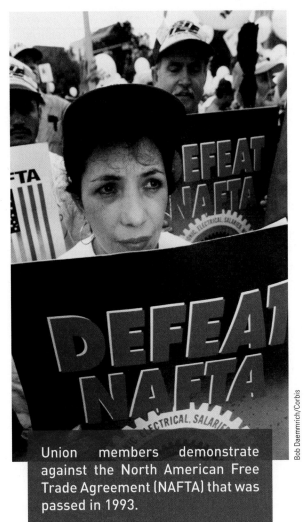

Union members demonstrate against the North American Free Trade Agreement (NAFTA) that was passed in 1993.

Bob Daemmrich/Corbis

The effect of these interest group claims is clearly shown in the debate over trade restriction. Usually the economic health of the nation affects everyone in pretty much the same way—we are all hurt by inflation or helped by stable prices; the incomes of all of us tend to grow (or remain stagnant) together. In these circumstances, the politics of economic health is majoritarian.

Suppose, however, that most of us are doing pretty well but that the people in a few industries or occupations are suffering. That is sometimes the result of foreign competition. In many countries, labor costs are much lower than in the United States. That means these countries can ship to American buyers goods—such as shoes, textiles, and beef—that sell at much lower prices than American producers can afford to charge. By contrast, if the price of a product is based chiefly on having advanced technology rather than low labor costs, American manufacturers can beat almost any foreign competitor.

When Congress passes laws governing foreign trade, it is responding to interest group politics. Industries that find it easy to sell American products abroad want free trade—that is, they want no taxes or restrictions on international exchanges. Industries that find it hard to compete with foreign imports oppose free trade—that is, they want tariffs and other limitations on imports.

When the North American Free Trade Agreement (NAFTA) was passed by Congress in 1993, the free traders won, and tariffs on our commerce with Canada and Mexico were largely abolished. But when the government later suggested creating free trade with all of Latin America, the critics of free trade opposed

the idea, and it died. This is a good example of how people who bear the costs of a policy are often much more effective in influencing the votes on it than are those who stand to benefit from it.

Not only has the United States not extended the NAFTA idea to other countries, but it has done things that reward certain economic interest groups. Even though Republicans tend to support free trade, President George W. Bush imposed sharp increases in the taxes that must be paid on imported steel. The reason is not hard to find. Steel is produced in certain states, such as Ohio and Pennsylvania, that the president wanted to carry in 2004.

GLOBALIZATION

Trying to block free trade is a part of the opposition of some people to **globalization,** the growing integration of the economies and societies of the world.

globalization The growing integration of the economies and societies of the world.

You can experience globalization easily: if your computer develops a problem and you call technical support, you are likely to speak with a technician based in India.

Supporters of globalization argue that it has increased the income, literacy, and standard of living of people in almost every country involved in the worldwide process of economic growth. These supporters favor free trade because it makes products cheaper. Opponents of globalization make several different and not always consistent arguments. Some (such as labor union leaders) argue that free trade undercuts the wages of American workers as less expensive foreign workers make things that are sold here. Others argue that globalization is driven by selfish corporate interests that exploit people in poor countries when they work for American firms. Still others feel that globalization means imposing one culture on everyone in ways that hurt local cultures.

Spending Money

If only the economic health of the nation mattered, then majoritarian politics would dominate, and the president and Congress would both work to improve economic conditions. Although they still might work at cross-purposes because they held to different economic theories, the goal would be the same.

But the government must also respond to the demands of voters and interest groups. While these demands are no less legitimate than the voters' general interest in economic health, they produce not majoritarian but client and interest group politics.

The sources of this conflict can be seen in public opinion polls. Voters consistently say they want a balanced budget and lower government spending. They believe the government spends too much and that if it wanted to, it could cut spending. When the government runs a deficit, the reason in the voters' eyes is that it is spending too much, not that it is taxing too little. But these same polls show that the voters believe the government should spend more on education, homelessness, childcare, and crime control.

The voters are not irrational, thinking they can have more spending and less spending simultaneously. Nor are they hypocrites, pretending to want less spending overall but more spending for particular programs. They are simply expressing a variety of concerns. They want a limited government with no deficit; they also want good schools, cleaner air, better health care, and less crime. They believe a frugal government could deliver what they want by cutting out waste. They may be wrong about that belief, but it is not obviously silly.

What this means for the government is easy to imagine. Politicians have an incentive to make two kinds of appeals: The first is, "Vote for me and I will keep government spending down and cut the deficit." The second is, "Vote for me and I will make certain that your favorite program gets more money." Some people will vote for the candidate because of the first appeal; some will vote for him or her because of the second. But acting on these two appeals is clearly going to lead to inconsistent policies. These inconsistencies become evident in the budget.

The Budget

A **budget** is a document that announces how much the government will collect in taxes and spend in revenues and how those expenditures will be allocated among various programs. (Each budget covers a **fiscal year,** which runs from October 1 of one year through September 30 of the next. A fiscal year is named after the year in which it *ends:* thus, "fiscal 2009" or "FY 2009" means the year ending on September 30, 2009.

In theory, the federal budget should be based on *first* deciding how much money the government is going to spend and *then* allocating that money among different programs and agencies. That is the way a household makes up its budget: "We have this much in the paycheck, and so we will spend X dollars on rent, Y dollars on food, and Z dollars on clothing, and what's left over on entertainment. If the amount of the paycheck goes down, we will cut something out—probably entertainment."

In fact, the federal budget is a list of everything the government is going to spend money on, with only slight regard (sometimes no regard at all) for how much money is available to be spent. Instead of being a way of *allocating* money to be spent on various purposes, it is a way of *adding up* what is being spent.

Indeed, there was no federal budget at all before 1921, and there was no unified presidential budget until the 1930s. Even after the president began submitting a single budget, the committees of Congress acted on it separately, adding to or subtracting from the amounts he proposed. (Usually they followed his

budget A document that states tax collections, spending levels, and the allocation of spending among purposes.

fiscal year For the federal government, October 1 through the following September 30.

lead, but they were certainly free to depart from it as they wished.) If one committee wanted to spend more on housing, no effort was made to take that amount away from the committee that was spending money on health (in fact, there was no machinery for making such an effort).

The Congressional Budget Act of 1974 changed this somewhat. Now after the president submits his budget in February, two budget committees—one in the House, one in the Senate—study his overall package and obtain an analysis of it from the Congressional Budget Office (CBO). Each committee then submits to its house a **budget resolution** that proposes a total budget ceiling and a ceiling for each of several spending areas (such as health or defense). Each May, Congress is supposed to adopt, with some modifications, these budget resolutions, intending them to be targets to guide the work of each legislative committee as it decides what should be spent in its area. During the summer Congress then takes up the specific appropriations bills, informing its members as it goes along whether or not the spending proposed in these bills conforms to the May budget resolution. The object, obviously, is to impose some discipline on the various committees. After each committee approves its appropriations bill and Congress passes it, it goes to the president for his signature.

These appropriations bills, however, can rarely make big changes in government spending. About two-thirds of what the government spends is mandatory—that is, the money goes to people who are entitled to it. **Entitlements** include Social Security and Medicare payments, veterans' benefits, food stamps, and money the government owes investors who have bought Treasury bonds (that is, the interest on the national debt). In theory, the government could change these entitlements by, for example, cutting Social Security payments, but that would be a political disaster. In reality, the government can change only about one-third of federal spending in any year.

There is a big loophole in the current budget process: nothing in the process requires Congress to tighten the government's financial belt. It can pass a budget resolution authorizing spending that is more or less than what the president has proposed. Nonetheless, the process has made a difference. Congress is now conscious of how its spending decisions match up with estimates of tax revenues.

When President Reagan took office, he and his allies in Congress took advantage of the Congressional Budget Act to start the controversial process of cutting federal spending. The House and Senate budget committees, with the president's support, used the first budget resolution in May 1981 not simply to set a budget ceiling that, as in the past, looked pretty much like the previous year's budget but to direct each committee of Congress to make *cuts*—sometimes deep cuts—in the programs for which it was responsible. These cuts were to be made in the authorization legislation (see Chapter 15) as well as in the appropriations.

budget resolution A congressional decision that states the maximum amount of money the government should spend.

entitlements A claim for government funds that cannot be changed without violating the rights of the claimant.

The object was to get members of Congress to vote for a total package of cuts before they could vote on any particular cut. Republican control of the Senate and an alliance between Republicans and conservative southern Democrats in the House allowed this strategy to succeed. The first budget resolution ordered Senate and House committees to reduce federal spending during fiscal 1982 by about $36 billion—less than the president had first asked, but a large sum nonetheless. Then the individual committees set to work trying to find ways of making these cuts.

Note how the *procedures* used by Congress can affect the *policies* adopted by Congress. If the Reagan plan had been submitted in the old piecemeal way, it is unlikely that cuts of this size would have occurred in so short a time, or at all. The reason is not that Congress would have wanted to ignore the president but that, then as now, Congress reflects public opinion on economic policy. As stated at the beginning of the chapter, the public wants less total federal spending but more money spent on specific federal programs. Thus, if you allow the public or Congress to vote first on specific programs, spending is bound to rise. But if you require Congress to vote first on a budget ceiling, then (unless it changes its mind as it goes along) total spending will go down, and tough choices will have to be made about the component parts of the budget. That, at least, is the theory. It worked once, in 1981, but it did not work very well thereafter.

Reducing Spending

Because the 1974 Congressional Budget Act did not automatically lead to spending cuts, people concerned about the growing federal deficit decided

Figure 18.2
Federal Outlays in 2008

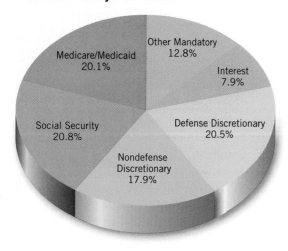

Figure 18.2
Federal Revenues in 2008

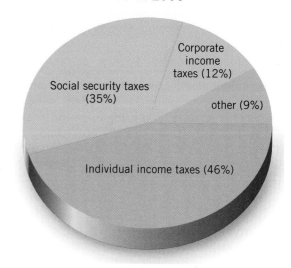

Source: Office of Management and Budget, *Mid-Season Review, 2009.*

to find ways to put a cap on spending. The first such cap was the Balanced Budget Act of 1985, now called the Gramm-Rudman Act after two of its sponsors, Senators Phil Gramm (R-Tex.) and Warren Rudman (R-N.H.). The law required that each year from 1986 to 1991 the budget would automatically be cut until the federal deficit had disappeared. What made the cuts automatic, its authors hoped, was a provision in the bill, called a **sequester,** that required across-the-board percentage cuts in all federal programs (except for entitlements) if the president and Congress failed to agree on a total spending level that met the law's targets. No one liked this plan, but it seemed necessary. Senator Rudman called it a "bad idea whose time has come."

But the plan failed. By various devices that people began to call "smoke and mirrors," Congress and the president found ways to get new spending that was higher than the targeted amounts. By 1990, it was evident that a new strategy was needed if the government was going to help eliminate the deficit.

That strategy had two parts. First, Congress voted for a tax increase. Second, it passed the Budget Enforcement Act of 1990 that set limits on **discretionary spending.** This phrase refers to those government expenditures that are

sequester Automatic spending cuts.

discretionary spending Spending that is not required to pay for contracts, interest on the national debt, or entitlement programs such as Social Security.

not required by existing contracts, payments on the national debt, or entitlement programs such as Social Security. (Only about one-third of the budget involves discretionary spending.) According to the 1990 act, if Congress were to spend more on a discretionary program, it would have to cut spending on another discretionary program or raise taxes. The law expired in 2001, but in 2007 some members of Congress hoped to revive it. As Figure 18.3 makes clear, something has to be done to manage huge future increases in spending on Social Security and Medicare.

Figure 18.3
Social Security and Medicare Cost as a Percentage of GDP

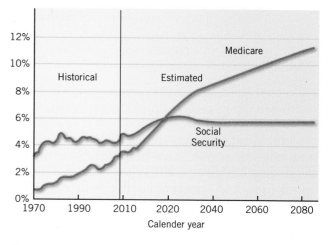

Source: *Trustees' Report,* 2009.

Levying Taxes

Tax policy reflects a mixture of majoritarian politics ("What is a 'fair' tax law?") and client politics ("How much is in it for me?"). In the United States, a fair tax law generally has been viewed as one that keeps the overall tax burden rather low, requires everyone to pay something, and requires the better-off to pay at a higher rate than the less-well-off. The law, in short, was viewed as good if it imposed modest burdens, prevented cheating, and was mildly progressive.

Americans have had their first goal satisfied. The tax burden in the United States is lower than it is in most other democratic nations (see Figure 18.4). There is some evidence that they have also had their second goal met—there is reason to believe that Americans evade their income taxes less than do citizens of, say, France or Italy. (That is one reason why many nations rely more on sales taxes than we do—they are harder to evade.) Just how progressive our tax rates are is a matter of dispute; to determine whether the rich really pay at higher rates than the poor, one has to know not only the official rates but also the effect of deductions, exemptions, and exclusions (that is, of loopholes).

Keeping the burden low and the cheating at a minimum are examples of majoritarian politics: most people benefit, most people pay. The loopholes, however, are another matter—all manner of special interests can get some special benefit from the tax law that the rest of us must pay for but, given the complexity of the law, rarely notice. Loopholes are client politics par excellence.

Because of that, hardly any scholars believed tax reform (dramatically reducing the loopholes) was politically possible. Every interest that benefited from a loophole—and these included not just corporations but universities, museums, states, cities, and investors—would lobby vigorously to protect it.

Nevertheless, in 1986 a sweeping tax reform act was passed. Many of the most cherished loopholes were closed or reduced. What happened? It is as if scientists who had proved that a bumblebee could not fly got stung by a flying bumblebee.

THE RISE OF THE INCOME TAX

To understand what happened in 1986, one must first understand the political history of taxation in the United States. Until almost the end of the nineteenth century, there was no federal income tax (except for a brief period during the Civil War). The money the government needed came mostly from tariffs (that is, taxes on goods imported into this country). And when Congress did enact a peacetime income tax, the Supreme Court in 1895 struck it down as unconstitutional.[10] To change this, Congress proposed, and in 1913 the states ratified, the Sixteenth Amendment, which authorized such a tax.

For the next 40 years or so, tax rates tended to go up during wartime and down during peacetime (see Figure 18.5). The rates were progressive—that is, the wealthiest individuals paid at a higher rate than the less affluent. For example, during World War II incomes in the highest bracket were taxed at a rate of 94 percent. (The key tax rate is called by economists the "marginal rate." This is the percentage of the last dollar you earn that must be paid out in taxes.)

An income tax offers the opportunity for majoritarian politics to become class politics. The majority of the citizenry earn average incomes and control most of the votes. In theory there is nothing to prevent the mass of people from voting for legislators who will tax only the rich, who, as a minority, will always be outvoted. During the early decades of this century, that is exactly what the rich feared would

Figure 18.4

Tax Burdens in Democratic Nations (Taxes as a Percentage of Income of a Family with Two Children)

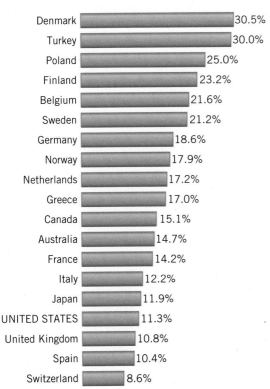

Denmark	30.5%
Turkey	30.0%
Poland	25.0%
Finland	23.2%
Belgium	21.6%
Sweden	21.2%
Germany	18.6%
Norway	17.9%
Netherlands	17.2%
Greece	17.0%
Canada	15.1%
Australia	14.7%
France	14.2%
Italy	12.2%
Japan	11.9%
UNITED STATES	11.3%
United Kingdom	10.8%
Spain	10.4%
Switzerland	8.6%

Source: *Statistical Abstract of the United States, 2003*, Table 1344.

Figure 18.5

Federal Taxes on Income, Top Percentage Rates, 1913–2002

Source: Updated from *Congressional Quarterly Weekly Report* (September 18, 1993), 2488.

happen. Since the highest marginal tax rate was 94 percent, you might think that is in fact what did happen.

You would be wrong. Offsetting the high rates were the deductions, exemptions, and exclusions by which people could shelter some of their income from taxation. These loopholes were available for everyone, but they particularly helped the well-off. In effect, a political compromise was reached during the first half of the 20th century. The terms were these: the well-off, generally represented by the Republican party, would drop their bitter opposition to high marginal rates provided that the less-well-off, generally represented by the Democratic party, would support a large number of loopholes. The Democrats (or more accurately, the liberals) were willing to accept this compromise because they feared that if they insisted on high rates with no loopholes, the economy would suffer as people and businesses lost their incentive to save and invest.

For at least 30 years after the adoption of the income tax in 1913, only a small number of high-income people paid any significant amount in federal income taxes. The average citizen paid very little in such taxes until World War II. After the war, taxes did not fall to their prewar levels.

Most people did not complain too much, because they, too, benefited greatly from the loopholes. They could deduct from their taxable income the interest they paid on their home mortgages, the state and local taxes they paid, much of what they paid in medical insurance premiums, and the interest they paid on consumer loans (such as those used to buy automobiles). On the eve of the Tax Reform Act of 1986, an opinion poll showed that more people favored small cuts in tax rates coupled with many large deductions than favored big cuts in tax rates coupled with fewer and smaller deductions.[11]

Interest groups organized around each loophole. Home builders organized to support the mortgage-interest deduction; universities supported the charitable-contribution deduction; insurance companies supported the deduction for medical insurance premiums; and automakers supported the deduction for interest on consumer loans.

In addition to these well-known loopholes, there were countless others, not so well known and involving much less money, that were defended and enlarged through the efforts of other interest groups: for instance, oil companies supported the deduction for drilling costs, heavy industry supported the investment tax credit, and real estate developers supported special tax write-offs for apartment and office buildings.

WHAT WOULD YOU DO?

MEMORANDUM

To: *Elizabeth Gilbert, chairperson, Council of Economics*

From: *Edward Larson, White House speechwriter*

Subject: *Flat tax proposal*

The President would like your advice on whether to endorse a flat tax. His likely opponent is pushing this issue.

Arguments for:

1. A flat tax is fair because it treats all income groups the same. We could leave the lowest income group with no taxes.

2. With a flat tax, we could eliminate almost all deductions and loopholes from the tax code.

3. Countries with a flat tax, such as Lithuania, have achieved great economic prosperity.

Arguments against:

1. A flat tax is unfair because it treats all income groups the same. The rich should be taxed more heavily.

2. Many tax deductions, such as the one for home mortgages, are desirable.

3. We could eliminate undesirable tax loopholes without creating a flat tax.

Friday,

Should We Have a Flat Tax?

January 31
BOSTON, MA

White House candidate David Wilson declared yesterday that he would seek a fundamental overhaul of the nation's tax system by creating a single rate for all taxpayers. The President is expected to respond to this in his State of the Union…

Your decision:

Support _____   Oppose _____

© Tribune Media Services, Inc. All rights reserved. Reprinted by permission.

Until 1986, the typical tax fight was less about rates than about deductions. Rates were important, but not as important as tax loopholes. "Loophole politics" was client politics. When client groups pressed for benefits, they could take advantage of the decentralized structure of Congress to find well-placed advocates who could advance these interests through low-visibility bargaining. In effect, these groups were getting a subsidy from the federal government equal to the amount of the tax break. However, the tax break was even better than a subsidy, because it did not have to be voted on every year as part of an appropriations bill: once part of the tax code, it lasted for a long time, and given the length and complexity of that code, scarcely anyone would notice it was there.

Many of these loopholes could be justified by arguments about economic growth. Low tax rates on a certain kind of investment encouraged more investment of that kind. Deductions for mortgage interest and property taxes encouraged people to own their own homes and boosted the construction industry.

Then the Tax Reform Act of 1986 turned the decades-old compromise on its head: instead of high rates with big deductions, we got low rates with much smaller deductions. The big gainers were individuals; the big losers were businesses.

But soon the old system began to reassert itself. Not long after the 1986 bill became law, tax rates started to go up again, this time with far fewer of the deductions that had once made it easy for affluent citizens to keep their rates low. In 1990, President Bush, after having campaigned on the slogan "Read my lips, no new taxes," signed a tax increase. The top rate was 31 percent. In 1993 President Clinton proposed another tax increase, one that would raise the top rate to over 39 percent (it had been 28 percent in 1986) and make most Social Security benefits taxable for upper-income retirees. His bill narrowly passed by a vote of 218 to 216 in the House, a vote of 51 to 50 in the Senate, with Vice President Al Gore casting the deciding vote. Not a single Republican voted for it. It was the first time since 1945 that the majority party in Congress had passed a major bill without one vote from the minority party.

When President George W. Bush got his tax cut plan through Congress in 2002, many Democrats as well as most Republicans voted for it. The next issue is clear: should the tax cuts, now expiring at the end of 2010, be made permanent?

SUMMARY

Three economic factors make a difference to voters; the policies for each are formulated by a distinctive type of policy making. The first is the economic health of the nation, the second the amount and kinds of government spending, and the third is the level and distribution of taxes.

National economic health has powerful effects on the outcome of elections, as much through people's perception of national conditions as from their worries about their own finances. The politics of inflation, unemployment, and economic growth tend to be majoritarian. The president is held responsible for national conditions. But he must meet that responsibility by using imperfect economic theories to manage clumsy government tools controlled by divided political authorities.

When economic ill health occurs in some industries and places but not others (as a result of such forces as foreign competition), the politics of economic health are shaped by interest group politics.

Firms that import foreign products or sell to foreign nations try to avoid trade restrictions, while firms and unions hurt by foreign competition try to impose such restrictions.

The amount of spending is theoretically determined by the budget, but in fact the nation has no meaningful budget. Instead the president and Congress struggle over particular spending bills whose amounts reflect interest group and client pressures. In the 1980s those pressures, coupled with a large tax cut, led to a sharp increase in the size of the federal debt.

The general shape of federal tax legislation is determined by majoritarian politics, but the specific provisions (especially the deductions, exemptions, and exclusions) are the result of client group politics. The Tax Reform Act of 1986 was a remarkable example of the reassertion of majoritarian politics over client group pressures made possible by policy entrepreneurs and political incentives.

RECONSIDERING WHO GOVERNS?

1. Who in the federal government can make our economy strong?

Nobody. The president, the Congress, the Federal Reserve Board, and countless small agencies play a role. And opinions as to what is the correct course of action (cut or increase taxes, decrease or increase regulations, spend more or less money) are deeply divided. The party that controls the White House usually must take the blame if the economy is in bad shape, but it is limited in what it can do to make it better.

2. How do you end a recession?

Who knows? The government has pumped billions of dollars into the economy with only slight effects. Somehow banks must become willing to make loans, borrowers must be willing to repay loans, and big investments firms (including government-sponsored ones) must stop buying up dubious mortgages.

RECONSIDERING TO WHAT ENDS?

1. Why does the federal government ever have a budget deficit?

It is not because politicians like deficits, it is because events may cause them while

leaders disagree over how to fix them. Since the 1930s we have had deficits whenever the economy went into a depression or we had to take part in a war. In fact, a lot of things the government buys, such as new buildings and military supplies, ought to be considered as investments to be paid for over time, just as when private citizens buy cars and houses. And when the deficit goes up, some politicians will want to cut it by raising taxes while others will prefer cutting spending.

2. Who was responsible for the 2007–2009 recession?

Everybody. Borrowers, banks, credit rating agencies, investment firms, and two big government-sponsored enterprises, Fannie Mae and Freddie Mac.

WORLD WIDE WEB RESOURCES

Internal Revenue Service: **www.irs.gov**

Tax Foundation: **www.taxfoundation.org**

SUGGESTED READINGS

Birnbaum, Jeffrey H., and Alan S. Murray. *Showdown at Gucci Gulch*. New York: Random House, 1987. Lively journalistic account of the passage of the Tax Reform Act of 1986.

Kiewiet, D. Roderick. *Macroeconomics and Micropolitics*. Chicago: University of Chicago Press, 1983. Argues that citizens vote on the basis of their estimate of national economic conditions as well as their own financial circumstances.

Samuelson, Robert J. *The Good Life and Its Discontents*. New York: Times Books/ Random House, 1995. A readable, intelligent account of American economic life since the Second World War.

Schick, Allen. *The Federal Budget*. Washington, D.C.: Brookings Institution, 2000. Excellent overview of how Washington allocates money.

Shlaes, Amity. *The Greedy Hand*. New York: Random House, 1999. Spirited attack on federal tax policy.

Stein, Herbert, and Murray Foss. *The New Illustrated Guide to the American Economy*. 3rd ed. Washington, D.C.: American Enterprise Institute, 1999. A vivid collection of graphs, all clearly explained, that describes the American economy and government spending from the 1950s through the 1990s.

Tufte, Edward R. *Political Control of the Economy*. Princeton, N.J.: Princeton University Press, 1978. Argues that there is a "political business cycle" caused by politicians' trying to stimulate the economy just before an election.

19

Social Welfare

WHO GOVERNS?

1. How, if at all, have Americans' views of government's responsibility to help the "deserving poor" changed over time?
2. Why are some government social welfare programs politically protected while others are politically imperiled?

TO WHAT ENDS?

1. What does the Constitution mean by "promote the general Welfare"?
2. Should religious groups be eligible to administer some federal welfare programs?

Many groups of senior citizens take day trips from Philadelphia to Atlantic City, New Jersey, where they stroll or gamble. On the bus ride, they are usually relaxed and talkative, but this wasn't the case in 2005. Then they had their noses buried in a booklet sent to them by the federal government. Entitled *Medicare & You,* it explained that if they were old enough to be on Medicare, then starting in January 2006, Uncle Sam would help them pay for their prescription drugs. The new program had a lot of complicated choices, but seniors were helped by a massive government-sponsored public relations program that explained everything to them. By 2009, most eligible senior citizens had signed up, and even with robust enrollments, the program actually was costing taxpayers a little less than the government had projected it would cost—a rarity since most social welfare programs end up costing far more than was originally predicted.

Jerry Tobias/Corbis

Two Kinds of Welfare Programs

Another welfare program is for certain poor people who get help to buy food by acquiring Food Stamps. Mary Summers, an expert on this program at the University of Pennsylvania, discovered that even bright college students with easy access to computer- based information systems required nearly four hours to figure out who could apply. She described it as "an administrative maze." Unlike with the Medicare prescription drug benefit, however, there has never been a massive public relations campaign to explain how to sign up for the Food Stamps program.

The key difference in this regard involves *who* benefits. Two kinds of social welfare programs exist in this country: those that benefit most or all of the people and those that help only a small number of them. In the first category are Social Security and Medicare, programs that provide retirement benefits or medical assistance to almost every citizen who has reached a certain age. In the second are programs such as Medicaid and Food Stamps that offer help only to people with low incomes.

Legally, the difference between the two kinds of programs is that the first have no *means test* (they are available to everyone without regard to income) while the second are *means tested* (you must fall below a certain income level to enjoy them). Politically, the programs differ in how they get money from the government. The first kind of welfare program represents **majoritarian politics:** nearly everyone benefits, nearly everyone pays. The second kind represents **client politics:** a (relatively) few number of people benefit, but almost everyone pays. The biggest problem facing majoritarian welfare programs is their cost: who will pay, and how much will they pay? The biggest problem facing client-oriented programs is their legitimacy: who should benefit, and how should they be served?

majoritarian politics A policy in which almost everybody benefits and almost everybody pays.

client politics A policy in which one small group benefits and almost everybody pays.

This political difference between these programs has a huge impact on how the government acts in regard to them. Social Security and Medicare are sacrosanct. The thought of making any changes that might lower the benefits these programs pay is so politically risky that most politicians never even discuss them. When programs such as these run into trouble because of rising expenses (Medicare is in deep trouble today, and Social Security will be in even deeper trouble in a few decades), politicians scramble to look for ways of maintaining benefits while hiding the rising costs or postponing dealing with them. As we shall see later in this chapter, there has been a sharp growth in the proportion of people who are retired and are thus entitled to Social Security and Medicare. To keep benefits flowing to these individuals, people who are not retired will have to pay more and more in taxes. No politician wants to raise taxes or cut benefits, so they adopt a variety of halfhearted measures (like slowly increasing the age at which people can get these benefits) designed to postpone the tough decisions until they are out of office.

Client-based welfare programs—those that are means tested—are a very different matter. Like many other client-based programs, their political appeal changes as popular opinion about them changes. Take the old Aid to Families with Dependent Children (AFDC) program. When it was started in 1935, people thought of it as a way of helping poor women whose husbands had been killed in war or had died in mining accidents. The goal was to help these women support their children, who had been made fatherless by death or disaster. Most people thought of these women as the innocent victims of a tragedy. No one thought that they would take AFDC for very long. It was a program to help smooth things over for them until they could remarry.

About 30 years later, however, the public's opinion of AFDC had begun to change. People started to think AFDC was paying money to women who had never married and had no intention of marrying. The government, according to this view, was subsidizing single-parent families, encouraging out-of-wedlock births, and creating social dependency. Moreover, some people thought that African Americans were taking undue advantage of the program. (In fact, when this opinion emerged, African Americans were still a minority among AFDC recipients.) From the mid-1960s, through the mid-1990s, these views became stronger. AFDC had lost the legitimacy it needed, as a client program, to survive politically.

Whenever a client program loses political legitimacy, the program is in trouble. Client politics depends on the beneficiaries' being thought of as legitimate. Almost any means-tested program risks losing its political legitimacy, because some people will always wonder whether the program itself causes people to avoid working in order to claim the benefits. Some people think that about Food Stamps, the program that gives low-income people free stamps that they can exchange for food. There have been a few publicized cases of people using food stamps to buy luxury items. But no powerful opposition to the program has developed, because in general the only thing the beneficiaries have in common is that they have low incomes. Many Americans can imagine becoming poor, and so they probably are willing to allow such a program to operate as part of a government-supplied safety net that might, someday, help them.

But AFDC was a different matter. Having to accept AFDC was not something the typical taxpayer thought would ever happen to him or her. Moreover, the beneficiaries weren't just poor; some of them did things—such as having babies without getting married—that most Americans thought were simply wrong. The legitimacy of AFDC was thus in jeopardy, because it either made possible or actually encouraged behavior that most Americans found improper. As a result, something happened to AFDC that almost never happens to decades-old government programs: it was abolished.

In this chapter, we provide examples of both majoritarian and client welfare programs and describe how they have been reformed over the years. There are far too many social welfare programs to describe them all here; rather the main purpose of this chapter is to explain the key features of the two main kinds of programs.

Social Welfare in the United States

Before analyzing how these programs came into being, it is first necessary to understand that social welfare policy in the United States is shaped by four factors that make it different from what exists in many other nations. First, Americans generally have taken a more restrictive view of who is entitled to government assistance. Second, America has been slower than other countries to embrace the welfare state. Third, we have insisted that the states (and to a degree private enterprise) play a large role in running welfare programs. Fourth, nongovernmental organizations play a large role in welfare.

The first distinctive feature of the American welfare state involves who benefits. To Americans, who benefits has been a question of who *deserves* to benefit. We usually have insisted that public support be given only to those who cannot help themselves. But what does it mean to say that a person cannot help himself or herself? Surely a disabled, blind, elderly woman

Handicapped parking signs are a common reminder of the government's interest in social welfare.

deserted by her family cannot do much to help herself, but would she still be deserving of public aid were she merely disabled? Or merely elderly? And to what extent should we require that her family support her? As we shall see, American welfare policy since the 1930s has been fundamentally shaped by a slow but steady change in how we have separated the "deserving" from the "undeserving" poor.

That we have always thought this way may make us forget there are other ways of thinking about welfare. The major alternative view is to ask not who deserves help but what each person's "fair share" of the national income is. Seen this way, the role of government is to take money from those who have a lot and give it to those who have only a little, until each person has, if not the same amount, then at least a fair share. But defining a "fair share" is even more difficult than defining the "deserving poor." Moreover, Americans have generally felt that giving money to people who are already working, or who could work if they chose to, is unfair. In some nations—Sweden is an example—government policy is aimed at redistributing income from better-off to not-so-well-off persons, without regard to who "deserves" the money.

Thus Americans base welfare policy on the concept of "help for the deserving poor" rather than "redistribution to produce fair shares."[1] They have done so, one suspects, because they believe citizens should be encouraged to be self-reliant, people who work hard will get what they deserve, and giving money to people who could help themselves will produce a class of "welfare chiselers." If Americans believed success at work was a matter of luck rather than effort or was dictated by forces over which they had no control, they might support a different concept of welfare.

Moreover, we have always been a bit uneasy about giving money to people. Though we recognize that many people through no fault of their own cannot buy groceries and thus need funds, we would prefer that, to the extent possible, people who deserve help be given *services* (education, training, medical care) rather than money. Throughout much of our history, our welfare policies have reflected a general philosophical disposition in favor of providing services to deserving persons.

The second striking fact about American welfare policy is how late in our history it arrived (at least at the national level) compared to other nations. By 1935, when Congress passed the Social Security Act, at least 22 European nations already had similar programs, as did Australia and Japan.[2] Germany was the first to create a nationwide social security program when it developed sickness and maternity insurance in 1883. Six years later, it added old-age insurance and in 1927 unemployment insurance.

England offers perhaps the clearest contrast with the United States. In 1908, a national system of old-age pensions was set up, followed three years later by a plan for nationwide health and unemployment insurance.[3] England had a parliamentary regime in which a political party with liberal sentiments and a large majority had come to power. With authority concentrated in the hands of the prime minister and his cabinet, there was virtually no obstacle to instituting measures, such as welfare programs, that commended themselves to party leaders on grounds of either principle or party advantage. Furthermore, the British Labour party was then beginning to emerge. Though the party was still small (it had only 30 seats in Parliament in 1908), its leaders included people who had been influential in formulating welfare programs that the leaders of the dominant Liberal party backed. And once these programs were approved, they were in almost all cases nationally run: there were no state governments to which authority had to be delegated or whose different experiences had to be accommodated.

Moreover, the British in 1908 were beginning to think in terms of social classes, to accept the notion of an activist government, and to make welfare the central political issue. Americans at that time also had an activist leader, Theodore Roosevelt; there was a progressive movement; and labor was well along in its organizing drives. But the issues were defined differently in the United States.

Progressives, or at least most of them, emphasized the reform of the political process—by eliminating corruption, by weakening the parties, and by improving the civil service—and attacked bigness by breaking up industrial trusts. Though some progressives favored the creation of a welfare state, they were a distinct minority. They had few allies in organized labor (which was skeptical of public welfare programs) and could not overcome the general distrust of big government and the strong preference for leaving matters of welfare in state hands. In sum, what ordinary politics brought to England in 1908–1911, only the crisis politics of 1935 would bring to the United States. But once started, the programs grew. By 1983, almost one-third of all Americans received benefits from one or more social welfare programs.

The third factor involves the degree to which federalism has shaped national welfare policy. Since the Constitution was silent on whether Congress had the power to spend money on welfare and since powers not delegated to Congress were reserved to the states, it was not until the constitutional reinterpretation of the 1930s (see Chapter 16) that it became clear that the federal government could do anything in the area of social policy. At the same time, federalism meant that any state so inclined could experiment with welfare programs. Between 1923 and 1933, thirty states enacted some form of an old-age pension. By 1935 all but two states had adopted a "mother's pension"—a program whereby a widow with children was given financial assistance, provided that she was a "fit mother" who ran a "suitable home." The poor were given small doles by local governments, helped by private charities, or placed in almshouses. Only one state, Wisconsin, had an unemployment insurance program.

Politically the state programs had a double-edged effect: they provided opponents of a federal welfare system with an argument (the states were already providing welfare assistance), but they also supplied a lobby for federal financial assistance (state authorities would campaign for national legislation to help them out). Some were later to say that the states were the laboratories for experimentation in welfare policy. When the federal government entered the field in 1935, it did so in part by spending money through the states, thereby encouraging the formation in the states of a strong welfare bureaucracy whose later claims would be difficult to ignore.

A fourth distinctive feature of welfare policy in the United States is that much of it is administered via grants and contracts to nongovernmental institutions, both for-profit firms and nonprofit organizations. For example, many large national nonprofit organizations, such as Big Brothers Big Sisters of America, Youth Build, Jewish Federation, and Catholic Charities, have received large federal grants and long participated in the administration of federal social programs. The 1996 law that abolished the Aid to Families with Dependent Children program contained a provision directing that religious nonprofit organizations, including small community-based groups, be permitted to compete for government grants with which to administer federal welfare-to-work and related policies. The latter provision, known as **charitable choice,** enjoyed bipartisan support. The provision prohibited religious organizations from using any public funds for proselytizing, religious instruction, or worship services, but also prohibited the government from requiring them to remove religious art or iconography from buildings where social service delivery programs funded in whole or in party by Washington might be administered.

In 2001, President George W. Bush's call to expand the role of religious organizations in administering federal social programs led to a political firestorm.[4] Some religious conservatives demanded that the Bush administration act to permit faith-based organizations to proselytize with public funds and

also allow them to hire only coreligionists if they wished. But some civil libertarians sought to reduce or eliminate most existing public-private partnerships involving religious organizations.

Between 2002 and 2003, HHS and HUD grants to faith-based groups increased 41 percent and 16 percent, respectively, and five federal agencies awarded $1.17 billion to such organizations.[5] Today, faith-based organizations figure ever more prominently in the administration of welfare-to-work programs in many big cities, from about 14 percent of all such programs in Los Angeles to about 41 percent in Philadelphia.[6] Fewer than one in 10 of these urban faith-based organizations give preferences to coreligionists in hiring, and virtually all accept beneficiaries without regard to religion.[7] This approach reflects mass opinion on the subject: three-quarters want government to help fund community-serving, faith-based organizations and deem them to be "more caring and compassionate" than professional providers of the same services; but the same

charitable choice Name given to four federal laws passed in the late 1990s specifying the conditions under which nonprofit religious organizations could compete to administer certain social service delivery and welfare programs.

Major Social Welfare Programs

Insurance, or "Contributory," Programs
Old Age, Survivors, and Disability Insurance (OASDI) Monthly payments to retired or disabled people and to surviving members of their families. This program, popularly called Social Security, is paid for by a payroll tax on employers and employees. *No means test.*

Medicare Federal government pays for part of the cost of medical care for retired or disabled people covered by Social Security. Paid for by payroll taxes on employees and employers. *No means test.*

Assistance, or "Noncontributory," Programs
Unemployment Insurance (UI) Weekly payments to workers who have been laid off and cannot find work. Benefits and requirements determined by states. Paid for by taxes on employers. *No means test.*

Temporary Assistance for Needy Families (TANF) Payments to needy families with children. Replaced

the old AFDC program. Partially paid for by block grants from the federal government to the states. *Means test.*

Supplemental Security Income (SSI) Cash payments to aged, blind, or disabled people whose income is below a certain amount. Paid for from general federal revenues. *Means test.*

Food Stamps Vouchers, given to people whose income is below a certain level, that can be used to buy food at grocery stores. Paid for out of general federal revenues. *Means test.*

Medicaid Pays medical expenses of persons receiving TANF or SSI payments. *Means test.*

Earned Income Tax Credit Pays cash or tax credit to poor working families. *Means test.*

three-fourths majority opposes government support for faith-based programs that require beneficiaries to "take part in religious practices" or "only hire people of the same faith."[8]

The 2008 Democratic National Convention featured "faith caucus" meetings. In 2009, President Barack Obama established the White House Office of Faith-Based and Neighborhood Partnerships, building on the charitable choice legislation first signed by Clinton and acknowledging the role that religions nonprofits continue to play in delivering diverse social welfare programs.

MAJORITARIAN WELFARE PROGRAMS: SOCIAL SECURITY AND MEDICARE

Today, tens of millions of Americans receive food, money, or medicine through programs funded largely by the federal government (see Figure 19.1).

At the time the Great Depression began, in 1929, the job of providing relief to needy people fell almost entirely to state and local governments or to private charities, and even these sources were primarily concerned with widows, orphans, and the elderly.[9] Hardly any state had a systematic program for

In 1932, unemployed workers line up at a soup kitchen during the Great Depression.

Topham/The Image Works

Figure 19.1

AFDC/TANF, Food Stamps, and SSI Recipients, 1975–2006

Note: AFDC/TANF refers to Aid to Families with Dependent Children/Temporary Assistance for Needy Families; TANF replaced AFDC after 1996. SSI refers to Supplemental Security Income.

Source: Adapted from U.S. Department of Health and Human Services, *Indicators of Welfare Dependence: Annual Report to Congress,* 2006.

supporting the unemployed, though many states provided some kind of help if it was clear that the person was out of work through no fault of his or her own. When the economy suddenly ground to a near standstill and the unemployment rate rose to include one-fourth of the work force, private charities and city relief programs nearly went bankrupt.

The election of 1932 produced an overwhelming congressional majority for the Democrats and placed Franklin D. Roosevelt in the White House. Almost immediately, a number of emergency measures were adopted to cope with the depression by supplying federal cash to bail out state and local relief agencies and by creating public works jobs under federal auspices. These measures were recognized as temporary expedients, however, and were unsatisfactory to those who believed the federal government had a permanent and major responsibility for welfare. Roosevelt created the Cabinet Committee on Economic Security to consider long-term policies. The committee drew heavily on the experience of European nations and on the ideas of various American scholars and social workers, but it understood that it would have to adapt these proposals to the realities of American politics. Chief among these was the widespread belief that any direct federal welfare program might be unconstitutional. The Constitution nowhere explicitly gave to Congress the authority to set up an unemployment compensation or old-age retirement program. And even if a welfare program were constitutional, many believed, it would be wrong because it violated the individualistic creed that people should help themselves unless they were physically unable to do so.

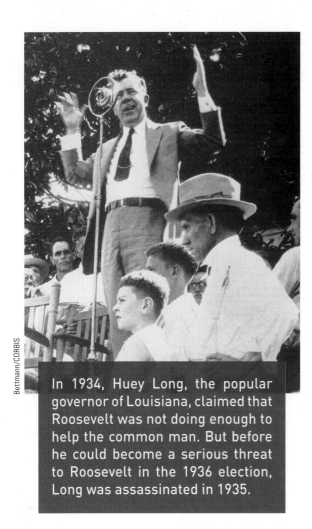

Bettmann/CORBIS

In 1934, Huey Long, the popular governor of Louisiana, claimed that Roosevelt was not doing enough to help the common man. But before he could become a serious threat to Roosevelt in the 1936 election, Long was assassinated in 1935.

as providing "insurance" for the aged was necessary because for the first few years the insurance program would not pay out any benefits.) The federal government would use its power to tax to provide the funds, but all of the programs (except for old-age insurance) would be administered by the states. Everybody, rich or poor, would be eligible for the insurance programs. Only the poor, as measured by a **means test** (a measure to determine that incomes are below a certain level), would be eligible for the assistance programs. Though bitterly opposed by some, the resulting Social Security Act passed swiftly and virtually unchanged through Congress. It was introduced in January 1935 and signed by President Roosevelt in August of that year.

The idea of having the government pay the medical and hospital bills of the elderly and the poor had been discussed in Washington since the drafting of the Social Security Act. President Roosevelt and his Committee on Economic Security sensed that medical care would be very controversial, and so health programs were left out of the 1935 bill in order not to jeopardize its chances of passage.[10]

The proponents of the idea did not abandon it, however. Working mostly within the executive branch, they continued to press, sometimes publicly, sometimes behind the scenes, for a national health care plan. Democratic presidents, including Truman, Kennedy, and Johnson, favored it; Republican president Eisenhower opposed it; Congress was deeply divided on it. The American Medical Association attacked it as "socialized medicine." For thirty years key policy entrepreneurs, such as Wilbur Cohen, worked to find a formula that would produce a congressional majority.

The first and highest hurdle to overcome, however, was not Congress as a whole but the House Ways and Means Committee, especially its powerful chairman from 1958 to 1975, Wilbur Mills of Arkansas. A majority of the committee members opposed a national health care program. Some members believed it wrong in principle; others feared that adding a costly health component to the Social Security system would jeopardize the financial solvency and administrative integrity of one of the most popular government

But failure by the Roosevelt administration to produce a comprehensive social security program, his supporters felt, might make the president vulnerable in the 1936 election to the leaders of various radical social movements. Huey Long of Louisiana was proposing a "Share Our Wealth" plan; Upton Sinclair was running for governor of California on a platform calling for programs to "End Poverty in California"; and Dr. Francis E. Townsend was leading an organization of hundreds of thousands of elderly people on whose behalf he demanded government pensions of $200 a month.

The plan that emerged from the cabinet committee was carefully designed to meet popular demands within the framework of popular beliefs and constitutional understandings. It called for two kinds of programs: (1) an **insurance program** for the unemployed and elderly, to which workers would contribute and from which they would benefit when they became unemployed or retired; and (2) an **assistance program** for the blind, dependent children, and the aged. (Giving assistance as well

insurance program
A self-financing government program based on contributions that provide benefits to unemployed or retired persons.

assistance program
A government program financed by general income taxes that provides benefits to poor citizens without requiring contribution from them.

means test An income qualification program that determines whether one is eligible for benefits under government programs reserved for lower-income groups.

How Things Work

Medicare ABCDs

Medicare is a federal health insurance program that covers most senior citizens 65 or older, some younger people with disabilities, and people with end-stage renal disease. Today, it covers about 45 million elderly and disabled persons.

Medicare does not provide benefits for annual physicals, eyeglasses, hearing aids, long-term nursing home care, or in-home care.

Part A

Is hospital insurance. Some people pay a monthly premium; others do not.

Part B

Is medical insurance. The standard monthly premium in 2009 was $96.40. It gets deducted automatically from your Social Security check.

Part C

Is called Medicare Advantage Plus. Basically, it sets the terms under which companies that contract with the Medicare program must provide benefits.

Part D

Is prescription-drug coverage. Participation is voluntary, and the monthly premium depends on how much coverage you have.

---

programs. By the early 1960s, a majority of the House favored a health care plan, but without the approval of Ways and Means it would never reach the floor.

The 1964 elections changed all that. The Johnson landslide produced such large Democratic majorities in Congress that the composition of the committees changed. In particular, the membership of the Ways and Means Committee was altered. Whereas before it had three Democrats for every two Republicans, after 1964 it had two Democrats for every one Republican. The House leadership saw to it that the new Democrats on the committee were strongly committed to a health care program. Suddenly the committee had a majority favorable to such a plan, and Mills, realizing that a bill would pass and wanting to help shape its form, changed his position and became a supporter of what was to become Medicare.

The policy entrepreneurs in and out of the government who drafted the Medicare plan attempted to anticipate the major objections to it. First, the bill would apply only to the aged—those eligible for Social Security retirement benefits. This would reassure legislators worried about the cost of providing tax-supported health care for everybody. Second, the plan would cover only hospital expenses, not doctors' bills. Since doctors were not to be paid by the government, they would not be regulated by it;

thus, presumably, the opposition of the American Medical Association would be blunted.

Unexpectedly, however, the Ways and Means Committee broadened the coverage of the plan beyond what the administration had thought was politically feasible. It added sections providing medical assistance, called Medicaid, for the poor (defined as those already getting public assistance payments) and payment of doctors' bills for the aged (a new part of Medicare). The new, much-enlarged bill passed both houses of Congress with ease. The key votes pitted a majority of the Democrats against a majority of the Republicans.

REFORMING MAJORITARIAN WELFARE PROGRAMS

Both Social Security and Medicare are changing. What a majority of the people want will soon cost them more money than they can afford. But not every citizen is prepared to do what is necessary to fix this problem, and so the politicians are left in a bind: they must "save" Social Security and Medicare without changing Social Security and Medicare. It will not be easy.

Social Security costs about $700 billion a year. The key problem for Social Security is that, as

President Lyndon Johnson (left) signs the Medicare Act in 1965 in the company of Vice President Hubert Humphrey (standing) and former president Harry S Truman (right).

Lyndon Baines Johnson Library/National Archives

the population ages, soon there will not be enough people paying Social Security taxes to provide benefits for every retired person. By 2020, there will be fewer than two workers for every retiree, and the payroll taxes on these workers would have to more than double to pay that retiree's bills.

At present, Social Security faces a nearly $4 trillion shortfall over the next 75 years. There are many different ideas about how to close the gap and save the system. Here are a half-dozen proposals that have been analyzed and debated, some of them more popular than others with U.S. citizens (see Table 19.1):

1. *Raise the retirement age:* Under existing law, the age at which a citizen received full or partial Social Security benefits is rising to 67 for people born after 1959. By or before the year 2090, raise it to 70. This would close the long-term funding gap by about 20 percent.
2. *Reduce benefits for high-earners:* Today, a retiree in the program's highest wage bracket is eligible for a maximum monthly payment of about $2,120. Over the next several decades, reduce the maximum monthly benefit by about 10 percent. This change would close the gap by about 25 percent.

3. *Raise payroll taxes:* Now both workers and their employers pay 6.2% of the worker's wages up to $97,500 in Social Security payroll taxes. Over the next generation or two, increase that tax to 6.7%. This would eliminate about half of the projected funding gap.
4. *Increase the wage cap:* Presently workers and employers pay Social Security taxes on the first $97,500 of wages. Over the next several decades, increase the wage cap to $150,000. This would close the gap by about half.
5. *Have government make investments:* Let the government invest 15 percent of the fund in U.S. Treasury bonds or certain low-risk stock funds. If begun soon, this could reduce the gap by about 15 percent.
6. *Let individuals make investments:* Let people invest some of their Social Security tax payments in private retirement accounts like stocks or mutual funds, with benefits higher or lower than expected depending on stock market performance. There is no consensus on how this proposal might affect the gap.

A national advisory commission proposed the sixth option—private investment accounts—to President Clinton, but he did not embrace it. Another commission recommended three versions of the option

Table 19.1 Public Opinion on Social Security Reform Options

Reform Option	Consider	Favor
Raise the retirement age	47%	33%
Reduce benefits for higher-earners	43	28
Raise payroll taxes	72	59
Increase the wage cap	81	71
Have government make investments	54	40
Let individuals make investments	—	46

Source: Knowledge Networks; January 19-29, 2007, as reported in *Retirement Security Survey Report* (Washington, D.C. American Association of Retired Persons, Feb 2007), and Public Agenda Foundation, "Society Security: Bills and Proposals," 2007, at http://www.publicagenda.org/issues/major_proposals, citing a January 2005 survey by the Pew Research Center.

to President George W. Bush, but he received the report just a few months after September 11, 2001. Bush revived the plan in 2004, and the 109th Congress began to debate it in 2005. In 2007, the Democratic-led 110th Congress rebuffed Bush's attempts to bring it up yet again. In 2009, President Barack Obama reiterated what he said during the 2008 presidential campaign about opposing private investment accounts.

Medicare now costs about $450 billion a year. The key problems with Medicare are that it costs a huge amount of money and is not a very efficient

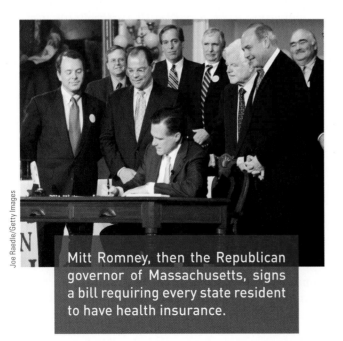

Mitt Romney, then the Republican governor of Massachusetts, signs a bill requiring every state resident to have health insurance.

Joe Raedle/Getty Images

way of paying for health care. When Medicare was enacted in 1965, the government said that by 1990 it would cost $12 billion a year. When 1990 rolled around, Medicare actually cost $110 billion. Today, it costs over $300 billion a year. As the population gets older and new (and expensive) life-prolonging technologies are developed, the cost of the program will rise even faster. Post–1970 growth in government health care spending has been higher in the United States than in many other countries (see Table 19.2), a fact for which Medicare's growth is largely responsible.

Medicare allows people to visit the doctor or go to the hospital whenever they feel they need to (see the box on page 514). The doctor or hospital is paid a fee for each visit. This creates three problems: (1) a lot of people use medical services when they don't really need them; (2) some doctors and hospitals overcharge the government for their services; and (3) doctors and hospitals are paid on the basis of a government-approved payment plan that can change whenever the government wants to save money.

In 1997, a bipartisan commission was formed to solve the problem of Medicare, but President Clinton, who had helped create it, repudiated its report. Few politicians are willing to propose cost-cutting measures for fear of being burned at the voting booth.

One possible cure is to get rid of Medicare and instead have doctors and hospitals work for the government. That is done in several countries, and as a result the citizens of these countries pay less for health care than do U.S. citizens. But many critics argue that government-run health care provides fewer benefits and slower care and discourages aggressive new health care innovations.

A second solution to the problem is to let the elderly take their Medicare money and buy health insurance from private suppliers, including health maintenance organizations (HMOs). This may or may not be an affordable alternative for individuals.

During the 2008 presidential campaign, Both Barack Obama and John McCain made detailed health care policy proposals. In February 2009, President Obama announced his "guiding principles" for "comprehensive health care reform," which included cutting health care costs for businesses, guaranteeing citizens their choice of doctors and health plans, ending barriers to coverage for people with preexisting medical conditions, and several others.

In mid-2009, opinion polls indicated that health care reform was considered "very important" by half of all voters and "somewhat important" by nearly a third of all voters; and, asked which party they trusted

Table 19.2 Post–1970 Government Health Care Spending in Ten Countries

Country	Average Annual Real Per-Capita Increase (%)
Australia	4.1
Austria	4.0
Canada	3.1
Germany	3.6
Japan	4.9
Norway	5.3
Spain	5.1
Sweden	2.6
United Kingdom	3.7
United States	5.1
Average	4.1

Source: Laurence Kotlilkoff and Christian Hagist, National Bureau of Economic Research, Working paper no. 11833, 2005, reporting OECD data and rounded averages for the period 1970–2002, as cited in National Center for Policy Analysis, *Health Care Spending Trends*, 2004, table 1.

more to handle the issue, voters favored Democrats (47 percent) over Republicans (37 percent).[11] The major concern expressed by people was that reform might result in a government-run health plan that would displace private ones.

By no means, however, is the legislative success of the Obama administration's health reform plans, or, for that matter, any competing plans, thereby assured. Even within the Democratic majorities in Congress, the same sorts of wide intraparty differences on the

When members of Congress went home in August 2009, they encountered a long line of voters angry over the health care debate.

Bradley C Bower/AP Photo

issue that surfaced during President Clinton's ill-fated push for comprehensive health care reform still exist.

Intraparty rifts aside, forming a winning bipartisan legislative coalition for any major new federal health policy will be especially difficult, in part because the public consensus on the need for "reform," when tested in Congress, usually proves far wider than it is deep.

For example, by over 2 to 1, people want Washington to enact sweeping health reform, but also fear that if it happens the cost of health care will go up, not down, and oppose "reform" if it means changing their own insurance coverage.[12] Indeed, half the public doubts it is even possible to "provide health insurance for anyone."[13] We shall see.

CLIENT WELFARE PROGRAMS: AID TO FAMILIES WITH DEPENDENT CHILDREN

One part of the Social Security Act of 1935 created what came to be called Aid to Families with Dependent Children (AFDC). It was scarcely noticed at the time. The federal government, in response to the depression, promised to provide aid to states that were, in many cases, already running programs to help poor children who lacked a father.

Because AFDC involved giving federal aid to existing state programs, it allowed the states to define what constituted "need," to set benefit levels, and to administer the program. Washington did set (and, over the years, continued to increase) a number of rules governing how the program would work, however. Washington told the states how to calculate applicants' incomes and required the states to give Medicaid to AFDC recipients. The states had to establish mandatory job-training programs for many AFDC recipients and to provide child-care programs for working AFDC parents. Washington also required that women on AFDC identify their children's fathers.

In addition to the growing list of requirements, Washington created new programs for which AFDC recipients were eligible, such as Food Stamps, the Earned Income Tax Credit, or EITC, (a cash grant to poor parents who were working), free school meals, various forms of housing assistance, and certain other benefits. But while all this was happening, public opinion moved against the AFDC program.

The combination of souring public opinion, increasing federal regulations, and a growing roster of benefits produced a program that irritated almost

A girl looks on as her mother displays food stamps.

everyone. The states disliked having to conform to a growing list of federal regulations. The public disliked the program because it was viewed as weakening the family by encouraging out-of-wedlock births (since AFDC recipients received additional benefits for each new child). The public worried that AFDC recipients were working covertly on the side; the data proved that this was true of at least half of them in several large cities. AFDC recipients saw the actual (inflation-adjusted) value of their AFDC checks was going down. Critics countered that if you added together all the benefits they were receiving (Food Stamps, Medicaid, housing assistance, and so on), benefit levels were actually going up. Politicians complained that healthy parents were living off AFDC instead of working. The AFDC law was revised many times, but never in a way that satisfied all, or even most, of its critics. Though AFDC recipients were only a small fraction of all Americans, they had become a large political problem.

> ***Earned Income Tax Credit (EITC)*** A provision of a 1975 law that entitles working families with children to receive money from the government if their total income is below a certain level. The program was expanded in the early 1990s.

What made matters worse was that the composition of the people in the program had changed. In 1970, about half of the mothers on AFDC were there because their husbands had died or divorced them; only a quarter had never been married. By 1994, the situation had changed dramatically: only about a quarter of AFDC mothers were widowed or divorced, and over half had never been married at all. And though most women on AFDC for the first time got off it after just a few years, almost two-thirds of the women on AFDC at any given moment had been on it for eight years or more.

These facts, combined with the increased proportion of out-of-wedlock births in the country as a whole, made it virtually impossible to sustain political support for what had begun as a noncontroversial client program. In 1996 the program was abolished. It was replaced by a block grant program, Temporary Assistance for Needy Families (TANF), that set strict federal requirements about work and limited how long families can receive federally funded benefits. Under TANF, by 2006, welfare caseloads nationally had declined by 62 percent.

Majoritarian versus Client Politics

The programs just described illustrate two patterns of policymaking. The old-age pensions created by the Social Security Act of 1935 and the health care benefits created by the Medicare Act of 1965 are examples of *majoritarian politics*: almost everybody benefits, and almost everybody pays. The TANF program is an example of *client politics*: a relatively few people benefit, but everybody pays.

Majoritarian Politics

When both the benefits and the costs of a proposed program are widely distributed, the proposal will be adopted if the beneficiaries believe their benefits will exceed their costs *and* if political elites believe it is legitimate for the federal government to adopt the program.

Initially, the benefits people received from the retirement program greatly exceeded its costs to them. Older people were able to get an old-age pension or health care even though they had paid in taxes only a small fraction of what these benefits cost. Social Security and Medicare seemed initially like the nearest thing to a free lunch.

The big debate in 1935 and 1965 was not over whether the people wanted these programs—the polls showed that they did—but over whether it was legitimate for the federal government to provide them.[14] In 1935, conservatives argued that as desirable as Social Security might be, nothing in the Constitution authorized the federal government to spend money for this purpose; welfare, they said, was a policy area reserved to the states. Liberals rejoined that the federal government had an obligation to help people avoid poverty in their old age. Besides, they said, as an "insurance" program, retirement benefits were not really a federal expenditure at all: Washington was merely collecting payments and holding them in a trust fund until the people who paid them were ready to retire. In the

Who Governs? To What Ends?

Reforming Majoritarian Education Programs

America is home to about 50 million public school children. Most citizens, even the elderly and young adults with no children in public schools, tend to think of public education in majoritarian terms: everyone benefits, everyone pays.

Until recently, Democrats pretty much owned this majoritarian issue. With the exception of some Democratic mayors, most Democratic leaders have opposed plans to give parents school vouchers (public monies that can be used to pay for private or religious school tuitions). Meanwhile, most Republican leaders have favored vouchers. In 2000, voucher referenda were defeated soundly in California and Michigan.

Three days after taking office in January 2001, Republican president George W. Bush proposed an education reform plan that he then described as "the cornerstone of my administration." It contained voucher language and related provisions that would have effected sweeping changes in the Elementary and Secondary Education Act (ESEA). But just a few months into negotiations on the bill with Senate Democrats, virtually every aspect of the original Bush plan that could not be credibly couched in majoritarian terms, reconciled with existing ESEA programs, or otherwise justified as "recruiting high-quality teachers,"

"promoting informed parental choice," or "improving the academic achievement of the disadvantaged" was abandoned.

On January 8, 2002, Congress easily passed the No Child Left Behind Act of 2001. The president's major ally in getting the 670-page education reform plan into law was Democratic senator Ted Kennedy of Massachusetts. Democrats applauded the act mainly for increasing federal education funding under the ESEA by 49 percent over 2000 levels, to over $22 billion a year. Republicans, led by House conservatives, complained about the increased ESEA spending and lamented that the new law did nothing to advance the cause of school vouchers.

On February 17, 2009, President Barack Obama signed the American Recovery and Reinvestment Act. It had something in it for just about everyone: about $5 billion for early learning programs like Head Start, $30 billion for college loans and other support for higher education, and federal grants totaling nearly $50 billion for elementary and secondary schools, among other provisions.

In the several years after Bush's No Child Left Behind bill became law, Republicans pulled even with Democrats on public trust with respect to education policy; but just a few months after the Obama administration's majoritarian push for education reform, by mid-2009, Democrats had regained a big edge on the issue.

---

midst of the Great Depression and at a time when liberals had large majorities in Congress, it was an easy argument to make, and so the Social Security bill readily crossed over the legitimacy barrier.

In 1965, the same issues were raised. Conservatives argued that medical care was a private, not a governmental, matter and that any federal involvement would subject doctors and hospitals to endless red tape and harm the quality of the doctor-patient relationship. Liberals rejoined that the elderly had health needs they could not meet without help and that only the federal government had the resources to provide that assistance. Because the 1964 elections, when Lyndon Johnson defeated Barry Goldwater, had swept into the House and Senate large majorities of liberal Democrats, there was no

chance that a conservative coalition of Republicans and southern Democrats could defeat Medicare, and so it passed.

The votes in Congress on Social Security and Medicare followed party lines. Since the Democratic opponents of these bills typically were conservative southerners, the vote followed ideological lines even more closely.

Client Politics

When the benefits of a proposal are to go to a relatively small group but the public at large pays, we have client politics. Proposals to benefit clients will pass if the cost to the public at large is not perceived to be great *and* if the client receiving the benefit is thought to be "deserving."

WHAT WOULD YOU DO?

MEMORANDUM

To: *Ursula Marx, Senate Committee chair*

From: *Cindy Fried, senior staff member*

Subject: *Universal Health Care Legislation*

You and the committee have two fairly distinct sets of options on this universal health care package.

Arguments for:

1. With more than 47 million Americans, or one in seven, lacking health care coverage, the government needs to enact far-reaching reform to ensure that everyone receives quality medical care.

2. The soaring cost of health care (which is expected to reach approximately one-fifth of the federal budget in the next decade) can be contained only by a public system that has the power to set prices and control costs.

3. Universal health care is a logical expansion of the Medicare and Medicaid programs created in 1965; nearly half a century later, health care should be a fundamental right guaranteed for everyone who lives in the United States.

Arguments against:

1. Though many people lack health insurance, most of them get health care in hospital emergency rooms and from doctors who donate their services.

2. Medical services in the United States are the best in the world, and government controls on costs will serve only to reduce the quality of care available.

Friday,

Universal Health Care Gets Strong Backing in Senate

July 9
WASHINGTON, D.C.

A bill sponsoring universal health care in the United States is likely to be reviewed by the full Senate next week. After vigorous hearings over coverage and costs, the chair of the Senate Committee on Health, Education, Labor, and Pensions said the committee would approve the bill. But it faces an uphill battle in the main chamber, as forty-two senators say they will not support such drastic reform. Public opinion is divided, with a recent poll showing that Americans want everyone to have basic health care, but they do not want a new "health" tax to fund the program.

3. In an era of budget deficits and trillions of dollars in national debt, the United States cannot afford to expand social welfare programs.

Your decision:

Support _____   Oppose _____

As noted previously, when AFDC was first enacted, it was relatively noncontroversial. Originally, it seemed intended to help deserving people. In 1935, the typical welfare mother was perceived to be a woman living in a small town, whose husband had been killed in a mining accident. Who could object to giving some modest help to a person who was the victim of circumstances?

Right or wrong, American values on this subject changed. Today, most Americans believe that able-bodied people on welfare should be made to work for their benefits. The work-based welfare provisions of TANF plainly reflect this belief. In 2002, during the largely consensual congressional debate over reauthorizing TANF, even many who had opposed these strategies in 1996 (when TANF replaced AFDC) now supported them. There remains, however, some popular sentiment for giving welfare recipients job training or even creating government jobs for them. This **service strategy** (providing training and education) is strongly preferred to an **income strategy** (giving people money)—unless, of course, the income can be called "insurance."[15]

Indeed, some critics of welfare, such as Charles Murray, have argued that AFDC actually increased the number of people living in poverty. Murray claimed that high welfare benefits made it more attractive for some people to go on welfare than to look for a job and more attractive for some women to have babies than to get married. This kept them poor. Other scholars have criticized Murray's thesis. They have argued that there is no direct evidence that welfare encourages family breakup and have suggested that the rise in the number of illegitimate children occurred during a period (the 1970s) when welfare benefits, in real (that is, inflation-adjusted) dollars, were going down.[16]

In short, the clients of these programs never acquired in the public's mind the legitimacy necessary for their programs to prosper. As a result, whereas for 40 years it was thought to be good politics to increase old-age benefits, it increasingly became considered bad politics to do anything but attack, investigate, and curtail "welfare" programs.

service strategy A policy providing poor people with education and job training to help lift them out of poverty.

income strategy A policy giving poor people money to help lift them out of poverty.

Still, as we stressed in Chapter 17, the politics of policy issues can be affected by changes in people's perceptions concerning who bears the burdens and who receives the benefits. Thus, under TANF, after 1996, able-bodied adults had a harder time getting welfare benefits, but welfare-related child-care spending in most states rose significantly. The average AFDC (and later TANF) benefit amount, adjusted for inflation, has fallen since 1980. In addition, many poor parents who are eligible for an EITC grant are unaware of the program and so do not receive benefits.

The politics of the policy process is always hard to predict, but in the years just ahead, needy children and other at-risk youth might well prove more politically popular, and be more widely perceived as "deserving" government aid, than baby-boomer retirees.

SUMMARY

We can explain the politics of social welfare policy in America principally in terms of two factors: who benefits and who pays, and the beliefs citizens have about social justice. Neither factor is static: gainers and losers vary as the composition of society and the workings of the economy change, and beliefs about who deserves what are modified as attitudes toward work, the family, and the obligations of government change.

The federal government spends far more on majoritarian social welfare programs (such as Social Security and Medicare) than on client ones (such as Food Stamps and EITC). It also promotes the majoritarian programs and encourages people to participate; it does much less of either with the client programs.

The congressional (as opposed to the parliamentary) system of government means that greater political effort and more time are required for the adoption of a new welfare policy. Federalism means the states will play a large role in determining how any welfare program is administered and at what level benefits are set.

RECONSIDERING WHO GOVERNS?

1. How, if at all, have Americans' views of government's responsibility to help the "deserving poor" changed over time?

American welfare policy since the 1930s has undergone a slow but steady change in how it has separated the "deserving" from the "undeserving" poor. In essence, today we separate them less and are more willing to have people rely solely on the government for help. For example, even before the New Deal, most Americans would surely have counted a poor, disabled, blind, elderly woman deserted by her family as deserving of public aid. Today, however, many citizens would also favor giving her aid even if she were only disabled, without regard to her income or family situation. Likewise, whereas once most Americans were inclined to provide public aid only if the beneficiary's family helped too, today most citizens do not believe in strictly conditioning public aid on family support.

2. Why are some government social welfare programs politically protected while others are politically imperiled?

Majoritarian programs (nearly everyone benefits, nearly everyone pays) like Social Security and Medicare are politically sacrosanct. Client-based programs (a relatively few number of people benefit, but almost everyone pays) like the now-defunct Aid to Families with Dependent Children (AFDC) are politically shaky. Debates about the former normally concern only how to keep the benefits flowing; debates about the latter often concern *whether* to keep the program ongoing. But certain client-based programs are less politically vulnerable than others—it all depends on who the clients are, or are widely perceived to be. Medicaid was protected largely because its clients included middle-class retirees who received nursing home benefits and medically needy low-income children. AFDC was targeted because its clients were perceived by many to include ablebodied adults who chose to receive public aid rather than go to work.

RECONSIDERING TO WHAT ENDS?

1. What does the Constitution mean by "promote the general Welfare"?

The Framers of the Constitution did not mean by this phrase that government has a duty to provide cash assistance or other benefits to citizens in economic need, or that the president or Congress has to manage the economy. Rather, they undoubtedly meant something closer to "protect private property and promote public safety and morals." It is difficult, however, to be sure about what they meant by those words. Some present-day advocates for the poor have suggested that the federal government, by enacting laws intended to lift low-income citizens out of poverty, to provide health care at public expense, and to guarantee access to affordable housing, has thereby established a constitutional right to such social welfare programs, services, or supports. There is little constitutional case law to support that view.

2. Should religious groups be eligible to administer some federal welfare programs?

Under four Charitable Choice laws the federal government may not discriminate against community-serving faith-based organizations in the grant-making process, but these organizations are strictly prohibited from using any public funds to proselytize, provide religious instruction, or perform worship services; may not hire only coreligionists; and must serve all eligible persons without regard to religion. The courts have consistently upheld its legality and constitutionality.

WORLD WIDE WEB RESOURCES

Social welfare programs
    Medicare: **www.medicare.gov**
    Social Security: **www.ssa.gov**
    TANF: **www.acf.dhhs.gov/programs/ofa/**
Views on Social Security reform
    www.socialsecurityreform.org
    www.socialsecurity.org
    www.socsec.org

SUGGESTED READINGS

Derthick, Martha. *Policymaking for Social Security*. Washington, D.C.: Brookings Institution, 1979. A detailed analysis of how the Social Security program grew.

Eberstadt, Nicholas. *The Poverty of "The Poverty Rate": Measure and Mismeasure of Want in Modern America*. Washington, D.C.: American Enterprise Institute, 2008. A searching analysis of the official poverty rate as a measure of social welfare in America.

Heclo, Hugh. *Modern Social Politics in Britain and Sweden*. New Haven, Conn.: Yale University Press, 1974. Comparative analysis of how social welfare programs came to Britain and Sweden.

Monsma, Stephen V. *Putting Faith in Partnerships: Welfare-to-Work in Four Cities*. Ann Arbor: The University of Michigan Press, 2004. Careful study of the six different types of organizations that administer welfare-to-work programs in big cities today.

Moynihan, Daniel Patrick. *Family and Nation*. New York: Harcourt Brace Jovanovich, 1986. Argument for the importance of federal policy to aid families.

Murray, Charles. *Losing Ground: American Social Policy, 1950–1980*. New York: Basic Books, 1984. An argument that federal spending on the poor actually increased poverty during the 1960s and 1970s.

Wilson, William J. *The Truly Disadvantaged*. Chicago: University of Chicago Press, 1987. Disputes Murray's explanation, arguing instead that ghetto poverty has been the result of the movement of jobs out of cities.

20

Foreign and Military Policy

WHO GOVERNS?

1. Is American foreign policy set by public wishes or elite views?
2. If only Congress can declare war, why has the president become so powerful in military affairs?

TO WHAT ENDS?

1. Why do we go to war against some dictatorships and not others?
2. Should our foreign policy be based on American interests or some conception of human rights?

When you heard about the 9/11 attacks by hijacked aircraft against the World Trade Center and the Pentagon, you were witnessing the most lethal destruction of American lives and property since the Japanese bombed Pearl Harbor on December 7, 1941. But 9/11 was different from Pearl Harbor: the attack on Pearl Harbor had, so to speak, a return address: we knew who did it and where they lived. But 9/11 had no return address: it was a terrorist attack waged by small groups that could be located anywhere.

The public response was impressive, as was evident in an outburst of patriotism and a heightened sense of confidence in the national government. Valuable as these reactions were, they left unanswered some fundamental questions:

- How can America wage war in remote nations that harbor terrorists?
- If terrorists are sheltered or supported by nations that are otherwise friendly to the United States, what do we do about these countries?
- Should the United States allow other nations (for example, Israel) to wage war against terrorists (for example, those in neighboring Palestine), or should we try to be mediators?
- How can the military, designed to fight big, conventional land wars in Europe, be redesigned to make it effective in small, long-lasting struggles against terrorists?

And terrorism is not our only foreign or military problem. It is a new and very important one added to a long list of other issues. Among them are two questions:

- Do we support any nation that goes along with us, or only those that are reasonably free and democratic?
- Are we the world's policeman? We did not intervene to prevent China from occupying Tibet, to end the massacre of thousands of Tutsis in Rwanda, or to help Bosnia when

WISSAM AL-OKAILI/AFP/Getty Images

it was attacked by Serbs. But we did intervene to try to end a dictatorship in Haiti, to help starving people in Somalia, to turn back an Iraqi invasion of Kuwait, and to punish Serbs who were attacking Kosovo.

These choices must be made in a democracy, and some observers think democratic politics makes managing foreign and military policy harder. Tocqueville said the conduct of foreign affairs requires precisely those qualities most lacking in a democratic nation: "A democracy can only with great difficulty regulate the details of an important undertaking, persevere in a fixed design, and work out its execution in spite of serious obstacles. It cannot combine its measures with secrecy or await their consequences with patience."[1] In plain language, a democracy is forced to play foreign policy poker with its cards turned up. As a result, aggressors from Hitler to Saddam Hussein can bluff or misjudge us.

But other writers disagree. To them, the strength of democracy is that, though it rarely if ever wages an unjustified war on another country, its people, when mobilized by the president, will support our overseas engagements even when many deaths occur.[2]

Others find fault not with the system but with what they view as the reckless policies of American presidents. If Congress had been more involved, they say, we would not have gotten bogged down in Vietnam, tried to trade arms for hostages in Iran, or supported the rebels in Nicaragua.

Happily, most foreign policy issues are not matters of war or peace. But the same issues can be found in them all: How great are the powers of the president? What role should Congress play? How important is public opinion? When do interest groups make a difference? To answer those questions, we must first distinguish among foreign policy issues that involve majoritarian, interest group, and client politics.

Kinds of Foreign Policy

The majoritarian component of foreign policy includes those decisions (and nondecisions) perceived to confer widely distributed benefits and impose widely distributed costs. The decision to go to war is an obvious example of this. So, too, are the establishment of military alliances with Western Europe, the negotiation of a nuclear test ban treaty or a strategic arms limitation agreement, the response to the crisis posed by the Soviet blockade of West Berlin or the placement of Soviet offensive missiles in Cuba, the decision to aid the contras in Nicaragua, and the opening up of diplomatic relations with the People's Republic of China. These may be good or bad policies, but such benefits and such costs as they have accrue to the nation generally. Some argue that the costs of many of these policies are in fact highly concentrated—for example, soldiers bear the burden of a military operation—but that turns out, on closer inspection, not to shape the positions that people take on issues of war and peace. Though soldiers and their immediate families may feel the costs of a war to an especially high degree, public opinion surveys taken during the Vietnam War showed that having a family member in the armed forces did not significantly affect how people evaluated the war.[3] There is a sense that, during wartime, we are all in this together.

Foreign policy decisions may also reflect interest group politics. Tariff decisions confer benefits on certain business firms and labor unions and impose costs on other firms and unions. If the price of Japanese steel imported into this country is increased by tariffs, quotas, or other devices, this

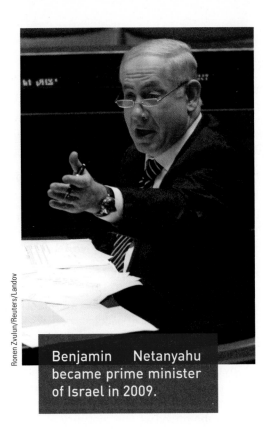

Ronen Zvulun/Reuters/Landov

Benjamin Netanyahu became prime minister of Israel in 2009.

helps the American steel industry and the United Steel Workers of America. On the other hand, it hurts those firms (and associated unions) that had been purchasing the once-cheap Japanese steel.

Examples of client politics also occur in foreign affairs. Washington often provides aid to American corporations doing business abroad because the aid helps those firms directly without imposing any apparent costs on an equally distinct group in society. Our policy toward Israel has in part reflected the fact that Jews in this country feel strongly about the need to support a Jewish state abroad and are well organized to make those concerns felt. (Other factors also help explain our support of Israel; it is by no means a pure case of client politics.) Arab Americans have begun to organize and to press on the government concerns very different from the pro-Israel arguments. We may in fact be witnessing a change of our policy toward Israel from one chiefly influenced by client politics to one more subject to interest group politics.

Who has power in foreign policy depends very much on what kind of foreign policy we have in mind. Where it is of a majoritarian nature, the president is clearly the dominant figure, and much, if not everything, depends on his beliefs and skills and on those of his chief advisers. Public opinion will ordinarily support this presidential leadership, but it

will not guide it. As we shall see, public opinion on majoritarian foreign policy issues usually reflects a disposition to trust the president. But woe to the president who by his actions forfeits that trust.

When interest group or client politics is involved, Congress plays a much larger role. Although Congress has a subsidiary role in the conduct of foreign diplomacy, the decision to send troops overseas, or the direction of intelligence operations, it has a large one in decisions involving foreign economic aid, the structure of the tariff system, the shipment of weapons to foreign allies, the creation of new weapons systems, and the support of Israel.

And Congress is the central political arena on those occasions when entrepreneurial politics shapes foreign policy. If a multinational corporation is caught in a scandal, congressional investigations shake the usual indifference of politicians to the foreign conduct of such corporations. If presidential policies abroad lead to reversals, as when in 1986 presidential aides sought to trade arms for U.S. hostages in Iran and then use some profits from the arms sales to support the anti-Marxist contras fighting in Nicaragua, Congress becomes the forum for investigations and criticism. At such moments Congress often seeks to expand its power over foreign affairs.

In this chapter, we will be chiefly concerned with foreign policy insofar as it displays the characteristics of majoritarian politics. Limiting the discussion in this way permits us to focus on the grand issues of foreign affairs—war, peace, and global diplomacy. It allows us to see how choices are made in a situation in which public majorities support but do not direct policy, in which opinion tends to react to events, and in which interest groups are relatively unimportant.

The Constitutional and Legal Context

The Constitution defines the authority of the president and of Congress in foreign affairs in a way that, as Edward Corwin put it, is an "invitation to struggle."[4] The president is commander in chief of the armed forces, but Congress must authorize and appropriate money for those forces. The president appoints ambassadors, but they must be confirmed by the Senate. The president may negotiate treaties, but the Senate must ratify these by a two-thirds vote. Only Congress may regulate commerce with other nations and "declare" war. (In an early draft of the

Constitution, the Framers gave Congress the power to "make" war but changed this to "declare" so that the president, acting without Congress, could take military measures to repel a sudden attack.) Because power over foreign affairs is shared by the president and Congress, conflict between them is to be expected.

Yet almost every American thinks instinctively that the president is in charge of foreign affairs, and what popular opinion supposes, the historical record confirms. Presidents have asserted the right to send troops abroad on their own authority in more than 125 instances. Only six of the 13 major wars that this country has fought have followed a formal declaration of war by Congress.[5] The State Department, the Central Intelligence Agency, and the National Security Agency are almost entirely "presidential" agencies, with only modest congressional control. The Defense Department, though keenly sensitive to congressional views on weapons procurement and the location of military bases, is very much under the control of the president on matters of military strategy. While the Senate has since 1789 ratified well over a thousand treaties signed by the president, the president during this period has also signed around 7,000 executive agreements with other countries that did not require Senate ratification and yet have the force of law.[6]

PRESIDENTIAL BOX SCORE

When the president seeks congressional approval for foreign policy matters, he tends to win more often than when he asks for support on domestic matters. One student of the presidency, Aaron Wildavsky, concluded that the American political system has "two presidencies"—one in domestic affairs that is relatively weak and closely checked, and another in foreign affairs that is quite powerful.[7] As we shall see, this view considerably overstates presidential power in certain areas.

When it comes to international diplomacy and the use of American troops, the president is indeed strong, much stronger than the Framers may have intended and certainly stronger than many members of Congress would prefer. Examples abound:

- 1861: Abraham Lincoln blockaded southern ports and declared martial law.

- 1940: Franklin D. Roosevelt sent 50 destroyers to England to be used against Germany, with which we were then technically at peace.

- 1950: Harry Truman sent American troops into South Korea to help repulse a North Korean attack on that country.

- 1960s: John F. Kennedy and Lyndon Johnson sent American forces into South Vietnam without a declaration of war.

- 1983: Ronald Reagan sent troops to overthrow a pro-Castro regime in Grenada.

- 1989: George H.W. Bush ordered the U.S. invasion of Panama to depose dictator Manuel Noriega.

- 1990: Bush ordered troops to Saudi Arabia in response to Iraq's invasion of Kuwait.

- 1999: Bill Clinton ordered the military to attack, with bombs and cruise missiles, Serbian forces that were trying to control Kosovo.

- 2001: George W. Bush sent U.S. troops to liberate Afghanistan from the Taliban, a regime supportive of Osama bin Laden, the architect of the September 11 terrorist attacks.

- 2003: Bush, with some allies, invaded Iraq.

However, by the standards of other nations, even other democratic ones, the ability of an American president to act decisively often appears rather modest. England was dismayed at the inability of Woodrow Wilson in 1914–1915 and Franklin Roosevelt in 1939–1940 to enter into an alliance when England was engaged in a major war with Germany. Wilson was unable to bring this country into the League of Nations. Gerald Ford could not intervene covertly in Angola in support of an anti-Marxist faction. Ronald Reagan was heavily criticized in Congress for sending fifty-five military advisers to El Salvador and a few hundred Marines to Lebanon. After George H.W. Bush sent U.S. troops to the Persian Gulf in 1990, he began a long debate with Congress over whether he would need a formal declaration of war before the troops were sent into combat. George W. Bush's decision to invade Iraq in 2003 became bitterly controversial in the 2004 and 2006 elections.

Furthermore, a treaty signed by the president is little more than his promise to try to get the Senate to go along. He can sign executive agreements without Senate consent, but most of these are authorized in advance by Congress.[8]

By contrast, the leaders of other democratic nations (to say nothing of totalitarian ones) often are able to act with much greater freedom. While Reagan was arguing with Congress over whether we should assign any military advisers to El Salvador, the president of France, François Mitterrand, ordered 2,500 combat troops to Chad with scarcely a ripple of opposition. A predecessor of Mitterrand, Charles de Gaulle, brought France into the European Common Market over the explicit opposition of the French Assembly

Shifting Patterns of Leadership in Foreign Policy

Depending on the personalities, skills, and interests of those involved, leadership in making American foreign policy may be found centered in the White House (the president and his national security adviser) or in the State Department (the secretary of state).

Periods of White House Dominance

President	Secretary of State
Franklin D. Roosevelt	Cordell Hull (1933–1944)
John F. Kennedy(and National Security Adviser McGeorge Bundy)	Dean Rusk (1961–1969)
Richard M. Nixon (and National Security Adviser Henry A. Kissinger)	William P. Rogers (1969–1973)

Periods of Leadership by the Secretary of State

Secretary of State	President
George C. Marshall (1947–1949) and Dean Acheson (1949–1953)	Harry S Truman
John Foster Dulles (1953–1959)	Dwight D. Eisenhower
Henry A. Kissinger (1973–1977)	Gerald R. Ford
Warren Christopher (1993–1996)	Bill Clinton

Periods of Tension between the White House and Secretary of State

President	Secretary of State
Jimmy Carter	Cyrus Vance (1977–1980)
Ronald Reagan	George Shultz (1982–1989)

and granted independence to Algeria, then a French colony, without seriously consulting the Assembly.[9] The British prime minister brought his country into the Common Market despite popular opposition and can declare war without the consent of Parliament.[10]

EVALUATING THE POWER OF THE PRESIDENT

Whether one thinks the president is too strong or too weak in foreign affairs depends not only on whether one holds a domestic or international point of view but also on whether one agrees or disagrees with his policies. Historian Arthur M. Schlesinger, Jr., thought that President Kennedy exercised commendable presidential vigor when he made a unilateral decision to impose a naval blockade on Cuba to induce the Soviets to remove missiles installed there. However, he viewed President Nixon's decision to extend U.S. military action in Vietnam into neighboring Cambodia as a deplorable example of the "imperial presidency."[11] To be sure, there were important differences between these two actions, but that is precisely the point: a president strong enough to do something that one thinks proper is also strong enough to do something that one finds wrong.

The Supreme Court has fairly consistently supported the view that the federal government has powers in the conduct of foreign and military policy beyond those specifically mentioned in the Constitution. The leading decision, rendered in 1936, holds that the right to carry out foreign policy is an inherent attribute of any sovereign nation:

> *The power to declare and wage war, to conclude peace, to make treaties, to maintain diplomatic relations with other sovereignties, if they had never been mentioned in the Constitution, would have vested in the Federal Government as necessary concomitants of nationality.[12]*

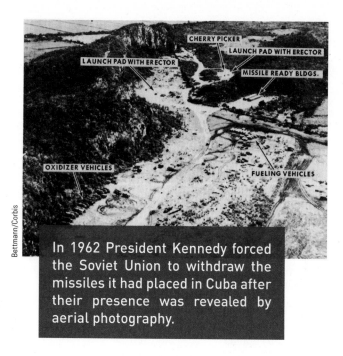

In 1962 President Kennedy forced the Soviet Union to withdraw the missiles it had placed in Cuba after their presence was revealed by aerial photography.

The individual states have few rights in foreign affairs.

Moreover, the Supreme Court has been reluctant to intervene in disputes over the conduct of foreign affairs. When various members of Congress brought suit challenging the right of President Nixon to enlarge the war in Vietnam without congressional approval, the court of appeals handled the issue, as one scholar was later to describe it, with all the care of porcupines making love. The Court said it was a matter for the president and Congress to decide and that if Congress was unwilling to cut off the money to pay for the war, it should not expect the courts to do the job for it.[13]

The Supreme Court upheld the extraordinary measures taken by President Lincoln during the Civil War and refused to interfere with the conduct of the Vietnam War by Presidents Johnson and Nixon.[14] After Iran seized American hostages in 1979, President Carter froze Iranian assets in this country. To win the hostages' freedom the president later agreed to return some of these assets and to nullify claims on them by American companies. The Court upheld the nullification because it was necessary for the resolution of a foreign policy dispute.[15]

How great the deference to presidential power may be is vividly illustrated by the actions of President Franklin Roosevelt in ordering the army to move over 100,000 Japanese Americans—the great majority of them born in this country and citizens of the United States—from their homes on the West Coast to inland "relocation centers" for the duration of World War II. Though this action was

a wholesale violation of the constitutional rights of U.S. citizens and was unprecedented in American history, the Supreme Court decided that with the West Coast vulnerable to attack by Japan, the president was within his rights to declare that people of Japanese ancestry might pose a threat to internal security; thus the relocation order was upheld.[16] (No Japanese American was ever found guilty of espionage or sabotage.) One of the few cases in which the Court denied the president broad wartime powers occurred in 1952, when by a 5 to 4 vote it reversed President Truman's seizure of the steel mills—a move that he had made in order to avert a strike that, in his view, would have imperiled the war effort in Korea.[17]

CHECKS ON PRESIDENTIAL POWER

If there is a check on the powers of the federal government or the president in foreign affairs, it is chiefly political rather than constitutional. The most important check is Congress's control of the purse strings. In addition, Congress has imposed three important kinds of restrictions on the president's freedom of action, all since Vietnam:

Limitations on the President's Ability to Give Military or Economic Aid to Other Countries

For example, between 1974 and 1978 the president could not sell arms to Turkey because of a dispute between Turkey and Greece over control of the island of Cyprus. The pressure on Congress from groups supporting Greece was much stronger than that from groups supporting Turkey. In 1976, Congress prevented President Ford from giving aid to the pro-Western faction in the Angolan civil war. Until the method was declared unconstitutional, Congress for many years could use a legislative veto, a resolution disapproving of an executive decision (see Chapter 15), to block the sale by the president of arms worth more than $25 million to another country.

The War Powers Act

Passed in 1973 over a presidential veto, this law placed the following restrictions on the president's ability to use military force:

- He must report in writing to Congress within 48 hours after he introduces U.S. troops into areas where hostilities have occurred or are imminent.

- Within 60 days after troops are sent into hostile situations, Congress must, by declaration of war or other specific statutory authorization, provide for the continuation of hostile action by U.S. troops.

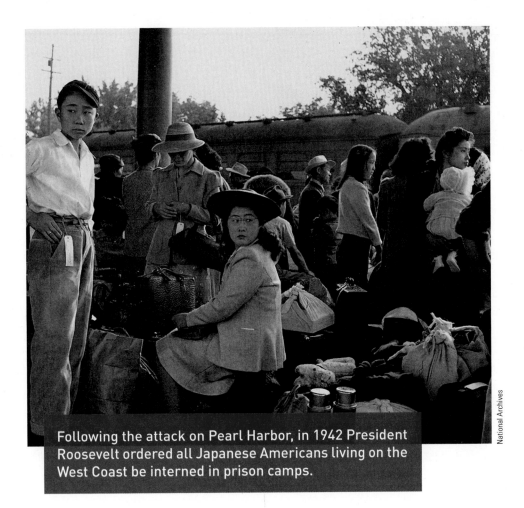

National Archives

Following the attack on Pearl Harbor, in 1942 President Roosevelt ordered all Japanese Americans living on the West Coast be interned in prison camps.

- If Congress fails to provide such authorization, the president must withdraw the troops (unless Congress has been prevented from meeting as a result of an armed attack).

- If Congress passes a concurrent resolution (which the president may not veto) directing the removal of U.S. troops, the president must comply.

The War Powers Act has had very little influence on American military actions. Since its passage every president—Ford, Carter, Reagan, Bush, Clinton, and Bush the younger—has sent American forces abroad without any explicit congressional authorization. (Bush the elder asked for that support when he attacked Iraq and, by a narrow margin, received it.) No president has acknowledged that the War Powers Act is constitutional. In its 1983 decision in the *Chadha* case, the Supreme Court struck down the legislative veto, which means that this section of the act is already in constitutional trouble.[18]

Even if the act is constitutional, politically it is all but impossible to use. Few members of Congress would challenge a president who carried out a successful military operation (for example, those in Grenada, Panama, and Afghanistan). More might challenge the president if, after a while, the military action were in trouble, but the easiest way to do that would be to cut off funding for the operation. But even during the Vietnam War, a conflict that preceded the War Powers Act, Congress, though it contained many critics of U.S. policy, never stopped military appropriations.

Intelligence Oversight

Owing to the low political stock of President Nixon during the Watergate scandal and the revelations of illegal operations by the Central Intelligence Agency (CIA) within the United States, Congress required that the CIA notify appropriate congressional committees about any proposed covert action (between 1974 and 1980 it had to notify *eight* different committees). Today it must keep two groups, the House and the Senate Intelligence Committees, "fully and currently informed" of all intelligence activities,

Rivalry versus Cooperation: The President and the Senate

Because the Senate must ratify treaties and consent to the appointment of ambassadors and other high foreign policy officials, it has the opportunity to play a large role in the conduct of foreign affairs. The key figure in the Senate is usually the chairman of the Senate Foreign Relations Committee.

Depending on personalities and circumstances, the president and the chairman have sometimes been able to work together closely but at other times have been bitter, outspoken rivals. In general, cooperation occurs when there is a widely shared foreign policy worldview; rivalry erupts when worldviews diverge.

Periods of Shared Worldviews and Political Cooperation

President	Chairman of Foreign Relations Committee
Franklin D. Roosevelt	Tom Connally (1941–1947, 1949–1953)
Harry S Truman	Arthur H. Vandenberg (1947–1949)

Periods of Competing Worldviews and Political Rivalry

President	Chairman of Foreign Relations Committee
Woodrow Wilson	Henry Cabot Lodge (1919–1924)
Lyndon B. Johnson	J. William Fulbright (1959–1975)
Richard M. Nixon	J. William Fulbright (1959–1975)
Bill Clinton	Jesse Helms (1995–1999)

including covert actions. The committees do not have the authority to disapprove such actions.

However, from time to time Congress will pass a bill blocking particular covert actions. This happened when the Boland Amendment (named after its sponsor, Representative Edward Boland) was passed on several occasions between 1982 and 1985. Each version of the amendment prevented, for specifically stated periods, intelligence agencies from supplying military aid to the Nicaraguan contras. After the surprise terrorist attack on September 11, there was an investigation to find out why the CIA had not warned the country of this risk.

The 9/11 terrorist attacks left everyone wondering why our intelligence agencies had not foreseen them. In an effort to improve matters, Congress passed and President Bush signed a law creating the Office of the Director of National Intelligence

(DNI). It was designed to coordinate the work of the CIA, the FBI, the Defense Intelligence Agency (DIA), and the intelligence units of several other government agencies. The DNI replaced the director of the CIA as the president's chief adviser. It is too early to tell how much real coordination will occur; the DNI's office is another large bureaucracy placed on top of other big ones.

The Machinery of Foreign Policy

From the time that Thomas Jefferson took the job in Washington's first administration until well into the 20th century, foreign policy was often made and almost always carried out by the secretary of state. No more. When America became a major world power during and after World War II, our commitments overseas expanded dramatically. With that expansion two things happened. First, the president began to put foreign policy at the top of his agenda and to play a larger role in directing it. Second, that policy was shaped by the scores of agencies (some brand-new) that had acquired overseas activities.

Today Washington, D.C., has not one State Department but many. The Defense Department has military bases and military advisers abroad. The Central Intelligence Agency has intelligence officers abroad, most of them assigned to "stations" that are part of the American embassy but not under the full control of the American ambassador there. The Departments of Agriculture, Commerce, and Labor have missions abroad. The Federal Bureau of Investigation and the Drug Enforcement Administration have agents abroad. The Agency for International Development has offices to dispense foreign aid in host countries. The United States Information Agency runs libraries, radio stations, and educational programs abroad.

Every new secretary of state bravely announces he or she is going to "coordinate" and "direct" this enormous foreign policy establishment. He or she never does. The reason is partly that the job is too big for any one person and partly that most of these agencies owe no political or bureaucratic loyalty to the secretary of state. If anyone is to coordinate them, it will have to be the president. But the president cannot keep track of what all these organizations are doing in the more than 190 nations and 50 international organizations where we have representatives, or in the more than 800 international conferences that we attend each year.

So he has hired a staff to do the coordinating for him. That staff is part of the National Security Council (NSC), a committee created by statute and chaired by the president, whose members include by law the vice president and the secretaries of state and defense, by custom the director of national intelligence (DNI), the chairman of the Joint Chiefs of Staff, and often the attorney general. Depending on the president, the NSC can be an important body in which to hammer out foreign policy. Attached to it is a staff headed by the national security adviser. That staff, which usually numbers a few dozen men and women, can be (again, depending on the president) an enormously powerful instrument for formulating and directing foreign policy.

Presidents Truman and Eisenhower made only limited use of the NSC staff, but beginning with President Kennedy it has grown greatly in influence. Its head, the national security adviser, has come to rival the secretary of state for foreign policy leadership, especially when the adviser is a powerful personality such as Henry Kissinger. President Reagan attempted to downgrade the importance of the national security adviser, but ironically it was one of his relatively low-visibility appointees, Admiral John Poindexter, and his subordinate, Lieutenant Colonel Oliver North, who precipitated the worst crisis of the Reagan presidency when, allegedly without informing the president, they tried to use cash realized from the secret sale of arms to Iran to finance guerrillas fighting against the Marxist government of Nicaragua. The sale and the diversion became known, North was fired, a congressional investigation ensued, criminal charges were filed against Poindexter and North, and the president's political position was weakened.

But even in ordinary times the NSC staff has been the rival of the secretary of state, except during that period in the Ford administration when Henry Kissinger held *both* jobs.

The way in which the machinery of foreign policy making operates has two major consequences for the substance of that policy. First, as former secretary of state George Shultz asserted, "It's never over." Foreign policy issues are endlessly agitated, rarely settled. The reason is that the rivalries *within* the executive branch intensify the rivalries *between* that branch and Congress. In ways already described, Congress has steadily increased its influence over the conduct of foreign policy. Anybody in the executive branch who loses out in a struggle over foreign policy can take his or her case (usually by means of a well-timed leak) to a sympathetic member of Congress, who then can make a speech, hold a hearing, or introduce a bill.

Second, the interests of the various organizations making up the foreign policy establishment profoundly affect the positions that they take. Because the State Department has a stake in diplomacy, it tends to resist bold or controversial new policies that might upset established relationships with other countries. Part of the CIA has a stake in gathering and analyzing information; that part tends to be skeptical of the claims of other agencies that their overseas operations are succeeding. Another part of the CIA conducts covert operations abroad; it tends to resent or ignore the skepticism of the intelligence analysts. The air force flies airplanes and so tends to be optimistic about what can be accomplished through the use of air power in particular and military power in general; the army, on the other hand, which must fight in the trenches, is often dubious about the prospects for military success. During the

Landmark Cases

Foreign Affairs

- **Curtiss-Wright Export Corp. v. United States (1936):** American foreign policy is vested entirely in the federal government where the president has plenary power.

- **Korematsu v. United States (1944):** Sending Japanese Americans to relocation centers during World War II was based on an acceptable military justification.

- **Youngstown Sheet & Tube Co. v. Sawyer (1952):** The president may not seize factories during wartime without explicit congressional authority even when they are threatened by a strike.

- **Hamdi v. Rumsfeld (2004):** An American citizen in jail because he allegedly joined the Taliban extremist group should have access to a "neutral decision maker."

- **Rasul v. Bush (2004):** Foreign nationals held at Guantanamo Bay because they are believed to be terrorists have a right to bring their cases before an American court.

American war in Iraq, the conflict between the CIA and the Defense Department was great, with each side leaking information to the press.

Americans often worry that their government is keeping secrets from them. In fact, there are no secrets in Washington—at least not for long.

Foreign Policy and Public Opinion

These organizational conflicts shape the details of foreign policy, but its broad outlines are shaped by public and elite opinion.

World War II was the great watershed event in American foreign policy. Before that time, a clear majority of the American public opposed active involvement in world affairs. The public saw the costs of such involvement as being substantially in excess of the benefits, and only determined, skillful leaders were able, as was President Roosevelt during 1939–1940, to affect in even a limited fashion the diplomatic and military struggles then convulsing Europe and Asia.

In 1937, 94 percent of the American public preferred the policy of doing "everything possible to keep out of foreign wars" to the policy of doing "everything possible to prevent war, even if it means threatening to fight countries that fight wars." In 1939, after World War II had begun in Europe but before Pearl Harbor, was attacked, only 13 percent of Americans polled thought that we should enter the war against Germany. Just a month before Pearl Harbor, only 19 percent felt that the United States should take steps, at the risk of war, to prevent Japan from becoming too powerful.[19] Congress reflected the non-interventionist mood of the country: in the summer of 1941, with war breaking out almost everywhere, the proposal to continue the draft passed the House of Representatives by only one vote.

The Japanese attack on Pearl Harbor on December 7 changed all that. Not only was the American war effort supported almost unanimously, not only did Congress approve the declaration of war with only one dissenting vote, but World War II—unlike World War I—produced popular support for an active assumption of international responsibilities that continued after the war had ended.[20] Whereas after World War I a majority opposed U.S. entry into the League of Nations, after World War II a clear majority favored our entry into the United Nations.[21]

This willingness to see the United States remain a world force persisted. Even during the Vietnam War the number of people thinking that we should "keep independent" in world affairs as opposed to "working closely with other nations" rose from 10 percent in 1963 to only 22 percent in 1969.[22] In 1967, after more than two years of war in Vietnam, 44 percent of Americans believed that this country had an obligation to "defend other Vietnams if they are threatened by communism."[23]

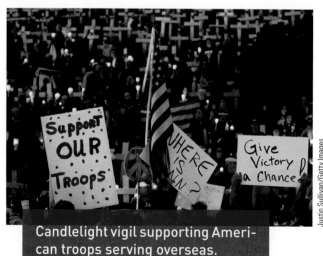

Candlelight vigil supporting American troops serving overseas.

Justin Sullivan/Getty Images

Before 9/11, hardly any American thought we should fight a war in Afghanistan, but after that attack we fought exactly that war in order to get rid of the Taliban regime. The Taliban, a group of radical young Muslims, had taken control of that country and allowed Osama bin Laden, the head of al Qaeda, to use the nation as a place to train and direct terrorists. Though al Qaeda designed and carried out the 9/11 attacks on America, it is not a single organization located in one place and thus easily defeated. It is instead a network of terrorist cells found all over the world that is allied with other terrorist groups.

But the support for an internationalist American foreign policy was, and is, highly general and heavily dependent on the phrasing of poll questions, the opinions expressed by popular leaders, and the impact of world events. Public opinion, while more internationalist than once was the case, is both mushy and volatile. Just prior to President Nixon's decision to send troops into Cambodia, only 7 percent of the people said they supported such a move. After the troops were sent and Nixon made a speech explaining his move, 50 percent of the public said they supported it.[24] Similarly, only 49 percent of the people favored halting the American bombing of North Vietnam before President Johnson ordered such a halt in 1968; afterward 60 percent of the people said they supported such a policy.[25]

BACKING THE PRESIDENT

Much of this volatility in specific opinions (as opposed to general mood) reflects the already-mentioned deference to the "commander in chief" and a desire to support the United States when it confronts other nations. Table 20.1 shows the proportion of people who said that they approved of the way the president was doing his job before and after various major foreign policy events. Each foreign crisis increased the level of public approval of the president, often dramatically. The most vivid illustration of this was the Bay of Pigs fiasco: an American-supported, American-directed invasion of Cuba by anti-Castro Cuban émigrés was driven back into the sea. President Kennedy accepted responsibility for the aborted project. His popularity *rose*. (Comparable data for domestic crises tend to show no similar effect.)

This tendency to "rally round the flag" operates for some but not all foreign military crises.[26] The rally not only helped Kennedy after the Bay of Pigs, but it also helped Ronald Reagan when he invaded Grenada and George Bush the elder when he sent troops to fight Iraq. But it did not help Bill Clinton when he sent forces to Bosnia or launched bombing attacks on Iraq. If there is an attack on America, the president will do very well. Just before September 11, 2001, George Bush's favorability rating was 51 percent; just after the attack, it was 86 percent.

Table 20.1 Popular Reactions to Foreign Policy Crises

Percentage of public saying that they approve of the way the president is handling his job

Foreign Policy Crisis		Before	After
1960	American U-2 spy plane shot down over Soviet Union	62%	68%
1961	Abortive landing at Bay of Pigs in Cuba	73	83
1962	Cuban missile crisis	61	74
1975	President Ford sends forces to rescue the American ship	40	51
1979	American embassy in Teheran seized by Iranians	32	61
1980	Failure of military effort to rescue hostages in Iran	39	43
1983	U.S. invasion of Grenada	43	53
1989	U.S. invasion of Panama	71	80
1990	U.S. troops to Persian Gulf	60	75
1995	U.S. troops to Bosnia	59	54
1999	U.S. troops to Kosovo	55	51
2001	U.S. combat in Afghanistan	51	86
2003	U.S. invasion of Iraq	58	71

Source: Updated from Theodore J. Lowi, *The End of Liberalism* (New York: Norton, 1969), 184. Poll data are from Gallup poll. Time lapse between "before" and "after" samplings of opinion was in no case more than one month.

Sometimes people argue that whatever support a president gets during a military crisis will disappear once dead soldiers in body bags begin returning home. There are two things wrong with this statement. First, dead soldiers do not come home in body bags; they come home in coffins. Second, a close study of how casualty rates affect public opinion showed that although deaths tend to reduce how "favorable" people are toward a war, what they then support is not withdrawal but an *escalation* in the fighting so as to defeat the enemy more quickly. This was true during Korea, Vietnam, and the Persian Gulf War.[27]

In sum, people tend to be leery of overseas military expeditions by the United States—until they start. Then they support them and want to win, even if it means more intense fighting. When Americans began to dislike our involvement in Korea and Vietnam,[28] they did not conclude that we should pull out; they concluded instead that we should do whatever was necessary to win. The invasion of Iraq did not raise large questions for Americans until terrorist attacks on the American military continued after the Iraqi army had been defeated.

Despite the tendency for most Americans to rally round the flag, there has been for many decades some public opposition to almost any war in which the United States participates. About one-fifth of Americans opposed our invading Iraq, about the same level of opposition to our wars in Korea and Vietnam. Opposition has generally been highest among Democrats, African Americans, and people with a postgraduate degree.[29]

MASS VERSUS ELITE OPINION

The public is poorly informed about foreign affairs. It probably has only a vague idea where Kosovo is, how far it is from Baghdad to Kuwait, or why the Palestinians and the Jews disagree about the future of Israel. But that is to be expected. Foreign affairs are, well, foreign. They do not have much to do with the daily lives of American citizens, except during wartime.

But the public, since World War II, has consistently felt that the United States should play an important international role.[30] And if our troops go abroad, it is a foolish politician who will try to talk the public out of supporting them.

Political elites, however, have a different perspective. They are better informed about foreign policy issues, but their opinions are more likely to change rapidly. Initially, college-educated people gave *more* support to the war in Vietnam than those without

college training; by the end of the war, however, that support had decreased dramatically. Whereas the average citizen was upset when the United States seemed to be on the *defensive* in Vietnam, college-educated voters tended to be more upset when the United States was on the *offensive*.[31]

Though the average citizen did not want our military in Vietnam in the first place, he or she felt that we should support our troops once they were there. The average person also was deeply opposed to the antiwar protests taking place on college campuses. When the Chicago police roughed up antiwar demonstrators at the 1968 Democratic convention, public sentiment was overwhelmingly on the side of the police.[32] Contrary to myths much accepted at the time, younger people were *not* more opposed to the war than older ones. There was no "generation gap."

By contrast, college-educated citizens, thinking at first that troops should be involved, soon changed their minds, decided that the war was wrong, and grew increasingly upset when the United States seemed to be enlarging the war (by invading Cambodia, for example). College students protested against the war largely on moral grounds, and their protests received more support from college-educated adults than from other citizens.

Elite opinion changes more rapidly than public opinion. During the Vietnam War, upper-middle-class people who regularly read several magazines and newspapers underwent a dramatic change in opinion between 1964 (when they supported the war) and 1968 (when they opposed it). But the views of blue-collar workers scarcely changed at all.[33]

The cleavage between mass and elite opinion is even wider if you restrict the definition of *elite* to only those involved in making foreign policy rather than including all college-educated people. In Table 20.2, we see the differences in foreign policy views of a cross section of American citizens and a group of 450 leaders active in government, academia, the mass media, and various organizations concerned with foreign affairs.[34]

In general the leaders have a more liberal and internationalist outlook than the public: they are more likely to favor giving economic aid to other countries and defending our allies. The public, on the other hand, wants the United States to be less active overseas and worries about protecting the jobs of American workers. Accordingly, it wants the United States to protect American jobs from foreign competition and give less economic aid to other nations.

Table 20.2 How the Public and the Elite See Foreign Policy 2004

	Percentage Agreeing	
	Public	Leaders
Combating international terrorism should be very important	71	84
Protect jobs of American workers	78	41
Reduce illegal immigration	59	21
Support U.S. troops in Afghanistan	60	92
Use U.S. troops to defend South Korea if attacked by North	43	82
Take Israel's side in conflicts with Palestinians	17	15
Expand economic aid to other countries	8	61

Source: *Global Views 2004* (Chicago: Chicago Council on Foreign Relations, 2004).

Cleavages among Foreign Policy Elites

As we have seen, public opinion on foreign policy is permissive and a bit mushy: it supports presidential action without giving it much direction. Elite opinion therefore acquires extraordinary importance. Of course events and world realities are also important, but since events have no meaning except as they are perceived and interpreted by people who must react to them, the attitudes and beliefs of those people in and out of government who are actively involved in shaping foreign policy often assume decisive importance. Contrary to the views of people who think that some shadowy, conspiratorial group of insiders runs our foreign policy, the foreign policy elite in this country is deeply divided.

That elite consists not only of those people with administrative positions in the foreign policy field—the senior officials of the State Department and the staff of the National Security Council—but also the members and staffs of the key congressional committees concerned with foreign affairs (chiefly the Senate Foreign Relations Committee and the House International Relations Committee) and various private organizations that help shape elite opinion, such as the members of the Council on Foreign Relations and the editors of two important

publications, *Foreign Affairs* and *Foreign Policy*. To these must be added influential columnists and editorial writers whose work appears regularly in the national press. One could extend the list by adding ever-wider circles of people with some influence (lobbyists, professors, leaders of veterans' organizations); this would complicate without changing the central point: elite beliefs are probably more important in explaining foreign policy than in accounting for decisions in other policy areas.

HOW A WORLDVIEW SHAPES FOREIGN POLICY

These beliefs can be described in simplified terms as **worldviews** (or, as some social scientists put it, as paradigms)—more or less comprehensive mental pictures of the critical problems facing the United States in the world and of the appropriate and inappropriate ways of responding to these problems. The clearest, most concise, and perhaps most influential statement of one worldview that held sway for many years was in an article published in 1947 in *Foreign Affairs,* titled "The Sources of Soviet Conduct."[35] Written by a "Mr. X" (later revealed to be George F. Kennan, director of the Policy Planning Staff of the State Department and thereafter ambassador to Moscow), the article argued that the Russians were pursuing a policy of expansion that could only be met by the United States' applying "unalterable counterforce at every point where they show signs of encroaching upon the interests of a peaceful and stable world." This he called the strategy of "containment," and it became the governing principle of American foreign policy for at least two decades.

> *worldviews* A comprehensive opinion of how the United States should respond to world problems.

There were critics of the containment policy at the time—Walter Lippmann, in his book *The Cold War,* argued against it in 1947[36]—but the criticisms were less influential than the doctrine. A dominant worldview is important precisely because it prevails over alternative views. One reason why it prevails is that it is broadly consistent with the public's mood. In 1947, when Kennan wrote, popular attitudes toward the Soviet Union, favorable during World War II when Russia and America were allies, had turned quite hostile. In 1946, less than one-fourth of the American people believed Russia could be trusted to cooperate with this country,[37] and by 1948 over three-fourths were convinced the Soviet

Union was trying not simply to defend itself but to become the dominant world power.[38]

Such a worldview was also influential because it was consistent with events at the time: Russia had occupied most of the previously independent countries of Eastern Europe and was turning them into puppet regimes. When governments independent of both the United States and the Soviet Union attempted to rule in Hungary and Czechoslovakia, they were overthrown by Soviet-backed coups. A worldview also becomes dominant when it is consistent with the prior experiences of the people holding it.

Four Worldviews

Every generation of political leaders comes to power with a foreign policy worldview shaped, in large measure, by the real or apparent mistakes of the previous generation.[39] This pattern can be traced back, some have argued, to the very beginnings of the nation. Frank L. Klingberg traces the alteration since 1776 between two national "moods" that favored first "extroversion" (or an active, internationalist policy) and then "introversion" (a less active, even isolationist posture).[40]

Since the 1920s, American elite opinion has moved through four dominant worldviews: isolationism, containment (or antiappeasement), disengagement, and human rights. **Isolationism** was the view adopted as a result of our unhappy experience in World War I. Our efforts to help European allies had turned sour: thousands of American troops had been killed in a war that had seemed to accomplish little and certainly had not made the world, in Woodrow Wilson's words, "safe for democracy." As a result, in the 1920s and 1930s elite opinion (and popular opinion) opposed getting involved in European wars.

The **containment** (or antiappeasement) paradigm was the result of World War II. Pearl Harbor was the death knell for isolationism. Senator Arthur H. Vandenberg of Michigan, a staunch isolationist before the attack, became an ardent internationalist not only during but after the war. He later wrote of the Japanese attack on Pearl Harbor on December 7, 1941, "that day ended isolationism for any realist."[41] At a conference in Munich, efforts of British and French leaders to satisfy Hitler's territorial demands in Europe had led not to "peace in our time," as Prime Minister Neville Chamberlain of Britain had claimed, but to ever-greater territorial demands and ultimately to world war. This crisis brought to power men determined not to repeat their predecessors' mistakes: "Munich" became a synonym for weakness, and leaders such as Winston Churchill made antiappeasement the basis of their postwar policy of resisting Soviet expansionism. Churchill summed up the worldview that he had acquired from the Munich era in a famous speech delivered in 1946 in Fulton, Missouri, in which he coined the term *iron curtain* to describe Soviet policy in Eastern Europe.

The events leading up to World War II were the formative experiences of those leaders who came to power in the 1940s, 1950s, and 1960s. What they took to be the lessons of Pearl Harbor and Munich were applied repeatedly—in building a network of defensive alliances in Europe and Asia during the late 1940s and 1950s, in operating an airlift to aid West Berlin when road access to it was cut off by the Russians, in coming to the aid of South Korea, and finally in intervening in Vietnam. Most

A meeting that named an era: In Munich in 1938, British prime minister Neville Chamberlain attempted to appease the territorial ambitions of Hitler. Chamberlain's failure brought World War II closer.

isolationism The opinion that the United States should withdraw from world affairs.

containment The belief that the United States should resist the expansion of aggressive nations especially the former Soviet Union.

of these applications of the containment worldview were successful in the sense that they did not harm American interests, they proved welcome to allies, or they prevented a military conquest.

The **disengagement** (or "Vietnam") view resulted from the experience of the younger foreign policy elite that came to power in the 1970s. Unlike previous applications of the antiappeasement view, our entry into Vietnam had led to a military defeat and a domestic political disaster. There were three ways of interpreting that crisis: (1) we applied the correct worldview in the right place but did not try hard enough; (2) we had the correct worldview but tried to apply it in the wrong place under the wrong circumstances; (3) the worldview itself was wrong. By and large, the critics of our Vietnam policy tended toward the third conclusion, and thus when they supplanted in office the architects of our Vietnam policy, they inclined toward a worldview based on the slogan "no more Vietnams." Critics of this view called it the "new isolationism," arguing that it would encourage Soviet expansion.

The language of Vietnam colored many discussions of foreign policy. Almost every military initiative since then has been debated in terms of whether it would lead us into "another Vietnam": sending the Marines to Lebanon, invading Grenada, dispatching military advisers to El Salvador, supporting the contras in Nicaragua, helping South American countries fight drug producers, and sending troops to invade Iraq.

How elites thought about Vietnam affected their foreign policy views for many years. If they thought the war was "immoral," they were reluctant to see American military involvement elsewhere. They played a large role in the Carter administration but were replaced by rival elites—those more inclined to a containment view—during the Reagan presidency.[42] When George H.W. Bush sought to expel Iraqi troops from Kuwait, the congressional debate pitted those committed to containment against those who believed in disengagement. The Senate vote on Bush's request for permission to use troops was narrowly carried by containment advocates.

When Clinton became president in 1992, he brought to office a lack of interest in foreign policy coupled with advisers who were drawn from the ranks of those who believed in disengagement. His strongest congressional supporters were those who had argued against the Gulf War. But then a remarkable change occurred. When Slobodan Milosevic, the Serbian leader, sent troops into neighboring Kosovo to suppress the ethnic Albanians living there, the strongest voices for American military intervention

The battleship *West Virginia* burns after being hit by Japanese warplanes at Pearl Harbor on December 7, 1941.

U.S. Navy

came from those who once advocated disengagement. During the Gulf War 47 Senate Democrats voted to oppose U.S. participation. A few years later, 42 Senate Democrats voted to support our role in Kosovo.

What had happened? The change was inspired by the view that helping the Albanians was required by the doctrine of **human rights.**

> *disengagement* The belief that the United States was harmed by its war in Vietnam and so should avoid supposedly similar events.
>
> *human rights* The view that we should try to improve the lives of people in other countries

Liberal supporters of U.S. air attacks on Serbian forces believed that we were helping Albanians escape mass killing. By contrast, many conservative members of Congress who had followed a containment policy in the Gulf War now felt that disengagement ought to be followed in Kosovo. Of course, politics also mattered. Clinton was a Democratic president; Bush had been a Republican one.

But politics was not the whole story. American liberal elites had persuaded themselves that the attack in Kosovo resembled the genocide—that is, the mass murder of people because of their race or ethnicity—that the Jews had suffered in Nazi Germany. They held that we must "never again" permit a whole people to be killed.

There are some problems with this view. Hardly any human rights advocates had called for U.S. intervention in Rwanda, China, or Iraq—all countries that massacred millions of their own citizens. In addition, the historical record suggests that the Serbs and the Albanians have been killing each other for centuries. Now that the Serbian army has withdrawn from Kosovo, Serbian civilians who stayed behind are being killed by the Albanians whom they once killed. The response that some human rights advocates would give to these criticisms is that America owes a special obligation to Europe and that even if Albanians kill Serbs, a Western military presence there will at least prevent organized military killing.

In the aftermath of 9/11, a new issue has arisen that may divide foreign policy elites in the future. Should the United States "go it alone" against its enemies abroad, or do so only on the basis of a broad coalition of supporting nations? President Bush the elder assembled just such a coalition to force Iraq out of Kuwait, but President Bush the younger acted without UN support in invading Afghanistan and later Iraq, though he received crucial support from Great Britain, Australia, and Poland.

POLITICAL POLARIZATION

For as long as we have records, public opinion has been slow to favor our military actions overseas in the abstract but quick to support them once they occur. However, that pattern ended with our invasion of Iraq in 2003. Public opinion became deeply divided about that war, with most Democrats strongly opposing it and most Republicans favoring it.

That was not how things worked out during our wars in Korea and Vietnam. The war in Korea produced angry divisions in Congress, especially after General Douglas MacArthur, the allied commander in Korea, was fired in 1951 for having disobeyed the president. He received a hero's welcome when he returned to this country and gave an emotional speech to a joint session of Congress. Many Republicans demanded that President Truman be impeached. Despite this public support for MacArthur and these angry congressional words, the country was not split along partisan lines. Slightly more Republicans than Democrats said the war was a mistake (roughly half of each party), but the differences between these voters was not great.

The war in Vietnam split American political elites even more deeply. Journalists and members of Congress took sharply opposing sides, and some Americans traveled to North Vietnam to express their support for the Communist

polarization A deep and wide conflict over some government policy.

cause. When the North Vietnamese launched a major offensive to destroy American and South Vietnamese troops during the Tet holidays in 1968, it failed, but the American press reported it as a Communist victory, and demands to bring our troops home were heard during the presidential campaign that year. But public opinion did not divide along party lines; in 1968, Democratic and Republican voters had just about the same views (a little over half thought the war was a mistake, about a third thought it wasn't).

Our invasion of Iraq was a different story. From the very first , Democratic voters strongly opposed it and Republican ones favored it. By 2006, 76 percent of Democrats said we should have stayed out of Iraq, while 71 percent of Republicans said that the invasion was the right thing to do.[43]

American public opinion has become more polarized by our foreign policy. **Polarization** means a deep and wide conflict, usually along party lines, over some government policy. It has replaced the bipartisan foreign policy of the Second World War and the modest differences in public opinion during Korea and Vietnam.[44]

The Use of Military Force

Foreign policy takes many forms—discussions are held, treaties are signed, organizations are joined—but in many cases it depends on the ability to use military force. Troops, ships, and aircraft are not the only ways of influencing other countries; international trade and foreign aid are also useful. But in modern times, as in the past, the nations of the world know the difference between a "great power" (that is, a heavily armed one) and a weak nation.

With the collapse of the Soviet Union and the end of the cold war, one might think that military power has become less important. But in fact it remains as important as ever. Since the Soviet Union was dissolved and the Berlin Wall came down in 1989, the United States has used military force to attack Iraq, maintain order in Bosnia, defend Kosovo, and go to war in Afghanistan. Various rogue nations, such as Iran and North Korea, have acquired or are about to acquire long-range rockets and weapons of mass destruction (that is, nuclear, chemical, and biological arms). Many nations that feel threatened by their neighbors, such as China, India, Pakistan, and Israel, have nuclear bombs. And Russia still has many of the nuclear weapons that the old Soviet

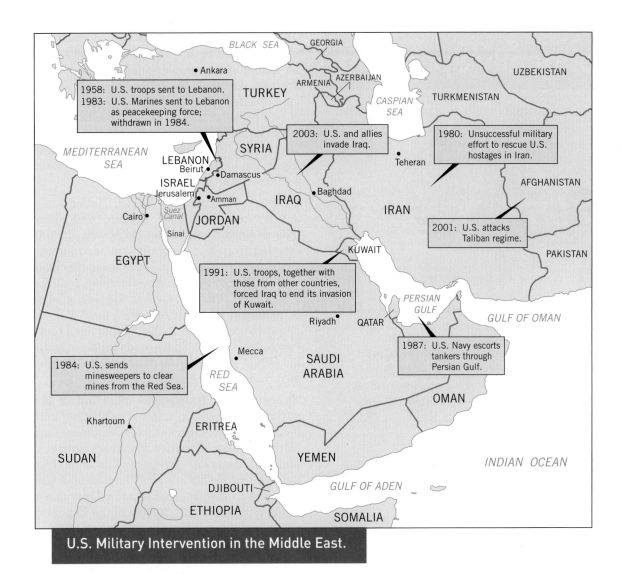

1958: U.S. troops sent to Lebanon.
1983: U.S. Marines sent to Lebanon as peacekeeping force; withdrawn in 1984.

2003: U.S. and allies invade Iraq.

1980: Unsuccessful military effort to rescue U.S. hostages in Iran.

2001: U.S. attacks Taliban regime.

1991: U.S. troops, together with those from other countries, forced Iraq to end its invasion of Kuwait.

1987: U.S. Navy escorts tankers through Persian Gulf.

1984: U.S. sends minesweepers to clear mines from the Red Sea.

U.S. Military Intervention in the Middle East.

Union built. It would be foolish to assume that the end of the cold war means the end of war.

There are two views about the role of the military in American life. One is majoritarian: the military exists to defend the country or to help other nations defend themselves. When troops are used, almost all Americans benefit and almost all pay the bill. (Some Americans, such as those who lose a loved one in war, pay much more than the rest of us.) The president is the commander in chief, and Congress plays a largely supportive role.

Although the other view does not deny that the armed forces are useful, it focuses on the extent to which the military is a large and powerful client. The real beneficiaries of military spending are the generals and admirals, as well as the big corporations and members of Congress whose districts get fat defense contracts. Everyone pays, but these clients get most

of the benefits. What we spend on defense is shaped by the **military-industrial complex,** a supposedly unified bloc of Defense Department leaders and military manufacturers.

military-industrial complex An alleged alliance between military leaders and corporate leaders.

WAR IN IRAQ

After the Iraqi army under Saddam Hussein had invaded neighboring Kuwait in 1990, the United Nations passed a resolution demanding that Iraq withdraw and authorizing force to expel it. In January 1991 the United States led a coalition of forces from several nations that attacked Iraq; within one hundred days, the Iraqi army had retreated from Kuwait and fled home. The U.S.-led military ended its attack, allowing Saddam to remain in power in Baghdad, the Iraqi capital.

Politically Speaking

Third World

Originally a French term (*tiers monde*) referring to nations neutral in the cold war between the United Nations and the Soviet Union, the **Third World** now means almost any underdeveloped nation in Africa, Asia, Latin America, or the Middle East.

When the oil-producing nations, such as Saudi Arabia, became wealthy after having succeeded in raising oil prices in the early 1970s, some observers began to use a new phrase, the **Fourth World,** to refer to underdeveloped nations that had no oil reserves and thus had to pay heavily for imported oil.

And some nations, such as Taiwan and the Republic of Korea, once thought to be part of the Third World because they were underdeveloped have made such startling economic progress that they are now referred to as the "newly industrialized nations" (NINs).

Source: Adapted from *Safire's Political Dictionary* by William Safire. Copyright © 1968, 1972, 1978 by William Safire. Reprinted by permission of Random House, Inc. and the author.

After the war, a no-fly zone was established under which Iraqi flights in certain areas were prohibited. This ban was enforced for twelve years by U.S., British, and French planes that shot down Iraq aircraft violating the rule.

Throughout this time, UN inspectors were sent to Iraq to look for weapons of mass destruction (WMDs): chemical, biological, and nuclear materials that could be used to attack others. There was no doubt such weapons existed, as Saddam had dropped chemical weapons on people living in his own country. The UN inspectors found evidence of such a program, but in 1997 Saddam expelled them from his country, only to allow them to return a few years later. Saddam's misleading statements led American and British leaders to conclude that his regime was a threat to peace.

Unable to convince the United Nations to support a war, America, Great Britain, and other countries decided to act alone. On March 30, 2003, they invaded Iraq in a campaign called Operation Iraqi Freedom; within about six weeks, the Iraqi army was defeated and the American-led coalition occupied all of the country. After the war, a large group of inspectors toured Iraq looking for WMDs, but they found virtually none. Later a bipartisan commission concluded that Saddam had apparently cancelled his WMD program, but had told hardly any of his own military leaders about this.[45]

The newly freed Iraqi people voted first for an interim parliament, then for a new constitution, and finally for a regular government. But this process was offset by the terrorist activities of various insurgents, first aimed at American troops and later at Iraqi civilians, killing several tens of thousands of them. The situation in Iraq became a major American political issue, contributing to the loss of the Republican congressional majority in the 2006 elections.

As we shall see (page 551), a new military strategy began in 2007 that improved conditions in Iraq.

The Defense Budget

To sort out these competing claims, one has to understand how America raises and spends its defense dollars. There are two important things to know: how much money we spend and how it is divided up. The first reflects majoritarian politics, the second, interest group bargaining.

TOTAL SPENDING

Throughout most of our history the United States has not maintained large military forces during peacetime. For instance, the percentage of the gross national product (GNP) spent on defense in 1935, on the eve of World War II, was about the same as it was in 1870, when we were on the eve of nothing in particular. We armed when a war broke out, then we disarmed when the war ended. But all of that changed after World War II, when defense spending declined sharply but did not return to its prewar

UNITED STATES

GULF OF MEXICO

ATLANTIC OCEAN

1962: U.S. naval blockade of Cuba to prevent installation of Soviet missiles.

BAHAMAS

Havana

2004: U.S. troops quell uprising in Haiti

1965: U.S. troops occupy Dominican Republic to block takeover by Communist regime.

1961: U.S.– sponsored invasion of Cuba fails at Bay of Pigs.

MEXICO

CUBA

JAMAICA

HAITI DOMINICAN REPUBLIC

VIRGIN ISLANDS (U.S.)

PUERTO RICO (U.S.)

GUATEMALA BELIZE

HONDURAS

1980–?: U.S. conducts joint military operations with Honduras.

CARIBBEAN SEA

1954: U.S. helps overthrow Marxist government in Guatemala.

EL SALVADOR

NICARAGUA

1982–1989: CIA supports anti-government guerrillas in Nicaragua.

GRENADA

1981: U.S. military advisers sent to help government of El Salvador.

COSTA RICA

Panama Canal Zone

1983: U.S. troops invade Grenada to oust pro-Cuba government.

PACIFIC OCEAN

PANAMA

1989: U.S. invades Panama, ousts dictator Manuel Noriega.

COLOMBIA

VENEZUELA

U.S. Military Intervention in Central America and the Caribbean Since 1950.

levels. And in 1950, our defense expenditures soared again.

In that year, we rearmed to fight a war in Korea, but when it was over, we did not completely disarm. The reason was our containment policy toward the Soviet Union. For about 40 years—from the outbreak of the Korean War in 1950 to the collapse of the Soviet Union in 1991—American military spending was driven by our desire to contain the Soviet Union and its allies. The Soviet Union had brought under its control most of Eastern Europe; would it also invade Western Europe? Russia had always wanted access to the oil and warm-water ports of the Middle East; would the Soviets someday invade or subvert Iran or Turkey? The Soviet Union was willing to help North Korea invade South Korea and North Vietnam to invade South Vietnam; would it next use an ally to threaten the United States? Soviet leaders supported "wars of national liberation" in Africa and Latin America; would they succeed in turning more and more nations against the United States?

To meet these threats, the United States built up a military system designed to repel a Soviet invasion of Western Europe and at the same time help allies resist smaller-scale invasions or domestic uprisings. Figure 20.1 depicts the dramatic increase in military spending in 1950. It also shows that even after we decided to have a large military force, there were many ups and downs in the actual level of spending. After the Korean War was over, we spent less; when we became involved in Vietnam, we spent more; when the Soviet Union invaded Afghanistan and we invaded Iraq, we spent more again. These changes in spending tended to reflect changes in public opinion about the defense budget.

As Figure 20.2 shows, a majority of Americans have said that our defense program is either "about right" or "not strong enough," but other studies show that popular support for spending more money on defense changes from year to year.

After the collapse of the Soviet Union, there has been a debate about defense strategy. Liberals demanded sharp cuts in defense spending, weapons procurement, and military personnel, arguing that with the Soviet threat ended, it was time to the collect our "peace dividend" and divert funds from the military to domestic social programs. Conservatives agreed that some military cuts were in order, but they argued that the world was still a dangerous

Figure 20.1

Trends in Military Spending (outlays in constant dollars)

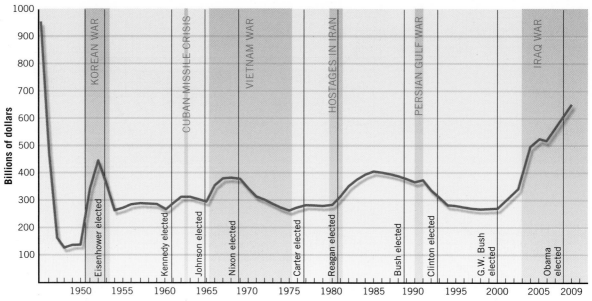

Source: Office of the Under Secretary of Defense (Comptroller), "National Defense Budget Estimates for FY 2007."

Figure 20.2

Most Americans Think National Defense Is Either "About Right" or "Not Strong Enough"

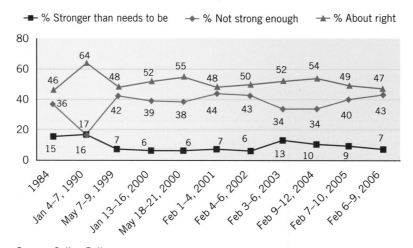

Source: Gallup Poll.

place and therefore that a strong (and well-funded) military remained essential to the nation's defense. This disagreement reflected different predictions about what the future would be like. Many liberals (and some conservatives, such as Pat Buchanan, who believed that America should "stay at home") argued that we could not afford to be the "world's policeman." Many conservatives (and some liberals) responded by saying that Russia was still a military powerhouse that might once again fall under the control of ruthless leaders and that many other nations hostile to the United States (such as North Korea, Iran, and Iraq) were becoming potential adversaries as they tried to build or acquire nuclear weapons and missile systems.

American campaigns in Afghanistan and Iraq made clear that whether or not the United States was the "world's police officer," there was no escaping its need to use military force. They also made clear that the United States had reduced its armed forces so sharply since Desert Storm (there were half a million fewer people in the military in 1996 than in 1991) that it was hard-pressed to carry out any sustained military campaign (see Table 20.3). When the national budget deficit was eliminated in 1999, both President Clinton and the Republican Congress called for more military spending.

But that increase did not pay for what the military had been authorized to buy, and did little to get us ready for the war in Afghanistan against Osama bin Laden. But once the battle began, the federal purse strings loosened and the defense budget grew.

WHAT DO WE GET WITH OUR MONEY?

We get people, of course—soldiers, sailors, airmen, and airwomen. They are the most expensive part of the defense budget. Then we get hardware of roughly two kinds—big-ticket items, like aircraft carriers and bombers, and small-ticket items, like hammers and screwdrivers. Each of these kinds of hardware has its own politics. Finally, we get "readiness"—training, supplies, munitions, fuel, and food.

Personnel

Efforts to develop our military forces before World War II reflected the considerable American discomfort with a strong central government. The United States did not institute a peacetime draft until 1940, when the rest of the world was already at war, and the draft was renewed the following year (only a few months before Pearl Harbor) by only a one-vote margin in the House. Until 1973, the United States relied on the draft to obtain military personnel. Then, at the end of the Vietnam War, it replaced the draft with the all-volunteer force (AVF). After getting off to a rocky start, the AVF began to improve thanks to increases in military pay and rising civilian unemployment. Abolishing the draft had been politically popular: nobody likes being drafted, and even in congressional districts that otherwise are staunch supporters of a strong defense, the voters tell their representatives that they do not want to return to the draft.

There has been a steady increase in the percentage of women in the military (in 2005, they constituted 20 percent of the total). For a long time, however, women were barred by law from serving in combat roles. (What constitutes a "combat role" is a bit difficult to say, since even personnel far from the main fighting can be hit by an enemy bomb or artillery shell.) In 1993 Congress ended the legal ban on assigning women to navy combat ships and air force

Table 20.3 U.S. Military Forces Before and After the Breakup of the Soviet Union

Service	Before 1991	End FY 1998
Army		
Active divisions	18	10
National Guard divisions	10	8
Navy		
Aircraft carriers	15	11
Training carriers	1	2
Ships	546	346
Air Force		
Active fighter wings	24	13
Reserve fighter wings	12	7
Marine Corps		
Active divisions	3	3
Reserve divisions	1	1
Strategic Nuclear Forces		
Ballistic missile submarines	31	18
Strategic bombers	324	182
ICBMs	1,000	550

Source: Statistical Abstract of the United States, 1998, 363.

fighter jets, and soon women were serving on three aircraft carriers. Congress must still be consulted in advance if women are to serve in ground combat forces (such as in front-line infantry or tank units).

The presence of homosexuals in the military has proved much harder to resolve. Until 1993, it was the long-standing policy of the U.S. armed forces to bar homosexuals from entering the military and to discharge them if they were discovered serving. Gay and lesbian rights organizations had long protested this exclusion. In 1993, a gay soldier won a lawsuit against the army for having discharged him; he settled for back pay and retirement benefits in exchange for a promise not to reenlist. In 1993, a judge ordered the navy to reinstate a discharged sailor who had revealed on national television that he was a homosexual. In response to the growing controversy, presidential candidate Bill Clinton promised to lift the official ban on gays and lesbians serving in the military if he were elected to office.

Once in office, he discovered that it was not that easy. Many members of the armed forces believed that knowingly serving alongside and living in close quarters with gays and lesbians would create unnecessary tension and harm military morale and troop

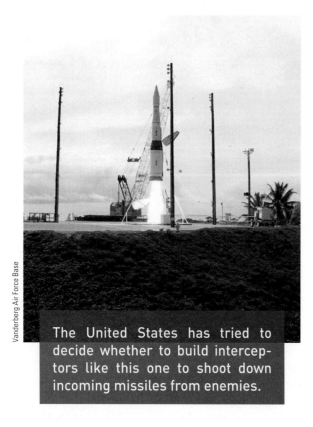

Vanderberg Air Force Base

The United States has tried to decide whether to build interceptors like this one to shoot down incoming missiles from enemies.

1960s, things were only slightly better—actual costs were twice estimated costs.

There are five main reasons for these overruns. First, it is hard to know in advance what something that has never existed before will cost once you build it. People who have remodeled their homes know this all too well. So do government officials who build new subways or congressional office buildings. It is no different with a B-2 bomber.

Second, people who want to persuade Congress to appropriate money for a new airplane or submarine have an incentive to underestimate the cost. To get the weapon approved, its sponsors tell Congress how little it will cost; once the weapon is under construction, the sponsors go back to Congress for additional money to cover "unexpected" cost increases.

Third, the Pentagon officials who decide what kind of new aircraft they want are drawn from the ranks of those who will fly it. These officers naturally want the best airplane (or ship or tank) that money can buy. As air force general Carl "Tooey" Spaatz once put it, "A second-best aircraft is like a second-best poker hand. No damn good."[46] But what exactly is the "best" airplane? Is it the fastest one? Or the most maneuverable one? Or the most reliable one? Or the one with the longest range? Pentagon officials have a tendency to answer, "All of the above." Of course, trying to produce all of the above is incredibly expensive (and sometimes impossible). But asking for the expensive (or the impossible) is understandable, given that the air force officers who buy it will also fly it. This tendency to ask for everything at once is called **gold plating.**

Fourth, many new weapons are purchased from a single contractor. This is called sole-sourcing. A contractor is hired to design, develop, and build an airplane. As a result there is no competition, and so

solidarity. The Joint Chiefs of Staff opposed lifting the ban, and several key members of Congress said they would try to pass a law reaffirming it. President Clinton was forced to settle for a compromise: "don't ask, don't tell." Under this policy, persons entering or serving in the military will not be asked to reveal their sexual orientation and will be allowed to serve, provided they do not engage in homosexual conduct. If a person says he or she is a homosexual, it will not be automatic grounds for discharge, but it may be grounds for launching an investigation to see whether rules against homosexual conduct have been violated.

In 1994, the new Pentagon rules designed to implement "don't ask, don't tell" went into effect, but they created their own problems. What if heterosexuals harass gays without asking if they are gay? What if a gay or lesbian doesn't tell but his or her commanding officer finds out anyway?

Big-Ticket Items
Whenever the Pentagon buys a new submarine, airplane, or missile, we hear about **cost overruns.** In the 1950s, actual costs were three times greater than estimated costs; by the

cost overruns When the money actually paid to military suppliers exceeds the estimated costs.

gold plating The tendency of Pentagon officials to ask weapons contractors to meet excessively high requirements.

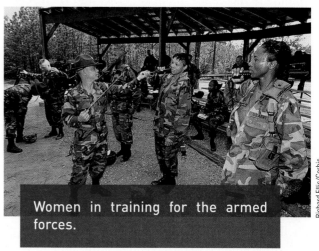

Richard Ellis/Corbis

Women in training for the armed forces.

Gays campaign for greater acceptance in the armed forces.

C. Nicklas Hill

the manufacturer has no strong incentive to control costs. And if the sole manufacturer gets into financial trouble, the government, seeking to avoid a shutdown of all production, has an incentive to bail the company out.

Fifth, when Congress wants to cut the military budget, it often does so not by canceling a new weapons system but by stretching out the number of years during which it is purchased. Say that Congress wants to buy one hundred F-22s, twenty-five a year for four years. To give the appearance of cutting the budget, it will decide to buy only fifteen the first year and take five years to buy the rest. Or it will authorize the construction of twenty now and then ask again next year for the authority to build more. But start-and-stop production decisions and stretching out production over more years drives up the cost of building each unit. If Toyota built cars this way, it would go broke.

There are ways to cope with four of these five problems. You cannot do much about the first, ignorance, but you can do something about low estimates, gold plating, sole-sourcing, and stretch-outs. If the Pentagon would give realistic cost estimates initially (perhaps verified by another agency); if it would ask for weapons that meet a few critical performance requirements instead of every requirement that can be thought of; if two or more manufacturers were to compete in designing, developing, and manufacturing new weapons; and if Congress were to stop trying to "cut" the budget using the smoke-and-mirrors technique of stretch-outs, then we would hear a lot less about cost overruns.

Some of these things are being done. There is more competition and less sole-sourcing in weapons procurement today than once was the case. But the political incentives to avoid other changes are very powerful. Pentagon officers will always want "the best." They will always have an incentive to understate costs. Congress will always be tempted to use stretch-outs as a way of avoiding hard budget choices.

Readiness

Presumably, we have a peacetime military so that we will be ready for wartime. Presumably, therefore, the peacetime forces will devote a lot of their time and money to improving their readiness.

Not necessarily. The politics of defense spending is such that readiness often is given a very low priority. Here is why.

Client politics influences the decision. In 1990, Congress was willing to cut almost anything, provided it wasn't built or stationed in some member's district. That doesn't leave much. Plans to stop producing F-14 fighters for the navy were opposed by members from Long Island, where the Grumman manufacturing plant was located. Plans to kill the Osprey aircraft for the Marines were opposed by members from the places where it was to be built. Plans to close bases were opposed by every member with a base in his or her district.

That leaves training and readiness. These things, essential to military effectiveness, have no constituencies and hence few congressional defenders. When forced to choose, the services themselves often prefer to allocate scarce dollars to developing and buying new weapons than to spending for readiness. Moreover, the savings from buying less fuel or having fewer exercises shows up right away, while the savings from canceling an aircraft carrier may not show up for years. Not surprisingly, training and readiness are usually what get the ax.

Bases

At one time, the opening and closing of military bases was pure client politics, which meant that a lot of bases were opened and hardly any were closed. Almost every member of Congress fought to get a base in his or her district, and *every* member fought to keep an existing base open. Even the biggest congressional critics of the U.S. military, people who would vote to take a gun out of a soldier's hand, would fight hard to keep bases in their districts open and operating.

In 1988, Congress finally concluded that no base would ever be closed unless the system for making decisions was changed. It created a Commission on Base Realignment and Closure (BRAC), consisting of private citizens (originally 12, later eight) who would consider recommendations from the secretary of defense. By law Congress would have to vote within 45 days for or against the commission's list as a whole, without having a chance to amend it.

Since 1988, there have been five BRAC reports. Congress approved each one, resulting in the closing of over 350 bases.

Congress, it appears, has finally figured out how to make some decisions that most members know are right but that each member individually finds it politically necessary to oppose.

The Structure of Defense Decision Making

The formal structure within which decisions about national defense are made was in large part created after World War II, but it reflects concerns that go back at least to the time of the Founding. Chief among these is the persistent desire by citizens to ensure civilian control over the military.

The National Security Act of 1947 and its subsequent amendments created the Department of Defense. It is headed by the secretary of defense, under whom serve the secretaries of the army, the air force, and the navy as well as the Joint Chiefs of Staff. The secretary of defense, who must be a civilian (though one former general, George C. Marshall, was allowed by Congress to be the secretary), exercises, on behalf of the president, command authority over the defense establishment. The secretary of the army, the secretary of the navy,* and the secretary of the air force also are civilians and are subordinate to the secretary of defense. Unlike him, they do not attend cabinet meetings or sit on the National Security Council. In essence, they manage the "housekeeping" functions of the various armed services, under the general direction of the secretary of defense and his deputy and assistant secretaries of defense.

The four armed services are separate entities; by law, they cannot be merged or commanded by a single military officer, and each has the right to communicate directly with Congress. There are two reasons for having separate uniformed services functioning within a single department: the fear of

many citizens that a unified military force might become too powerful politically, and the desire of each service to preserve its traditional independence and autonomy. The result, of course, is a good deal of interservice rivalry and bickering, but this is precisely what Congress intended when it created the Department of Defense. Rivalry and bickering, it was felt, would ensure that Congress would receive the maximum amount of information about military affairs and would enjoy the largest opportunity to affect military decisions.

Since the end of World War II, Congress has aimed both to retain a significant measure of control over the military's decision making and to ensure the adequacy of the nation's defenses. Congress does not want a single military command headed by an all-powerful general or admiral, but neither does it want the services to be so autonomous or their heads so equal that coordination and efficiency suffer. In 1986, Congress passed and the president signed a defense reorganization plan known as the Goldwater-Nichols Act, which increased the power of the officers who coordinate the activities of the different services. The 1947 structure was left in place, but with revised procedures.

JOINT CHIEFS OF STAFF

The Joint Chiefs of Staff (JCS) is a committee consisting of the uniformed heads of each of the military services (the army, navy, air force, and Marine Corps), plus a chairman and a (nonvoting) vice chairman, also military officers, who are appointed by the president and confirmed by the Senate. The JCS does not have command authority over troops, but it plays a key role in national defense planning. Since 1986, the chairman of the joint chiefs has been designated the president's principal military adviser, in an effort to give him more influence over the JCS.

Assisting the JCS is the Joint Staff, consisting of several hundred officers from each of the four services. The staff draws up plans for various military contingencies. Before 1986, each staff member was loyal to the service whose uniform he or she wore. As a result, the staff was often "joint" in name only, since few members were willing to take a position opposed by their service for fear of being passed over for promotion. The 1986 law changed this in two ways: first, it gave the chairman of the JCS control over the Joint Staff; now it works for the chairman, not for the JCS as a group. Second, it required the secretary of defense to establish guidelines to ensure that officers assigned to the Joint Staff (or to other interservice bodies) are promoted at the same rate as officers whose careers are spent entirely with their own services.

---

* The secretary of the navy manages two services, the navy and the Marine Corps.

THE SERVICES

Each military service is headed by a civilian secretary—one for the army, the navy (including the Marine Corps), and the air force—plus a senior military officer: the chief of staff of the army, the chief of naval operations, the commandant of the Marine Corps, and the chief of staff of the air force. The civilian secretaries are in charge of purchasing, auditing, congressional relations, and public affairs. The military chiefs oversee the discipline and training of their uniformed forces and in addition represent their services on the Joint Chiefs of Staff.

THE CHAIN OF COMMAND

Under the Constitution the president is the commander in chief of the armed forces. The chain of command runs from him to the secretary of defense (also a civilian), and from him to the various unified and specified commands. These orders may be transmitted through the Joint Chiefs of Staff or its chairman, but by law the chairman of the JCS does not have command authority over the combat forces. Civilians are in charge at the top to protect against excessive concentration of power.

No one yet knows how well the 1986 changes will work, though many analysts viewed the quick victory in the 1991 Persian Gulf War as evidence of its success. Critics of the Pentagon have been urging changes along these lines at least since 1947. But others say that unless the armed services are actually merged, interservice rivalry will continue. Still others argue that even the coordination achieved by the 1986 act is excessive. The country, in their view, is better served by having wholly autonomous services. What is striking is that so many members of Congress who once would have insisted on the anticoordination view voted for the 1986 law, thereby indicating a greater willingness to permit some degree of central military leadership.

The New Problem of Terrorism

Since 9/11, both our foreign policy and our military policy have had to focus on terrorism and what to do with nations we have conquered that harbored terrorists. When the cold war was on, this was easy. For a half century, each president, operating through the National Security Council, made it clear that our chief goal was to prevent the Soviet Union from overrunning Western Europe, bombing the United States, or invading other nations.

But the Soviet Union has disappeared and no other nation has acquired the power to take its place. During the cold war, we lived in a **bipolar world** made up of two superpowers. Now we live in a **unipolar world** made up of the United States as the only superpower. But our superpower status, though it means no other country can challenge us militarily, still leaves us vulnerable here and abroad to terrorist attacks, as 9/11 amply confirms.

bipolar world A political landscape with two superpowers.

unipolar world A political landscape with one superpower.

To respond, President George W. Bush in September 2002 issued a document that emphasized a new view of our policies. Instead of waiting to be attacked, the president said that America "will act against such emerging threats before they are fully formed" because we "cannot defend America and our friends by hoping for the best." We will identify and destroy a terrorist threat "before it reaches our borders" and "we will not hesitate to act alone."[47] In the case of Iraq, this meant a commitment to "regime change"; that is, getting rid of a hostile government, even if the United Nations did not support us.

This has been called a doctrine of preemption; that is, of attacking a determined enemy before it can launch an attack against us or an ally. In fact, it is not really new. President Bill Clinton launched cruise missile strikes against training camps that followers of Osama Bin Laden were using in the aftermath of their bombing of American embassies in Kenya and Tanzania in 1998. President Bush elevated the policy of preemption into a clearly stated national doctrine.

Supporters of this view hailed it as a positive step to defeat terrorists abroad before they could attack us at home. Critics attacked the argument as justifying preemptive and possibly unjust wars and abandoning the United Nations. This debate has divided Congress in a way that puts an end to the old adage that partisanship ends at the water's edge.

Since the end of the cold war, we have not had a common enemy that, in the opinion of critics of our overseas efforts, should justify a nonpartisan view. Most liberal Democrats opposed both our effort to get Iraq out of Kuwait in 1991 and our invasion of Iraq in 2003; most Republicans supported both efforts.[48] But when President Clinton launched

WHAT WOULD YOU DO?

MEMORANDUM

To: *The president*

From: *National security adviser*

Subject: *Hostages*

The six Americans held hostage in the Middle East are beginning their second year of captivity. One, a CIA officer, is undergoing torture. It has been the policy of this administration not to negotiate with terrorists. Criticism of this refusal is being heard from hostage families and their sympathizers. The terrorist groups are demanding that we end our support of Israel. A government in the region has secretly indicated that, in exchange for military supplies, it may be able to help win the release of "some" hostages.

Friday,

American Hostages Begin Second Year of Captivity

Families Urge President to Negotiate Freedom

July 13
WASHINGTON, D.C.

The families of the six American hostages held captive in the Middle East today criticized the president for failing to win their release…

Your options:

1. Maintain the "no-negotiations" policy but use quiet diplomacy with friendly nations in the region to see whether they can intercede with the terrorist groups on behalf of the hostages.

   Advantages: (a) Our "no-negotiations" policy remains credible, and this will deter other terrorist groups from thinking that they can win concessions by capturing Americans. (b) This policy is consistent with our insistence that U.S. allies not negotiate with terrorists.

   Disadvantages: (a) There is no evidence that our traditional policy will get the hostages released. (b) Public sympathy for the hostages may increase, and this will lead to more criticism of this administration for failing to free captive Americans.

2. Secretly exchange arms for the release of Americans.

   Advantages: (a) Some or all hostages may be released. (b) We may earn the goodwill of more moderate elements in the area and thereby increase our influence there.

   Disadvantages: (a) We may deliver arms and no hostages will be released. (b) If secret arms deliveries become public, we will be heavily criticized for abandoning our "no-negotiations" policy.

3. Use military units to find and free the hostages.

   Advantage: The hostages may be freed without our having to make any concessions.

   Disadvantages: (a) The military is not optimistic that it can find and free the hostages, who are being kept in hidden, scattered sites. (b) The hostages may be killed during the rescue effort.

Your decision:

Option 1 _____   Option 2 _____   Option 3 _____

The Paradoxes of Fighting Insurgents

The U.S. Army Field Manual lists some paradoxes of fighting terrorists and insurgents. It is the manual used by Petraeus in Iraq.

Sometimes, the more you protect your force, the less secure you are.
You may be safe staying barricaded in compounds but you lose contact with the people

Some of the best weapons for fighting insurgents do not shoot.
Diplomacy, communications, and economic development can be more effective than guns.

Many important decisions are not made by generals.
Teaching lower ranking personnel how to think and adapt is more important than teaching them what to think.

Sometimes the more force is used, the less effective it is.
Using too much force can hurt civilians and generate sympathy for insurgents.

---

attacks on hostile forces in Kosovo, he was supported by many liberal Democrats and opposed by many conservative Republicans.[49] Party differences and political ideology now make a big difference in foreign policy.

Sometimes we have sought and obtained United Nations support, as we did when going to war in Korea (1950) and in launching our effort to force Iraqi troops out of Kuwait (1991). We did not seek it in fighting against North Vietnam (in the 1960s), in occupying Haiti (1994), or in going to the assistance of friendly forces in Bosnia (1994) or Kosovo (1999). When we invaded Iraq in 2003, we asked for but did not get United Nations support; we went anyway, aided by allies, such as Britain and Australia, that joined with us.

After we conquered Afghanistan and Iraq, we faced the problem of rebuilding these nations. The United States has had a lot of experience, some good and some bad, with this problem. We helped put Germany and Japan back on their feet after World War II. From 1992 to 1994, we tried to bring peace among warring factions to Somalia. From 1994 to 1996, we worked to install a democratically elected president and rebuild the local police force in the Caribbean country Haiti. Starting in 1995, we worked with European allies to restore order to Bosnia and Kosovo, located in what used to be Yugoslavia. In 2001, we began helping Afghans create a new government and economy, and in 2003 we started doing the same thing in Iraq.

We succeeded in Germany and Japan, failed in Somalia and Haiti, and made progress in Bosnia and Kosovo.[50]

IRAQ AND AFGHANISTAN

After easily defeating the Iraqi army in 2003, we tried to bring stability and democracy to the country in mistaken ways. We abolished the Iraqi army (and so had no native defense force), relied on too few American troops (and so could not pacify the country), and kept these troops when they were not fighting in American compounds (thus leaving Iraqi civilians unprotected). Iran funneled arms and terrorists into the country to help attack American soldiers. Public opinion in this country, though deeply divided along party lines, became hostile to our efforts there.

To deal with this problem, President Bush (over the objections of many subordinates) announced a new strategy. We would send another 30,000 troops to Iraq (the "surge") and instruct these troops to work in Iraqi neighborhoods and build alliances with local groups. He assigned General David Petraeus to be our military leader.

The surge worked. Deaths of American forces and Iraqi civilians fell dramatically, an elected Iraqi government began to function effectively, and new Iraqi elections in 2009 were held peacefully. The American government negotiated an agreement with Iraqi leaders that called for withdrawing American troops from the country by 2011. Because of this progress and because our economy went into a recession, American public opinion began to lose interest in Iraq.

Afghanistan is a more difficult problem. Unlike Iraq, it has never been a unified nation and lacks a large middle class or many populous cities. We easily defeated the Taliban regime and managed to put in office a moderate leader. Troops from other nations arrived to help out. But creating an effective central government in a country that has rarely had one and ending terrorist attacks has proved to be a difficult assignment. During the 2008, presidential campaign, Barack Obama promised to send more forces to that country, and beginning in 2009 he did so. By the middle of the year we had 60 thousand troops there, but they were not enough. In 2009 the general leading our forces there asked President Obama for another 40,000 troops.

SUMMARY

The great issues of national diplomacy and military policy are shaped by majoritarian politics. The president is the dominant figure, political ideology is important, and interest groups are central only to those issues—such as free trade and the allocation of military contracts—that engage their interests.

Majority opinion is weakly defined. In general, it approves of the United States playing an international role but in particular cases would like Americans to stay home and mind their own business. But when America is caught up in a crisis or the president sends troops overseas, the country and the troops are strongly supported.

Elite opinion plays a more powerful role, but it is divided into four worldviews: isolationism, containment, disengagement, and human rights. The first is less common now than once was the case.

Proponents of the remaining three would be deeply at odds if they were confronted today with a decision of whether we should stay in Vietnam, drive Iraqi troops out of Kuwait, give aid to Bosnia, or launch an air campaign in Kosovo.

Foreign and military decision-making is organized to give civilians control. The president is assisted chiefly by the National Security Council and the secretaries of state and defense. Civilian control of the military is vested in the president, who issues orders not through military officers but through the secretary of defense. The Joint Chiefs of Staff is a planning and advisory body.

When the military budget is developed, it tends to abide by majoritarian politics. But when it is spent on the armed services and military contractors, interest group politics intervenes.

RECONSIDERING WHO GOVERNS?

1. Is American foreign policy set by public wishes or elite views?

Elite views matter greatly because most Americans pay little attention to foreign affairs most of the time. And on many key issues, the public disagrees with the elite. But when the president sends troops overseas to fight, the public will rally around him.

2. If only Congress can declare war, why has the president become so powerful in military affairs?

The Constitution makes him the commander in chief of the military, and the Supreme Court has made it clear that he has great powers on foreign affairs. The president often has sent troops to fight without a declaration of war, but Congress has invariably supported him. Technically, he should get Congress's approval under the War Powers Act, but if Americans are already fighting it would be very hard for Congress to say no.

RECONSIDERING TO WHAT ENDS?

1. Why do we go to war against some dictatorships and not others?

Some threaten our interests directly and some do not. And even when they do not threaten us, as in Bosnia, Haiti, Kosovo, and Somalia, we may intervene to protect citizens from brutality. Or we may not, as in Rwanda. Everything depends on how the government assesses each situation.

2. Should our foreign policy be based on American interests or some conception of human rights?

Sometimes this is not a problem because in a few cases a threat to our interests and a violation of human rights coincide. But at other times, they do not. This is a continuing issue that divides American foreign policy elites. In Congress, liberal members supported and conservative ones opposed our intervention in Bosnia and Kosovo even though neither country threatened us; in Iraq, conservative ones supported and many liberal ones opposed our intervention.

WORLD WIDE WEB RESOURCES

U.S. Army: **www.army.mil**

U.S. Air Force: **www.af.mil**

U.S. Navy: **www.navy.mil**

Central Intelligence Agency: **www.odci.gov**

Department of State: **www.state.gov**

SUGGESTED READINGS

Allison, Graham T. *Essence of Decision: Explaining the Cuban Missile Crisis.* Boston: Little, Brown, 1971. Shows how the decision made by a president during a major crisis was shaped by bureaucratic and organizational factors.

Barnett, Thomas P. M. *The Pentagon's New Map: War and Peace in the Twenty-First Century.* New York: Berkley Books, 2004. Discusses what America's foreign and military policy should be in the global war against terror.

Commission on the Intelligence Capabilities of the United States Regarding Weapons of Mass Destruction. *Report to the President of the United States.* Washington, D.C.: Government Printing Office, 2005. Thorough examination by a bipartisan group of why American intelligence agencies did not understand Iraq's WMD efforts.

Kissinger, Henry. *White House Years.* Boston: Little, Brown, 1979. A brilliant insider's account of the politics and tactics of "high diplomacy" during the Nixon administration.

Mead, Walter Russell. *Special Providence.* New York: Knopf, 2001. Argues that American foreign policy, though often criticized, has been remarkably successful.

Mueller, John E. *War, Presidents, and Public Opinion.* New York: Wiley, 1973. Best summary of the relationship between presidential foreign policy decisions and public opinion.

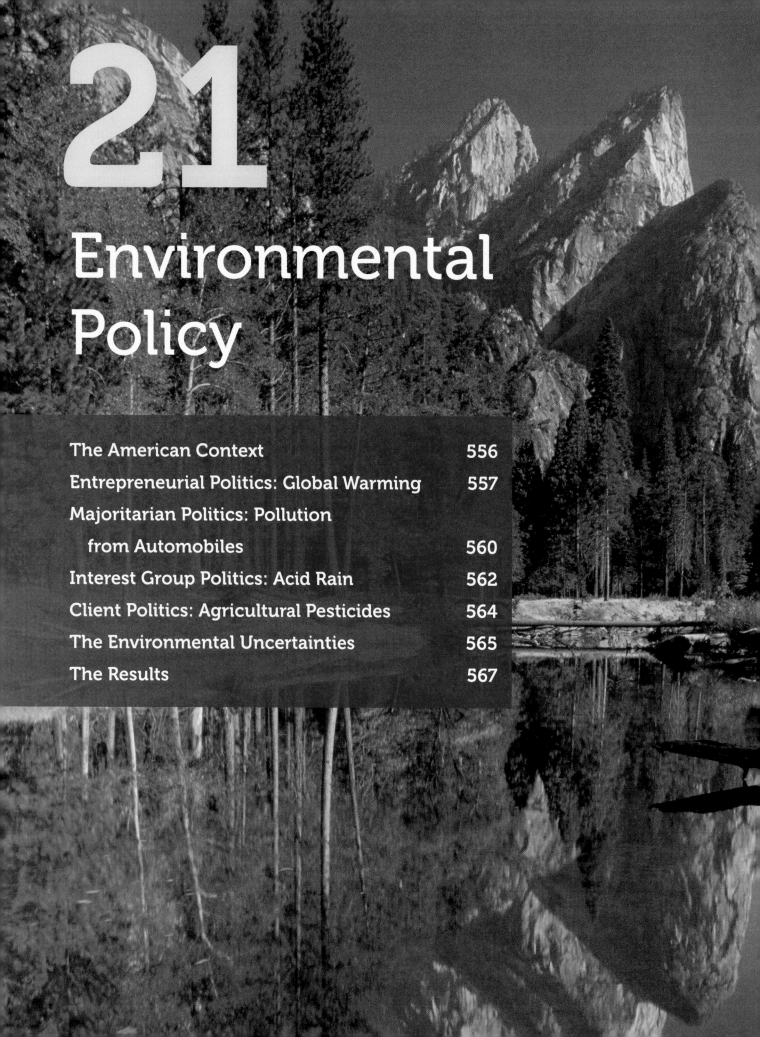

21

Environmental Policy

Elvele Images Ltd/Alamy

WHO GOVERNS?

1. Why have environmental issues become so important in American politics and policymaking?
2. Does the public get the environmental laws it wants?

TO WHAT ENDS?

1. If we wish to have cleaner air and water, how far should we go in making them cleaner when the cost of each additional gain goes up?
2. What is the best way for the government to achieve an environmental goal: by issuing orders or offering incentives?

Everybody loves the environment. A large majority of the American public believes the government should do more to protect it. Over 80 percent of college freshmen believe the government is not doing enough to control pollution, far more than the number who think the government is doing too little about disarmament, protecting the consumer, or controlling handguns.[1] No one wants to be called a "polluter." A staff member in the George W. Bush administration briefed the president over 200 times. When asked what issue got the most attention in Washington, his answer was clear: the environment.[2]

Why, then, is environmental policy so controversial? There are four reasons. First, every governmental policy, including one established to protect the environment, creates both winners and losers. The losers are the people who must pay the costs without getting enough of the benefits. Sometimes those losers are influential interest groups. But sometimes the losers are average citizens. They may love the environment, but not enough to change the way they live in order to enhance it. For example, automobile exhausts are a major cause of smog, but not many people like the idea of being told to leave their cars at home and take the bus to work.

Second, many environmental issues are enmeshed in scientific uncertainty: the experts either do not know or they disagree about what is happening and how to change it. For example, many scientists worry that society is burning so much fuel (thus producing a lot of carbon dioxide) and cutting down so many trees (thus reducing the plants available to convert carbon dioxide back into oxygen) that the earth will soon become a greenhouse: the excess carbon dioxide in the earth's atmosphere will prevent heat from escaping, and so the earth will get warmer with disastrous effects for humanity. But there are some scientists who say human activity is not a major cause of global warming; instead, they argue, it is the result of natural changes in the earth's temperature.[3]

Third, much environmental policy takes the form of entrepreneurial politics—mobilizing decision makers with strong, often emotional appeals in order to overcome the political advantages of the client groups that oppose a change. To make these appeals, people who want change must stir up controversy and find villains. Many times this produces desirable changes. But it can also lead to distorted priorities. For example, it is much easier to make dramatic and politically powerful arguments about a pesticide that causes a minute increase in the risk of cancer than it is to dramatize the runoff into our rivers and oceans of polluted water from farms and city streets.

Finally, environmental politics profoundly affect how the federal government deals with states and with other nations. The states have passed more than three dozen laws to lower the emission of various greenhouse gases and have influenced how Washington handles cleaning up toxic waste sites.[4] During the Clinton administration, the government participated in drafting the 1997 Kyoto Protocol that called for a 5 percent reduction worldwide in greenhouse gases, but aware that the Senate was strongly opposed to this treaty President Clinton never pushed for its ratification. Senators had noted that the treaty would allow several countries, such as China and India, to keep generating greenhouse gases but would require that the United States cut energy use by 25 percent by 2012.[5] The George W. Bush administration scrapped the treaty.

The American Context

Environmental policy, like welfare policy, is shaped by the unique features of American politics. Almost every industrialized nation has rules to protect the environment, but in this country those rules are designed and enforced in a way that would be baffling to someone in, say, Sweden or England.

First, environmental policy making in the United States is much more adversarial than it is in most European nations. In this country, there have been bitter and lasting conflicts over the contents of the Clean Air Act. Minimum auto emissions standards are uniform across the nation, regardless of local conditions (states can set higher standards if they wish). Many rules for improving air and water quality have strict deadlines and require expensive technology. Hundreds of inspectors enforce these rules, and hundreds of lawyers bring countless lawsuits to support or challenge this enforcement. Government and business leaders have frequently denounced each other for being unreasonable or insensitive. So antagonistic are the interests involved in environmental policy that it took 13 years, from 1977 to 1990, to agree on a congressional revision of the Clean Air Act.

In England, by contrast, rules designed to reduce air pollution were written by government and business leaders acting cooperatively. The rules are neither rigid nor nationally uniform; they are flexible and allow plenty of exceptions to deal with local variations in business needs. Compliance with the rules depends mostly on voluntary action, not formal enforcement. Lawsuits are rare. Business and government officials do not routinely accuse each other of being unreasonable. You might think all this sweetness and light were the result of having meaningless rules, but not so. As David Vogel has shown, the improvement in air and water quality in England has been at least as great as, if not greater than, that in the United States.[6]

A second feature of environmental policy here is that, as in so many other policy areas, what is done depends heavily on the states. Though there are uniform national air quality standards, how those standards are achieved is left to the states (subject to certain federal controls). Though sewage treatment plants are in large measure paid for by Washington, they are designed, built, and operated by state and local governments. Though the federal government decrees that radioactive waste must be properly disposed of somewhere, the states have a big voice in where that is. When Congress decided in 1982 to select places in which to dispose of such waste, it announced that sites would be chosen on the basis of "science." But of course no state wanted to get such waste, so all objected. In the congressional committee that made the final decision in 1988, Nevada had the least influence, and so Nevada got the waste. In a federal system of government, "science" rarely makes allocative decisions; local politics usually does.

Federalism reinforces adversarial politics: one of the reasons environmental issues are so contentious in this country is that cities and states fight over what standards should apply where. But federalism is not the whole story. The separation of powers guarantees that almost anybody who wants to wield influence over environmental policy will have an opportunity to do so. In England and in most European nations, the centralized, parliamentary form of government means that the opponents of a policy have less leverage.*

It would take a book almost as long as this one to describe all the environmental laws and regulations now in effect in this country and to discuss the endless controversies over how those rules should be changed or expanded. Since 1963, over three dozen major federal environmental laws have been enacted. This is not a book about environmental policy; it is only one about the politics of that policy.

In this chapter, we want to explain how environmental policy is made. Controversies over controlling pollution from stationary sources, such as factories and power plants, take the form of *entrepreneurial politics*—many people hope to benefit from rules that impose costs on a few firms. Policies intended to reduce air pollution caused by automobiles involve *majoritarian politics*—many people hope to benefit, but many people (anyone who owns a car) will have to pay the cost. The fight over acid rain has largely been a case of *interest group politics*—regions hurt by acid rain (mainly in the Northeast) argue with regions that produce a lot of acid rain (mainly in the Midwest) about who should pay. Finally, there are examples of *client politics* at work—for example, when farmers manage to minimize federal controls over the use of pesticides. Most people are unaware of what food contains what pesticide or which, if

any, are harmful; farmers are keenly aware of the economic benefits of pesticides and are well organized to defend them.

Entrepreneurial Politics: Global Warming

When an offshore well spewed thousands of gallons of oil onto the beaches of Santa Barbara, California, at the very time (January 1969) when protest politics was in the air, it became difficult or impossible for the government or business firms to resist the demand that threats to our natural surroundings be curtailed. The emerging environmental movement created an occasion—Earth Day, first celebrated on April 22, 1970—to celebrate its beginning.

The movement was hugely successful. In 1970, President Nixon created the Environmental Protection Agency (EPA) and Congress toughened the existing Clean Air Act and passed the Water Quality Improvement Act. Two years later, it passed laws designed to clean up the water; three years later, it adopted the Endangered Species Act. New laws were passed right into the 1990s. Existing environmental organizations grew in size, and new ones were formed. Public opinion rallied around environmental issues. One was global warming.

The phrase means that gases, such as carbon dioxide, produced by people when they burn fossil fuels—wood, oil, or coal—get trapped in the atmosphere and cause the earth's temperature to rise. When the temperature goes up, bad things may follow—floods on coastal areas as the polar ice caps melt, wilder weather as more storms are created, and the spread of tropical diseases to North America.

Kansas Gets It: Coal is Dirty

The fight over climate change pits people who use coal with those who oppose burning it.

Robert Nickelsberg/Getty Images

---

* Here, environmental pressures are brought by interest groups; in Europe, where such groups have less influence, environmentalists form political parties, such as the Green party, so as to be represented in the legislature.

WHAT WOULD YOU DO?

MEMORANDUM

To: *Senator Diane Gray*

From: *Keith Mays, legislative assistant*

Until recently, you could get a tax cut if you bought a hybrid car. But it was only available for the first 60,000 cars built by any manufacturer.

Arguments for incentives:

1. We need to reduce gasoline consumption and our dependence on foreign oil.

2. Hybrid cars consume much less gasoline.

3. A tax break to buyers of hybrid vehicles that rely on both electric and gasoline engines will provide a stable market that will encourage sales.

Arguments against incentives:

1. We can more easily cut fuel consumption by raising taxes on gasoline.

2. Many hybrids get worse gas mileage than several conventional cars.

3. The past tax breaks, with the 60,000 car cap, were essentially a support for domestic car builders who were being beaten in the market by Japanese producers.

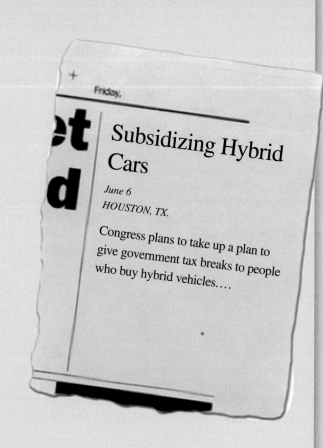

Friday,

Subsidizing Hybrid Cars

June 6
HOUSTON, TX.

Congress plans to take up a plan to give government tax breaks to people who buy hybrid vehicles....

Your decision:

Support _____   Oppose _____

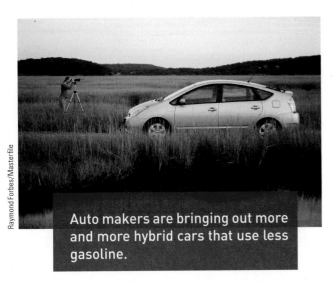

Raymond Forbes/Masterfile

Auto makers are bringing out more and more hybrid cars that use less gasoline.

But our natural concern for global warming must address three difficult questions. First we need to know by how much greenhouse gases cause the earth's temperature to rise. Various scientific groups, such as a panel from the National Science Foundation (NSF), and certain government organizations, such the Intergovernmental Panel on Climate Change (IPCC), have argued that it is "very likely" that greenhouse gases produced by humans have made and will continue to make the earth warmer.

But other organizations, such as the Nongovernmental International Panel on Climate Change (NIPCC), have produced reports arguing that greenhouse gases have not caused the earth to warm. The NIPCC argues that the IPCC neglects the effect of the sun and other natural forces have had in making the earth warmer and ignores periods in the past when, long before greenhouse gases had been produced, people were managing farms in Greenland.

Second, if human activity has caused global warming, what would it cost in lost productivity and income to reduce greenhouse gases? Since America acting alone cannot eliminate greenhouse gases, we have to figure out how to get other countries, especially rapidly growing ones such as China and India, to absorb their share of the cost.

Third, how large would be the gains to humankind, and when would they occur? On the one hand, a warmer globe will cause sea levels to rise, threatening coastal communities; on the other hand, greater warmth will make it easier and cheaper to grow crops and avoid high heating bills.[7]

As with most kinds of entrepreneurial politics, global warming has resulted in a conflict among elites who often base their arguments on ideology as much as on facts. Environmental activists raise money with scary statements about the harm global warming will cause; conservatives raise money with scary statements about the economic pain an American cut in greenhouse gases will cause.[8]

Major Environmental Laws

Smog Clean Air Act (passed in 1970; amended in 1977 and 1990)

- **Stationary sources:** EPA sets national air quality standards; states must develop plans to attain them. If the state plan is inadequate, EPA sets a federal plan. Local sources that emit more than a certain amount of pollutants must install pollution control equipment.

- **Gasoline-powered vehicles:** Between 1970 and 1990, pollution from cars was cut by between 60 and 80 percent. Between 1991 and 1998 there was another 30 percent reduction. All states must have an auto pollution inspection system.

- **Cities:** Classifies cities in terms of how severe their smog problem is and sets deadlines for meeting federal standards.

Water Clean Water Acts of various years state that there is to be no discharge of wastewater into lakes and streams without a federal permit; to get a permit, cities and factories must meet federal discharge standards.

Toxic Wastes EPA is to clean up abandoned dump sites with money raised by a tax on the chemical and petroleum industries and from general revenues. (Many thousands of such sites exist.)

Environmental Impact Statements Since 1969, any federal agency planning a project that would significantly affect the human environment must prepare in advance an environmental impact statement (EIS).

Acid Rain The Clean Air Act of 1990 requires a reduction of 10 million tons of sulfur dioxide (mostly from electric-generating plants that burn coal) by 1995. The biggest sources must acquire government allowances (which can be traded among firms) setting emission limits.

Another environmental example of entrepreneurial politics is the Endangered Species Act (ESA). Passed in 1973, it forbids buying or selling a bird, fish, animal, or plant the government regards as "endangered"—that is, likely to become extinct unless it receives special protection—or engaging in any economic activity (such as building a dam or running a farm) that would harm an endangered species. Currently there are more than 600 species on the protected list; about half are plants. The regulations forbid not only killing a protected species but also adversely affecting its habitat.

The ESA is run by the Fish and Wildlife Service and the National Oceanic and Atmospheric Administration. They can add species to the endangered or threatened list or in response to a private petition. Trafficking in an endangered species can lead to criminal penalties; fines may be imposed for managing private land in ways that might harm a species. Several species, (such as bald eagles, grizzly bears, gray wolves, and sea otters) have increased in number since being listed and a few, such as bald eagles and gray wolves, have been taken off the list.

Firms and government agencies that wish to build a dam, bridge, factory, or farm in an area where an endangered species lives must comply with federal regulations. The complaints of such clients about these regulations are outweighed by the public support for the law. Sometimes the law preserves a creature, such as the bald eagle, that almost everyone admires; sometimes it protects a creature, such as the snail darter, that no one has ever heard of.

Majoritarian Politics: Pollution from Automobiles

The Clean Air Act of 1970 imposed tough restrictions on the amount of pollutants that could come out of automobile tail pipes. Indeed, most of the debate over that bill centered on this issue.

Initially, the auto emissions control rules followed the pattern of entrepreneurial politics: an aroused public with media support demanded that automobile companies be required to make their cars less polluting. It seemed to be "the public" against "the interests," and the public won: by 1975, new cars would have to produce 90 percent less of two pollutants (hydrocarbons and carbon monoxide), and by 1976 achieve a 90 percent reduction in another

(nitrous oxides). This was a tall order. There was no time to redesign automobile engines or to find an alternative to the internal combustion engine; it would be necessary to install devices (called catalytic converters) on exhaust pipes that would transform pollutants into harmless gases.

But a little-noticed provision in the 1970 law soon shoved the battle over automobile pollution into the arena of majoritarian politics. That provision required states to develop land-use and transportation rules to help attain air quality standards. What that meant in practice was that in any area where smog was still a problem, even after emission controls had been placed on new cars, there would have to be rules restricting the public's use of cars.

There was no way cities such as Denver, Los Angeles, and New York could get rid of smog just by requiring people to buy less-polluting cars—the increase in the number of cars or in the number of miles driven in those places outweighed the gain from making the average car less polluting. That meant the government would have to impose such unpopular measures as bans on downtown parking, mandatory use of buses and carpools, and even gasoline rationing.

Efforts to do this failed. Popular opposition to such rules was too great, and the few such rules put into place didn't work. Congress reacted by postponing the deadlines by which air quality standards in cities would have to be met; the EPA reacted by abandoning any serious effort to tell people when and where they could drive.[9]

Even the effort to clean up the exhausts of new cars ran into opposition. Some people didn't like the higher cost of cars with catalytic converters; others didn't like the loss in horsepower these converters caused (many people disconnected them). The United Auto Workers union began to worry that antismog rules would hurt the U.S. auto industry and cost them their jobs. Congress took note of these complaints and decided that despite a lot of effort, new cars could not meet the 90 percent emission reduction standard by 1975–1976, and so in 1977 it amended the Clean Air Act to extend these deadlines by up to six years.

The Clean Air Act, when revised again in 1990, set new, tougher auto emission control standards—but it pushed back the deadline for compliance. It reiterated the need for getting rid of smog in the smoggiest cities and proposed a number of ways to do it—but it set the deadline for compliance in the worst area (Los Angeles) at 20 years in the future.

Highway congestion in California gets worse and uses up a lot of fuel.

Hendrik Holler/PhotoLibrary

Most clean-air laws passed since 1990 have targeted particular industries. For example, in 2004 the Bush administration approved a new measure to dramatically reduce emissions from heavy-use diesel engines used in construction, agricultural, and other industrial machinery. The public will support such tough environmental laws when somebody else pays or when the costs are hidden (as in the price of a car); it will not give as much support when it believes it is paying, especially when the payment takes the form of changing how and when it uses the family car. Here are more examples of each kind of majoritarian politics.

Majoritarian Politics When People Believe the Costs Are Low

The National Environmental Policy Act (NEPA), passed in 1969, contained a provision requiring that an **environmental impact statement** (EIS) be written before any federal agency undertakes an activity that will "significantly" affect the quality of the human environment. (Similar laws have been passed in many states, affecting not only what government does but what private developers do.) Because it required only a "statement" rather than some specific action and because it was a pro-environment law, NEPA passed by overwhelming majorities.

As it turned out, the EIS provision was hardly innocuous. Opponents of virtually any government-sponsored project have used the EIS as a way of blocking, changing, or delaying the project. Hundreds of lawsuits have been filed to challenge this or that provision of an EIS or to claim that a project was not supported by a satisfactory EIS. In this way, environmental activists have challenged

Landmark Cases

Government and the Environment

- *Union Electric Co. v. Environmental Protection Agency* (1976): EPA rules must be observed without regard to their cost or technological feasibility.

- *Chevron v. National Resources Defense Council* (1984): States should comply with EPA decisions, even if not explicitly authorized by statute, provided they are reasonable efforts to attain the goal of the law.

- *Whitman v. American Trucking Associations* (2001): Allows Congress to delegate broad authority to regulatory agencies.

- *Massachusetts v. Environmental Protection Agency* (2207): The EPA must hear a petition asking it to regulate greenhouse gases.

the Alaska pipeline, a Florida canal, and several nuclear power plants, as well as countless dams, bridges, highways, and office buildings. Usually the agency's plan is upheld, but this does not mean the EIS is unimportant: the EIS induces the agency to think through what it is doing, and it gives critics a chance to examine, and often to negotiate, the content of those plans.

Despite the grumbling of many people adversely affected by fights over an EIS (someone once complained that Moses would never have been able to part the Red Sea if he had had to file an EIS first), popular support for it remains strong because the public at large does not believe it is paying a high price and does believe it is gaining a significant benefit.

environmental impact statement A report required by federal law that assesses the possible effect of a project on the environment if the project is subsidized in whole or part by federal funds.

Majoritarian Politics When People Believe the Costs Are High

From time to time, someone proposes that gasoline taxes be raised sharply. Such taxes would discourage driving, and this not only would conserve fuel but also would reduce smog. Almost everyone would pay, but almost everyone would benefit. However, it is only with great difficulty that the public can be persuaded to support such taxes. The reason is that the people pay the tax first, and the benefit, if any, comes later. Unlike Social Security, where the taxes we pay now support cash benefits we get later, gasoline taxes support noncash benefits (cleaner air, less congestion) that many people doubt will ever appear or, if they do, will not be meaningful to them.[10]

When gasoline taxes have been raised, it has usually been because the politicians did not push the tax hike as an environmental measure. Instead, they promised that in return for paying higher taxes the public would receive some concrete benefits—more highways, more buses, or a reduction in the federal deficit (as happened with the gas tax hike of 1990 and again in 1993).

Since it cannot easily cut gasoline use by raising taxes, the government has turned to other approaches. One is to provide tax breaks and other incentives to companies that seek to develop alternative energy sources. Another is to offer incentives to car manufacturers to build vehicles that consume less fuel by relying in whole or in part on electricity.

Interest Group Politics: Acid Rain

Sometimes the rain, snow, or dust particles that fall onto the land are acidic. This is called *acid rain*. One source of that acid precipitation is burning fuel, such as certain types of coal, that contains a lot of sulfur. Some of the sulfur (along with nitrogen) will turn into sulfuric (or nitric) acid as it comes to earth. Steel mills and electric power plants that burn high-sulfur coal are concentrated in the Midwest and Great Lakes regions of the United States. The prevailing winds tend to carry those sulfurous fumes eastward, where some fall to the ground.

That much seems certain. Everything else has been surrounded by controversy. Many lakes and rivers in the eastern United States and in Canada have become more acidic, and some forests in these areas have died back. Some part of this is the result of acid rain from industrial smokestacks, but some part of it is also the result of naturally occurring acids in the soils and rainfall. How much of the acidification is man-made and how much is a result of the actions of Mother Nature is unclear. Some lakes are not affected by acid rain; some are. Why some are affected more than others is unclear. The long-term effects of higher acid levels in lakes and forests are also unclear.

These scientific uncertainties were important because they provided some support for each side in a fierce interest group battle. Residents of Canada and New England complained bitterly of the loss of forests and the acidification of lakes, blaming it on midwestern smokestacks. Midwestern businesses, labor unions, and politicians denied that their smokestacks were the major cause of the problem (if, indeed, there was a problem) and argued that, even if they were the cause, they shouldn't have to pay the cost of cleaning up the problem.

An attempt to deal with the issue in 1977 reflected the kind of bizarre compromises that sometimes result when politically opposed forces have to be reconciled. There were essentially two alternatives. One was to require power plants to burn low-sulfur coal. This would undoubtedly cut back on sulfur emissions, but it would cost money, because low-sulfur coal is mined mostly in the West, hundreds of miles away from the midwestern coal-burning industries. The other way would be to require power plants to install scrubbers—complicated and very expensive devices that would take sulfurous fumes out of the gas before it came out of the smokestack. In addition to their cost, the trouble with scrubbers was that they didn't always work and that they generated a lot of unpleasant sludge that would have to be hauled away and buried somewhere. Their great advantage, however, was that they would allow midwestern utilities to continue their practice of using cheap, high-sulfur coal.

Congress voted for the scrubbers for all new coal-burning plants, even if they burned low-sulfur coal. In the opinion of most economists, this was the wrong decision,[11] but it had four great political advantages. First, the jobs of miners in high-sulfur coal mines would be protected. They had powerful allies in Congress. Second, environmentalists liked scrubbers, which they seemed to regard as a definitive, technological "solution" to the problem, an approach far preferable to relying on incentives to induce power plants to buy low-sulfur coal. Third, scrubber manufacturers liked the idea, for obvious reasons. Finally, some eastern governors liked scrubbers because if all new plants had to have them, it would be more costly, and thus less likely, for existing factories in their states to close down and move into the West.

The 1977 law in effect required scrubbers on all new coal-burning plants—even ones located right next to mines where they could get low-sulfur coal. As two scholars later described the law, it seemed to produce "clean coal and dirty air."[12]

The 1977 bill did not solve much. Many of the scrubbers, as predicted, didn't work very well. And there remained the question of what to do about existing power plants and factories.

When a solution was finally agreed upon, it was a compromise. President Bush the elder proposed a two-step regulation. In the first phase, 111 power plants would be required to reduce their emission of sulfur by a fixed amount. They could decide for themselves how to do it: buy low-sulfur coal, install scrubbers, or use some other technology. This would be done by 1995. In the second phase, with a deadline in the year 2000, there would be sharper emission reductions for many more plants, and this would probably require the use of scrubbers. To create some flexibility in how much each utility must cut its emissions, a system of sulfur dioxide allowances that could be bought and sold was established. This compromise became part of the Clean Air Act of 1990. By 2005, interest groups, advocates, and experts on all sides of the issue were once again poised to battle each other.

Interest group politics permeates many aspects of environmental policy making. When cities or states consider land-use controls and zoning ordinances, they are weighing the competing demands of established residents (who often want as little new growth in their communities as possible) against demands of developers who want to build additional housing.

The heady victories of the early 1970s are hard to duplicate today because groups that were once unorganized are now well organized.

For example, there is now a large and growing industry that makes products designed to improve the environment. As we saw in the acid rain controversy, industry can play an important role in supporting laws that favor their machines, whether or not they are the best solution to the problem. Industry is far better organized today than in 1970 to use its employees and political allies to defend its interests. Similarly, public-interest groups, such as the Environmental Defense Fund, that did not exist in 1965 now compete with other environmental groups for money and publicity. Labor unions, such as the United Auto Workers, that once fought for tough air pollution laws now are worried about whether some of these laws may cost them their jobs.

When the public is asked which should be more important, economic growth or environmental protection, their answers change. In the 1980s and 1990s, they overwhelmingly preferred environmental protection, but by the mid-2000s, a preference for economic growth had risen (see Figure 21.1). However, overall, citizens are environmentalists first.

Figure 21.1

Which Should Take Precedence: Environmental Protection or Economic Growth?: 1984–2007

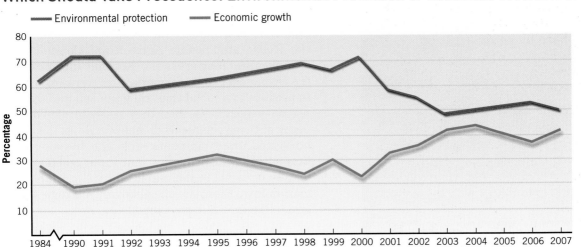

Source: Gallup Poll.

Client Politics: Agricultural Pesticides

Some client groups have so far escaped this momentum. One such group is organized farmers, who have more or less successfully resisted efforts to restrict, sharply, the use of pesticides or to control the runoff of pesticides from farmlands.

For a while, it seemed as though farmers would also fall before the assaults of policy entrepreneurs. When Rachel Carson published *Silent Spring* in 1962, she set off a public outcry about the harm to wildlife caused by the indiscriminate use of DDT, a common pesticide. In 1972, the EPA banned the use of DDT.

That same year, Congress directed the EPA to evaluate the safety of all pesticides on the market; unsafe ones were to be removed. However, that is easier said than done. One reason is that there are over 50,000 pesticides now in use, with 5,000 new ones introduced every year.[13] Testing all of these chemicals is a huge, vastly expensive,

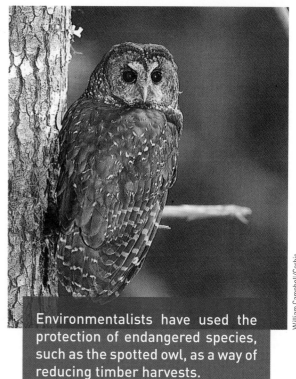

William Campbell/Corbis

Environmentalists have used the protection of endangered species, such as the spotted owl, as a way of reducing timber harvests.

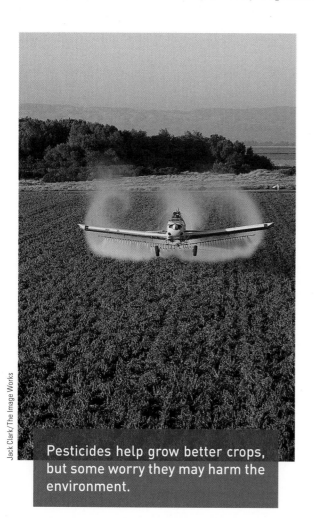

Jack Clark/The Image Works

Pesticides help grow better crops, but some worry they may harm the environment.

and very time-consuming job, especially since any health effects on people may not be observed for several years.[14] Another reason is that pesticides have many beneficial uses; therefore, someone has to balance the gains and the risks of using a given pesticide and compare the relative gains and risks of two similar pesticides.

But even if the science were easy, the politics would not be. American farmers are the most productive in the world, and most of them believe they cannot achieve that output (and thus their present incomes) without using pesticides. These farmers are well organized to express their interests and well represented in Congress (especially on the House and Senate Agricultural Committees). Complicating matters is the fact that the subsidies the taxpayers give to farmers often encourage them to produce more food than they can sell and thus to use more pesticides than they really need. Though many of these chemicals do not remain in the crops harvested, large amounts sink into the soil, contaminating water supplies. But these problems are largely invisible to the public and are much harder to dramatize than, say, the discovery of a toxic waste dump like that at Love Canal, New York.

Though attacked by environmental organizations, farm groups have been generally successful at practicing client politics. The EPA's budget for reviewing pesticides has been kept small.[15] Very few pesticides have been taken off the market, and those that have been removed have tended to be ones that, because they were involved in some incident receiving heavy media coverage (such as the effect of DDT on birds), easily fell prey to entrepreneurial politics.

One of the reasons client politics has been able to protect the use of pesticides despite a political atmosphere that heavily favors environmental safety is that in fact pesticides have trivial effects on long-term human health problems, such as cancer. The most scholarly studies of the tendency of pesticides to cause cancer suggest that they are "unimportant" because "there is no convincing evidence" that they produce cancer.[16]

A similar kind of client politics exists in the timber industry. Wood product companies and loggers want access to forests under the control of the U.S. Forest Service. Though only 13 percent of all cut timber comes from these forests and two-thirds of the U.S. forest system is already off-limits to logging, environmentalists want further restrictions, especially to prevent clear-cutting (cutting down all the trees in a given area) and to prevent harvesting trees from the old-growth forests of Oregon and Washington. But Congress has generally supported the timber industry, ordering the Forest Service to sell harvesting rights at below-market prices, in effect subsidizing the industry. Some activists hope to convert this client politics into entrepreneurial politics by demanding that clear-cutting in certain forests be stopped in order to protect endangered species, such as the spotted owl.

The Environmental Uncertainties

Making environmental policy strikes many people as easy—identify a problem, raise a fuss, defeat "the interests," and enjoy the benefits. In fact it is much harder than that to have a sane environmental policy.

First, what is the problem? Nobody likes smog, and human waste or oil slicks floating off our beaches are obviously bad. But many other problems are much less clear-cut. Science doesn't know how bad the greenhouse effect is. Pesticides that cause cancer in animals when given in megadoses may or may not cause cancer in people when absorbed in nominal amounts.

Second, if there is a problem, what goals do we want to achieve? We want reasonably clean air and water, of course, but how clean is reasonably clean? Since

the cost of removing from the air the last 10 percent of some pollutants often is greater than the cost of removing the first 90 percent, how clean is clean enough? If making air and water cleaner is costly in terms of jobs, energy, and economic growth, how big a price are we willing to pay?

Third, how do we want to achieve our goals? Issuing rules and enforcing them in court often seem the easiest things to do, but they are not always the wisest. That **command-and-control strategy** assumes that the rule makers and rule enforcers know how to achieve the greatest environmental gain at the least cost. In fact, no one knows how to do that, because local circumstances, technological problems, and economic costs are so complex. Under what circumstances can we use incentives and market prices to get people voluntarily to clean up their act by using their own imagination?

> **command-and-control strategy** A strategy to improve air and water quality, involving the setting of detailed pollution standards and rules.

All of these uncertainties have become part of the endless political controversies surrounding the administration of the Environmental Protection Agency. For example:

What Is the Problem?

The EPA was given the responsibility to administer certain laws governing air, water, and pesticides (among others). But it is rarely left alone to define these problems; any new environmental scandal leads to popular and congressional demands that it drop everything and solve that crisis. When toxic chemicals were found at Love Canal and Virginia Beach, these dramatic discoveries put other, less

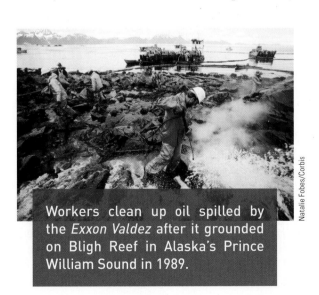

Workers clean up oil spilled by the *Exxon Valdez* after it grounded on Bligh Reef in Alaska's Prince William Sound in 1989.

Natalie Fobes/Corbis

Who Governs? To What Ends?

Superfund: Cleaning Up Toxic Wastes

During the 1970s, hazardous waste sites were discovered all across America. Dangerous chemicals, many used decades before anybody worried about the environment and in some cases involving substances no one knew to be toxic, were found in the soil and near drinking water. These new investigations understandably alarmed many people. They and their legislators wanted this junk cleaned up.

What could be simpler? Find the dangerous stuff and take it out. In 1980, President Carter signed the Comprehensive Environmental Response, Compensation, and Liability Act (CERCLA), commonly known as Superfund. The law did two things: First, it taxed chemical and petroleum industries and put the proceeds, along with general tax revenues, into a trust fund to pay for cleaning up abandoned hazardous waste sites. Second, the law gave the government the power to sue any person or company (if they could be found) that had dumped the waste. In 1986, the law was strengthened when President Reagan signed a bill that gave the Environmental Protection Agency (EPA) more power and increased the size of Superfund to $8.5 billion.

But a decade later, the results were mixed. Superfund and related laws were associated with steep reductions in levels of toxic chemical releases (few new hazardous waste sites were created), but only 14 of 1,200 known hazardous waste sites had been cleaned up. By 2005, there were still more than 2,000 waste sites that had not been treated. What had gone wrong?

First, finding and suing the responsible parties was very difficult. These "potentially responsible parties" included present and past owners of a site, their insurance companies, and any firm that deposited waste long before a law had been passed saying it was illegal. Some companies had dumped the junk knowingly, others by accident; still others had long since gone out of business or were bankrupt. Finding them and getting them to pay were slow and difficult processes. As a result a lot of the Superfund money went to hire lawyers, not waste removers.

Second, it is complicated and time-consuming to clean up a site. Some sites had become big industrial plants or suburban housing developments. The EPA never had a staff equal to these high demands. There was a rapid turnover in EPA Superfund managers.

Third, as the environmental lobby got stronger, it put more and more pressure on the EPA to expand the list of hazardous sites and raise the standard for what constituted a cleaned-up site. No one seemed to be interested in developing a clear list of top-priority sites; instead, the whole list just got longer.

Nobody wants to live on a toxic waste site. But how do you clean it up? Just by hiring more lawyers to sue more people? The Superfund problem highlights the difficulty of designing an effective strategy and a good administrative system for doing what almost everyone wants done.

---

dramatic, but often more important problems on the back burner.

What Are the Costs and Benefits?

Everyone wants a healthy environment, but people do not distinguish accurately between realistic and unrealistic threats or between reasonable and unreasonable costs. The biggest scare is cancer, even though every form of cancer has been steadily declining for many years (except lung cancer, which is caused primarily by smoking, not environmental hazards). People fear the unknown—many are afraid of flying, for example, even though flying is vastly safer than driving. People fear strange threats, such as toxic chemicals, even though they may never hurt anyone. People applaud dramatic governmental steps without asking whether they actually help anyone. For example, the government has mandated that all asbestos must be removed from public school buildings. Though intense exposure to asbestos can cause health problems, removing all the asbestos from old school buildings helps almost no one and may hurt the asbestos removers. The problem for government officials is to keep policies aimed at real risks—they do exist—and not to be diverted by popular concerns over unreal ones. In a free society, that is not easy.

What Are Our Goals?

When the EPA was told by Congress to eliminate *all* pollutants entering our waterways by 1985, to cut auto emissions by 90 percent within five years, and to eliminate smog in *all* cities, Congress should have known that these goals were utterly unrealistic. When the EPA realized it could not achieve these goals, it was forced to ask for extensions in deadlines and for revisions in laws. This gave it the appearance of knuckling under to industry pressure.[17]

How Do We Achieve Our Goals?

Initially, the EPA was zealous about using a command-and-control strategy to improve air and water quality. For example, to reduce water pollution discharged from factories, the EPA issued rules broken down into 642 industry subcategories, and even then there was a lot of local variation that it could not take into account. When the cost of doing this sort of thing got out of control, the EPA during the Carter administration began to devise incentives to replace some rules. These included offsets, bubbles, and banks:

- **Offsets.** If a company wants to open a new plant in an area with polluted air, it can do so if the pollution it generates is offset by a reduction in pollution from another source in that area. To achieve that reduction, the new company may buy an existing company and close it down.

- **Bubble standard.** A bubble is the total amount of air pollution that can come from a given factory. A company is free to decide which specific sources within that factory must be reduced in order to meet the bubble standard.

- **Pollution allowances (or banks).** If a company reduces its polluting emissions by more than the law requires, it can either use this excess to cover a future plant expansion or sell it to another company as an offset.

Once, only affected businesses complained about the high cost, slow progress, and legal complexity of environmental regulations. Increasingly, however, pro-environment interest groups and the government itself have become aware of the difficulties that arise when the government relies on a command-and-control strategy that is indifferent to costs and excessively reliant on lawsuits.

Cap and Trade

To deal with global warming, the House of Representatives in mid-2009 considered a bill that would set maximum emissions of carbon dioxide for most large firms. The emissions allowed imposed by these caps would decline as the years passed. If a firm produced less than the maximum emissions it could sell part of its permit to another firm. The theory was that firms would take the least costly way to meet the standards: either lowering their emissions or, if that was too expensive, buying an additional permit from another firm. This strategy was used in the 1990s to reduce the emission of sulphur dioxide that people believed caused acid rain.

This plan was similar to the cap-and-trade requirements imposed by the Kyoto Treaty of 1997, but the Senate had never ratified that bill in part because China, India, and other growing economies were not bound by it.

Some liberal critics of the 2009 bill argued that it allowed firms to pay money in order to pollute and was not an efficient method to reduce pollution. Many of them argued that it should be replaced by a tax on carbon. Some conservative critics said it would only work if the permits were auctioned off (instead, the plan allowed the government to give most away), that it required an unrealistically large decrease in carbon dioxide (85 percent by 2050), and that the decreased emissions would impose taxes on Americans and slow economic growth.

In mid-2009 the bill had not been passed by Congress but remained a key part of President Obama's program.

The Results

Though Americans think their environment has gotten worse, in fact many aspects of it have gotten better since 1970. There is now much less carbon monoxide, sulfur dioxide, and lead in the atmosphere than once was the case. It is less clear whether there have been equally noticeable improvements in water quality, in large part because much of the gunk that flows into our rivers, lakes, and oceans does not come from some fixed source (such as a sewer) that can be easily isolated; a lot comes from runoff from the ground as a result of rain washing pollutants off urban streets and farmlands and into the water.

Hazardous waste is found at thousands of known locations (and perhaps hundreds more unknown ones). The cleanup job is so great that it will be years before much progress can be shown. Getting big reductions in dangerous pesticides requires first reaching agreement on what is a dangerous pesticide and then finding a way of minimizing the harm to agriculture that would be caused by the reduction.

SUMMARY

Environmental issues illustrate all four styles of policymaking.

Entrepreneurial politics: an unorganized public is to benefit at the expense of a well-organized group. An example is the effort to reduce what some think is global warming. Such politics requires mobilizing the media, dramatizing the issue, and convincing members of Congress that their political reputations will suffer if they do not cast the right vote. To prevent client groups from taking over the implementation of these laws, the bills are written to make it easy to use the courts to force action.

Majoritarian politics: an unorganized public is to benefit at its own expense. Examples include reducing auto emissions by imposing transportation controls, raising gasoline taxes, and requiring environmental impact statements. Interest groups tend not to be the decisive players. Whether the proposal wins or loses depends on how the public generally evaluates the costs. They like environmental impact statements but oppose higher gasoline taxes and restrictions on private automobile use. Dramatizing a crisis tends to be less effective because the public at large, and not some small interest, must pay for any benefits.

Interest group politics: two organized groups with a material stake in the outcome fight over who will pay and who will benefit. An example is the controlling of acid rain. When faced with two or more powerful interests, Congress tends not to pass broad, sweeping bills but to find workable compromises.

Client politics: an organized group gets a benefit; an unorganized public must pay. Examples include the use of agricultural pesticides and timber cutting in U.S. forests. Client politics depends on the client group's having strategically placed allies in Congress and on its potential opponents' being unable to convert this policy system into a pattern of entrepreneurial politics (by dramatizing a crisis, for example).

In general, entrepreneurial politics has played the dominant role in most environmental issues. The prevalence of entrepreneurial politics in this arena is largely due to (1) the success of policy entrepreneurs in sensitizing public opinion to these matters and (2) the growth of a variety of public-interest lobbies with close ties to the media and with the ability to threaten recalcitrant legislators with attacks on their reputations.

Unlike economic or welfare issues, environmental issues lend themselves to entrepreneurial politics because the problems can be portrayed in life-threatening terms, the goals can be related to what most people believe is the good life, and the costs can be minimized, deferred, or (seemingly) placed on small groups.

RECONSIDERING WHO GOVERNS?

1. Why have environmental issues become so important in American politics and policymaking?

Today, almost everybody loves the environment and thinks government has a duty to protect and improve it. Despite post-1970 improvements in many environmental conditions, most people think the environment is getting worse, not better, and worry about acute environmental threats to public health and safety. Nevertheless, environmental issues have attracted the interest and energy of talented policy entrepreneurs. These issues figure prominently not only in Washington politics, but also at the state and local levels as well as in international relations.

2. Does the public get the environmental laws it wants?

Yes and no. Most people say they want the government to do whatever it takes to protect and improve the environment, and most support laws and regulations that force particular industries to reduce pollution or take other pro-environment actions at their own expense. Many such laws and regulations have been enacted and enforced since the early 1970s. But most people waver when it comes to laws and regulations that would impose substantial financial costs on them (substantially higher gasoline taxes, for example) or force them to change how they live (prohibiting them from driving their cars to work, for instance). Typically, politicians echo the public's pro-environment sentiments without, however, enacting policies or enforcing regulations that impose large and visible costs on most people.

RECONSIDERING TO WHAT ENDS?

1. If we wish to have cleaner air and water, how far should we go in making them cleaner when the cost of each additional gain goes up?

We have cut the pollutants coming out of cars dramatically, but it will cost a lot to cut them to zero. The key question is whether spending scarce dollars that way makes more sense than spending the same amount of money on something else, like preventing diseases or funding schools. Choosing between spending money on clean air, less disease, and better schools may strike some readers as wrongheaded; shouldn't we have all of these? But governing means using limited resources to deal with many different desires. It is almost impossible to have air that is entirely clean (natural fires and dust storms will make it dirty), and even reducing auto pollutants to zero will have to await the invention of engines powered by things like fuel cells that have as a waste product only water. If we spend huge sums on making air or water entirely pure, we will inevitably be spending less on something else that we also want. Americans love the environment, but even for things we love we have to worry about costs.

2. What is the best way for the government to achieve an environmental goal: by issuing orders or offering incentives?

For a lot of people, issuing orders makes sense. That way we tell people what they have to do and can punish them if they don't do it. But for most economists and policy analysts, incentives make more sense because they give people the opportunity to choose the most efficient way to help the environment. For example, we can tell utilities not to let any sulphur dioxide out of their smokestacks, but that may impose huge costs on utilities that already produce very little sulphur dioxide or even drive them out of business. If instead we tell utilities they will get rewards for reducing pollutants, those that can do so easily will make big changes and, if they reduce them by more than a specified amount, will be allowed to sell the extra gains to another company to help it meet its goals. Still, when the gains are huge and the costs minimal, issuing orders makes sense.

WORLD WIDE WEB RESOURCES

Environmental Protection Agency: **www.epa.gov**

Environmental activists

   Environmental Defense Fund: **www.edf.org**

   National Resources Defense Council: **www.nrdc.org**

   Sierra Club: **www.sierraclub.org**

Environmental skeptics

   American Enterprise Institute: **www.aei.org**

   Competitive Enterprise Institute: **www.cei.org**

SUGGESTED READINGS

Easterbrook, Gregg. *A Moment on Earth*. New York: Viking, 1995. A comprehensive account of what we have accomplished and what remains to be done regarding the environment, written by a hard-headed environmentalist.

Gore, Al. *Earth in the Balance*. Boston: Houghton Mifflin, 2000. Revised edition of a pro-environment argument first written when Gore was a senator.

Hayward, Steven F. *Index of Leading Environmental Indicators*. Washington, D.C.: American Enterprise Institute, 2005. Annual review of various measures of environmental change.

Intergovernmental Panel on Climate Change, *Fourth, Assessment Report* (2007). Latest study by the IPCC, created by two United Nations organizations.

Lomborg, Bjorn. *Cool It: The Skeptical Environmentalist's Guide to Global Warming*. New York: Knopf, 2007. A liberal agrees that global warming is occurring but urges more moderate steps to deal with it.

Nongovernmental International Panel on Climate Change, *Climate Change Reconsidered* (Chicago, IL: Heartland Institute, 2009). A lengthy argument by scientists who disagree with the IPCC report.

Rosenbaum, Walter A. *Environmental Politics and Policy*. 6th ed. Washington, D.C.: Congressional Quarterly Press, 2004. Analysis of the politics of environmental issues, including air and water pollution, the use of chemicals, nuclear power, and preserving outer space.

Vogel, David. *National Style of Regulation: Environmental Policy in Great Britain and the United States*. Ithaca, N.Y.: Cornell University Press, 1986. An explanation of why environmental politics in the United States is so adversarial.

Part 5

The Nature of American Democracy

Justice is the end of government. It is the end of civil society. It ever has been and ever will be pursued until it be obtained, or until liberty be lost in the pursuit.

* Federalist No. 51

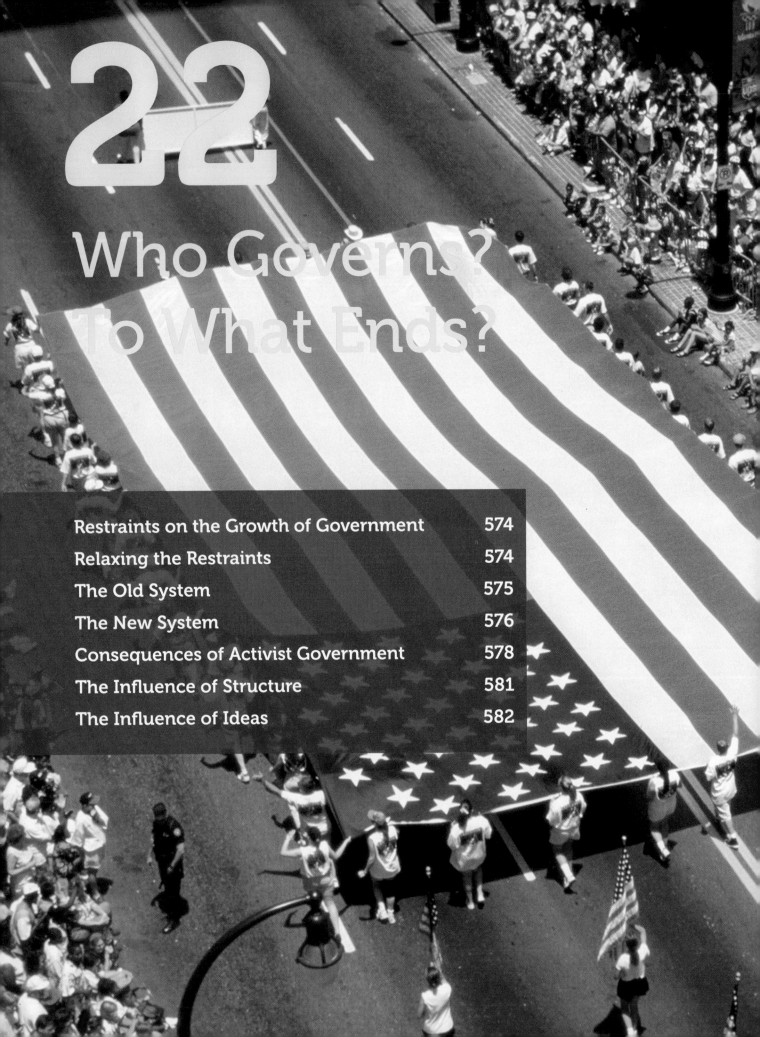

22

Who Governs?
To What Ends?

Ron Sherman/Getty Images

Like most Americans, you probably worry about some social problems. These might include abortion, crime, drug abuse, civil rights, gun control, homelessness, or school quality. Maybe you have argued about these matters with your friends, discussing what Washington should do about these things. While you argue, remember this: until about a half-century ago, when our parents were alive, all of this talk would have been nonsense. None of these things were matters that people believed the federal government could or should do anything about.

Restraints on the Growth of Government

When Dwight Eisenhower was president, none of these issues except civil rights was even thought to be a matter for federal policy, and on civil rights Congress didn't do very much. Our national political agenda was very short. During the Eisenhower administration, we decided to build an interstate highway system, admit Alaska and Hawaii into the union, and fight over the power of labor unions. For *eight years*, these were about the only major domestic political issues. The rest of the time, Washington worried about foreign affairs.

This was about what the Founders had expected, though many of them would have objected to some things that were done in the Eisenhower administration. Some would have thought Washington shouldn't build any highways because the Constitution did not authorize Congress to make laws about such matters. The federal government, in their view, should limit itself to war, peace, interstate commerce, establishing a national currency, and delivering the mail. And for a long time, the prevailing interpretation of the Constitution sharply limited what policies the federal government could adopt. The Supreme Court restricted the authority of the government to regulate business and prevented it from levying an income tax. Most important, the Supreme Court refused, with some exceptions, to allow the delegation of broad discretionary power to administrative agencies.

The Supreme Court could not have maintained this position for as long as it did if it had acted in the teeth of popular opposition. But popular opinion was also against the growth of government. It was not thought legitimate for the federal government to intervene deeply in the economy (even the American Federation of Labor, led by Samuel Gompers, resisted federal involvement in labor-management issues). It was certainly not thought proper for Washington to upset racial segregation as it was practiced in both the North and the South. It took constitutional amendments to persuade Congress that it had the authority to levy an income tax or to prohibit the sale of alcoholic beverages. Even in the 1930s, public opinion polls showed that as many as half the voters were skeptical of a federal unemployment compensation program.

That was the Old System. Today, under the New System, federal politics is not about some small list of problems thought to be truly national; it is about practically everything. It is almost impossible to think of a problem about which Washington has no policy at all or around which it does not carry on intense debates. Listen to radio talk shows, and they will be about why Washington has a good or bad policy about almost every issue you can imagine.

What is puzzling about this change from the Old System to the New System is that the Constitution is filled with arrangements designed to make it hard, not easy, for the federal government to act. The separation of powers permits the president, Congress, and the courts to check one another; federalism guarantees that states will have an important role to play; and the division of legislative authority between the House and the Senate ensures that each body will be inclined to block the other. To get a new law passed, you have to please a large number of political actors; to get a new one blocked, you only have to convince one congressional committee.

That system made the national government relatively unimportant for many decades. Until well into the 20th century, governors and mayors were more important than the president. Most members of Congress did not serve more than one or two terms in Washington; there didn't seem to be much point in becoming a career legislator because Congress didn't do much, didn't pay much, and wasn't in session for very long.

Relaxing the Restraints

As we have said, the constraints on federal action have now weakened or disappeared altogether. First, the courts have altered their interpretation of the Constitution in ways that have not only permitted but sometimes even required government action. The Bill of Rights has been extended so that almost all its important provisions are now regarded as applying to the states (by having been incorporated into the due process clause of the Fourteenth Amendment). This means that a citizen can use the federal courts to alter state policy to a greater degree than ever before. (Overturning state laws that ban abortions or require racially separate schools are two important examples of this change.) The special protection the courts once granted property rights has been substantially reduced so that business can be regulated to a greater degree than previously. The Court has permitted Congress to give broad discretionary powers to administrative agencies, allowing bureaucrats to make decisions that once only Congress could make.

Second, public opinion has changed in ways that support an expanded role for the federal government.

The public demanded action to deal with the Great Depression (the programs that resulted, such as Social Security, survived in part because the Supreme Court changed its mind about the permissible scope of federal action). Political elites changed their minds faster than the average citizen. Well-educated, politically active people began demanding federal policies regarding civil rights, public welfare, environmental protection, consumer safety, and foreign aid well before the average citizen became concerned with such things.

Once in place, most of these programs proved popular, so their continuance was supported by mass as well as elite opinion. The cumulative effect of this process was to blur, if not erase altogether, the line that once defined what the government had the authority to do. At one time, a new proposal was debated in terms of whether it was *legitimate* for the federal government to do it all. Federal aid to education, for example, usually was opposed because many people feared it would lead to federal control of local schools. But after so many programs (including federal aid to education) had been passed, people stopped arguing about whether a certain policy was legitimate and argued instead about whether it was *effective*.

Third, political resources have become more widely distributed. The number and variety of interest groups have increased enormously. The funds available from foundations for organizations pursuing specific causes have grown. It is now easier to get access to the federal courts than formerly was the case, and once in the courts the plaintiffs are more likely to encounter judges who believe that the law and the Constitution should be interpreted broadly to permit particular goals (for example, prison reform) to be attained by legal rather than legislative means. Hundreds of magazines, newsletters, and World Wide Web pages have arisen to provide policy information to specialized segments of opinion. The techniques of mass protest, linked to the desire of television to show visually interesting accounts of social conflict, have been perfected in ways that convey the beliefs of a few into the living rooms of millions.

Campaign-finance laws and court rulings have given legal status and constitutional protection to thousands of political-action committees (PACs) that raise and spend tens of millions of dollars from millions of small contributors. College education, once the privilege of a tiny minority, has become the common experience of millions of people, so that the effects of college—in encouraging political participation and in shaping political beliefs (usually in a liberal direction)—are now widely shared. The ability

of candidates to win nomination for office no longer depends on their ability to curry favor with a few powerful bosses; it now reflects their skill at raising money, mobilizing friends and activists, cultivating a media image, and winning a primary election.

So great have been the changes in the politics of policy-making in this country starting in the 1930s that we can refer, with only slight exaggeration, to one policy-making system having been replaced by another (see box on page 577).

The Old System

The Old System had a small agenda. Though people voted at a high rate and often took part in torchlight parades and other mass political events, political leadership was professionalized in the sense that the leadership circle was small, access to it was difficult, and the activists in social movements generally were kept out. Only a few major issues were under discussion at any time. A member of Congress had a small staff (if any at all), dealt with his or her colleagues on a personal basis, deferred to the prestige of House and Senate leaders, and tended to become part of some stable coalition (the farm bloc, the labor bloc, the southern bloc) that persisted across many issues.

When someone proposed adding a new issue to the public agenda, a major debate often arose over whether it was legitimate for the federal government to take action at all on the matter. A dominant theme in this debate was the importance of "states' rights." Except in wartime, or during a very

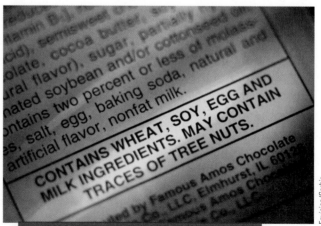

Food products now contain health warnings, such as nuts in this package of cookies.

brief period when the nation expressed interest in acquiring colonies, the focus of policy debate was on domestic affairs. Members of Congress saw these domestic issues largely in terms of their effect on local constituencies. The presidency was small and somewhat personal; there was only a rudimentary White House staff. The president would cultivate the press, but there was a clear understanding that what he said in a press conference was never to be quoted directly.

For the government to take bold action under this system, the nation usually had to be facing a crisis. War presented such crisis, and so the federal government during the Civil War and World Wars I and II acquired extraordinary powers to conscript soldiers, control industrial production, regulate the flow of information to citizens, and restrict the scope of personal liberty. Each succeeding crisis left the government bureaucracy somewhat larger than it had been before, but when the crisis ended, the exercise of extraordinary powers ended. Once again, the agenda of political issues became small, and legislators argued about whether it was legitimate for the government to enter some new policy area, such as civil rights or industrial regulation.

The New System

The New System began in the 1930s but did not take its present form until the 1970s. It is characterized by a large policy agenda, the end of the debate over the legitimacy of government action (except in the area of First Amendment freedoms), the diffusion and decentralization of power in Congress, and the multiplication of interest groups. The government has grown so large that it has a policy on almost every conceivable subject, and so the debate in Washington is less often about whether it is right and prudent to take some bold new step and more often about how the government can best cope with the strains and problems that arise from implementing existing policies. As someone once said, the federal government is now more concerned with managing than with ruling.

For example, in 1935 Congress debated whether the nation should have a Social Security system at all; in the 1980s, it debated whether the system could best be kept solvent by raising taxes or by cutting benefits; in 2004 and 2005, it debated whether some part of each person's Social Security payments could be invested in the stock market. In the 1960s, Congress argued over whether there should be any federal civil rights laws at all; by the 1980s and 1990s, it was arguing over whether those

laws should be administered in a way that simply eliminated legal barriers to equal opportunity for racial minorities or in a way (by affirmative action) that made up for the disadvantages that burdened such minorities in the past. As late as the 1950s, the president and Congress argued over whether it was right to adopt a new program if it meant the government had to borrow money to pay for it. As late as the 1960s, many members of Congress believed the federal government had no business paying for the health care of its citizens; today hardly anyone argues against having Medicare but many worry about how best to control its rising cost.

The differences between the Old and New Systems should not be exaggerated. The Constitution still makes it easier for Congress to block the proposals of the president, or for some committee of Congress to defeat the preferences of the majority of Congress, than in almost any other democratic government. The system of checks and balances operates as before. The essential differences between the Old and the New Systems are these:

1. Under the Old System, the checks and balances made it difficult for the federal government to *start* a new program, and so the government remained relatively small. Under the New System, these checks and balances made it hard to *change* what the government is already doing, and so the government remains large.
2. Under the Old System, power was *somewhat centralized* in the hands of party and congressional leaders. There was still plenty of conflict, but the number of people who had to agree before something could be done was not large. Under the New System, power is much more *decentralized,* and so it is harder to resolve conflict because so many more people—party activists, interest group leaders, individual members of Congress, heads of government agencies—must agree.

The transition from the Old to the New System occurred chiefly during two periods in American politics. The first was in the early 1930s when a catastrophic depression led the government to explore new ways of helping the needy, regulating business, and preventing a recurrence of the disaster. Franklin Roosevelt's New Deal was the result. The huge majorities enjoyed by the Democrats in Congress, coupled with popular demands to solve the problem, led to a vast outpouring of new legislation and the creation of dozens of new government agencies. Though initially the Supreme Court struck down some of these measures as unconstitutional, a key member of the Court changed his

How American Politics Has Changed

Old System		New System
	Congress	
Chairmen relatively strong		Chairmen relatively weak
Small staffs		Large staffs
Few subcommittees		Many subcommittees
	Interest Groups	
A few large blocs (farmers, business, labor)		Many diverse interests that form ad hoc coalitions
Rely on "insider" lobbying		Mobilize grassroots
	Presidency	
Small staff		Large staff
Reaches public via press conferences		Reaches public via radio and television
	Courts	
Allow government to exercise few economic powers		Allow government to exercise broad economic power
Take narrow view of individual freedoms		Take broad view of individual freedoms
	Political Parties	
Dominated by state and local party leaders meeting in conventions		Dominated by activists chosen in primaries and caucuses
	Policy Agenda	
Brief		Long
	Key Question	
Should the federal government enter a new policy area?		How can we fix and pay for an existing policy?
	Key Issue	
Would a new federal program abridge states' rights?		Would a new federal program prove popular?

mind and others retired from the bench; by the late 1930s, the Court had virtually ceased opposing any economic legislation.

The second period was in the mid-1960s, a time of prosperity. There was no crisis akin to the Great Depression or World War II, but two events helped change the face of American politics. One was an intellectual and popular ferment that we now refer to as the spirit of "the sixties"—a militant civil rights movement, student activism on college campuses aimed at resisting the Vietnam War, growing concern about threats to the environment, the popular

appeal of Ralph Nader and his consumer-protection movement, and an optimism among many political and intellectual leaders that the government could solve whatever problems it was willing to address. The other was the 1964 election that returned Lyndon Johnson to the presidency with a larger share of the popular vote than any other president in modern times. Johnson swept into office and with him, liberal Democratic majorities in both the House and Senate.

The combination of organized demands for new policies, elite optimism about the likely success of those

Auto manufacturers were particularly hard hit by the recent economic downturn, prompting government bailouts for both General Motors and Chrysler.

policies, and extraordinary majorities in Congress meant that President Johnson was able, for a few years, to get almost any program he wanted enacted into law. So large were his majorities in Congress that the conservative coalition of Republicans and southern Democrats was no longer large enough to block action; northern Democratic liberals were sufficiently numerous in the House and Senate to take control of both bodies. And so, much of Johnson's "Great Society" legislation became law. This included the passage of Medicare (to help pay the medical bills of retired people) and Medicaid (to help pay the medical bills of people on welfare), greatly expanded federal aid to the states (to assist them in fighting crime, rebuilding slums, and running transit systems), the enactment of major civil rights laws and of a program to provide federal aid to local schools, the creation of a "War on Poverty" that included various job-training and community-action agencies, and the enactment of a variety of laws regulating business for the purpose of reducing auto fatalities, improving the safety and health of industrial workers, cutting back on pollutants entering the atmosphere, and safeguarding consumers from harmful products.

These two periods—the early 1930s and the mid-1960s—changed the political landscape in America. Of the two, the latter was perhaps the more important, for not only did it witness the passage of so much unprecedented legislation, but also it saw major changes in the pattern of political leadership. It was during this time that the great majority of

the members of the House of Representatives came to enjoy relatively secure seats, the primary elections came to supplant party conventions as the decisive means of selecting presidential candidates, interest groups increased greatly in number, and television began to play an important role in shaping the political agenda and perhaps influencing the kinds of candidates nominated.

Consequences of Activist Government

One way of describing the New System is to call it an "activist" government. It is tempting to make a sweeping judgment about such a government, either praising it because it serves a variety of popular needs or condemning it because it is a bureaucratic affliction. Such generalizations are not entirely empty, but neither are they very helpful. The worth of any given program, or of any collection of programs, can be assessed only by a careful consideration of its costs and benefits, of its effects and side effects. But we may discover some general political consequences of the enlarged scope of government activity.

First, as the government gets bigger, its members must spend more time managing the consequences—intended and unintended—of existing programs and less time debating at length new ideas. As a result, all parts of the government, not just the executive agencies, become more bureaucratized. The White House Office and the Office of Management and Budget (OMB) grow in size and influence, as do the staffs of Congress. At the same time, private organizations (corporations, unions, universities) that deal with the government must also become more bureaucratic. The government hires more people when it is running 80 programs concerned with employment than when it is running two. By the same token, a private employer will hire (and give power to) more people when it is complying with 80 sets of regulations than when it is complying with two.

Second, the more government does, the more it will appear to be acting in inconsistent, uncoordinated, and cumbersome ways. When people complain of red tape, bureaucracy, stalemates, and confusion, they often assume these irritants are caused by incompetent or self-seeking public officials. There is incompetence and self-interest in government just as in every other part of society, but these character traits are not the chief cause of the problem. As citizens, we want many different and often conflicting things. The result is the rise of competing policies, the division of labor among separate administrative agencies, the diffusion of accountability and control, and the multiplication of paperwork. And because Americans are especially energetic about asserting their rights, we must add to the above list of problems the regular use of the courts to challenge policies that we do not like.

Third, an activist government is less susceptible to control by electoral activity than a passive one. When the people in Washington did little, elections made a larger difference in policy than when they began to do a lot. We have pointed out in this book the extent to which both political parties and voter turnout have declined. There are many reasons for this, but an important one often is forgotten. If elections make less of a difference—because the few people for whom one votes can do little to alter the ongoing programs of government—then it may make sense for people to spend less time on party or electoral activities and more on interest group activities aimed at specific agencies and programs.

The rapid increase in the number and variety of interest groups and their enlarged role in government are not pathological. They are a rational response to the fact that elected officials can tend to only a few things, and therefore we must direct our energies at the appointed officials (and judges) who tend to all other government matters. Every president tries to accomplish more, usually by trying to reorganize the executive branch. But no president and no reorganization plan can affect more than a tiny fraction of the millions of federal employees and thousands of government programs. "Coordination" from the top can at best occur selectively, for a few issues of exceptional importance.

Ronald Reagan learned this when he took office in 1981 after promising to reduce the size of government. He did persuade Congress to cut taxes, but his plans to cut domestic spending resulted in only small declines in some programs and actual increases in many others. Though some programs, such as public housing, were hard hit, most were not, and agricultural subsidies increased dramatically.

When George W. Bush became president in 2001, his philosophy was summarized by the phrase "compassionate conservatism," words that implied that, though he was a conservative, he was not much interested in simply cutting the size of the federal government. And while in office, he

proposed programs that would increase spending on many programs. His actions suggest a fact; cutting down on what Washington does is virtually impossible because the people want so much of what it does.

Finally, the more government tries to do, the more things it will be held responsible for and the greater the risk of failure. From time to time in the 19th century, the business cycle made many people unhappy with the federal government—recall the rise of various protest parties—though then the government did very little. If federal officials were lucky, popular support would rise as soon as economic conditions improved. If they were unlucky and a depression lasted into the election campaign, they would be thrown out of office. Today, however, the government—and the president in particular—is held responsible for crime, drug abuse, abortion, civil rights, the environment, the elderly, the status of women, the decay of central cities, the price of gasoline, and international tensions in half a dozen places on the globe.

No government and no president can do well on all or even most of these matters most of the time. Indeed, most of these problems, such as crime, may be totally beyond the reach of the federal government, no matter what its policy. It should not be surprising, therefore, that opinion surveys taken since the early 1960s have shown a steep decline in public confidence in government. There is no reason to believe that this represents a loss of faith in our form of government or even in the design of its institutions, but it clearly reflects a disappointment in, and even cynicism about, the performance of government.

It is too soon to know how, if at all, public sentiments about the performance of government will change as Washington (in response to the 2008–2009 economic crisis) expansioned government activity faster than it has grown in any periods since the late 1930s and the mid-1960s. In 2009, President Barack Obama proposed a budget for Fiscal Year 2010 that totaled $3.55 trillion and contemplated a deficit of $1.17 trillion. The large spending increases, however, are only half the story. The other half concerns the federal government taking on new responsibilities and challenges: It became the majority stockholder in what was once the world's largest automotive company, General Motors; it has more closely, controlled dozens of other companies and diverse financial markets; and it has proposed a large new government-regulated health care system.

WHAT WOULD YOU DO?

MEMORANDUM

To: *President Daniel Gilbert*

From: *Fowler Brown, legislative liaison*

Subject: *Replacing Social Security*

You face a difficult decision. Despite past reforms, the program can no longer be funded without large tax increases. Here are the arguments for and against allowing workers to invest their taxes in private mutual funds.

Arguments for:

1. Workers pay 15 percent of their salary to Social Security, with no guarantee that they will get their money back when they retire.

2. There are only two workers for every retired person (in the 1930s, there were 16 for every retiree). People must be encouraged to invest in their own retirement.

3. The federal government spends a quarter of its budget on Social Security, far more than it devotes to national defense.

Arguments against:

1. Workers will have no guarantee that the mutual funds in which they put their tax money will earn them enough.

2. We should raise taxes on all high-income workers to save Social Security.

3. Social Security is more important than national defense.

Policies for the Future

January 2021
WASHINGTON, D.C.

The President will make a major announcement about Social Security in his 2021 State of the Union message next week. The program, while popular, is running out of memory...

Your decision:

Approve _____   Oppose_____

Paul Brennan/shutterstock.com

The 2009 stimulus bill allowed people to get money if they traded in an old car that burned a lot of gas.

University of Maryland political scientist Donald F. Kettl has argued that the "financial meltdown accelerated our expectations that government will keep us safe. . . . We've gone from debates over privatizing the public sector to big steps toward governmentalizing the private sector."[1] The far-reaching changes include "more public money in the private economy, more rules to shape how the private sector behaves, and more citizen expectations that government will manage the risks we face."[2]

We cannot yet say whether multi-trillion-dollar budget deficits and policies that betoken government-guaranteed corporate capitalism will persist for years to come. But it seems a fair bet that the New System is entering a new era which, not unlike the expansion that began in the late 1930s, has been fueled by economic problems that afflicted or threatened most Americans.

It also seems likely that, if anything, public disenchantment with government performance will continue to grow along with government's role in people's lives. Such disenchantment is hardly unique to the United States; it appears to be a feature of almost every democratic political system. The disenchantment is in fact probably greater elsewhere. Americans who complain of high taxes might feel somewhat differently if they lived in Sweden, where taxes are nearly twice as high as here. Those who grouse about bureaucrats in this country probably have never dealt with the massive, centralized bureaucracies of Italy or France. People who are annoyed by congestion, pollution, and inflation ought to arrange a trip to Beijing, Mexico City, or Tokyo.

However frustrating private life and public affairs may be in this country, every year thousands living in other nations become immigrants to this country. Few Americans choose to emigrate to other places.

The enormous expansion of the scope and goals of the federal government has not been random or unguided. The government has tended to enlarge its powers more in some directions than in others; certain kinds of goals have been served more frequently than others. Though many factors shape this process of selection, two are of special importance. One is our constitutional structure, the other our political culture.

The Influence of Structure

To see the influence of structure, it is necessary to perform a mental experiment. Suppose the Founders had adopted a centralized, parliamentary regime instead of a decentralized, congressional one. They had the British model right before their eyes. Every other European democracy adopted it. What difference would it have made had we followed the British example?

No one can be certain, of course, because the United States and Great Britain differ in many ways, and not just in their political forms. At best, our mental experiment will be an educated guess. But the following possibilities seem plausible.

A parliamentary regime of the British sort centralizes power in the hands of an elected prime minister with a disciplined partisan majority in the legislature and frees him or her from most of the constraints created by independent congressional committees or independent, activist courts. Had the Framers adopted a parliamentary system, we might see these features in the political life of the United States today:

- *Quicker adoption of majoritarian policies, such as those in the area of social welfare.* Broad popular desires would be translated sooner into national policy when they are highly salient and conform to the views of party leaders.

- *More centralization of bureaucratic authority—more national planning, less local autonomy.* More decisions would be made bureaucratically, both because bureaucracies would be proportionately larger and because they would have wider discretionary authority delegated to them. (If the prime minister heads *both* the executive branch and the legislature, he or she sees no reason why decisions cannot be made as easily in one place as the other.) Local authorities would not have been able to prevent groups of citizens (such as African Americans) from voting or otherwise participating in public life by maintaining segregated facilities at the local level.

- *Fewer opportunities for citizens to challenge or block government policies of which they disapprove.* Without independent and activist courts, without local centers (state and city) of autonomous power, U.S. citizens would have less of a chance to organize to stop a highway or an urban-renewal project, for example, and hence fewer citizen organizations with these and similar purposes would exist.

- *Greater executive control of government.* If a situation like Watergate occurred, we would never know about it. No legislative investigating committees would be sufficiently independent of executive control to be able to investigate claims of executive wrongdoing.

- *Similar foreign policy.* We probably would have fought in about the same number of wars and under pretty much the same circumstances.

- *Higher and more centralized taxation.* Taxes would be higher, and a larger share of our tax money would be collected at the national level. Thus we would find it harder to wage a "tax revolt" (since it is easier to block local spending decisions than national ones).

If this list of guesses is even approximately correct, it means that you would get more of some things that you want and less of others. In general, it would have been easier for temporary majorities to govern and harder for individuals and groups to protect their interests.

The Founders would probably not be surprised at this list of differences. Though they could not have foreseen all the events and issues that would have led to these outcomes, they would have understood them, because they thought they were creating a system designed to keep central power weak and to enhance local and citizen power. They would have been amazed, of course, at the extent to which central power has been enhanced and local power weakened in the United States, but if they visited Europe, they would learn that by comparison American politics remains far more sensitive to local concerns than does politics abroad.

The Influence of Ideas

The broadly shared political culture of Americans has also influenced the policies adopted by the U.S. government. Paramount among these attitudes is

the preoccupation with rights. More than the citizens of perhaps any other nation, Americans define their relations with one another and with political authority in terms of rights. The civil liberties protected by the Bill of Rights have been assiduously defended and their interpretation significantly broadened even while the power of government has been growing.

For example, we expect the groups affected by any government program will have a right to play a role in shaping and administering that program. In consequence, interest groups have proliferated. We think citizens should have the right to select the nominees of political parties as well as to choose between the parties; hence primary elections have largely replaced party conventions in selecting candidates. Individual members of Congress assert their rights, and thus the power of congressional leaders and committee chairmen has steadily diminished. We probably use the courts more frequently than the citizens of any other nation to make or change public policy; in doing so, we are asserting one set of rights against a competing set. The procedural

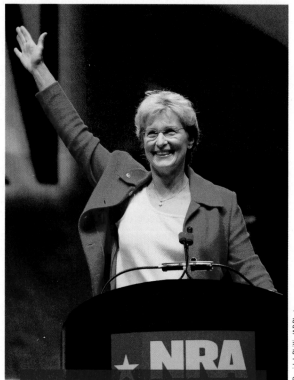

Not only do interest groups promote government policies, such policies stimulate interest groups. The National Rifle Association had little interest in federal regulations until gun control became a big issue.

David J. Phillip/AP Photo

rules that set forth how government is to act—the Freedom of Information Act, the Privacy Act, the Administrative Procedure Act—are more complex and demanding than the rules under which any other democratic government must operate. Each rule exists because it embodies what somebody has claimed to be a right: the right to know information, to maintain one's privacy, to participate in making decisions, and to bring suit against rival parties.

The more vigorously we assert our rights, the harder it is to make government decisions or to manage large institutions. We recognize this when we grumble about red tape and bureaucratic confusion, but we rarely give much support to proposals to centralize authority or simplify decision-making. We seem to accept whatever it costs in efficiency or effectiveness in order to maintain the capacity for asserting our rights.

We do not always agree on which rights are most important, however. In addition to the influence of the widely shared commitment to rights generally, government is also shaped by the views that certain political elites have about which rights ought to be given the highest priority. Elite opinion tends to favor freedom of expression over freedom to manage or dispose of property. Mass opinion, though it has changed a good deal in the last few decades, is less committed to the preferred position of freedom of expression. Rank-and-file citizens often complain that what the elite calls essential liberty should instead be regarded as excessive permissiveness. People who own or manage property often lament the extent to which the rights governing its use have declined.

The changes in the relative security of personal and property freedom are linked to a fundamental and enduring tension in American thought.

Tocqueville said it best: Americans, he wrote, "are far more ardently and tenaciously attached to equality than to freedom." Though democratic communities have a "natural taste for freedom," that freedom is hard to preserve, because its excesses are immediate and obvious and its advantages are remote and uncertain. The advantages of equality, on the other hand, are readily apparent, and its costs are obscure and deferred.[3] For example, Americans believe in free speech, but most of us rarely take advantage of that right and notice the problem only when somebody says something we don't like. We have to remind ourselves that freedom has to be

The "Rules" of Politics

Some "Rules" of Politics

Here are some generalizations about American politics, distilled from what has been said in this book, and offered in nervous awareness that our political system has a way of proving everybody wrong. (Before the 1960s, it was a "rule" of politics that no Catholic could be elected president. John F. Kennedy took care of that.)

- Policies, once adopted, tend to persist whatever their value. (It is easier to start new programs than to end old ones.)

- Almost all electoral politics is local politics. (Members of Congress who forget "home base" tend not to remain in Congress for long.)

- Whatever the size of their staff and budget, Congress and the White House will always be overworked. (More resources produce more work, which requires more resources.)

- Each branch of government tends to emulate the others. (Congress will become more bureaucratized to cope with an executive branch that becomes more bureaucratized; judges will become more activist as Congress becomes more activist.)

- Proposals that seem to confer widespread and immediate benefits will be enacted whatever their long-term costs.

- Proposals that seem to confer delayed benefits will be enacted only if their costs are unknown, concealed, or deferred.

- Nobody—business people, bureaucrats, members of Congress, judges, professors—likes competition, and everybody will do whatever he or she can to reduce or eliminate it.

- "Planning" in government takes place after a crisis takes place.

- The mass media never cover a story about things that are going well. Thus the number of "problems" in society is a function of the number of reporters.

- If you want something, you are claiming a right; if your opponent wants something, he or she is protecting a vested interest.

protected even when it does not help us directly. By contrast, we notice equality immediately, as when everybody of a certain age gets Social Security even when they are already rich. Equality makes us feel comfortable even if a few people don't need the benefits they are getting.

Tocqueville may have underestimated the extent to which political liberties would endure, because he did not foresee the determination of the courts to resist, in the long run if not the short, the passions of temporary majorities seeking to curtail such liberties. But he did not underestimate the extent to which in the economic and social realms Americans would decide that improving the conditions of life would justify restrictions on the right to dispose of property and to manage private institutions. At first, the conflict was between liberty and equality of opportunity; more recently it has become a conflict—among political elites if not within the citizenry itself—between equality of opportunity and equality of results.

The fact that decisions can be influenced by opinions about rights indicates that decisions can be influenced by opinions generally. As the political system has become more fragmented and more individualized as a result of our collective assertion of rights, it has come more under the sway of ideas. When political parties were strong and congressional leadership was centralized (as in the latter part of the 19th and the early part of the 20th centuries), gaining access to the decision-making process in Washington was difficult, and the number of new ideas that stood a chance of adoption was small. However, those proposals that could command leadership support were more easily adopted: though there were powerful organizations that could say no, those same organizations could also say yes.

Today, these and other institutions are fragmented and in disarray. Individual members of Congress are far more important than congressional leaders. Political parties no longer control nominations for office. The media have given candidates direct access to the voters; campaign finance laws have restricted, but not eliminated, the influence that interest groups can wield by spending money. Forming new, issue-oriented lobbying groups is much easier today than formerly, thanks to the capability of computers and direct-mail advertising.

These idea-based changes in institutions affect how policy is made. When there is widespread enthusiasm for an idea—especially among political elites but also in the public at large—new programs can be formulated and adopted with great speed. This happened when Lyndon Johnson's Great Society legislation was proposed, when the environmental and consumer protection laws first arrived on the public agenda, and when campaign finance reform was proposed in the wake of Watergate. So long as such symbols have a powerful appeal, so long as a consensus persists, change is possible. But when these ideas lose their appeal—or are challenged by new ideas—the competing pressures make change extremely difficult. Environmentalism today is challenged by concerns about creating jobs and economic growth; social legislation is challenged by skepticism about its effectiveness and concern over its cost; campaign finance reforms are, to some critics, merely devices for protecting incumbents.

This may all seem obvious to a reader raised in the world of contemporary politics. But it is different in degree if not in kind from the way in which politics was once carried out. In the 1920s, the 1930s, the 1940s, and even the 1950s, people described politics as a process of bargaining among organized interests, or "blocs," representing business, farming, labor, ethnic, and professional groups. With the expansion of the scope of government policy, there are no longer a few major blocs that sit astride the policy process. Instead, thousands of highly specialized interests and constituencies seek above all to protect whatever benefits, intangible as well as tangible, they get from government.

We have a large government—and large expectations about what it can achieve. But the government finds it increasingly difficult to satisfy those expectations. The public's acceptance of an activist role for government has been accompanied by a decline in public confidence in those who manage that government. We expect more and more from government but are less and less certain that we will get it, or get it in a form and at a cost that we find acceptable. This perhaps constitutes the greatest challenge to statesmanship in the years ahead: to find a way to serve the true interests of the people while restoring and retaining their confidence in the legitimacy of government itself.

Appendixes

The Declaration of Independence

In Congress, July 4, 1776

The Unanimous Declaration of the Thirteen United States of America

When, in the course of human events, it becomes necessary for one people to dissolve the political bands which have connected them with another, and to assume, among the powers of the earth, the separate and equal station to which the laws of nature and of nature's God entitle them, a decent respect to the opinions of mankind requires that they should declare the causes which impel them to the separation.

We hold these truths to be self-evident: That all men are created equal; that they are endowed by their Creator with certain unalienable rights; that among these are life, liberty, and the pursuit of happiness; that, to secure these rights, governments are instituted among men, deriving their just powers from the consent of the governed; that whenever any form of government becomes destructive of these ends, it is the right of the people to alter or to abolish it, and to institute new government, laying its foundation on such principles, and organizing its power in such form, as to them shall seem most likely to effect their safety and happiness. Prudence, indeed, will dictate that governments long established should not be changed for light and transient causes; and accordingly all experience hath shown that mankind are more disposed to suffer, while evils are sufferable, than to right themselves by abolishing the forms to which they are accustomed. But when a long train of abuses and usurpations, pursuing invariably the same object, evinces a design to reduce them under absolute despotism, it is their right, it is their duty, to throw off such government, and to provide new guards for their future security. Such has been the patient sufferance of these colonies; and such is now the necessity which constrains them to alter their former systems of government. The history of the present King of Great Britain is a history of repeated injuries and usurpations, all having in direct object the establishment of an absolute tyranny over these states. To prove this, let facts be submitted to a candid world.

He has refused to assent to laws, the most wholesome and necessary for the public good.

He has forbidden his governors to pass laws of immediate and pressing importance, unless suspended in their operation till his assent should be obtained; and, when so suspended, he has utterly neglected to attend to them.

He has refused to pass other laws for the accommodation of large districts of people, unless those people would relinquish the right of representation in the legislature, a right inestimable to them, and formidable to tyrants only.

He has called together legislative bodies at places unusual, uncomfortable, and distant from the depository of their public records, for the sole purpose of fatiguing them into compliance with his measures.

He has dissolved representative houses repeatedly, for opposing, with manly firmness, his invasions on the rights of the people.

He has refused for a long time, after such dissolutions, to cause others to be elected; whereby the legislative powers, incapable of annihilation, have returned to the people at large for their exercise; the state remaining, in the mean time, exposed to all dangers of invasions from without and convulsions within.

He has endeavored to prevent the population of these states; for that purpose obstructing the laws for naturalization of foreigners; refusing to pass others to encourage their migration hither, and raising the conditions of new appropriations of lands.

He has obstructed the administration of justice, by refusing his assent to laws for establishing judiciary powers.

He has made judges dependent on his will alone, for the tenure of their offices, and the amount and payment of their salaries.

He has erected a multitude of new offices, and sent hither swarms of officers to harass our people, and eat out their substance.

He has kept among us, in times of peace, standing armies, without the consent of our legislatures.

He has affected to render the military independent of, and superior to, the civil power.

He has combined with others to subject us to a jurisdiction foreign to our constitution, and unacknowledged by our laws, giving his assent to their acts of pretended legislation:

For quartering large bodies of armed troops among us:

For protecting them, by a mock trial, from punishment for any murders which they should commit on the inhabitants of these states;

For cutting off our trade with all parts of the world;

For imposing taxes on us without our consent;

For depriving us, in many cases, of the benefits of trial by jury;

For transporting us beyond seas, to be tried for pretended offenses;

For abolishing the free system of English laws in a neighboring province, establishing therein an arbitrary government, and enlarging its boundaries, so as to render it at once an example and fit instrument for introducing the same absolute rule into these colonies;

For taking away our charters, abolishing our most valuable laws, and altering fundamentally the forms of our governments;

For suspending our own legislatures, and declaring themselves invested with power to legislate for us in all cases whatsoever.

He has abdicated government here, by declaring us out of his protection and waging war against us.

He has plundered our seas, ravaged our coasts, burned our towns, and destroyed the lives of our people.

He is at this time transporting large armies of foreign mercenaries to complete the works of death, desolation, and tyranny already begun with circumstances of cruelty and perfidy scarcely paralleled in the most barbarous ages, and totally unworthy the head of a civilized nation.

He has constrained our fellow-citizens, taken captive on the high seas, to bear arms against their country, to become the executioners of their friends and brethren, or to fall themselves by their hands.

He has excited domestic insurrection among us, and has endeavored to bring on the inhabitants of our frontiers the merciless Indian savages, whose known rule of warfare is an undistinguished destruction of all ages, sexes, and conditions.

In every stage of these oppressions we have petitioned for redress in the most humble terms; our repeated petitions have been answered only by repeated injury. A prince, whose character is thus marked by every act which may define a tyrant, is unfit to be the ruler of a free people.

Nor have we been wanting in our attentions to our British brethren. We have warned them, from time to time, of attempts by their Legislature to extend an unwarrantable jurisdiction over us. We have reminded them of the circumstances of our emigration and settlement here. We have appealed to their native justice and magnanimity; and we have conjured them, by the ties of our common kindred, to disavow these usurpations, which would inevitably interrupt our connections and correspondence. They, too, have been deaf to the voice of justice and of consanguinity. We must, therefore, acquiesce in the necessity which denounces our separation, and hold them, as we hold the rest of mankind, enemies in war, in peace friends.

We, therefore, the representatives of the United States of America, in General Congress assembled, appealing to the Supreme Judge of the world for the rectitude of our intentions, do, in the name and by the authority of the good people of these colonies, solemnly publish and declare, that these United Colonies are, and of right ought to be, FREE AND INDEPENDENT STATES; that they are absolved from all allegiance to the British crown, and that all political connection between them and the state of Great Britain is, and ought to be, totally dissolved; and that, as free and independent states, they have full power to levy war, conclude peace, contract alliances, establish commerce, and do all other acts and things which independent states may of right do. And for the support of this declaration, with a firm reliance on the protection of Divine Providence, we mutually pledge to each other our lives, our fortunes, and our sacred honor.

JOHN HANCOCK [*President*]
[*and fifty-five others*]

The Constitution of the United States

Preamble

We the People of the United States, in Order to form a more perfect Union, establish Justice, insure domestic Tranquility, provide for the common defence, promote the general Welfare, and secure the Blessings of Liberty to ourselves and our Posterity, do ordain and establish this Constitution for the United States of America.

Article I.

Bicameral Congress

Section 1. All legislative Powers herein granted shall be vested in a Congress of the United States, which shall consist of a Senate and House of Representatives.

Membership of the House

Section 2. The House of Representatives shall be composed of Members chosen every second Year by the People of the several States, and the Electors in each State shall have the Qualifications requisite for Electors of the most numerous Branch of the State Legislature.

No person shall be a Representative who shall not have attained to the age of twenty five Years, and been seven Years a Citizen of the United States, and who shall not, when elected, be an Inhabitant of that State in which he shall be chosen.

Representatives and direct Taxes shall be apportioned among the several States which may be included within this Union, according to their respective Numbers, which shall be determined by adding to the whole Number of free Persons, including those bound to Service for a Term of Years, and excluding Indians not taxed, three fifths of all other Persons.[1] The actual Enumeration shall be made within three Years after the first Meeting of the Congress of the United States, and within every subsequent Term of ten Years, in such Manner as they shall by Law direct. The Number of Representatives shall not exceed one for every thirty Thousand, but each State shall have at Least one Representative; and until such enumeration shall be made, the State of New Hampshire shall be entitled to chuse three, Massachusetts eight, Rhode-Island and Providence Plantations one, Connecticut five, New-York six, New Jersey four, Pennsylvania eight, Delaware one, Maryland six, Virginia ten, North Carolina five, South Carolina five, and Georgia three.

When vacancies happen in the Representation from any State, the Executive Authority thereof shall issue Writs of Election to fill such Vacancies.

Power to impeach

The House of Representatives shall chuse their Speaker and other Officers; and shall have the sole Power of Impeachment.

Membership of the Senate

Section 3. The Senate of the United States shall be composed of two Senators from each State, *chosen by the Legislature thereof*,[2] for six Years; and each Senator shall have one Vote.

Immediately after they shall be assembled in Consequence of the first Election, they shall be divided as equally as may be into three Classes. The Seats of the Senators of the first class shall be vacated at

---

NOTE: The topical headings are not part of the original Constitution. Excluding the Preamble and Closing, those portions set in italic type have been superseded or changed by later amendments.
1. Changed by the Fourteenth Amendment, section 2.
2. Changed by the Seventeenth Amendment.

the Expiration of the second Year, of the second Class at the Expiration of the fourth Year, and of the third Class at the Expiration of the sixth Year, so that one third may be chosen every second Year; *and if Vacancies happen by Resignation, or otherwise, during the Recess of the Legislature of any State, the Executive thereof may make temporary Appointments until the next Meeting of the Legislature, which shall then fill such Vacancies.*[3]

No Person shall be a Senator who shall not have attained to the Age of thirty Years, and been nine Years a Citizen of the United States, and who shall not, when elected, be an Inhabitant of that State for which he shall be chosen.

The Vice President of the United States shall be President of the Senate, but shall have no Vote, unless they be equally divided.

Power to try impeachments

The Senate shall chuse their other Officers, and also a President pro tempore, in the Absence of the Vice President, or when he shall exercise the Office of President of the United States.

The Senate shall have the sole Power to try all Impeachments. When sitting for that Purpose, they shall be on Oath or Affirmation. When the President of the United States is tried the Chief Justice shall preside: And no Person shall be convicted without the Concurrence of two thirds of the Members present.

Judgment in Cases of Impeachment shall not extend further than to removal from Office, and disqualification to hold and enjoy any Office of honor, Trust or Profit under the United States: but the Party convicted shall nevertheless be liable and subject to Indictment, Trial, Judgment and Punishment, according to Law.

Laws governing elections

Section 4. The Times, Places and Manner of holding Elections for Senators and Representatives, shall be prescribed in each State by the Legislature thereof; but the Congress may at any time by Law make or alter such Regulations, except as to the Places of chusing Senators.

The Congress shall assemble at least once in every Year, and such Meeting shall be on the *first Monday in December, unless they shall by Law appoint a different Day.*[4]

Rules of Congress

Section 5. Each House shall be the Judge of the Elections, Returns and Qualifications of its own Members, and a Majority of each shall constitute a Quorum to do Business; but a smaller number may adjourn from day to day, and may be authorized to compel the Attendance of absent Members, in such Manner, and under such Penalties as each House may provide.

Each House may determine the Rules of its Proceedings, punish its Members for disorderly Behaviour, and, with the Concurrence of two thirds, expel a Member.

Each House shall keep a Journal of its Proceedings, and from time to time publish the same, excepting such Parts as may in their Judgment require Secrecy; and the Yeas and Nays of the Members of either House on any question shall, at the Desire of one fifth of those Present, be entered on the Journal.

Neither House, during the Session of Congress, shall, without the Consent of the other, adjourn for more than three days, nor to any other Place than that in which the two Houses shall be sitting.

---

3. *Changed by the Seventeenth Amendment.*
4. *Changed by the Twentieth Amendment, section 2.*

Salaries and immunities of members

Section 6. The Senators and Representatives shall receive a Compensation for their Services, to be ascertained by Law, and paid out of the Treasury of the United States. They shall in all Cases, except Treason, Felony and Breach of the Peace, be privileged from Arrest during their Attendance at the Session of their respective Houses, and in going to and returning from the same; and for any Speech or Debate in either House, they shall not be questioned in any other Place.

Bar on members of Congress holding federal appointive office

No Senator or Representative shall, during the Time for which he was elected, be appointed to any civil Office under the Authority of the United States, which shall have been created, or the Emoluments whereof shall have been encreased during such time; and no Person holding any Office under the United States, shall be a Member of either House during his Continuance in Office.

Money bills originate in House

Section 7. All Bills for raising Revenue shall originate in the House of Representatives; but the Senate may propose or concur with Amendments as on other Bills.

Procedure for enacting laws; veto power

Every Bill which shall have passed the House of Representatives and the Senate, shall, before it become a Law, be presented to the President of the United States; If he approve he shall sign it, but if not he shall return it, with Objections to that House in which it shall have originated, who shall enter the Objections at large on their Journal, and proceed to reconsider it. If after such Reconsideration two thirds of that House shall agree to pass the Bill, it shall be sent, together with the Objections, to the other House, by which it shall likewise be reconsidered, and if approved by two thirds of that House, it shall become a Law. But in all such Cases the Votes of both Houses shall be determined by yeas and Nays, and the Names of the Persons voting for and against the Bill shall be entered on the Journal of each House respectively. If any Bill shall not be returned by the President within ten Days (Sundays excepted) after it shall have been presented to him, the Same shall be a Law, in like Manner, as if he had signed it, unless the Congress by their Adjournment prevent its Return, in which Case it shall not be a Law.

Every Order, Resolution, or Vote to which the Concurrence of the Senate and House of Representatives may be necessary (except on a question of Adjournment) shall be presented to the President of the United States; and before the Same shall take Effect, shall be approved by him, or being disapproved by him, shall be repassed by two thirds of the Senate and House of Representatives, according to the Rules and Limitations prescribed in the Case of a Bill.

Powers of Congress
—taxes

Section 8. The Congress shall have Power To lay and Collect Taxes, Duties, Imposts and Excises, to pay the Debts and provide for the common Defence and general Welfare of the United States; but all Duties, Imposts and Excises shall be uniform throughout the United States.

—borrowing

To borrow Money on the credit of the United States;

—regulation of commerce

To regulate Commerce with foreign Nations, and among the several States, and with the Indian Tribes;

—naturalization and bankruptcy

To establish an uniform Rule of Naturalization, and uniform Laws on the subject of Bankruptcies throughout the United States;

—money

To coin Money, regulate the Value thereof, and of foreign Coin, and fix the Standard of Weights and Measures;

—counterfeiting

To provide for the Punishment of counterfeiting the Securities and current Coin of the United States;

—post office
—patents and copyrights

To establish Post Offices and post Roads;

To promote the Progress of Science and useful Arts, by securing for limited Times to Authors and Inventors the exclusive Right to their respective Writings and Discoveries;

—create courts
—punish piracies

To constitute Tribunals inferior to the Supreme Court;

To define and punish Piracies and Felonies committed on the high Seas, and Offences against the Law of Nations;

—declare war

To declare War, grant Letters of Marque and Reprisal, and make Rules concerning Captures on Land and Water;

—create army and navy

To raise and support Armies, but no Appropriation of Money to that Use shall be for a longer Term than two Years;

To provide and maintain a Navy;

To make Rules for the Government and Regulation of the land and naval Forces;

—call the militia

To provide for calling forth the Militia to execute the Laws of the Union, suppress Insurrections and repel Invasions;

To provide for organizing, arming, and disciplining, the Militia, and for governing such Part of them as may be employed in the Service of the United States, reserving to the States respectively, the Appointment of the Officers, and the Authority of training the Militia according to the discipline prescribed by Congress;

—govern District of Columbia

To exercise exclusive Legislation in all Cases whatsoever, over such District (not exceeding ten Miles square) as may, by Cession of Particular States, and the Acceptance of Congress, become the Seat of the Government of the United States, and to exercise like Authority over all Places purchased by the Consent of the Legislature of the State in which the Same shall be, for the Erection of Forts, Magazines, Arsenals, dock-Yards and other needful Buildings;—And

—"necessary-and-proper" clause

To make all Laws which shall be necessary and proper for carrying into Execution the foregoing Powers, and all other Powers vested by this Constitution in the Government of the United States, or in any Department or Officer thereof.

Restrictions on powers of Congress
—slave trade

Section 9. The Migration or Importation of such Persons as any of the States now existing shall think proper to admit, shall not be prohibited by the Congress prior to the Year one thousand eight hundred and eight, but a Tax or duty may be imposed on such Importation, not exceeding ten dollars for each Person.

—habeas corpus

The Privilege of the Writ of Habeas Corpus shall not be suspended, unless when in Cases of Rebellion or Invasion the public Safety may require it.

—no bill of attainder or ex post facto law

No bill of Attainder or ex post facto Law shall be passed.

No Capitation, or other direct, Tax shall be laid, *unless in Proportion to the Census or Enumeration herein before directed to be taken.*[5]

—no interstate tariffs
—no preferential treatment for some states

No Tax or Duty shall be laid on Articles exported from any State.

No Preference shall be given by any Regulation of Commerce or Revenue to the Ports of one State over those of another; nor shall Vessels bound to, or from, one State, be obliged to enter, clear or pay Duties in another.

—appropriations

No Money shall be drawn from the Treasury, but in Consequence of Appropriations made by Law; and a regular Statement and Account of the Receipts and Expenditures of all public Money shall be published from time to time.

---

5. Changed by the Sixteenth Amendment.

—*no titles of nobility*

No Title of Nobility shall be granted by the United States: And no Person holding any Office of Profit or Trust under them, shall, without the Consent of the Congress, accept of any present, Emolument, Office, or Title, of any kind whatever, from any King, Prince, or foreign State.

Restrictions on powers of states

Section 10. No State shall enter into any Treaty, Alliance, or Confederation; grant Letters of Marque and Reprisal; coin Money; emit Bills of Credit; make any Thing but gold and silver Coin a Tender in Payment of Debts; pass any Bill of Attainder, ex post facto Law, or Law impairing the Obligation of Contracts, or grant any Title of Nobility.

No State shall, without the Consent of Congress, lay any Imposts or Duties on Imports or Exports, except what may be absolutely necessary for executing its inspection Laws; and the net Produce of all Duties and Imposts, laid by any State on Imports or Exports, shall be for the Use of the Treasury of the United States; and all such Laws shall be subject to the Revision and Controul of the Congress.

No State shall, without the Consent of Congress, lay any Duty of Tonnage, keep Troops, or Ships of War in time of Peace, enter into any Agreement or Compact with another State, or with a foreign Power, or engage in War, unless actually invaded, or in such imminent Danger as will not admit of delay.

Article II.

Office of president

Section 1. The executive Power shall be vested in a President of the United States of America. He shall hold his Office during the Term of four Years, and, together with the Vice President, chosen for the same Term, be elected, as follows:

Election of president

Each State shall appoint, in such Manner as the Legislature thereof may direct, a Number of Electors, equal to the whole Number of Senators and Representatives to which the State may be entitled in the Congress: but no Senator or Representative, or Person holding an Office of Trust or Profit under the United States, shall be appointed an Elector.

The Electors shall meet in their respective States, and vote by Ballot for two Persons, of whom one at least shall not be an Inhabitant of the same State with themselves. And they shall make a List of all the Persons voted for, and of the Number of Votes for each; which List they shall sign and certify, and transmit sealed to the Seat of the Government of the United States, directed to the President of the Senate. The President of the Senate shall, in the Presence of the Senate and House of Representatives, open all the Certificates, and the Votes shall then be counted. The Person having the greatest Number of Votes shall be the President, if such Number be a Majority of the whole Number of Electors appointed; and if there be more than one who have such Majority, and have an equal Number of Votes, then the House of Representatives shall immediately chuse by Ballot one of them for President; and if no Person have a Majority, then from the five highest on the List said House shall in like Manner chuse the President. But in chusing the President, the Votes shall be taken by States, the Representation from each State having one Vote; a quorum for this Purpose shall consist of a Member or Members from two thirds of the States, and a Majority of all the States shall be necessary to a Choice. In every Case, after the Choice of the President, the Person having the greatest Number of Votes of the Electors shall be the Vice President. But if there should remain two or more who have equal Votes, the Senate shall chuse from them by Ballot the Vice President.[6]

The Congress may determine the Time of chusing the Electors, and the Day on which they shall give their Votes, which Day shall be the same throughout the United States.

Requirements to be president

No Person except a natural born Citizen, or a Citizen of the United States, at the time of the Adoption of this Constitution, shall be eligible to the Office of President; neither shall any person be eligible to that Office who shall not have attained to the Age of thirty five Years, and been fourteen Years a Resident within the United States.

In Case of the Removal of the President from Office, or of his Death, Resignation, or Inability to discharge the Powers and Duties of the said Office, the Same shall devolve on the Vice President, and the Congress may by Law provide for the Case of Removal, Death, Resignation or Inability, both of the President and Vice President, declaring what Officer shall then act as President, and such Officer shall act accordingly, until the Disability be removed, or a President shall be elected.[7]

Pay of president

The President shall, at stated Times, receive for his Services, a Compensation, which shall neither be increased nor diminished during the Period for which he shall have been elected, and he shall not receive within that Period any other Emolument from the United States, or any of them.

Before he enter on the Execution of his Office, he shall take the following Oath or Affirmation:—"I do solemnly swear (or affirm) that I will faithfully execute the Office of President of the United States, and will to the best of my Ability preserve, protect and defend the Constitution of the United States."

**Powers of president
—*commander in chief***

Section 2. The President shall be Commander in Chief of the Army and Navy of the United States, and of the Militia of the several States, when called into the actual Service of the United States; he may require the Opinion, in writing, of the principal Officer in each of the executive Departments, upon any Subject relating to the Duties of their respective Offices, and he shall

—pardons

have Power to grant Reprieves and Pardons for Offences against the United States, except in Cases of Impeachment.

—*treaties and appointments*

He shall have Power, by and with the Advice and Consent of the Senate, to make Treaties, provided two thirds of the Senators present concur; and he shall nominate, and by and with the Advice and Consent of the Senate, shall appoint Ambassadors, other public Ministers and Consuls, Judges of the supreme Court, and all other Officers of the United States, whose Appointments are not herein otherwise provided for, and which shall be established by Law: but the Congress may by Law vest the Appointment of such inferior Officers, as they think proper, in the President alone, in the Courts of Law, or in the Heads of Departments.

The President shall have Power to fill up all Vacancies that may happen during the Recess of the Senate, by granting Commissions which shall expire at the End of their next Session.

Relations of president with Congress

Section 3. He shall from time to time give to the Congress Information of the State of the Union, and recommend to their Consideration such Measures as he shall judge necessary and expedient; he may, on extraordinary Occasions, convene both Houses, or either of them, and in Case of

---

6. *Superseded by the Twelfth Amendment.*
7. *Modified by the Twenty-fifth Amendment.*

Disagreement between them, with Respect to the Time of Adjournment, he may adjourn them to such Time as he shall think proper; he shall receive Ambassadors and other public Ministers; he shall take Care that the Laws be faithfully executed, and shall Commission all the Officers of the United States.

Impeachment

Section 4. The President, Vice President and all civil Officers of the United States, shall be removed from Office on Impeachment for, and Conviction of, Treason, Bribery, or other high Crimes and Misdemeanors.

Article III.

Federal courts

Section 1. The judicial Power of the United States, shall be vested in one supreme Court, and in such inferior Courts as the Congress may from time to time ordain and establish. The Judges, both of the supreme and inferior Courts, shall hold their Offices during good Behaviour, and shall, at stated Times, receive for their Services, a Compensation, which shall not be diminished during their Continuance in Office.

Jurisdiction of courts

Section 2. The judicial Power shall extend to all Cases, in Law and Equity, arising under this Constitution, the Laws of the United States, and Treaties made, or which shall be made, under their Authority;—to all Cases affecting Ambassadors, other public Ministers and Consuls;—to all Cases of admiralty and maritime Jurisdiction;—to Controversies to which the United States shall be a Party;—to Controversies between two or more States;—*between a State and Citizens of another State;*[8]— between Citizens of different States;—between Citizens of the same State claiming Lands under Grants of different States, and between a State, or the Citizens thereof, and foreign States, Citizens or Subjects.

—original

In all Cases affecting Ambassadors, other public Ministers and Consuls, and those in which a State shall be Party, the supreme Court shall have original Jurisdiction. In all the other Cases before mentioned, the supreme Court shall have appellate Jurisdiction, both as to Law and Fact, with such Exceptions, and under such Regulations as the Congress shall make.

—appellate

The Trial of all Crimes, except in Cases of Impeachment, shall be by Jury; and such Trial shall be held in the State where the said Crimes shall have been committed; but when not committed within any State, the Trial shall be at such Place or Places as the Congress may by Law have directed.

Treason

Section 3. Treason against the United States, shall consist only in levying War against them, or in adhering to their Enemies, giving them Aid and Comfort. No Person shall be convicted of Treason unless on the Testimony of two Witnesses to the same overt Act, or on Confession in open Court.

The Congress shall have Power to declare the Punishment of Treason, but no Attainder of Treason shall work Corruption of Blood, or Forfeiture except during the Life of the Person attainted.

Article IV.

Full faith and credit

Section 1. Full Faith and Credit shall be given in each State to the public Acts, Records, and judicial Proceedings of every other State. And the Congress may by general Laws prescribe the Manner in which such Acts, Records and Proceedings shall be proved, and the Effect thereof.

---

8. *Modified by the Eleventh Amendment.*

Privileges and immunities

Section 2. The Citizens of each State shall be entitled to all Privileges and Immunities of Citizens in the several States.

Extradition

A person charged in any State with Treason, Felony, or other Crime, who shall flee from Justice, and be found in another State, shall on Demand of the executive Authority of the State from which he fled, be delivered up, to be removed to the State having Jurisdiction of the Crime.

No Person held to Service or Labour in one State, under the Laws thereof, escaping into another, shall, in Consequence of any Law or Regulation therein, be discharged from such Service or Labour, but shall be delivered up on Claim of the Party to whom such Service or Labour may be due.[9]

Creation of new states

Section 3. New States may be admitted by the Congress into this Union; but no new State shall be formed or erected within the Jurisdiction of any other State; nor any State be formed by the Junction of two or more States, or Parts of States, without the Consent of the Legislatures of the States concerned as well as of the Congress.

Governing territories

The Congress shall have Power to dispose of and make all needful Rules and Regulations respecting the Territory or other Property belonging to the United States; and nothing in this Constitution shall be so construed as to Prejudice any Claims of the United States, or of any particular State.

Protection of states

Section 4. The United States shall guarantee to every State in this Union a Republican Form of Government, and shall protect each of them against Invasion; and on Application of the Legislature, or of the Executive (when the Legislature cannot be convened) against domestic Violence.

Article V.

Amending the Constitution

The Congress, whenever two thirds of both Houses shall deem it necessary, shall propose Amendments to this Constitution, or, on the Application of the Legislatures of two thirds of the several States, shall call a Convention for proposing Amendments, which, in either Case, shall be valid to all Intents and Purposes, as Part of this Constitution, when ratified by the Legislatures of three fourths of the several States, or by Conventions in three fourths thereof, as the one or the other Mode of Ratification may be proposed by the Congress; Provided that no Amendment which may be made prior to the Year One thousand eight hundred and eight shall in any Manner alter the first and fourth Clauses in the Ninth Section of the first Article; and that no State, without its Consent, shall be deprived of its equal Suffrage in the Senate.

Article VI.

Assumption of debts of Confederation

All Debts contracted and Engagements entered into, before the Adoption of this Constitution, shall be as valid against the United States under this Constitution, as under the Confederation.

Supremacy of federal laws and treaties

This Constitution, and the Laws of the United States which shall be made in Pursuance thereof; and all Treaties made, or which shall be made, under the Authority of the United States, shall be the Supreme Law of the Land; and the Judges in every State shall be bound thereby, any Thing in the Constitution or Laws of any State to the Contrary notwithstanding.

---

9. *Changed by the Thirteenth Amendment.*

No religious test

The Senators and Representatives before mentioned, and the Members of the several State Legislatures, and all executive and judicial Officers, both of the United States and of the several States, shall be bound by Oath or Affirmation, to support this Constitution; but no religious Test shall ever be required as a Qualification to any Office or public Trust under the United States.

Article VII.

Ratification procedure

The Ratification of the Conventions of nine States, shall be sufficient for the Establishment of this Constitution between the States so ratifying the Same.

Done in Convention by the Unanimous Consent of the States present the Seventeenth Day of September in the Year of our Lord one thousand seven hundred and Eighty seven and of the Independence of the United States of America the Twelfth In witness whereof We have hereunto subscribed our Names,

G^o. WASHINGTON—*Presid^t.*
and deputy from Virginia

New Hampshire	JOHN LANGDON NICHOLAS GILMAN	*Maryland*	JAMES M^CHENRY DAN OF S^T THO^S JENIFER DAN^L CARROLL
Massachusetts	NATHANIEL GORHAM RUFUS KING	*Virginia*	JOHN BLAIR— JAMES MADISON JR.
New Jersey	WIL: LIVINGSTON DAVID BREARLEY W^M PATERSON JONA: DAYTON	*North Carolina*	W^M BLOUNT RICH^D DOBBS SPAIGHT HU WILLIAMSON
Pennsylvania	B FRANKLIN THOMAS MIFFLIN ROB^T MORRIS GEO. CLYMER THO^S FITZSIMONS JARED INGERSOLL JAMES WILSON GOUV MORRIS	*South Carolina*	J. RUTLEDGE CHARLES COTESWORTH PINCKNEY CHARLES PINCKNEY PIERCE BUTLER
		Delaware	GEO: READ GUNNING BEDFORD JUN JOHN DICKINSON RICHARD BASSETT JACO: BROOM
Connecticut	W^M SAM^L JOHNSON ROGER SHERMAN		
New York	ALEXANDER HAMILTION	*Georgia*	WILLIAM FEW ABR BALDWIN

[The first ten amendments, known as the "Bill of Rights," were ratified in 1791.]

AMENDMENT I.

Freedom of religion, speech, press, assembly

Congress shall make no law respecting an establishment of religion, or prohibiting the free exercise thereof, or abridging the freedom of speech, or of the press; or the right of the people peaceably to assemble, and to petition the Government for a redress of grievances.

AMENDMENT II.

Right to bear arms

A well regulated Militia, being necessary to the security of a free State, the right of the people to keep and bear Arms, shall not be infringed.

AMENDMENT III.

Quartering troops in private homes

No Soldier shall, in time of peace be quartered in any house without the consent of the Owner, nor in time of war, but in a manner to be prescribed by law.

AMENDMENT IV.

Prohibition against unreasonable searches and seizures

The right of the people to be secure in their persons, houses, papers, and effects, against unreasonable searches and seizures, shall not be violated, and no Warrants shall issue, but upon probable cause, supported by Oath or affirmation, and particularly describing the place to be searched, and the persons or things to be seized.

AMENDMENT V.

Right when accused; "due-process" clause

No person shall be held to answer for a capital, or otherwise infamous crime, unless on a presentment or indictment of a Grand Jury, except in cases arising in the land or naval forces, or in the Militia, when in actual service in time of War or public danger; nor shall any person be subject for the same offence to be twice put in jeopardy of life or limb; nor shall be compelled in any criminal case to be a witness against himself, nor be deprived of life, liberty, or property, without due process of law, nor shall private property be taken for public use, without just compensation.

AMENDMENT VI.

Rights when on trial

In all criminal prosecutions, the accused shall enjoy the right to a speedy and public trial, by an impartial jury of the State and district wherein the crime shall have been committed, which district shall have been previously ascertained by law, and to be informed of the nature and cause of the accusation; to be confronted with the witnesses against him; to have compulsory process for obtaining witnesses in his favor, and to have the Assistance of Counsel for his defence.

AMENDMENT VII.

Common-law suits

In Suits at common law, where the value in controversy shall exceed twenty dollars, the right of trial by jury shall be preserved, and no fact tried by a jury, shall be otherwise reexamined in any Court of the United States, than according to the rules of the common law.

AMENDMENT VIII.

Bail; no "cruel and unusual" punishments

Excessive bail shall not be required, nor excessive fines imposed, nor cruel and unusual punishments inflicted.

AMENDMENT IX.

Unenumerated rights protected

The enumeration in the Constitution, of certain rights, shall not be construed to deny or disparage others retained by the people.

AMENDMENT X.

Powers reserved for states

The powers not delegated to the United States by the Constitution, nor prohibited by it to the States, are reserved to the States respectively, or to the people.

AMENDMENT XI.

[Ratified in 1795.]

Limits on suits against states

The Judicial power of the United States shall not be construed to extend to any suit in law or equity, commenced or prosecuted against one of the United States by Citizens of another state, or by Citizens or Subjects of any Foreign State.

AMENDMENT XII.

[Ratified in 1804.]

Revision of electoral-college procedure

The Electors shall meet in their respective states and vote by ballot for President and Vice President, one of whom, at least, shall not be an inhabitant of the same state with themselves; they shall name in their ballots the person voted for as President, and in distinct ballots the person voted for as Vice President, and they shall make distinct lists of all persons voted for as President, and of all persons voted for as Vice President, and of the number of votes for each, which lists they shall sign and certify, and transmit sealed to the seat of government of the United States, directed to the President of the Senate;—The President of the Senate shall, in the presence of the Senate and House of Representatives, open all the certificates and the votes shall then be counted;—The person having the greatest number of votes for President, shall be the President, if such number be a majority of the whole number of Electors appointed; and if no person have such majority, then from the persons having the highest numbers not exceeding three on the list of those voted for as President, the House of Representatives shall choose immediately, by ballot, the President. But in choosing the President, the votes shall be taken by states, the representation from each state having one vote; a quorum for this purpose shall consist of a member or members from two-thirds of the states, and a majority of all the states shall be necessary to a choice. *And if the House of Representatives shall not choose a President whenever the right of choice shall devolve upon them, before the fourth day of March next following, then the Vice President shall act as President, as in the case of the death or other constitutional disability of the President.*—[10] The person having the greatest number of votes as Vice President, shall be the Vice President, if such number be a majority of the whole number of Electors appointed, and if no person have a majority, then from the two

---

10. *Changed by the Twentieth Amendment, section 3.*

highest numbers on the list, the Senate shall choose the Vice President; a quorum for the purpose shall consist of two-thirds of the whole number of Senators, and a majority of the whole number shall be necessary to a choice. But no person constitutionally ineligible to the office of President shall be eligible to that of Vice President of the United States.

AMENDMENT XIII.
[*Ratified in 1865.*]

Slavery prohibited

Section 1. Neither slavery nor involuntary servitude, except as a punishment for crime whereof the party shall have been duly convicted, shall exist within the United States, or any place subject to their jurisdiction.

Section 2. Congress shall have power to enforce this article by appropriate legislation.

AMENDMENT XIV.
[*Ratified in 1868.*]

Ex-slaves made citizens

Section 1. All persons born or naturalized in the United States and subject to the jurisdiction thereof, are citizens of the United States and of the State wherein they reside. No State shall make or enforce any law which shall abridge the privileges or immunities of citizens of the United States; nor shall any State deprive any person of life, liberty, or property, without due process of law; nor deny to any person within its jurisdiction the equal protection of the laws.

"Due-process" clause applied to states "Equal-protection" clause
Reduction in congressional representation for states denying adult males the right to vote

Section 2. Representatives shall be apportioned among the several States according to their respective numbers, counting the whole number of persons in each State, excluding Indians not taxed. But when the right to vote at any election for the choice of electors for President and Vice President of the United States, Representatives in Congress, the Executive and Judicial officers of a State, or the members of the Legislature thereof, is denied to any of the male inhabitants of such State, being *twenty-one*[11] years of age and citizens of the United States, or in any way abridged, except for participation in rebellion, or other crime, the basis of representation therein shall be reduced in the proportion which the number of such male citizens shall bear to the whole number of male citizens twenty-one years of age in such State.

Southern rebels denied federal office

Section 3. No person shall be a Senator or Representative in Congress, or elector of President and Vice President, or hold any office, civil or military, under the United States, or under any State, who, having previously taken an oath, as a member of Congress, or as an officer of the United States, or as a member of any State legislature, or as an executive or judicial officer of any State, to support the Constitution of the United States, shall have engaged in insurrection or rebellion against the same, or given aid or comfort to the enemies thereof. But Congress may by a vote of two-thirds of each House, remove such disability.

---

11. *Changed by the Twenty-sixth Amendment.*

Rebel debts repudiated

Section 4. The validity of the public debt of the United States, authorized by law, including debts incurred for payment of pensions and bounties for services in suppressing insurrection or rebellion, shall not be questioned. But neither the United States nor any State shall assume or pay any debt or obligation incurred in aid of insurrection or rebellion against the United States, or any claim for the loss or emancipation of any slave; but all such debts, obligations and claims shall be held illegal and void.

Section 5. The Congress shall have power to enforce, by appropriate legislation, the provisions of this article.

AMENDMENT XV.

[*Ratified in 1870.*]

Blacks given right to vote

Section 1. The right of citizens of the United States to vote shall not be denied or abridged by the United States or by any State on account of race, color, or previous condition of servitude.

Section 2. The Congress shall have power to enforce this article by appropriate legislation.

AMENDMENT XVI.

[*Ratified in 1913.*]

Authorizes federal income tax

The Congress shall have power to lay and collect taxes on incomes, from whatever source derived, without apportionment among the several States, and without regard to any census or enumeration.

AMENDMENT XVII.

[*Ratified in 1913.*]

Requires popular election of senators

The Senate of the United States shall be composed of two Senators from each State, elected by the people thereof, for six years; and each Senator shall have one vote. The electors in each State shall have the qualifications requisite for electors of the most numerous branch of the State legislatures.

When vacancies happen in the representation of any State in the Senate, the executive authority of such State shall issue writs of election to fill such vacancies: Provided, That the legislature of any State may empower the executive thereof to make temporary appointments until the people fill the vacancies by election as the legislature may direct.

This amendment shall not be so construed as to affect the election or term of any Senator chosen before it becomes valid as part of the Constitution.

AMENDMENT XVIII.

[*Ratified in 1919.*]

Prohibits manufacture and sale of liquor

Section 1. *After one year from the ratification of this article the manufacture, sale, or transportation of intoxicating liquors within, the importation thereof into, or the exportation thereof from the United States and all territory subject to the jurisdiction thereof for beverage purposes is hereby prohibited.*

Section 2. The Congress and the several States shall have concurrent power to enforce this article by appropriate legislation.

Section 3. This article shall be inoperative unless it shall have been ratified as an amendment to the Constitution by the legislatures of the several States, as provided in the Constitution, within seven years from the date of the submission hereof to the States by the Congress.[12]

AMENDMENT XIX.

[*Ratified in 1920.*]

Right to vote for women

The right of citizens of the United States to vote shall not be denied or abridged by the United States or by any State on account of sex.

Congress shall have power to enforce this article by appropriate legislation.

AMENDMENT XX.

[*Ratified in 1933.*]

Federal terms of office to begin in January

Section 1. The terms of the President and Vice President shall end at noon on the 20th day of January, and the terms of Senators and Representatives at noon on the 3d day of January, of the years in which such terms would have ended if this article had not been ratified; and the terms of their successors shall then begin.

Section 2. The Congress shall assemble at least once in every year, and such meeting shall begin at noon on the 3d day of January, unless they shall by law appoint a different day.

Emergency presidential succession

Section 3. If, at the time fixed for the beginning of the term of the President, the President elect shall have died, the Vice President elect shall become President. If a President shall not have been chosen before the time fixed for the beginning of his term, or if the President elect shall have failed to qualify, then the Vice President elect shall act as President until a President shall have qualified; and the Congress may by law provide for the case wherein neither a President elect nor a Vice President elect shall have qualified, declaring who shall then act as President, or the manner in which one who is to act shall be selected, and such person shall act accordingly until a President or Vice President shall have qualified.

Section 4. The Congress may by law provide for the case of the death of any of the persons from whom the House of Representatives may choose a President whenever the right of choice shall have devolved upon them, and for the case of the death of any of the persons from whom the Senate may choose a Vice President whenever the right of choice shall have devolved upon them.

Section 5. Sections 1 and 2 shall take effect on the 15th day of October following the ratification of this article.

---

12. *Repealed by the Twenty-first Amendment.*

Section 6. This article shall be inoperative unless it shall have been ratified as an amendment to the Constitution by the legislatures of three-fourths of the several States within seven years from the date of its submission.

AMENDMENT XXI.
[*Ratified in 1933.*]

Repeals Prohibition

Section 1. The eighteenth article of amendment to the Constitution of the United States is hereby repealed.

Section 2. The transportation or importation into any State, Territory, or possession of the United States for delivery or use therein of intoxicating liquors, in violation of the laws thereof, is hereby prohibited.

Section 3. This article shall be inoperative unless it shall have been ratified as an amendment to the Constitution by conventions in the several States, as provided in the Constitution, within seven years from the date of submission hereof to the States by the Congress.

AMENDMENT XXII.
[*Ratified in 1951.*]

Two-term limit for president

Section 1. No person shall be elected to the office of the President more than twice, and no person who has held the office of President, or acted as President, for more than two years of a term to which some other person was elected President shall be elected to the office of President more than once. But this Article shall not apply to any person holding the office of President when this Article was proposed by the Congress, and shall not prevent any person who may be holding the office of President, or acting as President, during the term within which this Article becomes operative from holding the office of President or acting as President during the remainder of such term.

Section 2. This Article shall be inoperative unless it shall have been ratified as an amendment to the Constitution by the legislatures of three-fourths of the several States within seven years from the date of its submission to the States by the Congress.

AMENDMENT XXIII.
[*Ratified in 1961.*]

Right to vote for president in District of Columbia

Section 1. The District constituting the seat of Government of the United States shall appoint in such manner as the Congress may direct:

A number of electors of President and Vice President equal to the whole number of Senators and Representatives in Congress to which the District would be entitled if it were a State, but in no event more than the least populous State; they shall be in addition to those appointed by the States, but they shall be considered, for the purposes of the election of President and Vice President, to be electors appointed by a State; and they shall meet in the District and perform such duties as provided by the twelfth article of amendment.

Section 2. The Congress shall have power to enforce this article by appropriate legislation.

AMENDMENT XXIV.
[*Ratified in 1964.*]

Prohibits poll taxes in federal elections

Section 1. The right of citizens of the United States to vote in any primary or other election for President or Vice President, for electors for President or Vice President, or for Senator or Representative in Congress, shall not be denied or abridged by the United States or any State by reason of failure to pay any poll tax or other tax.

Section 2. The Congress shall have the power to enforce this article by appropriate legislation.

AMENDMENT XXV.
[*Ratified in 1967.*]

Presidential disability and succession

Section 1. In case of the removal of the President from office or of his death or resignation, the Vice President shall become President.

Section 2. Whenever there is a vacancy in the office of the Vice President, the President shall nominate a Vice President who shall take office upon confirmation by a majority vote of both Houses of Congress.

Section 3. Whenever the President transmits to the President pro tempore of the Senate and the Speaker of the House of Representatives his written declaration that he is unable to discharge the powers and duties of his office, and until he transmits to them a written declaration to the contrary, such powers and duties shall be discharged by the Vice President as Acting President.

Section 4. Whenever the Vice President and a majority of either the principal officers of the executive departments or of such other body as Congress may by law provide, transmit to the President pro tempore of the Senate and the Speaker of the House of Representatives their written declaration that the President is unable to discharge the powers and duties of his office, the Vice President shall immediately assume the powers and duties of the office as Acting President.

Thereafter, when the President transmits to the President pro tempore of the Senate and the Speaker of the House of Representatives his written declaration that no inability exists, he shall resume the powers and duties of his office unless the Vice President and a majority of either the principal officers of the executive department[s] or of such other body as Congress may by law provide, transmit within four days to the President pro tempore of the Senate and the Speaker of the House of Representatives their written declaration that the President is unable to discharge the powers and duties of his office. Thereupon Congress shall decide the issue, assembling within forty-eight hours for that purpose if not in session. If the Congress, within twenty-one days after receipt of the latter written declaration, or, if Congress is not in session, within twenty-one days after Congress is required to assemble, determines by two-thirds vote of both Houses that the President is unable to discharge the powers and duties of his office, the Vice

President shall continue to discharge the same as Acting President; otherwise, the President shall resume the powers and duties of his office.

AMENDMENT XXVI.
[*Ratified in 1971.*]

Voting age lowered to eighteen

Section 1. The right of citizens of the United States, who are eighteen years of age or older, to vote shall not be denied or abridged by the United States or by any State on account of age.

Section 2. The Congress shall have power to enforce this article by appropriate legislation.

AMENDMENT XXVII.
[*Ratified in 1992.*]

Congressional pay raises

No law varying the compensation for the services of the Senators and Representatives shall take effect, until an election of Representatives shall have intervened.

The Federalist No. 10

November 22, 1787

James Madison

TO THE PEOPLE OF THE STATE OF NEW YORK.

Among the numerous advantages promised by a well constructed Union, none deserves to be more accurately developed than its tendency to break and control the violence of faction. The friend of popular governments, never finds himself so much alarmed for their character and fate, as when he contemplates their propensity to this dangerous vice. He will not fail therefore to set a due value on any plan which, without violating the principles to which he is attached, provides a proper cure for it. The instability, injustice and confusion introduced into the public councils, have in truth been the mortal diseases under which popular governments have every where perished; as they continue to be the favorite and fruitful topics from which the adversaries to liberty derive their most specious declamations. The valuable improvements made by the American Constitutions on the popular models, both ancient and modern, cannot certainly be too much admired; but it would be an unwarrantable partiality, to contend that they have as effectually obviated the danger on this side as was wished and expected. Complaints are everywhere heard from our most considerate and virtuous citizens, equally the friends of public and private faith, and of public and personal liberty; that our governments are too unstable; that the public good is disregarded in the conflicts of rival parties; and that measures are too often decided, not according to the rules of justice, and the rights of the minor party; but by the superior force of an interested and over-bearing majority. However anxiously we may wish that these complaints had no foundation, the evidence of known facts will not permit us to deny that they are in some degree true. It will be found indeed, on a candid review of our situation, that some of the distresses under which we labor, have been erroneously charged on the operation of our governments; but it will be found, at the same time, that other causes will not alone account for many of our heaviest misfortunes; and particularly, for that prevailing and increasing distrust of public engagements, and alarm for private rights, which are echoed from one end of the continent to the other. These must be chiefly, if not wholly, effects of the unsteadiness and injustice, with which a factious spirit has tainted our public administrations.

By a faction I understand a number of citizens, whether amounting to a majority or minority of the whole, who are united and actuated by some common impulse of passion, or of interest, adverse to the rights of other citizens, or to the permanent and aggregate interests of the community.

There are two methods of curing the mischiefs of faction: the one, by removing its causes; the other, by controlling its effects.

There are again two methods of removing the causes of faction: the one by destroying the liberty which is essential to its existence; the other, by giving to every citizen the same opinions, the same passions, and the same interests.

It could never be more truly said than of the first remedy, that it is worse than the disease. Liberty is to faction, what air is to fire, an aliment without which it instantly expires. But it could not be a less folly to abolish liberty, which is essential to political life, because it nourishes faction, than it would be to wish the annihilation of air, which is essential to animal life, because it imparts to fire its destructive agency.

The second expedient is as impracticable, as the first would be unwise. As long as the reason of man continues fallible, and he is at liberty to exercise it, different opinions will be formed. As long as the connection subsists between his reason and his self-love, his opinions and his passions will have a reciprocal influence on each other; and the former will be objects to which the latter will attach themselves. The diversity in the faculties of men from which the rights of property originate, is not less an insuperable obstacle to a uniformity of interests. The protection of these faculties is the first object of Government. From the protection of different and unequal faculties of acquiring property, the possession of different degrees and kinds of property immediately results: and from the influence of these on the sentiments and views of the respective proprietors, ensues a division of the society into different interests and parties.

The latent causes of faction are thus sown in the nature of man; and we see them every where brought into different degrees of activity, according to the different circumstances of civil society. A zeal for different opinions concerning religion, concerning Government and many other points, as well of speculation as of practice; an attachment to different leaders ambitiously contending for pre-eminence and power; or to persons of other descriptions whose fortunes have been interesting to the human passions, have in turn divided mankind into parties, inflamed them with mutual animosity, and rendered them much more disposed to vex and oppress each other, than to cooperate for their common good. So strong is this propensity of mankind to fall into mutual animosities, that where no substantial occasion presents itself, the most frivolous and fanciful distinctions have been sufficient to kindle their unfriendly passions, and excite their most violent conflicts. But the most common and durable source of factions, has been the various and unequal distribution of property. Those who hold, and those who are without property, have ever formed distinct interests in society. Those who are creditors, and those who are debtors, fall under a like discrimination. A landed interest, a manufacturing interest, a mercantile interest, a monied interest, with many lesser interests, grow up of necessity in civilized nations, and divide them into different classes, actuated by different sentiments and views. The regulation of these various and interfering interests forms the principal task of modern Legislation, and involves the spirit of party and faction in the necessary and ordinary operations of Government.

No man is allowed to be judge in his own cause; because his interest would certainly bias his judgment, and, not improbably, corrupt his integrity. With equal, nay with greater reason, a body of men, are unfit to be judges and parties, at the same time; yet, what are many of the most important acts of legislation, but so many judicial determinations, not indeed concerning the rights of single persons, but concerning the rights of large bodies of citizens, and what are the different classes of legislators, but advocates and parties to the causes which they determine? Is a law proposed concerning private debts? It is a question to which the creditors are parties on one side, and the debtors on the other. Justice ought to hold the balance between them. Yet the parties are and must be themselves the judges; and the most numerous party, or, in other words, the most powerful faction must be expected to prevail. Shall domestic manufactures be encouraged, and in what degree, by restrictions on foreign manufactures? are questions which would be differently decided by the landed and the manufacturing classes; and probably by neither, with a sole regard to justice and the public good. The apportionment of taxes on the various descriptions of property, is an act which seems to require the most exact impartiality; yet, there is perhaps no legislative act in which greater opportunity and temptation are given to a predominant party, to trample on the rules of justice. Every shilling with which they over-burden the inferior number, is a shilling saved to their own pockets.

It is in vain to say, that enlightened statesmen will be able to adjust these clashing interests, and render them all subservient to the public good. Enlightened statesmen will not always be at the helm: Nor, in many cases, can such an adjustment be made at all, without taking into view indirect and remote considerations, which will rarely prevail over the immediate interest which one party may find in disregarding the rights of another, or the good of the whole.

The inference to which we are brought, is, that the *causes* of faction cannot be removed; and that relief is only to be sought in the means of controlling its *effects*.

If a faction consists of less than a majority, relief is supplied by the republican principle, which enables the majority to defeat its sinister views by regular vote: It may clog the administration, it may convulse the society; but it will be unable to execute and mask its violence under the forms of the Constitution. When a majority is included in a faction, the form of popular government on the other hand enables it to sacrifice to its ruling passion or interest, both the public good and the rights of other citizens. To secure the public good, and private rights, against the danger of such a faction, and at the same time to preserve the spirit and the form of popular government, is then the great object to which our inquiries are directed: Let me add that it is the great desideratum, by which alone this form of government can be rescued from the opprobrium under which it has so long labored, and be recommended to the esteem and adoption of mankind.

By what means is this object attainable? Evidently by one of two only. Either the existence of the same passion or interest in a majority at the same time, must be prevented; or the majority, having such co-existent passion or interest, must be rendered, by their number and local situation, unable to concert and carry into effect schemes of oppression. If the impulse and the opportunity be suffered to coincide, we well know that neither moral nor religious motives can be relied on as an adequate control. They are not found to be such on the injustice and violence of individuals, and lose their efficacy in proportion to the number combined together; that is, in proportion as their efficacy becomes needful.

From this view of the subject, it may be concluded, that a pure Democracy, by which I mean, a Society, consisting of a small number of citizens, who assemble and administer the Government in person, can admit of no cure for the mischiefs of faction. A common passion or interest will, in almost every case, be felt by a majority of the whole; a communication and concert results from the form of Government itself; and there is nothing to check the inducements to sacrifice the weaker party, or an obnoxious individual. Hence it is, that such Democracies have ever been spectacles of turbulence and contention; have ever been found incompatible with personal security, or the rights of property; and have in general been as short in their lives, as they have been violent in their deaths. Theoretic politicians, who have patronized this species of Government, have erroneously supposed, that by reducing mankind to a perfect equality in their political rights, they would, at the same time, be perfectly equalized and assimilated in their possessions, their opinions, and their passions.

A republic, by which I mean a government in which the scheme of representation takes place, opens a different prospect, and promises the cure for which we are seeking. Let us examine the points in which it varies from pure democracy, and we shall comprehend both the nature of the cure and the efficacy which it must derive from the union.

The two great points of difference, between a democracy and a republic, are, first, the delegation of the government, in the latter, to a small number of citizens, elected by the rest; secondly, the greater number of citizens, and greater sphere of country, over which the latter may be extended.

The effect of the first difference is, on the one hand, to refine and enlarge the public views, by passing them through the medium of a chosen body of citizens, whose wisdom may best discern the true interest of their country, and whose patriotism and love of justice, will be least likely to sacrifice it to temporary or partial considerations. Under such a regulation, it may well happen, that the public voice, pronounced by the representatives of the people, will be more consonant to the public good, than if pronounced by the people themselves, convened for the purpose. On the other hand the effect may be inverted. Men of factious tempers, of local prejudices, or of sinister designs, may by intrigue, by corruption, or by other means, first obtain the suffrages, and then betray the interest of the people. The question resulting is, whether small or extensive republics are most favorable to the election of proper guardians of the public weal, and it is clearly decided in favor of the latter by two obvious considerations.

In the first place, it is to be remarked that, however small the republic may be, the representatives must be raised to a certain number, in order to guard against the cabals of a few; and that however large it may be, they must be limited to a certain number, in order to guard against the confusion of a multitude. Hence, the number of representatives in the two cases not being in proportion to that of the constituents, and being proportionally greatest in the small republic, it follows, that if the proportion of fit characters be not less in the large than in the small republic, the former will present a greater option, and consequently a greater probability of a fit choice.

In the next place, as each Representative will be chosen by a greater number of citizens in the large than in the small Republic, it will be more difficult for unworthy candidates to practise with success the vicious arts, by which elections are too often carried; and the suffrages of the people being more free, will be more likely to center on men who possess the most attractive merit, and the most diffusive and established characters.

It must be confessed, that in this, as in most other cases, there is a mean, on both sides of which inconveniences will be found to lie. By enlarging too much the number of electors, you render the representatives too little acquainted with all their local circumstances and lesser interests; as by reducing it too much, you render him unduly attached to these, and too little fit to comprehend and pursue great and national objects. The Federal Constitution forms a happy combination in this respect; the great and aggregate interests being referred to the national, the local and particular, to the state legislatures.

The other point of difference is, the greater number of citizens and extent of territory which may be brought within the compass of Republican, than of Democratic Government; and it is this circumstance principally which renders factious combinations less to be dreaded in the former, than in the latter. The smaller the society, the fewer probably will be the distinct parties and interests composing it; the fewer the distinct parties and interests, the more frequently will a majority be found of the same party; and the smaller the number of individuals composing a majority, and the smaller the compass within which they are placed, the more easily they will concert and execute their plans of oppression. Extend the sphere, and you take in a greater variety of parties and interests; you make it less probable that a majority of the whole will have a common motive to invade the rights of other citizens; or if such a common motive exists, it will be more difficult for all who feel it to discover their own strength, and to act in unison with each other. Besides other impediments, it may be remarked, that where there is a consciousness of unjust or dishonorable purposes, communication is always checked by distrust, in proportion to the number whose concurrence is necessary.

Hence it clearly appears, that the same advantage, which a Republic has over a Democracy, in controlling the effects of factions, is enjoyed by a large over a small Republic—is enjoyed by the Union over the States composing it. Does this advantage consist in the substitution of Representatives, whose enlightened views and virtuous sentiments render them superior to local prejudices, and to schemes of injustice? It will not be denied, that the Representation of the Union will be most likely to possess these requisite endowments. Does it consist in the greater security afforded by a greater variety of parties, against the event of any one party being able to outnumber and oppress the rest? In an equal degree does the increase variety of parties, comprised within the Union, increase this security? Does it, in fine, consist in the greater obstacles opposed to the concert and accomplishment of the secret wishes of an unjust and interested majority? Here, again, the extent of the Union gives it the most palpable advantage.

The influence of factious leaders may kindle a flame within their particular States, but will be unable to spread a general conflagration through the other States: a religious sect, may degenerate into a political faction in a part of the Confederacy but the variety of sects dispersed over the entire face of it, must secure the national Councils against any danger from that source: a rage for paper money, for an abolition of debts, for an equal division of property, or for any other improper or wicked project, will be less apt to pervade the whole body of the Union, than a particular member of it; in the same proportion as such a malady is more likely to taint a particular county or district, than an entire State.

In the extent and proper structure of the Union, therefore, we behold a Republican remedy for the diseases most incident to Republican Government. And according to the degree of pleasure and pride, we feel in being Republicans, ought to be our zeal in cherishing the spirit, and supporting the character of Federalists.

PUBLIUS

The Federalist No. 51

February 6, 1788

James Madison

TO THE PEOPLE OF THE STATE OF NEW YORK.

To what expedient then shall we finally resort for maintaining in practice the necessary partition of power among the several departments, as laid down in the constitution? The only answer that can be given is, that as all these exterior provisions are found to be inadequate, the defect must be supplied, by so contriving the interior structure of the government, as that its several constituent parts may, by their mutual relations, be the means of keeping each other in their proper places. Without presuming to undertake a full development of this important idea, I will hazard a few general observations, which may perhaps place it in a clearer light, and enable us to form a more correct judgment of the principles and structure of the government planned by the convention.

In order to lay a due foundation for that separate and distinct exercise of the different powers of government, which to a certain extent, is admitted on all hands to be essential to the preservation of liberty, it is evident that each department should have a will of its own; and consequently should be so constituted, that the members of each should have as little agency as possible in the appointment of the members of the others. Were this principle rigorously adhered to, it would require that all the appointments for the supreme executive, legislative, and judiciary magistracies, should be drawn from the same fountain of authority, the people, through channels, having no communication whatever with one another. Perhaps such a plan of constructing the several departments would be less difficult in practice than in it may in contemplation appear. Some difficulties however, and some additional expense, would attend the execution of it. Some deviations therefore from the principle must be admitted. In the constitution of the judiciary department in particular, it might be inexpedient to insist rigorously on the principle; first, because peculiar qualifications being essential in the members, the primary consideration ought to be to select that mode of choice, which best secures these qualifications; secondly, because the permanent tenure by which the appointments are held in that department, must soon destroy all sense of dependence on the authority conferring them.

It is equally evident that the members of each department should be as little dependent as possible on those of the others, for the emoluments annexed to their offices. Were the executive magistrate, or the judges, not independent of the legislature in this particular, their independence in every other would be merely nominal.

But the great security against a gradual concentration of the several powers in the same department, consists in giving to those who administer each department, the necessary constitutional means, and personal motives, to resist encroachments of the others. The provision for defense must in this, as in all other cases, be made commensurate to the danger of attack. Ambition must be made to counteract ambition. The interest of the man must be connected with the constitutional right of the place. It may be a reflection on human nature, that such devices should be necessary to control the abuses of government. But what is government itself but the greatest of all reflections on human nature? If men were angels, no government would be necessary. If angels were to govern men, neither external nor internal controls on government would be necessary. In framing a government which is to be administered by men over men, the great difficulty lies in this: You must first enable the government to control the governed; and in the next place, oblige it to control itself. A dependence on the people is no doubt the primary control on the government; but experience has taught mankind the necessity of auxiliary precautions.

This policy of supplying by opposite and rival interests, the defect of better motives, might be traced through the whole system of human affairs, private as well as public. We see it particularly displayed in all the subordinate distributions of power; where the constant aim is to divide and arrange the several offices in such a manner as that each may be a check on the other; that the private interest of every individual, may be a sentinel over the public rights. These inventions of prudence cannot be less requisite in the distribution of the supreme powers of the state.

But it is not possible to give each department an equal power of self defense. In republican government the legislative authority, necessarily, predominates. The remedy for this inconvenience is, to divide the legislative into different branches; and to render them by different modes of election, and different principles of action, as little connected with each other, as the nature of their common functions, and their common dependence on the society, will admit. It may even be necessary to guard against dangerous encroachments by still further precautions. As the weight of the legislative authority requires that it should be thus divided, the weakness of the executive may require, on the other hand, that it should be fortified. An absolute negative, on the legislature, appears at first view to be the natural defense with which the executive magistrate should be armed. But perhaps it would be neither altogether safe, nor alone sufficient. On ordinary occasions, it might not be exerted with the requisite firmness, and on extraordinary occasions, it might be prefidiously abused. May not this defect of an absolute negative be supplied, by some qualified connection between this weaker department, and the weaker branch of the stronger department, by which the latter may be led to support the constitutional rights of the former, without being too much detached from the rights of its own department?

If the principles on which these observations are founded be just, as I persuade myself they are, and they be applied as a criterion, to the several state constitutions, and to the federal constitution, it will be found, that if the latter does not perfectly correspond with them, the former are infinitely less able to bear such a test.

There are moreover two considerations particularly applicable to the federal system of America, which place the system in a very interesting point of view.

First. In a single republic, all the power surrendered by the people, is submitted to the administration of a single government; and usurpations are guarded against by a division of the government into distinct and separate departments. In the compound republic of America, the power surrendered by the people, is first divided between two distinct governments, and then the portion allotted to each, subdivided among distinct and separate departments. Hence a double security arises to the rights of the people. The different governments will control each other; at the same time that each will be controlled by itself.

Second. It is of great importance in a republic, not only to guard the society against the oppression of its rulers; but to guard one part of the society against the injustice of the other part. Different interests necessarily exist in different classes of citizens. If a majority be united by a common interest, the rights of the minority will be insecure. There are but two methods of providing against this evil: The one by creating a will in the community independent of the majority, that is, of the society itself, the other by comprehending in the society so many separate descriptions of citizens, as will render an unjust combination of a majority of the whole, very improbable, if not impracticable. The first method prevails in all governments possessing an hereditary or self appointed authority. This at best is but a precarious security; because a power independent of the society may as well espouse the unjust views of the major, as the rightful interests, of the minor party, and may possibly be turned against both parties. The second method will be exemplified in the federal republic of the United States. While all authority in it will be derived from and dependent on the society, the society itself will be broken into so many parts, interests and classes of citizens, that the rights of individuals or of the minority, will be in little danger from interested combinations of the majority. In a free government, the security for civil rights must be the same as for religious rights. It consists in the one case in the multiplicity of interests, and in the other, in the multiplicity of sects. The degree of security in both cases will depend on the number of interests and sects; and this may be presumed to depend on the extent of country and number of people comprehended under the same government. This view of the subject must particularly recommend a proper federal system to all the sincere and considerate friends of republican government: Since it shows that in exact proportion as the territory of the union may be formed into more circumscribed confederacies or states, oppressive combinations of a majority will be facilitated, the best security under the republican form, for the rights of every class of citizens, will be diminished; and consequently, the stability and independence of some member of the government, the only other security, must be proportionally increased. Justice is the end of government. It is the end of civil society. It ever has been, and ever will be pursued, until it be obtained, or until liberty be lost in the pursuit. In a society under the forms of which the stronger faction can readily unite and oppress the weaker, anarchy may as truly be said to reign, as in a state of nature where the weaker individual is not secured against the violence of the stronger: And as in the latter state even the stronger individuals are prompted by the uncertainty of their condition, to submit to a government which may protect the weak as well as themselves: So in the former state, will the more powerful factions or parties be gradually induced by a like motive, to wish for a government which will protect all parties, the weaker as well as the more powerful. It can be little doubted, that if the state of Rhode Island was separated from the confederacy, and left to itself, the insecurity of rights under the popular form of government within such narrow limits, would be displayed by such reiterated oppressions of factious majorities, that some power altogether independent of the people would soon be called for by the voice of the very factions whose misrule had proved the necessity of it. In the extended republic of the United States, and among the great variety of interests, parties and sects which it embraces, a coalition of a majority of the whole society could seldom take place on any other principles than those of justice and the general good; and there being thus less danger to a minor from the will of the major party, there must be less pretext also, to provide for the security of the former, by introducing into the government a will not dependent on the latter; or in other words, a will independent of the society itself. It is no less certain than it is important, notwithstanding the contrary opinions which have been entertained, that the larger the society, provided it lie within a practicable sphere, the more duly capable it will be of self government. And happily for the *republican cause*, the practicable sphere may be carried to a very great extent, by a judicious modification and mixture of the *federal principle*.

PUBLIUS

PRESIDENTS AND CONGRESSES, 1789–2009

Year	President and vice president	Party of president	Congress	House Majority party	House Minority party	Senate Majority party	Senate Minority party
1789–1797	**George Washington** John Adams	None	1st 2d 3d 4th	38 Admin 37 Fed 57 Dem-Rep 54 Fed	26 Opp 33 Dem-Rep 48 Fed 52 Dem-Rep	17 Admin 16 Fed 17 Fed 19 Fed	9 Opp 13 Dem-Rep 13 Dem-Rep 13 Dem-Rep
1797–1801	**John Adams** Thomas Jefferson	Federalist	5th 6th	58 Fed 64 Fed	48 Dem-Rep 42 Dem-Rep	20 Fed 19 Fed	12 Dem-Rep 13 Dem-Rep
1801–1809	**Thomas Jefferson** Aaron Burr (to 1805) George Clinton (to 1809)	Dem-Rep	7th 8th 9th 10th	69 Dem-Rep 102 Dem-Rep 116 Dem-Rep 118 Dem-Rep	36 Fed 39 Fed 25 Fed 24 Fed	18 Dem-Rep 25 Dem-Rep 27 Dem-Rep 28 Dem-Rep	13 Fed 9 Fed 7 Fed 6 Fed
1809–1817	**James Madison** George Clinton (to 1813) Elbridge Gerry (to 1817)	Dem-Rep	11th 12th 13th 14th	94 Dem-Rep 108 Dem-Rep 112 Dem-Rep 117 Dem-Rep	48 Fed 36 Fed 68 Fed 65 Fed	28 Dem-Rep 30 Dem-Rep 27 Dem-Rep 25 Dem-Rep	6 Fed 6 Fed 9 Fed 11 Fed
1817–1825	**James Monroe** Daniel D. Tompkins	Dem-Rep	15th 16th 17th 18th	141 Dem-Rep 156 Dem-Rep 158 Dem-Rep 187 Dem-Rep	42 Fed 27 Fed 25 Fed 26 Fed	34 Dem-Rep 35 Dem-Rep 44 Dem-Rep 44 Dem-Rep	10 Fed 7 Fed 4 Fed 4 Fed
1825–1829	**John Quincy Adams** John C. Calhoun	Nat-Rep	19th 20th	105 Admin 119 Jack	97 Jack 94 Admin	26 Admin 28 Jack	20 Jack 20 Admin
1829–1837	**Andrew Jackson** John C. Calhoun (to 1833) Martin Van Buren (to 1837)	Democrat	21st 22d 23d 24th	139 Dem 141 Dem 147 Dem 145 Dem	74 Nat Rep 58 Nat Rep 53 AntiMas 98 Whig	26 Dem 25 Dem 20 Dem 27 Dem	22 Nat Rep 21 Nat Rep 20 Nat Rep 25 Whig
1837–1841	**Martin Van Buren** Richard M. Johnson	Democrat	25th 26th	108 Dem 124 Dem	107 Whig 118 Whig	30 Dem 28 Dem	18 Whig 22 Whig
1841	**William H. Harrison*** John Tyler	Whig					
1841–1845	**John Tyler** (VP vacant)	Whig	27th 28th	133 Whig 142 Dem	102 Dem 79 Whig	28 Whig 28 Whig	22 Dem 25 Dem
1845–1849	**James K. Polk** George M. Dallas	Democrat	29th 30th	143 Dem 115 Whig	77 Whig 108 Dem	31 Dem 36 Dem	25 Whig 21 Whig
1849–1850	**Zachary Taylor*** Millard Fillmore	Whig	31st	112 Dem	109 Whig	35 Dem	25 Whig
1850–1853	**Millard Fillmore** (VP vacant)	Whig	32d	140 Dem	88 Whig	35 Dem	24 Whig
1853–1857	**Franklin Pierce** William R. King	Democrat	33d 34th	159 Dem 108 Rep	71 Whig 83 Dem	38 Dem 40 Dem	22 Whig 15 Rep
1857–1861	**James Buchanan** John C. Breckinridge	Democrat	35th 36th	118 Dem 114 Rep	92 Rep 92 Dem	36 Dem 36 Dem	20 Rep 26 Rep

NOTES: Only members of two major parties in Congress are shown; omitted are independents, members of minor parties, and vacancies. Party balance as of beginning of Congress.

Congresses in which one or both houses are controlled by party other than that of the president are shown in color.

During administration of George Washington and (in part) John Quincy Adams, Congress was not organized by formal parties; the split shown is between supporters and opponents of the administration.

ABBREVIATIONS: **Admin** = Administration supporters; **AntiMas** = Anti-Masonic; **Dem** = Democratic; **Dem-Rep** = Democratic-Republican; **Fed** = Federalist; **Jack** = Jacksonian Democrats; **Nat Rep** = National Republican; **Opp** = Opponents of administration; **Rep** = Republican; **Union** = Unionist; **Whig** = Whig.

* Died in office.

Year	President and vice president	Party of president	Congress	House		Senate	
				Majority party	Minority party	Majority party	Minority party
1861–1865	**Abraham Lincoln***	Republican	37th	105 Rep	43 Dem	31 Rep	10 Dem
	Hannibal Hamlin (to 1865) Andrew Johnson (1865		38th	102 Rep	75 Dem	36 Rep	9 Dem
1865–1869	**Andrew Johnson**	Republican	39th	149 Union	42 Dem	42 Union	10 Dem
	(VP vacant)		40th	143 Rep	49 Dem	42 Rep	11 Dem
1869–1877	**Ulysses S. Grant**	Republican	41st	149 Rep	63 Dem	56 Rep	11 Dem
	Schuyler Colfax (to 1873)		42d	134 Rep	104 Dem	52 Rep	17 Dem
	Henry Wilson (to 1877)		43d	194 Rep	92 Dem	49 Rep	19 Dem
			44th	169 Dem	109 Rep	45 Rep	29 Dem
1877–1881	**Rutherford B. Hayes**	Republican	45th	153 Dem	140 Rep	39 Rep	36 Dem
	William A. Wheeler		46th	149 Dem	130 Rep	42 Dem	33 Rep
1881	**James A. Garfield***	Republican	47th	147 Rep	135 Dem	37 Rep	37 Dem
	Chester A. Arthur						
1881–1885	**Chester A. Arthur**	Republican	48th	197 Dem	118 Rep	38 Rep	36 Rep
	(VP vacant)						
1885–1889	**Grover Cleveland**	Democrat	49th	183 Dem	140 Rep	43 Rep	34 Dem
	Thomas A. Hendricks		50th	169 Dem	152 Rep	39 Rep	37 Dem
1889–1893	**Benjamin Harrison**	Republican	51st	166 Rep	159 Dem	39 Rep	37 Dem
	Levi P. Morton		52d	235 Dem	88 Rep	47 Rep	39 Dem
1893–1897	**Grover Cleveland**	Democrat	53d	218 Dem	127 Rep	44 Dem	38 Rep
	Adlai E. Stevenson		54th	244 Rep	105 Dem	43 Rep	39 Dem
1897–1901	**William McKinley***	Republican	55th	204 Rep	113 Rep	47 Rep	34 Dem
	Garret A. Hobart (to 1901) Theodore Roosevelt (1901)		56th	185 Rep	163 Rep	53 Rep	26 Dem
1901–1909	**Theodore Roosevelt**	Republican	57th	197 Rep	151 Dem	55 Rep	31 Dem
	(VP vacant, 1901–1905)		58th	208 Rep	178 Dem	57 Rep	33 Dem
	Charles W. Fairbanks		59th	250 Rep	136 Dem	57 Rep	33 Dem
	(1905–1909)		60th	222 Rep	164 Dem	61 Rep	31 Dem
1909–1913	**William Howard Taft**	Republican	61st	219 Rep	172 Dem	61 Rep	32 Dem
	James S. Sherman		62d	228 Dem	161 Rep	51 Rep	41 Dem
1913–1921	**Woodrow Wilson**	Democrat	63d	291 Dem	127 Rep	51 Dem	44 Rep
	Thomas R. Marshall		64th	230 Dem	196 Rep	56 Dem	40 Rep
			65th	216 Dem	210 Rep	53 Dem	42 Rep
			66th	240 Rep	190 Dem	49 Rep	47 Dem
1921–1923	**Warren G. Harding***	Republican	67th	301 Rep	131 Dem	59 Rep	37 Dem
	Calvin Coolidge						
1923–1929	**Calvin Coolidge**	Republican	68th	225 Rep	205 Dem	51 Rep	43 Dem
	(VP vacant, 1923–1925)		69th	247 Rep	183 Dem	56 Rep	39 Dem
	Charles G. Dawes (1925–1929)		70th	237 Rep	195 Dem	49 Rep	46 Dem
1929–1933	**Herbert Hoover**	Republican	71st	267 Rep	167 Dem	56 Rep	39 Dem
	Charles Curtis		72d	220 Dem	214 Rep	48 Rep	47 Dem
1933–1945	**Franklin D. Roosevelt***	Democrat	73d	310 Dem	117 Rep	60 Dem	35 Rep
	John N. Garner (1933–1941)		74th	319 Dem	103 Rep	69 Dem	25 Rep
			75th	331 Dem	89 Rep	76 Dem	16 Rep
	Henry A. Wallace (1941–1945)		76th	261 Dem	164 Rep	69 Dem	23 Rep
			77th	268 Dem	162 Rep	66 Dem	28 Rep
	Harry S Truman (1945)		78th	218 Dem	208 Rep	58 Dem	37 Rep
1945–1953	**Harry S Truman**	Democrat	79th	242 Dem	190 Rep	56 Dem	38 Rep
	VP vacant, 1945–1949		80th	245 Rep	188 Dem	51 Rep	45 Dem
	Alben W. Barkley (1949–1953)		81st	263 Dem	171 Rep	54 Dem	42 Rep
			82d	234 Dem	199 Rep	49 Dem	47 Rep

* Died in office.

Year	President and vice president	Party of president	Congress	House Majority party	House Minority party	Senate Majority party	Senate Minority party
1953–1961	**Dwight D. Eisenhower**	Republican	83d	221 Rep	211 Dem	48 Rep	47 Dem
	Richard M. Nixon		84th	232 Dem	203 Rep	48 Dem	47 Rep
			85th	233 Dem	200 Rep	49 Dem	47 Rep
			86th	283 Dem	153 Rep	64 Dem	34 Rep
1961–1963	**John F. Kennedy***	Democrat	87th	263 Dem	174 Rep	65 Dem	35 Rep
	Lyndon B. Johnson						
1963–1969	**Lyndon B. Johnson**	Democrat	88th	258 Dem	177 Rep	67 Dem	33 Rep
	(VP vacant, 1963–1965)		89th	295 Dem	140 Rep	68 Dem	32 Rep
	Hubert H. Humphrey (1965–1969)		90th	247 Dem	187 Rep	64 Dem	36 Rep
1969–1974	**Richard M. Nixon†**	Republican	91st	243 Dem	192 Rep	57 Dem	43 Rep
	Spiro T. Agnew†† Gerald R. Ford§		92d	254 Dem	180 Rep	54 Dem	44 Rep
1974–1977	**Gerald R. Ford**	Republican	93d	239 Dem	192 Rep	56 Dem	42 Rep
	Nelson A. Rockefeller§		94th	291 Dem	144 Rep	60 Dem	37 Rep
1977–1981	**Jimmy Carter**	Democrat	95th	292 Dem	143 Rep	61 Dem	38 Rep
	Walter Mondale		96th	276 Dem	157 Rep	58 Dem	41 Rep
1981–1989	**Ronald Reagan**	Republican	97th	243 Dem	192 Rep	53 Rep	46 Dem
	George Bush		98th	269 Dem	165 Rep	54 Rep	46 Dem
			99th	253 Dem	182 Rep	53 Rep	47 Dem
			100th	257 Dem	178 Rep	54 Dem	46 Rep
1989–1993	**George Bush**	Republican	101st	262 Dem	173 Rep	55 Dem	45 Rep
	Dan Quayle		102d	267 Dem	167 Rep	56 Dem	44 Rep
1993–2000	**Bill Clinton**	Democrat	103d	258 Dem	176 Rep	57 Dem	43 Rep
	Albert Gore, Jr.		104th	230 Rep	204 Dem	53 Rep	47 Dem
			105th	228 Rep	206 Dem	55 Rep	45 Dem
			106th	223 Rep	211 Dem	54 Rep	46 Dem
2000–2009	**George W. Bush**	Republican	107th	220 Rep	215 Dem	50 Rep	50 Dem
	Dick Cheney		108th	229 Rep	204 Dem	51 Rep	48 Dem
			109th	233 Rep	206 Dem	55 Rep	44 Dem
			110th	229 Dem	196 Rep	51 Dem	49 Rep
2009–2012	**Barack Obama**	Democrat	111th	256 Dem	179 Rep	60 Dem	40 Rep
	Joe Biden						

*Died in office. †Resigned from the presidency. ††Resigned from the vice presidency. §Appointed vice president.

Glossary

activist approach The view that judges should discern the general principles underlying laws or the Constitution and apply them to modern circumstances. (16)

activists People who tend to participate in all forms of politics. (8)

ad hoc structure Several subordinates, cabinet officers, and committees report directly to the president on different matters. (14)

adversarial press The tendency of the national media to be suspicious of officials and eager to reveal unflattering stories about them. (12)

affirmative action Programs designed to increase minority participation in some institution (businesses, schools, labor unions, or government agencies) by taking positive steps to appoint more minority-group members. (6)

amendment A new provision in the Constitution that has been ratified by the states. (2)

amicus curiae A brief submitted by a "friend of the court." (16)

Antifederalists Those who favor a weaker national government. (2)

appropriation A legislative grant of money to finance a government program or agency. (15)

Articles of Confederation A weak constitution that governed America during the Revolutionary War. (2)

assistance program A government program financed by general income taxes that provides benefits to poor citizens without requiring contribution from them. (19)

Australian ballot A government-printed ballot of uniform dimensions to be cast in secret that many states adopted around 1890 to reduce voting fraud associated with party-printed ballots cast in public. (8)

authority The right to use power. (1)

authorization legislation Legislative permission to begin or continue a government program or agency. (15)

background A public official's statement to a reporter given on condition that the official not be named. (12)

benefit A satisfaction people believe they will enjoy if a policy is adopted. (17)

bicameral legislature A lawmaking body made up of two chambers or parts. (13)

bill of attainder A law that declares a person, without a trial, guilty of a crime. (2)

Bill of Rights First ten amendments to the Constitution. (2)

bipolar world A political landscape with two superpowers. (20)

blanket primary A primary election in which each voter may vote for candidates from both parties. (10)

blog A series, or log, of discussion items on a page of the World Wide Web. (12)

brief A written statement by an attorney that summarizes a case and the laws and rulings that support it. (16)

budget A document that states tax collections, spending levels, and the allocation of spending among purposes. (18)

budget resolution A congressional decision that states the maximum amount of money the government should spend. (18)

bully pulpit The president's use of his prestige and visibility to guide or enthuse the American public.(14)

bureaucracy A large, complex organization composed of appointed officials. (15)

bureaucratic view View that the government is dominated by appointed officials. (1)

cabinet The heads of the fifteen executive branch departments of the federal government. (14)

categorical grants Federal grants for specific purposes, such as building an airport. (3)

caucus A meeting of party members to select delegates backing one or another primary candidate. (9, 10, 13)

charitable choice Name given to four federal laws passed in the late 1990s specifying the conditions under which non-profit religious organizations could compete to administer certain social service delivery and welfare programs. (19)

checks and balances Authority shared by three branches of government. (2)

circular structure Several of the president's assistants report directly to him. (14)

civic competence A belief that one can affect government policies. (4)

civic duty A belief that one has an obligation to participate in civic and political affairs. (4)

civil disobedience Opposing a law considered unjust by peacefully disobeying it and accepting the resultant punishment. (6)

civil rights The rights of people to be treated without unreasonable or unconstitutional differences. (6)

civil society Voluntary action that makes cooperation easier. (4)

class consciousness A belief that you are a member of an economic group whose interests are opposed to people in other such groups. (4)

class-action suit A case brought by someone to help him or her and all others similarly situated. (16)

class view View that the government is dominated by capitalists. (1)

clear-and-present-danger test Law should not punish speech unless there was a clear and present danger of producing harmful actions. (5)

client politics A policy in which one small group benefits and almost everybody pays. (17, 19)

closed primary A primary election in which voting is limited to already registered party members. (10)

closed rule An order from the House Rules Committee that sets a time limit on debate; forbids a bill from being amended on the floor. (13)

cloture rule A rule used by the Senate to end or limit debate. (13)

coalition An alliance of factions. (2)

coattails The alleged tendency of candidates to win more votes in an election because of the presence at the top of the ticket of a better-known candidate, such as the president. (10)

command-and-control strategy A strategy to improve air and water quality, involving the setting of detailed pollution standards and rules. (21)

committee clearance The ability of a congressional committee to review and approve certain agency decisions in advance and without passing a law. (15)

competitive service The government offices to which people are appointed on the basis of merit, as ascertained by a written exam or by applying certain selection criteria. (15)

concurrent powers Powers shared by the national and state governments. (2)

concurrent resolution An expression of opinion without the force of law that requires the approval of both the House and the Senate, but not the president. (13)

concurring opinion A signed opinion in which one or more members agree with the majority view but for different reasons. (16)

conditions of aid Terms set by the national government that states must meet if they are to receive certain federal funds. (3)

conference committees A joint committee appointed to resolve differences in the Senate and House versions of the same bill. (13)

congressional campaign committee A party committee in Congress that provides funds to members and would-be members. (9)

conservative coalition An alliance between Republican and conservative Democrats. (13)

Constitutional Convention A meeting in Philadelphia in 1787 that produced a new constitution. (2)

constitutional court A federal court authorized by Article III of the Constitution that keeps judges in office during good behavior and prevents their salaries from being reduced. They are the Supreme Court (created by the Constitution) and appellate and district courts created by Congress. (16)

containment The belief that the United States should resist the expansion of aggressive nations, especially the former Soviet Union. (20)

cost A burden people believe they must bear if a policy is enacted. (17)

cost overruns When the money actually paid to military suppliers exceeds the estimated costs. (20)

courts of appeals Federal courts that hear appeals from district courts; no trials. (16)

critical or realignment period Periods when a major, lasting shift occurs in the popular coalition supporting one or both parties. (9)

de facto segregation Racial segregation that occurs in schools, not as a result of the law, but as a result of patterns of residential settlement. (6)

de jure segregation Racial segregation required by law. (6)

deficit What occurs when the government in one year spends more money than it takes in from taxes. (18)

democracy The rule of the many. (1)

direct or participatory democracy A government in which all or most citizens participate directly. (1)

discharge petition A device by which any member of the House, after a committee has had the bill for thirty days, may petition to have it brought to the floor. (13)

discretionary authority The extent to which appointed bureaucrats can choose courses of action and make policies that are not spelled out in advance by laws. (15)

discretionary spending Spending not required to pay for contracts, interest on the national debt, or entitlement programs such as Social Security. (18)

disengagement The belief that the United States was harmed by its war in Vietnam and so should avoid supposedly similar events. (20)

dissenting opinion A signed opinion in which one or more justices disagree with the majority view. (16)

district courts The lowest federal courts; federal trials can be held only here. (16)

diversity cases Cases involving citizens of different states who can bring suit in federal courts. (16)

divided government One party controls the White House and another party controls one or both houses of Congress. (14)

division vote A congressional voting procedure in which members stand and are counted. (13)

double-tracking A procedure to keep the Senate going during a filibuster in which the disputed bill is shelved temporarily so that the Senate can get on with other business. (13)

dual federalism Doctrine holding that the national government is supreme in its sphere, the states are supreme in theirs, and the two spheres should be kept separate. (3)

due process of law Denies the government the right, without due process, to deprive people of life, liberty, and property. (5)

earmarks "Hidden" congressional provisions that direct the federal government to fund specific projects or that exempt specific persons or groups from paying specific federal taxes or fees. (13)

Earned Income Tax Credit (EITC) A provision of a 1975 law that entitles working families with children to receive money from the government if their total income is below a certain level. The program was expanded in the early 1990s. (19)

economic planning The belief that government plans, such as wage and price controls or the direction of investment, can improve the economy. (18)

electoral college The people chosen to cast each state's votes in a presidential election. Each state can cast one electoral vote for each senator and representative it has. The District of Columbia has three electoral votes, even though it cannot elect a representative or senator. (14)

elite People who have a disproportionate amount of some valued resource, like money or power. (1, 7)

entitlements A claim for government funds that cannot be changed without violating the rights of the claimant. (18)

entrepreneurial politics A policy in which almost everybody benefits and a small group pays the cost. (17)

enumerated powers Powers given to the national government alone. (2)

environmental impact statement A report required by federal law that assesses the possible effect of a project on the environment if the project is subsidized in whole or part by federal funds. (21)

equal protection of the law A standard of equal treatment that must be observed by the government. (5)

equal time rule An FCC rule that if a broadcaster sells time to one candidate, it must sell equal time to other candidates. (12)

equality of opportunity Giving people an equal chance to succeed. (6)

equality of result Making certain people achieve the same result. (6)

establishment clause First Amendment ban on laws "respecting an establishment of religion." (5)

ex post facto law A law that makes an act criminal although the act was legal when it was committed. (2)

exclusionary rule Improperly gathered evidence may not be introduced in a criminal trial. (5)

exit polls Polls based on interviews conducted on Election Day with randomly selected voters. (7)

faction A group with a distinct political interest. (2)

feature stories Media stories about events that, though public, are not regularly covered by reporters. (12)

federalism Government authority shared by national and local governments. (2, 3)

Federalists Those who favor a stronger national government. (2)

federal-question cases Cases concerning the Constitution, federal laws, or treaties. (6)

fee shifting A rule that allows a plaintiff to recover costs from the defendant if the plaintiff wins. (16)

filibuster An attempt to defeat a bill in the Senate by talking indefinitely, thus preventing the Senate from taking action on the bill. (13)

fiscal policy Managing the economy by the use of tax and spending laws. (18)

fiscal year For the federal government, October 1 through the following September 30. (18)

527 organizations Organizations that, under section 527 of the Internal Revenue Code, raise and spend money to advance political causes. (10)

franking privilege The ability of members to mail letters to their constituents free of charge by substituting their fac-simile signature for postage. (13)

freedom of expression Right of people to speak, publish, and assemble. (5)

freedom of religion People shall be free to exercise their reli-gion, and government may not establish a religion. (5)

free-exercise clause First Amendment requirement that law cannot prevent free exercise of religion. (5)

gender gap Difference in political views between men and women. (7)

general election An election held to choose which candidate will hold office. (10)

gerrymandering Drawing the boundaries of legislative dis-tricts in bizarre or unusual shapes to favor one party. (10)

globalization The growing integration of the economies and societies of the world. (18)

gold plating The tendency of Pentagon officials to ask weapons contractors to meet excessively high requirements. (20)

good-faith exception An error in gathering evidence suffi-ciently minor that it may be used in a trial. (5)

government by proxy Washington pays state and local gov-ernments and private groups to staff and administer federal programs. (15)

grandfather clause A clause in registration laws allowing people who do not meet registration requirements to vote if they or their ancestors had voted before 1867. (8)

grants-in-aid Money given by the national government to the states. (3)

Great Compromise Plan to have a popularly elected House based on state population and a state-selected Senate, with two members for each state. (2)

gridlock The inability of the government to act because rival parties control different parts of the government. (14)

gross domestic product The total of all goods and services produced in the economy during a given year. (18)

habeas corpus An order to produce an arrested person before a judge. (2)

human rights The view that we should try to improve the lives of people in other countries. (20)

ideological interest groups Political organizations that at-tract members by appealing to their political convictions or principles. (11)

ideological party A party that values principled stands on issues above all else. (9)

impeachment Charges against a president approved by a majority of the House of Representatives. (14)

in forma pauperis A method whereby a poor person can have his or her case heard in federal court without charge. (16)

incentive Something of value one cannot get without joining an organization. (11)

income strategy A policy giving poor people money to help lift them out of poverty. (19)

incumbent The person already holding an elective office. (10)

independent expenditures Spending by political action com-mittees, corporations, or labor unions done to help a party or candidate but done independently of them. (10)

initiative Process that permits voters to put legislative mea-sures directly on the ballot. (3)

insider stories Media stories about events that are not usually made public. (12)

insurance program A self-financing government program based on contributions that provide benefits to unemployed or retired persons. (19)

interest group An organization of people sharing a common interest or goal that seeks to influence public policy. (17)

interest group politics A policy in which one small group benefits and another small group pays. (17)

iron triangle A close relationship between an agency, a con-gressional committee, and an interest group. (15)

isolationism The opinion that the United States should with-draw from world affairs. (20)

issue network A network of people in Washington, D.C.– based interest groups, on congressional staffs, in universi-ties and think tanks, and in the mass media, who regularly discuss and advocate public policies. (15)

joint committees Committees on which both senators and representatives serve. (13)

joint resolution A formal expression of congressional opinion that must be approved by both houses of Congress and by the president; constitutional amendments need not be signed by the president. (13)

judicial restraint approach The view that judges should decide cases strictly on the basis of the language of the laws and the Constitution. (16)

judicial review The power of courts to declare laws unconsti-tutional. (2, 16)

Keynesianism The belief the government must manage the economy by spending more money when in a recession and cutting spending when there is inflation. (15)

laissez-faire An economic theory that government should not regulate or interfere with commerce. (15)

lame duck A person still in office after he or she has lost a bid for reelection. (14)

legislative courts Courts created by Congress for specialized purposes whose judges do not enjoy the protections of Article III of the Constitution. (16)

legislative veto The authority of Congress to block a presiden-tial action after it has taken place. The Supreme Court has held that Congress does not have this power. (14, 15)

legitimacy Political authority conferred by law or by a state or national constitution. (1)

libel Writing that falsely injures another person. (5)

line-item veto An executive's ability to block a particular pro-vision in a bill passed by the legislature. (2, 14)

literacy test A requirement that citizens show they can read before registering to vote. (8)

litmus test An examination of the political ideology of a nominated judge. (16)

loaded language Words that imply a value judgment, used to persuade a reader without having made a serious argument. (12)

logrolling A legislator supports a proposal favored by another in return for support of his or hers. (17)

majoritarian politics A policy in which almost everybody benefits and almost everybody pays. (17, 19)

majority leader The legislative leader elected by party members holding the majority of seats in the House or the Senate. (13)

malapportionment Drawing the boundaries of legislative districts so they are unequal in population. (10)

mandates Terms set by the national government that states must meet whether or not they accept federal grants. (3)

marginal districts Political districts in which candidates elected to the House of Representatives win in close elections, typically by less than 55 percent of the vote. (13)

material incentives Money or things valued in monetary terms. (11)

means test An income qualification program that determines whether one is eligible for benefits under government programs reserved for lower-income groups. (19)

military-industrial complex An alleged alliance between military leaders and corporate leaders. (20)

minority leader The legislative leader elected by party members holding a minority of seats in the House or the Senate. (13)

monetarism The belief that inflation occurs when too much money is chasing too few goods. (18)

monetary policy Managing the economy by altering the supply of money and interest rates. (18)

mugwumps or progressives Republican party faction of the 1890s to the 1910s composed of reformers who opposed patronage. (9)

multiple referral A congressional process whereby a bill may be referred to several important committees. (13)

name-request job A job filled by a person whom an agency has already identified. (15)

national chairman Day-to-day party manager elected by the national committee. (9)

national committee Delegates who run party affairs between national conventions. (9)

national convention A meeting of party delegates held every four years. (9)

national debt The total deficit from the first presidency down to the present. (18)

"necessary and proper" clause Section of the Constitution allowing Congress to pass all laws "necessary and proper" to its duties, and which has permitted Congress to exercise powers not specifically given to it (enumerated) by the Constitution. (3)

New Jersey Plan Proposal to create a weak national government. (2)

norm A standard of right or proper conduct. (7)

nullification The doctrine that a state can declare null and void a federal law that, in the state's opinion, violates the Constitution. (3)

office-bloc ballot A ballot listing all candidates of a given office under the name of that office; also called a "Massachusetts" ballot. (9)

open primary A primary election in which voters may choose in which party to vote as they enter the polling place. (10)

open rule An order from the House Rules Committee that permits a bill to be amended on the floor. (13)

opinion of the court A signed opinion of a majority of the Supreme Court. (16)

orthodox A belief that morality and religion ought to be of decisive importance. (4)

party polarization A vote in which a majority of Democratic legislators oppose a majority of Republican legislators. (13)

party-column ballot A ballot listing all candidates of a given party together under the name of that party; also called an "Indiana" ballot. (9)

per curiam opinion A brief, unsigned court opinion. (16)

personal following The political support provided to a candidate on the basis of personal popularity and networks. (9)

plaintiff The party that initiates a lawsuit. (16)

pluralist view The belief that competition among all affected interests shapes public policy. (1)

plurality system An electoral system in which the winner is the person who gets the most votes, even if he or she does not receive a majority; used in almost all American elections. (9)

pocket veto A bill fails to become law because the president did not sign it within ten days before Congress adjourns. (14)

polarization A deep and wide conflict over some government policy. (20)

police power State power to enact laws promoting health, safety, and morals. (3, 6)

policy entrepreneurs Activists in or out of government who pull together a political majority on behalf of unorganized interests. (17)

political action committee (PAC) A committee set up by a corporation, labor union, or interest group that raises and spends campaign money from voluntary donations. (10)

political agenda Issues that people believe require governmental action. (17)

political cue A signal telling a legislator what values are at stake in a vote, and how that issue fits into his or her own political views on party agenda. (11)

political culture A patterned and sustained way of thinking about how political and economic life ought to be carried out. (4)

political elites Persons with a disproportionate share of political power. (7)

political ideology A more or less consistent set of beliefs about what policies government ought to pursue. (7)

political machine A party organization that recruits members by dispensing patronage. (9)

political party A group that seeks to elect candidates to public office (9)

political question An issue the Supreme Court will allow the executive and legislative branches decide. (16)

political socialization Process by which background traits influence one's political views. (7)

poll A survey of public opinion. (7)

poll tax A requirement that citizens pay a tax in order to register to vote. (8)

pork-barrel legislation Legislation that gives tangible benefits to constituents in several districts or states in the hope of winning their votes in return. (13, 17)

position issues An issue about which the public is divided and rival candidates or political parties adopt different policy positions. (10)

power The ability of one person to get another person to act in accordance with the first person's intentions. (1)

power elite view View that the government is dominated by a few top leaders, most of whom are outside of government. (1)

primary election An election held to choose candidates for office. (10)

prior restraint Censorship of a publication. (5)

private bill A legislative bill that deals only with specific, private, personal, or local matters. (13)

probable cause Reasonable cause for issuing a search warrant or making an arrest; more than mere suspicion. (5)

process regulation Rules governing commercial activities designed to improve consumer, worker, or environmental conditions. Also called *social regulation*. (17)

progressive A belief that personal freedom and solving social problems are more important than religion. (4)

prospective voting Voting for a candidate because you favor his or her ideas for handling issues. (10)

public bill A legislative bill that deals with matters of general concern. (13)

public-interest lobby A political organization whose goals will principally benefit nonmembers. (11)

public opinion How people think or feel about particular things. (7)

purposive incentive A benefit that comes from serving a cause or principle. (11)

pyramid structure A president's subordinates report to him through a clear chain of command headed by a chief of staff. (14)

quorum The minimum number of members who must be present for business to be conducted in Congress. (13)

quorum call A roll call in either house of Congress to see whether the minimum number of representatives required to conduct business is present. (13)

random sample Method of selecting from a population in which each person has an equal probability of being selected. (7)

ratings Assessments of a representative's voting record on issues important to an interest group. (11)

Reaganomics The belief that a combination of monetarism, lower federal spending, and supply-side economics will stimulate the economy. (18)

recall Procedure whereby voters can remove an elected official from office. (3)

red tape Complex bureaucratic rules and procedures that must be followed to get something done. (15)

referendum Procedure enabling voters to reject a measure passed by the legislature. (3)

registered voters People registered to vote. (8)

remedy A judicial order enforcing a right or redressing a wrong. (16)

representative democracy A government in which leaders make decisions by winning a competitive struggle for the popular vote. (1)

republic A government in which elected representatives make the decisions. (2)

reserved powers Powers given to the state government alone. (2)

restrictive rule An order from the House Rules Committee that permits certain kinds of amendments but not others to be made into a bill on the floor. (13)

retrospective voting Voting for a candidate because you like his or her past actions in office. (10)

reverse discrimination Using race or sex to give preferential treatment to some people. (6)

roll-call vote A congressional voting procedure that consists of members answering "yea" or "nay" to their names. (13)

routine stories Media stories about events regularly covered by reporters. (12)

runoff primary A second primary election held when no candidate wins a majority of the votes in the first primary. (10)

safe districts Districts in which incumbents win by margins of 55 percent or more. (13)

sampling error The difference between the results of random samples taken at the same time. (7)

search warrant A judge's order authorizing a search. (5)

select committees Congressional committees appointed for a limited time and purpose. (13)

selective attention Paying attention only to those news stories with which one already agrees. (12)

selective incorporation Court cases that apply Bill of Rights to states. (5)

separate-but-equal doctrine The doctrine established in *Plessy v. Ferguson* (1896) that African Americans could constitutionally be kept in separate but equal facilities. (6)

separation of powers Constitutional authority is shared by three different branches of government. (2)

sequential referral A congressional process by which a Speaker may send a bill to a second committee after the first is finished acting. (13)

sequester Automatic spending cuts. (18)

service strategy A policy providing poor people with education and job training to help lift them out of poverty. (19)

Shays's Rebellion A 1787 rebellion in which ex-Revolutionary War soldiers attempted to prevent foreclosures of farms as a result of high interest rates and taxes. (2)

signing statement A presidential document that reveals what the president thinks of a new law and how it ought to be enforced. (14)

simple resolution An expression of opinion either in the House or Senate to settle procedural matters in either body. (13)

social movement A widely shared demand for change in some aspect of the social or political order. (11)

soft money Funds obtained by political parties that are spent on party activities, such as get-out-the-vote drives, but not on behalf of a specific candidate. (10)

solidary incentives The social rewards (sense of pleasure, status, or companionship) that lead people to join political organizations. (9, 11)

sophomore surge An increase in the votes congressional candidates usually get when they first run for reelection. (10)

sound bite A radio or video clip of someone speaking. (12)

sovereign immunity The rule that a citizen cannot sue the government without the government's consent. (16)

split ticket Voting for candidates of different parties for various offices in the same election. (9)

sponsored party A local or state political party largely supported by another organization in the community. (9)

standing A legal rule stating who is authorized to start a lawsuit. (16)

standing committees Permanently established legislative committees that consider and are responsible for legislation within a certain subject area. (13)

stare decisis "Let the decision stand," or allowing prior rulings to control the current case. (16)

straight ticket Voting for candidates who are all of the same party. (9)

superdelegates Party leaders and elected officials who become delegates to the national convention without having to run in primaries or caucuses. (9)

supply-side theory The belief that lower taxes and fewer regulations will stimulate the economy. (18)

symbolic speech An act that conveys a political message. (5)

teller vote A congressional voting procedure in which members pass between two tellers, the "yeas" first and the "nays" second. (13)

trial balloon Information leaked to the media to test public reaction to a possible policy. (12)

trust funds Funds for government programs collected and spent outside the regular government budget. (15)

two-party system An electoral system with two dominant parties that compete in national elections. (9)

unalienable A human right based on nature or God. (2)

unified government The same party controls the White House and both houses of Congress. (14)

unipolar world A political landscape with one superpower. (20)

valence issue An issue about which the public is united and rival candidates or political parties adopt similar positions in hopes that each will be thought to best represent those widely shared beliefs. (10)

veto message A message from the president to Congress stating that he will not sign a bill it has passed. Must be produced within ten days of the bill's passage. (14)

Virginia Plan Proposal to create a strong national government. (2)

voice vote A congressional voting procedure in which members shout "yea" in approval or "nay" in disapproval, permitting members to vote quickly or anonymously on bills. (13)

voting-age population Citizens eligible to vote after reaching the minimum age requirement. (8)

waiver A decision by an administrative agency granting some other part permission to violate a law or rule that would otherwise apply to it. (3)

wall of separation Court ruling that government cannot be involved with religion. (5)

whip A senator or representative who helps the party leader stay informed about what party members are thinking. (13)

white primary The practice of keeping blacks from voting in the southern states' primaries through arbitrary use of registration requirements and intimidation. (8)

worldviews A comprehensive opinion of how the United States should respond to world problems. (20)

writ of certiorari An order by a higher court directing a lower court to send up a case for review. (16)

Notes

Chapter 1
The Study of American Government

1. Aristotle, *Politics*, iv, 4, 1290[b]. More precisely, Aristotle's definition was this: Democracy is a "constitution in which the free-born and poor control the government—being at the same time a majority." He distinguished this from an oligarchy, "in which the rich and well-born control the government—being at the same time a minority." Aristotle listed several varieties of democracy, depending on whether, for example, there was a property qualification for citizenship.
2. Joseph A. Schumpeter, *Capitalism, Socialism, and Democracy*, 3d ed. (New York: Harper Torchbooks, 1950), 269. (First published in 1942.)
3. John Locke, *Second Treatise of Civil Government* (New York: Hafner Publishing Co., 1956). First published in 1690.
4. Thomas Hobbes, *Leviathan* (Oxford: Basil Blackwell, 1957). First published in 1651.
5. Karl Marx and Friedrich Engels, "The Manifesto of the Communist Party," in *The Marx-Engels Reader*, 2d ed., ed. Robert C. Tucker (New York: Norton, 1978), 469–500.
6. C. Wright Mills, *The Power Elite* (New York: Oxford University Press, 1956).
7. H. H. Gerth and C. Wright Mills, eds., *From Max Weber: Essays in Sociology* (London: Routledge and Kegan Paul, 1948), 232–235.
8. Among the authors whose interpretations of American politics are essentially pluralist is David B. Truman, *The Governmental Process*, 2d ed. (New York: Knopf, 1971).
9. Alexis de Tocqueville, *Democracy in America*, vol. 2, ed. Phillips Bradley (New York: Knopf, 1951), book 2, ch. 8, 122.

Chapter 2
The Constitution

1. Quoted in Bernard Bailyn, *The Ideological Origins of the American Revolution* (Cambridge: Harvard University Press, 1967), 61, n. 6.
2. Quoted in Bailyn, ibid., 135–137.
3. Quoted in Bailyn, ibid., 77.
4. Quoted in Bailyn, ibid., 160.
5. *Federalist* No. 37.
6. Gordon S. Wood, *The Creation of the American Republic* (Chapel Hill: University of North Carolina Press, 1969). See also *Federalist* No. 49.
7. Letter of George Washington to Henry Lee (October 31, 1787), in *Writings of George Washington*, vol. 29, ed. John C. Fitzpatrick (Washington, D.C.: Government Printing Office, 1939), 34.
8. Letters of Thomas Jefferson to James Madison (January 30, 1787) and to Colonel William S. Smith (November 13, 1787), in *Jefferson Himself*, ed. Bernard Mayo (Boston: Houghton Mifflin, 1942), 145.
9. *Federalist* No. 51.
10. *Federalist* No. 48.
11. *Federalist* No. 51.
12. Ibid.
13. Ibid.
14. "The Address and Reasons of Dissent of the Minority of the State of Pennsylvania to Their Constituents," in *The Anti-Federalist*, ed. Cecelia Kenyon (Indianapolis: Bobbs-Merrill, 1966), 39.
15. Max Farrand, *The Framing of the Constitution of the United States* (New Haven, Conn.: Yale University Press, 1913), 185.
16. See, for example, John Hope Franklin, *Racial Equality in America* (Chicago: University of Chicago Press, 1976), ch. 1, esp. 12–20.
17. Max Farrand, *The Records of the Federal Convention of 1787*, 4 vols. (New Haven, Conn.: Yale University Press, 1911–1937).
18. Theodore J. Lowi, *American Government: Incomplete Conquest* (Hinsdale, Ill.: Dryden Press, 1976), 97.
19. Article I, section 2, para. 3.
20. Gary Wills, *"Negro President": Jefferson and the Slave Power* (Boston: Houghton Mifflin, 2003).
21. Article I, section 9, para. 1.
22. Article IV, section 2, para. 3
23. Charles A. Beard, *An Economic Interpretation of the Constitution* (New York: Macmillan, 1913), esp. 26–51, 149–151, 324–325.
24. Forrest McDonald, *We the People* (Chicago: University of Chicago Press, 1958); Robert E. Brown, *Charles Beard and the Constitution* (Princeton: Princeton University Press, 1956).
25. Robert A. McGuire, "Constitution Making: A Rational Choice Model of the Federal Convention of 1787," *American Journal of Political Science* 32 (May 1988): 483–522. See also Forrest McDonald, *Novus Ordo Seclorum* (Lawrence: University of Kansas Press, 1985), 221.
26. McDonald, *Novus Ordo Seclorum*, 202–221.
27. Robert A. McGuire and Robert L. Ohsfeldt, "Economic Interests and the American Constitution: A Quantitative Rehabilitation of Charles A. Beard," *Journal of Economic History* 44 (June 1984): 509–519.
28. Lloyd N. Cutler, "To Form a Government," *Foreign Affairs* (Fall 1980): 126–143.

Chapter 3
Federalism

1. Woodrow Wilson, *Constitutional Government in the United States* (New York: Columbia University Press, 1961), 173. (First published in 1908.)
2. Martin Diamond, "The Federalists' View of Federalism," in *Essays in Federalism*, ed. George C. S. Benson (Claremont, Calif.: Institute for Studies in Federalism, 1961), 21–64; and Samuel H. Beer, "Federalism, Nationalism, and Democracy in America," *American Political Science Review* 72 (March 1978): 9–21.
3. *United States v. Sprague*, 282 U.S. 716 (1931).
4. *Garcia v. San Antonio Metropolitan Transit Authority*, 105 S. Ct. 1005 (1985), overruling *National League of Cities v. Usery*, 426 U.S. 833 (1976).
5. *McCulloch v. Maryland*, 4 Wheat. 316 (1819).
6. *Pollock v. Farmers' Loan & Trust Co.*, 157 U.S. 429 (1895); *South Carolina v. Baker*, No. 94 (1988).
7. *Texas v. White*, 7 Wall. 700 (1869).
8. *Champion v. Ames*, 188 U.S. 321 (1903).
9. *Hoke v. United States*, 227 U.S. 308 (1913).
10. *Clark Distilling Co. v. W. Md. Ry.*, 242 U.S. 311 (1917).
11. *Hipolite Egg Co. v. United States*, 220 U.S. 45 (1911).
12. *United States v. E. C. Knight Co.*, 156 U.S. 1 (1895).

13. *Paul v. Virginia*, 8 Wall. 168 (1869).
14. *Veazie Bank v. Fenno*, 8 Wall. 533 (1869).
15. *Brown v. Maryland*, 12 Wheat. 419 (1827).
16. *Wickard v. Filburn*, 317 U.S. 111 (1942); *NLRB v. Jones & Laughlin Steel Corp.*, 301 U.S. 58 (1937).
17. *Kirschbaum Co. v. Walling*, 316 U.S. 517 (1942).
18. *Goldfarb v. Virginia State Bar*, 421 U.S. 773 (1975); *Flood v. Kuhn*, 407 U.S. 258 (1972); *Gonzales v. Raich* (03-1454), 2005.
19. David B. Truman, "Federalism and the Party System," in *Federalism: Mature and Emergent,* ed. Arthur McMahon (Garden City, N.Y.: Doubleday, 1955), 123.
20. Harold J. Laski, "The Obsolescence of Federalism," *New Republic* (May 3, 1939), 367–369.
21. William H. Riker, *Federalism: Origin, Operation, Significance* (Boston: Little Brown, 1964), 154.
22. Daniel J. Elazar, *American Federalism: A View from the States* (New York: Crowell, 1966), 216.
23. Martha Derthick, *Keeping the Compound Republic: Essays on American Federalism* (Washington, D.C.: Brookings Institution, 2001), 140.
24. Donald F. Kettl, ed., *The Department of Homeland Security's First Year: A Report Card* (New York: Century Foundation Report, 2004), 18, 102.
25. Samuel H. Beer, "The Modernization of American Federalism," *Publius* 3 (Fall 1973): esp. 74–79; and Beer, "Federalism," 18–19.
26. Congressional Budget Office, *Federal Constraints on State and Local Government Actions* (Washington, D.C.: Government Printing Office, 1979).
27. William T. Gormley, Jr., "Money and Mandates: The Politics of Intergovernmental Conflict," *Publius: The Journal of Federalism* 36 (4): 527.
28. Ibid., 535–537.
29. U.S. Advisory Commission on Intergovernmental Relations, *Federally Induced Costs Affecting State and Local Governments*, September 1994.
30. Paul Teske, *Regulation in the States* (Washington, D.C.: Brookings Institution, 2004).
31. Stephen V. Monsma, *Putting Faith in Partnerships: Welfare-to-Work in Four Cities.* (Ann Arbor: University of Michigan Press, 2004).
32. Baylor University Institute for Studies of Religion, *Ohio Governor's Office of Faith-Based and Community Initiatives: A Case Study*, January 2007.

Chapter 4
American Political Culture

1. *The Public Perspective* (November/December 1991): 5, 7: reporting survey data from the Roper Center for Public Opinion Research.
2. Fred I. Greenstein, "The Benevolent Leader Revisited: Children's Images of Political Leaders in Three Democracies," *American Political Science Review* 69 (December 1975): 1387.
3. Alexis de Tocqueville, *Democracy in America*, ed. Phillips Bradley (New York: Knopf, 1951), vol. 1, 288. (First published in 1835.)
4. Donald J. Devine, *The Political Culture of the United States* (Boston: Little, Brown, 1972), 185; Herbert McClosky and John Zaller, *The American Ethos: Public Attitudes Toward Capitalism and Democracy* (Cambridge: Harvard University Press, 1984), ch. 3, esp. 74–75.
5. McClosky and Zaller, *The American Ethos*, 74–77.
6. Ibid., 66.
7. Gunnar Myrdal, *An American Dilemma: The Negro Problem in Modern Democracy* (New York: Harper, 1944), intro. and ch. 1.
8. Frank R. Westie, "The American Dilemma: An Empirical Test," *American Sociological Review* 30 (August 1965): 536–537.
9. Samuel P. Huntington, *American Politics* (Cambridge, Mass.: Harvard University Press, 1983), 202.
10. Eric L. McKitrick, "Party Politics and the Union and Confederate War Efforts," in *The American Party Systems*, ed. William Nisbet Chambers and Walter Dean Burnham, 2d ed. (New York: Oxford University Press, 1975), 117–121.
11. Russell J. Dalton, *The Good Citizen* (Washington, D.C.: CQ Press, 2008), 38, 71, 168–171.
12. McClosky and Zaller, *The American Ethos*, 174.
13. Sidney Verba and Gary R. Orren, *Equality in America: The View from the Top* (Cambridge: Harvard University Press, 1985), 146–147.
14. McClosky and Zaller, *The American Ethos*, 82–84, 93, 95.
15. Verba and Orren, *Equality in America*, 72, 254.
16. Donald Kinder and David Sears, "Symbolic Racism Versus Racial Threats to the Good Life," *Journal of Personality and Social Psychology* 40 (1981): 414–431.
17. Paul M. Sniderman and Michael Gray Hagen, *Race and Inequality: A Study in American Values* (Chatham, N.J.: Chatham House, 1985), 111.
18. Ibid., 37–38.
19. Theodore Caplow and Howard M. Bahr, "Half a Century of Change in Adolescent Attitudes: A Replication of a Middletown Survey by the Lynds," *Public Opinion Quarterly* 43 (1979): 1–17, table 1.
20. Thomas J. Anton, "Policy-Making and Political Culture in Sweden," *Scandinavian Political Studies* 4 (1969): 88–100; M. Donald Hancock, *Sweden: The Politics of Post-Industrial Change* (Hinsdale, Ill.: Dryden Press, 1972); Sten Johansson, "Liberal-Democratic Theory and Political Processes," in *Readings in the Swedish Class Structure*, ed. Richard Scarse (New York: Pergamon Press, 1976); Steven J. Kelman, *Regulating America, Regulating Sweden: A Comparative Study of Occupational Safety and Health Policy* (Cambridge, Mass.: MIT Press, 1981), 118–123.
21. Lewis Austin, *Saints and Samurai: The Political Culture of American and Japanese Elites* (New Haven, Conn.: Yale University Press, 1975).
22. Gabriel Almond and Sidney Verba, *The Civic Culture* (Princeton, N.J.: Princeton University Press, 1963), 169, 185. See also Gabriel Almond and Sidney Verba, eds., *The Civic Culture Revisited* (Boston: Little, Brown, 1980).
23. Sidney Verba et al., *Voice and Equality: Civic Voluntarism in American Politics* (Cambridge: Harvard University Press, 1995), 69, 70.
24. Kenneth Newton and Pipa Norris, "Confidence in Public Institutions: Faith, Culture or Performance?," paper presented at the Annual Meeting of the American Political Science Association, Atlanta, Ga., September 1999, tables 8.1 and 8.3.
25. Paul M. Sniderman, *A Question of Loyalty* (Berkeley: University of California Press, 1981).
26. Verba and Orren, *Equality in America*, 255.

27. Pippa Norris and Ronald Ingelhart, *Sacred and Secular: Religion and Politics Worldwide* (Cambridge: Cambridge University Press, 2004); George Gallup, Jr., and Thomas Jones, *The Next American Spirituality* (Colorado Springs, Colo.: Cook, 2000).

28. Arthur C. Brooks, *Who Really Cares? America's Charity Divide* (New York: Basic Books, 2006), ch. 2; Ram A. Cnaan, *The Other Philadelphia Story: How Local Congregations Support Quality of Life in Urban America* (Philadelphia: University of Pennsylvania Press, 2006).

29. Max Weber, *The Protestant Ethic and the Spirit of Capitalism*, trans. Talcott Parsons (New York: Scribner's, 1930). (First published in 1904.)

30. Erik H. Erikson, *Childhood and Society* (New York: Norton, 1950), ch. 8.

31. James Davison Hunter, *Culture Wars: The Struggle to Define America* (New York: Basic Books, 1991), and Hunter, *Before the Shooting Begins* (New York: Macmillan, 1994).

32. Morris P. Fiorina, *Culture War? The Myth of a Polarized America*, rev. ed. (New York: Pearson Longman, 2006), and Fiorina and Matthew S. Levendusky, "Disconnected: The Political Class Versus the People," in Pietro S. Nivola and David W. Brady, eds., *Red and Blue Nation?* (Washington, D.C.: Brookings Institution, 2006), 49–71.

33. Alan I. Abramovitz, "Comment," in Nivola and Brady, op. cit., 72–85, 111–114; Gary C. Jacobson, "Comment," in Nivola and Brady, op. cit., 85–95.

34. Philip D. Zelikow and David C. King, eds., *Why People Don't Trust Government* (Cambridge, Mass.: Harvard University Press, 1997).

35. Marc J. Hetherington, *Why Trust Matters* (Princeton, N.J.: Princeton University Press, 2005).

36. Robert D. Putnam, *Bowling Alone: The Collapse and Revival of American Community* (New York: Simon & Schuster, 2000), and Putnam, et al., *Better Together: Report of the Saguaro Seminar* (Cambridge, Mass.: Ken-nedy School of Government, Harvard University), 2001.

37. James Q. Wilson, "Bowling with Others," *Commentary* (Oct., 2007), 30–33.

38. James W. Prothro and Charles M. Grigg, "Fundamental Principles of Democracy: Bases of Agreement and Disagreement," *Journal of Politics*, 22 (Spring 1960): 275–294.

39. Gallup Poll data compiled by Professor John Zaller, Department of Political Science, UCLA.

40. *The American Enterprise* (January/February 1999): 37; reporting data from various polls.

41. John L. Sullivan, James Piereson, and George F. Marcus, *Political Tolerance and American Democracy* (Chicago: University of Chicago Press, 1982), 194–202.

Chapter 5
Civil Liberties

1. *Zamora v. Pomeroy*, 639 F.2d 662 (1981); *Goss v. Lopez*, 419 U.S. 565 (1975); *Tinker v. Des Moines Community School District*, 393 U.S. 503 (1969); *Smith v. Goguen*, 415 U.S. 566 (1974); *New Jersey v. T.L.O.*, 469 U.S. 325 (1985); Morse v. Frederick, 06-278 (2007).

2. *Sheppard v. Maxwell*, 384 U.S. 333 (1966); *New York Times Co. v. United States*, 403 U.S. 713 (1971); *Kunz v. New York*, 340 U.S. 290 (1951).

3. *Barron v. Baltimore*, 7 Pet. 243 (1833).

4. *Chicago, Burlington, and Quincy Railroad Co. v. Chicago*, 166 U.S. 226 (1987); *Gitlow v. New York*, 268 U.S. 652 (1925); *Palko v. Connecticut*, 302 U.S. 319 (1937).

5. *District of Columbia v. Heller*, 07–290 (2008).

6. William Blackstone, *Commentaries*, vol. 4 (1765), 151–152.

7. Jefferson's remarks are from a letter to Abigail Adams (quoted in Walter Berns, *The First Amendment and the Future of American Democracy* [New York: Basic Books, 1976], 82 and from a letter to Thomas McKean, governor of Pennsylvania, February 19, 1803 (Paul L. Ford, ed., *The Writings of Thomas Jefferson: 1801–1806*, vol. 8 [New York: Putnam, 1897], 218.

8. *Schenck v. United States*, 249 U.S. 47 (1919), 52.

9. *Gitlow v. New York*, 268 U.S. 652 (1925), 666.

10. *Fiske v. Kansas*, 274 U.S. 380 (1927); *Stromberg v. California*, 283 U.S. 359 (1931); *Near v. Minnesota*, 283 U.S. 697 (1931); *De Jonge v. Oregon*, 299 U.S. 353 (1937).

11. *Dennis v. United States*, 341 U.S. 494 (1951), 510ff. The test was first formulated by Judge Learned Hand of the court of appeals: see *Dennis v. United States*, 183 F.2d 201 (1950), 212.

12. *Yates v. United States*, 354 U.S. 298 (1957).

13. *Brandenburg v. Ohio*, 395 U.S. 444 (1969).

14. *Village of Skokie v. National Socialist Party*, 432 U.S. 43 (1977); 366 N.E.2d 349 (1977); and 373 N.E.2d 21 (1978).

15. *R.A.V. v. City of St. Paul*, 112 S. Ct. 2538 (1992).

16. *Wisconsin v. Mitchell*, No. 92–515 (1993).

17. C. Herman Pritchett, *Constitutional Civil Liberties* (Englewood Cliffs, N.J.: Prentice-Hall, 1984), 100.

18. *New York Times v. Sullivan*, 376 U.S. 254 (1964); but compare *Time, Inc. v. Firestone*, 424 U.S. 448 (1976).

19. Henry J. Abraham, *Freedom and the Court*, 4th ed. (New York: Oxford University Press, 1982), 193, fn 189.

20. Justice Stewart's famous remark was made in his concurring opinion in *Jacobellis v. Ohio*, 378 U.S. 184 (1964), 197.

21. *Miller v. California*, 413 U.S. 15 (1973).

22. *Jenkins v. Georgia*, 418 U.S. 153 (1974).

23. *Schad v. Borough of Mt. Ephraim*, 452 U.S. 61 (1981).

24. *Barnes v. Glen Theatre*, 111 S. Ct. 2456 (1991).

25. *American Booksellers Association v. Hudnut*, 771 F.2d 323 (1985), affirmed at 475 U.S. 1001 (1986).

26. *Renton v. Playtime Theatres*, 475 U.S. 41 (1986). See also *Young v. American Mini-Theatres, Inc.*, 427 U.S. 50 (1976).

27. *Reno v. American Civil Liberties Union*, 521 U.S. 844 (1997); *Ashcroft v. Free Speech Coalition*, 122 S. Ct. 1389 (2002).

28. *United States v. O'Brien*, 391 U.S. 367 (1968).

29. *Texas v. Johnson*, 109 S. Ct. 2533 (1989).

30. *U.S. v. Eichman*, 496 U.S. 310 (1990).

31. *First National Bank of Boston v. Bellotti*, 435 U.S. 765 (1978); *Federal Election Commission v. Massachusetts Citizens for Life, Inc.*, 479 U.S. 238 (1986).

32. *44 Liquormart v. Rhode Island*, 517 U.S. 484 (1996); *Greater New*

Orleans Broadcasting Association v. United States, 527 U.S. 173 (1999).

33. *Pacific Gas and Electric Co. v. Public Utilities Commission*, 475 U.S. 1 (1986). Some limitations on corporate speech have been upheld, including a state law prohibiting a firm from spending money on candidates for elective office. *Austin v. Michigan Chamber of Commerce*, 100 S. Ct. 1391 (1990).

34. *Board of Trustees of the State University of New York v. Fox*, 492 U.S. 469 (1989).

35. *Bates v. State Bar of Arizona*, 433 U.S. 350 (1977); *Edenfield v. Bane*, 113 S. Ct. 1792 (1993).

36. *McConnell v. Federal Election Commission*, 124 S. Ct. 619 (2003); *Federal Election Commission v. Wisconsin Right to Life*, 06-969 (2007).

37. *Hazelwood School District v. Kuhlmeier, et al.*, 484 U.S. 260 (1988).

38. *Murdock v. Pennsylvania*, 319 U.S. 105 (1943).

39. *Church of the Lukumi Babalu Aye v. City of Hialeah*, 508 U.S. 520 (1993).

40. *Reynolds v. United States*, 98 U.S. 145 (1878).

41. *Jacobson v. Massachusetts*, 197 U.S. 11 (1905).

42. *Employment Division, Department of Human Resources of Oregon v. Smith*, 110 S. Ct. 1595 (1990).

43. *Society for Krishna Consciousness v. Lee*, 112 S. Ct. 2701 (1992).

44. *Welsh v. United States*, 398 U.S. 333 (1970); Pritchett, *Constitutional Civil Liberties*, 140–141.

45. *Sherbert v. Verner*, 374 U.S. 398 (1963); *Wisconsin v. Yoder*, 406 U.S. 205 (1972); *Hobbie v. Unemployment Appeals Commission of Florida*, 480 U.S. 136 (1987); *Estate of Thornton v. Caldor, Inc.*, 472 U.S. 703 (1985).

46. Berns, *The First Amendment*.

47. Pritchett, *Constitutional Civil Liberties*, 145–147.

48. *Everson v. Board of Education*, 330 U.S. 1 (1947).

49. *Engel v. Vitale*, 370 U.S. 421 (1962).

50. *Lubbock Independent School District v. Lubbock Civil Liberties Union*, 669 F.2d 1038.

51. *School District of Abington Township v. Schempp*, 374 U.S. 203 (1963).

52. *Lee v. Weisman*, 112 S. Ct. 2649 (1992); *Santa Fe Independent School District v. Jane Doe*, 530 U.S. 290 (2000).

53. *Epperson v. Arkansas*, 393 U.S. 97 (1968); *McLean v. Arkansas Board of Education*, 529 F. Supp. 1255 (1982).

54. *McCollum v. Board of Education*, 333 U.S. 203 (1948); *Zorach v. Clauson*, 343 U.S. 306 (1952).

55. *Tilton v. Richardson*, 403 U.S. 672 (1971).

56. *Board of Education v. Allen*, 392 U.S. 236 (1968).

57. *Walz v. Tax Commission*, 397 U.S. 664 (1970).

58. *Mueller v. Allen*, 463 U.S. 388 (1983).

59. *Zobrest v. Catalina Foothills School District*, 509 U.S. 1 (1993); *Mitchell v. Helms*, 2000 Lexis 4485.

60. *Lemon v. Kurtzman*, 403 U.S. 602 (1971).

61. *Committee for Public Education v. Nyquist*, 413 U.S. 756 (1973).

62. *Meek v. Pittenger*, 421 U.S. 349 (1975); *Wolman v. Walter*, 433 U.S. 229 (1977).

63. *Edwards v. Aguillard*, 482 U.S. 578 (1987); *Board of Education of Kiryas Joel Village School v. Louis Grumet*, 114 S. Ct. 2481 (1994).

64. *Agostini v. Felton*, 521 U.S. 203 (1997) overruled *Aguilar v. Felton*, 473 U.S. 402 (1985).

65. *Zelman v. Simmons-Harris*, 536 U.S. 639 (2002).

66. *Lemon v. Kurtzman*, 403 U.S. 602 (1971).

67. *Lynch v. Donelly*, 465 U.S. 668 (1984); *Allegheny v. ACLU*, 109 S. Ct. 3086 (1989); *McCreary County, Kentucky, v. ACLU*, 125 S. Ct. 2722 (2005); *Van Orden v. Perry*, 125 S. Ct. 2854 (2005).

68. *Marsh v. Chambers*, 492 U.S. 573 (1983).

69. Yale Kamisar, "Does (Did) (Should) the Exclusionary Rule Rest on a 'Principled Basis' Rather Than an 'Empirical Proposition'?" *Creighton Law Review* 16 (1982–1983): 565–667.

70. *Wolf v. Colorado*, 338 U.S. 25 (1949).

71. *Mapp v. Ohio*, 367 U.S. 643 (1961).

72. *Chimel v. California*, 395 U.S. 752 (1969).

73. *Washington v. Chrisman*, 455 U.S. 1 (1982).

74. *Oliver v. United States*, 466 U.S. 170 (1984).

75. *Arkansas v. Sanders*, 442 U.S. 753 (1979); *Robbins v. California*, 453 U.S. 420 (1981).

76. *United States v. Ross*, 456 U.S. 798 (1982); *Maryland v. Dyson*, 199 S. Ct. 2013 (1999); *Wyoming v. Houghton*, 119 S. Ct. 1297 (1999);

Whren v. United States, 517 U.S. 806 (1996).

77. *Winston v. Lee*, 470 U.S. 753 (1985).

78. *South Dakota v. Neville*, 459 U.S. 553 (1983); *Schmerber v. California*, 384 U.S. 757 (1966).

79. *United States v. Dunn*, 480 U.S. 294 (1987); *California v. Ciraolo*, 476 U.S. 207 (1986); *California v. Carney*, 471 U.S. 386 (1985).

80. *O'Connor v. Ortega*, 480 U.S. 709 (1987).

81. *Escobedo v. Illinois*, 378 U.S. 478 (1964); *Miranda v. Arizona*, 384 U.S. 436 (1966).

82. *Malloy v. Hogan*, 378 U.S. 1 (1964).

83. *Miranda v. Arizona*, 384 U.S. 436 (1966).

84. *Gilbert v. California*, 388 U.S. 263 (1967); *Kirby v. Illinois*, 406 U.S. 682 (1972).

85. *Estelle v. Smith*, 451 U.S. 454 (1981).

86. *Brewer v. Williams*, 430 U.S. 387 (1977).

87. *Illinois v. Perkins*, 496 U.S. 292 (1990).

88. *Missouri v. Seibert*, 542 U.S. 600 (2004).

89. *Dickerson v. U.S.*, 530 U.S. 428 (2000).

90. *Fare v. Michael C.*, 442 U.S. 707 (1979).

91. *United States v. Leon*, 468 U.S. 897 (1984); *Massachusetts v. Sheppard*, 468 U.S. 981 (1984); *Herring v. United States* (07–513, 2008).

92. *New York v. Quarles*, 467 U.S. 649 (1984); *Arizona v. Fulminante*, 499 U.S. 279 (1991).

93. *Nix v. Williams*, 467 U.S. 431 (1984).

94. *Ex Parte Quirin*, 317 U.S. 1 (1942).

95. *Rasul v. Bush*, 542 U.S. 466 (2004).

96. *Hamdi v. Rumsfeld*, 542 U.S. 507 (2004).

97. Military Commissions Act, Public Law 109–366 (2006).

98. Public Law 109-13 (2005).

99. *In Re: Sealed Case*, Foreign Intelligence Review Court, 02-001 (2001).

Chapter 6
Civil Rights

1. *United States v. Carolene Products Co.*, 304 U.S. 144 (1938); *San Antonio Independent School District v. Rodriguez*, 411 U.S. 1 (1973).

2. Gunnar Myrdal, *An American Dilemma* (New York: Harper, 1944), ch. 27.

3. Richard Kluger, *Simple Justice* (New York: Random House/Vintage Books, 1977), 89–90.

4. Paul B. Sheatsley, "White Attitudes Toward the Negro," in *The Negro*

American, ed. Talcott Parsons and Kenneth B. Clark (Boston: Houghton Mifflin, 1966), 305, 308, 317.

5. *Strauder v. West Virginia*, 100 U.S. 303 (1880).

6. *Civil Rights Cases*, 109 U.S. 3 (1883).

7. *Plessy v. Ferguson*, 163 U.S. 537 (1896).

8. *Cumming v. Richmond County Board of Education*, 175 U.S. 528 (1899).

9. *Missouri ex rel. Gaines v. Canada*, 305 U.S. 337 (1938).

10. *Sipuel v. Board of Regents of the University of Oklahoma*, 332 U.S. 631 (1948).

11. *Sweatt v. Painter*, 339 U.S. 629 (1950); *McLaurin v. Oklahoma State Regents for Higher Education*, 339 U.S. 637 (1950).

12. *Brown v. Board of Education of Topeka*, 347 U.S. 483 (1954).

13. *Brown v. Board of Education of Topeka*, 349 U.S. 294 (1955). This case is often referred to as "Brown II."

14. Frederick S. Mosteller and Daniel P. Moynihan, eds., *On Equality of Educational Opportunity* (New York: Random House, 1972), 60–62.

15. *Brown v. Board of Education of Topeka*, 347 U.S. 483 (1954).

16. C. Herman Pritchett, *Constitutional Civil Liberties* (Englewood Cliffs, N.J.: Prentice-Hall, 1984), 250–251, 261.

17. *Green et al. v. County School Board of New Kent County*, 391 U.S. 430 (1968).

18. *Swann v. Charlotte-Mecklenburg Board of Education*, 402 U.S. 1 (1971).

19. Busing *within* the central city was upheld in *Armour v. Nix*, 446 U.S. 930 (1980); *Keyes v. School District No. 1*, Denver, 413 U.S. 189 (1973); *Milliken v. Bradley*, 418 U.S. 717 (1974); *Board of School Commissioners of Indianapolis v. Buckley*, 429 U.S. 1068 (1977); and *School Board of Richmond v. State Board of Education*, 412 U.S. 92 (1972). Busing *across* city lines was upheld in *Evans v. Buchanan*, 423 U.S. 963 (1975), and *Board of Education v. Newburg Area Council*, 421 U.S. 931 (1975).

20. *Pasadena City Board of Education v. Spangler*, 427 U.S. 424 (1976).

21. See, for example, Herbert McClosky and John Zaller, *The American Ethos* (Cambridge: Harvard University Press, 1984), 92, 100; and data reported in Chapter 5 of this text.

22. NES, *1952–1990 Cumulative Data File, 1992 NES Pre/Post Election Study* (1992).

23. *Freeman v. Pitts*, 112 S. Ct. 1430 (1992); *Parents v. Seattle School District*, 05-908 (2007).

24. Robert S. Erikson and Norman R. Luttbeg, *American Public Opinion* (New York: Wiley, 1973), 49; Hazel Erskine, "The Polls: Demonstrations and Race Riots," *Public Opinion Quarterly* 31 (Winter 1967–1968): 654–677.

25. Howard Schuman, Charlotte Steeh, and Lawrence Bobo, *Racial Attitudes in America* (Cambridge: Harvard University Press, 1985), 69, 78–79.

26. Ibid., 102, 110, 127–135.

27. *Grove City College v. Bell*, 465 U.S. 555 (1984).

28. *United States v. Armstrong*, 116 S. Ct. 1480 (1996).

29. *Promoting Cooperative Strategies to Reduce Racial Profiling: A Technical Guide*, chap. 9 (Santa Monica, CA: RAND, April 2004).

30. *Mueller v. Oregon*, 208 U.S. 412 (1908).

31. Equal Pay Act of 1963; Civil Rights Act of 1964, Title VII, and 1978 amendments thereto; Education Amendments of 1972, Title IX.

32. *Reed v. Reed*, 404 U.S. 71 (1971).

33. *Frontiero v. Richardson*, 411 U.S. 677 (1973).

34. *Stanton v. Stanton*, 421 U.S. 7 (1975).

35. *Craig v. Boren*, 429 U.S. 190 (1976).

36. *Dothard v. Rawlinson*, 433 U.S. 321 (1977).

37. *Cleveland Board of Education v. LaFleur*, 414 U.S. 632 (1974).

38. *Fortin v. Darlington Little League*, 514 F.2d 344 (1975).

39. *Roberts v. United States Jaycees*, 468 U.S. 609 (1984); *Board of Directors Rotary Interna-tional v. Rotary Club of Duarte*, 481 U.S. 537 (1987).

40. *Arizona Governing Committee for Tax Deferred Annuity and Deferred Compensation Plans v. Norris*, 463 U.S. 1073 (1983).

41. *E.E.O.C. v. Madison Community Unit School District No. 12*, 818 F.2d 577 (1987).

42. *Michael M. v. Superior Court*, 450 U.S. 464 (1981).

43. *Vorchheimer v. School District of Philadelphia*, 430 U.S. 703 (1977).

44. *Kahn v. Shevin*, 416 U.S. 351 (1974).

45. *Schlesinger v. Ballard*, 419 U.S. 498 (1975).

46. *Bennett v. Dyer's Chop House*, 350 F. Supp. 153 (1972); *Morris v. Michigan State Board of Education*, 472 F.2d 1207 (1973); *Fitzgerald v. Porter Memorial Hospital*, 523 F.2d 716 (1975); *Kruzel v. Podell*, 226 N.W.2d 458 (1975).

47. *United States v. Virginia*, 116 S. Ct. 2264 (1996).

48. *Rostker v. Goldberg*, 453 U.S. 57 (1981).

49. *Gebser v. Lago Vista School District*, 118 S. Ct. 1989 (1998); *Faragher v. Boca Raton*, 118 S. Ct. 2275 (1998); *Burlington Industries v. Ellerth*, 118 S. Ct. 2257 (1998).

50. *Griswold v. Connecticut*, 381 U.S. 479 (1965).

51. *Roe v. Wade*, 410 U.S. 113 (1973).

52. Though the constitutionality of the Hyde Amendment was upheld in *Harris v. McRae*, 448 U.S. 297 (1980), other limitations on access to abortions were struck down in *Planned Parenthood Federation of Central Missouri v. Danforth*, 428 U.S. 52 (1976); *Akron v. Akron Center for Reproductive Health*, 462 U.S. 416 (1983); and *Thornburgh v. American College of Obstetricians and Gynecologists*, 476 U.S. 747 (1986).

53. *Planned Parenthood v. Casey*, 112 S. Ct. 2791 (1992).

54. *Gonzales v. Carhart* (05-380), 2007.

55. For an argument in support of a color-blind Constitution, see Andrew Kull, *The Color-Blind Constitution* (Cambridge: Harvard University Press, 1992).

56. *Regents of the University of California v. Bakke*, 438 U.S. 265 (1978).

57. *Fullilove v. Klutznick*, 448 U.S. 448 (1980).

58. *City of Richmond v. J.A. Croson Co.*, 488 U.S. 469 (1989).

59. *Metro Broadcasting v. FCC*, 497 U.S. 547 (1990).

60. *Northeastern Florida Contractors v. Jacksonville*, 508 U.S. 656 (1993).

61. *Firefighters Local Union No. 1784 v. Stotts*, 467 U.S. 561 (1984); *Wygant v. Jackson Board of Education*, 476 U.S. 267 (1986); *City of Richmond v. J.A. Croson Co.*, 488 U.S. 469 (1989).

62. *Local No. 28 of the Sheet Metal Workers' International Association v. Equal Employment Opportunity Commission*, 478 U.S. 421 (1986); *Wards Cove Packing Co. v. Atonio*, 490 U.S. 642 (1989); *Price*

Waterhouse v. Hopkins, 490 U.S. 228 (1989). (Note: *Wards Cove* and *Price* were both superseded in part by the Civil Rights Act of 1991.)

63. *Fullilove v. Klutznick*, 448 U.S. 448 (1980); *Metro Broadcasting v. FCC*, 497 U.S. 547 (1990).

64. *United Steelworkers of America v. Weber*, 443 U.S. 193 (1979); *Johnson v. Santa Clara County Transportation Agency*, 480 U.S. 616 (1987).

65. *Wygant v. Jackson Board of Education*, 476 U.S. 267 (1986); *U.S. v. Paradise*, 480 U.S. 149 (1987).

66. Seymour Martin Lipset and William Schneider, "An Emerging National Consensus," *The New Republic* (October 15, 1977): 8–9.

67. John R. Bunzel, "Affirmative Re-Actions," *Public Opinion* (February/March 1986): 45–49; *New York Times* (December 14, 1997).

68. *Adarand Constructors v. Pena*, 515 U.S. 200 (1995).

69. *Hopwood v. Texas*, 78 F. 3d 932 (1996).

70. *Gratz v. Bollinger*, 539 U.S. 244 (2003).

71. *Grutter v. Bollinger*, 539 U.S. 306 (2003).

72. *Bowers v. Hardwick*, 478 U.S. 186 (1986).

73. *Romer v. Evans*, 517 U.S. 620 (1996).

74. *Lawrence v. Texas*, 539 U.S. 558 (2003).

75. *Goodridge v. Department of Public Health*, 440 Mass. 309 (2003) and 440 Mass. 1201 (2004).

76. *Boy Scouts of America v. Dale*, 530 U.S. 640 (2000).

Chapter 7
Public Opinion

1. Darlene Superville, "Americans See Gloom, Doom in 2007," Associated Press, December 31, 2006.

2. Nancy Benac, "Americans Optimistic for 2007," Associated Press, December 31, 2006.

3. George W. Bishop, Alfred J. Tuchfarber, and Robert W. Oldendick, "1984: How Much Can We Manipulate and Control People's Answers to Public Opinion Surveys?" paper delivered at the 1984 annual meeting of the American Political Science Association; Howard Schuman and S. Presser, *Questions and Answers in Attitude Surveys* (New York: Academic Press, 1981), ch. 5.

4. For example, see Bernard Berelson, et al., *Voting: A Study of Opinion Formation in a Presidential Campaign* (Chicago: University of Chicago Press, 1954), and Phillip E. Converse, "The Nature of Belief Systems in Mass Publics," in *Ideology and Discontent*, ed. David E. Apter (New York: Free Press, 1964).

5. For example, see V. O. Key, *The Responsible Electorate* (Cambridge: Harvard University Press, 1966); Samuel Popkin, *The Reasoning Voter: Communication and Persuasion in Presi-dential Campaigns* (Chicago: University of Chicago Press, 1991); Benjamin I. Page and Robert Y. Shapiro, *The Rational Public: Fifty Years of Trends in Americans' Policy Preferences* (Chicago: University of Chicago Press, 1991).

6. Terry M. Moe, *Schools, Vouchers, and the American Public* (Washington, D.C.: Brookings Institution, 2001), 253.

7. James Q. Wilson, "The Press at War," *City Journal* (Autumn 2006): 54–63.

8. M. Kent Jennings and Richard G. Niemi, "The Transmission of Political Values from Parent to Child," *American Political Science Review* 62 (March 1968): 173; Robert D. Hess and Judith V. Tomey, *The Development of Political Attitudes in Children* (Chicago: Aldine, 1967), 90.

9. John R. Alford, Carolyn L. Funk, and John R. Hibbing, "Are Political Orientations Genetically Transmitted?" *American Political Science Review*, 99 (May 2005), 153–167; James Q. Wilson, "The DNA of Politics," *City Journal* (Winter 2009), 83–87; Thomas J. Bouchard, et al., "Evidence for the Construct Validity and Heritability of the Wilson–Patterson Conservatism Scale," *Personality and Individual Differences*, 24 (2003) 959–969.

10. Several studies of child-parent agreement on party prefer-ence are summarized in David O. Sears, "Political Behavior," in *The Handbook of Social Psychology*, ed. Gardner Lindzey and Elliot Aronson, 2d ed. (Reading, Mass.: Addison-Wesley, 1969), vol. 5, 376.

11. Norman H. Nie, Sidney Verba, and John R. Petrocik, *The Changing American Voter* (Cambridge: Harvard University Press, 1976), ch. 4.

12. Elizabeth Humel, et al., "Younger Voters," *Public Perspective* (May/June 2003): 11.

13. Pew Forum on Religion and Public Life, Survey: More Americans Question Religion's Role in Politics, August 21, 2008.

14. Pew Forum on Religion and Public Life, Survey: Religious Groups Agree—Fixing the Nation's Economy Is Job One, March 4, 2009.

15. V. O. Key, Jr., *Public Opinion and American Democracy* (New York: Knopf, 1961), 122–138.

16. Richard E. Dawson, *Public Opinion and Contemporary Disarray* (New York: Harper & Row, 1973), ch. 4.

17. David Bositis, *Public Opinion 1998: Political Attitudes* (Washington, D.C.: Joint Center for Political and Economic Studies, 1998), table 18A.

18. "The Black and White of Public Opinion," Pew Research Center on the People and the Press (October 31, 2005).

19. Ibid.

20. Lisa J. Montoya, et al., "Latina Politics: Gender, Participation, and Leadership," *PS: Political Science and Politics* 33 (September 2000): 557.

21. Bruce Cain and Roderick Kiewit, "California's Coming Minority Majority," *Public Opinion* (February/March 1986): 50–52.

22. Ibid.

23. Pew Hispanic Center, *Survey of Latino Attitudes on the War in Iraq*, Pew Research Center, February 7, 2005.

24. Richard Frey, et al., *Hispanics and the Social Security Debate*, Pew Research Center, March 16, 2005.

25. Ibid.

26. Nie, Verba, and Petrocik, *The Changing American Voter*, 247–250.

27. Robert S. Erikson and Kent L. Tedin, *American Public Opinion*, 7th ed. (New York: Longman, 2004).

28. Adam J. Berinsky, *Silent Voices: Public Opinion and Political Participation in America* (Princeton, N.J.: Princeton University Press, 2004); Berinsky, "Two Faces of Public Opinion," *American Journal of Political Science* (October 1999): 1209–1230.

29. Ibid.

30. John Zaller, *The Nature and Origins of Mass Opinion* (Cambridge: Cambridge University Press, 1992).

31. Ibid.

32. Lawrence R. Jacobs and Robert Y. Shapiro, "Debunking the Myth of the Pandering Politician," *Public Perspective* (April/May 1997): 3–5.

Chapter 8
Political Participation

1. U.S. Bureau of the Census, Current Population Survey, "Reported Voting and Registration," June 2008, Table 4a.
2. Nonprofit Voter Engagement Network, *America Goes to the Polls: The 2008 General Election*, "Average Turnout in Established Democracies, 1945–2007," Figure 1, March 1, 2009.
3. Donald P. Green and Alan S. Gerber, *Get Out the Vote: How to Increase Voter Turnout* (Washington, D.C.: Brookings Institution Press, 2008).
4. Alan S. Gerber, Donald P. Green, and Christopher W. Larimer, "Social Pressure and Voter Turnout: Evidence from a Large-Scale Field Experiment," *American Political Science Review* 102, February 2008, p. 38.
5. U.S. Bureau of the Census, Current Population Survey, "Reasons for Not Voting," June 2008, Table 6.
6. John P. DiIulio, "The Liberalization of Absentee and Mail-In Voting, 1996–2008," unpub. paper, November 2008.
7. Raymond E. Wolfinger and Jonathan Hoffman, "Registering and Voting with Motor Voter," *PS: Political Science and Politics*, 34 (March 2001): 90.
8. Morton Keller, *Affairs of State* (Cambridge: Harvard University Press, 1977), 523.
9. *United States v. Reese*, 92 U.S. 214 (1876); *United States v. Cruikshank*, 92 U.S. 556 (1876); and *Ex parte Yarbrough*, 110 U.S. 651 (1884).
10. *Guinn and Beall v. United States*, 238 U.S. 347 (1915).
11. *Smith v. Allwright*, 321 U.S. 649 (1944).
12. *Schnell v. Davis*, 336 U.S. 933 (1949).
13. *Historical Statistics of the United States: Colonial Times to 1970*, part 2, 1071–1072.
14. Walter Dean Burnham, "The Changing Shape of the American Political Universe," *American Political Science Review* 59 (March 1965): 11; and William H. Flanigan and Nancy H. Zingale, *Political Behavior of the American Electorate*, 3d ed. (Boston: Allyn and Bacon, 1975), 15.
15. Burnham, "The Changing Shape"; E. E. Schattschneider, *The Semisovereign People* (New York: Holt, Rinehart and Winston, 1960), chs. 5, 6.
16. Philip E. Converse, "Change in the American Electorate," in *The Human Meaning of Social Change*, ed. Angus Campbell and Philip E. Converse (New York: Russell Sage Foundation, 1972), 263–338.
17. Michael P. McDonald and Samuel L. Popkin, "The Myth of the Vanishing Voter," *American Political Science Review* 95 (December 2001): table 1, 966.
18. Ibid.
19. Raymond Wolfinger and Benjamen Highton, "What If They Gave an Election and Everyone Came?" Public Affairs Report, Institute of Governmental Studies, University of California at Berkeley, June 1999, 11–13.
20. Sidney Verba and Norman H. Nie, *Participation in America* (New York: Harper & Row, 1972), 30. See also Aage R. Clausen, "Response Validity: Vote Report," *Public Opinion Quarterly*, 32 (1968–1969): 588–606.
21. Sidney Verba, et al., *Voice and Equality: Civic Voluntarism in American Politics* (Cambridge: Harvard University Press, 1995), 79.
22. Ibid., 77.
23. Verba and Nie, *Participation in America*, ch. 6.
24. Catherine E. Wilson, *The Politics of Latino Faith: Religion, Identity and Urban Community* (New York: New York University Press, 2008).

Chapter 9
Political Parties

1. American Enterprise Institute, *AEI Political Report*, November 2006, 1; reporting data from a Fox News/Opinion Dynamics survey conducted October 10–11, 2006.
2. Leon D. Epstein, "Political Parties," in *Handbook of Political Science*, ed. Fred I. Greenstein and Nelson W. Polsby (Reading, Mass.: Addison-Wesley, 1975), vol. 4, 230.
3. Quoted in Henry Adams, *History of the United States of America During the Administrations of Jefferson and Madison*, ed. Ernest Samuels, abridged edition (Chicago: University of Chicago Press, 1967), 147.
4. Walter Dean Burnham, *Critical Elections and the Mainsprings of American Politics* (New York: Norton, 1970), 10.
5. James L. Sundquist, *Dynamics of the Party System* (Washington, D.C.: Brookings Institution, 1973), ch. 7.
6. Edward G. Carmines and James A. Stimson, "Issue Evolution, Population Replacement, and Normal Partisan Change," *American Political Science Review* 75 (March 1981): 107–118; and Gregory Markus, "Political Attitudes in an Election Year," *American Political Science Review* 76 (September 1982): 538–560.
7. Ray Wolfinger and Michael G. Hagen, "Republican Prospects: Southern Comfort," *Public Opinion* (October/November 1985): 8–13. But compare Richard Scammon and James A. Barnes, "Republican Prospects: Southern Discomfort," *Public Opinion* (October/November 1985): 14–17.
8. Jerold G. Rusk, "The Effect of the Australian Ballot Reform on Split-Ticket Voting: 1876– 1908," *American Political Science Review* 64 (December 1970): 1220–1238.
9. Morton Keller, *Affairs of State* (Cambridge: Harvard University Press, 1977), 239.
10. Quoted in Keller, ibid., 256.
11. Martin Shefter, "Parties, Bureaucracy, and Political Change in the United States," in *The Development of Political Parties*, Sage Electoral Studies Yearbook, vol. 4, ed. Louis Maisel and Joseph Cooper (Beverly Hills, Calif.: Sage, 1978).
12. James Q. Wilson, *The Amateur Democrat: Club Politics in Three Cities* (Chicago: University of Chicago Press, 1962).
13. Samuel J. Eldersveld, *Political Parties: A Behavioral Analysis* (Chicago: Rand McNally, 1964), 278, 287.
14. Robert H. Salisbury, "The Urban Party Organization Member," *Public Opinion Quarterly* 29 (Winter 1965–1966): 550–564.
15. Ibid., 557, 559.
16. Eldersveld, *Political Parties*; and J. David Greenstone, *Labor in American Politics* (New York: Knopf, 1969), 187.
17. David R. Mayhew, *Placing Parties in American Politics* (Princeton, N.J.: Princeton University Press, 1986), chs. 2, 3.
18. *Boston Globe* (July 9, 1984): 1.
19. William Nisbet Chambers and Walter Dean Burnham, eds., *The

American Party Systems: Stages of Political Development, 2d ed. (New York: Oxford University Press, 1975), 6.

20. American National Election Studies, November 27, 2005, table 2B.4; reporting data for the period 1952–2004.

21. For example, see *The Public Perspective* (April/May 1998).

22. American National Election Survey, November 27, 2005, table 2B.3; reporting data for the period 1972–2000.

23. *Williams v. Rhodes,* 393 U.S. 23 (1968).

24. James Q. Wilson, *Political Organizations* (New York: Basic Books, 1973), ch. 12; and Samuel Stouffer, *Communism, Conformity, and Civil Liberties* (Garden City, N.Y.: Doubleday, 1955).

25. Updated from Jeane Kirkpatrick, *The New Presidential Elite* (New York: Russell Sage Foundation and Twentieth Century Fund, 1976), 297–315.

26. Nelson W. Polsby, *Consequences of Party Reform* (New York: Oxford University Press, 1983), 9–11, 64.

27. Ibid., 158. But compare John G. Geer, "Voting in Presidential Primaries," paper delivered to the 1984 annual meeting of the American Political Science Association.

28. Center for the Study of the American Electorate, April 2000.

29. Michael J. Malbin, "Democratic Party Rules Are Made to Be Broken," *National Journal* (August 23, 1980): 1388.

Chapter 10
Elections and Campaigns

1. The Center for Public Integrity, *Campaign Consultants,* Georgetown University, Washington, D.C., September 26, 2006, 1.

2. Ted Bader, *Campaigning for Hearts and Minds: How Emotional Appeals Work in Political Ads* (Chicago: University of Chicago Press, 2006).

3. Ibid., 140–143.

4. Steven Levy, " Every Voter a 'Microtarget'," *Washington Post,* April 23, 2008, D1.

5. Joe Klein, *Politics Lost: How American Democracy Was Trivialized by People Who Think You're Stupid* (New York: Doubleday, 2006), 54.

6. Ibid., 14–16; and Bader, op. cit., 19–20.

7. Bader, op. cit., chap. 2, endnote 5, reporting data from AAPC, 220.

8. *Wesberry v. Sanders,* 376 U.S. 1 (1964).

9. Richard F. Fenno, Jr., "U.S. House Members and Their Constituencies: An Exploration," *American Political Science Review* 71 (September 1977): 883–917, esp. 914.

10. John A. Ferejohn, *Pork Barrel Politics* (Stanford, Calif.: Stanford University Press, 1974).

11. Douglas Arnold, *Congress and the Bureaucracy* (New Haven, Conn.: Yale University Press, 1979).

12. Arthur H. Miller et al., "A Majority Party in Disarray: Policy Polarization in the 1972 Election," *American Political Science Review* 70 (1976): 757.

13. Donald E. Stokes and John J. DiIulio, Jr., "Valence Politics in Modern Elections," in *The 1992 Elections,* ed. Michael J. Nelson (Washington, D.C.: Congressional Quarterly Press, 1993), ch. 1.

14. Michael Kelley, "The Making of a First Family: A Blueprint," *New York Times* (November 14, 1992): 1, 9.

15. Ibid.

16. Thomas E. Patterson and Robert D. McClure, *The Unseeing Eye: The Myth of Television Power in National Politics* (New York: Putnam, 1976); and Xandra Kayden, *Campaign Organization* (Lexington, Mass.: D. C. Heath, 1978), ch. 6.

17. Gerald M. Pomper et al., *The Election of 1980* (Chatham, N.J.: Chatham House, 1981), 75, 105–107.

18. *Public Opinion Strategies: American Monitor* (November 2004).

19. Gary C. Jacobson, *The Politics of Congressional Elections,* 2d ed. (Boston: Little, Brown, 1987), 49.

20. Donald Philip Green and Jonathan S. Krasno, "Salvation for the Spendthrift Incumbent: Reestimating the Effects of Campaign Spending in House Elections," *American Journal of Political Science* 32 (1988): 884–960; Stephen Ansolabehre, "Winning Is Easy but It Sure Ain't Cheap," Working Paper 90–1, Center for American Politics and Public Policy, UCLA, 1990; Robert S. Erickson and Thomas R. Palfrey, "The Puzzle of Incumbent Spending in Congressional Elections," Social Science Working Paper 806, California Institute of Technology, August 1992.

21. Angus Campbell, Philip E. Converse, Warren E. Miller, and Donald E. Stokes, *The American Voter* (New York: Wiley, 1960), ch. 8.

22. V. O. Key, Jr., *The Responsible Electorate* (Cambridge: Harvard University Press, 1966).

23. Morris P. Fiorina, *Retrospective Voting in American National Elections* (New Haven, Conn.: Yale University Press, 1981).

24. Jay P. Greene, "Forewarned Before Forecast: Presidential Election Forecasting Models and the 1992 Election," *P.S.: Political Science and Politics* (March 1993): 20.

25. Paul Freedman and Ken Goldstein, "Measuring Media Exposure and the Effects of Negative Campaign Ads," *American Journal of Political Science* 43 (October 1999): 1189–1208.

26. Robert Axelrod, "Where the Votes Come From: An Analysis of Electoral Coalitions, 1952–1968," *American Political Science Review* 66 (1972): 11–20; and Axelrod, "Communication," *American Political Science Review* 68 (1974): 718–719.

27. Gerald M. Pomper, *Elections in America* (New York: Dodd, Mead, 1971), 178.

28. Benjamin Ginsberg, "Elections and Public Policy," *American Political Science Review* 70 (March 1976): 41–49.

Chapter 11
Interest Groups

1. Kay Lehman Schlozman and John T. Tierney, "More of the Same: Washington Pressure Group Activity in a Decade of Change," *Journal of Politics* 45 (1983): 356.

2. The use of injunctions in labor disputes was restricted by the Norris-LaGuardia Act of 1932; the rights to collective bargaining and to the union shop were guaranteed by the Wagner Act of 1935.

3. *Historical Statistics of the United States, Colonial Times to 1970,* vol. 1, 386.

4. The distinction is drawn from Kay Lehman Schlozman and John T. Tierney, *Organized Interests and American Democracy* (New York: Harper and Row, 1985).

5. Jeffrey M. Berry, *The Interest Group Society* (Boston: Little, Brown, 1984), 20–21.

6. Ibid., 24, 130.
7. Gabriel A. Almond and Sidney Verba, *The Civic Culture* (Princeton, N.J.: Princeton University Press, 1963), 302; Derek C. Bok and John T. Dunlop, *Labor and the American Community* (New York: Simon and Schuster, 1970), 49; *Statistical Abstract of the United States, 1975*, 373.
8. Almond and Verba, *The Civic Culture*, 194.
9. Ibid., 207.
10. Mancur Olson, Jr., *The Logic of Collective Action* (Cambridge: Harvard University Press, 1965), 153–157.
11. Ellen Nakashima, "Study: Contracts Given to Repeat Violators," *Washington Post* (May 7, 2002): A19.
12. Bok and Dunlop, *Labor*, 134.
13. Jane J. Mansbridge, *Why We Lost the ERA* (Chicago: University of Chicago Press, 1986), ch. 10.
14. Joyce Gelb and Marian Lief Palley, *Women and Public Choices* (Princeton, N.J.: Princeton University Press, 1982), ch. 3; Jo Freeman, *The Politics of Women's Liberation* (New York: McKay, 1975), ch. 3; Maren Lockwood Carden, "The Proliferation of a Social Movement: Ideology and Individual Incentives in the Contemporary Feminist Movement," *Research in Social Movements* 1 (1978): 179–196; and Dom Bonafede, "Still a Long Way to Go," *National Journal* (September 13, 1986): 2175–2179.
15. Jeffrey M. Berry, *Lobbying for the People* (Princeton, N.J.: Princeton University Press, 1977), 71–76.
16. Berry, *Interest Group Society*, 88.
17. Schlozman and Tierney, *Organized Interests and American Democracy*, table 5-4.
18. Robert G. Kaiser, *So Damn Much Money* (New York: Knopf, 2009).
19. Raymond A. Bauer, Ithiel de Sola Pool, and Lewis Anthony Dexter, *American Business and Public Policy* (New York: Atherton, 1963), ch. 30.
20. Berry, *Lobbying for the People*, 136–140.
21. Margaret Ann Latus, "Assessing Ideological PACs: From Outrage to Understanding," in *Money and Politics in the United States*, ed. Michael J. Malbin (Chatham, N.J.: Chatham House, 1984), 143; data supplied by the Federal Election Commission, March 1992.
22. Latus, *Assessing*, 144.

23. Malbin, *Money and Politics*, table A.8, 290–291.
24. Michael J. Malbin, "Looking Back at the Future of Campaign Finance Reform: Interest Groups and American Elections," in Malbin, *Money and Politics*, 248; James B. Kau and Paul H. Rubin, *Congressmen, Constituents and Contributors* (Boston: Martinus Nijhoff, 1982); Henry W. Chappell, Jr., "Campaign Contributions and Voting on the Cargo Preference Bill: A Comparison of Simultaneous Models," *Public Choice* 36 (1981): 301–312; W. P. Welch, "Campaign Contributions and Voting: Milk Money and Dairy Price Supports," *Western Political Quarterly* 35 (1982): 478–495; John R. Wright, "PACs, Contributions, and Roll Calls: An Organizational Perspective," *American Political Science Review* 79 (1985): 400–414. But compare Benjamin Ginsberg and John C. Green, "The Best Congress Money Can Buy," in *Do Elections Matter?*, ed. Benjamin Ginsberg and Alan Stone (Armonk, N.Y.: M. E. Sharpe, 1986), 75–89.
25. William T. Gormley, "A Test of the Revolving Door Hypothesis at the FCC," *American Journal of Political Science* 23 (1979): 665–683; Paul J. Quirk, *Industry Influence in Federal Regulatory Agencies* (Princeton, N.J.: Princeton University Press, 1981); Jeffrey E. Cohen, "The Dynamics of the 'Revolving Door' on the FCC," *American Journal of Political Science* 30 (1986): 689–708.
26. Robert O'Harrow and Scott Higham, "Report Finds DHS Lax on Contracting Procedures," *Washington Post*, November 22, 2006.
27. Suzanne Weaver, *Decision to Prosecute* (Cambridge, Mass.: MIT Press, 1977), 154–163.
28. *United States v. Harriss*, 347 U.S. 612 (1954).
29. *United States Code*, Title 26, section 501(c)(3).

Chapter 12
The Media

1. Pew Research Center for the People and the Press, 2005.
2. Karin Deutsch Karlekar, ed. *Freedom of the Press, 2004* (New York: Freedom House, 2004).
3. David E. Butler, "Why America's Political Reporting Is Better than England's," *Harper's* (May 1963): 15–25.
4. Gerard Alexander, "Illiberal Europe," *Weekly Standard*, April 10, 2006.
5. Quoted in F. L. Mort, *American Journalism, 1690–1960*, 3rd ed. (New York: Macmillan, 1962), 529.
6. Center for Media and Public Affairs, "The Incredible Shrinking Sound Bite," Press release, Washington, D.C., September 28, 2000.
7. U.S. Census Bureau, *Home Computers and Internet Use in the United States: August 2000* (Washington, D.C.: Census Bureau, 2001).
8. Updated from Times Mirror Center for the People and the Press, June 28, 1990.
9. Edward J. Epstein, *News from Nowhere: Television and the News* (New York: Random House, 1973), 37.
10. *Near v. Minnesota*, 283 U.S. 697 (1931).
11. *New York Times v. United States*, 403 U.S. 713 (1971).
12. *New York Times v. Sullivan*, 376 U.S. 254 (1964).
13. *Miami Herald Publishing Co. v. Tornillo*, 418 U.S. 241 (1974).
14. *Yates v. United States*, 354 U.S. 298 (1957).
15. *Branzburg v. Hayes*, 408 U.S. 665 (1972).
16. *Zurcher v. Stanford Daily*, 436 U.S. 547 (1978), overturned by the Privacy Protection Act of 1980 (P.L. 96–440).
17. S. Robert Lichter, Stanley Rothman, and Linda S. Lichter, *The Media Elite* (Bethesda, Md.: Adler and Adler, 1986); Stanley Rothman and Amy Black, "Elites Revisited: American Social and Political Leadership in the 1990s," *International Journal of Public Opinion Research* 11 (1999): 169–195; William Schneider and I. A. Lewis, "Views on the News," *Public Opinion* (August/September 1985): 7.
18. Rothman and Black, "Elites Revisited," 182.
19. Ibid., 177.
20. Gallup Poll, February 2003; Pew Research Center for the People and the Press poll, July 2003.
21. William G. Mayer, "Why Talk Radio Is Conservative," *The Public Interest* (Summer 2004): 86–103.
22. David W. Brady and Jonathan Ma, "Spot the Difference," *Wall Street Journal* (November 12, 2003).

23. Lichter, Rothman, and Lichter, *Media Elite.*

24. John R. Lott, Jr., and Kevin A. Hassett, "Is Newspaper Coverage of Economic Events Politically Biased?" unpublished paper, American Enterprise Institute (September 1, 2004). See also Tim Groseclose and Jeff Milyo, "A Measure of Media Bias," *Quarterly Journal of Economics,* 120 (November 2005): 1191–1237.

25. Matthew Gentzkow and Jesse M. Shapiro, "What Drives Media Slant?" NBER paper 1207 (Cambridge, Mass.: National Bureau of Economic Research, 2006).

26. David O. Sears and Richard E. Whitney, "Political Persuasion," in Pool, *Handbook of Communication,* 253–289.

27. Robert S. Erickson, "The Influence of Newspaper Endorsements in Presidential Elections: The Case of 1964," *American Journal of Political Science* 20 (May 1976): 207–233.

28. Kim Fridkin Kahn and Patrick J. Kenney, "The Slant of the News: How Editorial Endorsements Influence Campaign Coverage and Citizens' Views of Candidates," *American Political Science Review* 96 (2002): 381–394; James N. Druckman and Michael Parkin, "The Impact of Media Bias," *Journal of Politics* 67 (2005): 1030–1049.

29. Stefano Della Vigna and Ethan Kaplan, "The Fox News Effect: Media Bias and Voting," Working paper 12160 (Cambridge, Mass.: National Bureau of Economic Research, 2006).

30. Alan Gerber, Dean Karlan, and Daniel Berigan, "Does the Media Matter? A Field Experiment," Unpub. paper, Department of Political Science, Yale University, January 2006.

31. Maxwell E. McCombs and Donald R. Shaw, "The Agenda Setting Function of the Mass Media," *Public Opinion Quarterly* 36 (Summer 1972): 176–187; Shanto Iynegar and Donald R. Kinder, *News That Matters* (Chicago: University of Chicago Press, 1987).

32. G. Ray Funkhouser, "The Issues of the Sixties," *Public Opinion Quarterly* 37 (Spring 1973): 62–75.

33. Benjamin I. Page, Robert Y. Shapiro, and Glenn R. Dempsey, "What Moves Public Opinion?" *American Political Science Review* 81 (March 1987): 23–43; Benjamin I. Page, "The Media as Political Actors," *PS: Political Science and Politics* (March 1996): 21.

34. Pew Research Center for the People and the Press, "Media Seen as Fair, But Tilting to Gore," Press Release, Washington, D.C., October 15, 2000.

35. Center for Media and Public Affairs, "Public to Press: Keep in Touch!," Press Release, Washington, D.C., 1996.

36. Pew Center for the People and the Press, "Terror Coverage Boost News Media's Images," Press Release, November 28, 2001.

37. Will Lester, "Poll: Interest in News Stabilizes," *The Macon Telegraph* (June 9, 2002).

Chapter 13
Congress

1. H. Douglas Price, "Careers and Committees in the American Congress," in *The History of Parliamentary Behavior,* ed. William O. Aydelotte (Princeton, N.J.: Princeton University Press, 1977), 28–62; John F. Bibby, Thomas E. Mann, and Norman J. Ornstein, *Vital Statistics on Congress, 1980* (Washington, D.C.: American Enterprise Institute, 1980), 53–54; Thomas E. Cavanaugh, "The Dispersion of Authority in the House of Representatives," *Political Science Quarterly* 97 (1982–1983): 625–626; *Congressional Quarterly Weekly Reports.*

2. David R. Mayhew, *Congress: The Electoral Connection* (New Haven, Conn.: Yale University Press, 1974); Bibby, Mann, and Ornstein, *Vital Statistics,* 14–15.

3. Mayhew, *Congress;* Morris P. Fiorina, *Congress: Keystone of the Washington Establishment* (New Haven, Conn.: Yale University Press, 1977).

4. Rhodes Cook, "House Republicans Scored a Quiet Victory in '92," *Congressional Quarterly* (April 17, 1993): 966.

5. Bruce E. Cain and David Butler, "Redrawing District Lines: What's Going On and What's at Stake," *The American Enterprise* (July/August 1991): 37.

6. Warren E. Miller and Donald E. Stokes, "Constituency Influence in Congress," in *Elections and the Political Order,* ed. Angus Campbell et al. (New York: Wiley, 1966), 359.

7. John E. Jackson, *Constituencies and Leaders in Congress* (Cambridge: Harvard University Press, 1974).

8. Jerrold E. Schneider, *Ideological Coalitions in Congress* (Westport, Conn.: Greenwood Press, 1979), 134, 195.

9. Michael Foley, *The New Senate: Liberal Influence on a Conservative Institution, 1959–1972* (New Haven, Conn.: Yale University Press, 1980), 242.

10. "A Polarized Congress," *National Journal,* January 21, 2006, 21.

11. Tim Groseclose, Steven D. Levitt, and James M. Snyder, Jr., "Comparing Interest Group Scores Across Time and Chambers," *American Political Science Review* 93 (1999): 33–50.

12. *Congressional Quarterly Weekly Report* (December 3, 1994): 3430–3435.

13. In 1993 the 103rd Congress also contained a lot of newly elected Democratic members eager to change House rules. They voted for the old rules and procedures, however, because that is what their party leaders wanted.

14. Barbara Sinclair, *The Transformation of the United States Senate* (Baltimore: Johns Hopkins University Press, 1989).

15. Norman J. Ornstein, Thomas E. Mann, and Michael J. Malbin, *Vital Statistics on Congress, 1995–1996* (Washington, D.C.: Congressional Quarterly Press, 1996), 199–200.

16. Gary C. Jacobson, "The Electoral Basis of Partisan Polarization in Congress," paper delivered at the annual meeting of the American Political Science Association, August 31– September 3, 2002; Larry M. Bartels, "Partisanship and Voting Behavior, 1952–1996," *American Journal of Political Science* 44 (2000): 35–50.

17. Marc J. Hetherington, "Resurgent Mass Partisanship: The Role of Elite Polarization," *American Political Science Review* 95 (2001): 619–631.

18. Damon M. Cann, "Modeling Committee Selection in the U.S. House of Representatives," *Political Analysis* 16 (2008): 274–289.

19. Keith T. Poole and Howard Rosenthal, *Congress: A Political Economic History of Roll Call Voting* (New York: Oxford University Press, 1997), 8.

20. Nolan McCarty, Keith T. Poole, and Howard Rosenthal, "The Hunt for Party Discipline in Congress," *American Political Science Review* 95, no. 3 (September 2001): 686.

21. Susan Webb Hammond, "Congressional Caucuses in the 104th Congress," in *Congress Reconsidered*, ed. Lawrence C. Dodd and Bruce I. Oppenheimer, 6th ed. (Washington, D.C.: Congressional Quarterly Press, 1997), 6.

22. Steven S. Smith, "Revolution in the House: Why Don't We Do It on the Floor?" discussion paper no. 5, Brookings Institution, Washington, D.C., September 1986.

23. Richard F. Fenno, Jr., *Congressmen in Committees* (Boston: Little, Brown, 1973).

24. Michael J. Malbin, "Delegation, Deliberation, and the New Role of Congressional Staff," in *The New Congress*, ed. Thomas E. Mann and Norman J. Ornstein (Washington, D.C.: American Enterprise Institute, 1981), 134–177, esp. 170–171.

25. Lawrence H. Chamberlain, "The President, Congress, and Legislation," in *The Presidency*, ed. Aaron Wildavsky (Boston: Little, Brown, 1969), 444–445; Ronald C. Moe and Steven C. Teel, "Congress as a Policy-Maker: A Necessary Reappraisal," *Political Science Quarterly* 85 (September 1970): 443–470.

26. Joshua D. Clinton and John S. Lapinski, "Measuring Legislative Accomplishment, 1977–1944," *American Journal of Political Science* 50 (2006): 232–249; J. Tobin Grant and Nathan J. Kelly, "Legislative Productivity of the U.S. Congress, 1789–2004," *Political Analysis* 16 (2008): 303–323.

27. Thomas E. Mann and Norman J. Ornstein, *Broken Branch: How Congress Is Failing America and How to Get It Back on Track*, 2nd edition (New York: Oxford University Press, 2008).

28. David Mayhew, *Divided We Govern: Party Control, Lawmaking, and Investigations, 1946–1990* (New Haven, Conn.: Yale University Press, 1991); Grant and Tobin, "Legislative Productivity," op. cit.

29. Data from Congressional Research Service and Congressional Budget Office as reported by Tom Coburn, "The Spending Process Is Broken," *Extensions: Journal of the Carl Albert Congressional Research and Studies Center* (Spring 2007): 16.

30. Continuity of Government Commission, *Preserving Our Institutions: The Continuity of Congress–First Report*, Washington, D.C. (June 4, 2003): 3, 4.

31. National Commission on Terrorist Attacks Upon the United States, *The 9/11 Commission Report: Final Report of the National Commission on Terrorist Attacks Upon the United States* (New York and London: W.W. Norton & Company, 2004).

32. Richard E. Cohen, "Challenging the House's Traffic Cop," *National Journal* (April 4, 1993): 1002.

33. Thomas E. Mann and Norman J. Ornstein, *Renewing Congress: A Second Report* (Washington, D.C.: American Enterprise Institute, 1993), 49.

34. Diana Evans, "Appropriations in the Republican Era," *Extensions: Journal of the Carl Albert Congressional Research and Studies Center* (Spring, 2007): 13.

Chapter 14
The Presidency

1. Jean Blondel, *An Introduction to Comparative Government* (New York: Praeger, 1969), as cited in Nelson W. Polsby, "Legislatures," in *Handbook of Political Science*, ed. Fred I. Greenstein and Nelson W. Polsby (Reading, Mass.: Addison-Wesley, 1975), vol. 5, 275.

2. Donald F. Kettl, *Deficit Politics: Public Budgeting in Its Institutional and Historical Context* (New York: Macmillan, 1992), 13.

3. Morris P. Fiorina, *Divided Government* (New York: Macmillan, 1992), 86–111.

4. David Mayhew, *Divided We Govern: Party Control, Lawmaking, and Investigations, 1946–1990* (New Haven, Conn.: Yale University Press, 1991), 76.

5. Mark A. Peterson, *Legislating Together: The White House and Congress from Eisenhower to Reagan* (Cambridge: Harvard University Press, 1990).

6. Richard E. Cohen, *Washington at Work: Back Rooms and Clean Air* (New York: Macmillan, 1992), 154–155.

7. Ibid., 169.

8. Kettl, *Deficit Politics*, 138.

9. Woodrow Wilson, *Congressional Government* (New York: Meridian Books, 1956), 167–168, 170. (First published in 1885.)

10. Stephen Hess, *Organizing the Presidency* (Washington, D.C.: Brookings Institution, 1976), 3; R. W. Apple, "Clinton's Refocusing," *New York Times* (May 6, 1993): A22; Michael K. Frisby, "Power Switch," *Wall Street Journal* (March 26, 1993): A1, A7.

11. David T. Stanley et al., *Men Who Govern* (Washington, D.C.: Brookings Institution, 1967), 41–42, 50.

12. Daniel J. Elazar, "Which Road to the Presidency?" in *The Presidency*, ed. Aaron Wildavsky (Boston: Little, Brown, 1969), 340.

13. Richard E. Neustadt, *Presidential Power*, rev. ed. (New York: Wiley, 1976), ch. 4.

14. Walter D. Burnham, "Insulation and Responsiveness in Congressional Elections," *Political Science Quarterly* 90 (Fall 1975): 412–413; George C. Edwards III, *Presidential Influence in Congress* (San Francisco: Freeman, 1980), 70–78; Warren E. Miller, "Presidential Coattails: A Study in Political Myth and Methodology," *Public Opinion Quarterly* 19 (Winter 1955–1956): 368; and Miller, "The Motivational Basis for Straight and Split Ticket Voting," *American Political Science Review* 51 (June 1957): 293–312.

15. *Clinton v. City of New York*, 118 S.Ct. 2091 (1998).

16. *Marbury v. Madison*, 1 Cranch 137 (1803).

17. *United States v. Nixon*, 418 U.S. 683 (1974).

18. *Clinton v. Jones*, 520 U.S. 681 (1997); *In Re Grand Jury Subpoena Duces Tecum*, 112 F.3d 910 (1997); *In Re Sealed Case*, 121 F.3d 729 (1997).

19. Christopher S. Kelley, "A Comparative Look at the Constitutional Signing Statement," paper presented at the Midwest Political Science Association meeting, April 2003.

20. Walter Dellinger, "Memorandum for Bernard N. Nussbaum, Counsel to the President," Office of Legal Counsel, U.S. Department of Justice, November 3, 1993.

21. *Chevron v. NRDC*, 467 U.S. 837 (1984).

22. Edwin S. Corwin, *The Presidency: Office and Powers* (New York: New York University Press, 1957), 171.

23. Marcus Cunliffe, *American Presidents and the Presidency* (New York: American Heritage Press/ McGraw-Hill, 1972), 63, 65.
24. Ibid., 214.
25. Adapted from Paul C. Light, *The President's Agenda* (Baltimore, Md.: Johns Hopkins University Press, 1982), 217–225.

Chapter 15
The Bureaucracy

1. Charles E. Lindblom, *Politics and Markets* (New York: Basic Books, 1977), 114.
2. Donald F. Kettl, *Government by Proxy: (Mis?) Managing Federal Programs* (Washington, D.C.: Congressional Quarterly Press, 1988); John J. DiIulio, Jr., "Government by Proxy: A Faithful Overview," *Harvard Law Review* (March 2003): 1272–1284.
3. Mark Hemmingway, "Warriors for Hire," *Weekly Standard*, December 18, 2006, 25.
4. Ibid., 26.
5. Martha Derthick, *Keeping the Compound Republic: Essays on American Federalism* (Washington, D.C.: Brookings Institution, 2001), 63.
6. Donald F. Kettl, *The Next Government of the United States: Why Our Institutions Fail Us and How to Fix Them* (New York: W.W. Norton, 2008), 1–14.
7. Article II, section 2, para. 2.
8. Article II, section 3.
9. Calculated from data in *Historical Statistics of the United States: Colonial Times to 1970* (Washington, D.C.: Government Printing Office, 1975), vol. 2, 1102–1103.
10. *Panama Refining Co. v. Ryan*, 293 U.S. 388 (1935).
11. *Hampton Jr. & Co. v. United States*, 276 U.S. 394 (1928).
12. Edward S. Corwin, *The Constitution and What It Means Today*, 13th ed. (Princeton, N.J.: Princeton University Press, 1973), 151.
13. Bruce D. Porter, "Parkinson's Law Revisited: War and the Growth of American Government," *Public Interest* (Summer 1980): 50–68.
14. See the cases cited in Corwin, *The Constitution*, 8.
15. *U.S. Statutes*, vol. 84, sec. 799 (1970).
16. *Historical Statistics of the United States*, vol. 2, 1107.

17. Kettl, *The Next Government* op. cit., 52.
18. Donald F. Kettl et al., *Civil Service Reform: Building a Government That Works* (Washington, D.C.: Brookings Institution, 1996), 15.
19. Hugh Heclo, "Issue Networks and the Executive Establishment," in *The New American Political System*, ed. Anthony King (Washington, D.C.: American Enterprise Institute, 1978), 87–124.
20. Quoted in Hugh Heclo, *A Government of Strangers* (Washington, D.C.: Brookings Institution, 1977), 225.
21. Alexis Simendinger, "Of the People, for the People," *National Journal* (April 18, 1998): 852–855. Data from the Pew Charitable Trusts Research Center for the People and the Press.
22. Kenneth Meier and Lloyd Nigro, "Representative Bureaucracy and Policy References: A Study of the Attitudes of Federal Executives," *Public Administration Review* 36 (July/August 1976): 458–467; Bernard Mennis, *American Foreign Policy Officials* (Columbus: Ohio State University Press, 1971).
23. David Stockman, *The Triumph of Politics* (New York: Harper and Row, 1986).
24. James Q. Wilson, *Bureaucracy* (New York: Basic Books, 1989), ch. 6.
25. Heclo, "Issue Networks and the Executive Establishment," 87–124.
26. Richard F. Fenno, Jr., *The Power of the Purse* (Boston: Little, Brown, 1966), 450, 597.
27. John E. Schwartz and L. Earl Shaw, *The United States Congress in Comparative Perspective* (Hinsdale, Ill.: Dryden Press, 1976), 262–263; *National Journal* (July 4, 1981): 1211–1214.
28. *Immigration and Naturalization Service v. Chadha*, 462 U.S. 919 (1983); *Maine v. Thiboutot*, 448 U.S. 1 (1980).
29. See cases cited in Corwin, *The Constitution*, 22.
30. Steven Kelman, "The Grace Commission: How Much Waste in Government?" *Public Interest* (Winter 1985): 62–87.
31. Daniel Katz et al., *Bureaucratic Encounters* (Ann Arbor: Survey Research Center, University of Michigan, 1975), 63–69, 118–120, 184–188.

32. U.S. Government Accountability Office, *Government Performance Lessons Learned*, GAO Report, July 24, 2008, as cited in Kettl, *The Next Government*, op. cit., 173, 255.

Chapter 16
The Judiciary

1. Henry J. Abraham, *The Judicial Process*, 3d ed. (New York: Oxford University Press, 1975), 279–280.
2. Robert G. McCloskey, *The American Supreme Court* (Chicago: University of Chicago Press, 1960), 27.
3. *Marbury v. Madison*, 5 U.S. 137 (1803); and *McCulloch v. Maryland*, 17 U.S. 316 (1819).
4. *Martin v. Hunter's Lessee*, 14 U.S. 304 (1816); and *Cohens v. Virginia*, 19 U.S. (1821).
5. *Gibbons v. Ogden*, 22 U.S. (1824).
6. Quoted in Albert J. Beveridge, *The Life of John Marshall* (Boston: Houghton Mifflin, 1919), vol. 4, 551.
7. *Dred Scott v. Sandford*, 60 U.S. 393 (1857).
8. Abraham, *The Judicial Process*, 286.
9. *In re Debs*, 158 U.S. 564 (1895).
10. *Pollock v. Farmers' Loan & Trust Co.*, 157 U.S. 429 (1895).
11. *United States v. Knight*, 156 U.S. 1 (1895).
12. *Cincinnati, N.O. & T.P. Railway Co. v. Interstate Commerce Commission*, 162 U.S. 184 (1896).
13. *Hammer v. Dagenhart*, 247 U.S. 251 (1918).
14. *Lochner v. New York*, 198 U.S. 45 (1905).
15. McCloskey, *The American Supreme Court*, 151.
16. *Munn v. Illinois*, 94 U.S. 113 (1877).
17. *Dayton-Goose Creek Railway Co. v. United States*, 263 U.S. 456 (1924).
18. *Atchison, Topeka, and Santa Fe Railroad Co. v. Matthews*, 174 U.S. 96 (1899).
19. *Mugler v. Kansas*, 123 U.S. 623 (1887).
20. *St. Louis Consolidated Coal Co. v. Illinois*, 185 U.S. 203 (1902).
21. *New York Central Railroad Co. v. White*, 243 U.S. 188 (1917).
22. *German Alliance Insurance Co. v. Lewis*, 233 U.S. 389 (1914).
23. Morton Keller, *Affairs of State* (Cambridge: Harvard University Press, 1977), 369. See also Mary Cornelia Porter, "That Commerce Shall Be Free: A New Look at the Old Laissez-Faire Court," in *The Supreme Court Review*, ed. Philip

B. Kurland (Chicago: University of Chicago Press, 1976), 135–159.

24. *Chief of Capitol Police v. Jeannette Rankin Brigade*, 409 U.S. 972 (1972).

25. *Aptheker v. Secretary of State*, 378 U.S. 500 (1964).

26. *Trop v. Dulles*, 356 U.S. 86 (1958); *Afroyim v. Rusk*, 387 U.S. 253 (1967); and *Schneider v. Rusk*, 377 U.S. 163 (1964).

27. *Lamont v. Postmaster General*, 381 U.S. 301 (1965); and *Blount v. Rizzi*, 400 U.S. 410 (1971).

28. *Richardson v. Davis*, 409 U.S. 1069 (1972); *U.S. Department of Agriculture v. Murry*, 413 U.S. 508 (1973); *Jimenez v. Weinberger*, 417 U.S. 628 (1974); and *Washington v. Legrant*, 394 U.S. 618 (1969).

29. *United States v. Lopez*, 514 U.S. 549 (1995).

30. *Seminole Tribe of Florida v. Florida*, 517 U.S. 44 (1996); *Alden v. Maine*, 527 U.S. 706 (1999); *Florida v. College Savings Bank*, 527 U.S. 627 (1999).

31. Daniel R. Pinello, "Linking Party to Judicial Ideology in American Courts: A Meta-analysis," *Justice System Journal* 20 (1999): 219–254.

32. An opinion survey of federal judges shows how party affects ideology: see Althea K. Nagai, Stanley Rothman, and S. Robert Lichter, "The Verdict of Federal Judges," *Public Opinion* (November/December 1987): 52–56.

33. *United States v. Lanza*, 260 U.S. 377 (1922). Cf. *Abbate v. United States*, 359 U.S. 187 (1959), and *Bartkus v. Illinois*, 359 U.S. 121 (1989).

34. *Gideon v. Wainwright*, 372 U.S. 335 (1963). The story is told in Anthony Lewis, *Gideon's Trumpet* (New York: Random House, 1964).

35. Erwin Griswold, "Rationing Justice: The Supreme Court's Case Load and What the Court Does Not Do," *Cornell Law Review* 60 (1975): 335–354.

36. Joseph Weis, Jr., "Disconnecting the Overloaded Circuits—A Plan for a Unified Court of Appeals," *St. Louis University Law Journal* 39 (1995): 455.

37. *Alyeska Pipeline Service Co. v. Wilderness Society*, 421 U.S. 240 (1975).

38. *Flast v. Cohen*, 392 U.S. 83 (1968), which modified the earlier *Frothingham v. Mellon*, 262 U.S. 447

(1923); *United States v. Richardson*, 418 U.S. 166 (1947).

39. *Brown v. Board of Education of Topeka*, 347 U.S. 483 (1954).

40. *Baker v. Carr*, 369 U.S. 186 (1962).

41. See Louise Weinberg, "A New Judicial Federalism?" *Daedalus* (Winter 1978): 129–141.

42. Quoted in Abraham, *The Judicial Process*, 330.

43. Carolyn D. Richmond, "The Rehnquist Court: What Is in Store for Constitutional Precedent?" *New York Law Review* 39 (1994): 511.

44. *Colegrove v. Green*, 328 U.S. 549 (1946).

45. The Court abandoned the "political question" doctrine in *Baker v. Carr*, 369 U.S. 186 (1962), and began to change congressional-district apportionment in *Wesberry v. Sanders*, 376 U.S. 1 (1964).

46. Donald L. Horowitz, *The Courts and Social Policy* (Washington, D.C.: Brookings Institution, 1977), 6.

47. *Gates v. Collier*, 349 F. Supp. 881 (1972).

48. *Lau v. Nichols*, 414 U.S. 563 (1974).

49. Jane Burnbaum, "Guilty! Too Many Lawyers and Too Much Litigation," *Business Week* (April 13, 1992), 60–61.

50. Joel B. Grossman and Austin Sarat, "Litigation in the Federal Courts: A Comparative Perspective," *Law and Society Review* 9 (Winter 1975): 321–346.

51. Administrative Office of the U.S. Courts, *Annual Report, 1988*, 109.

52. Jack W. Peltason, *Fifty-eight Lonely Men: Southern Federal Judges and School Desegregation* (New York: Harcourt Brace, 1961).

53. Anthony Patridge and William B. Eldridge, *The Second Circuit Sentencing Study* (Washington, D.C.: Federal Judicial Center, 1974).

54. *Abington School District v. Schempp*, 374 U.S. 203 (1963).

55. Robert H. Birkby, "The Supreme Court and the Bible Belt," *Midwest Journal of Political Science* 10 (1966): 3.

56. Cass R. Sunstein, "Impeaching the President," *University of Pennsylvania Law Review* 147 (1998): 279.

57. *United States v. Butler*, 297 U.S. 1 (1936).

58. *Ex parte McCardle*, 74 U.S. 506 (1869).

59. Walter F. Murphy, *Congress and the Court* (Chicago: University

of Chicago Press, 1962); and C. Herman Pritchett, *Congress Versus the Supreme Court* (Minneapolis: University of Minnesota Press, 1961).

60. Gregory A. Caldeira, "Neither the Purse nor the Sword: Dynamics of Public Confidence in the U.S. Supreme Court," *American Political Science Review* 80 (1986): 1209–1226. See also Joseph T. Tannenhaus and Walter F. Murphy, "Patterns of Public Support for the Supreme Court: A Panel Study," *Journal of Politics* 43 (1981): 24–39.

Chapter 17
The Policy-Making Process

1. E. E. Schattschneider, *The Semisovereign People* (New York: Holt, Rinehart and Winston, 1960), 68.

2. Jack L. Walker, "Setting the Agenda in the U.S. Senate: A Theory of Problem Selection," *British Journal of Political Science* 7 (1977): 343, 441.

3. *Statistical Abstract of the United States, 1975* (Washington, D.C.: Government Printing Office, 1975), 342–343, 349.

4. Alexis de Tocqueville, *The Old Regime and the French Revolution*, trans. Gilbert Stuart (Garden City, N.Y.: Doubleday Anchor Books, 1955), 176–177. (First published in 1856.)

5. David O. Sears and J. B. McConahay, *The Politics of Violence* (Boston: Houghton Mifflin, 1973). Compare Abraham H. Miller et al., "The New Urban Blacks," Ethnicity 3 (1976): 338–367.

6. Daniel Patrick Moynihan, *Maximum Feasible Misunderstanding* (New York: Free Press, 1969), ch. 2.

7. Nelson W. Polsby, "Goodbye to the Senate's Inner Club," in *Congress in Change: Evolution and Reform*, ed. Norman J. Ornstein (New York: Praeger, 1975), 208–215.

8. *Federalist* No. 62.

9. Walker, "Setting the Agenda," 434, 439, 441.

10. This is a revised version of a theory originally presented in James Q. Wilson, *Political Organizations* (New York: Basic Books, 1973), ch. 16. There are other ways of classifying public policies, notably that of Theodore J. Lowi, "American Business, Public Policy, Case

Studies, and Political Theory," *World Politics* 16 (July 1964).

11. Donald F. Kettl, *Sharing Power: Public Governance and Private Markets* (Washington, D.C.: Brookings Institution, 1993); Lawrence J. Hajna, "Superfund: Costly Program Under Fire," *Courier-Post* (February 13, 1994): 6A.

12. Edward S. Greenberg, *Serving the Few: Corporate Capitalism and the Bias of Government Policy* (New York: Wiley, 1974).

13. Charles E. Lindblom, *Politics and Markets* (New York: Basic Books, 1977).

14. Joseph Schumpeter, *Capitalism, Socialism, and Democracy* (New York: Harper and Row, 1950).

15. Louis Galambos, *The Public Image of Big Business in America, 1880–1940* (Baltimore: Johns Hopkins University Press, 1975).

16. Suzanne Weaver, *Decision to Prosecute: Organization and Public Policy in the Antitrust Division* (Cambridge, Mass.: MIT Press, 1977); Robert H. Bork, *The Antitrust Paradox* (New York: Basic Books, 1978).

17. Richard A. Posner, *Antitrust Law: An Economic Perspective* (Chicago: University of Chicago Press, 1976), 25.

18. Alan L. Seltzer, "Woodrow Wilson as 'Corporate-Liberal': Toward a Reconsideration of Left Revisionist Historiography," *Western Political Quarterly* 30 (June 1977): 183–212.

19. Weaver, *Decision to Prosecute*; and Robert A. Katzmann, *Regulatory Bureaucracy: The Federal Trade Commission and Antitrust Policy* (Cambridge, Mass.: MIT Press, 1980).

20. Charles R. Plott, "Occupational Self-Regulation: A Case Study of the Oklahoma Dry Cleaners," *Journal of Law and Economics* 8 (October 1965): 195–222.

21. Paul H. MacAvoy, ed., *Federal Milk Marketing Orders and Price Supports* (Washington, D.C.: American Enterprise Institute, 1977).

22. Ibid., 111.

23. *Congressional Quarterly Weekly Report* (April 21, 1990): 1184–1188.

24. Pietro Nivola, "The New Pork Barrel," *Brookings Review* (Winter 1998): 6–13.

25. Upton Sinclair, *The Jungle* (New York: Doubleday, Page and Co., 1906).

26. Mark V. Nadel, *The Politics of Consumer Protection* (Indianapolis, Ind.: Bobbs-Merrill, 1971), 143–144.

27. Alfred A. Marcus, *Promise and Performance: Choosing and Implementing an Environmental Policy* (Westport, Conn.: Greenwood Press, 1980).

28. Nadel, *Politics*, 66–80.

29. Martha Derthick and Paul J. Quirk, *The Politics of Deregulation* (Washington, D.C.: Brookings Institution, 1985).

30. Executive Orders 11821 (1974), 12044 (1978), and 12291 (1981).

Chapter 18
Economic Policy

1. Edward R. Tufte, *Political Control of the Economy* (Princeton, N.J.: Princeton University Press, 1978): 84; Douglas A. Hibbs, Jr., "The Mass Public and Macroeconomic Performance: The Dynamics of Public Opinion Toward Unemployment and Inflation," *American Journal of Political Science* 23 (1979): 705–731.

2. D. Roderick Kiewiet, *Macroeconomics and Micropolitics: The Electoral Effect of Economic Issues* (Chicago: University of Chicago Press, 1983); Morris P. Fiorina, "Economic Retrospective Voting in American National Elections: A Micro-Analysis," *American Journal of Political Science* 22 (1978): 426–443; Donald R. Kinder and D. Roderick Kiewiet, "Sociotropic Politics: The American Case," *British Journal of Political Science* 11 (1981): 129–161.

3. *New York Times*/CBS News poll cited in Douglas A. Hibbs, Jr., "President Reagan's Mandate from the 1980 Elections: A Shift to the Right?" *American Politics Quarterly* 10 (1982): 387–420.

4. Hibbs, "The Mass Public."

5. Ibid.

6. Kiewiet, *Macroeconomics and Micropolitics*.

7. Michael S. Lewis-Beck, "Comparative Economic Voting: Britain, France, Germany, Italy," *American Journal of Political Science* 30 (1986): 315–346.

8. Douglas A. Hibbs, Jr., "Political Parties and Macroeconomic Policy," *American Political Science Review* 71 (1977): 1467–1487.

9. Kiewiet, *Macroeconomics and Micropolitics*, 69.

10. *Pollock v. Farmers' Loan & Trust Co.*, 157 U.S. 429, 158 U.S. 601 (1895).

11. NBC News/*Wall Street Journal* poll, as reported in *National Journal* (July 12, 1986): 1741.

Chapter 19
Social Welfare

1. For a general discussion see Charles E. Gilbert, "Welfare Policy," in *Handbook of Political Science*, ed. Fred I. Greenstein and Nelson W. Polsby (Reading, Mass.: Addison-Wesley, 1975), vol. 6, ch. 4.

2. *Congress and the Nation, 1945–1964* (Washington, D.C.: Congressional Quarterly Service, 1965), 1225.

3. Harold E. Raynes, *Social Security in Britain: A History* (London: Pitman, 1960), ch. 18. See also Hugh Heclo, *Modern Social Politics in Britain and Sweden* (New Haven, Conn.: Yale University Press, 1974).

4. Amy E. Black, Douglas Koopman, and David K. Ryder, *Of Little Faith: The Politics of George W. Bush's Faith-Based Initiatives* (Washington, D.C.: Georgetown University Press, 2004).

5. Anne Farris, Richard P. Nathan, and David Wright, *The Expanding Administrative Presidency: George W. Bush and the Faith-Based Initiative* (Albany, New York: Nelson A. Rockefeller Institute of Government, 2004), Executive Summary, 2.

6. Stephen V. Monsma, *Putting Faith in Partnerships: Welfare-to-Work in Four Cities* (Ann Arbor, Mich.: University of Michigan Press, 2004), ix, 70.

7. Ibid., x.

8. Surveys by Pew Forum on Religion and Public Life: *American Views on Religion, Politics, and Public Policy* (Washington, D.C.: Pew Forum, 2001); *Lift Every Voice: A Report on Religion in American Public Life* (Washington, D.C.: Pew Forum, 2002); *Americans Struggle with Religion's Role at Home and Abroad* (Washington, D.C.: Pew Forum, 2002).

9. Histories of the 1935 act include Edwin E. Witte, *The Development of the Social Security Act* (Madison: University of Wisconsin Press, 1962). A different view, offering a neo-Marxist interpretation of the act, can be found in Frances Fox

Piven and Richard A. Cloward, *Regulating the Poor* (New York: Pantheon, 1971).

10. The development of Medicare is described in Theodore Marmor, "Doctors, Politics, and Health Insurance for the Aged: The Enactment of Medicare," in *Cases in Contemporary American Government*, ed. Allan Sindler (Boston: Little, Brown, 1969).

11. Rasmussen Reports, national surveys conducted June 3–4, 2009 and May 28–31, 2009.

12. Rasmussen Reports, national surveys conducted December 5–6, 2008.

13. Ibid.

14. Michael E. Schiltz, *Public Attitudes Toward Social Security, 1935–1965*, Research Report No. 3, Social Security Administration, U.S. Department of Health, Education, and Welfare (Washington, D.C.: Government Printing Office, 1970), 36, 98, 128, 140.

15. Ibid., ch. 4, 154–165

16. Charles Murray, *Losing Ground: American Social Policy, 1950–1980* (New York: Basic Books, 1984). A critique of Murray is William J. Wilson, *The Truly Disadvantaged* (Chicago: University of Chicago Press, 1987), esp. chs. 3 and 4.

17. Richard P. Nathan and Thomas L. Gais, "The Devolution Revolution," *Blueprint* (January/ February 2002): 32.

Chapter 20
Foreign and Military Policy

1. Alexis de Tocqueville, *Democracy in America, vol. 1*, ed. Phillips Bradley (New York: Knopf, 1951), 235.

2. See Victor Davis Hanson, *Carnage and Culture* (New York: Anchor Books, 2002) and Hanson, *The Soul of Battle* (New York: Free Press, 1999).

3. Richard Lau, Thad A. Brown, and David O. Sears, "Self-Interest and Civilians' Attitudes Toward the Vietnam War," *Public Opinion Quarterly* 42 (1978): 464–481.

4. Edward S. Corwin, *The President: Office and Powers* (New York: New York University Press, 1940), 200.

5. Louis W. Koenig, *The Chief Executive*, 3d ed. (New York: Harcourt Brace Jovanovich, 1975), 217.

6. Louis Fisher, *President and Congress* (New York: Free Press, 1972), 45;

7. Aaron Wildavsky, "The Two Presidencies," in *The Presidency*, ed. Wildavsky (Boston: Little, Brown, 1969), 231.

8. Loch Johnson and James M. McCormick, "The Making of International Agreements: A Reappraisal of Congressional Involvement," *Journal of Politics*, 40 (1978), 468–478.

9. Bernard E. Brown, "The Decision to End the Algerian War," in *Cases in Comparative Politics*, ed. James B. Christoph (Boston: Little, Brown, 1965), 154–180; Roy C. Macridis, "De Gaulle and NATO," in *Modern European Governments*, ed. Macridis (Englewood Cliffs, N.J.: Prentice-Hall, 1968), 92–115; and John E. Schwartz and L. Earl Shaw, *The United States Congress in Comparative Perspective* (Hinsdale, Ill.: Dryden Press, 1976), 235–236.

10. Peter G. Richards, *Parliament and Foreign Affairs* (London: George Allen and Unwin, 1967), 37–38; Schwartz and Shaw, *The United States Congress in Comparative Perspective*, 235.

11. Arthur M. Schlesinger, Jr., *A Thousand Days: John F. Kennedy in the White House* (Boston: Houghton Mifflin, 1965), chs. 30, 31. Schlesinger, at p. 841, described Kennedy's actions as a "brilliantly controlled," "matchlessly calibrated" combination of "nerve and wisdom." His view of Nixon's actions was a good deal less charitable in *The Imperial Presidency* (Boston: Houghton Mifflin, 1974), ch. 7.

12. *United States v. Curtiss-Wright Export Co.*, 299 U.S. 304 (1936).

13. *Mitchell v. Laird*, 488 F.2d 611 (1973).

14. *Prize Cases*, 67 U.S. 635 (1863); *Mora v. McNamara*, 389 U.S. 934 (1964); *Massachusetts v. Laird*, 400 U.S. 886 (1970).

15. *Dames and Moore v. Regan*, 435 U.S. 654 (1981).

16. *Korematsu v. United States*, 323 U.S. 214 (1944).

17. *Youngstown Sheet & Tube Co. v. Sawyer*, 343 U.S. 579 (1952).

18. *Immigration and Naturalization Service v. Chadha*, 103 S. Ct. 2764 (1983).

19. Robert S. Erikson and Norman R. Luttbeg, *American Public Opinion* (New York: Wiley, 1973), 50–51.

20. William R. Caspary, "The 'Mood Theory': A Study of Public Opinion and Foreign Policy," *American Political Science Review* 64 (June 1970): 536–547.

21. Erikson and Luttbeg, *American Public Opinion*, 52.

22. John E. Mueller, *War, Presidents, and Public Opinion* (New York: Wiley, 1973), 110.

23. Ibid., 112.

24. Milton J. Rosenberg, Sidney Verba, and Philip E. Converse, *Vietnam and the Silent Majority* (New York: Harper and Row, 1970), 26–27.

25. Erikson and Luttbeg, *American Public Opinion*, 155.

26. John R. Oneal and Brad Lian, "Presidents, the Use of Military Force, and Public Opinion," Working Papers in International Security I–92–8, Hoover Institution, Stanford, Calif. (July 1992).

27. Benjamin C. Schwarz, *Casualities, Public Opinion, and U.S. Military Intervention* (Santa Monica, Calif.: RAND, 1994).

28. Mueller, *War, Presidents, and Public Opinion*, 45–47, 169.

29. James Q. Wilson and Karlyn Bowman, "Defining the Peace Party," *The Public Interest* (Fall 2003): 69–78.

30. Everett Carll Ladd, "Since World War II, Americans Have Persistently Looked Outward," *The Public Perspective* (August/September 1997): 5–34.

31. Howard Schuman, "Two Sources of Antiwar Sentiment in America," *American Journal of Sociology* 78 (1973): 513–536.

32. Philip E. Converse, Warren E. Miller, Jerrold G. Rusk, and Arthur C. Wolfe, "Continuity and Change in American Politics," *American Political Science Review* 63 (December 1969): 1083–1105; John P. Robinson, "Public Reaction to Political Protest: Chicago, 1968," *Public Opinion Quarterly* 34 (Spring 1970): 1–9.

33. James D. Wright, "Life, Time, and the Fortunes of War," *Transaction* 9 (January 1972).

34. John E. Rielly, *American Public Opinion and U.S. Foreign Policy, 1999* (Chicago: Chicago Council on Foreign Relations, 1999).

35. X, "The Sources of Soviet Conduct," *Foreign Affairs* 25 (July 1947): 566.

36. Walter Lippmann, *The Cold War* (New York: Harper Brothers, 1947).

37. Erikson and Luttbeg, *American Public Opinion*, 52.
38. Mueller, *War, Presidents, and Public Opinion*, 40.
39. Michael Roskin, "From Pearl Harbor to Vietnam: Shifting Generational Paradigms and Foreign Policy," *Political Science Quarterly* 89 (Fall 1974): 567.
40. Frank L. Klingberg, "The Historical Alternation of Moods in American Foreign Policy," *World Politics* 4 (1952): 239–273.
41. Roskin, "From Pearl Harbor," 567.
42. *American Public Opinion and U.S. Foreign Policy, 1987* (Chicago: Chicago Council on Foreign Relations, 1987), 33.
43. Carl M. Cannon, "Comment," in Pietro S. Nivola and David W. Brady, eds., *Red and Blue Nation?* (Washington, D.C.: Brookings Institution, 2006), 168; and Cannon, "Administration: A New Era of Partisan War," *National Journal,* March 18, 2006.
44. For a lively debate over the extent of political polarization, see Morris Fiorina and Matthew S. Levendusky, "Disconnected: The Political Class Versus the People"; Alan I. Abramowitz, "Comment"; and Gary C. Jacobson, "Comment,"—all in Nivola and Brady, op. cit.
45. Commission on the Intelligence Capabilities of the United States Regarding Weapons of Mass Destruction, *Report to the President* (Washington, D.C.: Government Printing Office, 2005), 43–249.
46. Quoted in Robert J. Art, *The TFX Decision* (Boston: Little, Brown, 1968), 126.
47. *The National Security Strategy of the United States of America*, September 2002, cover letter and p. 6.
48. The vote on the Persian Gulf War as reported in *Congress and the Nation*, vol. 8 (Washington, D.C.: Congressional Quarterly Press, 1993), 310; the vote on the war in Iraq as reported in the *New York Times* (October 12, 2002): A11.
49. There were no congressional votes on our military efforts in Bosnia and Kosovo, but speeches supporting them were made by (among others) Democratic Senators Barbara Boxer, Carl Levin, and Paul Wellstone and Representative David Bonior; speeches opposing them were made by (among others) Republican Senators Don Nickles and John Warner and by Representatives Robert Barr and Dan Burton. In the vote on the invasion of Iraq, each group took the opposite position.
50. James Dobbins et al., *America's Role in Nation Building* (Santa Monica, Calif.: RAND, 2003).

Chapter 21
Environmental Policy

1. Alexander W. Astin et al., *The American Freshman: National Norms for 1989* (Los Angeles: UCLA Graduate School of Education, 1989), 89.
2. John W. Bridgeland, speaking at the Robert A. Fox Leadership Forum, University of Pennsylvania, September 30, 2004.
3. Sallie Baliunas, "The Koyoto Protocol and Global Warming," *Imprimis* 31 (March 2002); *Climate Change: An Analysis of Some Key Questions* (Washington, D.C.: National Academy of Sciences, 2000); Bjo/rn Lomborg, *The Skeptical Environmentalist* (Cambridge: Cambridge University Press, 2001), ch. 24.
4. Barry G. Rabe, "Statehouse and Greenhouse: The States Are Taking the Lead on Climate Change," *Brookings Review* 20 (Spring 2002): 11–13.
5. Baliunas, "Koyoto Protocol," 2.
6. David Vogel, *National Styles of Regulation* (Ithaca, N.Y.: Cornell University Press, 1986), 19–30.
7. For arguments by activists, see Albert Gore, *Earth in the Balance* (Boston: Houghton Mifflin, 1992), and Stephen Schneider, *Global Warming* (San Francisco: Sierra Club Books, 1989). For arguments by skeptics, see Gregg Easterbrook, *A Moment on the Earth* (New York: Viking, 1995), ch. 17; Frederick Seitz et al., "Environmental Effects of Increased Atmospheric Carbon Dioxide," on the World Wide Web at www.oism.org/project; and Patrick J. Michaels, "Global Deception," Policy Study 146, Center for the Study of American Business, Washington University (1998).
8. Easterbrook, *A Moment*, 309.
9. R. Shep Melnick, *Regulation and the Courts: The Case of the Clean Air Act* (Washington, D.C.: Brookings Institution, 1983), ch. 9.
10. Pietro S. Nivola, *The Politics of Energy Conservation* (Washington, D.C.: Brookings Institution, 1986), 11–12, 244–247.
11. Robert W. Crandall, "Pollution, Environmentalists, and the Coal Lobby," in *The Political Economy of Deregulation*, ed. Roger G. Noll and Bruce M. Own (Washington, D.C.: American Enterprise Institute, 1983), 84–96; Crandall, *Controlling Industrial Pollution* (Washington, D.C.: Brookings Institution, 1983).
12. Bruce A. Ackerman and William T. Hassler, *Clear Coal/Dirty Air* (New Haven, Conn.: Yale University Press, 1981).
13. Robert Dorfman, "Lessons of Pesticide Regulation," in *Reform of Environmental Regulation*, ed. Wesley A. Magat (Cambridge, Mass.: Ballinger, 1982), 13–30.
14. Easterbrook, *A Moment*, 386–395.
15. *Congressional Quarterly Weekly Report* (January 12, 1990): 166–170.
16. Richard Doll and Richard Peto, "The Causes of Cancer," *Journal of the National Cancer Institute* 66 (1981); World Cancer Research Fund, *Food, Nutrition, and the Prevention of Cancer* (Washington, D.C.: American Institute for Cancer Research, 1997).
17. R. Shep Melnick, "Deadlines, Cynicism, and Common Sense," *The Brookings Review* (Fall 1983): 21–24.

Chapter 22
Who Governs? To What Ends?

1. Donald F. Kettl, "Heading for Disaster, "*Government Executive*, February 1, 2009.
2. Ibid.
3. Alexis de Tocqueville, *Democracy in America*, vol. 2, ed. Phillips Bradley (New York: Knopf, 1951), book 2, ch. 1.

Index

AMERICAN GOVERNMENT: POLICIES

The Politics of Public Policy

Cabinet
http://www.whitehouse.gov/administration/cabinet/

Fifteen executive departments comprise the Cabinet of the United States, including State, Defense, Energy, Homeland Security, and Education.

Federal Reserve
http://www.federalreserve.gov/

As the central bank of the United States, the Federal Reserve oversees the American monetary and financial system.

Internal Revenue Service
http://www.irs.gov/

The Internal Revenue Service is responsible for federal tax collection and enforcement of the nation's tax laws.

Social Security
http://www.ssa.gov/

The Social Security Administration oversees distribution of funding for retirement, Supplemental Security Income, and Medicare.

Temporary Assistance for Needy Families
http://www.acf.hhs.gov/ programs/ofa/tanf/index.html

The U.S. Department of Health and Human Services oversees the Temporary Assistance for Needy Families Program, popularly known as "welfare."

Environmental Protection Agency
http://www.epa.gov/

The Environmental Protection Agency is responsible for protecting people's health and their environment.